lonely planet

Belize
Guatemala & Yucatán

Ben Greensfelder
Carolyn Miller
Conner Gorry
Sandra Bao

LONELY PLANET PUBLICATIONS
Melbourne • Oakland • London • Paris

BELIZE, GUATEMALA & YUCATÁN

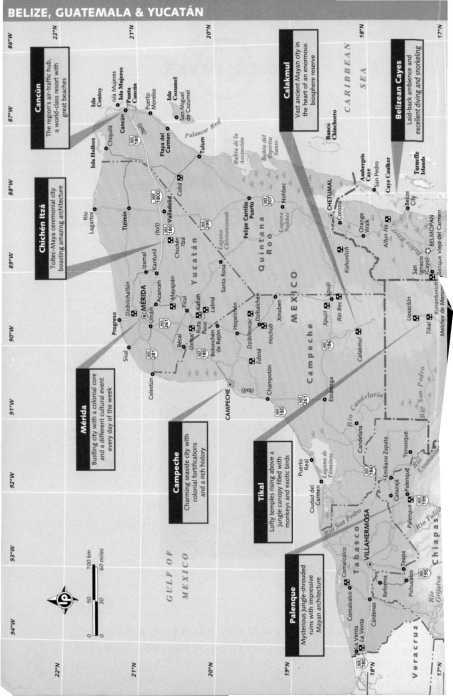

Cancún
The region's air-traffic hub, a world-class resort with great beaches

Chichén Itzá
Toltec-Maya ceremonial city boasting amazing architecture

Calakmul
Vast ancient Mayan city in the heart of an enormous biosphere reserve

Belizean Cayes
Laid-back ambience and excellent diving and snorkeling

Mérida
Bustling city with a colonial core and a different cultural event every day of the week

Campeche
Charming seaside city with colonial fortifications and a rich history

Tikal
Lofty temples rising above a jungle canopy filled with monkeys and exotic birds

Palenque
Mysterious jungle-shrouded ruins with impressive Mayan architecture

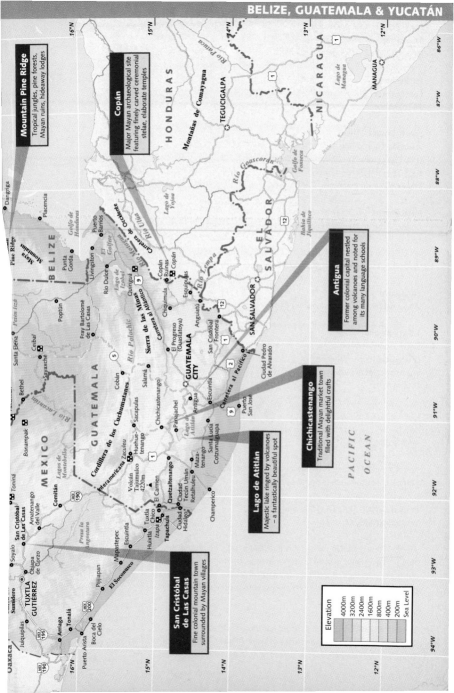

BELIZE, GUATEMALA & YUCATÁN

Mountain Pine Ridge
Tropical jungles, pine forests, Mayan ruins, hideaway lodges

Copán
Major Mayan archaeological site featuring finely carved ceremonial stelae, elaborate temples

Antigua
Former colonial capital nestled among volcanoes and noted for its many language schools

Chichicastenango
Traditional Mayan market town filled with delightful crafts

Lago de Atitlán
Majestic lake ringed by volcanoes – a fantastically beautiful spot

San Cristóbal de Las Casas
Fine colonial mountain town surrounded by Mayan villages

Elevation
4000m
3200m
2400m
1600m
800m
400m
200m
Sea Level

MEXICO

Oaxaca
Juquipilas
Sumidero
Tuxtla Gutiérrez
Chiapa de Corzo
Soyaló
San Cristóbal de Las Casas
Amatenango del Valle
Comitán
Toniná
Lagos de Montebello
Bonampak
Bethel
Santa Elena
Ceibal
Sayaxché
Arriaga
Tonalá
Mapastepec
Escuintla
Pijijiapan
El Suconusco
Boca del Cielo
Puerto Arista
Huixtla
Tuxtla Chico
Izapa
Tapachula
Ciudad Hidalgo
El Carmen
Ciudad Tecún Umán
Volcán Tajumulco 4220m
Quetzaltenango
Champerico
Retalhuleu
Maza-tenango
Santa Lucía Cotzumalguapa
Huehue-tenango
Sacapulas
Salamá
Cobán
Fray Bartolomé de Las Casas
Poptún
Chichicastenango
Panajachel
Lago Atitlán
Antigua
GUATEMALA CITY
El Progreso (Guastatoya)
San Cristóbal Frontera
Anguiatú
SAN SALVADOR
Ciudad Pedro de Alvarado
Puerto San José
Escuintla

GUATEMALA

Cordillera de los Cuchumatanes
Interamericana
Zaculeu
Sierra de las Minas
Río Polochic
Río Motagua
Carretera al Atlántico
Chiquimula
Esquipulas
Copán Ruinas
Copán
Quiriguá
Río Dulce
Lago de Izabal
Livingston
Punta Gorda
Golfo de Honduras
El Golfete
Puerto Barrios
Carretera de Occidente

BELIZE

Pine Ridge
Maya Mountains
Dangriga
Placencia

HONDURAS

Montañas de Comayagua
TEGUCIGALPA
Lago de Yojoa
Río Ulúa

EL SALVADOR

Río Lempa
Río Goascorán
Golfo de Fonseca
Bahía de Jiquilisco

NICARAGUA

Lago de Managua
MANAGUA

PACIFIC OCEAN

Presa la Angostura
Río Lacantún
Río Usumacinta
Petén Itzá

Belize, Guatemala & Yucatán
4th edition – March 2001
First published – October 1991

Published by
Lonely Planet Publications Pty Ltd ABN 36 005 607 983
90 Maribyrnong St, Footscray, Victoria 3011, Australia

Lonely Planet Offices
Australia Locked Bag 1, Footscray, Victoria 3011
USA 150 Linden St, Oakland, CA 94607
UK 10a Spring Place, London NW5 3BH
France 1 rue du Dahomey, 75011 Paris

Photographs
Many of the images in this guide are available for licensing from
Lonely Planet Images.
email: lpi@lonelyplanet.com.au
Web site: www.lonelyplanetimages.com

Front cover photograph
Water drops on curling vine (Stone/Art Wolfe)

Title page photographs
Belize (John Elk III)
Guatemala (Eric L Wheater)
Yucatán (John Elk III)

ISBN 1 86450 140 5

text & maps © Lonely Planet Publications Pty Ltd 2001
photos © photographers as indicated 2001

Printed by SNP SPrint (M) Sdn Bhd
Printed in Malaysia

Contents

GETTING THERE & AROUND 199

GUATEMALA CITY 206

ANTIGUA 221

THE HIGHLANDS 239

THE PACIFIC SLOPE 290

CENTRAL & EASTERN GUATEMALA 302

EL PETÉN 347

FACTS ABOUT THE YUCATÁN 380

FACTS FOR THE VISITOR 386

GETTING THERE & AROUND 396

QUINTANA ROO 399

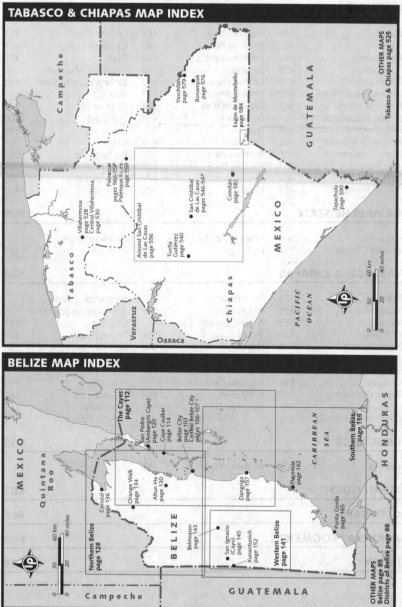

TABASCO & CHIAPAS MAP INDEX

OTHER MAPS
Tabasco & Chiapas page 525

Campeche

GUATEMALA

Yaxchilán
page 579

Bonampak
page 576

Lagos de Montebello
page 584

Palenque
pages 565–9
Palenque Ruins
page 568

Villahermosa
page 528
Central Villahermosa
page 530

San Cristóbal
de Las Casas
pages 546–54

Comitán
page 582

Tapachula
page 590

Around San Cristóbal
de Las Casas
page 556

MEXICO

Tuxtla
Gutiérrez
page 540

Tabasco

Chiapas

PACIFIC
OCEAN

Veracruz

Oaxaca

0   30   60 km
0   20   40 miles

BELIZE MAP INDEX

MEXICO

Quintana
Roo

The Cayes
page 112

San Pedro
(Ambergris Caye)
page 120

Caye Caulker
page 114

Belize City
page 103
Central Belize City
pages 106–107

CARIBBEAN
SEA

Southern Belize
page 155

HONDURAS

Corozal
page 136

Orange Walk
page 134

Altun Ha
page 130

Dangriga
page 157

Placencia
page 162

Northern Belize
page 128

Belmopan
page 143

San Ignacio
(Cayo)
page 145
Xunantunich
page 152

Western Belize
page 141

Punta Gorda
page 165

BELIZE

OTHER MAPS
Belize page 85
Districts of Belize page 88

0   30   60 km
0   20   40 miles

Campeche

GUATEMALA

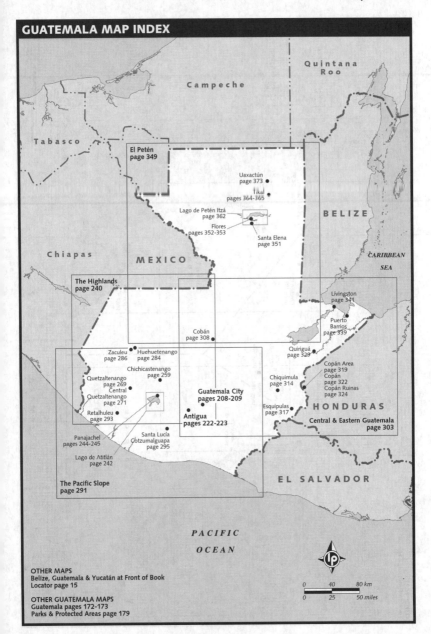

GUATEMALA MAP INDEX

Quintana Roo

Campeche

Tabasco

El Petén
page 349

Uaxactún
page 373

Tikal
pages 364-365

Lago de Petén Itzá
page 362

Flores
pages 352-353

Santa Elena
page 351

BELIZE

Chiapas

MEXICO

CARIBBEAN
SEA

The Highlands
page 240

Livingston
page 341

Puerto
Barrios
page 339

Cobán
page 308

Zaculeu
page 286

Huehuetenango
page 284

Quiriguá
page 329

Chichicastenango
page 259

Quetzaltenango
page 269

Central
Quetzaltenango
page 271

Guatemala City
pages 208-209

Copán Area
page 319
Copán
page 322
Copán Ruinas
page 324

Chiquimula
page 314

Retalhuleu
page 293

Antigua
pages 222-223

Esquipulas
page 317

HONDURAS

Panajachel
pages 244-245

Santa Lucía
Cotzumalguapa
page 295

Central & Eastern Guatemala
page 303

Lago de Atitlán
page 242

The Pacific Slope
page 291

EL SALVADOR

PACIFIC

OCEAN

OTHER MAPS
Belize, Guatemala & Yucatán at Front of Book
Locator page 15

OTHER GUATEMALA MAPS
Guatemala pages 172-173
Parks & Protected Areas page 179

0   40   80 km
0   25   50 miles

YUCATÁN PENINSULA MAP INDEX

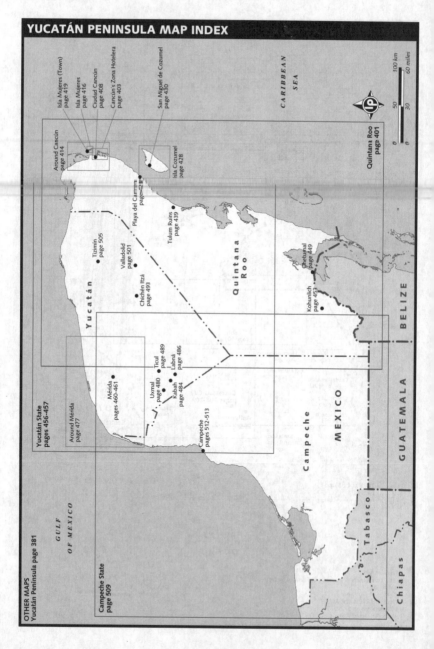

CARIBBEAN SEA

100 km

60 miles

50

30

0

Yucatán

Quintana Roo

BELIZE

Campeche

MEXICO

GUATEMALA

Tabasco

Chiapas

GULF OF MEXICO

The Authors

Ben Greensfelder

Ben Greensfelder was born and raised in Marin County, California. After high school he spent 11 years alternating university attendance with various jobs (many of them in forestry in California's Sierra Nevada), finally graduating from UC Santa Cruz with a degree in language studies. He first visited Mexico in 1964, on a family road trip to Álamos, and has returned to the country several times since then. His wide-ranging world travels have also included extended stays in Greece and South Korea. Ben has worked as an editor since 1986 and as a Lonely Planet editor since 1997. He and his wife, Sandra Bao, make their home in Oakland.

Carolyn Miller

California native Carolyn Miller has been lucky enough to both live and work for travel since graduating from the University of California at Berkeley. She now runs the US marketing department for Lonely Planet and has contributed to a number of the company's projects, including Lonely Planet's *San Francisco*. Happiest in the heat, she has traveled in some of the world's best tropical destinations in Central America, Southeast Asia and the South Pacific. She enjoys scuba diving, hiking and swimming almost as much as reading a good book in a shady hammock. She lives in Oakland with her husband.

Conner Gorry

It all started in Vieques, Puerto Rico, more than 20 years ago. On that seminal trip, it dawned on Conner that there was a world outside of suburban strip malls and prepubescent pap. The Dominican Republic and Culebra followed (islands kick ass!) and it wasn't long before she was hooked. The habit took hold and between adventures, she got a BA in Latin American Studies and an MA in International Policy. Conner currently lives among all those dot commies in San Francisco with her partner Koch (somebody save us!). Day by day the Siren song of Manhattan and Havana grow mightier. She wrote Lonely Planet's *Read This First: Central & South America* and *Guatemala* and has contributed to *South America on a shoestring* and other LP titles.

Sandra Bao

Born and raised in Buenos Aires, Argentina, to Chinese parents, Sandra reluctantly came to the US when she was nine. Her introduction to America was Toledo, Ohio, in winter (it had been summer in South America). She attended UC Santa Cruz with a major in psychology, which she finds useful except when seeking employment. Sandra has traveled extensively around the world and even taught introductory English to a 90-student class at Cheju National University in Korea. These days she spends her time hanging out in her cute Oakland pad, doing odd jobs and activities, and searching for people to challenge at racquetball. This is her first 'official' (paid) writing gig.

FROM THE AUTHORS

Ben Greensfelder In Mérida, many thanks go to Raúl Lí Causí, Geovanna Campos, Roger Lynn and Jorge Manzanero Góngora, for their kindness and mountains of information. Thanks to Mike Hesson, Molly Roth and Elinor in Valladolid, for excellent company and continuing updates. In Cancún, I thank Sra Araceli Domínguez for her time and her tireless struggle to protect the environment.

I thank my mother-in-law, Fung-Lin Lee de Bao, for her endless optimism and support. To my parents, Bob and Jean, thank you for raising me with an appreciation of other cultures. Finally, to Sandra Bao – my wife, coauthor and traveling companion – thanks for your help and support on this project, for seven mostly excellent years of marriage and for always being eager to hit the road!

Carolyn Miller In Belize, special thanks to Shakira Oxley and Rudy Borges for setting me off in the right directions, the Crooked Tree folks for showing me all those birds, and Allan Forman for talking me into the Blue Hole.

In Oakland thanks to Kate Hoffman, Mariah Bear and Eric Kettunen for encouraging me to jump the fence, Heather Harrison and the LP marketeers for graciously filling in while I was away, the Matter family for exceptional pet care and Paul Carlstroem for making it so nice to come home. Finally, thanks to Joan and Rich Miller for showing me early on the joys of an open book and an open road.

Conner Gorry To my partner/co-conspirator/travel-king Koch, who makes life so damn fun and fulfilling: Thanks baby, for being you and always loving the sometimes intolerable me.

In Antigua, thanks go to Nancy Hoffman and Luis Ramirez of Vision Travel; Gunther Blauth supplied good info on the 'jungle route.' Tom Lingenfelter in Xela was a terrific help. Dr Bill in Todos Santos kept me healthy in body and spirit. Thanks doc! Heartfelt appreciation goes to Molly Harlow and Rosario Martin Chavez for helping with the Mam language section. In Momos, thanks to Kermit Frazier and Rigoberto Itzep Chanchavac. Rosie and Bill Fogerty rock on all fronts; the time we spent at their place in Jaibalito was ethereal. Christine and Aimee saved my sanity in Fray. Words can barely capture the trial and triumph that was our hike to El Mirador. Gerd Unni Rougnø was a paragon of courage, good humor and insight on that trip. Unni, you're fantastic! I'd also like to shout out to our guide Calistro from Carmelita, who taught me an important life lesson with three short words: *poco a poco.*

Finally, if anyone reading this knows Lourdes and/or Elyse (last seen in Monterey), tell them to email me!

Sandra Bao Thanks to my husband, Ben, for enduring endless questions and putting up with two writers in one household; to the many expats I met (including Dana Gay, Glen Wersch and Ellen Jones) for their hospitality and opinions; to the helpful people at the tourist offices and on the street corners (who also endured myriad questions); and finally to my parents, Fung and David, for the love and support to let me be myself and someone else I'm trying to find.

This Book

The 1st and 2nd editions of this book were researched and written by Tom Brosnahan. Nancy Keller helped Tom with the 3rd edition, contributing the updated Guatemala section. For this 4th edition, Ben Greensfelder updated the introductory chapters and the Quintana Roo, Yucatán State and Campeche chapters; Carolyn Miller handled the Belize chapters; Conner Gorry updated the Guatemala chapters; and Sandra Bao revised the Tabasco & Chiapas chapter. Portions of the text were updated from material written by Scott Doggett and John Noble for Lonely Planet's *Mexico*.

FROM THE PUBLISHER

This 4th edition was produced deep in the pyramid-free asphalt jungle of Oakland, California, by a dedicated staff of *dzules*. On the lookout for stray 'tapers' and 'peckeries' roaming the wild text were big-game editors Don Root and Kevin Anglin, supervised by editorial *caciques* Laura Harger, David Zingarelli and Kate Hoffman. The proofreading was in the *pizote* pudding for Rachel Bernstein, Paul Sheridan and Vivek Wagle. Find the indexer under D for DellaPenta, Ken. Support-staff starring roles were played by Carl 'Kukulcán' Bruce and John 'Hernán Cortés' Spriggs, while Stella Breslin turned in a fine cameo appearance as 'the gringa.'

The book's masterfully drawn maps were handcrafted (using traditional indigenous software programs) by lead cartographer Eric Thomsen, with help from Sean Brandt, Justin Colgan, Matthew DeMartini, Chris Gillis, Dion Good, Heather Haskell, Annette Olson, Tessa Rottiers, Kat Smith and Ed Turley, all overseen by Tracey 'La Jefa' Croom and Alex 'King Carto' Guilbert.

Carved-stone hieroglyphs being deemed impractical, we opted to illustrate the book with far lighter but equally beautiful drawings by Hugh D'Andrade, Hayden Foell, Jun Jalbuena, Rini Keagy, Beca Lafore, Justin Marler, Henia Miedzinski, Hannah Reineck, Jennifer Steffey and Lisa Summers.

All these elements were laid out and artfully assembled in Extremely Late Postclassic style by expert designer Henia Miedzinski (who also put together the colorwraps), with help from all-star *aluxes* Josh Schefers and Wendy Yanagihara. Design of the cover was well covered by cover girl Rini Keagy, and design manager Susan Rimerman appeased the production gods to accomplish this heroic feat in well under two *uinals*.

Foreword

ABOUT LONELY PLANET GUIDEBOOKS

The story begins with a classic travel adventure: Tony and Maureen Wheeler's 1972 journey across Europe and Asia to Australia. Useful information about the overland trail did not exist at that time, so Tony and Maureen published the first Lonely Planet guidebook to meet a growing need.

From a kitchen table, then from a tiny office in Melbourne (Australia), Lonely Planet has become the largest independent travel publisher in the world, an international company with offices in Melbourne, Oakland (USA), London (UK) and Paris (France).

Today Lonely Planet guidebooks cover the globe. There is an ever-growing list of books, and there's information in a variety of forms and media. Some things haven't changed. The main aim is still to help make it possible for adventurous travelers to get out there – to explore and better understand the world.

At Lonely Planet we believe travelers can make a positive contribution to the countries they visit – if they respect their host communities and spend their money wisely. Since 1986 a percentage of the income from each book has been donated to aid projects and human-rights campaigns.

Updates Lonely Planet thoroughly updates each guidebook as often as possible. This usually means there are around two years between editions, although for more unusual or more stable destinations the gap can be longer. Check the imprint page (following the color map at the beginning of the book) for publication dates.

Between editions, up-to-date information is available in two free newsletters – the paper *Planet Talk* and email *Comet* (to subscribe, contact any Lonely Planet office) – and on our website at www.lonelyplanet.com. The *Upgrades* section of the website covers a number of important and volatile destinations and is regularly updated by Lonely Planet authors. *Scoop* covers news and current affairs relevant to travelers. And, lastly, the *Thorn Tree* bulletin board and *Postcards* section of the site carry unverified, but fascinating, reports from travelers.

Correspondence The process of creating new editions begins with the letters, postcards and emails received from travelers. This correspondence often includes suggestions, criticisms and comments about the current editions. Interesting excerpts are immediately passed on via newsletters and the website, and everything goes to our authors to be verified when they're researching on the road. We're keen to get more feedback from organizations or individuals who represent communities visited by travelers.

> Lonely Planet gathers information for everyone who's curious about the planet – and especially for those who explore it firsthand. Through guidebooks, phrasebooks, activity guides, maps, literature, newsletters, image library, TV series and website, we act as an information exchange for a worldwide community of travelers.

Research Authors aim to gather sufficient practical information to enable travelers to make informed choices and to make the mechanics of a journey run smoothly. They also research historical and cultural background to help enrich the travel experience and allow travelers to understand and respond appropriately to cultural and environmental issues.

Authors don't stay in every hotel because that would mean spending a couple of months in each medium-size city and, no, they don't eat at every restaurant because that would mean stretching belts beyond capacity. They do visit hotels and restaurants to check standards and prices, but feedback based on readers' direct experiences can be very helpful.

Many of our authors work undercover; others aren't so secretive. None of them accept freebies in exchange for positive write-ups. And none of our guidebooks contain any advertising.

Production Authors submit their raw manuscripts and maps to offices in Australia, the USA, the UK or France. Editors and cartographers – all experienced travelers themselves – then begin the process of assembling the pieces. When the book finally hits the shops, some things are already out of date, we start getting feedback from readers and the process begins again....

WARNING & REQUEST

Things change – prices go up, schedules change, good places go bad and bad places go bankrupt – nothing stays the same. So, if you find things better or worse, recently opened or long since closed, please tell us and help make the next edition even more accurate and useful. We genuinely value all the feedback we receive. A well-traveled team reads and acknowledges every letter, postcard and email and ensures that every morsel of information finds its way to the appropriate authors, editors and cartographers for verification.

Everyone who writes to us will find their name listed in the next edition of the appropriate guidebook. They will also receive the latest issue of *Planet Talk*, our quarterly printed newsletter, or *Comet*, our monthly email newsletter. Subscriptions to both newsletters are free. The very best contributions will be rewarded with a free guidebook.

We may edit, reproduce and incorporate your comments in all Lonely Planet products, such as guidebooks, Web sites and digital products, so let us know if you don't want your comments reproduced or your name acknowledged.

Send all correspondence to the Lonely Planet office closest to you:

Australia: Locked Bag 1, Footscray, Victoria 3011
USA: 150 Linden St, Oakland, CA 94607
UK: 10a Spring Place, London NW5 3BH
France: 1 rue du Dahomey, 75011 Paris

Or email us at: talk2us@lonelyplanet.com.au

For news, views and updates, see our Web site: www.lonelyplanet.com

HOW TO USE A LONELY PLANET GUIDEBOOK

The best way to use a Lonely Planet guidebook is any way you choose. At Lonely Planet, we believe the most memorable travel experiences are often those that are unexpected, and the finest discoveries are those you make yourself. Guidebooks are not intended to be used as if they provided a detailed set of infallible instructions!

Contents All Lonely Planet guidebooks follow the same format. The Facts about the Country chapters or sections give background information ranging from history to weather. Facts for the Visitor gives practical information on issues like visas and health. Getting There & Away gives a brief starting point for researching travel to and from the destination. Getting Around gives an overview of the transport options available when you arrive.

The peculiar demands of each destination determine how subsequent chapters are broken up, but some things remain constant. We always start with background, then proceed to sights, places to stay, places to eat, entertainment, getting there and away, and getting around information – in that order.

Heading Hierarchy Lonely Planet headings are used in a strict hierarchical structure that can be visualized as a set of Russian dolls. Each heading (and its following text) is encompassed by any preceding heading that is higher on the hierarchical ladder.

Entry Points We do not assume guidebooks will be read from beginning to end, but that people will dip into them. The traditional entry points are the list of contents and the index. In addition, however, some books have a complete list of maps and an index map illustrating map coverage.

There may also be a color map that shows highlights. These highlights are dealt with in greater detail later in the book, along with planning questions. Each chapter covering a geographical region usually begins with a locator map and another list of highlights. Once you find something of interest in a list of highlights, turn to the index.

Maps Maps play a crucial role in Lonely Planet guidebooks and include a huge amount of information. A legend is printed on the back page. We seek to have complete consistency between maps and text, and to have every important place in the text captured on a map. Map key numbers usually start in the top left corner.

Although inclusion in a guidebook usually implies a recommendation, we cannot list every good place. Exclusion does not necessarily imply criticism. In fact, there are a number of reasons why we might exclude a place – sometimes it is simply inappropriate to encourage an influx of travelers.

Introduction

The Mayan lands of Guatemala, Belize and southern Mexico were home to the Western Hemisphere's greatest ancient civilization. Travelers to this region today come to see the huge pyramids and temples, the great stelae covered in hieroglyphic inscriptions and the broad ball courts where mysterious athletic contests were held.

But Mayan lore is more than the forgotten culture of a long-dead empire. As you travel here, the Maya are all around you. Modern descendants of the ancient Maya drive your bus, catch the fish you dine upon, work in the bank where you change money and greet you as you trudge up the side of a smoking volcano. The Mayan kingdoms may be dead, but the Maya people – some 2 million of them – are very much alive in their ancient land.

The land is varied, from the flat limestone shelf of Yucatán to the cool pine-clad mountains of Chiapas and Guatemala, from the steamy jungles of El Petén, rich with tropical bird life, to the swamps and fens of northern Belize. It is also threatened. The dense tropical forest is disappearing at an alarming rate as farmers and ranchers, responding to personal need and world market conditions, slash and burn to carve out new fields for subsistence farming or pastureland for high-profit herds of beef cattle.

The rich heritage of Mayan civilization and the environmental integrity of Mayan lands have their defenders, however. Both governments and private organizations are instituting programs to preserve and protect the Mayan heritage and its natural setting. Tourism is one of the most important forces in these plans.

La Ruta Maya (the Mayan Route) was a plan conceived and championed by Wilbur E Garrett, former editor of *National Geographic* magazine. Its intent is to develop tourism in the region as an economic alternative to slash-and-burn agriculture and

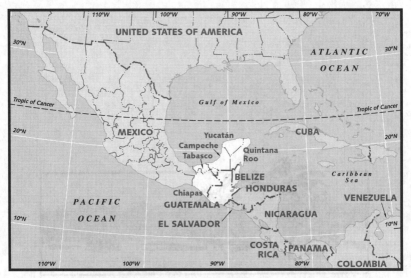

other environmentally unsound practices, yet carefully control that development to ensure minimal adverse impact on the land, the people and the Maya's heritage. Income from increased tourism may also be used to preserve and protect Mayan archaeological sites and jungle biosphere reserves. The governments of Mexico, Guatemala, Belize, Honduras and El Salvador have subscribed to the plan and have established an intergovernmental organization known as El Mundo Maya to make tourism work to the benefit of the Maya and their land. The organization works to highlight the cultural, ecological and archaeological significance

of the Mayan lands, to provide direction and resources for protection and conservation and to help the Maya preserve their ancient culture while improving the conditions under which they live.

This guidebook emphasizes Mayan culture, both ancient and modern, but it also provides information on other regional highlights, including diving off Mexico's Caribbean coast, sunbathing and snorkeling on the Belizean cayes, exploring Mérida's beautiful colonial architecture, investigating Campeche's pirate history, climbing volcanoes in Guatemala and more. In short, it is a complete guide to the lands of the Maya.

Facts about the Region

HISTORY

Archaic Period
(20,000 to 2000 BC)

The great glaciers that blanketed northern Europe, Asia and North America in the Pleistocene epoch robbed earth's oceans of a lot of water, lowering the sea level. The receding waters exposed enough land so that wandering bands of Asiatic people could find their way on dry land from Siberia to Alaska, and then southward through the Western Hemisphere.

They made this journey perhaps as early as 23,000 years ago, establishing themselves throughout every part of North and South America, down to the Strait of Magellan. When the glaciers melted (about 7000 BC) and the sea level rose, the land bridge over which they crossed was submerged beneath what is now the Bering Strait.

The early inhabitants hunted mammoths, fished and gathered wild foods. After the Ice Age came a hot, dry period in which the mammoths' natural pastureland (and, consequently, the mammoths themselves) disappeared. Wild harvests of nuts and berries became scarce. The primitive inhabitants had to find some other way to get by, so they sought out favorable microclimates and invented agriculture.

The ancients cultivated beans, tomatoes, squash and especially maize (corn), which became the Mayan staff of life – a status that it enjoys to this day. They wove baskets to carry in the crops, and they domesticated turkeys and dogs for food. Artifacts left behind by these early cultures include crude stone tools, primitive pottery and simple clay fertility figurines.

Early Preclassic Period
(2000 to 800 BC)

The improvement in the food supply led to an increase in population, a higher standard of living and more time to fool around with such things as decorating pots and growing ever-plumper ears of corn. Even at the beginning of the Early Preclassic period, people here spoke an early form of the Mayan language. These early Maya also decided that living in caves and under palm fronds was old-fashioned, so they invented the *na*, or thatched Mayan hut; this ancient architecture is still used today, some 4000 years later, throughout much of the region. Where spring floods were a problem, a family would build its na on a mound of earth. When a family member died, burial took place right there in the living room, and the Dear Departed attained the rank of honored ancestor.

The Copán Valley (in present-day Honduras) had its first proto-Mayan settlers by about 1100 BC, and a century later the settlements on the Pacific coast of what is now Guatemala were developing a hierarchical society.

Olmecs Without question, the most significant event of the Early Preclassic period took place about 1000 BC, not in the traditional Mayan lands, but in nearby Tabasco and Veracruz (both in modern Mexico). The mysterious Olmec people developed a writing system of hieroglyphics, perhaps based on knowledge borrowed from the Zapotecs of Oaxaca. They also developed what is known as the Vague Year calendar of 365 days (see the Mayan Calendar System section at the end of this chapter).

The Olmecs' jaguar-god art became widespread through Mesoamerica. The huge, mysterious basalt heads they carved weighed up to 60 tons. How the heads were hewn without metal tools and moved some 100km from basalt quarries to the Olmecs' capital city of La Venta remains a mystery to this day.

Eventually the Olmecs disappeared; historians assume they were trampled by waves of invaders. But aspects of Olmec culture lived on among their neighbors, paving the way for the later accomplishments of Mayan art, architecture and science.

Middle Preclassic Period
(800 to 300 BC)

By this time there were rich villages in Honduras' Copán Valley, and settlers had founded villages at Tikal. Trade routes developed, with coastal peoples exchanging salt for highland tribes' tool-grade obsidian. Everybody happily traded pots.

Late Preclassic Period
(300 BC to AD 250)

As the Maya got better at agriculture, the food surpluses they generated allowed them time for other activities. Their society diversified into various classes, and they began to build temples. The first temples consisted of raised platforms of earth topped by a thatch-roofed shelter very much like a normal na.

As with a na, the local potentate was buried beneath the shelter. In the lowlands, where limestone was abundant, the Maya began to build platform temples from stone. As each succeeding local potentate had to have a bigger temple, more and larger platforms were put over other platforms, forming huge step pyramids with a na-style shelter on top. The potentate was buried deep within the stack of platforms. Sometimes the pyramids were decorated with huge stylized masks.

More and more pyramids were built around large plazas, much as the common people clustered their thatched houses in family compounds facing a common open space. The stage was set for the flourishing of Classic Mayan civilization.

Early Classic Period
(AD 250 to 600)

Armies from Teotihuacán (near modern Mexico City) invaded the Mayan highlands, conquered the Maya and imposed their rule and their culture for a time, but they were finally absorbed into Mayan daily life. The so-called Esperanza culture, a blend of Mexican and Mayan elements, was born of this conquest.

The great ceremonial centers at Copán, Tikal, Yaxchilán, Palenque and especially Kaminaljuyú (near present-day Guatemala City) flourished during this time. Mayan as-

tronomers used the elaborate Long Count calendar to date all of human history.

Late Classic Period
(AD 600 to 900)

At the height of this period, the Mayan lands were ruled not as an empire but as a collection of independent but interdependent city-states. Each city-state had its noble house, headed by a king who was the social, political and religious focus of the city's life. The king propitiated the gods by shedding his blood in ceremonies where he pierced his tongue and/or penis with a sharp instrument. He also led his city's soldiers into battle against rival cities, capturing prisoners for use in human sacrifices. Many a king perished in a battle he was too old to fight; but the king, as sacred head of the community, was required to lead in battle for religious as well as military reasons.

King Pacal ruled at Palenque and King Bird-Jaguar at Yaxchilán during the early part of this period, marking the height of civilization and power in these two cities. Mayan civilization in Tikal was also at its height during the Late Classic period. By the end of the period, however, the great Mayan cities of Tikal, Yaxchilán, Copán, Quiriguá, Piedras Negras and Caracol had reverted to little more than villages. The focus of Mayan civilization shifted to northern Yucatán, where a new civilization developed at Chichén Itzá, Uxmal and Labná, giving us the artistic styles known as Maya-Toltec, Puuc, Chenes and Río Bec.

Early Postclassic Period
(900 to 1200)

The collapse of Classic Mayan civilization is as surprising as it was sudden. It seems as though the upper classes demanded ever more servants, acolytes and laborers, and though the Mayan population was growing rapidly, it did not furnish enough farmers to feed everyone. Thus weakened, the Maya were prey to the next wave of invaders from central Mexico.

The Toltecs of Tula (near Mexico City) conquered Teotihuacán, then marched and sailed eastward to Yucatán. They were an extremely warlike people, and human sacrifice was a regular practice. Legend has it that the Toltecs were led by a fair-haired, bearded king named Quetzalcóatl (Plumed Serpent), who established himself in Yucatán at Uucil-abnal (Chichén Itzá). The story was told that he would one day return from the direction of the rising sun. The culture at Uucil-abnal flourished after the late 10th century, when all of the great buildings were constructed, but by 1200 the city was abandoned.

Late Postclassic Period (1100 to 1350)

Itzáes After the abandonment of Toltec Uucil-abnal, the site was occupied by a people called the Itzáes. Probably of Mayan race, the Itzáes had lived among the Putún Maya near Champotón in Campeche until the early 13th century. Forced by other invaders to leave their traditional homeland, they headed southeast into El Petén to the lake that became known as Petén Itzá after their arrival. Some continued to Belize, later making their way north along the coast and into northern Yucatán, where they settled at Uucil-abnal. The Itzá leader styled himself Kukulcán, as had the city's Toltec founder, and recycled lots of other Toltec lore as well. But the Itzáes strengthened the belief in sacred cenotes (the natural limestone caves that provided the Maya with their water supply on the riverless plains of the northern Yucatán Peninsula), and they even named their new home Chichén Itzá (Mouth of the Well of the Itzáes).

The Itzáes were overthrown by the Cocomes, based in the city of Mayapán to the west of Chichén Itzá. Claiming descent from Kukulcán (who supposedly founded Mayapán), the Cocom group ruled a fractious collection of Yucatecan city-states from the late 12th to mid-15th centuries. They were in turn overthrown by a subject people called the Xiú, from Uxmal. Mayapán was pillaged, ruined and never repopulated. For the next century, until the coming of the conquistadors, northern Yucatán was alive with battles and power struggles among its city-states.

The Coming of the Spaniards The Spaniards had been in the Caribbean since Christopher Columbus arrived in 1492, with their main bases on the islands of Santo Domingo (Hispaniola, now home to Haiti and the Dominican Republic) and Cuba. While searching for a passage to the East Indies through the landmass to their west, they heard tales of an empire rich in gold and silver. Trading, slaving and exploring expeditions from Cuba were led by Francisco Hernández de Córdoba in 1517 and Juan de Grijalva in 1518. When these expeditions attempted to penetrate inland from Mexico's Gulf Coast, they were driven back by hostile natives.

In 1518 the governor of Cuba, Diego Velásquez, asked Hernán Cortés to lead a new expedition westward. As Cortés gathered ships and men, Velásquez became uneasy about the costs of the venture and about Cortés' questionable loyalty, so he canceled the expedition. Cortés ignored the governor and set sail on February 15, 1519, with 11 ships, 550 men and 16 horses.

Landing first at Cozumel, off Yucatán, the Spaniards were joined by Jerónimo de Aguilar, a Spaniard who had been shipwrecked there several years earlier. With

Hernán Cortés (1485-1547)

Aguilar acting as translator and guide, Cortés' force moved west along the coast to Tabasco. After defeating an Indian group there, the expedition headed inland, winning more battles and some converts to Christianity as it went.

At this time, central Mexico was dominated by the Aztec empire from its capital of Tenochtitlán (now Mexico City). The Aztecs, like many other cultures in the area, believed that Quetzalcóatl (Kukulcán), the fair-skinned god, would one day return from the east. The time of Cortés' arrival coincided with their prophecies of Quetzalcoatl's return. Fearful of angering these strangers who might be gods, the Aztecs allowed the small Spanish force into the capital rather than slaughtering them outright.

By this time thousands of members of the Aztecs' subject peoples had allied with Cortés, eager to throw off the harsh rule imposed by their overlords. Many Aztecs died of smallpox brought by the Spanish, and by the time they resolved to make war against Cortés and their own erstwhile subjects they found themselves outnumbered and were defeated.

Detailed firsthand accounts can be found in *True History of the Conquest of New Spain* by one of Cortés' soldiers, Bernal Díaz del Castillo.

Cortés went on to conquer central Mexico, after which he turned his attentions to the Yucatán.

Conquest & Colonial Period (1530 to 1821)

Yucatán Despite the political infighting among the Yucatecan Maya, conquest by the Spaniards was not easy. The Spanish monarch commissioned Francisco de Montejo (El Adelantado, the Pioneer) with the task, and he set out from Spain in 1527 accompanied by his son, also named Francisco de Montejo (El Mozo, the Lad). Landing first at Cozumel off the Caribbean coast, then at Xel-Há on the mainland, the Montejos discovered (perhaps not to their surprise) that the local people wanted nothing to do with them. The Maya made it

quite clear that the two would-be conquerors should go conquer somewhere else.

The father-and-son team then sailed around the peninsula, conquered Tabasco (1530) and established their base near Campeche, which could easily be supplied with provisions, arms and troops from New Spain (central Mexico). They pushed inland to conquer, but after four long, difficult years they were forced to retreat and return to Mexico City in defeat.

The younger Montejo took up the cause again, with his father's support, and in 1540 he returned to Campeche with his cousin named (guess what?) – Francisco de Montejo. The two Francisco de Montejos pressed inland with speed and success, allying themselves with the Xiús against the Cocomes, defeating the Cocomes and gaining the Xiús as converts to Christianity.

When the Xiú leader was baptized, he was made to take a Christian name, so he chose what must have appeared to him to be the most popular name of the entire 16th century and became Francisco de Montejo Xiú.

The Montejos founded Mérida in 1542 and within four years had almost all of Yucatán subjugated to Spanish rule. The once proud and independent Maya became peons, working for Spanish masters without hope of deliverance except in heaven. The attitude of the conquerors toward the indigenous peoples is graphically depicted in the reliefs on the facade of the Montejo mansion in Mérida: In one scene, armor-clad conquistadors are shown with their feet holding down ugly, hairy, club-wielding savages.

Chiapas & Guatemala The conquest of Chiapas and Guatemala fell to Pedro de Alvarado (1485–1541), a clever but cruel soldier who had been Cortés' lieutenant at the conquest of Aztec Tenochtitlán. Several towns in highland Guatemala had sent embassies to Cortés, offering to submit to his control and protection. In response, Cortés dispatched Alvarado in 1523, and his armies roared through Chiapas and the highland kingdoms of the Quiché and Cakchiquel Maya, crushing them. The Mayan lands were divided into large estates, or *encomiendas*, and the Maya living on the lands were mercilessly exploited by the landowning *encomenderos*.

With the coming of Dominican friar Bartolomé de Las Casas and groups of Franciscan and Augustinian friars, things got a bit better for the Maya. However, although in many cases the friars were able to protect the local people from the worst abuses, exploitation was still the rule.

The capital city of the Captaincy-General of Guatemala was founded as Santiago de los Caballeros de Guatemala at the site now called Ciudad Vieja, near Antigua (also known as Antigua Guatemala), in 1527. Destroyed by a mud slide less than two decades later, the capital was then moved to Antigua (1543). After a devastating earthquake (1773), the capital was moved to the present site of Guatemala City.

Friar Diego de Landa The Maya recorded much information about their history, customs and ceremonies in beautiful 'painted books' made of beaten-bark paper coated with fine lime. These 'codices' must have numbered in the hundreds when the conquistadors and missionary friars first arrived in the Mayan lands. Unfortunately, the Franciscans ordered the priceless books destroyed, considering them a threat to the domination of Christianity in the region. Only a handful of painted books survive, but these provide valuable insight into ancient Mayan life.

Among those Franciscans directly responsible for the burning of the Mayan books was Friar Diego de Landa, who, in July of 1562 at Maní (near present-day Ticul in Yucatán), ordered the destruction of 27 'hieroglyphic rolls' and 5000 idols. Landa went on to become Bishop of Mérida from 1573 until his death in 1579.

Ironically, it was Friar Diego de Landa, the great destroyer of Mayan cultural records, who wrote the most important book on Mayan customs and practices – the source for much of what we know about the Maya. Landa's book, *Relación de las Cosas de Yucatán*, was written about 1565. It covers virtually every aspect of Mayan life as it was in the 1560s, from Mayan houses, food, drink and wedding and funeral customs to the calendar and the counting system.

Landa's book is available in English as *Yucatán Before and After the Conquest* (see the Books section of the Facts for the Visitor chapter). You can buy it in a number of bookstores and shops at archaeological sites in Yucatán and Guatemala.

The Last Mayan Kingdom The last region of Mayan sovereignty was the city-state of Tayasal, in Guatemala's department of El Petén. Making their way south after being driven out of Chichén Itzá, a group of Itzáes settled on an island in Lago Petén Itzá, at what is now the town of Flores. They founded a city named Tayasal and enjoyed independence for over a century after the fall of Yucatán. The intrepid Cortés visited Tayasal in 1524, while on his way to conquer Honduras, but did not make war against King Canek, who greeted him peacefully. Only in the late 17th century did the Spanish decide that this last surviving Mayan state must be brought within the Spanish empire; in 1697 Tayasal fell to the latter-day conquistadors, some 2000 years after the founding of the first important Mayan city-states.

It's interesting to consider that the last independent Mayan king went down to defeat only a decade before the union of England and Scotland (1707) and at a time when Boston, New York and Philadelphia were small but thriving towns.

Independence Period

During the colonial period, society in Spain's New World colonies was rigidly and precisely stratified. Native Spaniards were at the very top; next were the *criollos*, people born in the New World of Spanish stock; below them were the *mestizos* or *ladinos*, people of mixed Spanish and Indian blood; and at the bottom were the Indians and blacks of pure race. Only the native Spaniards had real power – a fact deeply resented by the criollos.

The harshness of Spanish rule resulted in frequent revolts, none of them successful for long. In 1810, Mexico's Miguel Hidalgo y Costilla gave the Grito de Dolores, the 'Cry [of Independence] at Dolores,' at his church near Guanajuato, inciting his parishioners to revolt. With his lieutenant, a mestizo priest named José María Morelos, he brought large areas of central Mexico under his control. But this rebellion, like earlier ones, failed. The power of Spain was too great.

Napoleon's conquests in Europe changed all that, destabilizing the Spanish empire's foundations. When the French emperor deposed Spain's King Ferdinand VII and put his brother Joseph Bonaparte on the throne of Spain (1808), criollos in many New World colonies took the opportunity to rise in revolt. By 1821 both Mexico and Guatemala had proclaimed their independence.

Independent Mexico urged the peoples of Yucatán, Chiapas and Central America to join it in the formation of one large new state. At first Yucatán and Chiapas refused and Guatemala accepted, but all later changed their minds. Yucatán and Chiapas joined the Mexican union, and Guatemala led the 1823 formation of the United Provinces of Central America, which included Guatemala, El Salvador, Nicaragua, Honduras and Costa Rica. Their union, torn by civil strife from the beginning, lasted only until 1840 before breaking up into its constituent states.

Central American independence has been marred from the beginning by civil war and conflicts among the various countries of the region, a condition that persists today.

Though independence brought new prosperity to the criollos, it worsened the lot of the Maya. The end of Spanish rule meant that the Crown's few liberal safeguards, which had afforded the Indians minimal protection from the most extreme forms of exploitation, were abandoned. Mayan claims to ancestral lands were largely ignored and huge plantations were created for the cultivation of tobacco, sugarcane and henequen (a plant yielding rope fiber). The Maya, though legally free, were enslaved by debt peonage to the great landowners.

Modern Nations

Following independence from Spanish colonial rule, each of the countries in the region went its own way. For the histories of these modern nations, see the respective 'Facts about' chapters for Belize, Guatemala and the Yucatán, later in this book.

CLIMATE

The hottest month in the region is April, and the coolest is February. The most rain falls in June.

Hurricane season in the Caribbean is from July to November, with most of the ac-

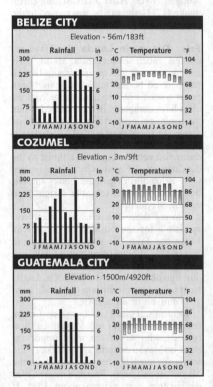

tivity from mid-August to mid-September; about once every decade, some part of the region gets clobbered. In 1998, Hurricane Mitch killed more than 10,000 people in Central America and southeastern Mexico.

If a full-blown hurricane is predicted for where you are, go somewhere else – fast! Sitting out a hurricane may look exciting in the movies, but hurricanes are almost always followed by shortages of housing, transportation, electricity, water, food, medicine, etc, which can be unpleasant if not perilous. At the very least, go inland – far from the dangerous sea swell that usually accompanies hurricanes.

At least a few tropical storms also blow through the area each year and may or may not affect your travel plans. For more detailed climate information, see the section on each country.

ECOLOGY & ENVIRONMENT

Tropical forests have been called the 'lungs of the planet' – by converting carbon dioxide into oxygen, they purify and enrich the air we breathe. The forests are also storehouses of chemical and biological substances and genetic material that have yet to be extensively explored. The thousands of organisms in the forest may contain the materials needed to cure dreaded diseases and develop new forms of life. But if the forests disappear – and they are disappearing at an alarming rate worldwide – humankind will lose this great storehouse and may not be able to breathe.

Steps have been taken to preserve vast tracts of tropical forest in the region. Mexico, Guatemala and Belize, sometimes with funding help from the United Nations, have established biosphere reserves in which the cutting or burning of forest and the hunting of animals is restricted.

A huge protected area now lies where the three countries meet, in the southern central part of the Yucatán Peninsula. It comprises Mexico's 7231-sq-km Calakmul Biosphere Reserve; the adjacent Maya Biosphere Reserve, covering all of the northern Petén in Guatemala (some 16,000 sq km); and, to the east, Belize's Río Bravo Conservation Area, more than 2000 sq km of tropical forests, rivers, ponds and Mayan archaeological sites.

Other biosphere reserves protect coral reefs and breeding grounds for rare and endangered species of birds and mammals. Unfortunately, oversight in many of these reserves is limited or nonexistent, and illegal fishing, hunting and logging (in addition to poor boating and diving practices resulting in damage to reefs) are common occurrences. In Chiapas' Montes Azules Biosphere Reserve, created to protect the remnants of the Lacandón Jungle, indigenous settlers fleeing violence in other parts of the state have cleared approximately 6 sq km and live on them illegally.

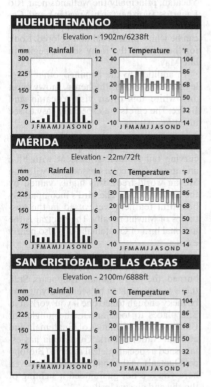

But the reserves on the whole fare better than other land, which is subject to assaults by developers and agriculturalists. Driving through the countryside around Tizimín in Mexico's Yucatán state, you'll see huge tracts of land smoldering from the fires used to clear the forest for the farmer's plow and the herder's cattle. And along the 'Riviera Maya' to the east, reefs, mangrove forests and turtle hatcheries have been ruined by rampant development.

FLORA & FAUNA

As you might expect, the lush jungles of Chiapas, Guatemala and Belize are teeming with fascinating plants and animals. But the drier forests of Yucatán also provide habitat for a surprising number and variety of living things.

Plants

The region's forests are numerous and varied. In one place or another you can find coastal mangrove forest, dense low-growing deciduous forest, rain forest, cloud forest and quintessential jungle, with its multilayered canopy, climbing vegetation and epiphytes (air plants).

Many lowland areas contain a wide variety of palms and tropical fruit trees, such as mango, avocado and papaya, and lots of annuals and perennials, such as the red-orange–flowering flamboyant tree and the purple-flowering jacaranda. On the southern half of the Yucatán Peninsula, the taller trees support 75 known species of orchid. But for the really spectacular blooms, the avid orchid hunter will need to head into the highlands of Chiapas and Guatemala, where the exotic plants thrive at elevations around 1000m.

Birds

As you might imagine, birds are numerous and varied throughout the region. In fact, bird-watching in itself is enough reason to plan an extended stay here. In addition to the more well-known species listed below, such ornithological wonders as the acorn woodpecker and keel-billed toucan, the endangered horned guan and an abundance of macaws, parrots, hummingbirds, songbirds and aquatic birds inhabit the region – there are 500 recorded species on the Yucatán Peninsula alone. Habitat destruction is taking its steady toll, however. In Guatemala, for instance, the giant pie-billed grebe once endemic to the shores of Lago de Atitlán is now believed to be extinct.

Turkeys The 'pheasant' of Mayan lore is actually the ocellated turkey, a beautiful bird that looks something like a peacock. Turkeys are native to the Yucatán and the New England and Middle Atlantic regions of the USA.

Flamingos These long, lanky but graceful birds inhabit certain areas of northern Yucatán, principally the wetlands near Río Lagartos (northeastern Yucatán) and Celestún (northwestern Yucatán). Flamingos can be white, pink or salmon-colored. Look for them when the rainy season begins in late May.

In addition to the flamingo, other long-legged birds such as the heron, snowy egret and white ibis often visit Yucatán and Belize. The egrets are especially easy to see in cattle pastures.

Quetzals The gorgeous quetzal, its long, curving tail feathers iridescent with blue and green (the colors associated with the Mayan world-tree), was highly valued by the ancient Maya. The bird's incomparably beautiful feathers were used in the costumes of Mayan royalty. The quetzal is the national bird of Guatemala. It is also nearly extinct.

As the quetzal becomes scarcer, its value rises; and as the rain forests are slashed and burned, the bird's habitat disappears. Still, there are quetzals to be seen, and you may be lucky enough to see one if you work at it. The places to look are in the jungles of Chiapas, in the highlands of Guatemala and at Tikal National Park. Guatemala has established a special quetzal reserve (Biotopo del Quetzal) on the road to Cobán, but even here you are not guaranteed a sighting of the shy and elusive bird.

Guatemala's national bird, the quetzal

Mammals

Cats Mayan culture, and that of the Olmecs preceding it, could hardly get along without the jaguar, symbol of power, stealth, determination…and bloodletting. Jaguars still roam the forests of the Mayan lands. You are unlikely to see one except in a cage, but that won't change your opinion of it. You'll realize at once that the jaguar is an animal worthy of respect.

The jaguar lives on deer, peccary and tapir, which may help explain why the tapir,

when attacked, sprints away blindly in any direction – anything to escape.

The ocelot and puma also live in the jungles here, but are just as rare as the jaguar these days. Other seldom-seen cat species include the jaguarundi and the margay.

Deer Deer are plentiful enough in Yucatán for deer hunting to be still popular both as sport and as a way of getting a cheap dinner. Venison appears on many restaurant menus in the tourist resorts. Deer multiply rapidly, love eating corn and don't seem to be in danger of depopulation.

Monkeys Spider monkeys inhabit some forested areas of the region, but you're most likely to see one of these expert tree-swingers kept as a pet. They look something like a smaller, long-tailed version of the gibbon, an ape native to southwest Asia. The howler monkey is another elusive primate, frequenting forest around the ruins of Palenque, Tikal and other southern areas of the region. Howlers are more often heard than seen, but you have a good chance of doing both at the 'baboon sanctuary' in Bermudian Landing (see the Northern Belize chapter).

Armadillos & Anteaters Armadillos are creatures about 25 to 30cm long with prominent ears, snouts and tails and hard bony coverings for protection. Though they look fearsome, they are dangerous only to insects, which is what they live on. Their sharp claws help them to dig for fat, tasty grubs and to hollow out the underground burrows where they live. You might see armadillos in northern Yucatán, but unfortunately, they'll likely be roadkill.

The anteater is a cousin of the armadillo, though it's difficult to see the resemblance. There are several species, all with very long, flexible snouts and sharp-clawed, shovel-like front paws – the two tools needed to seek out and enjoy ants and other insects. Unlike the armadillo, the anteater is covered in hair and has a long bushy tail. Its slow gait and poor eyesight make it another common roadkill victim.

Tapirs & Peccaries Short of leg and tail, stout of build, small of eye, ear and intelligence, the tapir eats plants, bathes daily and runs like mad when approached. If you're wandering the leafy paths of Tikal and you hear something crashing through the underbrush nearby, you've probably frightened a tapir. Or it could have been a peccary, a sort of wild pig that can weigh 30kg or more. If the crashing is particularly noisy, it's probably peccaries (also called javelinas), as they tend to travel in groups.

Reptiles

Iguanas One animal you can see at any Yucatecan archaeological site is the iguana, a harmless lizard of fearsome appearance. Of the many different kinds of iguanas, most are green with black bands encircling the body. The iguana can grow to 1m in length, including its long, flat tail. But many of the ones you'll see will be shorter than 30cm (about 1 foot). Iguanas love to bask in the sun on the warm rocks of old Mayan temples, but they'll shoot away from their comfy perches and hide when you approach them.

Sea Turtles Giant sea turtles are found in the waters off Yucatán and Belize. They're protected by law, especially during mating and nesting seasons. Though there are legal methods for hunting small numbers of the turtles, most of the casualties come as the result of poaching and egg-hunting, as sea turtle eggs are believed by the uninformed to be an aphrodisiac. Coastal development has also taken a huge toll on the turtle population, by destroying the beaches where they lay their eggs. You may see turtle or turtle eggs on a menu, and there's a chance they may have been taken legally. But they're best avoided.

Other Reptiles The region is home to several varieties of snakes, including the deadly coral snake, the fer-de-lance and tropical rattlesnakes. These beasts do not look for trouble and will slither away from you if they can. It's unlikely that you'll meet one, and if you do, it's unlikely that you'll do

something to anger it, and if you do, it's not likely that you'll get bitten. But if you do, you'll need help quickly, as they are deadly poisonous. Watch where you step.

Another dangerous reptile is the crocodile, plentiful in the Sian Ka'an Biosphere Reserve on Mexico's Caribbean coast and in areas of Belize. A few remain near the town of Río Lagartos on the northern coast of Yucatán state. These beasts are fascinating to look at but unpleasant, even deadly, to meet up close. Keep your distance.

POPULATION & PEOPLE

Many of the Maya you meet today are the direct descendants of the people who built the marvelous temples and pyramids. To confirm this, all you need to do is compare their appearance with that of the ancient Maya shown in inscriptions and drawings. For information on the people of each part of the region, see the respective 'Facts about' chapters for Belize, Guatemala and the Yucatán, later in this book.

ARCHITECTURE & ARCHAEOLOGY

Mayan architecture is amazing for its achievements but perhaps even more amazing for what it did not achieve. Mayan architects never seem to have used the true arch (a rounded arch with a keystone), and they never thought to put wheels on boxes and use them as wagons to move the thousands of tons of construction materials needed in their tasks. They had no metal tools – they were technically a Stone Age culture – yet they could build breathtaking temple complexes and align them so precisely that windows and doors were used as celestial observatories of great accuracy.

The arch used in most Mayan buildings is the corbeled arch (or, when used for an entire room rather than a doorway, corbeled vault). In this technique, large flat stones on either side of the opening are set progressively inward as they rise. The two sides nearly meet at the top, and this 'arch' is then topped by capstones. Though they served the purpose, the corbeled arches limited severely the amount of open space beneath them. In effect, Mayan architects were limited to long, narrow vaulted rooms.

The Maya also lacked draft animals (horses, donkeys, mules, oxen). All the work had to be done by humans, on their feet, with their arms and with their backs, without wagons or even wheelbarrows.

The Celestial Plan

Every major work of Mayan architecture had a celestial plan. Temples were aligned in such a manner as to enhance celestial observation, whether of the sun, moon or certain stars and planets, especially Venus. The alignment might not be apparent except at certain conjunctions of the celestial bodies (eg, an eclipse), but the Maya knew each building was properly 'placed' and that this enhanced its sacred character.

Temples usually had other features that linked them to the stars. The doors and windows might be aligned in order to frame a celestial body at a certain exact point in its course on a certain day of a certain year. This is the case with the Palacio del Gobernador (Governor's Palace) at Uxmal, which is aligned in such a way that, from the main doorway, Venus would have been visible exactly on top of a small mound some 3.5km away, in the year AD 750. At Chichén Itzá, the observatory building called El Caracol was aligned in order to sight Venus exactly in the year AD 1000.

Furthermore, the main door to a temple might be decorated to resemble a huge mouth, signifying entry to Xibalbá (the secret world or underworld). Other features might relate to the numbers of the Calendar Round, as at Chichén Itzá's El Castillo. This pyramid has 364 stairs to the top; with the top platform, this makes 365, the number of days in the Mayan Vague Year. On the sides of the pyramid are 52 panels, signifying the 52-year cycle of the Calendar Round. The terraces on each side of each stairway total 18 (nine on either side), signifying the 18 'months' of the solar Vague Year. The alignment of El Castillo catches the sun and makes a shadow of the sacred sky-serpent descending into the earth on the vernal equinox (March 21) each year. The serpent

is formed perfectly only on that day, and it descends during a period of only 34 minutes.

Mayan temples were often built atop smaller, older temples. This increased their sacredness and preserved the temple complex's alignment.

Mayan Architectural Styles

Mayan architecture's 1500-year history has seen a fascinating progression of styles. The style of architecture changed not just with the times, but with the particular geographic area of Mesoamerica in which the architects worked.

Late Preclassic Late Preclassic architecture is perhaps best exhibited at Uaxactún, north of Tikal in Guatemala's Petén department. At Uaxactún, Pyramid E-VII-sub is a fine example of how the architects of what is known as the Chicanel culture designed their pyramid-temples in the time from around 100 BC to AD 250. E-VII-sub is a square stepped-platform pyramid with central stairways on each of the four sides, each stairway flanked by large jaguar masks. The entire platform was covered in fine white stucco. The top platform is flat and probably bore a temple *na* made of wooden poles topped with palm thatch. This temple was well preserved because others had been built on top of it; these later structures were ruined by the ages and were cleared away to reveal E-VII-sub. Chicanel-style temples similar to this one were built at Tikal, El Mirador and Lamanai (in Belize) as well.

By the end of the Preclassic period, simple temples such as E-VII-sub were being aligned and arranged around plazas, and all was prepared for the next phase of Mayan architecture.

Early Classic The Esperanza culture typifies this phase. In Esperanza-style temples, the king was buried in a wooden chamber beneath the main staircase of the temple; successive kings were buried in similar places in the pyramids built on top of the first one. Among the largest Early Classic Esperanza sites is Kaminaljuyú near Guatemala City; unfortunately, most of the site was destroyed by construction crews or covered by their buildings, and urban sprawl engulfed the site before archaeologists could complete their work.

Of the surviving Early Classic pyramids, perhaps the best example is the step-pyramid at Acanceh, a few kilometers south of Mérida.

Late Classic The most important Classic sites flourished during the latter part of the period. By this time the Mayan temple-pyramid had a masonry building on top, replacing the use of wood poles and thatch. Numbers of pyramids were built close together, sometimes forming contiguous or even continuous structures. Near them, different structures now called palaces were built. These palaces sat on lower platforms and held many more rooms, perhaps a dozen or more.

In addition to pyramids and palaces, Classic sites have carved stelae and round 'altar-stones' set in the plaza in front of the pyramids. Another feature of the Classic and later periods is the ball court, with sloping playing surfaces of stone covered in stucco. Among the purest of the Classic sites is Copán in Honduras, which can be reached on a day's excursion from Guatemala's Motagua Valley. Along the eastern reaches of the Motagua is Quiriguá (Guatemala), where the pyramids are unremarkable but the towering stelae and mysterious zoomorphs are unique.

Of all the Classic sites, however, Tikal is the grandest restored so far. Here the pyramids reached their most impressive heights and were topped by superstructures (called roofcombs by archaeologists) that made them even taller. As in earlier times, these monumental structures were used as the burial places of kings.

If Tikal is the most impressive Classic Mayan city, Palenque (Chiapas) is certainly the most beautiful. Mansard roofs and large relief murals characterize the great palace, with its unique watchtower and the harmonious Temple of the Inscriptions. Palenque exhibits the perfection of the elements of the Classic Mayan architectural style. The great stairways, the small sanctuaries on top of pyramids, the lofty roofcombs – all were brought to their finest proportions here. The tomb of King Pacal in the Temple of the Inscriptions, reached by a buried staircase, is unique in its two Egyptian-like features: a secret chamber accessible without dismantling the pyramid and a great carved slab covering the sarcophagus.

Puuc, Chenes & Río Bec Among the most distinctive of the Late Classic Mayan architectural styles are those that flourished in the western and southern regions of the Yucatán Peninsula. These styles valued exuberant display and architectural bravado more than they did proportion and harmony.

The Puuc style, named for the low Puuc Hills near Uxmal, used facings of thin limestone 'tiles' to cover the rough stone walls of buildings. The tiles were worked into geometric designs and stylized figures of monsters and serpents. Minoan-style columns and rows of engaged columns (half-round cylinders) were also a prominent feature of the style; they were used to good effect on facades of buildings at Uxmal and at the Puuc sites of Kabah, Sayil, Xlapak and Labná. Puuc architects were crazy about Chac, the rain god, and stuck his grotesque face on every temple, many times. At Kabah, the facade of the Templo de los Mascarones is completely covered in Chac masks.

The Chenes style, prevalent in areas to the south of the Puuc Hills in Campeche, is very similar to the Puuc style, but Chenes architects seem to have enjoyed putting huge masks as well as smaller ones on their facades.

The Río Bec style, epitomized in the richly decorated temples at the archaeological sites between Escárcega and Chetumal, used lavish decoration, as in the Puuc and Chenes styles, but added huge towers to the corners of its low buildings, just for show. Río Bec buildings look like a combination of the Governor's Palace of Uxmal and Temple I at Tikal.

Early Postclassic The collapse of Classic Mayan civilization created a power vacuum that was filled by the invasion of the Toltecs from central Mexico. The Toltecs brought with them their own architectural ideas, and in the process of conquest these ideas were assimilated and merged with those of the Puuc style.

The foremost example of what might be called the Toltec-Maya style is Chichén Itzá. Elements of Puuc style – the large masks and decorative friezes – coexist with Toltec warrior *atlantes* (male figures used as supporting columns) and *chac-mools*, odd reclining statues that are purely Toltec and have nothing to do with Mayan art. Platform pyramids with broad bases and spacious top platforms, such as the Temple of the Warriors, look as though they might have been imported from the ancient Toltec capital of Tula (near Mexico City) or by way of Teotihuacán, with its broad-based pyramids of the sun and moon. Because Quetzalcóatl (called Kukulcán in Mayan) was so important to the Toltecs, feathered serpents are used extensively as architectural decoration.

Late Postclassic After the Toltecs came the Cocomes, who established their capital at Mayapán, south of Mérida, and ruled a confederation of Yucatecan states. After the golden age of Tikal and Palenque, even after the martial architecture of Chichén Itzá, the architecture of Mayapán is a disappointment. The pyramids and temples are small and crude compared to the glorious Classic structures. Mayapán's only architectural distinction comes from its vast defensive city wall, one of the few such walls ever discovered in a Mayan city. The fact that the wall exists testifies to the weakness of the Cocom rulers and the unhappiness of their subject peoples.

Tulum, another walled city, is also a product of this time. The columns of the Puuc style are used here, and the painted decoration on the temples must have been colorful. But there is nothing here to rival Classic-age architecture.

Cobá has the finest architecture of this otherwise decadent period. The stately pyramids here had new little temples built atop them in the style of Tulum.

In Guatemala, the finest and best preserved Late Postclassic sites are Mixco Viejo, north of Guatemala City; Utatlán (or K'umarcaaj), the old Quiché Maya capital on the outskirts of Santa Cruz del Quiché; and Iximché, the last Cakchiquel capital, near Tecpan. All of these sites show pronounced central-Mexican influences in their twin-temple complexes, which probably descend from similar structures at Teotihuacán.

Spanish Colonial Architecture

The conquistadors, Franciscans and Dominicans brought with them the architecture of their native Spain and adapted it to the conditions they met in the Mayan lands. Churches in the largest cities were decorated with baroque elements, but in general the churches are simple and fortresslike. The exploitation of the Maya by the Spaniards led to frequent rebellions, and the strong, high stone walls of the churches worked well in protecting the upper classes from the wrath of the indigenous people.

As you travel through the region, you'll see that many churches are plain, both inside and out. These crude and simple borrowings from Spanish architecture are eclipsed by the richness of the religious pageantry that takes place inside the buildings – including many half-Mayan, half-Catholic processions, rituals, decorations and costumes.

SOCIETY & CONDUCT

With only a few exceptions, the people you encounter throughout the region will be friendly, good-humored and willing to help. Language difficulties can obscure this fact. Some people are shy or will ignore you because they haven't encountered foreigners before and don't imagine a conversation is possible. But just a few words of Spanish will often bring you smiles and warmth, not to mention lots of questions. Then someone who speaks a few words of English will pluck up the courage to try them out on you, and conversation is under way.

Some Indian peoples adopt a cool attitude to visitors; they have learned to mistrust outsiders after five centuries of exploitation by Spaniards and mestizos. They don't like being gaped at by crowds of tourists and can be sensitive about cameras, particularly in churches and at religious festivals.

If you have white skin and speak a foreign language, you'll be referred to as a *gringo* or *gringa*, depending upon whether you're male or female, and you'll often be assumed to be a citizen of the USA. Your presence may provoke any reaction from curiosity or wonder to reticence or, occasionally, hostility. If you're not a citizen of the USA and you make it known, you may get little reaction at all, or you may be treated as an even greater curiosity, perhaps even as a freak of nature.

The classic Mexican attitude to the USA is the combination of envy and resentment that a poorer, weaker neighbor feels for a richer, more powerful one. The *norteamericanos* have also committed the sins of sending their soldiers into Mexican territory three times and taking huge chunks of it by force (Texas, California, Colorado and more!).

Any hostility toward individual Americans usually evaporates as soon as you show that you're human too. And although 'gringo' isn't exactly a compliment, it can also be used with a brusque friendliness.

In Guatemala and Belize, however, it's Mexico that's the richer, more powerful 'neighbor to the north.' Guatemalan and Belizean attitudes toward North Americans are usually more intensely friendly when they're friendly and more intensely hostile when they're hostile.

Traditional Culture

Traditional Dress One of the most intriguing aspects of Indian life throughout the Mayan lands is the colorful, usually handmade traditional clothing. This comes in infinite and exotic variety, often differing dramatically from village to village. Under the onslaught of modernity, such clothing is less common in everyday use than a few decades ago, but in some areas – notably around San Cristóbal in Chiapas – it's actually becoming more popular as Mayan pride reasserts itself and the commercial potential of handicrafts is developed. In general, Mayan women have kept to traditional dress longer than men.

Some styles still in common use go back to precolonial times. Among these (all worn by women) are the *huipil*, a long, sleeveless tunic; the *quechquémitl*, a shoulder cape; and the *enredo*, a wraparound skirt. Blouses are colonial innovations. Mayan men's garments owe more to Spanish influence; nudity was discouraged by the church, so shirts, hats and *calzones*, long baggy shorts, were introduced.

The most eye-catching feature of these costumes is their colorful embroidery – often entire garments are covered in a multicolored web of stylized animal, human, plant and mythological shapes that can take months to complete. Each garment identifies the group and village from which its wearer comes. *Fajas*, waist sashes, which bind the garments and hold what we would put in pockets, are also important in this respect.

The designs often have multiple religious or magical meanings. In some cases the exact significance has been forgotten, but in others the traditional associations are still alive. To the Mayan weavers of Chiapas, diamond shapes represent the universe (the ancient Maya believed the earth was a cube), and wearing a garment with saint figures on it is a form of prayer.

Materials and techniques are changing, but the pre-Hispanic backstrap loom is still widely used. The warp (long) threads are stretched between two horizontal bars, one of which is fixed to a post or tree, and the other is attached to a strap that goes round the weaver's lower back. The weft (cross) threads are then woven in.

Yarn is hand-spun in many villages. Vegetable dyes are not yet totally out of use, and natural indigo is employed in several areas. Red dye from cochineal insects and purple dye from sea snails are used by some groups. Modern luminescent dyes go down very well with the Maya, who are happily addicted to bright colors, as you will see.

Music & Dance You're likely to hear live music at any time on streets, plazas or even buses. The musicians are playing for their living and range from marimba teams (with big wooden 'xylophones') and mariachi bands (violinists, trumpeters, guitarists and a singer, all dressed in 'cowboy' costume) to ragged lone buskers with out of tune guitars and hoarse voices. Marimbas are particularly popular in Guatemala's highlands and on Mexico's Gulf Coast.

Music and traditional dances are important parts of the many colorful festivals on the Mayan calendar. Performances honor Christian saints, but in many cases they have pre-Hispanic roots and retain traces of ancient ritual. There are hundreds of traditional dances; some are popular in many parts of the country, but others can be seen only in a single town or village. Nearly all of them feature special costumes, often including masks. Some tell stories of clear Spanish or colonial origin; one widespread dance, *Moros y Cristianos*, reenacts the victory of Christians over Moors in medieval Spain.

Dos & Don'ts

Politeness is a very important facet of social interaction in Latin America. When beginning to talk to someone in Spanish-speaking areas of the region, even in such routine situations as in a store or bus, it's polite to preface your conversation with a greeting – a simple *'Buenos días'* or *'Buenas tardes'* and a smile, answered by a similar greeting on the other person's part, gets a conversation off to a positive start. When you enter a room, such as a restaurant or waiting room, it's polite to make a general greeting to everyone in the room – a simple *'Buenos días'* or *'Buenas tardes'* will do. When leaving a restaurant, it is common to wish the other diners *'buen provecho.'* Friendly handshakes are also used frequently.

Pay attention to your appearance when traveling. Latin Americans, on the whole, are very conscious of appearance, grooming and dress; it's difficult for them to understand why a foreign traveler, who is naturally assumed to be rich, would go around looking scruffy when even poor people in Latin America do their best to look neat. Try to present as clean an appearance as possible, especially if you're dealing with officialdom (police, border officials, immigration officers, etc); in such cases it's a good idea to look not only clean, but also as conservative and respectable as possible. (Most of Belize is more laid-back in this respect.)

Standards of modesty in dress are becoming more relaxed in recent years; you may see women wearing mini-skirts in the largest cities, where just a few years ago this would have been unthinkable. Nevertheless, not everyone appreciates this type of apparel, and many locals still find it offensive. Take particular care not to offend local people with your attire.

Dress modestly when entering churches, as this shows respect for local people and their culture. Some churches in heavily touristed areas will post signs at the door asking that shorts and tank tops (singlets) not be worn in church, but in most places such knowledge is assumed.

Shorts are usually worn by both sexes only at the beach and in coastal towns, or where foreign tourists are plentiful. (See the Women Travelers section in the following chapter for further tips specifically for women travelers.)

Special Considerations The traditional Maya people are wonderfully welcoming to strangers. Even so, you should take care to be sensitive to local cultural norms.

The most serious conflicts arise over photography. Although many local people don't mind being captured on film or video, others see it as highly offensive. The solution is simple: Ask before you shoot. Sign language – pointing at your camera, then at the subject – will usually suffice. Abide by the response. (Also see Photography & Video in the following Facts for the Visitor chapter.)

Note that many Maya, especially in rural areas, speak only their indigenous language. Where this is the case, it's futile to try to engage them in conversation in Spanish, though sign and body language are always viable options. (Also see the Modern Mayan section in the Language chapter at the end of this book.)

Many Mayan women prefer to avoid contact with foreign men; in their culture, talking with strange men is not something that a virtuous woman does. With this in mind, male travelers in need of directions or information should instead approach another man for help.

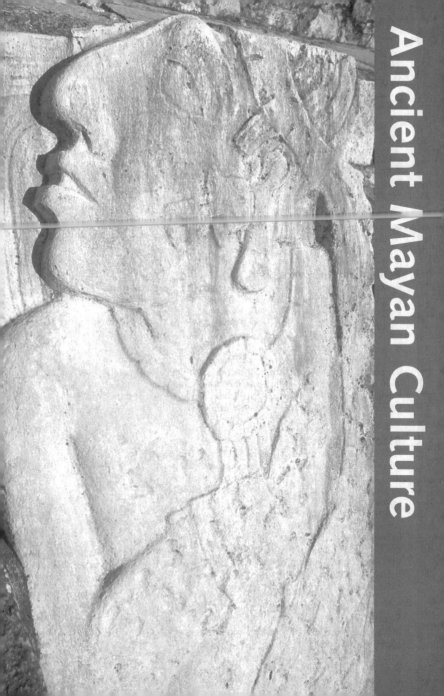

RELIGION
World-Tree & Xibalbá

JOHN ELK III

For the Maya, the world, the heavens and the mysterious 'unseen world' or underworld called Xibalbá (shi-bahl-**bah**) were all one great, unified structure that operated according to the laws of astrology and ancestor worship. The towering ceiba tree was considered sacred. It symbolized the Whack Chan, or world-tree, which united the 13 heavens, the surface of the earth and the nine levels of the underworld of Xibalbá. The world tree had a sort of cruciform shape and was associated with the color blue-green. In the 16th century, the Franciscans friars arrived and required the Indians to venerate the cross; this Christian symbolism meshed easily with established Maya beliefs.

Points of the Compass

In Mayan cosmology, each point of the compass had special religious significance. East was most important, as it is where the sun is reborn each day; its color was red. West was black because it is where the sun disappears. North was white and is the direction from which the all-important rains come, beginning in May. South was yellow because it is the 'sunniest' point of the compass.

Everything in the Mayan world was seen in relation to these cardinal points, with the world-tree at the center. But the cardinal points were only the starting point for the all-important astronomical and astrological observations that determined fate. (See 'Calendar System,' later in this section, for more on Mayan astrology.)

Bloodletting

Humans had certain roles to play within this great system. Just as the great cosmic dragon shed its blood, which fell to the earth as rain, so humans had to shed blood to link themselves with Xibalbá.

Bloodletting ceremonies were the most important religious ceremonies, and the blood of kings was seen as the most acceptable for these rituals. Thus when the friars said that the blood of Jesus, the King of the Jews, had been spilled for the common people, the Maya could easily understand the symbolism.

Sacred Places

Mayan ceremonies were performed in natural sacred places as well as in their human-made equivalents.

Title page: El Palacio relief, Palenque (photo by John Elk III)

Above: Tzompantil (Temple of Skulls), Chichén Itzá

Left: Mayan bust, Palenque

Mountains, caves, lakes, cenotes, rivers and fields were all sacred and had special importance in the scheme of things. Pyramids and temples were thought of as stylized mountains; sometimes they had secret chambers within them, like the caves in a mountain. A cave was the mouth of the creature that represented Xibalbá, and to enter it was to enter the spirit of the secret world. This is why some Mayan temples have doorways surrounded by huge masks: As you enter the door of this 'cave,' you are entering the mouth of Xibalbá.

The plazas around which the pyramids were placed symbolized the open fields or the flat land of the tropical forest. What we call stelae were to the Maya 'tree-stones'; that is, sacred tree-effigies echoing the sacredness of the world-tree. These tree-stones were often carved with the figures of great Mayan kings, for the king was the world-tree of Mayan society.

As there places were sacred, it made sense for succeeding Mayan kings to build new and ever grander temples directly over older temples, as this enhanced the sacred character of the spot. The temple being covered over was not seen as mere rubble to be exploited as building material, but as a sacred artifact to be preserved. Certain features of these older temples, such as the large masks on the facades, were carefully padded and protected before the new construction was placed over them.

Ancestor worship and genealogy were very important to the Maya, and when they buried a king beneath a pyramid, or a commoner beneath the floor or courtyard of his or her na, the sacredness of the location was increased.

The Mayan 'Bible'

Of the painted books destroyed by Friar Landa and other Franciscans, no doubt some were books of sacred legends and stories similar to the Bible. Such sacred histories and legends provided a worldview to believers and guidance in belief and daily action.

One such Mayan book, the *Popol Vuh*, survived not as a painted book but as a transcription into the Latin alphabet of a Mayan narrative text; that is, it was written in Quiché Maya, but in Latin characters, not hieroglyphs. The *Popol Vuh* was apparently written by Quiché Maya Indians of Guatemala who had learned Spanish and the Latin alphabet from the Dominican friars. The authors showed their book to Francisco Ximénez, a Dominican who lived and worked in Chichicastenango from 1701 to 1703. Friar Ximénez copied the Indians' book word for word, then translated it into Spanish. Both his copy and the Spanish translation survive, but the Indian original has been lost.

For a translation of the Spanish version into English, see *Popol Vuh: Ancient Stories of the Quiché Indians of Guatemala*, by Albertina Saravia E (Guatemala City: Editorial Piedra Santa, 1987), on sale in many bookshops in Guatemala for about US$4.

According to the *Popol Vuh*, the great god K'ucumatz created humankind first from earth (mud), but these 'earthlings' were weak and dissolved in water. K'ucumatz tried again, using wood. The wood people had no hearts or minds and could not praise their Creator. These too were destroyed, all except the monkeys who live in the forest, who are the descendants of the wood people. The Creator tried once again, this time successfully, using substances recommended by four animals – the gray fox, coyote, parrot and crow. The substances were white and yellow corn, ground into meal to form the flesh and stirred into water to make the blood.

After the devastating earthquake of 1976 in Guatemala, the government rebuilding program included the printing and distribution of posters bearing a picture of an ear of corn and the words ¡Hombre de maíz, levántate! (Man of corn, arise!)

The Popol Vuh legends include some elements that made it easier for the Maya to understand certain aspects of Christian belief, including virgin birth and sacrificial death, followed by a return to life.

Shamanism & Catholicism

The ceiba tree's cruciform shape was not the only correspondence the Maya found between their animist beliefs and Christianity. Both traditional Mayan animism and Catholicism have rites of baptism and confession, days of fasting and other forms of abstinence, religious partaking of alcoholic beverages, burning of incense and the use of altars.

Today, the Mayan practice of Catholicism is a fascinating fusion of shamanist-animist and Christian ritual. The traditional religious ways are so important that often a Maya will try to recover from a malady by seeking the advice of a shaman-healer rather than a medical doctor. Use of folk remedies linked with animist tradition is widespread in Mayan areas.

CALENDAR SYSTEM

In some ways, the ancient Mayan calendar – still used in certain parts of the region – is more accurate than the Gregorian calendar we use today. Without sophisticated technology, Mayan astronomers were able to ascertain the length of the solar year, the lunar month and the Venus year. Their calculations enabled them to pinpoint eclipses with uncanny accuracy. Their lunar cycle was a mere seven minutes off today's sophisticated technological calculations, and their Venus cycle errs by only two hours for periods covering 500 years.

Time and the calendar, in fact, were the basis of the Mayan religion, which resembled modern astrology in some respects. Astronomical observations played such a pivotal role in Mayan life that astronomy and religion were linked and the sun and moon were worshiped. Most Mayan cities were constructed in strict accordance with celestial movements (see Architecture & Archaeology, in the Facts about the Region chapter).

How the Calendar Worked

Perhaps the best analogy to the Mayan calendar is the gears of a mechanical watch, where small wheels mesh with larger wheels, which in turn mesh with other sets of wheels to record the passage of time.

Tzolkín The two smallest wheels in this Mayan calendar 'watch' were two cycles of 13 days and 20 days. Each of the 13 days bore a number from one to 13; each of the 20 days bore a name such as Imix, Ik, Akbal or Xan. As these two 'wheels' meshed, the passing days received unique names. For example, Day 1 of the 13-day cycle meshed with the day named Imix in the 20-day cycle to produce the day named 1 Imix. Next came 2 Ik, then 3 Akbal, 4 Xan, etc. After 13 days, the first cycle began again at one, even though the 20-day name cycle still had seven days to run, so the 14th day was 1 Ix, then 2 Men, 3 Cib, etc. When the 20-day name cycle was finished, it began again with 8 Imix, 9 Ik, 10 Akbal, 11 Xan, etc. The permutations continued for a total of 260 days, ending on 13 Ahau, then beginning again on 1 Imix.

The two small 'wheels' of 13 and 20 days the created a larger 'wheel' of 260 days, called a tzolk'i... Let's leave the 13 day and 20-day 'wheels' and the larger 260-day wheel whirling as we look at another set of gears in the watch.

Vague Year (Haab) Another set of wheels in the Mayan calendar watch comprised 18 'months' of 20 days each, which formed the basis of the Mayan solar Vague Year calendar, or *haab*. Each month had a name – Pop, Uo, Zip, Zotz, Tzec, and so on – and each day had a number from zero (the first day, or 'seating,' of the month) to 19, much as our Gregorian

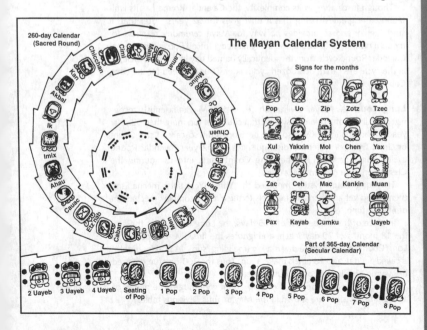

260-day Calendar (Sacred Round)

The Mayan Calendar System

Signs for the months

Pop   Uo   Zip   Zotz   Tzec

Xul   Yakxin   Mol   Chen   Yax

Zac   Ceh   Mac   Kankin   Muan

Pax   Kayab   Cumku   Uayeb

Part of 365-day Calendar (Secular Calendar)

2 Uayeb   3 Uayeb   4 Uayeb   Seating of Pop   1 Pop   2 Pop   3 Pop   4 Pop   5 Pop   6 Pop   7 Pop   8 Pop

solar calendar does. There was 0 Pop (the 'seating' of the month Pop), 1 Pop, 2 Pop, etc, up to 19 Pop, then 0 Uo, 1 Uo and so forth.

Eighteen months, each of 20 days, equals 360 days; the Maya added a special omen-filled five-day period called the *uayeb* at the end of this cycle in order to produce a solar calendar of 365 days. Anthropologists today call this the Vague Year, its vagueness coming from the fact that the solar year is actually 365.24 days long. To account for this extra quarter day, we add an extra day to our Gregorian calendars every four years in Leap Year. The Maya did not do this.

Calendar Round The huge wheels of the tzolkín and the haab also meshed, so that each day actually had two names and two numbers, a tzolkín name-number and a haab name-number, used together: 1 Imix 5 Pop, 2 Ik 6 Pop, 3 Akbal 7 Pop, and so on. By the time the huge 260-day wheel of the tzolkín and 365-day wheel of the Vague Year had finished completely, exhausting all the 18,980 day-name permutations, a period of 52 solar years had passed.

This bewilderingly complex meshing of the tzolkín and the haab is called the Calendar Round, and it was the dating system used throughout Mesoamerica by the Olmecs, the Aztecs, the Zapotecs and the Maya. In fact, it is still in use in some traditional mountain villages of Chiapas and highland Guatemala.

Though fascinating in its complexity, the Calendar Round has its limitations, the greatest being that it only goes for 52 years. After that, it starts again, and so provides no way for Maya ceremony planners (or modern historians) to distinguish a day named 1 Imix 5 Pop in this 52-year Calendar Round cycle from the identically named day in the next cycle, or in the cycle after that, or a dozen cycles later. Thus the need for the Long Count.

Long Count As Mayan civilization developed, Mayan scientists recognized the limits of a calendar system that could not run more than 52 solar years without starting over, so they developed the so-called Long Count or Great Cycle, a system of distinguishing the 52-year Calendar Round cycles from one another. The Long Count came into use during the Classic period of Mayan civilization.

The Long Count system modified the Vague Year solar mechanism, then added yet another set of wheels to the already complex mechanism of Mayan time.

In place of the Vague Year of 365 days, the Long Count uses the *tun*, the 18 months of 20 days each, and ignores the final five-day period. In Long Count terminology, a day is a *kin* (meaning 'sun'). A 20-kin 'month' is called a *uinal*, and 18 uinals make a tun. Thus the 360-day tun replaced the Vague Year in the Long Count system.

The time wheels added by the Long Count were huge. The names of all the time divisions are shown in the Mayan Time Divisions table.

Mayan Time Divisions

unit	same as	days	Gregorian years*
kin	—	1	—
uinal	20 kins	20	—
tun	20 uinals	360	0.99
katún	20 tuns	7200	19.7
baktún	20 katúns	14,000	394
(Great Cycle)	13 baktúns	1.872 million	5125
pictún	20 baktúns	2.88 million	7885
calabtún	20 pictúns	57.6 million	157,705
kinchiltún	20 calabtúns	1.152 billion	3,154,091
alautún	20 kinchiltúns	23.04 billion	63,081,809

*approximate

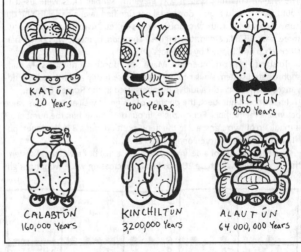

KATÚN
20 Years

BAKTÚN
400 Years

PICTÚN
8000 Years

CALABTÚN
160,000 Years

KINCHILTÚN
3,200,000 Years

ALAUTÚN
64,000,000 Years

In practice, the gigantic units above *baktún*, (*pictún calabtún* etc) were not used except for grandiose effect, as when a very self-important king wanted to note exactly when his extremely important reign took place in the awesome expanse of time. The largest unit in use in monument inscriptions was usually the baktún. There were 13 baktúns (1,872,000 days, or 5125 Gregorian solar years) in a Great Cycle.

When a Great Cycle was completed a new one would begin, but for the Maya of the Classic period this was unimportant, as Classic Mayan civilization died out long before the end of the first Great Cycle. For them, the Great Cycle began on August 11, 3114 BC (some authorities say August 13), and it will end on December 23, AD 2012. The end of a Great Cycle was a time fraught with great significance – usually fearsome. Keep that date in mind, and let's see how this Great Cycle finishes up!

Right: Mayan time-period pictographs

Even the awesome *alautún* was not the largest unit used in the Long Count. In order to date everything in proper cosmic style, one date found at Cobá is equivalent to 41,341,050,000,000,000,000,000,000,000 of our years! (In comparison, the Big Bang that is said to have formed our universe is estimated to have occurred a mere 15,000,000,000 years ago.)

It's important to remember that to the Maya, time was not a continuum but a cycle, and even this incomprehensibly large cycle of years would be repeated, over and over, infinitely, in infinitely larger cycles. In effect, the Mayan 'watch' had an unlimited number of gear wheels, and they kept ticking around and around forever.

COUNTING SYSTEM

The Mayan counting system was elegantly simple: Dots were used to count from one to four; a horizontal bar signified five; a bar with one dot above it was six, with two dots was seven, etc. Two bars signified 10, three bars 15. Nineteen, the highest common number, was three bars stacked up and topped by four dots.

To signify larger numbers the Maya used positional numbers – a fairly sophisticated system similar to the one we use today and much more advanced than the crude additive numbers used in the Roman Empire.

In positional numbers, the position of a sign as well as the sign's value determine the number. For example, in our decimal system the number 23 is made up of two signs: a 2 in the 'tens' position and a 3 in the 'ones' position; two tens plus three ones equals 23.

The Maya used not a decimal system (base 10) but a vigesimal system, that is, a system with base 20; positions of increasing value went not right

Left: Bars and dots formed the basis of the Mayan counting system.

to left (as ours do) but from bottom to top. So the bottom position showed values from one to 19; the next position up showed values from 20 to 380. The bottom and upper positions together could show up to 19 twenties plus 19 ones (ie, 399). The third position up showed values from one four hundred to 19 four hundreds (ie, 7600). The three positions together could signify numbers up to 7999. By adding more positions one could count as high as needed.

Such positional numbers depend upon the concept of zero, a concept that the Romans never developed but the Maya did. The zero in Mayan numbering was represented by a stylized picture of a shell or some other object – anything except a bar or a dot.

The Mayan counting system was used by merchants and others who had to add up many things, but its most important use – and the one you will encounter during your travels – was in writing calendar dates

The Museo de la Cultura Maya in Chetumal (see the Quintana Roo chapter) has excellent interactive exhibits that demonstrate clearly the Mayan calendar and counting system.

LANGUAGE

During the Classic period, the Mayan lands were divided into two linguistic areas. In the Yucatán Peninsula and Belize, people spoke Yucatec, and in the highlands and Motagua Valley of Guatemala, they spoke a related language called Chol. People in El Petén were likely to speak both languages, as this was where the linguistic regions overlapped. Yucatec and Chol were similar – about as similar as Spanish and Italian – a fact that facilitated trade and cultural exchange.

In addition, both Yucatec and Chol were written using the same hieroglyphic system, so a written document or inscription could be understood by literate members of either language group.

The written language of the Classic Maya was complex. Glyphs could signify a whole word or just a syllable, and the same glyph could be drawn in a variety of ways. Sometimes extra symbols were appended to a glyph to help indicate pronunciation. Reading ancient Mayan inscriptions and texts accurately takes a great deal of training and experience. In fact, many aspects of the written language are still not fully understood, even by the experts.

Regional Facts for the Visitor

HIGHLIGHTS

The top sights of La Ruta Maya are among the most fascinating on the planet, but some of the most enjoyable and memorable travel experiences happen in small towns and villages off the beaten track – places like Cobán (Guatemala), San Ignacio (Belize) or Xpujil (Campeche, Mexico). Just because these lesser-known spots are not mentioned below does not mean they are unworthy of your time.

Cities & Towns

The first rank for charm, ambience and interesting things to do includes Mérida, San Cristóbal de Las Casas and Antigua Guatemala (usually just called Antigua). They are, however, on the tourist track. Should you want to get off that track, spend a few days in the city of Campeche, an attractive, authentic, very untouristy place with a rich history, beautiful architecture and a scenic seaside setting. Another good choice would be Valladolid, on the highway between Cancún and Chichén Itzá.

Pleasant small towns? First has to be Panajachel, on Guatemala's Lago de Atitlán, in the highlands. It's very touristy, and for good reason: The lake is breathtakingly beautiful, and the villages on its shores offer fascinating possibilities for meeting and getting to know the modern Maya. In Belize, the most pleasant place to spend a few days – apart from the wonderful cayes – is San Ignacio, on the banks of the peaceful Macal River in western Belize.

Mayan Archaeological Sites

Without a doubt the top four Mayan archaeological sites are Chichén Itzá and Uxmal in Yucatán; Palenque, near the city of Villahermosa in Chiapas; and Tikal in Guatemala. These sites have the tallest pyramids, the most buildings, the boldest architecture and the best restoration. Tulum, on the coast south of Cancún, is not architecturally impressive, but its unique location on the edge of the Caribbean Sea and its proximity to Cancún draw many visitors.

If you enjoy having archaeological sites more or less to yourself, consider the following among the 'second rank': Kabah, Sayil and Labná on the Puuc Route south of Uxmal; Cobá, inland from Tulum; Edzná, near Campeche; Uaxactún, north of Tikal; and Quiriguá off Guatemala's Carretera al Atlántico. Copán, just across the border from Guatemala in Honduras, is among the most important Mayan sites and falls somewhere in between the first and second rank.

Museums

The region's only top-class museums are in Guatemala City and Villahermosa, Tabasco. For Olmec lore – including the enormous basalt heads – the Parque Museo La Venta in Villahermosa is worth the detour if you get as far as Palenque; the two are only an hour or so apart by bus. And while you're in Villahermosa, take a tour through the good Museo Regional de Antropología Carlos Pellicer Cámara, which offers a competent introduction to Olmec and Mayan culture.

In Guatemala City, don't miss the Museo Popol Vuh – a superb private collection of pre-Columbian and colonial artifacts next to the university – and the Museo Ixchel, famous for its displays of exquisite traditional hand-woven textiles and other crafts still thriving in Guatemala.

SUGGESTED ITINERARIES

Most travelers arrive at Cancún, as that resort city has the busiest airport and the most frequent, far-reaching and cheapest air services. Other possible approaches are via Mexico City, Guatemala City or Belize City. See the introductory Getting There & Away chapter.

The Top Sights in a Week

Spend your first night in Cancún or Isla Mujeres, changing money, getting used to Mexico and enjoying the beaches. Start for

42

Chichén Itzá on the morning of the second day, visit the ancient city and spend the night in the nearby town of Pisté. On the third day, return to the ruins in the relative cool of the morning, then drive to Mérida for the afternoon and overnight. On the fourth day, visit Uxmal, south of Mérida, either staying overnight at the ruins or returning to Mérida. On the fifth day, head back toward Cancún, via Valladolid or via Felipe Carrillo Puerto and Tulum; spend the night in either of these cities, or in Cancún. On the sixth or seventh day, take a flight from Cancún to Tikal, Guatemala, for a visit to the most magnificent of Mayan cities, stay overnight in nearby Flores, returning to Cancún the following day.

This itinerary is rushed, and you may want to go by rented car rather than by bus to make it more comfortable. The rented car and the flights would make it expensive but allow you to see all the top sights – Cancún, Chichén Itzá, Mérida, Uxmal, Tulum, Tikal – and a good deal of the countryside in the shortest possible time.

It is also possible to see the top archaeological sites – Chichén Itzá, Uxmal and Tikal – on day trips or overnight excursions by air from Cancún. If you're addicted to the beaches, or if you've signed up for a package vacation that provides a hotel in Cancún, you may want to see them that way.

Two Weeks

This itinerary gives you a good look at the Mayan sites in Mexico, the highlands of Guatemala, the fabulous ruins of Tikal and a glimpse of Belize, all in 14 or 15 days. It includes one or two flights, but the rest can be done by bus. If you have 15 or 16 days, or if you move at a slightly faster pace, you can do it all by bus, which brings the cost down considerably.

Day 1 – Cancún or Isla Mujeres, arrive and find your hotel.

Day 2 – Ride to Chichén Itzá, visit the ruins and stay overnight.

Day 3 – To Mérida and overnight.

Day 4 – Spend another day in Mérida if you like, or take a day trip to Dzibilchaltún and Progreso, or head south to Mayapán, Ticul and Uxmal.

Day 5 – Uxmal; overnight near the ruins.

Day 6 – Visit Kabah near the Puuc Route and perhaps Sayil, then on to Campeche for the night; or, if you like, go directly to Palenque.

Day 7 – To Palenque and overnight.

Day 8 – Visit the ruins at Palenque, then onward to San Cristóbal de Las Casas.

Day 9 – From San Cristóbal, cross the border into Guatemala and get as far as Huehuetenango or, preferably, Quetzaltenango.

Day 10 – If it's Wednesday or Saturday, go to Chichicastenango and find a hotel room in preparation for the market (Thursday and Sunday). If it's Tuesday or Friday, go to Sololá and catch the market there before continuing to Panajachel on Lago de Atitlán for the night.

Day 11 – Depending upon market days, visit Chichicastenango, Sololá or Antigua (markets every day, but especially Monday, Thursday and Saturday).

Day 12 – Start early from Antigua to the airport at Guatemala City for a flight to Flores, then on to Tikal.

Day 13 – Visit Tikal. Return to Flores for the night, or head to Guatemala City.

Day 14 – From Flores, fly to Guatemala City or to Belize City for a flight back to Cancún, or fly directly home.

Day 15 – If you have an extra day, go by bus from Flores to Belize City on Day 14, then from Belize City to Chetumal and back to Cancún on Day 15. This is a lot of bus time, but it saves the cost of a flight and gives you a look at Belize.

Three Weeks

An itinerary of three weeks would follow the same general course as the one for two weeks but would include more time in several spots. You'd have time to see all the Puuc Route sites, including Kabah, Sayil, Labná, Xlapak and the Grutas de Loltún, and you could take a detour to Villahermosa to visit the Parque Museo La Venta.

You would also have time for visits to Quiriguá, on Guatemala's Carretera al Atlántico, and to Copán (in Honduras), as well as more time in Belize.

Three weeks would also give you an extra day or two to spend basking on the beach, perhaps on the sunny Belizean cayes or in the Yucatán on the Caribbean isle of Cozumel.

Four Weeks
A month is enough time to include interesting but seldom-visited places in your itinerary, such as Toniná, near Ocosingo in Chiapas; Cobá, inland from Tulum; Kohunlich near Chetumal; Laguna de Bacalar, the gorgeous and virtually untouristed lake just north of Chetumal; Mountain Pine Ridge in Belize, and the southern part of that country. You'd have lots of time for treks on horseback into the forests surrounding San Cristóbal de Las Casas, time to look for pink flamingos at Río Lagartos in northern Yucatán, and time to relax in a cabaña on the beach south of Tulum. In fact, one could easily spend months traveling the lands of the Maya.

PLANNING
When to Go
You can travel the region at any time of year; there is no off-season. The Caribbean's pellucid waters are always invitingly warm, the beaches always good for sunning. But the topography of the region is varied, from low-lying Yucatán to the lofty volcanoes of Chiapas and Guatemala, so you will encounter a variety of climatic conditions whenever you go.

The height of the tourist season is in winter, from Christmas to the end of March; the other high-season month is August. During these times you should reserve middle and top-end hotel rooms in advance for Mérida, Uxmal, Cancún, Cozumel, Isla Mujeres, Belize's cayes and the resorts of Mexico's Caribbean Coast. For bottom-end rooms, try to get to your destination as early in the day as possible so you can nail down a room at the price you want.

Maps
ITMB Publishing (☎ 604-879-3621, fax 604-879-4521, itmb@itmb.com, www.itmb.com), 530 W Broadway, Vancouver BC, V5Z 1E9, Canada, publishes a series of Traveler's Reference Maps. Titles include *Guatemala* (1:500,000), which also covers neighboring portions of Chiapas, Tabasco, Belize and Honduras; *Yucatán Peninsula* (1:1 million),

which extends to Tabasco, Chiapas, Belize and El Petén (northern Guatemala); and *Belize* (1:350,000). They're available from many travel-book and map stores. For information on other maps relevant to the countries of the region, see the respective Facts for the Visitor chapters later in this book.

What to Bring
Clothing Local people of the Mayan lands tend to dress informally but conservatively. Most men of all classes, from taxi drivers to business executives, wear long trousers and sports shirts or *guayaberas*, the fancy shirts decorated with tucks and worn outside the belt, which substitute for jacket and tie in this warm climate. Women dress traditionally, in long white Mayan dresses with embroidered collars or bodices, or stylishly in dresses or blouses and skirts. The local people do not expect you to dress in the same manner. They allow for foreign ways, but you should know that shorts and T-shirts mark the tourist.

In lowland areas, you should always have a hat, sunglasses and sunblock cream. If your complexion is particularly fair or if you burn easily, consider wearing light cotton shirts with long sleeves and light cotton trousers. Otherwise, men can wear light cotton shorts, tennis shoes or sandals and T-shirts, although more conservative wear is in order when visiting churches. Women can dress similarly except off the beaten track in villages unaccustomed to tourists. In general, it is better for women to dress somewhat more conservatively when in town – no shorts, tank tops etc. Cancún is the exception; in Cancún, wear whatever you like. Bring a light sweater or jacket for evening boat rides. Denim is uncomfortably heavy in these warm, humid areas.

Clothing made from the new weaves of synthetic blends (usually some combination of polyester and nylon) offers several advantages. It is lightweight, wrinkles less than cotton clothing when packed, wicks perspiration away from the body to evaporate in the air, and dries quickly after washing. The downside is high cost.

Sport sandals of the type developed for river rafting are an excellent item to bring on a lowlands trip. They can be worn at the beach, climbing pyramids or snorkeling cenotes.

In the highlands of Chiapas and Guatemala you will need warmer clothing – a pair of trousers or jeans, for sure, plus a sweater or jacket (or both if you plan to be out for long periods in the evening or early morning). A light rain jacket, preferably a loose-fitting poncho, is good to have from October to May and is a necessity from May to October.

Many travelers like to pack clothing that they can discard or give away toward the end of their trip or as they travel into a region where it is no longer needed. Whatever you bring, don't bring too much of it. Pack ahead of time and carry your bag around the block once or twice on a trial run. If it feels heavy now, just imagine how it will be in a hot, humid climate when you're walking for blocks. Remember too that you can usually buy clothing as needed after you arrive (shoes, especially larger sizes, being the exception).

Other Items Toiletries such as shampoo, soap, toothpaste, toilet paper, razors and shaving cream are readily available in all but the smallest villages. You should bring your own contact lens solution, tampons, contraceptives and deodorant.

Don't forget the all-important insect repellent containing DEET (see the Health section), which may be easier to find at home. Besides, if you buy it before you leave home, you'll have it when you need it. The aforementioned sunblock cream is a good thing to buy at home as well. Be aware that many private swimming areas (such as Xel-Há, Xcaret and certain cenotes in the Yucatán) allow only biodegradable sunblock to be used by visitors. They will confiscate (temporarily) the nonbiodegradable kind. Some places issue their own; at others you must buy what they have.

Other items you might find useful are a flashlight (torch) for exploring caves, pyramids and your hotel room when the power goes out, a disposable lighter (for the same reasons), a pocket knife, two to three meters of cord, diving or snorkeling equipment, fishing equipment, a small sewing kit, a money belt or pouch, lip balm and a small Spanish-English dictionary.

RESPONSIBLE TOURISM

Many souvenirs sold in the region are made from endangered plants and animals that have been acquired illegally. By collecting or purchasing these items you aid in their extinction. Avoid purchasing any items made from turtle shell or coral. The sale and purchase of jaguar teeth and pelts is not only illegal, it's ethically criminal. Same goes for crocodile and ocelot and margay skins. Orchids are endemic and are also protected by domestic and international law; view but don't pick.

Don't take home anything that you pick up at the site of an ancient city or out on a coral reef. And please be careful what you touch and where you place your feet when you're snorkeling and scuba diving; not only can coral cut you, but it's extremely fragile and takes years to grow even a finger's length; see 'Considerations for Responsible Diving' in this chapter.

Many areas in the region, especially on the Yucatán Peninsula, have limited water reserves, and in times of drought the situation can become serious. Additionally, wastewater-treatment facilities (where they exist) can't always keep up with the strain placed on them by local residents, let alone tourists. Contamination of groundwater is becoming a serious problem.

Please do your part by keeping water use down, especially in areas that have signs requesting you to do so. Limit the length of your showers and the number of toilet flushes. And as Mom always said, don't run the water while you're brushing your teeth or shaving!

VISAS & DOCUMENTS

See the individual country sections for information on passports and visas. Make sure you know when your passport expires; some countries may not let you in when you're close to the expiration date. If you are traveling the region by private car, you will need motor-vehicle insurance and a valid import permit, as well as a driver's license. See the Getting There & Away chapter for details.

Student & Hostel Cards

If you have a student card, you may find it useful for reductions in admission fees at a few museums, but not for much else.

Hostel cards are a bit more useful along La Ruta Maya, at least in Mexico. More hostels affiliated with HI or AMAJ have been opening, and most of these offer discounts of about US$1 for card-carriers. For more detail, see Accommodations later in this chapter.

Copies

All important documents (passport data page and visa page, credit cards, travel insurance policy, air/bus/train tickets, driver's license etc) should be photocopied before you leave home. Leave one copy with someone at home and keep another with you, separate from the originals.

It's also a good idea to store details of your vital travel documents in Lonely Planet's free online Travel Vault in case you lose the photocopies or can't be bothered with them. Your password-protected Travel Vault can be accessed online from anywhere in the world. To create it, log onto www.ekno.lonelyplanet.com.

EMBASSIES & CONSULATES

For lists of embassies and consulates, see each country's Facts for the Visitor chapter.

An embassy is a diplomatic mission from one government to another. A consulate is a mission in a foreign country that promotes the home country's business interests and protects its citizens. If you need help from your home government while in a foreign country, call upon your nearest consulate or the consular section of your embassy.

If you plan to travel in unstable areas or to stay in a country longer than a month or two, it's a good idea to register with your consulate so that they can warn you of dangers if necessary.

Your Own Embassy

It's important to realize what your own embassy – the embassy of the country of which you are a citizen – can and can't do to help you if you get into trouble. Generally speaking, it won't be much help in emergencies if the trouble you're in is remotely your own fault. Remember that you are bound by the laws of the country you are in. Your embassy will not be sympathetic if you end up in jail after committing a crime locally, even if such actions are legal in your own country.

In genuine emergencies you might get some assistance, but only if other channels have been exhausted. For example, if you need to get home urgently, a free ticket home is exceedingly unlikely – the embassy would expect you to have insurance. If you have all your money and documents stolen, it might assist with getting a new passport, but a loan for onward travel is out of the question. Most embassies and consulates, however, can help you by contacting relatives or friends, or by suggesting reliable doctors, clinics etc.

Some embassies used to keep letters for travelers or have a small reading room with home newspapers, but these days the mail holding service has usually been stopped and even newspapers tend to be out of date.

CUSTOMS

Customs officers only get angry and excited about a few things: drugs, weapons, large amounts of currency, automobiles and other expensive items that might be sold while you are in the country. Do not take illegal drugs or any sort of firearms across any of the region's borders.

Normally the customs officer will not look seriously in your luggage and may not look at all. At some border points the amount of search is inversely proportional to the amount of 'tip' you have provided; that is, big tip no search, no tip big search. As for valuable items, if you have an expensive camera, electronic gizmos, or jewelry, there is a risk that they may be seen as leverage or be deemed as liable for duty at the discretion of the customs officer. Be prepared and be firm but flexible. (See the section on Crossing Borders in the following Getting There & Away chapter for more information.)

Whatever you do, keep it all formal and polite. Anger, surliness or impoliteness can get you thrown out of the country or into jail, or worse.

MONEY

For details on the currencies of Guatemala, Belize and Mexico, see Money in the respective Facts for the Visitor chapters.

Exchanging Money

Cash & Traveler's Checks Carry your money in US dollars or US-dollar traveler's checks. Though you should be able to change other sorts of currency (especially Canadian dollars) in major banks in large cities and resorts (for example, Cancún), it can require some time-consuming hassles and may be supremely difficult in smaller cities and towns. In many parts of the region (especially Mexico) it can take a lot of time in a bank just to change US dollars, let alone some currency that is, to a local bank teller, highly exotic.

It is often difficult or impossible to exchange traveler's checks on weekends. Friday should be one of your routine money-changing days so that you'll be supplied with cash for the weekend.

ATMs Automated teller machines can now be found in many cities along La Ruta Maya, especially in Mexico. (Those in Belize don't yet accept foreign ATM cards.) They often provide instructions in English as well as in Spanish and issue local currency debited against your home cash-card account or credit card. The machines offer fast, hassle-free service at exchange rates better than at most banks or *casas de cambio* (money exchange offices).

Don't depend on ATMs to supply all your local cash needs. Have traveler's checks and/or a credit card for backup.

Money Changers This region has no black market to speak of, as currencies are freely convertible. The best rates of exchange – for US dollars only – are often from freelance money changers at border crossing points. However, it's probably best to avoid the money changers working on the street in cities; when you deal with them you're showing them where you keep your money and how much you have. They might end up with it all.

Banks exchange foreign currencies, but often only at limited hours, sometimes at disadvantageous rates, and subject to fees and commissions. Casas de cambio often have poorer rates of exchange, but they usually don't charge commission, and they offer fast, hassle-free service.

Try to spend all of your local currency before you cross a border, as the exchange rates between countries are often terrible. For example, if you exchange pesos for quetzals in Guatemala the rate will be abysmal; the same thing happens if you exchange quetzals for pesos in Mexico, and ditto for quetzals or pesos to Belizean dollars.

Security

As pickpockets and robbers are not uncommon in the cities of this region, it's important to carry your money, passport and other valuables in a pouch or belt underneath your clothing. A neck pouch is preferable to a money belt as a neck pouch can be retrieved and the contents extracted without disrobing in public.

Costs

See the Facts for the Visitor chapter in each country section. At the time of writing, Mexico is the cheapest country in the region, followed by Guatemala, with Belize being substantially overpriced.

Tipping & Bargaining

Tipping practices vary throughout the region. Staff in some of the smaller, cheaper eating places don't expect much in the way of tips, but in others it may be all they earn. In many areas it's customary to leave the small change you receive from the bill. Watch what others do.

In the expensive resort establishments, tourists are expected to be lavish in their largesse. Tipping in Cancún and Cozumel is up to US standards of 15% to 20%; elsewhere, 10% is usually sufficient.

In the Yucatán, it is customary to give a couple of pesos to: the gas-station attendant who fills up your tank (and/or anyone who washes your windshield in the station); the young person who bags your groceries; and the official person who watches over a parking area and guides your car out of its spot (in cities, that is – not the mobs of children at archaeological sites offering to do so).

For handicrafts and other souvenirs, and for anything in an open-air market, bargaining is the rule, and you may pay many times the going price if you pay the first price quoted. The exception to this rule comes when you buy handicrafts from some Chiapan and Guatemalan artisans' cooperatives, which use fixed prices.

Taxes & Refunds
European-style VAT-refund plans are not available.

POST & COMMUNICATIONS
Sending & Receiving Mail
Almost every city and town in the region has a post office where you can buy postage stamps and send or receive mail. Most villages do not.

If you are sending something by airmail from Mexico or Guatemala, be sure to clearly mark it with the words 'Por Avión.' An airmail letter sent from this part of the world to Canada or the USA may take anywhere from four to 14 days. Airmail letters to Europe can take anywhere from one to three weeks.

If you can arrange for a private address to receive mail, do so. There's less chance of your mail getting put aside, lost or returned to the sender if you're late in picking it up.

See each country's individual Post & Communications section for details on the post office.

Telephone
Local calls are cheap, and international calls are generally expensive. Don't go to the post office looking for telephones, as telephone companies in these countries are quasi-independent corporations separate from the post office. For details on calling from each country, see that country's section.

To call establishments listed in this guide from your home, follow the international calling procedures for your home telephone company, which will include dialing an access code for international service, then the country code, the area or city code, and then the local number. City codes are given for most telephone numbers in this guide. Country codes are (☎ 52) for Mexico, (☎ 502) for Guatemala and (☎ 501) for Belize.

International phone cards that can be used in the region are available. Lonely Planet's eKno Communication Card is aimed specifically at independent travelers and provides budget international calls, a range of messaging services, free email and travel information. Check it out online at www.ekno.lonelyplanet.com for joining procedures, access numbers and updates on new features. Or, in the US, call ☎ 800-707-0031.

Fax, Email & Internet Access
Many mid-range and most top-end hotels have facsimile machines, as do airlines, car-rental companies, tourist offices and other businesses. Many of these establishments have email addresses as well. Email and fax are the best methods of making reservations or asking for information. The recipient gets written instructions, which makes translations easier and minimizes the chance of errors. At the same time, slow and sometimes unreliable postal service is avoided.

Some hotels have websites that allow for online booking of rooms, but more often they contain only contact and room information.

Public Internet access in the region is expanding rapidly, and as more cybercafes open (many are mentioned in the text), prices continue to fall. Connection quality

Internet access is expanding in the region.

varies from slow as molasses to satellite fast, and prices range from about US$1.50 to US$8 an hour.

BOOKS

Many aspects of Mayan life and culture remain shrouded in mystery. New discoveries are being made every year by Mayanists and released to the world in books and magazine articles. The University of Oklahoma Press, Norman, OK 73019-0445, USA, has a particularly strong Mesoamerican list.

Most books are published in different editions by different publishers in different countries. As a result, a book might be a hardcover rarity in one country while it's readily available in paperback in another. Fortunately, bookstores and libraries search by title or author, so your local bookstore or library is best placed to advise you on the availability of the following recommendations.

Lonely Planet

Lonely Planet's encyclopedic *Mexico* guidebook covers the entire country in great detail, as the *Guatemala* guide does for that

country. *Central America on a shoestring* is your guide if you're traveling through the rest of the region on a tight budget. *Read This First: Central & South America* is a know-before-you-go book that covers trip-planning essentials and provides maps, capsule overviews and suggested itineraries for the 22 countries in the region. *Healthy Travel in Central America* provides tips on keeping you alive and well in your travels through the area – including how to recognize and avoid such wildlife hazards as leeches piranhas and tarantulas – and offers an illustrated guide to useful plants of the rain forest.

In *Green Dreams: Travels in Central America* (Lonely Planet Journeys series), Stephen Benz takes a witty look at the myths and realities of ecotourism, focusing on the Ruta Maya tourist track and its effect on the region's Maya.

Mayan Life & Culture

In preparation for your journey, find a copy of *Maya: The Riddle and Rediscovery of a Lost Civilization*, by Charles Gallenkamp. It's the best available general introduction to Mayan life and culture. Equally good but more scholarly is *The Maya*, by eminent Mayanist Michael D Coe.

Prehistoric Mesoamerica, by Richard EW Adams, is a scholarly survey of the history, culture and peoples of Mesoamerica. Another entertaining and academically accurate book is *A Forest of Kings: The Untold Story of the Ancient Maya*, by Linda Schele & David Freidel (Morrow, 1990), a much more detailed look at Mayan history and beliefs.

If you have access to back issues of *National Geographic*, get hold of 'La Ruta Maya,' Volume 176, No 4 (October 1989), pp 424–505, for the best short introduction to the concept of La Ruta Maya. Other *National Geographic* articles worth reading are 'Jade, Stone of Heaven,' 'Exploring a Vast Maya City, El Mirador,' Volume 172, No 3 (September 1987), pp 282–339, and 'The Royal Crypts of Copán,' Volume 196, No 2 (December 1997), pp 68–93.

Archaeological Guides

For an exhaustive survey of archaeological sites in the region, read Joyce Kelly's comprehensive and authoritative paperbacks: *An Archaeological Guide to Mexico's Yucatán Peninsula* (1993) and/or *An Archaeological Guide to Northern Central America: Belize, Guatemala, Honduras and El Salvador* (1996). Unfortunately, so far no comparable handbook exists for the ruins of Tabasco or Chiapas.

Tikal: A Handbook of the Ancient Maya Ruins, by William R Coe, is available at Tikal but may be cheaper if you buy it at home before you leave. If you expect to spend several days exploring Tikal, you'll want this excellent guide.

Travelogues

Most important of all are the delightful travel books written by John L Stephens and beautifully illustrated by Frederick Catherwood more than a century and a half ago. Stephens, a New York lawyer, sometime diplomat and amateur archaeologist, and Catherwood, a patient and skilled draftsman, traveled extensively in the Mayan lands in the mid-19th century. The descrip-

tions of their journeys, published soon after their return, were instant transatlantic bestsellers, entertaining readers throughout North America and Britain. More than just travelogues, their discoveries and painstaking explorations produced the first extensive and serious look at many Mayan archaeological sites. Their detailed descriptions and drawings are now the only evidence we have for some features of the sites that have been lost, destroyed or stolen.

The books *Incidents of Travel in Central America, Chiapas and Yucatan*, in two volumes (1969 and later reprints of the original 1041 edition), and *Incidents of Travel in Yucatan*, in two volumes (1963 and later reprints of the 1843 edition), are available in paperback at some bookstores in the region, among other places.

Aldous Huxley traveled through Mexico, too; *Beyond the Mexique Bay*, first published in 1934, has interesting observations on the Maya. Also interesting, if extremely negative and skewed entirely by the author's feelings about the anticlerical violence occurring at the time, is Graham Greene's *The Lawless Roads*, chronicling the writer's travels through Chiapas and Tabasco in 1938.

Contemporary writers have also found the lands of the Maya to be inspiring. *Sweet Waist of America*, by Anthony Daniels (Arrow/Hutchinson, 1990), is a fine book telling about the author's travels, mostly in Guatemala but also in Honduras, El Salvador and Nicaragua.

So Far from God: A Journey to Central America, by Patrick Marnham, was the winner of the 1985 Thomas Cook Travel Book Award. It's an insightful and often amusing account of a leisurely meander from Texas down to Mexico City and on through Oaxaca and San Cristóbal de Las Casas into Central America.

Around the Edge, otherwise entitled *Tekkin a Waalk* (Viking Penguin, 1991; Flamingo, 1993), is by Peter Ford, who traveled by foot and boat along the Caribbean Coast from Belize to Panama.

Time Among the Maya: Travels in Belize, Guatemala, and Mexico, by Ronald Wright, is a thoughtful account of numerous journeys made in recent years among the descendants of the ancient Maya and will certainly help you to 'feel' Mayan culture as you travel the region.

History

Friar Diego de Landa's book *Yucatán Before and After the Conquest* can be bought in a number of bookstores and shops at archaeological sites in the Yucatán. Landa played a major role in wiping out Mayan culture and civilization, including the burning of many Mayan texts. But he also wrote a superb book describing Mayan ceremonial festivals, daily life, history, clothing, human sacrifices, the Spanish conquest and more.

Ambivalent Conquests: Maya and Spaniard in Yucatan, 1517-1570, by Inga Clendinnen, covers the formative years of the relationship between the Maya and their Spanish overlords, years that set the tone of Indian-Hispanic relations for the rest of Yucatecan history.

The multivolume *Handbook of Middle American Indians*, edited by Robert Wauchope, is an encyclopedic work that covers both the pre-Hispanic and more recent stages of Indian history and culture in great detail.

Culture, Art & Architecture

The basic text of Mayan religion is the *Popol Vuh*, which recounts the Mayan creation myths. A version easily available in Guatemala is *Popol Vuh: Ancient Stories of the Quiche Indians of Guatemala*, by Albertina Saravia E.

The Flayed God: The Mythology of Mesoamerica, by Roberta H Markman and Peter T Markman, is a fascinating exploration of the religious and cultural myths of the Maya from the earliest times to the present.

Maya Missions: Exploring the Spanish Colonial Churches of Yucatan, by Richard and Rosalind Perry, is an excellent guide to the more prominent fortresslike churches of the Yucatán. Order it through your bookstore or from the publisher: Espadaña Press,

PO Box 31067, Santa Barbara, CA 93130, USA; www.colonial-mexico.com.

The Blood of Kings: Dynasty & Ritual in Maya Art, by Linda Schele and Mary Ellen Miller, is a heavily illustrated guide to the art and culture of the Mayan period with particular emphasis on sacrifices, bloodletting, torture of captives, the ball game and other macabre aspects of Mayan culture. The illustrated analyses of Mayan art are fascinating.

The incredibly complex and portentous Mayan calendrical system makes a fascinating study. *The Book of the Year: Middle American Calendrical Systems*, by Munro S Edmonson, is an excellent but fairly expensive book.

NEWSPAPERS & MAGAZINES

Some major US newspapers such as *USA Today*, the *Miami Herald* and the *Los Angeles Times* are sold in luxury-hotel newsstands and some big-city and airport bookshops in the region. *Newsweek* and *Time* magazines are also sometimes available, along with *The New York Times* and the *Wall Street Journal*. The better hotel shops also have good selections of European newspapers and magazines in French, German, Italian and Spanish.

The quarterly *Mundo Maya* (Maya World) contains articles in Spanish and English about the Mayan culture and natural attractions found in the Mayan-populated regions of Mexico, Belize, Honduras, Guatemala and El Salvador. The current edition of this excellent magazine can be read online at www.mayadiscovery.com, and back issues and upcoming issues can also be ordered via the website.

RADIO & TV

Local radio broadcasting, both AM and FM, is all in Spanish except in Belize (where it's in English) and in Cancún, where a few hours of English programming are broadcast each day. In the evening you may be able to pick up US stations on the AM band.

Many mid-range hotel rooms in the Yucatán and Guatemala have TV sets, often with satellite hookups that can receive some

Internet Resources

The World Wide Web is a rich resource for travelers. You can research your trip, hunt down bargain airfares, book hotels, check on weather conditions or chat with locals and other travelers about the best places to visit (or avoid!).

There's no better place to start your Web explorations than the Lonely Planet website (www.lonelyplanet.com). Here you'll find succinct summaries on traveling to most places on earth, postcards from other travelers and the Thorn Tree bulletin board, where you can ask questions before you go or dispense advice when you get back. You can also find travel news and updates to many of our most popular guidebooks, and the subWWWay section links you to the most useful travel resources elsewhere on the Web.

Information on country-specific websites can be found in the respective Facts for the Visitor chapters of this book. Other general sites worth noting include:

Mundo Maya Online www.mayadiscovery.com – features articles about topics of interest in the Mayan lands of Mexico, Guatemala, Belize, Honduras and El Salvador. Via the website, you can also order a subscription to the quarterly print version of the magazine.

US Department of Health, Centers for Disease Control & Prevention www.cdc.gov/travel – provides region-specific information on health risks and preventative health measures (including recommended vaccinations).

US Department of State, Bureau of Consular Affairs travel.state.gov – lists up-to-date travel warnings, consular services available to Americans abroad, passport and visa information and links to numerous other resources for travelers.

Magic Bus.com www.magic-bus.com/buslinks.shtml – offers regional bus schedules, other transportation information and related links.

You might also take a look at:

Arenal Lesbigay Homepage www.indiana.edu/~arenal/ingles.html

Explore Worldwide Ltd www.explore.co.uk

International Travel Maps & Books www.itmb.com

Journey Latin America www.journeylatinamerica.co.uk

La Ruta Maya Online larutamayaonline.com

Latin American Travel Consultants www.amerispan.com/lata

South American Explorers www.samexplo.org

US stations. Most popular are ESPN (the sports channel) and UNO (the Spanish-language US network). Spanish-language programming includes hours and hours of talk shows and soap operas, some sports and reruns of old US movies dubbed in Spanish. In Belize, the local TV station broadcasts in English.

PHOTOGRAPHY & VIDEO

Camera stores, pharmacies and hotels are the most common outlets for buying film. Be suspicious of film that is being sold at prices lower than what you might pay in the US or Canada – it is often outdated.

Print film, both B&W and color, is easily found, though you may not find the brand you like without a search. Processing is not particularly expensive and can be done in a day or two, even quicker in the large cities. Print film prices are US$1 or US$2 higher than in the USA.

Slide (transparency; in Spanish, *diapositivo*) film is more difficult to find outside of Cancún, especially in smaller locales. Kodachrome is not sold in these countries because they have no facilities to process it, though you may some of the various E-6 process films (Ektachrome, Velvia etc), at premium prices.

Restrictions & Etiquette

Most people in the region do not mind having their photographs taken – if you ask first. Just as you might not enjoy having someone photograph you without your permission, you should ask permission before opening fire.

Increasingly, you will be asked to pay for the photo. This is especially true in areas that see heavy tourist traffic. Many locals have grown tired of being treated like objects of art or zoo animals and have taken the attitude that they deserve compensation for being 'framed.'

If you intend to take lots of photos of people, consider bringing a Polaroid camera in addition to your 35mm camera. Presenting strangers with photos of themselves can ease the tension they may feel about being photographed.

Of course one must use common sense and decency: Ask permission before snapping away at anything military, religious or close-up personal. And keep in mind that there are a few locations – the village of San Juan Chamula outside San Cristóbal de Las Casas, other villages nearby, the church of Santo Tomás in Chichicastenango – where photography is forbidden. If local people make any sign of being offended, you should put your camera away and apologize immediately, both out of decency and for your own safety.

It is illegal to take pictures in Mexican airports and of police stations and penal institutions. Also, many police officers do not like being photographed, and they have the authority to arrest you for photographing them without authorization. When in doubt, it's best to ask before you shoot.

Video

Video cameras and tapes are widely available at photo supply stores in the largest cities and in towns that receive many foreign visitors. Prices are significantly higher than you may be used to in the US, Canada or Europe. VHS is standard.

Be forewarned that there's a 'video fee' at many of the ruins and other attractions. In some instances, the user will be expected to pay US$20 or more if he/she intends to use a video camera while at a tourist site.

TIME

North American central standard time (GMT/UTC minus six hours) is the basis of time throughout the region. Belize and Guatemala do not observe daylight saving (or 'summer') time. Mexico does, though some villages throughout the country refuse to comply with the time change. In the Yucatán, the main areas of resistance are villages around Felipe Carrillo Puerto.

ELECTRICITY

Outlets (points) take the same flat-pronged plugs as in the USA and Canada. Electrical current is also the same: 115V to 125V, 60Hz.

WEIGHTS & MEASURES

Guatemala and Mexico use the metric system. For conversion information, see the inside back cover of this book. Because of the great commercial influence of the USA, you may find that ounces *(onzas)*, pounds *(libras)*, feet *(pies)*, miles *(millas)* and US gallons *(galones)* are used informally, at village markets for instance. Officially, however, everything's metric.

In Belize, both systems are used – and confused. For example, your rental car odometer and speedometer will be in kilometers and kilometers per hour, but the few road signs indicate distances in miles. When you see quarts and gallons, they are the smaller American measure, not the larger British Imperial measure.

LAUNDRY

The largest cities have laundries and dry-cleaning shops where you can leave your clothes to be cleaned. Often you can have your laundry back in a day; dry cleaning usually takes at least overnight. Addresses of convenient laundries are given in this guidebook for each city that has them.

TOILETS

In a hot climate, where your body loses lots of moisture through perspiration, you have less frequent need of toilets. This is good, as public toilets are virtually nonexistent. Use the ones in cafes, restaurants, your hotel and at archaeological sites.

Don't throw anything into the toilet, including toilet paper. The plumbing in most places in the region cannot handle toilet paper and will clog; if there's a trash receptacle anywhere near the toilet, put your used paper in it. If there's no basket, and paper is tossed on the floor, you can follow suit. Toilet paper is rarely provided, so always carry your own.

HEALTH
Predeparture Preparations

Ideally, you should make sure you're as healthy as possible before you start traveling. If you're going for more than a couple of weeks, make sure your teeth are OK; there are lots of places in the region where a visit to the dentist would be the last thing you'd want to do. If you wear glasses, take a spare pair and your prescription.

Health Insurance Purchasing a travel insurance policy to cover medical problems (as well as theft or other loss) is a wise idea. Travel agencies sell them; STA Travel and other student travel organizations usually offer good values.

Some policies specifically exclude 'dangerous activities,' which can include scuba diving, motorcycling, even trekking. If such activities are on your agenda, you don't want that sort of policy.

Medical Kit Take a small first-aid kit with adhesive bandages, a sterilized gauze bandage, cotton, a thermometer, tweezers and scissors.

Consider taking these: an antiseptic agent (Dettol or Betadine), burn cream (Caladryl is good for sunburn, minor burns and itchy bites), aspirin, ibuprofen or acetaminophen (paracetamol) for pain or fever, and insect repellent containing DEET. Antihistamine (such as Benadryl) is useful for colds and allergies; it will also ease the itch from insect bites and help prevent motion sickness. A rehydration mixture for treatment of severe diarrhea is particularly important if you're traveling with children.

Don't forget a full supply of any medication you're already taking; the prescription might be difficult to match abroad. If you're traveling off the beaten track, it may be wise to include antimalarial medication and antibiotics, which must be prescribed – make sure you carry the prescription with you.

Illness Prevention Specific immunizations are not normally required for travel anywhere in Guatemala, Mexico or Belize. All the same, it's a good idea to be up to date on your tetanus, typhoid-paratyphoid and polio immunizations; if you were born in the US after 1957, you should also make sure that you're immune to measles (ask your doctor). You should also get vaccinated against hepatitis A. And you'll need a yellow fever certificate to enter the region if, within the last six months, you have been to a country where yellow fever is present.

Food spoils easily in the tropics, mosquitoes roam freely, and sanitation is not always the best, so you must take special care to protect yourself from illness. The most important steps you can take are to be careful about what you eat and drink, stay away from mosquitoes (or at least make them stay away from you) and practice safe sex. These measures are particularly important for adventurous travelers who enjoy getting off the beaten track, mingling with the locals and trekking into remote areas.

As you read the following catalog of potential illnesses, bear in mind that many people have traveled throughout the region staying in the cheapest accommodations and eating every manner of food without getting anything more serious than traveler's diarrhea.

If you come down with a serious illness, be careful to find a competent doctor and don't be afraid to get second opinions. You may want to telephone your doctor at home for consultation as well. In some cases it may be best to end your trip and fly home for treatment, difficult as this may be.

Basic Rules

Food & Water Food can be contaminated by bacteria, viruses and/or parasites when it is harvested, shipped, handled, washed (if the water is contaminated) or prepared. Cooking, peeling and/or washing food in pure water is the way to get rid of the germs. To avoid gastrointestinal diseases, avoid salads, uncooked vegetables and unpasteurized milk or milk products (including cheese). Make sure the food you eat has been freshly cooked and is still hot. Do not eat raw or rare meat, fish or shellfish. Peel fruit yourself with clean hands and a clean knife.

As for beverages, don't trust any water except that which has been boiled for at least five minutes (longer if you're much above sea level), has been treated with purifiers or comes in an unopened bottle labeled *agua purificada*. Most hotels have large bottles of purified water from which you can fill your carafe or canteen; some will put smaller capped bottles of purified water in your room. Local people may drink the water from the tap or the well, or rainwater from the cistern, and their systems may be used to it; or they may have chronic gastric diseases! Inexpensive purified water is available at supermarkets, grocery stores, liquor stores and often from street vendors.

Use only pure water for drinking, washing food, brushing your teeth and making ice. Tea, coffee and other hot beverages should be made with boiled water. If the waiter swears that the ice in your drink is made from agua purificada, you may feel you can take a chance with it.

Canned or bottled carbonated beverages, including carbonated water, are usually safe, as are beer, wine and liquor.

If you plan to travel off the beaten track, you may have to purify water yourself. Water purification drops or tablets containing tetraglycine hydroperiodide (Globaline, Potable Aqua and Coghlan's are some brand names) are sold in pharmacies and US sporting-goods stores such as REI (☎ 800-426-4840), LL Bean (☎ 800-441-5713) and Campmor (☎ 800-526-4784). Alternatively, you can use a 2% tincture of iodine.

In Mexico or Guatemala ask for *gotas* (drops) or *pastillas* (tablets) *para purificar agua* (for purifying water) in pharmacies and supermarkets. For tincture of iodine, four drops per liter or quart of clear water is the recommended dosage; let the treated water stand for 20 to 30 minutes before drinking. Vigorously boiling water for five minutes is another way to purify the water, but at high altitudes water boils at a lower temperature, so germs are less likely to be killed. Boil it for longer in those environments.

Protection Against Mosquitoes Many serious tropical diseases are spread by infected mosquitoes. If you protect yourself against mosquito bites, your travels will be both safer and more enjoyable.

Some mosquitoes feed during the day, others at night. In general, they're most bothersome when the sun is not too hot, in the evening and early morning, and on overcast days. There are many more mosquitoes in lowland and coastal regions and in the countryside than there are in cities or in highland areas, and many more during the rainy season (May to October) than during the rest of the year. Avoid going to mosquito-infested places during these times and seasons if you can.

You can avoid many mosquito bites by:

- wearing light-colored clothing, long pants and long-sleeved shirts
- using mosquito repellents containing the compound DEET on exposed areas
- avoiding highly scented perfume or aftershave
- making sure your room has properly fitting mosquito screens over the windows
- using a mosquito net (it may be worth taking your own)

Use insect repellent that has at least a 20% but no more than a 30% concentration of DEET (N,N diethyl-metatoluamide) on clothing and exposed skin. Repellents with higher concentrations of DEET work longer but are also more likely to cause allergic reactions.

It's best to buy repellent before leaving home as repellents bought in Mexico, Guatemala or Belize may not have this most effective ingredient. To avoid reactions to the repellent, apply it sparingly only to exposed skin or to clothing, don't inhale the stuff or get it in your eyes or mouth or on broken or irritated skin, and wash it off soon after you enter a mosquito-free area.

Be particularly careful with children: Don't apply repellent to infants or young children; don't put it on hands, which may be put in the mouth or eyes; use as little as possible; and wash it off as soon as you're out of mosquito country.

Medical Problems & Treatment

Diarrhea A change of water, food or climate can all cause the runs, but diarrhea caused by contaminated food or water can be more serious. Despite precautions, you may still have a mild bout of traveler's diarrhea (TD, known informally among travelers as Montezuma's revenge or *turista*), but a few rushed toilet trips with no other symptoms are not generally indicative of a serious problem.

Moderate diarrhea, involving half a dozen loose movements in a day, is more of a nuisance. Dehydration is the main danger with any diarrhea, particularly for children, in whom it can occur quite quickly, and fluid replacement is the mainstay of management. Soda water, weak black tea with a little sugar, or soft drinks allowed to go flat and diluted 50% with water are all good.

With severe diarrhea, a rehydrating solution is necessary to replace lost minerals and salts. Commercially available oral rehydration salts are useful; add the contents of one packet to a liter of boiled or bottled water. In an emergency, you can make up a solution of six teaspoons of sugar and a half teaspoon of salt to a liter of boiled or bottled water. Stick to a bland diet as you recover.

Lomotil or Imodium can be used to bring relief from the symptoms, though they do not cure the problem. Use these drugs only if absolutely necessary – for example, if you *must* travel. Do not use them if you have a high fever or are severely dehydrated.

In the following situations, antibiotics may be necessary (and gut-paralyzing drugs such as Imodium or Lomotil should be avoided):

- watery diarrhea with blood and mucus
- watery diarrhea with fever and lethargy
- persistent diarrhea for more than five days
- severe diarrhea, if it is logistically difficult to stay in one place

Remember that you can walk into a pharmacy in Mexico, Guatemala or Belize and buy medicines – often without a prescription – that might be banned for good reason in your home country. Well-meaning but incompetent doctors or pharmacists might recommend certain medicines for gastrointestinal ailments, but such medicines may be worse than no medicine at all. Though they may bring some relief from the symptoms of TD, they may cause other sorts of harm such as neurological damage. Medicines called halogenated hydroxyquinoline derivatives are among these, and may bear the chemical names clioquinol or iodoquinol, or brand names EnteroVioform, Mexaform or Intestopan, or something similar. It's best not to take these medicines without consulting a trusted physician, preferably your regular doctor at home.

Diarrhea can also be a sign of giardiasis, dysentery, cholera or typhoid; see the following sections on those diseases.

Giardiasis The parasite causing this intestinal disorder is present in contaminated water. The symptoms are stomach cramps, nausea, a bloated stomach, frequent gas and watery, foul-smelling diarrhea. Giardiasis can appear several weeks after you have been exposed to the parasite. The symptoms may disappear for a few days and then return; this can continue for several weeks. Tinidazole, known as Fasigyn, and metronidazole (Flagyl) are recommended treatments.

Dysentery This serious illness is caused by contaminated food or water and is characterized by severe diarrhea, often with blood or mucus in the stool.

Bacillary dysentery is characterized by a high fever and rapid onset of illness; headache, vomiting and stomach pains are also symptoms. It generally does not last longer than a week, but it is highly contagious.

Amoebic dysentery ('amoebas') is often more gradual in onset, with cramping abdominal pain and vomiting less likely; fever may not be present. It will persist until treated and can recur and cause long-term health problems.

A stool test is necessary to diagnose which kind of dysentery you have, so you should seek medical help urgently. In an emergency, norfloxacin 400mg twice daily for three days or ciprofloxacin 500mg twice daily for five days can be used as presumptive treatment for bacillary dysentery.

For amebic dysentery, metronidazole (Flagyl) can be used as presumptive treatment in an emergency. An alternative is Fasigyn. Avoid alcohol during treatment and for 48 hours afterward.

Heat Exhaustion & Heatstroke In hot regions, exercising excessively or failing to replace lost fluids and electrolytes can result in heat exhaustion, characterized by dizziness, weakness, headaches, nausea and profuse sweating. Salt tablets or rehydration formulas may help, but rest and shade are essential.

Heatstroke is more serious and can be fatal. It results from prolonged, continuous exposure to high temperatures. In this condition the victim sweats very little or not at all and has a high body temperature (39°C to 41°C, or 102°F to 106°F). Where sweating has ceased, the skin becomes flushed and red. Severe, throbbing headaches and lack of coordination will occur. The victim will become delirious or convulse. Hospitalization is essential, but meanwhile get victims

out of the sun, remove their clothing, cover them with a wet sheet or towel and fan them continually.

Protect yourself against heat-related diseases by taking special care to drink lots of fluids. If you urinate infrequently and in small amounts, you're not drinking enough fluids. If you feel tired and have a headache, you're not drinking enough fluids. Don't just drink when you're thirsty; make it a habit to drink frequently, whether you're thirsty or not. It's so easy to prevent dehydration that you should feel foolish if you succumb to it.

Alcohol, coffee and tea are diuretics; they make you urinate and lose fluids. They are not a cure for dehydration, they're part of the problem. Drink pure water, fruit juices and soft drinks instead; go easy on the beer. Salty food is good to eat in hot climates as the salt helps your body to retain fluids.

To further protect against the heat, don't overdo it. Take it easy climbing pyramids and trekking through the jungle. Wear light cotton clothing that breathes and cools you or synthetics designed to do the same; wear a hat and sunglasses. Allow yourself frequent rest breaks in the shade, and give your body a chance to balance itself. Use sunblock to prevent bad sunburn. Be doubly cautious if you spend time near or on the water, as the sun's glare from sand and water can double your exposure. You may want to swim or go boating wearing a T-shirt and hat.

Fungal Infections Hot weather fungal infections are most likely to occur on the scalp, between the toes or fingers (athlete's foot), in the groin (jock itch or crotch rot) and on the body (ringworm). You get ringworm (which is a fungal infection, not a worm) from infected animals or by walking on damp areas, like shower floors.

Other Illnesses
Though you're unlikely to contract anything more than an unpleasant bout of traveler's diarrhea, you should be informed about the symptoms and treatments of these other diseases just in case.

Cholera This serious disease now seems epidemic in Mexico and Central America. Like dysentery, it is a disease of poor sanitation and spreads quickly in areas, urban and rural, where sewage and water supplies are rudimentary. It can also be spread in foods that are uncooked, such as the popular *ceviche*, which is made from marinated raw fish, as well as salads and raw vegetables.

The disease is characterized by a sudden onset of acute diarrhea with 'rice water' stools, vomiting, muscular cramps and extreme weakness. You need medical help – but first treat for dehydration, which can be extreme. If there is an appreciable delay in getting to the hospital, begin taking tetracycline (adults one 250mg capsule four times a day; children over eight 125mg; children under eight 80mg). The disease does respond to treatment if caught early.

Dengue Fever Symptoms include the fast onset of high fever, severe frontal headache and pain in muscles and joints; there may be nausea and vomiting, and a skin rash may develop about three to five days after the first symptoms, spreading from the torso to arms, legs and face. It is possible to have subclinical dengue (that is, a 'mild' case of it) and also to contract dengue hemorrhagic fever (DHF), a potentially fatal disease.

Dengue is spread by mosquitoes. Risk of contraction, though low for the average traveler, is highest during the summer (July to September), several hours after daybreak and before dusk, and on overcast days. The disease occurs mostly in populated areas, especially in urban centers.

There are four different dengue viruses but no medicines to combat them. The disease is usually self-limiting, which means that the body cures itself. If you are generally healthy and have a healthy immune system, the disease may be unpleasant but is rarely serious. To guard against getting dengue, see the earlier section on Protection against Mosquitoes.

Hepatitis Hepatitis is a general term for inflammation of the liver. It has many causes; drugs, alcohol and contaminated injections are but a few.

The letters A, B, C, D, E and a rumored G identify specific agents that cause viral hepatitis, which is an infection of the liver that can lead to jaundice (yellow skin), fever, lethargy and digestive problems. It can have no symptoms at all, with the infected person not knowing he or she has the disease. Hepatitis D, E and G are fairly rare (so far), and following the same precautions as for A, B and C should be all that's necessary to avoid them.

Hepatitis A is common in countries with poor sanitation. It's transmitted by contaminated water or food, including shellfish contaminated by sewage. Taking care with what you eat and drink can go a long way toward preventing hepatitis A, but it's a very infectious virus, so additional precautions are recommended. Protection can be provided in two ways – either with the antibody immunoglobulin or with the vaccine Havrix 1440, which provides long-term immunity (possibly longer than 10 years) after an initial injection and boosters at six and 12 months. Immunoglobulin should not be given until at least 10 days after the administration of any other vaccine you'll be getting before traveling. It does not provide complete protection against hepatitis, and it is at its most effective in the first few weeks after administration. Havrix takes about three weeks to provide good protection.

The symptoms of hepatitis A are fever, chills, headache, fatigue, aches and pains, followed by loss of appetite, nausea, vomiting, abdominal pain, dark urine, light-colored feces and jaundiced skin. The whites of the eyes may turn yellow. You should seek medical advice, but in general there is not much you can do apart from rest, drink lots of fluids, eat lightly and avoid fatty foods. People who have had hepatitis must forgo alcohol for six months after the illness.

Incidence of hepatitis B is fairly low in the region, and vaccination is not considered necessary. It's spread through contact with infected blood, blood products or bodily fluids – for example through sexual contact, unsterilized needles or blood transfusions. Other risk situations include getting a shave or tattoo or getting your ears pierced.

The symptoms are much the same as for hepatitis A, except that they are more severe and may lead to irreparable liver damage or even liver cancer. Although there is no treatment for hepatitis B, an effective prophylactic vaccine is readily available in most countries. The immunization schedule requires two injections at least a month apart followed by a third dose five months after the second. Persons who should receive a hepatitis B vaccination include anyone who anticipates contact with blood or other bodily secretions, either as a health-care worker or through sexual contact with the local population, and particularly those who intend to stay in the region for a long period of time.

Hepatitis C is a concern because it seems to lead to liver disease more rapidly than does hepatitis B. The virus is spread by contact with blood, usually via contaminated transfusions or shared needles. Avoiding both is the only means of prevention, as there is no available vaccine.

Leishmaniasis This group of parasitic diseases is transmitted by sand flies, which are found in many parts of Central America. Cutaneous leishmaniasis affects the skin tissue, causing ulceration and disfigurement, and visceral leishmaniasis affects the internal organs. Seek medical advice, as laboratory testing is required for diagnosis and correct treatment. Avoiding sand-fly bites is the best precaution. Bites are usually painless, itchy and yet another reason to cover up and apply repellent.

Malaria This is the one disease that everyone fears and the one about which you must make an important decision.

Symptoms might include jaundice (a yellow cast to the skin and/or eyes), general malaise, headaches, fever and chills, bed sweats and anemia. Symptoms of the disease may appear as early as eight days after infection, or as late as several months after you return from your trip. You can contract malaria even if you've taken medicines to protect yourself.

Malaria is spread by mosquitoes that bite mostly between dusk and dawn. In this part of the world it is primarily present in rural areas. Risk of infection is low in the major resort areas and in the highlands, and lower in the dry season (October to May) than in the rainy season (May to October). But it is fair to say that somewhere in the region you will encounter mosquitoes. They may or may not carry infectious diseases, but the best way to protect yourself against malaria is to protect yourself against mosquito bites (see Protection Against Mosquitoes, earlier in this section).

You can also take medicines to protect against malarial infection, usually chloroquine phosphate (Aralen) or hydroxychloroquine sulfate (Plaquenil), though other medicines may be indicated for specific individuals. (To date, there have been no reports of chloroquine-resistant strains of malaria in Mexico, Guatemala or Belize.) You must consult a doctor on the use of these medicines, and get a prescription to buy them. Begin taking the medicine *one or two weeks before you arrive* in a malarial area, continue taking it while you're there, and also for a month after you leave the area, according to your doctor's instructions. Taking medicine does not absolutely guarantee that you will not contract malaria, though.

The choice you must make is whether to take preventive medicine, which can have unpleasant side effects. As an adventurous

traveler, you are more at risk than a person who buys a package tour to Cancún. Although most visitors to Mexico, Guatemala and Belize do not take malaria medicine, and most do not get malaria, you must decide for yourself.

Talk to your doctor. Check with the Health Information Sources listed at the end of this section. Call a hospital or clinic that specializes in tropical diseases. Whether or not you take medicine, do be careful to protect yourself against mosquito bites.

Rabies The rabies virus is spread through bites by infected animals, or (rarely) through broken skin (scratches, licks) or the mucous membranes (as from breathing rabid-bat-contaminated air in a cave, for instance). Typical signs of a rabid animal are mad or uncontrolled behavior, inability to eat, biting at anything and everything and frothing at the mouth.

If any animal (but especially a dog) bites you, assume you have been exposed to rabies until you are certain this is not the case – there are no second chances. First, immediately wash the wound with lots of soap and water – this is very important! If it is possible and safe to do so, try to capture the animal alive, then give it to local health officials who can determine whether or not it's rabid. Begin rabies immunization shots as soon as possible; if you are taking anti-malarial medicine, be sure to mention this to the doctor because antimalarial medicines can interfere with the effectiveness of rabies vaccine. Rabies is a potentially fatal disease, but it can be cured by prompt and proper treatment.

Sexually Transmitted Diseases Sexual contact with an infected sexual partner spreads these diseases. While abstinence is the only 100% preventative, using condoms and otherwise observing safe-sex procedures is usually effective.

Gonorrhea and syphilis are the most common of these diseases; sores, blisters or rashes around the genitals, discharges or pain when urinating are common symp-

toms. Symptoms may be less marked or not observed at all in women.

Syphilis symptoms eventually disappear completely, but the disease continues and can cause severe problems in later years. The treatment of gonorrhea and syphilis is by antibiotics.

There are numerous other sexually transmitted diseases, for most of which effective treatment is available. However, there is no cure for herpes and there is also no cure for AIDS.

AIDS can be spread through infected blood transfusions; most developing countries cannot afford to screen blood for transfusions properly. AIDS can also be spread by dirty needles – vaccinations, acupuncture and tattooing can potentially be as dangerous as intravenous drug use if the equipment is not clean. If you do need an injection, it may be a good idea to buy a new syringe from a pharmacy and ask the doctor to use it.

Tetanus This potentially fatal disease is found in undeveloped tropical areas. It is difficult to treat, but preventable with immunization. Tetanus occurs when a wound becomes infected by a germ that lives in the feces of animals or people, so clean all cuts, punctures and animal bites well. Tetanus is also known as lockjaw, and its first symptom may be discomfort in swallowing, or stiffening of the jaw and neck; this is followed by painful convulsions of the jaw and body.

Typhoid Fever This serious disease is spread by contaminated food and beverages and has symptoms similar to those of traveler's diarrhea. If you get it, you should have close supervision by a competent doctor and perhaps spend a short time in the hospital. Inoculation can give you some protection but is not 100% effective. If diagnosed early, typhoid can be treated effectively.

Hospitals & Clinics

Almost every town and city now has either a hospital or medical clinic and Red Cross (Cruz Roja) emergency facilities, all of which are indicated by road signs that show a red cross. Hospitals are generally inexpensive for typical ailments (diarrhea, dysentery) and minor injuries (cuts and sprains). Clinics are often too understaffed and overburdened with local problems to be of much help, but they are linked to emergency services by a government radio network.

If you must use these services, try to ascertain the competence of the staff treating you. Compare their diagnoses and prescriptions to the information in this section. If you have questions, call your embassy and get a referral for a doctor, or call home and have your own doctor advise you.

Most hospitals have to be paid at the time of service, and doctors usually require immediate cash payment. Some facilities may accept credit cards. It's always a good idea to ask before service is rendered.

By the way, Guatemalans and Belizeans with serious illnesses often go to Mexican cities (Chetumal, Mérida, Cancún, Villahermosa or even Mexico City) for treatment in better medical facilities. People from all three countries look upon Miami, New Orleans and Houston as the medical centers of last resort.

Women's Health

Gynecological problems, poor diet, lowered resistance due to the use of antibiotics for stomach upsets and even contraceptive pills can lead to vaginal infections when traveling in hot climates. Wearing skirts or loose-fitting trousers or cotton underwear will help to prevent infections.

Yeast infections, characterized by a rash, itch and discharge, can be treated with a vinegar or lemon-juice douche, or with yogurt. Nystatin suppositories are the usual medical prescription. Trichomoniasis is a more serious infection; symptoms are a discharge and a burning sensation when urinating. Male sexual partners must also be treated, and if a vinegar-water douche is not effective medical attention should be sought. Metronidazole (Flagyl) is the prescribed drug.

Most miscarriages occur during the first three months of pregnancy, so this is the most risky time to travel. The last three months should also be spent within reasonable distance of good medical care, as serious problems can develop at this time. Pregnant women should avoid all unnecessary medication, but vaccinations and malarial prophylactics should still be taken where possible. Additional care should be taken to prevent illness and particular attention should be paid to diet and nutrition.

Health Information Sources

In the USA, the Centers for Disease Control and Prevention (CDC) maintains a toll-free Travelers Hotline (☎ 877-394-8747). General health information can be obtained by calling ☎ 800-311-3545. The CDC's website offers good information and guidance for travelers: www.cdc.gov/travel. In the UK, the Medical Advisory Service for Travellers Abroad (MASTA) of the London School of Hygiene and Tropical Medicine has a Travellers' Health Line, ☎ 0906-8-224100, from which you can order 'Health Briefs' mailed to you for up to six countries at a time. Calls are charged at 60p per minute. MASTA's website is at www.masta.org. In Australia, try the Traveller's Medicine and Vaccination Centre in Sydney (toll-free ☎ 1300-65-88-44, www.tmvc.com.au).

WOMEN TRAVELERS

In general, the local men aren't great believers in the equality of the sexes, and women alone have to expect numerous attempts to chat them up. It's commonly believed that foreign women without male companions are easy game for local men. This can get tiresome at times; the best discouragement is a cool, unsmiling but polite initial response and a consistent, firm 'No.'

Avoid situations in which you might find yourself alone with one or more strange men, at remote archaeological sites, on empty city streets or on secluded stretches of beach.

GAY & LESBIAN TRAVELERS

Anything goes in Cancún, but throughout the rest of the region machismo rules, and the quiet, private enjoyment of your preference is the best policy.

Gay and lesbian travelers may want to contact the International Gay Travelers Association (☎ 800-448-8550), PO Box 4974, Key West, FL 33041, USA, to locate a travel agent familiar with gay and gay-friendly tours and lodgings.

DISABLED TRAVELERS

Much of Cancún can be negotiated by wheelchair, and sidewalk ramps are found in central Mérida, but in general the unstandardized sidewalks, streets and colonial buildings make access difficult. Mobility International USA (☎ 541-343-1284, www.miusa.org), PO Box 10767, Eugene, OR 97440, USA, runs exchange programs and publishes *A World of Options: A Guide to International Educational Exchange, Community Service & Travel for People with Disabilities*. In Europe, Mobility International (☎ 02-201-5608, mobint@arcadis.be) is at Boulevard Baudouin 18, Brussels B-1000, Belgium.

The Council on International Educational Exchange (CIEE; ☎ 888-268-6245, 212-822-2600, www.ciee.org), 205 E 42nd St, New York, NY 10017, USA, can help disabled people interested in working, studying or volunteering outside their home countries.

An excellent website for disabled travelers to check is www.access-able.com.

SENIOR TRAVELERS

Senior travelers should pay particular heed to the medical advice given above on the dangers of dehydration and exposure to excessive heat and sun.

The American Association of Retired Persons (AARP; ☎ 800-424-3410), 601 E St NW, Washington, DC 20049, USA, is an advocacy group for Americans 50 years and older and a good resource for travel bargains. Annual membership costs US$8.

Also in the USA, membership in the National Council of Senior Citizens (☎ 301-578-8800), 8403 Colesville Rd, Silver Spring, MD 20910, USA, gives access to discount information and travel-related advice.

TRAVEL WITH CHILDREN

Children are highly regarded throughout the region and can often break down the barriers and open the doors to local hospitality. For a wealth of good ideas, pick up a copy of Lonely Planet's *Travel with Children*, by Maureen Wheeler.

DANGERS & ANNOYANCES
Safety

Guatemala, and to a lesser extent, Belize and Mexico, demand caution. Up-to-date travel advisories are available from the US Department of State's website at www.travel.state.gov/travel_warnings.html. Those without Internet access can telephone the department's Office of American Citizens Services at ☎ 202-647-5225. British subjects can contact the UK Foreign Office's Travel Advisory Service (☎ 020-7238-4503, 193.114.50.10/travel).

The 36-year-long guerrilla war in Guatemala is supposedly over, but this danger has been replaced by an alarming rise in the general crime rate. There have been incidents of rape, robbery, car-jacking and even murder of foreign tourists. These incidents occur at random and are not predictable. See the Guatemala Facts for the Visitor chapter for specific warnings.

In Belize, the problem is mostly petty theft and robbery in Belize City. See that section for details. Generally, Mexico is quite safe, though you must take normal precautions against pickpockets, purse-snatchers and thieves. Special caution is necessary when traveling in eastern and southern Campeche state, especially on the road east from Escárcega, which has been the scene of repeated robberies of buses, mostly at night though also in daylight. The road between Palenque and San Cristóbal de Las Casas via Ocosingo has also been subject to roadblocks by bandits who say they are guerrillas resisting the government. They make you pay a 'tax,' which may be small or may equal all of your valuables. Your best bet here is to travel these roads in the morning with a major bus company.

Will you run into trouble? No one can say. Tens of thousands of foreign visitors enjoy the incomparable beauties of the region and the friendliness of its people every year, the huge majority without untoward incidents of any kind. But then there are the unlucky few.

Your best defenses against trouble are up-to-date information and reasonable caution. You should make the effort to contact your government and inquire about current conditions and trouble spots, then follow the advice offered.

Robbery & Theft

Robbery is a danger in Guatemala City, Antigua, Chichicastenango and Belize City. Petty theft, particularly pocket-picking and purse-snatching, is also not unusual in cities, such as Mérida and Antigua, and in beach areas. Foreign tourists are particularly singled out for theft as they are presumed to be 'wealthy' and to be carrying valuables.

To protect yourself, take these common-sense precautions:

- Unless you have immediate need of them, leave most of your cash and traveler's checks, your passport, jewelry, airline tickets, credit cards, expensive watch, camera and other valuables in a sealed, signed envelope in your hotel's safe; obtain a receipt for the envelope. Virtually all hotels except the very cheapest provide a safe for guests' valuables. You may have to provide the envelope (buy some at a *papelería*, or stationery store). Your signature on the envelope and a receipt from the hotel clerk will help to ensure that hotel staff won't pilfer your things.

- Leaving valuable items in a locked suitcase in your hotel room is often safer than carrying them with you on the streets of Guatemala City.

- Have a money belt or a pouch on a string around your neck, place your remaining valuables in it and wear it *underneath your clothing*. You can carry a small amount of ready money in a pocket or bag.

- Be aware that any purse or bag in plain sight may be slashed or grabbed. Often two thieves work together, one cutting the strap, the other grabbing the bag in a lunge past you, even as you walk along a street or stand at a bus stop. At ticket counters in airports and bus stations, keep your bag between your feet, particularly when you're busy talking to a ticket agent.

- Be wary if anyone points out a foreign substance soiling your clothes. A ploy used increasingly by pickpockets (sometimes operating in teams) in many parts of the world is to distract the victim by 'accidentally' soiling him or her (with mustard, ice cream or the like), then helping to clean the victim off. In a variation on this ploy, a setup person will spit at or throw a noxious substance (such as dog shit) on the victim.

- Do not wander alone down empty city streets or in isolated areas, particularly at night.

- Do not leave any valuables visible in your vehicle when you park it in a city, unless it is in a guarded parking lot.

- On beaches and in the countryside, do not camp overnight in lonely places unless you can be sure it's safe.

- When paying for something, wait until all of the change has been counted out before picking it up. A favorite ruse of dishonest ticket clerks in particular is to hand over the change slowly, bit by bit, in the hope that you'll pick it up and go before you have it all.

There's little point in going to the police after a robbery unless your loss is insured, in which case you'll need a statement from the police to present to your insurance company. Outside of Belize, you'll probably have to communicate with them in Spanish, so if your own is poor take a more fluent speaker along. Say, *Yo quisiera poner una acta de un robo* (I'd like to report a robbery). This should make it clear that you merely want a piece of paper and aren't going to ask the police to do anything inconvenient like look for the thieves or attempt to recover your goods. With luck you should get the required piece of paper without too much trouble. You may have to write it up yourself, then present it for official stamp and signature.

LEGAL MATTERS

Police officers in these countries are sometimes (if not often) part of the problem rather than of the solution. The less you have to do with the law, the better.

Whatever you do, *don't* get involved in any way with illegal drugs: Don't buy or sell, use or carry, or associate with people who do – even if the locals seem to do so freely. As a foreigner, you are at a distinct disadvantage, and you may be set up by others. Drug laws in all of these countries are strict, and though enforcement may be uneven, penalties are severe.

PUBLIC HOLIDAYS & SPECIAL EVENTS

You will notice that Sunday is indeed a day of rest. Local people put on their best clothes, go to church, then spend the afternoon relaxing in the parks or strolling along the streets. Most businesses are closed, though some towns and villages have Sunday markets. Bus services may be curtailed. In the big resorts (Cancún, Cozumel, Isla Mujeres), Sundays are not observed so strictly.

The big national holidays are dictated by the Roman Catholic Church calendar. Christmas and Holy Week (Semana Santa),

leading up to Easter, are the region's most important events, though the celebrations are often as much Mayan shamanist in spirit as Christian. Hotels and buses are busy in Mexico and packed throughout Guatemala during Holy Week, especially in the towns that have particularly elaborate and colorful celebrations, such as Antigua.

January

Though the first two weeks of January see somewhat fewer hordes of tourists flocking to Cancún after the Christmas rush, the busy winter sun-and-fun season begins in earnest by mid-January. The weather is dry.

January 1 *New Year's Day* is a legal holiday in Mexico, Guatemala and Belize.

January 6 *Día de los Reyes Magos*, or Day of the Three Wise Men. Mexicans exchange Christmas presents on this day, in memory of the kings who brought gifts to baby Jesus.

Last Sunday in January *Día de la Inmaculada Concepción*, or Festival of the Immaculate Conception. In the Yucatán, nine days of devotions lead up to a secular festival including a dance that features a pig's head decorated with offerings of flowers, ribbons, bread, liquor and cigarettes. The traditional *jaranas* (Yucatecan dances) are usually performed as well. Note that Yucatecans also celebrate the Immaculate Conception on December 8, with the rest of the Catholic world.

February

The height of the tourist season, February sees most hotel rooms filled, most rental cars rented and most other activities in full swing.

Religious Holidays Late February or early March is when *Carnival (Carnaval* in Spanish) comes, preceding Lent, which starts 46 days before Easter. Carnival festivities are important throughout the region and include parades with fantastic floats, folk dancing, athletic competitions and everybody dressing up in costumes. Carnival begins in earnest on the weekend preceding the beginning of Lent. The final day of Carnival, known as *Martes de Carnaval* (Carnival Tuesday) or *Mardi Gras* (Fat Tuesday), is the last day on which observant Catholics are allowed to eat meat. Fat Tuesday is followed by *Ash Wednesday*, first of the 40 days of Lent leading up to Easter. On Ash Wednesday the Carnival party is over; fasting and prayers are the rule. Fat Tuesday falls on February 27, 2001; February 12, 2002; and February 24, 2004.

Religious procession, Guatemala

ERIC L WHEATER

February 5 *Constitution Day* is observed as a legal holiday in Mexico.

March

The tourist season continues at its height.

Religious Holidays *Carnival* (see February) usually falls in late February and early March, ending on Fat Tuesday, which is March 4, 2003.

March 9 *Baron Bliss Day* is a legal holiday in Belize. It honors the English nobleman who dropped anchor in Belizean waters in the 1920s, fell in love with the place and willed his considerable fortune (several million dollars) to the people of Belize. His bequest, held in trust and earning interest, has been funding worthwhile projects such as roads, schools, market halls etc ever since.

March 21 *Birthday of Benito Juárez*, a legal holiday in Mexico, celebrates the plucky Indian president who fought off the French intervention headed by Emperor Maximilian of Hapsburg in the 1860s. Also on March 20 or 21 is the vernal equinox, celebrated at Chichén Itzá as the sun creates the 'serpent' on the stairway of El Castillo.

April

The rainy season may start by late April. The few weeks before it does are often the hottest of the year. Everyone and everything swelters in the lowlands, while high in the mountains the weather is delightful.

Religious Holidays During *Holy Week (Semana Santa)*, the week before Easter Sunday, things are especially busy in the lands of the Maya, particularly in the towns of highland Guatemala. Holy Week begins on *Palm Sunday*, the Sunday before Easter, which is April 8, 2001; March 24, 2002; and April 13, 2003. *Good Friday, Holy Saturday* and *Easter Sunday* are official holidays in all three countries. In Guatemala *Holy Thursday* is a holiday. *Easter Monday* is a holiday in Belize.

April 21 *Queen's Birthday* is a legal holiday in Belize.

May

The rainy season begins, with heavy rains during the first few weeks of the season. No place escapes the rains, though they are heaviest to the west, in Chiapas and in Guatemala's highlands. In the Yucatán the rains may be limited to an hour's downpour in the afternoon.

May 1 *Labor Day* is a legal holiday in Mexico, Guatemala and Belize.

May 5 *Cinco de Mayo* is a legal holiday in Mexico commemorating the Battle of Puebla (1862), when Juárez' forces defeated French armies decisively, ending the European-sponsored occupation of Mexico.

May 24 *Commonwealth Day* is a legal holiday in Belize.

June

Rains may continue to be heavy during June.

June 30 *Army Day* and commemoration of the revolution of 1871 is observed as a legal holiday in Guatemala.

July

Rains are less bothersome, and the summer tourist season is in full swing. The hurricane season officially begins in July, though historically not many storms blow in this month. Summer visitors are usually more interested in archaeology and local culture than the sun-and-sea crowd that comes in winter.

August

The summer tourist season peaks, and rooms in some places may be difficult to find. Hurricane season comes to the Caribbean; this is one of the most active months for tropical storms.

August 15 *Festival of Guatemala* in Guatemala City; offices and shops close for the day.

August 29 *Postal Workers' Holiday*; all post offices close in Guatemala.

September

The summer crowd thins out, but it's still hot and humid. Hurricane season continues, and tropical storms are common.

Religious Holidays *El Señor de las Ampollas*, a festival in Mérida celebrating the 'Christ of the Blisters' in the cathedral, runs from the end of September into mid-October.

September 1 *President's Message to Congress* (Mexico).

September 10 *Belize National Day* is a legal holiday in Belize. It commemorates the Battle of St George's Caye fought in 1798 between British buccaneers and Spanish naval forces. The victory prize was Belize itself. The British won. Celebrations begin today and continue until Independence Day on the 21st.

September 15 *Independence Day* is a legal holiday in Guatemala.

September 16 *Independence Day* is a legal holiday in Mexico.

September 21 *Independence Day* is a legal holiday in Belize. The colony of British Honduras gained its independence from the UK in 1981.

October

The rains cease sometime during October, as does most danger of hurricanes. The number of visitors drops off, facilities are less crowded and many bargains are available. It's a great time to travel here.

Religious Holidays The festival of *las Ampollas* continues in Mérida (see September). In late October (18 to 28) Izamal (east of Mérida) is the place to be. The *Día del Cristo de Sitilpech* is celebrated as a venerated statue of Christ comes in procession from the village of Sitilpech to the great monastic church in Izamal. On the evenings of October 25 and 28, *jaranas* are performed in the plazas.

October 12 *Día de la Raza* (Day of the Race; Mexico); *Columbus Day* is a legal holiday in Belize.

October 20 Commemoration of the revolution of 1944 (Guatemala).

November

A low season for travel, it's wonderful for the person who wants uncrowded beaches, empty hotels, quiet restaurants, an unhurried pace and discount travel-service prices. Hurricane season officially comes to an end.

November 1 *Todos Santos*, or All Saints' Day (Guatemala). In Mexico, visitors place flowers on graves of the deceased and light candles in their memory. Celebrations and observances continue into November 2.

November 2 *Día de los Muertos*, or Day of the Dead (Mexico). Every cemetery in the country comes alive with festive visitors.

November 19 *Garífuna Settlement Day* (Belize) commemorates the Garinagus' (Black Caribs') arrival to settle in Belize in 1823.

November 20 *Anniversary of the Mexican Revolution* (Mexico).

December

Until the Christmas rush to the resorts begins, December is an excellent month to visit, with little rain, good temperatures, low prices and uncrowded facilities. The crowds begin to arrive – and prices rise substantially – after December 15.

December 8 *Día de la Inmaculada Concepción* (Feast of the Immaculate Conception) takes place in many towns of Mexico and Guatemala. The festivities in Izamal, Yucatán, are particularly lively.

December 11 to 12 *Day of the Virgin of Guadalupe*, a legal holiday in Mexico, honors the country's patron saint.

December 24 to 25 *Christmas Eve* is a holiday in the afternoon in Mexico and Guatemala; *Christmas Day* is a holiday in all three countries.

December 26 *Boxing Day* is a legal holiday in Belize.

December 31 *New Year's Eve* afternoon is a holiday in Guatemala.

ACTIVITIES
Swimming

The Caribbean Coast from Cancún and Isla Mujeres in the north to the Belizean cayes in the south is a paradise for water sports, including swimming, snorkeling, scuba diving, fishing, sailing and sailboarding.

Guatemala's Pacific Coast is relatively undeveloped, and water sports possibilities are not nearly as attractive as they are along the Caribbean. Likewise, the beaches and waters along Mexico's Gulf Coast often leave something to be desired (usually cleanliness). The north coast of the Yucatán peninsula has some beaches, most notably at Progreso and Celestún, but it also has mangrove swamps, shallow waters and – in certain places – crocodiles and caimans.

Diving & Snorkeling

Cancún has the most water-sports facilities, but Cozumel and the Belizean cayes have the barrier reef and thus the best diving, replete with tropical fish, coral and undersea flora. If you plan to dive, bring evidence of your certification to show the dive-shop people, and check the rental equipment over carefully before you dive.

Rafting & Kayaking

Guatemala is the place to go for paddling adventures. A number of rivers there offer anything from frothing Class IV whitewater to easy Class II floats. See that country's Facts for the Visitor chapter for details.

Hiking & Climbing

Much of the region is flat, flat, flat, and tropical jungle to boot, not the most interesting

Considerations for Responsible Diving

The popularity of diving is placing immense pressure on many sites. Please consider the following tips when diving, and help preserve the ecology and beauty of reefs:

- Do not use anchors on the reef, and take care not to ground boats on coral. Encourage dive operators and regulatory bodies to establish permanent moorings at popular dive sites.

- Avoid touching living marine organisms with your body or dragging equipment across the reef. Polyps can be damaged by even the gentlest contact. Never stand on corals, even if they look solid and robust. If you must hold on to the reef, only touch exposed rock or dead coral.

- Be conscious of your fins. Even without contact, the surge from heavy fin strokes near the reef can damage delicate organisms. When treading water in shallow reef areas, take care not to kick up clouds of sand. Settling sand can easily smother the delicate organisms of the reef.

- Practice and maintain proper buoyancy control. Major damage can be done by divers descending too fast and colliding with the reef. Make sure that you are correctly weighted and that your weight belt is positioned so that you stay horizontal. If you have not dived for a while, do a practice dive in a pool before taking to the reef. Be aware that buoyancy can change over the period of an extended trip: Initially, you may breathe harder and need more weight; a few days later, you may breathe more easily and need less weight.

- Take great care in underwater caves. Spend as little time within them as possible, as your air bubbles may be caught within the roof and thereby leave previously submerged organisms high and dry. Taking turns to inspect the interior of a small cave lessens the chances of damaging contact.

- Resist the temptation to collect or buy corals or shells. Aside from the ecological damage, taking home marine souvenirs depletes the beauty of a site and spoils the enjoyment of others. The same goes for marine archaeological sites (mainly shipwrecks). Respect their integrity; some sites are even protected from looting by law.

- Ensure that you take home all your rubbish and any litter you may find as well. Plastics in particular are a serious threat to marine life. Turtles can mistake plastic for jellyfish and eat it.

- Resist the temptation to feed fish. You may disturb their normal eating habits, encourage aggressive behavior or feed them food that is detrimental to their health.

- Minimize your disturbance of marine animals. In particular, do not ride on the backs of turtles, as this causes them great anxiety.

trekking country. The exceptions are the highlands of Chiapas and Guatemala, which have excellent hiking possibilities and many picturesque volcanoes to climb. The best base for hikes into the forests and jungles of Chiapas is San Cristóbal de Las Casas. Treks on horseback may be organized here as well. In Guatemala you can climb the volcanoes bordering Lago de Atitlán, though caution is in order as rural areas hereabouts

harbor robbers. The volcanoes near Antigua in Guatemala also offer excellent possibilities, but see the warning in the Guatemala's Highlands chapter for information on how to find out whether or not it is currently safe to climb.

Cycling
See Bicycle under Local Transportation in the introductory Getting Around chapter.

Highway robbers have beset several cyclists, so you must use caution.

COURSES

Spanish-language courses are popular in Antigua and Quetzaltenango (Guatemala) and to a lesser extent in San Cristóbal de Las Casas (Chiapas, Mexico). See those sections for details.

WORK

According to law you must have a work permit to work in any of these countries. In practice you may get paid under the table or through some bureaucratic loophole, if you can find suitable work. The most plentiful work for native English speakers is teaching their language. Consult the classified advertisements in local newspapers (both English- and Spanish-language papers), browse the bulletin boards in spots where gringos gather, and ask around. Big cities offer the best possibilities. Pay may be low, but it's better than a negative cash flow.

More-lucrative teaching positions may be available tutoring business and bank executives. It takes a while to establish a network of contacts and referrals, so you should not plan to tutor for just a month or two. If you get a good reputation, however, you can be paid quite well, as your students will be among the commercial elite.

ACCOMMODATIONS

Accommodations range from luxury resort hotels, tourist vacation hotels, budget hotels and motels to *casas de huéspedes* (guesthouses), *albergues de juventud* (youth hostels) and simple spots to hang a hammock. Prices vary from city to city; Cancún, for example, is more expensive across the board than other cities in the region. All prices quoted in this book are approximate, not guaranteed.

It's important to note that many establishments (more frequently mid-range and top-end places) are open to negotiation when business is slow. In the months following the arrival of the year 2000, for example, in what should have been the busy winter/spring season, some hotels in the Yucatán would offer walk-in customers large discounts on the posted rates with no prompting. Many others stated their rates were negotiable, and some advertised promotions that included a free breakfast or other perk combined with lowered rates.

Discounts can often be negotiated for multinight stays, groups, and sometimes, at upper-end places, payment in cash. If prices seem high anywhere, it's always worth asking for a discount or *promoción*.

Reservations

It's advisable to reserve a room in advance at particularly popular hotels or if you plan to visit busy areas either during the Christmas-New Year holidays or during July and August. In tourist areas of Guatemala and Mexico, it's essential to book ahead for Semana Santa (Easter Week); in addition to foreign guests, many Mexicans head for vacation spots at this time, and prices can double in some places.

You should request a reservation by email, telephone or fax, asking whether a deposit is required and how to send it, and requesting confirmation in writing.

Camping

You can camp for free on many beaches, but this can be risky. Wherever facilities are available for campers, expect to pay from US$3 to US$15 per night, depending upon the facilities and the desirability of the location. Most equipped campgrounds are trailer parks designed for campers or travel trailers.

Cabañas & Hammocks

These are the two cheapest forms of accommodations, usually found in low-key beach spots. You can rent a hammock and a place to hang it for less than US$3 in some beach places – usually under a thatched roof outside a small casa de huéspedes or a fishing family's hut. If you bring your own hammock, the cost may be even less. It's easy enough to buy hammocks in Mexico; Mérida has many shops specializing in them, and they are widely available in other towns throughout Yucatán as well.

Cabañas are palm-thatched huts with wooden walls. Some have dirt floors and nothing inside but a bed; others are more solidly built with electric light, mosquito nets, fans, even a hot plate. Prices range from US$8 up to US$30; the most luxurious (think air-con) in the choicest spots can run much more.

Casas de Huéspedes

The next-cheapest option is the casa de huéspedes, a home converted into simple guest lodgings. A double room at one of these can cost anywhere from US$5 to US$20, with or without meals.

Youth Hostels

Mexico's albergues de juventud, formerly organized by the federal government, are now mostly run by local or state governments or youth groups. The charge per night for two dormitory beds often equals or even exceeds the cost of a simple double room in a hotel or pension. As hostels are often located away from the town center, you may find a cheap hotel the better option.

The situation is improving, however, with the establishment of a handful of independent hostels aimed toward travelers. Most have gained affiliation with Hostelling International. Look for new hostels in Valladolid, Cancún (sounding particularly promising) and Tulum. Guatemala and Belize do not have any usable official hostels.

Hotels & Motels

Budget lodgings, those costing US$6 to US$25 double, come in many varieties and degrees of comfort and cleanliness. Guatemala has the cheapest and simplest budget hotels and pensions, although as the country becomes more popular prices are rising. Belize has the most expensive ones, with quality not much higher than the Guatemalan ones. Mexico has a good range of options in all price ranges.

In the middle range are comfortable hotels and motels, some with appealing colonial ambience, others modern with green lawns, tropical flowers and swimming pools shaded by palm trees. Still others are urban high-rise buildings with many services and comforts. These range in price from about US$25 to US$120 or so, the higher prices being charged in the major cities.

The luxury resort hotels are mainly found in Cancún, though there are upper-class hostelries in Villahermosa, Guatemala City and Belize City as well. Some of the resorts on the Belizean cayes are positively sybaritic, with prices to match. They are all expensive but most offer excellent values for what you get. Double room rates start at about US$80 per night and go well beyond US$250. Most of the guests at these palatial hotels do not pay these rack rates, however, but are booked in ahead of time through travel agents who can obtain good discounts. You can dig up some good deals from home through the websites of those hotels that have them.

FOOD

The various cuisines found throughout the region have similarities as well as unique elements. Traditional Yucatecan cuisine features several distinctive ingredients – turkey and venison, for example – not used in the rest of Mexico. Guatemalan cooking, though derived from the same roots as Mexican, has regional specialties and variations. Belizean cooking tends to the rough and ready.

Three staples are found throughout the region. *Tortillas* are thin round patties of pressed corn dough cooked on griddles. They may be wrapped around or topped with various foods. Fresh handmade tortillas are best, followed by fresh machine-made ones bought at a *tortillería*. Most restaurants serve fairly fresh ones kept warm in a hot, moist cloth.

Frijoles are beans, served boiled, fried, refried, in soups, spread on tortillas or with eggs. If you simply order frijoles they may come in a bowl swimming in their own dark sauce, as a runny mass on a plate, or as a thick and almost black paste. No matter how they come, they're usually delicious and nutritious. The only bad ones are refried beans that have been fried using too much or low-quality fat.

Chiles (peppers) come in many varieties and are consumed in hundreds of ways. Some chiles such as the *habanero* and *serrano* are always spicy-hot, while others such as the *poblano* vary in spiciness according to when they were picked. If you are unsure about your tolerance for hot chiles, ask if the chile is *picante* (spicy-hot) or *muy picante* (very spicy-hot).

For full lists of menu items with translations, see the Menu Guide at the back of this book. For details on each country's cuisine, look under Food in the Facts for the Visitor chapter of each country.

Meals

The standard three meals a day are breakfast *(el desayuno)*, lunch *(la comida, el almuerzo)* and supper *(la cena)*.

Breakfast The morning meal can be either continental or US-style. A light, continental-style breakfast can be made of sweet rolls *(pan dulce)* or toast, and coffee. In Mexico a basket of pan dulce may be placed on your breakfast table when your coffee is served. When the time comes to pay, you tell the clerk how many you have eaten.

US-style breakfasts are often available and might include bacon or sausage and eggs, pancakes (called hot cakes in Mexico, *panqueques* in Guatemala), cold cereal such as corn flakes or hot cereal such as oatmeal (porridge), cream of wheat, fruit juice and coffee. You may order eggs in a variety of ways (see the Menu Guide).

Lunch This is the biggest meal of the day and is served about 1 or 2 pm. In restaurants that do not cater primarily to tourists, menus might change daily, weekly or not at all. Meals might be ordered à la carte or table d'hôte. A fixed-price meal of several courses called a *comida corrida* (the bargain or daily special meal) is sometimes offered. It might include from one to six courses; choices and price are often displayed near the front door of the restaurant. Simple comidas corridas may consist of a plain soup or pasta, a garnished main course plate and coffee; more expensive versions may have a fancy soup or

ceviche, a choice main course such as steak or fish, salad, dessert and coffee. Another term for comida corrida is *menú*, though in tourist-oriented restaurants using this word may get you the written list of offerings (usually known as *la carta*).

Supper Served about 7:30 pm, *la cena* is a lighter version of lunch. In beach resorts the evening meal tends to be the big one, as everyone is out at the beach during the day.

DRINKS

Because of the hot climate in many parts of the region, you will find yourself drinking lots of fluids. Indeed, you must remember to drink even if you don't feel particularly thirsty, in order to prevent dehydration and heat exhaustion (see the Health section in this chapter).

Nonalcoholic Drinks

Water & Soft Drinks Bottled or purified water is widely available in hotels and shops (see Food & Water in the Health section). You can also order safe-to-drink fizzy mineral water by saying 'soda.'

Besides the easily recognizable and internationally known brands of *refrescos* (soft drinks) such as Coca-Cola and Pepsi, you will find interesting local flavors. Orange-flavored *(naranja)* soda is popular, and grapefruit *(toronja)* is even better, though less readily available. Squirt (pronounced eh-**skweert**) is a brand of lemon-flavored soda that is a bit drier than 7-Up. Also in Mexico, try the two apple-flavored drinks named Sidral and Manzanita.

Coffee, Tea & Cocoa The Pacific coastal plain of Chiapas and Guatemala has many large coffee plantations that produce excellent beans, including those typed as Guatemalan Antigua and Maragogipes. Some hotels in Antigua have coffee bushes growing right on their grounds (no pun intended). Coffee is available everywhere – strong and flavorful in Mexico, surprisingly weak and sugary in parts of Guatemala.

Black tea *(té negro)*, usually made from bags (often locally produced Lipton), tends to be a major disappointment to devoted tea drinkers. It's best to bring your own supply of loose tea and a tea infuser, then just order *una taza de agua caliente* (a cup of hot water) and brew your own.

Herbal teas are much better. Chamomile tea *(té de manzanilla)*, a common item on restaurant and cafe menus, is a specific remedy for problems with a queasy stomach or gripy gut.

Hot chocolate or cocoa was the royal stimulant during the Classic period of Mayan civilization, when kings and nobility drank it on ceremonial occasions. Their version was unsweetened and dreadfully bitter. Today it's sweetened and, if not authentic, at least more palatable.

Fruit & Vegetable Juices Fresh fruit and vegetable juices *(jugos)*, shakes *(licuados)* and flavored waters *(aguas frescas)* are popular drinks, particularly in Mexico. Almost every town has a stand serving one or more of these, and Mérida seems to have one every few blocks. All of the fruits and a few of the squeezable vegetables are used either individually (as in jugos or aguas frescas) or in some combination (as in licuados).

The basic licuado is a blend of fruit or juice with water and sugar. Other items can be added or substituted: raw egg, milk, ice, and flavorings such as vanilla or nutmeg. The delicious combinations are practically limitless.

Aguas frescas are made by mixing fruit juice or a syrup made from mashed grains or seeds with sugar and water. You will usually see them in big glass jars on the counters of juice stands. Try the *agua fresca de arroz* (literally rice water), which has a sweet nutty taste.

Alcoholic Drinks

Supermarkets, grocery stores and liquor stores stock both beer and wine, both imported and locally made. Some of the local stuff is quite good. You certainly won't go thirsty, and drinking will not bust your budget. But remember that excessive alcohol intake is a good way to become dehydrated in the region's hot climate.

Beer Breweries were first established in Mexico and Guatemala by German immigrants in the late 19th century. European techniques and technology have been used ever since the beginning, which may explain why Mexico has so many delicious beers, both light and dark. Most beers *(cervezas)* are light lagers, served cold from bottles or cans, but there are also a few flavorful dark beers such as Negra Modelo (Mexico) and Moza (Guatemala).

Mexico's breweries now produce more than 25 brands of beer, including major labels such as Modelo, Superior, Corona, Bohemia and Carta Blanca. Local beers made in Yucatán include the lagers Carta Clara and Montejo, and the excellent dark León Negra.

Guatemala's two nationally distributed beers are Gallo (**gah**-yoh, rooster) and Cabro (goat). The distribution prize goes to Gallo – you'll find it everywhere.

In Belize, Belikin virtually owns the beer market. Belikin Export, the premium version, comes in a larger bottle, is much tastier, costs more and is worth it. When you get sick of Belikin you can readily find US and European beers, but they cost considerably more.

In restaurants and bars unaccustomed to tourists, beer is sometimes served at room temperature. If you want to be sure of getting a cold beer, ask for *una cerveza fría.* Sometimes the waiter or bartender will hand you the bottle or can and let you feel it for proper coldness. This usually means it's not very cold, and your choice is then the dismal one of 'this beer or no beer at all.'

Wine Wine is not the local drink of choice. That distinction goes to beer and liquor made from sugarcane, by far. But as foreign wine-lovers spread through the region, so does the availability of wine.

Mexico's few large wine growers, all near Ensenada in Baja California, produce some drinkable vintages. Pedro Domecq, which also owns Sauza, one of the two big tequila firms, has the highest profile. Its Cabernet Sauvignon XA, costing US$15 to US$20 in restaurants, is probably the most popular

Mexican red. Its Zinfandel XA is of similar quality. Domecq's Calafia and Los Reyes reds and whites cost little over half that.

The top three wineries in quality are generally considered to be Chateau Camou, Bodegas de Santo Tomás and Monte Xanic. The very best wines fetch US$60 a bottle in upmarket restaurants.

The situation in Guatemala and Belize is much worse. Local wines are no thrill to drink, and imported wines are fairly expensive, but at least they're available. In all but the best places you may have to specify that you want your red wine at room temperature and your white wine chilled.

Spirits The traditional Mayan spirit in Yucatán is *xtabentún* (shtah-behn-**toon**), an anise-flavored brandy that, when authentic, is made by fermenting honey. The modern version has a goodly proportion of grain neutral spirits, however. It is made to be either dry *(seco)* or sweet *(crema)*. The seco tastes much like the Greek ouzo or French pastis; the crema is like the sweeter Italian sambuca. It is served in some restaurants as an after-dinner drink; you can find it readily

in many liquor shops in Mérida, Cancún and other Yucatecan towns.

Many other famous liquors, liqueurs and brandies are made in Mexico: Bacardi rum, Pedro Domecq brandy, Controy (orange liqueur, a knock-off Cointreau), Kahlúa (coffee-flavored liqueur) and Oso Negro vodka. All are of good quality and inexpensive. Tequila and mezcal, which are made from the maguey plant, come from 'mainland' Mexico.

Rum and *aguardiente* (sugarcane liquor, also known as *caña)* are the favorite strong drinks in Guatemala and Belize as well, and though most are of low price and matching quality, some local products are exceptionally fine. Zacapa Centenario is a smooth aged Guatemalan rum made in Zacapa, off the Carretera al Atlántico. It should be sipped slowly, neat, like fine cognac. Cheaper rums and brandies are often mixed with soft drinks to make potent but cooling drinks, like the *Cuba libre* of rum and Coke.

Other drinks include gin – mixed with tonic water, ice and lime juice to make what many consider the perfect drink for the hot tropics – and whiskey, mostly from the USA.

Getting There & Away

The easiest approach to the region, and the one most travelers use, is by air. The region's major international airports are at Cancún and Guatemala City, with a small amount of international traffic heading for Belize City. Mexico City also receives a large number of flights from all parts of the world, with connecting flights to Cancún, Chetumal, Guatemala City, Mérida, Palenque, Tuxtla Gutiérrez and Villahermosa.

Approaches by road from Mexico and Central America (El Salvador and Honduras) are easy, with fairly good roads and frequent service in comfortable (though not luxurious) buses.

Amtrak, the US rail service (☎ 800-872-7245 in the USA, www.amtrak.com), runs trains to some cities on the US side of the Mexican border, but it offers no service across the border. Recently, regular passenger service in Mexico had been severely curtailed and faces an uncertain future.

Warning

The information in this chapter is particularly vulnerable to change: Prices for international travel are volatile, routes are introduced and canceled, schedules change, special deals come and go, and rules and visa requirements are amended. Airlines and governments seem to take a perverse pleasure in making price structures and regulations as complicated as possible. You should check directly with the airline or a travel agent to make sure you understand how a fare (and any ticket you may buy) works. In addition, the travel industry is highly competitive and there are many hidden costs and benefits.

The upshot of this is that you should get opinions, quotes and advice from as many airlines and travel agents as possible before you part with your hard-earned cash. The details given in this chapter should be regarded as pointers and are not a substitute for your own careful, up-to-date research.

Belize has no trains, and no passenger train service connects Guatemala with the rest of Central America.

There is no regular car or passenger ferry service between the region and the USA.

AIR
Routes

International air routes are structured so that virtually all flights into the region from the rest of the world pass through half a dozen 'hub' cities: Dallas/Fort Worth, Houston, Los Angeles, Miami, Mexico City or San Salvador. You might have to change planes in one of these cities.

Mayan Route Tickets

The national airlines of the Central American countries, including Aviateca, COPA, LACSA, NICA and TACA, have formed a marketing organization named America Central Corporation that offers special Mayan Route fare plans. Such fares allow you to fly from a gateway (usually Miami, New Orleans or Houston) to the region, make stops in several places, then fly home. Call the airlines or your travel agent for details on current pricing.

Travelers with Special Needs

Most international airlines can cater to people with special needs – travelers with disabilities, people with young children and even children traveling alone.

Travelers with special dietary preferences (vegetarian, kosher etc) can request appropriate meals with advance notice. If you are traveling in a wheelchair, most international airports can provide an escort from check-in desk to plane when needed, and ramps, lifts, toilets and phones are generally available.

Airlines usually allow babies up to two years of age to fly for 10% of the adult fare, although a few may allow them free of charge. Reputable international airlines usually provide diapers (nappies), tissues, talcum and all the other paraphernalia

Air Travel Glossary

Baggage Allowance This will be written on your ticket and usually includes one 20kg item to go in the hold, plus one item of hand luggage.

Bucket Shops These are unbonded travel agencies specializing in discounted airline tickets.

Cancellation Penalties If you have to cancel or change a discounted ticket, there are often heavy penalties involved; insurance can sometimes be taken out against these penalties. Some airlines impose penalties on regular tickets as well, particularly against 'no-show' passengers.

Check-In Airlines ask you to check in a certain time ahead of the flight departure (usually one to two hours on international flights). If you fail to check in on time and the flight is overbooked, the airline can cancel your booking and give your seat to somebody else.

Confirmation Having a ticket written out with the flight and date you want doesn't mean you have a seat until the agent has checked with the airline that your status is 'OK' or confirmed. Meanwhile you could just be 'on request.'

Consolidator The US equivalent of a bucket shop: A consolidator buys seats in bulk from airlines at considerable discounts and resells them to the public through travel agents or published ads.

ITX An ITX, or 'independent inclusive tour excursion,' is often available on tickets to popular holiday destinations. Officially, it's a package deal combined with hotel accommodations, but many agents will sell you one of these for the flight only and give you phony hotel vouchers in the unlikely event that you're challenged at the airport.

Lost Tickets If you lose your airline ticket, an airline will usually treat it like a traveler's check and, after inquiries, issue you another one. Legally, however, an airline is entitled to treat it like cash: If you lose it, it's gone forever. Take good care of your tickets.

No-Shows Full-fare passengers who fail to turn up for their flights are sometimes entitled to travel on a later flight. Others are penalized (see Cancellation Penalties).

---

needed to keep babies clean, dry and half-happy. For children between the ages of two and 12, the fare on international flights is usually 50% of the regular fare or 67% of a discounted fare.

The USA & Canada

American, Continental, Delta, Northwest and United are the US airlines with the most service to La Ruta Maya. Aeroméxico, Aeronica, Aeroquetzal, Aviateca, COPA, LACSA, Mexicana and TACA are the Latin American airlines with flights to the USA.

You can fly nonstop on a major scheduled airline to Cancún from any of these North American cities: Atlanta, Chicago, Dallas/Fort Worth, Houston, Los Angeles, Miami, New Orleans, New York, San Francisco and Tampa/St Petersburg.

Dozens of airfares can apply to any given air route. They vary with each company,

class of service, season of the year, length of stay, dates of travel, date of purchase and type of reservation. Your ticket may cost more or less depending upon the flexibility you are allowed in changing your plans. The price of the ticket is even affected by how you buy it and from whom.

Travel agents are the first people to consult about fares and routes. Once you've discovered the basics of the airlines flying to your destination, the routes taken and the various discounted tickets available, you can consult your favorite bucket shop, consolidator or charter airline to see if their fares are better.

Here are some sample fixed-date round-trip fares (also called excursion fares) from various cities to Cancún: Chicago, US$386; Dallas/Fort Worth, US$322; Los Angeles, US$366; Miami, US$284; New York, US$389; Toronto, US$359.

Air Travel Glossary

On Request This is an unconfirmed booking for a flight.

Open-Jaw Tickets These are return tickets on which you fly to one place but return from another. If available, these can save you backtracking to your arrival point.

Overbooking Airlines hate to fly with empty seats, and because every flight has some passengers who fail to show up, airlines often book more passengers than they have seats. Usually excess passengers make up for the no-shows, but occasionally somebody gets bumped. Guess who it's most likely to be? The passengers who check in late.

Reconfirmation At least 72 hours prior to departure time of an onward or return flight, you must contact the airline and 'reconfirm' that you intend to be on the flight. If you don't do this, the airline can delete your name from the passenger list and you could lose your seat.

Restrictions Discounted tickets often have various restrictions on them, such as advance payment, minimum and maximum periods you must be away (for example, a minimum of two weeks or a maximum of one year) and penalties for changing the tickets.

Round-the-World Tickets RTW tickets give you a limited period (usually a year) in which to circumnavigate the globe. You can go anywhere the carrying airlines go, as long as you don't backtrack. The number of stopovers or total number of separate flights is decided before you set off, and they usually cost a bit more than a basic return flight.

Stand-By This is a discounted ticket on which you fly only if there is a seat free at the last moment. Stand-by fares are usually available only on domestic routes.

Travel Periods Ticket prices vary with the time of year. There is a low (off-peak) season and a high (peak) season, and often a low-shoulder season and a high-shoulder season as well. Usually the fare depends on your outward flight. If you depart in the high season and return in the low season, you pay the high-season fare.

Besides these excursion fares, many package tours from the USA typically provide roundtrip airfare, transfers and accommodations for a few days or a week. These are by far the most economical way to visit Cancún. Some of these tour packages allow you to extend your stay in order to tour the region on your own.

Package tours change in price and features as the seasons change. For a cheap flight to Cancún, read the advertisements in the travel section of your local newspaper and find a package-tour operator or a travel agent who sells such tours. Then call and ask if you can buy 'air only' (just the roundtrip air transportation, not the hotel or other features). Often this is possible, and usually it is cheaper than buying a discounted excursion ticket.

Sometimes, though, the difference between air-only and a tour package including hotels is so insignificant that it makes sense just to accept the hotel along with the flight. To a limited extent, this is also true of package tours to Guatemala and Belize.

Consolidators (called bucket shops in Europe) are organizations that buy bulk seats from airlines at considerable discounts and then resell them to the public, often through travel agents, sometimes directly through newspaper and magazine ads. Though there are some shady dealers, many consolidators are legitimate.

Ask your travel agent about buying a consolidator ticket, or look for the consolidator ads in the travel section of your local newspaper. (The consolidator ads are the ones with tables of destinations and fares and a toll-free number to call).

Cancún is easy to reach cheaply; it's a bit more difficult to find air-only fares to Guatemala City and Belize.

The Caribbean & Central & South America

America Central Corporation airlines (see Mayan Route Tickets, above) predominate in the region. Mexicana and Cubana fly between Cancún and Havana.

Europe

The cheapest fares are on charter flights to Cancún, such as those run by Air Europa from Spain and Martinair from Amsterdam. Most of the scheduled airlines' routes take you to one of the US hub cities, where you change to a plane of a US, Mexican, Guatemalan or other Central American airline before reaching your final destination.

The UK For cheap tickets from London, pick up a copy of *City Limits, Time Out, TNT* or any of the other magazines that advertise discount (bucket shop) flights, and check out a few of the advertisers. The Sunday Times is also a good resource, and the magazine *Business Traveller* has lots of good advice on airfare bargains. Most bucket shops are trustworthy and reliable, but the occasional sharp operator appears – *Time Out* and *Business Traveller* give some useful advice on precautions to take.

Agents offering cheap fares to Mexico include Journey Latin America (☎ 020-8747-3108, www.journeylatinamerica.co.uk), 12-13 Heathfield Terrace, London W4 4JE (this company also runs small-group tours to Mexico); STA Travel (☎ 020-7361-6145, www.statravel.co.uk), 86 Old Brompton Rd, London SW7 3LQ, and 117 Euston Rd, London NW1 2SX (among other branches); and Usit Campus (☎ 0870-240-1010, www.usitcampus.co.uk), 52 Grosvenor Gardens, London SW1W 0AG.

A typical fixed-date return (excursion) fare from London to Cancún at the time of writing was US$690.

Continental Europe Discount tickets are available at prices similar to London's in several European cities. Amsterdam, Paris and Frankfurt are among the main cheap flight centers. Air France, KLM, Iberia and the Colombian airline Avianca are some

of the airlines whose tickets are handled by discount agents.

Here are some typical fixed-date return (excursion) fares to Cancún valid at the time of writing: Amsterdam, US$412; Frankfurt, US$632; Paris, US$583.

Australia & New Zealand

No direct flights from Australia to the region are available. The cheapest way of getting there is via the USA – often Los Angeles. Discount roundtrip flights from Sydney to Los Angeles cost around US$900 and up. Cheap flights from the USA to the region are hard to find in Australia. The cheapest Los Angeles-Cancún fare is around US$366 roundtrip (see North America, above).

Travelers looking to combine a visit to the Mayan region with a South American excursion will find that the cheapest roundtrip tickets from Sydney to Lima or Rio de Janeiro are about US$1174. Santiago and Buenos Aires are cheaper at about US$988. If you want to fly into South America and out of the USA, or vice-versa, the best option is to get a roundtrip ticket to South America on an airline that flies there via the USA (United, for example), then simply don't use one of the legs you paid for. Fortunately, at the time of writing, United's fares for this route were much the same as those of airlines that go directly to South America – discount returns via the USA from Sydney to Buenos Aires, Lima, Santiago or Rio de Janeiro were all available at around US$1200.

Round-the-world tickets with a Mexico/Guatemala option are sometimes available in Australia. STA Travel (www.statravel .com.au), with more than 80 offices around the country, is one of the most popular discount travel agents in Australia. It also has sales offices or agents all over the world.

Departure Tax

A departure tax of about US$17 is charged on international flights from Mexico, US$30 from Guatemala and US$15 from Belize. This tax may already be included in your ticket price; the letters XD on your ticket show the tax has been paid.

LAND
Border Crossings

Most of the time and at most entry points, crossing the border is a breeze. If you fly into any of these countries you should have few, if any, hassles. If you cross at land border points, you may run into other situations. There are a few things that you ought to know.

For details on land border crossings, see the Getting There & Around sections for each country.

Border officials in Latin American countries sometimes request unofficial 'fees' from travelers at the border; these are called *la mordida*, or the 'bite.' There are some things you can try to do to avoid paying.

You can scowl quietly and act important or cosmopolitan (dressing nicely helps). Scowl all you want, but whatever you do, keep everything formal. Never *ever* raise your voice, mumble a curse, get angry or verbally confront a Latin American official. You'll get farther acting quietly superior and unruffled at all times.

If you really like to play the game, offer some weird currency such as Thai baht or Norwegian kroner or Dutch guilders. At the sight of strange money the officer may drop the request. If he doesn't, or if the fee turns out to be legitimate, 'search' for several minutes in your belongings and come up with the dollars you need. If the official will accept the unusual currency, inflate its value; tell him a low note is actually worth big bucks.

You can also ask for a receipt, *un recibo*. Some fees are indeed official and legitimate. If the fee is proper, you'll get an official-looking receipt.

Bus

For details on bus travel, see the Getting There & Away chapter for each country.

Car

For US and Canadian visitors, taking your own vehicle across the USA/Mexico border is a practical and convenient option. The most apparent difficulty in driving your own vehicle is that most North American cars now have catalytic converters, which

require unleaded fuel. Though unleaded is widely available in Mexico, it is not yet sold in Guatemala or Belize. You can arrange to have your catalytic converter disconnected and replaced with a straight piece of exhaust pipe soon after you cross into Mexico (it's illegal to have it done in the USA). Save the converter and make sure to have it replaced before recrossing the border into the USA.

Another consideration is that in Guatemala and Belize it may be difficult to find mechanics and parts for newer-model US and Canadian cars with sophisticated electronics and pollution-control systems. If your vehicle breaks down and needs parts, those parts may have to be ordered from the USA or Canada.

Coming from overseas, you may want to buy a used car or van in the USA, where they're relatively cheap, drive through the USA to Mexico and travel the entire Ruta Maya.

Motor Vehicle Insurance You'd be wise to buy local liability insurance in this region; in case of an accident, no matter whose fault, you could be 'detained' indefinitely until all claims are settled. If you drive your vehicle into all three countries, you'll need three separate policies; rates depend on your vehicle's value. See each country's Getting There & Around chapter for details.

Driver's License To drive any motor vehicle in this region, you need a valid driver's license from your home country. Police will be familiar with US and Canadian licenses; those from other countries may be scrutinized more closely, but they are still legal. International Driver's Licenses, provided by auto clubs, generally are not considered valid driver's licenses by local authorities.

Importing Motor Vehicles The rules for taking a vehicle into this region (and especially Mexico), described in the sections that follow, have in the past changed from time to time. You can check current laws with the American Automobile Association (AAA) and any local consulate or government tourist office.

You will need a temporary import permit if you want to take a vehicle more than 25km into Mexico. The permits are available at the *aduana* (customs) office near border crossings.

In addition to a passport and tourist card, you'll need the following documents, which must be in your own name: a certificate of title or ownership for the vehicle; a current registration card; and a driver's license. Have at least one photocopy of each of these documents as well as the original.

One person cannot bring in two vehicles. If, for example, you have a motorcycle attached to your car, you'll need another adult traveling with you to obtain a permit for the motorcycle, and that person will need to have all the right papers for it. If the motorcycle is registered in your name, you'll need a notarized affidavit authorizing the other person to take it into Mexico.

As a rule, the owner cannot leave Mexico without the vehicle. If it's wrecked completely, you must obtain permission to leave it in the country from either the Registro Federal de Vehículos (Federal Registry of Vehicles) in Mexico City, or an Hacienda (Treasury Department) office in another city or town. If you have to leave the country in an emergency, the vehicle can be left in temporary storage at an airport or seaport or with an aduana or Hacienda office. Similar rules apply in Guatemala and Belize.

Getting Around the Region

Bus travel has always been the most dependable means of travel within the region, but air routes are expanding, allowing travelers with more money than time to get to the major sights quickly.

Unfortunately, car-rental companies have yet to join this 'easy access' campaign. Hire cars are expensive in the Yucatán, more expensive in Guatemala and very expensive in Belize. In most cases you may not drive a rental car outside the national territory of the country in which you rented it (that is, you cannot drive it across a border). In those cases where you may drive across borders, you usually need permission in writing from the car-rental company. Thus a plan to tour most of the region by hire car often involves different rentals in three countries and bus or plane in between.

AIR

You can avoid some long, hot and even dangerous bus trips by taking a plane between these points:

Palenque/Villahermosa-Mérida	US$135
Cancún-Chetumal	US$88
Chetumal-Villahermosa	US$75
Belize City-Flores (Tikal)	US$85

BUS

The prevalent means of transportation is bus. You can travel on a bus to 95% of the sites described in this book (the other 5% can be reached by boat or on foot). Bus travel can be luxurious or uncomfortable, but it is usually cheap.

In general, bus traffic is most intense in the morning (beginning as early as 4 or 5 am), tapering off by mid- or late afternoon. In many places within the region, no buses run in the late afternoon or evening.

Routes to remote towns and villages serve villagers going to market in larger towns. This often means that the only bus departs from the village early in the morning and returns from the larger market town by midafternoon. If you want to visit the village, you may find that you must take this late afternoon bus and stay the night in the village, catching the bus back to the market town the next morning. Remote villages rarely have hotels, so you should be prepared to camp.

For details on getting around by bus, see each country's section.

CAR & MOTORCYCLE

Driving in this region is not for everyone – you should know some Spanish and have basic mechanical aptitude, lots of patience and access to extra cash for emergencies. You should also note which stretches of highway have reputations for crime, especially at night. Also, police are sometimes known to cite motorists for bogus moving violations. Motorists should limit their driving to daylight hours (this is partly a security issue and partly a matter of livestock and wild animals on the roadways) and obey speed-limit signs.

Motorcycling in this region is not for the fainthearted. Chickens, dogs, iguanas, and even boa constrictors can appear on roads. Pedestrians cross highways with abandon. Roads can be rough, and parts and mechanics are generally hard to come by. The only parts you'll find at all will be for Kawasaki, Honda and Suzuki bikes.

Private car, camper van or trailer (caravan) is perhaps the best way to travel the region. You can go at your own pace and easily reach many areas not served by frequent public transportation. The major roads and many of the minor roads are easily passable by any sort of car, and border crossings are fairly easy. But you need private motor vehicle insurance, an import permit and you may need a car that uses leaded fuel or has had its unleaded-fuel catalytic converter removed. See the previous chapter (Getting There & Away) for details on bringing vehicles into the region.

Car rental is a bit more expensive in Guatemala, Belize and Mexico than in the USA, averaging about US$30 to US$45 per day, all-inclusive, for a basic car such as a Volkswagen Beetle or Nissan Tsuru.

Information on fuel costs in each country is given in the respective Getting There & Around chapters. When you buy fuel, many station attendants – especially in Mexico – may try to overcharge you. There are numerous scams. To avoid them, follow these steps:

- Get out of your car and stand by the gas pump
- Learn to estimate how much fuel you'll need *in local currency*, and ask for so-and-so many pesos' worth of fuel. (Don't just say 'fill it up.')
- Watch to be sure that the attendant resets the pump to zero before pumping, then note the amount immediately when he stops pumping. (Attendants commonly reset the meter immediately after pumping. Another ploy to watch for is an attendant hitting the emergency stop button at the pumps, which resets the display to a different amount that he then attempts to add to your bill.)
- Pay in exact change if you can. If not, tell the attendant out loud the amount of money you're offering as you hand it to him. (This prevents him from claiming you gave him 50 pesos when in fact you gave him a 100-peso bill.)

HITCHHIKING

People hitch at a few places, such as the Puuc Route south of Uxmal in the Yucatán, where transportation is infrequent. But hitching in Mexico can be dangerous, and it's very dangerous in Guatemala and Belize.

Hitchhiking is not necessarily free transportation. In most cases, if you are picked up by a truck, you will be expected to pay a fare similar to that charged on the bus, if there is one. (In some areas, pickup and flatbed stake trucks *are* the 'buses' of the region, and every rider pays.) Your best bet for free rides is with other foreign tourists who have their own vehicles.

Hitching is never entirely safe in any country in the world, and we don't recommend it. Travelers who decide to hitch should understand that they are taking a potentially serious risk. People who do

choose to hitch will be safer if they travel in pairs or groups.

BOAT

Though no long-distance sea transportation serves the region, boats are used for public transportation in a surprising number of places.

Motor launches are the favored means of transportation on Guatemala's Lago de Atitlán, and dugout canoes take you up the Río Dulce and El Golfete to Lago de Izabal for a look at the wildlife. Dugouts are also used for excursions on Lago Petén Itzá around Flores (near Tikal).

Belize has the most transportation by sea. Fast motor launches connect Belize City, Caye Chapel, Caye Caulker and Ambergris Caye several times daily. Other boats go to the many other cayes several times a week on scheduled services or by charter. Boat service connects Punta Gorda, in southern Belize, with Lívingston and Puerto Barrios in Guatemala, and charter service to Puerto Cortés, Honduras, may be available as well. In western Belize, boat, canoe or kayak trips along the rivers of the Mountain Pine Ridge area are mostly for fun, but also sometimes for transportation when the rainy season has turned the unpaved roads to sloughs of mud.

In Mexico, ferryboats and hydrofoils connect the island of Cozumel to the mainland, and ferries run to Isla Mujeres as well. In Chiapas, you can take a boat ride through the stupendous Cañon del Sumidero. Boats also transport adventurous travelers down rivers on the route between Palenque (Mexico) and Flores (Guatemala).

LOCAL TRANSPORTATION
Bus

Except for Belize City, all major cities and towns have public bus service. Buses are always the US school bus type of vehicle, usually rattly and uncomfortable but always cheap; fares are as low as US$0.10 in Guatemala City. In many places the number of available buses is insufficient to meet demand, so they tend to be packed solid at rush hour and perhaps at other times as well.

Jitney

Guatemala City has an extensive jitney cab network that becomes important at night after the city buses stop running. Jitneys also ply some popular tourist routes, such as Tulum to Cobá and Belize City to San Ignacio, offering the comfort and speed of a car at only slightly more than bus fare.

Taxi

Taxis are expensive, charging rates equal to or exceeding those in places like New York City. None has a meter, so it's necessary to determine the price of the trip before setting out. Rates are set, but drivers will often try to rip you off by quoting a higher price. This means that you must usually resort to bargaining or asking several drivers.

Bicycle

Sport cycling is not yet popular in the region. Roads are often not the smoothest, the sun can be relentless, and you may have to travel long distances between towns. Often there's not much to look at except the verdant walls of jungle that hem in the road. Insects – both those that hit you in the face and those that eat you for lunch – are another disincentive.

This having been said, certain areas are beautiful for biking. The Guatemalan highlands have light traffic, decent roads and manageable distances between towns, but they also present danger from robbers. Highland Chiapas is similar. Unless you like pedaling in the rain, though, it's wise to plan your trip for the dry season (from October to May). At least two cities in the Yucatán – Valladolid and Campeche – have constructed bike paths. Hopefully other cities and towns will follow suit.

Horse

Horseback riding is not so much a means of transportation here as a means of pleasure, though in the backcountry of western Belize it is also eminently practical. Treks on horseback are possible in many places, including San Cristóbal de Las Casas, Lago de Atitlán, Flores and Mountain Pine Ridge.

Facts about Belize

This English-speaking tropical country embraces a beguiling mixture of Caribbean and Latin cultures. The people are friendly, open and relaxed – everyone here seems to know how to have a good time – and though tourism is big business, travelers rarely feel commodified. Belizeans readily offer visitors help and advice, and they're committed to avoiding the pitfalls of mass-market tourism. The preservation of the country's many natural wonders is a high-priority item here; some pioneers of the ecotravel movement started their work in Belize, and the local tourism industry boasts many earth-friendly innovations.

Belize is a tiny country. Its entire population numbers only about 250,000 (the size of a small city in Mexico, Europe or the USA), and its 23,300-sq-km area is only slightly larger than that of Wales or Massachusetts. Yet despite its diminutive size, the country offers a variety of terrain and plenty of opportunity for adventure. You can go snorkeling and diving in the cayes; hiking and caving inland; bird and wildlife viewing in the country's robust network of unspoiled national parks; or exploring at any of several Mayan ruins, which you're likely to have to yourself outside peak tourism hours.

Many visitors opt for a 'surf and turf' vacation, dividing their time between the cayes or the beach at Placencia and the mountainous regions of Cayo. Travelers who wish to get off the beaten track – to get to know Belize and its people beyond the lodges and tours – need only travel a couple of hours out from Belize City, heading north to, say, Corozal or south to Punta Gorda. The country is an independent traveler's dream – an efficient network of buses making frequent runs in all directions means that it's easy to get from point to point without much waiting around or advance planning.

Those looking for relaxation, adventure and wildlife in a small, easy-to-get-around package will be enamored by Belize, and indeed, many travelers return year after year. But while good values, comfortable lodges and wholesome cheap meals are available here, travelers interested in bargain-basement prices will be happier in Guatemala or Mexico.

HISTORY
Colonial Times

In the opinion of its Spanish conquerors, Belize was a backwater good only for its harvestable logwood, which was used to make dye. The country had no obvious riches to exploit and no great population to convert for the glory of God and the profit of the conquerors. Far from being profitable, Belize was dangerous, because the barrier reef tended to tear the keels from Spanish ships attempting to approach the shore.

Though Spain 'owned' Belize, it did little to rule it, as there was little to rule. The lack of effective government and the safety afforded by the barrier reef attracted English and Scottish pirates to Belizean waters during the 17th century. The pirates operated mostly without serious hindrance, capturing Spanish galleons heavily laden with gold and other riches taken from Spain's American empire. In 1670, however, Spain convinced the British government to clamp down on the pirates' activities. The pirates, now unemployed, mostly went into the logwood business, becoming lumberjacks instead of buccaneers. By today's standards, the erstwhile pirates made bad timber managers, cutting logwood indiscriminately and damaging the jungle ecosystem.

During the 18th century, the Spanish wanted the British loggers out of Belize. But with little control over the country and more important things to attend to in other parts of its empire, Spain mostly ignored Belize.

The British did not.

As British economic interests in the countries of the Caribbean increased, so too

BELIZE

did British involvement in Belize. In the 1780s the British actively protected the former pirates' logging interests, at the same time assuring Spain that Belize was indeed a Spanish possession. This was a fiction. By this time, Belize was already British by tradition and sympathy, and it was with relief and jubilation that Belizeans received the news, on September 10, 1798, that a British force had defeated the Spanish armada off St George's Caye. Belize had been delivered from Spanish rule, a fact that was ratified by treaty some 60 years later.

The country's new status did not bring prosperity, however. Belize was still essentially one large logging camp, not a balanced society of farmers, artisans, merchants and traders. When the logwood trade collapsed, killed by the invention of synthetic dyes, the colony's economy crashed. It was revived by the trade in mahogany during the early 19th century, but this collapsed, too, when African sources of the wood brought fierce price competition.

Belize's next trade boom was in arms, ammunition and other supplies sold to the Maya rebels in Yucatán, who fought the War of the Castes during the mid-19th century. The war also brought a flood of refugees to Belize. First came the whites and their mestizo lieutenants, driven out by the wrath of the Maya; then came the Maya themselves when the whites regained control of Yucatán. The Maya brought farming skills that were of great value in expanding the horizons and economic viability of Belizean society.

In 1862, while the USA was embroiled in the Civil War and unable to enforce the terms of the Monroe Doctrine, Great Britain declared Belize its colony, calling it British Honduras. The declaration encouraged people from many parts of the British Empire to settle in Belize, which helps account for the country's present-day ethnic diversity.

Modern Times

The Belizean economy worsened after WWII, leading to agitation for independence from the UK. Democratic institutions and political parties were established over the years, and self-government eventually became a reality. On September 21, 1981, the colony of British Honduras officially became the independent nation of Belize, but it remained a member of the British Commonwealth.

Belizean independence was not celebrated by neighboring Guatemala, which had long claimed Belize as part of its national territory. The Guatemalans threatened war, but British troops stationed in Belize kept the territorial dispute to a diplomatic squabble. In 1992, a new Guatemalan government signed a treaty recognizing Belize's independence but not relinquishing claim to some 7500 square miles of land. Intermittent border flare-ups continued. In July 2000, the two countries began formal talks to resolve the longstanding territorial dispute. So far, Belize refuses to let any land go, but has stated that it is willing to explore options for allowing Guatemala expanded access to the sea.

Though the logwood and mahogany trades brought some small measure of prosperity in the late 18th and early 19th centuries, Belize has never been a rich country. Its economic history in the past hundred years has been one of getting by, benefiting from economic aid granted by the UK and the USA, from money sent home by Belizeans living and working abroad and from the foreign currency generated by its small agricultural sector.

Increasingly, Belize is relying on tourism to increase the standard of living. The government has invested heavily in foreign public-relations campaigns while working to improve the travel infrastructure on the home front. Because of these efforts, the country has seen record increases in visitors and tourist dollars.

GEOGRAPHY & CLIMATE

Belize, like Yucatán, is mostly tropical lowland, typically hot and humid day and night for most of the year. Rainfall is lightest in the north, heaviest in the south. The southern rain forests receive almost 4m of precipitation annually, helping to make the south the country's most humid region.

An exception to Belize's low-lying topography and hot, sticky climate can be found in the Maya Mountains, which traverse western and southern Belize at elevations approaching 1000m. The mountains enjoy a more pleasant climate than the lowlands – comfortably warm during the day, cooling off a bit at night. But even here the forests are lush, well watered and humid year round.

The country's coastline and northern coastal plain are largely covered in mangrove swamp, which indistinctly defines the line between land and sea. Offshore, the limestone bedrock extends eastward into the Caribbean for several kilometers at a depth of about 5m. At the eastern extent of this shelf is the longest barrier reef in the Western Hemisphere, second longest in the world (behind Australia's).

Many islands, called cayes, lie offshore; most are ringed by mangroves, and sandy beaches are few and far between. Out on the cayes, tropical breezes waft constantly through the shady palm trees, providing natural air-conditioning when sweltering temperatures plague the mainland.

Mangroves line much of the Belize coast.

GOVERNMENT

British colonial rule left a tion of representative de tinued after independenc country did not succumb to pattern of political development America, where bullets often h more influence than ballots. Despite tablishment by pirates, Belize's poli scene is surprisingly nonviolent, thoug hardly incorrupt.

As a member of the Commonwealth, Belize recognizes the British monarch as its head of state. The Crown is represented on Belizean soil by the governor-general, who is appointed by the monarch with the advice of the Belizean prime minister. The Belizean legislature is bicameral, with a popularly elected House of Representatives and a nominated Senate similar in function to the British House of Lords.

The prime minister is the actual political head of Belize, and since independence the prime minister has usually been George Price, a founder of the People's United Party (PUP). The PUP was born in the 1950s during the early movement for independence. For the first decade of its existence, the PUP was seen as anti-British, and the colonial authorities harassed its leaders.

But by 1961 the British government saw that Belizean independence was the wave of the future. Price went from being considered a thorn in the British side to being the prospective leader of a fledgling nation.

In 1964 Belize got a new constitution for self-government, and the PUP, led by Price, won the elections of 1965, 1969, 1974 and 1979. The PUP was the leading force for full independence, achieved in 1981. Despite this success, the party did not fulfill Belizeans' dreams of a more prosperous economy, a failure due in part to world market conditions beyond the party's control. The party was also seen as having been

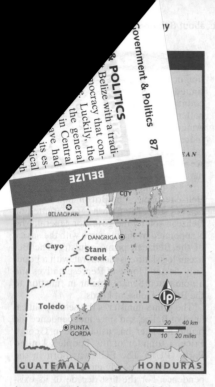

... Belize with a tradi-
...mocracy that con-
... Luckily, the
... in general
... the
... ve had
... its es-
...ical
...th

BELIZE

BELMOPAN

BELIZE CITY

DANGRIGA

Cayo · Stann Creek

Toledo

PUNTA GORDA

0   20   40 km
0   10   20 miles

GUATEMALA   HONDURAS

in power too long and was widely accused of complacency and corruption.

The PUP's main opposition, a conservative, multiparty coalition later named the United Democratic Party (UDP), won the elections of 1984 under the slogan 'It's time for a change,' and Manuel Esquivel replaced George Price as prime minister. Priding itself on its handling of the economy, the UDP gained more ground in municipal elections held at the end of the decade. But the early national election of September 1989 held a surprise: The PUP took 15 seats in the House of Representatives while the UDP took only 13. The venerable George Price changed places with Manuel Esquivel, taking the prime minister's seat while Esquivel resumed his old seat at the head of the opposition.

In 1993 the PUP called early elections, secure in its popularity and intent on extending its mandate for an additional three years. To most Belizeans, a PUP victory was

a foregone conclusion. Many of the PUP adherents didn't bother to vote, but UDP supporters did, and the UDP squeaked to victory by the slimmest of margins – a single vote in some districts. Manuel Esquivel became prime minister again, while PUP supporters looked on in disbelief.

In 1996 George Price announced his retirement as head of the PUP, opening the way to a noisy power struggle among his lieutenants. Said Musa won the struggle and led the PUP to a stunning sweep of town board seats in the March 1997 by-elections. In the 1998 election, Said Musa defeated Esquivel, and the PUP now has control of the central and local governments.

ECONOMY

In the lands west and south of Belize City, cattle ranching is a prime economic component, along with farming (corn, other vegetables and citrus fruits) and, in the Maya Mountains, forestry. In the north, cattle ranches share the land with large sugarcane plantations and their attendant refineries. The cayes depend on tourism and fishing for their income, but these two pursuits are sometimes in conflict. The spiny lobster and some types of fish have been seriously overexploited.

In the 1980s and 1990s Belize developed something of a reputation as a transshipment point for the illicit drug trade, especially around Belize City. This industry seems to have died down, reducing the dangers associated with high-volume drug transportation. Recreational drug use is still prevalent, but it happens discreetly.

POPULATION & PEOPLE

For such a tiny country, Belize enjoys a fabulous, improbable ethnic diversity. Creoles – descendants of the African slaves and British pirates who first settled here to exploit the country's forest resources – make up the country's largest ethnic group. Racially mixed and proud of it, Creoles speak a fascinating, unique dialect of English that, though it sounds familiar at first, is not easily intelligible to a speaker of standard English. Most of the people you will meet and deal with in Belize City and Belmopan will be Creole.

Fully one-third of Belize's people are mestizos, or persons of mixed European and Central American Indian ancestry, some of whose ancestors immigrated from Yucatán during the 19th century.

The Maya of Belize make up about 10% of the population and are divided into three linguistic groups. The Yucatec live in the north near the Yucatán border, the Mopan live in western Belize around the border town of Benque Viejo del Carmen, and the Kekchi inhabit far southern Belize in and around Punta Gorda. In recent years, political refugees from Guatemala and El Salvador have contributed to Belize's Maya population. Use of the Mayan language is decreasing, and both Spanish and English – the official language of Belize – are becoming more widespread among the Maya.

Southern Belize is the home of the Garífunas (or Garinagus, also called Black Caribs), who account for less than 10% of the population. The Garífunas are of South American Indian and African descent. They look more African than Indian, but they speak a language that's much more Indian than African, and their unique culture combines aspects of both peoples.

Other ethnic groups in Belize include small populations of Europeans, North Americans, Chinese and East Indians.

RELIGION

Belize's mixture of religions follows its ethnic composition. Anglicans, Buddhists, Catholics, Hindus, Muslims, Mennonites and evangelical Protestants are all represented, and some communities still observe traditional Mayan rites.

LANGUAGE

Belize is officially English-speaking. But the Creoles, the country's largest ethnic group (over half of the population), speak their own colorful dialect as well as standard English flavored with the Caribbean's musical lilt. Spanish is the first language in the north and in some towns in the west. You may also hear Mayan, Chinese, Mennonite German, Hindi and Garífuna.

Facts for the Visitor

PLANNING
When to Go
The busy winter season is between mid-December and April, and a second peak occurs during the North American summer, June through August. As with the rest of the Ruta Maya area, the dry season (November to May) is the better time to travel, but prices are lower and lodgings on the cayes easier to find in summer (July to November). If you do visit in summer, be aware that this is hurricane season. Belize City was badly damaged by hurricanes, with heavy loss of life, in 1931, 1961 and 1978.

Maps
If you're driving, pick up a copy of Emory King's annual *Driver's Guide to Beautiful Belize*, sold in bookstores and gift shops in Belize City. The guide has basic maps and detailed route descriptions – helpful since road markers in Belize are few and far between.

The various British Ordnance Survey maps (1:750,000 to 1:1000) are the most detailed and accurate of the country. In North America, order them from OMNI Resources (☎ 910-227-8300, fax 227-8374), PO Box 2096, Burlington, NC 27216; or Map Link (☎ 805-692-6777, fax 692-6787), 30 S La Patera Lane, Unit 5, Santa Barbara, CA 93117.

More readily accessible in Belize is the *Belize Facilities Map* issued by the Belize Tourism Board, PO Box 325, Belize City. Derived from the Ordnance Survey maps, it has plans of all major towns in Belize, a road map, plans of the archaeological sites at Altun-ha and Xunantunich and a list of facts about Belize. If you write to the Board in advance you may be able to get one free; in Belizean shops the map is sold for US$4.

TOURIST OFFICES
Belize Tourism Board (☎ 2-31910, 2-31913, fax 2-31943, btbb@btl.net, www.travelbelize.org) is headquartered in the Central Bank Building on Gabourel Lane in Belize City. It also maintains a branch in Germany: Belize Tourism Board (☎ 711-233-947), Bopserwaldstrasse 40-G, D-70184, Stuttgart.

Belize Tourism Industry Association (☎ 2-75717, 2-71144, fax 2-78710, btia@btl.net), 10 N Park St, Belize City, is Belize's private-sector tourism organization. This association publishes Destination Belize, a helpful visitor's guide available from information kiosks and hotels throughout the country.

VISAS & DOCUMENTS
Citizens of many countries (among them Australia, Canada, France, Germany, Ireland, Italy, Mexico, New Zealand, the UK, the USA and many Caribbean nations) do not need to obtain a Belizean visa in advance, provided they have a valid passport and an onward or roundtrip airline ticket from Belize. A visitor's permit valid for 30 days will be stamped in their passport at a border crossing or at the airport. Details on visa requirements for other visitors are available from any Belizean embassy or consulate (see Embassies & Consulates, below).

If you plan to drive in Belize, you'll need to bring a valid driver's license from your home country.

EMBASSIES & CONSULATES
Belizean Embassies & Consulates
Because Belize is a small country and far from rich, its diplomatic affairs overseas are usually handled by the British embassies and consulates.

Some consulates mentioned below are actually honorary consulates or consular agencies. These posts can usually issue visas, but they refer more complicated matters to the nearest full consulate or the Belizean embassy's consular section.

The following are Belize's diplomatic posts abroad:

Canada Honorary Consul (☎ 514-871-4741, fax 514-397-0816), 1080 Beaver Hall Hill, Suite 1720,

Montréal, QC H2Z 1S8; Honorary Consul
(☎ 416-865-7000, fax 416-865-7048), Suite 3800,
South Tower, Royal Bank Plaza, Toronto, ON
M5J 2J7

Germany Honorary Consul (☎ 71-423-925, fax 71-
423-225), Lindenstrasse 46-48, 74321 Beitigheim,
Bissingen

Guatemala Embassy (☎ 334-5531, 331-1137, fax
334-5536), Avenida La Reforma 1-50, Zona 9,
Edificio El Reformador, Suite 803, Guatemala
City

Honduras Consulate (☎ 504-551-6191, fax 504-
551-6460), 2 Avenida 7 Calle No 102, Colonia
Bella Vista San Pedro Sula

Mexico Embassy (☎ 5-520-12-74, fax 5-520-00-03),
Calle Bernardo de Gálvez 215, Colonia Lomas
de Chapultepec, Mexico, DF 11000; Consulate
(☎ 9-832-77-28), Avenida Obregón 226, Chetumal; c/o British Consulate (☎ 928-39-62), Calle
58 No 450, at Calle 53, Fraccionamiento del
Norte, Mérida

UK Belize High Commission to London (☎ 020-
7499-9728, fax 020-7491-4139), 22 Harcourt
House, 19 Cavendish Square, London W1M
9AD

USA Embassy (☎ 202-332-9636, fax 202-332-
6888), 2535 Massachusetts Ave NW, Washington,
DC 20008; Consulate General (☎ 323-469-7343,
fax 323-469-7346), 5825 Sunset Blvd, Suite 206,
Hollywood, CA 90028

Embassies & Consulates in Belize

A few countries have ambassadors stationed
in Belize. Many others appoint nonresident
ambassadors who handle Belizean affairs
from their home countries. Embassies and
consulates tend to be open from about 9 am
to noon Monday to Friday. Unless otherwise mentioned, all the offices listed below
are in Belize City.

Denmark Consulate (☎ 2-72172, fax 2-77280), 13
Southern Foreshore
European Union Commission of the European
Union (☎ 2-72785, 2-32070), Eyre St at Hutson St
France Honorary Consul (☎ 2-32708, fax 2-32416),
109 New Rd
Germany Honorary Consul (☎ 2-24371, fax 2-
24375), 3½ Miles, Western Hwy
Guatemala Embassy (☎ 93-2531, fax 93-2532),
Church St, Benque Viejo del Carmen
Israel Honorary Consul (☎ 2-73991, fax 2-30463),
4 Albert St

Italy Honorary Consul (☎ 2-78449, fax 2-73056),
18 Albert St
Mexico Embassy (☎ 2-30194, 2-31388, fax 2-
78742), 20 N Park St; also an office in Belmopan
Netherlands Honorary Consul (☎ 2-73612, fax 2-
75936), 14 Central American Blvd
Norway Honorary Consul (☎ 2-77031, fax 2-
77062), 1 King St
Panama Consulate (☎ 2-34282, fax 2-30653), 5481
Princess Margaret Dr
Sweden Honorary Consul General (☎ 2-30623), 11
Princess Margaret Dr
UK British High Commission (☎ 8-22146, fax 8-
22761), Embassy Square, Belmopan
USA Embassy (☎ 2-77161, fax 2-30802), 29
Gabourel Lane

MONEY
Currency

The Belizean dollar (BZ$) bears the por-
trait of Queen Elizabeth II and is divided
into 100 cents. Coins come in denominations of one, five, 10, 25 and 50 cents, and
one dollar; bills (notes) are all of the same
size but differ in color and come in denominations of two, five, 10, 20, 50 and 100
dollars.

The Belizean dollar's value has been
fixed for many years at US$0.50. Prices are
generally quoted in Belizean dollars, written
as '$30 BZE,' though you will also occasion-
ally see '$15 US.' To avoid surprises, be sure
to confirm with service providers whether
they are quoting prices in US or Belizean
dollars. Often people will quote prices as
'20 dollars Belize, 10 dollars US' just to be
clear.

The smaller the town you're in, the more
difficult it is to exchange large bills, so be
sure to have small denominations around if
you're heading off the tourist trail.

Exchanging Money

Most businesses accept US currency in cash
without question. They usually give change
in Belizean dollars, though they may return
US change if you ask for it and they have it.
Many also accept US-dollar traveler's
checks.

Canadian dollars and UK pounds ster-
ling are exchangeable at any bank, although
traveler's checks in currencies other than
US dollars are not consistently accepted

by Belizean banks. It's very difficult to exchange currencies of other foreign countries in Belize.

Moneychangers around border-crossing points will change your US cash for Belizean dollars legally at the standard rate of US$1=BZ$2. If you change money or traveler's checks at a bank, you may get only US$1=BZ$1.97; they may also charge a fee of BZ$5 (US$2.50) to change a traveler's check.

ATMs & Credit Cards ATMs for Belizean banks are becoming common, but they don't yet accept foreign ATM cards. If you depend upon your ATM card for money, stock up on cash in Mexico or Guatemala before entering Belize.

Major credit cards such as Visa and MasterCard are accepted at all airline and car-rental companies and at the larger hotels and restaurants everywhere; American Express is often accepted at higher-end places and is becoming more common among the smaller establishments. Most businesses add a surcharge (usually 5%) to your bill when you pay by card.

Belize has Western Union offices where you can arrange wire transfers.

Costs

Though a poor country, Belize is more expensive than you might anticipate. A small domestic economy and a large proportion of imports keep prices high. A fried-chicken dinner that costs US$3 in Guatemala goes for US$5 in Belize. A very basic, waterless pension room, cheap in Guatemala and Mexico, costs US$8 to US$10 per person on Caye Caulker. Budget travelers will find it difficult to spend less than US$15 per day for a room and three meals; US$20 is a more realistic bottom-end figure, and US$25 makes life a lot easier. Mid-range

travelers will be fine on between US$50 and US$60 a day.

Tipping & Bargaining

In highly touristed areas, tipping tour leaders, dive operators and waitstaff is becoming more common, but this should be done only if you feel the service warrants it. Tips need go no higher than 10%.

Bargaining is not a huge part of the culture in Belize, because shops generally have set prices on goods.

Taxes & Refunds

Belize levies an 8% value-added tax (VAT) on retail sales, as well as a 7% tax on hotel rooms, meals and drinks. The rates listed in this book for accommodations in Belize do not include the 7% room tax. If you stay in a small hotel or guesthouse just one night and don't insist on a receipt, you may not be charged the hotel tax. Foreign visitors do not get a refund of the VAT.

POST & COMMUNICATIONS
Post

By airmail to Canada or the USA, a postcard costs BZ$0.30, a letter BZ$0.60. To Europe it's BZ$0.40 for a postcard or BZ$0.75 for a letter.

Address poste restante (general delivery) mail to: (name), c/o Poste Restante, (town), Belize. To claim poste restante mail, present a passport or other identification; there's no charge.

Telephone

The telephone system is operated by Belize Telecommunications Ltd (BTL), with offices in major towns (open 8 am to noon and 1 to 4 pm Monday to Friday and 8 am to noon Saturday).

Local phone calls cost BZ$0.25. Telephone debit cards can be purchased in denominations of BZ$10, BZ$20 and BZ$50.

To call one part of Belize from another, dial 0 (zero), then the one- or two-digit area code, then the four- or five-digit local phone number. You must also dial 0 and the area code when you're making a local call with a phone card.

Here are Belize's area codes:

Ambergris Caye	☎ 26
Belize City	☎ 2
Belmopan	☎ 8
Benque Viejo del Carmen	☎ 93
Burrell Boom	☎ 28
Caye Caulker	☎ 22
Corozal	☎ 4
Dangriga	☎ 5
Independence/Placencia	☎ 6
Ladyville	☎ 25
Orange Walk	☎ 3
Punta Gorda	☎ 7
San Ignacio	☎ 92
Cell phones	☎ 14

Here are some useful numbers:

Directory assistance	☎ 113
Local & regional operator	☎ 114
Long-distance (trunk) operator	☎ 110
International operator	☎ 115
Fire & ambulance	☎ 90
Police	☎ 911

The country code is 501. The large American long-distance companies provide international service as well. Their rates may not be much different than BTL's, however. AT&T's USADirect and WorldConnect services can be requested through the international operator.

Fax, Email & Internet Access

Fax service is available at many hotels and businesses. BTL provides Internet access to local residents with accounts, charging by the hour. Most hotels will send email messages for guests. Internet cafés are starting to crop up in Belize's tourist centers; rates average around US$3 for 15 minutes. BTL's service is crashy – the joke in the country is that BTL stands for 'Betta Try Later' – but it only goes down for short periods of time. CompuServe and America Online do not have nodes in Belize at the time of this writing.

INTERNET RESOURCES

Several helpful websites offer information for travelers to Belize. The best starting points are www.belizetravel.org, the Belize Tourism Board's official website, and www .belizenet.com, which provides excellent travel and accommodations information and links to regional websites. Belizenet .com operates the Belize Forums, a top-notch travelers' bulletin board monitored by Belize travel experts who can help answer your trip-planning questions.

The online version of *Belize First Magazine* can be found at www.turq.com/belizefirst.

The entertaining www.belizeans.com offers a quirky look at Belizean lifestyle and culture, with content provided by both resident and expat Belizeans.

NEWSPAPERS & MAGAZINES

Belizean newspapers are small in size, circulation and interest. Most are supported by one political party or another, so much space is devoted to political diatribe. The PUP-leaning *Amandala* (www.belizemall.com/amandala) has the largest circulation. *Belize Times* (www.belizetimes.com) represents the UDP perspective. The *Reporter* (www .reporterbelize.com) appears to present the most neutral coverage.

Belize's Number Change

Belize Telecommunications Ltd (BTL) was scheduled to change all Belizean phone numbers to seven digits as of May 2002. The change means that callers will be required to dial all digits whether calling from outside an area or city or within it.

For an initial period following the number changes, callers will be immediately forwarded to the new number. After that, a recording should provide you with information. The new numbers will also be reflected in BTL's April 2002 phone directory.

For number conversions, go to the BTL Web site, ⓦ www.btl.net. You can also check the Lonely Planet Web site (ⓦ www .lonelyplanet.com/upgrades; see *Belize, Guatemala & Yucatán*), where we will post new information as it becomes available.

Foreign newspapers such as the *Miami Herald* are difficult to find. Few newsstands – even those in the luxury hotels and resorts – carry current foreign periodicals. *Belize First Magazine*, published by Belize expert Lan Sluder, has information of interest to travelers as well as retirees and other expats. Especially helpful are the reader recommendations on lodging, restaurants and tours. An online version is available at www.turq.com/belizefirst. The print version is published quarterly and sold for US$29 per year. To order, fax a request to 828-667-1717, email bzefirst@aol.com, or write Equator Travel Publications/Asheville, 280 Beaverdam Rd, Candler, NC 28715 USA.

RADIO & TV
Love-FM serves as the nation's national radio station. Showing up at various spots on the radio dial, it's a charming mix of local news, public-service announcements and the world's best love songs.

Channel 5 is Belize's primary TV station. Programming consists mainly of rebroadcast US satellite feeds and a few hours of local content, such as local news, ceremonies and special sporting events. Most hotels with TVs in their guest rooms provide cable service with several dozen channels, including CNN, BBC, Discovery, HBO and the major US networks (ABC, NBC, CBS and Fox).

BUSINESS HOURS
Banking hours vary from bank to bank, but most are open 8 am to 1:30 pm Monday to Thursday and 8 am to 4:30 pm Friday. Most banks and many businesses and shops close on Wednesday afternoon. Shops are usually open 8 am to noon Monday to Saturday and 1 to 4 pm Monday, Tuesday, Thursday and Friday. Some shops have evening hours from 7 to 9 pm on those days as well. Most businesses, offices and city restaurants close on Sunday. Note that in smaller towns, the popular Belizean restaurants usually close before 6 pm.

FOOD
Being a young, small, somewhat isolated and relatively poor country, Belize never developed an elaborate native cuisine. Recipes in Belize are mostly borrowed – from the UK, the Caribbean, Mexico and the USA. Each community has its own local favorites, but Garífuna and Mayan dishes and traditional favorites such as *boil-up* rarely appear on restaurant menus. Even so, there is some good food to be had, especially the fresh fish options available in seaside locales.

Rice and beans prevail on Belizean menus and plates. They're usually served with other ingredients – chicken, pork, beef, fish, vegetables, even lobster – plus some spices and condiments such as coconut milk. 'Stew beans with rice' is stewed beans on one side of the plate, boiled rice on the other side and chicken, beef or pork on top. For garnish, sometimes you'll get coleslaw or fried plantain.

Some restaurants serve wild game such as armadillo, venison and the guinea-pig-like gibnut (also called 'paca'). Conservationists frown on this practice. Lobsters are in season from mid-June to mid-February (to discourage poaching, don't order them the rest of the year), and conch season begins when lobster season ends.

SHOPPING
Belizeans do not trade in handicrafts at the level of Mexicans and Guatemalans; instead, most gift shops in the country do a booming business in T-shirts, imported sarongs and Belikin Beer paraphernalia. Some useful and valuable goods made in Belize can be picked up for souvenirs. Among these are Rainforest Remedies (a line of all-natural health products – digestive aids, insect repellents, salves etc – produced by IxChel farms in San Ignacio); Marie Sharp's hot sauce; and Rasta Pasta spice packets, for creating traditional Belizean dishes at home. Books and recordings by Belizean artists can be purchased from Cubola Productions (cubolabz@btl.net, www.belizemall.com/cubola).

Getting There & Around

Getting There & Away

AIR

Major airlines serving Belize include American (from Miami and Dallas), Continental (from Houston) and Grupo TACA (from Los Angeles). Most international air routes to Belize City go through these gateways.

Grupo TACA also offers direct flights between Belize City and Guatemala City (Guatemala), San Salvador (El Salvador), and Roatan and San Pedro Sula (Honduras), as well as connecting flights from Panama, Nicaragua and Costa Rica. Mexicana Airlines (in the US ☎ 800-531-7921, www.mexicana.com, no ticket agent in Belize) flies between Cancún (Mexico) and Belize City on Thursday, Saturday and Sunday. South American and European flights connect through Miami or Texas.

American Airlines (☎ 2-32522, fax 2-31730, in the US ☎ 800-433-7300), New Rd at Queen St, Belize City

Continental Airlines (☎ 2-78309, 2-78223, fax 2-78114, in the US and Canada ☎ 800-231-0856), 80 Regent St, Belize City

Grupo TACA (☎ 2-72332, 2-77257, fax 2-75213, in the US ☎ 800-535-8780, www.grupotaca.com), 41 Albert St, Belize City

Philip SW Goldson International Airport (BZE) at Ladyville, 9 miles (16km) northwest of the city center, handles all international flights.

Departure taxes and airport-use fees of BZ$30 (US$15) are levied on non-Belizean travelers departing Goldson International Airport for foreign destinations.

Flights to Tikal (Guatemala)

Tropic Air offers day and overnight tours by air from San Pedro on Ambergris Caye to Tikal in Guatemala. The tours leave at 8 am and 2 pm Monday to Friday, stopping at Belize City's Goldson International Airport at 8:30 am and 2:30 pm and leaving Flores

on the return trip at 9:30 am and 3:30 pm. A one-way flight with no tour services costs US$85. A tour package including airfare, ground transportation to Tikal, lunch and a guided tour of the archaeological site at Tikal costs US$280; departure taxes and overnight stays are extra.

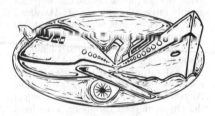

LAND

Several companies, including Batty Brothers and Venus, operate direct buses from Chetumal (Mexico) to Belize City. Companies including Batty Brothers and Novelo's run between Belize City and Benque Viejo del Carmen on the Guatemalan border, connecting with Guatemalan buses headed for Flores. Some of these lines arrange connections so that you can travel between Flores and Chetumal directly, with only brief stops in Belize to change buses. For details, see Chetumal in the Yucatán section and Flores in the Guatemala section. For information on Belizean buses, see Getting Around, later this chapter.

Exit tax at Belizean land border-crossing points is US$7.50.

SEA

The *Gulf Cruza* runs between Belize City and Puerto Cortés (Honduras), with stops in Placencia and Big Creek, every Friday, returning Monday morning.

Scheduled boats and occasional small passenger boats ply the waters between Punta Gorda in southern Belize and Lívingston and Puerto Barrios in eastern Guatemala. Another service runs from Punta

Gorda to Puerto Cortés (Honduras). Refer to the Southern Belize chapter for details. These boats can usually be hired for special trips between countries, and if enough passengers split the cost, the price per person can be reasonable.

Getting Around

AIR

With few paved roads, Belize depends greatly on small airplanes (de Havilland Twin Otters, Cessnas etc) for fast, reliable transportation within the country.

Belize City has two airports. All international flights use Philip SW Goldson International Airport (BZE), 9 miles (16km) northwest of the city center. The Municipal Airport (TZA) is 1.5 miles (2.5km) north of the city center, on the shore. Most local flights will stop and pick you up at either airport, but fares are almost always lower from Municipal, so unless you're connecting to an international flight, use that one.

Two airlines operate along two main domestic air routes: Belize City-Caye Caulker-San Pedro-Corozal, returning along the reverse route; and Belize City-Dangriga-Placencia-Punta Gorda, also returning along the reverse route. Sometimes planes will not stop at a particular airport if they have no passengers to drop off or reservations for passengers to pick up, so be sure to reserve your seat in advance whenever possible. Tickets for both airlines can be booked through most of the hotels and tour agencies within the country.

Local Belizean airlines include:

Maya Island Air (in Belize City ☎ 2-31140, miatza@btl.net; in San Pedro ☎ 26-2435, miaspr@btl.net; in the USA and Canada ☎ 800-521-1247; www.mayaairways.com)

Tropic Air (in San Pedro ☎ 26-2012, fax 26-2338; in the USA and Canada ☎ 800-422-3435; tropicair@btl.net, www.tropicair.com)

The following list provides information on flights from Belize City to various points. Fares are one way from Municipal/Goldson International airports (note that prices are always higher flying into and out of Goldson):

Caye Caulker (CLK/CKR) – 10 minutes, US$24/43. Tropic Air flights to San Pedro stop at Caye Caulker on request. Maya Island Air has flights (continuing to San Pedro) at 6:45, 7:15, and 8:30 am and 2, 3, 3:30 and 4:25 pm.

Corozal (CZL) – 1 to 1½ hours, US$61/80. Tropic Air's 9:40 am and 2:30 pm flights from Belize City to San Pedro continue to Corozal, then return to Belize City from Corozal at 10:30 am and 3:30 pm via San Pedro. There's also a San Pedro-Corozal flight at 7:10 am, returning at 7:30 am. Maya Island Air has flights from San Pedro to Corozal at 7:15 am, noon and 4 pm, returning at 7:45 am and 12:30 and 4:35 pm.

Dangriga (DGA) – 20 minutes, US$31/45. Maya Island Air flies to Dangriga from Belize City at 10 am and 12:30, 2:30 and 4:30 pm. Tropic Air flights leave at 8:30 and 11 am and 12:30, 2:30 and 4:50 pm.

Flores (Guatemala) – 1 hour, US$85. Tropic Air has flights from Goldson International Airport daily at 8:30 am and 2:30 pm.

Placencia (PLA) – 25 to 35 minutes, US$54/64. Maya Island Air flies to Placencia from Belize City at 8 and 10 am and 12:30, 2:30 and 4:30 pm. Tropic Air flights leave at 8:30 and 11 am and 12:30, 2:30 and 4:50 pm. All flights stop first in Dangriga.

Punta Gorda (PND) – 55 minutes, US$73/85. Departures from Belize City are the same as for Placencia. Return flights on Tropic Air depart from Punta Gorda for Belize City at 7 and 9:35 am and 12:15, 1:35 and 4 pm; return flights on Maya Island Air leave Punta Gorda at 6:45, 9:20 and 11:20 am and 4:05 pm.

San Pedro, Ambergris Caye (SPR) – 15 minutes, US$24/43. Tropic Air offers hourly flights from 7 am to 5 pm. Maya Island Air has 12 flights between 6:45 am and 5:30 pm daily. Maya will run flights later in the evening if major flights from the US to Belize City have been delayed.

Note: Fares for the individual legs of the routes average about US$30.

BUS

Most Belizean buses are used US school buses, although a few 1st-class services are available. The larger companies operate frequent buses along the country's three main roads. Smaller village lines tend to be run on

Bus Line Update

As this book was going to press, the Batty Brothers bus company was taken over by Novelo's Bus Lines. Novelo's reports that all schedules and contact information will remain the same; only the name has changed. All mentions of Batty in this book now refer to Novelo's.

local work and school schedules: buses run from a smaller town to a larger town in the morning and return in the afternoon. Fares average about US$1.50 per hour's ride.

Each major bus company has its own terminals. Belize City's bus terminals are located near the Pound Yard Bridge, along or close to the Collett Canal on W Collett Canal St, E Collett Canal St or neighboring streets. This is a rundown area not good for walking at night; take a taxi. Outside Belize City, bus drivers will usually pick up and drop off passengers at undesignated stops if requested. If in doubt about this on certain routes, check with a local or your hotel.

Visit www.belizetravel.org for an automated bus schedule.

Batty Brothers Bus Service (☎ 2-72025, fax 2-78991), 15 Mosul St, Belize City, operates buses along the Northern Hwy to Orange Walk, Corozal and Chetumal (Mexico) and has westward runs from Belize City to San Ignacio and through to Melchor de Mencos on the Guatemalan border.

Novelo's Bus Lines (☎ 2-77372), 19 W Collett Canal St, runs to Belmopan, San Ignacio, Xunantunich, Benque Viejo del Carmen and Melchor de Mencos.

Urbina's Bus Service (☎ 3-22048), based on Main St in Orange Walk; and Escalante's Bus Service, based out of the Batty Brothers terminal in Orange Walk, both run between Belize City and Corozal via Orange Walk.

Venus Bus Lines (☎ 2-73354, 2-77390), on Magazine Rd, operates buses between Belize City and Chetumal.

Z-Line Bus Service (☎ 2-73937), operating from the Venus Bus Lines terminal on Magazine Rd in Belize City, runs buses south to Dangriga, Big Creek, Placencia and Punta Gorda.

James Bus Service (☎ 7-22049) operates out of Punta Gorda and has daily Punta Gorda-Mango Creek-Dangriga-Belmopan-Belize City runs.

Ritchie's Bus Service (☎ 5-22130), 58 St Vincent St, Dangriga, runs between Placencia, Dangriga and Belize City.

Pilferage of luggage has been a problem, particularly on the Punta Gorda route. Give your luggage only to the bus driver or conductor, and watch as it is stored. Be there when the bus is unloaded and retrieve your luggage at once.

Here are details on buses from Belize City to major destinations. Travel times are approximate, as the length of a ride depends upon how many times the driver stops to pick up and drop off passengers along the way:

Belmopan 52 miles (84km), 1 hour. See Benque Viejo del Carmen.

Benque Viejo del Carmen 81 miles (131km), 3 hours. Novelo's operates daily buses from Belize City to Belmopan, San Ignacio and Benque Viejo del Carmen on the hour and half hour from 11 am to 9 pm. Batty Brothers operates nine westbound buses between 4 and 10:15 am daily. Several of these go all the way to Melchor de Mencos (Guatemala). Returning from Benque/Melchor, buses to San Ignacio, Belmopan and Belize City start at 11:30 am; the last bus leaves at 4 pm.

Chetumal (Mexico) 100 miles (160km), 4 hours. Batty Brothers runs 11 northbound buses from Belize City to Chetumal's Nuevo Mercado via Orange Walk and Corozal from 4 am to noon; afternoon runs are at 3, 5 and 6 pm. Twelve southbound buses from Chetumal's Nuevo Mercado run from 4 am to 6:30 pm. Venus Bus Lines has buses departing from Belize City for Chetumal at 11:30 am and 1, 2, 3, 4, 5:20, 6:30 and 7 pm; departures from Chetumal are on the hour from 5 to 10 am.

Corozal 96 miles (155km), 3 hours. All Batty Brothers and Venus buses to and from Chetumal stop in Corozal. Venus runs additional southbound buses on the half hour from 4 to 11:30 am.

Dangriga 195 miles (170km), 3 to 4 hours. Z-Line has hourly buses from Belize City to Dangriga from 8 am to 5 pm. Most buses go via Belmopan and the Hummingbird Hwy, although some take the shorter but unpaved Manatee Hwy. James Bus Service has a daily 7 am Belize

City-Belmopan-Dangriga-Punta Gorda route. A northern bus returns through Dangriga at 9:30 am Monday, Wednesday, Thursday and Saturday; 4 pm Tuesday and Friday; and 11 am Sunday. Ritchie's Bus Service has Belize City-Dangriga runs at 2:30 and 4:30 pm, and Dangriga-Belize City runs at 5:15 and 8:30 am.

Flores (Guatemala) 146 miles (235km), 5 hours. Take a bus to Melchor de Mencos (see Benque Viejo del Carmen) and transfer to a Guatemalan bus. Some hotels and tour companies organize minibus trips, which are more expensive but much faster and more comfortable.

Melchor de Mencos (Guatemala) 84 miles (135km), 3¼ hours. See Benque Viejo del Carmen

Orange Walk 58 miles (92km), 2 hours. See Chetumal and Corozal schedules for Batty Brothers and Venus lines. Escalante's makes six runs from Belize City to Orange Walk from 4:15 to 5:30 pm and 6 southbound runs between the cities from 5 to 6:30 am. Urbina's runs hourly from noon to 6 pm between Belize City and Orange Walk, and at 6:30, 7, 7:30 and 8 am between Orange Walk and Belize City.

Placencia 161 miles (260km), 4 hours. Take a morning Z-Line bus to Dangriga, then catch the connector bus to Placencia. A bus returns from Placencia to Dangriga at 5:30 and 8 am; there may be others as well, depending upon the number of customers. Ritchie's bus leaves Belize City at 2:30 pm. Northern routes leave Placencia at 5:30 and 6 am. The 5:30 am bus stops in Hopkins.

Punta Gorda 210 miles (339km), 8 to 10 hours. Z-Line has buses from Belize City to Punta Gorda at 6 and 8 am and 3 pm, northern routes at 5 and 9 am, noon and 3 pm. James Bus Service has a daily 7 am Belize City-Belmopan-Dangriga-Punta Gorda route. A northern bus leaves at 4:30 am on Monday, Wednesday, Thursday and Saturday; 11 am on Tuesday and Friday; 6 am on Sunday.

San Ignacio 72 miles (116km), 2½ hours; see Benque Viejo del Carmen.

CAR

Belize has three good asphalt-paved two-lane roads: the Northern Hwy between the Mexican border near Corozal and Belize City; the Western Hwy between Belize City and the Guatemalan border at Benque Viejo del Carmen; and the Hummingbird Hwy from Belmopan to Dangriga. Most other roads are narrow one- or two-lane dirt roads; many are impassable after heavy rains. The Southern Hwy is paved in patches but remains slow going.

Anyone who drives a lot in Belize has a 4WD vehicle or a high-clearance pickup truck. If you plan on sticking to the main roads and you're traveling during the dry season, you will be fine renting a high-clearance pickup, which will cost about US$20 a day less than a 4WD.

Sites off the main roads may be accessible only by 4WD vehicles, especially between May and November. After heavy rains in Belize, you can get profoundly stuck in floodwaters or mud even with 4WD, and getting winched out is expensive. Wet conditions aren't the only challenge; in mountain regions the dry soil is loose and rocky, making it hard to keep traction on steep roads.

Fuel stations are available in the larger towns and along the major roads. At last report, leaded gasoline was going for between US$2.50 and US$3 per US gallon (US$0.66 to US$0.79 per liter). Unleaded fuel is currently unavailable in Belize.

Mileposts and highway signs record distances in miles and speed limits in miles per hour, although many vehicles have odometers and speedometers that are calibrated in kilometers.

Road Rules

Although Belize is a former British colony, cars drive on the right side of the road here. Except in Cayo District in western Belize, road signs pointing the way to towns and villages are few and far between. Keep track of your mileage so you know when your turnoff is approaching, and don't be afraid to ask people for directions.

Watch out for sudden changes in road conditions, especially in the south; an overly quick transition from pavement to dirt could cause you to lose control of your vehicle. Be prepared to slow down for double speed-control bumps (called 'sleeping policemen') along the approaches to towns and intersections.

All roads in Belize are two-lane (one in each direction), and you'll soon learn that

Belizeans aren't timid about passing, even on busy stretches of road. Next you'll learn that if you want to get anywhere, you're going to have to play the passing game too. Major roads are used by vehicles of all sizes and speeds – from lumbering sugarcane trucks to swift new SUVs.

Be safe by using your turn signals when you're ready to pass, always heeding no-passing zones (double solid lines) and keeping an eye out for fast-approaching vehicles behind you. Consider driving with your lights on during the day so you'll be visible to oncoming traffic. And if you're in doubt about whether you have room to pass, don't take a risk – there will be other opportunities.

Note: When making a left turn, you must pull over to the right, let oncoming cars pass and make your turn when traffic is clear in both directions.

Use of seat belts is required. If you are caught not wearing yours, the fine is US$12.50.

Petty theft can be an issue – keep your car or truck locked at all times and do not leave valuables in it, especially not in plain view where thieves could be tempted.

Rental

Generally, renters must be at least 25 years old, have a valid driver's license and pay by credit card or leave a large cash deposit. You must obtain a release from the car-rental agency if you plan to drive a rental out of Belize.

Most car-rental companies have representatives at Belize City's Goldson International Airport; many will also deliver or take return of cars at Belize City's Municipal Airport. Rates are around US$80 to US$88 per day (US$482 to US$498 per week), 15% tax included, with unlimited mileage. A Loss Damage Waiver (LDW, loosely known as 'insurance') costs an additional US$14 per day, tax included.

Budget Rent-a-Car (☎ 2-32435, 2-33986, in the USA ☎ 800-283-4387, jmagroup@btl.net), 771 Bella Vista, Belize City. Most of the company's Suzuki and Vitara cars have 4WD, AM-FM radio and air-con.

National Rental Car (☎ 2-31587, 2-31650), 12 N Front St, Belize City.

Crystal Auto Rental (☎ 3-31600, crystal@btl.net), 1½ Miles, Northern Hwy. Offers good prices on 2WD pickups as well as 4WDs. You can arrange pick-ups or drop-offs from your hotel or the airports.

Note that you won't need to rent a car for travel on any of the cayes. Bicycles and electric golf carts are available for rent on Ambergris Caye and Caye Caulker, and these are sufficient.

Insurance

Liability insurance is required in Belize, and you must have it for the customs officer to approve the temporary importation of your car into Belize. You can usually buy the insurance from booths at the border for about US$1 per day. The booths are generally closed Sunday, meaning no insurance is sold that day and no temporary import permits are issued. If you're crossing the border with a car, try to do it on a weekday morning.

BOAT

Fast motor launches zoom between Belize City, Caye Caulker and Ambergris Caye frequently every day.

Preparations

This boat trip is usually fast, windy and bumpy; it is not particularly comfortable. You will be in an open boat with no shade for at least 30 minutes, so provide yourself with sunscreen, a hat and clothing to protect you from the sun and the spray. If you sit in the bow, there's less spray, but you bang down harder when the boat goes over a wave. Sitting in the stern gives a smoother ride, but you may get dampened. If it rains, the mate will drag out a plastic tarp that passengers may hold above their heads.

Schedules

The Belize Marine Terminal (☎ 2-31969), on N Front St at the north end of the Swing Bridge in Belize City, is the main dock for boats to the northern cayes. The terminal building also holds the small Maritime Museum, open 8 am to 5 pm (closed Monday).

Tips on Tours

Most of the tours you'll take in Belize will be fun, interesting and much more fulfilling than if you visited a place by yourself. Following are some tips to help you choose the best tour operators and get the best value from your tour.

- Make sure that your tour guide (not just your tour operator) is licensed by the Belize Tourism Board (BTB).
- Find out what's included in the cost of your tour. Often entry fees and lunch are not included in the quoted price. If lunch is not included, consider bringing your own to save money.
- Restaurants pay tour guides commissions to bring them patrons, and the commission is often built into the price of your meal. Do not feel obligated to eat at the place recommended by your tour operator. Also, do not feel obligated to buy your tour operator lunch; his or her lunch will be provided by the restaurant. If you want to reward your guide for a job well done, a tip is fine compensation.
- Ask how many others will be on the tour. An overcrowded vehicle can be misery. Also, the larger the group, the more waiting around you do.
- Ask to see the boat or the vehicle you will be spending the day in. Make sure it meets your comfort and safety standards.
- Tipping is not mandatory, but if you feel compelled to do so, 10% is a fair amount.

The efficient Caye Caulker Water Taxi Association (☎ 2-31969 in Belize City, ☎ 22-2992 on Caye Caulker, ☎ 26-2036 in San Pedro) operates fast, frequent launches between Belize City, Caye Caulker and San Pedro on Ambergris Caye, with stops on request at Caye Chapel and St George's Caye. Against the wind, the trip to Caulker takes 30 to 45 minutes. The San Pedro ride takes 45 minutes to an hour. See the Cayes chapter for details.

Slightly cheaper is a ride from Triple J Boating Service (☎ 2-33464, fax 2-44375), which runs boats to Caye Caulker and San Pedro from the Court House Wharf behind the Supreme Court building.

ORGANIZED TOURS

Belize has a well-developed network of tour providers, and organized tours can be arranged through local hotels or tour offices at great prices. Additionally, a number of international organizations conduct adventure tours or nature-watching tours in the country. A few of these are listed below:

International Zoological Expeditions (☎ 5-22119, fax 5-23152, in the USA ☎ 508-655-1461, fax 508-655-4445, www.ize2belize.com) runs wildlife expeditions and university research projects from base lodges on South Water Caye and in Blue Creek Rainforest Preserve near Punta Gorda.

Island Expeditions (☎ 5-23328, in North America ☎ 800-667-1630, www.islandexpeditions.com) also offers multiactivity adventure-travel packages, including tours from Belize to Tikal.

Slickrock Adventures (in the USA ☎ 800-390-5715, fax 435-259-6996, www.slickrock.com) offers a variety of sea- and river-kayaking tours, augmented with diving, snorkeling, mountain-biking and hiking.

Belize City

- **population 80,000**

Colorful, ramshackle and alive with Caribbean-style hustle and bustle, Belize City is a great place to explore. Here, unlike in more tourist-oriented areas, you'll have a good opportunity to meet Belizeans going about their everyday lives.

In the past, travelers to Belize have joked that the best thing to do in Belize City is leave. Stories of street crime and harassment have caused many to skip the city altogether and head straight to a safe haven in the cayes or the Cayo District. But much has been done in recent years to make the streets safer. And though Belize City isn't a picture-postcard seaside village, as the country's commercial, cultural and social center it has its own rewards.

HISTORY

Originally the nation's capital, Belize City was built on landfill on the site of a Mayan fishing village. During its tenure as capital, the city endured many natural disasters, including smallpox and cholera epidemics, tidal waves and hurricanes. After the city was ravaged by Hurricane Hattie in 1961, the government moved inland to Belmopan, the country's current capital. That said, the prime minister still lives in Belize City, and most events and announcements of nationwide significance still originate here, usually from the conference rooms of the Radisson Hotel.

ORIENTATION

Haulover Creek, a branch of the Belize River, runs through the middle of the city, separating the commercial center (bounded by Albert, Regent, King and Orange Sts) from the slightly more genteel residential and hotel district of Fort George to the northeast. Hotels and guesthouses are found on both sides of Haulover Creek.

The Swing Bridge joins Albert St with Queen St, which runs through the Fort George district and its pleasant King's Park

Highlights

- Take in the colonial architecture and cooling sea breezes of the Fort George district.
- Soak up urban Belize in the town center, and check out the Swing Bridge – the only working bridge of its type in the world.
- Enjoy traditional Belizean cuisine – from the ubiquitous rice and beans with stewed chicken to lobster and other seafood.

neighborhood. It seems as though everything and everybody in Belize City crosses the Swing Bridge at least once a day. The bridge, a product of Liverpool's ironworks, was built in 1923 and is the only known working bridge of its type in the world. Its operators manually rotate the bridge open at 5:30 am and 5:30 pm daily, just long enough to let tall boats pass and to bring most of the traffic in the city center to a halt. It's quite a procedure, and if you're in the right place at the right time, you might even get to help out.

The Belize Marine Terminal, used by motor launches traveling to Caye Caulker and Ambergris Caye, is at the north end of the bridge.

Each of Belize's bus companies has its own terminal. Most are on the west side of W Collett Canal St, near Cemetery Rd. See the Belize Getting There & Around chapter for details.

INFORMATION
Tourist Offices
The Belize Tourism Board (BTB; ☎ 2-31910/13, fax 2-31943, btbh@btl.net), in the Central Bank Building on Gabourel Lane, is open 8 am to noon and 1 to 5 pm Monday to Friday (until 4:30 pm on Friday).

The Belize Tourism Industry Association (☎ 2-75717, 2-71144, fax 2-78710, btia@btl.net), 10 N Park St, on the north side of Memorial Park in the Fort George district, can provide information about its members, including most of the country's hotels, restaurants, tour operators and other travel-related businesses. Hours are 8:30 am to noon and 1 to 4:30 pm Monday to Friday (until 4 pm on Friday).

Money
Scotiabank (☎ 2-77027), on Albert St at Bishop St, is open 8 am to 1 pm Monday to Friday and 3 to 6 pm on Friday afternoon.

Nearby, the Atlantic Bank Limited (☎ 2-77124), 6 Albert St at King St, is open 8 am to noon and 1 to 3 pm Monday, Tuesday and Thursday, 8 am to 1 pm Wednesday and 8 am to 4:30 pm Friday.

Also on Albert St you'll find the prominent Belize Bank (☎ 2-77132), 60 Market Square (facing the Swing Bridge), and Barclay's Bank (☎ 2-77211), 21 Albert St.

Post & Communications
The main post office is in the Paslow Building at the north end of the Swing Bridge, at the intersection of Queen and Front Sts. Hours are 8 am to noon and 1 to 5 pm Monday to Saturday.

Belize City hasn't caught the Internet café wave yet. You can check your email at Angelus Press (☎ 2-35777), 10 Queen St, for US$5 an hour, but you'll have to do without coffee.

Travel Agencies
Belize Adventures (☎ 2-77257, fax 2-75213, bzeadventure@btl.net), 41 Albert St, is an experienced agency that works with the major airlines. You might also try G&W Holiday Tours (☎ 2-52461, fax 2-52645, gholiday@btl.net) at Goldson International Airport.

Bookstores
Books are sold at Angelus Books, 10 Queen St. Thrift & Book Town, 4 Church St (the book department is upstairs); and Papagayo Gift Shop, Belize Biltmore Plaza Hotel, Mile 3, Northern Hwy.

Laundry
Stan's Laundry, 22 Dean St, between Albert and Canal Sts, charges US$5 per load. Most hotels can arrange laundry service for you at similar prices.

Medical Services
Karl Heusner Memorial Hospital (☎ 2-31548) is on Princess Margaret Dr in the northern part of town. For the treatment of serious illnesses, many Belizeans fly to Houston, Miami or New Orleans.

Business Hours
Offices are usually open Monday to Friday, shops usually Monday to Saturday. Many business establishments close for lunch between noon and 1 pm, and most close for the day by 6 pm. Restaurants in tourist areas generally stay open later.

Emergency
Belize City's emergency police number is ☎ 911. For the fire department or ambulance call ☎ 90.

Dangers & Annoyances
Yes, there is petty crime in Belize City, but it's not necessary to run for your room at the stroke of dusk, as some doomsayers will tell you. Take the same commonsense precautions that you would in any major city.

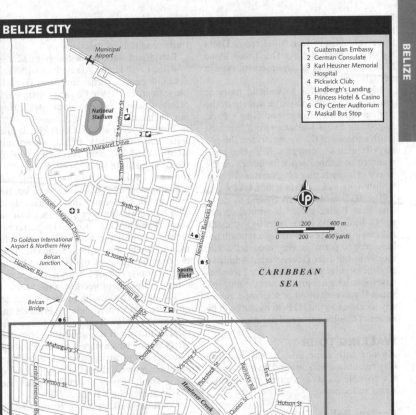

BELIZE CITY

1 Guatemalan Embassy
2 German Consulate
3 Karl Heusner Memorial
  Hospital
4 Pickwick Club;
  Lindbergh's Landing
5 Princess Hotel & Casino
6 City Center Auditorium
7 Maskall Bus Stop

Municipal
Airport

National
Stadium

St Matthew St

Thomas St

Princess Margaret Drive

Princess Margaret Drive

Sixth St

St Joseph St

To Goldson International
Airport & Northern Hwy

Haulover Rd

Belcan
Junction

Belcan
Bridge

Freetown Rd

Main St

Newtown Barracks Rd

Sports
Field

CARIBBEAN
SEA

0   200   400 m
0   200   400 yards

Mahogany St

Central American Blvd

Vernon St

To Western
Hwy

Cemetery Rd

Roger's
Stadium

Orange St

King St

Allenby St

Neal's Pen Rd

Faber's Rd

Caesar Ridge Rd

Douglas-Jones St

Haulover Creek

Victoria St

Pickstock St

Swing
Bridge

Albert St

Regent St

Queen St

Barracks Rd

Eve St

Hutson St

**Fort George
District**

Belize
Harbour

Bird
Island

see Central Belize City map

BELIZE

Don't flash wads of cash, expensive camera equipment or other signs of wealth. Don't leave valuables in your hotel room. Don't use or deal in illicit drugs. Don't walk alone at night, and avoid deserted streets, even in daylight.

It's always better to walk in pairs or groups and to stick to major streets in the city center, Fort George and King's Park. Especially avoid walking along Front St south and east of the Swing Bridge; this is a favorite area for muggers. Ask your hotel operator or a shopkeeper for advice on the safety of a particular neighborhood or establishment, and when in doubt, take a cab.

The BTB is deeply motivated to make sure that Belize builds a reputation for safety. To this end it was recently successful in lobbying for the creation of a tourism police force to patrol heavily touristed areas, mostly in the Fort George area. Additionally, the regular municipal police force has developed a higher profile over the past few years. If you're hassled or scammed, report any incidents to the BTB so its staff will be aware of trouble spots and patterns.

WALKING TOUR

Anyone with some time to kill in Belize City can have a walk around. In a few hours it's possible to take in many of the city's sights and sounds.

Central Belize City

Starting at the Swing Bridge, first take in the **Maritime Museum** (☎ 2-31969), in the Belize Marine Terminal, where exhibits focus on fishing, boats, the reef and other sea-related topics. It's open 8 am to 5 pm daily; US$4 (US$2 for students with ID).

From the Marine Terminal, cross the Swing Bridge and walk south along Regent St, one block inland from the shore. The large, modern **Commercial Center** to the left, just off the Swing Bridge, replaced a ramshackle market dating from 1820. The ground floor holds a food market; offices and shops are above.

As you start down Regent St, you can't miss the prominent **Court House**, built in

1926 as the headquarters for Belize's colonial administrators. It still serves administrative and judicial functions.

Battlefield Park is on the right across from the Court House. Always busy with vendors, loungers, con artists and other slice-of-life segments of Belize City society, the park offers welcome shade in the sweltering midday heat.

Turn left just past the Court House and walk one long block to the waterfront street, called Southern Foreshore, to find the **Bliss Institute** (☎ 2-72458). Baron Bliss was an Englishman with a happy name and a Portuguese title who came here on his yacht to fish. He seems to have fallen in love with Belize without ever having set foot on shore. When he died – not too long after his arrival – he left the bulk of his wealth in trust to the people of Belize. Income from the trust has paid for roads, market buildings, schools, cultural centers and many other worthwhile projects over the years.

The Bliss Institute is open 8:30 am to noon and 2 to 8 pm Monday to Friday, 8 am to noon Saturday. Belize City's prime cultural institution, it is home to the National Arts Council, which stages periodic exhibits, concerts and theatrical works. The Institute also houses the **National Library** (upstairs) and a small display of artifacts from the Mayan archaeological site at Caracol.

Continue walking south to the end of Southern Foreshore, then south on Regent St to reach the **House of Culture** (☎ 2-73050), built in 1814. Formerly called the Government House, this was the residence of the governor-general until Belize attained independence within the British Commonwealth in 1981. Today it holds the tableware once used at the residence, along with exhibits of historic photographs and occasional special exhibits. Open 8:30 am to 4:30 pm Monday to Friday; US$5. The admission price is a bit steep to look at old crockery, but you can stroll around the pleasant grounds for free.

Down beyond the House of Culture you'll come to **Albert Park**, which gets nice sea breezes and has a well-maintained playground, and **Bird Island**, a recreation area with a basketball court (US$2.50 per hour) and an open-air restaurant that serves snacks and cool drinks. Bird Island is accessible only on foot.

Inland from the House of Culture, at the corner of Albert and Regent Sts, is **St John's Cathedral**, the oldest Anglican church in Central America, dating from 1847.

A block southwest of the cathedral is **Yarborough Cemetery**, whose gravestones outline the turbulent history of Belize going back to 1781.

Walk back to the Swing Bridge northward along Albert St, the city's main commercial thoroughfare. Note the unlikely little **Hindu temple** between South and Dean Sts, with offices for Amerijet and FedEx on its 1st floor.

Northern Neighborhoods

Cross the Swing Bridge heading north and you'll come face-to-face with the wood-frame **Paslow Building**, which houses the city's main post office. Go straight along Queen St to see the city's quaint wooden **central police headquarters**. At the end of Queen St, look left to see the old Belize prison, rumored to be the future site of a national museum, and then turn right onto Gabourel Lane.

Down Gabourel you'll pass by the **US embassy**, set among some pretty Victorian houses. A left at Hutson St will take you to the sea, where if you head south (a right turn) on Marine Parade you'll pass breezy **Memorial Park**, the Chateau Caribbean Hotel and the Radisson Fort George Hotel. At the southern tip of the peninsula you'll reach the **Baron Bliss Memorial**, next to the Fort George lighthouse. A small park here offers good views of the water and the city.

Walking back to the Swing Bridge along Fort St (which eventually turns into Front St) you'll pass the **Belize Audubon Society** (☎ 2-35004), 12 Fort St, offering information on national parks and wildlife reserves throughout the country. The **Image Factory Art Foundation** (☎ 2-34151), 81 N Front St, near the Marine Terminal, displays work by Belizean artists.

ORGANIZED TOURS

From Belize City you can book tours to all the country's major sites. Most mid-range and top-end hotels can arrange half- and full-day guided tours to Altun Ha, the Baboon Sanctuary, Belize Zoo, the barrier reef, Cockscomb Basin Wildlife Sanctuary (also called the Jaguar Reserve), Xunantunich and other attractions, usually at prices ranging from US$60 to US$150 per person per tour.

The Belize Audubon Society (☎ 2-35004) offers presentations on bird-watching and environmental awareness the second Tuesday of each month at 7.30 pm in the Maritime Museum. The organization also leads nature walks in Belize City and sponsors other nature-related activities; call for a schedule of events.

Hugh Parkey's Belize Dive Connection (☎ 2-34526, fax 2-78808, www.belizediving .com) specializes in dive trips but also arranges inland excursions.

PLACES TO STAY

Note: A 7% lodging tax will be added to the cost of your room. In addition, some hotels will tack on a service charge, often around 10%. Prices listed here (and throughout the Belize section of this book) are base prices, exclusive of tax and service charge; when settling on the cost of a room, be sure to ask about additional charges.

Budget

The BTB keeps an eye on the city's lowest-budget lodgings and occasionally shuts down those it deems unworthy. Travelers on a flophouse budget should call first to make sure the place they're thinking of staying is open for business.

Seaside Guest House (☎ 2-78339, fax 2-71689, jself@ucb.edu.bz, 3 Prince St) is operated by Friends Services International, a Quaker service organization. The six clean, simple rooms share baths and rent for US$16.50/24/33 single/double/triple. A bunk in the seven-bed dorm room costs US$10. Breakfast is available, as is valuable information on travel in Belize City and beyond.

CENTRAL BELIZE CITY

PLACES TO STAY
3   Freddie's Guest House
4   Glenthorne Guesthouse
6   Mira Rio Hotel
7   North Front Street Guest House
8   Bonaventure Hotel
24 Isabel Guest House
35 Fort Street Guest House
36 Chateau Caribbean Hotel
45 Colton House
46 Radisson Fort George Hotel
47 Great House
52 Bellevue Hotel
53 Seaside Guest House
59 Hotel Mopan

PLACES TO EAT
11 Phil & Barbie's
11 Macy's
47 Smokey Mermaid Restaurant
48 Dit's Restaurant
51 Three Amigos
58 Ocean Restaurant & Bakery

OTHER
1   Ghane Clock Tower
2   Methodist Church
5   Belize Tourism Board
9   American Airlines
10 French Consulate
12 Catholic Church
13 Angelus Press (Internet Access)
14 Central Police Headquarters
15 US Embassy
16 Venus Bus Station; Z-Line Bus Station
17 Fuel Station
18 James Bus Station; Ritchie's Bus Station; Urbina's Bus Station
19 Batty Brothers Bus Station
20 Belize Marine Terminal; Maritime Museum
21 Post Office (Paslow Building)
22 Belize Tourism Industry Association
23 Mexican Embassy
25 Big Daddie's; Commercial Center
26 Image Factory
27 Novelo's Bus Station
28 Barclay's Bank
29 Belize Bank
30 Thrift & Book Town
31 Taxi Stand
32 Court House
33 Boat Dock for Triple J & Gulf Cruza
34 National Handicrafts Centre
37 Ro-Mars
38 Brodie's
39 BTL Telephone Office
40 Bliss Institute
42 Scotiabank
43 Atlantic Bank Limited
44 Belize Audubon Society
49 Belize Adventures; TACA Airlines
50 Italian Consular Agency
54 Baron Bliss Memorial
55 Stan's Laundry
56 Methodist Church
57 Hindu Temple; FedEx
60 Continental Airlines Office
61 Playground
62 St John's Cathedral
63 House of Culture

BelChina Bridge

Douglas Jones St

Unidos Alley

Vernon St

Logwood St

Magazine Rd

Johnson St

Woods St

W Collet Canal St

E Collet Canal St

Bagdad St

Mosul St

 16

17 18

Banak St

Constitution Park

Cemetery Rd

27

 Roger's Stadium

Gibnut St

King St

Hiccatee St

Amara Ave

Euphrates Ave

Tigris St

West St

George St

Iguana St

Dean St

Dolphin St

Bocatora St

Raccoon St

Basra St

Allenby St

Armadillo St

Kut Ave

Rocky Lane

Tanzmoush Canal

Kut Ave

Mex Ave

Southside Canal

Racecourse St

Villa Boscardi B&B
223-1691

CENTRAL BELIZE CITY

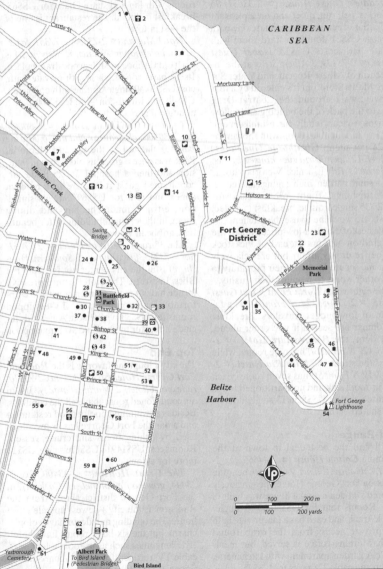

BELIZE

This is the most popular budget guesthouse in Belize City, and it's usually necessary to book well in advance.

Freddie's Guest House (☎ 2-33851, *86 Eve St*) is well run, quiet and on a pleasant residential street. Two rooms share one bath and cost US$21 double; a third room with private bath costs US$23. *Isabel Guest House* (☎ 2-73139, *3 Albert St*) is at the intersection of Albert, Regent, and Water Sts, above Matus Store, but it's entered by a rear stairway; walk around the Central Drug Store to the back of the building and follow the signs. A clean, family-run establishment, it offers three double rooms with shower for US$24 per night. *Glenthorne Guesthouse* (☎ 2-44212, *glenthorneguesthouse@btl.net, 27 Barracks Rd*) is a nice Victorian house with a small garden, high ceilings and eclectic furnishings. Eight rooms rent for US$28/35 single/double, breakfast included. Guests are welcome to use the kitchen.

The best of the ultra-low-priced hotels are clustered on N Front St, east of Pickstock St. They're dreary affairs but are relatively clean and secure. Perhaps their proximity to each other works to monitor their quality.

The eight-room *North Front Street Guest House* (☎ 2-77595, *124 N Front St*) is a favorite of low-budget travelers. Breakfast and dinner are served if you order ahead. Next door, the *Bonaventure Hotel* (☎ 2-44248, 122 N Front St*) has nine rooms, while across the street, the *Mira Rio Hotel* (☎ 2-34147, 59 N Front St*) has seven rooms, each with in-room sink and nonpartitioned toilet. All three charge US$8.50/13 single/double, with shared bath.

Mid-Range

You'll find the best deal in town at the charming *Colton House* (☎ 2-44666, fax 2-30451, *coltonhse@btl.net, 9 Cork St*), near the Radisson Fort George Hotel. The graciously restored wooden colonial house was built in 1928. Rooms rent for US$50/60/70 single/double/triple, and each has a fan, private bath and private access from the wraparound porch. Morning coffee is served, but meals aren't. A garden apartment with kitchenette, air-con and cable TV rents for US$75.

Just up the street, the *Fort Street Guest House* (☎ 2-30116, fax 2-78808, *fortst@ btl.net, 4 Fort St*) has six comfortable guest rooms with fan and shared bath for US$65, breakfast included. The restaurant is one of the best in town.

Hotel Mopan (☎ 2-73356, 2-77351, fax 2-75383, *hotelmopan@btl.net, 55 Regent St*) is a big old Caribbean-style wood-frame place. Its 12 basic rooms, each with private bath, cost US$30/40 single/double with only a fan, US$40/50 with air-con. Add US$10 for each additional person.

Chateau Caribbean Hotel (☎ 2-30800, fax 2-30900, *chateaucar@btl.net, 6 Marine Parade*), flanked by the sea and Memorial Park, was once a gracious old Belizean mansion and then a hospital. Its 25 basic, air-conditioned guest rooms are in a modern annex and rent for US$69/79/89/95 single/double/triple/quad. The bar and dining room, in the original building, offer beautiful Caribbean views.

The 35-room *Bellevue Hotel* (☎ 2-77051, fax 2-73253, *fins@btl.net, 5 Southern Foreshore*) is in the city center not far from the Bliss Institute. The hotel's unimpressive facade hides a modern interior with 35 comfortable, air-conditioned, TV-equipped rooms for US$33 per person. Amenities include a restaurant, bar and swimming pool.

Top End

The city's longtime favorite is the *Radisson Fort George Hotel* (☎ 2-33333, fax 2-73820, *radexec@blt.net, 2 Marine Parade*). Its 76 air-conditioned rooms have all the comforts. Besides a swimming pool, a good restaurant and a bar, the Fort George has its own dock used by fishing boats and cruise vessels. Rooms cost US$149 to US$176 single, US$11 more for a double.

The Great House (☎ 2-33400, fax 2-33444, *greathouse@btl.net, 13 Cork St*), in the Fort George district across from the Radisson, is the city's newest upscale guest house. The building and decor have colonial charm, but the six large rooms have hotel-style amenities such as in-room telephones, cable TV, refrigerator and air-con. Suitably priced at US$100 double.

No 116009

B
$0.75

TOWER HILL BRIDGE TOLL

Private Cars not exceeding 4,000 lbs.
Omnibuses not more than 12 passengers
Taxis not exceeding 4,000 lbs.

$0.75

Northeast of city center in the King's Park neighborhood, the 120-room *Princess Hotel* (☎ 2-32670, fax 2-32660, princessbz@ btl.net), on Newtown Barracks Rd, was formerly the Fiesta Inn Belize and before that the Ramada Royal Reef. It has a swimming pool, marina and casino, and rates are US$120/130 single/double.

Belize Biltmore Plaza (☎ 2-32302, fax 2-32301, biltmore@btl.net), Mile 3 (Km 5) Northern Hwy, is 3.5 miles (4.5km) north of the city center on the way to Ladyville and Goldson International Airport. The 90 air-conditioned rooms have no sea views and thus offer a good value at US$77 to US$88 single or double. Amenities include a pool, air-con and cable TV.

PLACES TO EAT

Belize City's restaurants present a well-rounded introduction to Belizean cuisine, as well as options for reasonable and tasty foreign meals. The basic and ubiquitous Belizean dish of rice and beans with stewed chicken is inexpensive and usually delicious. Lobster (when in season) and shrimp will be at the high end of the price spectrum. Conch (when in season), snapper and other fish fillets are good moderately priced choices.

Belizeans usually eat their large meal in the afternoon, so later in the day you may find that restaurants have run out of, or are no longer serving, their traditional menu items.

The Three Amigos (☎ 2-74378, 2-B King St), formerly GG's Café and Patio, is a favorite with travelers for its tasty food, friendly staff and clean, comfortable dining areas. You'll have a choice of sitting in the cool, tiled dining room – perfect for escaping the midday heat – or out on the patio, best for the evening meal. For lunch, a burger or a big plate of rice and beans with beef, chicken or pork will cost about US$4. Imaginative dinner courses range from US$8 to US$14, and soups and salads run US$5 to US$6. It's open 11:30 am to 2:30 pm and 5:30 to 9 pm daily (until 10 pm Friday and Saturday).

Macy's (☎ 2-73419, 18 Bishop St) offers consistently good Caribbean Creole cook-ing, friendly service and decent prices. Fish fillet with rice and beans costs about US$5, armadillo or wild boar a bit more. Hours are 11:30 am to 10 pm daily. *Dit's Restaurant* (☎ 2-33330, 50 King St) is a homey place with a loyal local clientele. It offers huge portions at low prices; rice and beans with beef, pork or chicken costs US$3, and burgers are US$1.75. Cakes and pies make a good dessert at US$1 per slice. Dit's is open 8 am to 9 pm daily.

Ocean Restaurant & Bakery (☎ 2-70597, 46 Regent St) is a good bet for Chinese food. The chef/proprietor makes his own noodles, eschews lard and serves delicious stir fried rice and noodle dishes for US$3.50 to US$7.50. *Big Daddie's* (☎ 2-70932, 2nd floor, Commercial Center) serves hearty meals at low prices. Lunch is served cafeteria-style starting at 11 am and lasting until the food is gone. Prices vary by size of portions from US$2.50 to US$4. Breakfasts of fry jacks, eggs, beans and bacon are US$3.50, burgers about US$2.

Pete's Pastries (☎ 2-44974, 41 Queen St), near Handyside St, serves good pies (of fruit or meat), cakes and tarts. A slice and a soft drink costs US$1. You might try Pete's famous cowfoot soup, served on Saturday only (US$1.75), or a ham and cheese sandwich (US$1.50). Pete's is open 8:30 am to 7 pm Monday to Saturday, 8 am to 6 pm Sunday.

The high-end *Fort Street Restaurant* (☎ 2-30116, 4 Fort St) offers the best combination of atmosphere and fine dining. Tables are set on the 1st floor and the wraparound verandah of the Fort Street Guesthouse. The cuisine is nouvelle, with California inspiration and strengths in Belizean seafood. Prices are not low – a full dinner with wine or beer might cost US$30 – but the setting can't be beat and it's your best bet for the money. Open daily 7 to 10 am for breakfast, 11 am to 2 pm for lunch, 5:30 to 10 pm for dinner. No lunch on Sunday. Call to reserve a verandah seat.

St George's Dining Room (☎ 2-77400), at the Radisson Fort George Hotel, offers a broad à la carte menu as well as buffet dinners and theme nights. Main courses run from US$20 to US$25, so a complete meal could be up in the US$40 range. Less formal with similar prices is the **Smokey Mermaid** (☎ 2-34759), across the street at the Great House Hotel. Its terraced patio is a lovely place to relax at the end of the day, and the menu offers plenty to choose from. Both are open 6:30 am to 10 pm daily.

ENTERTAINMENT

Nightfall in Belize City brings lots of interesting action, much of it illegal or dangerous. Be judicious in your choice of nightspots. If drugs are in evidence, there's lots of room for trouble, and as a foreigner you'll have a hard time blending into the background.

The bars at the upscale hotels – **Radisson Fort George**, **Great House**, **Chateau Caribbean** – are safe and pleasant, and they draw foreigners and Belizeans alike. The Friday happy hour at the Radisson is especially lively. The **Bellevue Hotel Bar** has a great sea view and is popular with travelers staying south of the Swing Bridge.

The casino at the **Princess Hotel** (☎ 2-32670), on Newtown Barracks Rd, is open from noon until 4 am. Across the street are **Lindbergh's Landing** and the **Pickwick Club**, popular spots for music and dancing.

SHOPPING

Brodie's, 2 Albert St, and Ro-Mars, 27 Albert St, are good places to load up on groceries and other supplies. Brodie's has some English-language books and magazines. For souvenirs, visit the National Handicrafts Centre (☎ 2-33636), 3 Fort St. It's small but offers a good selection of Belizean crafts.

GETTING THERE & AROUND

Buses, boats and planes are available to take you from Belize City to any other part of the country, and car rentals are available. For additional information, see the Belize Getting There & Around chapter. In town, most people get around on foot.

To/From the Airport

The taxi fare to or from the international airport is US$15. You might want to approach other passengers about sharing a cab to the city center.

It takes about half an hour to walk from the air terminal 2 miles (3km) out the access road to the Northern Hwy, where it's easy to catch a bus going either north or south.

Taxi

Trips by taxi within Belize City (including to and from Municipal Airport) cost US$2.50 for one person, US$6 for two or three and US$8 for four. Be aware that if you phone for a cab instead of hailing one on the street, the price may go up, as it will if you're going outside the city center. Secure the price in advance with your driver and, if in doubt, check with hotel staff about what the cost should be before setting out.

The Cayes

Belize's 180-mile-long barrier reef, the longest in the Western Hemisphere, is the eastern edge of the limestone shelf that underlies most of the Mayan lands. To the west of the reef the sea is very shallow – usually not much more than 15 feet (around 5m) deep – allowing for numerous islands called cayes (pronounced 'keys') to bask in warm waters.

Of the dozens of cayes, large and small, that dot the blue waters of the Caribbean off the Belizean coast, the two most popular with travelers are Caye Caulker and Ambergris Caye. Caulker is commonly thought of as the low-budget island, where hotels and restaurants are less expensive than on resort-conscious Ambergris, though with Caulker's booming popularity its residents are fighting to keep the distinction.

Both islands have an appealing, laid-back Belizean atmosphere. No one's in a hurry here. Stress doesn't figure in the lives of many islanders. Pedestrian traffic along the sandy, unpaved streets moves at an easy tropical pace.

Island residents include Creoles, mestizos and a few transplanted North Americans and Europeans. They operate lobster- and conch-fishing boats, hotels and pensions, little eateries and island businesses supplying the few things necessary in a benevolent tropical climate.

Water sports are the name of the game on both islands, especially on Ambergris. The streets of San Pedro tend to be deserted in early afternoon, filling up again after the dive and snorkeling boats return in late afternoon. These cayes aren't so much about hanging out at the beach – Placencia's for that. Visitors here tend to stay active and scheduled during the day, but return home smiling and ready for more fun.

CAYE CAULKER
• population 800

Approaching Caye Caulker on the boat from Belize City, you glide along the eastern

Highlights

• Dive and snorkel off the barrier reef – don't miss Hol Chan Reserve and Shark Ray Alley – or head farther out to sea to find unmatched diving through pristine coral fields.

• Enjoy the freewheeling, sun-dappled Caribbean lifestyle at Ambergris Caye – with its active, resort-style ambience and nightlife – or at Caye Caulker, a laid-back and budget-oriented hideout.

• Take a boat trip to remote Boca Bacalar Chico, a new national park and marine reserve in an area once frequented by seafaring Maya.

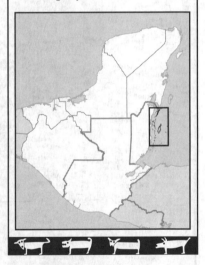

shore, which is overhung with palm trees. Dozens of wooden docks jut out from the shore to give moorings to boats. Off to the east, about a mile (1.6km) away, the barrier reef is marked by a thin white line of surf.

Caye Caulker (called Hicaco in Spanish and sometimes Corker in English) lies some 20 miles (32km) north of Belize City and

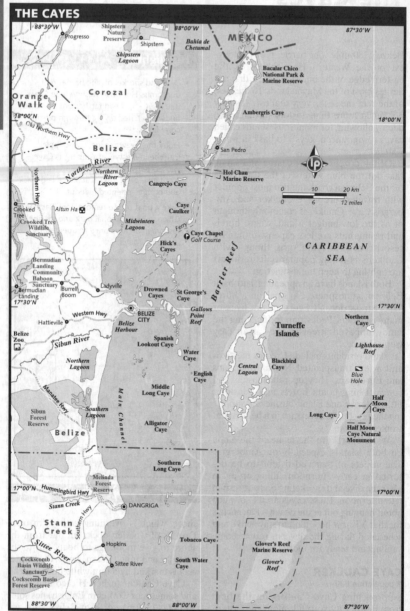

THE CAYES

88°30'W   88°00'W   87°30'W

Progresso
Shipstern Nature Preserve
Shipstern
Shipstern Lagoon
Bahía de Chetumal
MEXICO
Corozal
Bacalar Chico National Park & Marine Reserve
Orange Walk
Old Northern Hwy
18°00'N
Ambergris Caye
18°00'N
Belize
Northern River
San Pedro
Northern River Lagoon
Hol Chan Marine Reserve
Cangrejo Caye
Crooked Tree
Altun Ha
Crooked Tree Wildlife Sanctuary
Midwinters Lagoon
Caye Caulker
Caye Chapel Golf Course
CARIBBEAN SEA
Hick's Cayes
Bermudian Landing Community Baboon Sanctuary
Bermudian Landing
Burrell Boom
Ladyville
Drowned Cayes
St George's Caye
Barrier Reef
17°30'N
Gallows Point Reef
Northern Caye
17°30'N
Hattieville
Western Hwy
BELIZE CITY
Belize Harbour
Turneffe Islands
Lighthouse Reef
Belize Zoo
Sibun River
Spanish Lookout Caye
Water Caye
Blue Hole
Northern Lagoon
English Caye
Central Lagoon
Blackbird Caye
Half Moon Caye
Middle Long Caye
Manatee Hwy
Main Channel
Sibun Forest Reserve
Southern Lagoon
Belize
Alligator Caye
Long Caye
Half Moon Caye Natural Monument
17°00'N
Hummingbird Hwy
Melinda Forest Reserve
Southern Long Caye
17°00'N
Stann Creek
DANGRIGA
Southern Hwy
Stann Creek
Sittee River
Hopkins
Tobacco Caye
Glover's Reef Marine Reserve
Cockscomb Basin Wildlife Sanctuary
Cockscomb Basin Forest Reserve
Sittee River
South Water Caye
Glover's Reef

0   10   20 km
0   6   12 miles

88°30'W   88°00'W   87°30'W

15 miles (24km) south of Ambergris Caye. The island is about 4 miles (6.5km) long from north to south and is only about 650 yards (600m) wide at its widest point. Mangrove covers much of the shore and coconut palms provide shade. The village is on the southern portion of the island. Actually Caulker is two islands, since Hurricane Hattie split the island just north of the village. The split is called, simply, the Split (or the Cut). It has a tiny beach, with swift currents running through it. North of the Split is mostly undeveloped land, and part of it has just been declared a nature reserve.

You disembark and wander ashore to find a place of sandy unpaved 'streets,' which are actually more like paths. The government has carefully placed 'Go Slow' and 'Stop' signs at the appropriate places, even though there are usually no vehicles in sight and everyone on Caulker naturally goes slow and stops frequently. Virtually constant sea breezes keep the island comfortable even in Belize's sultry heat. If the wind dies, the heat immediately becomes noticeable, as do the sand flies and mosquitoes.

Many gardens and paths on the island have borders of conch shells, and every house has its catchment, or large cistern, to catch rainwater for drinking.

Orientation & Information

The village has two principal streets: Front St to the east and Back St to the west. The distance from the Split in the north to the village's southern edge is little more than a half mile (0.8km).

South of the village is the Belize Tourism Industry Association office, on the site of the **Caye Caulker Mini Reserve** (☎ 22-2251). Here you can get information on what to see and do on the island, then stroll an interpretive trail identifying the island's flora and fauna. Call first, as hours are irregular.

Atlantic Bank, on Back St, is open 8 am to 2 pm Monday to Friday and 8:30 am to noon Saturday.

Caye Caulker has its own website: www .gocayecaulker.com. An Internet café on the dock street charges about US$1.50 for 15 minutes. Mike's Movie House, on the east shore, screens videos for US$7.50 for one to three people and offers Internet access at US$2.50 for 15 minutes.

Water Sports

The surf breaks on the barrier reef and is easily visible from the eastern shore of Caye Caulker. Don't attempt to swim out to it, however – the local boaters speed their powerful craft through these waters and are completely heedless of swimmers. Swim only in protected areas.

A short boat ride takes you out to the reef to enjoy some of the world's most exciting snorkeling, diving and fishing. Boat trips are big business on the island, so you have many operators to choose from. Virtually all of the island residents are trustworthy boaters, but it's still good to discuss price, number of people on the boat (they can become crowded), duration, areas to be visited and the seaworthiness of the boat. Boat and motor should be in good condition. Even sailboats should have motors in case of emergency (the weather can change quickly here).

For **dive trips**, contact Belize Diving Service, ☎ 22-2143, fax 22-2217; Blue Water Divers, ☎ 22-2046, fax 22-2239; or Frenchie's Diving, ☎ 22-2234, fax 22-2074. Two-tank dives with gear included range from US$55 to US$90; three-tank dives should cost between US$95 and US$165, all depending on the distance to the site.

Snorkeling trips to Hol Chan and Shark Ray Alley cost around US$20 for a full day or US$13 for a half day, after factoring in cost for gear rental and entry fee. Full-day tours include a stop in San Pedro for lunch. The best guides will get in the water with you to point out interesting coral formations. They also know where to find the best critters, since many of the animals have territories and favorite spots.

Also available are snorkeling trips combined with **manatee-watching** for around US$30. Be sure to bring a sun hat, as this involves a lot of waiting and bubble-watching. Another short excursion typically offered is to a shark- and ray-viewing point off the reef at Caye Caulker. For snorkeling or

BELIZE

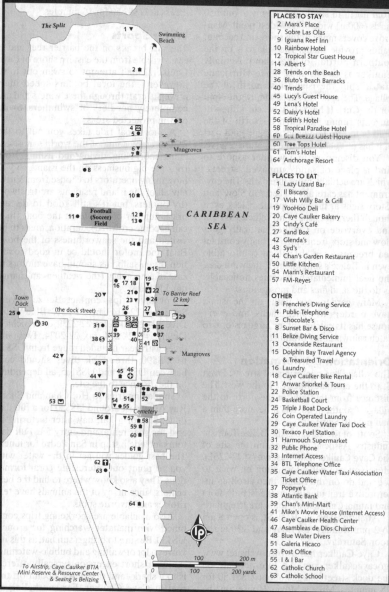

CAYE CAULKER

PLACES TO STAY
2 Mara's Place
7 Sobre Las Olas
9 Iguana Reef Inn
10 Rainbow Hotel
12 Tropical Star Guest House
14 Albert's
28 Trends on the Beach
36 Bluto's Beach Barracks
40 Trends
45 Lucy's Guest House
49 Lena's Hotel
52 Daisy's Hotel
56 Edith's Hotel
58 Tropical Paradise Hotel
60 Sea Beezzz Guest House
60 Tree Tops Hotel
61 Tom's Hotel
64 Anchorage Resort

PLACES TO EAT
1 Lazy Lizard Bar
6 Il Biscaro
17 Wish Willy Bar & Grill
19 YooHoo Deli
20 Caye Caulker Bakery
23 Cindy's Café
27 Sand Box
42 Glenda's
43 Syd's
44 Chan's Garden Restaurant
50 Little Kitchen
54 Marin's Restaurant
57 FM-Reyes

OTHER
3 Frenchie's Diving Service
4 Public Telephone
5 Chocolate's
8 Sunset Bar & Disco
11 Belize Diving Service
13 Oceanside Restaurant
15 Dolphin Bay Travel Agency
    & Treasured Travel
16 Laundry
18 Caye Caulker Bike Rental
21 Anwar Snorkel & Tours
22 Police Station
24 Basketball Court
25 Triple J Boat Dock
26 Coin Operated Laundry
29 Caye Caulker Water Taxi Dock
30 Texaco Fuel Station
31 Harmouch Supermarket
32 Public Phone
33 Internet Access
34 BTL Telephone Office
35 Caye Caulker Water Taxi Association
    Ticket Office
37 Popeye's
38 Atlantic Bank
39 Chan's Mini-Mart
41 Mike's Movie House (Internet Access)
46 Caye Caulker Health Center
47 Asambleas de Dios Church
48 Blue Water Divers
51 Galeria Hicaco
53 Post Office
55 I & I Bar
62 Catholic Church
63 Catholic School

The Split
Swimming Beach
Mangroves

CARIBBEAN SEA

Football (Soccer) Field

Town Dock

(the dock street)

To Barrier Reef (2 km)

Back St

Front St

Mangroves

Cemetery

To Airstrip, Caye Caulker BTIA
Mini Reserve & Resource Center
& Seaing is Belizing

0   100   200 m
0   100   200 yards

LP

manatee-watching tours, contact Carlos Ayala, ☎ 22-2093; Chocolate's (specializing in manatee tours), ☎ 22-2151; or Anwar Snorkel & Tours, ☎ 22-2327.

A handful of **sailboats** take travelers out to the various sites. Ask other visitors to the island for recommendations for tours. Or check by the boat dock before 10 am or in the evening to speak to the boat skippers themselves.

Several places in town rent water-sports equipment. Snorkeling gear and beach floats each cost around US$5 per day, sit-on sea kayaks U0020 per half day, and a Hobie Cat sailboat US$20 per hour or US$50 per half day.

Beachgoers will find the water warm, clear and blue, but will not find much in the way of beach. Though there's lots of sand, it doesn't seem to arrange itself in nice, long, wide stretches along the shore. Most of your sunbathing will be on docks or in deck chairs at your hotel. Caulker's public beach, north of the village at the Split, is tiny, crowded and nothing special.

Organized Tours

A variety of inland trips can be arranged from the cayes. The most popular is the Altun Ha river trip, which stops at Maruba Resort for lunch, swimming and horseback riding. Cost is US$60. This can be arranged through Carlos Ayala, Chocolate's, Anwar Snorkel & Tours (all listed under Water Sports) or your hotel.

Nature and bird-watching tours can be arranged through Ellen McRae at Cari-Search/Galleria Hicaco (☎ 22-2178) or Dorothy Beveridge at Seaing is Belizing (☎ 21-2079). Cost is US$13. Beveridge starts with the interpretive trail at the Caye Caulker Mini Reserve (☎ 22-2251) and combines bird-watching with a mangrove tour.

Places to Stay

Budget Hotels surrounded by trees, or with some grounds, or on the beach cost slightly more than those without such amenities. The rates listed below (and throughout the Belize section of this book) do not include the 7% room tax.

The two-story wood-and-masonry *Tropical Star Guest House* (☎ 22-2374), toward the village's north side, has a porch for sitting and rooms with private shower. Rooms range from US$15 to US$20. *Lena's Hotel* (☎ 22-2106) has 11 rooms in an old waterfront building with no grounds to speak of. Rates are high for what you get: US$25/30 single/double with private shower.

Daisy's Hotel (☎ 22-2123) offers 11 rooms with shared bath for US$10/13/18 single/double/triple. Rooms at the tidy and proper *Edith's Hotel* are tiny, but each has a private shower; US$18 double. *Albert's* (☎ 22-2294) rents six clean rooms for a reasonable US$12/16 single/double.

Mid-Range & Top End Terry and Doris Creasey's tidy, friendly *Tree Tops Hotel* (☎ 22-2008, fax 22-2115) is a gem. Each of its four bright rooms has a fridge and TV. Two rooms share a bath and cost US$25 double (no sea view); the other two have private baths and rent for US$30. *Lucy's Guest House* (no phone) is not on the shore, but it has some trees and gardens, as well as porches off the bungalows for hanging hammocks. Prices are good: A double with shared bath costs US$22; with a private shower it's US$32.

Well-kept *Tom's Hotel* (☎ 22-2102) features nice white buildings on the beach. The 20 cheapest rooms – simple and waterless – cost US$12/18 single/double; bigger rooms in the newer building go for US$23/30; and the comfortable cabins, each with private shower, cost US$30. *Mara's Place* (☎ 22-2156) is in a good location near the Split and has rooms for US$25.

Sobre Las Olas (☎ /fax 22-2243) has 12 rooms, including four with fan at US$25 double and eight with two beds and air-con at US$30 double. Some rooms have cable TV. *Tropical Paradise Hotel* (☎ 22-2124, fax 22-2225) has standard rooms from US$25 (with fan) to US$35 (with air-con); individual cabins – tightly packed together – for US$40 (fan) to US$50 (air-con and cable TV); and suites with air-con and cable TV for US$70, single or double. Amenities include

Diving & Snorkeling from Caye Caulker & Ambergris Caye

The following is a sampling of tours and destinations you can book from either of the cayes.

The Must-See Spots: Hol Chan Marine Reserve and Shark-Ray Alley Hol Chan (Mayan for 'little channel') was the first marine reserve established in Central America. It's the most popular diving site in Belize, and rightly so, because it's swarming with fish of all shapes and sizes. The park encompasses about 5 sq miles (13 sq km) of protected area. It's 100 feet (30m) deep in parts and dotted with coral formations.

Shark-Ray Alley is usually visited in combination with Hol Chan and is now considered part of the marine reserve. Here is an amazing chance to get up close and personal with nurse sharks and southern stingrays, who will swim right up to greet you in 6½ feet (2m) of water.

You'll notice that the boat operators will feed the fish, necessary to keep them in this protected area and on view. This makes for a more exciting visit, but can also lead to sharks and rays getting aggressive with divers, since they're expecting to be fed.

Most dive shops make day and afternoon trips to these sites, and night dives are also an option. Entrance fee is US$5.

Note: Because of the popularity of these sites, the coral has taken quite a beating. Do your part for conservation by not touching any coral; if you're unsure in your flippers, give it a wide berth.

Other Nearby Sites These sites are close by and usually one or two will be visited in combination.

Caye Caulker North Island is the relatively uninhabited northern part of Caulker, with good snorkeling, swimming and places for a beach barbecue. Part of it has recently been designated a marine reserve.

Mexico Rocks is a cluster of boulder coral inland from the reef and therefore protected and calm. Living with the coral are lobster, shrimp, scallops, anemones and eels.

Punta Arena (also known as Small Cut) is an area of dramatic underwater canyons and sea caves teeming with fish, rays, turtles, sponges and coral.

Mata Cut is just north of Punta Arena and the home of *Chaga's Wreck*, the remains of an old barge.

Tres Cocos Cut is a series of deep and narrow furrows creating a natural break in the barrier reef. An astonishing variety of coral formations and marine life can be seen here, and it's only a five-minute boat ride from San Pedro.

Day Trips These trips require long boat rides across choppy seas, but the farther you go, the more pristine your surroundings will be.

Turneffe Atoll, 19 miles (30km) east of Belize City, is alive with coral, fish and large rays. The terrain is quite varied. You can enjoy wreck, wall and current diving, as well as protected shallow areas abundant with coral (perfect for novice divers and snorkelers). Most of the dive sites are at the atoll's southern end.

---

a good restaurant and bar and a big dock for boats or sunning.

The *Sea Beezzz Guest House* (☎ 22-2176) is a solid two-story house on the shore with a nice patio garden in front. It's safe, secure and comfortable, and it offers hot water in the private showers as well as dining-room

service for all three meals. Unfortunately, it's closed May through October. Rates are US$40 to US$60 per room. *Rainbow Hotel* (☎ 22-2123, fax 22-2172), just north of the boat docks, is a two-story concrete building. Plain, clean, cell-like rooms go for US$30 to US$35. Rooms with air-con are US$43. In

BELIZE

Diving & Snorkeling from Caye Caulker & Ambergris Caye

Lighthouse Reef is the farthest atoll from the shore, 62 miles (100km) east of Belize City. Its sites offer some of the best underwater visibility in the country. Half Moon Caye is a small island on Lighthouse Reef, 70 miles (113km) east of Belize City. It has a lighthouse, excellent beaches and spectacular submerged walls teeming with marine flora and fauna. Underwater visibility can extend more than 200 feet (60m) here. The caye is a bird sanctuary and home to the rare pink-footed booby.

Also within Lighthouse Reef, the Blue Hole is the country's best known dive site and often appears in tourist brochures touting Belize's marine wonders. It's a sinkhole of vivid blue water around 400 feet (122m) deep and 1000 feet (305m) across. The dive itself is somewhat gimmicky – you drop quickly to 130 feet (40m), where you swim beneath an overhang, observing stalactites above you and, usually, a school of reef sharks below you. Ascent begins after eight minutes because of the depth.

This trip is usually combined with other dives at Lighthouse Reef, and experienced divers will tell you that those other dives are the real highlight of the trip out. But judging from the popularity of this trip – all the dive shops make a run to the Blue Hole once or twice a week – plenty are willing to make the deep descent, gimmick or not. Snorkelers don't despair: The shallows around Blue Hole are interesting as well.

On day trips the Blue Hole will be your first dive, which can be nerve-racking if you're unfamiliar with the divemaster and the other divers or if you haven't been underwater for a while. An alternative is to take an overnight trip to the reef. Coral Beach Divers offers a five-dive overnight trip for US$220.

Bacalar Chico National Park & Marine Reserve (aka Boca Bacalar Chico) is a newly created national marine park at the northern tip of Ambergris Caye. The park, accessed through a channel dug 1500 years ago by sea-trading Maya, has a nature trail and a Mayan site to explore on land and pristine coral and plentiful marine life under the sea. It's intended to be developed as an alternative to the increasingly crowded Hol Chan Marine Reserve, but its distance – about 90 minutes from San Pedro – has kept the tours from developing. To arrange a trip to the site, ask at your hotel or contact San Pedro's Bacalar Chico National Park & Marine Reserve office (☎ 26-2420, 14-7308, www.bacalar.org), on Carabeña St, west of Pescador Dr. Bacalar Chico can also be visited from Corozal.

addition, two kitchen-equipped apartments rent for US$150 for up to four people.

At **Bluto's Beach Barracks** (☎ 22-2398), just south of the Water Taxi Dock, six new dark-wood bungalows range from US$10 per person for a dorm bunk to US$100 for deluxe accommodations. **Anchorage Resort** (☎ 22-2304), constructed on the site of Caye Caulker's first resort, has comfortable, hotel-style rooms on the sea. Rooms have two double beds, private balconies, private bath and cable TV. A bargain at US$45 double.

The Iguana Reef Inn (☎ 22-2213, fax 22-2000, iguanareef@btl.net), on the island's west side, is Caulker's first luxury resort. Its two-room suites in a new, modern building go for US$90 single or double. Packages are available. *Trends* (☎ 22-2094) has two locations, one on the beach and one on Front St. Rooms start at US$25.

Places to Eat

You'll find prices higher here than on the mainland, though not as high as the restaurants in San Pedro. Seafood is your best bet.

Do your part to avoid illegal lobster fishing: don't order lobster outside its mid-June to mid February season, and complain if you're served a 'short' (a lobster below the legal harvest size).

Glenda's, on the island's west side, is the in spot for breakfast (7 to 10 am): eggs, bacon or ham, bread and coffee for US$3. Get there early, as they usually run out of menu items – and interest – around 9 am. Closed on weekends. Another good place for breakfast and good coffee is *Cindy's Café*, opposite the basketball court on Front St.

The *Caye Caulker Bakery*, on Back St, is the place to pick up fresh bread, rolls and similar goodies. Other picnic supplies are available at *Harmouch Supermarket* and *Chan's Mini-Mart*. For box lunches (US$3 to US$5) try the *YooHoo Deli* (☎ 22-2232), on Front St near the police station, or *FM-Reyes* (☎ 22-2125), next to the Tropical Paradise Hotel. If you're leaving early in the morning for a tour, it's best to call the day before to arrange for a meal.

Serving all three meals (and gallons of Belikin), the *Sand Box* (☎ 22-2200) is perhaps the island's most popular place to dine and drink. For dinner, try the fish with spicy banana chutney (US$7) or the less-expensive barbecued chicken or pastas (including vegetarian lasagna).

Il Biscaro (☎ 22-2045), Caulker's Italian restaurant, serves up plates of pasta and seafood for dinner (until 10 pm) and hearty breakfasts with espresso drinks in the morning. *The Lazy Lizard*, at the Split, mainly serves beer to swimmers and other hangers-about, but it has some menu items as well. The faithful stay here until long after dark.

Marin's Restaurant (☎ 22-2104) serves hearty Belizean fare and seafood dishes priced around US$5. *Little Kitchen* is a slightly cheaper alternative. *Syd's* is popular for seafood and Mexican dishes. Try a couple of tostadas for lunch (US$0.50 each) or the steamed fish for dinner (US$4). *Chan's Garden Restaurant* serves reasonably authentic Chinese food (the owner is from Hong Kong) at moderate prices.

The restaurant at the *Tropical Paradise Hotel* is busy all day because it serves the island's most consistently good food in big portions at decent prices. The light, cheerful dining room serves breakfast 8 am to noon, lunch 11:30 am to 2 pm and dinner 6 to 10 pm. You can order curried shrimp or lobster for US$12 or choose from among many lower-priced items.

Entertainment

The *Oceanside* often hosts live bands, *I&I* is the happening reggae bar, and the *Sand Box*, *Wish Willy* and *Popeye's* attract their fair share of thirsty travelers. The *Sunset Disco*, on the west side of the island, has weekend dances and a rooftop bar with snacks.

Getting There & Away

Air Maya Island Air (☎ 22-2012) and Tropic Air (☎ 22-2040) offer regular flights between Caye Caulker, Ambergris Caye and the Belize City airports. See the Belize Getting There & Around chapter for details.

Boat The Caye Caulker Water Taxi Association (on Caulker ☎ 22-2992; in Belize City ☎ 2-31969) runs boats from Caulker to Belize City at 6:30, 7:30, 8:30 and 10 am, noon and 3 pm (also at 5 pm on weekends and holidays). Boats leave Belize City's Marine Terminal for Caye Caulker at 9 and 10:30 am, noon, 1:30, 3 and 5 pm. The ride takes 30 to 40 minutes, depending on the weather. Fare is US$7.50 one way, US$12.50 roundtrip.

Boats to San Pedro on Ambergris Caye run at 7, 8:30 and 10 am and 1 and 4 pm, returning at 8, 9:30 and 11:30 am and 2:30 pm (also 4:30 pm on weekends and holidays).

The ride takes 20 to 30 minutes. Fare is US$7.50 one way, US$12.50 roundtrip.

Water taxis also run to St George's Caye and Caye Chapel.

Getting Around

Caulker is so small that most people walk everywhere. If need be, you can rent a bicycle or golf cart or use the golf-cart taxi service, which costs US$2.50 for a one-way trip anywhere on the island.

AMBERGRIS CAYE & SAN PEDRO
• population 2000

The largest of Belize's cayes, Ambergris (pronounced am-**ber**-griss) lies 36 miles (58km) north of Belize City. It's about 25 miles (40km) long, and its northern side almost adjoins Mexican territory.

Most of the island's population lives in the town of San Pedro, near the southern tip. The barrier reef is only a half mile (0.8km) east of San Pedro. In the morning, before the workday noises begin, stand on one of the docks on the town's east side – you can hear the low bass roar of the surf breaking over the reef.

San Pedro started life as a fishing town but is now Belize's prime tourist destination. More than half of the tourists who visit Belize fly straight to San Pedro and use it as their base for excursions elsewhere. Even so, San Pedro is certainly no Cancún, though there has been some small-scale development in recent years.

Like Caye Caulker, Ambergris has an engaging, laid-back atmosphere. You'll see plenty of 'no shirt, no shoes – no problem!' signs. San Pedro has sandy streets, lots of Caribbean-style wooden buildings (some on stilts) and few people who bother to wear shoes. Everyone is friendly and, for the most part, each visitor is welcomed as a person, not a source of income.

Orientation

Most of San Pedro's services are walking distance from each other in the town center, within a half mile of the airstrip, but to reach the hotels and resorts to the south

and north of the center you'll need to use wheeled or water transportation. Minivan taxis cost US$2.50 for a one-way trip anywhere in town.

San Pedro has three main north-south streets, which used to be called Front St (to the east), Middle St and Back St (to the west). Now these streets have tourist-class names – Barrier Reef Dr, Pescador Dr and Angel Coral Dr – but some islanders still use the old names.

The river at the end of Pescador Dr is as far as you can go by car. From there, you can cross by hand-drawn ferry to reach a bike and golf-cart trail that runs north to Journey's End resort. Most take the road only as far as Sweet Basil (☎ 26-3870) for lunch, or the Palapa Bar for drinks, before heading back to San Pedro.

The far north resorts are accessed by water taxi.

Information
Tourist Offices The BTB office (☎ 26-2605) is at the smallish Ambergris Museum, in the Island Sun Shopping Center at Barrier Reef Dr and Pelican St. (Admission to the museum is US$2.50.) Tourist information is also available on the caye's own website: www.ambergriscaye.com.

Money You can exchange money easily in San Pedro, and US cash and traveler's checks are accepted in most establishments.

Atlantic Bank Limited (☎ 26-2195), on Barrier Reef Dr, is open 8 am to noon and 1 to 3 pm Monday, Tuesday and Thursday; 8 am to 1 pm Wednesday; 8 am to 1 pm and 3 to 6 pm Friday; and 8:30 am to noon Saturday. Across the street and one block down is Belize Bank, open 8 am to 3 pm Monday to Thursday, 8 am to 1 pm and 3 to 6 pm Friday and 8:30 am to noon Saturday.

Post & Communications The post office is on Buccaneer St off Barrier Reef Dr. Hours are 8 am to noon and 1 to 5 pm Monday to Friday (until 4:30 pm on Friday). It's closed on Saturday and Sunday.

The Cyber Café (☎ 26-3015), 25 Barrier Reef Dr, provides its customers with free

SAN PEDRO (AMBERGRIS CAYE)

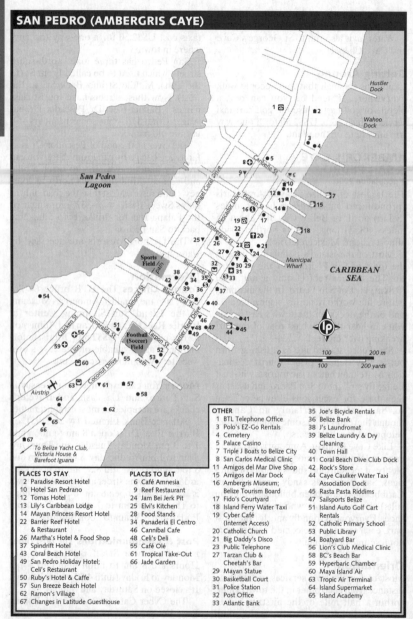

Hustler Dock

Wahoo Dock

San Pedro Lagoon

CARIBBEAN SEA

Municipal Wharf

Sports Field

Football (Soccer) Field

Airstrip

To Belize Yacht Club, Victoria House & Barefoot Iguana

0   100   200 m
0   100   200 yards

PLACES TO STAY
2   Paradise Resort Hotel
10 Hotel San Pedrano
12 Tomas Hotel
12 Lily's Caribbean Lodge
14 Mayan Princess Resort Hotel
22 Barrier Reef Hotel & Restaurant
26 Martha's Hotel & Food Shop
37 Spindrift Hotel
43 Coral Beach Hotel
49 San Pedro Holiday Hotel; Celi's Restaurant
50 Ruby's Hotel & Caffe
57 Sun Breeze Beach Hotel
62 Ramon's Village
67 Changes in Latitude Guesthouse

PLACES TO EAT
6   Café Amnesia
9   Reef Restaurant
24 Jam Bei Jerk Pit
25 Elvi's Kitchen
28 Food Stands
34 Panadería El Centro
46 Cannibal Cafe
48 Celi's Deli
55 Café Olé
61 Tropical Take-Out
66 Jade Garden

OTHER
1   BTL Telephone Office
3   Polo's EZ-Go Rentals
4   Cemetery
5   Palace Casino
7   Triple J Boats to Belize City
8   San Carlos Medical Clinic
11 Amigos del Mar Dive Shop
15 Amigos del Mar Dock
16 Ambergris Museum; Belize Tourism Board
17 Fido's Courtyard
18 Island Ferry Water Taxi
19 Cyber Café (Internet Access)
20 Catholic Church
21 Big Daddy's Disco
23 Public Telephone
27 Tarzan Club & Cheetah's Bar
29 Mayan Statue
30 Basketball Court
31 Police Station
32 Post Office
33 Atlantic Bank
35 Joe's Bicycle Rentals
36 Belize Bank
38 J's Laundromat
39 Belize Laundry & Dry Cleaning
40 Town Hall
41 Coral Beach Dive Club Dock
42 Rock's Store
44 Caye Caulker Water Taxi Association Dock
45 Rasta Pasta Riddims
47 Sailsports Belize
51 Island Auto Golf Cart Rentals
52 Catholic Primary School
53 Public Library
54 Boatyard Bar
56 Lion's Club Medical Clinic
58 BC's Beach Bar
59 Hyperbaric Chamber
60 Maya Island Air
63 Tropic Air Terminal
64 Island Supermarket
65 Island Academy

cookies and coffee while they're using the equipment. The rates are US$0.75 for five minutes, US$10 per hour or all day, with in-and-out privileges.

Laundry Several laundromats lie at the southern end of Pescador Dr, among them Belize Laundry & Dry Cleaning and J's Laundromat.

Medical Services The San Carlos Medical Clinic, Pharmacy & Pathology Lab (☎ 26-2918, 26-3649, in emergencies ☎ 14-9251), on Pescador Dr just south of Caribeña St, treats ailments and does blood tests.

The Lion's Club Medical Clinic is across the street from the Maya Island Air terminal at the airport. Right next door is the island's hyperbaric chamber for diving accidents.

Water Sports

Ambergris is good for all water sports: scuba diving, snorkeling, sailboarding, boating, swimming, deep-sea fishing and sunbathing. Many island hotels have their own dive shops, which rent equipment, provide instruction and organize diving excursions. In fact, just about any local can put you in touch with someone organizing water-sports trips.

Amigos del Mar Dive Shop (☎ 26-2706, fax 26-6264, amigosdive@btl.net), on the dock east of Lily's Restaurant, rents scuba and snorkeling gear and leads diving and fishing trips.

Coral Beach Dive Club (☎ 26-2013, fax 26-2864, forman@btl.net) arranges a variety of trips, including overnight boat excursions on its Off-shore Express. It's not the island's fanciest dive operation, but it gets high marks from experienced divers.

Blue Hole Dive Center (☎ 26-2982, fax 26-2981, bluehole@btl.net) offers a variety of snorkeling and diving trips, including overnight excursions, and is known for the competence and professionalism of its staff. A boat, guide and equipment for a two-tank dive costs around US$70. A diving certification course runs about US$350.

Snorkeling and picnicking excursions cost about US$40. You can choose to travel by powerboat or sailboat. The going rental rate for a snorkel, mask and fins is US$8.

Manatee-watching off Goff's Caye can be added to a snorkeling trip (US$75). Hire a fishing boat for US$165 a day (deep-sea fishing for US$650 a day for six people). Sailsports Belize (☎ 14-8070) rents sailboards for US$20 per hour and sailboats for US$30 per hour; lessons are available.

All beaches are public, and most waterside hotels and resorts are generous with their lounge chairs on slow days. While sandy beaches are plentiful, protected sea grass at the waterline makes entry from shore not terribly pleasant, so you'll be swimming from piers. Swimming is best off the pier at Ramon's.

Organized Tours

Boat Tours The Winnie Estelle (☎ 26-2394), a 66-foot island trader moored at the Paradise Resort Hotel pier, goes out on daily snorkeling trips to Caye Caulker.

The Reef Seeker glass-bottom boat, based at the San Pedro Holiday Hotel, makes daily reef trips for US$20 per adult (half price for kids). The aptly named Rum Punch II, a wooden sailboat, runs sunset cocktail cruises for US$20.

Mainland Tours Many visitors to Belize fly to Ambergris and make it their base for excursions by plane or boat to other parts of the country. Tours are available to the Mayan ruins at Altun Ha (US$75) and Lamanai (US$125) or beyond to the Belize Zoo, Xunantunich, Crooked Tree Bird Sanctuary, the Baboon Sanctuary, Mountain Pine Ridge and Tikal (Guatemala). Any hotel, travel agency or dive shop can fill you in on tours, or contact Excaliber Tours (☎ 26-3235), Seaduced by Belize (☎ 26-2254) or Hustler Tours (☎ 26-4137).

Places to Stay

Wherever you stay, you'll never be more than a minute's walk from the water. All but the cheapest hotels accept major credit cards, usually for a 5% surcharge. Listed below are winter, peak-season rates. Rates usually drop 15% to 20% May through November, although some hotels may consider June through August high season as well, since it coincides with summer break for North American schools. The rates listed below do not include the 7% room tax.

Competition for guests on San Pedro is fierce, and taxi drivers are often rewarded commissions for bringing guests to hotels. Often this commission is tacked on to the cost of your room, so you're likely to save money if you make reservations in advance or show up unescorted. You'll also avoid being taken on a lodging tour of the island if you tell your cab driver that you have reservations. Most hotels on the island now have a 24-hour cancellation policy to discourage reservation pirating by cab drivers.

Budget Right on the water, *Ruby's Hotel* (☎ 26-2063, fax 26-2434), at the south end of Barrier Reef Dr, attracts return visitors year after year. Five of the nine rooms have a private shower; not all rooms overlook the sea. Rates are US$15/20 single/double with shared bath and US$25 to US$45 double with private bath. The choice waterfront rooms must be reserved in advance.

Tomas Hotel (☎ 26-2061), on Barrier Reef Dr, offers a very good value. This family-run place offers eight light, airy rooms with private bath (some with tub) for US$25 double, or US$35 with air-con.

Martha's Hotel (☎ 26-2053, fax 26-2589), Ambergris St at Pescador Dr, has 16 rooms, all with private bath; sometimes the sink is in the room because the bathroom is so small. Rates are US$24/35/47/59 single/double/triple/quad.

Hotel San Pedrano (☎ 26-2054, fax 26-2093, sanpedrano@btl.net), Barrier Reef Dr at Caribeña St, has six rooms, all with private bath and three with air-con. Most rooms don't have ocean views, but you can always sit out on the wraparound porch. Fan-only rooms rent for US$25/30/38/43. Add US$10 per room for air-con.

Mid-Range Note that some of these hotels charge an additional 10% or 15% for service along with the 7% government room tax.

The *Barrier Reef Hotel* (☎ 26-2075, fax 26-2719, barriereef@btl.net), on Barrier Reef Dr in the center of town, is a landmark, its

attractive Caribbean wood-frame construction captured by countless tourist cameras daily. The hotel's eight guest rooms are not in this structure, however, but in a newer and less charming concrete-block addition at the back. Rates are US$55/75/85 single/double/triple with air-con and cable TV.

Changes in Latitude B&B (☎/fax 26-2986), south of the airport on Coconut Dr, just north of the Belize Yacht Club, is a trim two-story guesthouse offering six ground-floor rooms with private bath and air-con. Rates are US$80/85 single/double; $20 lower in the off season. It's just a short block inland from the beach and has a nice garden area.

Coral Beach Hotel (☎ 26-2013, fax 26-2864), on Barrier Reef Dr, is a simple diver's hotel charging US$45/65/85 for air-conditioned rooms. Good-value dive packages are available.

Lily's Caribbean Lodge (☎ 26-2059, fax 26-2673), off the east end of Caribeña St, faces the sea and offers 10 clean, pleasant rooms with air-con; several (especially those on the top floor) have good sea views. Rates are US$45/50/60.

San Pedro Holiday Hotel (☎ 26-2014, fax 26-2295, holiday@btl.net) is on Barrier Reef Dr in the south part of the town center. Rooms are in three cheery, pink-and-white wooden buildings, all facing the sea. The rooms are basic (with air-con, ceiling fans and patios), and the walls can be thin. Rates range from US$103 to US$115 double; the more expensive rooms have refrigerators. You're paying for the location – if you want to be on the beach in the thick of things, this is your place.

Spindrift Hotel (☎ 26-2018, 26-2174, fax 26-2251), on Buccaneer St at Barrier Reef Dr, has a good location right in the center of town on the beach. It's a modern concrete affair with 30 rooms of various sizes. Each of the small rooms has one double bed, a ceiling fan and a view of the street (US$47 double). Larger ones have two double beds, air-con and sea views (US$83). Several apartments are also available (US$110).

Paradise Resort Hotel (☎ 26-2083, fax 26-2232), at the north end of Barrier Reef

Dr, has 25 rooms, cabañas and villas for US$90 to US$110 double.

Top End The *Mayan Princess Resort Hotel* (☎ 26-2778, fax 26-2784, mayanprin@ btl.net), on Barrier Reef Dr, is a modern condominium building in the town center on the beach. Suites with kitchenettes, aircon and cable TV rent for US$125 double.

Sun Breeze Beach Hotel (☎ 26-2191, fax 26-2346, sunbreeze@btl.net), across Coconut Dr from the airport, is a generic two-story concrete building with a sandy inner court and swimming pool opening toward the beach. Shady tiled porticos set with easy chairs are great for lounging. Each of the 34 air-conditioned rooms has two double beds, cable TV and private bath. Rates range from US$110 to US$140 single, US$120 to US$150 double.

Ramon's Village (☎ 26-2071, fax 26-2214), south of town on Coconut Dr at the sea, offers 60 rooms in two-story cabañas, thatched Tahitian-style, facing a good beach and a nice dock for swimming. A dive shop, excursion boats, jet skis, sailboards, lounge chairs for sunbathing, a swimming pool with bar surrounded by coconut palms…this place has everything, and it's very well kept. Some cabañas have sea views, many have sitting porches, and all come with at least a king-size bed or two double beds. Rates range from US$140 to US$175 double; the higher-priced rooms have kitchenettes and sitting rooms. This is among the island's best places to stay.

Victoria House (☎ 26-2067, fax 26-2429, in the USA ☎ 800-247-5159, victoria@btl .net) is an elegant resort hotel 2 miles (3km) south of the airport, on the beach. The beach, the lawns and the 31 rooms are beautifully kept, and amenities include a dining room, bar and dive shop. Here you're away from it all, but San Pedro is a quick 10-minute bike, shuttle van or golf cart ride away (use of bikes is free for hotel guests; golf carts can be rented). Rates range from US$150 to US$240 double mid-December to mid-April; lower rates at other times.

The *Belize Yacht Club* (☎ 26-2777, fax 26-2768, bychotel@btl.net), on Coconut Dr

south of the airport, has several two-story Spanish-style buildings arranged around a swimming pool and set amid lawns stretching down to the beach. Its air-conditioned one- to three-bedroom suites have full kitchens and cost US$165 to US$500.

Mata Chica (☎ 21-3010, fax 21-3012, matachica@btl.net), at the north end of Ambergris, is perhaps the chicest place on the island, with its 11 luxurious thatch-roofed casitas, each decorated in a tropical-fruit theme. Rooms range from US$210 to US$275 double, and a luxury villa rents for US$550 a night. You can also visit for dinner at Mambo, Mata Chica's restaurant (see Places to Eat).

Journey's End (☎ 26-2173, 26-2397, in the US ☎ 800-460-5665, info@journeysendresort .com, ambergriscaye.com/journeysend) is a large, all-inclusive-style resort on a northern narrow strip of the island. It's popular with divers and families and bills its offering 'a barefoot adventure.' Room rates range from US$114 to US$176 off the seafront, US$206 on the beach, single or double occupancy. In addition, a three-bedroom villa is available for $513 a night.

Places to Eat

Several small cafés in the town center serve cheap, simple meals. The best places for low-budget feasting are the stands in front of the park, where you can pick up a plate of stewed chicken with beans and rice, barbecue and other delicacies for under US$2, then enjoy it while watching a rousing game of pick-up basketball.

Ruby's Caffe, next to Ruby's Hotel on Barrier Reef Dr, is a tiny place with good cakes and pastries but unpredictable hours. For simpler take-out pastries and bread, try the *Panadería El Centro*, on Buccaneer at Pescador Dr. *Celi's Deli*, on Barrier Reef Dr just north of the San Pedro Holiday Hotel, serves food to go – fried chicken, sandwiches, ice cream and their own banana bread – at prices ranging from US$1.50 to US$5.

Café Olé, across from the airport, has a deli offering olive oils, cheeses and wine, and it's open for all three meals. *Tropical Take-Out*, across the street from the Tropic

Air terminal at the airport, has daily specials as well as the usual list of sandwiches and light meals. Taco plates are US$2.50, and most other meals are US$4.

Hotel staff will recommend *Elvi's Kitchen* (☎ 26-2176), on Pescador Dr near Ambergris St, for seafood and traditional Belizean dishes. You can spend US$5 for a hamburger or as much as US$30 for a full lobster dinner with wine. Mixed drinks are available but expensive. Be sure to ask about items not priced on the menu – they're sometimes out of scale and you may get a surprise.

If you're yearning for traditional Belizean fare at traditional prices, try *The Reef*, on Pescador Dr between Pelican and Caribeña Sts. Meals run around US$5 to US$7 at this thatched-roof place with sand-covered floors. *Jade Garden* (☎ 26-2506), on Coconut Dr, a 10-minute walk south of the airport, is San Pedro's Chinese restaurant, with a long menu and prices from US$5 to US$18.

Jam Bei Jerk Pit, next to Big Daddy's disco, serves spicy hot Jamaican dishes at reasonable prices. It also has a nice rooftop patio. The beachside *Cannibal Café*, on Barrier Reef Dr at Black Coral St, serves moderately priced breakfasts, lunches and early dinners. *Café Amnesia* (☎ 26-2806), on the north end of Barrier Reef Dr, serves an imaginative meld of European and Caribbean cuisines in a cozy, candlelit dining room. Pizza specials are served daily.

The latest thing in fine dining is to take a moonlight water-taxi ride up to one of the resort restaurants at the island's north end. Meals are usually pricey at these places, but menus are often unusual and feature excellent seafood preparations. *Mata Chica's Mambo Café* (☎ 21-3010) has a Mediterranean flair, *Rendezvous* (☎ 26-3426) is pan-Asian, and *Capricorn* (☎ 26-2809) has been described as nouvelle.

Entertainment

Sipping, sitting, talking and dancing are parts of everyday life on Ambergris. Many hotels have comfortable bars, often with sand floors, thatched roofs and reggae music.

Rasta Pasta Riddims, on the wharf at the east end of Black Coral Dr (in the former location of the beloved, departed Tackle Box Bar), frequently presents live reggae. *Fido's Courtyard Bar*, on Barrier Reef Dr near Pelican St, is the landlubbers' favorite.

BC's Beach Bar, on the beach in a palapa between Ramon's Village and the Sea Breeze Hotel, stays open late and is usually filled with sun-crisped expatriates enjoying Jimmy Buffett on the jukebox. The Sunday afternoon barbecue is a hot ticket. It starts at noon and continues until the food runs out, usually around 2:30 pm.

Big Daddy's Disco, right next to San Pedro's church, is a hot nightspot, often featuring live reggae, especially during the winter. Across Barrier Reef Dr, the *Tarzan Club & Cheetah's Bar*, a jungle-themed bar, is often closed off-season, but it rocks in the winter. The recently opened *Barefoot Iguana*, on Coconut Dr south of the airstrip, is giving the older establishments a run for their money.

The Boatyard Bar is west of the airstrip on the lagoon in an enormous palapa. Wednesday night is ladies' night, but the whole town tends to show up. The *Palace Casino*, on Pescador Dr at Carabeña, opens at 2 pm daily and has blackjack tables, slots and smoky, low-ceilinged ambience.

Shopping

Plenty of gift shops in the hotels and on Barrier Reef Dr sell key chains, T-shirts and beachwear. One of the best shopping spots is Belizean Arts (☎ 26-3019), in Fido's Courtyard, which sells ceramics, woodcarvings and paintings alongside affordable and tasteful knickknacks. Also in Fido's Courtyard is Amber (☎ 26-3101), selling handmade jewelry produced on the island.

Getting There & Away

Air Both Maya Island Air (☎ 26-2435 in San Pedro) and rival Tropic Air (☎ 26-2012 in San Pedro) offer several flights daily between San Pedro and the Belize City airports and to Corozal. See the Belize Getting There & Around chapter for details.

Boat The Caye Caulker Water Taxi Association (San Pedro ☎ 26-2036; Caye Caulker main office ☎ 22-2992) runs boats between San Pedro, Caye Caulker and Belize City. Boats to Belize City via Caye Caulker leave from the Rasta Pasta Riddims dock in San Pedro at 8, 9:30 and 11:30 am and 2:30 pm (also 4:30 pm on weekends and holidays). Boats leave Belize City for San Pedro at 9 am, noon and 3 pm. Cost is US$12.50 one way, US$23 roundtrip. Boats leave Caye Caulker for San Pedro at 7, 8:30 and 10 am and 1 and 4 pm; fare is US$7.50 each way, US$12.50 roundtrip.

Getting Around
You can walk into town from the airport in 10 minutes or less, and the walk from the boat docks is even shorter. A taxi ride from the airport costs US$2.50 to any place in town, US$5 to the hotels south of town.

San Pedranos get around on foot or by bicycle, golf cart, pickup truck or minivan. You can rent golf carts at Polo's EZ-Go Rentals (☎ 26-2467, 26-3542), at the northern end of Barrier Reef Dr, or at Island Auto Golf Cart Rentals (☎ 26-2790), on Coconut Dr across from the airstrip. Golf carts rent for US$10 per hour, US$30 for four hours, US$35 for eight hours, US$50 for 24 hours or US$225 per week. Rent bikes at Polo's EZ-Go or Joe's Bicycle Rentals (☎ 26-2982, 26-3776); rates are around US$6 for a half day, US$9 for 24 hours.

The Island Ferry (☎ 26-3231) operates an Ambergris-only water-taxi service north and south from the Fido's Courtyard dock.

OTHER CAYES
Though Ambergris and Caulker are the most easily accessible and popular cayes, it is possible to arrange visits to the others. Serious divers are the usual customers at camps and resorts on the smaller cayes. Often a special flight or boat charter is necessary to reach these cayes; you can make arrangements for transportation when you book your lodgings. Most booking offices are in Belize City, as the smaller cayes have infrequent mail service and no telephones (only radios).

Caye Chapel
Just south of Caye Caulker, Caye Chapel holds an 18-hole golf course (☎ 2-28250) and a superdeluxe corporate retreat center. Golfing is open to the public when there are no retreaters. Cost is US$50 for nine holes, US$75 for 18 holes, clubs and cart included. You must also arrange boat transportation to the island, which will probably cost about US$50 from San Pedro or Caye Caulker.

St George's Caye
Nine miles (14km) offshore of Belize City, St George's Caye was the Belize settlement's first capital (1650–1784) and site of the decisive 1798 battle between British settlers and a Spanish invasion force. Today it holds vacation homes for the Belize elite and two resorts perfect for those looking to get away from it all: *St George's Lodge* (☎/fax 21-2121, in the US ☎ 800-678-6871), a 16-room, moderately priced resort, and *Cottage Colony Resort* (☎ 21-2020, fax 2-73253), which caters to divers.

Turneffe Islands
This coral atoll 19 miles (30km) east of Belize City is a magnet for divers and fishers. Divers will find walls and wrecks to explore and rewarding sites for all experience levels. Fishing enthusiasts are attracted by the flats, which are ideal for saltwater fly-fishing. The *Turneffe Islands Lodge* (☎/fax 21-2011, ☎ 14-9564, info@turneffeislandlodge.com) offers dive packages for US$1395 per person, including transfers from the mainland.

Half Moon Caye
This caye in Lighthouse Reef is protected as the Half Moon Caye Natural Monument. Standing less than 10 feet (3m) above sea level, the caye's 45 acres (18 hectares) hold two distinct ecosystems. To the west is lush vegetation fertilized by the droppings of thousands of seabirds, including some 4000 red-footed boobies, the wonderfully named magnificent frigate bird and some 98 other bird species; the east side has less vegetation but more coconut palms. Loggerhead and hawksbill turtles, both endangered, lay their eggs on the southern beaches.

A nature trail weaves through the southern part of the island to an observation platform that brings viewers eye level with nesting boobies and frigate birds. Along the path you'll see thousands of seashells, many inhabited by hermit crabs (unnerving when you first notice them moving!). Entrance fee is US$5. Accommodations are unavailable,

but camping is allowed in designated areas and showers and toilets are provided. Organized boat trips stop at Half Moon Caye and the nearby Blue Hole.

Southern Cayes

For details on cayes off the southern Belizean coast, see the Southern Belize chapter.

Northern Belize

The northern Belize most commonly seen by visitors is farmland. Sugarcane fields grow alongside the paved, swift Northern Hwy, and off on the side roads, Mennonites, Maya and mestizos tend efficient multipurpose farms. Head deeper into the region and you'll hit jungle in the hilly west and mangrove swamp along the convoluted Caribbean shoreline.

Orange Walk and Corozal are the region's two major towns. Orange Walk is the commercial center for area farming as well as the starting point for river tours to Lamanai, a Mayan ruin site known for its historical interest and for the exotic river journey that most travelers take to reach it.

Corozal is Belize's northernmost town of appreciable size and is a gateway for travelers going to and from Mexico's Yucatán Peninsula. It's a pleasant seaside town offering an eclectic combination of Mayan, Mexican and Caribbean cultures, and its sea breezes are a refreshing escape from the area's inland heat. At Cerros, across the bay from Corozal, a small Mayan fishing settlement became a powerful kingdom in Late Preclassic times.

The north has several significant biosphere reserves. Largest is the Río Bravo Conservation Area, around 400 sq miles (1000 sq km) of tropical forests, rivers, ponds and Mayan archaeological sites in the western part of Orange Walk District.

The Crooked Tree Wildlife Sanctuary, midway between Orange Walk and Belize City, is an excellent place for bird-watching, as is Shipstern Nature Reserve, south of Sarteneja on the large peninsula southeast of Corozal.

Highlights

- Take the picturesque river tour to the ruins of Lamanai, one of the Mayan world's most famous ancient centers.

- Fall in step with traditional lifestyles in the northern seaside towns of Corozal and Sarteneja, where Mexican and Mayan cultures meet.

- Experience Belize's abundant wildlife at Bermudian Landing Community Baboon Sanctuary, Crooked Tree Wildlife Sanctuary or Shipstern Nature Reserve.

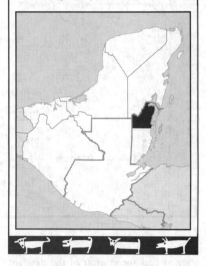

BERMUDIAN LANDING COMMUNITY BABOON SANCTUARY

No real baboons inhabit Belize, but Belizeans use that name for the country's indigenous black howler monkeys. Though howler monkeys live throughout South and Central America, the endangered black howler exists only in Belize.

In 1985 local farmers organized to help preserve the black howler and its habitat. Care is taken to maintain the forests along the banks of the Belize River, where the black howler feeds, sleeps and – at dawn and dusk – howls (loudly and unmistakably).

At the Community Baboon Sanctuary (☎ 21-2181), in the village of Bermudian Landing, you can learn all about the black

127

NORTHERN BELIZE

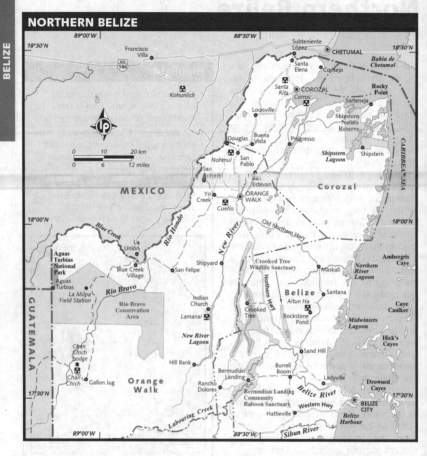

howler and the 200 other species of wildlife found in the reserve. Black howlers are vegetarians and spend most of the daylight hours cruising the treetops in groups of four to eight, led by a dominant male. Various fruits, flowers, leaves and other tidbits keep them happy, and they don't seem to mind visitors lurking below.

A guided nature walk is included with your price of admission (US$5) and can be arranged at the visitors center. Tours of the villages surrounding the sanctuary are available for US$20, as are canoe trips and night hikes.

For more information about the reserve, check with the Belize Audubon Society (☎ 2-35004, fax 2-34985, base@btl.net), 12 Fort St, Belize City.

Places to Stay & Eat

Rustic accommodations are available at the reserve, but it's best to arrange these in advance.

Nature Resort (☎ *2-33668, fax 21-2197, naturer@btl.net*), next to the visitors center, rents refurbished cabañas for US$25 double with shared bath, US$35 with private bath, US$50 with private bath and kitchenette.

Caribbean accents flavor the bustling streets of Belize City.

Speedy water taxis whisk visitors from Belize City to the cayes.

Oceanfront guesthouses, Caye Caulker, Belize

Sunrise on the New River, northern Belize

Mayan ruins at Lamanai, on New River Lagoon

JOHN ELK III

JOHN ELK III

The ***Howler Monkey Resort*** (*☎ 21-2158, jungled@btl.net*), formerly the Jungle Drift Lodge, rents cabañas for US$12.50 per person, but appears to be more interested in catering to group tours than individuals.

Camping (US$5 per person) and village homestays (US$12.50) can be arranged at the visitors center.

Getting There & Away

The Community Baboon Sanctuary lies 26 miles (42km) west of Belize City in the village of Bermudian Landing – an easy day trip from Belize City or the cayes. You can book an organized tour or arrange for a taxi in Belize City (roundtrip taxi fare should be about US$45).

If you're driving, turn west off the Northern Hwy at the Burrell Boom turnoff (Mile 13). From there it's another 12 miles (20km) of dirt road to the sanctuary. Note: If you're heading to western Belize after visiting the sanctuary, you'll save time by taking the 8-mile (13km) cut from Burrell Boom south to Hattieville on the Western Hwy, avoiding Belize City traffic.

Russell's and McFadzean's both operate bus routes to Bermudian Landing, but the schedules are such that it's necessary to spend the night and leave early the next morning. Another option is to catch one of the frequent northern highway buses heading to the Mexican border, get off at Burrell Boom and hitch the 13 miles (8km) into the sanctuary.

ALTUN HA

Northern Belize's most famous Mayan ruin is Altun Ha, 34 miles (55km) north of Belize City along the Old Northern Hwy. The site is near the village of Rockstone Pond, 10 miles (16km) south of Maskall.

Altun Ha (Mayan for 'Rockstone Pond') was undoubtedly a small (population about 3000) but rich and important Mayan trading town, with agriculture also playing an essential role in its economy. Altun Ha had formed as a community by at least 600 BC, perhaps several centuries earlier, and the town flourished until the mysterious collapse of Classic Mayan civilization around AD 900. Most temples you will see in Altun Ha date from Late Classic times, though burials indicate that

The endangered black howler monkey is found only in Belize.

Altun Ha's merchants were trading with Teotihuacán in Preclassic times.

Altun Ha is open 9 am to 5 pm daily; US$2.50. Modern toilets and a drinks shop are on site.

Of the grass-covered temples arranged around the two plazas here, the largest and most important is the Temple of the Masonry Altars (Structure B-4), in Plaza B. The restored structure you see dates from the first half of the 7th century and takes its name from altars on which copal was burned and beautifully carved jade pieces were smashed in sacrifice. Excavation of the structure in 1968 revealed many burial sites of important officials. Most sites had been looted or desecrated, but two were intact. Among the jade objects found in one of these was a unique mask sculpture portraying Kinich Ahau, the Mayan sun god; as of now, this is the largest well-carved jade object ever uncovered from a Mayan archaeological site.

In Plaza A, Structure A-1 is sometimes called the Temple of the Green Tomb. Deep within it was discovered the tomb of a priest-king dating from around AD 600.

Tropical humidity had destroyed the king's garments and the paper of the Mayan 'painted book' that was buried with him, but many riches were intact: shell necklaces, pottery, pearls, stingray spines used in bloodletting rites, jade beads and pendants, and ceremonial flints.

Places to Stay & Eat

Camping, though not strictly legal, is sometimes permitted; ask at the site.

Mayan Wells Restaurant (☎ 21-2039), on the road to Altun Ha, is a popular stop for lunch or refreshments. Traditional Belizean lunches of rice, beans and stewed chicken are served for US$5 in a pleasant outdoor setting. Camping is allowed on the premises for US$5; bathroom and shower facilities are available.

Two miles (3km) north of Maskal is the luxury Maruba Resort *(☎ 3-22199, in the USA ☎ 713-799-2031)*, Mile 40.5, Old Northern Hwy. This 'jungle spa' is decorated with

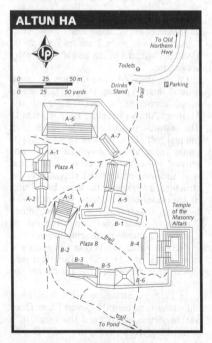

an artist's fine eye. The grounds are very well kept and the staff is exceedingly welcoming. Rooms rent for US$155 double, US$255 if you opt for a meal package. Many day tours stop here for lunch (about US$20) and horseback riding.

Getting There & Away

The easiest way to visit Altun Ha is on one of the many tours running daily from Belize City or San Pedro on Ambergris Caye.

To get there in your own vehicle, take the Northern Hwy 19 miles (31km) northwest from Belize City to the town of Sand Hill, where the highway divides – the new paved highway continues northwest and the old one heads northeast to the ruins. The old road is narrow and potholed, passing through jungle and the occasional village. The ruins are about 2 miles (3km) west off the road, 10.5 miles (17km) from the junction. Note that the Old Northern Hwy is not busy; a breakdown could be problematic, and hitch-hiking is usually disappointing.

If you're firmly committed to public transportation, you can catch an afternoon bus departing from Douglas Jones St (see the Belize City map) for the town of Maskall, north of Altun Ha.

CROOKED TREE WILDLIFE SANCTUARY

Midway between Belize City and Orange Walk, 3.5 miles (5.5km) west of the Northern Hwy, lies the fishing and farming village of Crooked Tree. In 1984 the Belize Audubon Society was successful in having 5 sq miles (12 sq km) around the village declared a wildlife sanctuary, principally because of the area's wealth of bird life. Migrating birds flock to the rivers, swamps and lagoons here each year during the dry season (November to May). The best time of year for wildlife-watching is in May, when the water in the lagoon drops to its lowest level and the animals must come farther out into the open to reach their food supply.

Herons, ducks, kites, egrets, ospreys, kingfishers and hawks are among the 275 bird species seen here. In winter, a large group of jabiru storks comes here to nest. With a wingspan of over 8 feet (2.5m), the jabiru is the largest flying bird in all the Western Hemisphere.

Black howler monkeys, Morelet's crocodiles, coatis, iguanas and turtles also live among the mango and cashew trees at Crooked Tree.

Day trips to Crooked Tree are possible, but it's best to stay the night so you can be here at dawn, when the birds are most active. Trails weave through the villages and you can spot plenty of species on your own, but you'll get farther and see more on a guided tour. In fact, for those interested in viewing birds and other wildlife, a guided nature tour of this sanctuary is among the most rewarding experiences in Belize.

Admission to the sanctuary is US$5. Tours cost US$60 to US$70 for groups of four (less per person for larger groups) and usually include a boat trip through the lagoon, a walk along the elevated boardwalk and viewing time atop the observation towers. Arrangements can be made through the visitors center or your hotel. More information can be obtained from the Belize Audubon Society (☎ 2-35004, fax 2-34985, base@btl.net), 12 Fort St, Belize City.

The hotels in Crooked Tree can also arrange day trips to Altun Ha, the Community Baboon Sanctuary or Lamanai for US$20 to US$40 per person, depending on the size of the group.

Places to Stay & Eat
Sam Tillett's Hotel & Tour (☎ 21-2026, samhotel@btl.net) rents one budget room with shared bath for US$10, rooms with private bath for US$20/30 single/double and the luxury Jabiru Suite for US$50. Meals are also available. Sam's bird tours are in demand – he's known throughout the country as the 'king of birds.'

Also enjoying a considerable reputation among birders is the Crawford family, owners of the *Paradise Inn* (☎ 25-2535, fax 25-2534). The inn rents simple cabañas with nice lagoon views and private baths for US$35/45 single/double, and the restaurant gets high marks with travelers. Breakfast is US$3, lunch US$4, dinner US$10.

The *Bird's Eye View Lodge* (☎ 2-32040, birdseye@btl.net) is in Crooked Tree village facing the lagoon. Rooms, all with private bath, cost US$40/60/70 single/double/triple. Meals are available, as are campsites.

Getting There & Away
The road to Crooked Tree village is 30 miles (48km) up the Northern Hwy from Belize City, 25 miles (40km) south of Orange Walk. The village is 3.5 miles (5km) west of the highway via a causeway over Crooked Tree Lagoon.

If you want to take a bus roundtrip to Crooked Tree, you'll have to spend the night there. Jex Bus offers service daily departing Belize City for Crooked Tree village at 10:30 am and 4:30 and 5:30 pm daily; return trips leave Crooked Tree at 6:00, 6:30 and 7:00 am. A Batty Brothers bus leaves Belize City at 4 pm and departs Crooked Tree at 6 am.

If you start early from Belize City, Corozal or Orange Walk, you can bus to Crooked Tree Junction and then walk the 3.5 miles (5.5km) to the village (about an hour).

CHAN CHICH LODGE
In western Orange Walk District, Chan Chich Lodge is truly a destination unto itself. Its setting is incredible: thatched cabañas share space with partially excavated ruins in the central plaza of a Mayan archaeological site. Each of the 12 cabañas has a private bath, fan, two queen-size beds and a verandah. Rooms cost US$130/145 single/double, with meal package available for US$40. Package deals are also available. The lodge offers guided walks and activities throughout the day, and 9 miles (15km) of trails invite independent exploration. While you may not see jaguars during your visit, you'll definitely feel their presence, and you are likely to see coatis, warries, deer, howler and spider monkeys and an array of bird life. Resident ornithologists have identified more than 350 species of birds here. One of Belize's first ecolodges, Chan Chich remains among the most luxurious.

The lodge lies between the settlement of Gallon Jug and the Guatemalan border. It's best reached by chartered plane from Belize City, though you can also drive in on an all-weather road (130 miles/210km, 3½ hours from Belize City). For more information on the lodge or to make reservations, call ☎/fax 2-34419.

RÍO BRAVO CONSERVATION AREA & LA MILPA FIELD STATION

Protecting 240,000 acres of tropical forest and its inhabitants, the Río Bravo Conservation Area is the flagship project of the Programme for Belize (PFB). The long-term goal of PFB is to create a sustainable reserve that allows for income from timber but provides for rehabilitation and conservation. To that end PFB conducts research, conservation education and training and promotes environmental awareness among visitors.

In addition to the wealth of plant and animal life here, over 60 Mayan sites have been discovered on the land. The preeminent site is La Milpa, the third-largest Mayan site in Belize, believed to have been founded in the Late Preclassic period.

Two field stations are in the reserve. La Milpa Field Station is intended for tourism, archaeology and environmental education, while Hill Bank Field Station is devoted primarily to the research and development of sustainable forest management.

La Milpa Field Station is near Gallon Jug on the road to Chan Chich Lodge. Visiting and transportation arrangements must be made in advance through Programme for Belize (☎ 2-75616, fax 2-75635, pfbel@btl.net), 1 Eyre St, Belize City. Cost for a cabaña is US$90 per person, meals and two guided tours included.

LAMANAI

By far the most impressive site in this part of the country is Lamanai, in its own archaeological reserve on the New River Lagoon near the small settlement of Indian Church. Though much of the site remains unexcavated and unrestored, the trip to Lamanai, by motorboat up the New River, is an adventure in itself.

Take a sun hat, sunblock, insect repellent, shoes (rather than sandals), lunch and a beverage (unless you plan to take a tour that includes lunch).

History

As with most sites in northern Belize, Lamanai ('Submerged Crocodile,' the original Mayan name of the place) was occupied as early as 1500 BC, with the first stone buildings appearing between 800 and 600 BC. Lamanai flourished in Late Preclassic times, growing into a major ceremonial center with immense temples long before most other Mayan sites.

Unlike many other sites, Maya lived here until the coming of the Spanish in the 16th century. The ruined Indian church (actually two of them) nearby attests to the fact that there were Maya here for the Spanish friars to convert. Convert them they did, but by 1640 the Maya had reverted to their ancient forms of worship. British interests later built a sugar mill, now in ruins, at Indian Church. The archaeological site was excavated by David Pendergast in the 1970s and '80s.

New River Voyage

Most visitors opt to reach Lamanai on a spectacular boat ride up the New River from the Tower Hill toll bridge south of Orange Walk. On this trip, available only as part of an organized tour (see Getting There & Away), you motor 1½ hours up-river, between riverbanks crowded with dense jungle vegetation. En route, your skipper/guide points out the many local birds and will almost certainly spot a crocodile or two. Along the way you pass the Mennonite community at Shipyard. Finally you come to New River Lagoon – a long, broad expanse of water that can be choppy during the frequent rainstorms – and the boat dock at Lamanai.

Touring Lamanai

Landing at Lamanai (open 9 am to 5 pm daily), you'll sign the visitors' book, pay the admission fee (US$2.50) and wander into the dense jungle, past gigantic guanacaste, ceiba and *ramón* (breadnut) trees, strangler figs, allspice, epiphytes and examples of Belize's national flower, the black orchid. In the canopy overhead you might see one of the groups of howler monkeys resident at Lamanai.

A tour of the ruins takes 90 minutes minimum, more comfortably two or three hours. Of the 60 significant structures identified here, the grandest is Structure N10-43, a huge, Late Preclassic building rising more than 111 feet (34m) above the jungle canopy. Other buildings along La Ruta Maya are taller, but this one was built well before the others. It's been partially uncovered and restored. Not far from N10-43 is Lamanai's ball court, a smallish one, partially uncovered.

To the north along a jungle path is Structure P9-56, built several centuries later, with a huge stylized mask of a man in a crocodile-mouth headdress 13 feet (4m) high emblazoned on its southwest face. Archaeologists have dug deep into this structure (from the platform level high on the east side) to look for burials and to document the several earlier structures that lie beneath.

Near this structure are a small temple and a ruined stela that once stood on the temple's front face. Apparently some worshipers built a fire at the base of the limestone stela and later doused the fire with water. The hot stone stela, cooled too quickly by the water, broke and toppled. The stela's bas-relief carving of a majestic figure is extremely fine.

A small museum near the boat landing exhibits some interesting figurative pottery and large flint tools.

Places to Stay

Lamanai Outpost Lodge (☎/*fax 2-33578, lamanai@btl.net*) is a five-minute boat ride south of the archaeological zone. Perched on a hillside sloping down to the lagoon, the well-kept lodge, bar and open-air dining room enjoy panoramic views. Guests stay in one of 18 thatch-roof bungalows, each with fan, private bath and verandah.

Archaeologists, ornithologists, botanists and naturalists in residence at the lodge lead tours and provide information and programs

for guests. Activities include river excursions (the nighttime spotlight safari is a highlight), wildlife walks and tours of Lamanai.

Rooms cost US$105/125 single/double, tax and service included. Meals cost US$8 for breakfast, US$12 for lunch and US$22 for dinner. All-inclusive multiday packages are available, as are education-adventure programs that allow guests to participate in archaeological or jungle-habitat research. Transfers from Belize City can be arranged by land or air.

Getting There & Away

Though the river voyage is much more convenient and enjoyable, Lamanai can be reached by road (36 miles/58km) from Orange Walk via Yo Creek and San Felipe. Bus service from Orange Walk is available but limited (it's primarily for village people coming to town for marketing); buses depart Orange Walk on Tuesday at 3 pm and Thursday at 4 pm.

The Novelo brothers (Antonio and Herminio) have excellent reputations as guides and naturalists. Their company, Jungle River Tours (☎ 3-22293, fax 3-23749), 20 Lovers' Lane, Orange Walk (near the southeast corner of the central park), offers excursions to Lamanai for US$40 per person (minimum of four persons), which includes lunch, beverages and the guided tour along the river and at the ruins. The tour group meets at 9 am at the office in Orange Walk, though by prior arrangement the boat will pick you at the New River Park Hotel at 9:30 am. The tour returns at 4 pm. Reservations required.

Reyes & Sons (☎ 3-23327) runs tours departing Jim's Cool Pool (just north of the toll bridge) at 9 am daily (be there by 8:30 am). The boat ride and guided tour costs US$25 per person; boxed lunch is another US$5. Note: Lamanai entrance fee (US$2.50) is not included in the price of either tour.

It's possible to get an early Batty Brothers bus from Belize City to Orange Walk, get out at the Tower Hill toll bridge and be in time for the morning departure of the boats to Lamanai. In the evening you can catch a return bus to Belize City at the bridge or, preferably, in Orange Walk.

ORANGE WALK
- **population 10,000**

The agricultural and social center of northern Belize, Orange Walk is 58 miles (94km) north of Belize City. The town serves the region's farmers (including many Mennonites), who raise sugarcane and citrus fruits primarily. It's not highly developed for tourism but does have a few modest hotels and good restaurants. (Another option, if you're spending a few days in the region, is to base

in Corozal about 41 miles/66km north. Buses between the two towns are plentiful.)

The Northern Hwy, called Queen Victoria Ave in town, serves as the main road. The center of town is shady Central Park, on the east side of Queen Victoria Ave. The town hospital is in the northern outskirts, readily visible on the west side of the Northern Hwy.

Cuello & Nohmul Archaeological Sites

Near Orange Walk is Cuello, a Mayan site with a 3000-year history but little to show for it. Archaeologists have found plenty

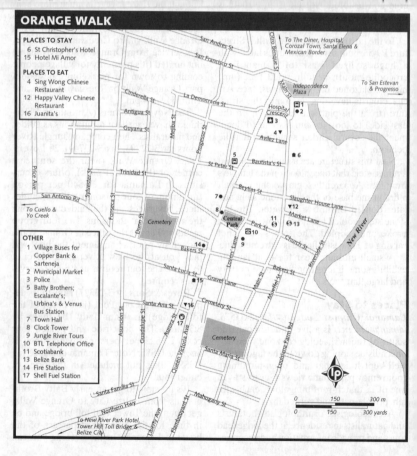

ORANGE WALK

PLACES TO STAY
6 St Christopher's Hotel
15 Hotel Mi Amor

PLACES TO EAT
4 Sing Wong Chinese Restaurant
12 Happy Valley Chinese Restaurant
16 Juanita's

OTHER
1 Village Buses for Copper Bank & Sarteneja
2 Municipal Market
3 Police
5 Batty Brothers; Escalante's; Urbina's & Venus Bus Station
7 Town Hall
8 Clock Tower
9 Jungle River Tours
10 BTL Telephone Office
11 Scotiabank
13 Belize Bank
14 Fire Station
17 Shell Fuel Station

here, but only Structure 350, a nine-tiered stepped pyramid, will draw your interest. The site is on private property owned by the Cuello Brothers Distillery (☎ 3-22141), 2.5 miles (4km) west of Orange Walk along San Antonio (Yo Creek) Rd. The distillery, on the left (south) side of the road, is unmarked; the site is through and beyond it. Ask permission at the distillery gate.

Nohmul ('Great Mound' in Mayan), 7 miles (12km) north of Orange Walk and 1 mile (2km) west of the village of San Pablo, was a much more important site. Structure ? the site's tallest building, is a lofty acropolis looming over the surrounding countryside. Though the vast site covers more than 7 sq miles (18 sq km), most of it is now overgrown by grass and sugarcane. The site is owned by Steven Itzab, who lives in the northern part of San Pablo village, opposite the water tower. Stop at Itzab's house for permission to visit; a guide will be sent with you.

Places to Stay
St Christopher's Hotel (☎ 3-21064, 10 Main St) is simple, relatively quiet and decently priced. Rooms with fan, private bath and cable TV cost US$23/28/33/38 single/double/triple/quad. Rooms with air-con start at US$35. The riverside rooms are the nicest.

Hotel Mi Amor (☎ 3-22031, fax 3-23462, 19 Queen Victoria Ave) has doubles for US$25 with fan, US$38 with TV and air-con. A noisy disco is on the ground floor.

Juanita's (☎ 3-22677, 8 Santa Ana St), popular for its restaurant, rents five basic but clean and sunny rooms, all with shared bath, for US$8.50 single or double.

New River Park Hotel (☎ 3-23987), on the east side of the Northern Hwy, 4 miles (7km) south of Orange Walk, just north of the Tower Hill toll bridge, is convenient if you're taking the boat trip to Lamanai. Double rooms cost US$25 with fan, US$50 with air-con. The terrace restaurant offers meals from US$4 to US$9.

Places to Eat
Juanita's, on Santa Ana St near the Shell fuel station, is a simple place with tasty local fare at low prices; breakfast and lunch from US$2.50.

Orange Walk has several Chinese restaurants. *Happy Valley* (☎ 3-22554, 32 Main St) and *Sing Wong*, Main St at Avilez Lane, are about the nicest.

The Diner (☎ 3-22131, 34 Clark St) is the favorite local hangout for breakfast, lunch and dinner. It's off the beaten track a bit but worth it for its creative menu and cool, leafy setting. Go north and turn left just before the hospital, then bear right (follow the signs) and go about a quarter mile (400m). Closes at 10pm Sunday to Thursday, midnight Friday and Saturday.

Getting There & Away
Four bus lines – Batty Brothers, Venus, Escalante's and Urbina's – compete for the traffic on the route between Orange Walk and Belize City. Buses run hourly in both directions, and additional southbound runs in early morning and northbound runs in late afternoon accommodate work and school schedules. All four services use the bus stop on Queen Victoria Ave at St Peter St. By bus, it takes about two hours to reach Belize City (58 miles, 92km) and an hour to get to Corozal (41 miles, 66km). For more details see the Belize Getting There & Around section.

COROZAL
• **population 9000**
Corozal is a prosperous farming town blessed with fertile land and a favorable climate for agriculture (sugarcane is the area's leading crop). It's a popular stop with travelers busing their way to or from Mexico, and many choose to base here when exploring northern Belize. A small North American expatriate community centers around the retirement developments in Consejo Shores, south of Tony's Inn.

History
Corozal's Mayan history is long and important. On the town's northern outskirts are the ruins of a Mayan ceremonial center once called Chetumal, now called Santa Rita. Across the bay at Cerros is one of the

BELIZE

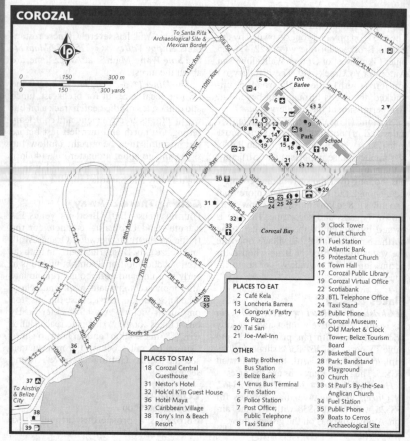

COROZAL

To Santa Rita
Archaeological Site &
Mexican Border

Corozal Bay

PLACES TO EAT
2 Café Kela
13 Loncheria Barrera
14 Gongora's Pastry
& Pizza
20 Tai San
21 Joe-Mel-Inn

OTHER
1 Batty Brothers
Bus Station
3 Belize Bank
4 Venus Bus Terminal
5 Fire Station
6 Police Station
7 Post Office;
Public Telephone
8 Taxi Stand

9 Clock Tower
10 Jesuit Church
11 Fuel Station
12 Atlantic Bank
15 Protestant Church
16 Town Hall
17 Corozal Public Library
19 Corozal Virtual Office
22 Scotiabank
23 BTL Telephone Office
24 Taxi Stand
25 Public Phone
26 Corozal Museum;
Old Market & Clock
Tower; Belize Tourism
Board
27 Basketball Court
28 Park; Bandstand
29 Playground
30 Church
33 St Paul's By-the-Sea
Anglican Church
34 Fuel Station
35 Public Phone
39 Boats to Cerros
Archaeological Site

PLACES TO STAY
18 Corozal Central
Guesthouse
31 Nestor's Hotel
32 Hok'ol K'in Guest House
36 Hotel Maya
37 Caribbean Village
38 Tony's Inn & Beach
Resort

To Airstrip
& Belize
City

most important Late Preclassic sites yet to be discovered.

Maya have been living around Corozal since 1500 BC. Modern Corozal dates from only 1849, however. In that year, refugees from the War of the Castes in Yucatán fled across the border to safe haven in British-controlled Belize. They founded a town and named it after the cohune palm, a symbol of fertility. For years it had the look of a typical Caribbean town, until Hurricane Janet roared through in 1955 and blew away many of the old wooden buildings on stilts.

Much of Corozal's cinderblock architecture dates from the late 1950s.

Orientation & Information
Though founded by the Maya, Corozal is now arranged around a town square in the traditional style of a Mexican town. You can walk easily to any place in town.

The main road is 7th Ave, which briefly skirts the sea before veering inland through town. The old town market and custom-house has recently been converted to a museum and houses the BTB information office (☎ 4-23176). A colorful mural depicting Corozal's history enlivens the lobby of town hall.

The Belize Bank on the north side of the plaza is open for currency exchange 8 am to 1 pm Monday to Friday and 3 to 6 pm Friday afternoon.

Internet services are provided at Corozal Virtual Office (☎ 4-22010), 6 Park St S.

Santa Rita Archaeological Site

Called Chetumal by the Maya, this city sat astride important riverine trade routes and had its share of wealth. The jade and pottery artifacts found here have been dispersed to museums, and the site's important frescoes have been destroyed.

Santa Rita's one restored Mayan temple is in a small, tidy park just over a half mile (1km) northwest of the Venus bus terminal in Corozal. Go north on the main highway just under half a mile (800m) and bear right just before the statue. After about another 100 yards (90m) turn left and go straight for about two-tenths of a mile (320m) to the site. The 'hill' on the right is actually a temple. The site is open during daylight hours and is free. There is no visitors center.

Cerros Archaeological Site

Cerros (also called Cerro Maya) flourished in Late Preclassic times. Its proximity to the New River made it a valuable trade center for Lamanai and other inland Mayan communities. Unlike at other Mayan sites, little subsequent construction from the Classic and Postclassic periods covers the original structures here. Thus the site has given archaeologists important insights into Mayan Preclassic architecture.

Climb Structure 4, a temple more than 65 feet (20m) high, for stunning panoramic views. Though the site is still mostly a mass of grass-covered mounds, the center has been cleared and consolidated and it's easy to see how the plaza structures were designed to fit together. Also notable are the canals that ring the site, which have remained mysteriously clear of vegetation through the ages.

Stefan Moerman conducts guided tours of the site that also include a boat trip on the New River to search for manatees and crocodiles. Tours can be arranged through your hotel, or contact Stefan directly at ☎ 4-22833. The cost for one to four people is US$60. You can also charter a boat (US$50) or arrange for a fisherman to take you over to the site to explore independently. The boat trip takes about 15 minutes; then you walk 10 minutes to the site.

Bacalar Chico

Stefan Moerman also runs a snorkeling and bird-watching tour to Bacalar Chico (aka Boca Bacalar Chico), a national marine park at the northern tip of Ambergris Caye. The park, accessed through a channel dug 1500 years ago by sea-trading Maya, is a splendid alternative to the congested snorkeling spots visited from San Pedro. Marine life is plentiful, the coral pristine. Tours cost US$200 for one to two people, US$250 for three to four, US$300 for five to six.

Places to Stay

Budget The *Hotel Maya* (☎ 4-22082, fax 4-22827, hotelmaya@btl.net), on 7th Ave (the main road) between 9th and 10th Sts S, is the longtime budget favorite. The 17 aged but clean rooms with private shower cost US$25 double with fan, US$30 with fan and TV and US$43 with air-con and cable TV. The adjoining eatery serves good, cheap meals.

Corozal Central Guesthouse (☎ 4-22335, cghczl@yahoo.com, 22 6th Ave), a short walk from the plaza, is simpler and cheaper, with waterless rooms going for US$15 double. Bonuses include a cooking area and a large common area.

Caribbean Village (☎ 4-22752), south of town across the main road from the sea, has large swaths of lush grass shaded by coconut palms. Basic palapas rent for US$15/20 single/double. Campsite rates are US$2.50 per person for a tent.

Nestor's Hotel (☎ 4-22354, 125 5th Ave S) makes a large part of its money from its restaurant-bar and video machines. Rooms are cheap at US$15/18, but they're noisy.

Mid-Range The *Hok'ol K'in Guest House* (☎ 4-23329, fax 4-23569), 4th St S at 4th Ave, is a small, modern hotel with a nice dining room and patio. The comfortable rooms are designed to catch sea breezes, and each has two double beds, a bathroom and cable TV. At US$32/44 single/double, this is the best value in town.

About 1 mile (1.6km) south of the plaza on the shore road is *Tony's Inn & Beach Resort* (☎ 4-22055, fax 4-22829, tonys@btl.net), with landscaped grounds and lawn chairs set to enjoy the view of the bay. It has its own swimming lagoon, cable TV, restaurant and bar. The 26 rooms, in a motel-style building, come with fan or air-con and cost US$65 to US$70 double.

Places to Eat

The *Hok'ol K'in Guest House*, *Hotel Maya* and *Tony's Inn & Beach Resort* have pretty good restaurants. *Nestor's Hotel* is a popular watering hole for travelers.

Tai San, on Park St between 1st and 2nd Aves, is the favored Chinese restaurant. *Joe-Mel-Inn*, 4th Ave at 2nd St S, serves terrific Belizean food but isn't open for dinner. Also for lunch, *Lonchería Barrera*, off the west corner of the square, offers delicious Mexican dishes at unbeatable prices. Next door is *Gongora's Pastry & Pizza*.

Le Café Kela (☎ 4-22833, 37 1st Ave), set in a palapa with lovely landscaping, blends traditional Belizean dishes with French cuisine. Here you'll find the best crepes in Belize. Belizean dishes, pastas and crepes are around US$4; steak and seafood run US$6 to US$8. With 24-hour notice you can get a traditional cassoulet (US$4.50). The restaurant is open for all three meals.

Getting There & Away

Air Corozal has its own airstrip (code CZL) south of the town center, reached by taxi (US$4). It is only an airstrip, with no shelter or services, so there's no point in arriving too early for your flight. Taxis meet all incoming flights.

Maya Island Air (☎ 4-22874) and Tropic Air (☎ 4-20356) each have three flights daily between Corozal and San Pedro (20 minutes, US$30 one way). From San Pedro you connect with flights to Belize City and onward to other parts of the country. For details, see the Belize Getting There & Around chapter.

Bus Corozal is 8 miles (13km) south of the border-crossing point at Santa Elena/Subteniente López. Most of the frequent Venus and Batty Brothers buses traveling between Chetumal (Mexico) and Belize City stop at Corozal. (For details, see Chetumal in the Yucatán's Quintana Roo chapter and also the Belize Getting There & Around chapter). Otherwise, hitch a ride or hire a taxi (expensive at US$12) to get to Santa Elena. From Subteniente López, minibuses shuttle the 7 miles (12km) to Chetumal's Minibus Terminal all day. You'll have to pay a tourist fee of around US$18.50 to cross into Mexico (see the Yucatán Facts for the Visitor chapter for details).

Buses leave Corozal and head south via Orange Walk for Belize City at least every hour from 4 am to 7:30 pm, with extra buses in the morning. Likewise, buses travel between Belize City and Corozal hourly (96 miles/155km, 2¼ to 2¾ hours), with extra runs in the afternoon to accommodate work and school schedules.

SARTENEJA & SHIPSTERN NATURE RESERVE

Sarteneja is a tiny traditional fishing village east of Corozal. It's possible but costly (US$75) to charter a boat from Corozal to reach the village. By car, you'll have to backtrack south along the Northern Hwy to Orange Walk to pick up the road. Then it's a bumpy but scenic two-hour drive back north and east through farm country to get there. Because of this difficult route, Sarteneja doesn't make it onto many itineraries – it's a great option for travelers who really want to get away from it all. In town there's not much to do but gaze at the sea and make friends with the townspeople, although it's possible to arrange boating and fishing trips.

Shipstern Nature Reserve covers approximately 22,000 acres of forest, wetlands and mangrove shoreline. Some 250 bird species are known to exist in the reserve, and coatis, peccaries, tamanduas and other wild creatures put in frequent appearances. You might even see jaguar tracks. A butterfly breeding farm is on the premises. The entrance fee of US$5 includes a guided nature walk and a tour of the butterfly center. Tours farther into the reserve can be arranged starting at US$50. This area is heavy with mosquitoes; long sleeves and pants are recommended.

Places to Stay & Eat

The recently remodeled *Fernando's Seaside Guesthouse* (☎ 4-32085), on N Front St, has three rooms, each with a sparkling private bathroom, for US$30 double. Down the road, *Krisami's Bayview Lodge* (☎ 4-32283) rents modern, tiled cabañas with private baths for US$38. Both of these places have restaurants that serve meals to their guests. Another dining option is *Richie's* (☎ 4-32031), in a palapa south of Fernando's. Its official hours are 3 to 11 pm, but Richie will cook for you at other times by special arrangement. Meals include stewed chicken, rice and beans, and various Mexican dishes for around US$4.

West of Sarteneja, in Copper Bank village, is the *Last Resort* (☎ 4-12009). Here Enrique Flores and Donna Noland have created a low-key, low-budget getaway. Cabins, arranged at the mouth of a lagoon, rent for US$13 without electricity, US$15 to US$18 with electricity. Baths are shared. Weekly rates are available. The resort is remote and best for visitors who are planning to stay and sit awhile. A bus route serves the village from Orange Walk, and you can get to the resort by boat from Corozal for US$50.

Getting There & Away

Sarteneja is 40 miles (64km) northeast of Orange Walk, where the road starts in the north part of town at the bridge near the village bus station. The road will take you through the village of San Estevan and the Mennonite community of Little Belize. At Mile 23 (Km 37), veer right to reach Sarteneja and Shipstern. The left road will take you through Progresso to Copper Bank and the Last Resort. Village buses run from Orange Walk to Sarteneja and Copper Bank Monday to Saturday. A charter boat from Corozal to Sarteneja will take 45 minutes and cost US$75.

Western Belize

Western Belize – the Cayo District – is the country's highlands, with peaks rising to over 3000 feet (900m). This beautiful, unspoiled mountain terrain is dotted with waterfalls, caves and Mayan ruins and teeming with wild orchids, colorful parrots, keel-billed toucans and other exotic flora and fauna – prime territory for adventure seekers. The area's numerous and popular forest lodges make great base camps for your explorations of the region.

STARTING DOWN THE WESTERN HIGHWAY

Heading west from Belize City along Cemetery Rd, you'll pass right through Lords Ridge Cemetery and soon find yourself headed out of town on the Western Hwy. In 15 miles (25km) you'll pass Hattieville, founded in 1961 after Hurricane Hattie wreaked destruction on Belize City, and in another 13 miles (21km) you'll come to the Belize Zoo.

Buses run at least hourly along the Western Hwy and upon request will drop you at the zoo, by Guanacaste National Park or anywhere else along the highway. (See the Belize Getting There & Around chapter for details.)

Belize Zoo

The Belize Zoo & Tropical Education Centre (☎ 92-3310), Mile 29, Western Hwy, began in 1983, when Sharon Matola was in charge of 17 Belizean animals during the shooting of a wildlife film entitled *Path of the Raingods*. By the time filming was over, the animals had become partly tame. Concerned that her charges would not likely survive if released back into the wild, Matola founded this zoo, which displays native Belizean wildlife in natural surroundings on 29 acres (12 hectares). On a self-guided tour (45 to 60 minutes) you'll see over 125 native animals, including jaguars, ocelots, howler monkeys, peccaries, vultures, storks, crocodiles, tapirs and gibnuts.

Highlights

- Get your bearings and plan your explorations in the lovely hillside town of San Ignacio, the center for travelers to the Cayo District.

- Go hiking, horseback riding or caving in and around the Mountain Pine Ridge Forest Reserve.

- Float the Mopan and Macal Rivers by tube or canoe.

- Take a day trip to the Mayan ruins of Caracol, adding a midday swim at Río On Pools or Thousand Foot Falls.

- Get away from it all at a secluded jungle lodge – they're available for all budgets.

- Take a day or overnight tour to the magnificent ruins of Tikal, right over the border in Guatemala.

One of the zoo's central goals is to make Belizeans sensitive to the value of preserving native wildlife. To this end, there are signs throughout the park imploring visitors not

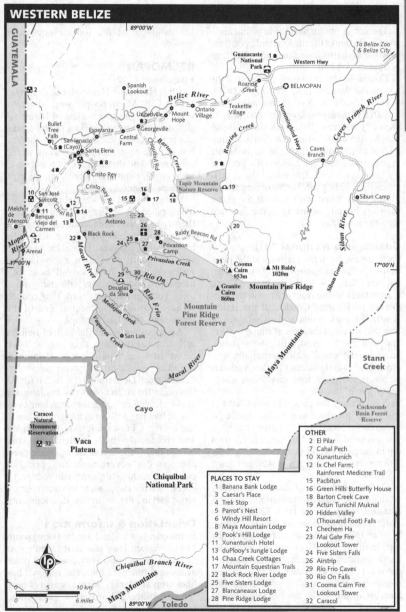

WESTERN BELIZE

PLACES TO STAY
1 Banana Bank Lodge
3 Caesar's Place
4 Trek Stop
5 Parrot's Nest
6 Windy Hill Resort
8 Maya Mountain Lodge
9 Pook's Hill Lodge
11 Xunantunich Hotel
13 duPlooy's Jungle Lodge
14 Chaa Creek Cottages
17 Mountain Equestrian Trails
22 Black Rock River Lodge
25 Five Sisters Lodge
27 Blancaneaux Lodge
28 Pine Ridge Lodge

OTHER
2 El Pilar
7 Cahal Pech
10 Xunantunich
12 Ix Chel Farm; Rainforest Medicine Trail
15 Pacbitun
16 Green Hills Butterfly House
18 Barton Creek Cave
19 Actun Tunichil Muknal
20 Hidden Valley (Thousand Foot) Falls
21 Chechem Ha
23 Mai Gate Fire Lookout Tower
24 Five Sisters Falls
26 Airstrip
29 Rio Frio Caves
30 Rio On Falls
31 Cooma Cairn Fire Lookout Tower
32 Caracol

to hunt, skin or eat the wild relatives of the zoo's residents.

The zoo is on the north side of the highway (a sign marks the turnoff) and open 8 am to 4:30 pm daily (closed on major Belizean holidays); US$7.50.

Competing for customers just west of the zoo on the Western Hwy are *Cheer's* (☎ 14-9311), Mile 31.25 (Km 50) Western Hwy, and *JB's Watering Hole* (☎ 14-8098), Mile 32 (Km 52) Western Hwy. Each serves Belizean, Mexican and American dishes accompanied by ice-cold Belikins, all at moderate prices. Traditionalists prefer JB's because it's been there longer, although the eponymous JB is long gone. Both are fun, festive places often filled with just-off-the-plane travelers happily adjusting to the fact that they're on holiday.

Guanacaste National Park

Farther west down the highway, at the junction with the Hummingbird Hwy, is Guanacaste National Park, a small 52-acre (21-hectare) nature reserve around the confluence of Roaring Creek and the Belize River. The park holds a giant guanacaste tree that survived the axes of canoe makers and still rises majestically in its jungle habitat. Festooned with bromeliads, epiphytes, ferns and dozens of other varieties of plants, the great tree supports a whole ecosystem of its own.

A hike along the park's 2 miles (3km) of trails will introduce you to the abundant and colorful local bird life. After your hike, you can head down to the Belize River for a dip in the park's good, deep swimming hole. The reserve is open 8 am to 4:30 pm daily; US$2.50.

On the north side of the Western Hwy (turn off near Guanacaste National Park) is *Banana Bank Lodge* (☎ 8-12020, fax 8-12026, bbl@btl.net, www.bananabank.com), Mile 46 (Km 74), Western Hwy, which sits astride the Belize River and is reached by hand-operated ferry. Each of the thatched cabañas here has a private bath and a unique two-bedroom design. All are decorated with local art, including the work of lodge owner Carolyn Carr. Rates are US$89/89/119/139

single/double/triple/quad, including breakfast. Horseback tours and unguided riding are available at the lodge's equestrian center.

BELMOPAN
• population 4000

In 1961, Hurricane Hattie all but destroyed Belize City. Many people were skeptical when in 1970 the government of Belize declared its intention to build a model capital city in the geographic center of the country, but certain that killer hurricanes would come again and that Belize City could never be properly defended from them, the government decided to move.

During its first decade Belmopan was a lonely place. Weeds grew through cracks in the streets, a few bureaucrats dozed in new offices, and insects provided most of the town's traffic. Today the capital has begun to come to life. Its population is growing and some embassies have moved here. But unless you have business with the government, you'll probably stay only long enough to have a snack or a meal at one of the restaurants near the bus stops.

An important aside: The bulk of Belize's architectural treasures that haven't been taken from the country are in Belmopan, stored in a vault at the government's Archaeological Department (☎ 8-22106). At this point the collection is not available for public viewing, although there has long been talk of building a national museum to house the artifacts. Preservationists, tour guides, and archaeology buffs in Belize are concerned that without continuing public pressure on the government, this priceless collection might disappear. So do your part – check with the department to voice your interest and inquire about new developments.

Orientation & Information

Belmopan, just under 2.5 miles (4km) south of the Western Hwy and about a mile east of the Hummingbird Hwy, is a small place easily negotiated on foot. The regional bus lines stop at Market Square, which is near the post office, police station, market and telephone office.

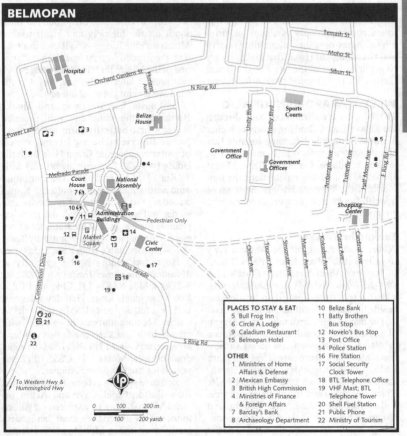

BELMOPAN

PLACES TO STAY & EAT
5 Bull Frog Inn
6 Circle A Lodge
9 Caladium Restaurant
15 Belmopan Hotel

OTHER
1 Ministries of Home
   Affairs & Defense
2 Mexican Embassy
3 British High Commission
4 Ministries of Finance
   & Foreign Affairs
7 Barclay's Bank
8 Archaeology Department

10 Belize Bank
11 Batty Brothers
    Bus Stop
12 Novelo's Bus Stop
13 Post Office
14 Police Station
16 Fire Station
17 Social Security
    Clock Tower
18 BTL Telephone Office
19 VHF Mast; BTL
    Telephone Tower
20 Shell Fuel Station
21 Public Phone
22 Ministry of Tourism

Places to Stay & Eat

Belmopan is a town for bureaucrats and diplomats, not one for budget travelers. The 14-room *Circle A Lodge* (☎ 8-22296, fax 8-23616, 35-37 Half Moon Ave) is perhaps the town's oldest hotel, but it's still serviceable at US$25 double with fan or US$30 with air-con.

The neighboring *Bull Frog Inn* (☎ 8-22111, fax 8-23155, bullfrog@btl.net, 25 Half Moon Ave), also with 14 rooms, is Belmopan's nicest place to stay. Its cheerful air-conditioned rooms, each with bathroom and cable TV, cost US$48/63 single/double. The restaurant at the inn is one of the town's best; dinners are around US$7, breakfast and lunch US$3 to US$4.

The 20-room *Belmopan Hotel* (☎ 8-22130, fax 8-23066, 2 Bliss Parade) is convenient to the Market Square bus stops. Rooms with air-con, TV and private bath cost US$44/50.

Caladium Restaurant (☎ 8-22754), on Market Square just opposite the Novelo's bus station, offers daily special plates for US$4. Another option is the market, which features plenty of snack carts selling tasty, low-cost munchies.

Getting There & Away

Thanks to its location near a major highway intersection, Belmopan is a stop for virtually all buses operating along the Western and Hummingbird Hwys. That makes it easy to get in and out of the city. See the Belize Getting There & Around chapter for details.

WEST TOWARD SAN IGNACIO

The Western Hwy continues west through the Cayo District, climbing slowly to higher altitudes through lush farming country. Tidy country towns with odd names such as Teakettle Village, Ontario Village, Mount Hope and Unitedville appear along the way. North of the Western Hwy is the town of Spanish Lookout, a prosperous Mennonite community.

Teakettle Village

A dirt road leading off the Western Hwy from Teakettle Village leads 6 miles (10km) to Ray and Vicki Snaddon's *Pook's Hill* (☎ 8-12017, fax 8-22948, pookshill@btl.net), a 300-acre estate nestled in wilderness beside the Tapir Mountain Nature Reserve.

The main lodge surrounds a small Mayan plaza, and the round, thatch-and-stucco cabañas sport wraparound windows and immaculate tile bathrooms. The rates are US$88/125/153 single/double/triple. Breakfast costs US$6, lunch US$9, dinner US$16. River swimming and forest hiking are free, and horseback riding, river tubing and mountain biking are available for a reasonable charge. Tours can be arranged to all the Mountain Pine Ridge and Cayo attractions at rates similar to those charged in San Ignacio. Pook's Hill is around 12 miles (20km) southwest of Belmopan.

Georgeville

Continuing west down the highway, around Georgeville you'll come to *Caesar's Place* (☎ 92-2341), Mile 60 (Km 96.6), Western Hwy, which rents a couple of rooms with private baths for rates of US$40/50/55 single/double/triple. Caesar's has one of the country's best gift shops, with a wide selection of Belizean souvenirs and Guatemalan handicrafts at good prices.

Chiquibul Road

At Mile 61 (Km 98), Chiquibul Rd turns south off the highway and heads toward Mountain Pine Ridge – you'll take this road if you're headed straight from Belize City to one of the Mountain Pine Ridge lodges (see that section later in this chapter). Up the road are several points of interest.

Biologists Jan Meerman and Tineke Boomsma (the same duo who founded Belize's first butterfly farm at Shipstern Nature Reserve) raise a staggering variety of butterfly species at **Green Hills Butterfly House** (☎ 91-2017, meerman@btl.net), Mile 8 (Km 13), Chiquibul Rd. The butterflies bred here are exported to butterfly houses outside of the country. Knowledgeable guides will walk you through the farm, explaining the life cycle of the butterfly – from egg to caterpillar to pupa to butterfly. Tours (US$4) are available from 8 am to 5:30 pm.

Horseback riding is the specialty at *Mountain Equestrian Trails* (☎ 8-23180, fax 8-23505), Mile 8 (Km 13), Chiquibul Rd, a four-room jungle lodge. Half-day rides cost US$55; a full day costs US$75 and includes lunch. Accommodations in cabañas with private bath and kerosene lamps – there's no electricity – cost US$100/120/140 single/double/triple. Meals cost US$5/10/12 per person for breakfast/lunch/dinner.

Two cave systems accessed via Chiquibul Rd – Barton Creek Cave and Actun Tunichil Muknal – can be explored on guided tours, usually undertaken from San Ignacio (see Caves under Mountain Pine Ridge Area, later this chapter).

SAN IGNACIO (CAYO)
• population 8000

San Ignacio, also called Cayo, is a prosperous farming and holiday center in the lovely, tropical Macal River valley. Together with neighboring Santa Elena across the river, this is the chief population center of Cayo District. That said, it's still small, and during the day it's quiet. At night the quiet disappears and the jungle rocks to music from the town's bars and restaurants.

There's nothing much to do in town, but San Ignacio is a good base from which to

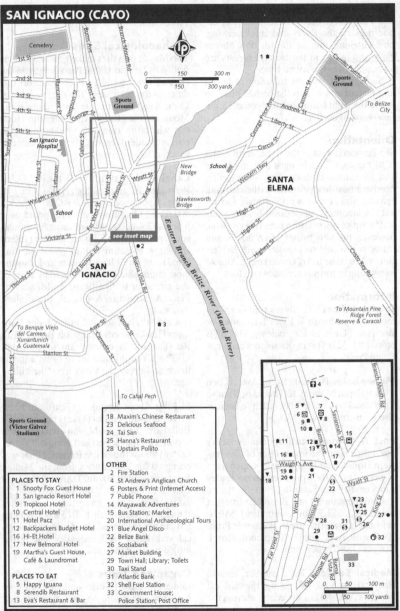

SAN IGNACIO (CAYO)

0   150   300 m
0   150   300 yards

To Belize
City

SANTA
ELENA

To Mountain Pine
Ridge Forest
Reserve & Caracol

To Benque Viejo
del Carmen,
Xunantunich
& Guatemala

To Cahal Pech

SAN
IGNACIO

Sports Ground
(Victor Galvez
Stadium)

PLACES TO STAY
1   Snooty Fox Guest House
3   San Ignacio Resort Hotel
9   Tropicool Hotel
10 Central Hotel
11 Hotel Pacz
12 Backpackers Budget Hotel
16 Hi-Et Hotel
17 New Belmoral Hotel
19 Martha's Guest House,
    Café & Laundromat

PLACES TO EAT
5   Happy Iguana
8   Serendib Restaurant
13 Eva's Restaurant & Bar

18 Maxim's Chinese Restaurant
23 Delicious Seafood
24 Tai San
25 Hanna's Restaurant
28 Upstairs Pollito

OTHER
2   Fire Station
4   St Andrew's Anglican Church
6   Posters & Print (Internet Access)
7   Public Phone
14 Mayawalk Adventures
15 Bus Station; Market
20 International Archaeological Tours
21 Blue Angel Disco
22 Belize Bank
26 Scotiabank
27 Market Building
29 Town Hall; Library; Toilets
30 Taxi Stand
31 Atlantic Bank
32 Shell Fuel Station
33 Government House;
    Police Station; Post Office

0   50   100 m
0   50   100 yards

explore the natural beauties of the Mountain Pine Ridge area. Horseback treks, canoe trips on the rivers and creeks, caving, bird-watching, touring the region's Mayan ruins and hiking in the tropical forests are all popular ways to spend time.

San Ignacio, with its selection of hotels and restaurants, is also the logical place to spend the night before or after you cross the Guatemalan border.

Orientation

San Ignacio is west of the river; Santa Elena is to the east. Two bridges join the towns and are usually both one-way – the newer, northernmost bridge leads traffic into San Ignacio, and Hawkesworth Bridge, San Ignacio's landmark suspension bridge, leads traffic out of town. During the rainy season, however, the new bridge often floods, and traffic is diverted to Hawkesworth Bridge. Burns Ave is the town's main street. Almost everything in town is accessible on foot.

Information

Tourist Offices The town's traditional information exchange is Eva's Restaurant & Bar (see Places to Eat, below). The BTB office (☎ 9-32318) is in the visitors center at Cahal Pech.

Money Belize Bank, on Burns Ave, is open 8 am to 1 pm Monday to Thursday, 8 am to 1 pm and 3 to 6 pm Friday. Atlantic Bank is also on Burns Ave.

Post & Communications San Ignacio's post office is on the upper floor of Government House, near the bridge. It's open 8 am to noon and 1 to 5 pm Monday to Friday and 8 am to 1 pm Saturday.

Eva's Restaurant and Bar offers Internet access for US$2.50 for 15 minutes, US$9.50 per hour. Down the street, Posters & Print, 30 Burns Ave, above Tropicool Hotel, charges US$7.50 per hour.

Medical Services The basic San Ignacio Hospital (☎ 92-2066) is up the hill off Waight's Ave, west of the center. Across the river in Santa Elena is the Hospital La

Loma Luz (☎ 92-2087, fax 92-2674), an Adventist hospital and clinic.

Archaeological Sites

Two Mayan ruin sites make good excursions from San Ignacio. Cahal Pech is right on the edge of town, while El Pilar is a short distance to the northwest. The nearby ruins of Caracol and Pacbitun are covered under the Mountain Pine Ridge Area, later this chapter, while the ruins of Xunantunich are covered under West to Guatemala later this chapter.

Cahal Pech Mayan for 'Tick City,' Cahal Pech (not its original name) was a city of some importance from 900 BC through AD 800. The 34 buildings here are spread over 6 acres (2.4 hectares) and grouped around seven plazas. Plaza B, about 500 feet (150m) from the museum building and parking area, is the site's largest plaza and also the most impressive. It's surrounded by some of the site's most significant buildings. Off Plaza A, Structure A-1 is the site's tallest pyramid.

Cahal Pech is about 1 mile (under 2km) from Hawkesworth Bridge off Buena Vista Rd. The site is open 9 am to 4:30 pm; US$2.50. You might want to bring a picnic lunch and enjoy the views from the hilltop site.

El Pilar About 12 miles (19km) northwest of San Ignacio, 7 miles (11km) northwest of Bullet Tree Falls, the Mayan archaeological site of El Pilar is perched almost 900 feet (275m) above the Belize River. El Pilar was occupied for 15 centuries, from the Middle Preclassic (about 500 BC) through the Late Classic (about AD 1000) periods. With 25 plazas, the city was more than three times the size of Xunantunich. El Pilar has been left largely uncleared, and five archaeological and nature trails meander among the jungle-covered mounds.

Organized Tours

Lodges in Cayo District operate their own tours and excursions on foot, by canoe and on horseback. But you can also take similar excursions using a cheap hotel in San Ignacio as your base. Every hotel and most restaurants in town will want to sign you up. Compare offerings and talk to other travelers before making your choice.

Many guides and tour operators advertise their services at Eva's Restaurant & Bar (☎/fax 92-2267, evas@btl.net), 22 Burns Ave, or at nearby shops on Burns Ave. Drop by and see what's available. To be assured the best tour for your money, sign on only with a licensed tour operator. Always check to see if entrance fees and lunch are included in the tour price – you don't want to get caught short, or hungry! (See Tips on Tours in the Cayes chapter.)

Easy Rider (☎ 92-3734), a stable on the outskirts of town, will pick you up in San Ignacio and take you on a horseback excursion into the jungle for US$40 per person, lunch included. Shorter rides can be had for US$25.

Tours can be arranged through the Maya Mountain Lodge (☎ 92-2164, fax 92-2029, jungle@mayamountain.com), even if you're not a guest. Another reputable tour operator is International Archaeological Tours (☎ 92-3991, iatours@btl.net), on West St near Martha's Guest House.

Following are some of the widely offered tours in and around San Ignacio, along with some sample prices:

- Voyages by boat or canoe along the Macal, Mopan and Belize Rivers; favorite goals on the Macal River include the Rainforest Medicine Trail at Ix Chel Farm and the butterfly farm at Chaa Creek. US$20.

- A trip to the Mountain Pine Ridge area, which usually includes a picnic and a swim in the pools at Río On, a walk to Thousand Foot (Hidden Valley) Falls and a tour of the Río Frio Caves. US$50.

- An overland trip to the Mayan ruins at Caracol with quick stops at the above Mountain Pine Ridge sites. US$75.

- Cave tours to Chechem Ha, Barton Creek Caves or Tunichil Muknal – Mayan ceremonial caves where you'll see pottery shards, skulls and other evidence of the Maya. US$25 to US$60.

- An excursion to Tikal (Guatemala), either for the day or overnight. US$85 and up.

Places to Stay – San Ignacio

Budget A good option is *Martha's Guest House* (☎ 92-2732, marthas@btl.net, 10 West St), a modern home with a family atmosphere. Rooms rent for US$17.50 double with shared bath and fan, US$20 with private bath. Some rooms have cable TV. Amenities include a laundromat (US$5 per load) and a ground-floor café serving good food.

Hotel Pacz (☎ /fax 92-2110, 402 Far West St) rents five basic but sparkling clean rooms for US$10/17.50/20 single/double/triple; bathrooms are shared.

Hi-Et Hotel (☎ 92-2828, 12 West St), at Waight's Ave, is a rickety old house with thinly partitioned rooms, clean beds and low rates of US$5/10 single/double for rooms with shared bath.

New Belmoral Hotel (☎ 92-2024, 17 Burns Ave), at Waight's Ave, has 11 recently remodeled rooms with private bath and cable TV for US$12.50/20 with fan or US$30/40 with air-con.

Tropicool Hotel (☎ 92-3052, 30A Burns Ave) has pleasant ground-floor rooms facing a garden for US$10/12.50 with shared bath.

Central Hotel (☎ 92-2253, 24 Burns Ave) is among San Ignacio's cheapest hotels at US$8/12 for rooms without running water. The neighboring *Backpackers Budget Hotel* competes fiercely for the same clientele.

The tidy *Snooty Fox Guest House* (☎ 92-2150, fax 92-3556, 64 George Price Ave), just across the river in Santa Elena, has clean rooms with shared bath for US$20 double, cabins that have private bath for US$35 and an apartment with two bedrooms and kitchen for US$50. A long stairway leads down to the river.

Mid-Range The *San Ignacio Resort Hotel* (☎ 92-2034, fax 92-2134, sanighot@btl.net), on Buena Vista Rd about a half mile (1km) uphill from Government House, has 25 basic rooms with timeworn bathrooms. Rates are US$65/91/104 single/double/triple or about US$20 more for deluxe air-conditioned units. The hotel has a pool, restaurant, bar and disco, and it often fills up with tour groups.

BELIZE

Cahal Pech Village (☎ 92-3740, fax 92-2225, daniels@btl.net), about 1½ miles (2.5km) uphill from the town center, has a large thatched main building surrounded by 14 small thatched cabins with private bath; US$45 double. Perched atop Cahal Pech Hill, the cabins enjoy fine views of the town and valley, but without a car the walk to and from town can get tedious. On Saturday night the road can get downright treacherous with traffic running to and from the Cahal Pech bar – be prepared to dodge cars.

Places to Stay – Around San Ignacio

The *Parrot's Nest* (☎ 9-37008, cellular ☎ 14-6083, parrot@btl.net), 3 miles (5km) north-west of San Ignacio, near Bullet Tree Falls, is aptly named: Guests stay in treehouselike thatched cabins built high on stilts. Baths are mostly shared, but there's electricity all the time and the price is right: US$25 to US$28 double; one cabin with private toilet for US$33. The site is beautiful, surrounded by the river on three sides. Hiking, canoeing and horseback riding are available, and shuttles to San Ignacio can be arranged.

Maya Mountain Lodge (☎ 92-2164, fax 92-2029, jungle@mayamountain.com, 9 Cristo Rey Rd) is just over 1.5 miles (3.5km) from San Ignacio. The six rooms and eight thatched cottages all have fan and private bath with hot water. Delicious meals are served in the verandah restaurant. Bart and Suzi Mickler, the owners, are walking encyclopedias of Belizean jungle lore. In fact, they pioneered many of the tours that are widely offered throughout the region. Rates are US$49 to US$89 single or double. Home-style meals cost US$8/8/16 for breakfast/lunch/dinner.

Windy Hill Resort (☎ 92-2017, fax 92-3080, windyhill@btl.net), about 1.5 miles (2.5 km) west of San Ignacio on the Western Hwy, has all the facilities: swimming pool, riding horses, nature trail, canoes ready for a paddle on the Mopan River and a full program of optional tours. Accommodations in cozy wooden cabins with private bath, cable TV and ceiling fan cost US$60/80/95 single/double/triple, meals not included.

The *Trek Stop* (☎ 9-32265, susa@btl.net), Mile 71 (Km 114), Western Hwy, 6 miles (10km) west of San Ignacio, is ideal for backpackers. Basic cabins rent for US$10 per person. A campsite costs US$3.50 with your tent (or no tent), US$6 with their tent. Meal packages are available for US$15 per day, and kitchen facilities are available. Nature trails are on the site, as is the Tropical Wings Nature Center, which houses an interpretive center and a small butterfly farm.

For other lodges near San Ignacio, see Mountain Pine Ridge Area, later in this chapter.

Places to Eat

Eva's Restaurant & Bar (☎ /fax 92-2267, evas@btl.net, 22 Burns Ave) is the information and social center of the expatriate set – temporary and permanent – in San Ignacio. Daily special plates at US$4 to US$6 are the best value.

The popular terrace café at *Martha's* (10 West St) serves freshly prepared food for all three meals. You can get breakfast for US$4 to US$5, pizzas for US$9 to US$11 and sandwiches for US$2 to US$3.

Happy Iguana (27 Burns Ave) has a cheerful patio setting and serves stewed chicken, burgers and sandwiches for US$3 to US$5. *Upstairs Pollito*, on Missiah St, is another popular spot for cheap, good eats.

Maxim's Chinese Restaurant, at Far West St and Waight's Ave, is recommended by the locals. Prices range from US$2.50 to US$5. The small, dark restaurant is open 11:30 am to 2:30 pm and 5 pm until midnight. Other choices for Chinese food are *Tai San* and *Delicious Seafood*, both on Burns Ave.

Across Burns Ave from Eva's and a short distance north is the *Serendib Restaurant*, serving – of all things – Sri Lankan dishes. The service is friendly, the food is good, and the prices are not bad, ranging from US$3.50 for the simpler dishes up to US$10 for steak or lobster. Lunch is served 9:30 am to 3 pm, dinner 6:30 to 11 pm.

Hanna's (☎ 92-3014, 5 Burns Ave) serves Indian, Belizean and vegetarian dishes priced from US$4.50 to US$6. Open from 6:30 am to 3 pm and 6:30 to 10 pm daily.

Entertainment

The **Blue Angel**, on Waight's Ave, regularly has big-name live music on the weekends. The **Cahel Pech Bar** sometimes schedules weekend dances. Benque Viejo del Carmen, the small town just east of the Guatemala border, often holds weekend dances attracting people from all over the country. Ask in San Ignacio to see if anything's on for the weekend.

Getting There & Away

Batty Brothers and Novelo's buses run to and from Belize City, Belmopan and Benque Viejo del Carmen nearly every half hour. For details, see the Belize Getting There & Around chapter.

The taxi stand for the Cayo Taxi Drivers Association (☎ 92-2196) is on the traffic circle opposite Government House. Rates can be surprisingly high for short trips out of town (a trip of a few miles can easily cost US$5 to US$10), but a jitney cab ride to Benque Viejo del Carmen costs only US$1.50.

MOUNTAIN PINE RIDGE AREA

South of the Western Hwy, between Belmopan and the Guatemala border, the land begins to climb toward the heights of the Maya Mountains, whose arcing crest forms the border separating Cayo District from Stann Creek District to the east and Toledo District to the south.

In the heart of this highland area – land of macaws, mahogany, mangoes and jaguars – over 300 sq miles (777 sq km) of tropical pine forest has been set aside as the **Mountain Pine Ridge Forest Reserve**. The high elevations and cooler climate here create an environment where pine and palm trees share a forest; you'll hear much exclaiming from foreign visitors about the incongruity of this arrangement. The reserve and its surrounding area are full of rivers, pools, waterfalls and caves to explore.

Roads into the Mountain Pine Ridge area are few. The most important are (from east to west) Chiquibul Rd, which intersects the Western Hwy at Mile 61 (Km 98), near Georgeville, about 6 miles (10km) east of San Ignacio; Cristo Rey Rd, which turns south off the Western Hwy in Santa Elena (across the river from San Ignacio); and Chial Rd, a rough, unpaved road that turns south off the Western Hwy about 5 miles (8km) southwest of San Ignacio or roughly 2 miles (3km) northeast of Benque Viejo del Carmen.

Of these, Chiquibul Rd penetrates deepest into the mountains; the unpaved but graded road runs all the way through the forest reserve and continues south as far as the Caracol archaeological site. All roads in the area may sometimes be impassable between May and late October. Always check with tour operators in San Ignacio about road conditions; you don't want to drive deep into the jungle only to be turned back.

Rainforest Medicine Trail

Formerly called the Pantí Medicine Trail, this herbal-cure research center is at **Ix Chel Farms** (☎ 92-3870), 8 miles (13km) southwest of San Ignacio up Chial Rd.

Dr Eligio Pantí, who died in 1996 at age 103, was a healer in San Antonio village who used traditional Mayan herb cures. Dr Rosita Arvigo, an American, studied medicinal plants with Dr Pantí, then began several projects to spread the wisdom of traditional healing methods and to preserve the rain forest habitats, which harbor an incredible 4000 plant species.

One of her projects was the establishment of the Rainforest Medicine Trail, a self-guiding path among the jungle's natural cures. It's open 8 am to noon and 1 to 5 pm daily; US$5.

At the farm's shop you can buy Rainforest Remedies – herbal cures drawn from the farm's resources and marketed by the Ix Chel Tropical Research Foundation. Ix Chel Farm has recently established a wellness center and guesthouse (see Places to Stay).

Caves

See the map for the general location of these caves, which are usually visited on organized tours out of San Ignacio.

Chechem Ha is a Mayan cave complete with ancient ceremonial pots. Members of the Morales family, who discovered the cave, act as guides, leading you up the steep slope to the cave mouth, then down inside, walking and sometimes crouching, to see what the Maya left. A fee of US$25 pays for one to three people. Take water and a flashlight. You can also camp at Chechem Ha or sleep in one of the simple bunks.

The **Río Frio Caves** are the region's most famous and visited caverns, usually included on Mountain Pine Ridge tours. But gaining on Río Frio in popularity is **Barton Creek Cave**, accessible only by tour prearranged with Barton Creek Ranch. One of the more popular day trips offered out of San Ignacio, the cave holds spooky skulls and bones and pottery shards from the ancient Maya. To see them you'll have to negotiate some very narrow passages. This cave is less visited than the Río Frio Caves, which makes it feel more adventurous.

The latest cave system to be opened for tours is **Actun Tunichil Muknal**. In an effort to prevent looting of the Mayan bones and artifacts within, and to keep general wear and tear to a minimum, only a couple of tour operators are allowed to run tours here at this point. To arrange a tour (around US$65 per person), check with your hotel or with Mayawalk Adventures (☎ 92-3070, cellular ☎ 14-4352), 19 Burns Ave in San Ignacio.

Pools & Waterfalls

Most Mountain Pine Ridge tours stop at one of two popular swimming-hole sites. At **Río On Pools**, small waterfalls connect a series of pools that the river has carved out of granite boulders. Some of the falls double as water slides. The pools at tranquil **Five Sisters Falls**, accessible by an outdoor-elevator ride (small charge, usually US$2) at Five Sisters Lodge, are connected by five falls cascading over a short drop-off. Travelers and locals alike visit this site.

The region's aquatic highlight is **Thousand Foot Falls** (or Hidden Valley Falls), southeast of San Antonio. Hiking trails surround the falls, and a viewing platform at the top of the cascade is a great spot for catching a Mountain Pine Ridge vista. The

falls actually are around 1500 feet high, but they aren't spectacular in the dry season.

Archaeological Sites

The highlands here hold two Mayan ruins of interest, one small and one huge.

Pacbitun This small Mayan archaeological site, approximately 12 miles (20km) south of San Ignacio via Cristo Rey Rd, near San Antonio, seems to have been occupied continuously through most of Mayan history, from 900 BC to AD 900. Today only lofty Plaza A has been uncovered and partially consolidated. Structures 1 and 2, on the east and west sides of the plaza, respectively, are worth a look. Within them archaeologists discovered the graves of Maya women of nobility, buried with a variety of musical instruments, perhaps played at their funerals.

Caracol Some 53 miles (86km) south of San Ignacio via Chiquibul Rd lies Caracol, a vast Mayan city hidden in the jungle. The site covers some 35 sq miles (88 sq km), with 36,000 structures marked so far.

Caracol was occupied in the Postclassic period from around 300 BC until AD 1150. At its height, between AD 650 and 700, Caracol is thought to have had a population of 150,000 – not much less than the entire population of Belize today.

Highlights of the site include Caana (Sky-Palace) in Plaza B, Caracol's tallest structure at 138 feet (42m); the Temple of the Wooden Lintel, dating from AD 50, in Plaza A; the ball court with a marker commemorating Caracol's defeat of rivals Tikal in AD 562 and Naranjo in AD 631; and the central acropolis, containing a royal tomb. The south acropolis, residential area, reservoir and causeway are also worth a look.

You can sign up for a tour (US$50 to US$75 per person) in San Ignacio or at one of the lodges. Those who opt to visit Caracol on their own can reach it on a long day trip in a 4WD or high-clearance vehicle; check road conditions before you go. No services are available at the site, so bring your own food, water and motor fuel.

Places to Stay

The forests and mountains of the greater Mountain Pine Ridge area are dotted with small inns, lodges and ranches offering accommodations, meals, hiking, horseback trips, caving, swimming, bird-watching and similar outdoor activities.

A few of these lodges are for the budget traveler; the rest are more expensive, though they offer a good value for the money. Standard room rates are listed below, but most of the lodges also offer money-saving packages that include lodging, meals and tours. It never hurts to ask if discounts and specials are available.

Although you can sometimes show up unannounced and find a room, these are small, popular places, so it's best to write or call for reservations as far in advance as possible. Most lodges have websites accessible through www.belizenet.com.

Unless you have your own transportation, you'll have to depend on taxis or the hospitality of your lodge hosts to transport you between San Ignacio and the lodges. Sometimes the lodges will shuttle you at no extra cost; sometimes they'll arrange a taxi for you. The Mountain Pine Ridge lodges are served by the Blancaneaux Lodge airstrip; charter flights are arranged by the lodge.

Macal River Lodges Several lodges, some quite famous, lie along the Macal River, reached by Chial Rd. If you drive in yourself, your host lodge will give you exact directions.

Ix Chel Farms (☎ 92-3870, ixchel@btl .net), 8 miles (13km) up Chial Rd, offers comfortable and basic rooms for US$53 double. The focus here is on wellness and healing; massages, facials and aquatherapy are on the menu, along with dietary, health and lifestyle consultations. The atmosphere is calm, and the vegetarian restaurant is one of the country's best.

Chaa Creek Cottages (☎ 92-2037, fax 92-2501, chaacreek@btl.net), the most luxurious of the Cayo lodges, is on the bank of the Macal River right next to Ix Chel Farm and the Rainforest Medicine Trail. Its beautifully kept thatch-roofed cottages are set in tropical gardens and richly decorated with Mayan textiles and local crafts; all have fan and private bath. A state-of-the-art spa has recently been added. Rates are US$135/160/190 single/double/triple. Luxury suites rent for US$180. Breakfast costs US$8, a box lunch is US$7, and dinner is US$22. Chaa Creek also operates *Macal River Camp*, a budget alternative offering platformed safari-style tents for US$42 per night, meals included, bathrooms shared. Guests at Macal River Camp have access to the grounds at Chaa Creek Cottages.

The lodge complex at *duPlooy's Jungle Lodge* (☎ 92-3101, fax 92-3301, duplooys@btl.net) lies largely on a fairly steep hill; the rooms look out over the tree canopy and are accessed by boardwalk, giving the place a treehouse appeal. Guests can enjoy swimming in the Macal River or sunbathing on the resort's white, sandy beach. Three levels of accommodations are available. Rooms in the Pink House have fan and shared bath and cost US$33/43 single/double. Standard bungalows and rooms in the Jungle Lodge have fans and private baths and go for US$100/120. The high-end bungalows cost US$130/155. Meal packages cost US$35 per day for three meals.

Remote *Black Rock River Lodge* (☎ 92-2341, 92-3296, fax 92-3449, blackrock@btl.net) is a simpler place with thatched-roof tent cottages, solar electricity and solar-heated hot water. Rates are US$36/42/46/50 single/double/triple/quad with shared bath, US$60/70/75/80 with a private bath. For details, ask at Caesar's Place, near Georgeville on the Western Hwy, described in West Toward San Ignacio earlier in this chapter.

Mountain Pine Ridge Lodges See the map for a general idea of the location of the following lodges. If you decide to drive in on your own, your lodge will provide you with exact directions.

Pine Ridge Lodge (☎ 92-3310, prlodge@mindspring.com) rents out spacious, well-maintained cottages with private baths for

US$75 double. The restaurant serves lunch (US$7) and dinner (US$17.50).

Blancaneaux Lodge (☎ *92-3878, fax 92-3919, blodge@btl.net*) offers 14 rooms in thatched cabins and luxury villas overlooking waterfalls deep in the Mountain Pine Ridge reserve. Formerly a private writing retreat for the resort's owner, director Francis Ford Coppola, the lodge features beautiful tiled bathrooms, open-air living rooms (in the villas) and a decor filled with handicrafts from Belize, Guatemala, Mexico and Thailand. The restaurant serves Italian cuisine and wines from California's Napa Valley. Cabañas (including light breakfast) cost US$120 to US$150 single, US$150 to US$180 double. Villas cost US$200/300/325/340 single/double/triple/quad.

West of Blancaneaux is *Five Sisters Lodge* (☎ *92-3184, fax 91-2024, fivesislo@btl.net*), named for the five waterfalls that cascade through the property. Cozy hillside cabañas rent for US$60 double with shared bath, US$105 with private bath. A hydro-powered tram runs guests down to the river for swimming and sunbathing. Meals cost US$6/7.50/17.50 breakfast/lunch/dinner.

WEST TO GUATEMALA
From San Ignacio it's another 10 miles (16km) southwest down the Western Hwy to the Guatemala border.

Xunantunich
Belize's most accessible Mayan site of significance, Xunantunich (pronounced soo-**nahn**-too-neech) is reached via a free ferry crossing at San José Succotz, on the Western Hwy about 7 miles (12km) west of San Ignacio. From the ferry it's a walk of 1 mile (2km) uphill to the ruins.

Set on a leveled hilltop overlooking Río Mopán, Xunantunich (Stone Maiden) controlled the riverside track that led from the hinterlands of Tikal down to the Caribbean. During the Classic period, a ceremonial center flourished here. Archaeologists have uncovered evidence that an earthquake damaged the city badly about AD 900, after which the place may have been largely abandoned.

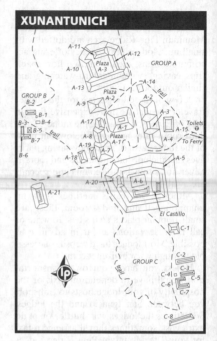

The site's dominant structure, El Castillo (Structure A-6), rises 130 feet (40m) above the jungle floor. The stairway on its northern side – the side you approach from the courtyard – goes only as far as the temple building. To climb to the roofcomb you must go around to the southern side and use a separate set of steps. On the temple's east side, a few of the many masks that once surrounded the structure have been restored.

Xunantunich is open 9 am to 5 pm; US$2.50. Guides can be hired for a one-hour tour for US$13, but the site can easily be navigated independently. The *Xunantunich Hotel & Saloon*, across the road, is a good stop for lunch and refreshments. It also rents rooms at rates ranging from US$20 double (fan, shared bath) to US$63 (air-con, private bath).

Buses on their way between San Ignacio and Benque Viejo del Carmen will drop you at the ferry for the fare of US$0.50. Jitney taxis shuttling the same route cost US$1.50.

Ferry hours are 8 am to noon and 1 to 5 pm; crossing is on demand and free for both foot passengers and cars.

Benque Viejo del Carmen

A sleepy town 2 miles (3km) east of the border, Benque Viejo del Carmen holds few services for travelers, and you're better off eating and sleeping in San Ignacio. The town stirs from its normal tropical somnolence in mid-July, when the Benque Festival brings three days of music and revelry.

Crossing the Border

Cross early in the morning to have the best chance of catching buses onward. Get your passport (and, if applicable, your car papers) stamped at the Belizean station, then cross into Guatemala. The border station is supposedly open 24 hours a day, but most travelers try to cross during daylight hours. If you need a Guatemalan visa (see the Visas & Documents and Embassies & Consulates sections in the Guatemala Facts for the Visitor chapter), obtain it before you reach the border. Guatemalan tourist cards (US$5) are obtainable at the border. Be prepared to pay a US$3.75 Protected Areas Conservation Trust fee when crossing the border. This fee is valid for 30 days if you cross another border from Belize.

Two banks at the border will change money, but the itinerant moneychangers often give you a better deal – for US cash. The rates for exchanging Belizean dollars to Guatemalan quetzals and vice versa are poor. Use up your local currency before you get to the border, then change hard foreign currency, preferably US dollars.

Both Transportes Pinita and Transportes Rosalita buses westward to Santa Elena (Guatemala) depart town early in the morning. Sometimes available are more comfortable – and more expensive – minibuses (US$10 per person); many travelers feel this is money well spent.

To go on to Tikal, get off the bus at El Cruce (Puente Ixlu), 22 miles (36km) east of Flores, and wait for another bus, minibus or obliging car or truck to take you the final 21 miles (35km) north to Tikal. Note that the flow of traffic from El Cruce to Tikal drops dramatically after lunch.

Southern Belize

If you want to explore off the tourist track, southern Belize is the place. The region's biggest draw is Placencia, attracting beach-loving budget travelers for whom life in the cayes is just too hectic. Dangriga, in the Stann Creek District, is a lively seaside town and the center of Garífuna culture in Belize. Out to sea you'll find Tobacco and South Water Cayes and Glover's Reef, offering divers nearly virgin reef to explore.

The Southern Hwy – long, bumpy and dusty – carries travelers through the region to its final destination, the Toledo District. Toledo's main town, Punta Gorda, is a wild mixture of all the cultures of Belize and lies near several unrestored ruins and natural wonders. This is the most remote, least explored part of the country and getting around can be an expensive hassle, but it's a wonderland for the truly adventurous.

HUMMINGBIRD HIGHWAY

Both roads to southern Belize are reached via the Western Hwy. The mostly unpaved Manatee (or Coastal) Hwy goes southeast from the Western Hwy at the village of La Democracia, a short distance past the Belize Zoo. Though the countryside along this route is lush, there's nothing to stop for, and during the rainy summer months the road is often flooded and impassable. The Hummingbird Hwy is the all-weather route.

Heading south from Belmopan, the Hummingbird Hwy stretches 49 miles (79km) to the junction of the Southern Hwy and the turnoff to Dangriga. It's almost all paved, but be ready to slow for roadworks or sudden transitions to dirt road. Mile counters on the Hummingbird Hwy run from Mile 55 at the Western Hwy junction to Mile 0 at the Dangriga city limits.

Blue Hole National Park & St Herman's Cave

The Blue Hole, focus of the like-named national park, is a cenote (water-filled limestone sinkhole) some 328 feet (100m) in diameter and 108 feet (33m) deep. Fed by underground tributaries of the Sibun River, it's deliciously cool on the hottest days and makes an excellent swimming hole.

The park visitors center is about 11 miles (18km) south of Belmopan on the Hummingbird Hwy. At the center is the trailhead to St Herman's Cave, a large cavern once used by the Maya during the Classic period. This is one of the few caves in Belize you can visit independently, although a guide is required if you wish to venture in farther than 150 yards. Also here are a series of nature trails and an observation tower.

Highlights

- Enjoy Placencia's easy beach life.
- Soak up Garífuna culture in Dangriga, Hopkins or Sittee River.
- Snorkel the reefs of Glover's Atoll, accessible from Dangriga.
- Get off the beaten track to the southernmost outpost of Punta Gorda

154

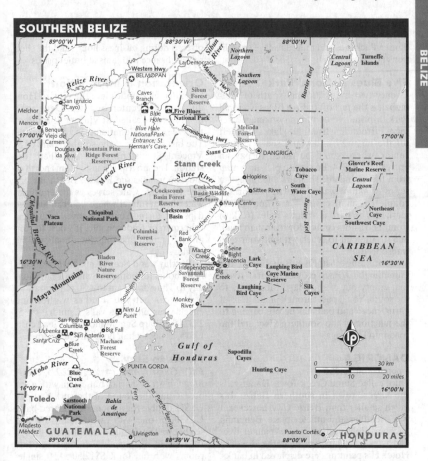

SOUTHERN BELIZE

The trail to the Blue Hole itself starts at a parking area about a mile farther down the highway. (Break-ins are not unheard of here, so be cautious with your belongings.) You don't have to stop at the visitors center if you're just going for a swim; an attendant is posted at the trail to the Blue Hole to collect your money. The park is open 8 am to 4 pm daily; US$4.

Between the two entrances, a road on the left leads to Ian Anderson's Caves Branch Adventure Company & Jungle Camp (☎/fax 8-22800, caves@pobox.com), featuring adventure tours to caves on a privately owned

estate. Day trips cost US$60 to US$95 per person and require various levels of activity – you can choose a leisurely tub float down the Caves Branch River or go for a harder adventure where you'll hike, climb and even rappel to reach your destination.

Caves Branch offers lodging for a range of budgets, from spacious screened cabaña suites with private baths (US$97 double) or cabañas with shared baths (US$58 double) to bunks (US$15 per person) or camping (US$5 per person). The jungle has been cleared just enough to allow room for the buildings, giving the grounds an exotic feel, especially at night when the tiki torches are lit. Meals cost US$12/12/17 breakfast/lunch/dinner. Packages and multiday cave expeditions are available.

Five Blues National Park

Twenty-two miles (36km) south of Belmopan is the turnoff to Five Blues National Park, a primitive community-managed reserve surrounding five (blue) lakes. Turn left off the highway and you'll see a visitors center, where you'll be asked to pay an entry fee of US$4. Be sure to pick up a map from the attendant. The park's features – a series of nature walks, a diving platform, a couple of small caves – are not clearly marked. The park is about 4 miles (6.5km) from the visitors center down a rough road, and it's difficult to reach without your own transportation.

Continuing past Five Blues park, the Hummingbird Hwy crosses several rivers that empty out of the Maya Mountains to the south. You'll pass through plantations of citrus, cacao and bananas before coming to the junction of the Southern Hwy and the road into Dangriga.

DANGRIGA
• population 10,000

Once called Stann Creek Town, Dangriga is the largest town in southern Belize. It's much smaller than Belize City, however it is a friendlier and quieter place. Benjamin Nicholas, Belize's most famous painter, lives and works in Dangriga near the Bonefish Hotel. His paintings are displayed in banks, hotel lobbies and public buildings throughout the country. Stop in at his studio and have a look. Popular diving and fishing spots off Glover's Reef and Tobacco Caye are accessed from Dangriga; hire a boat at the Riverside Café.

There's not a lot to do in town except spend the night and head onward – unless you're here on Garífuna Settlement Day (November 19), a major celebration. Eight miles (13km) northwest of town on Melinda Rd is **Marie Sharp's Factory** (☎ 5-22370), the source of Belize's beloved hot sauce. The primary ingredients are habanero peppers and carrots, purchased from local farmers. Casual tours, often led by Marie herself, are offered during business hours, and the shop sells hot sauce and jams at outlet prices.

Orientation & Information

Stann Creek empties into the Gulf of Honduras at the center of town. Dangriga's main street is called St Vincent St south of the creek and Commerce St to the north. The bus station is at the southern end of St Vincent St just north of the Shell fuel station. The airstrip is a mile (2km) north of the center, near the Pelican Beach Resort. The Riverside Café serves as the unofficial water-taxi terminal where you can arrange trips out to the southern cayes with local fishermen or tradespeople. It's best to stop in by 10 am to find out when boats will be leaving.

Barclay's and Scotiabank have branches here; hours for both are 8 am to 1 pm Monday to Thursday, 8 am to 4:30 pm Friday.

You can get your clothes washed and check your email at Val's Laundry (☎ 5-23324), 1 Sharp St at Mahogany. A load costs US$5, as does a half hour on the Internet.

Places to Stay

Pal's Guest House (☎ /fax 5-22095, 868-A Magoon St) is spartan but clean, with a sea breeze and the sound of the surf. You pay US$15 double for a room with shared bath, US$30 for one with private bath, TV and sea view. The family-run *Bluefield Lodge* (☎ 5-22742, 6 Bluefield Rd) has seven tidy rooms with fan for US$12.50/14.50 single/double with shared bath, US$17.50 double with private bath.

Chaleanor Hotel (☎ 5-22587, 35 Magoon St) has clean, comfortable rooms with private baths at US$30 double. The rooftop deck offers views of the Caribbean. *Bonefish Hotel* (☎ 5-22165, bonefish@btl.net, 15 Mahogany Rd) rents 10 bunkerlike rooms with fan, air-con, TV and private bath for US$50 to US$75 double. The hotel caters to divers and also operates the Blue Marlin Lodge on South Water Caye.

Pelican Beach Resort (☎ 5-22044, fax 5-22570, pelicanbeach@btl.net), at the north

BELIZE

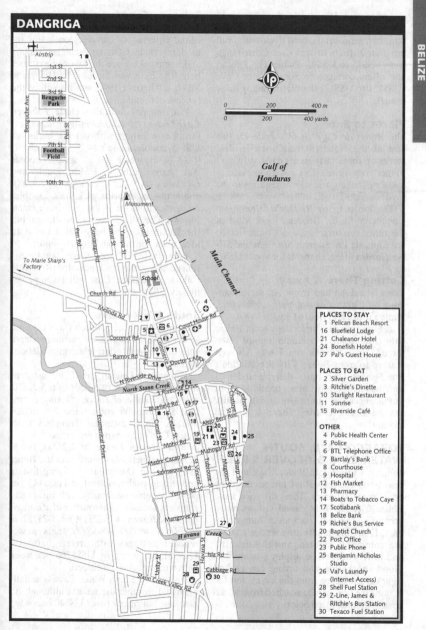

DANGRIGA

Airstrip

1st St
2nd St
3rd St
Benguche Park
5th St
7th St
Football Field
10th St

Benguche Ave
Pen St

Monument

To Marie Sharp's Factory

Gulf of Honduras

0   200   400 m
0   200   400 yards

Pen Rd
Gumaragu Rd
Sawai St
Yampa St
From St

School

Church Rd
Melinda Rd

Main Channel

Coconut Rd
Ramos Rd
Plum St
Commerce St

Doctor's Alley

N Riverside Drive
North Stann Creek
S Riverside Drive

Bluefield Rd
Cedar St
Canal St
Maho Rd

Alejo Beni St
S Foreshore St
Oak St

Ecumenical Drive

Madre Cacao Rd
Salmwood Rd
Yemeri Rd

Mahogany Rd
Tubroose St
St Vincent St
Magoon St
Sharp St

Mangrove Rd

Havana Creek

Isla Rd
Cabbage Rd

Havana St
Unity St

Stann Creek Valley Rd

PLACES TO STAY
1 Pelican Beach Resort
16 Bluefield Lodge
21 Chaleanor Hotel
24 Bonefish Hotel
27 Pal's Guest House

PLACES TO EAT
2 Silver Garden
3 Ritchie's Dinette
10 Starlight Restaurant
11 Sunrise
15 Riverside Café

OTHER
4 Public Health Center
5 Police
6 BTL Telephone Office
7 Barclay's Bank
8 Courthouse
9 Hospital
12 Fish Market
13 Pharmacy
14 Boats to Tobacco Caye
17 Scotiabank
18 Belize Bank
19 Richie's Bus Service
20 Baptist Church
22 Post Office
23 Public Phone
25 Benjamin Nicholas Studio
26 Val's Laundry (Internet Access)
28 Shell Fuel Station
29 Z-Line, James & Ritchie's Bus Station
30 Texaco Fuel Station

end of town, is Dangriga's upmarket hotel. It's on the waterfront and boasts a restaurant, bar, sand beach, boat dock and a full program of tours to area sites. Costs range from US$75 to US$97 double. The Pelican also offers cottages on South Water Caye (US$151 to US$171 double, including three meals).

Places to Eat

The *Riverside Café*, on Riverside Dr just east of the North Stann Creek Bridge, serves up three tasty meals daily at budget to moderate prices. This is a good place to ask about fishing and snorkeling trips to the cayes or treks inland.

The locals favor *Ritchie's Dinette*, on Commerce St, for Belizean food. Most of the other restaurants along Commerce St are Chinese: The *Sunrise*, *Starlight* and *Silver Garden* offer full meals for about US$6.

Getting There & Away

Maya Island Air and Tropic Air serve Dangriga on flights also stopping at Placencia, Punta Gorda and Belize City.

Z-Line runs five buses daily from Belize City (four hours via Hummingbird Hwy, three hours via the Coastal Hwy). Also operating to/from Belize City are Ritchie's Bus Service (two buses daily) and James (one bus daily). Most buses continue south to Placencia and Punta Gorda. For details, see the Belize Getting There & Around chapter.

TOBACCO CAYE, SOUTH WATER CAYE & GLOVER'S REEF

Tobacco Caye, South Water Caye and the resorts of Glover's Reef are accessed by boat from Dangriga. Their distance from Belize City has kept casual visitors away, protecting the reef from much human impact. Dolphins, manta rays and manatees are commonly sighted, and the quantity and variety of coral on display is incredible. Good snorkeling and diving can be had right off the shore from the cayes, and the major dive sites can be reached from all accommodations listed below.

Tobacco Caye

Tint Tobacco Caye is a 5-acre (2-hectare) island catering to travelers on a low-to-moderate budget. Diving, fishing, snorkeling and hammocking are the favorite pastimes here. The caye was hit hard by Hurricane Mitch in October 1998, and it's still in the process of rebuilding.

Lodging possibilities include *Tobacco Caye Lodge* (☎ 5-12033, tclodge@btl.net), offering new cabins with private baths for US$75 double; *Lana's* (☎ 5-22571, cellular ☎ 14-7451), which has 10 spartan rooms with shared baths for US$30 double; and *Gaviota's* (☎ 5-22294, cellular ☎ 14-9763), about the same price as Lana's. Double-occupancy rates for all lodges include meals for two. The island has no restaurants, but the Tobacco Caye Lodge has a bar – an ideal place for the watching the sunset.

Passage to Tobacco Caye can be arranged along the river near the Riverside Café in Dangriga. Cost will be approximately US$15 one way.

South Water Caye

Five miles south of Tobacco Caye is South Water Caye, a much more exclusive island, with dive resorts offering accommodations packages.

Dangriga's Pelican Beach Resort runs the *Pelican's Pouch* (☎ 5-22044, fax 5-22570, sales@pelicanbeach.com), offering rooms for US$183 double and cottages for US$207 double, meals included. Transfers from Belize City or Dangriga are extra.

Blue Marlin Lodge (☎ 5-22243, fax 5-22296, marline@btl.net) also runs the Bonefish Hotel in Dangriga. Weeklong fishing and diving packages start at US$1443 per person, double occupancy, with meals and transfers included. *International Zoological Expeditions* (☎ 5-22119, fax 5-23152, in the USA ☎ 800-548-5843) rents newer wooden cottages with private baths for US$951 per week, or US$1266 per week with a dive package included.

Passage to South Water Caye is usually arranged through the resorts, although it's possible, but pricey (over US$40 one way), to pick up a boat at the Riverside Café in Dangriga.

Glover's Reef
Named for the pirate John Glover, Glover's Reef holds a handful of secluded lodges, each on its own atoll. The well-run *Manta Resort* (☎ *2-32767, fax 2-32764, info@ mantaresort.com, www.mantaresort.com)*, on Southwest Caye, offers weeklong diving and fishing packages ranging from US$1500 to US$2000, including meals and transportation. Its elegant cabins, each with dark-wood interior, fan and air-con, are spaced well for privacy. The food here is excellent.

Glover's Atoll Resort (☎ *5-12016, cellular ☎ 14-8351, glovers@btl.net)*, on Northeast Caye, offers budget accommodations on a 9-acre (3.6-hectare) atoll about 20 miles (32km) from the mainland. Weekly rates are US$80 for camping, US$99 for a dorm bunk and US$149 double for a cabin. Facilities are rustic, but the 360-degree Caribbean view can't be beat. It's a good deal for budget travelers, but extras – water, food, equipment – can add up. A sailboat departs for the island every Sunday morning at 8 am from the Sittee River Guesthouse (see Sittee River in the next section). The trip costs US$30 and takes three to four hours, depending on the weather.

Slickrock Adventures and Island Expeditions also have camps on Glover's Reef for members of their countrywide expeditions (see Organized Tours in the Belize Getting There & Around chapter).

SOUTHERN HIGHWAY
The Southern Hwy, south of Dangriga, is unpaved and can be rough, especially in the rainy months, but along the way are some great opportunities for experiencing off-the-beaten-track Belize. Some southern reaches of the highway, near Punta Gorda, are being paved.

Hopkins
• **population 1100**
The farming and fishing village of Hopkins is 4 miles (7km) east of the Southern Hwy,

on the coast. Most of its people are Garífunas, living as the coastal inhabitants of Belize have lived for centuries.

A handful of thatch cabaña lodges lie south of town. The best is *Sandy Beach Lodge* (☎ *5-37006, t-travels@btl.net)*, owned and operated by the Sandy Beach Women's Cooperative. Its six simple dorm-style rooms rent for US$9/10 single/double with shared bath. Cabins with private bath cost US$13/18. North of town center, the *Swinging Armadillo*, a cheery restaurant and bar, also has bunks available for US$10 per person.

More expensive accommodations are offered at *Jaguar Reef Lodge* (☎/*fax 2-12041, jaguarreef@btl.net)*, with 14 rooms in luxury cabañas right on the beach for US$185 double.

Sittee River
Another small coastal village where you can get away from it all is Sittee River. *Sittee River Guesthouse* rents bunks for US$5 a night (and not worth a penny more). Call Glover's Atoll Resort for more information. The boat to Glover's Reef picks up passengers here. Next door is the more gracious, good-value *Toucan Sittee* (☎ *5-37039)*, offering riverside rooms at US$8 to US$12 per person, shared baths, as well as two apartments at US$40 and US$55 double.

Cockscomb Basin Wildlife Sanctuary
Almost halfway between Dangriga and Independence is the village of Maya Centre, where a track goes 6 miles (10km) west to the Cockscomb Basin Wildlife Sanctuary (sometimes called the Jaguar Reserve), a prime place for wildlife-watching.

The varied topography and lush tropical forest within the 98,000-acre (39,000-hectare) sanctuary make it an ideal habitat for a wide variety of native Belizean fauna. Several species of wild cats – including jaguarundis, jaguars, pumas, ocelots and margays – inhabit the reserve. Among the other resident animals, many the prey of the cats, are agoutis, anteaters, armadillos,

Baird's tapirs, brocket deer, coatis, kinkajous, otters, pacas, peccaries and the weasel-like tayras. Snakes here include the boa constrictor and the deadly poisonous fer-de-lance. There are birds galore.

Visitor facilities at the reserve include a campsite (US$2.50 per person), several simple shared rental cabins with solar electricity (US$15 per person, kitchen use US$1 per person), a visitors center and numerous hiking trails. The walk through the lush forest is a pretty one, and though you cannot be assured of seeing a jaguar, you will certainly enjoy seeing many of the hundreds of other species of birds, plants and animals in this rich environment. No public transportation to the reserve is available.

Tapirs are among the many exotic species inhabiting Cockscomb Basin Wildlife Sanctuary.

For information, contact the Belize Audubon Society (☎ 2-35004, fax 2-34985, base@btl.net), 12 Fort St, Belize City, or the Cockscomb Basin Wildlife Sanctuary, PO Box 90, Dangriga.

At the start of the road into the reserve, in Maya Centre, are the **Nuch Che'il Cottages** (☎ 5-12021), Mile 14 (Km 23) Southern Hwy, and the Hmen Herbal Center Medicinal Trail (entrance fee US$2). Aurora Saqui, a relative and apprentice of the legendary Dr Eligio Pantí of the Rainforest Medicine Trail at Ix Chel Farms, runs both. Bunks in the cheery dorm cost US$8, rooms are US$18/20 single/double. Three meals a day are served (not included in rates).

PLACENCIA
• population 600

Perched at the southern tip of a long, narrow, sandy peninsula, Placencia is 'the caye you can drive to.' Not too long ago, the only practical way to get here was by boat from the mainland. Now a road runs all the way down the peninsula and an airstrip lies just north of town. But Placencia still has the wonderful laid-back ambience of the cayes, along with varied accommodations and friendly local people.

As on the cayes, plenty of activities are available here, including water sports and excursions to many points of interest both onshore and off. Unlike most of the cayes, however, Placencia has good palm-lined beaches on its east side. The beaches attract an international crowd looking for sun and sand, and they make low-key pastimes such as swimming, sunbathing and lazing-about the preferred 'activities' for many visitors.

Orientation & Information

The town owes its layout to years gone by, when all commerce and activity was carried out by boat so streets were of little use. The village's main north-south 'street' is actually a narrow concrete footpath about 3 feet (1m) wide that threads its way among simple wood-frame houses (some on stilts) and beachfront lodges. An unpaved road skirts the town to the west, ending at the peninsula's southern tip, which is the bus stop.

An easy walk takes you anywhere in town. From the airstrip, it's about a half mile (0.8km) south to the village and a mile (1.6km) farther to the peninsula's southern tip. North of the airstrip, past various resorts scattered along the coast, lie the villages of Seine Bight and Maya Beach, both of which are struggling to develop their own tourism infrastructures.

The village has no central landmark or town square. At its south end you'll find the wharf, fuel station, bus stop and icehouse. Atlantic Bank, also on the south end of town, is open 9 am to 2 pm Monday to Thursday,

Blancaneaux Lodge, Mountain Pine Ridge area, western Belize

El Castillo dominates the Mayan ruins at Xunantunich.

Fountain, Benque Viejo del Carmen

Dockside boat repair, Glover's Reef, Belize

Omar's Fast Food, Placencia, southern Belize

Southwest Caye on Glover's Reef, a popular dive center

9 am to noon and 1 to 4 pm Friday. You can check your email at The Purple Space Monkey Internet Café (☎ 6-24094) for US$2.50 for 15 minutes, US$6 for one hour. It's open 7 am to midnight and has an espresso machine – a rare and welcome sight in southern Belize.

Laundry service is available from most of the hotels and guesthouses on the peninsula for US$5 a load.

Organized Tours

Vying to sign up customers for tours of the sort listed below are Ocean Motion Guide Service (☎ 6-23363, 6-23162) and Nite Wind Guide Service (☎ 6-23487, 6-23176), both operating out of small offices near the boat dock. Next door, and offering dive trips in addition to the rest, is Natural Mystic Dive Shop & Aquatic Adventures (☎ 6-23182).

For inland tours, check with Toadal Adventure (☎ 6-23207, fax 6-23334), operating out of Deb and Dave's Last Resort, or with Kitty's Place (☎ 6-23227, kittys@btl.net).

Below are some of the tours available from Placencia, along with ballpark prices:

• Snorkeling or sea kayaking around Laughing Bird, Ranguana or Silk Cayes. Usually includes a beach barbecue. US$35 to US$40. Diving these areas costs around US$80, equipment included.

• Bird-watching and a tube float in the Cockscomb Basin Wildlife Sanctuary. US$50.

• A trip up the Monkey River, which includes a short sea cruise south to the river's mouth, then nature-watching and a walk through Monkey River Village. US$35.

• A long day trip to the Mayan ruins of Nim Li Punit or Lubaantun, possibly with a stop at Blue Creek caves. US$65.

• A trip to the forests surrounding the village of Red Bank to see a seasonal population of scarlet macaws, an increasingly rare site in Central America. For more information, contact the Programme for Belize office in Belize City (☎ 2-75616, fax 2-75635) or inquire at hotels or guide services in Placencia.

Places to Stay

Placencia has lodgings in all price ranges. Budget and mid-range accommodations are in the village (you're likely to get a beach-side cabaña, but your neighbor will be just a couple of feet away); top-end places are north along the beach.

Village Center The *Julia & Lawrence Guesthouse* (☎ 6-23478) is central and clean. Rooms with shared bath go for US$13/18 single/double; ones with private baths rent for a bit more. *Sunrider Guest House* (☎ 6-23486) has good, clean rooms with private bath for US$16/21/25 single/double/triple. The rooms face a beach with shady palms.

Deb & Dave's Last Resort (☎ 6-23297, fax 6-23334, debanddave@btl.net) has rooms with shared baths for US$16/22. It's on the lagoon side of the peninsula and stays quieter than the beach places.

To the south, *Sonny's Resort* (☎ 6-23103, fax 2-32819) has well-spaced but expensive rooms with cable TV (US$22 double). A restaurant and bar are on site. *Barracuda & Jaguar Inn* (☎ 6-23330, fax 6-23250, wende@btl.net) rents two hardwood cabañas with refrigerator and coffeemaker for US$45, light breakfast included. A number of other places offer one or two cabañas for rent, including *Coconut Cottages* (☎ /fax 6-23234), with cottages on the beach for US$28.

Sea Spray Hotel (☎ 6-23148), right in the village center on the beach, has rooms and cabins with shared or private bath (and hot water) priced from US$25 to US$40 double. The more expensive rooms are larger and have porches and sea views. *Ranguana Lodge* (☎ /fax 6-23112) has attractive, good-sized mahogany cabins, but they're packed tightly together; US$50 to US$60 double with private shower. Each room has a fan, refrigerator, coffeemaker and balcony. The more expensive rooms have beach views.

North of the Village The lodgings north of the village tend to be more expensive destination-style resorts, but they're very satisfying, with tropical-isle ambience. All offer various water sports, activities and local excursions.

Kitty's Place (☎ 6-23227, fax 6-23226, kittysbtl.net), 1.5 miles (2.5km) north of the village, is a Caribbean Victorian beachfront

BELIZE

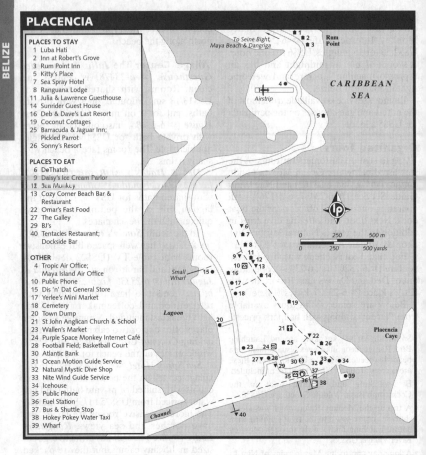

PLACENCIA

PLACES TO STAY
1 Luba Hati
2 Inn at Robert's Grove
3 Rum Point Inn
5 Kitty's Place
7 Sea Spray Hotel
8 Ranguana Lodge
11 Julia & Lawrence Guesthouse
14 Sunrider Guest House
16 Deb & Dave's Last Resort
19 Coconut Cottages
25 Barracuda & Jaguar Inn;
   Pickled Parrot
26 Sonny's Resort

PLACES TO EAT
6 DeThatch
9 Daisy's Ice Cream Parlor
12 Sea Monkey
13 Cozy Corner Beach Bar &
   Restaurant
22 Omar's Fast Food
27 The Galley
29 BJ's
40 Tentacles Restaurant;
   Dockside Bar

OTHER
4 Tropic Air Office;
   Maya Island Air Office
10 Public Phone
15 Dis 'n' Dat General Store
17 Yerlee's Mini Market
18 Cemetery
20 Town Dump
21 St John Anglican Church & School
23 Wallen's Market
24 Purple Space Monkey Internet Café
28 Football Field; Basketball Court
30 Atlantic Bank
31 Ocean Motion Guide Service
32 Natural Mystic Dive Shop
33 Nite Wind Guide Service
34 Icehouse
35 Public Phone
36 Fuel Station
37 Bus & Shuttle Stop
38 Hokey Pokey Water Taxi
39 Wharf

To Seine Bight,
Maya Beach & Dangriga

Rum
Point

CARIBBEAN
SEA

Airstrip

Small
Wharf

Lagoon

Channel

Placencia
Caye

0   250   500 m
0   250   500 yards

lodge with rooms (US$95/115 single/double), garden cabins (US$95/115) and beachfront cabins (US$135/155). This is perhaps Placencia's best place to stay.

Nautical Inn (☎ 6-23595, fax 6-23594, nautical@btl.net) is a small, modern resort in Seine Bight, north of Placencia. Proprietors Ben and Janie Ruoti are equipped for all adventures. They rent motorcycles, run diving and coastal tours and provide guests with free use of bikes, snorkels, sailboats and kayaks. The 12 comfortable rooms cost US$105/125. Meal packages and weekly rates are available.

At **The Green Parrot** (☎/fax 6-22488, www.greenparrot-belize.com), in Maya Beach, split level cabañas with kitchenettes cost US$125 double. Rates include breakfast and airport transfers. Open since 1974, **Rum Point Inn** (☎ 6-23239, fax 6-23240, rupel@btl.net) is Placencia's oldest resort. Guests can stay in mushroom-shaped stucco cabañas or choose more conventional hotel-style rooms, all renting for US$123/144/173 single/double/triple. Meal packages are available for US$30 more per person. Amenities include a library and pool.

The Inn at Robert's Grove (☎ 6-23565, fax 6-23567, www.robertsgrovebelize.com) has modern and spacious rooms, beautiful grounds, a swimming pool and rooftop hot tubs. Prices range from US$150 double for standard rooms to US$175 for suites. A dive shop is on site, and tours to all local attractions can be arranged.

Luba Hati (☎ 6-23402, fax 6-23403, lubahati@btl.net) is designed as an Italian villa, built with Caribbean hardwoods, stucco and ceramic tile. Rooms in the main building have their own terrace and sea view. Cabañas offer more privacy and have open-air showers. Franco's restaurant combines Italian and Caribbean cuisines. Rates range from US$120 to US$150 single, US$150 to US$180 double. A meal plan is available for US$40 per person.

Places to Eat

Omar's Fast Food offers homemade food at low prices. Try the cheap, good burritos or higher-priced menu items like conch steak (US$9). Open 7 am to 10 pm. A good stop for low-priced Belizean food is *BJ's*, in the southern part of town off the main road. *Daisy's Ice Cream Parlor*, in the center of town, west off the central pathway, serves meals as well as desserts and has a pleasant patio area. Burgers cost US$2; meals run from US$7 to US$10.

The best of the beachside places is *Sea Monkey Bar (☎ 6-24060)*, where the staff is friendly and the setting simple and comfortable. The menu is limited, but the offerings are delicious, with bar snacks such as nachos and black bean chili for US$2 to US$3.

Nearby, the *Cozy Corner Beach Bar & Restaurant (☎ 6-23280)* is open for lunch and dinner daily and stays open for drinks until around 10 pm, later on the weekends. Another good place to hang out late is the *Pickled Parrot*, the restaurant and bar at the Barracuda & Jaguar Inn. *DeThatch (☎ 6-24011)* is a small bar on the beach serving drinks and some meals. Fish burritos cost US$3.50.

The Galley, west of the main part of the village, is a favorite for long dinners with good conversation. A full meal with drinks

costs about US$10 to US$15. *Tentacles Restaurant (☎ 6-23333)* is another evening favorite – a breezy, atmospheric place with its popular *Dockside Bar* built on a wharf out over the water.

Getting There & Away

Air Maya Island Air and Tropic Air offer daily flights linking Placencia with Belize City and Dangriga to the north and Punta Gorda to the south. For details see the Belize Getting There & Around chapter. The village begins a half mile (0.8km) south of the airstrip; taxis meet most flights. If you're staying at one of the pricier resorts, ask to be picked up.

Bus Ritchie's and Z-Line each run two buses from Belize City to Placencia via Dangriga. See the Belize Getting There & Around chapter for details.

Boat Daily except Sunday, the *Hokey Pokey Water Taxi* (US$5) departs Placencia at 10 am for Mango Creek, and departs Mango Creek at 2:30 pm on the return trip. The water taxi departs Placencia again at 4 pm. Many boats will do a charter run to/from Mango Creek for US$20 for up to six persons.

The *Gulf Cruza (☎ 2-24506)* makes a Belize City-Placencia-Big Creek-Puerto Cortés (Honduras) run on Friday, leaving Placencia at 9:30 am, arriving at Puerto Cortés at 11 am. It takes the same route north on Monday, leaving Placencia at 2:30 pm, arriving at Belize City at 5 pm. The boat takes passengers only, no vehicles.

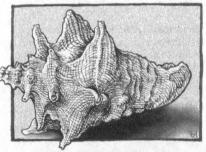

Getting Around

Placencia Shuttle Service makes six daily runs in each direction between Maya Beach, Seine Bight and Placencia from 6 am to 8 pm, stopping at the resorts along the way. Schedules are posted at most hotels and restaurants en route.

You can rent bicycles for US$15 a day at the Purple Space Monkey (☎ 6-24094) or call John (☎ 14-4087) for a bike.

PUNTA GORDA
• population 3000

The Southern Hwy ends at Punta Gorda, the southernmost town in Belize. Rainfall and humidity are at their highest and the jungle at its lushest here in the Toledo District. Prepare yourself for at least a short downpour almost daily and some sultry weather in between.

Known throughout Belize simply as 'PG,' this sleepy town was founded for the Garífunas who emigrated from Honduras in 1832. In 1866, after the US Civil War, some Confederate veterans received land grants from the British government and founded a settlement here, but it didn't endure.

Though still predominantly Garífuna, PG is also home to the typical bewildering variety of Belizean citizenry: Creoles, Kekchi Maya, and expat Americans, Brits, Canadians, Chinese and East Indians.

Fishing was the town's major livelihood for almost two centuries, but now farming is important as well. Tourism is building, as PG is the base for excursions inland to the Mayan archaeological sites at Lubaantun and Nim Li Punit, to the Mayan villages of San Pedro Columbia and San Antonio, and to Blue Creek Cave.

Orientation & Information

The town center is a triangular park with a bandstand and a distinctive blue-and-white clock tower. Saturday is market day, when area villagers come to town to buy, sell and barbecue. It's a fascinating and colorful mix-up.

Nature's Way Guest House (☎ 7-22119), 65 N Front St, is the unofficial information center for travelers. The Belize Tourism Board office (☎ 7-22531) and the Toledo Visitors' Information Center (☎ 7-22470), run by the BTIA, are off Front St and open Monday to Wednesday, Friday and Saturday 9 am to 1 pm. Tours can be arranged through your hotel, or contact Galvez Taxi, Tours & Travel Service (☎ 7-22402, cellular ☎ 14-3931), which leads tours of the area for around US$100 a day.

Belize Bank, at Main and Queen Sts across from the town square, is open 8 am to 1 pm Monday to Thursday, 8 am to 4:30 pm Friday. Punta Gorda Laundry Service is at 2 Prince St and charges US$1.50 per pound.

Places to Stay

Punta Gorda's lodging is resolutely budget-class, with only a few places rising above basic shelter.

Nature's Way Guest House (☎ 7-22119, 65 Front St) is the intrepid travelers' gathering place. This converted house charges US$8/13/18 single/double/triple in rooms with clean shared showers. Trips by minibus and boat can be arranged to all points of interest around PG.

St Charles Inn (☎ 7-22149, 23 King St) offers a good value for the money. Clean and well kept, it has rooms with private bath and fan for US$15/20 single/double. Small groups sometimes fill it. **Pallavi's Hotel** (☎ 7-22414, 19 N Main St) has rooms for US$11 double.

Punta Caliente Hotel (☎ 7-22561, 108 José María Núñez), near the Z-Line bus station, has a good restaurant on the ground floor and rooms above. Each room has good ventilation as well as a fan and private bath. Prices are good: US$20/25.

The **Tidal Waves Retreat** (☎ 7-22111, bills_tidalwaves@yahoo.com), on the sea at the south edge of town, rents two rooms for US$19/24, including access to a kitchenette. A cabaña rents for US$49, including breakfast. Camping is available for US$5 per person, US$9 with breakfast.

The **Traveller's Inn** (☎ 7-22568, fax 7-22814) is at the southern end of José María Núñez St, next to the Z-Line bus station. For US$50/60 you get a modern – if stodgy – air-conditioned room with private bath and

BELIZE

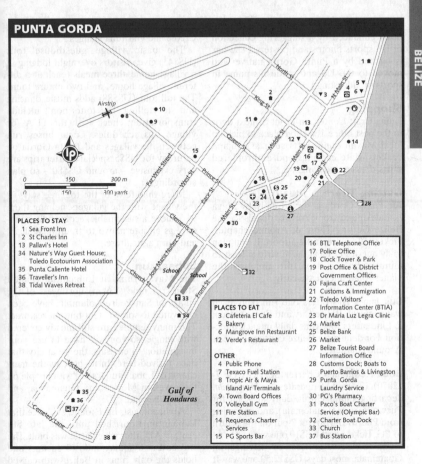

PUNTA GORDA

North St

King St

Airstrip

Queen St

Far West Street

West St

Prince St

Pace St

Clement St

Main St

Church St

Jose Maria Nunez St

Victoria St

Cemetery Lane

*Gulf of
Honduras*

0   150   300 m
0   150   300 yards

PLACES TO STAY
1 Sea Front Inn
2 St Charles Inn
13 Pallavi's Hotel
34 Nature's Way Guest House;
   Toledo Ecotourism Association
35 Punta Caliente Hotel
36 Traveller's Inn
38 Tidal Waves Retreat

School
School

PLACES TO EAT
3 Cafeteria El Cafe
5 Bakery
6 Mangrove Inn Restaurant
12 Verde's Restaurant

OTHER
4 Public Phone
7 Texaco Fuel Station
8 Tropic Air & Maya
   Island Air Terminals
9 Town Board Offices
10 Volleyball Gym
11 Fire Station
14 Requena's Charter
   Services
15 PG Sports Bar

16 BTL Telephone Office
17 Police Office
18 Clock Tower & Park
19 Post Office & District
   Government Offices
20 Fajina Craft Center
21 Customs & Immigration
22 Toledo Visitors'
   Information Center (BTIA)
23 Dr Maria Luz Legra Clinic
24 Market
25 Belize Bank
26 Market
27 Belize Tourist Board
   Information Office
28 Customs Dock; Boats to
   Puerto Barrios & Livingston
29 Punta Gorda
   Laundry Service
30 PG's Pharmacy
31 Paco's Boat Charter
   Service (Olympic Bar)
32 Charter Boat Dock
33 Church
37 Bus Station

cable TV; breakfast is included. There's secured parking as well.

The *Sea Front Inn* (☎ 7-22300, fax 7-
22682, seafrontinn@btl.net), north of the
town center on Front St, is the town's
newest hotel but nonetheless a ramshackle
arrangement of wood and stone, towering
above the rest of the town's buildings. The
rooms have private baths and cable TV and
cost US$50 double.

Places to Eat
The restaurant at the *Punta Caliente Hotel*
serves stew pork, fish fillet, beans and rice

with chicken and similar dishes for US$3.50
to US$5, and it's all good.

Cafeteria El Café is a tidy place open for
breakfast and lunch. *Verde's Restaurant*, on
Main St, offers standard Belizean family
cooking and good breakfasts.

Mangrove Inn Restaurant (☎ 7-39910)
serves up daily fresh-fish specials, good
Mexican food and quite possibly the best
fried chicken in Belize for US$6 to US$8.

Entertainment
The *PG Sports Bar*, West and Prince Sts., is
a good bet for live music on weekends. It's

a good-sized, fairly standard bar, incongruously enhanced by a staggering collection of US sports photos and posters. (The bar is backed by a Punta Gorda native who moved to the US and made his name in sports broadcasting.)

Shopping

Fajina Craft Center, on Front St next door to the post office, is a good place to pick up local Mayan handicrafts such as jipijapa baskets, slate carvings and embroidered shirts, dresses and hangings.

Getting There & Away

Air Punta Gorda is served daily by Maya Island Air and Tropic Air. For details see the Belize Getting There & Around chapter. Ticket offices are at the airport. If you plan to fly out of PG, be at the airstrip at least 15 minutes before departure time, as the planes sometimes leave early.

Bus James Bus offers one run daily each way between Belize City and Punta Gorda; Z-Line offers four runs daily in each direction. For details see Belize Getting There & Around chapter.

Boat Requena's Charter Services (☎ 7-22070), 12 Front St, operates the *Mariestela*, departing Punta Gorda daily at 9 am for Puerto Barrios (Guatemala), and departing from Puerto Barrios' at 2 pm on the return to PG. Tickets cost US$10 one way.

Paco's Boat cruises to Lívingston, Guatemala, most days; US$12.50 one way. If you have a large enough group, you can also arrange for passage to Honduras. Ask for details at the Olympic Bar (☎ 7-22164), 3 Clements St. On Tuesday and Friday, another boat to Lívingston leaves from the customs dock at 10:30 am.

AROUND PUNTA GORDA
Toledo Ecotourism Association

The Toledo Ecotourism Association (☎ 7-22119, fax 7-22199, ttea@btl.net), at Nature's Way Guest House, 65 Front St, runs a Village Guesthouse and Ecotrail Program that takes participants to any of

13 traditional Mopan Maya, Kekchi Maya, Creole and Garífuna villages.

The basic village guesthouse tour (US$43) gives visitors overnight lodging in a village home, three meals (each at a different village home) and two nature tours. The full tour (US$88) adds music, dancing and storytelling. The tours don't include transportation; check with the TEA for village bus schedules. Local buses run between the villages and Punta Gorda on Saturday for US$5; special charter trips are very expensive – around US$80 – so plan accordingly.

More than 85% of the tour fee stays in the village with the villagers, helping them to achieve a sustainable, ecofriendly economy as an alternative to traditional slash-and-burn agriculture.

Lubaantun

The Mayan ruins at Lubaantun (Fallen Stones), 1 mile (1.6km) northwest of the village of San Pedro Columbia, have been excavated to some extent but not restored. The many temples are still mostly covered with jungle, so you will have to use your imagination to envisage the great city that once thrived here. In its heyday, the merchants of Lubaantun traded with people on the cayes, in Mexico and Guatemala, and perhaps beyond.

Archaeologists have found evidence that Lubaantun flourished until the late 8th century AD, after which little was built. The site covers a square mile (3 sq km) and holds the only ruins in Belize with curved stone corners. Of its 18 plazas, only the three most important (Plazas III through V) have been cleared. Plaza IV, the most important of all, is built along a ridge of hills and surrounded by the site's most impressive buildings: Structures 10, 12 and 33. A visitors center on the site exhibits Mayan pottery and other artifacts.

Down the road is the *Fallen Stones Butterfly Ranch and Jungle Lodge* (☎/fax 7-22167, www.fallenstones.co.uk), which offers eight cabins looking out across 60 miles (96km) of virgin jungle, with views to the Maya Mountains. It's a splendid, if remote, setting. Cabins rent for US$105 double. Meals cost US$8/13/23 for breakfast/lunch/dinner. If you can't stay, consider visiting for a tour of the Butterfly Ranch (US$5) and lunch.

Nim Li Punit

About 24 miles (38km) northwest of Punta Gorda, just west of the Southern Hwy, stand the ruins of Nim Li Punit (Big Hat). Named for the headgear worn by the richly clad figure on Stela 14, Nim Li Punit may have been a tributary city to larger, more powerful Lubaantun.

The South Group of structures was the city's ceremonial center and is of the most interest. The plaza has been cleared, but the structures surrounding it are largely unrestored. Have a look at the stelae, especially Stela 14, at 33 feet (10m) the longest Mayan stela yet discovered, and Stela 15, which dates from AD 721 and is the oldest work recovered here so far.

San Antonio & Blue Creek

The Mopan Maya of San Antonio are descended from former inhabitants of the Guatemalan village of San Luis Petén, just across the border. The San Antonians fled oppression in their home country to find freedom in Belize. They brought their ancient customs with them, however, and you can observe a traditional lowland Mayan village on a short visit here. If you are here during a festival, your visit will be much more memorable.

About 4 miles (6km) west of San Antonio, near the village of Santa Cruz, is the archaeological site of **Uxbenka**, which has numerous carved stelae.

About 12 miles (20km) south of San Antonio lies the village of Blue Creek, and beyond it the **nature reserve** of Blue Creek Cave. Hike into the site (less than 1 mile/1.6km) along the marked trail and enjoy the rain forest around you and the pools, channels, caves and refreshingly cool waters of the creek system. Guided nature walks – including a canopy walk and a climb to an observation deck accessed by rope ladder (you must wear helmet and harness) – are available for US$15 per hour.

International Zoological Expeditions (☎ 14-3967, bluecreek@btl.net) operates a *guesthouse* on the site. Its seven cabins rent for US$45 per person, including meals.

Getting There & Away

Village buses serve the sites listed above, but the schedules are somewhat erratic. Your best bet is to book a tour or taxi to take you to these sites.

Guatemala

Facts about Guatemala

At the very heart of the Mayan world, Guatemala is a beautiful, mystical land with a tragic history. From conquistadors and almighty earthquakes to death squads and guerilla cadres, Guatemala has been locked in a centuries-long struggle for tranquility and equality.

This dynamic was most evident in Guatemala's 36-year civil war (1960–96), a particularly brutal and dark time in the country's history. The war pitted the armed forces against guerilla troops, and the vicious fighting dragged many innocent by-standers (mostly Maya) into the fray.

Since peace was struck in 1996, the Maya have continued their call for basic rights (including access to education and health care) with some success. New school curricula taught in indigenous languages, conservation efforts spearheaded and run by local communities, and Maya representatives in public office mean little by little Guatemalans are creating a more balanced national reality.

Throughout it all, Maya culture has persevered: holidays and ceremonies are still filled with ancient pageantry and animism, and the weekly markets are ablaze with the vivid colors of traditional handmade clothing, known as *traje*. Maintaining this traditional culture in our modern age is a new and different struggle facing the Maya, but one which promises a lot less bloodshed.

HISTORY

Guatemala's history since becoming an independent nation in 1847 has been one of rivalry and struggle between the forces of left and right. Unfortunately, both sides have benefited the social and economic elite and done little for the people of the countryside, mostly Maya.

The 19th Century

Early in Guatemala's history as a republic, the liberals, who had been the first to advocate independence, opposed the vested interests of the elite conservatives, who had the church and the large landowners on their side.

During the short existence of the United Provinces of Central America, liberal president Francisco Morazán (1830–39) instituted reforms aimed at correcting three persistent problems: the overwhelming economic, political and social power of the church; the division of society into a Hispanic upper class and an Indian lower class; and the region's impotence in world markets. This liberal program was echoed by Guatemalan chief of state Mariano Gálvez (1831–38).

But unpopular economic policies, heavy taxes and a cholera epidemic in 1837 led to an Indian uprising that brought conservative pig farmer Rafael Carrera to power. Carrera ruled until 1865 and undid much of what Morazán and Gálvez had achieved. His government allowed Great Britain to take control of Belize in exchange for construction of a road between Guatemala City and Belize City. The road called for in the treaty was never built, and Guatemala's claims for compensation were never resolved. This dispute between Belize and Guatemala persists and is revived every so often – usually when one of the nations needs a distraction from domestic problems.

The liberals came to power again in the 1870s under Justo Rufino Barrios, a rich, young coffee *finca* (plantation) owner who held the title of president but ruled as a dictator (1873–79). During his tenure, the country made great strides toward modernization, constructing roads, railways, schools and a modern banking system. Not surprisingly, Barrios also did everything possible to encourage coffee production. Peasants in good coffee-growing areas were forced off their lands to make way for coffee fincas, and many Maya were forced to contribute seasonal labor on the plantations. Most of the policies of the liberal reform movement benefited the finca owners and the traders in the cities.

Succeeding governments generally pursued the same policies. Economic control of the country was held by a small group of land-owning and commercial families; foreign companies were given generous concessions; dissenters were censored, imprisoned or exiled by the extensive police force; and the government apparatus remained beholden to economic interests despite a liberal constitution.

The Early 20th Century

Manuel Estrada Cabrera ruled from 1898 to 1920 in a dictatorial style. He fancied himself a bestower of light and culture to a backward land, and he wanted to turn Guatemala into a 'tropical Athens.' At the same time, however, he looted the treasury, ignored the schools and spent millions on the armed forces.

When Estrada Cabrera was overthrown, Guatemala entered a period of instability that ended in 1931 with the election of General Jorge Ubico. President Ubico insisted on honesty in government, and he modernized the country's health and social welfare infrastructure. Debt peonage was outlawed, releasing the Indians from this servitude, but was replaced by a new servitude of labor contributions to the government road-building program.

In the 1940s Ubico dispossessed and exiled the German coffee finca owners and otherwise assumed a pro-Allied stance during the war, but at the same time he openly admired Spain's Generalissimo Francisco Franco. In 1944 he was forced to resign and go into exile.

The elections of 1945 brought a philosopher – Juan José Arévalo – to power. Arévalo established the nation's social security system, a government bureau of Indian affairs, a modern public-health system and liberal labor laws. During his six years as president there were 25 coup attempts by conservative military forces – an average of one coup attempt every three months or so.

Arévalo was succeeded by Colonel Jacobo Arbenz Guzmán in 1951. Arbenz instituted an agrarian reform law designed to break up the large estates and foster high productivity on small, individually owned farms. He also expropriated vast lands conceded to the United Fruit Company during the Estrada and Ubico years, announcing that the lands were to be distributed to peasants and replanted for food cultivation. But the expropriation set off alarms in Washington, which (surprise, surprise!) supported the interests of United Fruit. In 1954 the USA, in one of the first documented covert operations by the Central Intelligence Agency, orchestrated an invasion from Honduras led by two exiled Guatemalan military officers; Arbenz was forced to step down and the land reform never took place.

After Arbenz, the country had a succession of military presidents and violence became a staple of political life. Government opponents regularly turned up dead. The land-reform measures were reversed, voting was made dependent on literacy (disenfranchising around 75% of the population), the secret police force was revived and military repression was common. As a result, guerrilla groups began to form, and the seeds of civil strife took root.

Civil War

During the 1960s and '70s, Guatemalan industry developed at a fast pace, but most profits from the boom flowed upward. In addition, labor union organization challenged the political fabric, and migration from the countryside to the cities produced urban sprawl and slums. All these factors exacerbated political tensions, and protest and repression became rampant. Amnesty International has estimated that 50,000 to 60,000 people were killed in Guatemala during the political violence of the 1970s alone.

As if that weren't enough, a severe earthquake in 1976 killed about 22,000 people and left about a million people homeless. Most of the aid sent to help the people in need never reached them.

The military suppression of antigovernment elements in the countryside peaked under the presidency of General José Efraín Ríos Montt, an evangelical Christian who came to power in a coup in 1982. In the name of anti-insurgency, stabilization and

GUATEMALA

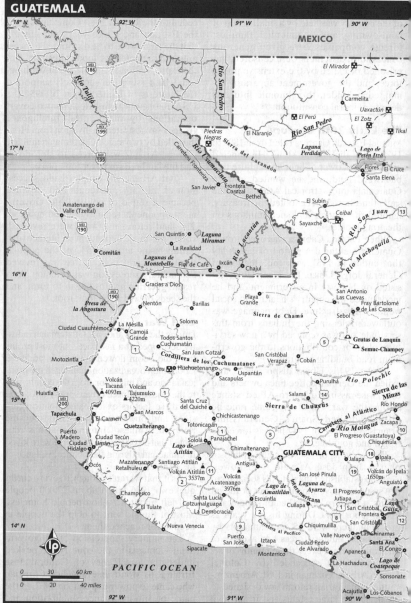

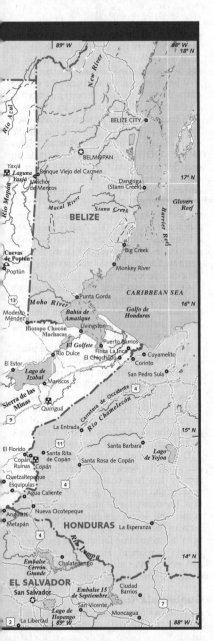

anticommunism, Ríos Montt initiated a 'scorched earth' policy that exterminated entire populations of villages in suspected rebel areas, hoping such tactics would not only get rid of some opposition forces but also dissuade the peasantry from joining or supporting the guerrillas. Over 400 villages were razed, and alarming numbers of people, mostly Maya men, were massacred (often tortured as well). It was later estimated that 15,000 civilian deaths occurred as a result of counterinsurgency operations during Ríos Montt's reign, and an estimated 100,000 refugees (again, mostly Maya) fled over the border to Mexico.

Despite the government's heavy-handed tactics, perhaps half a million people, mostly peasants in the western and central highlands and in the northern El Petén region, actively supported the guerrilla movement. In February 1982 four powerful guerrilla organizations united to form the URNG (Guatemalan National Revolutionary Unity).

In August 1983 Ríos Montt was deposed by a coup led by General Oscar Humberto Mejía Victores, but the abuses continued. It was estimated that over 100 political assassinations and 40 abductions occurred every month under the new ruler. The bloodbath led the US to suspend military assistance to the Guatemalan government, which led in turn to the 1985 election of a civilian president, Marco Vinicio Cerezo Arévalo, the candidate of the Christian Democratic Party.

Before turning over power to the civilians, however, the military ensured that its earlier activities would not be examined or prosecuted, and it established formal mechanisms for military control of the countryside. Though many hoped that Cerezo Arévalo's administration would temper the excesses of the power elite and the military and establish a basis for true democracy, in fact, little progress was made.

The 1990s

Cerezo Arévalo was succeeded as president by Jorge Serrano Elías (1990–93), an evangelical Christian who reopened dialogue with the URNG, hoping to bring the decades-long civil war to an end. But the talks collapsed, Serrano's popularity declined, and he came to depend more on the army for support. On May 25, 1993, Serrano carried out an *autogolpe* (autocoup), attempting to take control of the country by suspending the constitution and ruling by decree. Though supported by the military, the coup was unsuccesful and Serrano was forced into exile. Congress elected Ramiro de León Carpio, the Solicitor for Human Rights and an outspoken critic of the army's strong-arm tactics, to complete Serrano's term.

In March 1995 the USA announced it was suspending aid to Guatemala yet again due to the government's failure to investigate the murder or disappearance of US citizens in Guatemala. These cases included the 1990 murder of Michael Devine, who had operated Finca Ixobel in Poptún, and URNG leader Efraín Bámaca Velásquez, whose wife, US attorney Jennifer Harbury, had been conducting a protest (covered in the international media) since his disappearance in 1992. Eventually it was revealed that he had been murdered. Charges were made that the CIA had been instrumental in both murders, but after investigating the claims, the US government declared them unfounded.

The Signing of the Peace Accords

In 1996, Álvaro Enrique Arzú Irigoyen of the middle-right PAN (Partido de Avanzada Nacional) party was elected and continued negotiations between the government and the URNG. In December of that year, the two parties came to agreement and signed peace accords ending the 36-year civil war – a war in which an estimated 200,000 Guatemalans were killed, a million were made homeless and untold thousands 'disappeared.'

The accords contained provisions calling for accountability for the human-rights violations perpetrated by the armed forces during the war and the resettlement of Guatemala's one million refugees. The accords also addressed the identity and

rights of indigenous peoples, health care, education and other basic social services, women's rights, the abolition of obligatory military service and the incorporation of the ex-guerrillas into civilian life.

It has been a rocky road since the signing of the peace accords. Violence against critics of the ruling elite continues. In a particularly tragic flouting of peace and democracy, Bishop Juan Gerardi, coordinator of the Guatemalan Archbishop's Human Rights Office (ODHAG), was beaten to death outside his home on April 26, 1998, only two days after making public his findings concerning human-rights violations by the armed forces during the civil war. (Three suspects were finally arrested for the murder in January 2000.) And in May 1999, a minuscule 18% of the population came out to vote down referenda that would have permitted constitutional reforms integral to the peace process.

On an encouraging note, the country's Maya population has developed a more sophisticated political organization and has become better mobilized since the signing of the peace accords.

The greatest challenge to a lasting peace in Guatemala stems from great inequities in the social and economic power structure of Guatemalan society. It's estimated that 70% of the country's arable land is owned by less than 3% of the population. According to a United Nations report, the top 20% of the population has an income 30 times (that's 3000%) greater than the bottom 20%.

Discrimination against indigenous people, which has been deeply ingrained in the society for five centuries, manifests in poverty and misery for most of the population. The desire for an improvement in economic and social conditions, basic social services, land reform and labor rights has been the motivation for much of the revolutionary movement. How these needs are met may be the most important factor in creating a true and lasting peace.

Guatemala Today

Guatemala's future hangs in the balance. In November 1999, the country held its first peacetime elections in nearly 40 years. The race came down to a runoff between the former mayor of Guatemala City, Oscar Berger of the incumbent PAN party, and conservative and admitted murderer Alfonso Portillo of the Frente Republicano Guatemalteco (FRG).

Portillo appealed to voters by promising to be tough on criminals, citing his murders as proof; he claimed they were committed in self-defense, and if he could defend himself, he could defend his people. For many human-rights observers, more disturbing than this muddy logic was the fact that Ríos Montt (executor of the 'scorched earth' policy under which tens of thousands of indigenous people were killed) was also running on the FRG ticket and advising Portillo. (Ríos Montt actually went on to become the leader of Congress.) In the end, voters responded to Portillo's anticrime platform and elected him as Guatemala's new president.

Portillo has vowed to clean up the judicial system, crack down on crime, tax the rich and respect human rights. In March 2000, he invited the UN observers responsible for overseeing implementation of the peace accords to stay beyond their targeted December 2000 departure date. Still, it's action, not rhetoric, that counts, and only time will determine Portillo's ultimate place in Guatemalan history. His recent moves, including bolstering municipal police squads with national armed troops and sending most of his family to Canada in self-imposed exile, are particularly worrisome.

GEOGRAPHY & GEOLOGY

Guatemala covers an area of 109,000 sq km, its terrain consisting primarily of mountainous forest highlands and jungle plains. The western highlands hold 30 volcanoes (many active) reaching heights of 3800m in the Cuchumatanes range northwest of Huehuetenango. Here land that has not been cleared for Mayan *milpas* (cornfields) is covered in pine forests, though these are dwindling rapidly as trees are felled for cooking and heating.

The Pacific Slope holds rich coffee, cacao, fruit and sugar plantations. Down along the shore the volcanic slope meets the sea, yielding vast beaches of black volcanic sand. The sweltering climate here is almost unbearable. Grass grows profusely and is fed to cattle.

Guatemala City lies at an altitude of around 1500m. North of the city, the highlands of Alta Verapaz gradually give way to the lowlands of El Petén, an extension of the southern Yucatán. El Petén's climate and topography is like that of Yucatán: hot and humid or hot and dry, depending upon the season. Southeast of the Petén is the valley of the Río Motagua, dry in some areas, moist in others. Bananas thrive in the Motagua Valley.

Guatemala is at the confluence of three tectonic plates. When these plates get frisky, earthquakes and volcanic eruptions ensue. Major quakes struck in 1773, 1917 and 1976.

Guatemala's dynamic geology also includes a tremendous system of aboveground and subterranean caves. Millions of years ago, when the sea level fell and exposed the landmass that now comprises Guatemala and the Yucatán, mollusks perished on the surface, eventually becoming limestone. Over the millennia, water coursing over and through this limestone base created subterranean caves and sinkholes. This type of terrain – known as karst – riddles the Verapaces region and has made Guatemala a popular spelunking destination. In addition, surface-level caves have been used for Mayan ceremonies since ancient times.

CLIMATE

Although Guatemala's official motto is the 'Land of Eternal Spring,' that only tells part of the story. In fact, temperatures can get down to freezing at night in the highland mountains. Days can be dank and chill during the rainy season, but in the dry season – from late October to May – the highlands are warm and delightful. Even in the dry season, however, nights are less than torrid here.

Guatemala's coasts are tropical, rainy, hot and almost constantly humid. Temperatures often reach 32°C to 38°C (90°F to 100°F), and the high humidity abates only slightly in the dry season. Although the rainy and dry seasons are distinct on the Pacific coast and in the highlands, on the Caribbean side rain is possible anytime. Cobán has only about one month of strictly dry weather (in April), though you can catch some less-than-soggy spells between November and March as well.

The vast jungle lowland of El Petén has a tropical climate that is seasonally either hot and humid or hot and dry. December and January are the coolest months, while March and April – the hottest months – are like hell on earth.

ECOLOGY & ENVIRONMENT

As is true almost everywhere else on the planet, deforestation is a big problem in Guatemala. This is especially true in the Petén, where jungle is being felled at an alarming rate to make way for cattle ranches. Colonization by returning refugees and Guatemalans migrating from other, more crowded, areas are also taxing the region's resources. Only a few years ago, the government required anyone buying tracts of land in the Petén to clear a certain portion of it – presumably in the name of 'progress.'

Most of the Petén is now officially protected; in addition to the 576-sq-km Tikal National Park, there's the nearly 2-million-hectare Maya Biosphere Reserve, which includes most of the northern Petén region. The Maya Biosphere Reserve is split into three spheres: the multiple-use zone on the outer fringe permits settlements and agriculture, including the slash-and-burn variety; the buffer zone allows only minimal-impact activities such as gathering forest products; the smallest core zone at the center of the reserve allows no human activity other than limited ecotourism.

Unfortunately, these spheres are only theoretical. The forest is still being ravaged by timber poachers; looters continue to desecrate Mayan tombs deep in the jungle; and tourists, no matter how ecology-conscious, have a negative impact on the fragile ecosystem the reserve is trying to protect. The hope for the Guatemalan rain forest lies with local communities, which are gaining an awareness of the threat and learning to generate income from alternative forest products and activities like ecotourism.

On Guatemala's Pacific side, which holds most of the country's population, the land is devoted mostly to agriculture or industry. The remaining forests of the Pacific coastal and highland areas are not long for this world, as local communities exhaust the trees for heat and cooking purposes.

Another immediate environmental problem facing Guatemala is garbage and its disposal. Open dumps are common sights outside of towns and cities with garbage collection. Where collection doesn't exist, people burn what they can, creating noxious fumes. What can't be burned is thrown in rivers or alongside the road. If garbage is ignored long enough, it will turn into a health, as well as an environmental, issue.

Environmental Organizations

The following organizations in Guatemala City are good resources for finding out more about Guatemala's natural and protected areas:

Asociación Amigos del Bosque (☎ 238-3486), 9a Calle 2-23, Zona 1

Centro de Estudios Conservacionistas de la Universidad de San Carlos (CECON; ☎ 331-0904, 334-6064, 334-7662), Avenida La Reforma 0-63, Zona 10

Comisión Nacional del Medio Ambiente (CONAMA; ☎ 334-1708, 331-2723), 5a Avenida 8-07, Zona 10

Consejo Nacional de Areas Protegidas (CONAP; ☎ 332-0465, 332-0464), Via 5 4-50, Edificio Maya, 4th floor, Zona 4

Fundación Defensores de la Naturaleza (Defensores; ☎ 334-1885, fax 361-7011, defensores@pronet.net.gt), 14 Calle 6-49, Zona 9; Defensores also maintains an office in El Estor.

Fundación Solar (☎ 360-1172, 332-2548, fax 332-2548, funsolar@guate.net), 15a Avenida 18-78, Zona 13

Fundación para el Ecodesarrollo y la Conservación (FUNDAECO; ☎ 472-4268), 7a Calle A 20-53, Zona 11, Colonia El Mirador

For current information on conservation efforts in the Petén, check out some of the organizations concentrating solely on that region. The following are all in Flores:

Asociación Alianza Verde (☎/fax 926-0718, alianza verde@conservation.org.gt), north side of plaza

Centro de Información sobre la Naturaleza, Cultura y Artesanía de Petén (CINCAP), north side of plaza

ProPetén (☎ 926-1370, fax 926-0495, propeten@ guate.net, www.conservation.org), Calle Central

FLORA

Guatemala has over 8000 species of plants in 19 different ecosystems ranging from the mangrove forests on both coasts to the pine forests of the mountainous interior to the cloud forests at higher altitudes. In addition, the Petén region supports a variety of trees, including mahogany, cedar, ramón and sapodilla.

The national flower, the *monja blanca* or white nun orchid, is said to have been picked so much that it's now rarely seen in the wild. Nevertheless, the country holds around 600 species of orchid (a third of them endemic), so you shouldn't have any trouble finding some. If you're interested in orchids and you're in Cobán, check out the large orchid nursery there.

Guatemala also holds the dubious honor of having the perfect climatic conditions for a plant called *xate* (**sha**-tay). Xate is a low-growing palm that thrives in the Petén and is prized in the developed world as flower arrangement filler. *Xateros* – the men who collect the plant – live in the jungle for months at a time, affecting the fragile ecosystem there in the process. The same type of degradation is perpetuated in the Petén by *chicleros*, men who harvest chicle for chewing gum.

FAUNA

With 19 ecosystems, Guatemala also has an abundance of animals. So far, estimates point to 250 species of mammals, 600 species of birds, 200 species of reptiles and amphibians and many species of butterflies and other insects.

The national bird, the resplendent quetzal, is often used to symbolize Central America as well. (Guatemala's national monetary unit, the quetzal, is named for the bird.) Though small, the quetzal is exceptionally beautiful. The males sport a bright red breast, brilliant blue-green across most of the rest of the body and a spot of bright white on the underside of the tail (which is several times as long as the bird's body). The females, alas, are decidedly less dramatic.

Other colorful birds in Guatemala include toucans, macaws and parrots. If you visit Tikal, you can't miss the ocellated turkey (also called the Petén turkey), a large, impressive, multicolored bird reminiscent of a peacock. Tikal is a birding hot spot, with some 300 tropical and migratory species sighted to date. Several woodpecker species, nine types of hummingbirds and four trogon species are just the beginning. Also in the area are large white herons, hawks, warblers, kingfishers, harpy eagles (rare) and a plethora of other feathered beasts.

Although Guatemala's forests still host many types of mammal and reptile species, many remain hidden from the casual observer. Still, visitors to Tikal can enjoy the antics of the omnipresent *pizotes* (coatis) and might also spy howler and spider monkeys. Other mammals deeper in the Petén forest

The entertaining *pizote* (coati)

include jaguars, ocelots, pumas, peccaries, kinkajous, *tepezcuintles* (pacas), opossums, agoutis, tapirs, white-tailed and red brocket deer and armadillos. The forests also harbor some very large rattlesnakes. Reptiles and amphibians in the rest of Guatemala include at least three species of sea turtles (leatherback, *tortuga negra* and olive ridley) and at least two species of crocodile (one found in the Petén, the other in the Río Dulce). Manatees also frequent the waters around Río Dulce.

PARKS & PROTECTED AREAS

Guatemala has more than 30 protected areas, including *parques nacionales* (national parks) and *biotopos* (biological reserves). Over 40 more areas have been proposed for protection. Many of the protected areas are remote; the ones mentioned here are some of the most easily accessible and interesting to visitors. Many are covered more fully in the appropriate regional chapters later in this book.

National Parks & Biosphere Reserves

Reserva de la Biósfera Maya Covering the northern half of the Petén, this 1,844,900-hectare reserve is Guatemala's largest protected area. Within its boundaries are many important Mayan archaeological sites, including Tikal, Uaxactún, El Zotz, El Mirador and Río Azul. Tours and access information are available in Flores.

Reserva de la Biósfera de Sierra de Las Minas In the eastern part of the country, Guatemala's most important cloud forest reserve protects a mountainous area ranging in elevation from 150m to over 3000m above sea level. Before entering, visitors must obtain permission from the Fundación Defensores de la Naturaleza (see the Ecology & Environment section).

Parque Nacional Tikal Guatemala's principal tourist attraction, this park within the larger Maya Biosphere Reserve contains the magnificent Tikal archaeological site as well as 57,600 hectares of pristine jungle. It's also one of the easiest places to observe wildlife in Guatemala.

Parque Nacional Ceibal This archaeological site tucked in the jungle near Sayaxché is accessible only by boat for most of the year. Ceibal is noted for its carved stelae and has several temples, in-

cluding a rare circular one. Tours are available from Flores or Sayaxché.

Parque Nacional Río Dulce In eastern Guatemala, between Lago de Izabal and the Caribbean, this 7200-hectare reserve protects the canyon of the Río Dulce, one of the country's most beautiful rivers. Boat trips on the river can be taken from either Lívingston or Río Dulce.

Parque Nacional Laguna Lachuá In the northeast of the department of Alta Verapaz, this 10,000-hectare park contains a beautiful, circular, turquoise-colored lake that is only 5km in surface area but over 220m deep and holds a great variety of fish. The park has hiking trails, a camping area and visitors center.

Parque Nacional Sierra del Lacandón In the western Petén region, this large park includes the southern portion of the Sierra del Lacandón and abuts the Río Usumacinta, which forms part of the border between Guatemala and Mexico. It's accessible from El Naranjo or by boat along the Río Usumacinta.

Biological Reserves

Biotopo del Quetzal This 1000-hectare cloud forest reserve, also called Biotopo Mario Dary Rivera, was established to protect quetzals. Well-maintained trails snake through a forest of broad-leaf and coniferous trees, climbing plants, ferns, mosses, orchids and bromeliads. This reserve is one of the easiest to access and, as a result, has very few (if any) quetzals in residence.

Biotopo Cerro Cahuí On the northeast shore of Lago Petén Itzá, this well-protected 650-hectare reserve has campgrounds and hiking trails with fine views. Over 300 species of birds have been documented here, including toucans, kingfishers, woodpeckers and herons.

Biotopo Chocón Machacas This 7600-hectare reserve is within Río Dulce National Park on the north bank of the river.

Biotopo Punta de Manabique This 50,000-hectare reserve is on the Caribbean. The only access is by boat, which can be arranged from the piers at either Puerto Barrios or Lívingston.

Biotopo San Miguel-La Pelotada-El Zotz Part of the Maya Biosphere Reserve, this is west of and contiguous with Tikal National Park. It protects a dense forest, bat caves (*zotz* means 'bat' in many Mayan languages) and the archaeological site El Zotz.

Biotopo Laguna del Tigre/Río Escondido Situated within the Maya Biosphere Reserve in the northwest of the Petén, this 46,300-hectare

PARKS & PROTECTED AREAS

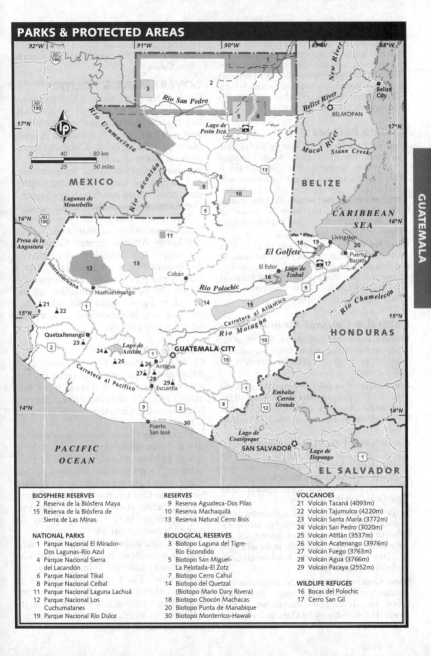

BIOSPHERE RESERVES
2 Reserva de la Biósfera Maya
15 Reserva de la Biósfera de
   Sierra de Las Minas

NATIONAL PARKS
1 Parque Nacional El Mirador-
  Dos Lagunas-Río Azul
4 Parque Nacional Sierra
  del Lacandón
6 Parque Nacional Tikal
8 Parque Nacional Ceibal
11 Parque Nacional Laguna Lachuá
12 Parque Nacional Los
   Cuchumatanes
19 Parque Nacional Río Dulce

RESERVES
9 Reserva Aguateca-Dos Pilas
10 Reserva Machaquilá
13 Reserva Natural Cerro Bisís

BIOLOGICAL RESERVES
3 Biotopo Laguna del Tigre-
  Río Escondido
5 Biotopo San Miguel-
  La Pelotada-El Zotz
7 Biotopo Cerro Cahuí
14 Biotopo del Quetzal
   (Biotopo Mario Dary Rivera)
18 Biotopo Chocón Machacas
20 Biotopo Punta de Manabique
30 Biotopo Monterrico-Hawaii

VOLCANOES
21 Volcán Tacaná (4093m)
22 Volcán Tajumulco (4220m)
23 Volcán Santa María (3772m)
24 Volcán San Pedro (3020m)
25 Volcán Atitlán (3537m)
26 Volcán Acatenango (3976m)
27 Volcán Fuego (3763m)
28 Volcán Agua (3766m)
29 Volcán Pacaya (2552m)

WILDLIFE REFUGES
16 Bocas del Polochic
17 Cerro San Gil

reserve is one of Guatemala's most remote protected areas. It conserves the largest freshwater wetlands in Central America, a refuge for countless bird species. Organized tours are available in Flores. Boat trips can also be arranged at the preserve's administration office in El Naranjo, with prior permission from the Centro de Estudios Conservacionistas de la Universidad de San Carlos (CECON) in Guatemala City.

Wildlife Refuges

Bocas del Polochic On the western side of Lago de Izabal, the Río Polochic forms a marshy delta where it empties into the lake; this is Guatemala's second largest freshwater wetland area. It's especially attractive for birders since it attracts more than 300 bird species, 40% of which are migratory. It's accessible only by water; boats are easily arranged in El Estor.

Cerro San Gil On the south side of El Golfete, east of Lago de Izabal, this refuge occupies the highest part of the Montañas del Mico, the continuation of the Sierra de las Minas. It has many endemic species and great biodiversity. Two parts of the refuge are open to the public.

Natural & Cultural Monuments

Quiriguá This archaeological site, 2km off of the Carretera al Atlántico and easily accessible, is famous for its giant stelae, the tallest in the Mayan world.

Iximché Capital of the Cakchiquel Maya at the time of the Spanish conquest, this is one of the few archaeological sites with a documented history. There is easy access to this site, 2km from Tecpán.

Aguateca-Dos Pilas This monument protects several important archaeological sites and the forest around them. It's in the Río La Pasión valley, in the southwestern Petén municipality of Sayaxché, and accessible from Sayaxché or by tour from Flores/Santa Elena.

Yaxjá On the shores of Lake Petexbatún in eastern Petén, this site is thought by archaeologists to have been a vacation getaway for the Maya nobility. The Topoxté site in the middle of the lake was an observatory. Tours are available from Flores/Santa Elena.

Semuc Champey On the Río Cahabón in the municipality of Lanquín, Alta Verapaz, this site is a series of pristine pools surrounded by rain forest. It's accessible by 4WD, on foot or by tour from Cobán.

Grutas de Lanquín Serviced by frequent buses, these caves 61km from Cobán are at least several kilometers long. You can camp outside the entrance to the caves. Tours are available from Cobán.

GOVERNMENT & POLITICS

Guatemala is a republic with 22 departments. Executive power is held by a president who is elected by direct universal adult suffrage to a term of four years. He is assisted by a vice president and an appointed cabinet. The unicameral national congress consists of 80 members (64 departmental representatives and 16 national seats) also elected to four-year terms. Judicial power rests in a Supreme Court and associated courts.

With a few notable exceptions, such as the administrations of Juan José Arévalo and Jacobo Arbenz Guzmán, Guatemala's government has always been controlled for the benefit of the commercial, military, landowning and bureaucratic classes. Although the niceties of democracy are observed, real government often takes place by means of intimidation and secret military activities (see History).

ECONOMY

Coffee is the country's biggest export crop, followed by sugar, cotton, bananas and cardamom. Other exports include fruits, vegetables, natural rubber and flowers. Tourism is the second-largest income producer after coffee.

Guatemala City is the country's industrial and commercial center and is similar in sprawl and bustle to Mexico City, its great sister to the north. Like Mexico City and many other Latin American urban centers, Guatemala City has problems of immigration, pollution, congestion and crime that arise from its virtual monopoly on the country's commercial life.

The Guatemalan highlands are given over to agriculture, particularly corn, with some mining and light industry around the larger cities. The Pacific Slope has large coffee, citrus and sugarcane plantations worked by migrant labor from the highlands, and the Pacific coast has cattle ranches and some fishing villages.

The Motagua Valley holds some mining operations, but agriculture – primarily vast banana and sugarcane plantations – is most important here. The lush green hills of Alta Verapaz have dairy farms, cardamom and coffee plantations and timber-producing forests.

El Petén depends upon tourism and farming for its livelihood. The rapid growth of agriculture and cattle ranching poses a serious threat to the ecology of the Petén, a threat that will have to be controlled if the forests of this vast jungle province are to survive. Tourism, on the other hand, is a mostly positive factor here, providing alternative sources of income that depend upon the preservation of the ecology for success. Still, not all tour outfits wearing the ecotourism label are promoting environmentally responsible adventures; in such a fragile environment, low-impact tourism may be an oxymoron.

POPULATION & PEOPLE

According to 1999 estimates, Guatemala's population is nearing 12.5 million. Official census statistics list 56% of the population as *ladino* and 44% as indigenous. In fact, Mayans probably make up more than half of the total population, but this doesn't register in the census because that survey defines 'indigenous' as only those people who wear traditional dress and speak their Mayan language. Obviously, this excludes all people who may be full-blooded Maya but who also speak Spanish and wear jeans.

About 40% of all Guatemalans live in cities, the biggest of which are Guatemala City, Quetzaltenango and Escuintla. The Petén and Izabal regions are the most sparsely populated, though internal migration to both those areas is on the rise. On average, the country has a population density of 170 inhabitants per square kilometer. The Guatemalan population is due to double by the year 2020 if it continues to grow at its current rate of 2.68% annually.

EDUCATION

Education in Guatemala is free and compulsory between the ages of seven and 14. Primary education lasts for six years; it's es-timated that 79% of children of this age are actually in school. Secondary education begins at age 13 and lasts for up to six years, with two cycles of three years each; it's estimated that only 23% of children of the relevant age group are in secondary school. Note that not all secondary education is free – a considerable deterrent for the average Guatemalan student. Guatemala has five universities; the University of San Carlos, founded in 1676 in Antigua (and later moved to Guatemala City), was the first university in Central America.

Overall adult literacy is around 65%, but literacy rates vary widely among different ethnic groups. For example, some estimates indicate that up to 95% of Guatemala's rural Mayan women can't read. Maya children who do seasonal migrant work with their families find it difficult to get an education, as the time the families go away to work falls during the normal school year.

ARTS

The Maya of Guatemala still make various traditional handicrafts. Most striking are their weavings, embroidery and other textile arts, but they also produce basketry, ceramics and wood carving.

A number of well-known Maya painters work in a primitivist style depicting scenes from daily life. Known as Tz'utuhil oil painting, this genre is typified by vibrant colors and is centered in Lago de Atitlán. Accomplished artists of this style include Rafael González y González, Pedro Rafael González Chavajay and Mariano González Chavajay. For more on Mayan oil painting, visit the Arte Maya website at www.artemaya.com.

Music is an important part of Guatemalan society, and it is a source of pride that the marimba may have been invented here. This xylophone-type instrument might have already existed in Africa before slaves brought it to Guatemala, or it might have been created and/or refined in the New World – whatever the case may be, marimba music can still be heard throughout the country. The Maya also play traditional instruments including the *chirimía* (of Arabic origin and related to the oboe) and reed flute.

GUATEMALA

The Guatemalan novelist Miguel Ángel Asturias won the Nobel Prize in literature in 1967 – another great source of national pride. Best known for his thinly veiled vilification of Latin American dictators in *El Señor Presidente*, Asturias also wrote poetry (collected in *Sien de Alondra*, published in English as *Temple of the Lark*). Other celebrated Guatemalan writers include poet Luis Cardoza y Aragón and short-story master Augusto Monterroso, who was born in Honduras but raised in Guatemala.

The ancient Maya ruins and the Spanish colonial structures in Antigua are both impressive works of architecture. Interestingly, Mayan embellishments can be found on many colonial buildings (such as the lotus flowers adorning Antigua's La Merced) – an enduring testament by the Maya laborers forced to carry out the Europeans' architectural concepts.

SOCIETY & CONDUCT

Guatemalan society is divided between the ladino and Maya peoples, both pursuing pathways that are sometimes convergent but often at odds. While the ladino culture proceeds into the modern world, in many ways the Maya are holding fast to their traditional culture and identity despite five centuries of European domination and occupation of their land.

The Mayan culture expresses itself in many ways. The most noticeable to visitors is the beautiful traditional clothing worn by Maya women. In most parts of Guatemala the Maya men now wear western clothing, but in some places, such as Sololá and Todos Santos Cuchumatán, the men also still wear traditional *traje*. Each village has its own unique style of dress, and variations within that style can denote social status. When all of the different variations are taken into account, the Maya have something like 500 distinctive clothing designs, each with its own particular significance.

Twenty different Mayan languages are spoken in Guatemala; most Maya still speak one of them as their everyday language. Mayan religion, firmly based in nature, is also still practiced.

Unfortunately, in Guatemala the Maya suffer vicious (and often violent) discrimination. While a tiny minority of Maya are going to universities, working in the business world and joining modern society, those continuing the traditional way of life are the poorest sector of Guatemalan society.

The plight of these people has attracted international attention. Many nongovernmental organizations from around the world are working in Guatemala to assist the indigenous people. Travelers can help by patronizing Maya-owned businesses and buying traditional Mayan handicrafts. If the Maya can sell their wares to tourists and receive fair prices, it helps to make their craft an economically viable occupation.

Ladino culture is most strongly felt in literature, dance and music (particularly mariachis), anything cowboy – from firearms to exquisite leatherwork – and, of course, soccer. A medley of North American and European influences have wended their way into Guatemalan culture over the years; for tourists this will be most evident at the dinner table, where spaghetti and tacos often show up.

Dos & Don'ts

See the Dos & Don'ts section in this book's Facts about the Region chapter for general tips on conduct in Latin America.

Nobel laureate Miguel Ángel Asturias

In recent years, stories circulated through Guatemala that some foreign visitors (particularly white women) were kidnapping Maya children, perhaps for the grisly purpose of selling their organs. A twist on the tale held that the foreign women were kidnapping Guatemalan children to raise as their own. Do be aware that some people are extremely suspicious of foreigners who make friendly overtures toward local children.

When planning your wardrobe, note that while Mayan women are extremely eager to sell their traditional clothing to foreigners, especially the beautiful embroidered *huipiles* (blouses), it is considered bad form for a visitor to wear these things in Guatemala. Indeed, travelers sporting *traje* stick out like sore thumbs; better save them for home.

Also think about safety in connection with your appearance. Particularly in the capital, locals will warn you against wearing even cheap imitation jewelry: You could be mugged for it. If you have any wealth, take care not to flaunt it.

RELIGION

Roman Catholicism is the predominant religion in Guatemala, but it is not the country's only religion. Since the 1980s, evangelical Protestant sects, most of them rabidly Pentecostal, have surged in popularity, and now

an estimated 30% of Guatemalans are of this faith.

When Catholicism was thrust upon Guatemala it did not wipe out the traditional Mayan religion, and it still has not today. Many aspects of Catholicism easily blended with Mayan beliefs, and the Maya still worship at many places where they have worshiped since ancient times, bringing offerings and making sacrifices to gods that predate the arrival of the Spanish.

Various Catholic saints hold a double meaning for the Maya; often the Catholic identity of the saint was superimposed over a deity or saint the Maya people already had when the Spanish arrived. The Maya also have some of their own saints independent of the Catholic church, such as Maximón in Santiago Atitlán and San Simón in Zunil.

LANGUAGE

Spanish is the official national language, but in practice 23 different languages are spoken in Guatemala, including Spanish, Garífuna, a Pipil-based language spoken by the Xinka people and 20 Mayan languages. Many Maya people speak Spanish, but you can't assume for sure that they do; some Maya elders, women and children do not. Maya children often start to learn Spanish only after they start school.

Facts for the Visitor

PLANNING

When to Go

There is really no bad time for a Guatemalan adventure, although rain may limit access to certain areas. The rainy season, from May to October, turns the lowland jungles muddy and brings cold temperatures to the highlands, especially at night. The dry season, from late October or early November through the end of April, means sweltering heat in the Petén, possible rain in the Caribbean and comfortably warm days and cool nights in the highlands.

High tourist season is from the end of December to the beginning of April, with the crunch becoming acute around Christmas, New Year's and Easter. A secondary high season occurs between June and August, when throngs of foreigners descend on Guatemala to study Spanish.

Maps

ITMB Publishing (☎ 604-879-3621, fax 604-879-4521, itmb@itmb.com, www.itmb.com), 530 W Broadway, Vancouver BC, Canada V5Z 1E9, publishes international travel maps and books. The *Guatemala-El Salvador* (1:500,000) map in the company's Traveler's Reference Maps series is good and covers neighboring portions of Mexico (Tabasco and Chiapas), Belize and Honduras. These maps are available from many travel-book and map stores.

A letter to the Instituto Guatemalteco de Turismo (INGUAT), 7 Avenida 1-17, Zona 4, Guatemala City, Centro America, sent well in advance of your departure, will yield a useful map of the country. You can buy the same map, called the *Mapa Vial Turístico*, in Guatemala at shops or from street vendors (US$2) or over the Internet from Latin American Travel Consultants at www.amerispan.com/lata.

In Guatemala, the Instituto Geográfico Militar (☎ 332-2611), Avenida Las Américas 5-76, Zona 13, Guatemala City, is the best resource for good topographical maps.

What to Bring

Many travelers fall into the tropical trap while packing for a Guatemalan trip, when in fact, the country can be downright cold. You'll want a sweater, jacket and a pair of warm pants to keep out the chill of the highland evenings. If you're visiting during the rainy season or plan to spend time in the mountains, bring a heavier jacket – fleece works particularly well here – and dress in layers.

You can bring shorts and tank tops if you want, but be aware that the country has few beaches, and you'll stick out big time wearing shorts anywhere else; except in the most casual places, locals don't expose much skin.

For rainy-season travels, bring a poncho or similar raingear and have a strategy for keeping your pack dry; line the inside with plastic bags, buy or make a pack cover (or get a poncho big enough to cover you and your pack) and carry an umbrella.

RESPONSIBLE TOURISM

Tourism and the intrusion that goes with it is a fairly touchy subject in a country just emerging from 36 years of civil war. The Maya have suffered terribly during this period and travelers should refrain from probing into wartime tragedies. Let your hosts offer information, don't dig.

New areas are accessible to tourists since peace broke out, and many companies, local and foreign, peg Guatemala as the next ecotourism jewel. While some outfits are running genuinely ecofriendly tours, others are simply exploiting the enthusiasm for low-impact travel and are harming the environment more than helping it. Just the presence of people in ecologically sensitive areas can disrupt the balance. This is a growing problem with some jungle tours, especially those visiting remote areas (see 'Responsible Tourism' in the Petén chapter).

Another unfortunate trend is the serving of 'exotic' fare – sometimes including endangered or threatened species – at some restaurants. By ordering these dishes you may be contributing to the extinction of endemic fauna.

TOURIST OFFICES
Local Tourist Offices
The main outpost of the national tourist office, Instituto Guatemalteco de Turismo (INGUAT; ☎ 331-1333, fax 331-8893, inguat@guate.net), is in Guatemala City at 7a Avenida 1-17, Centro Cívico, Zona 4. Another office is in Zone 9 of the capital. Branch offices are in Antigua, Flores (on the plaza; quite helpful), Panajachel, Quetzaltenango and at the international airports in Guatemala City and Flores/Santa Elena.

Tourist Offices Abroad
INGUAT's central information source (in the USA ☎ 888-464-8281, inguat@guate.net, www.travel-guatemala.org.gt) is OK for the most basic queries. The following INGUAT contacts (most at Guatemalan embassies or consulates) should be able to answer more detailed questions:

Canada Guatemalan Embassy (☎ 613-233-7188, 233-7237), 130 Albert St, Suite 1010, Ottawa, ON K1P 5G4

France Guatemalan Embassy (☎ 14-227-7863, fax 14-754-0206), 73 rue de Courcelles, 75008 Paris

Germany Guatemalan Embassy (☎ 228-351-579, fax 228-354-940), Zietenstrasse 16, 53173 Bonn; Guatemalan Consulate (☎ 40-430-6051, fax 40-430-4274), Fruchtalle 17, 2059 Hamburg; Guatemalan Consulate (☎ 89-406-214), Grafinger Strasse 2, 81671 Munich

Mexico Guatemalan Embassy (☎ 5-540-7520, 520-9249, fax 5-202-1142), Avenida Explanada 1025, Lomas de Chapultepec 11000, México 4, DF

UK Guatemalan Embassy (☎ 0171-351-3042, fax 0171-376-5708, 13 Fawcett St, London SW10 9HN

USA Guatemalan Embassy (☎ 202-745-3873, fax 202-745-1908), 2220 R St NW, Washington, DC 20008; Guatemalan Tourist Commission (☎ 305-443-0343, fax 305-443-0699), 300 Sevilla Ave, Suite 210-A, Coral Gables, FL 33134

VISAS & DOCUMENTS
Visas
Guatemala changed its visa requirements in 1999 and is revising other regulations (especially for extensions), so you should check with the nearest Guatemalan embassy or consulate before heading off.

Most travelers can enter Guatemala without a visa. If you need a visa and arrive at the border without one, however, you will be turned back; if you're flying into Guatemala, you probably won't be allowed to board the plane without having the necessary entry visa.

As of early 2000, citizens of many countries – among them Australia, Canada, El Salvador, France, Germany, Honduras, Ireland, Mexico, the Netherlands, New Zealand, the USA and the UK – need no visa or tourist card and may stay up to 90 days in Guatemala after arrival. Officials don't always give you the 90-day maximum; ask for the maximum or you may end up with a 30-day stamp.

Citizens of Belize and a few other countries do not need a visa or tourist card but may stay a maximum of only 30 days in Guatemala after arrival.

Citizens of many other countries must obtain a visa; contact the Guatemalan embassy or a Guatemalan consulate in your home country for more information.

If you want to cross into Honduras on a day (or two) pass to visit Copán, Guatemalan immigration officials will usually allow you to return to Guatemala and continue your journey without interrupting your original entry stamp. For information on this, refer to the section on Copán.

Visa Extensions Guatemala is cracking down on visa extensions. Whereas unlimited extensions used to be the norm, most foreigners are now permitted a total of 180 days – 90 on entering and 90 upon renewal.

Extensions must be applied for in person at the Dirección General de Migración in Guatemala City. Plans are afoot to establish another immigration office in Antigua to handle extension requests. To apply for an extension you'll need your passport, a recent photo, proof of funds and an onward ticket.

Onward Tickets
Theoretically, Guatemala requires all visitors to show proof of funds and an onward

GUATEMALA

ticket before they're permitted entry. Very rarely will you be asked to produce either, though if pressed, you can present a credit card as proof of funds and an international bus ticket as proof of onward passage.

Minors Traveling Alone

If you are under 18 and traveling alone, to enter Guatemala you (technically) must have a letter of permission signed by both your parents and witnessed by a Guatemalan consular official.

EMBASSIES & CONSULATES

Some of the consulates mentioned here are actually honorary consuls or consular agencies. These posts can issue visas, but they usually refer more complicated matters to the nearest full consulate or to the embassy's consular section. All the listings are for embassies unless noted.

Guatemalan Embassies & Consulates

Guatemala's diplomatic offices abroad include the following:

Belize (☎ 2-33150, 2-33314, fax 2-35140), 6A St Matthew St, near Municipal Airport, Belize City

Canada (☎ 613-233-7188, 233-7237), 130 Albert St, Suite 1010, Ottawa, ON K1P 5G4; also consulates in Vancouver and Montreal

Costa Rica (☎ 314074, fax 316645), Avenida Primera, Calles 24 y 28, No 2493, San José

El Salvador (☎ 271-2225, fax 271-3019), 15 Avenida Norte 135, San Salvador

France (☎ 14-227-7863, fax 14-754-0206), 73 rue de Courcelles, 75008 Paris; also consulates in Ajaccio, Bordeaux, Le Havre, Strasbourg and Marseilles

Germany (☎ 228-351-579, fax 228-354-940) Zietenstrasse 16, 53173 Bonn; also consulates in Dusseldorf, Hamburg, Munich and Stuttgart

Honduras (☎ 32-9704, 32-1543, fax 32-1580) 4a Calle & Avenida Juan Lindo, No 2421, Colonia Las Minitas, Tegucigalpa; also a consulate in San Pedro Sula (☎ 53-3560, fax 55-7748), 8a Calle between 14a and 15a Avenida NO, No 148 B, Barrio Los Andes

Japan (☎ 3-3400-1830, fax 3-3400-1820), 38 Kowa Bldg, Room 905, 4-12-24 Nichi-Azabu, Tokyo 106; also a consulate in Osaka

Mexico (☎ 5-540-7520, fax 5-202-1142) Avenida Explanada 1025, Lomas de Chapultepec 11000, México 4, DF. Consulates in: Chetumal, Quintana Roo (☎ 9-832-3045), Retorno No 4, Casa 8, Fraccionamiento Bahía; in Ciudad Hidalgo, Chiapas (☎ 962-8-01-84, fax 962-8-01-93), Avenida Central Norte, No 12; in Comitán, Chiapas (☎ 963-2-26-69), Avenida 2 Pte Sur at Calle 1 Sur Pte, No 28; in Guadalajara, Jalisco (☎ 36-11-15-03, fax 36-10-12-46), Callejón de Los Claveles 127, Colonia de Buganvillas; in Monterrey, Nuevo León (☎ 8-375-7248), Belisario Domínguez 2005, Colonia Obispado; and in Tapachula, Chiapas (☎ 962-6-12-52), 2 Calle Ote No 33

Netherlands (☎ 55-55-74-21, fax 55-21-17-68), 2e Beukelaán 3, 7313 Apeldoorn

Nicaragua (☎ 279-697, fax 279-478), Km 11.5, Carretera a Masaya, Managua; also a consulate in León

Panama (☎ 769-3475, fax 723-1922), Edificio ADIR, Piso 6, Apartamento 6B, El Cangrejo, Panama City

UK (☎ 0171-351-3042, fax 0171-376-5708), 13 Fawcett St, London SW10 9HN.

USA (☎ 202-745-4952, fax 202-745-1908), 2220 R St NW, Washington, DC 20008; also consulates in Atlanta, Baltimore, Chicago, Fort Lauderdale, Houston, Leavenworth, Los Angeles, Memphis, Miami, Minneapolis, Montgomery, New Orleans, New York, Philadelphia, Pittsburgh, Providence, San Antonio, San Diego, San Francisco and Seattle

Guatemala does not maintain embassies in Australia or New Zealand; contact the Guatemalan embassy in Tokyo.

Embassies & Consulates in Guatemala

All of the following offices are in Guatemala City, except where noted. Australia, Ireland and New Zealand do not maintain diplomatic representation in Guatemala.

Belize (☎ 334-5531, 331-1137, fax 334-5536), Avenida La Reforma 1-50, Zona 9, Edificio El Reformador, Office 803

Canada (☎ 333-6102, fax 363-4208), 13a Calle 8-44, Zona 10, Edificio Plaza Edyma (8th floor)

Costa Rica (☎ 331-9604, ☎/fax 332-0531), Avenida La Reforma 8-60, Zona 9, Edificio Galerías Reforma, Office 702

El Salvador (☎ 366-2240, fax 366-7960), 4a Avenida 13-60, Zona 10

France (☎ 337-3639, 337-3180), 16a Calle 4-53, Zona 10, Edificio Marbella, 11th floor

Germany (☎ 337-0028), 20a Calle 6-20, Edificio Plaza Marítima, Zona 10

Honduras (☎ 335-3281, 338-2068, fax 338-2073), 12a Calle 1-25, Edificio Géminis, 12th floor, Zona 10; also a consulate in Esquipulas (☎ 943-2027, 943-1547, fax 943-1371), 2a Avenida in the Hotel Payaquí

Japan (☎ 367-2244, fax 367-2245), Avenida la Reforma 16-85, 10th floor, Zona 10

Mexico (☎ 333-7254/5/6/7/8), 15a Calle 3-20, Edificio Centro Ejecutivo, 7th floor, Zona 10; also consulates in Guatemala City (☎ 331-8165, 331-9573), 13a Calle 7-30, Zona 9; Huehuetenango, 5a Avenida 4-11, Zona 1; and Quetzaltenango (☎ 763-1312/3/4/5), 9a Avenida 6-19, Zona 1

Netherlands (☎ 367-4761, fax 367-5024, nlgovgua@infovia.com.gt), 16a Calle 0-55, Torre Internacional, 13th floor, Zona 10

Nicaragua (☎ 368-0785, fax 337-4264), 10a Avenida 14-72, Zona 10

Panama (☎ 333-7182/3, 337-2495, fax 337-2445), 5a Avenida 15-45, Edificio Centro Empresarial, Torre II, Office 702, Zona 10

UK (☎ 367-5425/6/7/8/9, fax 367-5430, embassy@infovia.com.gt), 16a Calle 0-55, Torre Internacional, 11th floor, Zona 10

USA (☎ 331-1541 to -1555), Avenida La Reforma 7-01, Zona 10

CUSTOMS

Customs limits are the usual two cartons of cigarettes and up to three liters of alcohol. Tourists are allowed to take out US$100 in goods duty-free. International treaties stipulate harsh penalties for trafficking in Mayan artifacts. Limit your legal and karmic liability by not participating in this activity.

MONEY
Currency

The Guatemalan *quetzal* (Q) is named for the country's gorgeous national bird; the quetzal is divided into 100 *centavos*. There are coins of one (useless), five, 10 and 25 centavos and bills (notes) of 50 centavos, one, five, 10, 20, 50 and 100 quetzals. In 1999 the government introduced new coins of one and 50 centavos and one quetzal. Wildly unpopular, the coins may not be in circulation when you arrive.

Exchange Rates

Currency exchange rates at the time of writing were as follows:

country	unit		quetzals
Australia	A$1	=	Q4.57
Belize	BZ$1	=	Q3.89
Canada	C$1	=	Q5.23
El Salvador	ES¢1	=	Q0.90
France	FF1	=	Q1.08
Germany	DM1	=	Q3.61
Honduras	L1	=	Q0.52
Japan	¥100	=	Q7.46
Mexico	N$10	=	Q8.40
Netherlands	f1	=	Q3.21
New Zealand	NZ$1	=	Q3.49
UK	UK£1	=	Q11.55
USA	US$1	=	Q7.70
Euro	€1	=	Q7.07

Exchanging Money

Bring US dollars to Guatemala. Any other currencies – even those of neighboring Honduras, El Salvador and Mexico – will probably prove impossible to exchange. The banks at the airports in Guatemala City and Flores/Santa Elena are among the few places that exchange other currencies.

Many establishments accept cash dollars as well as quetzals, usually at the bank exchange rate but sometimes at lower rates. Even so, you'll need quetzals because businesses may not want to deplete their quetzals and take on dollars. Carry a stash of small bills, as many towns suffer from a change shortage.

Traveler's checks are usually easy to exchange, though some banks – particularly in small or rural towns – won't change them. The rate for traveler's checks is sometimes slightly lower than that for cash.

Automated teller machines *(cajeros automáticos)* are available in the biggest cities and tourist towns. The ATMs at the international airport in Guatemala City also accept Visa and MasterCard.

The majority of ATMs in Guatemala are on the Visa/Plus system, and your life will be a whole lot easier if you have a Visa credit card. MasterCard is completely useless in most of Guatemala, and some banks impose a 500 quetzal ($65) daily withdrawal limit on MasterCard. Credomatic branches in Guatemala City and Quetzaltenango give cash advances on Visa and MasterCard.

Guatemalan ATMs accept only personal identification numbers (PINs) of four digits, so before you leave home, contact your bank to get a compatible PIN.

Costs

Prices in Guatemala are among the region's best. Beds in little pensions may cost US$6 double, and camping can be even cheaper. Markets sell fruits and snacks for pennies, cheap eateries called *comedores* offer one-plate meals for about US$2, and bus trips cost less than US$1 per hour. It's not unrealistic to spend less than US$15 a day in Guatemala without too much hardship. If you want a little more comfort, you can upgrade to rooms with private showers and meals in nicer restaurants and still pay only US$25 per day for room and board.

Solo travelers get few bargains as the price differential between single and double rooms is negligible; if practical, hook up with other travelers to defray costs. Prices for everything are higher around Tikal.

Tipping & Bargaining

A 10% tip is expected at restaurants. In small comedores, leaving some spare change is the local practice. Tour guides are generally tipped around 10% (more if the tour was truly outstanding), especially on longer trips.

Bargaining is standard practice at handicrafts markets or any other time you're buying handicrafts; the first price you're told will often be double or triple what the seller really expects. Remember that bargaining is not a fight to the death; the object is to arrive at a price agreeable to you and the seller. Be friendly about it, keep your sense of humor and have patience.

You can sometimes bargain for better rates at hotels, especially when business is slow. Often you can get a discount if you take the room for a few days or more; ask about this when you check in.

Taxes

Guatemala's IVA (national sales tax) is 10%, and there's also a 10% tax on hotel rooms to pay for the activities of INGUAT, so a total tax of 20% will be added to your hotel bill. (In this book, tax is included in the prices quoted.) The very cheapest places don't usually charge tax.

POST & COMMUNICATIONS

Post

The Guatemalan postal service was privatized in 1999. Generally, letters from Guatemala take a week to arrive in the US and Canada and about twice that to Europe. Almost every city and town has a post office where you can buy stamps and send mail. A letter sent to North America costs around US$0.40, to anywhere else in the world around US$0.50.

Although it's possible to ship packages through the Guatemalan postal service, it's more efficient to use an international shipping service. Companies like DHL and Federal Express have offices in Guatemala, as do businesses specializing in international shipping, like International Bonded Couriers.

The Guatemalan postal service no longer holds post restante mail. The easiest way to receive mail is through a private address; American Express will hold mail for card-members, and some travel agencies in Antigua hold mail for clients. It is important to address mail clearly; the last lines should read 'Guatemala – Centro America.'

Telephone & Fax

Telgua, the Guatemalan phone system, was also recently privatized and has experienced a jump in reliability, technology and price. Coin-operated phones are nearly obsolete – the newfangled units accept cards only. Phone cards are available in denominations of 20, 30 and 50 quetzals wherever the phones are found. These cards work domestically and internationally.

A local call costs about US$0.12 a minute; long distance is twice that. Using the phones is very straightforward as you just dial direct. In cities and towns without these phones, you have to go to the Telgua office to make calls. In towns where there is no Telgua office, there will likely be a *teléfono comunitario* (community telephone) that will place calls. Guatemala's country code is 502. There are no area codes. The number for directory assistance is ☎ 124, and the correct time is available at ☎ 126.

You can send faxes with Telgua, but it will be much cheaper with an agency catering to the communication needs of tourists.

International Calls The best way to call internationally is through agencies offering phone services. These are common in cities and tourist spots, and they typically charge around US$0.75 a minute to the US and US$1.50 to Europe. Using public phones is not much more expensive, but if you use an agency, your party can call you back.

Unless it's an emergency, don't use the phones placed strategically around tourist towns that say 'Press 2 to call the US free!' This is a bait-and-switch scam whereby the operator quotes you one price (or no operator comes on at all), you put the call on your credit card and get bilked for US$8 to US$20 per minute.

Telgua offices charge an arm and a leg for international calls, starting with a US$4 connect fee and exorbitant per-minute rates thereafter. Telgua does allow you to make free collect calls, but only to certain countries and at usurious rates to the other party.

Sprint, MCI and AT&T have deals for calls to the USA: preface the numbers listed below with 99-99 to receive the reduced rate.

There are also numerous 'direct line' services, such as AT&T's *USADirect*: Dial 190 and you will be connected with an AT&T operator in the USA who will complete your collect or credit-card call. Below are the direct line numbers:

Intercity long-distance calls	☎ 121
International calls (by operator)	☎ 171
MCI Call USA	☎ 189

USADirect (AT&T)	☎ 190
España Directo	☎ 191
Italia Directo	☎ 193
Sprint Express	☎ 195
Costa Rica Directo	☎ 196
Canada Direct	☎ 198

Cellular Phones Long-term travelers may consider leasing a cellular phone. Many companies offer the equipment and service – be sure to read the contractual fine print before signing on. One company to try is Cellular Rent (☎/fax 331-6251), 6a Avenida 6-45, Zona 10 in Guatemala City.

Emergency Emergency telephone numbers include the following:

Ambulance	☎ 125 or 128
Fire department	☎ 122
Red Cross (Cruz Roja)	☎ 125
Tourism police	☎ 110 or 120

Email & Internet Access

Travelers will have little problem getting their email fix in Guatemala. All cities and most tourist towns have Internet capabilities. Cybercafés are popular, and some hotels have email services for their guests. Access can be slow, and many places have only Spanish keyboards, which can be frustrating if you're unfamiliar with them. Prices for Internet access range from US$1.50 an hour in Antigua to an incredible US$7.75 in Cobán.

INTERNET RESOURCES

Among the comprehensive sites that will keep you busy are the Guatemalan Web Page Directory (mars.cropsoil.uga.edu/trop-ag/guatem.htm), which stands out for its in-depth cultural information and terrific kids' page, and the Guatemala Web (www.guatemalaweb.com). The University of Texas, known for its Latin American expertise, also has a Guatemala resource page (lanic.utexas.edu/la/ca/guatemala).

Several cities and regions support their own informative websites. One of the best is the Quetzaltenango Pages (www.xelapages.com), with information on everything from job openings to legal services in Xela. Similar

Online Services

The following are some websites that you might find helpful:

Antigua Pages
www.theantiguajournal.com

Arte Maya
www.artemaya.com

Central American Report
www.worldcom.nl/inforpress

Fiestas of Guatemala
www.mayaparadise.com/
fiestas/fiestas.htm

Guatemala Web
www.guatemalaweb.com

Guatemala Weekly
www.pronet.net.gt/gweekly

INGUAT
www.travel-guatemala.org.gt

Lake Atitlán Pages
www.atitlan.com

Learn Spanish
www.studyspanish.com

Momostenango Pages
www.geocities.com/momostenango

Mundo Maya online
www.mayadiscovery.com

Quetzaltenango Pages
www.xelapages.com

Revue
www.revue.conexion.com

Río Dulce Pages
www.mayaparadise.com

The Siglo News
www.sigloxxi.com

**University of Texas
Guatemala Resource Page**
lanic.utexas.edu/la/ca/guatemala

**WWWanderer
CA Volunteer guide**
www.tmn.com/wwwanderer/
Volguide/projects.html

pages are available for Antigua (www.theantiguajournal.com), Lago de Atitlán (www.atitlan.com) and the Río Dulce area (www.mayaparadise.com).

If you're planning to study Spanish in Guatemala, check out the Learn Spanish website (www.studyspanish.com) for a list of schools. Volunteer opportunities can be found in the WWWanderer CA Volunteer guide (www.tmn.com/wwwanderer/volguide/projects.html).

Travelers interested in Mayan ceremonial life are encouraged to visit www.geocities.com/momostenango.

BOOKS

Guatemala in the Spanish Colonial Period, by Oakah L Jones Jr, is a comprehensive assessment of 300 years of Spanish dominance. Where this book leaves off, Paul J Dosal's *Doing Business with the Dictators: A Political History of United Fruit in Guatemala, 1899-1944* takes over. *Bitter Fruit: The Story of the American Coup in Guatemala*, by Stephen Schlesinger et al, is a readable analysis of US dirty-pool politics.

I, Rigoberta Menchú: An Indian Woman in Guatemala, by 1992 Nobel Peace Prize laureate Rigoberta Menchú, is highly recommended. This book tells of Menchú's life among the highland Maya and the birth of her social consciousness during the brutal civil-war period. Almost single-handedly, Menchú brought the world's plight of Guatemala's Maya to the world's attention. Her follow-up effort, *Crossing Borders*, was published in 1998. Menchú's work has also generated controversy: David Stoll shocked the world with the 1999 publication of *Rigoberta Menchú and the Story of All Poor Guatemalans*, in which he contests the autobiographical veracity of Menchú's first book.

Jennifer Harbury's book, *Searching for Everardo: A Story of Love, War and the CIA in Guatemala*, tells how she attracted the world's attention by conducting three hunger strikes, two in front of Guatemala's National Palace and one in front of the White House in Washington, DC, seeking information on her husband, a URNG commander who disappeared mysteriously in 1992. Her earlier book, *Bridge of Courage: Life Stories of the Guatemalan Compañeros and Compañeras*, focuses on people who fought in the Guatemalan guerrilla movement.

Unfinished Conquest: The Guatemalan Tragedy, by Victor Perera, explores the current situation of the Maya in their homeland and the long history preceding it. A fascinating account of the war's aftermath is presented in *Return of Guatemala's Refugees: Reweaving the Torn*, by Taylor Clark. *Guatemala: A Guide to the People, Politics and Culture*, by Trish O'Kane, is a well-written book on modern Guatemala.

Many travelers may want a more in-depth guide exploring a particular area of interest. *Orchids of Guatemala and Belize*, by Oakes Ames and Stewart Donovan (Dover Publications), remains one of the best handbooks on orchids available internationally. *Birds of Guatemala*, by Hugh C Land (Livingston, 1970), is a field guide to bird-watching in Guatemala. *The Birds of Tikal: An Annotated Checklist for Tikal National Park and Petén, Guatemala*, by Randell A Beavers, is a must-have for birders.

Guatemalan Journey, by Stephen Benz, lends a traveler's eye to an honest and funny account of modern Guatemala, making for good on-the-road reading. *Bird of Life, Bird of Death*, by Jonathan Evan Maslow, tells of the author's travels in Guatemala, where he went to see the resplendent quetzal (the 'bird of life'). What he found was the quetzal becoming increasingly endangered, while the *zopilote* (vulture), the 'bird of death,' was flourishing.

FILMS

Though Guatemalan films are few, those that exist are poignant. *El Silencio de Neto* is a coming-of-age story set in 1954 that follows the development of a boy during the Arbenz coup. *La Hija del Puma* is a powerful drama about the displacement,

torture and genocide suffered by the Guatemalan Maya during the civil war.

Several documentaries have been made about Guatemala. Check out *Dirty Secrets: Jennifer, Everardo & the CIA in Guatemala*, the abbreviated story of Jennifer Harbury and her disappeared husband during the civil war, and the great film *Todos Santos*, difficult to find outside Guatemala, which tells the story of that mountain town.

NEWSPAPERS & MAGAZINES

Among Guatemala's many daily newspapers are *La Prensa Libre, El Gráfico, La República, Siglo Veintiuno, El Periódico* and *Al Día. La Prensa Libre* is the most widely respected and read. The weekly paper *El Regional*, written in both Spanish and Mayan languages, is read by many Maya people. *La Cuerda*, a well-written monthly discussing Guatemalan women's issues, appears in *El Periódico* and *El Regional.*

Newspapers in English include two free weeklies published in Guatemala City and distributed in major hotels and tourist spots around the country: the *Guatemala Weekly* (☎ 337-1061, fax 337-1076, gweekly@pronet .net.gt), 14 Calle 3-27, Zona 10, Local 8, Guatemala City, or in the USA, PO Box 591999-F-69, Miami, FL 33159-1999; and *The Siglo News* (☎ 332-8101/2/3, fax 332-8119, in the USA ☎ 888-287-4921, sales@sigloxxi.com, www.sigloxxi.com), 11 Calle 0-65, Zona 10, Edificio Vizcaya, 4th floor, Guatemala City, or in the USA, NotiNET SA, Worldbox Gu-0147, PO Box 379012, Miami, FL 33137-9012.

The *Revue* is Guatemala's English-language magazine, published monthly; you can read and order back issues online at www.revue.conexion.com.

Some major US newspapers, such as *USA Today*, the *Miami Herald* and the *Los Angeles Times*, are sold in luxury hotels and some city and airport bookstores in the region. *Newsweek* and *Time* magazines are also sometimes available.

RADIO & TV

Guatemala has 11 radio and five TV stations. The radio waves are dominated by

Latin American pop and evangelical crusaders. Because you'll probably get enough of these on the bus, consider bringing a shortwave radio.

TV programming and reception in Guatemala leave something to be desired, so most folks with a television also have cable. A number of stations from the USA, including CNN news, come in by cable, as do movies and sports in both English and Spanish.

LAUNDRY

Laundries are everywhere in Guatemala, offering wash, dry and fold service for around US$2 per load; drop it off and pick it up a few hours later. Cheaper lodgings usually have a *lavadero*, where you can wash your clothes by hand, and a clothesline.

HEALTH

Tap water is not safe to drink in Guatemala, so you must either purify water yourself or drink bottled water. Bottled water is widely available; it's what most locals drink.

Malaria is present in Guatemala, especially in lowland rural areas, but there is no malaria risk in the highlands. Chloroquine is the recommended antimalarial. Dengue fever is also present, as is cholera. See the Health section in the introductory Facts for the Visitor chapter for more about protecting your health while traveling.

WOMEN TRAVELERS

Women should encounter no special problems traveling in Guatemala. In fact, women (and men) will be surprised by how helpful most locals are. The primary thing you can do to make it easy for yourself is to dress modestly; most Guatemalan women do. Modesty in dress is highly regarded here, and if you practice it, you will usually be treated with respect.

Specifically, shorts should be worn only at the beach, not in town, and especially not in the highlands. Skirts should be at or below the knee. Be sure to wear a bra, as going braless is considered provocative. Many local women swim with T-shirts over their swimsuits; in places where they do

this, you may want to do the same to avoid stares.

Women traveling alone can expect plenty of attempts by men to chat them up. Often they are just curious and not out for a foreign conquest. Try to sit next to women or children on the bus, if that makes you more comfortable.

The catcalls, hisses and howls so frequently directed at women in some other parts of the region are less common in Guatemala but are still occasionally heard – just do what the local women do and ignore them completely.

Nasty rumors about foreign women kidnapping Guatemalan children for a variety of sordid ends not limited to organ harvesting have died down. Still, women travelers should be cautious around children, especially in Alta Verapaz.

Although there's no need to be paranoid, you must be aware that the possibility of rape, mugging and other crime does exist. Use your normal traveler's caution – avoid walking alone in isolated places or through city streets late at night, avoid hitchhiking, don't camp alone etc. Taking a self-defense class for women is a good way to prepare for your trip and bolster your confidence.

See Society & Conduct in Facts about Guatemala for more tips to help smooth your way while traveling here.

GAY & LESBIAN TRAVELERS

Few places in Latin America are genuinely gay friendly, and that includes Guatemala (where, by the way, homosexuality is legal for persons 18 years and older). Though Antigua has an active, subdued scene, affection and action are kept behind closeted doors; the exception is The Casbah on Thursday nights, which is so hopping it's become more of a mixed than gay crowd. In Guatemala City, Pandora's Box and Eclipso are the current hot spots. In large part though, gay folks traveling here will find themselves pushing the twin beds together – a tired but workable compromise.

Toto Tours (☎ 800-565-1241, 773-274-8686, fax 773-274-8695, info@tototours.com, www.tototours.com), 1326 W Albion Ave,

Chicago, IL 60626 USA, runs all-gay-men adventure trips to Guatemala and other parts of Central America.

DISABLED TRAVELERS

Guatemala is not the easiest country to negotiate with a disability; provisions for the hearing- or sight-impaired are nonexistent, and wheelchair-bound travelers will face some serious challenges.

Many hotels in Guatemala are old converted houses with rooms around a courtyard, which is a good layout for wheelchair accessibility. The most expensive hotels have facilities such as ramps, elevators and accessible toilets. Transportation will be the biggest hurdle for disabled travelers. Travelers in wheelchairs may consider renting a car and driver, as the buses will prove especially challenging. If bus is your preferred way to go, arrive early for the best spot.

Transitions/Guatemala (☎ 832-4261, email transitions@guate.net), Colonia Candelaria No 80 in Antigua, is an outstanding organization aiming to increase awareness and access for disabled persons in Guatemala.

SENIOR TRAVELERS

Senior travelers should consult a doctor before venturing to Guatemala and take particular care with food and drink while in the country. Older adventurers may have problems negotiating the tight seats on Guatemalan chicken buses, and the stairs up Tikal's temples are hard on all but the strongest knees. Consider renting a car or joining an organized tour to cover long distances, and spread a Tikal visit over a few days to minimize the physical stress and maximize the experience.

TRAVEL WITH CHILDREN

Children are highly regarded in Guatemala and can often break down barriers and open doors to local hospitality. Logistically, traveling here with children is not a problem. However, Guatemala travel so heavily emphasizes history and archaeology that children can easily get bored here. Parents should be creative and make a point of visiting kid-friendly sites such as the Auto Safari Chapín, south of the capital. Water parks, recreation centers with pools, games and playgrounds (called Turicentros) and hands-on activities like weaving are all available in Guatemala. Most Spanish courses are open to kids, too.

DANGERS & ANNOYANCES

The civil war is over, but that ugliness has been replaced by a precipitous rise in the general crime rate. Armed thieves roam the highlands; avoid stopping by the roadside in lonely places. Guatemala City has seen incidents of armed robbery, purse-snatching and carjacking. Don't wander around Guatemala City (or any other city) late at night. If you're driving, keep valuables out of sight and keep the car windows rolled up at least halfway. And if you are approached by armed carjackers, embassies suggest relinquishing your vehicle without resistance, rather than risking injury or worse.

If you plan to travel by road in the highlands or El Petén, ask other travelers about current conditions. Don't rely solely on information from local newspapers, government officials or businesspeople, as they often cover up 'unpleasant' incidents that could affect tourist revenue. Incidents of bandits pouncing on tourists along lonely roads are rare nowadays, however.

In past years there have been a few bizarre incidents in which foreign visitors have been unjustly suspected of kidnapping Guatemalan children in order to use their organs in transplant operations. One woman taking photographs of children in a town on Guatemala's Pacific Slope was nearly murdered by a hysterical crowd, and in April 2000 a mob stoned another tourist to death in similar circumstances. Be careful not to put yourself in any situation that might be thus misinterpreted.

The popular hike up the active Volcán Pacaya can be unpredictable and dangerous; tourists have been injured by flaming rocks and debris exploding from the cone. In January 2000, this volcano was upgraded to orange alert status, meaning eruption was more likely. Keep abreast of developments before you go.

GUATEMALA

See the Facts for the Visitor chapter for general comments on theft and other crimes.

BUSINESS HOURS

Guatemalan businesses are generally open 8 am to noon and 2 to 6 pm daily. A two-hour siesta is the norm, especially in smaller towns, and hours may be curtailed on Sunday. Government offices keep shorter hours; usually they are open 8 am to 4 pm Monday to Friday. Official business is always better conducted in the morning.

PUBLIC HOLIDAYS & SPECIAL EVENTS

The following are public holidays:

January 1 – New Year's Day

March/April – Holy Thursday, Holy Friday and Easter Sunday

May 1 – Labor Day

June 30 – Army Day

August 15 – Fiesta de Guatemala City

September 15 – Independence Day

October 20 – Revolution of 1944

November 1 – All Saints' Day

December 24 – Christmas Eve

December 25 – Christmas Day

December 31 – New Year's Eve

Certain special events throughout the year are well worth experiencing. Semana Santa (Holy Week, the week before Easter) in Antigua is an unforgettable spectacle. Intricate, colorful carpets made of dyed sawdust are created in the street to mark the route of a procession. Then a robed *cofradía* (religious brotherhood) carries the image of crucified Christ down the route on a large, heavy litter, accompanied by swinging censers and music. The events leading up to Christ's crucifixion and resurrection are reenacted in impressive ceremonies.

Semana Santa is celebrated in other places, too – each indigenous group has its own religious and folkloric traditions. Huehuetenango and Totonicapán also have processions and enactments of the passion of Christ, held on Wednesday through Easter Sunday.

Traditional celebrations also take place on All Saints' Day (November 1) and All Souls' Day (November 2). Since it's believed that this is when the souls of the dead are nearest, throughout Guatemala people spruce up the graveyards, painting tombs and pulling weeds. Families bring flowers and picnic at the graves of their dearly departed. It's not a sad occasion, but a time for the living to visit with those they miss.

On November 1, giant, colorful *barriletes* (kites) are flown in the cemeteries of Santiago Sacatepéquez and Sumpango, both near Antigua. Traditionally, it's believed that the soaring kites provide communication with dead loved ones. Thousands of participants come to fly kites and gorge on food, especially the traditional *fiambre*, a salad-type dish heavy on the beets, assorted meats, seafood and vegetables.

On the same day, in Todos Santos Cuchumatán, local men dressed in traditional costumes hurtle through town in the drunken horse race – the culmination of a week of debauchery (October 21 through November 1) that reaches a fevered pitch the night before.

Each town celebrates the day of its patron saint with a fiesta including social, cultural and sporting events; Chichicastenango's famous fiesta – honoring Santo Tomás – begins December 13 and peaks on December 21 with the *palo volador* derring-do, in which a tall pole is set up in the plaza and costumed *voladores* (fliers) swing around the top of it.

In late July, Q'eqchi' Indians throughout the Verapaces celebrate Rabin Ajau with folkloric festivals featuring traditional costumes and foods. Perhaps the most impressive of these is in Cobán, where festivities culminate with the traditional Paabanc, a medley of the most impressive folkloric dances including the Dance of the Devils and the Dance of the Moors and the Christians.

Visitors interested in the Mayan lifecycle should head to one of the towns still observing the traditional Mayan calendar (eg, Momostenango or Todos Santos) for Wajshakib Batz, the sacred Mayan New Year. It will fall on the following dates: July

23, 2001; April 9, 2002; December 25, 2002; September 11, 2003; and May 28, 2004. Outsiders are not necessarily invited to join in the sacred ceremonies, but it's still a good time to be in a traditional town.

Other interesting festivals include the birthday of San Simón (also known as Maximón and Ry Laj Man) on October 28, celebrated with an all-out party in San Andrés Iztapa, near Antigua, and a fiesta in Zunil; and Quema del Diablo, the Burning of the Devil, celebrated on December 7 throughout the country but particularly noteworthy in Chichicastenango, where a 12-piece band accompanies an extravagant pyrotechnic affair.

ACTIVITIES

While Mayan culture, art and archaeology are of great interest and accessible to most travelers, Guatemala has more going for it than ruins.

Mountaineering

Guatemala is a climber's paradise, with formidable peaks rising amid breathtaking scenery. Facilities and services for climbers are limited, so you'll need to be self-sufficient or guided. Volcán Tajumulco (at 4220m, the tallest peak in Central America) is one of the most challenging ascents in the country, and good climbing can also be found in the Cuchumatanes Range. Popular day trips include hiking the active Volcán Pacaya, south of Guatemala City, or Volcán San Pedro, on Lago de Atitlán.

Spelunking

A caving mecca, Guatemala attracts spelunkers from the world over. The Verapaces are riddled with caves and among the most frequented spots. While the caves of Lanquín and Poptún have long been popular, new discoveries such as the Gruta Rey Marcos, the Chicoy Cave and the caves at Candelaria are broadening the spelunking opportunities here.

White-Water Rafting & Kayaking

From placid Class II to raging Class IV rapids, Guatemala has some excellent river rafting and kayaking in the most majestic settings. The Río Cahabón can be run year-round, while the Esclavos, Motagua and Naranjo are rushing from June to October. Kayaking is excellent on the Ríos Lanquín, Sauce and Esclavos in September and October and on the Río Cahabón any time of year. Quality equipment and guides are available.

Wildlife-Watching

National parks and biospheres here have few facilities, but they do offer excellent wildlife-watching opportunities. Sites such as Tikal, El Mirador and the Biotopo Cerro Cahuí in the Petén have an abundance of wildlife. The Bocas de Polochic on Lake Izabal and the mangroves near Monterrico are among the best places to go birding. And you can see lots of wildlife even on day trips to Lake Chicabal near Xela or the Atitlán Nature Reserve in Panajachel.

LANGUAGE COURSES

Spanish-language courses are wildly popular in Antigua and Quetzaltenango; together those cities boast over 100 Spanish schools. Students wanting something a little farther off the beaten track will easily find a school and situation to suit their taste. There are schools on Lago de Atitlán (in San Pedro La Laguna and Panajachel), on Lago Petén Itzá (in San Andrés and San José) and in Todos Santos, Huehuetenango and Cobán. Schools typically provide one-on-one instruction, homestays with Guatemalan families, electives such as dancing or weaving and volunteer opportunities. Some highland schools also offer instruction in Mayan languages such as Mam and Quiché.

WORK

Guatemala is a poor country, and work is hard to come by. You might find work teaching English, but don't count on it. Service jobs are probably easier to land because hostels, bars and restaurants catering to travelers are always looking for worldly help. Xela, Antigua, Monterrico and Panajachel are likely spots to find service jobs. Skilled guides such as alpinists may find

GUATEMALA

work as the tourism industry continues to blossom. If you do find work, wages will be low; expect to cover your expenses, but that's about it.

Volunteer Work
If you really want to get to the heart of Guatemalan matters, consider volunteering. Opportunities abound here, from caring for abandoned animals to teaching orphans. Travelers with specific skills – nurses, doctors, teachers etc – are particularly encouraged to investigate volunteering in Guatemala.

To learn more about Guatemalan volunteer positions, visit the AmeriSpan volunteer website (www.amerispan.com/volunteer/default.htm) or the WWWanderer CA Volunteer Guide (www.tmn.com/wwwanderer/volguide/projects.html). Most positions require Spanish skills and a minimum time commitment. Volunteers may have to pay for room and board. See the boxed text 'Volunteer Opportunities in Guatemala.'

ACCOMMODATIONS
All levels of accommodations are available in Guatemala, from basic pensions to luxury five-star hotels and resorts. If you'll be studying Spanish, you may prefer a homestay with a local family, which costs less than a hotel; virtually all Spanish language schools offer this option. Camping and hammock-slinging are rock-bottom budget options.

ROBERT REID

Gallo is Guatemala's most popular beer.

FOOD
Guatemalan food is basic. Try to develop a taste for corn tortillas before your trip because you'll be seeing stacks of them at every meal. Maintaining a vegetarian diet will be challenging here, but you can usually wrangle up some rice and steamed vegetables at the very least.

Mostly you will encounter *bistec* (tough grilled or fried beef), *pollo asado* (grilled chicken), *chuletas de puerco* (pork chops) and lighter fare such as *hamburguesas* (hamburgers) and *salchichas* (sausages similar to hot dogs). Of the simpler food, *frijoles con arroz* (beans and rice) is cheapest and often best. A few Mexican standards such as *enchiladas* (tortillas topped with beans, meat or cheese), *guacamole* (a salad of mashed avocados, onions and tomatoes) and *tamales* (steamed corn dough rolls with a meat or other filling) are usually available as well.

One of the surprising things about Guatemala is the omnipresence of Chinese restaurants (good sources for vegetarian food). All the cities and some large towns have them – usually small places serving cheap, if not overly authentic, Chinese food.

For full lists of menu items with translations, see the Menu Guide at the back of this book.

DRINKS
Even though Guatemala grows some of the world's richest coffee, it's rarely available because most of the quality beans are cultivated for export; living on instant coffee in light of this is frustrating. In the tourist towns you can find delicious brewed coffee, but everywhere else it's of the weak and overly sweet instant variety. If you like milk in your coffee, ask for *café con leche*.

As elsewhere throughout the region, sweetened fruit juice mixed with water is a popular and refreshing beverage. It's usually made with purified water, but ask before you drink it. All the usual brands of soft drinks are available everywhere.

Limonadas are delicious and addicting drinks made with lime juice, water and sugar. Try a *limonada con soda*, which adds

Volunteer Opportunities in Guatemala

The following well-established organizations in Guatemala are always in search of volunteers:

ARCAS (Asociación de Rescate y Conservación de Vida Silvestre – the Wildlife Rescue and Conservation Association; ☎/fax 591-4731, arcas@pronet.net.gt), 1a Calle 50-37, Zona 11, Colonia Molino de las Flores, Guatemala City (in the USA, write: ARCAS, Section 717, PO Box 52-7270, Miami, FL 33152-7270). Operates a wildlife rescue center near Flores and a sea turtle hatchery east of Monterrico. See the Monterrico and Flores sections for details. ARCAS also has other volunteer projects, including education and health projects.

Asociación Hogar Nuevos Horizontes (☎ 761-2608, fax 761-4328), 3a Calle 6-51, Zona 2, Quetzaltenango. Runs a battered women's shelter, legal and medical clinics and a child-care center. The organization is dedicated to ending domestic violence. Men are encouraged to apply. A minimum one-month commitment is required.

Casa Alianza (☎ 253-2965, 251-2569, fax 253-3003, guatemala@casa-alianza.org, www.casa-alianza.org/en/help/volunteer2.shtml), 3a Avenida 11-28, 5th floor, Zona 1, Guatemala City. Runs a shelter for street children in Guatemala City. Volunteers can work in the shelter or administrative offices. Working in the shelter requires a minimum six-month commitment.

Casa Guatemala (☎ 232-5517, casaguatemal@guate.net, www.mayaparadise.com/casaguae.htm), 14a Calle 10-63, Zona 1, Guatemala City. Helps abandoned, orphaned and malnourished children. A second facility and the main administrative offices (☎/fax 331-9408) are at 5a Avenida 7-22, Zona 10. Programs in Guatemala City include a clinic, food-distribution program and temporary home for teenage orphans and pregnant teens. It also has an orphanage on the Río Dulce (☎ 902-0612, 208-1779, fax 902-0612), in eastern Guatemala. Short-term opportunities are available.

Escuela de la Calle (☎ 761-1521, fax 763-2104, edelac@usa.net, beef.brownrice.com/streetschool/home.htm), Diagonal 15, 7-61, Zona 5, Quetzaltenango. Helps at-risk children in Xela with a variety of programs, including a school and dorm. A two-month commitment is required. In the US, contact Michael Shorr (☎ 505-820-0114, mhshorr@earthlink.net), 2003 Hopi Rd, Santa Fe, NM 87505-2401. Information is also available at Quetzaltrekkers (☎ 761-2470, quetzaltrekkers@hotmail.com), Diagonal 12 8-37, Zona 1, Quetzaltenango, which donates all its proceeds to Escuela de la Calle.

Kuinik Ta'ik Volunteer Program (email Kermit Frazier at momostenango@conexion.com.gt, www.geocities.com/momostenango). Has opportunities in the Momostenango area for teachers, medical personnel and agricultural specialists. Minimum commitment of three months is required except for medical personnel, who need only commit to a month; homestays are available.

Proyecto Ak' Tenamit (☎/fax 254-1560), 11a Avenida A 9-39, Zona 2, Guatemala City. Works with the Q'eqchi' Maya near Río Dulce. Programs include a medical volunteer project, a dental clinic, a school, potable-water projects and a women's cooperative. A one-year commitment is preferred. In Río Dulce call ☎ 902-0608. In the USA, contact the Guatemalan Tomorrow Fund (☎ 407-747-9790, fax 407-747-0901), PO Box 3636, Tequesta, FL 33469.

Red International (email Volunteer Coordinator Alex Morales at redidh@yahoo.com). Sends human-rights observers for a three-week minimum to villages in Chiapas, Mexico. Observers conduct interviews with villagers and file reports about the human-rights situation in Chiapas. Information is also available at Quetzaltrekkers (☎ 761-2470), Diagonal 12 8-37, Zona 1, Quetzaltenango.

a fizzy dimension. *Naranjadas* are the same thing made with orange juice. *Jamaica* (pronounced 'hah-**my**-cah') is a refreshing juice made from hibiscus flowers.

Gallo is Guatemala's most popular light beer. Moza, a dark beer, is what some travelers prefer. Dorado is lighter than Gallo.

Guatemala grows plenty of sugarcane, and rum is also made here. Ron Zacapa Centenario, a dark rum that comes in a bottle with a wicker basket around it, is said to be the best. Ron Botrán Añejo, another dark rum, is also good. Venado is a light, locally produced rum. Then there's Quetzalteca Especial, a white firewater made of sugarcane that comes in a tiny bottle with a saucy label.

ENTERTAINMENT

Guatemala City has some nightclubs, and Antigua and Panajachel both have discos, but that's about it for nightlife. Awards go to Guatemala City for its burgeoning hip, creative scene that supports coffeehouses, open-mic performances, poetry readings and live music.

Traditional cinemas and movie houses showing multiple titles on big-screen televisions are common in the biggest towns and cities. Theater companies in Guatemala City and Xela put up consistently good productions. Soccer games are popular; seats range from US$3 to US$7.

SHOPPING

Guatemala's brilliantly colorful weavings and textiles are world famous. Weaving is a traditional and thriving art of the Maya people here. Wall hangings, clothing – especially the beautiful embroidered *huipiles* (blouses) and *cortes* (skirts) of the Mayan women – purses, belts, sashes, friendship bracelets, tablecloths, bedspreads and many other woven items are ubiquitous and good value.

Guatemalan craftspeople make sublime leather goods, which is not surprising given that much of the arable land is devoted to cattle and cowboy culture. Fine briefcases, duffel bags, backpacks and belts are sold in most handicrafts markets. Cowboy boots and hats can be custom made in some areas.

Although most of the finest coffee beans are earmarked for export, some are (thankfully) held back for the tourist trade. While most tourist shops sell coffee in cute bags made of traditional cloth, it's woefully overpriced, and some is even sold already ground – java blasphemy! To ensure you're getting the finest, freshest coffee available, visit one of the several farms and/or roasters and buy from them directly. Cobán and Antigua produce some of the world's greatest coffee; both towns have growers and roasters. There are also roasters in Xela and Panajachel; see those sections for details.

In 1958 an ancient Mayan jade quarry near Nebaj, Guatemala, was rediscovered. Today it produces jade (pronounced 'hahdeh' in Spanish) both for gemstone use and for carving. Jade is sold in many markets countrywide and in specialty jade shops in Antigua. Beautiful well-carved stones can cost US$100 or much more. Look for translucency, purity and intensity of color and absence of flaws. Ask the merchant if you can scratch the stone with a pocketknife; if it scratches, it's not jade but an inferior stone.

The largest markets are the Thursday and Sunday blowouts in Chichicastenango and the permanent market in Panajachel (which has many wholesalers). If you're serious about buying handicrafts, it's worth a trip to one of these places. Many fine textiles are also available in Antigua, but the prices are higher.

All villages also have market days, when you can buy textiles directly from the weaver. The weavers of Todos Santos are famed for their vibrant red *traje* (traditional woven cloth), and Sololá and Santa Catarina Palopó on Lago de Atitlán are great towns in which to buy typical textiles. Momostenango is justly famed for its thick woolen blankets, coveted in many a cold clime, including Guatemala.

When buying textiles, it's normal practice to bargain. (See Tipping & Bargaining under Money, earlier this chapter, for more about bargaining.)

Getting There & Around

Getting There & Away

AIR

Guatemala's two major international airports are in Guatemala City (Aeropuerto Internacional La Aurora) and Flores, near Tikal in El Petén. Limited international service is also provided at the airports in Puerto Barrios (eastern Guatemala) and Quetzaltenango (the highlands).

Scheduled Flights

Belize City TACA offers four flights weekly via El Salvador. Tikal Jets flies five times per week via Flores. Aerovías flies three times a week, also by way of Flores.

Cancún Aerocaribe, Aviateca, TACA and Tikal Jets have daily flights.

Chetumal (Mexico) Aeroméxico has flights four times weekly via Flores.

Flores, El Petén (for Tikal) Mayan World has three flights daily. Tikal Jets, Racsa, TACA and Aviateca have daily direct flights.

Havana Aviateca has two direct flights a week. Cubana Air has three a week.

Houston Continental has two direct flights daily. Aviateca has three direct flights per week. TACA has daily flights via El Salvador and Belize City.

Los Angeles Aviateca, United and TACA all have daily direct flights. Mexicana has daily flights via Mexico City.

Madrid Iberia has daily flights via Miami.

Managua TACA and COPA both have two daily flights via San Salvador.

Mérida Aviateca has a morning flight three days per week.

Mexico City Mexicana, United and Aviateca have daily nonstop flights.

Miami American has three daily flights. Aviateca and Iberia each have one direct flight daily. TACA has daily flights via El Salvador.

New York TACA has flights daily via Washington, DC. Delta and American have one daily flight.

Palenque Tikal Jets and Aerocaribe have daily flights from Flores.

Panama City COPA has three flights daily; two are via San José, Costa Rica.

San Francisco United and Continental have daily flights via Houston. TACA has direct flights four times weekly.

San José (Costa Rica) United and COPA have direct flights daily. TACA, Aviateca and LACSA have daily flights.

San Pedro Sula (Honduras) TACA and COPA have daily flights.

San Salvador Several daily nonstops by TACA, COPA and Aviateca.

Tapachula (Mexico) Tikal Jets has daily flights from Guatemala City, some connect through Quetzaltenango.

Airline Contacts in Guatemala City

Aerocaribe See Mexicana

Aeroméxico See Mexicana

Aerovías (☎ 332-7470, 361-5703, fax 334-7935), La Aurora International Airport

Alitalia (☎ 331-1276, www.alitalia.com/english/index.html), 10a Calle 3-17, Zona 10

American Airlines (☎ 334-7379, www.americanair.com), Hotel El Dorado, 7a Avenida 15-45, Zona 9

Aviateca See TACA

British Airways (☎ 332-7402/3/4, fax 332-7401, www.british-airways.com), 1a Avenida 10-81, Zona 10, Edificio Inexsa, 6th floor

Continental Airlines (☎ 335-3341, 366-9985, fax 335-3444, www.continental.com), 12a Calle 1-25, Zona 10, Edificio Géminis 10, Torre Norte, 12th floor, office 1210; La Aurora International Airport (☎ 331-2051/2/3/4, fax 331-2055)

COPA (Compañía Panameña de Aviación; ☎ 361-1567, 361-1607, fax 331-8314, www.copaair.com), 1a Avenida 10-17, Zona 10

Delta Airlines (☎ 337-0642, fax 337-0588), 15a Calle 3-20, Zona 10, 2nd floor

Iberia (☎ 334-3816/7, fax 334-3715, www.iberia.com), Avenida La Reforma 8-60, Zona 9, Edificio Galerías Reforma, Local 204; La Aurora International Airport (☎ 332-5517/8, fax 332-3634)

LACSA (Líneas Aéreas Costarricenses) see TACA

Lufthansa (☎ 336-5526, fax 339-2995, www.lufthansa.com), Diagonal 6 10-01, Zona 10, Centro Gerencial Las Margaritas, Torre II, 8th floor

Mayan World (☎ 334-2067, 339-1519), 7a Avenida 6-53, Zona 4, Edificio El Triángulo, 2nd floor

Mexicana (☎ 333-6048), 13a Calle 8-44, Zona 10; La Aurora International Airport (☎ 332-1924, 331-3291, www.mexicana.com)

Nica – see TACA

TACA (reservations ☎ 334-7722; main office ☎ 331-8222, fax 334-2775), Avenida Hincapié 12-22, Zona 13; Centro de Servicio (☎ 332-2360, 332-4640), 7 Avenida 14-35, Zona 9; Hotel Ritz Continental (☎ 238-1415, 238-1479), 6a Avenida A 10-13, Zona 1; La Aurora International Airport (☎ 331-8222); Plaza Biltmore (☎ 331-2520, 337-3462), 14 Calle 0-20, Zona 10

Tapsa (☎ 331-4860, 331-9180, fax 334-5572), La Aurora International Airport

Tikal Jets (☎ 334-5631, 334-5568, fax 361-3343, www.tikaljets.centroamerica.com), La Aurora International Airport

United Airlines (☎ 332-2995, fax 332-3903, www.ual.com), Avenida La Reforma 1-50, Zona 9, Edificio El Reformador, 2nd floor; La Aurora International Airport (☎ 332-1994/5, fax 332-2795)

Departure Tax
A US$30 departure tax is charged to passengers on all international flights leaving Guatemala.

LAND
Guatemala is linked to Chiapas (Mexico) by two official highway routes and three road-and-river routes; to Belize by one road route and one sea route; and to Honduras and El Salvador by numerous overland routes.

For the road routes from Chiapas, refer to the Tabasco & Chiapas chapter (in Yucatán); for the road-and-river routes, see the El Petén chapter (in Guatemala); for the routes from Belize, see the Western Belize and Southern Belize chapters.

Most obscure border crossings between Guatemala and neighboring countries are now well trodden, including the so-called jungle route from eastern Guatemala to Honduras and the road-and-river routes between El Petén and Chiapas (see the Central & Eastern Guatemala and El Petén chapters for details).

Bus
Several international bus routes connect Guatemala with Mexico, Belize, El Salvador and Honduras. When traveling between Guatemala and neighboring countries, you will often have the choice of a direct, 1st-class bus or a series of chicken buses (that is, buses with lots of rowdy animal cargo). The latter option usually takes longer but is always cheaper and infinitely more interesting. International bus routes from Guatemala City include the following:

Belize City US$55, 12 hours, 684km. Autopullman Línea Dorada (☎ 232-9658, 220-7990, lineadorada@intelnet.net.gt), 16a Calle 10-55, Zona 1, has Thursday and Sunday departures at 8 pm, leaving Belize City on the return trip Friday and Monday at 4 pm.

El Carmen/Talismán (Mexican border) US$6, five to six hours, 275km. Transportes Galgos (☎ 232-3661, 253-4868), 7a Avenida 19-44, Zona 1, runs direct buses to this border crossing at 5:30 and 10 am and 1:30 and 3:30 pm. It also operates buses going all the way to Tapachula (Mexico); see Tapachula.

El Florido/Copán (Honduras) US$3.50, six hours, 227km to El Florido. Bus to Chiquimula (daily departures every 30 minutes; see Chiquimula under Getting Around, later this chapter), where you change buses to continue on to the border at El Florido.

La Mesilla/Ciudad Cuauhtémoc (Mexican border) US$4.50, seven hours, 345km. Transportes Velásquez, 20a Calle at 2a Avenida, Zona 1, has hourly buses from 8 am to 4 pm.

Managua US$25, 14 hours, 667km. 'Chicken' bus leaves from 9a Avenida 15-10, Zona 1, daily at 1 pm. It's crowded; be there at least three hours early.

People and poultry share the ride on chicken buses.

Melchor de Mencos (Belizean border) 10 to 12 hours, 588km. Buses of Transportes Rosita (☎ 251-7351) leave from 15a Calle 9-58, Zona 1 at 3, 5 and 8 pm (US$8). Autopullman Línea Dorada (☎ 232-9658, 220-7990, lineadorada@intelnet.net.gt), 16a Calle 10-55, Zona 1, has 1st-class buses departing at 8 pm daily to Melchor de Mencos via Santa Elena (US$30). They make the return trip every day at 6 pm.

San Salvador (El Salvador) five hours, 268km. Melva Internacional (☎ 331-0874), 3a Avenida 1-38, Zona 9, runs buses via Cuilapa, Oratorio and Jalpatagua to the Salvadoran border at Valle Nuevo and onward to San Salvador (US$6.50 one way), hourly from 5 am to 4 pm. Tica Bus (☎ 261-1773, 331-4279, ticabus@ticabus.com, www.ticabus.com), 11a Calle 2-72, Zona 9, has a daily departure at 1 pm (US$8.50 one way, US$17 roundtrip); from San Salvador, Tica buses continue to all the other Central American capitals except Belize City. Confort Lines (☎ 332-6702), Avenida Las Américas at 2a Calle, Zona 13, Edificio El Obelisco, Nivel 1, has luxury buses daily at 8 am and 2 pm (US$15 one way, US$25 roundtrip). Transportes King Quality (☎ 331-1761), 7a Avenida 14-44, Zona 9, Edificio La Galería, has luxury buses departing at 6:30 am and 3:30 pm (US$20 one way, US$35 roundtrip), with connections to Tegucigalpa. Pulmantur (☎ 332-9797) has luxury bus departures at 6:15 am and 3:15 pm daily from the Radisson Suites Villa Magna Hotel, 1a Avenida 12-43, Zona 10 (US$23 one way, US$45 roundtrip).

Tapachula (Mexico) US$22, seven hours, 291km. Transportes Galgos (☎ 253-4868, 232-3661), 7a Avenida 19-44, Zona 1, has direct buses at 7:30 am and 1:30 pm. (From Tapachula, they depart for Guatemala City at 9:30 am and 1:30 pm.) These buses cross the border at El Carmen/Talismán and go into Mexico as far as Tapachula, where they connect with Mexican buses.

Tecún Umán/Ciudad Hidalgo (Mexican border) US$4.50, five hours, 248km. Transportes Fortaleza (☎ 232-3643, 251-7994), 19 Calle 8-70, Zona 1, has 30 daily departures between 1:30 am and 7:15 pm.

Shuttle Minibus

Zippy, comfortable minivans called shuttle buses are becoming increasingly popular as Guatemala begins to attract independent travelers with more money than time. International routes include Antigua-Copán (Honduras), Flores-Belize City, Flores-Chetumal (Mexico) and Panajachel-La Mesilla or Tecún Umán, both on the Mexican border. Shuttle transportation is most easily arranged in Antigua, Panajachel or Flores. See those respective sections for more information.

SEA & RIVER

Ocean approaches to Guatemala are few. On the Caribbean coast, boats leave Punta Gorda (Belize) for Puerto Barrios daily and for Lívingston twice weekly. Passage from Omoa, Honduras, to Lívingston is also possible twice a week, though it may be difficult to arrange in the low season. Generally, sea passage is easiest to and from Puerto Barrios, as this is an active transit point. No car ferries are available.

Three river crossings connect Chiapas, Mexico, to El Petén, Guatemala. These are good, adventurous alternatives for travelers wishing to visit the ruins of Palenque and Tikal in one trip. All three involve a not-too-arduous combination of bus and boat travel. Tour operators in Palenque and Flores offer these trips at a cost (see the El Petén chapter for details).

If arriving or departing by river or sea, make sure you get your exit and entry stamps at the appropriate immigration offices in both countries.

Getting Around

AIR

Guatemala has several active airports. Not all operate year-round, but during the high season, flights should be available to any of them. In addition to the international airports in Guatemala City and Santa Elena/Flores, there are airports in Coatepeque, Cobán, Huehuetenango, Playa Grande, Puerto Barrios, Quetzaltenango, Quiché, Retalhuleu and Río Dulce. You can also fly into an airstrip near Copán in Honduras. For schedules and prices, see the individual regional sections. A US$0.65 tax, payable at the airport, is charged to all passengers on domestic flights.

BUS

The overwhelming majority of Guatemalan buses are resurrected school buses from the USA and Canada. It is not unusual for a local family of five to squeeze into seats designed for two child-size butts. These chicken buses (so called due to the live cargo accompanying many passengers) are frequent, crowded and cheap. Expect to pay US$1 (or less) for an hour of bus travel. Popular routes are served by more luxurious *especial* buses. These may have bathrooms, TVs and, in some cases, food service.

Guatemala City has no central bus terminal, though if you ask, locals will probably refer you to the Terminal de Autobuses in Zona 4. Ticket offices and departure points are different for each company. Many are near the huge, chaotic market in Zona 4. If the bus you want is one of these, go to the market and ask until you find it. The following Guatemala City bus information should get you most places in Guatemala you may want to go:

Amatitlán US$0.30, 30 minutes, 25km. Buses depart from 20a Calle at 2a Avenida, Zona 1, every half-hour from 7 am to 7 pm. Also see Puerto San José.

Antigua US$0.50, one hour, 45km. Transportes Unidos (☎ 232-4949, 253-6929), 15 Calle 3-65, Zona 1, has departures every half hour from 7 am to 7 pm, stopping in San Lucas Sacatepéquez. Other buses depart more frequently, every 15 minutes from around 4 am to 7 pm, from the lot at 18a Calle and 4a Avenida, Zona 1. Several shuttle minibus companies also offer services; see that section below.

Autosafari Chapín US$1, 1½ hours, 88km. Delta y Tropical, 1a Calle at 2a Avenida, Zona 4, has buses every 30 minutes via Escuintla.

Biotopo del Quetzal US$2.25, three hours, 156km. Escobar y Monja Blanca, 8a Avenida 15-16, Zona 1, has hourly buses from 4 am to 5 pm via El Rancho and Purulhá. (Any bus heading for Cobán will stop here.)

Chichicastenango US$1.50, 3½ hours, 144km. Veloz Quichelense, Terminal de Buses, Zona 4, runs buses every half hour from 5 am to 6 pm, stopping in San Lucas, Chimaltenango and Los Encuentros. Many continue to Quiché and beyond.

Chiquimula US$3, three hours, 169km. Rutas Orientales (☎ 253-7282, 251-2160), 19 Calle 8-18, Zona 1, runs buses via El Rancho, Río Hondo and Zacapa to Chiquimula every 30 minutes from 5 am to 6 pm. Next door, Transportes Guerra has five daily departures (US$2.50). If you're heading for Copán, Honduras, change buses at Chiquimula to continue to the border at El Florido.

Cobán US$3.75, four hours, 213km. Escobar Monja Blanca (☎ 251-1878), 8a Avenida 15-16, Zona 1, has deluxe buses hourly from 4 am to 5 pm, stopping at El Rancho, the Biotopo del Quetzal, Purulhá, Tactic and San Cristóbal. Special (US$3.25) and regular (US$2.25) buses are also available.

El Estor US$7.75, four hours, 216km. Fuentes del Norte (☎ 238-3894, 251-3817), 17a Calle 8-46, Zona 1 has one daily departure, at 10 am.

Escuintla US$1.25, one hour, 57km. See Autosafari Chapín, La Democracia, Monterrico, Puerto San José and Tecún Umán.

Esquipulas US$3.25, four hours, 222km. Rutas Orientales (☎ 253-7282, 251-2160), 19a Calle 8-18, Zona 1, has buses every half hour from 5 am to 6 pm, with stops at El Rancho, Río Hondo, Zacapa and Chiquimula.

Flores (Petén) 488km. Fuentes del Norte (☎ 238-3894, 251-3817), 17a Calle 8-46, Zona 1, runs more than a dozen daily buses departing from the capital and stopping at Río Dulce and Poptún (US$10.50, 12 hours). Its Maya del Oro luxury service (US$19.50, 10 hours) departs at 8 pm daily. Máxima (☎ 232-2495, 238-4032), 9a Avenida 17-28, Zona 1, has buses departing at 4, 6 and 8 pm. Autopullman Línea Dorada (☎ 232-9658, 220-7990, lineadorada@intelnet.net.gt), 16a Calle 10-55, Zona 1, operates three luxury buses daily at 9 am and 8 and 9 pm (US$30, eight hours); buses make stops at Río Dulce and Poptún (buses usually leave Guatemala City and Santa Elena full; anyone getting on midway stands). Transportes Rosita, 15a Calle 9-58, Zona 1, has departures at 3, 5 and 8 pm (US$6.50, 12 hours).

Huehuetenango US$3.75, five hours, 266km. Los Halcones, 7a Avenida 15-27, Zona 1, runs three buses a day (7 am and 2 and 5 pm) up the Interamericana to Huehue, stopping at Chimaltenango, Patzicía, Tecpán, Los Encuentros, San Cristóbal and Totonicapán. Buses to La Mesilla also stop here; see La Mesilla.

La Democracia US$1, two hours, 92km. Chatla Gomerana, Muelle Central, Terminal de Autobuses, Zona 4, has buses every half hour from 6 am to 4:30 pm, stopping at Escuintla, Siquinalá (change for Santa Lucía Cotzumalguapa), La Democracia, La Gomera and Sipacate.

La Mesilla/Ciudad Cuauhtémoc (Mexican border)
US$4.50, seven hours, 345km. Transportes Velásquez, 20a Calle at 2a Avenida, Zona 1, has buses going to La Mesilla, on the Interamericana at the border with Mexico, hourly from 8 am to 4 pm. Stops are at Los Encuentros, Totonicapán and Huehuetenango.

Lívingston See Puerto Barrios.

Monterrico US$1.50, four hours, 124km. Transportes Cubanita, Muelle Central, Terminal de Buses, Zona 4, has buses departing at 10:30 am and 12:30 and 2:30 pm, stopping at Escuintla, Taxisco and La Avellana.

Panajachel US$1.75, three hours, 148 km. Transportes Rébuli (☎ 251-3521), 21a Calle 1-34, Zona 1, departs hourly from 7 am to 4 pm, stopping at Chimaltenango, Patzicía, Tecpán Guatemala (for the ruins of Iximché), Los Encuentros and Sololá. It also has one daily departure from Antigua (US$3.25, two hours, 146km).

Poptún See Flores.

Puerto Barrios US$5.25, five hours, 295km. Transportes Litegua (☎ 232-7578, 253-8169), 15a Calle 10-40, Zona 1, has *especial* buses at 6, 6:30, 7:30, 10, 10:30 and 11:30 am and 12:30, 2, 2:30, 4, 4:30 and 5 pm, with stops at El Rancho, Teculután, Río Hondo, Los Amates and Quiriguá. There are also a dozen regular buses (US$4) a day. Boats run from Puerto Barrios to Lívingston until about 5 pm.

Puerto San José Two hours, 106km. Transportes Esmeralda (☎ 471-0327), Trebol, Zona 12, operates buses every 10 minutes from 5 am to 8 pm, stopping at Amatitlán, Palín and Escuintla.

Quetzaltenango US$3.75, four hours, 206km. Transportes Alamo (☎ 253-0219), 21a Calle 1-14, Zona 1, has buses at 8 and 10 am and 12:45, 3 and 5:45 pm. Líneas América (☎ 232-1432), 2a Avenida 18-47, Zona 1, has buses at 5:15 and 9:15 am, noon, and 3:15, 4:40 and 7:30 pm. Transportes Galgos (☎ 253-6312, 232-3661), 7a Avenida 19-44, Zona 1, makes this run at 5:30, 8:30 and 11 am and 12:30, 2:30, 5 and 7 pm. All these buses stop at Chimaltenango, Los Encuentros and San Cristóbal.

Quiché Three hours, 163km; see Chichicastenango.

Quiriguá See Puerto Barrios.

Retalhuleu US$3.75, three hours, 186km. See El Carmen and Tecún Umán.

Río Dulce US$4.50, five hours, 274km. Transportes Litegua (☎ 232-7578, 253-8169), 15a Calle 10-40, Zona 1, has daily departures at 6 and 9 am and 1 pm; also see Flores.

Río Hondo See Chiquimula, Esquipulas and Puerto Barrios.

San Pedro La Laguna (Lago de Atitlán) US$2.75, three to four hours, 170km. Ruta Méndez, 21a Calle & 5a Avenida, Zona 1, has buses at 10 and 11 am, noon and 1 pm.

Santa Elena See Flores.

Santa Lucía Cotzumalguapa See El Carmen, La Democracia and Tecún Umán.

Sayaxché US$9, 11 hours, 397km. Fuentes del Norte (☎ 238-3894, 251-3817), 17a Calle 8-46, Zona 1, has one daily departure, at 4:30 pm.

Tecún Umán/Ciudad Hidalgo (Mexican border) US$4.50, five hours, 248km. Transportes Fortaleza (☎ 232-3643, 251-7994), 19 Calle 8-70, Zona 1, has hourly buses from 1:30 am to 7:15 pm, stopping at Escuintla (change for Santa Lucía Cotzumalguapa), Mazatenango, Retalhuleu and Coatepeque.

Tikal See Flores.

Shuttle Minibus

Various companies offer minibus services on the main tourist routes (Guatemala City-Aeropuerto La Aurora-Antigua-Panajachel-Chichicastenango). Shuttles depart from La Aurora International Airport for Antigua every hour until around 8 pm; the same buses offer door-to-door transportation between Antigua and Guatemala City. Expect to pay US$10 per person.

Most of these operators have their offices in Antigua; check that section for contact information. TURANSA has an office in Guatemala City (☎ 595-3574, fax 595-3583) in the Supercentro Metro, Carretera Roosevelt Km 15, Zona 11, Local 68-69.

CAR & MOTORCYCLE

Driving a car or motorcycle in Guatemala means you can travel where you want, when you want. Before setting off, consider whether you can make repairs, how you'll secure your vehicle and how comfortable you are driving in a foreign country with screwy road rules. See this book's introductory Getting There & Away chapter to familiarize yourself with the paperwork rigmarole for this type of trip.

There are three types of fuel available in Guatemala. Regular (87 octane) costs around US$1.75 a gallon; Premium or Super (91 octane) costs US$1.90 a gallon; and

GUATEMALA

diesel fuel, widely available, costs about US$1.25 a gallon.

Road Rules

Local driving etiquette may be different from what you're used to back home. Expect no road signs in Guatemala. A tree branch or other foreign matter in the middle of the road signals trouble up ahead – a breakdown or rock slide perhaps – and you should slow down and drive carefully in this situation. A driver coming uphill always has the right of way.

Speaking Spanish will go a long way toward making a driving trip more enjoyable. At least learn some car and directional lingo. Driving at night is a bad idea for many reasons, including armed bandits, drunk drivers and decreased visibility.

Rental

Rental cars are expensive: expect to pay around US$50 to US$75 a day, not including gas. Trucks, minivans and 4WD vehicles are also available. Insurance policies accompanying rental cars may not protect you from loss or theft, in which case you can be liable for US$600 to US$1500 or more in damages. Be careful where you park, especially in Guatemala City and at night. Motorcycles can be rented in Antigua and Panajachel.

To rent a car or motorcycle you need to show your passport, driver's license and a major credit card. Usually, the person renting the vehicle must be 25 years or older. If you are not the holder of a valid credit card, you may still be able to rent by leaving a large cash deposit. Obviously, an official receipt is needed in this event. Guatemala has both international and local rental car companies.

BICYCLE

Cycling is coming into its own in Guatemala. You can join biking tours or take to the hills independently. Bikes can be rented in Antigua, Flores, Panajachel and Quetzaltenango.

Long-distance road cycling can be dangerous as few drivers are accustomed to sharing the roads with bikes; be aware at all times and equip your bike with the proper mirrors, reflectors and other safety equipment.

HITCHHIKING

Hitchhiking in the strict sense of the word (meaning free lifts) is not practiced in Guatemala. However, where bus services are sporadic, pickup trucks and other vehicles serve as public transportation. Stand by the side of the road, hold your arm out and someone will stop. You are expected to pay the driver as if it were a bus, and the fare will be similar. This is a safe and reliable system used by locals and travelers, and the only inconvenience you're likely to encounter is severe overcrowding – get used to it.

BOAT

Speedy motorboats called *lanchas* are becoming the norm for transportation on Lago de Atitlán and between the towns of Puerto Barrios, Lívingston and Río Dulce. Bigger, cheaper ferries run sporadically on these routes but have been largely discontinued in favor of the faster motorboats.

Dugout canoes and motorboats are used on Lago Petén Itzá near Flores and within the mangrove forests near Monterrico. A few of Guatemala's natural reserves (eg, Bocas de Polochic) and archaeological sites (eg, Ceibal) are accessible only – or preferably – by water (see Parks & Protected Areas in the Facts about Guatemala chapter).

LOCAL TRANSPORTATION

The local buses are crowded and cheap. Guatemala City and Quetzaltenango are the only cities boasting local buses. In either place, expect to pay around US$0.15 for an inner-city jaunt in an overflowing jalopy.

Few Guatemalan taxis are metered, and as fares are exorbitant (equal to or exceeding those in places like New York City), deft Spanish and negotiating skills are a must for getting a fair price. Determine the price of the trip before setting out, writing it on a slip of paper as proof, if necessary. Rates are set, but drivers will often try to rip you off by quoting a higher price, especially from the airport, where you are most vulnerable.

If you don't like the price quote, walk away. There's almost always another cab to be found.

ORGANIZED TOURS

Guatemala is becoming a hot spot with travelers, and the quantity and quality of locally organized tours reflects this growing popularity. White-water rafting, visits to obscure archaeological sites and general tours of the country's highlights are all easily arranged from Guatemala City, Antigua or Flores. The following is a selection of recommended tour operators:

Area Verde Expeditions (☎/fax 832-3383, 832-6506, in the USA ☎/fax 719-583-8929, anthonyjosh@hotmail.com, www.adventuresports .com/kayak/areaverd/welcome.htm), 1a Avenida Sur 15 in Antigua, offers white-water rafting trips and general tours of the country.

Aventuras Turísticas (☎ 951-4213, ☎/fax 951-4214), 3a Calle 2-38, Zona 3 in Cobán, offers a host of tours in the Verapaces and El Petén, plus custom tours.

AVINSA Tikal Travel (☎ 926-0808, fax 926-0807, info@tikaltravel.com, www.tikaltravel.com), 4a Calle, Santa Elena, runs horseback riding, hiking and camping trips to the more inaccessible sites in the Petén, including Yaxjá and Nakum. It can also arrange sailing trips from Río Dulce to Belize.

Clark Tours (☎ 339-2888, fax 339-2909, clark@ guate.net, www.clarktours.com.gt), Centro Gerencial Las Margaritas, Diagonal 6 10-01, Torre II, Zona 10, Guatemala City, is the oldest tour operator in the country, offering high-end luxury trips to the most popular destinations.

Ecotourism & Adventure Specialists (☎ 361-3104, fax 334-0453, info@ecotourism-adventure.com, www.ecotourism-adventure.com), Avenida Reforma 8-60, Zona 9, Guatemala City, offers extreme sports tours and jungle adventures to remote sites. It employs archaeologists and ornithologists as guides and coordinates trips with its offices in Belize, Mexico and Honduras. English, Spanish and Hebrew are spoken.

EcoMaya (☎ 926-1363, 926-3321, fax 926-3322, ecomaya@guate.net, www.ecomaya.com), Calle 30 de Junio, Flores, runs hardcore adventure trips to the jungle and archaeological sites of El Mirador, El Perú, El Zotz and Tikal.

Guatemalan Birding Resource Center (☎ 767-7339, birdguatemala@latinmail.com, www.xelapages .com/gbrc), 7a Calle 15-18, Zona 1, Quetzaltenango, offers birding tours to the Pacific coast and the highlands. In the USA contact Anne M Berry (☎ 317-842-1494), 7361 Hawthorne Lane, Indianapolis, IN 46250.

Maya Expeditions (☎ 363-4955, 363-4965, ☎/fax 337-4666, mayaexp@guate.net), 15a Calle 1-91, Zona 10, Local 104, Guatemala City, runs whitewater rafting trips. In Antigua, Maya Expeditions is represented by Sin Fronteras (☎ 832-1017, ☎/fax 832-2674), 3a Calle Pte 12.

Monkey Eco Tours (☎ 201-0759, fax 926-0807, in the USA fax 978-945-6486, nitun@nitun.com, www.nitun.com), run by the Ni'tun Ecolodge, San Andrés, Petén, operates luxury adventure jungle trips with specialist guides including archaeologists, biologists and ecologists.

Old Town Outfitters (☎ 832-4243, trvlnlite@ hotmail,com), 6a Calle Pte 7, Antigua, specializes in mountain biking, hiking and volcano tours. 'We summit any volcano' is its motto.

Proyecto EcoQuetzal (☎/fax 952-1047, bidaspeq@ guate.net, www.granjaguar.com/peq), 2a Calle 14-36, Zona 1 in Cobán, arranges full immersion trips to Q'eqchi' villages and builds quetzalviewing platforms; available from March to June; one month prior reservation required.

Quetzalventures (☎ 761-2470, info@quetzalventures .com, www.quetzalventures.com), Diagonal 12 8-37, Zona 1, Quetzaltenango, offers traditional tours, adventure tours and budget adventures. Options include scuba diving, rafting, bungee jumping, Spanish classes and more. All profits go to Xela's nonprofit Escuela de la Calle.

Vision Travel & Information Services (☎ 832-3293, 832-1962, fax 832-1955, vision@guatemalainfo .com, www.guatemalainfo.com), 3a Avenida Nte 3, Antigua, offers all manner of tours, both packaged and customized, including trips to the highlands, Tikal, Copán and Lago de Atitlán. In addition, it offers special event tours for Día de Todos los Santos and Easter.

Guatemala City

• **population 2 million** • **elevation 1500m**
Guatemala's capital city, the largest urban agglomeration in Central America, spreads across a flattened mountain range run through by deep ravines. Initially, the sprawl and smog may remind you of Mexico City. But Guatemala City (more often referred to as simply Guatemala or Guate) has a distinct flavor. Its huge chaotic market bursts with dazzling smells, sounds and colors. Rickety buses chug along in clouds of diesel,

Highlights

- Hanging out at Parque Minerva with its Mapa en Relieve; great for children
- Visiting the local museums; try the Museo Ixchel del Traje Indígena or the Museo Popol Vuh for starters
- Exploring the ruins at Kaminaljuyú
- Checking out Torre del Reformador, the world's only accurate scale replica of the Eiffel Tower
- Shopping in the Mercado Central

trolling for ever more passengers, and street urchins eke out a tenuous existence in the city's poverty-stricken outlying areas.

The city's few interesting sights can be seen in a day or two, and many travelers skip the capital altogether, preferring to make Antigua their base. Still, you may need to get acquainted with the city since it's a transportation and service hub.

HISTORY

Earthquakes are a fact of life here; a devastating temblor on July 29, 1773, resulted in the city's founding. Prior to that event, the Spanish capital of Central America was at La Ciudad de Santiago de los Caballeros de Guatemala, known today as Antigua Guatemala (or simply Antigua). The earthquake razed much of Antigua, and in hopes of escaping further destruction, the government decided to move its headquarters to the present site of Guatemala City. On September 27, 1775, King Carlos III of Spain signed a royal charter for the founding of La Nueva Guatemala de la Asunción, and Guatemala City was officially born.

Unfortunately, colonial planners didn't move the capital far enough; earthquakes in 1917, 1918 and 1976 rocked Guatemala City, reducing buildings to rubble. The 1976 quake killed nearly 23,000, injured another 75,000 and left an estimated one million homeless. The city's comparatively recent founding and its history of earthquakes have left little to see in the way of colonial churches, palaces or quaint old neighborhoods.

ORIENTATION
Street Grid System

Guatemala City, like all Guatemalan towns, is laid out according to a street grid system that is logical and easy to use. Avenidas run north-south; calles run east-west. Streets are usually numbered from north and west (lowest) to south and east (highest); building numbers run in the same directions, with odd numbers on the left-hand side and even on the right as you head south or east. However, Guatemala City is divided into 15 *zonas*, and each zona has its own version of this grid system. Thus 14a Calle in Zona 10 is a completely different street several miles distant from 14a Calle in Zona 1, though major thoroughfares such as 6a Avenida and 7a Avenida cross through several zones while maintaining the same name.

Addresses are given in this form: '9a Avenida 15-12, Zona 1,' which means '9th Avenue above 15th Street, No 12, in Zone 1.' The building you're looking for (in this case the Hotel Excel) will be on 9th Ave between 15th and 16th Sts, on the right side of the street as you walk south. Beware though of Guatemala City's street grid anomalies, such as diagonal streets called *rutas* and *vías* and wandering boulevards called *diagonales*.

Short streets may be suffixed 'A,' as in 14a Calle A, a short street running between 14a Calle and 15a Calle.

Landmarks

The ceremonial center of Guatemala City is Plaza Mayor (sometimes called Parque Central). It's at the heart of Zona 1, surrounded by the Palacio Nacional, the Catedral Metropolitana and the Portal del Comercio. Beside Plaza Mayor to the west is Parque Centenario, the city's central park. Zona 1 is also the retail commercial district, where shops sell clothing, crafts, film and myriad other things. Behind the cathedral, the Mercado Central (Central Market) features lots of crafts. Most of the city's good budget and mid-range hotels are in Zona 1.

Around the Zona 1-Zona 4 border is the Centro Cívico (Civic Center), which holds various government buildings, including the main office of the national tourist bureau. Southwestern Zona 4 is the city's major market district and holds frenetic bus terminals.

South of Zona 4, 10a Avenida becomes Avenida La Reforma and divides Zonas 9 and 10, a pair of tony residential areas boasting several interesting small museums. Zona 10, east of Avenida La Reforma, is the poshest, its Zona Viva (Lively Zone) arrayed around the deluxe Camino Real Guatemala and Guatemala Fiesta hotels. Many of the city's fancier restaurants and nightclubs are in the Zona Viva. In Zona 9, landmarks include the mini-Eiffel Tower (called the Torre del Reformador), at 7a Avenida and 2a Calle, and the Plazuela España traffic roundabout at 7a Avenida and 12a Calle.

Zona 13, just south of Zona 9, holds large Parque Aurora, several museums and Aeropuerto Internacional La Aurora.

Maps

The INGUAT tourist office sells a useful country map for US$1. This map has an inset of greater Guatemala City, as well as a close-up of the downtown area. The Librería de Pensativo (see Bookstores & Libraries later in this chapter) sells International Travel Maps' Guatemala map.

Detailed topographical maps can be purchased at the Instituto Geográfico Militar (☎ 332-2611, Avenida Las Américas 5-76, Zona 13).

INFORMATION

Official tourist publications claim the tap water in Guatemala City is safe to drink. Unless you're hell-bent on testing this assertion, stick to bottled water.

Tourist Offices

The tourist office is in the lobby of the INGUAT headquarters (☎ 331-1333, fax 331-8893, inguat@guate.net), 7a Avenida 1-17, Centro Cívico, Zona 4. Look for the blue-and-white sign with the letter 'i' on the east side of the street; it's next to a flight of stairs, a few meters south of the railway viaduct that crosses above 7a Avenida. Hours are 8 am to 4 pm Monday to Friday, 8 am to 1 pm Saturday. Staff members are friendly and helpful. A second office is at Avenida La Reforma 13-70, Zona 9.

INGUAT's office at La Aurora International Airport (☎ 331-4256 ext 294) is open 6 am to 9 pm daily.

Immigration

Extensions must be applied for in person at the Dirección General de Migración office

GUATEMALA

GUATEMALA CITY

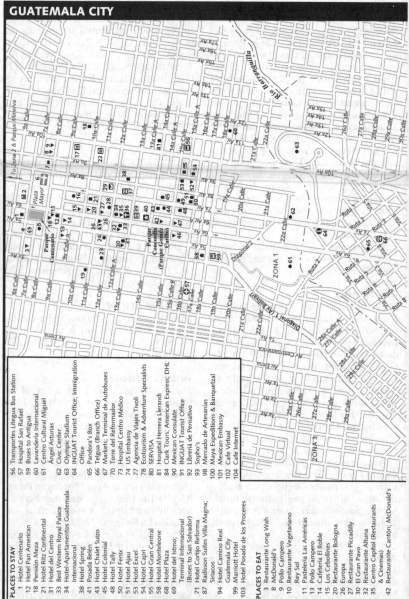

PLACES TO STAY
1   Hotel Centenario
12 Hotel Pan American
18 Pensión Meza
21 Hotel Ritz Continental
31 Hotel del Centro
33 Best Western Royal Palace
34 Hotel-Apartamentos Guatemala
    Internacional
38 Hotel Spring
41 Posada Belén
43 Hotel Chalet Suizo
45 Hotel Colonial
48 Hotel Tally
50 Hotel Fenix
51 Hotel Ajau
53 Hotel Excel
54 Hotel Capri
55 Hotel Gran Central
58 Hotel Monteleone
68 Hotel Plaza
69 Hotel del Istmo;
    Terminal Internacional
    (Buses to San Salvador)
71 Hotel Cortijo Reforma
87 Radisson Suites Villa Magna;
    Siriacos
94 Hotel Camino Real
    Guatemala City
99 Marriott Hotel
103 Hotel Posada de los Proceres

PLACES TO EAT
3   Restaurante Long Wah
8   McDonald's
9   Pollo Campero
10 Restaurante Vegetariano
    Rey Sol
11 Pastelería Las Américas
13 Pollo Campero
14 Cafetería El Roble
15 Los Cebollines
20 Restaurante Bologna
26 Europa
27 Restaurante Piccadilly
30 El Gran Pavo
32 Restaurante Altuna
35 Centro Capitol (Restaurants
    & Cinemas)
42 Restaurante Cantón; McDonald's

56 Transportes Litegua Bus Station
57 Hospital San Rafael
59 Buses to Antigua
60 Lavandería Internacional
61 Centro Cultural Miguel
    Ángel Asturias
62 Civic Center
63 Olympic Stadium
64 INGUAT Tourist Office; Immigration
    Office
65 Pandora's Box
66 Telgua (Branch Office)
67 Markets; Terminal de Autobuses
70 Torre del Reformador
73 Hospital Centro Médico
77 Agencia de Viajes Tivoli
78 Ecotourism & Adventure Specialists
80 SERVISA
81 Hospital Herrera Llerandi
84 Clark Tours; American Express; DHL
90 Mexican Consulate
91 INGUAT Tourist Office
92 Librería de Pensativo
93 Sopho's
98 Mercado de Artesanías
101 Maya Expeditions & Banquetzal
101 Mexican Embassy
102 Cafe Virtual
104 Cafe Internet

GUATEMALA CITY

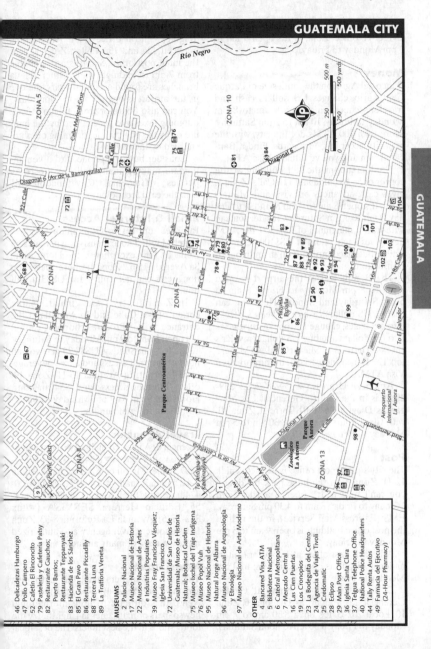

GUATEMALA

46 Delicadezas Hamburgo
47 Pollo Campero
52 Cafetín El Rinconcito
79 Pastelería y Cafetería Patsy
82 Restaurante Gauchos;
   Puerto Barrios;
   Restaurante Teppanyaki
83 Hacienda de los Sánchez
85 El Gran Pavo
86 Restaurante Piccadilly
88 Tercera Luna
89 La Trattoria Veneta

MUSEUMS
2 Palacio Nacional
17 Museo Nacional de Historia
22 Museo Nacional de Artes
   e Industrias Populares
39 Museo Fray Francisco Vásquez;
   Iglesia San Francisco
72 Universidad de San Carlos de
   Guatemala; Museo de Historia
   Natural; Botanical Garden
75 Museo Ixchel del Traje Indígena
76 Museo Popol Vuh
95 Museo Nacional de Arqueología
   y Etnología
96 Museo Nacional Jorge Albarra
   Natural
97 Museo Nacional de Arte Moderno

OTHER
4 Bancared Visa ATM
5 Biblioteca Nacional
6 Catedral Metropolitana
7 Mercado Central
16 Las Cien Puertas
19 Los Cronopios
23 La Bodeguita del Centro
24 Agencia de Viajes Tívoli
25 Credomatic
28 Eclipso
29 Main Post Office
36 Iglesia Santa Clara
37 Telgua Telephone Office
40 National Police Headquarters
44 Tally Renta Autos
49 Farmacia del Ejecutivo
   (24-Hour Pharmacy)

(☎ 634-8476/7/8), 7a Avenida 1-17, Piso 2, INGUAT office, Zona 4. It's open 9 am to 3 pm Monday to Friday.

Money

Banco del Agro, on the south side of Parque Centenario, changes US dollars cash and traveler's checks; it's open 9 am to 8 pm Monday to Friday, 10 am to 2 pm Saturday. More than 100 ATMs dot the city, with the majority accepting Visa cards. Find a Bancared sign and you've found a Visa ATM.

Credomatic, in the tall building at the corner of 3a Avenida and 11a Calle, Zona 1, gives cash advances on Visa and Master-Card. It's open 8 am to 7 pm Monday to Friday, 9 am to 1 pm Saturday. Inside, you can withdraw a maximum of US$500; the ATM here gives a maximum of US$100 per transaction, but places no limit on the number of transactions.

The Banquetzal at the airport is open 7 am to 8 pm Monday to Friday, 8 am to 6 pm Saturday and Sunday. Here you can change US dollars cash or traveler's checks into quetzales, change European currencies into US dollars and buy US dollar traveler's checks. There is a MasterCard ATM here too. The Banco Industrial at the airport has a Visa ATM.

American Express (☎ 339-2877, fax 339-2882) is in the Centro Gerencial Las Margaritas, Diagonal 6 10-01, Torre II, Zona 10, with Clark Tours. It's open 8:30 am to 5 pm Monday to Friday.

Post

The city's main post office is at 7a Avenida 12-11, Zona 1, in the huge pink building – you can't miss it. It's open 8 am to 7 pm Monday to Friday, 8 am to 4:30 pm Saturday. EMS (Express Mail Service), in the rear of the post office building, is open 9 am to 5 pm Monday to Friday.

A branch post office at La Aurora International Airport is open from 7 am to 3 pm Monday to Friday.

DHL has a pick-up point at Centro Gerencial Las Margaritas, Diagonal 6, Zona 10, Local 202-B. It's open 8:30 am to 7 pm Monday to Friday, 8:30 am to noon Saturday.

Telephone & Fax

Telgua's central office is on 7a Avenida, between 12a and 13a Calles, Zona 1, near the main post office. Services are available from 7 am to midnight daily. Other Telgua branches are found around the city; the one in the airport is open 7 am to 7 pm daily. You can also fax to or from Telgua offices; outgoing faxes may be charged by the minute or by the page, while incoming ones are charged by the page.

Consider buying a phone card if you anticipate making many calls, as most pay phones in Guatemala City function only with the card technology.

Email & Internet Access

Internet services in Guatemala City are largely limited to expensive cybercafés in Zona 10. One exception is the Hotel Ajau, 8a Avenida 15-62, Zona 1, where guests and nonguests can get online for US$3 a half hour.

In Zona 10, try Cafe Virtual, on the corner of 16a Calle and 2a Avenida at the entrance to Los Proceres shopping center. It's open 8 am to 9 pm Monday to Saturday, 10 am to 8 pm Sunday; US$5.25 gets you an hour of Internet access and a free beverage. Cafe Internet, 5a Avenida 16-11, Zona 10, offers Internet access for US$4 an hour. Hours are 9 am to 9 pm Monday to Saturday, 10 am to 7 pm Sunday.

Travel Agencies

Agencia de Viajes Tivoli has two convenient locations: in Zona 9 (☎ 339-2260/1/2, fax 334-3297, viajes@tivoli.com.gt) at 6a Avenida 8-41; and in Zona 1 (☎ 238-4771/2/3, fax 220-4744, centro@tivoli.com.gt) at 12a Calle 4-55, Edificio Herrera. SERVISA (☎/fax 332-7526), Avenida La Reforma 8-33, Zona 10, is another travel agency and authorized representative of many airlines.

Newspapers

The two newspapers available in English are the *Guatemala Weekly* and the *Siglo News*. It is difficult to find international newspapers or magazines in English. Try the lobby shops in the best hotels. The best local

Guatemalan newspaper is *La Prensa Libre*, available everywhere.

Bookstores & Libraries

The Arnel bookstore, Edificio El Centro, No 108, at the corner of 9a Calle and 7a Avenida, Zona 1, sells a variety of books in English and French, including general fiction, Latin American literature in translation, travel guides, Spanish-language instructional texts and books about the region and Mayan civilization.

Sopho's (☎ 332-3242), in the Zona Viva at Avenida La Reforma 13-89, El Portal No 1, Zona 10, offers a good selection of books and magazines in English. It's a relaxed place to have a coffee and read. Librería de Pensativo (☎ 332-5055), Avenida La Reforma 13-01, Zona 9, has a selection of Lonely Planet guidebooks and titles about Guatemala in English. It also sells maps. The Europa bar/restaurant (see Places to Eat) has used books in English for sale or trade. Vista Hermosa Book Shop (☎ 269-1003), 2a Calle 18-50, Zona 15, stocks Lonely Planet travel guides.

The Biblioteca Nacional (☎ 232-2443), on the west side of Parque Centenario, is open 9 am to 6 pm Monday to Friday.

Laundry

Laundries can be found throughout the city. In Zona 1, try the Lavandería Internacional on 18a Calle between 11a and 12a Avenidas.

Medical Services

Guatemala City has many private hospitals and clinics. One is the Hospital Centro Médico (☎ 332-3555, 334-2157), 6a Avenida 3-47, Zona 10; another is Hospital Herrera Llerandi (☎ 334-5959, emergencies ☎ 334-5955), 6a Avenida 8-71, Zona 10, which is also called Amedesgua.

Hospital San Rafael (☎ 230-5048, 232-5352), 16a Calle 2-42, is recommended and cheap, though most of its doctors speak only Spanish. The Guatemalan Red Cross (☎ 125) is at 3a Calle 8-40, Zona 1.

Guatemala City uses a duty-chemist (*farmacia de turno*) system with designated pharmacies remaining open at night and on weekends. Ask at your hotel for the nearest farmacia de turno, or look for the farmacia de turno sign in pharmacy windows. The Farmacia del Ejecutivo, on 7a Avenida at the corner of 15a Calle, Zona 1, is open 24 hours; it accepts Visa and MasterCard.

Emergency

Emergency telephone numbers are as follows:

Ambulance	☎ 125, 128
Fire	☎ 122, 123
Police	☎ 120, 137, 138

Dangers & Annoyances

Street crime is increasing in Guatemala City. Use normal urban caution; don't walk around with your wallet hanging out, and avoid walking downtown late at night. It's safe to walk downtown in early evening, as long as you stick to well-lit and populated streets. In Zona 1, 18a Calle (the red-light district) is notoriously dangerous at night, especially near the bus stations; if you are arriving by bus at night or must go to 18a Calle at night, take a taxi.

The city's more affluent sections, such as Zona 9 and Zona 10, are much safer. Still, even in these areas, traveling in pairs is advised, and you should leave your documents and the bulk of your cash in the hotel safe.

All buses, especially local ones, are the turf of adroit pickpockets. Stay alert and try to take the more expensive *servicio preferencial* buses plying local routes in the capital.

ZONA 1
Plaza Mayor

Most of the city's notable sights are in Zona 1 near the Plaza Mayor, which is bounded by 6a and 8a Calles and 6a and 7a Avenidas.

According to the standard colonial town-planning scheme, every town in the New World had to have a large plaza for military exercises, reviews and ceremonies. On this plaza's north side was the *palacio de gobierno*, or colonial government headquarters. On another side, preferably the east, was a church (if the town was large enough to merit a bishop, it was a cathedral). The other sides of the square could hold additional civic buildings or the large and imposing mansions of wealthy citizens. Plaza Mayor is a prime example of this classic town plan.

To appreciate the Plaza Mayor, visit on Sunday, when the locals come out in their best to stroll, play in the fountains, take the air, gossip, neck and groove to salsa music on boom boxes. If you can't make it on a Sunday, try for lunchtime or late afternoon. You'll be besieged by shoeshine boys and sellers of kitsch; ignore or indulge them as is your wont.

Palacio Nacional

On Plaza Mayor's north side is the magnificent Palacio Nacional, built at enormous cost during the dictatorial presidency of General Jorge Ubico (1931–44). It's the third palace to stand here, and it's currently being restored to house a Guatemalan-history museum.

Free tours are given between 9 am and 5:30 pm Monday to Friday and between 8 am and 3 pm Saturday and Sunday. The tour takes you through a labyrinth of gleaming brass, polished wood, carved stone and frescoed arches (painted by Alberto Gálvez Suárez). Notable features include the gold, bronze and Bohemian-crystal chandelier in the reception salon (which weighs around 2000kg) and the two Moorish-style inner courtyards.

Catedral Metropolitana

Built between 1782 and 1809 (the towers were finished later, in 1867), the restored Metropolitan Cathedral is not a particularly beautiful building, inside or out. It's supposedly open 8 am to 7 pm daily, though you may find it closed, especially during siesta.

Mercado Central

Until it was destroyed by the quake of 1976, the central market on 9a Avenida between 6a and 8a Calles, behind the cathedral, was the place locals bought food and other necessities. Reconstructed in the late 1970s, the new market specializes in touristy items such as cloth (handwoven and machine-woven), carved wood, worked leather and metal, basketry and other handicrafts. Vegetables and other daily needs have been moved to the streets surrounding the market. When you visit Plaza Mayor, you can stroll around here, though there are better places to buy crafts. Market hours are 7 am to 6 pm Monday to Saturday, 6 am to noon Sunday.

The city's true 'central' food market is in Zona 4.

Museums

Museums in Zona 1 include **Museo Fray Francisco Vásquez** (☎ 232-3023), Iglesia San Francisco, 6a Avenida at 13a Calle, which houses a Franciscan friar's belongings. The museum is open 9 am to noon and 3 to 6 pm daily.

The **Museo Nacional de Artes e Industrias Populares** (☎ 238-0334), 10a Avenida 10-72, is the national popular arts museum, exhibiting paintings, ceramics, masks, musical instruments, metalwork and gourds. It's open 9 am to 5 pm Monday to Friday.

The collection of the **Museo Nacional de Historia** (☎ 253-6149), 9a Calle 9-70, is a jumble of historical relics but is strong on photography. It's open 9 am to 4 pm Tuesday to Friday, 9 am to noon and 2 to 4 pm Saturday and Sunday. Entrance is US$1.25. This museum may be moved to the Palacio Nacional after that building is restored.

ZONA 2

Zona 2 is north of Zona 1. Though mostly a middle-class residential district, its northern end holds the large Parque Minerva, which is surrounded by golf courses, sports grounds and the buildings of the Universidad Mariano Gálvez.

Parque Minerva

Minerva, goddess of wisdom, technical skill and invention, was a favorite of President Manuel Estrada Cabrera (served 1898–1920; see History in the Facts about Guatemala chapter).

Parque Minerva is a placid place, good for relaxing, walking among the eucalyptus trees and sipping a cool drink. Still, be on the alert for pickpockets and purse-snatchers who target tourists. The prime sight in the park is the **Mapa En Relieve**, a huge relief map of Guatemala. Constructed in 1904 under the direction of Francisco Vela, the map shows the country at a scale of 1:10,000, but the height of the mountainous terrain has been exaggerated to 1:2000 for dramatic effect. The map was fully restored in late 1999, so it's in fine shape these days. Little signs indicate major towns and topographical features. Viewing towers afford a panoramic view. This place is odd but fun. Hours are 9 am to 5 pm daily; US$2. Nearby are carnival rides and games for children.

The Mapa En Relieve and Parque Minerva are 2km north of Plaza Mayor along 6a Avenida, but that street is one-way heading south. Catch a northbound bus (No 1, 45 or 46) on 5a Avenida in Zona 1 and take it to the end of the line.

CIVIC CENTER AREA
The Centro Cívico complex, constructed during the 1950s and '60s, lies around the junction of Zonas 1, 4 and 5. Here you'll find the Palace of Justice, the headquarters of the Guatemalan Institute of Social Security (IGSS), the Banco del Quetzal, city hall and INGUAT headquarters. The Banco del Quetzal building bears high-relief murals by Dagoberto Vásquez depicting the history of his homeland. City hall holds a huge mosaic by Carlos Mérida.

Behind INGUAT is the Olympic Stadium, and across the street from the Centro Cívico, on a hilltop, is the Centro Cultural Miguel Ángel Asturias, which holds the national theater, a chamber theater, an open-air theater and a small museum exhibiting old armaments.

Other than the Civic Center, this area is known mostly for its markets and bus stations, all thrown together in the chaotic southwestern corner of Zona 4 near the railway.

ZONA 10
East of Avenida La Reforma, Zona 10 is an upscale district of posh villas, luxury hotels and embassies. It also holds two of the city's most important museums, both in large new buildings at the Universidad Francisco Marroquín, on the east end of 6a Calle.

Museo Ixchel del Traje Indígena (☎ 331-3634, 331-3638) is named for Ixchel, wife of Maya sky god Itzamná and goddess of the moon, women, reproduction and textiles (among other things). Photographs and exhibits of indigenous costumes, textiles and other crafts show the incredible richness of traditional arts in Guatemala's highlands. If you enjoy seeing Guatemalan textiles at all, you must make a visit to this museum. It's open 8 am to 5:50 pm Monday to Friday, 9 am to 12:50 pm Saturday; US$2.

Behind it is the **Museo Popol Vuh** (☎/fax 361-2301), where well-chosen polychrome pottery, figurines, incense burners, burial urns, carved wooden masks and traditional textiles fill several exhibit rooms. Other rooms hold colonial paintings and wood and silver objects. A faithful copy of the Dresden Codex, one of the precious 'painted books' of the Maya, is among the most interesting pieces. This is an important collection, especially given its precolonial emphasis. The Museo Popol Vuh is open from 9 am to 5 pm Monday to Friday, and 9 am to 1 pm Saturday; US$2.

The biology department at the Universidad de San Carlos de Guatemala (☎ 476-2010), Calle Mariscal Cruz 1-56, has a fine **natural history museum** and a large **botanical garden**. Hours are 8 am to 3 pm Monday to Friday; US$1.25.

ZONA 13
The major attraction in the city's southern reaches is the Parque Aurora, with its zoo, children's playground, fairgrounds and several museums. The last are housed on grounds called the Finca Nacional La Aurora.

One of the museums, the Moorish-looking **Museo Nacional de Arqueología y Etnología** (☎ 472-0478), has a collection of Mayan artifacts from all over Guatemala, including stone carvings, jade, ceramics, statues, stelae and a tomb. Models depict the ruins at Tikal and Zaculeu. Exhibits in the ethnology section highlight the various indigenous peoples and languages in Guatemala, with emphasis on traditional costumes, dances and implements of daily life. The museum is open 9 am to 4 pm Tuesday to Friday, 9 am to noon and 2 to 4 pm Saturday. Admission is a stiff US$4.

Facing the Museo Nacional de Arqueología y Etnología is the **Museo Nacional de Arte Moderno** (☎ 472-0467), which holds a collection of 20th-century Guatemalan art, especially painting and sculpture. Hours are 9 am to 4 pm Tuesday to Friday, 9 am to noon and 2 to 4 pm Saturday and Sunday; US$1.25. Nearby is the **Museo Nacional de Historia Natural Jorge Albarra** (☎ 472 0168), which claims fame for its large collection of dissected animals. The museum is open 9 am to 4 pm Tuesday to Friday, 9 am to noon and 2 to 4 pm Saturday and Sunday; US$1.50.

Several hundred meters east from the museums is the city's official handicrafts market, the **Mercado de Artesanías** (☎ 472-0208), on 11a Avenida, just off the access road to the airport. Like most official handicrafts markets it's a sleepy place where shopkeepers display the same items available in hotel gift shops. It's open 8 am to 6 pm Monday to Saturday, 8:30 am to 2 pm Sunday.

The pleasant **Zoológico La Aurora** (☎ 472-0507) is open Tuesday to Sunday 9 am to 5 pm. Admission to the zoo costs US$1 for adults, US$0.50 for children.

KAMINALJUYÚ

Several kilometers west of the center, in Colonia Kaminaljuyú, Zona 7, lie the extensive ruins of Kaminaljuyú (☎ 253-1570), a Late Preclassic/Early Classic Mayan site displaying both Mexican and Mayan influences.

Unfortunately, much of Kaminaljuyú has been covered by urban sprawl. Though you can visit from 9 am to 4 pm daily and pay US$1.25 for the privilege, your time would be better spent looking at the artifacts recovered here that are on display in the city's museums. Bus Nos 35 and 37 come here from 4a Avenida, Zona 1.

PLACES TO STAY

As you would expect from a capital city, Guatemala City has accommodations for every budget. The cheapest rooms, as well as the most expensive, tend to fill up fast, but there are usually plenty to be had at prices in between. Prices are higher here than anywhere else in the country.

Budget

Many decent budget hotels and cheap, convenient little restaurants lie several blocks south of the Plaza Mayor, near National Police Headquarters and the post office in an area bounded by 4a and 9a Avenidas and 12a and 16a Calles. Keep street noise in mind as you look for a room. All the places listed below are in Zona 1.

Hotel Spring (☎ 230-2858, 230-2958, fax 232-0107, 8a Avenida 12-65) is a clean and comfortable old hotel that's often *completo* (full) because of its good location, sunny courtyard and decent prices: US$10/14/20 single/double/triple with shared, hot bath; US$14/20/24 with private bath and cable TV; US$22/28/34 for fancier rooms in the new *anexo*. Some of the annex rooms are wheelchair accessible. The cafeteria serves meals from 6:30 am to 1:30 pm. You can do laundry here and store luggage.

Hotel Ajau (☎ 232-0488, 251-3008, fax 251-8097, hotajaugua.gbm.net, 8a Avenida 15-62) is fairly clean and also somewhat cheaper and quite a bit quieter than many hotels on 8a Avenida. Rooms cost US$7/7.75/9.25 single/double/triple with shared bath; US$11.50/12.50/14.75 with private bath. All rooms have cable TV. Laundry and email services are available.

Hotel Chalet Suizo (☎ 251-3786, fax 232-0429, 14a Calle 6-82) has been a travelers' favorite for decades. The 47 rooms around plant-filled courtyards are comfortable and exceptionally clean. Rates are US$12/16 single/double with shared bath, or US$24/28 with private bath. A safe and luggage storage are available. Book in advance.

Hotel Excel (☎ 253-2709, 230-0140, fax 238-4071, 9a Avenida 15-12) is a bright, modern place with 17 rooms on three levels around a courtyard-cum-car park. It has a cafeteria. Rooms with bath and cable TV are US$20/23/27 single/double/triple. Across the street in a sprawling three-story building is the superbudget *Hotel Gran Central* (☎ 232-9514), where cleanish, basic, dark rooms are US$3.50/4.75/6. Hot water may be available. The nearby *Hotel Capri* (☎ 232-8191, 251-3737, 9a Avenida 15-63) has rooms with private bath and cable TV for US$11.50/16 single/double. It also has a safe and parking.

Several hotels have long been popular with savvy travelers. *Pensión Meza* (☎ 232-3777, 10a Calle 10-17) has drab rooms but is busy with international backpackers who like the sunny courtyard, camaraderie, helpful proprietor and low prices. Rooms with shared bath are US$6.50/7.75 with one bed, US$8.50 with two beds; dorm bunks are US$4.50 per person. The restaurant serves cheap meals, and there's a good book swap here. *Hotel Fenix* (☎ 251-6625, 7a Avenida 15-81) has been a reliable budget standby for years due to the friendly atmosphere and clean rooms. This is one of Guatemala's best cheapies. Basic rooms with shared, hot bath are US$5.50 single or double, US$9.50/11 triple/quad. The hotel also has a cafeteria and spacious hangout areas.

If you're arriving by bus from San Salvador, the *Hotel del Istmo* (☎ 332-4389, 3a Avenida 1-38, Zona 9), at the Terminal Internacional, will be convenient. It's clean and comfortable and has an inexpensive cafeteria. Rooms with private hot bath are US$10.50/13/15.50 single/double/triple.

The recommended *Hotel Monteleone* (☎ 238-2600, fax 253-9205, 18a Calle 4-63, Zona 1) is conveniently located across from the Antigua bus stop. Clean rooms in an amicable environment are US$7.50 single or double with shared bath, US$11.75 double with private bath.

Mid-Range

Guatemala City's mid-range lodgings are good values. All are comfortable and some are even charming. All these places are in Zona 1, except for the Hotel Plaza and the Hotel Posada de los Proceres.

Posada Belén (☎ 232-9226, 253-4530, fax 251-3478, pbelen@guatemalaweb.com, 13a Calle A 10-30) is on a quiet side street. A converted colonial home, the Belén is a quaint hostelry offering 11 rooms with private bath, a dining room serving all meals and laundry service. Rooms accommodate one (US$36), two (US$43), three (US$48) or four (US$53) people.

Hotel Pan American (☎ 232-6807/8/9, fax 251-8749, panamhot@infovia.com.gt, 9a Calle 5-63) was Guatemala City's luxury hotel before WWII. It still attracts many faithful return visitors who like its faded charm. The 55 rooms, all art deco and Biedermeier, are pleasant and comfortable, with cable TV, telephone, private bath (with tub) and fan. Avoid rooms facing the noisy street. Rates are US$41/43/46/48 single/double/triple/quad; rooms with six beds go for US$53. Amenities include a restaurant and many guest services, including email.

Hotel del Centro (☎ 232-5980, 238-1519, fax 230-0208, hotelcentro@guate.net, 13a Calle 4-55) is a good, solid hotel that has been dependable for decades. The 55 large, comfortable rooms come with shiny baths and cable TV; some have two double beds and some have street noise. Rates are US$42/48/54 single/double/triple. The hotel has a restaurant, a bar with music on Friday nights and a rooftop terrace.

Hotel Colonial (☎ 232-6722, 232-2955, fax 232-8671, colonial@infovia.com.gt, 7a Avenida 14-19) is in a large converted old house with heavy, dark colonial decor. The covered interior court is inviting and the 42 rooms are clean. Four rooms have shared bath for US$18/24 single/double; the rest have private bath for US$24/32/41 single/double/triple. A restaurant serves meals from 6:30 am to 2 pm.

Attractive for long stays or families is the conveniently located *Hotel-Apartamentos Guatemala Internacional* (☎ 238-4441/2, fax 232-4350, 6a Avenida 12-21). Each of its 27 furnished apartments has a TV, telephone and fully equipped kitchen. One-bedroom apartments run US$24/30/36 single/double/triple or quad; two-bedroom units are US$27/33/40. A few larger apartments sleep six. Studios (like the apartments but without a kitchen) are US$18/20 single/double.

Hotel Centenario (☎ 230-4005/7, fax 238-2039, 6a Calle 5-33), centrally located on the north side of Parque Centenario, has 42 rooms with well-worn but clean showers. Many have a double and a single bed. Prices are US$25/32/40/45 single/double/triple/quad.

Hotel Tally (☎ 232-9845, 251-7082, fax 253-1749, 7a Avenida 15-24) is a terrific new place with a convenient location. Each of its plain but sparkling rooms has a private hot bath, cable TV and air-con; US$23/29/33/37 single/double/triple/quad. This place is often full, so reservations are recommended.

Hotel Plaza (☎ 331-6173, 331-0396, fax 331-6824, Vía 7, No 6-16, Zona 4), with colonial appointments, is 1km south of the Centro Cívico and a 15-minute walk east of the market and bus station area. The 64 ample rooms, each with private bath, telephone and cable TV, cost US$55/61 single/double.

Hotel Posada de los Proceres (☎ 363-0744, 363-4423, fax 368-1405, posadazv@guate.net, 16a Calle 2-40) is in a tranquil residential district in upmarket Zona 10, near Los Proceres shopping center. Rates are US$49/59/69 single/double/triple. Most of the other hotels around here are much more expensive; this one is a find.

The brand-spanking-new **Best Western Royal Palace** (☎ 232-5125/6/7, fax 238-3715, 6a Avenida 12-66, Zona 1) has all the amenities of a posh chain hotel, with the character of a smaller, family-owned outfit. Each huge room is unique and carpeted, with small balconies, a phone, fan and cable TV. All rooms are wheelchair accessible. Facilities include a restaurant, bar, gym and sauna. Rates are US$65/70/75 single/double/triple.

Top End

Most luxurious of this city's hotels is the **Camino Real Guatemala City** (☎ 333-4633, fax 337-4313, in the USA ☎ 800-937-8461, caminor@guate.net, Avenida La Reforma at 14a Calle, Zona 10), in the heart of the Zona Viva. Part of the Westin chain, this is the capital's international-class hotel, with 400 rooms and five-star amenities, including swimming pools and lush gardens. Rates are US$168/192 double for standard/deluxe rooms (deluxe rooms are better located).

Hertz and American Express have offices in the lobby.

Another excellent luxury hotel in the Zona Viva is the four-star **Radisson Suites Villa Magna** (☎ 332-9797, fax 332-9772, in the USA ☎ 800-333-3333, radisson@gold.guate.net, 1a Avenida 12-46, Zona 10). The upper-floor suites (US$169 double) have one bedroom and beautiful views from full-wall windows. Junior suites (US$139) have one big room. Rates include buffet breakfast.

The modern, five-star **Marriott Hotel** (☎ 331-7777, fax 332-1877, in the USA or Canada ☎ 800-228-9290, 7a Avenida 15-45, Zona 9) has 385 rooms for US$114 single, double or triple, including breakfast. Facilities include a pool, spa, gym and every other perk befitting a luxury hotel.

Several hundred meters north of the Zona Viva stands the **Hotel Cortijo Reforma** (☎ 332-0712, fax 331-8876, Avenida La Reforma 2-18, Zona 9). Each of the hotel's 120 suites features a bedroom, living room, minibar, kitchenette, tiny balcony and a tiled bathroom with tub and shower. Rates are a good value at US$72/78/84 single/double/triple.

Downtown, the four-star **Hotel Ritz Continental** (☎ 238-1671/75, fax 238-1527, hotritz@medianet.com.gt, 6a Avenida A 10-13, Zona 1) has recently been renovated. Junior suites are US$96 for one or two people, master suites are US$120; rates include breakfast. The hotel has a swimming pool and a quiet convenient location three blocks south of the Plaza Mayor. Deals are offered by the hotel's desk on the lower level of the airport.

Near the Airport

A couple of good budget hotels are near the airport, and **Dos Lunas** (☎ /fax 334-5264, lorena@pronet.gt, www.xelapages.com/doslunas, 21a Calle 10-92, Zona 13, Aurora II) is far and away the current favorite. Clean, secure and quiet rooms are US$10 per person, including free airport transfer and breakfast. Reservations are required. Another option near the airport is **Economy Dorms** (☎ 331-8029, 8a Avenida

17-74, Zona 13, Aurora I), which has rooms for US$10, including breakfast and airport shuttle.

For mid-range accommodations, try the recommended *Hotel El Aeropuerto Guest House* (☎ 332-3086, fax 362-1264, 15a Calle A 7-32, Zona 13). Here doubles with private hot bath, breakfast and airport transfers are US$30. The *Hotel Hincapie* (☎ 332-7721, aruedap@infovia.com.gt, Avenida Hincapié 18-77, Zona 13) is another alternative, with doubles for US$25 including breakfast and airport transfers.

About a mile from the airport is the five-star *Crowne Plaza Las Américas* (☎ 339-0676, fax 339-0690, in the USA ☎ 800-227-6963, Avenida Las Américas 9-08, Zona 13). Operated by Holiday Inn, this hotel has newly renovated rooms for US$108/132 single/double.

PLACES TO EAT
Budget
Cheap eats are not hard to find, as fast-food and snack shops abound. To really save money, head for Parque Concordia, in Zona 1 around 5a and 6a Avenidas and 14a and 15a Calles. The park's west side is lined with open-air food stalls serving sandwiches and snacks at rock-bottom prices from early morning to late evening. A meal for US$2 is the rule here.

Delicadezas Hamburgo (5a Calle 5-34, Zona 1), on the south side of Parque Concordia, features a long list of sandwiches at lunch and dinner. It's open 7 am to 9:30 pm daily.

Restaurante Cantón (☎ 251-6331, 6a Avenida 14-29, Zona 1), on the east side of the park, is the place to go for Chinese food; US$5 to US$8 per platter. It's open 9 am to 9:30 pm daily. Numerous other Chinese restaurants lie near the corner of 6a Avenida and 14a Calle, Zona 1.

The city's other rich concentration of Chinese restaurants is in the blocks west of Parque Centenario along 6a Calle, where you'll find the *Restaurante Long Wah* (☎ 232-6611, 6a Calle 3-70, Zona 1) and several other places such as the *Palacio Real*, *Palacio Dorado* and *Jou Jou*.

Along 6a Avenida between 10a and 15a Calles, you'll find dozens of restaurants of all types: hamburgers, pizzas, pasta, Chinese, fried chicken. You won't have any trouble eating well around here for US$3 to US$4. *Pastelería Las Américas* (6a Avenida 8-52), near Plaza Mayor, is a chill place to stop for coffee and a European-style pastry or cake.

Several good little restaurants are on 9a Avenida between 15a and 16a Calles. The *Cafetín El Rinconcito* (9a Avenida 15-74), facing the Hotel Capri, is good for tacos and sandwiches; breakfast, lunch and dinner each cost around US$1.50 to US$2. The restaurant in the Hotel Capri (9a Avenida 15-63, Zona 1) serves more substantial meals.

Cafetería El Roble (9a Calle 5-46, Zona 1), facing the Hotel Pan American entrance, is a clean little café popular with local office workers for lunch (US$1.75) as well as for breakfast and dinner (US$1.25).

Europa (☎ 253-4929, 11a Calle 5-16, Zona 1) is a comfortable restaurant, bar and gathering place for locals and foreigners alike. A sign on the door says 'English spoken, but not understood.' Inside you'll find cable TV, a book exchange and good, inexpensive food; it's open 8 am to 1 am Monday to Saturday. A block and a half north is *Los Cebollines* (6a Avenida 9-75, Zona 1), a casual, recommended place for Mexican food.

Pastelería y Cafetería Patsy, on the corner of 8a Calle and Avenida La Reforma in Zona 10, is a bustling, popular place. The chicken, pasta, sandwiches and other light meals here are cheap – especially for the Zona Viva.

For coffee in Zona 10, head over to *Tercera Luna* (☎ 362-5030, 1a Avenida 12-70), where the java rocks and art exhibits and poetry readings are often happening. *Sopho's* (Avenida La Reforma 13-89, El Portal No 1, Zona 10) is a bookstore with a nice outdoor café.

Pollo Campero is Guatemala's KFC clone. You can find branches of the chain on the corner of 9a Calle and 5a Avenida, at 6a Avenida and 15a Calle and at 8a Calle 9-29,

GUATEMALA

all in Zona 1. Two pieces of chicken, french fries (chips) and a beverage cost US$2.50.

Many branches of American fast-food chains like **McDonald's, Wendy's, Burger King** and **Pizza Hut** are sprinkled around the city. They're open long hours, often from 7 am to 10 pm. Pizza Hut has free delivery (☎ 230-3490 in Zona 1; ☎ 332-0939 in Zona 9).

Restaurante Vegetariano Rey Sol (8a Calle 5-36), on the south side of Parque Centenario, has a long cafeteria line with a good selection: whole-grain breads, sandwiches, soya products, fruit and vegetable salads, hot foods and more. It's open 7:15 am to 8:45 pm Monday to Saturday.

Restaurante Piccadilly (☎ 230-2866, 253-9223, 6a Avenida 11-01, Zona 1) is among the capital's most popular eateries, with a multinational menu heavy on Italian fare. Most main courses cost US$3 or less. Another branch is on Plazuela España at 7a Avenida 12-00, Zona 9. Down the block, the Centro Capitol is a mall popular with teens who like hanging about the myriad casual restaurants and multiscreen cinema here.

Mid-Range

Most mid-range hotels in Zona 1 offer excellent set lunches for US$6 to US$10. Try **Hotel Del Centro, Hotel Ritz Continental** or the popular **Hotel Pan American** (9a Calle 5-63, Zona 10), which many travelers favor for its ambience, though the waitstaff wandering around in full traditional regalia are a bit much.

Restaurante Altuna (☎ 232-0669, 251-7185, 5a Avenida 12-31, Zona 1), just a few steps north of Hotel del Centro, is a large restaurant with the atmosphere of a private club. Specialties are seafood and Spanish dishes, with meals about US$7 to US$14 per person. It's open noon to 11 pm Tuesday to Saturday, noon to 4:30 pm Sunday.

Small but attractive **Restaurante Bologna** (☎ 251-1167, 10a Calle 6-20, Zona 1), just around the corner from Hotel Ritz Continental, is very small but attractive and serves tasty pizza and pasta dishes for US$3 to US$4. It's open 10 am to 9:30 pm daily except Tuesday.

El Gran Pavo (☎ 232-9912, 13a Calle 4-41, Zona 1) is a big place just west of Hotel del Centro's entrance (other branches around town include one at 12a Calle 5-54, Zona 9). The menu seems to include every Mexican dish imaginable, including birria, a spicy-hot soup of meat, onions, peppers and cilantro, served with tortillas – a meal in itself for US$3.75. The restaurant is open 10 am to midnight daily, with mariachi music on Friday and Saturday starting around 10 pm.

Top End

Guatemala City's most elegant dining is in the Zona Viva, in the area around the Hotel Camino Real Guatemala.

La Trattoria Veneta (☎ 331-0612, 334-3718, 13a Calle 1-55, Zona 10) is the place to go for good Italian specialties. Service is attentive. Expect to spend US$12 to US$15 per person for dinner with wine.

Hacienda de los Sánchez (☎ 331-6240, 334-8448, 12a Calle 2-25, Zona 10) is where Guatemalan meat-eaters come to pig out. The ambience is aggressively ranchero. Steaks and ribs cost about US$11 to US$12.50. The parking lot is full of shiny American pickup trucks. Open noon to midnight daily.

Puerto Barrios (☎ 334-1302, 7a Avenida 10-65, Zona 9) is awash in nautical theme: waiters in knee breeches and frogged coats, oil paintings of buccaneers, portholes for windows and a big compass by the door. You can easily spend US$16 to US$30 per person here. Open 11 am to 3 pm and 7 to 11 pm daily.

In the same little complex, open the same hours, are **Restaurante Gauchos** (☎ 334-1302), an Argentinean steak-and-seafood restaurant, and **Restaurante Teppanyaki** (☎ 332-4646), offering Japanese cuisine.

Siriacos (☎ 334-6316, 1a Avenida 12-12, Zona 10), near the Radisson Suites Villa Magna, is flashy but informal, with a sunken dining room and bar, a skylighted patio courtyard and a menu of continental specialties. Expect to spend around US$15 per person for dinner. Open for lunch Monday to Friday, dinner Monday to Saturday.

ENTERTAINMENT

Many visitors enjoy wining and dining the night away in the Zona Viva. If that's beyond your budget, take in a movie at one of the cinemas along 6a Avenida between Plaza Mayor and Parque Concordia. Tickets sell for about US$1.50. Or check out the cultural events at the *Centro Cultural Miguel Ángel Asturias* (☎ 232-4041/2/3/4/5, 253-1743), in Zona 4.

Guatemala City has a hopping creative scene, so if you're itching for some urban culture, check out some of the bars and clubs in Zona 1.

Bars

La Bodeguita del Centro (☎ 230-2976, 12a Calle 3-55, Zona 1) is a huge, bilevel, bohemian hangout with live music, poetry readings and performances. Hundreds of posters featuring the likes of Ché, Van Gogh and Bob Marley cover the walls. Pick up a schedule of events. Lunch and dinner are served.

Las Cien Puertas, in Zona 1 on Pasaje Aycincena between 6a and 7a Avenidas and 9a and 10a Calles, has to be one of the coolest bars in Guatemala. This hip (but not studiously so) hangout is a gathering place for all manner of local creative types. The alley has a hundred doors (hence the name) and is sometimes closed off for live bands. Similar is *Los Cronopios*, on the corner of 11a Calle and 3a Avenida in Zona 1, which attracts a good crowd for live music, poetry readings and open-mic performances.

Gay & Lesbian Venues

Guatemala City is not known for its gay scene, so don't get too excited about this section. However, a couple of places are worth mention. *Pandora's Box*, Vía 3 at Ruta 4 in Zona 4, is the old standby that has been hosting the capital's gay crowd for years. Zona 4 holds other gay clubs as well, but as this isn't the greatest area, don't go wandering around here alone or late at night. *Eclipso* (12a Calle 6-61, Zona 1) is a newer, edgier place, with sex toys for sale and a (reportedly) palatable S&M scene.

GETTING THERE & AWAY

Air

International flights arrive and depart from La Aurora International Airport. At the airport you'll find banks, a post office, snack shops and knickknack peddlers. Taxis and shuttle buses depart from the lower (arrivals) level. A US$30 departure tax is charged to visitors leaving Guatemala by air. La Aurora is also served by smaller regional and domestic carriers (see this book's Getting There & Around chapter).

Bus & Shuttle Minibus

It is possible to travel overland by bus between Guatemala and the rest of the region. See the Getting There & Around chapter for more information on international buses, including details for Copán and Honduras.

Shuttle minibuses serve the most popular international routes frequented by tourists. See Getting There & Around in the Antigua, Panajachel and Flores sections for detailed information.

Car

Major international rental companies have offices both at La Aurora International Airport and in the city center. Rental offices in Guatemala City include the following:

Ahorrent (☎ 361-5661, fax 361-5621), Boulevard Liberación 4-83, Zona 9; Hotel Cortijo Reforma (☎ 332-0712 ext 180), Avenida La Reforma 2-18, Zona 9; La Aurora International Airport (☎ 362-8921/2)

Avis (☎ 332-7744/7, fax 332-7448, avis@guate.net), 6a Avenida 11-24, Zona 9; La Aurora International Airport (☎ 331-0017, 361-5645)

Budget (☎ 332-2491), Avenida Hincapie 11-01, Zona 13; La Aurora International Airport (☎ 331-0273, 360-8639)

Dollar (☎ 232-3446, fax 238-1046), Hotel Ritz Continental, 6a Avenida A 10-13, Zona 1; La Aurora International Airport (☎ 331-7185, fax 362-5393)

Guatemala Rent (☎ 473-1330, email rentautos@centroamerica.com), 19a Calle 16-91 (Calle Real de Petapa), Zona 12; La Aurora International Airport (☎ 362-0205/6)

Hertz (☎ 334-2540/1, fax 331-7924, rentauto@guate.net), 7a Avenida 14-76, Zona 9; Hotel

Camino Real (☎ 368-0107); La Aurora International Airport (☎ 331-1711)

National (Interrent-Europcar-Tilden; ☎ 360-3963, 332-4702, fax 360-1404, national@pronet.net.gt), 12a Calle 7-69, Zona 9; La Aurora International Airport (☎ 331-8365, 361-5618)

Tabarini (☎ 332-2161, 334-5907, fax 334-1925), 2a Calle A 7-30, Zona 10; La Aurora International Airport (☎ 331-4755)

Tally (☎ 232-0421, fax 253-1749), 7a Avenida 14-60, Zona 1; La Aurora International Airport (☎ 332-6063, fax 334-5925)

Thrifty (☎ 332-1130, 332-1220, fax 332-1207), Avenida La Reforma 8-33, Zona 10; La Aurora International Airport (☎ 332-1265)

Tikal (☎ 332-4721, 361-0247), 2a Calle 6-56, Zona 10

GETTING AROUND
To/From the Airport

La Aurora International Airport (☎ 334-7680, 334-7689) is in Zona 13, the southern part of the city, 10 minutes from Zona 1 by taxi, half an hour by bus. Car rental offices and taxi ranks are outside the airport, downstairs from the arrivals level.

For the city bus, go upstairs to the departures level and walk across the airport parking lot to the bus stop. Bus No 83 comes by every 15 minutes, 6 am to 9 pm (US$0.15), and will take you through Zonas 9 and 4 to Zona 1. Going from town to the airport, No 83 goes south through Zona 1 on 10a Avenida, through Zona 9 on 6a Avenida, passes by the zoo and the museums on 7a Avenida and stops right in front of the international terminal.

Taxi fares to various points in the center are supposedly set but are actually negotiable, though quite high: from the airport to Zona 9 or 10, US$5; to Zona 1, US$7. A tip is expected. Be sure to establish the destination and price before getting into the taxi (see also Taxi).

Many companies offer shuttle service between the airport and Antigua, with door-to-door service on the Antigua end. They depart from the airport every hour or so until 8 pm and take an hour to reach Antigua (US$7). A taxi to Antigua costs around US$20; bargain hard and hook up with other travelers to cut costs.

Bus & Jitney

Buses in Guatemala City are frequent and cheap. In Zona 9, 6a Avenida (southbound) and 7a Avenida (northbound) are loaded with buses traversing the city; in Zona 1 these buses tend to swing away from the commercial district and travel along 4a, 5a, 9a and 10a Avenidas. The most useful north-south routes are bus Nos 2, 5 and 14. Note that modified numbers (such as 2A or 5-Bolívar) follow different routes and may not get you where you expect to go. Buses with 'Terminal' in the front window stop at the Terminal de Autobuses in Zona 4.

To get between Zona 1 and Zona 10, take bus Nos 82 or 101. You can catch these on the corner of 10a Avenida between 8a and 12a Calles. The 82 bus passes the Centro Cívico before turning onto Avenida La Reforma; this one is good for getting to INGUAT and several embassies.

City buses stop running at about 9 pm, and *ruteleros* (jitneys) begin to run up and down the main avenues. The jitneys run all night, until the buses resume their rattling rides at 5 am. Hold up your hand as the signal to stop a jitney or bus.

For information on buses from Guatemala City to the rest of the country, see the Getting There & Around chapter.

Taxi

Outside of Zona 1, you'll rarely see taxis cruising and will probably have to phone for one. Taxi Amarilla (☎ 332-1515) charges about half the price of most of the other taxi companies, and their cabs are metered.

Antigua

• **population 30,000** • **elevation 1530m**

Nestled between three volcanoes, Antigua Guatemala is among the oldest and most beautiful cities in the Americas. Its majestic setting, cobblestone streets, crumbling ruins and sprays of bougainvillea bursting from terra cotta roofs make Antigua a stunning town that even the most worldly traveler can appreciate. Seasoned Guatemala travelers spend as little time as possible in Guatemala City, preferring to make Antigua their base.

Highlights

- Visiting the Casa K'ojom museum and the convent ruins of La Merced
- Climbing active Volcán Pacaya on a day trip
- Hiking or horseback riding to the Cerro de la Cruz vista point
- Attending the town's wildly colorful Semana Santa celebrations
- Studying Spanish at one of the many schools in town

Antigua is one of Guatemala's most kid-friendly cities, with playgrounds, Spanish classes for children and food for the finicky.

Perhaps the most exciting time to visit Antigua is during Holy Week – especially on Good Friday. It takes planning however (make your hotel reservations at least four months in advance), as this is the busiest week of the year. Other busy tourist times are June through August and November to April.

Antigua is cold after sunset, especially between September and March, so bring warm clothes; you might even consider packing a sleeping bag or buying a blanket.

HISTORY

Antigua was founded on March 10, 1543, and it functioned as the colonial capital for 233 years. The capital was transferred to Guatemala City in 1776, after Antigua was largely destroyed in the great earthquake of July 29, 1773.

After that quake, Antigua was slowly rebuilt, retaining its traditional character, architecture and cobblestone streets. In 1944 the Legislative Assembly declared Antigua a national monument, and in 1979 UNESCO declared it a World Heritage Site.

Most of Antigua's buildings were constructed during the 17th and 18th centuries, when the city was a rich Spanish outpost and the Catholic church was ascending to power. Many handsome, sturdy colonial buildings remain, and several impressive ruins have been preserved and are open to the public.

ORIENTATION

Volcán Agua is southeast of the city and visible from most points; Volcán Acatenango is to the west; and Volcán Fuego (Fire) – easily recognizable by its plume of smoke and, at night, its red glow – is to the southwest. These three volcanoes (which appear on the city's coat of arms) provide easy reference points.

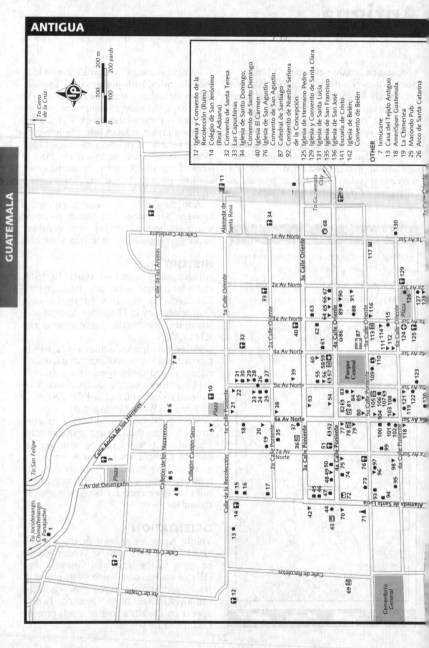

ANTIGUA

12 Iglesia y Convento de la Recolección (Ruins)
14 Colegio de San Jerónimo (Real Aduana)
32 Convento de Santa Teresa
33 Las Capuchinas
34 Iglesia de Santo Domingo; Convento de Santo Domingo
40 Iglesia El Carmen
76 Iglesia de San Agustín; Convento de San Agustín
87 Catedral de Santiago
92 Convento de Nuestra Señora de la Concepción
125 Iglesia de Hermano Pedro
129 Iglesia y Convento de Santa Clara
131 Iglesia de Santa Lucía
135 Iglesia de San Francisco
136 Iglesia de San José
141 Escuela de Cristo
142 Iglesia de Belén; Convento de Belén

OTHER
7   Ixmucane
13 Casa del Tejido Antiguo
18 AmeriSpan Guatemala
19 La Chimenea
25 Macondo Pub
26 Arco de Santa Catarina

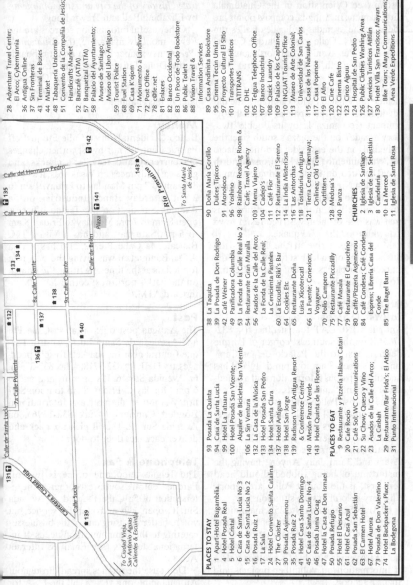

GUATEMALA

PLACES TO STAY
1 Apart-Hotel Bugambilia
4 Hotel Posada Real
5 Hotel Cristal
6 Casa de Santa Lucía No 3
15 Casa de Santa Lucía No 2
16 Posada Ruiz 1
17 La Sala
24 Hotel Convento Santa Catalina
27 The Cloister
30 Posada Asjemenou
35 Posada Ruiz 2
41 Hotel Casa Santo Domingo
45 Casa de Santa Lucía No 4
46 Posada Juma Ocag
47 Hotel la Casa de Don Ismael
50 Posada Refugio
55 Hotel El Descanso
61 Hotel Casa Azul
62 Posada San Sebastián
63 El Carmen Hotel
67 Hotel Aurora
73 Posada de Don Valentino
74 Hotel Backpacker's Place;
   La Bodegona
93 Posada La Quinta
94 Casa de Santa Lucía
99 Hotel La Tatuana
100 Hotel Posada San Vicente;
    Alquiler de Bicicletas San Vicente
106 La Sin Ventura
132 La Casa de la Música
133 Hotel Posada San Pedro
134 Hotel Santa Clara
137 Hotel Antigua
138 Hotel San Jorge
139 Radisson Villa Antigua Resort
    & Conference Center
140 Mesón Panza Verde
143 Hotel Quinta de las Flores

PLACES TO EAT
9 Restaurante y Pizzería Italiana Catari
20 Cafe Rocío
21 Café Sol; WC Communications
22 Su Chow; Queso y Vino
23 Asados de la Calle del Arco;
   La Casbah
29 Restaurante/Bar Frida's; El Ático
31 Punto Internacional
38 La Taquiza
39 La Posada de Don Rodrigo
42 Café Weiner
49 Panificadora Columbia
53 La Fonda de la Calle Real No 2
54 Restaurante Gran Muralla
56 Asados de la Calle del Arco;
   La Fonda de la Calle Real;
   La Cenicienta Pasteles
60 La Escudilla; Riki's Bar
64 Cookies Etc
65 Restaurante Doña
   Luisa Xicotencatl
66 La Fuente; Conexíon;
   Voyageur
70 Pollo Campero
75 Restaurante Piccadilly
77 Café Masala
79 Restaurante El Capuchino
80 Caffé/Pizzeria Asjemenou
84 Café Condesa; Café Condesa
   Express; Librería Casa del
   Conde
85 The Bagel Barn
90 Doña María Gordillo
   Dulces Típicos
91 Monoloco
96 Yoshino
98 Rainbow Reading Room &
   Cafe; Travel Agency
103 Menu Viajero
104 Cadejo's
111 Café Flor
112 Restaurante El Sereno
114 La India Misteriosa
116 Las Antorchas
118 Tostaduría Antigua
121 Tierra Cero; Cinemaya;
    Onlinea; Old Town
    Outfitters
128 Medusa's
140 Panza

CHURCHES
2 Iglesia de Santiago
3 Iglesia de San Sebastián
8 Candelaria
10 La Merced
11 Iglesia de Santa Rosa

28 Adventure Travel Center;
   El Arco; Cybermanía
36 Antigua Online
37 Sin Fronteras
43 Terminal de Buses
44 Market
48 Tabaquería Unicornio
51 Convento de la Compañía de Jesús;
   Handicrafts Market
52 Bancafé (ATM)
57 Banquetzal (ATM)
58 Palacio del Ayuntamiento;
   Museo de Santiago;
   Museo del Libro Antiguo
59 Tourist Police
68 Fuel Station
69 Casa K'ojom
71 Monumento a Landívar
72 Post Office
78 cafe.net
81 Enlaces
82 Banco Occidental
83 Un Poco de Todo Bookstore
86 Public Toilets
88 Vision Travel &
   Information Services
89 Casa Andinista Bookstore
95 Cinema Tecún Umán
97 Proyecto Cultural El Sitio
101 Transportes Turísticos
    ATITRANS
102 DHL
105 Telgua Telephone Office
107 Banco Industrial
108 Quick Laundry
109 Palacio de los Capitanes
110 INGUAT Tourist Office
113 Museo de Arte Colonial;
    Universidad de San Carlos
115 Casa de los Nahuales
117 Casa Popenoe
119 El Afro
120 Cine Cafe
122 Cinema Bistro
123 Cinco Aipnu
124 Hospital de San Pedro
126 Public Clothes Washing Area
127 Servicios Turísticos Atitlán
130 Hotel Villa San Francisco; Mayan
    Bike Tours; Maya Communications;
    Area Verde Expeditions

Antigua's street grid uses a modified version of the Guatemala City numbering system (see Orientation in the Guatemala City chapter). In Antigua, compass points are added to the avenidas and calles. Calles run east-west, so 4a Calle west of Parque Central is 4a Calle Pte; avenidas run north-south, so 3a Avenida north of Parque Central is 3a Avenida Nte.

Landmarks surrounding Parque Central include the Palacio de los Capitanes, the old headquarters of the Spanish colonial government (recognizable by its double, two-story arcade), on the plaza's south side; the cathedral, on the east side; and the Palacio del Ayuntamiento (Town Hall), on the north side. The **Arco de Santa Catarina**, spanning 5a Avenida Nte between 1a and 2a Calles, is another famous Antigua landmark. Built in 1694 (and rebuilt in the 19th century), this arch was one of the few structures in town that withstood the 1773 quake.

Most buses arrive at the Terminal de Buses, a large open lot just to the west of the market, four blocks west of Parque Central along 4a Calle Pte.

INFORMATION
Tourist Offices
Antigua's INGUAT tourist office (☎ 832-0763) is on the southeast corner of Parque Central, next to the Palacio de los Capitanes. It's open 8 am to 5 pm daily and has free city maps, bus information and a schedule of Semana Santa events.

The Tourist Police office (☎ 832-4131) is on the corner of 4a Calle Ote and 4a Avenida Nte. Officers provide free escorts to heretofore dangerous spots such as the cemetery and Cerro de la Cruz at 8:30 and 11 am and 3 pm daily. Anyone having the misfortune of being robbed should head here first, as the Tourist Police are reportedly very helpful in such situations.

El Arco, 5a Avenida Nte 25B, maintains a list of volunteer opportunities in Guatemala. AmeriSpan Guatemala (☎ 832-0164, 832-4846, fax 832-1896, amerispan@guate .net), 6a Avenida Nte 40A, is another source of information on volunteer projects and Spanish schools.

Visitors should look for the informative little book *Antigua Guatemala: An illustrated history of the city and its monuments*, by Elizabeth Bell and Trevor Long.

Other useful information sources are the *Revue* monthly magazine, the *Guatemala Weekly* newspaper and the bulletin boards at the Doña Luisa Xicotencatl restaurant, the Rainbow Reading Room & Cafe and the Casa Andinista bookstore, all described later in this chapter.

Money
Banco Occidental, on 4a Calle Pte just off Parque Central's northwest corner, changes US currency and traveler's checks and gives cash advances on Visa cards; it's open 8:30 am to 7 pm Monday to Friday, 9 am to 2 pm Saturday. Banco Industrial, on 5a Avenida Sur next to the Telgua office, is open 8 am to 7 pm Monday to Friday, 8 am to 5 pm Saturday, and has a Visa ATM. Bancafé, 4a Calle Pte 22, also has a Visa ATM. Banquetzal was giving the best rate for dollars at the time of writing; the branch on the park's northwest corner has a MasterCard ATM.

Post
The Antigua post office is at 4a Calle Pte and Alameda de Santa Lucía, west of Parque Central near the market. To ship packages, try DHL (☎ 832-3718, ☎/fax 832-3732), 6a Avenida Sur 16. It's open from 8 am to 6 pm Monday to Friday, 8 am to noon Saturday. Another alternative is International Bonded Couriers (☎/fax 832-1696), 6a Avenida Sur 12. They'll pick up, pack and deliver packages door-to-door.

Telephone & Fax
The Telgua telephone office is just off Parque Central's southwest corner, at the intersection of 5a Calle Pte and 5a Avenida Sur. It's open daily and offers fax service, but you're better off using one of the businesses catering to the communication needs of international tourists (see Email & Internet Access).

Don't use the phones spread throughout Antigua imploring you to call the USA for

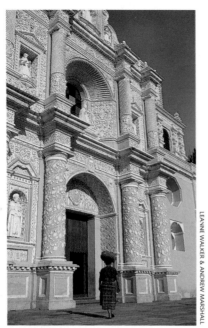

La Merced church, Antigua, Guatemala

Chillin' with the chicle, Antigua

5a Avenida Norte to La Merced, Antigua

Semana Santa parade, Antigua

Hanging out with the meat in San Rafael Petzal, Guatemala

Flower vendor, Chichicastenango

'Drab' is not in the Guatemalan vocabulary.

free; they charge usurious rates to your credit card – up to US$20 a minute in some cases!

Email & Internet Access

Antigua is awash in businesses supplying cheap, reliable Internet access. One of the oldest is Conexion (☎ 832-3768, fax 832-0082, users@conexion.com), 4a Calle Ote 14, inside La Fuente courtyard, where you can send and/or receive phone, fax, email and telex messages. Prices for sending are fairly high; receiving is cheap. Conexion also offers local dial-up access. It's open 8:30 am to 7 pm daily. Email, phone and fax services are also available at WC (☎ 832-5666, wwcall@infovia.com), 1a Calle Pte 9, by Café Sol, opposite La Merced church, and at Maya Communications, 1a Avenida Sur 15, in the Hotel Villa San Francisco, which claims 24-hour access, seven days a week.

Enlaces (☎ 832-0216, enlace@pobox.com), 6a Avenida Nte 1, offers competitively priced email, phone and fax services. It's open 8 am to 7:30 pm Monday to Saturday, 8 am to 1 pm Sunday. Other Internet places include Onlinea, 6a Calle Pte 7; c@fe.net, 6a Avenida Nte 14; Antigua Online, 3a Calle Pte 12; and Cybermannia, 5 Avenida Nte 25B.

Travel Agencies

Everywhere you turn in Antigua, you'll see travel agencies offering tours, flights, shuttle buses and more. Reputable agencies include, but are not limited to, the following:

Adventure Travel Center (☎/fax 832-0162, viareal@lguate.net), 5a Avenida Nte 25-B

Agencia de Viajes Tivoli (☎ 832-1370, 832-4274, fax 832-5690, antigua@tivoli.com), 4a Calle Ote 10, local 3

Gran Jaguar Travel Agency (☎ 832-2712), 4a Calle Pte 30, and Alameda de Santa Lucia Sur 3 (☎ 832-3149, evenings ☎ 832-3107); offers cheapest tours to Volcán Pacaya

Monarcas Travel (☎ 832-4779), 7a Avenida Nte 15-A, and 6a Avenida Nte 60-A (☎ 832-4305); offers trips to Mayan sites and shuttles to Copán

Rainbow Travel Center (☎ 832-4202/3/4/5/6/7, fax 832-4206, myers@gua.gbm.net), 7a Avenida Sur 8; English, French, German, Italian and Spanish spoken

Servicios Turísticos Atitlán (☎/fax 832-1493, turisticosatitlan@yahoo.com, www.atitlan.com), 2a Avenida Sur 4A

Sin Fronteras (☎ 832-1017, 832-1226, ☎/fax 832-2674, sinfront@sinfront.com), 3a Calle Pte 12; the representative for Maya Expedition rafting tours; also features many tour packages to Cuba

Transportes Turísticos ATITRANS (☎ 832-1381, 832-1297, ☎/fax 832-0644, after 8 pm ☎ 832-3371, atitrans@quick.guate.com), 6a Avenida Sur 7 and 8

TURANSA (☎/fax 832-2928), Calle Sucia at Carretera a Ciudad Vieja, in the Hotel Radisson Villa Antigua; and 5a Calle Pte 11-B (☎/fax 832-3316)

Vision Travel and Information Services (☎ 832-3293, 832-1962/64, fax 832-1955, vision@guatemalainfo.com, www.guatemalainfo.com), 3a Avenida Nte 3 (behind the cathedral); well-recommended company offering a guidebook library, shuttles, tours and phone service (will also hold mail and refill water bottles for cheap)

Voyageur (☎ 832-4237/38, fax 832-4247, info@travel.net.gt), 4a Calle Ote 14, inside La Fuente courtyard

Note: Several reports have alleged unprofessional behavior by the Eco Aventuras travel agency. There are many highly recommended agencies in Antigua, so you may be better off sticking with one of those.

Bookstores & Libraries

The Rainbow Reading Room & Cafe, 7a Avenida Sur at 6a Calle Pte, offers thousands of used books in English and Spanish for sale, rent or trade. Other excellent bookstores include Un Poco de Todo and the Librería Casa del Conde, both on the west side of Parque Central, as well as Casa Andinista, 4a Calle Ote 5. All carry new and used books in several languages and are open daily. One of the best collections of used books for sale or swap is at Monoloco (see Places to Eat). Hamlin y White, 4a Calle Ote 12A, boasts over 65 magazine titles and a Lonely Planet Travel Guide Center.

La Biblioteca Internacional de Antigua (International Library of Antigua), 5a Calle Pte 15 in the Proyecto Cultural El Sitio building, has a good book collection; temporary or long-term memberships available.

Laundry

Laundries are everywhere. The block of 6a Calle Pte between 5a and 7a Avenida Sur is packed with them. Quick Laundry (☎ 832-1976), 6a Calle Pte 14, is fast and reliable. It's open 9 am to 6 pm Monday to Saturday. The going rate is about US$1.75 per kilogram for wash and dry.

Toilets

Public toilets are on 4a Calle Ote near the corner of 4a Avenida Nte, off the northeast corner of Parque Central.

Medical Services

Hospital de San Pedro (☎ 832-0301) is at 3a Avenida Sur and 6a Calle Ote. Ixmucane (☎ 832-5539, houston@conexion.com.gt), 4a Avenida Nte 32, provides a complete range of gynecological services, from dispensing birth control to delivering babies. Herbal supplements are also available; German, English and Spanish are spoken.

Emergency

The National Police can be reached at ☎ 832-0251; the Tourism Police are at ☎ 832-4131. The municipal fire department is at ☎ 832-1075.

Dangers & Annoyances

Antigua seems like such a mellow town that you wouldn't think any misfortune could ever befall you. Think again. Although you probably will never have a problem, be wary when walking the streets late at night, as robberies have taken place. Armed robberies (and worse) have occurred on Cerro de la Cruz, on Volcán Pacaya and at the cemetery, which should be considered off-limits unless you are escorted by the Tourist Police. Crime against tourists has dropped precipitously since the formation of this agency; they will accompany you to the Cerro or the cemetery, for free (see Tourist Offices earlier in this chapter).

PARQUE CENTRAL

This plaza is the gathering place for locals and visitors alike. On most days the periphery is lined with villagers selling handicrafts to tourists; on Sunday it's mobbed and the streets on the park's east and west sides are closed to traffic. The best prices are to be had late Sunday afternoon, when the peddling is winding down.

The plaza's famous fountain was built in 1738. At night, you can hear mariachi or marimba bands in the park.

Palacio de los Capitanes

Built in 1543, the Palacio de los Capitanes has a stately double arcade on its facade, which marches proudly across the park's southern extent. Most of the facade is original, but the rest of the building was reconstructed a century ago. From 1543 to 1773, this building was the governmental center of all Central America, ruling Chiapas, Guatemala, Honduras and Nicaragua.

Catedral de Santiago

The Catedral de Santiago, on the park's east side, was founded in 1542, damaged by earthquakes many times, badly ruined in 1773 and only partially rebuilt between 1780 and 1820. In the 16th and early 17th centuries, Antigua's churches had lavish baroque interiors, but most – including this one – lost this richness when they were rebuilt after the earthquakes. The cathedral is being restored, but it will never regain its former grandeur. Inside, a crypt contains the bones of Bernal Díaz del Castillo, historian of the Spanish conquest, who died in 1581. If the front entrance is closed, you can enter at the rear or on the south side.

Palacio del Ayuntamiento

On the park's north side stands the Palacio del Ayuntamiento, Antigua's town hall, which dates mostly from 1743. In addition to town offices, it houses the **Museo de Santiago**, which exhibits colonial furnishings, artifacts and weapons. Museum hours are 9 am to 4 pm Tuesday to Friday, 9 am to noon and 2 to 4 pm Saturday and Sunday; US$1.25.

Next door are the colonial prison and the **Museo del Libro Antiguo** (Old Book Museum; same hours and admission price as the Museo de Santiago), which has exhibits of colonial printing and binding.

Universidad de San Carlos

The Universidad de San Carlos was founded in 1676. Its main building (built in 1763), 5a Calle Ote 5, half a block east of the park, houses the **Museo de Arte Colonial** (☎ 832-0429), which is known for its painting collection. Look for the Saint Francis series by notable colonial artist Cristóbal de Villapando. The museum keeps the same hours as the Museo de Santiago. Admission is US$0.75.

CHURCHES

Once glorious in their gilded baroque finery, Antigua's churches have suffered indignities from both nature and humankind. Rebuilding after earthquakes gave the churches thicker walls, lower towers and belfries and bland interiors, and moving the capital to Guatemala City deprived Antigua of the population needed to maintain the churches in their traditional richness. Still, the churches are impressive. Most are open 9 am to 5 pm daily; entrance costs under US$2. In addition to those noted below, you'll find many others scattered around town in various states of decay.

La Merced

From the park, walk three long blocks up 5a Avenida Nte, passing beneath the Arco de Santa Catarina. At the northern end of 5a Avenida is the Iglesia y Convento de Nuestra Señora de La Merced, known simply as La Merced – Antigua's most striking colonial church.

La Merced's construction began in 1548. Improvements continued to be made until 1717, when the church was ruined by earthquakes. Reconstruction was completed in 1767, but in 1773 yet another earthquake struck and the convent was totally destroyed. Repairs to the church were made from 1850 to 1855; its baroque facade dates from this period.

Inside the ruins is a fountain 27m in diameter – said to be the largest in Central America. There are pretty views from the upper level. Admission to the convent costs US$0.25 and is well worth it.

Iglesia de San Francisco

The next most notable church in town is the Iglesia de San Francisco, 7a Calle Ote at 1a Avenida Sur. It dates from the mid-16th century, but little of the original building remains. Rebuilding and restoration over the centuries has produced a handsome structure; reinforced concrete added in 1961 protected the church from suffering serious damage in the 1976 earthquake. All that remains of the original church is the Chapel of Hermano Pedro (not to be confused with the Iglesia de Hermano Pedro over on 3a Avenida Sur), resting place of Hermano Pedro de San José Betancourt, a Franciscan monk who founded a hospital for the poor and earned the gratitude of generations. He died here in 1667; his intercession is still sought by the ill, who pray here fervently.

Other Churches

The Iglesia y Convento de Nuestra Señora del Pilar de Zaragoza, usually called simply **Las Capuchinas**, at 2a Avenida Nte and 2a Calle Ote, was founded in 1736 by nuns from Madrid. Destroyed repeatedly by earthquakes, it is now a museum, with exhibits on religious life in colonial times. The building has an unusual structure of 18 concentric cells around a circular patio. Guided tours are available.

The **Iglesia y Convento de la Recolección**, a massive ruin at the west end of 1a Calle Pte, is among Antigua's most impressive monuments. Built between 1701 and 1708, it was destroyed in the 1773 earthquake.

Near La Recolección, at Alameda de Santa Lucía and 1a Calle Pte, **Colegio de San Jerónimo** (also called the Real Aduana) was built in 1757 by friars of the Merced order. Because it did not have royal authorization, it was taken over by Spain's Carlos III in 1761. In 1765 it was designated for use as the Real Aduana (Royal Customhouse), but it was destroyed in the 1773 earthquake. The ruins are open 9 am to 5 pm daily; US$1.25.

OTHER ATTRACTIONS
Casa K'ojom

In 1984, Samuel Franco Arce began photographing Mayan ceremonies and festivals and recording their music. By 1987 he had enough to establish Casa K'ojom (House of Music), a museum dedicated to Mayan music and the ceremonies in which it was used.

Some visitors to Guatemala are lucky enough to witness a parade of the *cofradías* or some other age-old ceremony. But everyone can experience some of this fascinating culture in a visit to Casa K'ojom. Besides the fine collection of photographs, Franco has amassed musical instruments, tools, masks and figures. Though small, the collection is cleverly displayed in two parts: the first room features traditional instruments that were in use before the Spanish arrived, and the second holds instruments that either evolved or survived beyond the conquest. Recordings of the music play softly in the background. Don't miss the Maximón exhibit, featuring the crafty folk-god venerated by the people of several highland towns.

The museum (☎ 832-3087) is at Calle de Recoletos 55, a block west of the bus station. It's open 9:30 am to 12:30 pm and 2 to 5 pm Monday to Friday, 9:30 am to 12:30 pm and 2 to 4 pm Saturday. The admission price of US$0.65 includes a superlative audiovisual show and a live demonstration of the instruments in the collection. The gift shop, worth a stop, sells instruments and compact discs.

Casa Popenoe
At the corner of 5a Calle Ote and 1a Avenida Sur stands this beautiful mansion built in 1636 by Don Luis de las Infantas Mendoza y Venegas. Ruined by the earthquake of 1773, the house stood desolate until it was bought in 1931 by Dr Wilson Popenoe and his wife, Dorothy. The Popenoes' painstaking and authentic restoration yields a fascinating glimpse of how the family of a royal official (Don Luis) lived in Antigua in the 17th century. The house is open 2 to 4 pm Monday to Saturday; a self-guided tour costs US$0.85.

Monumento a Landívar
At the west end of 5a Calle Pte is the Monumento a Landívar, a structure of five colonial-style arches set in a little park. Rafael Landívar, an 18th-century Jesuit priest and poet, lived and wrote in Antigua for some time. His poetry is esteemed as the colonial period's best, even though he wrote much of it in Italy after the Jesuits were expelled from Guatemala. Landívar's Antigua house was nearby on 5a Calle Pte.

Market
Down at the west end of 4a Calle Ote, across Alameda de Santa Lucía, sprawls the market – chaotic, colorful and always bustle. Mornings, when all the local villagers are actively buying and selling, is the best time to come. Official market days are Monday, Thursday and Saturday.

Cemetery
Antigua's Cementerio General, west of the market and bus terminal, is a beautiful conglomeration of tombs and mausoleums, all decked out with wreaths, exotic flowers and other signs of mourning. Unfortunately, it's also considered dangerous because thieves lay in wait for tourists to come strolling by. If you want to check out the cemetery, go with a Tourist Police escort (see Tourist Offices, earlier) or in a group, though even large groups have been robbed here.

Cerro de la Cruz
On the town's northeast side is Cerro de la Cruz (Hill of the Cross), offering fine views over Antigua and south toward Volcán Agua. Don't come here without a Tourism Police escort (see Tourist Offices), as this hill is famous for muggers waiting to prey on unsuspecting visitors. The Tourism Police was formed because of robberies at Cerro de la Cruz; reportedly no crime against tourists has taken place on the hill since.

ACTIVITIES
Horseback Riding
Several stables in Antigua rent horses and arrange day or overnight trips into the countryside. Establo Santiago has been recommended; contact the company through the Adventure Travel Center (see Travel Agencies).

Several readers recommend the Ravenscroft Riding Stables (☎ 832-6229, afternoons), 2a Avenida Sur 3, San Juan del Obispo. It's 3.2km south of Antigua, on the road to Santa María de Jesús; buses leave every half hour from the bus station behind the market. The stables offer English-style riding, with scenic rides of three to five hours in and around Antigua. Reservations and information are available through the Hotel San Jorge (☎ 832-3132), 4a Avenida Sur 13.

Another possibility is La Ronda Stables (☎ 832-1224), which leads tours of two to six hours for every level of experience. Reservations and information are also available at the Bagel Barn (see Places to Eat).

Bicycling

You can rent bicycles at several places in Antigua, including Alquiler de Bicicletas San Vicente (☎/fax 832-3311), 6a Avenida Sur 6 in the Hotel Posada San Vicente, and Aviatur (☎/fax 832-2642), 5a Avenida Nte 35, just north of the arch. Prices are around US$1.50 per hour, US$6 to US$8.50 per day, US$25 per week or US$35 for two weeks. Prices and equipment vary, so shop around.

Mayan Bike Tours (☎ 832-3383, 832-6506, email mayanbikeone@conexion.com.gt, www.mayanbike.com), 1a Avenida Sur 15, rents bikes and offers several area mountain-bike tours. Tours include all gear and cost US$19 for a half day, US$39 for a full day with lunch. The company also runs popular hike-and-bike tours to Acatenango volcano (US$49, 12 hours) and Lago de Atitlán (US$175, two days/one night).

Old Town Outfitters (☎ 832-4243, email trvlnlite@hotmail.com, www.bikeguatemala.com), 6a Calle Pte 7, rents high-quality standard bikes (US$7 a day) and premium bikes (US$14). It also offers tours, including a two-day/one-night pedal-and-paddle tour (bike and kayak) to Lago de Atitlán for US$125. You can rent camping gear here as well.

Climbing the Volcanoes

Climbing the volcanoes around Antigua used to be tempting fate, as armed robbers repeatedly intercepted groups of foreigners and relieved them of everything (including clothing). There were even incidents of rape and murder. Recent measures aimed at ensuring tourist safety have reduced the problem dramatically.

Volcán Pacaya Because of its status as the only active volcano near Antigua, Volcán Pacaya attracts the most tourists and the most bandits. The situation is improving, however, since each group climbing Pacaya is now accompanied by a security guard (little comfort when the guard turns out to be a toothless geezer with a machete!). Still, travelers these days are more likely to be hurt by flaming rocks and sulfurous fog than criminals.

Pacaya is temperamental and travelers have suffered serious, even fatal injuries when the volcano erupted unexpectedly while they were near the summit. In early 2000, Pacaya started getting *really* frisky, necessitating an escalation to orange alert status.

Get reliable advice about safety before you climb. Check with your embassy in Guatemala City or with the tourist office in Antigua. If you decide to go, make sure you go with reputable guides, arranged through an established agency.

Take sensible precautions. Wear adequate footwear (volcanic rock can shred shoes), warm clothing (it's very cold up there) and, in the rainy season, some sort of rain gear. Carry snacks, water and, in case it gets dark, a flashlight.

Other Volcanoes The volcanoes nearer Antigua (Agua, Fuego and Acatenango) are inactive, so they attract fewer tourists. Still, these volcanoes are impressive and offer magnificent views.

Volcán Agua (3766m) looms over Antigua, south of town. Various outfitters in Antigua can furnish details about the climb. To get to the mountain, follow 2a Avenida Sur or Calle de los Pasos south toward El Calvario (2km), then continue onward via San Juan del Obispo (another 3km) to Santa María de Jesús, a village of unpaved streets and bamboo fences. This is the jumping-off point for treks up the slopes of Volcán Agua, which rises dramatically right behind the village. The main plaza is also the bus terminal. *Comedor & Hospedaje El Oasis*, a tidy little pension, offers meals and beds.

You could also climb the other two volcanoes near Antigua: **Volcán Acatenango** and **Volcán Fuego**. Various companies offer guided tours. Mayan Bike Tours (see the Bicycling section, earlier) offers hike/bike tours on Acatenango, while Old Town Outfitters will take you to the summit of any volcano.

White-Water Rafting

Area Verde Expeditions (☎/fax 832-3383, in the USA ☎/fax 719-583-8929, mayanbike@guate.net) is at 1a Avenida Sur 15 in the Hotel Villa San Francisco. The company offers a variety of white-water rafting tours lasting from one to five days; rafting is possible year-round.

Maya Expeditions, represented in Antigua by Sin Fronteras (☎ 832-1017, ☎/fax 832-2674), 3a Calle Pte 12, also leads a variety of day trips and multiday tours on several rivers.

LANGUAGE COURSES

Antigua is famous for its many Spanish-language schools, which attract students from around the world. Price, teacher quality and student satisfaction vary greatly. Visit several schools before you choose one. Ask for references and talk to alumni. The INGUAT tourist office has a list of reputable schools, which include the following:

Academia de Español Guatemala (☎ 832-5057, 832-5060, fax 832-5058, aegnow@guate.net, www.travellog.com/guatemala/antigua/acadespanol/school.html), 7a Calle Ote 15

Academia de Español Sevilla (☎/fax 832-0442), 1a Avenida Sur 8

Academia de Español Tecún Umán (☎/fax 832-2792, etecun@centramerica.com, www.tecunuman.centroamerica.com), 6a Calle Pte 34

Centro de Español Don Pedro de Alvarado (☎/fax 832-4180), 1a Calle Pte 24

Centro Lingüístico La Unión (☎/fax 832-7337, launion@conexion.com, www.launion.conexion.com) 1a Avenida Sur 21

Centro Lingüístico Maya (☎ 832-1342, clmmaya@guate.net), 5a Calle Pte 20

Christian Spanish Academy (CSA; ☎ 832-3922, fax 832-3760, chspanac@infovia.com.gt), 6a Avenida Nte 15

Don Quijote Spanish Academy (☎ 832-2868, info central@donquijote.org, www.donquijote.org), Portal del Ayuntamiento 6, in the Museo del Libro Antiguo on Parque Central

Escuela de Español San José el Viejo (☎ 832-3028, fax 832-3029, in the USA ☎ 800-562-6274, spanish@guate.net, www.guate.net/spanish), 5a Avenida Sur 34 in the USA write Section 544, PO Box 02-5289, Miami, FL 33102

Proyecto Lingüístico Francisco Marroquín (☎/fax 832-2886, info@langlink.com), 7a Calle Pte 31 and three other locations in Antigua

Classes start every Monday at most schools, though you can usually be placed with a teacher any day of the week. Cost for four hours of one-to-one instruction daily, five days a week, ranges from around US$75 to US$100 per week; you can also enroll for up to seven hours a day. Most schools can arrange room and board with local families for around US$40 to US$60 per week.

Homestays are supposed to promote the 'total immersion' concept of language learning, but often several foreigners stay with a family at once, creating more of a hotel atmosphere than a family atmosphere. Sometimes, too, students and the family will have separate mealtimes. If you truly want to be totally immersed, inquire after such details.

Antigua is not for everyone who wants to study Spanish; with so many foreigners here, it takes real discipline to converse in Spanish rather than your native tongue. If you think this will bother you, consider studying in Xela or the Petén.

ORGANIZED TOURS

One of the most popular organized tours from Antigua is the day hike up Volcán Pacaya (see Activities). Though most agencies in Antigua offer this trip, the tours are all subcontracted by Gran Jaguar Travel Agency, which actually provides the transportation, guide and security for the hike. Booking the trip directly with Gran Jaguar costs around US$5, whereas it can be double or even triple elsewhere.

Author and Antigua aficionado Elizabeth Bell leads cultural tours of the town (in English and/or Spanish) on Tuesday, Wednesday, Friday and Saturday at 9:30 am. On Monday and Thursday, groups are led by Roberto Spillari and start at 2 pm. The tours take two hours and cost US$18. Reservations are recommended and can be made at Antigua Tours (☎ 832-0140 ext 341, elizbell@guate.net), in the lobby of the Hotel Casa Santo Domingo, 3a Calle Ote 28. (See Entertainment for information on Bell's slide shows.)

The Adventure Travel Center offers an interesting three-hour Villages & Farms Tour for US$25. Vision Travel leads a recommended Guatemala City museum tour for US$25. (See Travel Agencies, earlier this chapter, for contact details.)

Numerous travel agencies offer farther-flung tours to Tikal, Copán-Quiriguá-Río Dulce, Monterrico, Chichicastenango, Panajachel and other places.

SPECIAL EVENTS
By far the most interesting time to be in Antigua is during **Semana Santa** (Holy Week), when hundreds of people dress in violet robes to accompany daily religious processions in remembrance of the Crucifixion. Dense clouds of incense envelop the parade. Streets are covered in breathtakingly elaborate and colorful *alfombras* (carpets) of colored sawdust and flower petals. These beautifully fragile works of art are destroyed as the processions shuffle through them, but they're re-created the next morning for another parade.

Traditionally, the most interesting days are Palm Sunday, when a procession departs from La Merced (see Churches earlier in this chapter) in midafternoon; Holy Thursday, when a late-afternoon procession departs from the Iglesia de San Francisco; and Good Friday, when an early-morning procession departs from La Merced and a late-afternoon one leaves from the Escuela

de Cristo. Have ironclad hotel reservations well in advance of these dates, or plan to stay in another town and commute to the festivities.

The booklet *Lent and Easter Week in Antigua* by Elizabeth Bell gives explanations and a day-by-day schedule of processions, *velaciones* (vigils) and other events taking place throughout the Lenten season, the 40 days before Easter.

On a secular note, beware of pickpockets. It seems that Guatemala City's entire population of pickpockets (numbering perhaps in the hundreds) decamps to Antigua for Semana Santa. In the press of the emotion-filled crowds lining the processional routes, they target foreign tourists especially.

PLACES TO STAY
Antigua's climate, combined with the cement used in building construction, makes for some damp, musty and even moldy hotel rooms. Carpeted rooms and those on the ground floor seem to fare worse, so try to get an upstairs room, preferably with tile or linoleum floors.

Budget
When checking out budget hotels, look at several rooms, as some are much better than others.

Posada Refugio (4a Calle Pte 30) is the backpacker's supercheapie du jour. Basic rooms go for US$2.75/3.25/4 single/double/triple without bath, US$4/8/9.75 with bath. Rooms vary widely. *Posada Ruiz 2 (2a Calle Pte 25)* is a good deal for the price. Its small rooms go for US$2.25/4 single/double with shared bath. Lots of young international travelers stay here, congregating in the central courtyard in the evening. Not as nice is *Posada Ruiz 1 (Alameda de Santa Lucía 17)*, charging US$4 per person. Another hopping budget option is *La Sala* (☎ 832-6483) on the corner of Alameda de Santa Lucía and 2a Calle Pte, where a dorm bed is US$2.50.

The new *Hotel Backpacker's Place* (☎ 832-5023, 4a Calle Pte 27) is conveniently located for bus departures and has comfortable beds in spacious, if generic, rooms; US$6.50/7.75 single/double with shared bath, US$7.75/9.75 with private bath. South-facing rooms have views of Volcán Agua. Another great value is **Hotel la Casa de Don Ismael** (3a Calle Pte 6), down the unnamed alley off 3a Calle Pte, between 7a Avenida and Alameda de Santa Lucía. Clean, comfortable rooms with shared hot bath are US$5.25/7.75 single/double; try to get an upstairs room off the terrace. The hotel also has a pretty, compact courtyard. This is a safe, friendly place that fills up fast.

Posada Juma Ocag (☎ 832-3109, Alameda de Santa Lucía 13) is the superior budget hotel here. It's very quiet, despite being across from the market, and the four spotless, comfortable rooms have great mattresses, traditional appointments and private hot bath. Other amenities include a rooftop patio and small, well-tended garden. Touches like reading lamps and drinking water make this a killer value at US$10.50/12.50 double/triple. Unfortunately, reservations aren't accepted. **Hotel Cristal** (☎ 832-4177, Avenida del Desengaño 25) is also superlative for the price. Its 10 clean rooms surround a beautiful garden; US$6.50/9/11.50 single/double/triple with shared bath, US$9/11.50/13 with private bath. Students receive a discount.

With four locations, **Casas de Santa Lucía** is a mini-hotel chain. All charge US$10.25 double for clean, pleasant, attractive rooms with private hot bath, and all have rooftop terraces with views. Try the newly renovated original, at Alameda de Santa Lucía 9, between 5a and 6a Calles Pte; **Casa de Santa Lucía No 2** (Alameda de Santa Lucía 21); **Casa de Santa Lucía No 3** (6a Avenida Nte 43A); or **Casa de Santa Lucía No 4** (Alameda de Santa Lucía 5), which has nice rooms but can be loud. The first three have parking.

Hotel La Tatuana (☎ 832-1223, 7a Avenida Sur 3) has good, clean rooms with private bath for US$13/15 single/double. Try bargaining in the off-season. Similar in price is **Hotel Posada San Vicente** (☎ /fax 832-3311, 6a Avenida Sur 6), which has rooms with private bath for US$13 double; the up-

stairs rooms are better. Amenities include a pool table and bicycle rentals.

A step up in quality, **Posada de Don Valentino** (☎ 832-0384, 5a Calle Pte 28) has a nice patio, a pretty garden and bright, clean rooms with private bath for US$12/ 20/25 single/double/triple. Parking is available nearby.

Apart-Hotel Bugambilia (☎ /fax 832-2732, Calle Ancha de los Herreros 27) has 10 apartments, each with fully equipped kitchen, two or three double beds, cable TV and private hot bath. Daily rates are US$15/19/23 single/double/triple. Discounts are offered for weekly and monthly stays. Amenities include sitting areas, a beautiful patio garden, a fountain and a rooftop terrace.

Avoid the Arizona Hotel (2a Calle Pte 29A), which has an unsavory reputation.

Mid-Range

Antigua's mid-range hotels allow you to wallow in the city's colonial charms for a moderate cash outlay.

Posada Asjemenou (☎ 832-2670, 5a Avenida Nte 31), just north of the arch, is a beautifully renovated house built around a grassy courtyard with a fountain. It charges US$20/33 single/double for rooms with shared bath, US$26/40 for private bath. Discounts are available for stays of a week or more.

The convivial **Hotel Posada San Pedro** (☎ 832-3594, 3a Avenida Sur 15) comes highly recommended. Its 10 rooms are squeaky clean and nicely appointed; upstairs units have views. Guests have use of a communal kitchen and rooftop patio. This is a good choice at US$20/25 with private bath.

Hotel El Descanso (☎ 832-0142, 5a Avenida Nte 9) is friendly, clean and convenient. Its five rooms cost US$24/30 with private bath. There's a terrace upstairs in the rear. **Hotel Santa Clara** (☎ /fax 832-0342, 2a Avenida Sur 20) is quiet, proper and clean, with a relaxing garden. Rooms with terrific hot bath are US$21/25 in high season, US$13/16 in off-season; some large rooms with two double beds are available.

La Sin Ventura (☎ 832-0581, frontdesk@ lasinventura.com, www.lasinventura.com, 5a Avenida Sur 8) has a great location just off the park and sparkling rooms for US$19/30.
Hotel Posada Real (☎ 832-3396, Avenida del Desengaño 24) is a beautiful colonial hotel. Its nine rooms and suites, all with private hot bath and cable TV, are lovely, and many have fireplaces. Rooms can be noisy, however. Rates are US$25/35/45 single/double/triple.

Hotel San Jorge (☎ /fax 832-3132, 4a Avenida Sur 13) is a modern place where all 14 rooms have fireplace, cable TV and private bath with tub. Parking and laundry are available, and the guests (mostly older couples from the USA) may use the swimming pool and room-service facilities of the posh Hotel Antigua nearby. Rooms are US$30/35/40, and credit cards are accepted. Ask about discounts.

The *Posada San Sebastián (☎ /fax 832-2621, 3a Avenida Nte 4)* is like a museum where you get to spend the night. Each of the eight rooms is packed with Guatemalan antiques and laid with terra cotta tile, giving this place a historic, quirky ambience. The unique rooms, all with private hot bath and cable TV, cost US$36/46/56. Guests have use of the kitchen and rooftop terrace.

El Carmen Hotel (☎ 832-3850/1/2/3, fax 832-3847, 3a Avenida Nte 9) is tidy and quiet despite its location only 1½ blocks from the square. Twelve pleasant rooms with cable TV, phone, private bath and continental breakfast are US$44/50/60 for one to three beds. The hotel has a Jacuzzi, a courtyard sitting area and a rooftop terrace with a fine view.

La Casa de la Música (☎ 832-0335, fax 832-3690, ginger@guate.net, www.lacasade lamusica.centramerica.com, 7a Calle Pte 3) is a charming B&B with patios, fountains, gardens and a roof terrace. Rates for the five rooms and one suite range from US$125 to US$264 single or double per week, including a fabulous breakfast daily. A one-week minimum stay is required. This place is very kid-friendly.

The beautiful *Hotel Aurora (☎ 832-0217, 4a Calle Ote 16)* has a grassy courtyard graced by a fountain and flowers. Its 17 old-

fashioned rooms with bath are US$40/50/60 single/double/triple, including continental breakfast. Private parking available.
Hotel Convento Santa Catalina (☎ 832-3080, fax 832-3079, 5a Avenida Nte 28), just south of the arch, is a nicely renovated convent around a courtyard. Large rooms with bath, cable TV and telephone are US$50/72/82 single/double/triple, though you may be paying more for the history than the comfort at this price.

Top End
The beautiful *Mesón Panza Verde (☎ 832-2925, fax 832-1745, mpv@infovia.com.gt, 5a Avenida Sur 19)*, four blocks south of the park, is an elegant American-owned guesthouse with comfy, quiet rooms, each with its own private garden. Standard rooms are US$57 single or double, and suites with fireplace are US$100. The atmosphere and restaurant here are among the best in Antigua.

Hotel Quinta de las Flores (☎ 832-3721, fax 832-3726, Calle del Hermano Pedro 6) is a special place. The spacious grounds have beautiful gardens and fountains, a children's play area, swimming pool, sitting areas and a restaurant. The eight large, luxurious rooms, most with fireplace, are US$54/66 single/double. Five two-story houses, each with two bedrooms, a kitchen and living room, rent for US$120 for up to five people. Considerable discounts are offered if you stay by the week.

The new *Hotel Casa Azul (☎ 832-0961/2, fax 832-0944, 4a Avenida Nte 5)* is a gem. The upstairs units (US$90 double) are spectacular; each has sweeping views, a luxurious bath, telephone and minibar. Some have a fireplace. The downstairs rooms (US$78 double) are just as impressive but have no views. Amenities include a pool, Jacuzzi and sauna. Rates include breakfast.

The Cloister (☎ /fax 832-0712, cloister@ mailzone.com, www.thecloister.com, 5a Avenida Nte 23) is a renovated 16th-century cloister and one of the most romantic and exclusive hotels in Antigua. Bubbling fountains highlight the horticultural triumph that is the courtyard, and guests will likely spend a lot of time relaxing here. All rooms have antique furniture, bath, fireplace and library. Standard rooms cost US$90 single or double; suites are US$110/115/120 single/double/triple. All prices include breakfast. For reservations and information in the USA write: A-0026, PO Box 669004, Miami Springs, FL 33266.

Hotel Casa Santo Domingo (☎ 832-0140, 832-2628, fax 832-0102, 3a Calle Ote 28) is a wonderful luxury hotel set in the partially restored 1642 convent of Santo Domingo, which takes up an entire city block. Rooms are of an international five-star standard, but the public spaces are wonderfully colonial and include a swimming pool. Weekday rates are US$108 for one or two people, or US$136 for three; on weekends rates rise to US$125/146.

Hotel Antigua (☎ 832-2801/2/3/4, fax 832-0807, hainfo@hotelant.com.gt, 8a Calle Pte 1) is a large Spanish-colonial country club. The 60 rooms have private baths and fireplaces, and many have two double beds. Rates are US$102/114/126 single/double/triple; higher during Semana Santa and New Year's.

The five-star *Radisson Villa Antigua Resort & Conference Center* (☎ 832-0011, fax 832-0237, in the USA ☎ 800-333-3333, radisson@infovia.com.gt), Calle Sucia at Carretera a Ciudad Vieja, is the town's largest and most modern hotel, with 139 rooms and 45 suites. Rooms have balconies, fireplaces and modern baths, and the complex has every amenity. Rooms range from US$90 to US$180, depending on room size and location, time of the year and whether meals are included.

PLACES TO EAT
Budget
Eating cheaply is easy, even in touristy Antigua. Probably the cheapest food in town is the tasty fare served from midmorning to early evening at the stands on 4a Calle Pte, a block west of the park.

Restaurante Gran Muralla (4a Calle Pte 18) is a simple, inexpensive place serving a Guatemalan version of Chinese food. Perhaps better for Chinese food is *La Estrella* across the street, which has some of the most efficient, friendly service anywhere.

One of Antigua's best-known eateries is *Restaurant Doña Luisa Xicotencatl* (4a Calle Ote 12), 1½ blocks east of Parque Central. Tables are set around the central courtyard, with more on the upper level. The menu lists a dozen sandwiches (made with handmade bread), as well as yogurt, chili, burgers, stuffed potatoes, cakes and pies, all priced under US$4. Alcohol is served, as is excellent Antiguan coffee. The restaurant is open 7 am to 9:30 pm daily and is usually busy. The bakery here sells many kinds of breads, including whole-grain.

Rainbow Reading Room & Cafe, 7a Avenida Sur at 6a Calle Pte, is a lending library, bookstore, travelers' club and restaurant all in one. Healthy vegetarian dishes are a specialty, as is close camaraderie. The café is open 9 am to 11 pm daily.

Café Condesa, on the plaza's west side (walk through the Librería Casa del Conde bookstore to the rear), is a beautiful restaurant in the courtyard of an opulent Spanish mansion built in 1549. On the menu are excellent breakfasts, coffee, light meals and snacks. The Sunday buffet from 10 am to 2 pm, a lavish spread for US$6, is an Antigua institution. The café is open daily. For a quick java fix, hit the *Café Condesa Express*, next door; it's open 6:45 am to 7:45 pm daily.

La Fuente (4a Calle Ote 14) is another beautiful restaurant in the courtyard of an old Spanish home. The menu features lots of vegetarian selections, good coffee and desserts. Hours are 7 am to 7 pm daily. *Café Sol* (1a Calle Pte 9), opposite La Merced church, is a smaller, simpler, inexpensive patio restaurant with decent breakfasts.

Numerous restaurants line 5a Avenida Nte, north of Parque Central. *Asados de la Calle del Arco*, just off the park, has a simple but beautiful atmosphere, with candlelight in the evening and tables both inside and out on the back patio. It serves grilled meats and Tex-Mex food, though portions are small. Hours are 7 am to 10 pm daily. A second branch is farther north up 5a Avenida Nte, beside the Hotel Convento Santa Catalina.

La Fonda de la Calle Real *(5a Avenida Nte 5)* serves good and varied food in its upstairs dining room. The house specialty is *caldo real*, a hearty chicken soup that makes a filling meal (US$3.50). Grilled meats, *queso fundido* (melted cheese), *chiles rellenos* and nachos are priced from US$3 to US$8. The restaurant is open 7 am to 10 pm daily. Around the corner, *La Fonda de la Calle Real No 2* *(3a Calle Pte 7)* has the same menu and is open noon to 10 pm daily.

La Cenicienta Pasteles *(5a Avenida Nte 7)* serves mostly cakes, pastries, pies and coffee, but the blackboard menu often features yogurt, fruit, quiche lorraine and quiche chapín (Guatemalan-style) as well. A slice of something and a hot beverage will cost less than US$2. It's open daily. *Cookies Etc*, on 3a Avenida Nte at 4a Calle Ote, is another good place for sweets; it opens at 8 am daily and serves bottomless cups of coffee with breakfast. *The Bagel Barn*, on 5a Calle Pte just off the Parque Central, is popular for bagels, soups and coffee.

Near the arch, *Restaurante/Bar Frida's* *(☎ 832-0504, 5a Avenida Nte 29)* serves good Mexican fare and is jumping most evenings, sometimes with live music. It's open 12:30 pm to midnight daily. Nearby *Punto Internacional* *(5a Avenida Nte 35)* has been recommended by readers, as has *Su Chow* *(5a Avenida Nte 36)*, a Chinese place open late at night. Also on this strip is *Queso y Vino* *(5a Avenida Nte 32)*, a good choice for Italian food.

The best place in Antigua for breakfast is *Restaurante El Capuchino* *(6a Avenida Nte 10)*, where everything costs US$1.75. Check out the tasty omelet made with real cheese, olive oil and bell peppers. To top it off, the restaurant has an all-you-can-drink coffee policy. It's open 7 am to 10 pm daily except Monday and also serves lunch and dinner. The best coffee in town is at *Tostaduría Antigua* *(6a Avenida Sur 12A)*.

Antigua has an outlet of *Restaurante Piccadilly* *(4a Calle Pte 17)*, serving up the three p's: pasta, pollo and pizza. Two blocks away is *Cadejo's* *(6a Avenida Sur 1A)*, a popular place for pizza and beer; occasionally it presents live music. Also serving pizza is *Caffé-Pizzeria Asjemenou* *(5a Calle Pte 4)*. Some think this is the best pizza in town. It's open 7 am to 10 pm daily.

One of the current hot spots for good food and camaraderie is *La Escudilla* *(4a Avenida Nte 4)*. This place features simple, well-prepared meals and a set special for under US$3. Also here is Riki's Bar (see Entertainment). Another leader in the popularity contest is *Menu Viajero* *(6a Calle Pte 14A)*, which serves big plates of stir-fry or noodles, vegetarian or carnivore style, for as little as US$2.

Café Flor *(4a Avenida Sur 1)* serves huge portions of delicious food including Thai, Indonesian, Chinese and Indian dishes, each for around US$5. One dish can easily feed two people. Takeout is available. It's open 11 am to 11 pm Tuesday to Sunday; Friday and Saturday until midnight. The *Café Masala* *(6a Avenida Nte 14A)*, near 4a Calle Pte, has been recommended for Thai and Japanese food. It's open noon to 10 pm daily except Wednesday. Along the same pan-Asian gastronomic lines is *Cafe Rocio* *(6a Avenida Nte 34)*, which has a romantic garden area. It's open 7:30 am to 9:30 pm daily.

La Taquiza *(☎ 832-1560, 6a Avenida Nte 19)* serves fresh, satisfying meals combining Mexican and Guatemalan flavors. The atmosphere is relaxed and the service is friendly. For German food, try *Café Weiner* *(Alameda de Santa Lucía Portal 8)*, which boasts Antigua's only superschnitzel. The café makes decent breakfasts and has a patio upstairs.

If you're craving Japanese food, head straight to *Yoshino* *(☎ 832-6766, 5a Calle Pte 17A)*. Choose from sushi, tempura, teriyaki and more; the daily special includes soup, salad, appetizer and a main dish for US$4. It's open 12:30 to 4:30 pm and 6 to 9:30 pm Tuesday to Saturday, 12:30 to 3:30 pm Sunday.

Tierra Cero *(6a Calle Pte 7)* is a casual place set around a courtyard. The menu includes good salads and other veggie options.

GUATEMALA

Also here are a cinema, book exchange, internet café and bike rentals. *La India Misteriosa* *(3a Avenida Sur 4)* is recommended for vegetarian fare.

For good Italian food try *Restaurante y Pizzería Italiana Catari (6a Avenida Nte 52)*, opposite La Merced church. It's run by well-known chef Martedino Castrovinci. From noon to 4 pm the enormous lunch special is US$3, including beverage. Open daily.

Monoloco (2a Avenida Nte 6B), an upstairs restaurant/bar, serves tasty burgers, burritos and similar pub food for around US$3.50. This is a popular gathering place, with microbrews on tap and two satellite TVs showing the likes of the Rugby World Cup and the World Series. There's a great book swap too.

Antigua has two *Pollo Campero* outlets. The one by the bus terminal has a playground and is a favorite with kids.

Panificadora Columbia (4a Calle Pte 34) is a good stop for breads, coffee and breakfast before boarding the 7 am luxury bus to Panajachel (see Getting There & Away). Across the street, *La Bodegona* is a full-blown megamarket selling everything from underwear to bottled water.

Mid-Range

The dining room in the *Posada de Don Rodrigo (☎ 832-0291, 832-0387, 5a Avenida Nte 17)* is one of the city's most pleasant and popular places for lunch or dinner. Order the house favorite, the Plato Chapín (a platter of Guatemalan specialties), for US$11. A marimba band plays from noon to 4 pm and 7 to 9 pm daily.

The restaurant at *Mesón Panza Verde (☎ 832-2925, 5a Avenida Sur 19)* serves excellent continental cuisine in an appealing Antiguan atmosphere. The chef is Swiss, the food is divine, and the prices are moderate – about US$18 per person for a full dinner. *Café Terraza* is also here.

The owners of perennial favorite Frida's have recently opened *Medusa's (☎ 832-6951, 2a Avenida Sur 12)*, a ceviche and sushi place. The warm, comfortable restaurant does good seafood and snacks. Happy hour, from 7 to 10 pm daily, features free appetizers with each cocktail.

Doña María Gordillo Dulces Típicos (4a Calle Ote 11) is filled with traditional Guatemalan sweets for take-out, and a crowd of *antigüeños* often lines up to do just that. Local handicrafts are also sold here.

Top End

El Sereno (☎ 832-0501, 4a Avenida Sur 9) is Antigua's most exclusive restaurant. A colonial home has been nicely restored and modernized somewhat to provide a traditional wooden bar, plant-filled court and several small dining rooms hung with paintings. Cuisine is international, leaning heavily on French dishes; the menu changes weekly. The short wine list is good but expensive. Expect to pay US$17 to US$30 per person for dinner; reservations are recommended. It's open noon to 3 pm and 6:30 to 10 pm daily.

For steaks, head to *Las Antorchas (☎ 832-0806, 3a Avenida Sur 1)*, which has a beautiful courtyard to go with its mouthwatering beef. Open for breakfast, lunch and dinner daily.

The restaurant at the luxurious *Hotel Casa Santo Domingo* (see Places to Stay) is another beautiful spot for a splurge, with tables inside and out in the garden.

ENTERTAINMENT

Antigua has no shortage of nightlife, but weekends can be a bit crazed, as revelers pour in from Guatemala City for some action. In many cases, the bar with the most economical happy hour is the most popular; cocktail fans will have no trouble getting a bargain buzz here.

Bars & Discos

The town's hottest spot for chilling and swilling is *Riki's Bar (4a Avenida Nte 4)*, which attracts a hip crowd of locals and travelers. The big courtyard, decent food and low-key *Paris Bar Exclusivo* in the rear all make for a good night out. Another spot popular with students and Peace Corps types is *Monoloco* (see Places to Eat). Big sporting events are screened here.

La Chimenea, on the corner of 7a Avenida Nte and 2a Calle Pte, is a travelers' hangout with a decent happy hour from 6 to 9 pm. Down the block, *Latinos* is rougher around the edges, which may be just what you need if you've been in Antigua awhile.

El Atico (*5a Avenida Nte 29*), upstairs from Frida's, is a laid-back bar with a good pool table. Across the street, the *Macondo Pub* can be bustling or empty depending on when you turn up.

For dancing, try *La Casbah* (*5a Avenida Nte 30*), near Asados de la Calle del Arco restaurant and the Santa Catalina arch. It's open 7 pm to 1 am Wednesday to Saturday. This disco is quite a party most nights, but Thursday is gay night – the best time to drop in and boogie. *El Afro* (*6a Calle Pte 9*) is the place to go salsa dancing. It's open 6 pm to 1 am Tuesday to Sunday, but things don't heat up until around 10 pm.

Movies & Slide Shows

One of Antigua's most pleasant forms of entertainment is video-watching at cinema houses, where you can see a wide variety of international films. Try one of the following:

Cine Café 7a Calle Pte 22

Cinema Bistro 5a Avenida Sur 14

Cinema Tecún Umán 6a Calle Pte 34A

Cinemaya 6a Calle Pte 7

Proyecto Cultural El Sitio 5a Calle Pte 15

Most show several films a day, with the films changing daily; admission is around US$1.50. Check schedules posted at the door, or look for flyers advertising schedules around town.

Proyecto Cultural El Sitio (☎ 832-3037) also presents a variety of cultural events including live theater, concerts, video films and art exhibitions. Stop by to check the schedule, or look in the *Revue* monthly magazine for shows here and at other local venues.

Elizabeth Bell gives a fascinating slide show about Antigua called 'Behind the Walls' from 6 to 7 pm on Tuesday at the Christian Spanish Academy (see Language Courses, earlier in this chapter); US$2.50.

SHOPPING

Vendors flood Antigua to satisfy tourists' desires for colorful Guatemalan woven goods and other handicrafts. The sleepy **Mercado de Artesanías**, on the town's west side by the bus station, has plenty to choose from. A number of shops are on 4a Calle Pte, in the blocks between Parque Central and the market. And look for outdoor markets at the corner of 6a Calle Ote and 2a Avenida Sur, and at 4a Calle Pte at 7a Avenida Nte.

Be aware that prices for handicrafts tend to be much higher in Antigua than elsewhere in Guatemala. For a better selection at cheaper prices, try the markets in Chichicastenango, Panajachel and Guatemala City. Whenever buying handicrafts, be sure to bargain.

Antigua has several shops specializing in jade, including La Casa de Jade, 4a Calle Ote 3; Jades, SA, 4a Calle Ote 34; and the Jade Kingdom, 4a Avenida Nte 10. These places offer free tours of the jade factories behind their showrooms. Jades, SA has interesting exhibits and is open daily.

Galería El Sitio, 5a Calle Pte 15 (at the Proyecto Cultural El Sitio), specializes in paintings by modern Guatemalan artists. Ring the bell for admission. A number of other interesting galleries are along 4a Calle Ote, in the blocks to the east of Parque Central.

Nim Po't, 5a Avenida Nte 29, boasts 'the world's largest retail collection of Maya dress,' a claim hard to refute. This sprawling space is packed with traditional *huipiles, cortes, fajas* and more, all arranged according to region, so it makes for a fascinating visit whether you're buying or not. If you're pressed for time, this is a great place for one-stop shopping. It's open 9 am to 9 pm daily. Another intriguing place to buy textiles is Casa del Tejido Antiguo, 1a Calle Pte 51, which is like a museum, market and workshop rolled into one. It's open 8 am to 5 pm daily; US$0.65.

For coffee, head over to the Tostaduría Antigua (see Places to Eat), where a pound of beans, freshly roasted to your specifications, costs about US$3.

The Tabaquería Unicornio, 4a Calle Pte 38, sells a variety of fine tobacco, including Cuban cigars, as well as cigarettes and loose tobacco such as Drum and American Spirit.

GETTING THERE & AROUND
Bus
Buses arrive and depart from a large open lot beyond the market, on the town's west side. Bus connections with Guatemala City are frequent, and one direct bus daily runs to Panajachel. To reach other highland towns such as Chichicastenango, Quetzaltenango and Huehuetenango, or Panajachel at any other time of day, take one of the frequent buses to Chimaltenango, on the Interamericana, and catch an onward bus from there. Or take a bus heading toward Guatemala City, get off at San Lucas Sacatepéquez and change buses there – this takes a little more time, but it's a good road, and since you'll be boarding the bus closer to the capital you're more likely to get a seat (important if you want to avoid the possibility of standing for several hours).

Buses to outlying villages such as Santa María de Jesús (US$0.25, 30 minutes) and San Antonio Aguas Calientes (US$0.20, 25 minutes) depart from the bus area behind the market. It's best to make your outward trip early in the morning, returning by midafternoon, as bus services drop off dramatically as late afternoon approaches.

Chimaltenango US$0.30, one hour, 19km. Buses every 15 minutes, 6 am to 6 pm.

Escuintla US$0.65, 2½ hours, 102km. Two buses daily, 7 am and 1 pm.

Guatemala City US$0.50, one hour, 45km. Buses every 15 minutes, 4 am to 7 pm, stopping in San Lucas Sacatepéquez.

Panajachel US$3.25, 2½ hours, 146km. One *especial* bus daily, 7 am, departs from Hotel Backpacker's Place. Or take a bus to Chimaltenango and change there to a bus bound for Los Encuentros, Sololá or Panajachel. One of these buses passes every 20 minutes or so. The entire trip costs US$2.50 and takes longer.

Shuttle Minibus
Numerous travel agencies offer frequent and convenient shuttle services to places tourists go, including Guatemala City, La Aurora International Airport, Panajachel and Chichi. They also go less frequently (usually on weekends) to places further afield such as Río Dulce, Copán Ruinas (Honduras) and Monterrico. These services cost a lot more than ordinary buses (for example, from US$5 to US$10 to Guatemala City, as opposed to US$0.50 on a chicken bus), but they are comfortable and convenient, with door-to-door service on both ends. For recommendations, see Travel Agencies, earlier in the chapter.

Car & Motorcycle
Rental companies in Antigua include the following:

Ahorrent (☎ 832-0968, ahorrent@infovia.com.gt, www.infovia.com.gt/ahorrent), 5a Calle Ote 11B

Moto Servicio Antigua (☎ 511-8932), Carretera a Ciudad Vieja 90; rents motorcycles only

Sears Motorcycle Rental (☎ 832-6203), 3a Avenida Nte 3

Tabarini (☎/fax 832-3091, tabarini@centramerica .com, www.centramerica.com/tabarini), 2a Calle Pte 19A; Hotel Radisson Villa Antigua (☎/fax 832-7450)

Taxi
Taxis congregate at the bus station and on the east side of Parque Central. A ride in town costs around US$1.75.

Inexpensive buses run between Antigua and outlying areas.

TONY WHEELER

The Highlands

Guatemala's most dramatic region, the highlands stretch from Antigua to the Mexican border northwest of Huehuetenango. Here the verdant hills sport emerald green grass, cornfields and towering stands of pine, and every town and village has a story to tell.

The traditional values and customs of Guatemala's indigenous peoples are strongest in the highlands. Mayan dialects are the first language, Spanish a distant second. The age-old culture based on maize (corn) is still

Highlights

- Hiking, shopping, scuba diving, horseback riding, kayaking or plain chilling out on majestic Lago de Atitlán

- Shopping at the notoriously grand market in Chichicastenango

- Visiting the hot springs, steam baths, volcanic lakes and traditional towns near Quetzaltenango

- Exploring the Cuchumatanes Mountains

alive; a sturdy cottage set in the midst of a thriving *milpa* (cornfield) is a common sight, one as old as Maya culture itself. And on every road you'll see men, women and children carrying burdensome loads of *leña* (firewood), to be used for heating and cooking.

Visitors flock here, but the topography keeps certain places tucked away. If you visit during the rainy season, May to October, be prepared for some dreary, chilly, damp days; the region's lush vegetation comes from abundant rain. But when the sun comes out, this land is glorious to behold.

If you have only three or four days to spend in the highlands, spend them in Antigua, Panajachel and Chichicastenango. With more time you can make your way to Quetzaltenango and nearby sights such as Zunil, Fuentes Georginas, San Francisco El Alto, Momostenango and Totonicapán. Villages high in the Cuchumatanes Mountains north of Huehuetenango offer stellar scenery and adventures for intrepid travelers. Huehuetenango and the ruins nearby at Zaculeu are worth a visit if you're passing through or if you have lots of time.

Studying Spanish in this part of the country is increasingly popular. You'll find schools in Huehuetenango, Todos Santos, Quetzaltenango and around Lago de Atitlán.

Warning

Though most visitors never experience any trouble, there have been reported incidents of robbery, rape and murder of tourists in the highlands. These have occurred on trails up the volcanoes, on the outskirts of Chichicastenango and at lonely spots along country roads. Attacks are random. If you use caution and common sense and don't do much roaming or driving at night, you should have a fabulous time in this beautiful region. Traveling on chicken buses and pickups instead of tourist shuttles will make you less of a target.

Before traveling in the highlands, contact your embassy or consulate in Guatemala City for information on the current situation and advice on where to travel. Don't rely on local authorities for safety advice, as they may downplay the dangers. For a list of embassy phone numbers, see the Facts for the Visitor chapter.

Getting There & Around

The Interamericana, also known as Centroamérica 1 (CA-1), passes through the highlands on its way between Guatemala City and the Mexican border at La Mesilla. It's a curvy mountain road that must be negotiated slowly in many places. Driving the 266km between Guatemala City and Huehuetenango can take five hours, but the time passes pleasantly amid the beautiful scenery. The lower-elevation Carretera al Pacífico (CA-2), via Escuintla and Retalhuleu, is straighter and faster, and it's the better route if you're trying to reach Mexico as quickly as possible.

CA-1 is thick with bus traffic; for bus departures, refer to specific destinations in the Getting There & Around chapter. As most

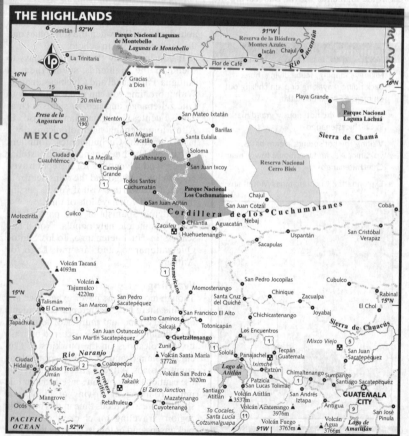

THE HIGHLANDS

of the places you'll want to reach are some distance off the Interamericana, you may find yourself waiting at major highway junctions such as Los Encuentros and Cuatro Caminos to connect with the right bus or a pickup. Travel is easiest on market days and in the morning. By mid- or late afternoon, buses may be difficult to find, and short-distance local traffic stops by dinnertime. You should follow suit. On remote routes, you'll probably be relying more on pickups than buses for transportation.

Lago de Atitlán

One of the most spectacular locales in Central America, Lago de Atitlán is a caldera (collapsed volcanic cone) filled with shimmering waters to a maximum depth of more than 320m. The lake covers an area of 128 sq km and is surrounded by fertile hills dotted with color. Three powerful volcanoes – Volcán Tolimán (3158m), Volcán Atitlán (3537m), and Volcán San Pedro (3020m) – loom over the entire landscape.

The lake is often still and beautiful early in the day. By noon the Xocomil, a south-easterly wind, may have risen to ruffle the surface, sometimes violently, making it a tough crossing for the small motorboats plying the shores.

Getting There & Away

Following CA-1 32km west from Chimaltenango, you'll reach the turnoff for the back road to Lago de Atitlán via Patzicía and Patzún. The area around these two towns has been notable for high levels of guerrilla and bandit activity in the past, so it's advisable to stay on the Interamericana to Tecpán Guatemala, the starting point for a visit to the ruined Cakchiquel capital city of Iximché.

Another 40km west along the Interamericana from Tecpán, is the **Los Encuentros** highway junction. A nascent town here serves all the people waiting to catch buses. The road to the right heads north to Chichicastenango and Santa Cruz del Quiché. From the Interamericana a road to the left

descends 12km to Sololá and another 8km to Panajachel, on the shores of Lago de Atitlán.

If you are not on a direct bus to these places, you can get off at Los Encuentros and catch another bus or minibus, or flag a pickup, from here down to Panajachel or up to Chichicastenango; it's a half-hour ride to either place.

The road from Sololá descends through pine forests, losing more than 500 meters in elevation on its 8km course to Panajachel. Sit on the right for breathtaking views of the lake and volcanoes.

IXIMCHÉ

Off CA-1 near the small dusty town of Tecpán Guatemala lie the ruins of Iximché (pronounced **eesh**-im-chay), capital of the Cakchiquel Maya. Set on a flat promontory surrounded by steep cliffs, Iximché (founded in the late 15th century) was easily defended against attack by the hostile Quiché Maya.

When the conquistadors arrived in 1524, the Cakchiquel formed an alliance with them against the Quiché and the Tz'utuhils. The Spaniards set up their headquarters next door to the Cakchiquel capital at Tecpán Guatemala, but Spanish demands for gold and other loot soured the alliance; the Cakchiquel were defeated in the ensuing battles.

Entering Tecpán, you'll see signs pointing to the unpaved road leading less than 6km south through fields and pine forests to Iximché. You can walk the distance, see the ruins and rest, then walk back to Tecpán in around three hours. If you do walk, do it in the morning so you can get back to the highway by early afternoon, before bus traffic dwindles.

The archaeological site has a small museum, four ceremonial plazas surrounded by grass-covered temple structures, and ball courts. Some of the structures have been cleaned and maintained; on a few the original plaster coating is still in place, and some traces of the original paint are visible. The site is open 9 am to 4 pm daily; US$3.25.

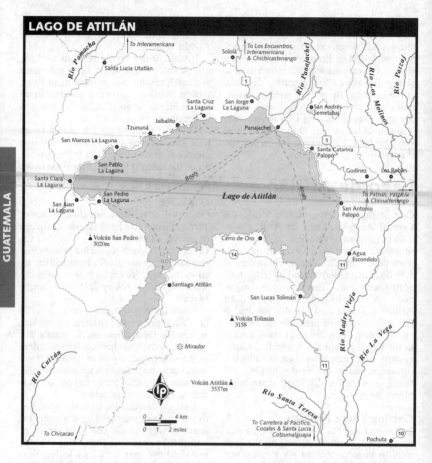

LAGO DE ATITLÁN

Tecpán has a couple of basic hotels and small eateries. Transportes Poaquileña runs buses between Tecpán and Guatemala City (1½ hours, 87km) every half hour, from 3 am to 5 pm eastbound and from 5 am to 7:30 pm westbound.

SOLOLÁ
• population 9000 • elevation 2110m

Sololá lies along trade routes between the *tierra caliente* (hot lands of the Pacific Slope) and *tierra fría* (the chilly highlands). All the traders meet here, and Sololá's big Friday market – a local, rather than a tourist, affair –

is one of the highlands' best. The plaza next to the cathedral comes ablaze with the colorful costumes of people from a dozen surrounding villages, and neatly arranged displays of meat, vegetables, fruit, housewares and clothing occupy every available space.

Every Sunday morning the officers of the traditional religious brotherhoods *(cofradías)* parade ceremoniously to the cathedral for their devotions. On other days, Sololá sleeps.

It's a pleasant walk from Sololá down to the lake, whether on the highway to Panajachel (9km) or on the path to Santa Cruz La Laguna (10km).

PANAJACHEL
• population 5000 • elevation 1560m

Nicknamed Gringotenango (Place of the Foreigners) by locals and foreigners alike, Pana is one of Guatemala's oldest tourist hangouts. In the hippie heyday of the 1960s and '70s, it was crowded with laid-back travelers in semipermanent exile. When the civil war made Panajachel a dangerous – or at least unpleasant – place to be in the late '70s and early '80s, many moved on. But the town's tourist industry is booming again and has even spread to lakeside villages.

Several different cultures mingle on the dusty streets of Panajachel: Ladinos and gringos control the tourist industry. The Cakchiquel and Tz'utuhil Maya from surrounding villages come to sell their handicrafts to tourists. The lakeside villa owners drive up on weekends from Guatemala City. Group tourists descend on the town by bus for a few hours, a day or overnight. And you'll still see hippies with long hair, bare feet, local dress and Volkswagen minibuses. The town itself is a small, not particularly attractive place that has developed haphazardly according to the demands of the tourist trade. But you need only go down to the lakeshore to understand why Pana attracts so many visitors.

Information

Tourist Offices The INGUAT tourist office (☎ 762-1392) is in the Edificio Rincón Sai on Calle Santander. It's supposedly open 8 am to 1 pm and 2 to 5 pm daily. An information-challenged tourist booth is near the bus stop.

Money Banco Industrial, on Calle Santander, changes US dollars cash and traveler's checks, gives cash advances on Visa cards and has an ATM. Banco Inmobiliario, on the corner of Calles Santander and Real, also changes money and maintains longer hours. BAM, on the same corner, changes money and is an agent for Western Union. The Bancared ATM at Calle Real 0-78 accepts Visa cards.

You can also change cash and traveler's checks at the INGUAT tourist office and at Hotel Regis, both on Calle Santander. The hotel will give cash advances on Visa and MasterCard, as will the adjacent Servicios Turísticos Atitlán (☎ 762-2075), for a 10% commission.

Post The post office is on the corner of Calles Santander and 15 de Febrero. Get Guated Out (☎ 762-0595, fax 762-2015, gguated@ quetzal.net), on Avenida Los Árboles, can ship your letters and parcels by air freight or international courier. They will also buy handicrafts for you and ship them for export – handy if you can't come to Panajachel yourself. Email services are also available here.

DHL has a drop-off location on Calle Santander in the complex with INGUAT. It's open 9 am to 6 pm Monday to Friday and 9 am to 1 pm Saturday.

Telephone The Telgua office on Calle Santander is open daily. Many other places along Calle Santander offer the same services cheaper. Check the ubiquitous travel agencies for phone, fax and email services.

Email & Internet Access As you'd expect given Pana's hip, international tenor, many places offer Internet access; the going rate is about US$1.50 an hour. MayaNet on Calle Santander, across from Hotel Regis, is open 9 am to 9 pm Monday to Saturday, 2:30 to 8 pm Sunday. Just down the block, adjacent to the Telgua office, is c@fe.net, open 9 am to 9 pm daily. Internet Access, in El Patio complex on Calle Santander, is another option.

Travel Agencies Full-service travel agencies offering trips, tours and shuttle buses are strung along Calle Santander. Among them are:

Rainbow Travel Center (☎ 762-1301/2/3, myers@ gua.gbm.net), Calle Santander, opposite the BAM bank

Toliman Excursions (☎/fax 762-2455, globalnet@ guate.net), Calle Santander 1-77

Transportes Turísticos ATITRANS (☎ 762-2336, 762-0146), Calle Santander, next to INGUAT

Travel Agency San Nicolas (☎ 762-0382, fax 762-0391), Calle Santander, next to Hotel Dos Mundos

PANAJACHEL

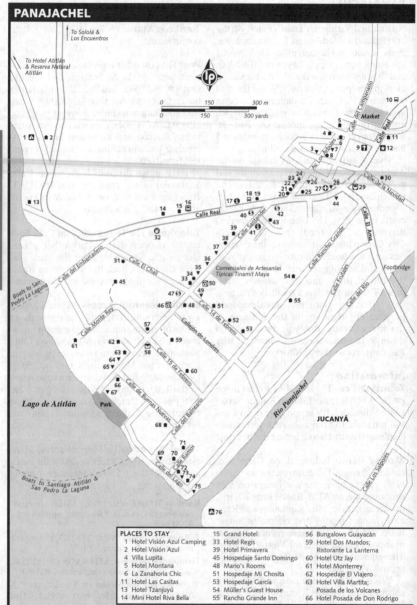

To Sololá &
Los Encuentros

To Hotel Atitlán
& Reserva Natural
Atitlán

Market

Calle del Campanario

Calle Real

Av Los Árboles

Calle de la Navidad

Boats to San
Pedro La Laguna

Calle del Embarcadero

Calle El Chali

Calle Real

Calle Santander

Comerciales de Artesanías
Típicas Tinamit Maya

Calle Rancho Grande

Calle El Amá

Calle Erutales

Calle del Río

Footbridge

Calle Monte Rey

Callejón de Londres

Calle 14 de Febrero

Calle 15 de Febrero

Río Panajachel

JUCANYÁ

Lago de Atitlán

Park

Calle de Buenas Nuevas

Calle del Balneario

Calle Ramos

Calle del Lago

Boats to Santiago Atitlán &
San Pedro La Laguna

Calle Los Salpores

PLACES TO STAY		
1 Hotel Visión Azul Camping	15 Grand Hotel	56 Bungalows Guayacán
2 Hotel Visión Azul	33 Hotel Regis	59 Hotel Dos Mundos;
4 Villa Lupita	39 Hotel Primavera	Ristorante La Lanterna
5 Hotel Montana	45 Hospedaje Santo Domingo	60 Hotel Utz Jay
6 La Zanahoria Chic	48 Mario's Rooms	61 Hotel Monterrey
11 Hotel Las Casitas	51 Hospedaje Mi Chosita	62 Hospedaje El Viajero
13 Hotel Tzanjuyú	53 Hospedaje García	63 Hotel Villa Martita;
14 Mini Hotel Riva Bella	54 Müller's Guest House	Posada de los Volcanes
	55 Rancho Grande Inn	66 Hotel Posada de Don Rodrigo

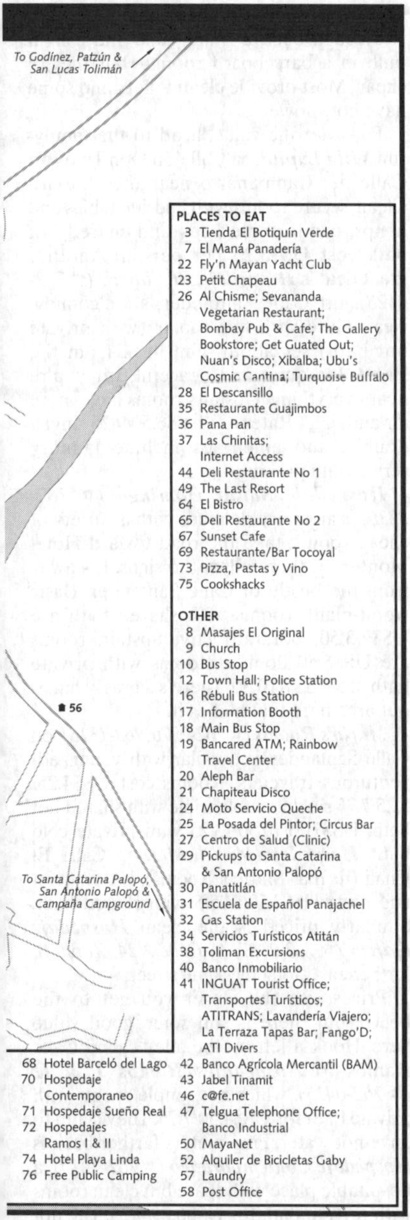

To Godínez, Patzún &
San Lucas Tolimán

☎ 56

To Santa Catarina Palopó,
San Antonio Palopó &
Campaña Campground

Bookstores Owner/author Jake Horsley vows to make Xibalba, in the Centro Comercial on Avenida Los Árboles, the best used bookstore in Central America. It's open 10 am to 7 pm daily and is a fun place to kick back.

Upstairs in the same complex is The Gallery Bookstore (☎ 762-0595, fax 762-2015), which sells new and used books and offers telephone/fax and travel service.

Laundry Among the handful of laundries in Pana is Lavandería Viajero, on Calle Santander in the complex with INGUAT; open 8 am to 6 pm daily.

Things to See & Do

One of Guatemala's most extensive **handicrafts** markets is the local Comerciales de Artesanías Típicas Tinamit Maya, on Calle Santander. It's got dozens of stalls, and you can get good deals if you're patient and bargain. Open 7 am to 7 pm daily.

The **Reserva Natural Atitlán** (☎ 762-2565) is down the spur leading to Hotel Atitlán and makes a good day trip. The well-designed nature reserve has trails, an interpretive center, butterfly farm, small shade coffee plantation, lots of monkeys and an aviary. It's open 8 am to 5 pm daily; US$3.

Lago de Atitlán offers phenomenal **hiking and biking** in a fantastic setting. You can walk from Panajachel to the lakeside village of Santa Catarina in about an hour, continuing to San Antonio in about another hour; it takes only half as long by bicycle, on hilly roads. Or take a bike on a boat to Santiago, San Pedro or another village to start a tour of the lake. Several places along Calle Santander rent bicycles; rates start around US$2.50 per half day. Equipment varies, so check out your bike before pedaling off.

ATI Divers (☎ 762-2646, santacruz@ guate.net, www.atidivers.com), on Calle Santander near INGUAT, leads **dive trips** from Santa Cruz La Laguna (see that section later in this chapter). A four-day PADI certification course costs US$160. The best time to dive here is between May and October, when the water is clear.

GUATEMALA

Visitors short on time are encouraged to take a **boat tour** to various towns around the lake. A typical tour lasts around seven hours and visits San Pedro, Santiago and San Antonio for US$7, depending on how many people are going. To arrange a tour, head to the pier at the foot of Calle del Balneario and start bargaining. Most travel agencies also arrange boat tours, which may include weaving demonstrations and visits to coffee plantations or the shrine of Maximón in Santiago.

Language Courses

Spanish courses are available from the Escuela de Español Panajachel (☎ 762-2637, fax 762-0092, nicholas_tr@latinmail.com), on Calle El Chali; the current favorite Jabel Tinamit (☎ 762-0238, spanishschool@hotmail.com), just off Calle Santander before INGUAT; and Panatitlán (☎ 762-0319, panatitlan@yahoo.com), Calle de la Navidad 0-40. Panatitlán will send the teacher to you, so you can study in the lakeside village of your choice. The cost for 30 hours of one-on-one study a week, including a homestay with a local family, is around US$130 per week.

Places to Stay – Budget

Camping A free public campground lies on the beach to the east side of Río Panajachel's mouth in Jucanyá. The site is more like a dirt patch than a campground, and safety can be a problem. A safer alternative is the campground on the spacious lakeside lawn at the *Hotel Visión Azul* (☎ 762-1426, ☎/fax 762-1419), on the town's western outskirts. It has electrical and water hookups for campers; US$1.50 per person, plus US$5 per tent and US$2.50 per vehicle.

Even better for its price and vibe is *Campaña Campground* (☎ 762-2479), on the road to Santa Catarina Palopó. For US$2 you can pitch a tent and use the kitchen. Amenities include a book exchange, luggage storage and pickup from Pana with advance notice.

Hospedajes & Hotels Low-budget travelers here will rejoice at the profusion of little family-run *hospedajes* (pensions).

They're as simple as they come – perhaps two rough beds, a small table and a light bulb in a bare board room – but they're cheap. Most provide clean toilets, and some have hot showers.

For a terrific value, head to the family-run *Villa Lupita*, on Callejón Don Tino (off Calle del Campanario near the church). Clean, secure rooms with bedside tables and lamps, comfortable beds and shared hot bath cost US$3.25 per person. Another great deal is *Hospedaje El Viajero* (☎ 762-0128), off Calle Santander, a welcoming, clean place with five rooms (with private hot bath) set about 40m back from the street. It's quiet and peaceful, yet you're near everything. Upstairs rooms have more air and light. Rates are US$6.50/9.25 single/double, and amenities include laundry service and parking.

Hospedaje Santo Domingo (☎ 762-0236) is an amicable place with a variety of cheap rooms; take the road toward Hotel Monterrey, then follow the signs. It's away from the bustle of Calle Santander. Basic wood-plank rooms with shared bath are US$2/3.50; more attractive upstairs rooms are US$6.50 double. Rooms with private bath are US$7/10.50. There's a grassy hang-out area here that makes it.

Mario's Rooms (☎ 762-2370, 762-1313), on Calle Santander, is popular with young, adventurous travelers. Rooms cost US$4.25/5.25/7.75 single/double/triple with shared hot bath; US$7.75/10.50/13.25 with private cold bath. *Hospedaje Mi Chosita*, on Calle El Chali (turn at Mario's Rooms), is tidy, quiet and costs US$3.50/4.25/5 with shared bath. Similarly priced is the clean *Hospedaje García* (☎ 762-2187, 4a Calle 2-24, Zona 2), farther east along the same street.

Prices rise the closer you get to the beach, but there is still some good value here. Hook a left up the alley called Calle Ramos to *Hospedajes Ramos I & II* (☎ 762-0413), which has simple rooms with private bath for US$4.50/7.75. They claim to have hot water. Fifty meters farther back is *Hospedaje Contemporaneo* (☎ 762-2214), a hospitable place with spare but clean rooms with private bath for US$6.25/9.25. The upstairs rooms have partial lake views. Just beyond the Contemporaneo is the new and recommended *Hospedaje Sueño Real* (☎ 762-0608), which has tasteful, clean rooms for US$5.25 per person with shared bath; US$7/11.75 with private bath. Bicycle rentals and phone and taxi services are available.

Grand Hotel (☎ 762-2940/1, granhotel@ infovia.com.gt) is the big, bright place at the bus stop. It's not as pretty inside as out, but the rooms are spacious and have decent beds; US$9/13/19.50/26 single/double/triple/quad. Amenities include a pool, restaurant and expansive grounds – a good place to stay if you're traveling with kids.

The standout *Hotel Utz Jay* (☎ /fax 762-1358, utzjay@atitlan.com) is on Calle 15 de Febrero near Calle Santander. Its four beautifully outfitted rooms are in adobe casitas. Each has a private hot bath, traditional fabrics and touches like candles and drinking water; US$13/15.50/18/21. Other amenities include gardens, hammocks, a communal kitchen and a *chuj*, or traditional Mayan sauna. The owners speak French and English and lead hiking and camping trips around the lake.

The new *Hotel Primavera* (☎/fax 762-2052, primavera@atitlan.com), on Calle Santander, is reader recommended. Upstairs rooms overlooking a lush garden are US$12.25/15.50 in high season; US$6.50/13 in low. *La Zanahoria Chic* (☎ 762-1249, fax 762-2138, Avenida Los Árboles 0-46), has seven clean rooms opening onto a communal sitting area with two shared baths. The rooms are simple, but comfortable, and the whole place has a cozy, lived-in feeling; US$4/7.75/11.50. *Posada de los Volcanes* (☎ 762-0244, ☎/fax 762-2367, posadavolcanes@ atitlan.com, www.atitlan.com/volcanes.htm, Calle Santander 5-51) is a beautiful place offering rooms with private bath and cable TV for US$20/25.

Places to Stay – Mid-Range

Mid-range lodgings are busiest on Friday and Saturday night. From Sunday to Thursday you may get a discount. All rooms in these lodgings have private hot showers.

Mini Hotel Riva Bella (☎ 762-1348, 762-1177, fax 762-1353), on Calle Real, is a collection of neat two-room bungalows, each with its own parking place, set around pleasant gardens. Rates are US$27/32 single/ double. The same owners operate *Bungalows Guayacán*, just across the river, where six apartments, each with kitchenette, one bedroom, living room and garden, go for US$42 for up to three people.

Hotel Monterrey (☎/fax 762-1126), on Calle Monte Rey (look for the sign), is a two-story motel-style building facing the lake across lawns and gardens extending down to the beach. Its 29 clean and cheerful rooms open onto a terrace with beautiful lake views; US$25/35.

Rancho Grande Inn (☎ 762-1554, 762-2255, fax 762-2247, hranchog@quetzal.net), Calle Rancho Grande, has 12 perfectly maintained country-style villas in a tropical setting amid bright green lawns. Some bungalows sleep up to five people, and a few have fireplaces. Marlita Hannstein, the congenial proprietor, charges a reasonable US$30 single, US$40 to US$60 double; rates include a delicious full breakfast. This is perhaps Pana's best place to stay. It's a good idea to reserve in advance.

Several meters north on Calle Rancho Grande is *Müller's Guest House* (☎ 762-2442, 762-2392, fax 363-1306), which has three nicely appointed, if dampish, rooms with bath around well tended gardens for US$45 for two or three people.

Hotel Visión Azul (☎ 762-1426, ☎/fax 762-1419), on the Hotel Atitlán road, is built into a hillside in a quiet location. Views look toward the lake through a grove of trees. The big, bright rooms in the main building have spacious terraces dripping with bougainvillea and ivy. Modern bungalows a few steps away provide more privacy. The hotel has a swimming pool. Rates are US$39/44/49/52 single/double/triple/quad.

Along the same road, *Hotel Tzanjuyú* (☎ /fax 762-1318) has large gardens and a private beach on a beautiful cove. All the rooms open onto small balconies with great lake views and cost US$31/35/39/43. A swimming pool and restaurant are on site.

Hotel Playa Linda (☎ /fax 762-1159, akennedy@gua.gbm.net, Calle del Lago 0-70), facing the beach, has an assortment of rooms, some wheelchair-accessible. Rooms 1 to 5 have large private balconies with tables, chairs and wonderful lake views; rooms 6 to 15 do not. All rooms have private bath, all but two have fireplaces, and some have satellite TV. Rates are US$54 double with balcony and view, US$40 without.

Set well back from the street, *Hotel Dos Mundos* (☎ 762-2078, 762-2140, fax 762-0127, dosmundos@atitlan.com, Calle Santander 4-72) is an attractive place with 16 bungalows amid tropical gardens. All have cable TV and nice decor; rates are US$45/55/65 single/double/triple. Also here are a swimming pool and a good Italian restaurant.

Hotel Regis (☎ 762-1149, fax 762-1152, regis@atitlan.com), on Calle Santander, is a group of colonial-style villas set back from the street across a lush, palm-shaded lawn. The 25 comfortable guest rooms are spread across ample grounds, which also hold a swimming pool, a children's playground and open-air mineral hot springs for guests only. Rooms are US$60/70/80 in the high season; less in low.

Places to Stay – Top End

At the lake end of Calle Santander, *Hotel Posada de Don Rodrigo* (☎ 762-2326/29, chotelera@c.net.gt) is another beautiful luxury hotel with a lakeside swimming pool, terrace and many other amenities. Rooms are US$84/93/102 single/double/triple.

The town's nicest lodging is the *Hotel Atitlán* (☎/fax 762-1416/29/41, hotinsa@infovia.com.gt, in Guatemala City ☎ 360-8405, fax 334-0640), on the lakeshore about 2km west of the town center. Spacious gardens surround this rambling three-story colonial-style hotel. Inside are gleaming tile floors, antique wood carvings and exquisite handicraft decorations. The patio has views across the swimming pools to the lake. The 65 rooms, each with private bath and lake-view balcony, cost US$84/96/118.

Hotel Barceló del Lago (☎ /fax 762-1555 to -1560, fax 762-1562, in Guatemala City ☎ 361-9683 or fax 361-9667, barcelo@infovia.com.gt),

at the junction of Calle de Buenas Nuevas and Calle del Balneario, is a modern six-story building woefully out of place in low-rise, laid-back Pana. The hotel has two swimming pools (one for children) set in nice gardens. Each of its 100 rooms has two double beds. Rates are US$182 double in high season, US$100 in low, including all meals.

Places to Eat

Budget The cheapest places to eat are down by the beach at the mouth of the Río Panajachel. The cookshacks on the shore have rock-bottom prices; the food stalls around the parking lot cost not much more. Across the street, you can fill up for US$4 at any of several little restaurants, all of which offer priceless lake views. *Pizza, Pastas y Vino* along here is open 24 hours.

At the lake end of Calle Santander, the open-air *Sunset Cafe* has a great lake vista. Meat or vegetarian meals start at US$3; snacks are less. The cafe has a bar with live music on weekends. It's open 11 am to 10 pm daily.

Nearby on Calle Santander, *Deli Restaurante No 2* is a tranquil garden restaurant serving a good variety of healthy, inexpensive foods to the strains of classical music. It's open 7 am to 5:45 pm daily except Tuesday; breakfast is served all day. *Deli Restaurante No 1*, on Calle Real near Calle El Amate, has the same menu and hours, except it's open on Tuesday and closed on Thursday.

El Bistro, on Calle Santander half a block from the lake, is another lovely, relaxing restaurant with tables both inside and out in the garden. It offers candlelight dining in the evening and sometimes live music. Open 7 am to 10 pm daily.

Las Chinitas, on Calle Santander in El Patio complex, serves unbelievably delicious, inexpensive Asian food. Ling, the friendly owner, is from Malaysia via New York and has been in Panajachel for many years.

Nearby on Calle Santander is the popular *Restaurante Guajimbos*, which has scores of menu items but is notable for its bottomless cup of coffee. Grab some whole-wheat bread or pastries at *Pana Pan*, next door, to go with the all-you-can-drink java.

The Last Resort restaurant/bar, just off Calle Santander on Calle 14 de Febrero, is famous for its good, inexpensive food. All meals on the varied menu are served with soup, salad, bread and coffee for US$3.50 to US$5; the buffet breakfast is US$2. Alcohol is served, there's table tennis in the rear, and on cool evenings the fireplace is a welcome treat. The restaurant is open daily.

The shady streetside patio at *Al Chisme*, on Avenida Los Árboles, is a favorite with locals and Pana regulars. Breakfasts of English muffins, Belgian waffles and omclets cost US$2 to US$4. For lunch and dinner, Al Chisme offers a variety of meat and vegetarian dishes, including Tex-Mex specialties. It's open daily except Wednesday.

Next door is the *Sevananda Vegetarian Restaurant*, offering sandwiches and vegetable plates for US$2 to US$4. It's open daily except Sunday. Next door again is *Bombay Pub and Cafe*, serving all vegetarian burritos, pastas and stir-fry in a pretty courtyard.

At the *Fly'n Mayan Yacht Club*, near the intersection of Calle Real and Calle Santander, the pizzas (US$3.50 to US$6.50) have a good reputation. It's open daily except Thursday.

Restaurante/Bar Tocoyal, near hotel Barceló del Lago, at the beach end of Calle Rancho Grande, is a tidy, modern thatch-roofed place serving good meals (including fish) for about US$8.

El Descansillo, on the corner of Calles Real and El Amate, features a relaxing garden courtyard where you can sit and enjoy breakfast or a light meal. The bread is homemade, the coffee is rich, and the numerous different salads are safe. It's open 7:30 am to 6 pm daily.

El Maná Panadería, on Avenida Los Árboles near La Zanahoria Chic, sells an awesome selection of fresh breads. Across the street, *Tienda El Botiquín Verde (naturalfoodpana@hotmail.com)* sells organic vegetables, free-range eggs, tofu, nut oils, juices, vitamins and herbal remedies. It's

open 9 am to 3 pm Monday to Friday, 9 am to 1 pm Saturday.

Fango'D, on Calle Santander in the complex with INGUAT, is a coffee roaster serving some of Pana's best coffee. It's open 6 am to 5 pm daily.

Mid-Range *Ristorante La Lanterna*, at Hotel Dos Mundos, set back from the street on Calle Santander, is a good, authentic Italian restaurant with both inside and garden tables; diners may use the hotel's swimming pool. It's open 7 am to 3 pm and 6 to 10 pm daily.

Upstairs in the same building with the INGUAT tourist office, *La Terraza Tapas Bar* (☎ 762-0041) is a lovely, upmarket open-air restaurant/bar open daily; locals consistently cite this as one of Pana's best restaurants.

The luxury *Hotel Barceló del Lago* offers lavish Sunday breakfast and dinner buffets when the hotel is fully occupied (on weekends and holidays mostly). The breakfast/dinner buffets cost US$7/13.

The even more luxurious *Hotel Atitlán* (☎ 762-1416/29/41) has a beautiful restaurant with inside and patio tables and magnificent lake views. If you come to eat here, you can use the swimming pool, beach and other hotel facilities free. Lunch or dinner buffets (US$11) are offered when occupancy is high and usually on Thursday afternoons; call ahead. Otherwise, choose the ample four-course prix fixe meal or an à la carte selection.

Entertainment

The recommended *Aleph Bar*, on Avenida Los Árboles, jumps with live music six nights a week. Other live-music venues include *Sunset Cafe* and *El Bistro* (see Places to Eat), as well as *La Posada del Pintor/Circus Bar*.

Pana's two discos – *Chapiteau* and *Nuan's* – are both on Avenida Los Árboles. The Chapiteau opens around 9 or 10 pm. Nuan's has an early evening happy hour. *Ubu's Cosmic Cantina* next to Nuan's, has a pool table, giant screen TV and couches for relaxed cocktail sipping.

GUATEMALA

Videos in English are shown at *Turquoise Buffalo*, on Avenida Los Árboles next to Al Chisme; it shows several films nightly and posts schedules out front. At *La Zanahoria Chic* video cafe, on Avenida Los Árboles, you can choose from a list of over a hundred films.

Shopping

Industrious bohemians used to come to Pana to get loads of textiles cheap, carry or ship them back to the USA or Europe and turn a nice profit on the resale. The loose infrastructure that developed around this trade still exists, and you can shop to your heart's content here and have the goods shipped to your door back home. There are even companies here that will do the shopping and shipping for you.

Calle Santander is lined with booths, stores and complexes; try the Comerciales de Artesanías Típicas Tinamit Maya, selling traditional clothing, jade, leather items, wood carvings and more. Freelance vendors also set up tables or blankets to display their wares here, especially on weekends. The approach to the beach at the end of Calle del Balneario is also lined with booths.

Getting There & Away

Bus The town's main bus stop is where Calles Santander and Real meet, across from the Banco Agrícola Mercantil. Rébuli buses depart from the Rébuli office on Calle Real (see map).

Antigua US$3.25, 2½ hours, 146km. Rébuli runs one direct deluxe bus at 11 am daily except Sunday. Or take the 10 am deluxe bus (US$2) to Chimaltenango and change there. Any Guatemala City bus will get you to Chimaltenango.

Chichicastenango US$1.75, 1½ hours, 37km. Mendoza has nine buses daily, 6:45 am to 4 pm. Rébuli buses (US$1.50) leave at 6:45 am Thursday and Sunday, Chichi's market days. Or take any bus to Los Encuentros and change there.

Cocales (Carretera al Pacífico) US$1, 2½ hours, 56km. Eight buses daily, from 6:30 am to 3 pm.

El Carmen/Talismán (Mexican border) via the Pacific route, take bus to Cocales and change buses there. Via the highland route, bus to Quetzaltenango and change buses there.

Guatemala City US$2.75, 3½ hours, 148km. Rébuli has 10 daily departures, 5:30 am to 3 pm. Or take a bus to Los Encuentros and change there.

Huehuetenango 3½ hours, 159km. Take bus to Los Encuentros and wait there for a bus bound for Huehue or La Mesilla (see the Getting There & Around chapter for a schedule). Or catch a Quetzaltenango bus and change at Cuatro Caminos. Buses run hourly from these junctions.

La Mesilla (Mexican border) seven hours, 241km. See Huehuetenango.

Los Encuentros US$0.50, 35 minutes, 20km. Take any bus heading toward Guatemala City, Chichicastenango, Quetzaltenango or the Interamericana.

Quetzaltenango US$1.75, 2½ hours, 99km. Six buses daily, 5:30, 6:15, 7:30, 10 and 11:30 am and 2 pm. Or take a bus to Los Encuentros and change there.

San Antonio Palopó US$0.40, 45 minutes, 9km. Daily buses via Santa Catarina Palopó, or grab one of the many pickups leaving from the corner of Calles Real and El Amate.

San Lucas Tolimán US$1, 1½ hours, 24km. Two buses daily, 6:45 am and 4 pm. Or take any bus heading for Cocales, get off at the crossroads to San Lucas, and walk about 1km into town.

Santa Catarina Palopó US$0.25, 20 minutes, 4km. Daily buses, or get a pickup at the corner of Calles Real and El Amate.

Sololá US$0.15, 10 minutes, 8km. Frequent direct local buses, or take any bus heading to Guatemala City, Chichicastenango, Quetzaltenango or Los Encuentros.

Shuttle Minibus Tourist shuttle buses usually take about half as much time as local buses. Many travel agencies on Calle Santander (see Travel Agencies) offer convenient shuttles to/from Antigua (US$10), Chichicastenango (US$7), Guatemala City (US$20), La Mesilla (US$35), Quetzaltenango (US$15) and Tecún Umán (US$35).

Car & Motorcycle Dalton Rent A Car (☎/fax 762-1275, 762-2251) has an office on Avenida Los Árboles. Moto Servicio Queche (☎ 762-2089), just past the intersection of Avenida Los Árboles and Calle Real, rents bicycles and off-road motorcycles.

Boat Passenger boats depart from the public beach at the foot of Calle del Balneario.

Head down there for a boat; you won't wait long as they typically leave when six passengers are ready to go. The big, slow ferries that used to make the trip around the lake have largely been discontinued in favor of fast, frequent motorboats called *lanchas*. Boats stop running around 6 pm.

One-way passage *anywhere* on Lago de Atitlán costs US$0.65, but the *lancheros* who drive the boats try to chisel gringos and will quote a price quadruple that. Generally, foreign visitors end up paying around US$1.50. You can hold out for the US$0.65 fare, but you may have to let a few boats go by before one accepts your offer.

The trip to Santiago Atitlán takes less than an hour, depending upon the winds. Another boat route stops in Santa Catarina Palopó, San Antonio Palopó and San Lucas Tolimán, though it's cheaper to go by bus to these nearby towns.

Another route goes counterclockwise around the lake, stopping in Santa Cruz La Laguna (15 minutes), Jaibalito, Tzununá, San Marcos La Laguna (30 minutes), San Juan La Laguna and San Pedro La Laguna (40 minutes). After departing Panajachel from the Calle del Balneario dock, the boats stop at another dock at the foot of Calle del Embarcadero before heading out (or vice versa, when arriving at Panajachel).

SANTA CATARINA PALOPÓ & SAN ANTONIO PALOPÓ

Four kilometers east of Panajachel along a winding road lies the picturesque, traditional village of Santa Catarina Palopó. Here narrow streets paved in stone blocks run past adobe houses with roofs of thatch or corrugated tin, and the gleaming white church commands the center of attention. Chickens cackle, dogs bark and the villagers go about their daily life dressed in their beautiful clothing.

Except for appreciating village life and enjoying the stunning views, there's little to do. Still, this is one of the best places to buy the luminescent indigo *huipiles* you see around Lago de Atitlán. Look for vendors on the path to the shore, or pop into one of the simple wooden storefronts hung thick

with the bright cloth. Several little *comedores* on the main plaza sell refreshments, and you can get a reasonably priced meal at the open-air **Restaurante Laguna Azul** on the lakeshore (take the path past the Villa Santa Catarina toward the water). If your budget allows, a drink or a meal at **Villa Santa Catarina**, the village's best hotel, is a treat.

The road continues past Santa Catarina 5km to San Antonio Palopó, a larger but similar village where men and women in traditional clothing tend their terraced fields and clean mountains of scallions by the lakeshore.

See the Panajachel section for details on buses, pickups and passenger or tour boats. From Panajachel, you can also walk to Santa Catarina in about an hour, continuing to San Antonio in about another hour. Bicycling is another option, but prepare for hills.

SANTIAGO ATITLÁN

South across the lake from Panajachel, on the shore of a lagoon squeezed between the towering volcanoes of Tolimán and San Pedro, lies Santiago Atitlán. Though it is the most visited village outside Panajachel, it clings to the traditional lifestyle of the Tz'utuhil Maya. The women of the town still weave and wear huipiles with brilliantly colored bunches of birds and flowers embroidered on them. The best days to visit are market days (Friday and Sunday, with a lesser market on Tuesday), but any day will do.

Santiago is also a curiosity because of its reverence for Maximón (mah-shee-**mohn**; see the boxed text 'A God Is a God Is a God'). Maximón is paraded around triumphantly during Semana Santa processions (see Public Holidays & Special Events in the Facts for the Visitor chapter for dates), which is a good excuse to head this way during Easter. The rest of the year, Maximón resides with a caretaker, receiving offerings. Local children will offer to take you to see him for a small tip.

As you disembark at the dock, children from Santiago greet you selling clay whistles and little embroidered strips of cloth.

They can act as guides, find you a taxi or lead you to a hotel, for a tip.

Orientation & Information

Walk to the left from the dock along the shore to reach the street into town, which is the main commercial strip. Every tourist walks up and down it between the dock and the town, so it's lined with shops selling woven cloth and other handicrafts.

Near the dock is the office of the Grupo Guías de Turismo Rilaj Maam, a guide cooperative offering trips to many nearby places, including the volcanoes and the Chutinamit archaeological site. The office is open 8 am to 5 pm daily. Martin Tzina is a recommended guide.

Santiago has a post office, a Telgua telephone/fax office and a bank where you can change US dollars and traveler's checks.

Things to See & Do

At the top of the slope is the main square, flanked by the town office and a huge centuries-old **church**. Within the stark, echoing church are wooden statues of the saints, each of whom gets new clothes made by local women every year. On the carved wooden pulpit, note the figures of corn (from which humans were formed, according

A God Is a God Is a God

The Spanish called him San Simón, the ladinos named him Maximón, and the Mayans knew him as Ry Laj Man (pronounced rhee-la-**mohn**). By any name, he's the revered deity found throughout the Guatemalan highlands. Assumed to be a combination of Mayan gods, Pedro de Alvarado (the fierce conquistador of Guatemala) and the biblical Judas, San Simón is an effigy to which Guatemalans of every stripe make offerings and ask for blessings. The effigy is usually cared for and housed by a *cofradía* member (town elder). The name, shape and ceremonies associated with this deity vary from town to town, but encountering him will be memorable regardless of where it occurs. For a small fee, photography is usually permitted. Offerings of cigarettes, rum or candles are always appreciated.

In Santiago Atitlán, locals worship Maximón, a wooden figure draped in colorful scarves, smoking a fat cigar and around which locals sing and manage the offerings made to him. His favorite gifts are Payaso cigarettes and Venado rum, but he often has to settle for the cheaper firewater Quetzalteca Especial. Each year, Maximón is moved to a new home, a custom anthropologists speculate was established to periodically redistribute the balance of power.

In Nahualá between Los Encuentros and Quetzaltenango, the effigy is also called Maximón. Instead of scarves and a human face, however, this is a god à la Picasso: Here Maximón is a simple wooden box with a cigarette protruding out of it. Still, the same offerings are made and simple blessings asked for, such as a good harvest and healthy days. In Zunil, near Xela, the deity is known as San Simón, but is similar to Santiago's Maximón in costume and form.

San Jorge La Laguna, on Lake Atitlán, is a very spiritual place for the Maya; here they worship Ry Laj Man. It is possible that the first effigy was made near here, carved from the *palo de pito* tree that spoke to the ancient shamans and told them to preserve their culture, language and traditions by carving Ry Laj Man. It should be noted that the flowers of the palo de pito can be smoked to induce hallucinations (don't try this at home, however!). The effigy in San Jorge looks like a joker, with an absurdly long tongue.

The residents of San Andrés Itzapa, near Antigua, also worship Ry Laj Man. Here he has a permanent home and is brought out on October 28 and paraded about in an unparalleled pagan festival. This is an all night, hedonistic party where cosmic dancers grab the staff of Ry Laj Man to harness his power and receive magical visions. San Andrés is less than 10km south of Chimaltenango, so you can easily make the party from Antigua.

ing to Mayan religion), of a quetzal bird reading a book and of Yum-Kax, the Maya god of corn. A similar carving is on the back of the priest's chair.

The walls of the church bear paintings, now covered by a thin layer of plaster. A memorial plaque at the back of the church commemorates Father Stanley Francis Rother, a missionary priest from Oklahoma; beloved by the local people, he was despised by ultrarightist 'death squads,' which murdered him in the church during the troubled year of 1981.

Among the several good **hikes** around Santiago is a four-hour walk to San Pedro. Take the path veering right just beyond the Posada de Santiago and continue around the San Pedro volcano saddle; get the last lancha back in the early afternoon. You can also catch a pickup to the small village of Cerro de Oro, between Santiago and San Lucas Tolimán. The village has a pretty church, and the eponymous hill provides great views. Pickups leave from in front of Hotel Chi-Nim-Yá.

A challenging 10km roundtrip hike to the **Mirador**, south of Santiago, is rewarding, taking you through cloud forest filled with parakeets, curassows, swifts and other birds. The path starts 1km beyond the Posada de Santiago (veer left at the fork) and leads to a lookout point with beautiful panoramic views. Plan on about five hours roundtrip, and start early, as clouds usually roll in by the afternoon. A guide costs US$13.

Recommended **Spanish classes** are offered by Cecilia and Rosa Archila (☎ 703-2562, fax 762-2466; in the USA write to PO Box 520972, Miami, FL 33152-0972). Follow signs from the dock or ask at the Grupo Guías office for more information.

Places to Stay & Eat

Near the dock, *Hotel Chi-Nim-Yá (☎ 721-7131)* is a simple hotel with 22 clean rooms around a central courtyard. Rates are US$2.75/4 single/double with shared bath; US$6.75/8 with private bath. The nicest room is No 106; it's large and airy, with lots of windows and outstanding lake views.

Nearby, *Restaurante Regiomontano* is open 7 am to 7 pm daily.

Hotel y Restaurante Tzutuhil (☎ 721-7174), about three blocks uphill on the road from the dock, is a modern five-story building – an anomaly in this little town. Many of the rooms have large windows with decent views; some have cable TV. Rooms vary widely, so look before committing. Clean rooms are US$2 per person with shared hot bath, US$3.25 per person with a private bath – a good deal. Go up on the rooftop for great sunsets. The restaurant here is open 6 am to 10:30 pm daily.

Along the eastern shore (left from the dock) is *Hotel-Restaurant Bambú (☎ 416-2122, bambu@virtualguatemala.com),* a new, comfortable place with freestanding bungalows, each with a private hot bath, for US$30/35/40/45 single/double/triple/quad. The grounds are pretty, and some rooms have views.

Restaurant Santa Rita, a few steps from the plaza's northeast corner, past Distribuidor El Buen Precio, boasts *deliciosos pays* (delicious pies).

One of the most charming hotels around the lake is *Posada de Santiago (☎ 721-7167, posdesantiagoguate.net).* Its half dozen bungalows and two suites, all with stone walls, fireplaces, porches and hammocks, are set around beautiful gardens stretching uphill from the lake. Rates are US$30/40/50/60/70 single/double/triple/quad/suite. It's 1km from the town center; to get there, walk out of town on the road past the Hospedaje Rosita, and keep walking along the lakeside road. The restaurant at the Posada de Santiago is special, too, with well-prepared food and cozy ambience.

Getting There & Away

Boats to Santiago from Pana take about an hour; from San Pedro La Laguna 20 minutes.

SAN PEDRO LA LAGUNA

The next most popular lakeside town to visit, after Santiago, is San Pedro La Laguna. It's heavily populated with bohemian travelers who liked it here so much they stayed.

GUATEMALA

Coffee is grown in San Pedro. You'll see coffee being picked and spread out to dry on wide platforms at the beginning of the dry season. Marijuana is also grown here; before long you'll smell the telltale blue smoke and be fielding purchase offers. Accommodations in San Pedro are among the cheapest in Guatemala. Try bargaining for longer stays and during the off season.

Orientation & Information

San Pedro has two docks. The one on the south side of town serves boats heading to/from Santiago Atitlán. Another dock, around on the east side of town, serves boats going to/from Pana. At either dock, walk straight ahead a few blocks on the road leading uphill from the dock to reach the center of town. Alternatively, from the Santiago dock, you can take your first right past the Ti Kaaj and follow the beaten path for about 15 minutes to the other side of town. Along this path are several hospedajes and simple eateries. To take this route coming from the Panajachel dock, take your first left and then a right into the little alley across from the Hospedaje Casa Elena; a sign painted on the wall says 'to El Balneario.'

San Pedro has a post office, a Telgua telephone/fax office and a Banrural where you can change US dollars and traveler's checks. The folks at Thermal Waters offer email services but no Internet access.

Most of the hotels, restaurants and other businesses here don't have private telephones. To reach them, you can phone the community telephone at Telgua (☎ 762-2486) and give them a time when you'll call back; the business will send someone over to receive your return call.

Volcán San Pedro

When you arrive by boat from Panajachel, boys will greet you, asking if you want a guide to ascend the San Pedro volcano, on foot or horseback. It's worth it to go with a guide; cost is around US$3 per person for the hiking trip, or slightly more on horseback. The hike takes around four hours. Bring water and snacks.

Thermal Waters

Thermal Waters (☎ 206-9658), right on the lakeshore between the two docks, has individual open-air solar-heated pools with great views. Reservations are a good idea, as it's a popular spot. Cost is US$2.75 per person. Antonio from California, the eccentric horticulturist inventor who built and operates Thermal Waters, also runs an organic vegetarian restaurant and a sweat lodge here.

Walking

Several nice walks between San Pedro and neighboring villages make terrific day trips. You can walk west to San Juan La Laguna (30 minutes), San Pablo La Laguna (1½ hours), San Marcos (three hours), Jaibalito (five hours) and finally, Santa Cruz (all day). From the last three you can easily hail a lancha back to San Pedro until around 3 pm. Walking southeast over and around the saddle of Volcán San Pedro, you can make it to Santiago Atitlán in around four hours.

Language Courses

Casa Rosario, a Spanish-language school, is operated by Professor Samuel Cumes, a well-known San Pedro teacher. It's very economical at US$55 per week for instruction and lodging (food not available). You can arrange weaving classes here as well. Another option is the San Pedro Spanish School, on the path between the two docks. The way to both these places is well signed.

Places to Stay & Eat

When you arrive at the dock serving boats to/from Pana, head up the main street and make your first right, walking along the trash-strewn path for about 75m to reach *Hotel & Restaurante Valle Azul* (☎ 207-7292). This cement behemoth has seen better days. Small, basic rooms with shared bath are US$2 per person (plus US$0.50 per shower). The restaurant is a great, inexpensive little place; it's open 7 am to 10 pm daily.

Continue on the path past Valle Azul and through the small cornfield for about five minutes to get to *Café Luna Azul*; you can see it from the dock and most boat drivers will drop you there if you ask. In-the-know travelers say this place has the best omelet-and-hash-browns breakfast going (US$2). The cafe also serves lunch.

Nearby, **Restaurante Nick's** is the vortex of the traveler scene. It has food and drink and hosts free movies nightly. Upstairs, **D'Noz** is another restaurant catering to backpackers.

Make a left just beyond Nick's to reach **Hospedaje Casa Elena**, a popular, family-run pension; US$2.50/3.50 single/double with shared bath. Several meters farther on is a simple comedor called **El Paisaje**. Take a right there and you'll see **Hospedaje Xocomil**, which rents quiet rooms around a cement courtyard for US$1.50 per person.

Continue to the alley opposite Hospedaje Casa Elena to reach several more pensions en route to the Santiago dock. The way is not always clear, so follow the signs for the Casa Rosario Spanish school. Make your first left and then another left to reach **Hospedaje Posada Xetawal** and **Posada Casa Domingo**; both have rooms for about US$1 a night. If you continue straight instead, toward the Santiago dock, you come to **Restaurant Pinocchio**, which serves good, homemade pastas and cakes; the breakfast here is a good value. **Thermal Waters** is a few minutes' walk beyond here; check out its organic vegetarian restaurant – you choose from the extensive menu, and Antonio goes out to the garden to gather the ingredients. Thermal Waters also offers beautiful and safe campsites with terrific views.

Next is the recommended **Hotelito El Amanecer Sak'cari**, which has rooms with private hot bath for US$4.50/9. Just past here the path takes a left and then a quick right to the friendly **Comedor Mata Hari**, a local place serving wholesome, cheap food.

Finally, you'll reach **Ti Kaaj**, a popular, inexpensive place with hammocks around the gardens and basic rooms with shared bath for US$1.75/3/4 single/double/triple. Its restaurant serves great coffee and simple pasta dishes, and you might also enjoy the disco and bar. From the Santiago dock, make your first right to get here.

Along and just off the road leading uphill from the Santiago dock are several more good places to stay, including Hospedaje Villa Sol, Hotel San Pedro, Hospedaje San Francisco and Hotel San Francisco; all offer rooms for rates of around US$2 to US$4 per person.

Heading left from the Santiago dock is the laid-back **Las Milpas** (lasmilpas@atitlan.com), which rents private bungalows for US$6.50/7.75; rooms with shared bath for US$9.50/14 (or simpler versions for US$6.50 per person); and larger rooms with private bath for US$20/24 double/triple. You can also camp here, and all guests have use of the hot tub, sauna and gardens.

Cafe Arte, on the road leading uphill from the Santiago dock, is a good, inexpensive cafe serving meat, fish and vegetarian dishes. It's operated by the family of internationally known primitivist artist Pedro Rafael González Chavajay; his paintings, and those of his students, are exhibited here. The cafe is open 7 am to 11 pm daily.

Shopping

A few doors away from Cafe Arte, on the road leading up from the Santiago dock, is Caza Sueños, a leather shop owned by the brothers González. Here they handcraft leather vests, shoes, boots, bags and more. They will make a pair of shoes to your specifications for an incredibly reasonable US$35; allow at least four days. It's open 9 am to 1 pm and 3 to 5 pm daily.

Getting There & Away

The paved road from San Lucas Tolimán to Santiago Atitlán continues 18km to San Pedro, making its way around the lagoon and behind Volcán San Pedro.

A newly paved road connects San Pedro with the Interamericana; the turnoff is at Km 148. The road meets the lake at Santa Clara La Laguna and turns right to San Pedro, left to San Marcos. From San Pedro it continues to Santiago Atitlán and San Lucas Tolimán. From San Marcos it continues to Tzununá, but beyond that it's a walking trail only, which continues to Santa Cruz La Laguna. Buses to Guatemala City depart from San Pedro at 3, 3:30, 4, 4:30 and 5 am; see the Getting There & Around chapter for return buses. The trip takes four hours and costs US$2.75.

Unless you want to bring a vehicle, it's easier to reach San Pedro by boat. Passenger boats come here from Panajachel (see that section for details) and from Santiago.

SAN MARCOS LA LAGUNA

San Marcos is a peaceful place, with houses set among shady coffee plants near the lakeshore. The shore is beautiful here, with several little docks for swimming.

The town's greatest claim to fame is **Las Pirámides** meditation center (☎ 205-7302, 205-7151), on the path heading inland from Posada Schumann. Every structure on the property is built in a pyramid shape and oriented to the four cardinal points. Among the many physical (for example, yoga, massage) and metaphysical (for example, Tarot readings, channeling) offerings here is a one-month lunar meditation course that begins every full moon and covers the four elements of human development (physical, mental, emotional and spiritual). Most sessions are held in English. Because the last week of the course requires fasting and silence by the participants, it is not recommended for novices. Nonguests can come for meditation or Hatha yoga sessions Monday to Saturday; US$4.

Accommodations are available in pyramid-shaped houses for US$10/9/8 per day by the day/week/month. This price includes the meditation course, use of the sauna and access to a fascinating library with books in several languages. A restaurant serves vegetarian fare. The best chance to get a space is just prior to the full moon, when the meditation program is finishing. Las Pirámides has a private dock; all the lancheros know it, so you can be dropped right here.

Places to Stay & Eat

Just to the left of the public dock is the **Hotel & Restaurante Arco Iris** (☎ 306-5039, arcoiris@atitlan.com), a comfortable hotel with good beds in clean rooms for US$5.25

per person. Hammocks are hung around the manicured grounds, and a restaurant overlooks the lake. Italian, English, French and German are spoken.

To get to the other hotels on foot, you have to walk for a few hundred meters along the inland street running parallel to the lake. Turn left onto the dirt path (look for the Posada Schumann sign), along which you'll find the rest of San Marcos' hotels.

The first one you come to is **Hotel Paco Real** (fax 762-1196), with nice gardens and simple, tastefully decorated rooms. Charming bungalows each with a loft bed, porch and shared bath are US$10.50 for two people. Clean rooms with tiled floors and shared bath are US$4.50/10.50/15 single/double/triple. Some rooms are musty. Also here is a restaurant run by a French chef; it's open 7 am to 9 pm daily.

Next on the strip is the mellow **Hotel La Paz** (☎ 702-9168), which offers basic little bungalows on rambling grounds that also hold organic gardens, a vegetarian restaurant and a traditional Mayan sauna. Each bungalow sleeps five people dorm-style and costs US$3.25 per person. One private double is available for US$9. Camping is allowed, and a common room above the restaurant has musical instruments and books. Gardeners, chefs, carpenters, masseurs and other folks good with their hands may have luck bartering.

Unicornio Rooms is another attractive place, with beautiful gardens, a sauna and a communal kitchen (but no electricity). Three small, thatch-roofed, A-frame bungalows, each with shared cold bath, cost US$2.75/5.25. One large two-story bungalow with private kitchen and bath is also available.

Right on the lakeside, **Posada Schumann** (☎ 202-2216, in Guatemala City ☎ 360-4049, 339-2683, fax 473-1326) has three stone bungalows – each with kitchen and private bath – a restaurant and a sauna. The bungalows run US$12/24; cheaper rooms are also available, US$7.75/15.50. You can save by renting weekly or monthly. Posada Schumann has a private pier for those arriving by lancha.

Volcanoes ring beautiful Lago de Atitlán, in Guatemala's highlands.

RICHARD I'ANSON

At home in Todos Santos Cuchumatán

KRAIG LIEB

Collecting water in Panajachel, on Lago de Atitlán

RICHARD I'ANSON

Canoeing the Río Dulce, eastern Guatemala

Garífuna resident in laid-back Lívingston

Soaking up the splendor at Tikal, in El Petén

Getting There & Away

You can drive to San Marcos from the Interamericana; the turnoff is at Km 148. See the San Pedro section, earlier. The walk or drive between Santa Clara La Laguna and San Marcos is incredible.

See Panajachel for information on passenger boats.

JAIBALITO

This tiny town is accessible only by boat or on foot. You can hike here along picturesque trails from San Marcos (three hours) or Santa Cruz (one hour), or you can come and go by lancha.

Perched on a secluded cliff here is Guatemala's most magical hotel: *La Casa del Mundo Hotel & Cafe* (☎ 204-5558, fax 762-1092, casamundo@yahoo.com). Designed and built by husband-and-wife team Bill and Rosie Fogarty, this place has gorgeous gardens, swimming holes and a hot tub overhanging the lake. Rooms with private bath are US$16.75 double; rooms with shared hot bath are US$6.50 per person. All rooms have views and are impeccably outfitted with comfortable beds, *típico* fabrics and fresh flowers. The restaurant is fantastic. You can rent kayaks or bikes here. Reservations are advisable.

Also in Jaibalito is the Norwegian-owned *Vulcano Lodge* (fax 762-0092, vulcanolodge@hotmail.com). This new place is set among pretty stands of banana and coffee and has spotless rooms with private hot bath for US$14/18. The bottom half of a house is available for US$25, or you can rent the family suite upstairs for US$50. The lodge also offers a verandah, hammocks and a reasonably priced restaurant.

From the public dock, head to your right on a shoreline trail to get to the steps leading to Casa del Mundo, or walk straight ahead and follow the signs to the Vulcano Lodge.

SANTA CRUZ LA LAGUNA

Santa Cruz La Laguna is another peaceful lakeside village. The vibe here is somewhere between the party scene of San Pedro and the spiritual feel of San Marcos. The main part of the village is up the hill from the dock; the hotels are on the shore.

Diving

ATI Divers (☎ 762-2646, fax 762-1196, santacruz@guate.net) conducts a four-day PADI open-water diving certification course (US$160), as well as a PADI high-altitude course and fun dives. It's based at La Iguana Perdida hotel.

Hiking

Good walks from Santa Cruz include the beautiful lakeside walking track between Santa Cruz and San Marcos, about four hours one way. You can stop for a beer and a meal at La Casa del Mundo en route (see Jaibalito). Or you can walk up the hill to Sololá, a 3½-hour walk one way.

Places to Stay & Eat

Three pleasant lakeside hotels provide accommodations and meals. Although electricity is available up the hill in town, the hotels by the shore have none. In the evening guests eat by candlelight and lantern light.

None of the following hotels has a telephone, but you can fax them at 762-1196 or try their email. It can take a few days to hear back from them.

Arca de Noé (thearca@yahoo.com) is recommended for its excellent food and for the beautiful lake views from its dense, colorful gardens. Standard rooms with shared bath go for US$6/10 single/double; plush rooms with private bath are US$20/21.75; dorm beds are US$3.50.

Popular with the backpacking set, *La Iguana Perdida* (santacruz@guate.net) has a restaurant and a variety of accommodations. Rates are US$2.50 per person for a dorm bed; US$5.50/7.75 for a private room; US$7.75/9.50 for a small cabaña with shared bath. Meals are served family-style; a three-course dinner is US$4.50, and a vegetarian choice is always available. There's also a sauna. The inn's friendly managers, Deedle Denman (from the UK) and Mike Kiersgard (from Greenland), also operate ATI Divers.

Posada Abaj Hotel (abaj@atitlan.com), also on the lakefront, is a nice big place that also has a restaurant. Rooms with shared bath are US$5 per person; bungalows with private bath are US$16.75 for two people. Spanish classes are offered and a sauna is on the nicely maintained grounds.

Getting There & Away
See Panajachel for details on passenger boats.

Quiché

The department of Quiché is famous mostly for the town of Chichicastenango, with its bustling Thursday and Sunday markets. Beyond Chichi to the north is Santa Cruz del Quiché, the capital of the department; on its outskirts lie the ruins of K'umarcaaj (or Gumarcaah), also called Utatlán, the last capital city of the Quiché Maya.

The road to Quiché leaves the Interamericana at Los Encuentros, winding its way north through pine forests and cornfields, down into a steep valley and up the other side. Women sit in front of their roadside cottages weaving gorgeous pieces of cloth on their simple backstrap looms. From Los Encuentros, it takes half an hour to travel the 17km to Chichicastenango.

CHICHICASTENANGO
• population 8000 • elevation 2030m
Surrounded by valleys, with nearby mountains looming overhead, Chichicastenango seems isolated from the rest of Guatemala. When its narrow cobbled streets and red-tiled roofs are enveloped in mists, as they often are, it seems magical.

Chichi is a beautiful, interesting place, with shamanistic and ceremonial undertones despite gaggles of camera-toting tour groups. Masheños (citizens of Chichicastenango) are famous for their adherence to pre-Christian religious beliefs and ceremonies. You can readily see versions of these old rites in and around the church of Santo Tomás and at the shrine of Pascual Abaj on the outskirts of town.

Chichi has always been an important trading town, and its Sunday and Thursday markets remain fabulous. If you have a choice of days, come on Sunday, when the cofradías (religious brotherhoods) often hold processions.

History
Once called Chaviar, this was an important Cakchiquel trading town long before the Spanish conquest. Just prior to the conquistadors arrival, the Cakchiquel and the Quiché (based at K'umarcaaj near present-day Santa Cruz del Quiché, 20km north) went to war. The Cakchiquel abandoned Chaviar and moved to Iximché, which was easier to defend. The conquistadors came and conquered K'umarcaaj, and many of the town's residents fled to Chaviar, which they renamed Chugüilá (Above the Nettles) and Tziguan Tinamit (Surrounded by Canyons). These names are still used by the Quiché Maya, although everyone else calls the place Chichicastenango, a foreign name given by the conquistadors' Mexican allies.

Information
Chichi has no official tourist office. Direct your questions to staff at the museum on the plaza or ask at one of the hotels. The Mayan Inn is among the most helpful and best informed.

Money Since Sunday is Chichi's biggest day of commerce, all the banks here are open on Sunday. Most banks change US dollars and traveler's checks; Bancafé, on 5a Avenida between 6a and 7a Calle, gives cash advances on Visa cards and has a Bancared ATM. The Hotel Santo Tomás (see Places to Stay) will change traveler's checks for guests and nonguests, at a lower rate than the banks.

Post & Communications The post office is at 7a Avenida 8-47, 3½ blocks south of Hotel Santo Tomás on the road into town. The Telgua telephone office is on 6a Calle between 5a and 6a Avenida.

Acses Computación, on 6a Calle in the same complex as Hotel Girón (see Places to Stay), offers email and Internet access when its network is up and running.

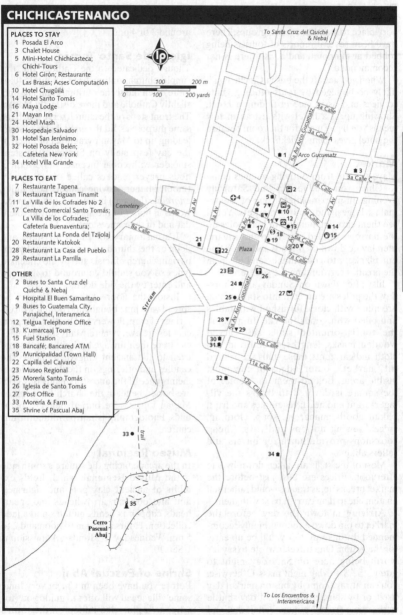

CHICHICASTENANGO

PLACES TO STAY
1 Posada El Arco
3 Chalet House
5 Mini-Hotel Chichicasteca;
   Chichi-Tours
6 Hotel Girón; Restaurante
   Las Brasas; Acses Computación
10 Hotel Chugüilá
14 Hotel Santo Tomás
16 Maya Lodge
21 Mayan Inn
24 Hotel Mash
30 Hospedaje Salvador
31 Hotel San Jerónimo
32 Hotel Posada Belén;
   Cafetería New York
34 Hotel Villa Grande

PLACES TO EAT
7 Restaurante Tapena
8 Restaurant Tziguan Tinamit
11 La Villa de los Cofrades No 2
17 Centro Comercial Santo Tomás;
   La Villa de los Cofrades;
   Cafetería Buenaventura;
   Restaurant La Fonda del Tzijolaj
20 Restaurante Katokok
28 Restaurant La Casa del Pueblo
29 Restaurant La Parrilla

OTHER
2 Buses to Santa Cruz del
   Quiché & Nebaj
4 Hospital El Buen Samaritano
9 Buses to Guatemala City,
   Panajachel, Interamerica
12 Telgua Telephone Office
13 K'umarcaaj Tours
15 Fuel Station
18 Bancafé; Bancared ATM
19 Municipalidad (Town Hall)
22 Capilla del Calvario
23 Museo Regional
25 Morería Santo Tomás
26 Iglesia de Santo Tomás
27 Post Office
33 Morería & Farm
35 Shrine of Pascual Abaj

To Santa Cruz del Quiché & Nebaj

0   100   200 m
0   100   200 yards

3a Calle
3a Calle A
5a Av Arco Gucumatz
Arco Gucumatz
3a Calle C
7a Calle
Cemetery
3a Av
8a Calle
5a Calle
7a Av
5a Calle
Plaza
7a Calle
8a Calle
Stream
9a Calle
10a Calle
11a Calle
12a Calle

Cerro
Pascual
Abaj

trail

To Los Encuentros &
Interamericana

GUATEMALA

Dangers & Annoyances The cemetery on the town's western edge is a decidedly unsavory place to wander, even in groups. There have been several reports of tourists being robbed at gunpoint, and a visit here is not recommended.

When you get off the bus in Chichi, you'll likely be besieged by touts offering guide services and assistance in finding a hotel. Showing up at a hotel with a tout in tow means you'll pay more for the room because the hotel gives them a kickback.

Market

Maya traders from outlying villages come to Chichi on Wednesday and Saturday evenings in preparation for one of Guatemala's largest indigenous markets. You'll see them carrying bundles of long poles up the narrow cobbled streets to the square, then laying down their loads and spreading out blankets to cook dinner and sleep in the arcades surrounding the square.

Just after dawn on Sunday and Thursday, the poles are erected into stalls, which are hung with cloth, furnished with tables and piled with goods for sale. In general, the tourist-oriented stalls sell carved wooden masks, lengths of embroidered cloth and garments; these stalls are around the market's outer edges in the most visible areas. Behind them, the center of the square is devoted to things the villagers want and need: vegetables and fruit, baked goods, macaroni, soap, clothing, spices, sewing notions and toys. Cheap cookshops provide lunch for buyers and sellers alike.

Most of the stalls are taken down by late afternoon. Prices are best just before the market breaks up, as traders would rather sell an item cheap than carry it back with them.

Arriving in town the day before the market to pin down a room is highly recommended. In this way, too, you'll be up early for the action. One traveler wrote to say it's worth being here on Saturday night to attend the Saturday night mass. Otherwise, you can always come by bus on market day itself, or by shuttle bus; market day shuttle buses come from Antigua, Panajachel and

Guatemala City, returning in early afternoon. The market starts winding down around 3 or 4 pm.

Iglesia de Santo Tomás

Though dedicated to the Catholic rite, this simple church, dating from about 1540, is more often the scene of rituals that are only slightly Catholic and more distinctly Mayan. The front steps of the church serve much the same purpose as did the great flights of stairs leading up to Mayan pyramids. For much of the day (especially on Sunday), the steps smolder with copal incense, while indigenous prayer leaders called *chuchkajaues* (mother-fathers) swing censers containing *estoraque* (balsam) incense and chant magic words in honor of the ancient Mayan calendar and of their ancestors.

It's customary for the front steps and door of the church to be used only by important church officials and by the chuchkajaues, so you should go around to the right and enter by the side door.

Inside, the floor of the church may be spread with pine boughs and dotted with offerings of corn, flowers and bottles of liquor; candles are everywhere. Many local families can trace their lineage back centuries, some even to the ancient kings of Quiché. The candles and offerings on the floor are in remembrance of the ancestors, many of whom are buried beneath the church floor just as Mayan kings were buried beneath pyramids. Photography is not permitted in this church.

Museo Regional

In the arcade facing the square's south side is the Museo Regional, which holds exhibits of ancient clay pots and figurines, flint and obsidian arrowheads and spearheads, copper ax heads, metates and a jade collection. Hours are 8 am to noon and 2 to 5 pm, Wednesday to Monday. Admission is US$0.10.

Shrine of Pascual Abaj

Before you have been in Chichi very long, some village lad will offer to guide you (for a tip) to a pine-clad hilltop on the town's outskirts to have a look at Pascual Abaj (Sacrifice Stone), which is the local shrine to Huyup Tak'ah, the Mayan earth god. Said to be hundreds – perhaps thousands – of years old, the stone-faced idol has suffered numerous indignities at the hands of outsiders, but locals still revere it. Chuchkajaues come here regularly to offer incense, food, cigarettes, flowers, liquor and Coca-Cola to the earth god. They may even sacrifice a chicken – all to express their thanks and hope for the earth's continuing fertility. The site also offers nice views of the town and valley.

Tourists have been robbed walking to visit Pascual Abaj, so the best plan is to go in a large group. To get there, walk down the hill on 5a Avenida from the Santo

Tomás church, turn right onto 9a Calle and continue downhill along this unpaved road, which bends to the left. At the bottom of the hill, when the road turns sharply right, bear left and follow a path through the cornfields, keeping the stream on your left. Signs mark the way. Walk to the buildings just ahead, which include a farmhouse and a workshop where masks are made. Greet the family here. If the children are not in school, you may be invited to see them perform a local dance in full costume on your return from Pascual Abaj (a tip is expected).

Walk through the farm buildings to the hill behind, then follow the switchbacking path to the top and along the ridge of the hill. Soon you'll reach a clearing and see the

GUATEMALA

Cofradías

Chichi's religious life is centered in traditional religious brotherhoods known as *cofradías*. Membership in the brotherhood is an esteemed civic duty; leadership is the greatest honor. Leaders are elected periodically, and the man who receives the honor of being elected must provide banquets and pay for festivities for the cofradía throughout his term. Though it is very expensive, a *cofrade* (member of the brotherhood) happily accepts the burden, even going into debt if necessary.

Each of Chichi's 14 cofradías has a patron saint. Most notable is the cofradía of Santo Tomás, Chichicastenango's patron saint. The cofradías march in procession to church every Sunday morning and during religious festivals, the officers dressed in costumes

RICHARD I'ANSON

Processions of *cofradías* mark religious festivals in the highlands.

showing their rank. Before them is carried a ceremonial staff topped by a silver crucifix or sun-badge that signifies the cofradía's patron saint. Indigenous drum and flute, and perhaps a few more modern instruments such as a trumpet, may accompany the procession, as do fireworks – the ubiquitous fireworks.

During major church festivals, effigies of the saints are brought out and carried in grand processions, and richly costumed dancers wearing the traditional carved wooden masks act out legends of the ancient Maya and of the Spanish conquest. For the rest of the year, these masks and costumes are kept in storehouses called *morerías*; you'll see them, marked by signs, around the town.

– Nancy Keller

idol in its rocky shrine. The idol looks like something from Easter Island. The squat stone crosses near it have many levels of significance for the Maya, only one of which pertains to Christ. The area of the shrine is littered with past offerings, and the bark of nearby pines has been stripped away in places to be used as fuel in the incense fires.

Special Events

December 7 is Quema del Diablo, the Burning of the Devil, when residents burn their garbage in the streets in an effort to release the evil spirits dwelling within. Highlights include a marimba band and a daring fireworks display that has observers running for cover. The following day is the Feast of the Immaculate Conception; be sure to see the early-morning dance of the giant cartoon characters in the plaza.

The Feast of Santo Tomás starts on December 13 and culminates on December 21, when pairs of brave (some would say maniacal) men fly about at high speeds suspended from a pole in the *palo volador* or flying pole extravaganza.

Places to Stay

Chichi has relatively few accommodations, so it's a good idea to arrive early on Wednesday or Saturday if you want to secure a room before market day. Parking is available in the courtyard of most hotels.

Budget The *Hotel Girón* (☎ 756-1156, fax 756-1226, 6a Calle 4-52) is a clean hotel around a courtyard/car park and offers reasonable value. Rooms cost US$5.50/7.75 single/double with shared cold bath, or US$12.50/15.50 with private hot bath.

Mini-Hotel Chichicasteca (☎ 756-1008, 5a Calle 4-42) is a good budget choice popular with locals. Rooms with shared bath are US$4 per person.

The *Hospedaje Salvador* (☎ 756-1329, 5a Avenida 10-09), two blocks southwest of the Santo Tomás church, is a large, mazelike building with 48 rooms on three floors. Rates are US$4/6.50/9 single/double/triple with

shared bath, US$9.75 double with private bath. Bargain hard.

Hotel Mash is a classic cheapie on 5a Avenida a half block from the plaza. Enter through the black door under the Tienda El Tzijhola sign and walk through the alley, past the simple residences to the staircase with the potted plants. Big, wood-plank rooms with shared bath are US$4 a night. This is about as close as you get to Guatemalan living, short of a homestay.

Hotel Posada Belén (☎/fax 756-1244, 12a Calle 5-55) is up a hill away from the market hubbub. Clean, comfortable rooms are US$4.50/7.75 with shared bath, US$6.50/10.50 with private bath. The showers aren't great, but this is offset by the friendly owners and killer views. You can pay US$1.75 more to get cable TV, and there's laundry service.

Posada El Arco (☎ 756-1255, 4a Calle 4-36), near the Arco Gucumatz, is a sweet guesthouse where you can chill in the rear garden and enjoy a great view north toward the mountains of Quiché. All the rooms are spacious and spotless, with attractive decor and private hot bath. The upstairs rooms (US$15.50 for one or two people) have fireplaces; the downstairs rooms (US$13.25 for one or two people) are larger but don't have fireplaces. The friendly owners, Emilsa and Pedro Macario, speak English and Spanish. Reservations are a good idea.

Another charming, recommended place owned by a friendly husband-and-wife team is *Hotel Chalet House* (☎ 756-1360, 3a Calle C 7-44). Cozy rooms with good beds and nice touches are US$14.25 double in high season, US$10.50 in low season. Breakfast is available.

Mid-Range The *Hotel Chugüilá* (☎ 756-1134, fax 756-1279, 5a Avenida 5-24) is pretty and a decent value. All of the 36 colonial-style rooms have private bath, and some have a fireplace. A few two-room suites and a restaurant are available. For what you get, the price is reasonable: US$31/36/40 single/double/triple. Certain rooms are noticeably better than others, as mildew has beset some.

On the main plaza in the very midst of the market, *Maya Lodge* (☎/fax 756-1167) has 10 rooms, some with fireplaces and all with clean showers. It's fairly plain, despite some colonial touches, but it's comfortable nonetheless. Rooms with private hot bath are US$25/31/39. The lodge has parking and a restaurant.

Top End The best hotel in town is the lovely old *Mayan Inn* (☎ 756-1176, fax 756-1212), 8a Calle A at 3a Avenida, in a quiet spot one long block southwest of the plaza. Founded in 1932 by Alfred S Clark of Clark Tours, it has grown to include several restored colonial houses, their courtyards planted with exuberant tropical gardens and their walls covered with brilliantly colored textiles. Not all of the 30 rooms are equally charming, so look at a few first. Each unit has a fireplace and antique furnishings, including carved wooden bedsteads, headboards painted with country scenes and heavily carved armoires. A staff member in traditional costume is assigned to help you carry your bags, answer any questions and even serve at your table in the dining room, as well as to look after your room – there are no door locks. Rates are US$90/98/108 single/double/triple.

Hotel Santo Tomás (☎ 756-1316, fax 756-1306, 7a Avenida 5-32), two blocks east of the plaza, is colonial in architecture and decor but modern in construction and facilities, and it is thus a favorite with tour operators. Each of the 43 rooms has a private bath (with tub) and fireplace; all the rooms are grouped around pretty courtyards with colonial fountains. Amenities include a swimming pool, Jacuzzi and a good bar and restaurant. Rates are US$66/78/96.

Hotel Villa Grande (☎ 756-1053, 756-1236, fax 756-1140, infos@villasdeguatemala .com), 1km south of Chichi's plaza along the road into town, is a resort with 75 modern rooms and suites in low tile-roofed buildings set into a hillside. It has fine views, a swimming pool and a restaurant. The regular rooms are stark, but the suites all have fireplaces and patios with a view. Rates are US$65/75/85 for the regular rooms, US$97/107/117 for the suites.

Places to Eat

Budget On Sunday and Thursday, eating at the *cookshops* set up in the center of the market is the cheapest way to go. Don't be deterred by the fried-food stalls crowding the fringe – dive in to the center for wholesome fare. On other days, look for the little comedores near the post office on the road into town.

Restaurant La Fonda del Tzijolaj, upstairs in the Centro Comercial Santo Tomás on the plaza's north side, has everything: good views, nice decor, decent food and reasonable prices – US$2 to US$3 for breakfast, twice that for lunch or dinner. It's closed Tuesday. Several other restaurants with portico tables are in the Centro Comercial; at *La Villa de los Cofrades* you can while away the hours playing checkers or backgammon while drinking the best coffee in town. It's a popular place, with breakfast for around US$2.50, lunch or dinner around US$4.

The inner courtyard of the Centro Comercial Santo Tomás is a vegetable market on market days, a basketball court the rest of the time. Upstairs, *Cafetería Buenaventura* is clean and economical.

La Villa de los Cofrades No 2, upstairs at the corner of 6a Calle and 5a Avenida (enter from 6a Calle), has tables inside and out on the balcony, overlooking the market street. It's run by the same owners as the original La Villa de los Cofrades and has the same good coffee and delicious food. An ample lunch or dinner with several courses and big portions costs around US$4 to US$6; simpler meals cost less. Down the block is the similar *Restaurante Katokok*, where pasta and meat dishes cost between US$4 and US$7. The coffee here is also good.

Restaurant Tziguan Tinamit, at the corner of 6 Calle and 5a Avenida, takes its name from the Quiché Maya name for Chichicastenango. It's popular with locals and foreigners for pizza, pasta and meat dishes; open daily.

On 6a Calle, upstairs from Hotel Girón, is *Restaurante Las Brasas*, which is open earlier than other places in Chichi. The breakfast here is a good value.

Restaurante Tapena, on 5a Avenida across the street from Hotel Chugüilá, is a gregarious, family-owned place with huge portions of tasty food for cheap. The service is very attentive.

Restaurant La Parrilla, at the corner of 5a Avenida Arco Gucumatz and 10a Calle, is a good, economical restaurant specializing in charcoal-grilled meats. Hearty meals of your choice of meat, served with rice, salad and soup are US$3 to US$5; breakfasts are cheaper.

Nearby, *Cafetería New York* is upstairs from Hotel Posada Belén; the owner is a Guatemalan who spent 14 years in New York and speaks English. Beans, rice and chicken are staples here.

Hotel Chugüilá (see Places to Stay) is one of the most pleasant places to eat. Main-course plates are priced at US$5.

Mid-Range The three dining rooms at the *Mayan Inn*, 8a Calle A at 3a Avenida, one block southwest of the plaza, have pale yellow walls, beamed ceilings, red-tiled floors, colonial-style tables and chairs and decorations of colorful local cloth. Waiters wear traditional costumes derived from the dress of colonial-era Spanish farmers; the outfits consist of a colorful headdress, sash, black tunic with colored embroidery, half-length trousers and squeaky leather sandals called *caítes*. The food here may not be as stellar as the costuming. The daily set-price meals are economical; US$6 for breakfast and US$12 for lunch or dinner, plus drinks and tip.

The *Hotel Santo Tomás* (7a Avenida 5-32) has a good dining room, but it's often crowded with tour groups. Try to get one of the courtyard tables, where you can enjoy the sun and the marimba band, which plays at lunchtime on market days.

Getting There & Away

Bus Chichi has no bus station. Buses heading south to Guatemala City, Panajachel, Quetzaltenango and all other points reached from the Interamericana arrive and depart from 5a Calle at 5a Avenida Arco Gucumatz, Zona 1, one block south of the arch. Buses heading north to Santa Cruz del Quiché and Nebaj arrive and depart from around the corner on 5a Avenida Arco Gucumatz. Any bus heading south can drop you at Los Encuentros, where you can catch a bus to your final destination.

Antigua 3½ hours, 108km. Take any bus heading for Guatemala City and change buses at Chimaltenango.

Guatemala City US$1.50, 3½ hours, 144km. Buses every 20 minutes, 3:30 am to 6 pm.

Los Encuentros US$0.35, 30 minutes, 17km. Take any bus heading for Guatemala City, Panajachel, Quetzaltenango and so on.

Nebaj US$2.50, 4½ hours, 103km. Two buses daily, or take a bus to Santa Cruz del Quiché and change buses there.

Panajachel US$1.75, 1½ hours, 37km. Eleven buses daily (approximately hourly), 4:30 am to 2:30 pm, or take any bus heading south and change buses at Los Encuentros.

Quetzaltenango US$1.50, three hours, 94km. Seven buses daily, mostly in the morning, or take any bus heading south and change at Los Encuentros.

Santa Cruz del Quiché US$0.50, 30 minutes, 19km. Buses every 20 minutes, 6 am to 9 pm.

Shuttle Minibus On market days, shuttle buses arrive en masse, bringing tourists from Pana, Antigua, Guatemala City and Xela. The shuttles arrive around midmorning, park in front of Hotel Santo Tomás and depart for the return trip around 2 pm. If you're in Chichi, you can usually catch a ride out on one of these.

Shuttle bus companies in Chichi offering services to these same places include Chichi-Tours (☎ 756-1134, 756-1008), at the corner of 5a Calle and 5a Avenida Arco Gucumatz, in the Mini-Hotel Chichicasteca, and K'umarcaaj Tours (☎/fax 756-1226), 6a Calle 5-70, Local 1. With a minimum of three passengers (or equivalent payment), Chichi-Tours will make trips to anyplace else you have in mind, including the ruins at K'umarcaaj (near Santa Cruz del Quiché).

SANTA CRUZ DEL QUICHÉ
• population 13,000 • elevation 2020m

The capital of the department of Quiché, Santa Cruz – which is usually called 'El

Quiché' or simply 'Quiché' – is 19km north of Chichicastenango. The small, dusty town is quieter and much more typical of the Guatemalan countryside than Chichi. Few tourists come here, but those who do come are treated well; friendly locals will direct you anywhere you need to go.

K'umarcaaj

The ruins of the ancient Quiché Maya capital are 3km west of El Quiché. Start out of town along 10a Calle and ask the way frequently. No signs mark the way and no buses ply the route. You can hire a taxi in town at the stand by the bus terminal; roundtrip fare, plus waiting time while you explore the ruins, is around US$6.50. Consider yourself lucky if you succeed in hitching a ride with other travelers who have their own vehicle. Admission to the site costs a few pennies.

The kingdom of Quiché was established in Late Postclassic times (about the 14th century) from a mixture of indigenous people and Mexican invaders. Around 1400, King Gucumatz founded his capital here at K'umarcaaj and conquered many neighboring cities. Eventually, the kingdom of Quiché extended its borders to Huehuetenango, Sacapulas, Rabinal and Cobán, even coming to influence the peoples of the Soconusco region in Mexico.

Pedro de Alvarado led his Spanish conquistadors into Guatemala in 1524, and it was the Quiché, under their king, Tecún Umán, who organized the defense of the territory. In the decisive battle fought near Quetzaltenango on February 12, 1524, Alvarado and Tecún locked in mortal combat. Alvarado won. The defeated Quiché invited the victorious Alvarado to visit their capital, where they secretly planned to kill him. Smelling a rat, Alvarado enlisted the aid of his Mexican auxiliaries and the anti-Quiché Cakchiquel, and together they captured the Quiché leaders, burnt them alive and destroyed K'umarcaaj (called Utatlán by his Mexican allies).

The history is more interesting than the ruined city, of which little remains but a few grass-covered mounds. Still, the site – shaded by tall trees and surrounded by defensive ravines (which failed to save the city from the conquistadors) – is a beautiful place for a picnic. It's also used by locals as a religious ritual site; a long tunnel beneath the plaza is a favorite spot for prayers and chicken sacrifices.

Places to Stay & Eat

Hotel San Pascual (☎ 755-1107, 7a Calle 0-43, Zona 1), a block south of the church, is a safe, clean hotel run by a dynamo señora. It's a friendly place, with guests gathering to watch TV in the evening. Rooms with private hot bath are US$5.25/6.50/9 single/double/triple.

The *Hotel Rey K'iche* (☎ 755-0824, 8a Calle 0-39, Zona 5) is two blocks from the bus terminal, toward the plaza. It's a clean, modern place with rooms with shared bath for US$5.25/7.75 single/double; rooms with private bath (some with color TV) are US$9/13. It also offers a decent restaurant, open daily until 9 pm.

Comedor Fliper (1a Avenida 7-31), 1½ blocks south of the church, is inexpensive, small, clean and friendly. Guests from Hotel San Pascual often walk around the corner to eat here. It's open 7 am to 9 pm daily.

Restaurante El Torito Steak House, on 4a Calle half a block west of the plaza, serves breakfast for US$2; burgers or sandwiches are the same. The house specialty, filet mignon, is US$4.50 for breakfast, US$6 for a full dinner with soup and more. It's open daily. *La Casona*, on 2a Calle between 4a and 5a Avenidas, a few blocks northwest of the church, is also popular.

Getting There & Away

Air Grupo TACA (reservations ☎ 334-7722, fax 334-2775) operates flights departing Guatemala City for El Quiché (US$55, 25 minutes) at 8:50 am, with an additional 2:25 pm departure on Thursday and Sunday. Return flights depart El Quiché at 10:15 am daily, with an additional 3 pm flight on Thursday and Sunday.

Bus Many buses from Guatemala City to Chichicastenango continue to El Quiché (look for 'Quiché' on the signboard). The last daily bus from El Quiché headed south to Chichi and Los Encuentros leaves in midafternoon, so don't tarry too long unless you want to spend the night.

El Quiché is the transportation hub for the sparsely populated and remote northern reaches of Quiché Department, which extends all the way to the Mexican border.

The bus station is about five blocks south and two blocks east of the plaza. Buses include:

Chichicastenango US$0.50, 30 minutes, 19km. Take any bus heading for Guatemala City.

Guatemala City US$1.75, 3½ hours, 163km. Buses every 20 minutes, 3 am to 4 pm.

Nebaj US$1.50, four hours, 84km. Buses at 8 and 10 am and 12:30, 1 and 3:30 pm. Or take a bus to Sacapulas and change there.

Sacapulas US$1, 1½ hours, 50km. Hourly buses, 9 am to 4 pm, or take any bus heading for Nebaj or Uspantán.

Uspantán US$2, six hours, 90km. Buses at 10 and 11 am, noon and 1 pm. Or take a bus to Sacapulas and change there; one bus a day leaves Sacapulas, at 10 am.

NEBAJ
• population 9000

High among the Cuchumatanes are the Ixil Maya villages of Nebaj, Chajul and Cotzal. The scenery is breathtakingly beautiful, and the local people, removed from the influences of TV and modern urbanity, proudly preserve their ancient way of life. They make excellent handicrafts, mostly textiles, and the Nebaj women wear beautiful huipiles.

Nebaj's remote location has been both a blessing and a curse. The Spaniards found it difficult to conquer, and they laid waste to the inhabitants when they finally did. In more recent times, guerrilla forces made the area a base of operations, drawing strong measures from the army to dislodge them – particularly during the short, brutal reign of Ríos Montt. The few surviving inhabitants of these villages either fled across the border into Mexico or were herded into 'strategic hamlets.' Refugees are still making their way back home here.

Travelers come to Nebaj for the scenery, local culture, excellent handicrafts, market (Thursday and Sunday) and, during the second week in August, the annual festival honoring La Virgen de la Asunción.

Bancafé is at 2a Avenida 46; it changes US dollars and traveler's checks. The post office is on 4a Calle; it's open 8:30 am to 5:50 pm Monday to Friday.

Hiking

Hiking in this area is breathtaking. Ask around for the location of nearby waterfalls and head off on your own, or track down Gaspar Terraza Ramos, a recommended local guide who knows the area and its history well. He can take you to see the beautiful countryside around Nebaj, towns destroyed by the war and new villages where former refugees struggle to resume their lives. The hikes start at US$3 an hour – you'll also be asked to donate to refugee programs championed by Gaspar, who's dedicated to that cause. Gaspar usually hangs about the bus station or plaza trying to drum up business.

Places to Stay & Eat

The new **Posada de Don Pablo** (*6a Avenida 5-15*) is the most comfortable place in town; rooms with private hot bath are US$6.50/ 9/9.75 single/double/triple. The current budget favorite is the friendly **Hotel Ixel**, where simple, clean rooms with shared bath are set around two courtyards. Each room is different. Rates are US$2.50/4/6; for something a bit more upscale, ask about the nearby *anexo*, where rooms with private warm bath are US$5 per person.

Pasabien, at the bus terminal, has garnered rave reviews from inveterate travelers for its great food, ample portions and low prices. It's open for dinner only. Near the plaza, **Comedor Irene** offers filling, nutritious dinners for just over US$1. **Maya-Inca**, on the plaza, serves reasonably priced Guatemalan and Peruvian dishes. A burgeoning cottage industry has developed around local women cooking meals for tourists. One reader had a terrific meal made by Juana 'Big Mama' Marcos; you may try to track her down or simply ask your hotel staff if they know any good cooks.

Getting There & Away

Buses come to Nebaj from Quiché, Huehue, Sacapulas and Cobán. More frequent pickup trucks provide transportation at a fare equivalent to that of the bus. Traffic is extremely light by late afternoon, and the earlier you're up and at 'em in this part of Guatemala, the better.

Coming from Cobán (9½ hours), you have to change buses several times, and it is nearly impossible to make it to Nebaj in one day. It's easier to reach Nebaj from Huehuetenango or from El Quiché, going via Sacapulas, as buses are more frequent.

Buses leave Nebaj for Quiché via Sacapulas (US$1.50) at 6 and 11:30 am and 2 pm daily. If you're headed toward Cobán, you must be on that first one to have any chance of making the connection to Uspantán in Sacapulas that same day. Sacapulas has a good hospedaje and restaurant.

SACAPULAS TO COBÁN

Heading east out of Sacapulas, the road winds its way up sadly deforested slopes before reaching the village of **Uspantán**. Rigoberta Menchú, the 1992 Nobel Peace Prize laureate, grew up a five-hour walk from Uspantán; Menchú is not universally loved around here, so don't be shocked if you get a chilly reaction should you mention her name.

If you're headed to Cobán by bus, you'll be spending the night in Uspantán, as the single daily eastbound bus leaves at 3 am (US$1.50, 4½ hours; this bus fills up fast, so get to the stop by 2:30 am). It can get very cold here – you'll be loving that sleeping bag if you brought it. *Pensión Galindo (5a Calle 2-09)*, three blocks from the plaza, charges US$2 per person and is a fine place to stay. A Banrural on the plaza will change US dollars.

Along with the Huehue to Sacapulas leg of the same highway (see East toward Cobán under Around Huehuetenango, later in this chapter), the Uspantán to Cobán road is one of the most gorgeous rides in Guatemala. Sit on the right side of the bus for the best views.

Western Highlands

The areas around Quetzaltenango, Totonicapán and Huehuetenango are more mountainous and less frequented by tourists than the regions closer to Guatemala City. The scenery here is just as beautiful and the indigenous culture just as fascinating. Travelers going to and from the border post at La Mesilla find these towns welcome breaks from long hours of travel, and the area offers some interesting excursion possibilities as well.

CUATRO CAMINOS

Heading westward from Los Encuentros, the Interamericana twists and turns ever higher into the mountains, bringing increasingly dramatic scenery and cooler temperatures. After 59km you come to the important highway junction known as Cuatro Caminos (Four Roads), where you can continue north (straight on) to Huehuetenango (77km), turn east to Totonicapán (12km) or turn southwest to Xela (13km). Buses pass through Cuatro Caminos about every half hour from 6 am to 6 pm, on their way between Totonicapán and Quetzaltenango.

TOTONICAPÁN
• population 9000 • elevation 2500m

San Miguel Totonicapán is a pretty Guatemalan highland town with few tourists. Buses between Totonicapán and Quetzaltenango (passing through Cuatro Caminos) run frequently throughout the day. Placards in the bus window say 'Toto.' The ride from Cuatro Caminos is along a beautiful pine-studded valley.

Flanking Totonicapán's *parque* (as the plaza is called) are the requisite large colonial church and a wonderful municipal theater, built in 1924 in the neoclassical style and restored in recent years. Buses drop you right at the parque.

Market days are Tuesday and Saturday; it's a locals' market, not a tourist affair, and it winds down by late morning. After that, you might want to check out Agua Caliente hot springs, a popular local bathing place 2km from the parque.

Casa de la Cultura Totonicapense

This cultural center (☎/fax 766-1575, email kiche78@hotmail.com, larutamayaonline .com/aventura.html), 8a Avenida 2-17, Zona 1, to the left of the Hospedaje San Miguel, holds displays on indigenous culture and crafts. It also administers a wonderful 'Meet the Artisans' program, which introduces tourists to artisans and local families. Starting at 10 am and lasting till about 4 pm, you'll meet local artisans, toy makers, potters, woodcarvers, weavers and musicians – watch them work, listen to their music, see their dances, experience their living conditions and eat a home-cooked lunch. Cost for the program depends on the size of group, with prices ranging from US$42 per person for four people to US$20 per person for 15 to 20 people; the money goes directly to the artists involved. An extended program includes a one-night stay with a local family for US$15 per person, including meals.

The Casa de la Cultura also offers a tour of Totonicapán-area workshops, community projects, schools and Mayan ceremonial sites (US$5 to US$13 per person) and leads guided hikes to local hot springs and altars. Reservations are requested; all tours are conducted in Spanish.

Special Events

Totonicapán celebrates the Fiesta de Esquipulas on January 15 in Cantón Chotacaj, 3km from the parque; the festival of the Apparition of the Archangel Michael on May 8, with fireworks and traditional dances; the Festival of Traditional Dance on the last Sunday in June; and the Feria Titular de San Miguel Arcángel (Name-Day Festival of the Archangel Saint Michael) September 24 to 30, with the principal celebration being on September 29.

Places to Stay & Eat

On the way into town, one block before the parque on the left is *Hospedaje San Miguel*

(☎ 766-1452, 3a Calle 7-49, Zona 1). It's a tidy place – not what you'd call Swiss-clean, but good for the price. Rooms cost US$4/7.75 single/double with shared hot bath, US$5.50/ 9.75 with private bath. Next door, *Cafe and Comedor Alex* is a clean and friendly place serving a hearty lunch for US$1.50. Continue on 3a Calle for a block toward the parque to *Restaurante La Hacienda*, which features steaks.

QUETZALTENANGO

* population 101,000 * elevation 2335m

Almost everyone calls Quetzaltenango by its Quiché Maya name: Xelajú, or simply Xela (**shay**-lah). The commercial center of southwestern Guatemala, Xela is Guatemala's second-largest city and the center of the Quiché Maya people. Towering over the city to the south is the 3772m Santa María volcano, which has the active 2488m Santiaguito volcano on its southwestern flank.

Xela's good selection of hotels in all price ranges makes it an excellent base for day trips to hot springs, lakes and traditional villages. In recent years, Xela has built a worldwide reputation for its Spanish-language schools. Many students prefer the schools in Xela over Antigua because the environment here more closely approaches the total-immersion ideal of language study.

History

Quetzaltenango came under the sway of the Quiché Maya of K'umarcaaj in the 14th century. Before that it had been a Mam Maya town. For the story of Tecún Umán, the powerful leader of the Quiché, and his archnemesis Pedro de Alvarado, see K'umarcaaj in the Santa Cruz del Quiché section, earlier this chapter.

When the Federation of Central America was founded in the mid-19th century, Quetzaltenango initially decided on federation with Chiapas and Mexico instead of with Central America. Later, the city switched alliances and joined the Central American Federation, becoming an integral part of Guatemala in 1840.

With the late 19th-century coffee boom, Quetzaltenango's wealth increased. Plantation

QUETZALTENANGO

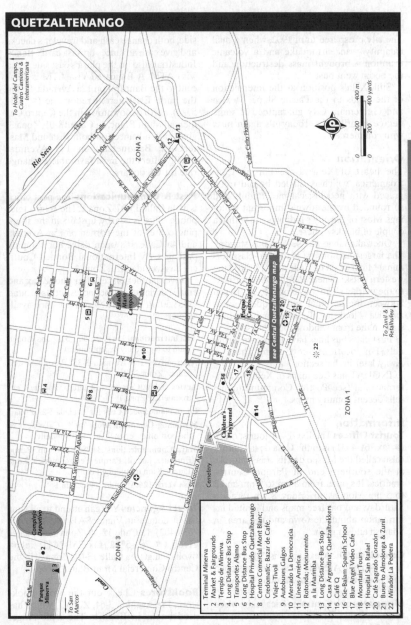

To Hotel del Campo,
Cuatro Caminos &
Interamericana

Río Seco

ZONA 2

ZONA 3

ZONA 1

Parque
Minerva

Complejo
Deportivo

To San
Marcos

Canal

Children's
Playground

Cemetery

Estadio
Mario
Camposeco

Parque
Centroamérica

see Central Quetzaltenango map

To Zunil &
Retalhuleu

Calle Rodolfo Robles

Calzada Sinforoso Aguilar

0   200   400 m
0   200   400 yards

1   Terminal Minerva
2   Market & Fairgrounds
3   Templo de Minerva
4   Long Distance Bus Stop
5   Transportes Alamo
6   Long Distance Bus Stop
7   Hospital Privado Quetzaltenango
8   Centro Comercial Mont Blanc;
     Credomatic; Bazar de Café;
     Viajes Tivoli
9   Autobuses Galgos
10 Mercado La Democracia
11 Líneas América
12 Rotonda; Monumento
     a la Marimba
13 Long Distance Bus Stop
14 Casa Argentina; Quetzaltrekkers
15 Café Q
16 Kie-Balam Spanish School
17 Blue Angel Video Cafe
18 Mountain Tours
19 Hospital San Rafael
20 Café Sagrado Corazón
21 Buses to Almolonga & Zunil
22 Mirador La Pedrera

GUATEMALA

owners came to the city to buy supplies, and the coffee brokers opened up warehouses. The city prospered until 1902, when a dual calamity – an earthquake and a volcanic eruption – brought mass destruction and the boom went bust.

Still, Xela's position at the intersection of the roads to the Pacific Slope, Mexico and Guatemala City guaranteed it some degree of affluence. Today it's again busy with commerce.

Orientation

The heart of Xela is the Parque Centroamérica, which is shaded by old trees, graced with neoclassical monuments and surrounded by the town's important buildings. Most of the city's lodgings are within a couple of blocks of here.

Quetzaltenango has several bus stations. The largest and busiest is the 2nd-class Terminal Minerva, on 6a Calle in Zona 3 (on the western outskirts near Parque Minerva, next to the market). City bus Nos 2, 6 and 10 run between the terminal and Parque Centroamérica – look for 'Terminal' and 'Parque' signs in the front windows of the buses.

First-class bus lines have their own terminals. For locations, see Getting There & Away, later in this section.

INGUAT has free maps of Xela. Alfa Internacional (see Post & Communications) sells decent country maps.

Information

Tourist Offices The INGUAT tourist office (☎/fax 761-4931) is in the Casa de la Cultura (also called the Museo de Historia Natural), at the southern end of Parque Centroamérica. It's open from 8 am to 1 pm and 2 to 5 pm Monday to Friday, 8 am to noon Saturday, and has free maps and limited information about the town and the area, in Spanish and English.

Consulates The Mexican consulate (☎ 763-1312/3/4/5), 9a Avenida 6-19, Zona 1, is open 8 to 11 am and 2 to 3 pm Monday to Friday.

Money Parque Centroamérica is the place to go for banks. Banco de Occidente, in the

beautiful building on the north side of the plaza, and Construbanco, on the plaza's east side, both change cash and traveler's checks and give cash advances on Visa cards. Banco Industrial, also on the plaza's east side, has a Visa ATM. A Bancared Visa ATM is adjacent to the Banrural on 12a Avenida, facing the park. Elsewhere, Credomatic (☎ 763-5722), north of downtown in the Centro Comercial Mont Blanc, 4a Calle 18-01, Zona 3, gives cash advances on both Visa and MasterCard. Banquetzal, on 14a Avenida, usually offers the most favorable exchange rate for US dollars.

Post & Communications The post office is at 4a Calle 15-07, Zona 1. The Telgua telephone office is nearby, upstairs in the shopping center at the corner of 15a Avenida and 4a Calle. It's open daily. For shipping packages, try International Bonded Couriers, 8a Avenida 6-23, Zona 1.

Several other places offer phone, fax and email services. Internet access costs around US$1.50 an hour. These services are available at:

Alfa Internacional 15a Avenida 3-51, Zona 1; open 9 am to 6 pm daily except Sunday

Alternativos 16a Avenida 3-35, Parque Benito Juárez, Zona 3

Arytex below Casa de la Cultura, Parque Centroamérica, Zona 1

International Speed Calls 15a Avenida 5-22, Zona 1

Marketing Communications on 4a Calle next to the post office; open 9 am to 10 pm daily

Maya Communications Bar/Salon Tecún, Pasaje Enríquez, just off Parque Centroamérica, Zona 1; open 8 am to midnight daily

Casa Verde 12a Avenida 1-40, Zona 1

Travel Agencies You can attend to all your travel details at Viajes SAB (☎ 765-0965, 763-6402), 1a Calle 12-35, Zona 1, or Viajes Tivoli (☎ 763-5792, fax 761-1447, xela@ tivoli.com.gt), 4a Calle 18-01, Zona 3, in the Centro Comercial Mont Blanc.

Bookstores Check out the Vrisa bookstore, 15a Avenida 3-64, Zona 1, which has used books in English. The Blue Angel

GUATEMALA

CENTRAL QUETZALTENANGO

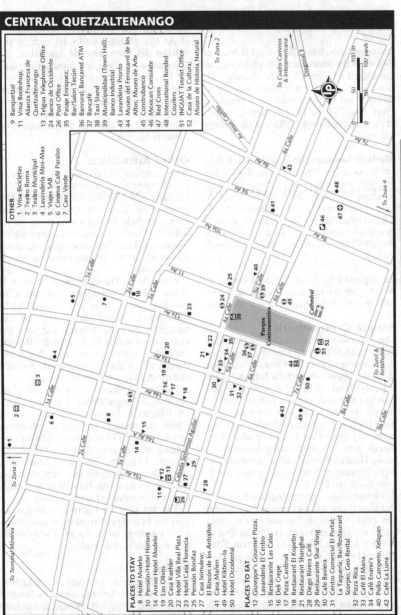

PLACES TO STAY
8 Hotel Modelo
10 Pensión/Hotel Horiani
14 Anexo Hotel Modelo
19 Los Olivos
20 Casa Kaehler
22 Hotel Villa Real Plaza
23 Hotel Casa Florencia
25 Pensión Bonifaz
27 Casa Ixmulew;
    El Rincón de los Antojitos
41 Casa Mañen
49 Hotel Kiktem-Ja
50 Hotel Occidental

PLACES TO EAT
12 Giuseppe's Gourmet Pizza;
    Lavandería El Centro
15 Restaurante Las Calas
16 Deli Crepe
17 Pizza Cardinali
18 Restaurant El Kopetin
21 Restaurant Shanghai
28 Diego Rivera Café
29 Restaurante Shai Shing
30 Cafe Baviera
31 Centro Comercial El Portal;
    La Taquería; Bar/Restaurant
    Scorpio; Geo Rental
32 Pizza Rica
33 Café El Mana
34 Café Enano's
40 Pollo Campero; Xelapan
42 Cafe La Luna

OTHER
1 Vrisa Bicicletas
2 Teatro Roma
3 Teatro Municipal
5 Lavandería Mini-Max
6 Cinema Café Paraíso
7 Casa Verde
9 Banquetzal
11 Vrisa Bookshop;
    Alianza Francesa de
    Quetzaltenango
13 Telgua Telephone Office
24 Banco de Occidente
26 Post Office
35 Pasaje Enriquez;
    Bar/Salon Tecún
36 Banrural; Bancared ATM
37 Bancafé
38 Taxi Stand
39 Municipalidad (Town Hall);
    Banco Industrial
43 Lavandería Pronto
44 Museo del Ferrocarril de los
    Altos; Museo de Arte
45 Construbanco
46 Mexican Consulate
47 Red Cross
48 International Bonded
    Couriers
51 INGUAT Tourist Office
52 Casa de la Cultura;
    Museo de Historia Natural

Video Cafe (see Places to Eat) sells international books and magazines.

Laundry Lavandería Mini-Max, 14a Avenida C47, faces the neoclassical Teatro Municipal. Lavandería El Centro is at 15a Avenida 3-51, Zona 1; it's open 9 am to 6 pm Monday to Friday, 9 am to 5 pm Saturday. Lavandería Pronto is at 7a Calle 13-25A, Zona 1. At each of these places it costs US$2 to wash and dry one load.

Medical Services The Hospital San Rafael (☎ 761-4414, 761-2956), 9a Calle 10-41, Zona 1, has 24-hour emergency service; Dr Oscar Rolando de León there speaks English. Hospital Privado Quetzaltenango (☎ 761-4381), Calle Rodolfo Robles 23-51, Zona 1, is another option. The Red Cross (Cruz Roja; ☎/fax 761-2746) is at 8a Avenida 6-62, Zona 1.

Emergency Call the national police at ☎ 761-2569; the municipal police at ☎ 761-5805; and the fire department at ☎ 761-2002.

Parque Centroamérica

This plaza and its surrounding buildings are pretty much all there is to see in Xela proper. At its southeast end, the Casa de la Cultura holds the **Museo de Historia Natural**, which has exhibits on the Maya, the liberal revolution in Central American politics and the Estado de Los Altos, of which Quetzaltenango was the capital. Marimbas, weaving, taxidermy and other local lore also claim places here. It's fascinating because it's funky. Hours are from 8 am to noon and 2 to 6 pm Monday to Friday, and from 9 am to 1 pm Saturday; US$1.

Continuing counterclockwise around the plaza, the once-crumbling **cathedral** has been rebuilt in the last few decades and was still being renovated at the time of writing. Up the block, the **Municipalidad** (Town Hall) follows the grandiose neoclassical style so favored as a symbol of culture and refinement in this wild mountain country. On the plaza's northwest side, the palatial **Pasaje Enríquez**, between 4a and 5a Calles, was built to be lined with elegant shops, but as Quetzaltenango has few elegant shoppers, it has suffered decline.

At the plaza's southwest corner, the **Museo del Ferrocarril de los Altos**, 12a Avenida at 7a Calle, is a museum focusing on the railroad that once connected Xela and Retalhuleu. Upstairs you'll find an **art museum** (mostly modern art) and schools of art, dance and marimba. Hours and admission are the same as at the Museo de Historia Natural.

Other Attractions

Walk north on 14a Avenida to 1a Calle to see the impressive neoclassical **Teatro Municipal**, which hosts regular performing-arts productions of all sorts, from international dance recitals to the coronation of La Señorita Quetzaltenango (recommended). Inside are three tiers of seating, the lower two of which have private boxes for prominent families.

Mercado La Democracia, in Zona 3, is about 10 blocks northwest of the plaza. To get there, walk along 14a Avenida to 1a Calle (to the Teatro Municipal), turn left, turn right onto 16a Avenida and cross the major street called Calle Rodolfo Robles; the market will be on your right. It's an authentic urban market with fresh produce and meat, foodstuffs and necessities.

Farther northwest, near the Terminal Minerva, is **Parque Minerva**. The neoclassical Templo de Minerva here was built to honor the classical goddess of education and to inspire Guatemalan youth to new heights of learning. Near the Templo de Minerva is Parque Zoológico Minerva, a zoo with a playground and carnival rides; it's open 9 am to 5 pm Tuesday to Sunday. A large outdoor market is also nearby.

The **Mirador La Pedrera**, a 15-minute walk (or $4 taxi ride) from the center, offers a fine view over the city. A small store at the top sells snacks and drinks.

Hiking

Volcán Tajumulco (4220m) is the highest point in Central America and a challenging two-day hike from Xela. Volcán Santiaguito (2488m) and Volcán Santa María (3772m) can also be ascended from Xela. Quetzaltrekkers (☎ 761-2470, quetzaltrekkers@hotmail.com, beef.brownrice.com/streetschool), Diagonal 12 8-37, Zona 1, is a recommended outfit specializing in these ascents. The Tajumulco trek costs US$35. All profits go to the nonprofit Escuela de la Calle, which works with street children in Xela.

For descriptions of day hikes around Xela; see Around Quetzaltenango, later in this section.

Cycling

Cycling is a great way to explore the surrounding countryside or commute to your Spanish class. Fuentes Georginas, San Andrés Xequl and the steam vents at Los Vahos (see Around Quetzaltenango) are all attainable day trips. Vrisa Bicicletas (☎ 761-3862), 15a Avenida 0-67, Zona 1, rents mountain and town bikes for US$2.75 a day, US$9.75 a week.

Language Courses

In recent years, Xela has become well known for its Spanish-language schools. Unlike Antigua, which has had a similar reputation for quite a bit longer, Xela is not overrun with foreigners, but it does have a small student social scene. The Xela Pages website, www.xelapages.com/schools.htm, has information on many of the schools here.

Xela seems to attract altruistic types. Most of the city's Spanish schools participate in social-action programs with the local Quiché people and provide students an opportunity to get involved. Prices for the schools vary a little; the standard price is around US$110/120/130 per week for four/five/six hours of daily instruction, Monday to Friday, including room and board with a local family, or around US$85 per week without homestay. Among the many reputable schools are:

Academia Latinoamericana Mayanse (ALM; ☎ 761-2877), 15a Avenida 6-75, Zona 1 (Apdo Postal 375)

Casa Xelajú (☎ 761-9954, fax 761-5953, office@casaxelaju.com, www.casaxelaju.com), Callejón 15, Diagonal 13-02, Zona 1; in the USA ☎ 512-416-6991 or write to PO Box 3275, Austin, TX

78764-3275; classes in Quiché and literature available

Celas-Maya (☎/fax 761-4342, celasmaya@yahoo.com), 6a Calle 14-55, Zona 1; also offers classes in Quiché

Centro Bilingüe Amerindia (CBA; ☎ 761-1613, fax 761-8773, cba@guate.net), 7a Avenida 9-05, Zona 1 (Apdo Postal 381); in the USA ☎ 508-896-7589 or write to c/o Martha Holden, 37 Run Hill Rd, Brewster MA 02631-2331; classes in Mayan languages offered

Centro de Estudios de Español Pop Wuj (☎/fax 761-8286, popwujxelpronet.net.gt, members.aol.com/popwuj/main.html), 1a Calle 17-72, Zona 1 (Apdo Postal 68); in the USA ☎/fax 707-869-1116, popwuj@juno.com, or write to PO Box 11127, Santa Rosa, CA 95406

Centro Maya de Idiomas (CMI; ☎ 767-0352, info@centromaya.org, www.centromaya.org), 21 Avenida 5-69, Zona 3; classes offered in Quiché, Mam, Q'anjob'al and Tz'utuhil

Desarrollo del Pueblo Spanish Language Institute (☎/fax 761-4624, desapu@hotmail.com), Diagonal 12 6-28, Zona 1

English Club International Language School (☎ 763-2198), Diagonal 4 9-71, Zona 9; classes in Spanish, Quiché and Mam

Escuela de Español Sakribal (☎/fax 761-5211), 10a Calle 7-17, Zona 1 (Apdo Postal 164); in the USA contact Kimberly Mueller (k_mueller@yahoo.com), 360 S Pleasant St No 2, Amherst, MA 01002

Guatemalensis Spanish School (☎/fax 765-1384, gssxela@infovia.com.gt, www.infovia.com.gt/gssxela), 19a Avenida 2-14, Zona 1 (Apdo Postal 53)

Instituto de Estudios de Español y Participación en Ayuda Social (INEPAS; ☎ 765-1308, fax 765-2584, iximulew@guate.net), 15a Avenida 4-59, Zona 1; in the USA contact Elliott Brown (☎ 607-273-8471); English and French spoken

Juan Sisay Spanish School (☎ 765-1318, fax 763-2104, info-sisay@trafficman.com), 15a Avenida 8-38, Zona 1 (Apdo Postal 392); in the USA contact Stacey Blankenbaker (☎ 650-312-7777, ext 7763, fax 650-312-7779, sblankenbaker@sfmc.k12.ca.us)

Kie-Balam Spanish School (☎ 761-1636, fax 761-0391), Diagonal 12 4-46, Zona 1; in the USA ☎ 847-888-2514, moebius@superhighway.net or write to c/o Martha Mora, 894 Patricia Dr, Elgin, IL 60120

Proyecto Lingüístico Quetzalteco de Español (☎/fax 763-1061, plq@c.net.gt, www.infoserve.net/hermandad/plqe.html), 5a Calle 2-42, Zona 1; in

GUATEMALA

the USA ☎ 800-963-9889, johnsond@televar.com or write to PO Box 452, Manson, WA 98831; the company also runs the Escuela de la Montaña, a school on a coffee *finca* in the mountains around Xela, where participation in local culture and volunteer work are strongly encouraged; enrollment limited to eight students

Spanish School Latin Arts (☎/fax 761-0204, latinartsxela@yahoo.com), 10a Avenida C-09, Zona 1

Ulew Tinimit (☎/fax 761-6242, utinimit@guate.net, www.unet.univie.ac.at/~a9509611/ut.html), 7a Avenida 3-18, Zona 1; Mayan language classes also offered

Utatlán Spanish School (☎ 761-0416, info@utatlan-trafficman.com), 12a Avenida 4-32, Zona 1, Pasaje Enríquez

Dance Lessons

Salsa and merengue lessons are popular here. Two recommended places offering one-on-one instruction are Latin Dance Lessons (☎ 763-0271), at the Casa Verde, 12a Avenida 1-46, Zona 1, and Latin Rhythm Dance Studio (☎ 761-2707, evenings ☎ 767-2104, latinrhythm@latinmail.com), inside the Diego Rivera Café, 15a Avenida 5-31, Zona 1. An hour of instruction costs from US$2 to $4.50; slightly more for couples or groups.

Volunteer Work

Xela has several organizations that work with the local Quiché people and need volunteers.

The Asociación Hogar Nuevos Horizontes, La Escuela de la Calle and Red International are all based in Quetzaltenango. See the Volunteer Work section in the Facts for the Visitor chapter for details. The Hogar de Esperanza, Diagonal 11 7-38, Zona 1, works with street children. Many of the Spanish-language schools also work with volunteer programs.

Organized Tours

Thierry Roquet and the folks at Casa Iximulew and the INEPAS school (☎ 765-1308, fax 765-2584, iximulew@trafficman.com), 15a Avenida 4-59, run several interesting tours. Half-day tours include Fuentes Georginas, Los Vahos and San Francisco El

Alto (US$32 for two people). Also offered are camping trips to Lake Atitlán and the Santa María and Santiaguito volcanoes, as well as longer tours to Flores, Tikal and El Zotz; these start at US$20 a day per person, with a minimum of three people. Spanish-, English- and French-speaking guides are available.

Mountain Tours (☎ 761-5993, 761-8650, mountaintours@hotmail.com), Diagonal 13 15-53, Zona 1, conducts tours to Fuentes Georginas, Zunil and San Francisco El Alto, and trips to more obscure sites like Laguna Chicabal and the hot springs at Aguas Amargas.

The Guatemala Birding Resource Center runs recommended birding trips from Xela; see Organized Tours in the Getting There & Around chapter for details.

Places to Stay

Budget The hot budget choice of the moment is *Casa Argentina* (☎ 761-2470, casaargentina@trafficman.com, Diagonal 12 8-37, Zona 1). This unpretentious, mellow place is a few minutes' walk from the park and has big, clean rooms with shared bath for US$3.25/5.25 single/double, US$18 per person by the week. Amenities include a communal kitchen and drinking water for guests. Quetzaltrekkers (see Hiking, earlier in this section) is also here.

Pensión/Hotel Horiani (☎ 763-5228, 12a Avenida 2-23, Zona 1) is a simple but clean family-run hospedaje with six rooms for US$4/6 with shared hot bath. The entrance is on 2a Calle.

Casa Kaehler (☎ 761-2091, 13a Avenida 3-33, Zona 1) is an old-fashioned European-style pension with seven rooms of various shapes and sizes. Room 7, with private bath, is the most comfortable; it's US$9/11. Otherwise, rooms with shared hot bath are US$8/10/12 single/double/triple. This is an excellent, safe place for women travelers; ring the bell to gain entry. Ask about tours in the region.

Across the street, the new *Los Olivos* (☎ 761-0215, 13a Avenida 3-32) is a good, friendly choice. Clean rooms with private hot bath, cable TV, towels and drinking water are US$13/19.50/24/28 single/double/triple/quad.

Casa Iximulew *(☎ 765-1308, fax 765-2584, iximulew@trafficman.com, 15a Avenida 4-59, Zona 1)* has one clean, spacious room with shared warm bath for US$4.75/6.75 or US$6/8.25 including breakfast at its adjoining restaurant, El Rincón de los Antojitos (see Places to Eat). The Casa also rents apartments, about a 10-minute walk from town center, for US$70/235 a week/month furnished. Each has two bedrooms, a fully equipped kitchen, living room, courtyard and cable TV. Unfurnished apartments rent for US$150 a month. The busy Casa also offers tours and runs the INEPAS Spanish school. French, English and Spanish are spoken.

The friendly ***Hotel Occidental*** *(☎ 765-4065, 7a Calle 12-23, Zona 1)* is right off the park and a good value. Clean and quiet rooms with quality beds are US$5.25/8.50 with shared hot bath, US$7/10.50 with private bath.

Southwest of the park is the huge old ***Hotel Kiktem-Ja*** *(☎ 761-4304, 13a Avenida 7-18, Zona 1)*. The 20 rooms, all with private bath and eight with fireplace, are on two levels around the courtyard, which also serves as a car park. Rooms hold one to eight people; US$15/20/25.

For long-term stays, check out ***Hospedaje Tecún*** *(☎ 765-1203, 761-2382, 4a Calle 10-55, Zona 3)*, about a 10-minute stroll from the center. This house has a kitchen, garden and communal space; private rooms rent for US$65 a month. Ask at the Bar/Salon Tecún (see Places to Eat) for information. You could also contact Señora Lidia de Mazariegos *(☎ 761-2166, 4a Calle 15-34, Zona 1)*, who rents fully furnished apartments with cable TV and free gas for the first month.

Mid-Range If you want to spend a little more for a lot more comfort, head straight for the family-run ***Hotel Modelo*** *(☎ 761-2529, 763-0216, fax 763-1376, 14a Avenida A 2-31, Zona 1)*. Pleasant small rooms with bath, cable TV and phone are US$25/28/31 single/double/triple inside the main hotel (where three of the rooms have a fireplace)

or US$17/20/24 in the equally comfortable *anexo* (☎ 765-1271). The hotel's good dining room serves breakfast, lunch and dinner. Parking is available.

Hotel Casa Florencia *(☎ 761-2326, 12a Avenida 3-61, Zona 1)*, a few steps from the plaza, is run by a pleasant señora who keeps everything spotless. The hotel's nine spacious rooms, all with bath, cable TV and carpet, are US$20/25/30. Breakfast (overpriced) is served in the dining room, and parking is available.

The comfortable ***Hotel Villa Real Plaza*** *(☎ 761-4045, 761-6036, fax 761-6780, 4a Calle 12-22, Zona 1)* is half a block west of the park. Its 60 large, airy rooms, all with bath, cable TV and phone, are US$32/36/41. Amenities include a restaurant, bar, sauna and parking.

Casa Mañen *(☎ 765-0786, fax 765-0678, casamannen@xela.net.gt, 9a Avenida 4-11, Zona 1)* is a quiet place with romantic atmosphere, beautifully outfitted rooms, tranquil gardens and distinguished service. All nine rooms have traditional appointments, hand-carved furniture, tile floors, TV and private bath. Some rooms have a fireplace, and upstairs units have balconies and views. The standard rooms are US$35/45 single/double; two suites go for US$50. Breakfast is available and there's a rooftop terrace.

The four-star ***Pensión Bonifaz*** *(☎ 761-2182, 761-2279, fax 761-2850, 4a Calle 10-50, Zona 1)*, near the northeast corner of Parque Centroamérica, is Xela's best-known hotel. Though it's a bit stuffy, Guatemalans and foreigners have been coming here for years. The 73 comfortably old-fashioned rooms all have private bath (some with tubs), cable TV and phone. Rooms in the original colonial-style building (the one you enter) are preferable to those in the adjoining modernized building. The hotel has a good dining room, a cheery bar and a car park. Rates are US$52/64.

The ***Hotel del Campo*** *(☎ 263-1665, fax 263-0074)*, Km 224, Camino a Cantel, is Xela's most modern hotel. Its 96 rooms have showers and TV and are decorated in wood and red brick. The hotel also boasts an all-weather swimming pool. Rooms on the lowest floor can be dark, so get a room numbered in the 50s. Prices are reasonable: US$25/31/37. The hotel is 4.5km (a 10-minute drive) east of the town center, a short distance off the main road between Quetzaltenango and Cuatro Caminos; watch for signs for the hotel and for the road to Cantel.

Places to Eat

As with hotels, Quetzaltenango has a good selection of places to eat in all price ranges. Cheapest are the food stalls in and around the small market to the left of the Casa de la Cultura, where snacks and substantial main-course plates are sold for US$1 or less.

An excellent place for Guatemalan home cooking is *Café Sagrado Corazón*, 9a Avenida at 9a Calle, Zona 1. The gregarious mother-daughter team here serves delicious breakfast, lunch and dinner and always offers a vegetarian option. Lunch plates start at US$1.75. It's open 9 am to 9 pm Monday to Saturday, 9 am to 3 pm Sunday.

Cafe Baviera, 13a Avenida at 5a Calle, is a European-style cafe serving good coffee roasted on the premises. Breakfast and other meals, pastries, snacks and alcoholic beverages are also served. It's open daily. Across the street, the friendly *Café El Mana* serves cheap and hearty breakfast, lunch and dinner. Down the block on 5a Calle and in the same vein is the recommended *Café Enano's*. Here you can dig in to economical, big meals in a family atmosphere.

A popular spot with good food is *El Rincón de los Antojitos*, 15a Avenida at 5a Calle, Zona 1. The menu features Guatemalan dishes, with a few concessions to international tastes and a variety of vegetarian dishes. The house specialty is *pepián* (chicken in a sesame sauce), a typical indigenous Guatemalan recipe, for US$5. Nearby, *Giuseppe's Gourmet Pizza (15a Avenida 3-68)* makes tasty and filling pizza and pasta at reasonable prices. It's open noon to 10 pm daily. Another place for pizza is the well-regarded *Pizza Rica (13a Avenida 5-42)*.

Cafe La Luna, 8a Avenida at 4a Calle, Zona 1, is a welcoming little place to hang out, drink coffee, write letters and socialize. Similar is *Diego Rivera Café (☎ 761-2707, 15a Avenida 5-31, Zona 1)*, a laid-back place for coffee or a meal.

Popular with students, *Blue Angel Video Cafe (7a Calle 15-22, Zona 1)* offers a good variety of excellent, healthy foods at economical prices. All the salads and veggies are sterilized. Alcohol is served. It's open 2 to 11:30 pm daily (see Entertainment). Nearby, *Café Q (Diagonal 12 4-46)* has an interesting menu featuring vegetarian options like falafel, soy burgers and lentil soup. It's open 1 pm to 'late,' Monday to Saturday.

The *Bar/Salon Tecún*, in Pasaje Enríquez, is another popular gathering spot for foreigners. It offers good Italian food, along with plenty of drinking and socializing, from noon to 3 pm and 5 pm to 1 am daily.

Pizza Cardinali (14a Avenida 3-41, Zona 1) serves savory pizza and pasta dishes. In the same block, *Restaurant El Kopetin* has a family atmosphere and a long and varied menu ranging from Cuban-style sandwiches to filet mignon. An average full meal costs around US$5; alcohol is served. Both are open daily. A few doors down is *Deli Crepe*, serving good portions of tasty food at great prices. Tacos, crepes, burritos and *licuados* come in an infinite variety here. Check out this place if you're traveling with children, as the atmosphere and food are kid-friendly.

A couple of other decent restaurants are in the Centro Comercial El Portal, 13a Avenida 5-38, Zona 1. *La Taquería* is a bright, cheerful Mexican restaurant with excellent prices; full meals are US$2 to US$4. *Bar/Restaurant Scorpio* has lunch specials or burgers for US$2.75, main dishes for US$4. The big fireplace is pleasant in the evening. Both have tables inside and out on the patio.

Restaurant Shanghai (4a Calle 12-22, Zona 1) features Guatemalan Chinese cuisine: *pato* (duck), *camarones* (shrimp) and other Chinese specialties cost about US$3.50 to US$5 per plate. Passable, cheap Chinese food is also served at *Restaurante Shai Shing (4a Calle 14-25)*, which has zero atmosphere but good service.

Pollo Campero, 5a Calle half a block east of the park, serves inexpensive fried chicken, burgers and breakfast daily. Next door, **Xelapan** is a good bakery open 5:15 am to 8 pm daily.

The new **Restaurante Las Calas** *(14a Avenida A 3-21)* is heaven sent, serving some of the best meals around. Satisfying portions of chicken, fish or beef are well prepared and cost US$3. Also featured are paella and four types of flan. The service is top notch and there's an art gallery through the courtyard. Hours are 8 am to 9:30 pm daily. Don't be surprised if the restaurant's prices rise with its growing popularity.

The dining room of **Hotel Modelo** *(14a Avenida A 2-31)* serves breakfast and has good set lunches and dinners (US$5.50).

The dining room of **Pensión Bonifaz** *(☎ 761-2182, 761-2279, 4a Calle 10-50, Zona 1)* is the best in town. This is where the local social set comes to dine and be seen. The food is good, and the prices, though high by Guatemalan standards, are low when compared to those even in Mexico. Soup, main course, dessert and drink can run to US$12, but you can spend about half that much if you order only a sandwich and a beer.

Entertainment

It gets chilly when the sun goes down, so you won't want to sit out in the Parque Centroamérica enjoying the balmy breezes – there aren't any. Nevertheless, it's softly lit and a pleasant place for an evening stroll.

Traditional Clothing

Anyone visiting the highlands can delight in the beautiful *traje indígena* (traditional clothing) of the local people. The styles, patterns and colors used by each village are unique, and each garment is the creation of its weaver, with subtle differences from all others.

The basic elements of the traditional wardrobe are the *tocoyal* (head-covering), *huipil* (blouse), *corte* or *refajo* (skirt), *calzones* (trousers), *tzut* or *kaperraj* (cloth), *paz* or *faja* (sash) and *caítes* or *xajap* (sandals).

Women's head-coverings are beautiful and elaborate bands of cloth up to several meters in length, wound about the head and decorated with tassels, pompoms and silver ornaments. In recent years they have been worn only on ceremonial occasions and for tourist photos.

Women's huipiles, however, are worn proudly every day. Though some machine-made fabrics are now being used, most huipiles are made completely by hand. The blouse is woven on a backstrap loom, then decorated with appliqué and embroidery designs and motifs common to the weaver's village. The unique designs helped oppressors (from colonial times and the civil war) monitor the movement of people. Many of the motifs are traditional symbols. No doubt all had religious or historical significance at one time, though today that meaning may be lost to memory.

Cortes (refajos) are pieces of cloth seven to 10 yards long that are wrapped around the body. Traditionally, girls wear theirs above the knee, married women at the knee and older women below the knee, though the style can differ markedly from region to region.

Both men and women wear fajas, long strips of woven cloth wrapped around the midriff as belts. Wrapped with folds upward like a cummerbund, the folds serve as pockets.

Tzutes (male) or kaperraj (female) are the all-purpose cloths carried by local people and used as head-coverings, baby-slings, produce sacks, basket covers and shawls. There are also shawls for women called *perraj*, probably a contraction of kaperraj.

Before the coming of the Spaniards, it was most common for simple leather thong sandals (caítes, xajap) to be worn only by men. Even today, many Highland women and children go barefoot, while others have thongs, more elaborate huarache-style sandals or modern shoes.

- **Tom Brosnahan**

Casa Verde (☎ /fax 763-0271, 12a Avenida 1-40, Zona 1) is a happening venue for concerts, live theater, poetry readings, films and other activities. Wednesday night features salsa dancing. It also offers billiards, chess, backgammon and other games and a restaurant/bar. Hours are 4 pm until around midnight, Tuesday to Saturday.

Performances and cultural events are also presented at the city's beautiful *Teatro Municipal*, on 1a Calle, and at *Casa de la Cultura* (☎ 761-6427), on the plaza's south side. *Teatro Roma*, on 14a Avenida A facing the Teatro Municipal, sometimes plays interesting movies.

The *Alianza Francesa de Quetzaltenango* (☎ /fax 761-4076, 15a Avenida 3-64, Zona 1) offers free French films with Spanish subtitles once a week, along with other activities.

Videos are shown at 8 pm nightly at *Blue Angel Video Cafe* (see Places to Eat); admission is US$1. The video schedule is posted on the door. The cafe here is popular for socializing in the evening. Also showing nightly videos is *Cinema Café Paraíso* (14a Avenida A 1-04). Admission is US$1.50. For cocktails and carousing, head to the ever popular *Bar/Salon Tecún,* in Pasaje Enríquez (see Places to Eat).

The bar at *Pensión Bonifaz* (see Places to Eat) is the place for more highbrow socializing.

Getting There & Away

Air Inter Group TACA flights leave Xela for Guatemala City at 8:50 am and 3:10 pm daily, and leave the capital for Xela at 8:10 am and 2:30 pm daily (US$30 Monday to Friday, US$35 on weekends; 30 minutes).

Bus For 2nd-class buses, head to Terminal Minerva, on 6a Calle in Zona 3 (on the western outskirts near Parque Minerva, next to the market). Bus Nos 2, 6 and 10 run between the terminal and Parque Centroamérica (look for 'Terminal' and 'Parque' signs in the bus window). You can catch the city bus (US$0.05) to the terminal from 8a Calle at 12a Avenida or from 13a Avenida at 4a Calle in the town center.

The city bus leaves you a short walk from where the long-distance buses depart. To get there, you must cross through the market; keeping the park and taxis on your left, head toward the market stalls. A passage leads to the other side of the busy terminal.

Buses that depart from Terminal Minerva headed for the Interamericana also pick up passengers at bus stops at the corner of 19a Avenida and 7a Calle, Zona 3, at the corner of 13a Avenida and 4a Calle, and at the corner of 7a Avenida (Calzada Independencia) and 8a Calle (Calle Cuesta Blanca) at the *rotonda* (traffic circle) and the Monumento a la Marimba. You can board them at any of these stops, though your chances of getting a seat are much better if you board at the terminal.

Transportes Alamo, Líneas América and Autobuses Galgos, three 1st-class lines operating buses between Guatemala City and Quetzaltenango, each have their own terminals. Transportes Alamo (☎ 761-2964) is at 4a Calle 14-04, Zona 3. Líneas América (☎ 761-2063, 761-4587) is at 7a Avenida 13-33, Zona 2. Autobuses Galgos (☎ 761-2248) is at Calle Rodolfo Robles 17-43, Zona 1.

All of the following buses depart from Terminal Minerva, unless otherwise noted:

Almolonga (for Los Vahos) US$0.35, 10 minutes, 6km. Buses every 15 minutes from 5:30 am to 5 pm, with a possible stop for additional passengers in Zona 4 southeast of the park.

Chichicastenango US$1.50, three hours, 94km. Buses at 6, 8:30, 9:30, 10:15 and 11 am and 12:30, 1:30, 2:30 and 4 pm. Or change at Los Encuentros.

Ciudad Tecún Umán (Mexican border) US$2, 2½ hours, 129km. Buses every half hour, 5:30 am to 4:30 pm.

El Carmen/Talismán (Mexican border) Take a bus to Coatepeque and change there for a bus to El Carmen. From Coatepeque it's about two hours to El Carmen (US$1.75).

Guatemala City US$3.75, four hours, 206km. First-class buses with Transportes Alamo five times daily, with Líneas América six times daily and with Autobuses Galgos eight times daily, each departing from its own terminal (see above). First-class buses stop at Totonicapán, Los Encuentros (change for Chichi or Pana) and Chimaltenango (change for Antigua). Second-class buses (US$2) depart from Terminal Minerva every half hour, 3 am to 4:30 pm; these make many stops and take longer.

Huehuetenango US$1, two hours, 90km. Buses every half hour, 5:30 am to 5:30 pm.

La Mesilla (Mexican border) US$2, 3½ hours, 170km. Buses every half hour, 5:30 am to 5:30 pm. Or bus to Huehuetenango and change there.

Momostenango US$0.45, 45 minutes, 35km. Hourly buses, 6:30 am to 5 pm.

Panajachel US$1.75, 2½ hours, 99km. Buses at 5, 6 and 8 am, noon, 3 and 4 pm. Or take any bus bound for Guatemala City and change at Los Encuentros.

Retalhuleu US$0.80, 1½ hours, 67km. Buses every 20 minutes, 4:30 am to 6 pm. Look for 'Reu' in the bus window.

San Andrés Xequl US$0.15, 40 minutes. Hourly buses, 6 am to 3 pm, or take any bus to San Francisco El Alto or Totonicapán, disembark at the Esso station at the Moreiria junction and flag a pickup.

San Francisco El Alto US$0.25, one hour, 17km. Buses every 15 minutes, 6 am to 6 pm.

San Martín Chile Verde (Sacatepéquez) US$0.25, 45 minutes, 25km. Xelajú buses every 30 minutes, 6:30 am to 4 pm. Placard in the bus window will say 'Colomba' or 'El Rincón.'

Totonicapán US$0.25, one hour, 30km. Buses every 15 minutes, 6 am to 5 pm.

Zunil US$0.25, 15 minutes, 10km. Buses every half hour, 7 am to 7 pm, departing from Terminal Minerva, with a possible additional stop in Zona 4, southeast of the park.

Shuttle Minibus Pana Tours (☎/fax 763-0606), 12a Avenida 12-07, Zona 1, offers shuttle service from Xela to Fuentes Georginas, Zunil, Guatemala City, Antigua, Chichicastenango, Panajachel and various other places around Guatemala.

Car Rental car companies in Xela include Geo Rental (☎ 763-0267), in the Centro Comercial El Portal, 13a Avenida 5-38, Zona 1; and Tabarini (☎/fax 763-0418), 9a Calle 9-21, Zona 1.

Getting Around

Quetzaltenango is served by a system of city buses, including those between Parque

Centroamérica and Terminal Minerva mentioned above. INGUAT has information on city bus routes. Taxis wait at the stand on the north end of Parque Centroamérica. Cab fare between Terminal Minerva and the city center is around US$3.

AROUND QUETZALTENANGO

The beautiful volcanic countryside around Quetzaltenango makes for many exciting day trips. Hot waters are a prime attraction. The natural steam baths at Los Vahos are primitive; the baths at Almolonga are basic, cheap and accessible; and the hot springs at Fuentes Georginas are idyllic. Take your pick or visit all three.

Other activities in the area can be equally rewarding. You can feast your eyes and soul on the wild church at San Andrés Xequl, hike to the shores of Laguna Chicabal from Xela, or simply hop on a bus and explore the myriad traditional villages that pepper this part of the highlands. Market days in the surrounding towns include Sunday in Momostenango, Monday in Zunil, Tuesday and Saturday in Totonicapán and Friday in San Francisco El Alto. Visit on these days to catch the locals in action.

Los Vahos

If you're a hiker and the weather is good, you'll enjoy a trip to the rough-and-ready sauna/steam baths at Los Vahos (The Vapors), 3.5km from Parque Centroamérica. Take a bus headed for Almolonga and ask to get out at the road to Los Vahos, which is marked with a small sign reading 'A Los Vahos.' From here it's a 2.3km uphill walk (around 1½ hours) to Los Vahos. The views are remarkable.

If you're driving, follow 12a Avenida south from the parque to its end, turn left, go two blocks and turn right up the hill; this turn is 1.2km from the parque. The remaining 2.3km of unpaved road is steep and rutted, with a thick carpet of dust in the dry season, mud in the rainy season (when you may want a 4WD vehicle). Take the first turn along the dirt road (it's an unmarked sharp right). At the second, bear left (this is badly marked).

The road ends at Los Vahos, where you can have a sauna/steam bath and a picnic. It's open 8 am to 6 pm daily; US$1.50.

San Andrés Xequl

About 10km northwest of Xela is San Andrés Xequl. Surrounded by fertile hills, this small town boasts perhaps the most bizarre **church** anywhere; Technicolor saints, angels, flowers and climbing vines share space with whimsical tigers and monkeys on its shocking-yellow facade. Clues as to why and how this church came into being have been lost. But contemplating the wild combination of iconography, it's hard to believe hallucinogens didn't somehow figure in. Inside, candles illuminate bleeding effigies of Christ while indigenous women pray furiously.

The annual festival here is November 29 and 30. The village has no visitor facilities. The quickest way to get here is to take any northbound bus from Xela and get off at the Esso station at the Moreiria crossroads, then hail a pickup or walk the 3km uphill to town. Alternatively, cool your heels in Xela's terminal until a direct bus is ready to leave. Buses returning to Xela leave from the plaza until about 3 pm.

Zunil

• population 6000 • elevation 2076m

Zunil is a pretty agricultural and market town in a lush valley framed by steep hills and dominated by a towering volcano. As you approach it on the downhill road from Quetzaltenango, you will see it framed as if in a picture, with its white colonial church gleaming above the red-tiled and rusted-tin roofs of the low houses.

On the way to Zunil the road passes **Almolonga**, a vegetable-growing town 6km from Quetzaltenango. Just over 1km beyond Almolonga is **Los Baños**, an area with natural hot sulfur springs. Several little places along here have bath installations; most are decrepit, but if a hot bath at low cost is your desire, you may want to stop. Tomblike enclosed concrete tubs rent for a few quetzals per hour.

Winding down the hill from Los Baños, the road skirts Zunil's fertile gardens before

intersecting the Cantel-to-El Zarco road. A bridge crosses a stream to lead the last 1km into town.

Zunil, founded in 1529 as Santa Catarina Zunil, is a typical Guatemalan highland town graced by a beautiful setting of mountains and farmland. The cultivated plots, divided by stone fences, are irrigated by canals; you'll see the indigenous farmers scooping up water from the canals with a shovel-like instrument and throwing it over their plants. Women wash clothes near the river bridge, in pools of hot water that emerges from the rocks.

Things to See & Do Another attraction of Zunil is its particularly pretty **church**; the ornate facade, with eight pairs of serpentine columns, is echoed inside by a richly worked silver altar. On market day (Monday) the plaza in front of the church is bright with the predominantly red traditional garb of locals buying and selling.

Half a block downhill from the church plaza, the **Cooperativa Santa Ana** is a handicrafts cooperative in which over 500 local women participate. Handicrafts are displayed and sold here, and weaving lessons are offered. It's open 8:30 am to 5 pm Monday to Saturday, 2 to 5 pm Sunday.

While you're in Zunil, visit the image of **San Simón**, an effigy of a local Maya hero venerated as a saint (though not of the church) by the local people. The effigy is moved each year to a different house; ask any local where to find San Simón, everyone will know (local children will take you for a small tip). You'll be charged a few quetzals to visit him and take pictures. See the boxed text 'A God Is a God Is a God' in this chapter.

The festival of San Simón is held each year on October 28, after which the image is moved to a new house. The festival of Santa Catarina Alejandrí, official patron saint of Zunil, is celebrated on November 25. Almolonga celebrates its annual fair on June 27.

Getting There & Away From Zunil, which is 10km from Quetzaltenango, you can continue to Fuentes Georginas (8km), return to Quetzaltenango via the Cantel road (16km), or alternately, take the jungle-bound toll road down the mountainside to El Zarco junction and the Carretera al Pacífico. Buses depart every 10 minutes, 6 am to 6:30 pm, for the return trip to Quetzaltenango (US$0.25, one hour).

Fuentes Georginas

Fuentes Georginas is the prettiest natural spa in Guatemala. Here, pools of varying temperatures are fed by hot sulfur springs and framed by a high wall of tropical vines, ferns and flowers. Fans of Fuentes Georginas were dismayed when a massive landslide caused by heavy rains in October 1998 destroyed several structures (including the primary bathing pool) and crushed the Greek goddess that previously gazed upon the pools. Still, after the site was restored, spa regulars realized the landslide had opened a new vent that feeds the pools. As a result, the water here is hotter than ever. Though the setting is intensely tropical, the mountain air currents keep it deliciously cool all day.

The site has a restaurant and three sheltered picnic tables with cooking grills (bring your own fuel). Down the valley a few dozen meters are seven rustic cottages that rent for US$4.50/6/7 single/double/triple. Each cottage has a shower, a BBQ area and a fireplace to ward off the mountain chill at night (wood and matches are provided). Big-time soakers will want to spend the night, as cottage rates include all-day, all-night pool access.

Trails here lead to two nearby volcanoes: Volcán Zunil (three hours each way) and Volcán Santo Tomás (five hours each way). Going with a guide is essential, so you don't get lost. Guides are available (ask at the restaurant) for US$10 for either trip, whatever the number of people in the group.

Fuentes Georginas is open 8 am to 6 pm daily; US$1.50, bathing suits required.

Take any bus to Zunil, where pickups wait to give rides the 8km up the hill to the springs (30 minutes). Negotiate the price for the ride. It's likely they'll tell you it's US$4 roundtrip, but when you arrive at the top they'll tell you it's US$4 *each way* – this is an irritating game the pickup drivers play. If there are many people in the group, they may charge US$1 per person. Unless you feel like walking back down the hill, arrange a time for the driver to return to pick you up.

You can walk from Zunil to Fuentes Georginas in about two hours. If you're the mountain-goat type, you may enjoy this; it's a strenuous 8km climb.

Hitchhiking is not good on the Fuentes Georginas access road, as the few cars that come down the road are often filled to capacity with Guatemalan families. The baths are busiest on weekends, when you might luck out with a free ride.

If you're driving, walking or hitching, go uphill from Zunil's plaza to the Cantel road (about 60m), turn right and go downhill 100m to a road on the left marked 'Turicentro Fuentes Georginas, 8km.' This road (near the bus stop on the Quetzaltenango-Retalhuleu road – note that there are three different bus stops in Zunil) heads off into the mountains; the baths are 9km from Zunil's plaza.

San Francisco El Alto
• population 3000 • elevation 2610m
High on a hilltop overlooking Quetzaltenango stands the town of San Francisco El Alto, Guatemala's garment district. Every inch of San Francisco is jammed with vendors selling sweaters, socks, blankets, jeans and more. Bolts of cloth spill from storefronts overstuffed with material, and this is on the quiet days! On Friday the town explodes with activity and the real market action kicks in. The large plaza, surrounded by the church and Municipalidad and centered on a cupola-like mirador (lookout), is covered in goods. Stalls crowd into neighboring streets, and the press of traffic is so great that a special system of one-way roads is established to avoid colossal traffic jams. Vehicles entering the town on market day must pay a small fee.

This is regarded as the country's biggest, most authentic market, but note that it's not nearly as heavy with handicrafts as are the markets in Chichicastenango and Antigua.

GUATEMALA

As with any crowded market situation, beware of pickpockets and stay alert.

Around midmorning when the clouds roll away, panoramic views can be had from throughout town, but especially from the roof of the church. The caretaker will let you up.

Most people come to San Francisco as a day trip from Quetzaltenango, 17km away. This is just as well, since the lodging situation here is dire. The big, new *Hospedaje Los Altos*, at 1a Avenida and 6a Calle, is your best bet. It charges US$6.50 per person for a room with private bath, and it has parking. For food try *Comedor San Cristóbal*, near the Hospedaje San Francisco de Asís. A Banco de Commercio on the corner of 2a Calle and 3a Avenida changes dollars and traveler's checks.

The town's annual festival day is October 5.

Momostenango
• population 7500

Beyond San Francisco El Alto, 35km from Quetzaltenango along a fairly smooth country road, Momostenango is Guatemala's famous center for *chamarras* – thick, heavy woolen blankets. The villagers also make ponchos and other woolen garments. As you enter the plaza, you'll see signs inviting you to watch the blankets being made and to purchase the finished products. The best time to do this is on Sunday, which is market day; haggle like mad. A basic good blanket costs around US$13, perhaps twice as much for an extra-heavy 'matrimonial.'

Momostenango is also noted for its adherence to the ancient Mayan calendar and traditional rites. Ceremonies coordinated with the important dates of the calendar round (see the Ancient Mayan Culture special section for details on the Mayan calendar) take place in the hills about 2km west of the plaza. Unfortunately, it's not easy to witness these rites, though Rigoberto Itzep Chanchavac (see Things to See & Do) hosts ceremonial workshops.

Picturesque *diablo* (devil) dances are held in the plaza a few times a year, notably on Christmas Eve and New Year's Eve. The homemade devil costumes can get elaborate; all have masks and cardboard wings, and some go whole hog with fake fur suits, heavily sequined outfits and more. Dance groups gather in the plaza, dancing to a five- to 13-piece band and drinking alcoholic refreshments during the breaks – they're most entertaining around 3 pm, but the festivities go on late into the night.

Information The Banrural on the plaza's south side changes dollars and traveler's checks. It's open 8:30 am to 5 pm Monday to Friday, 9 am to 1 pm Saturday. The post office is across the park on the eastern corner. Medical services are available at the hospital, on 1a Calle and 3a Avenida, near the bus stop.

Volunteer opportunities are also available here; for more information, see the Volunteer Work section of the Guatemala Facts for the Visitor chapter.

Things to See & Do Momostenango's **Los Riscos** (Crags) are peculiar geological formations on the edge of town. The eroded pumice spires rise into the air like something from Star Trek. To get there, take the left heading downhill from the bus stop at the Artesanía Palecom; look for the sign that says 'Entrada.' At the first intersection, you'll see another sign hanging from a corner store reading 'A Los Riscos.' Cross the bridge and head uphill about 50m and take a right onto 2a Calle, continuing about 120m to the formations.

The Takliben May (Misión Maya) Wajshakib Batz' (ritzep@hotmail.com, www.geocities.com/momostenango), 3a Avenida A 6-85, Zona 3, at the entrance to town, teaches classes in **Mayan ceremonies**. Its director, Rigoberto Itzep Chanchavac, is a Maya priest who offers horoscopes (US$3.50 to US$7) and private consultations and hosts ceremonial workshops. His traditional Mayan *tuj* (sauna) is open 2 to 5 pm Tuesday and Thursday; advance notice required.

Kieb Noj Language School (☎ 736-5196), 4a Avenida 4-49, Barrio Santa Isabel, offers **Spanish and Quiché classes**. Twenty-five hours of instruction a week is US$100, including a homestay and three meals a day.

Places to Stay & Eat The *Hotel Estiver* *(1a Calle 4-15, Zona 1),* four blocks downhill from the bus stop, has eight rooms sharing two large bathrooms for US$2.75 per person, and two rooms with private bath for US$3.25 per person.

Other places to stay in Momostenango are basic. The serviceable *Comedor y Hospedaje Paclom*, on 1a Calle just off the plaza, charges US$5.25 double for rooms sharing a hot bath and facing a courtyard crammed with birds and plants. Next door, *Comedor Santa Isabel* has been recommended for its good home cooking. *Hospedaje Roxana*, on the plaza, charges US$1.50, which may be too much, though guests and nonguests can use the hot shower for US$0.65. Of the several basic comedores on the plaza, *Comedor Aracely*, below the church, has received high marks.

Getting There & Away Catch an early bus from Quetzaltenango's Terminal Minerva, or at Cuatro Caminos, or at San Francisco El Alto. There are five or six buses daily; the last one back departs Momostenango by about 4 pm.

Another bus route departs from the plaza's west side and goes through Pologuá, which might be an advantage to travelers heading for Huehue or La Mesilla.

Laguna Chicabal

This magical lake is nestled in a crater of the Chicabal Volcano (2712m). The 'Center of Maya-Mam Cosmovision,' Laguna Chicabal is an intensely sacred place and a hotbed for Mayan ceremonies. Mayan priests come from all over to make offerings here, especially around May 3. Visitors are definitely *not* welcome at this time, so stay away from Laguna Chicabal the first week of May.

The lake is a two-hour hike from San Martín Chile Verde (also known as San Martín Sacatepéquez), a friendly, interesting village about 25km from Xela and notable for the traditional dress worn by the village men. To get to the lake, head down from the highway toward town and look for the sign on your right (you can't miss it). Hike 45 minutes uphill through

fields and past houses until you crest the hill. Continue hiking downhill for 15 minutes to the ranger station, where you pay a US$1.50 entrance fee. From there, it's another 30 minutes uphill to a mirador and then a whopping 615 steep steps down to the edge of the lake. Start early for best visibility; clouds and mists usually envelop the volcano and crater by early afternoon.

The thick vegetation ringing the lake hides picnic tables and sublime campsites. Campers and hikers are asked to treat the lake with the utmost respect due to its ceremonial significance.

Xelajú buses leave Quetzaltenango every 30 minutes until 4 pm for San Martín Chile Verde; hail a pickup to get back.

HUEHUETENANGO

• population 20,000 • elevation 1902m

Separated from the capital by mountains and a twisting road, Huehuetenango has that self-sufficient air exuded by many mountain towns. Coffee growing, mining, sheep raising, light manufacturing and agriculture are the region's main activities.

The lively Indian market is filled daily with traders who come down from the Cuchumatanes Mountains (highest in Central America). Surprisingly, the market area is about the only place you'll see colorful traditional costumes in this town, as most of its citizens are ladinos wearing modern clothes.

For travelers, Huehuetenango (or Huehue, pronounced **way**-way) is usually a leg on the journey to or from Mexico – the logical place to spend your first night in Guatemala after crossing the border. Its dusty, crowded streets are far from attractive, but the town is the perfect staging area for forays deeper into the Cuchumatanes or through the highlands on back roads.

Orientation

The town center is 5km north of the Interamericana. The bus station and new market are 3km from the highway along the road to the town center (6a Calle).

Almost every service of interest to tourists is in Zona 1 within a few blocks of the plaza. The old market, bordered by 1a

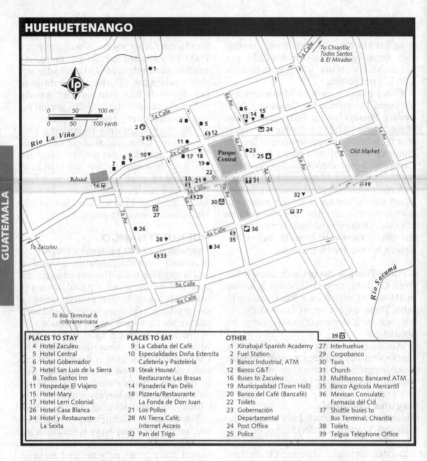

HUEHUETENANGO

To Chiantla;
Todos Santos
& El Mirador

Río La Viña

Parque
Central

Old Market

School

To Zaculeu

Río Sacumá

To Bus Terminal &
Interamericana

PLACES TO STAY	PLACES TO EAT	OTHER	
4 Hotel Zaculeu	9 La Cabaña del Café	1 Xinabajul Spanish Academy	27 Interhuehue
5 Hotel Central	10 Especialidades Doña Estercita	2 Fuel Station	29 Corpobanco
6 Hotel Gobernador		Cafetería y Pastelería	3 Banco Industrial; ATM	30 Taxis
7 Hotel San Luis de la Sierra	13 Steak House/	12 Banco G&T	31 Church
8 Todos Santos Inn		Restaurante Las Brasas	16 Buses to Zaculeu	33 Multibanco; Bancared ATM
11 Hospedaje El Viajero	14 Panadería Pan Delis	19 Municipalidad (Town Hall)	35 Banco Agrícola Mercantil
15 Hotel Mary	18 Pizzería/Restaurante	20 Banco del Café (Bancafé)	36 Mexican Consulate;
17 Hotel Lerri Colonial		La Fonda de Don Juan	22 Toilets		Farmacia del Cid
26 Hotel Casa Blanca	21 Los Pollos	23 Gobernación	37 Shuttle buses to
34 Hotel y Restaurante	28 Mi Tierra Café;		Departamental		Bus Terminal, Chiantla
	La Sexta		Internet Access	24 Post Office	38 Toilets
		32 Pan del Trigo	25 Police	39 Telgua Telephone Office

and 2a Avenidas and 3a and 4a Calles in
Zona 1, is still the busy one, especially on
Wednesday, market day.

Information

The post office is at 2a Calle 3-54, opposite
Hotel Mary, half a block east of the plaza.
The Telgua office is at the Edificio Triángulo, 4a Avenida 6-54, four blocks south of
Parque Central; this is its temporary address
while the regular office next to the post
office is being remodeled.

Just inside Mi Tierra Café (see Places to
Eat), 4a Calle 6-46, is a business that offers

Internet access for US$1.75 for 15 minutes.
It's open 9 am to 12:30 pm and 2:30 to 7 pm
Monday to Friday, 8 am to noon and 3 to
7 pm Saturday. Interhuehue, 3a Calle 6-
65B, offers access for the same price. It's
open 8 am to 12:30 pm and 2 to 6 pm daily.

A Bancared ATM accepting Visa cards is
at the Multibanco branch at 4a Calle 6-81.
Huehue has several other banks; most are
also Western Union agents.

The Mexican consulate is on 5a Avenida 4-
11, near the corner of 4a Calle, in the same
building as the Farmacia del Cid; it's open
9 am to noon and 3 to 5 pm Monday to Friday.

Parque Central

Huehuetenango's main plaza is shaded by nice old trees and surrounded by the town's imposing buildings: the Municipalidad (with its band shell on the upper floor) and the huge colonial church. The plaza has its own little relief map of the department of Huehuetenango.

Zaculeu

The Late Postclassic religious center of Zaculeu occupies a strategic defensive location. Surrounded by natural barriers – ravines and a river – on three sides, the site served its Mam Maya inhabitants well until 1525, when Gonzalo de Alvarado and his conquistadors laid siege to it. Good natural defenses are no protection against starvation, and it was this that defeated the Mam.

The buildings in this parklike archaeological zone show a great deal of Mexican influence and were probably designed and built originally with little innovation. Visitors accustomed to seeing archaeological sites with ruddy bare stones and grass-covered mounds may find the stark tidiness of Zaculeu unsettling. Some of the construction methods used in the restoration were not authentic to the buildings, but the work goes farther than others in trying to re-create the city's look from its glory days.

When Zaculeu flourished, its buildings were coated with plaster (Zaculeu means 'white earth' in the Mam language). In an attempt to be true to the original, the pyramids, ball courts and ceremonial platforms are today likewise covered in plaster – a thick graying coat of it. But missing is the fresco decoration that the Mam no doubt applied to the wet plaster.

Zaculeu is 4km north of Huehuetenango's main plaza. It's open 8 am to 5 pm daily; admission is free. Cold soft drinks and snacks are available. You're allowed to climb on the restored structures but not on the grassy mounds that await excavation.

From Huehue, jitney trucks to Zaculeu depart from in front of the school, on 2a Calle near the corner of 7a Avenida, every 30 minutes (or possibly hourly), 7:30 am to 7:30 pm (US$0.13, 20 minutes). Or you can take a taxi from the central plaza for US$5 roundtrip, with a half hour to spend at the ruins. To walk all the way from the main plaza takes about 45 minutes.

El Mirador

This lookout up in the Cuchumatanes, 12km from town, offers a great view of Huehuetenango and the entire region. A beautiful poem, 'A Los Cuchumatanes,' is mounted on plaques here. Getting to El Mirador is easiest with a private vehicle; a taxi from town costs around US$30 roundtrip.

Language Courses

The Xinabajul Spanish Academy (☎/fax 964-1518), 6a Avenida 0-69, offers one-to-one Spanish courses and homestays with local families.

Special Events

Special events in Huehue include the Fiestas Julias (July 13 to 20), held in honor of La

Potter at work in Huehuetenango

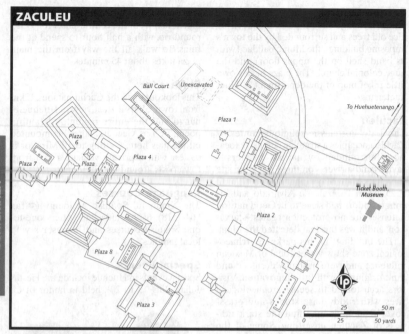

ZACULEU

Ball Court   Unexcavated

Plaza 1

To Huehuetenango

Plaza 6

Plaza 7   Plaza 5   Plaza 4

Ticket Booth,
Museum

Plaza 2

Plaza 8

Plaza 3

0   25   50 m
0   25   50 yards

Virgen del Carmen, Huehue's patron saint; and the Fiestas de Concepción (December 5 and 6), honoring the Virgen de Concepción. The Carrera Maratón Ascenso Los Cuchumatanes, a 12km run from Huehue's central plaza up to El Mirador, is held each fall and attracts hundreds of runners.

Places to Stay

Half a block northwest of the plaza, **Hotel Central** (☎ 764-1202, 5a Avenida 1-33) has 11 large, simple and well-used rooms with shared bath. Rates are US$2.50/4/5.50/7 single/double/triple/quad. The hotel's comedor serves cheap, hearty meals (US$1.75) daily except Sunday. It opens for breakfast at 7 am.

Hotel Lerri Colonial (☎ 764-1526, 2a Calle 5-49), near the plaza, has 21 superbasic rooms in a convenient location. Rates are US$2.75 per person with shared bath, $3.25 with private bath. The courtyard holds a comedor and parking. Across the street,

Hospedaje El Viajero (2a Calle 5-30) is not as good, but it's cheap. Rooms cost US$2 per person, shared bath with cold showers.

Hotel y Restaurante La Sexta, on 6a Avenida near 4a Calle, has a restaurant, parking, international phone service and decent rooms arranged around a courtyard; US$4 per person with shared bath, US$8/9.75/19.50 single/double/triple with private hot bath.

A block east of the plaza, **Hotel Mary** (☎ 764-1618, 2a Calle 3-52) is a cut above the other places. Its 25 small rooms have bedspreads and other nice touches. Rooms cost US$6.50 single or double with shared bath, or US$6.50/9.75/11.75 with private bath and cable TV. Hot water is available only three hours a day. A good cafeteria is attached.

Nearby, the friendly **Hotel Gobernador** (☎/fax 769-0765, 4a Avenida 1-45) is a good budget choice, with rooms for US$3.75/5.50/7.75 with extra-hot shared bath, US$5.50/8.50/12.25 with private bath. Some rooms are less damp than others. A decent cafeteria here serves breakfast, lunch and dinner.

The new *Hotel San Luis de la Sierra* (☎ 764-9216/17/18, fax 764-9219, 2a Calle 7-00) has spotless rooms with private bath and cable TV for US$16.25/24/30. Amenities include a restaurant and views from the roof terrace.

Next door, *Todos Santos Inn* (☎ 764-1241, 2a Calle 7-64) is among Huehue's best budget hotels. Simple rooms with nice touches such as towels, bedside tables and reading lamps are US$3.25 per person with shared bath or US$5.25 with private bath. There's hot water sometimes.

Hotel Zaculeu (☎ 764-1086, fax 764-1575, 5a Avenida 1-14), half a block northwest of the plaza, is a colonial-style place with a lovely garden courtyard, a good dining room, laundry service and 37 rooms, all with private bath and cable TV. Rooms in the older downstairs section (US$15/22/30/37) open onto the courtyard and are preferable to those at the back of the hotel. Rooms in the newer upstairs section are US$28/37/47.

Hotel Casa Blanca (☎/fax 769-0775 to -0781, 7a Avenida 3-41) is such a bright, pleasant hotel that it's tempting to say it's the best place in town. The 15 rooms, all with private bath and cable TV, cost US$23/29/35. Private parking is provided, and the hotel's two lovely restaurants are open 6 am to 10 pm daily.

Places to Eat

On 2a Calle, a block west of the plaza, is *Especialidades Doña Estercita Cafetería y Pastelería*, a tidy, cheerful place serving pastries and meals. Down the block, *La Cabaña del Café* serves Huehue's best coffee and is a popular dinner spot for pasta and other Italian fare. It's open 7 am to 9 pm daily.

The *Hotel San Luis de la Sierra* makes an excellent breakfast, replete with a full pot of coffee and a terrific view of the surrounding countryside.

The *Cafetería Mary* and *Panadería Pan Delis* are next to Hotel Mary, at 2a Calle 3-52. Another good bakery is *Pan del Trigo* (4a Calle 3-24), which usually has whole-grain breads; the cafeteria here offers breakfasts and dinners for US$2. Open daily.

Mi Tierra Café (4a Calle 6-46) is a casual, upbeat place serving tasty food in the Western vein. Breakfast features croissants, omelets, pancakes and good coffee. Dinner tends toward Tex-Mex, with fajitas and tacos sharing the menu with various chicken and seafood dishes.

The *Pizzería/Restaurante La Fonda de Don Juan* (2a Calle 5-35), a few steps from the park, is a clean, reliable place serving pizza and a variety of other dishes. It's open daily.

Los Pollos, 3a Calle between 5a and 6a Avenida, half a block west of the plaza, is open 24 hours a day. Two pieces of chicken with salad, chips and a beverage cost US$3. Burgers and smaller chicken meals are even cheaper.

One of Huehue's best restaurants is *Steak House/Restaurante Las Brasas*, on 4a Avenida just off 2a Calle, half a block from the Parque Central, where a full meal of Chinese food or steak (the specialties here) will cost about US$7. Alcohol is served. Open daily.

For lovely surroundings, you can't beat the two restaurants at *Hotel Casa Blanca* (see Places to Stay), one inside and the other out in the garden. Breakfasts are around US$3.50, burgers and sandwiches are US$2, and steaks are under US$6. Both restaurants are open 6 am to 10 pm daily.

Getting There & Away

Air TACA (reservations ☎ 334-7722) offers one daily flight between Guatemala City and Huehue (US$55; 50 minutes), via Quiché. The flight departs the capital for Huehue at 8:50 am; the flight leaves Huehue on the return at 9:50 am.

Bus The bus terminal is in Zona 4, 2km southwest of the plaza along 6a Calle. Buses from this terminal serve the following cities:

Aguacatán US$0.65, 1½ hours, 22km. A dozen daily departures, starting at 6 am.

Cuatro Caminos US$1, 1½ hours, 77km. Take any of the buses heading for Guatemala City or Quetzaltenango.

Guatemala City US$3.75, five hours, 266km. Buses at 2, 3, 8:30, 9:30 and 10 am.

La Mesilla (Mexican border) US$1.25, two hours, 79km. Buses every half hour, 3:30 am to 5 pm.

Nebaj US$1.75, six hours, 77km. One daily departure, at 11:30 am, via Aguacatán and Sacapulas.

Quetzaltenango US$1, two hours, 90km. Hourly buses, 4 am to 6 pm.

Sacapulas US$1.25, four hours, 50km. Buses at 11 am and 12:30 pm; sometimes there's a 9:30 am departure, which is convenient if you're going to Cobán via Uspantán.

Soloma US$1.75, four hours, 69km. Transportes Alicia has departures at 10:15 and 11 am.

Todos Santos Cuchumatán US$1, 2½ hours, 40km. Buses at 11:30 am and 12:30, 1 and 4 pm; sit on the left for views.

To reach Antigua, take any bus going to Guatemala City and change in Chimaltenango; for Lago de Atitlán, take the same bus and change at Los Encuentros.

Buses between the terminal and the center of town operate from 2 am to 11 pm; they depart from the corner of 4a Calle and 4a Avenida every five minutes in daytime, every half hour at night and before sunrise (US$0.06). Inner-city buses let you off two covered markets away from where the long-distance buses depart; walk through the markets to reach the terminal's other side. A taxi between the bus terminal and town center costs US$2.

Car Tabarini Rent A Car (☎ 764-1951, fax 764-2816) operates an office in Hotel Los Cuchumatanes, Zona 7. Amigos Rent-A-Car (☎ 769-0775), 7a Avenida 3-41, is in Hotel Casa Blanca. Cars start at US$52 a day, including unlimited mileage, taxes and insurance.

AROUND HUEHUETENANGO
Todos Santos Cuchumatán
• population 2000 • elevation 2450m

The picturesque mountain town of Todos Santos Cuchumatán is one of the few Guatemalan towns in which the Maya tzolkin calendar is still remembered and (partially) observed and in which both men and women still wear traditional Maya clothing.

Saturday is market day, with a smaller market on Wednesday. Hiking is good in the local hills, and the town is home to a couple of language schools: La Hermandad Educativa, Proyecto Lingüístico (in Xela ☎/fax 763-1061, proylingts@hotmail.com; in the USA ☎ 800-963-9889, johnsond@televar .com); and Nuevo Amanecer (mitierra@ c.net.gt). There's a bank here.

Todos Santos is famous for the annual **horse races** held on the morning of November 1, which cap a week of festivities and follow an all-night drinking spree the night before. Traditional foods are served throughout the day, and mask dances take place. **Christmas posadas** are held on each of the 10 days leading up to Christmas.

Note that if you'll be coming to Todos Santos in winter, bring warm clothes – it's cold at this high altitude, especially at night.

Places to Stay & Eat The *Hospedaje Casa Familiar*, 30m south of the plaza, is a friendly, family-owned place. It's clean but rustic, and there's hot water and a sauna. The rooms have plenty of blankets, windows and a fine view; cost is US$2.75 per person. For a similar price, you can try the new *Hotelito Todos Santos*, on the road leading east from the plaza. Villagers often rent rooms in their homes; ask around.

Comedor Karin, downhill from the plaza, serves tasty, wholesome meals for US$1.50. *Comedor Katy* is another decent choice. For gringo-style food, head to *Restaurant Cuchumatan* on the main road into town. Nearby, *Restaurant Tzolkin* is another bar/restaurant serving pancakes, pizza, and other Western fare.

Getting There & Away Buses operate between Huehuetenango and Todos Santos four times per day (US$0.90, 2½ hours, 40km). Ride on the top of the bus, if you like – the bus goes slow and the views are spectacular.

East Toward Cobán
The road from Huehuetenango to Cobán is rarely traveled, often rugged and always in-

spiring. It takes nearly three days of challenging travel and several transfers to make the 150km trip by bus, but it's well worth it for the views and tableaux of highland life. Adventure types craving more can continue the odyssey via the Cobán to Poptún route.

Starting high in the Cuchumatanes Mountains, you climb out of Huehuetenango en route to **Aguacatán** (services available), from where you'll have panoramic views of pine-pocked slopes and the fertile valleys below. The road then snakes down through the Río Blanco valley to **Sacapulas** (services available), along the Río Negro. This small town 50km from Huehue makes a good stopover en route to Cobán. For more on the eastward continuation of this route, see Sacapulas to Cobán in the Quiché section, earlier this chapter.

LA MESILLA

A distance of 4km separates the Mexican and Guatemalan immigration posts at La

Mesilla/Ciudad Cuauhtémoc, and you'll have to drive, walk, hitch or take a collective taxi (US$1) between them. The strip in La Mesilla leading to the border post has a variety of services including a police station, post office and a Banrural. Moneychangers at the border give a good rate if you're exchanging your dollars for their pesos or quetzals, a terrible one if you want dollars for your pesos or quetzals.

If you get marooned in La Mesilla, try *Hotel Mily's*, which has doubles with fan, cable TV and private hot bath for US$13. Though relatively pricey, this is the best place to bed down between here and Comitán in Mexico, some 85km down the road. Farther down the hill is the super-basic *Hotel El Pobre Simón*. A place to lay your head for the night here is US$1; the comedor attached is very popular with locals.

Good onward connections are available from the border post east to Huehuetenango and northwest to Comitán.

GUATEMALA

The Pacific Slope

Guatemala's steamy Pacific Slope is lush and tropical, with rich volcanic soil good for growing coffee at the higher elevations and palm oil seeds and sugarcane lower down. Along the coast, the temperature and humidity are uncomfortably high – day and night, rainy season and dry – and endless spoiled stretches of dark volcanic sand remind the visitor that beautiful beaches certainly are not Guatemala's strong suit.

A fast highway, the Carretera al Pacífico (CA-2), runs from the border crossings at Ciudad Hidalgo/Tecún Umán and Talismán/El Carmen to Guatemala City. The 275km between the Mexican border at Tecún Umán and Guatemala City takes about four hours by car, five by bus – much less than the Interamericana between La Mesilla and Guatemala. If speed is your goal, CA-2 is your route.

Most of the towns along the Carretera al Pacífico are muggy, chaotic and of little interest. And most of the beach villages are worse – unpleasantly hot and dilapidated. Still, visitors willing to hopscotch around a bit will find a few places worth checking out.

Retalhuleu, a logical stopping place if you're coming from the Mexican border, is pleasant and fun. Nearby is the active archaeological dig at Abaj Takalik. East of Retalhuleu, the pre-Olmec stone carvings at Santa Lucía Cotzumalguapa (8km west of Siquinalá) and La Democracia (9km south of Siquinalá) are unique.

The small beach village of Monterrico, with its nature reserve and wildlife preservation project, is buzzing with foreigners, who come from Antigua on weekends. Otherwise, the port town of Iztapa and its beach resort of Likín are fine if you simply must get to the beach.

CIUDAD TECÚN UMÁN

This is the preferable and busier of the two Pacific Slope border crossings; a bridge links Ciudad Tecún Umán (Guatemala) with Ciudad Hidalgo (Mexico). The border posts are open 24 hours a day, and banks here change dollars and traveler's checks. Several basic hotels and restaurants are available, but you'll want to cross the border and get on your way as soon as possible.

Minibuses and buses run frequently between Ciudad Hidalgo and Tapachula, 38km to the north. From Ciudad Tecún Umán,

---

Highlights

- Visiting the active archaeological dig at Abaj Takalik

- Exploring the Finca Bilbao, Finca Las Ilusiones and Finca El Baúl archaeological sites, tucked away in the sugarcane fields near Santa Lucía Cotzumalguapa

- Taking a beach vacation at Monterrico and ushering baby sea turtles hatched at the Tortugario Monterrico to their new life at sea

- Deep-sea fishing in Iztapa, where the fish are huge and plentiful and many a world record has been set

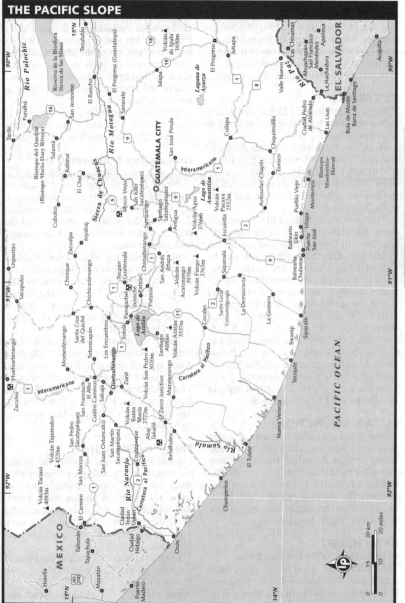

THE PACIFIC SLOPE

GUATEMALA

frequent buses head east along the Carretera al Pacífico, stopping at Coatepeque, Retalhuleu, Mazatenango and Escuintla before climbing into the mountains toward Guatemala City. If you don't find a bus to your destination, take any bus to Coatepeque or, preferably, Retalhuleu, and change there.

EL CARMEN

Though you can cross at El Carmen, you'll encounter much less hassle and expense if you cross at Tecún Umán.

A toll bridge across the Río Suchiate connects Talismán (Mexico) and El Carmen (Guatemala). The border-crossing posts are open 24 hours a day. Minibuses and trucks run frequently between Talismán and Tapachula, 20km away.

There are few services at El Carmen, and those that exist are basic. Buses run regularly from El Carmen to Malacatán, on the San Marcos-Quetzaltenango road, and to Ciudad Tecún Umán, 39km to the south. Fairly frequent 1st-class buses run to Guatemala City along the Carretera al Pacífico (US$6, five to six hours, 275km). Transportes Galgos (☎ 232-3661, 253-4868) is one company operating along this route. It runs five buses daily from El Carmen, stopping at Ciudad Tecún Umán, Coatepeque, Retalhuleu, Mazatenango and Escuintla (change for Santa Lucía Cotzumalguapa). Rutas Lima has a daily bus to Quetzaltenango via Retalhuleu and El Zarco junction.

EL ZARCO JUNCTION

About 40km east of the brash, ugly and chaotic commercial center of Coatepeque (many services if you get stuck) and 9km east of the turnoff for Retalhuleu on the Carretera al Pacífico is El Zarco, a major road junction. The toll road (under US$1) heading north from here climbs more than 2000m in its 47km run to Quetzaltenango.

RETALHULEU

• population 40,000 • elevation 240m

The Pacific Slope is a very rich agricultural region, and Retalhuleu – known simply as Reu (ray-oo) to most Guatemalans – is its clean, attractive capital. The balmy tropical air and laid-back attitude are restful, and the region's wealthy coffee traders come here to relax – splashing in the pool at the Posada de Don José or sipping a cool drink in the bar. The rest of the citizens get their kicks strolling through the palm-shaded plaza, flanked by the whitewashed colonial church and assorted wedding-cake government buildings.

Tourists are something of a curiosity in Reu and are treated well. If you can splurge for digs with a pool, you'll be happier for it.

Orientation & Information

The town center is 4km southwest of the Carretera al Pacífico along a grand boulevard lined with towering palms. The bus station is on 10a Calle between 7a and 8a Avenidas, Zona 1, northeast of the plaza. To find the plaza, look for the twin church towers and walk toward them.

Most services are within a few blocks of the plaza. There is no official tourist office, but people in the Municipalidad, on 6a Avenida facing the church, will do their best to help.

The post office is on 6a Avenida between 5a and 6a Calles. Telgua, at 5a Calle 4-50, is half a block from the park.

Banco Occidente, 6a Calle at 6a Avenida, and Banco Industrial, 6a Calle at 5a Avenida, both change US dollars or traveler's checks and give cash advances on Visa cards. Banco del Agro, on 5a Avenida facing the park, changes US dollars and traveler's checks and gives cash advances on MasterCard.

Things to See & Do

Located at 6a Avenida opposite the church, the **Museo de Arqueología y Etnología** is a small museum of archaeological relics. Upstairs are historical photos and a mural showing locations of 33 archaeological sites in the department of Retalhuleu. It's open 8 am to 1 pm and 2 to 5 pm Tuesday to Sunday; US$0.15.

Even nonguests can swim in the pools at the Siboney and La Colonia Hotels (see Places to Stay). Cost is US$0.65 at the Siboney, US$1.75 at the Colonia (which also has a poolside bar and food service).

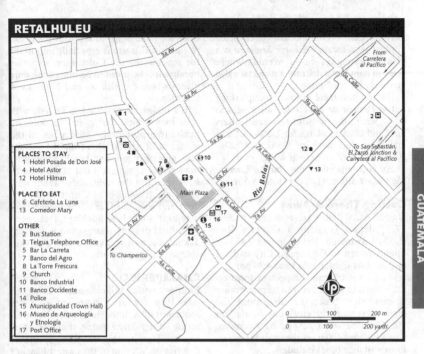

RETALHULEU

PLACES TO STAY
1 Hotel Posada de Don José
4 Hotel Astor
12 Hotel Hilman

PLACE TO EAT
6 Cafetería La Luna
13 Comedor Mary

OTHER
2 Bus Station
3 Telgua Telephone Office
5 Bar La Carreta
7 Banco del Agro
8 La Torre Frescura
9 Church
10 Banco Industrial
11 Banco Occidente
14 Police
15 Municipalidad (Town Hall)
16 Museo de Arqueología
   y Etnología
17 Post Office

GUATEMALA

Places to Stay

For a real cheapie, try **Hotel Hilman** *(7a Avenida 7-99)*, which has simple rooms with private bath and fan for US$3.25 per person.

Half a block west of the plaza, the remodeled **Hotel Astor** *(☎ 771-0475, 771-2780, fax 771-2562, 5a Calle 4-60, Zona 1)* has a charming courtyard and 27 well-kept rooms, each with ceiling fan, private bath and cable TV. The upstairs rooms are new, but the downstairs ones around the courtyard have more atmosphere. Rates are US$13/23 single/double; parking is available.

The nicest place in town is **Hotel Posada de Don José** *(☎ 771-0963, 771-0841, ☎/fax 771-1179, 5a Calle 3-67, Zona 1)*, across the street from the railway station and just two blocks northwest of the plaza. On weekends the Don José is often filled; at other times you can get an air-conditioned room with cable TV, a telephone and private bath for US$19.50/31/38 single/double/triple; discounts may be offered. Amenities include a swimming pool, cafe and restaurant.

Several other lodgings are out on the Carretera al Pacífico – convenient if you have a car and a hot hike from anywhere if you don't. **Hotel Siboney** *(☎ 771-0149, fax 771-0711)*, Cuatro Caminos, San Sebastian, is 4km east of town where Calzada Las Palmas meets the Carretera al Pacífico. The 25 rooms, all with air-con, cable TV, telephone and private bath, are US$26/29/31. **Hotel La Colonia** *(☎ 771-0054, fax 771-0191)*, Carretera al Pacífico Km 178, is 1km east of the Siboney. It has a fairly luxurious layout, with 44 bungalows around the swimming pool; US$40/50.

Places to Eat

Several little restaurants facing the plaza provide meals under US$3. **Cafetería La Luna**, 5a Calle at 5a Avenida, is a town favorite; open daily. Across from the Hotel

Hilman (see Places to Stay) is *Comedor Mary*, a classic Guatemalan lunch place popular with locals. *La Torre Frescura* is a giant supermarket on 5a Avenida where you can hunt and gather for a picnic; it's also invitingly air-conditioned.

For the best meal in town, try splashing out at *Posada de Don José* (see Places to Stay), where the pleasant restaurant offers beef and chicken plates for US$4 to US$6 and a big, full meal for US$7 to US$10. Breakfast is served here as well.

For cocktails, check out *Bar La Carreta (5a Calle 4-50)*, next to the Hotel Astor.

Getting There & Away
Daily TACA flights (reservations ☎ 334-7722) depart Guatemala City for Reu (US$40, 35 minutes) at 6 am and 3:45 pm. Flights return to Guatemala City daily at 6:45 am (via Coatepeque) and 4:30 pm.

As Reu is the most important town on the Carretera al Pacífico, bus transportation is easy. Most buses traveling along the highway stop at the city's bus station, on 10a Calle between 7a and 8a Avenidas, Zona 1, about 400m northeast of the plaza. Long-distance buses include:

Ciudad Tecún Umán US$1.75, 1½ hours, 78km. Buses every 20 minutes, 5 am to 10 pm.

Guatemala City US$3.75, three hours, 186km. Buses every 15 minutes, 2 am to 8:30 pm.

Quetzaltenango US$0.80, 1½ hours, 67km. Buses every 15 minutes, 3 am to 7 pm.

Santa Lucía Cotzumalguapa US$2.75, two hours, 97km. Take any bus headed to Guatemala City.

Local buses go to Champerico and El Asintal (for Abaj Takalik).

Tabarini Rent A Car (☎/fax 763-0418) has an office at 6a Calle 4-50, Zona 1.

ABAJ TAKALIK
About 30km west of Retalhuleu is the active archaeological dig at Abaj Takalik (ah-**bah**-tah-kah-**leek**), which is Quiché for 'standing stone.' Large 'Olmecoid' stone heads discovered here date the site as one of the earliest in the Mayan realm. The site has yet to be restored and prettified for tourists, so don't expect a Chichén Itzá or

Tikal. But if you're truly fascinated with archaeology and want to see it as it's done, pay a visit. This site is especially important for scholars of pre-Columbian societies because it is believed to be one of the only places where the Olmecs and Maya lived together.

It's easiest to reach Abaj Takalik with your own vehicle, but it can be done by public transportation. Catch a bus to the village of El Asintal, 4km from the site. Or take any early morning bus heading west toward Coatepeque, get out at the road to El Asintal (on the right, about 15km west of Retalhuleu along the Carretera al Pacífico), and walk the 5km to the village (you may have some luck hitching). Pickups at El Asintal provide transportation to Abaj Takalik. Spanish-speaking guides are available at the site entrance.

CHAMPERICO
Built as a coffee-shipping point during the late 19th century, Champerico, 38km southwest of Retalhuleu, is a tawdry, sweltering, dilapidated place that sees few tourists. Despite this icky (but accurate) description, it's one of the easiest beaches to access on a day trip from Xela, and beach-starved foreigners still try their luck here. The town has several cheap hotels and restaurants.

SANTA LUCÍA COTZUMALGUAPA
• population 24,000 • elevation 356m
About 100km east of Retahuleu is the unexciting but historically important town of Santa Lucía Cotzumalguapa. In the sugarcane fields and *fincas* near town stand great stone heads carved with grotesque faces and fine relief scenes. The question of who carved these ritual objects, and why, remains a mystery.

The local people are descended from the Pipil, an Indian culture known to have historic, linguistic and cultural links with the Nahuatl-speaking peoples of central Mexico. In Early Classic times, the Pipil grew cacao, the 'money' of the time. They were obsessed with the Mayan/Aztec ball game and with the rites and mysteries of death. Pipil art, unlike the flowery and almost romantic style of the Maya, is cold, grotesque and severe, but it's finely done.

What were these 'Mexicans' doing in the midst of Maya territory? How did they get here and where did they come from? Archaeologists do not have the answers.

Orientation

Santa Lucía Cotzumalguapa is northwest of the Carretera al Pacífico. In its main square, several blocks from the highway, are copies of some of the famous carved stones found in the region. Several basic hotels and restaurants are available in town.

The main archaeological sites to visit are: Finca Bilbao on the outskirts of town; Finca El Baúl, a large plantation farther from town, at which there are two sites (a hilltop site and the finca headquarters); and Finca Las Ilusiones, which has collected most of its findings into a museum near the finca headquarters. Of these sites, Bilbao and the hilltop site at El Baúl are far and away the most interesting.

If you don't have a car and you want to see the sites in a day, haggle with a taxi driver in Santa Lucía's main square. It's cloyingly hot and the sites are several kilometers apart, so you'll be really glad you rode at least part of the way. If you do it all on foot and by bus, pack a lunch; the hilltop site at El Baúl is perfect for a picnic.

Finca Bilbao

This ceremonial center flourished about AD 600. Plows have unearthed (and damaged) hundreds of stones during the last few centuries; thieves have carted off many others. In 1880 many of the finest stones were removed to museums abroad, including nine stones to the Dahlem Museum in Berlin.

Known locally as simply *las piedras* (the stones), this site actually consists of several separate sites deep within a sugarcane finca. The fields come right up to the edge of the town. From Santa Lucía's main square, go north uphill on 3a Avenida to the outskirts of town. Pass El Calvario church on your

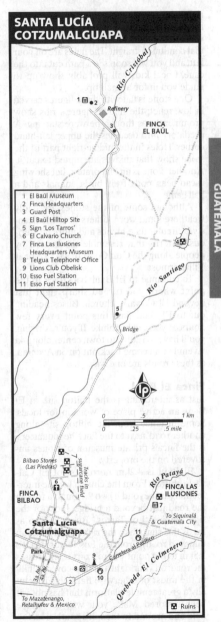

SANTA LUCÍA COTZUMALGUAPA

1   El Baúl Museum
2   Finca Headquarters
3   Guard Post
4   El Baúl Hilltop Site
5   Sign 'Los Tarros'
6   El Calvario Church
7   Finca Las Ilusiones
    Headquarters Museum
8   Telgua Telephone Office
9   Lions Club Obelisk
10 Esso Fuel Station
11 Esso Fuel Station

Rio Cristobal
Refinery
FINCA EL BAÚL
Rio Santiago
Bridge
Rio Pataya
Bilbao Stones (Las Piedras)
Tracks in sugarcane field
FINCA BILBAO
FINCA LAS ILUSIONES
Santa Lucía Cotzumalguapa
To Siquinalá & Guatemala City
Park
Carretera al Pacífico
Quebrada El Colmenero
To Mazatenango, Retalhuleu & Mexico

0   .5   1 km
0 .25 .5 mile

■ Ruins

GUATEMALA

right, and shortly thereafter turn sharply to the right. A hundred meters along, this road veers to the right, but take the unpaved road that continues straight. The fields are on your left, and you will soon see a path cut into the cane. Local kids will probably show up to guide you in for a small tip.

One stone is flat with three figures carved in low relief; the middle figure's ribs show prominently, as though he were starving. A predatory bird occupies the upper left-hand corner. Holes in the middle-right part of the stone show that thieves attempted to cut it. Another stone is an elaborate relief showing cacao bean pods, fruit, birds, animals and a ball game.

Although some of the stones are badly weathered and worn, others bear Mexican-style circular date glyphs and more mysterious patterns that resemble those used by people along the Gulf Coast of Mexico near Villahermosa.

To continue to El Baúl, backtrack to the point where you turned sharp right just beyond El Calvario church. Buses heading out to El Baúl pass this point every few hours, or you can hitchhike. If you're driving, you'll have to return to town center along 4a Avenida and come back out on 3a Avenida, as these roads are one way.

Finca El Baúl

Just as interesting is the hilltop site at El Baúl, an active place of worship for locals. Some distance from the hilltop site along another road, next to the finca headquarters, is the finca's private museum of stones uncovered on the property.

El Baúl is 4.2km northwest of El Calvario church. From the church (or the intersection just beyond it), go 2.7km to a fork in the road just beyond a bridge; look for the sign reading 'Los Tarros.' Buses will go as far as this sign. Take the right-hand fork (an unpaved road). From the Los Tarros sign it's 1.5km to the point where a dirt track crosses the road; on your right, the tree-covered 'hill' in the midst of otherwise flat fields is actually a great temple platform that has not yet been restored. Make your way across the field and around to the hill's south side, fol-

lowing the track to the top. If you have a car, you can drive to within 50m of the top. If you visit on a weekend, you may find worshipers here; people have been coming to pay homage to the idols for over 1400 years.

Of the two stones here, the great grotesque half-buried head is the most striking. The elaborate headdress, 'blind' eyes with big bags underneath, beaklike nose and shit-eating grin seem at odds with the blackened face and its position, half-buried in the ancient soil. The head is stained with candle wax, liquor and the smoke and ashes of incense fires – all part of worship. The other stone is a relief carving of a figure surrounded by circular motifs that may be date glyphs. A copy of this stone is in Santa Lucía's main square.

From the hilltop site, retrace your steps 1.5km to the fork with the Los Tarros sign. Take the other fork this time, and follow the paved road 3km to the headquarters of Finca El Baúl. (If you're on foot, you can walk from the hilltop site back to the unpaved road and straight across it, continuing on the dirt track. This will eventually bring you to the asphalt road that leads to the finca headquarters. When you reach the road, turn right.) Buses trundle along this road every few hours, shuttling workers between the refinery and the town center.

Approaching the finca headquarters (6km from Santa Lucía's main square), you cross a narrow bridge. Continue uphill and you will see the entrance on the left, marked by a machine-gun pillbox. Beyond this daunting entrance you pass workers' houses and a sugar refinery on the right and finally come to the headquarters building, guarded by several men with rifles. The smell of molasses is everywhere. Ask permission to visit the museum and a guard will unlock the gate just past the headquarters building.

Within the gates, sheltered by a palapa, are numerous sculpted figures and reliefs found on the plantation, some of which are very fine. Unfortunately, nothing is labeled.

Finca Las Ilusiones

The third site lies very close to Bilbao – indeed, this is the finca that controls the Bilbao cane fields – but, paradoxically, access is more difficult. Your reward is the chance to view hundreds of objects, large and small, that have been collected from the fields over the centuries.

Leave the town center heading east along Calzada 15 de Septiembre, the boulevard that joins the highway at an Esso fuel station. Go northeast for a short distance, then take an unpaved road on the left (just before another Esso station); this road leads a little over 1km to Finca Las Ilusiones and its museum. If the person with the museum key isn't around, you must be satisfied with the many stones collected around the outside of the museum.

Getting There & Away

Esmeralda 2nd-class buses shuttle between Santa Lucía Cotzumalguapa and Guatemala City (4a Avenida at 2a Calle, Zona 9) every half hour or so between 6 am and 5 pm, charging US$1.50 for the 90km, two-hour ride. You can also catch any bus traveling along the Carretera al Pacífico between Guatemala City and such points as Mazatenango, Retalhuleu or the Mexican border.

To travel between La Democracia and Santa Lucía, catch a bus running along the Carretera al Pacífico toward Siquinalá (8km) and change there for La Democracia.

Between Santa Lucía and Lago de Atitlán you will probably have to change buses at Cocales junction, 23km west of Santa Lucía and 58km south of Panajachel.

LA DEMOCRACIA

• population 4200 • elevation 165m

South of Siquinalá, 9.5km along the road to Puerto San José, is La Democracia, a nondescript Pacific Slope town that's hot all the time. Like Santa Lucía Cotzumalguapa, La Democracia is in the midst of a region populated from early times – according to some archaeologists – by cultures with mysterious connections to Mexico's Gulf Coast.

At the archaeological site called Monte Alto, on the outskirts of town, huge basalt heads have been found. Though cruder, the heads resemble those carved by the

Olmecs near Veracruz several thousand years ago.

Today these great Olmecoid heads are arranged around La Democracia's main plaza. As you come into town from the highway, follow signs to the museo, which will lead you left, then left again, and yet left again.

Facing the plaza, along with the church and the modest Palacio Municipal, is the small, modern Museo Rubén Chevez Van Dorne, with other fascinating archaeological finds. The star of the show is an exquisite jade mask. Smaller figures, 'yokes' used in the ball game, relief carvings and other objects make up the rest of this important small collection. On the walls are overly dramatic paintings of Olmecoid scenes. A rear room has more paintings and lots of potsherds only an archaeologist could love. The museum is open 8 am to noon and 2 to 5 pm; US$0.50.

La Democracia has no places to stay and only a few basic and ill-supplied eateries; it's best to bring your own food and buy drinks at the plaza. *Café Maritza*, next to the museum, is a picture-perfect hot-tropics hangout with a *rockola* (jukebox) blasting music and a small crew of locals sipping beers.

Chatla Gomerana, Muelle Central, Terminal de Buses, Zona 4, Guatemala City, has buses every half-hour from 6 am to 4:30 pm (US$1, two hours, 92km). Buses stop at Escuintla, Siquinalá (change for Santa Lucía), La Democracia and Sipacate.

ESCUINTLA

Surrounded by rich, green foliage, Escuintla should be a tropical idyll where people swing languidly in hammocks and concoct pungent meals of exotic fruit and vegetables. But it's not.

Escuintla is a hot, dingy, dilapidated commercial and industrial city that's important to the Pacific Slope's economy but not at all important to travelers, except to change buses. It's an old town, inhabited by Pipils before the conquest but now solidly ladino. It has some unexciting hotels and restaurants. If stranded, try *Hotel Costa Sur* (☎ 888-1819,

12a Calle 4-13), two blocks north of the bus terminal. Rooms with private hot bath are US$7.75/9.75 single/double. There's a restaurant and parking.

Most people know Escuintla for its bus terminal, in the southern part of town; this is where you catch buses to Antigua, at 7 am and 1 pm (US$0.65, three to four hours), Puerto San José, Pueblo Viejo and Iztapa. Buses for Guatemala City leave frequently from the main plaza. Most buses to the border with El Salvador go through Chiquimulilla (see Around Monterrico).

AUTOSAFARI CHAPÍN

Autosafari Chapín (☎ *363-1105, fax 337-1274),* Carretera al Pacífico Km 87.5, is a drive-through safari park and animal conservation project. Species here include white-tailed deer, peccaries, macaws and nonnative species such as lions, rhinos and leopards. The park has a restaurant and pool, and it makes a great day trip if you're traveling with kids; admission is US$4.50. Buses from Guatemala City go here (see the Getting There & Around chapter) or you can take any bus going from Escuintla to El Salvador. By car, the Autosafari is about 30km from Escuintla (toward Taxisco) on the Carretera al Pacífico.

PUERTO SAN JOSÉ, BALNEARIO LIKÍN & IZTAPA

Guatemala's most important seaside resort leaves a lot to be desired. But if you're eager to get into the Pacific surf, head south from Escuintla 50km to Puerto San José and neighboring settlements.

Puerto San José (population 14,000) was Guatemala's most important Pacific port in the latter half of the 19th century and well into the 20th. Now, superseded by the more modern Puerto Quetzal to the east, the city languishes and slumbers. Its beach, inconveniently located across the Canal de Chiquimulilla, is reached by boat. You'd do better to head west along the coast 5km to Balneario Chulamar, which has a nicer beach and a suitable hotel or two.

About 5km east of Puerto San José is **Balneario Likín,** Guatemala's only upmarket Pacific resort. Likín is much beloved by well-

to-do families from Guatemala City, who have seaside houses along the tidy streets and canals of this planned development.

Another 12km east of Puerto San José is **Iztapa,** Guatemala's first Pacific port, used by none other than Pedro de Alvarado in the 16th century. When Puerto San José was built in 1853, Iztapa's reign as the port of the capital city came to an end, and the city relaxed into a tropical torpor from which it has yet to emerge.

Iztapa has gained notoriety as a premier **deep-sea fishing** spot. World records have been set here and enthusiasts can fish for marlin, sharks and yellowfin tuna, among others. Aside from fishing, lounging about is the prime local pastime. The town has a post office but no bank.

Should you want to stay, check out *Sol y Playa Tropical (☎ 881-4365/6, 1a Calle 5-48),* which has a pool, restaurant and clean, airy rooms with fans and bath for US$10.75/21 single/double. Rates are lower in the off season. *Hotel Posada María del Mar (☎ 881-4055),* across from the post office, rents rooms for US$6.50 double without bath, US$11 with private bath.

The bonus about Iztapa is that you can catch a Transportes Pacífico bus from the market in Zona 4 in Guatemala City all the way here (four hours), or pick it up at Escuintla (one hour) or Puerto San José. You can also travel to Monterrico from Iztapa by catching one of the frequently scheduled *lanchas* (US$0.50) across the Canal de Chiquimulilla to Pueblo Viejo and transferring to a bus.

MONTERRICO

The coastal area around Monterrico is a totally different Guatemala, and life here is imbued with a sultry, tropical flavor that's more relaxed and inviting than anywhere else on the Pacific Slope. The architecture too, is different; wooden slat walls and thatched roofs prevail over the cement walls and corrugated-tin roofs common elsewhere.

Monterrico is probably the best spot in Guatemala for a weekend break at the beach. On weekdays it's relatively quiet, but on weekends and holidays, it teems with

Guatemalan families. It's also becoming popular with foreigners. The village has a post office (on Calle Principal) but no bank.

A few small, inexpensive hotels front the beach, which is dramatic here; powerful surf and riptides collide at odd angles (swim with caution). Behind the beach, on the other side of town, is an extensive network of mangrove swamps and canals, part of the 190km Canal de Chiquimulilla. Also in the area are a large wildlife reserve and a center for the hatching and release of sea turtles and caimans.

Things to See & Do

A big attraction around here is the **Biotopo Monterrico-Hawaii**, a 20-km-long nature reserve of coastal mangrove swamps filled with bird and aquatic life. The reserve is a breeding area for endangered leatherback and ridley turtles, who lay their eggs on the beach in many places along the coast.

Canals lace the swamps, connecting 25 lagoons hidden among the mangroves. Boat tours of the reserve, going through the swamps and visiting several of the lagoons, take around two hours and cost US$8 for two passengers. It's best to go early in the morning, when you'll see the most wildlife. Bring binoculars if you have them.

To arrange a boat tour, stop by the **Tortugario Monterrico** visitors center, a short walk east (left, if you're facing the sea) down the beach from the Monterrico hotels. Other villagers also offer boat tours, but the guides who work at the Tortugario are particularly

GUATEMALA

A Race to the Sea

Every Saturday from September to January, a delightful ritual takes place at sunset on Monterrico's beach. Workers from the Tortugario Monterrico walk out on the beach carrying big plastic tubs and two long ropes. They lay one rope out along the beach at a certain distance from the waterline and lay the other parallel to the first, several yards away. Tourists from the beach hotels gather around; come up to see what's going on and you'll find out the plastic tubs are full of baby sea turtles!

Pick a likely looking turtle out of the tub, make a small donation (less than US$2) to support the tortugario (turtle hatchery), and line up behind the rope farthest from the waves. It's an amazing feeling, to hold the baby sea turtle in your hand. When everyone is ready, on the count of three, everyone releases their sea turtles, which make a frantic scramble toward the sea. Keep an eye on your turtle; if yours is the first to reach the rope closer to the waves, you'll win a free meal for two at one of the Monterrico hotels. Eventually, all the turtles reach the water and are washed away by the waves, as the sun is sinking.

The race is not only a fun chance to win a free dinner, it's also poignant, as you consider the fate of 'your' little sea turtle. The turtles are released two to three days after they hatch. They're released in a group to give them a better chance of survival. Scientists say that on this race across the sand to the sea, the tiny turtles are being imprinted with information about their place of birth (the components of the sand, the water etc). This will enable them to return from the sea to this exact spot to lay eggs when they are adults. Most of them won't make it to adulthood. But the efforts of conservation groups such as the tortugario are giving the endangered turtles a better chance.

– Nancy Keller

concerned with wildlife. At the visitors center, you'll learn about the endangered species raised here, including leatherback, olive ridley and green sea turtles, caimans and iguanas. Also here is an interesting interpretive trail. The center is open 8 am to noon and 2 to 5 pm daily.

The **Reserva Natural Hawaii** is a nature reserve operated by the Asociación de Rescate y Conservación de Vida Silvestre (ARCAS; Association to Rescue and Conserve Wildlife), which operates a sea turtle hatchery on the beach 8km east of Monterrico. Volunteers are welcome year-round, but hatching season is from June to November, with August and September being the peak months. Volunteers are charged US$25 for a room; homestay options are available. See the boxed text 'Volunteer Opportunities in Guatemala' for further information about ARCAS.

Places to Stay & Eat

Monterrico has several simple hotels on or near the beach; most have restaurants attached. From where you alight from La Avellana boat, it's about a 15-minute walk through the village to the beach and hotels. Alternatively, if you take the bus from Pueblo Viejo, you'll have a five-minute walk down Calle Principal to the beach. If you brought a vehicle across on a car ferry, you can park it at any of the hotels. Coming from Calle Principal, head left to reach the following cluster of hotels, most of which offer discounts for stays of three nights or more.

Hotel Baule Beach (☎ 473-6196) is an insanely popular hotel run by former Peace Corps volunteer Nancy Garver. Throngs of foreign students choke the place on weekends, so it's not everyone's cup of tea. However, if you want to party with other travelers, head here. Ragged, cleanish rooms with private bath, right on the beach, cost US$7.50/12.75/17 single/double/triple. The bigger rooms accommodate up to six people. Meals are reasonably priced. Current schedules for every type of transportation serving Monterrico are posted here.

The next place over is the new *Hotel El Mangle* (☎ 369-7631), where the clean, comfortable rooms have fans, mosquito nets, private baths and quality beds – a good value at US$15.50 double. There's space for hanging out and it's quiet.

A favorite of vacationing Guatemalan families, *Johnny's Lodging* (☎ 337-4191, 633-0321) has clean rooms with fan and private bath for US$7.75 per person. It also offers seven bungalows, each with two bedrooms, a living room, private bath and fully equipped kitchen, for US$50 for four people. Two bungalows share a barbecue and small swimming pool (a second pool is available for the other guests). Also here is a restaurant.

Nearby, *Kaiman Inn* (☎ 334-6214, ☎/fax 334-6215) has eight rooms, each with fan, mosquito nets and private bath, for US$6.50 per person during the week, US$7.75 on weekends; rooms hold two to five people. The restaurant serves excellent Italian cuisine and seafood.

Farther down the beach, *Hotel Pez de Oro* (☎ 204-5249, ☎/fax 368-3684, laelegancia@ guate.net) is Monterrico's poshest hotel. It has nine clean, pleasant bungalows, each with fan, mosquito nets, private bath and a hammock out on the porch. Friday through Sunday, rooms are US$32/43/54 double/triple/quad (singles pay the same as doubles). Rooms are nearly US$10 cheaper on weekdays. Amenities include a swimming pool and a fine restaurant.

Down the beach in the opposite direction is *Hotel La Sirena*, which you'll know by the travelers lounging in the hammocks. This is one of Monterrico's best values, with a variety of rooms at different prices. Big, bare rooms with private bath, fan and three beds are US$11.75; rooms sleeping four with bath, refrigerator, stove and dining area are US$20; and simple rooms with shared bath are US$5.25 for one or two people. The hotel has a pool, and the restaurant here has the usual fish dishes that every other hotel on the beach is serving, but at half the price.

Nearby is the *Pig Pen Pub*, an open-air beachfront bar with good music and atmosphere. It's open from 8 pm 'until you're done drinking.' The gregarious expat owner knows the area well. Ask him about birding and mangrove tours.

Set back from the beach on the little paths that circumscribe the town are two recommended places. The first is the *Guest House*, a new hostel with four cozy, rustic rooms with mosquito nets, fans and shared bath for US$3.25/5.25 single/double. Stay here now while this introductory price lasts. You'll pass it if you're coming from La Avellana; from the beach, make a left at the first alley. Nearby, *Restaurant Neptune* garners rave reviews from repeat diners, and though it's not the cheapest place in town, it's worth a splash out.

Getting There & Away

There are two ways to get to Monterrico. You can take a bus to Iztapa (four hours from Guatemala City), catch a lancha across the canal to Pueblo Viejo and switch to another bus to Monterrico (US$0.65, one hour). This is the longer alternative, but it's a pretty journey that allows you to downshift and experience local life at a sane pace.

The other option is to head over to La Avellana, where lanchas and car ferries depart for Monterrico. About 10 direct buses daily run from Guatemala City to La Avellana (US$1.50, four hours, 124km); buses run

hourly from La Avellana to Guatemala City between 4 am and 4:30 pm. Or you can change buses at Taxisco, on CA-2 – buses operate hourly between Guatemala City and Taxisco (US$1.75, 3½ hours, 106km) and hourly between Taxisco and La Avellana (US$0.40, 20 minutes, 18km).

Shuttle buses also serve La Avellana. You can take a shuttle from Antigua for US$12 one way on weekdays, US$10 on weekends. From Antigua it's a 2½-hour trip. The Adventure Travel Center in Antigua (see the Antigua chapter) comes over every Saturday and returns every Sunday; other shuttle services also make the trip. Shuttle services depart from La Avellana for Antigua at 2:30 pm on Saturday and Sunday. Phone the Hotel Baule Beach in Monterrico to check the current schedule for buses and shuttles. During the week, the Hotel Baule Beach runs its own shuttle to Antigua (US$15 per person, minimum two people).

From La Avellana, *colectivo* lanchas charge US$0.35 per passenger for the half-hour trip along the Canal de Chiquimulilla, a long mangrove canal. They begin at 4:30 am and run every half hour. Car ferries (US$7) leave when a car and passengers are ready to go.

Those wishing to check out the Biotopo Monterrico-Hawaii can take a new road between Monterrico and the Biotopo; one bus a day runs between the two.

Central & Eastern Guatemala

North and east of Guatemala City, the topography ranges from misty, pine-covered mountains to hot, dry-tropic lowlands and coastal regions. Leaving the capital heading northeast on Carretera al Atlántico (CA-9), you'll climb into the mountains and get a tease of cool temperatures before descending into the Río Motagua valley, where dinosaurs once roamed.

Highlights

- Experiencing the natural wonders of Semuc Champey and the caves at Lanquín

- Visiting one of the most important Mayan sites at Copán, just across the border in Honduras

- Kicking back in the Garífuna town of Lívingston on Guatemala's Caribbean coast or in the equally relaxed riverside town of Río Dulce

- Hitting one of the off-the-beaten-track routes from Cobán to El Petén or from Cobán to Huehuetenango

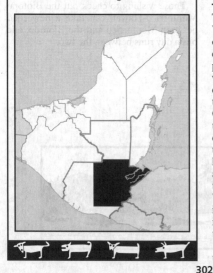

A turnoff at the valley's west end will lead you north into the Verapaces, a highland region that is the historical home of the Rabinal Maya people and the backdoor to the vast department of El Petén. If instead you continue east down the Río Motagua valley on the Carretera al Atlántico, you'll enter the department of Zacapa. This area and its neighbor to the south, the department of Chiquimula, hold a myriad of interesting destinations and provide access to the first-rate Mayan ruins at Copán, just across the border in Honduras.

Finally, east of Zacapa on the Carretera al Atlántico you'll enter Izabal, the country's easternmost department, which stretches to the Gulf of Honduras. The highway passes near tropical Lago de Izabal and ends at Puerto Barrios, Guatemala's Caribbean port. If you're not done moving yet, you can catch a boat here to Lívingston, a laid-back Garífuna hideaway.

The Verapaces

The mountainous highland region of the Verapaces is home to the Rabinal Maya, once noted for their warlike habits and merciless victories. The Rabinals battled the powerful Quiché Maya for a century but were never conquered. When the conquistadors arrived, they too had trouble defeating the Rabinals. It was Fray Bartolomé de Las Casas who convinced the Spanish authorities to give peace a chance. Armed with an edict that forbade Spanish soldiers from entering the region for five years, the friar and his brethren pursued their religious mission and succeeded in pacifying and converting the Rabinals. The region was renamed Verapaz (True Peace) and is now divided into the departments of Baja Verapaz, with its capital at Salamá, and Alta Verapaz, centered on Cobán.

The smooth and scenic asphalt road to the two capitals wends its way from the hot,

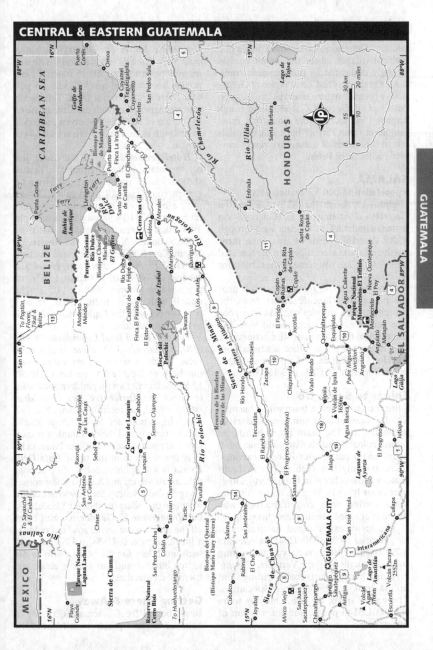

CENTRAL & EASTERN GUATEMALA

dry Río Motagua valley into the mountains through long stretches of coffee-growing country. The region holds many intriguing Rabinal villages, where the people remain strongly dedicated to their ancient traditions. On the way to Cobán is one of Guatemala's premier nature reserves, the Biotopo del Quetzal. Beyond Cobán, along rough unpaved roads, are the country's most famous caverns. Farther back still, on roads left to the whims of nature, are rarely traveled routes to El Petén.

SALAMÁ
* population 11,000 * elevation 940m

Highway 17, also marked CA-14, leaves the Carretera al Atlántico at El Rancho, 84km from Guatemala City. It heads west through a dry, desertlike lowland area, then turns north and starts ascending into the forested hills. After 47km you come to the turnoff for Salamá.

Services here are grouped around or near the plaza. The Bancafé across from the church changes traveler's checks at a poor rate and gives cash advances on Visa. The Banrural on the plaza may offer better rates. The Telgua telephone office is across from the Hotel Tezulutlán, and a police station is on the corner of 5a Calle and 9a Avenida.

Things to See & Do
Salamá is an attractive town with a bustling Sunday market and some reminders of colonial rule. The main plaza boasts an ornate colonial **church** with gold encrusted altars and a pulpit with Rococo carvings; there are only two such pulpits in Latin America (the other is in Lima, Peru). Don't miss Jesus lying in his glass coffin, his stigmata stuffed with cotton bunting and droplets of blood seeping from his scalp.

The local, experienced naturalists at EcoVerapaz (☎/fax 940-0294), 8a Avenida 4-77, Zona 1, offer a variety of interesting tours throughout Baja Verapaz. Caving, birding, hiking, horseback riding and orchid trips are among their specialties. The guides speak English. One-day tours start at US$40 per person for a group of five or more.

Places to Stay & Eat
Along the block directly behind the church, **Hospedaje Juárez** (☎ 940-0055, 10a Avenida 5-55, Zona 1) is a well-kept, safe and friendly place to stay. All 15 rooms have a private hot bath and cost US$5.25 per person. There's no sign out front. This family runs a cheaper place with the same name on the corner of 5a Calle, just down the block; rooms with shared bath there are US$4 per person.

Hotel Tezulutlán (☎/fax 940-0141), just off the main square behind the Texaco station, has 15 rooms arranged around a garden courtyard. All have cable TV and private bath (four rooms have hot water); rates are US$11/14/17 single/double/triple. Two other rooms with shared bath are US$6.50 double. Next door, the **Restaurant Happy Ranch** offers entire roasted chickens for US$3.25. Across the street, **Hotel San Ignacio** (☎ 940-0186) is a clean, family-run place where rooms cost US$4/5 single/double with shared bath, US$5/7.75 with private cold bath; the **Cafetería Apolo XI** is in the same building.

The new **Hotel Real Legendario** (☎ 940-0187, 8a Avenida 3-57, Zona 1) is a good value. Its clean, secure rooms with private hot bath and cable TV go for US$8.50/13.50/18. Travelers with children may want to check out **Turicentro Las Orquídeas** (☎ 940-0142), Carretera a Salamá Km 147, which has a pool and lots of room for the kids to run around. Rooms flank a restaurant and open spaces slung with hammocks.

A few doors from the plaza, **Cafe Deli-Donas** is a hospitable coffee shop serving light meals, sweets and Salamá's best coffee; it's open daily. Nearby, the **Cafetería Central** offers savory, filling lunches for US$3.25. At the **Restaurante El Ganadero**, a half block off the main square on the road out of town, a lunch might cost US$4 to US$6, a sandwich much less. On the plaza, **Pollo to Go** serves burgers and chicken in clean and friendly surroundings.

Getting There & Away
Buses bound for Guatemala City depart hourly, 3 am to 4 pm, from in front of the

Municipalidad (US$2, three hours, 151km). Buses originating in Guatemala City continue west from Salamá to Rabinal (US$1, one hour, 19km) and then 15km farther to Cubulco. Buses for San Jerónimo leave from in front of the church every half hour from 6 am to 4 pm (US$0.25, 20 minutes).

In Guatemala City, buses to Salamá depart hourly, 5 am to 5 pm, from the office of Transportes Unidos Baja Verapacenses (☎ 253-4618), 17a Calle 11-32.

AROUND SALAMÁ

Ten kilometers along the road to Salamá from the Cobán highway, you come to the turnoff for **San Jerónimo**. Behind the town's beautiful church, a former sugar mill is now a museum with a decent collection of unlabeled artifacts and photographs; admission is free. The museum's immaculate grounds also hold a playground. On the town plaza are some large stones that were carved in ancient times.

Nine kilometers west of Salamá along Hwy 5 is the village of **San Miguel Chicaj**, known for its weaving and traditional fiesta (September 25 to 29). Continue along the same road another 10km to reach the colonial town of **Rabinal**, founded in 1537 by Fray Bartolomé de Las Casas as a base for his proselytizing. Rabinal has gained fame as a center for pottery-making (look for the hand-painted chocolate cups) and citrus-growing (the harvest is in November and December). Rabinal is also known for its adherence to pre-Columbian traditions. If you can make it here for the annual fiesta of Saint Peter, between January 19 and 25 (things reach a fever pitch on January 21), or Corpus Cristi, do so. Market day here is Sunday. Two small hotels, the *Pensión Motagua* and the *Hospedaje Caballeros*, can put you up.

It's possible to continue from Rabinal another 15km west to the village of **Cubulco** or about 100km south to Guatemala City. Hwy 5 to Guatemala City passes through several small villages en route. It's best to tackle this road only with a 4WD vehicle. Buses do ply this remote route, albeit very slowly. Along the way you could pay a visit to the **ruins of Mixco Viejo**, near San Juan Sacatepéquez, about 25km from Guatemala City.

BIOTOPO DEL QUETZAL

Along the main highway (CA-14) 34km north of the turnoff for Salamá you reach the Biotopo Mario Dary Rivera nature reserve, commonly called the Biotopo del Quetzal; it's at Km 161, near the village of Purulhá (no services). The ride along here is sobering: entire hillsides are deforested and covered in huge sheets of black plastic meant to optimize the conditions in which to grow *xate*, a green palm exported for use in floral arrangements.

If you stop here intent on seeing a quetzal, Guatemala's national bird, you'll likely be disappointed – the birds are rare and elusive and their habitat is all but destroyed. You have the best chance of seeing them between February and September. Even if you don't spot one, it's still worth a visit to explore the lush high-altitude cloud forest that is the quetzal's natural habitat.

The two excellent, well-maintained nature trails that wind through the reserve's dense growth pass a number of waterfalls, most of which cascade into small pools where you can take a dip. Deep in the forest is Xiu Ua Li Che (Grandfather Tree), some 450 years old, which was alive when the conquistadors fought the Rabinals in these mountains.

Trail maps in English and Spanish can be purchased at the visitors center for US$0.50. They contain a checklist of 87 birds commonly seen here. Other resident animals include spider monkeys and *tigrillos*, which are similar to ocelots. Good luck spotting either of these.

The reserve is open 6 am to 4 pm daily (you must be in by 4 pm, but you can stay longer); admission costs US$5. Drinks (but no food) are available.

Camping is currently not allowed, though this may have changed by the time you read this. Services in the area include *Hotel y Comedor Ranchito del Quetzal* (☎ 953-9235), a rustic budget *hospedaje* with a restaurant, just north of the reserve; the more comfortable and more expensive *Posada Montaña del Quetzal* (☎ 208-5958), at Km 156.5, which has a restaurant and swimming pool;*and *Biotopín Restaurant*, at Km 160.5, a recommended place to eat.

The road between the Biotopo and Cobán is good – smooth and fast (though curvy), with light traffic. As you ascend into the evergreen forests, you'll still see tropical flowers here and there.

COBÁN

• population 20,000 • elevation 1320m

Cobán was once a stronghold of the Rabinal Maya. In the 19th century, German immigrants moved in, founding vast coffee and cardamom *fincas* and giving Cobán the look and feel of a German mountain town. The era of German cultural and economic domination ended during WWII, when the USA prevailed upon the Guatemalan government to deport the powerful finca owners, many of whom actively supported the Nazis.

Today Cobán is a pleasant town to visit, though the weather is less than ideal; most of the year it is chilly and either rainy or overcast. You can count on sunny days in Cobán for only about three weeks in April. In the midst of the 'dry' season (January to March) it can be misty and sometimes rainy, or bright and sunny with marvelous clear mountain air.

Guatemala's most impressive festival of indigenous rites, the Rabin Ajau folkloric festival, takes place at the end of July or in early August.

Information

Most services of interest to travelers are within a few blocks of the plaza. The heart of Cobán is built on a rise, so unless what you're looking for is in the town center, you'll be trudging uphill and down.

Though Cobán has no tourist office, the Casa D'Acuña and the Hostal de Doña Victoria (see Places to Stay) both have loads of information.

The post office is a block from the plaza on the corner of 2a Avenida and 3a Calle, Zona 3. The Telgua telephone office is on the plaza.

Access Computación (☎ 951-4040, inter cafe@c.net.gt), 1a Calle 3-13, Zona 1, offers email service for a steep US$7.75 an hour; at last check it was the only game in town.

It's open 8 am to noon and 2 to 7 pm Monday to Friday, 10 am to noon and 3 to 5 pm Saturday.

Banco Occidente, on the plaza, changes US dollars cash and traveler's checks and gives cash advances on Visa cards. Banco G&T, behind the cathedral, also changes money and gives cash advances on MasterCard. Banco Industrial, on 1a Calle, Zona 1, changes money and has a Visa ATM. Bancafé, 1a Avenida 2-66, Zona 2, also has a Visa ATM.

Laundry service is available from Lavandería Providencia on the plaza or from the Casa D'Acuña.

Templo El Calvario

You'll get a fine view over town from this church atop a long flight of stairs at the north end of 7a Avenida, in Zona 1. Indigenous people leave offerings at shrines and crosses in front of the church. You can walk around behind the church to enter the Parque Nacional Las Victorias, though this is not the park's main entrance.

Parque Nacional Las Victorias

This forested 82-hectare national park, right in town, has trails, ponds, barbecue/picnic areas, children's play areas, a lookout point and camping (US$1.50). It's open 8 am to 4:30 pm daily; admission is US$0.80. The entrance is at 9a Avenida and 3a Calle, Zona 1. Or you can enter by walking around to the rear of Templo El Calvario.

Vivero Verapaz

Orchid lovers mustn't miss a chance to see the many thousands of species at this famous nursery (☎ 952-1133). The rare *monja blanca*, or white nun orchid (Guatemala's national flower), grows here, as do hundreds of species of miniature orchids, some so small you actually need a magnifying glass to see them. The owners will take you on a tour for US$0.65. The national orchid show is held here each December.

Vivero Verapaz is on the Carretera Antigua de Entrada a Cobán, about 2km from the town center. It's a 20-minute walk southwest from the plaza on the heavily trafficked Carretera; you might prefer taking a taxi (US$1.50). Hours are 9 am to noon and 2 to 5 pm Monday to Saturday.

Finca Santa Margarita
Finca Santa Margarita (☎ 952-1286), 3a Calle 4-12, Zona 2, is a working coffee farm offering stellar guided tours. From propagation and planting to roasting and exporting, the 45-minute tour will tell you all you ever wanted to know about these powerful beans. You can purchase beans straight from the roaster for as little as US$3 a pound. Tours, in English or Spanish, are available 8 am to 12:30 pm and 1:30 to 5 pm Monday to Friday and 8 am to noon Saturday; US$2 per person.

Museo El Príncipe Maya
This private museum (☎ 952-1541), 6a Avenida 4-26, Zona 3, features an impressive collection of pre-Columbian artifacts, with an emphasis on jewelry, other body adornments and pottery. The displays are well designed and maintained. Open 9 am to 6 pm Monday to Saturday; US$1.50.

Language Courses
The Muq'b'ilb'e School (☎ 951-2459), at 6a Avenida 5-39, Zona 3, is run by Oscar Macz

The white nun orchid

and is well recommended for Spanish and Q'eqchi' instruction. The Instituto Internacional Cobán (INCO; ☎/fax 951-3113), 6a Avenida 3-03, Apdo 22, Zona 1, also offers Spanish classes.

Organized Tours
Aventuras Turísticas (☎ 951-4213, ☎/fax 951-4214), 3a Calle 2-38, Zona 3, in the Hostal de Doña Victoria, leads tours to Laguna Lachuá, the Rey Marco and Candelaria caves, Semuc Champey and Lanquín, Tikal, Ceibal and beyond. The company employs French, English and Spanish-speaking guides and will custom design itineraries for you.

The Casa D'Acuña (☎ 951-0482/84, fax 952-1547, uisa@infovia.com.gt), 4a Calle 3-11, Zona 2, also offers tours to Semuc Champey, the Grutas de Lanquín and other places farther afield.

The folks at Access Computación (see Information) offer day trips and overnight camping excursions to an idyllic lagoon and waterfall on Río Sachicha. The trips are not cheap (US$20 each for a day trip; US$27 for camping), but the river is on private land and not accessible to independent travelers. The company also runs cave tours and trips to El Salto waterfall.

Proyecto EcoQuetzal (☎/fax 952-1047, bidaspeq@guate.net, www.granjaguar.com/peq), 2a Calle 14-36, Zona 1, is a recommended outfit offering ethno-tourism trips. Participants hike to nearby villages nestled in the cloud forest, where they stay with a Q'eqchi' family. The price of US$11 a day includes three meals, lodging and guided hikes to interesting spots (the men of the host families serve as the guides, providing alternative income for their families). Reservations are required at least one day in advance. The office is open 8:30 am to 1 pm and 2 to 5:30 pm Monday to Friday. Participants should speak some Spanish.

Places to Stay
Camping is available at Parque Nacional Las Victorias, right in town. Facilities include water and toilets but no showers.

One of the cheapest places in town is the ***Pensión Familiar***, at the intersection of

GUATEMALA

GUATEMALA

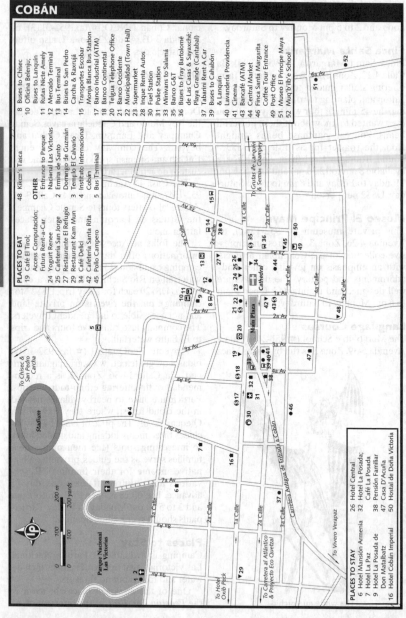

COBÁN

PLACES TO STAY
6 Hotel Mansión Armenia
7 Hotel La Paz
9 Hotel La Posada de
  Don Matalbatz
16 Hotel Cobán Imperial
26 Hotel Central
32 Hotel La Posada
38 Pensión Familiar
47 Casa D'Acuña
50 Hostal de Doña Victoria

PLACES TO EAT
19 Café El Tirol;
  Futura Rent-a-Car
  Access Computación;
24 Yogurt Renee
25 Cafetería San Jorge
27 Restaurante El Refugio
29 Restaurant Kam Mun
34 Café Delici
42 Cafetería Santa Rita
45 Pollo Campero
48 Kikec's Tasca

OTHER
1 Entrance to Parque
  Nacional Las Victorias
2 Ermita de Santo
  Domingo de Guzmán
3 Templo El Calvario
4 Instituto Internacional
  Cobán
5 Bus Terminal
8 Buses to Chisec
10 Oficina Belenju;
  Buses to Lanquín
11 Rutas Nicte Amely
12 Mercado Terminal
  Bus Terminal
14 Buses to San Pedro
  Carcha & Raxrujá
15 Transportes Escobar
  Monja Blanca Bus Station
17 Banco Industrial (ATM)
18 Banco Continental
20 Telgua Telephone Office
21 Banco Occidente
22 Municipalidad (Town Hall)
23 Supermarket
28 Inque Renta Autos
30 Fuel Station
31 Police Station
33 Minivans to Salamá
35 Banco G&T
36 Buses to Fray Bartolomé
  de Las Casas & Sayaxché;
  Playa Grande (Cantabal)
37 Tabarini Rent A Car
39 Buses to Cahabón
  & Lanquín
40 Lavandería Providencia
41 Cinema
43 Bancafé (ATM)
44 Central Market
46 Finca Santa Margarita
  Coffee Tour Entrance
49 Post Office
51 Museo El Principe Maya
52 Muq'b'ilb'e School

2a Calle and the Carretera de Entrada a Cobán, Zona 2. Basic rooms with saggy beds are US$2.75 per person.

Casa D'Acuña *(☎ 951-0482, 951-0484, fax 952-1547, uisa@infovia.com.gt, 4a Calle 3-11, Zona 2)*, down a steep hill from the plaza, is a clean, copacetic European-style hostel. Cost is US$4.50 per bunk, in rooms with two or four beds and shared bath (with incredible hot shower). One private room with shared bath is available for US$9 double. Amenities include a good restaurant, gift shop, laundry service and reasonably priced local tours.

Popular with Guatemalan families, the ***Hotel Cobán Imperial*** *(☎ 952-1131, 6a Avenida 1-12, Zona 1)* is 250m from the plaza. It's old but clean and has parking in the courtyard. Rooms with private bath are US$6/9/12.25 single/double/triple. Conveniently located for odd-hour bus travel is ***Hotel La Posada de Don Matalbatz*** *(☎/fax 951-0811, 3a Calle 1-46, Zona 1)*. This friendly place has big, clean rooms facing a pretty courtyard. Rooms with private hot bath and cable TV are US$8.50 per person. Rooms with clean, shared bath and little balconies are US$6.25 per person. Some rooms are mildewy, so sniff a few first. The hotel has a pool table, restaurant and parking, and you can make international calls here.

Hotel La Paz *(☎ 952-1358, 6a Avenida 2-19, Zona 1)* is cheerful, clean and an excellent deal for the price: US$3.25/6.25 with shared bath, US$4.75/9 with private bath. It has many flowers, courtyard parking and a good cafetería next door. It claims to have hot water.

The ***Hotel Central*** *(☎ 952-1118, ☎/fax 951-1442, 1a Calle 1-79, Zona 4)* is clean, with rooms (each with private bath) around a flowered courtyard. Rates are US$7/12.50/18 without TV, US$9.25/15/20 with TV. The Cafetería San Jorge is also here.

The comfortable ***Hotel Mansión Armenia*** *(☎ 951-4284, 951-0978, 7a Avenida 2-18, Zona 1)*, one block from Templo El Calvario, is clean, quiet and modern, with parking and a cafetería. Rooms with private bath and cable TV are US$11/20/27.

Hotel Oxib Peck *(☎ 951-3224, fax 952-1039, 1a Calle 12-11, Zona 1)* is 12 blocks

(750m) west of the plaza on the road out of town. The rooms are clean and pleasant, and the hotel has a dining room, laundry service and parking. Rooms with private bath and cable TV are US$15/22/29.

Hostal de Doña Victoria *(☎ 951-4213/4, 3a Calle 2-38, Zona 3)* occupies a restored mansion over 400 years old. Comfortable rooms with private bath surround a central courtyard that has plants and a restaurant/bar. Prices are US$17/24/30/33 single/double/triple/quad.

Best in town is the colonial-style ***Hotel La Posada*** *(☎ 952-1495, 951-0588, 1a Calle 4-12, Zona 2)*, just off the plaza in the very center of town. Its colonnaded porches are draped with tropical flowers and furnished with lounge chairs and hammocks from which you can enjoy the mountain views. The rooms have private baths, nice old furniture, fireplaces and wall hangings of local weaving; rates are US$23/29/34 single/double/triple.

Places to Eat

Most of Cobán's hotels have restaurants. The one at ***Casa D'Acuña*** is among the town's best, offering authentic Italian and other continental dishes in an attractive setting. Dinners start at around US$5. The restaurant opens at 7 am for breakfast. Also recommended is the restaurant at ***Hostal de Doña Victoria***.

Tiny ***Café Delicí***, 1a Calle at 2a Avenida, just behind the cathedral, serves awesome coffee, espresso and other java drinks in a friendly atmosphere. Try some pastries or the set lunch (US$1.50).

Café El Tirol, near the Hotel La Posada, advertises 'the best coffee' (try the specials) and offers several types of hot chocolate. It's a cozy little place to enjoy pastries and coffee for US$1 to US$2. Breakfast and light meals are served as well. It's closed on Sunday.

Café La Posada, at the Hotel La Posada on the plaza's west end, has tables on a verandah, overlooking the plaza. Inside is a comfortable sitting room with couches, coffee tables and a fireplace. All the usual café fare is served. Also facing the main square, ***Cafetería Santa Rita*** is small, tidy and popular with locals. Good typical Guatemalan meals go for around US$2.

Cafetería San Jorge, 1a Calle between 1a and 2a Avenidas, Zona 4, near the cathedral, has a varied menu and a dining room with views through large windows. Substantial meat dishes are offered (US$3), along with a variety of sandwiches (US$1 to US$2). Next door, **Yogurt Renee** makes delicious fruit yogurts and ice cream.

Pollo Campero has an outlet across from the post office on 2a Avenida at 3a Calle, Zona 3. **Restaurante El Refugio**, at the corner of 2a Avenida and 2a Calle, Zona 4, has rustic wooden decor and a menu with lots of game, seafood and meat options (grilled steaks are US$3 to US$8), and Mexican dishes.

Almost 500m from the plaza on the road out of town, **Restaurant Kam Mun** (1a Calle 8-12, Zona 2) serves Chinese fare in clean and pleasant surroundings. Full meals costs US$5 to US$8. **Kikoe's Tasca**, on the southern part of 2a Avenida, Zona 2, near the Casa D'Acuña, is a bar in the Bavarian vein. Cocktails, beer and bar food are served; it opens at 5 pm daily.

In the evening, food trucks park around the plaza, offering some of the cheapest dining in town. Some serve safe food, others don't.

Getting There & Away

Air TACA (reservations ☎ 334-7722) offers one daily flight from Guatemala City to Cobán at 9:50 am (US$45, 30 minutes). That same plane returns to Guatemala City from Cobán at 10:30 am daily.

Bus The CA-14/Carretera al Atlántico route is the most traveled circuit between Cobán and the outside world, but buses also serve other off-the-beaten-track routes. Consider taking the phenomenal Cobán to Huehuetenango route (see the Highlands chapter for details). Or head from Cobán to El Estor, on Lago de Izabel, or to Poptún in the Petén on the backdoor route via Fray Bartolomé de Las Casas.

Many buses leave from Cobán's new bus terminal, southeast of the stadium. Buses to

Guatemala City, Salamá, Lanquín and many other destinations depart from completely different stations. Bus stops are shown on the map. From Cobán, buses include the following:

Biotopo del Quetzal US$1, one hour, 58km. Any bus heading for Guatemala City will drop you at the entrance to the Biotopo.

Cahabón US$2, 4½ hours, 85km. Same buses as to Lanquín; more than a dozen departures daily.

Chisec 1½ hours, 66km. Six buses a day leave from the corner of 1a Avenida and 2a Calle between 6 am and 3 pm. The last bus returns to Cobán from Chisec at 12:30.

El Estor US$2.50, 7½ hours, 166km. Brenda Mercedes and Valenciana buses depart from the bus terminal 12 times daily; the first departure is at 4 am, the last at 3 pm.

Fray Bartolomé de Las Casas US$2, 5½ hours, 101km. Several buses daily, starting at 5 am. You can catch this bus on 2a Avenida, Zona 3, near Banco G&T.

Guatemala City US$2.25 to US$3.75, four hours, 213km. Transportes Escobar Monja Blanca (☎ 251-1878), 2a Calle 3-77, Zona 4, has buses leaving for Guatemala City every half hour from 2 to 6 am, then hourly from 6 am to 4 pm.

Lanquín US$1.25, 2½ hours, 61km. Buses depart at 6 am, noon, 1 and 3 pm from Oficina Belenju on 3a Calle, Zona 1. The return buses depart Lanquín at 5 am, 7 am and 3 pm. Rutas Nicte Amely buses leave at 5:15 am and 12:15 pm, returning at 4:30 am and 2 pm. You can catch these buses from 2a Calle, Zona 2, across from the Lavandería Providencia.

Playa Grande (sometimes called Cantabal) US$3, four hours, 141km. A few buses daily leave from 2a Avenida, Zona 3, near the Banco G&T; the first is at 4:30 am.

Puerto Barrios 6½ hours, 335km. Take any bus headed for Guatemala City and change at El Rancho junction. Do the same to get to Río Dulce, but transfer again at La Ruidosa junction (169km past El Rancho).

Salamá US$1.25, one hour, 57km. Frequent minivans leave from 2a Calle, across the street from the Lavandería Providencia.

San Pedro Carcha US$0.10, 20 minutes, 6km. Buses every 10 minutes, 6 am to 7 pm, from 2a Calle between 2a and 3a Avenidas, Zona 4.

Sayaxché US$5, seven hours, 184km. One daily departure, at 4:40 am, leaves from 2a Avenida near the Banco G&T.

Uspantán US$1.50, 4½ hours, 94km. Two buses daily, at 10 am and noon from the bus terminal south of the stadium.

Car Cobán's car rental places are small and may not have every type of vehicle available at every moment. It's a good idea to reserve one in advance. If you want to go to the Grutas de Lanquín or Semuc Champey, you'll need a 4WD.

Rental car companies include:

Futura Rent-a-Car (☎ 952-2059), 1a Calle 3-13, Zona 1, in the same building as the Café El Tirol, in the rear right corner of the courtyard

Inque Renta Autos (☎ 952-1994, 952-1172), 3a Avenida 1-18, Zona 4

Ochoch Pec Renta Autos (☎ 951-3474, 951-3214), opposite La Carrita el Viaje at the entrance to town

Tabarini Rent A Car (☎ 952-1504, ☎/fax 951-3282), 7a Avenida 2-27, Zona 2

AROUND COBÁN

Cobán (indeed all of Alta Verapaz) is becoming a hot destination for adventure travel. Not only does this area hold scores of villages where you can experience traditional Mayan culture in some of its purest extant form, it also harbors beautiful caves, waterfalls, pristine lagoons and many other natural wonders yet to be discovered. Go find them!

San Juan Chamelco

About 16km southeast of Cobán is the village of San Juan Chamelco, with swimming at the Balneario Chio. The church here, which dates back to the colonial period and may have been the first in Alta Verapaz, sits atop a small rise and has awesome views of the villages below. Mass is still held here in Spanish (Sunday 5 pm) and Q'eqchi' (Sunday 7 and 9:30 am).

In Aldea Chajaneb, Jerry Makransky (everyone knows him as 'Don Jerónimo'; sbrizuel@c.net.gt) rents comfortable, simple bungalows for US$25 per person (US$45 per couple) per day. Included in the price are three ample, delicious vegetarian meals fresh from the garden and many activities: tours to caves, to the mountains, inner tubing

on the Río Sotzil and more. Jerry dotes on his guests, and the atmosphere is friendly. To get there, take a bus from Cobán to San Juan Chamelco. From there, take a bus or pickup toward Chamil and ask the driver to let you off at Don Jerónimo's. Take the footpath to the left for 300m, cross the bridge and it's the first house on the right. Alternatively, you can hire a taxi from Cobán for about US$6.

Grutas de Lanquín

If you don't mind bumping over bad roads, the best excursion to make from Cobán is to the caves near Lanquín, a pretty village 61km east. If you get this far, make sure to visit Semuc Champey as well.

The Grutas de Lanquín are a short distance northwest of the town and extend for several kilometers into the earth. You must first stop at the police station in the Municipalidad (Town Hall) in Lanquín, pay the US$1.50 admission fee and ask them to open the caves for you; there is no attendant out at the caves. The caves have lights, but bring a powerful flashlight anyway. You'll also need shoes with good traction, as it's slippery inside.

Though the first few hundred meters of cavern has been equipped with a walkway and is lit by electric lights, most of this subterranean system is untouched. If you're a neophyte spelunker, think twice about wandering too far in – the entire extent of this cave has yet to be explored, let alone mapped. Aside from funky stalactites and stalagmites, these caves are crammed with bats; at sunset, they fly out of the mouth of the cave in formations so dense they obscure the sky. Sit at the entrance while they exit for a dazzling display of navigation skills. The river here gushes from the cave in clean, cool and delicious torrents; search out the hot pockets near the shore.

Camping is permitted near the cave entrance. In Lanquín, *La Divina Providencia* has simple rooms for about US$2 per person. *El Recreo* (☎ 952-2160), between the town and the caves, is more attractive and more expensive; US$15/20 single/double. The new *El Retiro* is a recommended place popular with backpackers. The four rooms

GUATEMALA

all share a bath and rent for US$2.75 per person. Meals are available for around US$1.50. The *Comedor Shalom* is also good for a meal.

Semuc Champey

Ten kilometers southeast of Lanquín along a rough, bumpy, slow road is Semuc Champey, famed for a natural wonder: a great limestone bridge 300m long, on top of which is a stepped series of pools of refreshing, flowing water good for swimming. The pools are fed by mountain stream runoff, while the powerful Río Cahabón rushes beneath the bridge underground. Though this bit of paradise is difficult to reach (and describe!), the gorgeous setting and the perfection of the pools, ranging from turquoise to emerald green, make it all worth it. Some people consider this the most beautiful spot in all Guatemala.

It's possible to camp at Semuc Champey, but be sure to camp only in the upper areas, as flash floods are common down below. It's risky to leave anything unattended, as it might get stolen. And solo travelers may feel uncomfortable in such a secluded spot.

Tours to the Grutas de Lanquín and Semuc Champey, offered in Cobán for around US$35 per person, are the easiest way to visit these places. On your own, if you're driving, you'll need a 4WD vehicle.

Several buses daily run between Cobán and Lanquín, continuing to Cahabón. Buses leave Lanquín on the return to Cobán at 4:30, 5 and 7 am and 2 and 3 pm. Since the last return bus departs so early, you should probably plan to stay the night. Occasional buses and trucks make the run from Lanquín to Semuc Champey; your chances of catching one are better in the early morning. Otherwise, it's a long, hot walk. Admission to the site is US$1.

BACKDOOR PETÉN ROUTES

The Cobán to Poptún route via Fray Bartolomé de Las Casas used to be a scratch of dirt road with one car passing a week. Nowadays, plenty of buses and pickups ply the decent roads. This is a great opportunity for getting off the Gringo Trail and into the heart of Guatemala.

The hospitable town of **Fray Bartolomé de Las Casas**, often referred to as Fray (pronounced 'fry'), is sizable for being in the middle of nowhere. You can't make it from Cobán to Poptún in one shot, so you'll be spending the night here. The friendly *Hotel y Restaurante Diamelas*, near the plaza, is the best place to stay in town. Its five rooms with private bath cost US$3.25 per person. The restaurant serves a terrific set lunch. Around the corner is the *Hospedaje Ralios*, but it's not as good. Here, dark, basic rooms around a neglected courtyard are US$2.50. (Note that a certain solo female traveler was harassed at Hotel & Restaurant Fontina, down the road to the market, so steer clear if you fall into that category.) The town has a bank, post office and police station.

One bus daily departs from the plaza at 3 am for Poptún (US$4, five hours, 100km). Buses for Cobán leave at 5, 6, 8, 10 and 11 am (US$2, 5½ hours, 101km).

Another backdoor trip you could take would be from **Cobán to Sayaxché and El Ceibal** – either by getting the one daily direct bus from Cobán (4:40 am) or one of the several departures to Chisec, where you transfer. See Getting There & Away in the Cobán section, above. You can also go via Raxrujá (many services), west of Fray Bartolomé de Las Casas. One bus daily leaves Fray for Sayaxché at 10 am (4½ hours, 117km).

Zacapa & Chiquimula

Visitors to these two departments will find no shortage of things to see and do. Highlights of the region include the paleontology museum at Estanzuela; the great basilica at Esquipulas, famous throughout Central America; and the impressive Mayan ruins of Copán, just over the border in Honduras.

RÍO HONDO

Río Hondo (Deep River) lies at the junction of CA-9 and CA-10, 42km east of El Rancho Junction and 126km from Guatemala City.

The center of town is northeast of the highway junction. By car, it's an hour from here to Quiriguá, half an hour to Chiquimula and 1½ hours to Esquipulas.

Places to Stay & Eat

Río Hondo's lodgings are used as weekend resorts by locals and Guatemala City residents, so they may be heavily booked on weekends. All of them are modern and have well-equipped bungalows (all with cable TV and private bath), spacious grounds and good restaurants. All except the Hotel Santa Cruz have giant swimming pools.

The following four motels are all near one another at Km 126 on the Carretera al Atlántico.

Cheapest of the four is *Hotel Santa Cruz* (☎ 934-7112, ☎/fax 934-7075), where rooms in duplex bungalows are US$9.75 per person with fan, US$12 with air-con. The popular restaurant here is cheaper than some of the others. Four apartments with kitchen are also available.

Hotel El Atlántico (☎ 934-7160, fax 934-7041) is probably the most attractive, with a large swimming pool, beautiful expansive grounds and a good restaurant. Large, well-equipped bungalows are US$16/27/32 single/double/triple. Reservations are wise.

Across the highway, the *Hotel Nuevo Pasabién* (☎/fax 934-7201, 934-7073/4) has large rooms with air-con for US$19.50/34 single/double, as well as less expensive rooms with fan.

Opposite the Hotel Santa Cruz and behind the 24-hour Shell gas station, *Hotel Longarone* (☎ 934-7126, fax 934-7035) is the old standard in this area. Some rooms are in a long row, others are in duplex bungalows. Simple rooms go for US$24/30/36 single/double/triple, or US$30/36/42 with cable TV and fridge; all have air-con. The hotel has two large swimming pools, two smaller ones for children and a tennis court.

Valle Dorado (☎ 941-2542, 933-1111, fax 941-2543), Carretera al Atlántico Km 149, 14km east of the CA-10 junction and 23km from the other Río Hondo hotels, is an enormous complex that includes an aquatic park with giant pools, waterslides, toboggans and

other entertainment. Rooms are US$45 for one to four people, or US$72 for six. Make reservations on weekends, when it fills up with families.

Many people prefer to stay at one of the other Río Hondo hotels and come to Valle Dorado for the day. Day use costs US$6/5 for adults/children on weekends, US$4.50/3.75 during the week. The park is open from 8 am to sunset daily.

ESTANZUELA
• **population 10,000**

Traveling south from Río Hondo along CA-10 you are in the midst of the Río Motagua valley, a hot, 'dry tropic' area that once supported a great number and variety of dinosaurs. Three kilometers south of the Carretera al Atlántico you'll see a small monument on the right-hand (west) side of the road commemorating the terrible earthquake of February 4, 1976.

Less than 2km south of the earthquake monument is the small town of Estanzuela, with its **Museo de Paleontología, Arqueología y Geología Roberto Woolfolk Sarvia**. This interesting museum holds most of the bones of dinosaurs, a giant ground sloth some 30,000 years old and a prehistoric whale. Also on display are early Mayan artifacts. The museum is open 8 am to noon and 1 to 5 pm daily; admission is free. To get there, go west from the highway directly through town for 1km, following the small blue signs pointing to the *museo*; anyone you see can help point the way.

CHIQUIMULA
• **population 24,000** • **elevation 370m**

Capital of the department of the same name, Chiquimula lies in a mining and tobacco-growing region on CA-10, 32km south of the Carretera al Atlántico. It's a major market town for eastern Guatemala, and lots of buying and selling activity takes place daily. It's also a transportation point and overnight stop for those en route to Copán in Honduras; this is the reason most travelers stop here. Among other things, Chiquimula is known for its sweltering climate and decent budget hotels.

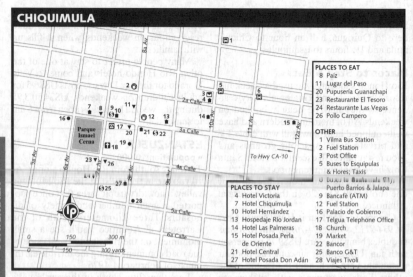

CHIQUIMULA

PLACES TO EAT
8 Paíz
11 Lugar del Paso
20 Pupusería Guanachapi
23 Restaurante El Tesoro
24 Restaurante Las Vegas
26 Pollo Campero

OTHER
1 Vilma Bus Station
2 Fuel Station
3 Post Office
5 Buses to Esquipulas & Flores; Taxis
6 Buses to Guatemala City, Puerto Barrios & Jalapa
9 Bancafé (ATM)
12 Fuel Station
16 Palacio de Gobierno
17 Telgua Telephone Office
18 Church
19 Market
22 Bancor
25 Banco G&T
28 Viajes Tivoli

PLACES TO STAY
4 Hotel Victoria
7 Hotel Chiquimulja
10 Hotel Hernández
13 Hospedaje Río Jordan
14 Hotel Las Palmeras
15 Hotel Posada Perla de Oriente
21 Hotel Central
27 Hotel Posada Don Adán

To Hwy CA-10

0   150   300 m
0   150   300 yards

Information

The post office, on 10a Avenida between 1a and 2a Calles, is in the dirt alley, around the building opposite the bus station. The Telgua telephone office is on 3a Calle, a few doors downhill from the plaza (Parque Ismael Cerna). The Hotel Hernández offers phone services and email for US$0.15 a minute. The Hotel Victoria, 2a Calle at 10a Avenida, has phone service, too. The busy market is near Telgua. Chiquimula is a small town and easily managed on foot.

Many banks will change US dollars cash and traveler's checks. Banco G&T, at 7a Avenida 4-75, changes both and also gives cash advances on Visa and MasterCard; it's open 9 am to 8 pm Monday to Friday, 10 am to 2 pm Saturday. Bancor, at 3a Calle 8-30, has longer Saturday hours, from 9 am to 6 pm. Bancafé, at 3a Calle and 7a Avenida, has a Visa ATM.

Viajes Tivoli (☎ 942-4915/33, fax 942-2258), 8a Avenida 4-71, can help you deal with any travel arrangements.

Places to Stay

On the plaza's north side is **Hotel Chiqui-mulja** (☎ 942-0387, 3a Calle 6-51). It was being remodeled at the time of writing, but will reopen with rooms with private bath and air-con.

Hotel Hernández (☎ 942-0708, 3a Calle 7-41) is clean, friendly and a great value; the owner speaks English, Spanish and some French. The hotel has parking and a sparkling swimming pool, and the rooms have fans and good beds. Rates are US$4/6.25 single/double with shared hot bath; US$7.75/10 with private bath and cable TV. Some rooms have air-con.

Hospedaje Río Jordan (☎ 942-0887, 3a Calle 8-91), a block farther downhill, has parking, a simple restaurant and rates of US$2 per person for rooms with shared bath, $3.25 per person for rooms with private bath.

Nearby is friendly **Hotel Central** (☎ 942-6352, 3a Calle 8-30, 2nd floor), which has five clean rooms with private bath, air-con, cable TV and small balconies overlooking all the action; US$7.75/12.50/15.50/18.50 single/double/triple/quad.

Near the bus station, **Hotel Las Palmeras** (☎ 942-4647, fax 942-0763, 10a Avenida 2-00) is a clean, family-run place that has rooms with private bath, cable TV and good beds for US$6.50/13 single/double with air-con, US$4/7.75 with fan.

Hotel Posada Perla de Oriente (☎ 942-0014, fax 942-0534, 12a Avenida 2-30), entrance on 2a Calle, has a small swimming pool, a children's play area and a restaurant. Simple rooms with private bath, fan and cable TV cost US$12/21/30/41.

Hotel Posada Don Adán (☎ 942-3924, 8a Avenida 4-30) is spotless. It's run by a friendly, efficient señora who charges US$13/17.50/22 single/double/triple for rooms with private bath, telephone, cable TV, fan and air-con.

Places to Eat

Chiquimula has lots of cheap little places to eat. Try *Pupusería Guanachapi*, on 3a Calle between 7a and 8a Avenidas, or *Lugar del Paso*, around the corner on 8a Avenida, which serves reasonably priced grilled meats, burgers and chicken dishes and has a full bar.

Restaurante El Tesoro, on the main plaza, serves Chinese food at fair prices. *Pollo Campero*, at 7a Avenida and 4a Calle, makes fried chicken, burgers and breakfasts. It's open daily, and its air-con is a treat.

For a step up in quality, try *Restaurante Las Vegas (7a Avenida 4-40)*, half a block from the plaza. It's perhaps Chiquimula's best, with fancy plants, jazzy music, a well-stocked bar and full meals for around US$6 (sandwiches less). It's open 7 am to midnight daily.

The *Paíz* grocery store on the park is huge. Stock up here for a picnic and enjoy the air-con. The *panadería* next door to the Hotel Hernández opens at 5:30 am – perfect for predawn bus departures.

Getting There & Away

Chiquimula is not a destination but a transit point. Your goal is probably the fabulous Mayan ruins at Copán in Honduras, just across the border from El Florido. The turnoff to Copán lies just south of Chiquimula. Beyond that, the road splits at Padre Miguel Junction. Take the left (east) branch to reach Esquipulas and Nueva Ocotepeque (Honduras); the right branch leads

to Anguiatú, a remote border crossing into El Salvador.

Several companies operate buses to Guatemala City and Puerto Barrios; all of them arrive and depart from the bus station area on 11a Avenida, between 1a and 2a Calles. Minivans to Esquipulas and buses to Flores arrive and depart from the bus station area a block away, on 10a Avenida between 1a and 2a Calles. Vilma (☎ 942-2253) operates buses to El Florido from its own bus station a couple of blocks north.

Agua Caliente (Honduras border) Take a minibus to Esquipulas and change there.

Anguiatú (El Salvador border) US$1, one hour, 54km. Hourly minibuses, 6 am to 3:30 pm.

El Florido (Honduras border) US$1, 2½ hours, 58km. Buses depart from the Vilma bus station at 6, 9, 10:30 and 11:30 am and 12:30, 1:30, 2:30 and 3:30 pm. Coming in the opposite direction, they depart hourly from El Florido, 5:30 am to 3:30 pm.

Esquipulas US$0.80, 45 minutes, 52km. Minibuses every 10 minutes, 4 am to 8 pm. Sit on the left for views.

Flores US$7, 10 hours, 385km. Transportes María Elena buses depart at 6 am and 3 pm.

Guatemala City US$3, three hours, 169km. Rutas Orientales, Transportes Guerra and Guatesqui operate buses departing every half hour, 3 am to 4:30 pm.

Puerto Barrios US$2.50, 4½ hours, 192km. Buses every 30 minutes, 4 am to 3 pm; take this bus for Quiriguá (US$1.50, two hours, 103km) and Río Dulce (change at La Ruidosa junction; US$2, three hours, 144km).

Quiriguá See Puerto Barrios.

Río Dulce See Puerto Barrios.

Río Hondo US$1, 35 minutes, 32km. Minibuses every half-hour, 5 am to 6 pm. Or take any bus heading for Guatemala City, Flores or Puerto Barrios.

PADRE MIGUEL JUNCTION & ANGUIATÚ

Between Chiquimula and Esquipulas is Padre Miguel Junction, the turnoff for Anguiatú (on the border with El Salvador, 30 minutes and 19km away). Minibuses pass by frequently, coming from Chiquimula,

Quezaltepeque and Esquipulas. The crossroads has a guard house, a bus stop shelter and little else.

The border at Anguiatú is open 6 am to 6 pm daily, though you might be able to get through on 'extraordinary service' until 9 pm. Across the border, buses run hourly to San Salvador, passing through Metapán, 12km from the border, and Santa Ana, 47km farther along.

ESQUIPULAS

From Chiquimula, CA-10 goes south into the mountains, where it's cooler and a bit more comfortable. After an hour's ride through pretty country, the highway descends into a valley ringed by mountains. Halfway down the slope, about a kilometer from town, a mirador provides a good view. As soon as you catch sight of the place you'll see the reason for coming: the great Basílica de Esquipulas that towers above the town, its whiteness shining in the sun.

History

This town may have been a place of pilgrimage even before the conquest. Legend has it that Esquipulas takes its name from a noble Mayan lord who ruled this region when the Spanish arrived.

With the arrival of the friars, a church was built, and in 1595 an image of Christ carved from black wood was installed in it. The steady flow of pilgrims to Esquipulas became a flood after 1737, when Pedro Pardo de Figueroa, Archbishop of Guatemala, came here on pilgrimage and went away cured of a chronic ailment. Delighted with this development, the prelate commissioned a huge new church to be built on the site. It was finished in 1758, and the pilgrimage trade has been the town's livelihood ever since.

Esquipulas is assured a place in modern history too. Beginning here in 1986, President Vinicio Cerezo Arévalo brokered agreements with the other Central American leaders on economic cooperation and peaceful conflict resolution. These negotiations became the seeds of the Guatemalan Peace Accords, which were finally signed in 1996.

Orientation & Information

The church and its adjacent park are the center of everything. Most of the good cheap hotels are within a block or two of here, as are numerous small restaurants. The highway does not enter town; 11a Calle, also sometimes called Doble Vía Quirio Cataño, comes in from the highway and is the town's 'main drag.'

The post office is at 6a Avenida 2-15, about 10 blocks north of the center. The Telgua telephone office, 5a Avenida at 9a Calle, is open daily. You can use phone cards in the town's public telephones.

A number of banks change US dollars cash and traveler's checks. Bancafé, 3a Avenida 6-68, Zona 1, changes both, gives cash advances on Visa and MasterCard and is the town's American Express agent.

The Honduran consulate (☎ 943-2027, 943-1547, fax 943-1371) is in the Hotel Payaquí. It's open 8:30 am to noon and 2 to 5 pm Monday to Saturday.

Basilica

A massive pile of stone that has resisted the power of earthquakes for almost 2½ centuries, the basilica is approached through a pretty park and up a flight of steps. The impressive facade and towers are floodlit at night.

Inside, the devout approach El Cristo Negro with extreme reverence, many on their knees. Incense, the murmur of prayers and the scuffle of sandaled feet fill the air. When throngs of pilgrims are here, you must enter the church from the side to get a close view of the famous Black Christ. Shuffling along quickly, you may get a good glimpse before being shoved onward by the press of the crowd behind you. On Sunday, religious holidays and (especially) during the festival around January 15, the press of devotees is intense. Otherwise, you may have the place to yourself.

Cueva de las Minas

The Centro Turístico Cueva de las Minas has a 50m-deep cave (bring your own light), grassy picnic areas, and the Río El Milagro, where people come for a dip and say it's

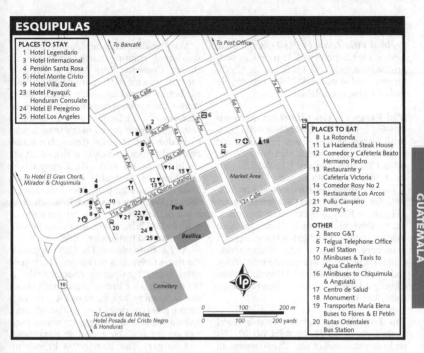

ESQUIPULAS

PLACES TO STAY
1 Hotel Legendario
3 Hotel Internacional
4 Pensión Santa Rosa
5 Hotel Monte Cristo
9 Hotel Villa Zonia
23 Hotel Payaquí;
    Honduran Consulate
24 Hotel El Peregrino
25 Hotel Los Angeles

To Bancafé

To Post Office

8a Calle

9a Calle

10a Calle

11a Calle (Doble Vía Quirio Cataño)

21 Calle

Market Area

Park

Basilica

To Hotel El Gran Chortí,
Mirador & Chiquimula

Cemetery

To Cueva de las Minas,
Hotel Posada del Cristo Negro
& Honduras

PLACES TO EAT
8 La Rotonda
11 La Hacienda Steak House
12 Comedor y Cafetería Beato
    Hermano Pedro
13 Restaurante y
    Cafetería Victoria
14 Comedor Rosy No 2
15 Restaurante Los Arcos
21 Pollo Campero
22 Jimmy's

OTHER
2 Banco G&T
6 Telgua Telephone Office
7 Fuel Station
10 Minibuses & Taxis to
    Agua Caliente
16 Minibuses to Chiquimula
    & Anguiatú
17 Centro de Salud
18 Monument
19 Transportes María Elena
    Buses to Flores & El Petén
20 Rutas Orientales
    Bus Station

0   100   200 m
0   100   200 yards

GUATEMALA

miraculous. The cave and river are half a kilometer from the entrance gate, which is behind the Basilica's cemetery, 300m south of the turnoff into town on the road heading toward Honduras. It's open 6:30 am to 4 pm daily; US$0.35. Refreshments are available.

Places to Stay

Esquipulas has an abundance of places to stay. On holidays and during the annual festival, every hotel in town is filled, whatever the price; weekends are fairly busy as well, with prices substantially higher. On weekdays when there is no festival, ask for a *descuento* (discount) and you'll probably get it.

Budget The area north of the basilica holds many cheap lodgings. The family-run *Pensión Santa Rosa* (☎ 943-2908), 10a Calle at 1a Avenida, is typical of these small places. It charges US$2.75 per person with shared bath, US$4 with private bath. Several others are on 10a Calle as well.

Hotel Monte Cristo (☎ 943-1453, fax 943-1042, 3a Avenida 9-12) is clean and OK, with parking and a restaurant. Rooms run US$6.25/11 single/double with shared bath, or US$13/19.50 with private bath.

Hotel El Peregrino (☎ 943-1054, 943-1859, 2a Avenida 11-94), on the southwest corner of the park, has simple rooms with private bath for US$6.50 per person, plus a new section in the rear where larger, fancier rooms with cable TV are US$23 double. Next door, *Hotel Los Angeles* (☎ 943-1254, 2a Avenida 11-94) has 20 rooms arranged around a bright inner courtyard. All have private bath, fan and cable TV; US$7.75/15. Both places have restaurants and parking.

In the same block, *Hotel Payaquí* (☎ 943-2025, fax 943-1371) is a large, attractive hotel with 55 rooms, all with private bath, cable TV, telephone and fridge. Rooms are US$19.50/32, with or without air-con. It has two restaurants, one in the rear by the swimming pool and one in front with a view of the park.

Hotel Villa Zonia (☎ *943-1133, 10a Calle 1-84)* is a bright hotel with 15 rooms, all with private bath and cable TV. Rates are US$22 for one double bed, US$25 for two double beds. Parking is available.

Mid-Range The clean *Hotel Internacional* (☎ *943-1131, 943-1667, 10a Calle 0-85)* has a small swimming pool, sauna, restaurant and parking. The 49 rooms, all with private bath, cable TV and phone, are US$15/19.50 with fan, US$19.50/23 with air-con.

Hotel Posada del Cristo Negro (☎ *943-1482, fax 943-1829)*, Carretera Internacional a Honduras Km 224, is 2km from the church, out of town on the way to Honduras. Nice touches include broad green lawns, a pretty swimming pool and a large dining room. Comfortable rooms with private bath, fridge and TV cost US$14/20/27/33 single/double/triple/quad. Two or three children (up to age eight) stay free.

Top End Modern and comfortable *Hotel Legendario* (☎ *943-1824/5, ☎/fax 943-1022)* is on 3a Avenida at 9a Calle. The 40 rooms all have private bath, fan, cable TV and large windows opening onto a grassy courtyard with a swimming pool; US$45/55 single/double. A restaurant and parking are on site.

Hotel El Gran Chorti (☎ *943-1148, 943-1560, fax 943-1551)*, Km 222, is 1km west of the church on the road to Chiquimula. The lobby floor is a hectare of black marble; behind it a serpentine swimming pool is set between umbrella-shaded café tables, lawns and gardens. Other amenities include a game room and a good restaurant, bar and cafeteria. The rooms have all creature comforts, and the rates reflect it: US$47/52, US$66 for a junior suite (sleeps four), US$81 for a master suite (sleeps six).

Places to Eat

Restaurants are more expensive here than in other parts of Guatemala. Low-budget restaurants are clustered at the park's north end, where hungry pilgrims can find them readily; ask in advance the price of each food item you order and add up your bill carefully.

Many small eateries lie along 3a Avenida, the street running north opposite the church. *Comedor Rosy No 2* is tidy and cheerful, with meals for around US$2.50 and big bottles of pickled chiles on the tables. Across the street, *Restaurante y Cafetería Victoria* is a bit fancier, with tablecloths, plants and higher prices. In the same block, *Comedor y Cafetería Beato Hermano Pedro* advertises set meals for around US$2.

On the park's west side, *Jimmy's* is a bright and clean cafeteria with big windows looking out onto the park. Prices are reasonable, and the menu is varied. Roast chicken is one of the specialties; you can get a whole chicken for US$6, or a quarter chicken with fries, salad and tortillas for US$2.

At *La Rotonda*, on 11a Calle opposite the Rutas Orientales bus station, chairs surround a circular open-air counter under a big awning. It's a breezy place that's clean and welcoming. The menu of the day, with soup, a main course, rice, vegetables, dessert and a drink is US$4, and plenty of other selections are available, including pizza, pasta and burgers. The Esquipulas branch of *Pollo Campero* is on 11a Calle and has a drive-thru.

All of these places are open from around 6 am until 9 or 10 pm daily.

The more expensive *La Hacienda Steak House*, 2a Avenida at 10a Calle, is an enjoyable place for grilled steaks, chicken and seafood; it's open 8 am to 10 pm daily. *Restaurante Los Arcos*, on 11a Calle opposite the park, is another upscale restaurant, open 7 am to 10 pm daily.

All of the mid-range and top-end hotels have dining rooms.

Getting There & Away

Buses to Guatemala City arrive and depart from the Rutas Orientales (☎ 943-1366) bus station on 11a Calle at 1a Avenida, near the entrance to town. Minibuses to Agua Caliente arrive and depart across the street; taxis also wait here. The taxis charge the same as the minibuses, and they leave when they have five passengers.

Minibuses to Chiquimula and to Anguiatú depart from the east end of 11a Calle; you'll see them hawking for passengers along the main street. Transportes María Elena operates buses to Flores from the far east side of town, beyond the market.

Agua Caliente (Honduras border) US$0.70, 30 minutes, 10km. Minibuses every half hour, 6 am to 5 pm.

Anguiatú (El Salvador border) US$1, one hour, 33km. Minibuses every half hour, 6 am to 4 pm.

Chiquimula US$0.80, 45 minutes, 52km. Minibuses every 10 minutes, 5 am to 5 pm.

Flores US$7.75, 11 hours, 437km. Transportes María Elena buses depart at 4:20 am and 1:30 pm.

Guatemala City US$3.25, four hours, 222km. Rutas Orientales' *servicio especial* buses depart at 6:30 and 7:30 am and 1:30 and 3:30 pm; ordinary buses depart at 3:30, 5, 6:30, 7:30, 8:15 and 11:30 am and 1, 1:30, 3, 3:30 and 5:30 pm.

COPÁN ARCHAEOLOGICAL SITE (HONDURAS)

The ancient city of Copán, 13km from the Guatemalan border in Honduras, is one of the most outstanding Mayan achievements, ranking in splendor with Tikal, Chichén Itzá and Uxmal. It's possible to visit on a long day trip by private car or organized tour, but it's better to take at least two days, staying the night in the town of Copán Ruinas, 1 km west of the ruins. This is a charming town, with good facilities, so unless you're in a huge rush, try to overnight here.

Pickup trucks coming from the border will usually take you on to the ruins after a stop in town. If not, you can always walk there on the *sendero peatonal* (footpath) alongside the road; it makes for a pretty walk, passing several stelae and unexcavated mounds on the way. Beyond the ruins, the path continues a couple of kilometers farther to Las Sepulturas archaeological site.

History

Pre-Columbian Ceramic evidence uncovered in the Copán valley places humans here as early as 1200 BC. Copán must have had substantial commercial activity since early times; graves showing significant Olmec influence have been dated to between 900 and 600 BC.

From AD 426 to 435, Copán was ruled by a mysterious king known as Mah K'ina Yax K'uk' Mo' (Great Sun Lord Quetzal

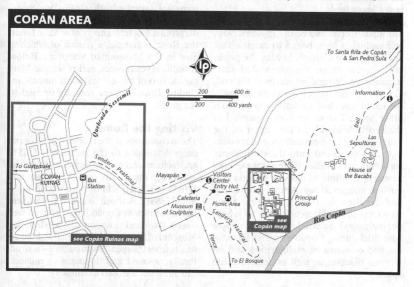

COPÁN AREA

Macaw). Archaeological evidence indicates that he was a great shaman; later kings revered him as the city's semidivine founder. The king's family dynasty ruled throughout Copán's Classic-period florescence.

Among the greatest of Copán's kings was Smoke Imix (Smoke Jaguar), who ruled from 628 to 695. Smoke Imix built Copán into a major military and commercial power in the region. He may have taken over the nearby princedom of Quiriguá, as one of the famous stelae there bears his name and image. By the time he died in 695, Copán's population had grown significantly.

Smoke Imix was succeeded by Uaxaclahun Ubak K'awil (18 Rabbit; 695–738), who pursued military conquest. In a war with his neighbor, King Cauac Sky, 18 Rabbit was captured and beheaded.

Another king, Smoke Shell (ruled 749–763), was one of Copán's greatest builders. He commissioned the construction of the city's most famous and important monument, the awesome Hieroglyphic Stairway, which immortalizes the achievements of the family dynasty from its establishment until 755, when the stairway was dedicated. It is the longest such inscription ever discovered in the Maya lands.

Until recently, the collapse of the civilization at Copán had been a mystery. Now, archaeologists have begun to surmise that near the end of Copán's heyday, the population grew at an unprecedented rate, straining agricultural resources; in the end, Copán was no longer agriculturally self-sufficient and had to import food from other areas. The urban core expanded in the fertile lowlands in the center of the valley, forcing both agriculture and residential areas to spread onto the steep slopes surrounding the valley. Wide areas were deforested, resulting in massive erosion that further hampered agricultural production and resulted in flooding during rainy seasons (not too different from what is happening today). Skeletal remains of people who died during Copán's final years show marked evidence of malnutrition and infectious diseases, as well as decreased life spans.

The Copán valley was not abandoned overnight – agriculturists probably continued to live in the ecologically devastated valley for another one or two centuries. But by around 1200 even the farmers had departed, and the royal city of Copán was reclaimed by the jungle.

Today The history of the ruins continues to unfold today. The remains of 3450 structures have been found in the 24 sq km surrounding the Principal Group, most of them within about half a kilometer of it. In a wider zone, 4509 structures have been detected in 1420 sites within the surrounding 135 sq km. These discoveries indicate that at the peak of civilization here, around the end of the 8th century, the valley of Copán had over 20,000 inhabitants – a population not reached again until the 1980s.

In addition to examining the area around the Principal Group, archaeologists are continuing to explore the Principal Group itself and making new discoveries. Five separate phases of building on this site have been identified; the final phase, dating from between AD 650 to 820, is what we see today. But buried underneath the visible ruins are layers of other ruins, which archaeologists are exploring by means of underground tunnels. This is how they found the Rosalila temple, a replica of which is now in the Museum of Sculpture. Below Rosalila is yet another, earlier temple, Margarita. Two of these excavation tunnels, including Rosalila, were recently opened to the public.

Visiting the Ruins

The archaeological site is open 8 am to 4 pm daily. Admission to the ruins costs US$10 and includes entry to the Sepulturas site. The excavation tunnels are open 8 to 11 am and 1 to 3 pm daily; admission costs an additional US$12. A touch of irony: The ancient Maya temples at Copán have survived well over a thousand years, but the modern-day Museum of Sculpture here – built to hold artifacts from the great Maya culture – is structurally unsound and threatens to collapse. The museum is closed indefinitely.

The visitors center *(centro de visitantes)* at the entrance to the ruins houses the ticket seller and a small exhibit about the site and its excavation. Nearby are a cafeteria and a souvenir and handicrafts shops. A picnic area lies along the path to the Principal Group. A nature trail *(sendero natural)*, entering the forest several hundred meters from the visitors center, passes by a small ball court.

Pick up a copy of the booklet *History Carved in Stone: A guide to the archaeological park of the ruins of Copán* by William L Fash and Ricardo Agurcia Fasquelle, available at the visitors center for US$1.75. It will help you understand and appreciate the ruins. It's also a good idea to go with a guide, who can help explain the ruins and bring them to life. Guides are US$20 no matter the size of the group and congregate at the visitors center.

Highlights

The path from the visitors center leads to the **Great Plaza** and the huge, intricately carved stelae portraying the rulers of Copán. Most of Copán's best stelae date from AD 613 to 738. All seem to have originally been painted; a few traces of red paint survive on Stela C.

Many of the stelae portray King 18 Rabbit. One of them, Stela D (736), at the north end of the Great Plaza at the base of Structure 2, is particularly interesting. On its back are two columns of hieroglyphs; at its base is an altar with fearsome representations of Chac, the rain god. In front of the altar is the burial place of Dr John Owen, an archaeologist with the expedition from Harvard's Peabody Museum who died during the work in 1893. Still, perhaps the most beautiful stela here is Stela A (AD 731); the one you see is a replica because the original was moved to the museum.

South of the Great Plaza, across what is known as the Central Plaza, is the **ball court**, the second largest in Central America. South of the ball court is Copán's most famous monument, the **Hieroglyphic Stairway** (743), the work of King Smoke Shell. The flight of 63 steps bears a history – in

several thousand glyphs – of the royal house of Copán. At the base of the stairway is Stela M (756), bearing a figure (probably King Smoke Shell) in a feathered cloak; glyphs tell of the solar eclipse in that year. Beside the stairway, a tunnel leads to the tomb of a nobleman, possibly the son of King Smoke Imix. The tomb, discovered in June 1989, held a treasure trove of painted pottery and beautiful carved jade objects that are now in Honduran museums.

The lofty flight of steps south of the Hieroglyphic Stairway is called the **Temple of the Inscriptions**, on the south side of which are the East and West Plazas. In the West Plaza, be sure to see Altar Q (776), among the most famous sculptures here. Around its sides, carved in superb relief, are the 16 great kings of Copán, ending with the altar's creator, Yax Pac. Behind the altar was a sacrificial vault in which archaeologists discovered the bones of 15 jaguars and several macaws, probably sacrificed to the glory of Yax Pac and his ancestors.

The East Plaza contains the tomb of Yax Pac, beneath Structure 18. Unfortunately, the tomb was discovered and looted long before archaeologists arrived. Both the East and West Plazas hold a variety of fascinating stelae and sculptured heads of humans and animals. The most elaborate relief carving is

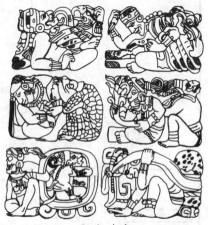

Copán glyphs

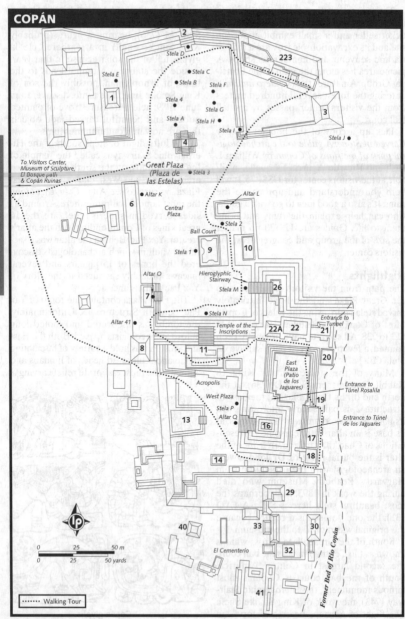

COPÁN

2

223

Stela D

Stela E

Stela C

1

Stela B

Stela F

Stela 4

Stela G

Stela A

Stela H

3

Stela I

Stela J

4

To Visitors Center,
Museum of Sculpture,
El Bosque path
& Copán Ruinas

Great Plaza
(Plaza de
las Estelas)

Stela 3

6

Central
Plaza

Altar L

Stela 2

Ball Court

10

Stela 1

9

Altar O

Hieroglyphic
Stairway

Stela M

26

7

Stela N

Entrance to
Tunnel

Altar 41

Temple of the
Inscriptions

21

22A   22

8

11

20

Acropolis

East
Plaza
(Patio
de los
Jaguares)

Entrance to
Túnel Rosalila

West Plaza

19

Stela P

Entrance to
Túnel
de los Jaguares

13

Altar Q

16

17

14

18

29

40

33

30

El Cementerio

32

0   25   50 m

0   25   50 yards

41

Former Bed of Río Copán

······· Walking Tour

atop Structure 22 on the north side of the East Plaza. Excavation and restoration is still underway.

Excavation Tunnels Excavation tunnels used to uncover the Rosalila temple below Structure 16 and the Galindo Tomb, in the southern part of the East Plaza (Patio de los Jaguares) below Structure 17, are now open to the public.

Descending into these tunnels is startling and more than a little claustrophobic. El Túnel Rosalila (Rosalila Tunnel) reveals the actual temple over which Structure 16 was built; you can still see traces of red paint, and all the carvings are remarkably crisp – especially the Sun God mask above the doorway. Some scholars consider this the best preserved stucco edifice in the Mayan world. Everything is behind Plexiglas to protect it from natural and human elements.

El Túnel de los Jaguares (Tunnel of the Jaguars) is longer and only slightly less dramatic with its niches for offerings and burial tombs. This was one of the first tombs discovered at Copán, in 1834. Bones, obsidian knives and beads were found here and archaeologists date the tomb's antebase mask to AD 540. The decorative macaw mask here is incredible. This tunnel is over 700m long, damp and somewhat foreboding.

Though the price of admission is high, these tunnels will not be open indefinitely and are worth a look for their historical, scientific and cultural significance.

Las Sepulturas & El Bosque

The excavations at the nearby sites of Las Sepulturas and El Bosque have shed light on the daily life of the Maya of Copán during its golden age.

Las Sepulturas, once connected to the Great Plaza by a causeway, may have been the residential area for the rich and powerful. One huge, luxurious compound seems to have housed some 250 people in 40 or 50 buildings arranged around 11 courtyards. The principal structure, called the House of the Bacabs (officials), had outer walls carved with full-size figures of 10 males in fancy feathered headdresses; inside was a huge hieroglyphic bench. To get to Las Sepulturas from the main Copán ruins you have to go back to the main road, turn right, then right again at the sign (2km).

The one-hour walk to El Bosque – down a path through foliage dense with birds – is more impressive than the site itself, which holds little of interest save for a small ball court. You may not see anyone along the way, and it's a powerful experience to have the thoroughfares of an ancient Mayan city all to yourself. To get to El Bosque, go right at the hut where they punch your ticket for the Copán ruins.

COPÁN RUINAS
• population 6000

The town of Copán Ruinas, often simply called Copán, is just over 1km from the famous Mayan ruins of the same name. It's a beautiful little village with cobblestone streets, white adobe buildings with red-tile roofs and a lovely colonial church on the plaza. This valley was inhabited by the Maya for around 2000 years before it was abandoned, and a feeling of timeless harmony fills the air. Copán has become a primary tourist destination, but this hasn't disrupted the town's peacefulness to the extent one might expect.

Orientation

Fortunately Copán Ruinas is small, because the town doesn't use street names. Parque Central is the heart of town; the church is on the park's east side. The ruins are 2km outside of town, on the road to La Entrada and San Pedro Sula. Las Sepulturas archaeological site is a few kilometers farther down this road.

Information

Banco de Occidente, on the plaza, changes US dollars and traveler's checks, Guatemalan quetzales and Salvadoran colones and gives cash advances on Visa and MasterCard. Banco Atlántida, also on the plaza, changes dollars and traveler's checks and gives cash advances on Visa. For US dollars, the banks offer a better rate than the moneychangers near the border but

GUATEMALA

GUATEMALA

COPÁN RUINAS

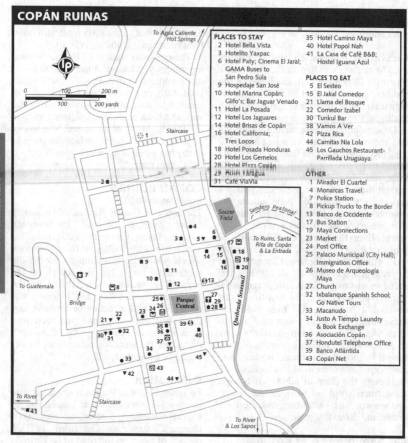

To Agua Caliente / Hot Springs

PLACES TO STAY
2   Hotel Bella Vista
3   Hotelito Yaxpac
6   Hotel Paty; Cinema El Jaral;
    GAMA Buses to
    San Pedro Sula
9   Hospedaje San José
10 Hotel Marina Copán;
    Glifo's; Bar Jaguar Venado
11 Hotel La Posada
12 Hotel Los Jaguares
14 Hotel Brisas de Copán
16 Hotel California;
    Tres Locos
18 Hotel Posada Honduras
20 Hotel Los Gemelos
28 Hotel Plaza Copán
29 Hotel Yaragua
31 Café ViaVia

35 Hotel Camino Maya
40 Hotel Popol Nah
41 La Casa de Café B&B;
    Hostel Iguana Azul

PLACES TO EAT
5   El Sesteo
15 El Jakal Comedor
21 Llama del Bosque
22 Comedor Izabel
30 Tunkul Bar
38 Vamos A Ver
42 Pizza Rica
44 Carnitas Nia Lola
45 Los Gauchos Restaurant-
    Parrillada Uruguaya

OTHER
1   Mirador El Cuartel
4   Monarcas Travel
7   Police Station
8   Pickup Trucks to the Border
13 Banco de Occidente
17 Bus Station
19 Maya Connections
23 Market
24 Post Office
25 Palacio Municipal (City Hall);
    Immigration Office
26 Museo de Arqueología
    Maya
27 Church
32 Ixbalanque Spanish School;
    Go Native Tours
33 Macanudo
34 Justo A Tiempo Laundry
    & Book Exchange
36 Asociación Copán
37 Hondutel Telephone Office
39 Banco Atlántida
43 Copán Net

slightly less than banks elsewhere in Honduras. Both banks are open 8 am to noon and 2 to 5 pm Monday to Friday, 8 am to noon Saturday. Café ViaVia (see Places to Stay) also changes traveler's checks.

The post office is a few doors from the plaza and Hondutel is around the corner. Next door to Hondutel, the Asociación Copán sells books and interpretive materials about the ruins. Hotel Los Gemelos offers international phone and fax services; it's open 7:30 am to 6 pm daily. Email services are available for around US$6 an hour at Copán Net, across the street from Justo a Tiempo; and at Maya Connections, adjacent to Hotel Los Gemelos.

A Honduran immigration office inside the Palacio Municipal can help you with visa issues. It's open 7 am to 4:30 pm Monday to Friday.

Justo A Tiempo offers laundry service and a book exchange; it's closed Sunday. The folks at Hotel Los Gemelos operate a cheaper laundry service.

Things to See & Do

The **Museo de Arqueología Maya** on the plaza is well worth a visit. It contains Copán's original Stela B, portraying King 18 Rabbit. Other exhibits include painted pottery, carved jade, Mayan glyphs, a calendar round and the 'Tumba del Brujo,' the tomb of a shaman or priest who died around AD 700 and was buried with many items under the Plaza de los Jaguares. The museum is open 8 am to noon and 1 to 4 pm Monday to Saturday; US$2.

About four blocks north of the plaza is the **Mirador El Cuartel**, the old jail, which affords a magnificent view over town. The building is now used as a school.

Organized Tours

Tours of the ruins and places farther afield are available from Go Native Tours (☎ 651-4432, ixbalan@hn2.com), sharing an office with Ixbalanque Spanish School; Xukpi Tours (☎ 651-4435, 651-4503), specializing in the ruins and bird-watching; reader-recommended Yaragua Tours (☎ 651-4464, fax 651-4050) in the Hotel Yaragua (see Places to Stay), offering horseback riding trips and caving tours; and Monarcas Travel (☎ 651-4361, monarcas@conexion.com), a block north of Banco de Occidente, which also offers shuttle service between Copán and Antigua (see Getting There & Away).

Aereo Ruta Maya/Jungle Flying Tours (in Guatemala City ☎ 360-4917, fax 331-4995, jungleflying@guate.net, in Copán ☎ 651-4023) offers flights from Guatemala City to an airstrip near Copán, from where you transfer to a bus for a short ride to the ruins (US$192 roundtrip without ruins tour; US$250 with tour).

Places to Stay

Budget The *Hostel Iguana Azul* (☎ 651-4620, fax 651-4623, casadecafe@mayanet.hn, www.todomundo.com/iguanaazul/index.html) is next door to La Casa de Café B&B and operated by the same friendly people. The colonial-style ranch house contains 12 dorm-style bunk beds (US$5 per person) in two rooms with a terrific shared hot bath. Three private rooms rent for US$11 each. The hostel also has a nice garden and a common area with books, magazines, travel guides and lots of travel information.

The *Hotel Los Gemelos* (☎ 651-4077), a long block northeast from the plaza, is a longtime favorite with budget travelers. Operated by a very friendly family, it has a garden patio, a place to wash your clothes (or laundry service if you prefer) and parking; coffee is always available. Rooms with shared cold bath are US$5/7 single/double.

Across the street, *Hotel California* has four attractive rooms that share a hot bath and are decorated with lots of bamboo and woven mats; US$7 per room.

In the same block, *Hotel Posada Honduras* (☎ 651-4082) has 13 simple fan-cooled rooms facing a courtyard full of mango, mamcy and lemon trees. Parking is out back. Rates are US$3/4.25 with shared cold bath, US$5/7 with private cold bath.

Tucked away on a residential street a block and a half from the plaza is the congenial *Hospedaje San José* (☎ 651-4195). The six rooms with shared bath and fan in a familial atmosphere cost US$3/5. The facilities are basic but brimming with authenticity.

Other simple decent places include *Hotelito Yaxpac* (☎ 651-4025) and *Hotel La Posada* (☎ 651-4070), which is half a block from the plaza.

The new *Café ViaVia* (☎ 651-4652, jncooman@lenz.unah.hondunet.net), next door to the Tunkul bar, is a great addition to the Copán hotel scene. This small European-style hotel has four spotless rooms with private hot bath, tiled floors and great beds (2m long) for US$10/13. Amenities include a café (see Places to Eat), hammocks, a small garden and plenty of space to hang out. Inquire about discounts for longer stays. English, French, German and Dutch are spoken.

Also in this price range is *Hotel Yaragua* (☎ 651-4464, fax 651-4050), a half block from the plaza, which has rooms with private bath and cable TV for US$10/17.50/25 single/double/triple. The beautiful, tropical courtyard provides a peaceful atmosphere that makes this place.

Hotel Popol Nah (☎ 651-4095) is a clean place with seven rooms for US$14/17.50/21, all with private hot bath and some with

GUATEMALA

air-con. The *Hotel Paty* (☎ 651-4021, fax 651-4019), near the soccer field, has rooms around a courtyard, all with private hot bath, for US$10.50/12.75.

The *Hotel Bella Vista* (☎ 651-4502, fax 651-4657) is up on a hill overlooking town, four blocks from the plaza. It has a beautiful view and large, comfortable rooms with cable TV and phone for US$11/14/18/24 single/double/triple/quad with private cold bath, US$14/18/21/28 with private hot bath. Parking is available.

Mid-Range The attractive *Hotel Brisas de Copan* (☎ 651-4118), near the soccer field, offers comfortable rooms with private hot bath. Upper rooms have cable TV, fan, shared terraces and plenty of light for US$21 double; larger rooms with two double beds but no TV are US$16.50.

For B&B accommodations try *La Casa de Café* (☎ 651-4620, fax 651-4623, casade cafe@mayanet.hn, www.todomundo.com/ casadecafe), four blocks from the plaza. It's a tasteful place, with loads of character in a beautiful setting – an outdoor area with tables and hammocks looks out past cornfields to the mountains of Guatemala. Five rooms with private hot bath and nice touches are US$30/38, including a hearty breakfast.

Right on the plaza is the new and lovely *Hotel Plaza Copán* (☎ 651-4274, fax 651-4039). All rooms have a private hot bath, both air-con and fan, good beds, cable TV, phone and some extras like private balconies and church views. Other amenities include a terrace, pool, restaurant and parking. Rates are US$40/45/50; rooms differ, so look at a few.

Other more expensive places in town include *Hotel Los Jaguares* (☎ 651-4451, fax 651-4075), US$35/41; *Hotel Camino Maya* (☎ 651-4578, 651-4646, fax 651-4517), US$48/54/60; and the large *Hotel Marina Copán* (☎ 651-4070/71/72, fax 651-4477, hmarinac@netsys.hn), which has a swimming pool, restaurant/bar and rates of US$75/85/95 (two kids stay free with accompanying adults). All of these places are beautiful, luxurious and right on the plaza.

Places to Eat

The *Tunkul Bar*, two blocks from the plaza, is a main gathering spot in town. It's an attractive covered-patio bar/restaurant with good food and music and a book exchange. Various meat and vegetarian meals cost around US$2.50. It's open 7 am to 11 pm or midnight daily; happy hour runs from 7 to 8 pm for beer, 8 to 9 pm for cocktails.

Next door, *Café ViaVia* serves all meals and cocktails in a convivial atmosphere, with tables overlooking the street and a replica of Copán's Altar Q behind the bar. The coffee is good and the prices reasonable. International newspapers and magazines are available, and horseback-riding trips can be arranged; it's open 7 am to 10 pm Sunday to Thursday, until midnight on Friday and Saturday.

Across the street, *Llama del Bosque* is another popular place, offering a good selection of meals and snacks; their *anafre* (fondue) is especially tasty. In the same block, *Comedor Izabel* is a cheap, typical comedor with decent food. Both are open 6:30 am to 9 pm daily.

Two simple comedores serving good, cheap eats are *El Jakal Comedor* and *El Sesteo*. They are across the street from each other, near the soccer field.

Another pleasant spot is *Vamos A Ver*, half a block from the plaza. It's a cozy, little covered-patio place with good, inexpensive foods that you don't always see while traveling in Central America: good homemade breads and soups, a variety of international cheeses, fruit and vegetable salads, good coffee, a wide variety of teas and always something for vegetarians. It's open 7 am to 10 pm daily.

Farther along, *Carnitas Nia Lola* is an open-air restaurant with a beautiful view over corn and tobacco fields toward the mountains. It's a relaxing place with simple and economical food; the specialties are charcoal-grilled chicken and beef. It's open 10 am to 10 pm daily.

On the road to the Hostel Iguana Azul is *Pizza Rica*, open 11 am to 11 pm daily. *Tres Locos*, in the Hotel California, also serves pizza, along with simple pasta dishes and salads. It's open 11:30 am to 8:30 pm daily.

Los Gauchos Restaurant-Parrillada Uruguaya is one of Copán's fancy restaurants. It's great for meat-eaters; meat and seafood main courses are around US$6.25 to US$11, or you can get the giant Parrillada Especial for four people for US$20. The restaurant enjoys a fine view outside and beautiful decor inside.

Glifo's, in the Hotel Marina Copán (see Places to Stay), is the best place in town according to locals. Expect to pay around US$10 per person for fine, international food in comfortable surroundings. It's open 6:30 am to 9 pm daily.

Entertainment
The *Tunkul Bar* and the bar in *Carnitas Nia Lola* are happening spots in the evening, though they're being rivaled by *Macanudo*, a new bar across the street from Pizza Rica. Macanudo has a good mix of locals and travelers; it's open 5 pm to midnight daily except Sunday. The *Bar Jaguar Venado*, in the Hotel Marina Copán, though not cheap, presents live marimba music 5 to 8 pm Friday and Saturday.

The only other thing to do in Copán after hours besides take cocktails is catch a movie. The *Cinema El Jaral*, at the Hotel Paty, shows typical Hollywood fare, which may be just what you're craving.

Getting There & Away
If you need a Honduran visa in advance, you can obtain it at the Honduran consulate in Esquipulas or Guatemala City.

Several Antigua travel agencies offer weekend trips to Copán, which may also include visits to other places, including the ruins at Quiriguá. All-inclusive day trips from Antigua to Copán cost around US$100 and are rushed. Check with the agencies in Antigua for details.

Bus It's 227km (seven hours) by bus from Guatemala City to El Florido, the Guatemalan village on the Honduran border. Buses from Guatemala City take you to Chiquimula, where you must change buses

and continue on to the border. See the Guatemala Getting There & Around chapter and the Chiquimula section for further details about these routes.

If you're coming from Esquipulas, you can get off the bus at Vado Hondo (the junction of CA-10 and the road to El Florido) and wait for a bus there. But as the bus may fill up before departure, you might as well go the extra 8km into Chiquimula and secure your seat before the bus pulls out.

Most buses between Copán Ruinas and points farther afield in Honduras depart from the tiny bus station near the soccer field. GAMA buses to San Pedro Sula leave from the Hotel Paty.

Shuttle Minibus Monarcas Travel (see Organized Tours, earlier in this section) in Copán Ruinas and Antigua runs a shuttle between those two towns. Scheduled shuttles leave Copán for Antigua daily at 2 pm with a minimum of four passengers (US$29) and continue to Guatemala City. Shuttles leave Antigua at 4 am and Guatemala City at 5 am.

Car & Motorcycle Traveling by organized tour or private vehicle is faster than going by bus. Theoretically, you can visit the ruins in a day trip from Guatemala City, but it's exhausting and far too harried. From Río Hondo, Chiquimula or Esquipulas, it takes a full day to get to Copán, tour the ruins and return, but it's easier. Still, it's best to spend at least one night at Copán if possible.

Drive south from Chiquimula 10km, north from Esquipulas 48km, and turn eastward at Vado Hondo (Km 178.5 on CA-10). A small motel just opposite the turnoff will do if you need a bed. A sign reading 'Vado Hondo Ruinas de Copán' marks the way on the two-hour, 50-km drive from this junction to El Florido.

Twenty kilometers northeast of Vado Hondo are the Chorti Maya villages of Jocotán and Camotán, set amid mountainous tropical countryside dotted with thatched huts in lush green valleys. The last bit of road from Camotán to El Florido is pretty terrible.

Crossing the Border Pickups going to the border depart from just before the small bridge and police station on the road to Guatemala. They leave every 40 minutes (or when full), 6 am to 6 pm, and charge around US$1.50. Make sure you're charged the correct price – ask around beforehand to find out what the price should be. On the Guatemala side, buses to Chiquimula (US$1, 2½ hours, 58km) depart from the border hourly, 5:30 am to 3:30 pm.

The village of El Florido, which has no services beyond a few soft-drink stands, is 1.2km west of the border. At the border crossing are a Banrural branch, a few snack stands and the basic *Hospedaje Las Rosas*, which can put you up in an emergency. The border crossing is open 7 am to 7 pm daily.

Moneychangers will approach you on both sides of the border to change Guatemalan quetzals for Honduran lempiras or either for US dollars. Usually they offer a decent rate because there's a Guatemalan bank right there and the current exchange rate is posted in the Honduran immigration office. Though quetzals and US dollars may be accepted at a few establishments in Copán Ruinas, it's best to change some money into Honduran currency. If the moneychangers give you a hard time, change enough at the border to get you into Copán Ruinas and then hit one of the banks there. Of course, if it's Sunday, you're beholden to the moneychangers – a situation they relish.

You must present your passport to the Guatemalan immigration and customs authorities, pay US$2.75, then cross the border and do the same thing with the Honduran authorities. If you just want a short-term permit to enter Honduras and plan to go only as far as Copán, tell this to the Honduran immigration officer; you'll be charged US$1 and receive a separate piece of paper that you have to produce upon crossing back into Guatemala. With such a permit you cannot go farther than the ruins and you must leave Honduras by the same route. If you want to travel farther in Honduras, you'll probably need a tourist card, which costs US$10 and may take a bit more time to get.

When you return through this border point, you must again pass through both sets of immigration and customs checkpoints (remitting your temporary permit to the authorities), but you pay *no* fees.

If you are driving a rented car, you have to present the Guatemalan customs authorities at the border with a special letter of permission to enter Honduras, written on the rental company's letterhead and signed and sealed by the appropriate company official. If you do not produce such a letter, you'll have to leave your rental car at El Florido and continue to Copán by pickup.

On the Honduran side of the border are several little cookshacks where you can get simple food and cool drinks while waiting for a pickup to come. Pickups depart from the border every 40 minutes throughout the day. They should charge around US$1.50 (payable in advance) for the 14km, 45-minute ride to Copán Ruinas.

Don't let the pickup guys bully you; some try to overcharge tourists on the ride from the border to Copán. Bus service has been suspended since the road between Copán and the border fell into disrepair, and though the road is being paved, bus service may not yet have resumed. If no bus is available, stand your ground with the pickup drivers and demand a fair price. Often the pickup drivers begin by asking for a ridiculous sum, but they'll eventually relent if they see you won't pay more than a reasonable price.

Izabal

About 60km east of Estanzuela you'll enter the department of Izabal, which holds the marvelous Mayan stelae and zoomorphs at Quiriguá; beautiful Lago de Izabal, the country's largest lake; the jungle waterway of Río Dulce; and Guatemala's only stretch of Caribbean coastline.

QUIRIGUÁ

Quiriguá's archaeological zone is famed for its intricately carved stelae – gigantic sandstone monoliths up to 10.5m tall – that rise like ancient sentinels in a quiet tropical park. Visiting the ruins is easy if you have your own transportation but more difficult if you're traveling by bus. From Río Hondo junction it's 67km along the Carretera al Atlántico to the village of Los Amates, which has a couple of hotels, a restaurant and a bank. The village of Quiriguá is 1.5km east of Los Amates, and the turnoff to the ruins is 1.5km farther east. Following the access road south from the Carretera al Atlántico, it's 3.4km through banana groves to the archaeological site.

History

Quiriguá's history parallels that of Copán, of which it was a dependency during much of the Classic period. The location lent itself to the carving of giant stelae. Beds of brown sandstone in the nearby Río Motagua had cleavage planes suitable for cutting large pieces. Though soft when first cut, the sandstone dried hard in the air. With Copán's expert artisans nearby for guidance, Quiriguá's stonecarvers were ready for greatness. All they needed was an eminent leader to inspire them – and to pay for the carving of the huge stelae.

That leader was Cauac Sky (725–84), who decided that Quiriguá should no longer be under the control of Copán. In a war with his former suzerain, Cauac Sky took Copán's King 18 Rabbit prisoner in 737 and later had him beheaded. Independent at last, Cauac Sky commissioned his stonecutters to go to work; for the next 38 years they turned out giant stelae and zoomorphs dedicated to the glory of King Cauac Sky.

In the early 1900s all the land around Quiriguá was sold off to the United Fruit Company and turned into banana groves. The company is gone, but the bananas and Quiriguá remain. In 1981, UNESCO declared Quiriguá a World Heritage Site.

Ruins

The beautiful parklike archaeological zone is open 7:30 am to 5 pm daily; US$0.65. A small stand near the entrance sells cold drinks and snacks, but you'll be better off bringing your own picnic.

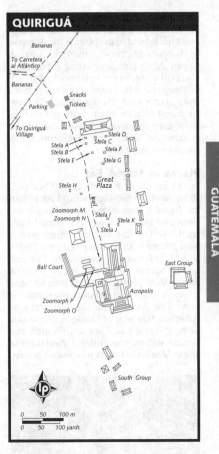

Despite the sticky heat and sometimes bothersome mosquitoes, Quiriguá is a wonderful place. The giant stelae on the Great Plaza are all much more worn than those at Copán, but they still inspire a sense of awe.

Seven of the stelae, designated A, C, D, E, F, H and J, were built during the reign of Cauac Sky and carved with his image. Stela E is the largest Mayan stela known, standing some 8m above ground, with another 3m or so buried in the earth. It weighs almost 60,000 kg. Note the exuberant, elaborate headdresses; the beards on some of the figures (an oddity in Mayan art and life); the staffs of office held in the kings' hands; and the glyphs on the stelae's sides.

At the far end of the plaza is the Acropolis, far less impressive than the one at Copán. At its base are several zoomorphs, blocks of stone carved to resemble real and mythic creatures. Frogs, tortoises, jaguars and serpents were favorite subjects. The low zoomorphs can't compete with the towering stelae in impressiveness, but as works of art, imagination and mythic significance, the zoomorphs are superb.

Places to Stay & Eat

In the center of the village of Quiriguá, 700m south of the Carretera al Atlántico, the **Hotel y Restaurante Royal** is simple, clean and quiet. Rooms with shared bath are US$4/6.50 single/double; larger rooms with private bath and five beds are US$6/9/13/17/20 for one to five people. The restaurant serves both meat and vegetarian meals. Most guests here are international travelers visiting the archaeological site.

At Los Amates, on the Carretera al Atlántico 3km west of Quiriguá village, is a 24-hour Texaco fuel station. Behind the Texaco station, the **Hotel y Restaurante Santa Mónica** has eight rooms with private

LEE FOSTER

Giant Mayan stela at Quiriguá

bath for US$6.50/9/11 single/double/triple. About 100m east of the Texaco station is the **Ranchón Chileño**, the area's best restaurant, where you can get good, filling meals for about US$6 and light meals for half that.

Comedor y Hospedaje Doña María, Carretera al Atlántico Km 181, is at the east end of the Doña María bridge, 20km west of Los Amates. The 10 rooms here, all with private bath, rent for US$6 per person; they're old but clean, lined up along an open-air walkway beside the river. Across the river is a large, grassy camping area with coconut palms and fruit trees, covered picnic tables and campsites for US$4 per vehicle or tent. Ask at the hotel and they'll open the gate for you. The open-air restaurant, open 6 am to 9 pm daily, has a great view of the river, and the swimming is good here. You're welcome to cross the footbridge for a picnic, but ask permission first.

Getting There & Away

The turnoff to Quiriguá is 205km (four hours) northeast of Guatemala City, 70km northeast of the Río Hondo junction, 43km southwest of the road to Flores in El Petén, and 90km southwest of Puerto Barrios.

Buses running Guatemala City-Puerto Barrios, Guatemala City-Flores, Esquipulas-Flores or Chiquimula-Flores drop you off or pick you up at the turnoff to Quiriguá town. Better yet, they'll drop you at the turnoff to the archaeological site if you ask.

The transportation center in this area is Morales, about 40km northeast of Quiriguá. It's not pretty, but it's where the bus for Río Dulce originates. If a seat isn't important to you, skip Morales and wait at the La Ruidosa junction for the Río Dulce bus.

Getting Around

From the turnoff on the highway, it's 3.4km to the archaeological site. Buses and pickups provide transportation between the turnoff and the site for US$0.25 each way. If you don't see one, don't fret; it's a nice walk on a dirt road through banana plantations to get there.

If you're staying in the village of Quiriguá or Los Amates and walking to and from the archaeological site, you can take a short cut along the railway branch line that goes from the village through the banana fields, crossing the access road near the entrance to the archaeological site.

LAGO DE IZABAL

This largest Guatemalan lake, north of the Carretera al Atlántico, is starting to register on travelers' radar screens. Most visitors here stay at the village of Río Dulce, on the north side of the bridge where CA-13, the road heading north to Flores and Tikal, crosses the lake's east end. East of this bridge is the beautiful Río Dulce, which opens into El Golfete before flowing into the Caribbean at Lívingston; a river trip is one of the highlights of a visit to eastern Guatemala.

Other lake highlights include El Castillo de San Felipe (an old Spanish fortress) and the Bocas del Polochic river delta. Many undiscovered spots in this area await exploration.

Río Dulce

East of Quiriguá at Km 245 on the Carretera al Atlántico (near the town of Morales) is La Ruidosa junction, where CA-13 turns off to the north en route to Flores. About 34km up CA-13 from the junction, the road crosses the Río Dulce, an outlet of Lago de Izabal. Straddling the river are a pair of villages: the village of Río Dulce, sometimes called Fronteras, is on the bridge's north side; El Relleno is on the south side. The communities both harbor a sizable population of foreign yachties – folks sailing around the world or some part thereof.

Orientation & Information Unless you're staying at Hotel Backpacker's (see Places to Stay) or volunteering at the adjacent Casa Guatemala, get off the bus on the north side of the bridge near the Río Bravo Restaurant. Otherwise you'll find yourself trudging over what is purported to be Central America's longest bridge – it's a steamy 30-minute walk.

Tijax Express, right by the river near where the bus drops you, is Río Dulce's unofficial tourist information center. Bus, boat,

hotel and other important travel details are available here. It's open daily and English is spoken. If you need to change money or traveler's checks, head for the Banrural or Banco de Comercio in town. Cap't Nemo's Communications (☎ 902-0616, rio@guate .net), beside Bruno's on the river, offers email and international phone/fax services. It's open 8 am to 6 pm Monday to Saturday, 9 am to 5 pm Sunday. It caters to contact-starved yachties, so it isn't cheap.

The minute you alight from the bus, young men will approach you and try to put you on a motorboat to Lívingston. This may be exactly what you want to do. (For details of this Río Dulce boat trip, see the Around Lívingston section, later.) However, you can spend some relaxing days around the lake if you're so inclined.

ATI Divers (santacruz@guate.net) offers seven-day excursions to Belize's barrier reef aboard the company's trimaran. The tours feature the same laid-back style that has made famous their Iguana Perdida hostel on Lago de Atitlán (see the Santa Cruz La Laguna section of the Highlands chapter). Trips include all taxes and meals; snorkeling costs US$370 and scuba diving starts at US$490. The ATI office is at Bruno's (see Places to Stay & Eat).

Places to Stay & Eat The *Hacienda Tijax* (☎ 902-0858, in Guatemala City ☎ 367-5563, tijax@guate.net, www.tijax.com, VHF channel 09), a 500-acre hacienda a two-minute boat ride across the cove from the Río Bravo Restaurant, is a special place to stay. Activities include horseback riding, hiking, birding, sailboat trips and tours around the rubber plantation. Small private rooms over the hacienda's restaurant are US$6/10 single/double. New cabañas built over the river with fans, nets and shared bath run US$13/17/22 single/double/triple. Thai-style thatch-roofed houses, each with private hot bath and kitchen, are US$50 single or double. You can pitch a tent in the camping area for US$2 per person. Access is by boat or by a road that turns off the highway about 1km north of the village. The folks here speak Spanish, English, Dutch, French and Italian, and they'll come pick you up from across the river; ask at the Tijax Express. The hacienda has a restaurant. Day passes are US$1.50. Travelers prone to getting stir-crazy might be uncomfortable with the isolation of this place.

Just up from the dock is *Las Brisas Hotel*, offering acceptable rooms for US$4.50 single with shared bath, US$6.50 per person with private bath and fan, US$10.75 with private bath and air-con.

Alongside the bridge, you'll see a path leading to *Bruno's* (☎ /fax 902-0610, rio@guate.net), a riverside hangout for yachties. Rooms with private hot bath and air-con are comfortable, clean and cost US$23 double. Cheaper rooms, also clean and comfortable, with a sink, fan and shared bath are US$7.75/15.50. A fully equipped apartment sleeping five is available for US$75.

Other places to stay in the village include: *Riverside Motel*, a simple place along the highway offering basic rooms with shared bath and fan for US$4 single or double; *Hotel Don Paco*, a yellow building with no sign, renting simple rooms with shared bath for US$4/7 single/double; and *Hotel Portal del Río*, among the better hotels in the village (which isn't saying much), offering rooms for US$5.25 with private bath and fan, US$13 to add air-con and cable TV.

Across the bridge is *Hotel Backpacker's*, (☎ 208-1779, casaguatemala@guate.net), a business run by Casa Guatemala and the orphans it serves. Foam dorm beds are US$4.50 with bath or US$4 without; space to hang your hammock is US$2, plus US$2.75 if you need to rent one; and basic private rooms are US$9.75 per person with bath, US$6.50 without – go for one overlooking the river. The hotel has a restaurant and bar right on the water and offers *lancha*, laundry, phone, fax and email services (US$5.25 an hour). If you're coming by lancha, ask the boat pilot to let you off here to spare yourself the walk across the bridge.

The best place to dine is *Restaurant Río Bravo*, which has an open-air deck over the lake, just on the north side of the bridge. Its menu offers a good variety of seafood (including ceviche) and pasta dishes; cocktails are available. Simple lunch and dinner plates

start at US$4; you can get a good breakfast for US$1.50.

Nearby, *Bruno's*, another open-air place beside the water, is a restaurant/sports bar with satellite TV and video. *Cafetería La Carreta*, off the highway on the road toward San Felipe, is often recommended by locals. *Hacienda Tijax* has a restaurant with a full bar and good coffee.

Several (more expensive) places to stay are on the waterfront farther from town. All have their own restaurants and are accessible only by boat. *Hotel Catamaran* (☎ 947-8361, fax 203 8860, hcatamaran@guate.net) is an upmarket place with rooms for US$36/41, bungalows for US$45/54/63. It has a fancy restaurant and sports bar. Also along the lakeshore, *Mario's Marina* has good food; it's a popular hangout for yachties.

Getting There & Away Grupo TACA flies from Guatemala City (US$50, one hour) on Friday, Saturday and Sunday at 11:30 am and 4 pm, with an additional morning flight at 6 am weekends. Flights from Río Dulce to the capital leave on Friday, Saturday and Sunday at 12:45 and 5:10 pm, with an additional weekend morning flight at 7:10 am.

Beginning at 7 am, eight buses a day head north along a paved road to Poptún (US$4, three hours, 99km) and Flores (US$6.50, five hours, 208km). The 8:30 and 10:30 pm departures continue all the way to Melchor de Mencos (US$9) on the Belize border. In the other direction, buses go to Guatemala City (US$4.50, five hours, 274km) 15 times a day. To get to Puerto Barrios, take any bus heading for Guatemala City and change at La Ruidosa.

The Atitlán Shuttle minibus operates from an office along the highway, near Tijax Express. Shuttles to Antigua cost around US$35.

Dilapidated Fuentes del Norte buses leave for El Estor (US$1.50, 1½ hours, 43km) from the highway in the middle of town, across from the Restaurant Costa Libre. They depart several times a day between 7:30 am and 4 pm. This bus does *not* go to San Felipe; you need to take one of the pickup trucks to get there.

Colectivo motorboats go down the Río Dulce to Lívingston whenever a minimum of six to eight people want to go. With plenty of stops, the trip takes about three hours and costs around US$7.75 per person (bargain for a fair price). Boats usually leave in the morning, but they may leave throughout the day.

The Road to Flores & Santa Elena

North across the bridge is the road into El Petén, Guatemala's vast jungle province. It's 208km to the towns of Flores and Santa Elena and another 71km to Tikal.

The entire stretch of road from the Carretera al Atlántico to Santa Elena has been recently paved, so it's a smooth ride all the way from Río Dulce to the Tikal ruins. You can make it there in a snappy five hours.

The forest here is disappearing at an alarming rate, falling to the machetes of subsistence farmers. Sections of forest are felled and burned off, crops are grown for a few seasons until the fragile jungle soil is exhausted, then the farmer moves deeper into the forest to slash and burn anew. Cattle ranchers – slashing and burning the forest to make pasture – have contributed to the damage, as has the internal migration of Guatemalans from the cities to the Petén.

Mariscos

Mariscos is the principal town on the lake's quiet south side. *Denny's Beach*, 10 minutes by boat from Mariscos, is a good place to get away from the tourist bustle. It offers cabañas (US$5 per person), tours, hiking and swimming and hosts full moon parties. You can camp here or sling a hammock for US$2 per person. Denny's is operated by Dennis Gulck and his wife, Lupe. When you arrive in Mariscos (or Río Dulce), you can radio them on VHF channel 63 – many people and businesses in the area use radios, so it isn't hard to find one – and they'll come to pick you up. Otherwise, you can hitch a *cayuco* (dugout canoe) at the Mariscos market for US$0.65. *Karlinda's* and *Marinita* are other places to stay in

Mariscos; both have restaurants and offer lake tours.

El Castillo de San Felipe

The fortress and castle of San Felipe de Lara, about 3km west of the bridge, was built in 1652 to keep pirates from looting the villages and commercial caravans of Izabal. Though it deterred the buccaneers a bit, a pirate force captured and burned the fortress in 1686. By the end of the next century, pirates had disappeared from the Caribbean and the fort's sturdy walls served as a prison. Eventually, though, the fortress was abandoned and became a ruin. The present fort was reconstructed in 1956.

Today the castle is protected as a park and is one of the lake's principal tourist attractions. In addition to the fort itself, the site has a large park, barbecue/picnic areas and swimming in the lake. It's open 8 am to 5 pm daily; US$1.

Near the Castillo, *Hotel Don Humberto* offers simple but clean rooms with private bath for US$4/7/10.50 single/double/triple. The hotel has a restaurant, or you could try *Cafetería Selva Tropical*. Nearby, *Viñas del Lago* (☎ *902-7505, fax 476-3042*) is a fancier hotel with rooms for US$60/70/80.

On the lakeshore, about a 10-minute walk from El Castillo, *Rancho Escondido* (☎/*fax 369-2681 in Guatemala City*) is a pleasant little hotel and restaurant. Downstairs rooms with shared bath are US$5/9 single/double; more attractive upstairs rooms with private bath are US$6.50/12.25, or you can stay in a hammock for US$2.50 per night. Hotel amenities include laundry service, good food, swimming in the lake and other activities. The owners will pick you up when you arrive in Río Dulce; ask at the Tijax Express and they'll radio for you.

It's a beautiful 45-minute walk between San Felipe and Río Dulce. Colectivo pickups provide transportation between the towns for US$0.35, running about every half-hour. In Río Dulce, pickups stop on the corner of the highway and the road to El Estor, across from Restaurant Costa Libre; in San Felipe they stop in front of Hotel Don Humberto, at the entrance to El Castillo.

Boats coming from Lívingston will drop you in San Felipe if you ask them. The Río Dulce boat trips usually come to El Castillo, allowing you to get out and visit the castle. Or you can come over from Río Dulce by private launch for US$5.

Finca El Paraíso

On the lake's north side, between San Felipe and El Estor, the Finca El Paraíso is a popular day trip from Río Dulce and other places around the lake. At the finca, which is a working ranch, you can walk to an incredibly beautiful spot in the jungle where a wide, hot waterfall drops about 12m into a clear, deep pool. You can bathe in the hot water, swim in the cool pool or duck under an overhanging promontory and enjoy a jungle-style sauna. Also on the finca are a number of interesting caves and good hiking. Admission is US$0.65; bungalows are rented for US$20 double.

To get to the finca, take an El Estor bus from Río Dulce (US$1, one hour). The last bus in either direction passes at around 5 pm, so don't dawdle past then unless you plan on spending the night.

El Estor

The major settlement on the northwest shore is El Estor. Once a nickel-mining town, it is now growing in popularity as a way station for adventurous travelers on the Cobán-Lago de Izabal route through the beautiful Panzós Valley. This is also the jumping-off point for explorations into the Bocas de Polochic, an area of extreme biodiversity supporting more than 300 species of birds and many varieties of butterflies and fish (visit now, before it attains ecotourism mecca status).

Orientation & Information El Estor is a friendly, somnolent town that is easy to negotiate. Banrural on 3a Calle at 5a Avenida changes US dollars, and the Corpobanco across the street is a Western Union agent. The police station is on 1a Calle at 5a Avenida, near the lakeshore. Phone calls can be made from Comedor Dalila #1 (see Places to Stay & Eat).

An office of the Fundación Defensores de la Naturaleza (☎ 949-7237, defensores@ pronet.net.gt) is next to the police station. Visitors interested in exploring the Reserva de la Biósfera de Sierra de las Minas or the Bocas del Polochic should stop in here. Ask for permission to stay at the foundation's scientific research station near Río Zarquito; the cost for transportation, a bunk and three meals a day is around US$15 per person.

Places to Stay & Eat Overlooking the lake, the *Hotel Vista al Lago* (☎ 949-7205, 6a Avenida 1-13, Zona 1) is airy and clean. Built between 1825 and 1830, the building was once a general store owned by an Englishman and a Dutchman; 'the store' gave the town of El Estor its name. The 21 rooms here, each with private bath and fan, are US$9/11/15 single/double/triple. The present owners can arrange tours and guides.

Hotel Santa Clara (☎ 949-7244, 5a Avenida 2-11) has clean rooms with private bath on the upper level for US$4.75/6.25/7.75 and worse rooms downstairs without bath for US$2 per person. *Hotel Villela* (6a Avenida 2-06) is another good place to stay, with clean, simple rooms arranged around a courtyard. Rooms with private bath and fan are US$3.25 per person.

Comedor Dalila #1, across from Transportes Valenciana, is a clean, cheap place serving huge plates of standard Guatemalan food. On the road into town, *Restaurante Centenario* has been locally recommended, as has *Ranchón Tipico Chaabil*, which is probably El Estor's best restaurant. It's across the street from the Fuentes del Norte bus office on the park. *Hugo's Restaurant* serves simple meals and has information about tours around the lake and cabañas on the Río Sauce.

Getting There & Away Brenda Mercedes and Transportes Valenciana buses operate between El Estor and Cobán (US$2.50, 7½ hours, 166km) several times daily. The first departure is at 5 am. The route is slow going but very beautiful. Fuentes de Polochic has three morning departures to Guatemala City (US$7, four hours, 216km), as does Fuentes del Norte. This company also has hourly buses to Río Dulce and Puerto Barrios from 6 am to 5 pm.

No public boat services operate between El Estor and other lake destinations. Private lanchas can be contracted, though this can be pricey, especially for solo travelers. Ask at your hotel or the Defensores office about hiring a boat or guide.

PUERTO BARRIOS
• population 35,000

Heading east from La Ruidosa junction toward Puerto Barrios, the country becomes even more lush, tropical and humid.

The powerful United Fruit Company owned vast plantations in the Río Motagua valley and many other parts of the country. The company built railways to ship its produce to the coast, and it built Puerto Barrios early in the 20th century to put that produce onto ships sailing for New Orleans and New York. Laid out as a company town, Puerto Barrios has long, wide streets arranged neatly on a grid plan. Many of its Caribbean-style wood-frame houses are on stilts.

When United Fruit's power and influence declined in the 1960s, the Del Monte company became successor to its interests. But the heyday of the imperial foreign firms was past, as was that of Puerto Barrios. A new, modern, efficient port was built a few kilometers to the southwest, at Santo Tomás de Castilla, and Puerto Barrios settled into tropical torpor.

For foreign visitors, Puerto Barrios is little more than the jumping-off point for boats to Punta Gorda (Belize) or Lívingston. As the boats for Lívingston leave at odd hours, you may find yourself (unfortunately) staying the night in Puerto Barrios; it's a rough, unfriendly place. And while the ships and sailors may have left for a new port, the dive bars and brothels remain. Most travelers will want to move on from here fast.

Orientation & Information

It's 800m from the Transportes Litegua bus terminal to the Muelle Municipal (Municipal Boat Dock) at the foot of 12a Calle, from which boats depart for Lívingston and Punta Gorda. You are liable to be in town just to take a boat, so you may want to select a hotel near the dock. However, avoid getting there via 9a Calle which is crawling with ruffians.

El Muñecón, at the intersection of 8a Avenida, 14a Calle and the Calzada Justo Rufino Barrios, is a statue of a *bananero* (banana worker); it's a favorite monument in the town.

The post office is on 6a Calle at 6a Avenida. Telgua is on 13a Calle, between 5a and 6a Avenidas.

Many banks change US dollars cash and traveler's checks. Banco G&T, 7a Calle between 5a and 6a Avenidas, changes both and gives cash advances on MasterCard and Visa; it's open 9 am to 8 pm Monday to Friday, 10 am to 2 pm Saturday. The Bancafé on 13a Calle near 6a Avenida has a Bancared ATM that accepts Visa cards.

The immigration office (☎ 948-0802, 948-0327) is at 9a Calle and 2a Avenida, a couple of blocks from the dock. Be sure to get your entry or exit stamp if you're entering or leaving the country.

In the evening, the noisy bars and brothels along 9a Calle really get going.

Places to Stay

A couple of good, clean hotels are on 3a Avenida between 11a and 12a Calles, one block from the dock. Both have rooms with private bath and fan arranged around a central courtyard. *Hotel Europa 2* (☎ 948-1292), perhaps the slightly more attractive, has rooms for US$4.75 per person; at the *Hotel Miami* (☎ 948-0537) rooms are US$5.25/10 single/double, or US$15 with air-con. If you're driving and need a safe place to leave your car while you visit Lívingston, you can park in the courtyard of either place for US$2.50 per day.

The original *Hotel Europa 1* (☎ 948-0127), on 8a Avenida between 8a and 9a Calles, is 1½ blocks from the cathedral (look for the openwork cross sitting atop the steeple). Fairly clean, comfortable and quiet, it has rooms with bath for US$4.75/9.50.

Hotel Lee (☎ 948-0685), on 5a Avenida around the corner from the Litegua bus

GUATEMALA

United Fruit Company

As late as 1870, the first year that bananas were imported to the USA, few Americans had ever seen a banana, let alone tasted one. By 1898 they were eating 16 million bunches annually.

In 1899 the Boston Fruit Company merged with the interests of Brooklyn-born Central American railroad baron Minor C Keith to form the United Fruit Company. Their aim was to own and cultivate large areas of Central American land by well-organized modern methods, providing predictable harvests of bananas that Keith, who controlled virtually all the railroads in Central America, would then carry to the coast for shipment to the US.

Central American governments readily granted United Fruit rights, at low prices, to large tracts of undeveloped jungle, for which they had no other use. The company provided access to the land by road and/or rail, cleared and cultivated it, built extensive port facilities for the export of fruit and offered employment to large numbers of local workers.

By 1930, United Fruit was capitalized at US$215 million and was the largest (though not the most equitable) employer in Central America. The company's Great White Fleet of transport ships was one of the largest private navies in the world. By controlling Puerto Barrios and the railroads serving it, all of which it had built, United Fruit effectively controlled all of Guatemala's international commerce, banana or otherwise.

The company soon came to be referred to as El Pulpo, The Octopus, by local journalists, who accused it of corrupting government officials, exploiting workers and, in general, exercising influence far beyond its role as a foreign company in Guatemala.

United Fruit's treatment of its workers was paternalistic. Although they worked long and hard for low wages, those wages were higher than those of the country's other farmworkers, and the

terminal, is a friendly, family-owned place offering great value. The rooms are a bit cramped but have private bath, good beds and fans for US$4.50 per person. A restaurant and bar are attached.

In a class by itself, the old *Hotel del Norte* (☎ 948-2116, ☎/fax 948-0087), 7a Calle at 1a Avenida, is at the waterfront end of 7a Calle, 1.2km from the dock (you must walk around the railway yard). In its airy dining room overlooking the Bahía de Amatique, you can almost hear the echoing conversation of turn-of-the-20th-century banana moguls and smell their pungent cigars. Spare, simple and

agreeably dilapidated, this is a real museum piece. Rooms with sea view, private bath and air-con are US$13/19.50/26 single/double/triple; less agreeable interior rooms with fan are US$9/14. Meals are served in the dining room; other amenities include a bar and two seaside swimming pools. Service is refined, careful and elegantly old-fashioned, but the food can be otherwise.

South of the streambed and west of the main road (Calzada Justo Rufino Barrios) are two fancier, more comfortable hotels. The 48-room *Hotel El Reformador* (☎ 948-0533, 948-5489, fax 948-1531, 7a Avenida

United Fruit Company

workers received housing, medical care and in some cases schooling for their children. Still, indigenous Guatemalans were required to 'give right of way to whites and remove their hats when talking to them.' And the company took out of the country far more in profits than it put in; between 1942 and 1952 the company paid stockholders almost 62 cents in dividends for every dollar invested.

The US government, responding to its rich and powerful constituents, saw its role as one of support for United Fruit and defense of the company's interests.

On October 20, 1944, a liberal military coup paved the way for Guatemala's first-ever free elections. Free at last from the repression of past military dictators, labor unions clamored for better conditions, with almost constant actions against la Frutera, United Fruit. The Guatemalan government, no longer willing to be bought off, demanded more equitable tax payments from the company and divestiture of large tracts of its unused land.

Alarm bells sounded in the company's Boston headquarters and in Washington, where powerful members of Congress and the Eisenhower administration – including Secretary of State John Foster Dulles – were convinced that Guatemala was turning communist. Several high-ranking US officials had close ties to United Fruit, and the company's effective and expensive public relations and lobbying campaign persuaded other politicians that Guatemala's leaders were a threat.

During the summer of 1954, the CIA planned and carried out an invasion from Honduras by 'anticommunist' Guatemalan exiles, which resulted in the resignation and exile of Guatemalan president Jacobo Arbenz. The CIA's handpicked 'liberator' was Carlos Castillo Armas, a military man of the old caste, who returned Guatemala to rightist military dictatorship. The tremendous power of the United Fruit Company, combined with the US government's meddling, had set back democratic development in Guatemala by at least half a century.

A few years after the coup, the US Department of Justice brought suit against United Fruit for operating monopolistically in restraint of trade. In 1958 the company signed a consent decree, and in the years following it surrendered some of its trade in Guatemala to local companies and some of its land to local owners. It yielded its monopoly on the railroads as well.

Caught up in the 'merger mania' of the 1960s, United Fruit merged with United Brands, which collapsed as the financial climate worsened in the early 1970s. In 1972 the company sold all of its remaining land in Guatemala to the Del Monte corporation.

– Tom Brosnahan

159), at 16a Calle, is a modern place offering rooms with TV and private bath for US$14/24 with fan, US$23/29 with air-con. Better located rooms with bath, air-con and TV are US$33/51. The hotel has its own restaurant. Around the corner, *Hotel Internacional* (☎ 948-7719/20), on 7a Avenida between 16a and 17a Calles, has a swimming pool, restaurant and parking. Rooms with private bath and TV are US$9/14 with fan, US$14/25 with air-con.

Fanciest place in town is *Hotel Puerto Libre* (☎ 948-3066, fax 948-3513), at the junction of the Carretera al Atlántico, the road into Puerto Barrios and the road to Santo Tomás de Castilla, 5km from the boat dock. Rebuilt after a fire in 1992, its 44 rooms come with private bath, air-con, cable TV and phone. It also has a swimming pool, restaurant and parking. Rates are US$51/58.

Places to Eat

The town's most enjoyable restaurant is *Restaurante Safari* (☎ 948-0568), on a thatch-roofed dock right over the water at the north end of 5a Avenida, about a kilometer from the town center. Locals and visitors alike love to eat here, catching the fresh sea breezes while mariachis stroll from table to table. Seafood meals of all kinds are the specialty (US$6 to US$10); burgers, sandwiches and chicken are also served. It's open 10 am to 9 pm daily.

Restaurante La Fogata, 6a Avenida between 6a and 7a Calle, is another fancy place, specializing in charcoal-grilled steaks and seafood. It offers a set lunch for US$3.50 and live music most nights.

Simpler places include *Restaurante Fogón Porteño*, opposite the bus station, which features charcoal-grilled chicken, steak and seafood; *Maxim*, a funky Chinese place on 6a Avenida at 8a Calle; and *La Habana Vieja*, attached to the Hotel Europa 1, which has a full bar and features tasty grilled meats, seafood and pasta dishes at reasonable prices.

Perhaps the oddest eatery in town is *Container*, a café and drinks stand at the foot of 7a Calle, near the Hotel del Norte. It's made of two steel shipping containers, and the chairs and tables set out in the street afford a fine bay view.

Restaurante Charrúa, at the Muelle Municipal, serves filling and cheap Guatemalan fare for breakfast, lunch and dinner.

Getting There & Away

Air The airport at Puerto Barrios receives a limited number of international flights, but it's served often by air from Guatemala City (US$50, one hour). TACA (reservations ☎ 334-7722) offers flights leaving the capital at 6 am and 4 pm daily, with an additional 11:35 am flight on Friday, Saturday and Sunday. Planes return to Guatemala City from Puerto Barrios at 7:10 am and 5:10 pm Monday to Thursday and at 1:05 and 5:30 pm Friday, Saturday and Sunday. An additional 7:30 am flight is offered on Saturday and Sunday.

Flights between Puerto Barrios and Santa Elena/Flores (US$65, 50 minutes) leave Puerto Barrios for Flores on Monday, Wednesday and Friday at 8:25 am and return the same days at 1:35 pm.

Bus The Transportes Litegua bus station (☎ 948-1172, 948-1002) is near the corner of 6a Avenida and 9a Calle. This is also the terminal for most other buses. Express buses bound for Guatemala City (US$5.25, five hours, 295km) leave at 1, 1:30, 2, 3, 7, 7:30 and 10 am, noon and 4 pm. Ordinary buses take several hours longer and leave Puerto Barrios more frequently.

Buses for Chiquimula (US$2.50, 4½ hours, 192km) leave every hour. Take this bus for Quiriguá and Río Dulce. You have to transfer at La Ruidosa.

You can store your luggage at the Transportes Litegua terminal for about US$0.25 per piece, per day.

Boat All boats depart from the Muelle Municipal at the foot of 12a Calle. Get to the dock at least 30 or 45 minutes prior to departure for a seat.

A ferry departs for Lívingston at 10 am and 5 pm daily; the trip takes 1½ hours and costs US$1.50. On the Lívingston side, it departs for Puerto Barrios at 5 am and 2 pm daily; if everything goes smoothly, the last ferry arrives in Puerto Barrios at 3:30 pm and the last bus to Guatemala City leaves at 4 pm, so you'll have to rush from the dock to the bus station.

Colectivo lanchas depart from both sides whenever 12 people are ready to go; they take 30 minutes and cost US$2.75. Especially in low season, don't count on 12 people getting together late in the day.

Small lanchas depart Puerto Barrios for Punta Gorda, Belize, at 10 am on Monday, Wednesday, Thursday and Saturday and at 8 am on Tuesday and Friday. Boats return from Punta Gorda at 4 pm Monday to Saturday; these take 50 minutes and cost US$7.75. Transportes El Chato (☎ 948-5525), at the Muelle Municipal in Puerto Barrios, is one company offering this service. You may also be able to contract a colectivo to Punta Manabique, north of Puerto Barrios.

The boats to Punta Gorda no longer stop in Lívingston. If you take one of these boats, you must pass through Guatemalan customs and immigration before boarding the boat. Allow some time, and have your passport handy.

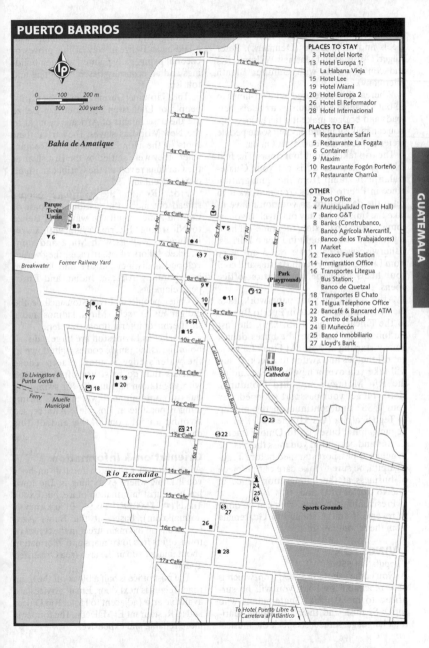

PUERTO BARRIOS

Bahía de Amatique

Parque
Tecún
Umán

Breakwater   Former Railway Yard

To Livingston &
Punta Gorda

Ferry   Muelle
Municipal

Río Escondido

Calzada Justo Rufino Barrios

Hilltop
Cathedral

Sports Grounds

To Hotel Puerto Libre &
Carretera al Atlántico

0   100   200 m
0   100   200 yards

1a Calle
2a Calle
3a Calle
4a Calle
5a Calle
6a Calle
7a Calle
8a Calle
9a Calle
10a Calle
11a Calle
12a Calle
13a Calle
14a Calle
15a Calle
16a Calle
17a Calle

1a Av
2a Av
3a Av
4a Av
5a Av
6a Av
7a Av
8a Av
6a Av

GUATEMALA

PLACES TO STAY
3   Hotel del Norte
13 Hotel Europa 1;
    La Habana Vieja
15 Hotel Lee
19 Hotel Miami
20 Hotel Europa 2
26 Hotel El Reformador
28 Hotel Internacional

PLACES TO EAT
1   Restaurante Safari
5   Restaurante La Fogata
6   Container
9   Maxim
10 Restaurante Fogón Porteño
17 Restaurante Charrúa

OTHER
2   Post Office
4   Municipalidad (Town Hall)
7   Banco G&T
8   Banks (Construbanco,
    Banco Agrícola Mercantíl,
    Banco de los Trabajadores)
11 Market
12 Texaco Fuel Station
14 Immigration Office
16 Transportes Litegua
    Bus Station;
    Banco de Quetzal
18 Transportes El Chato
21 Telgua Telephone Office
22 Bancafé & Bancared ATM
23 Centro de Salud
24 El Muñecón
25 Banco Inmobiliario
27 Lloyd's Bank

Overland to Honduras Information on this route is based on letters from Camille Geels and Anja Boye (Denmark), Peter Kügerl (Austria) and Matthew Willson (UK) and conversations with Gunther Blauth (Germany).

Whereas this route used to be off-limits to all but the most adventurous travelers, new roads and bridges make it a fairly easy trip. You can make it in one day, but some people prefer to break the journey at Omoa.

The trip takes about four hours. The first thing you need to do is get your Guatemalan exit stamp from the immigration office in Puerto Barrios. You may want to get it the day before, so you don't have to take the time on the day of travel. If you're coming from Lívingston, the trade-off here is you have to overnight in Puerto Barrios. Otherwise, you can take the 5 am ferry from Lívingston to Puerto Barrios and cool your heels until the immigration office opens.

After arranging your paperwork, take the bus from the market in Puerto Barrios to the Finca La Inca (US$0.50), the last station on the bus line; the buses depart hourly, starting at 7 am. At Finca La Inca, get off the bus and switch to a pickup that will take you over a new bridge spanning the Río Motagua and into Honduras. Here you get your passport stamped, pay your US$2 and continue on the pickup to Tegucigalpita (US $1, one hour). From Tegucigalpita, buses go to Omoa, Puerto Cortés and beyond. If you miss the chance to get your passport stamped before Tegucigalpita, be sure to take care of that piece of business at the immigration office in Puerto Cortés or Omoa.

Presumably, the same thing can be done in reverse if you're coming to Guatemala from the Honduran side.

LÍVINGSTON
- population 5500

As you come ashore in Lívingston, which is only reachable by boat, you will be surprised to meet black Guatemalans who speak Spanish and their traditional Garífuna language; some also speak the musical English of Belize and the islands. The town of Lívingston is an interesting anomaly, with a laid-back, Belizean way of life, groves of coconut palms, gaily painted wooden buildings and an economy based on fishing and tourism.

The Garífuna (Garinagu, or Black Carib) people of Lívingston and southern Belize are the descendants of Africans brought to the New World as slaves. They trace their roots to the Honduran island of Roatán, where they were settled by the British after the Garífuna revolt on the Caribbean island of St Vincent in 1795.

From Roatán the Garífuna people spread out along the Caribbean Coast of Central America all the way from Belize to Nicaragua. Intermarrying with Carib Indians as well as with Maya and shipwrecked sailors of other races, they've developed a distinct culture and language incorporating African, Indian and European elements.

Other people in Lívingston include the indigenous Q'eqchi' Maya, ladinos and a smattering of international travelers.

Beaches in Lívingston are largely disappointing, as the jungle comes right down to the water's edge in most places. Those beaches that do exist are often clogged with vegetation and unsafe for swimming due to contaminated water. Safe swimming is possible at Los Siete Altares; see Around Lívingston at the end of this chapter.

Orientation & Information

After being in Lívingston for half an hour you'll know where everything is. The town has no tourist information office, but Exotic Travel (π 947-0049/51, fax 947-0136, kjchew@hotmail.com), based at the Bahía Azul restaurant on the main street in the center of town, offers free town maps and information about things to do in the area (see Organized Tours).

The post office is half a block off the main road. Telgua is next door. Email services are available at @ (adjacent to Hotel Río Dulce) and at Restaurant El Malecón. The former is more reliable and expensive.

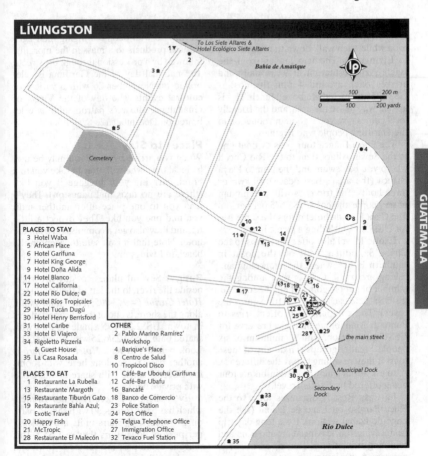

LÍVINGSTON

To Los Siete Altares &
Hotel Ecológico Siete Altares

Bahía de Amatique

Cemetery

the main street

Municipal Dock

Secondary
Dock

Rio Dulce

PLACES TO STAY
3 Hotel Waba
5 African Place
6 Hotel Garífuna
7 Hotel King George
9 Hotel Doña Alida
14 Hotel Blanco
17 Hotel California
22 Hotel Río Dulce; @
25 Hotel Ríos Tropicales
29 Hotel Tucán Dugú
30 Hotel Henry Berrisford
31 Hotel Caribe
33 Hotel El Viajero
34 Rigoletto Pizzería
   & Guest House
35 La Casa Rosada

PLACES TO EAT
1 Restaurante La Rubella
13 Restaurante Margoth
15 Restaurante Tiburón Gato
19 Restaurante Bahía Azul;
   Exotic Travel
20 Happy Fish
21 McTropic
28 Restaurante El Malecón

OTHER
2 Pablo Marino Ramírez'
   Workshop
4 Barique's Place
8 Centro de Salud
10 Tropicool Disco
11 Café-Bar Ubouhu Garifuna
12 Café-Bar Ubafu
16 Bancafé
18 Banco de Comercio
23 Police Station
24 Post Office
26 Telgua Telephone Office
27 Immigration Office
32 Texaco Fuel Station

Banco de Comercio and Bancafé change US dollars currency and traveler's checks. Several private businesses do too, including Restaurante Bahía Azul, which also changes the currencies of Belize and Honduras.

Laundry service is available at the Rigoletto Pizzería & Guest House and at La Casa Rosada (more expensive).

The immigration office is on the main street coming up from the dock. It's open 7 am to 9 pm daily.

Use mosquito repellent and other sensible precautions, especially if you go out into the jungle; remember that the mosquitoes

here on the coast carry both malaria and dengue fever.

Pablo Marino Ramírez has a workshop by the sea where he makes Garífuna drums and woodcarvings. You're welcome to visit.

Organized Tours

Exotic Travel, based at Restaurante Bahía Azul, offers various tours of the area's natural wonders. The Ecological Tour takes you for a walk through town, up to a lookout spot and on to the Río Quehueche, where you take a half-hour canoe trip down the river and then a jungle walk to

Los Siete Altares (Seven Altars). From there you walk down to the beach, hang out for a while, then walk down the beach back to Lívingston. The trip leaves from the Bahía Azul restaurant at 9 am daily and arrives back around 4 pm; the cost is US$7.75 and includes a boxed lunch. This is a great way to see the area, and the friendly local guides give you a good introduction to the Garífuna people who live here.

The Playa Blanca tour goes by boat first to the Seven Altars, then to the Río Cocolí where you can swim, and then on to Playa Blanca (the area's best beach) for two or three hours. The trip goes with a minimum of six people and costs US$7.75 per person. The Casa Rosada hotel offers the same trip for US$12.50, including a picnic lunch.

Exotic Travel also offers day trips to the Cayos Sapodillas, well off the coast in southern Belize, where the snorkeling and fishing are great. Cost is split among the number of people going (if eight people go, it's US$19.50 each, plus US$10 to enter the cayes). The company also offers trips to Punta de Manabique biological reserve for US$13 per person, with a minimum of six people. Smaller groups can do any of these tours if they're willing to pay the difference. Also ask about a new mountain-biking tour being offered by Exotic Travel.

La Casa Rosada organizes tours to the Finca Paraíso on Lago de Izabal (see the Lago de Izabal section). It's a long day trip from Lívingston, leaving at around 6 am and returning around 7 pm. This trip costs US$20 per person, maximum nine people. Lunch is included.

The folks at Rigoletto Pizzería & Guest House run tours stopping in eight different, picturesque spots, including the Castillo de San Felipe on Lago de Izabal. It's an all-day trip and costs US$15 for three or more people.

All of the above trips are also organized by the Happy Fish restaurant (☎ 902-7143), but not on any fixed schedule.

Special Events
Lívingston is packed with holidaymakers during Semana Santa. The day of San Isidro Labrador, who was a cultivator, is celebrated on May 15 with people bringing their agricultural products to a mass in the morning, followed by a procession through the streets. The national day of the Garífuna is celebrated on November 26 with a variety of cultural events. The day of the Virgin of Guadalupe, Mexico's patron saint, is celebrated on December 12.

Places to Stay
When you arrive by boat, you may be met by local boys who will offer to take you to a hotel, carrying your luggage if you like (there are no taxis in Lívingston). They'll lead you to one place after another until you find one you like. They expect a little tip, and they also get a commission from the hotel. Note that it isn't safe to sleep on the beach in Lívingston.

Budget Several places to stay are right beside the river, to the left of the boat dock. *Hotel Caribe* (☎ 947-0053), a minute's walk along the shore, is one of the cheapest places in town: US$2.50/4.75 single/double with shared bath, US$3.25/6.25 with private bath. Look before you rent. *Hotel El Viajero* is another basic place along here, with rooms for US$2.50 single with shared bath, US$3 with private bath.

Even cheaper is scruffy *Hotel Blanco*, which has basic rooms, all with shared bath, on two floors. Upstairs units are US$2.75 per person; downstairs they're US$2. This place is uphill past the center of town and popular with hardcore budget travelers.

Hotel Río Dulce, an authentic Caribbean two-story wood-frame place up the hill from the dock on the main street, is another cheapie. Upstairs rooms with shared bathrooms out in the backyard are US$3.25 per person; three rooms with private bath are US$6.50. The rooms here are none too clean, and you may hear mice at night. Still, many shoestring travelers like this funky old place. The wide balcony overlooking the street catches the breeze and is great for people-watching.

Next door, *Hotel Ríos Tropicales* (☎ 947-0158) is a good deal, with big, clean rooms with private bath and fan around a patio for US$6 per person. Rooms with shared bath are US$4.50. The hotel has hammocks and a restaurant, and you can hand-wash clothes. *Hotel California* is a clean, fine place with 10 simple rooms with private bath for US$5/8.

A few blocks from the center of town, *Hotel Garífuna* (☎ 947-0183, fax 947-0184) offers rooms with private bath for US$5.25/7.75/10.50 single/double/triple. It has international phone and fax service.

The *African Place* (☎ 948-0218/21), a large white building with Moorish arches, is an old favorite in Lívingston. The 25 rooms are clean and rent for US$4/6/7 with shared bath, US$6/10/12.50 with private bath. The hotel has a big flower-filled garden in back and a good restaurant. On the down side, it's a longish walk from town (10 or 15 minutes) and there have been reports of security problems (don't leave valuables in your room).

Turn right at the African Place and you come to *Hotel Waba* (☎ 947-0193), where clean rooms with a private bath are US$5.25/7.75. Two rooms with shared bath are US$2.75 per person. The balcony has a sea view, and an open-air palapa restaurant in the yard serves affordable meals.

For homey, friendly atmosphere, you can't beat *Rigoletto Pizzería & Guest House*, beside the river 300m left of the dock. Clean, simple rooms sharing a clean bathroom are US$10.50 double, and all three meals are served (the owner is a great cook). Other amenities include laundry service and a rear garden with tables and chairs right beside the river. Boats will drop you off here if you ask.

Beside the river, *Hotel Henry Berrisford* (☎/fax 948-1568) has clean, comfortable rooms with private bath and TV. Beware, though: the swimming pool is not always clean. Rooms with fan are US$7.50 per person, or US$10 per person with breakfast; with air-con and breakfast they are US$14 per person.

Hotel Doña Alida (☎/fax 947-0027), beside the sea a few blocks from town center, has a beautiful beach, a restaurant

and terraces with sea views. Doubles with shared bath are US$13; extra-large triple rooms with private bath, some with sea view, are US$39; a double bungalow is US$28. Breakfast is available.

La Casa Rosada (☎ 947-0303, fax 947-0304) is an attractive place right on the river, 800m to the left of the dock; boats will drop you here if you ask. Ample riverside gardens, a dock with a gazebo and refreshments available anytime all contribute to the relaxed, friendly ambience. For US$8 a person you can enjoy one of 10 freestanding, thatch-roofed bungalows, each with fan, screens and mosquito nets and sharing three clean bathrooms. Also available here are laundry service, daily tours and one of the town's best restaurants.

The *Hotel Ecológico Siete Altares* (☎ 332-7107, fax 478-2159, sietealtares@hotmail.com) is a welcoming cluster of riverside bungalows about an hour's walk from Lívingston. The rustic thatch bungalows have fans, sleep two, four or six people and cost US$10 per person. You can take a lancha from the dock in Lívingston or follow the shore north toward Siete Altares for an hour. A restaurant is nearby.

Top End Among all the town's laid-back, low-priced Caribbean lodgings, the 45-room *Hotel Tucán Dugú* (☎/fax 948-1588, in Guatemala City ☎ 334-7813, fax 334-5242, tukansa@guate.net), just up the hill from the dock, is a luxurious anomaly. Modern but still Caribbean in style, it has many conveniences and comforts, including tropical gardens, a swimming pool and a jungle bar where you might expect to see Hemingway or Bogart. Rooms are fairly large, with modern bathrooms, ceiling fans and little balconies overlooking the pool and gardens. Rates are US$60/66/90 single/double/triple.

Places to Eat

Food in Lívingston is more expensive than in the rest of Guatemala because most of it (except fish and coconuts) must be brought in from elsewhere. *Tapado*, a rich stew made from fish, shrimp, crab and other

GUATEMALA

seafood, coconut and plantain and spiced with coriander, is the special local dish.

The main street is also lined with little comedores. Your best plan may be to choose the place that is currently the most popular. At the time of writing, *Restaurante Tiburón Gato* was the titleholder and may still be hopping by the time you get to Livingston.

Restaurante Margoth has a full bar and offers filling, well-prepared fish and meat dishes at reasonable prices. Service can be slow. *Restaurante Bahía Azul* is a popular gathering spot in relaxed surroundings. It has good food, reasonable prices and live music some evenings. Open 7 am to 10 pm daily.

Other popular places on the main street include *Restaurante El Malecón*, just up the hill from the dock, on the left, where a full meal of Caribbean-inspired fare can be had for US$4 to US$7; the *McTropic*, a bit farther up the hill on the right-hand side, which is half restaurant, half shop and is favored by the thriftiest crowd; and *Happy Fish*.

The *African Place*, a few blocks from town center (see Places to Stay), serves a variety of exotic and local dishes. Full meals, including tapado, are available for US$6 or less.

On the road beside the river are a couple of other good restaurants. The *Rigoletto Pizzería* (see Places to Stay) has an international menu of Italian, east Indian, Chinese and other dishes, with many meat and veggie selections. The pizzas are made in a real pizza oven and are available for take-out.

Farther along, the restaurant at *La Casa Rosada* is another enjoyable riverside spot. All three meals are served, with good, ample dinners for around US$6 to US$8; dinner reservations are advisable. The coffee here is probably the best in town.

The dining room of *Hotel Tucán Dugú* is Livingston's most expensive spot; a good, complete dinner with drinks will set you back around US$15.

Entertainment

Garífuna people have a distinctive form of music and dance. The traditional Garífuna band, composed of three large drums, a turtle shell, maracas and a big conch shell, produces throbbing, haunting rhythms and melodies. The chanted words are like a litany, with responses often taken up by the audience. The dance is the *punta*, which features lot of gyrating hip movements.

Livingston is about the only place in Guatemala where Garífuna music and dance are easily accessible to visitors. *Restaurante Bahía Azul* has live music on weekends and sometimes on other evenings. *Café-Bar Ubafu* has live Garífuna music and dancing most evenings; it's liveliest on weekends. Across the street, *Café-Bar Ubouhu Garífuna* is another popular nightspot.

The disco *Barique's Place*, by the sea on the town's north side, is open weekends. This is a moonlit, beachy type of place thick with locals, where the liquor flows freely and things can get rough. It might not be the most recommendable place for travelers. The *Tropicool Disco*, on the other hand, is usually packed with foreigners getting down to disco beats. It's next to the Café-Bar Ubafu and liveliest on weekends.

Getting There & Away

The only way to get to Livingston is by boat. Frequent boats come downriver from Río Dulce and across the bay from Puerto Barrios; see those sections for further details. Boats also come here from Honduras and Belize.

Exotic Travel, based at Restaurante Bahía Azul, operates boats to Omoa (Honduras) and Punta Gorda (Belize). They run on a schedule, but will also go at any other time with a minimum of six people. Be sure to get your passport entry and exit stamps at the immigration offices on both ends of the journey.

The boats to Omoa depart Livingston at 7 am Tuesday and Friday, arriving about 10 am. In Omoa, the boat docks near the bus stop, where you can catch a bus to Puerto Cortés, San Pedro Sula or La Ceiba. The boat leaves Omoa for the return trip around noon or 1 pm, arriving back in Livingston around 3:30 pm. Cost is US$35 from Livingston to Omoa, or US$25 from Omoa to

Lívingston. The captain will take you to get your exit and entry stamps on both ends of the journey.

The boats to Punta Gorda (Belize) also leave Lívingston at 7 am Tuesday and Friday. This is a shorter trip, taking just 45 minutes; cost is US$13 each way. The boats depart Punta Gorda for the return trip at 9 am. Get your own exit stamp from the immigration office in Lívingston; the captain will take you to get your entry stamp in Punta Gorda.

Trips to Punta Gorda, Omoa and other places can also be arranged at the Happy Fish restaurant (☎ 902-7143).

AROUND LÍVINGSTON
Río Dulce Cruises

Lívingston is the starting point for boat rides on the Río Dulce. Passengers enjoy the tropical jungle scenery, have a swim and a picnic and explore the Biotopo Chocón Machacas, 12km west along the river.

Almost anyone in Lívingston can tell you who's currently organizing trips up the river. Exotic Travel makes trips daily, as do the Hotel La Casa Rosada and the Happy Fish restaurant. Or you can simply walk down to the dock and arrange a trip – many local boat captains are there, and it's good to support them.

Shortly after you leave Lívingston headed upriver, you'll enter a steep-walled gorge called **Cueva de la Vaca**, its walls hung with great tangles of jungle foliage and bromeliads. The humid air here is noisy with the cries of tropical birds. Just beyond that is **La Pintada**, a rock escarpment covered with graffiti. Farther on, a thermal spring forces sulfurous water out at the base of the cliff, providing a delightful place for a swim.

Emerging from the gorge, the river eventually widens into **El Golfete**, a lakelike body of water that presages the even vaster expanse of Lago de Izabal.

On the north shore of El Golfete is the **Biotopo Chocón Machacas**, a 7600-hectare reserve established to protect the beautiful river landscape, the valuable mangrove swamps and, especially, the manatees that inhabit the waters. A network of 'water trails' (boat routes around several jungle

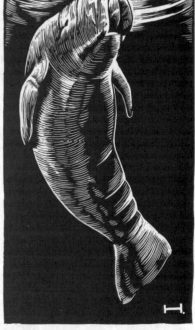

Manatees inhabit El Golfete on the Río Dulce.

lagoons) provide ways to see the reserve's flora and fauna. A nature trail begins at the visitors center and winds its way through forests of mahogany, palms and rich tropical foliage. Jaguars and tapirs live in the reserve, though your chances of seeing one are slight. The walruslike manatees are even more elusive. These huge mammals can weigh up to a ton, yet they glide effortlessly beneath the river's calm surface.

From El Golfete and the nature reserve, the boats continue upriver to the village of Río Dulce, where the road into El Petén crosses the river, and to the Castillo de San Felipe on Lago de Izabal (see the Lago de Izabal section, earlier).

The trip is also offered from Río Dulce; ask at the Tijax Express office. The fare is

US$7.75 one way or US$13 roundtrip. Trips are organized by Hotel La Casa Rosada and Rigoletto Pizzería.

Los Siete Altares

The Seven Altars is a series of freshwater falls and pools about 5km (1½-hour walk) northwest of Lívingston along the shore of Bahía de Amatique. It's a pleasant goal for a walk along the beach and a good place for a picnic and swim. Follow the shore northward to the river mouth. Ford the river and walk along the beach until it meets the path into the woods (about 30 minutes). Follow this path all the way to the falls. If you'd rather not do the ford, find a boat at the river mouth to ferry you across for a few quetzals.

Boat trips go to the Seven Altars, but locals say it's better to walk there in order to experience the natural beauty and the Garífuna people along the way. Although robberies on this walk were common in the past, Lívingston has beefed up its police force, so you should have an enjoyable, safe walk. The falls can be disappointing in the dry season, however.

Finca Tatin

A great B&B/Spanish school at the confluence of the Ríos Dulce and Tatin, Finca Tatin (☎ 902-0831, fincatatin@centramerica .com, www.centramerica.com/fincatatin) was built by husband-wife team Carlos and Claudia Simonini. Claudia holds a BA in Language & Literature and teaches the Spanish classes. A program of 20 hours of instruction in an open thatch bungalow overlooking the river, including room, is US$120 a week. Kitchen facilities are available to guests, or meals can be made for you (US$2.75 or cheaper vegetarian options). You can also skip the classes and just chill here; basic rooms in bungalows with shared bath are US$5 a day. There are trails, waterfalls and endless river tributaries that you can explore with one of the cayucos available for guest use. Or ask for suggestions on area camping. This is not a place for phobics of bugs or creeping fauna. Finca Tatin is easiest to reach by lancha from Lívingston (30 minutes). Hire a lanchero or call the Finca and they'll come pick you up (US$4). Spanish, English, French and Italian are spoken.

El Petén

In the dense jungle cover of Guatemala's vast northeastern department of El Petén, you may hear the squawk of parrots, the chatter of monkeys and the rustlings of strange animals moving through the bush. The landscape here is utterly different from that of Guatemala's cool mountainous high-

lands or the steamy Pacific Slope, and you should have plenty of bug repellent at the ready.

The monumental ceremonial center at Tikal is among the most impressive of the Mayan archaeological sites. Though it is possible to visit Tikal on a single-day excursion by plane from Guatemala City, travelers are strongly encouraged to stay over at least one night, whether in Flores, El Remate or Tikal itself. A day trip simply cannot do the place justice. The ruins of Uaxactún and Ceibal aren't as easily accessible, which perhaps makes them more exciting to visit. Several dozen other great Mayan cities hidden in El Petén that were previously only accessible to archaeologists with aircraft (or to artifact poachers) are now being opened for limited tourism.

In 1990 the Guatemalan government established the 1-million-hectare Maya Biosphere Reserve, which includes most of northern El Petén. The Guatemalan reserve adjoins the vast Calakmul Biosphere Reserve in Mexico and the Río Bravo Conservation Area in Belize, forming a huge multinational reserve of more than two million hectares.

Many travelers to the region linger in Poptún, a small town 113km southeast of Santa Elena that has been a popular backpacker layover for many years.

Warning

In years past, incidents of robbery of luxury and tourist buses on roads in El Petén were a concern, especially between Río Dulce and Flores and around the Belizean border at Melchor de Mencos/Benque Viejo del Carmen. Fortunately, things have quieted down considerably, and the overwhelming majority of visitors now enjoy safe visits. Still, contacting your embassy or consulate in Guatemala City for current information on the safety of roads in the region is a good idea; query other travelers as to latest developments as well.

GUATEMALA

Getting There & Around

The roads leading into El Petén have now all been paved, so travel here is now fast and smooth. Unfortunately, this improved access has encouraged the in-migration of farmers and ranchers from other areas of the country, increasing the pressure on the area's resources and leading to even more deforestation in a region whose forests had already been falling to the machete at an alarming rate.

The Guatemalan government long ago decided to develop the adjoining towns of Flores, Santa Elena and San Benito, on the shores of Lago de Petén Itzá, into the region's tourism base. Here you'll find an airport, hotels and other services. A few small hotels and restaurants are right at Tikal, but other services there will remain limited.

POPTÚN

• population 8000 • elevation 540m

The small town of Poptún is about halfway between Río Dulce and Flores and makes a good stopover en route to Tikal, especially if you're coming via Fray Bartolomé de Las Casas.

Several banks line 5a Calle. Bancafé gives cash advances on Visa cards; Master-Card users are out of luck in Poptún. The Telgua office is behind the police station near the market. Barring technical difficulties, email services are available at Fonda Ixobel II restaurant from 11 am to 1 pm daily; US$2.75 a half hour.

Places to Stay & Eat

The 400-acre **Finca Ixobel** (☎/fax 927-7363, fincaixobel@conexion.com.gt, fincaixobel .conexion.com) is a special place famous for its camaraderie – a friendly, relaxed spot for meeting other travelers from all parts of the globe. For several decades Carole DeVine has offered travelers tent sites, *palapas* for hanging hammocks, beds and good home-made meals with veggie selections galore. Swimming, horseback riding, camping trips, inner tubing on the river and a famous, thrilling cave trip (which even includes bodysurfing rapids inside a cave) are all or-

ganized on a daily basis, for a reasonable charge.

Accommodations run the gamut: Camping or hammock space costs US$2.25 per person; dorm beds are US$3; tree houses are US$6/7 single/double; a private room with shared bath is US$6.50/9/10.50 single/double/triple; a bungalow with private bath is US$11.75/16/21; and a big, private villa with bath is US$14.25/19.50/24. Meals offer stellar value, particularly the eat-all-you-like buffet dinner for US$4.50. You can cook in the campground, but bring all your own food as the finca has no store.

Volunteer opportunities exist for bilingual English-Spanish speakers; volunteers get free room and board. If the finca suits your style and you want to help/hang out for a month minimum, ask about volunteering.

Finca Ixobel also owns the Tierra Grande protected area and sanctuary, 16km from Poptún. This patch of rain forest supports a variety of tropical flora and fauna, and trips here are a valuable introduction to the jungle. Visitors sleep in hammocks, cook on an open fire and bathe in the river. Good-value multiday camping trips (starting at US$64.50, including transportation, guide, food and equipment) can be arranged at the finca or by calling ahead. Volunteers are also needed here, reintroducing captive animals into the wild. Two weeks minimum commitment is required.

The turnoff for the finca is marked on the highway, 5km south of town. In the daytime, you can ask the bus driver to let you off there; it's a 15-minute walk to the finca. At night, or if you don't feel like making the walk, get off the bus in town and go to the Fonda Ixobel II restaurant, near the bus stop. They will radio for a taxi to the finca (US$1 per person). It's important not to walk to the finca at night, as it's an isolated spot and robberies have been known to occur on the way. Indeed, robberies have also been attempted in broad daylight, so solo travelers might want to avail themselves of the taxi service.

Serviceable hotels in town include the good **Hotel Posada de los Castellanos** (☎ 927-7222), where clean rooms (some

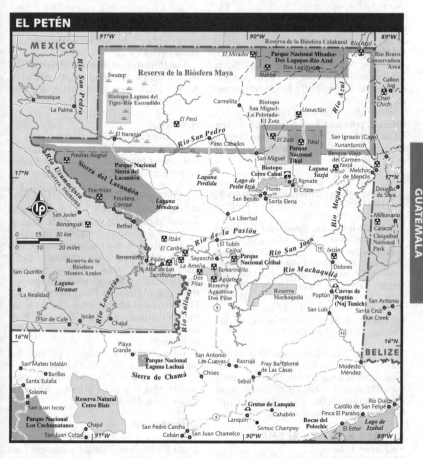

EL PETÉN

dark) with fan and private bath, arranged around a leafy courtyard, are US$4.50/6/7.75/9.25 single/double/triple/quad; and the *Pensión Izalco*, which has rooms with shared bath for US$3.25 single with fan, US$2.75 without.

Beyond Poptún, *Camping Cocay* (☎ 927-7024, birgitleistner@compuserve.com, ourworld.compuserve.com/homepages/birgitleistner), 7km north of town and then 700m from the highway, is a primitive campground in the forest beside the river, which is good for swimming, inner tubing and fishing. The prices of US$2.75 per person in a tent or

hammock, US$3.25 in a dorm, include breakfast; dinner is available for US$3.25. They also offer activities in the area. This place is primitive, remote and right in the jungle. Bring plenty of mosquito repellent; you'll need it.

The more upmarket *Hotel Ecológico Villa de los Castellanos* (☎ 927-7541/42, fax 927-7307) is just off the highway in Machaquila, 7km north of Poptún. It, too, is right beside the river and is great for swimming and inner tubing. Thatch-roofed cabins with electricity, private hot bath and two or three double beds are US$30/40/50.

The grounds hold a restaurant and acres of gardens.

Getting There & Away

All the Guatemala City–Flores buses stop in Poptún; see the section on Flores and the Guatemala Getting There & Around chapter for bus details.

Buses also traverse the remote route between Poptún and Fray Bartolomé de Las Casas on the way to Cobán. From Poptún it's five hours to Fray and another 5½ hours to Cobán.

Flores US$2.75, two hours, 113km; several buses daily. The first departures at 8 and 10:30 am do not pass Finca Ixobel (you must travel into town to catch the early buses).

Fray Bartolomé de Las Casas US$4, five hours, 100km; one bus at 11:30 am daily.

Guatemala City US$7.75, eight hours, 373km; buses at 9 and 10:30 am, noon, 1 and 4 pm daily, with an additional deluxe departure at 10 pm (US$16.75).

Melchor de Mencos (Belize border) US$4, four hours, 199km; Transportes Rosita (☎ 927-7413) buses leave at midnight, 2 and 4 am.

Río Dulce US$4, three hours, 99km; take any bus heading for Guatemala City.

If you're driving, fill your fuel tank before leaving Flores or Río Dulce, take some food, drink and a spare tire, and get an early start. The road is good in both directions, so drivers should have no problem driving between Poptún, Flores and Tikal.

FLORES & SANTA ELENA
• elevation 110m

The town of Flores (population 2000) is built on an island on Lago de Petén Itzá. A 500m causeway connects Flores to her sister town of Santa Elena (population 17,000) on the lakeshore. To the west of Santa Elena is the adjacent town of San Benito (population 22,000).

Flores, the departmental capital, is a dignified place. Its church, small government building and municipal basketball court surround the plaza, which sits atop a hill in the center of the island. The town's narrow streets, paved in cement blocks, are lined with charming, red-roofed houses. Santa

Elena is a disorganized town of dusty unpaved streets, and San Benito is even more disorganized, but its honky-tonk bars keep it lively.

The three towns form one large settlement usually referred to simply as Flores. All three have numerous small hotels and restaurants.

History

Flores was founded on an island (petén) by the Itzáes after their expulsion from Chichén Itzá. They named the place Tayasal. Cortés dropped in on King Canek of Tayasal in 1524 while on his way to Honduras, but the meeting was peaceable. Only in March 1697 did the Spaniards finally bring the Maya of Tayasal forcibly under their control.

At the time of its conquest, Flores was perhaps the last major functioning Mayan ceremonial center; it was covered in pyramids and temples, with idols everywhere. The God-fearing Spanish soldiers destroyed these 'pagan' buildings. Today when you visit Flores you will see not a trace of them, although the modern town is doubtless built on the ruins and foundations of the old city of Tayasal.

Tayasal's Mayan citizens fled into the jungle and may have started anew, giving rise to the myth of a 'lost' Mayan city; some believe this city is El Mirador, near the Guatemalan-Mexican border.

Orientation

The airport is on the eastern outskirts of Santa Elena, 2km from the causeway connecting Santa Elena and Flores. Each bus company has its own terminal in Santa Elena. No buses stop in Flores, so if you want to stay on the island, you'll have to walk, hire a taxi or hop a *lancha* to cross the lake.

Santa Elena's 'main drag' is 4a Calle. All the important hotels, restaurants and banks are on this street or just off it.

Information

Tourist Offices INGUAT staffs tourist information desks at the airport (☎ 926-0533) and on the plaza in Flores (☎ 926-0669).

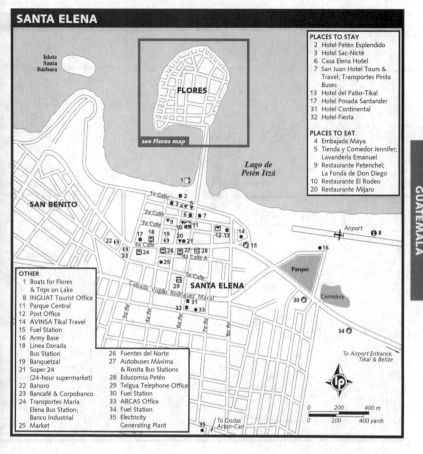

SANTA ELENA

FLORES

see Flores map

Islote
Santa
Bárbara

Lago de
Petén Itzá

SAN BENITO

Airport

SANTA ELENA

Parque

Cemetery

To Airport Entrance,
Tikal & Belize

To Grutas
Actun-Can

PLACES TO STAY
2 Hotel Petén Esplendido
3 Hotel Sac-Nicté
6 Casa Elena Hotel
7 San Juan Hotel Tours &
   Travel; Transportes Pinita
   Buses
13 Hotel del Patio-Tikal
17 Hotel Posada Santander
31 Hotel Continental
32 Hotel Fiesta

PLACES TO EAT
4 Embajada Maya
5 Tienda y Comedor Jennifer;
   Lavandería Emanuel
9 Restaurante Petenchel;
   La Fonda de Don Diego
10 Restaurante El Rodeo
20 Restaurante Mijaro

OTHER
1 Boats for Flores
   & Trips on Lake
8 INGUAT Tourist Office
11 Parque Central
12 Post Office
14 AVINSA Tikal Travel
15 Fuel Station
16 Army Base
18 Linea Dorada
   Bus Station
19 Banquetzal
21 Super 24
   (24-hour supermarket)
22 Banoro
23 Bancafé & Corpobanco
24 Transportes María
   Elena Bus Station;
   Banco Industrial
25 Market
26 Fuentes del Norte
27 Autobuses Máxima
   & Rosita Bus Stations
28 Educomsa Petén
29 Telgua Telephone Office
30 Fuel Station
33 ARCAS Office
34 Fuel Station
35 Electricity
   Generating Plant

GUATEMALA

0   200   400 m
0   200   400 yards

The offices are open from 7:30 to 10 am and 3 to 6 pm daily.

Useful Organizations The Centro de Información sobre la Naturaleza, Cultura y Artesanía del Petén (CINCAP), on the north side of the plaza in Flores, sells regional handicrafts and has exhibits on natural resources and forest conservation in the Petén. It's open 9 am to 1 pm and 2 to 7 pm Tuesday to Saturday. Sharing the same space is the Asociación Alianza Verde (☎/fax 926-0718, alianzaverde@conservation.org.gt), an organization dedicated to

responsible tourism in El Petén. It's open 9 am to noon and 2 to 6 pm Monday to Friday, 9 am to noon Saturday.

The Asociación de Rescate y Conservación de Vida Silvestre (ARCAS) has a wildlife rescue center about 12km east of Santa Elena, near Laguna Petenchel. Animals here include macaws, green and yellow parrots, jaguars, howler and spider monkeys, kinkajous and coatis that have been rescued from smugglers and the illegal pet trade. The animals are rehabilitated for release back into the wild. You are welcome to visit, but you should ask permission first (in

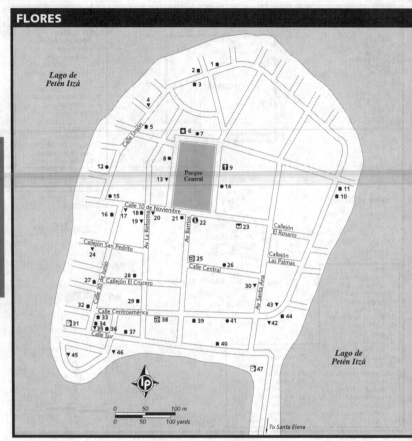

FLORES

Guatemala City ☎/fax 591-4731). Volunteers are welcome to stay at the center, paying US$50 per week for room and board and volunteering any amount of time. Contact ARCAS (see Work in the Guatemala Facts for the Visitor chapter) for further details.

The Proyecto Petenero para un Bosque Sostenible (ProPetén; ☎ 926-1370, fax 926-0495, propeten@guate.net) works with forest communities to promote tourism and other alternative uses of the Petén's natural resources. To this end, they've organized and trained Comités Comunitarios de Ecoturismo (Community Ecotourism Committees),

which take visitors into the jungle on tours to El Zotz (with an optional Tikal leg), El Perú and El Mirador. While none of these trips can be made independently, travelers wishing to arrange guide service through the Comités directly (rather than through a travel agency) should contact ProPetén.

Money Some hotels and travel agencies in Flores will change currency and traveler's checks, but at terrible rates – most people go to Santa Elena to do their banking.

Banks in Santa Elena are on 4a Calle. Banco Industrial has an ATM and gives cash

Currencies of the USA, Mexico and Belize can be changed at the Banquetzal at the airport, which also gives cash advances on MasterCard. It's supposedly open 8 am to noon and 2 to 5 pm daily.

Post & Communications In Flores, the post office is just off the plaza; Martsam Travel Agency, EcoMaya and Cahuí International Services offer domestic and worldwide telephone and fax facilities; and both TikalNet, on Calle Centroamérica, and café .net, on Avenida Barrios, offer reasonably priced Internet service.

In Santa Elena, the post office is on 2a Calle at 7a Avenida; the Telgua telephone office is on 5a Calle and open daily; and Educomsa Petén (☎ 926-0765) is at 4a Calle 6-76, Local B, Zona 1, and offers email and computer services.

Travel Agencies In Flores, Martsam Travel Agency (☎/fax 926-0493), next to the Restaurante y Hotel La Jungla, and Cahuí International Services (☎/fax 926-0494), next to the Hotel Santana, offer travel agency and telephone/fax services, tours, currency exchange and bicycle rental. EcoMaya (see Organized Tours) has similar services, plus international newspapers and magazines, a small book exchange and a message board; the company also runs organized tours to several archaeological sites in the jungle.

Most of the travel agencies in Flores lead trips to the more accessible sites such as Tikal, Uaxactún and Ceibal. For example, the Hotel Guayacán (see Places to Stay) offers trips to Ceibal (US$25) with an Aguateca option (US$60). Martsam offers transportation to sites such as Yaxjá for US$15 per person (great for independent travelers) or you can take a guided tour for US$40 per person, with a minimum of four people. There are other places, so shop and ask around.

San Juan Hotel Tours & Travel in Santa Elena and the San Juan de Isla Hotel & Travel Agency in Flores provide shuttle services to destinations of interest to travelers, including Belize City, Chetumal (near the Mexico/Belize border) and Palenque,

advances on Visa cards. Bancafé changes cash, traveler's checks and gives cash advances on Visa cards as well; it's open 8:30 am to 7 pm Monday to Friday, 9 am to 1 pm Saturday. Banoro changes cash and traveler's checks; it's open 8:30 am to 8 pm Monday to Friday, 9 am to 4 pm Saturday. Banquetzal has good rates and gives cash advances on MasterCard.

San Juan Hotel Tours & Travel in Santa Elena will give cash advances on Visa, MasterCard and American Express cards, as will EcoMaya in Flores (see Organized Tours).

among others (see Getting There & Away). Shuttles are efficient and convenient, if pricey.

Laundry In Flores, try the Lavandería Petenchel, open 8 am to 8 pm Monday to Saturday. In Santa Elena, Lavandería Emanuel, on 6a Avenida near the causeway, does a good job and the laundry is ready in an hour. It's open 8 am to 7 pm Monday to Saturday.

Emergency The national police can be reached at ☎ 926-1365; the national hospital is at ☎ 926-1333.

Grutas Actun-Can

The limestone cave of Actun-Can, also called La Cueva de la Serpiente (Cave of the Serpent), apparently holds no serpents, but the cave-keeper who turns on the lights for you may give you the rundown on the cave formations, which suggest animals, humans and various scenes. Bring a flashlight if you have one and adequate shoes – it can be slippery. Explorations take about 30 to 45 minutes. It's open 8 am to 5 pm daily; US$1.25. At the cave's entrance is a shady picnic area.

Actun-Can makes a good goal for a long walk from Santa Elena. Head south on 6a Avenida past the Telgua office. About 1km from the center of Santa Elena, turn left, go 300m and turn right at the electricity generating plant. Go another 1km to the site. A taxi from Santa Elena costs US$2.

Lago de Petén Itzá

As you stroll around town, particularly in Flores, locals will offer boat rides around the lake. Many are freelance agents who get a commission; it's better to talk with the boat owner directly. You should bargain over the price and inspect the boat. Or ask at the Restaurante/Bar Las Puertas in Flores; Carlos, the owner, offers boat trips around the lake and across to the other side, where he has land and a private dock for swimming and sunning. The travel agencies may also be able to arrange boat trips.

There's good birding on the Río Ixpop, which runs into the east side of the lake.

Boat trips along the river start from El Remate, on the lake's east side.

Organized Tours

Travel agencies in Flores offer a number of interesting tours to remote parts of the Petén region. EcoMaya (☎ 926-1363, 926-3321, fax 926-3322, in the USA ☎ 800-429-5660, ecomaya@guate.net, www.ecomaya .com), on Calle 30 de Junio, cooperates with the Comités Comunitarios to lead trips to El Mirador, El Zotz and El Perú (aka the Scarlet Macaw Trail). Three-day excursions start around US$110, including food, water, sleeping gear and a Spanish-speaking guide. These treks are demanding.

AVINSA Tikal Travel (☎ 926-0808, fax 926-0807, info@tikaltravel.com, www.tikal .com), on 4a Calle in Santa Elena, offers a well-recommended tour to Yaxjá and Nakum, with an optional Tikal extension. In addition to the sites themselves, horseback riding, hiking and wildlife viewing are highlights of this tour. Guides are available in English or Spanish.

Monkey Eco Tours (☎ 201-0759, fax 926-0808, in the USA fax 978-945-6486, nitun@ nitun.com, www.nitun.com), based at the Ni'tun Ecolodge on the lake's northwest side, specializes in deluxe adventure-camping tours. Transportation is via Land Cruisers; portable showers and inflatable mattresses are provided; and the guides are experts in their respective fields, be they birders, archaeologists or biologists. Tours run to El Mirador, Río Azul, Ceibal, Dos Pilas and Tikal, among other sites.

Places to Stay – Budget

Flores One of the town's best budget choices, *Hospedaje Doña Goya* (☎ 926-3538), on Calle Unión, is often full. Spotless rooms with comfortable beds and shared hot bath are US$4/6.50; doubles with private bath are US$7.75. The rooftop terrace has hammocks and lounge chairs from which you can enjoy lake views. Solo women travelers will do well to head here first.

Beside the lake, the cheerful, family-run *Hotel Villa del Lago* (☎ /fax 926-0629) is a good, clean place to stay – much nicer on the inside than its exterior appearance would suggest. Simple rooms with private bath are US$6.50 double. Bigger, nicer units with bath and TV are US$15.50 with fan, US$19.50 with air-con.

Facing the causeway is the new *Petenchel Hotel* (☎ 926-3359). This is a good value, with clean rooms with private hot bath and comfortable beds for US$6.50/9; some of the rooms are dark. The small courtyard is jammed with plants.

Next door is an entrance to the friendly *Restaurante & Hotel La Canoa* (☎ 926-0852/3). Rooms with private hot bath are US$4 per person; upstairs rooms are airier, and downstairs triples can be crowded. Two rooms with shared bath are available for US$2.75 per person. There's a good, popular restaurant here.

Hotel Guayacán (☎ 926-0351) has simple but serviceable rooms with shared bath for US$2.75 per person. *Hotel Posada Tayazal* (☎ 926-0568), on Calle Unión, has decent, cleanish doubles with private hot bath and fan for US$7.75. The upstairs rooms are hot but have partial lake views.

The simple but clean *Posada Tucán No 2* (☎ 926-1467) is OK. Rooms are US$4.50/5.25 with shared bath. Some rooms have lake views. Next door, the *Mirador del Lago* is a decent value, with rooms with private bath for US$7.75 double. The roof terrace has lake views.

Hotel Santa Rita (☎ 926-0710) is clean, friendly and family run; it's an excellent deal at US$6/9 with private bath. The adjacent *Restaurante and Hotel La Jungla* (☎ 926-0634) has clean, generic rooms with private cold bath for US$10/14/18 single/double/triple. This place will do in a pinch and it accepts credit cards.

The *Hotel y Restaurante Posada El Peregrino*, on Avenida La Reforma, has reasonable rooms for US$6.50 double with shared bath, US$9 with private hot bath and TV. The restaurant here is terrific.

Hotel y Restaurante La Mesa de los Mayas (☎/fax 926-1240) is a lovely place that is very clean and well kept. Rooms with private bath are US$15 double with fan, US$20 with air-con, US$20/25 triple/quad

for larger units with fan. The hotel accepts Visa and MasterCard.

Santa Elena The spotless *Hotel Posada Santander* (☎ 926-0574), on 4a Calle, is a simple hostelry in a convenient, but loud, location. The friendly family-run establishment offers ample rooms with private bath and two good double beds for US$5.25/6.50 single/double. Rooms with shared bath are US$3.25/4. The family also operates Transportes Inter Petén, a minibus service to Tikal and other places.

Nearer the lake, *Hotel Sac-Nicté* (☎ 926-0092) has clean, large upstairs rooms with private bath, balcony and views across the

Responsible Tourism

Visitors to any of the sites in the Petén forest should be conscious of traveling responsibly; increasing human presence here is already having a negative impact on the ecological balance. All inorganic garbage should be carried out, human waste and toilet paper should be buried in a pit at least 15cm deep and 100m from a water source, and only dead wood should be used to build fires. Observing these basic guidelines and insisting your guides do the same will help protect this fragile area.

One issue of particular concern is the use of pack animals on these trips. These animals eat copious amounts of sapodilla leaves, and nearly an entire mature tree will be stripped of its branches to feed four mules for one day. This is disturbing; if you can avoid using mules on your trip, do so. Otherwise, inquire about alternative food sources for the animals.

Another nagging problem is mud. There's lots of it between May and November, and guides hacking trails around mud patches kill new forest growth. Walking around mud holes makes them bigger, setting off an endless cycle of widening destruction. Hiking in these muddy conditions isn't much fun anyway, so try to arrange jungle trips for the dry season.

lake to Flores for US$10.50. Downstairs rooms have no view and cost US$7.75. The hotel has a restaurant, parking and transportation service.

Hotel Continental (☎ 926-0095), on 6a Avenida at Calzada Virgilio Rodríguez Macal, is a large hotel, relatively removed from everything. Rooms are US$2.75 per person with shared bath, US$4 with a private bath. Amenities include a restaurant and courtyard parking. Better is the *Hotel Fiesta*, next door, which also has a restaurant.

Places to Stay – Mid-Range

Flores On the island's north side, *Hotel Sabana* (☎/fax 926-1248) has a restaurant and sundeck over the water. Rooms with private bath, fan, air-con and cable TV are US$20/30/40 single/double/triple.

Hotel Casona de la Isla (☎ 926-0523, fax 926-0593, lacasona@guate.net) is a romantic place with a lakeside Jacuzzi and pool and an open-air bar/restaurant on the lakeshore. All 27 rooms have private bath, cable TV, phone, air-con and a balcony with chairs; US$33/37/47.

Hotel Petén (☎/fax 926-0692, lacasona@ guate.net) has a small courtyard with tropical plants, a pleasant lakeside terrace and restaurant and an indoor swimming pool. The 19 comfy-if-plain rooms, all with private bath, air-con and fan, are US$25/30/40 from April to June and September to November; all other times they're US$30/35/45. Try to get a top-floor room with a lake view.

The new *Casa Azul Guest House* (☎ 926-1138, fax 926-0593, lacasona@guate.net), on the north shore, is a comfortable, quiet place. Each room is unique and spotless and has a private hot bath, cable TV, fridge, phone, air-con and balcony for US$30/35. The ones facing the water are nicest.

At *Hotel Santana* (☎ 926-0491, ☎/fax 926-0662), most of the rooms have great lake views and large private balconies, and each has a private bath, cable TV, air-con and a fan; US$30/45/55/65 single/double/triple/quad. The hotel's restaurant has a lakeside terrace.

The *Hotel Isla de Flores* (☎ 926-0614, in Guatemala City ☎ 476-8775, fax 476-0294, reservaciones@junglelodge.guate.com, www .junglelodge.guate.com) is clean and attractive. The rooms are large and well equipped, with cable TV, air-con, ceiling fan, telephone and private bath with tub. Many have private balconies with a view of the lake. Rates are US$35/40.

Santa Elena The new *Casa Elena Hotel* (☎ 926-2238/39, fax 926-0097, in Guatemala City ☎ 472-4045, fax 472-1633), on the first block over the causeway, has nice, clean rooms that are short on character but long on comfort. Each has private hot bath, cable TV and telephone; US$35/45 single/double. Some rooms have park views, while others overlook the pool. Amenities include a bar, restaurant and roof terrace.

Places to Stay – Top End

In Santa Elena, *Hotel del Patio-Tikal* (☎ 926-0104, in Guatemala City ☎ 331-5720) looks severe from the outside but is actually a nice colonial-style hotel with a pretty central courtyard. The 22 rooms, all with air-con and ceiling fan, cable TV, telephone and private bath, are US$48 single or double, US$51 triple. The hotel has a bar, restaurant, pool and small gym.

Right on the water is the sparkling new *Hotel Petén Esplendido* (☎ 926-0880, fax 926-0866, in Guatemala City ☎ 360-8140, fax 332-3232, hpesplen@guate.net), a luxury lodging with every amenity, including a swanky poolside bar and two restaurants. The 62 rooms are modern, spotless, have little balconies and are wheelchair accessible. Rates are US$75/85/95. English, Italian and German are spoken.

Hotel Villa Maya (☎ /fax 926-0086, in Guatemala City ☎ 334-8136, fax 334-8134, stpvillas@pronet.net.gt), on Laguna Petenchel about 10km east of Santa Elena, has 40 double rooms in bungalows, each with private bath, ceiling fan, hot water, beautiful views of the lake and blissful quiet. Other amenities include a patio restaurant, tennis courts, two swimming pools, two private lagoons and a wildlife refuge. Rates at the hotel are US$77/85/93.

Places to Eat

As with hotels, the restaurants in Santa Elena tend to be cheaper than those in Flores. All are fairly simple and keep long hours. Beer, drinks and sometimes even wine are served, and most places offer a variety of local game, including *tepezcuintle* (a rabbit-sized jungle rodent known in English as the paca or cavy), *venado* (deer), armadillo and *pavo silvestre* (wild turkey).

Flores A popular hangout is *Restaurante/ Bar Las Puertas*, which has decent, pricey food and an interesting clientele. It's a good spot for friendly conversation. You can get real coffee here, and live music is presented on weekends. Hours are 9 am to 1 am Monday to Saturday.

The small *Restaurante Chal-tun-ha* has an open and fresh decor, with a terrace right over the water and a fine view across the lake. The menu offers a good selection of inexpensive dishes. It's open 9 am to 7:30 pm daily. *Restaurante Don Quijote*, in a small boat docked on the southern shore, serves affordable lunch and dinner.

Restaurante/Bar Posada El Tucán, next to the Villa del Lago, has a lakeside terrace that catches any breezes. Set breakfasts cost US$2 to US$3, lunches and dinners US$5 to US$8. Just across the street is the recommended *Restaurante & Pizzería Picasso*, offering pizza, pasta and salads at fair prices. *Restaurante La Canoa*, on Calle Centroamérica, is cheaper and plainer, but its decent food at low prices appeals to budget travelers. Don't miss the killer tortillas here.

La Hacienda del Rey, on the corner of Calles Sur and 30 de Junio, has a huge terrace, invitingly strung with lights. This place specializes in meat, and all manner of steaks fill the menu. It isn't cheap (US$11 for a hefty porterhouse), but it has a nice atmosphere and is open at 4:30 am for breakfast – perfect for a nip of coffee before the early Tikal shuttle.

Hotel y Restaurante La Mesa de los Mayas is a popular restaurant serving good traditional foods as well as local game. A mixed plate goes for US$9, a vegetarian plate is US$5, and chicken costs even less. It's open 7 am to 11 pm daily.

The *Restaurante Gran Jaguar* is often recommended by locals. It has a good variety of reasonably priced dishes, attractive decor and bar service. Hours are 11 am to 10 pm Monday to Saturday. *Restaurante La Unión*, on the northwestern bend of the island, serves chicken, pasta and seafood dishes at decent prices. The real reason to come here is the location, which is right on the water.

The *Mayan Princess Café, Bar & Cinema*, Calle 10 de Noviembre at Avenida La Reforma, serves surprisingly good traveler food along the lines of chicken florentine and pesto ravioli. The prices are reasonable (around US$4), though the portions are smallish and the service is spotty. Across the street is the very local, very friendly *Sala Maya*, serving set and à la carte meals at rock-bottom (for Flores!) prices. Try the *limonada con soda*, which will cure what ails you on a hot day.

Another place serving delicious food at great prices is *Hotel y Restaurante Posada El Peregrino*, on Avenida La Reforma. For US$3.25 you can dine on succulent roasted chicken, accompanied by french fries, salad and rice – highly recommended. A similar place long on atmosphere is *El Mirador*, on the plaza's west side. Here you can get a big, set lunch for US$1.50 while enjoying lake views.

Then there's the popular *La Luna*, on the corner of Calles 30 de Junio and 10 de Noviembre, where the food is delectable. The menu tempts with innovative chicken, fish and beef dishes the likes of which you'll be hard-pressed to find anywhere else in Guatemala. Expect to pay around US$8 for a meal, not including drinks. It's open for lunch and dinner Tuesday to Sunday.

Santa Elena Hotel Sac-Nicté, Hotel Fiesta, Hotel Continental, the Embajada Maya and

GUATEMALA

the Casa Elena Hotel all have restaurants. For a real splurge, try one of the restaurants at Hotel Petén Esplendido, overlooking the water.

Restaurante El Rodeo, 2a Calle at 5a Avenida, is often recommended by locals. It's open 11 am to 9 pm daily. In the same block, *Super 24* is a 24-hour supermarket. In the next block of 2a Calle, *Restaurante Petenchel* and *La Fonda de Don Diego* are also popular. *Restaurante Mijaro*, a simple *comedor* on the main road, is another place recommended by locals; it's open 7 am to 9 pm daily *Tienda y Comedor Jennifer* is a simple place near the causeway with good food, cold beer and great people-watching. A big plate of fried chicken with french fries costs US$2.

Entertainment

Flores is pretty dead at night, but a couple of hangouts can provide an escape from your hotel room. *Kayuko's*, on Calle Unión, is a copacetic bar with a pool table. It serves light meals at tables overlooking the lake and has satellite TV; closed Monday.

The *El Balcón del Cielo* bar offers awesome views of the lake and the church and is a great place to sip a cocktail while watching the sunset. The music is decent and the peanuts are free; light meals are available. The bar at *La Luna* is also popular.

The *Mayan Princess Café, Bar & Cinema* shows free movies (some of dubious quality) at 4 and 9 pm in its dining room. It has comfy chairs and imported beers, but the 9 pm screening can be a bit of a drag if you're trying to carry on a dinner conversation.

Getting There & Away

Air The airport at Santa Elena (usually called 'the airport at Flores') is busy these days. International flights include those to/from Belize City with Tropic Air, Island Air, Grupo TACA, Racsa, Tapsa and Aerovías; to/from Palenque, Chetumal, Cancún and Havana with Aerocaribe; and to/from Cancún with Aviateca (four times a week) and Grupo TACA (daily).

Flights between Flores and Guatemala City vary widely in price, ranging from around US$50 to US$85. Package tours including airfare and accommodations may work out to be cheaper and are available at many travel agencies. See the Tikal section, later, for more on this.

Flights between Santa Elena/Flores and Puerto Barrios (US$65, 50 minutes) depart on Monday, Wednesday and Friday at 1:35 pm.

More regional airlines will be opening up routes to and from Flores in the near future. Ask at travel agencies in Cancún, Mérida, Belize City and Guatemala City. Your travel agent at home may not be able to get up-to-date information on some of these small regional carriers. And travel agents in Flores and Santa Elena may charge more for a ticket than you would pay by buying it at the airport.

When you arrive at the airport in Flores you may be subjected to a cursory customs and immigration check, as this is a special customs and immigration district. You have to pay a US$30 departure tax if you're leaving Guatemala, US$0.65 if you're flying within the country.

Bus Travel by bus to or from Flores is fast and comfortable over new roads, except on the Bethel and Sayaxché routes. Each bus company has its own office. Transportes Pinita buses depart from the San Juan Hotel in Santa Elena (☎ 926-0041/2). The Transportes María Elena office (☎ 926-0574) is across the street from the Hotel Posada Santander in Santa Elena. Other bus companies in Santa Elena include Fuentes del Norte (☎ 926-0517), Línea Dorada (☎ 926-0070, 926-1817, lineadorada@intelnet.net.gt), Autobuses Máxima (☎ 926-0676) and Transportes Rosío. For several destinations you'll have the choice of taking a tourist shuttle or a local 'chicken bus.' The latter will always be slower and cheaper.

Belize City US$20, five hours, 222km; San Juan Hotel runs a daily shuttle that will pick you up from your hotel around 5 am and arrive in Belize City around 10 am (theoretically in time to connect with the boat to Caye Caulker and San Pedro, Ambergris Caye). Or take local buses from Santa Elena to Melchor de Mencos and change there (see Melchor de Mencos below).

Bethel (Mexico border) US$3.25, four hours, 127km; Transportes Pinita buses at 5 and 8 am and 1 pm; this is a rough road.

Ceibal See Sayaxché.

Chetumal (Mexico) US$35, seven hours, 350km; a special direct 1st-class San Juan bus departs from the San Juan Hotel and Hotel Continental in Santa Elena daily at 5 am, bypasses Belize City and goes straight to Chetumal. At Chetumal it connects with buses heading north along the coast to Tulum, Playa del Carmen and Cancún. Cheaper are Rosita buses leaving Santa Elena for Melchor de Mencos on the Belize border (see below), with a connection at the border to Chetumal.

El Naranjo See From El Petén to Chiapas, later in the chapter.

El Remate/Puente Ixlú 40 minutes, 35km; Tikal-bound buses and minibuses (see Tikal) will drop you here. Buses to/from Melchor de Mencos will drop you at Puente Ixlú/El Cruce, less than 2km south of El Remate.

Esquipulas US$7.75, 11 hours, 437km; two daily Transportes María Elena departures at 6 am and 2 pm. This bus goes via Chiquimula (US$6.50, 10 hours).

Guatemala City US$10.50, 12 hours, 488km; Fuentes del Norte operates buses all day from 7:30 am to 9:30 pm. Linea Dorada luxury buses (US$30, eight hours) depart at 10 am and 8 and 10 pm. Autobuses Máxima runs deluxe buses at 7 and 8 pm.

La Ruidosa (crossroads to Puerto Barrios) US$6, eight hours, 242km; take any bus bound for Guatemala City.

Melchor de Mencos (Belize border) US$2, two hours, 100km; 2nd-class Transportes Pinita buses at 5, 8 and 10:30 am. Rosita buses at 5, 7:30 and 11 am and 2, 4 and 6 pm. On the Belize side, buses (US$0.50) and share-taxis (US$2) leave for Benque Viejo and San Ignacio (30 minutes) every hour or so.

Palenque (Mexico) See From El Petén to Chiapas, later in the chapter.

Poptún US$2.75, two hours, 113km; take any bus heading for Guatemala City.

Río Dulce US$6.50, five hours, 208km; take any bus heading for Guatemala City.

San Andrés (around the lake) US$0.65, one hour, 20km; Transportes Pinita buses at 5:30 am and noon, departing San Andrés for the return trip at 7 am and 1:30 pm. Boats make this trip

more frequently (US$0.40, 30 minutes) departing from San Benito, on the west side of Santa Elena, and from Flores beside the Hotel Santana.

Sayaxché US$1.50, two hours, 61km; 2nd-class Transportes Pinita buses at 5:30, 7, 8, 9 and 10:30 am and 1 and 3:30 pm. There are also tours from Santa Elena via Sayaxché to the ruins at Ceibal, departing from the San Juan Hotel and Hotel Continental at 8 am, returning at 4 pm (US$30).

Tikal US$1.50, two hours, 71km; one Transportes Pinita bus daily at 1 pm, continuing to Uaxactún. It departs Tikal for the return trip at 6 am. It's quicker and more convenient to take a shuttle minibus to Tikal (see below).

Uaxactún US$2.50, three hours, 94km; Transportes Pinita, 1 pm. It departs from Uaxactún for the return trip at 5 am.

Shuttle Minibus Minibuses bound for Tikal pick up passengers in front of their hotel (5, 6, 8 and 10 am) and from the airport (meeting all flights). Any hotel can arrange a trip for you. The fare is US$5.25 per person roundtrip; the trip takes one to 1½ hours.

Return trips generally depart from Tikal at 2, 4 and 5 pm. Your driver will anticipate that you'll want to return to Flores that same afternoon; if you know which return trip you'd like to be on, they'll hold a seat for you or arrange a seat in a colleague's minibus. If you go out to Tikal and decide to stay overnight, it's a good idea to reserve a seat early the next morning for that afternoon's return trip; talk to one of the minibus drivers as soon as they arrive from Flores. Don't wait until departure time and expect to find a seat.

A taxi from Flores/Santa Elena or the airport to Tikal costs US$40 roundtrip (for up to four people).

Getting Around

Bus Buses and minibuses bound for the small villages around the lake and elsewhere in the immediate vicinity depart from the chaotic market area in Santa Elena.

Car Several hotels, car rental companies and travel agencies offer rentals, including cars, 4WDs, pickup trucks and minibuses.

Rental car companies are in the arrivals hall at Flores airport. They include:

Garrido	☎ 926-0092
Hertz	☎ 926-0332, 926-0415
Koka	☎ 926-0526, 926-1233
Los Compadres	☎ 926-0444
Los Jades	☎ 926-0734
Nesa	☎ 926-0082
Tabarini	☎/fax 302-5900

A basic car with unlimited *kilometraje* (distance allowance) costs a minimum of around US$50 per day. The travel agency at the San Juan Hotel in Santa Elena (☎ 926-0041/2, fax 926-0514) also has rental cars and there is a Hertz office inside the lobby of the Hotel Camino Real Tikal (☎ 929-0206 ext 2).

Bicycle In Flores, you can rent bicycles from Cahuí International Services (☎/fax 926-0494) for US$0.85 per hour or US$6.75 per day; or from Hotel Guayacán (☎ 926-0351) for US$0.75 an hour. Around the lake in El Remate, Casa Mobego (☎ 926-0269) also rents bicycles.

Boat Lanchas ferrying passengers between Santa Elena and Flores depart from both ends of the causeway (US$0.15, five minutes). Motor launches making tours around Lago de Petén Itzá depart from the Santa Elena end of the causeway. *Colectivo* boats to San Andrés and San José, villages across the lake, depart from San Benito, on the west side of Santa Elena and from alongside the Hotel Santana in Flores (US$0.40 if the boat is full, US$8 for one passenger). You can also contract the *lancheros* here for tours around the lake, but you'll need to bargain hard.

EL REMATE

Once little more than a few thatched huts 35km northeast of Santa Elena on the Tikal road, the village of El Remate keeps on growing, thanks to the tourist trade. Right on the lakeshore, El Remate is becoming a tertiary tourist center after Flores and Tikal. Halfway between the two places, it allows you to be closer to Tikal but still be on the lake.

El Remate is known for its wood carving. Several handicrafts shops on the lakeshore opposite La Mansión del Pájaro Serpiente sell local handicrafts and rent canoes, rafts and kayaks.

From El Remate an unpaved road snakes its way around the northeast shore of the lake to the Biotopo Cerro Cahuí, the luxury Hotel Camino Real Tikal and on to the villages of San José and San Andrés, on the northwest side of the lake. It's possible to go all the way around the lake by road.

With their newfound prosperity, *remate-cos* have built a *balneario municipal* (municipal beach) just off the highway; several cheap pensions and small hotels have opened here as well.

Biotopo Cerro Cahuí

At the northeast end of Lago de Petén Itzá, about 43km from Santa Elena and 3km from the Flores-Tikal road, the Biotopo Cerro Cahuí covers 651 hectares of subtropical forest. Within the reserve are mahogany, cedar, ramón, broom, sapodilla and cohune palm trees, as well as many species of lianas and epiphytes, including bromeliads, ferns and orchids. The hard sapodilla wood was used in Mayan temple door lintels, which have survived from the Classic period to our own time. And chicle is still sapped from the tree's innards.

Among the many animals found within the reserve are spider and howler monkeys, ocelots, white-tailed deer, raccoons, armadillos, numerous species of fish, turtles and snakes, and *Crocodylus moreletti*, the Petén crocodile. The bird life is rich and varied. Depending upon the season and migration patterns, you might see kingfishers, ducks, herons, hawks, parrots, toucans, woodpeckers and the famous ocellated (or Petén) turkey, a beautiful big bird resembling a peacock.

A network of loop trails starts at the road and goes up the hill, affording a view of the whole lake and of Lagunas Salpetén and Petenchel. A trail map is at the entrance.

Entrance to the reserve costs US$2.75 per person. The entrance gate is usually open 6 am to 4 pm (once in, you can stay as late as you like). If you find the gate closed, go to the administration center and they'll let you in. You can camp here for an additional US$2.75; toilets and showers are available, but El Remate is the closest place to get food and other necessities.

Places to Stay & Eat

El Remate has several small hotels and pensions, and more are opening all the time.

La Casa de Don David (☎ 306-2190), on the lakeshore about 10m from the Flores-Tikal road, is operated by American-born David Kuhn (the original 'gringo perdido') and his friendly Guatemalan wife. This place is more the haunt of organized tour groups than world travelers. Bland rooms with private bath in freestanding bungalows are pricey (even for this area) at US$15/20/25 single/double/triple. Disappointing meals are served on the wide upstairs terrace overlooking the lake. Organized activities include horseback riding and a two-hour boat ride across the lake and up the Río Ixpop to see crocodiles, birds and other wildlife (US$5.25 per person). Daily tours to Ceibal are also available for US$35, including lunch and transportation to the site. A shuttle to Tikal from here costs US$5 roundtrip.

Offering terrific value is *Casa de Don Luis*, on the east side of the Flores-Tikal road. This friendly, family-owned place has two spotless rooms with comfortable beds, fan and shared bath for US$6.50/7.75/9. It has no sign, but look for the slatted gate just before the *Casa de Juan*, which has super basic rooms with walls reaching partially to the ceiling for US$2 per person. Rooms do have fan and nets, however and the restaurant is pretty good.

Nearby on the path to the lake is the *Hotel Sun Breeze*, where simple, clean cement rooms with shared bath are US$2.75 per person. One or two simple *comedores* are nearby – try the Casa de Juan.

A couple of other decent places on the Flores-Tikal road offer great lake views. At the *Mirador del Duende* (☎ 926-0269, fax 926-0397) you can camp with your own hammock or tent for US$1.50 a person, sleep in a shelter (like a permanent tent)

for US$2.75 per person or stay in a bungalow for US$4.50 per person. Economical vegetarian food is served. Forest hiking tours are offered, and you can rent horses (US$10 a day) and canoes (US$4 a day).

Next door, *La Mansión del Pájaro Serpiente* (☎/fax 926-0065) has 10 attractive rooms with private hot bath for US$75, plus lovely gardens, a swimming pool and a reasonably priced restaurant/bar. Good discounts may be available if you just drop in.

A couple of other good places are about 3km west of El Remate on the road around the lake's north side, near the Biotopo Cerro Cahuí. First you'll come to a couple of laid-back cheapies, both with lake views. The *Casa de Doña Tonita* has six beds in a thatch *rancho* for US$3.25 per person. This is communal living in simple conditions (no fans or nets), but it could be a blast for a group. It has a restaurant. Nearby *Casa Mobego* (☎ 926-0269) has simple bungalows with outside bathrooms for US$4 per person. It's cheaper if you get meals here: US$9 per person covers accommodations, dinner and breakfast. A swimming dock is in front, and you can rent mountain bikes.

Farther along this road, right on the lakeshore, is the *Parador Ecológico El Gringo Perdido* (Guatemala City ☎/fax 334-2305). Shady, rustic hillside gardens hold a restaurant, bucolic camping area and simple but pleasant bungalows and dormitories. Per-person rates are US$3 to camp, US$6 for a camping bungalow with roof, beds and mosquito netting, US$10 for a dorm bunk and US$14 for rooms with private bath. Four-person bungalows, each with its own patio with hammocks and a small private dock for swimming and sunning on the lake, are US$25 per person, breakfast and dinner included. Two luxury bungalows with aircon are US$50. Overall cost is cheaper if you get a room-and-meals package. Activities include swimming, fishing, windsurfing, volleyball, basketball, bicycling and boat trips on the lake.

Farther around the lake is the luxury *Hotel Camino Real Tikal* (☎ 926-0207, caminor@infovia.com.gt), the fanciest hotel in El Petén. Located adjacent to the Biotopo

Cerro Cahuí 5km west of El Remate, the Camino Real has 120 air-conditioned rooms with all the comforts. Two restaurants and two bars keep guests happy, as do tennis courts, swimming pools, water sports on the lake, a gym and all the other top-class services. Rates are US$100/110, meals extra. (This hotel is rather remote, especially if you don't have your own wheels.)

Getting There & Away

Any bus or minibus going north from Santa Elena to Tikal can drop you at El Remate. Taxis from Santa Elena or the airport will cost US$20. Once you are in El Remate, you can hail any passing bus or minibus on the Flores-Tikal road to take you to Tikal or Flores, but traffic is light after midmorning.

AROUND LAGO DE PETÉN ITZÁ

San Andrés, a small town on the northwest side of the lake, is home to the Eco-Escuela de Español (☎/fax 928-8106, in the USA ☎ 800-429-5660 ext 264, ecoescuela@ conservation.org, www.conservation.org/ eco ecuela), a highly recommended Spanish school. Cost is US$200/220 per week for four/six hours of instruction daily, including room and board with a local family. Volunteer opportunities and excursions with this school are particularly rich, focusing heavily on cultural and ecological issues.

A few kilometers farther west, *Ni'tun Ecolodge* (☎ 201-0759, fax 926-0807, nitun@ nitun.com, www.nitun.com) is a beautiful place on 30 hectares of lakefront. Four spacious, attractive stone houses, each with three double beds, thatched roof and private patio, are US$40/60/80 single/double/triple. The restaurant here is also beautiful; a package of airport transfers, accommodations and three meals a day is US$55 per person per day. Bernie, who built and operates the hotel, is an adventurer who also runs Monkey Eco Tours (see Organized Tours under Flores).

In San José (population 3000), on the lake's northwest shore, the Bio-Itzá Spanish School (contact EcoMaya in Flores, ☎ 926-1363, 926-3321, fax 926-3322, in the USA ☎ 800-429-5660, ecomaya@guate.net, www.ecomaya.com) is another well-recommended program. The school offers 20 hours of instruction per week, with a homestay for US$200 a week, or with use of camping facilities (including hammock and mosquito net, shared kitchen

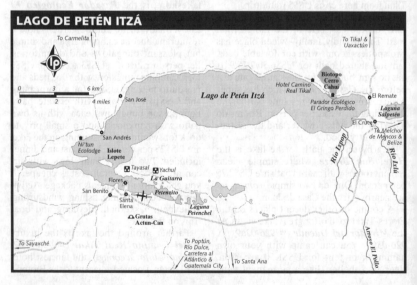

and bathroom) for US$125 a week. Students work closely with the Itzá community.

Both of these towns are most easily reached by boat from Flores. Lanchas leave when full for San Andrés (US$0.40, 30 minutes) and San José (US$0.65, 45 minutes), or you can bargain for a private boat. Buses also leave twice daily for these towns (5:30 am and noon), but it's a laborious ride and not nearly as enjoyable as going by boat.

TIKAL

Towering pyramids rise above the jungle canopy to catch the sun. Howler monkeys swing noisily through the branches of ancient trees as brightly colored parrots and toucans dart, squawking, from perch to perch. When the complex warbling song of some mysterious bird tapers off, the buzz of tree frogs provides background noise.

Certainly the most striking feature of Tikal is its architecture: steep-sided temples rise to heights of more than 44m. But Tikal is different from Chichén Itzá, Uxmal, Copán and most other great Mayan sites because it's nestled in the jungle. Its many plazas have been cleared of trees and vines, its temples uncovered and partially restored, but as you walk from one building to another you pass beneath the rain forest canopy. Rich smells of earth and vegetation, peacefulness and animal noises all contribute to an experience not offered by any other readily accessible Mayan site.

If you visit from December to February, expect some cool nights and mornings. March and April are the hottest and driest months. The rains begin in May or June, and with them come the mosquitoes – bring rain gear, repellent and if you plan on slinging a hammock, a mosquito net. July to November is muggy and buggy, though by October, the rains taper off and cooler temperatures return.

Day trips by air from Guatemala City to Tikal (landing in Flores/Santa Elena) are popular, as they allow you to get a glimpse of this spectacular site in the shortest possible time. Still, Tikal is so big, you'll need at least two days to see the major parts thoroughly.

History

Tikal is set on a small hill, which becomes evident as you walk up to the Great Plaza from the entry road. The hill, affording relief from the surrounding low-lying swampy ground, may be why the Maya settled here around 700 BC. Another reason was the abundance of flint, the valuable stone used by the ancients to make clubs, spearheads, arrowheads and knives. The wealth of flint meant good tools could be made, and flint could be exported in exchange for other goods. Within 200 years, the Maya of Tikal had begun to build stone ceremonial structures, and by 200 BC a complex of buildings stood on the site of the North Acropolis.

Classic Period The Great Plaza was beginning to assume its present shape and extent by the time of Christ. By the dawn of the Early Classic period, about AD 250, Tikal had become an important religious, cultural and commercial city with a large population. King Yax Moch Xoc, whose reign began around AD 230, is considered the founder of the dynasty that ruled Tikal thereafter.

Under a successor, King Great Jaguar Paw (who ruled in the mid-4th century), Tikal adopted a new and brutal method of warfare used by the rulers of Teotihuacán in central Mexico. Rather than meeting their adversaries on the plain of battle in hand-to-hand combat, the army of Tikal encircled their enemy and killed them by throwing spears. This first use of 'air power' among the Maya of Petén enabled Tikal to conquer Uaxactún and become the dominant kingdom in the region.

By the middle of the Classic period, in the mid-6th century, Tikal sprawled across 30 sq km and had a population of perhaps 100,000. In 553, Lord Water ascended to the throne of Caracol (in southwestern Belize), and by 562, using the same warfare methods learned from Tikal, he had conquered Tikal's king and sacrificed him. Tikal and other Petén kingdoms suffered under Caracol's rule until the late 7th century.

Tikal's Renaissance Around AD 700, a new and powerful king named Moon Double

GUATEMALA

TIKAL

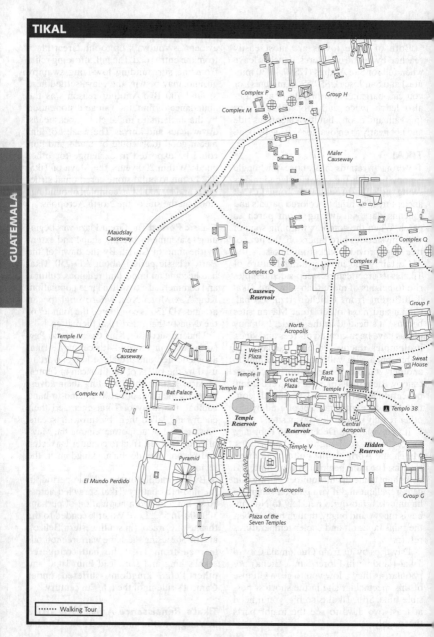

Complex P

Group H

Complex M

Maler
Causeway

Maudslay
Causeway

Complex Q

Complex R

Complex O

Causeway
Reservoir

Group F

Temple IV

North
Acropolis

Sweat
House

Tozzer
Causeway

West
Plaza

Complex N

Temple II

East
Plaza

Temple III

Bat Palace

Great
Plaza

Temple I

Templo 38

Temple
Reservoir

Palace
Reservoir

Central
Acropolis

Temple V

Hidden
Reservoir

Pyramid

El Mundo Perdido

South Acropolis

Group G

Plaza of the
Seven Temples

········· Walking Tour

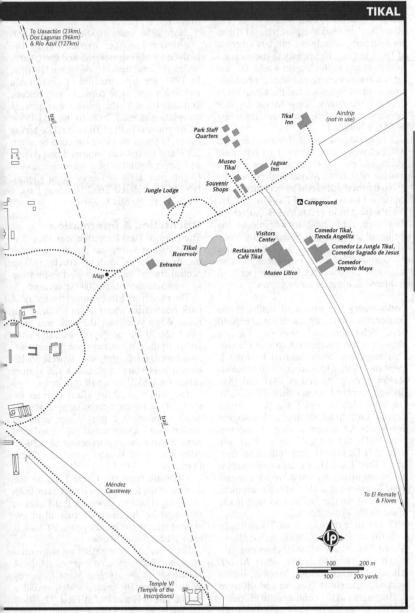

TIKAL

To Uaxactún (23km),
Dos Lagunas (96km)
& Río Azul (127km)

trail

Airstrip
(not in use)

Tikal Inn

Park Staff
Quarters

Jaguar
Inn

Museo
Tikal

Souvenir
Shops

Jungle Lodge

Campground

Visitors
Center

Comedor Tikal,
Tienda Angelita

Tikal
Reservoir

Restaurante
Café Tikal

Comedor La Jungla Tikal,
Comedor Sagrado de Jesus

Entrance

Comedor
Imperio Maya

Museo Lítico

Map

GUATEMALA

trail

Méndez
Causeway

To El Remate
& Flores

0   100   200 m
0   100   200 yards

Temple VI
(Temple of the
Inscriptions)

Comb (682–734), also called Ah Cacau (Lord Chocolate), 26th successor of Yax Moch Xoc, ascended the throne of Tikal. He restored not only the military strength of Tikal, but also its primacy as the most resplendent city in the Mayan world. He and his successors were responsible for building most of the temples around the Great Plaza that survive today. King Moon Double Comb was buried beneath the staggering height of Temple I.

The greatness of Tikal waned around 900, but it was not alone in its downfall, which was part of the mysterious general collapse of lowland Mayan civilization.

No doubt the Itzáes, who occupied Tayasal (now Flores), knew of Tikal in the Late Postclassic period (1200 to 1530). Perhaps they even came here to worship at the shrines of their old gods. Spanish missionary friars who moved through El Petén after the conquest left brief references to these junglebound structures, but these writings moldered in libraries for centuries.

Rediscovery It wasn't until 1848 that the Guatemalan government sent out an expedition, under the leadership of Modesto Méndez and Ambrosio Tut, to visit the site. This may have been inspired by John L Stephens' best-selling accounts of fabulous Mayan ruins, published in 1841 and 1843 (though Stephens never visited Tikal). Like Stephens, Méndez and Tut took an artist, Eusebio Lara, to record their archaeological discoveries. An account of their findings was published by the Berlin Academy of Science.

In 1877 Dr Gustav Bernoulli of Switzerland visited Tikal. His explorations resulted in the removal of carved wooden lintels from Temples I and IV and their shipment to Basel, where they are still on view in the Museum für Völkerkunde.

Scientific exploration of Tikal began with the arrival of English archaeologist Alfred P Maudslay in 1881; others continuing his work included Teobert Maler, Alfred M Tozzer and RE Merwin. Tozzer worked tirelessly at Tikal on and off from the beginning of the century until his death in 1954. The inscriptions at Tikal were studied and deciphered by Sylvanus G Morley.

Since 1956, archaeological research and restoration has been carried out by the University of Pennsylvania and the Guatemalan Instituto de Antropología e Historia. In 1991, the governments of Guatemala and Spain agreed to conserve and restore Temples I and V; the project was nearing completion in early 2000. In the mid-1950s an airstrip was built at Tikal to make access easier. In the early 1980s the road between Tikal and Flores was improved and paved, and direct flights to Tikal were abandoned (flights now land in Flores/Santa Elena). UNESCO declared Tikal National Park a World Heritage Site in 1979.

Orientation & Information

The ruins of Tikal lie within vast Tikal National Park, a 576-sq-km preserve containing thousands of ancient structures. The central area of the city occupied about 16 sq km and held more than 4000 structures.

The road from Flores enters the national park boundaries about 15km south of the ruins. When you enter the park you must pay US$6.50 for the day; if you enter after about 3 pm, you can have your ticket validated for the following day as well. Multilingual guides are available at the visitors center for US$20 for a half-day tour.

The area around the visitors center includes three hotels, a camping area, several small comedores, a post office, a police station, two museums and the abandoned airstrip. From the visitors center it's a 20- to 30-minute walk southwest to the Great Plaza.

The walk from the Great Plaza to the Temple of the Inscriptions is over 1km; from the Great Plaza to Complex P, it's 1km in the opposite direction. To visit all of the major building complexes you must walk at least 10km, probably more.

For complete information on the monuments at Tikal, pick up a copy of *Tikal – A Handbook of the Ancient Maya Ruins*, by William R Coe. The guide is widely available and on sale in Flores and at Tikal. *The Birds of Tikal* by Frank B Smithe (Natural History

Press, 1966), available at the Tikal museums, is a good resource for birders. For tips on birding in Tikal, see that section below.

The ruins are open from 6 am to 5 pm daily. You may be able to get permission to stay until 8 pm by applying to the Inspectorería to the west of the visitors center. Carry a flashlight if you stay after sunset or arrive before dawn, though this may be impractical, as park authorities have been cracking down on after-hours visitors.

Visitors should wear shoes with good traction. The ruins here can be slick from rain and organic matter, especially during the wet season. Also, bring adequate water, as dehydration is a real danger if you're walking around all day in the heat.

Great Plaza

Follow the signs to reach the Great Plaza. The path leads you into the plaza area around Temple I, the Temple of the Grand Jaguar. This was built to honor – and bury – King Moon Double Comb. The king may have worked out the plans for the building himself, but it was erected above his tomb by his son, who succeeded to the throne in 734. The king's rich burial goods included 180 beautiful jade objects, 90 pieces of bone carved with hieroglyphs, and pearls and stingray spines, which were used for ritual bloodletting. At the top of the 44m-high temple is a small enclosure of three rooms covered by a corbeled arch. The sapodillawood lintels over the doors were richly carved; one of them is now in a Basel museum. The lofty roofcomb that crowned the temple was originally adorned with reliefs and bright paint. It may have symbolized the 13 realms of the Mayan heaven.

Visitors were once permitted to make the dangerous climb to the top, but since at least two people tumbled to their deaths, the stairs up Temple I have been closed. Don't fret though: the views from Temple II just across the way are nearly as awe-inspiring. Temple II was once almost as high as Temple I, but now measures 38m without its roofcomb.

The North Acropolis, while not as immediately impressive as the twin temples, is of great significance. Archaeologists have un-

covered about 100 different structures, the oldest of which dates from before the time of Christ, with evidence of occupation as far back as 400 BC. The Maya built and rebuilt on top of older structures, and the many layers, combined with the elaborate burials, added sanctity and power to their temples. Look for the two huge, powerful wall masks, uncovered from an earlier structure and now protected by roofs. The final version of the Acropolis, as it stood around AD 800, had more than 12 temples atop a vast platform, many of them the work of King Moon Double Comb.

On the plaza side of the North Acropolis are two rows of stelae. Though hardly as impressive as the magnificent stelae at Copán or Quiriguá, these served the same purpose: to record the great deeds of the kings of Tikal, to sanctify their memory and to add 'power' to the temples and plazas that surrounded them.

Central Acropolis

On the south side of the Great Plaza, this maze of courtyards, little rooms and small temples is thought by many to have been a residential palace for Tikal's noble class. Others think the tiny rooms may have been used for sacred rites and ceremonies, as graffiti found within them suggest. Over the centuries the configuration of the rooms

Central Acropolis, Tikal

was repeatedly changed, suggesting perhaps that this 'palace' was in fact a noble or royal family's residence changed to accommodate different groups of relatives. A century ago, one part of the acropolis, called Maler's Palace, provided lodgings for archaeologist Teobert Maler when he worked at Tikal.

West Plaza

The West Plaza is north of Temple II. On its north side is a large Late Classic temple. To the south, across the Tozzer Causeway, is Temple III, 55m high. Yet to be uncovered, it allows you to see a temple the way the last Tikal Maya and first explorers saw them. The causeway leading to Temple IV was one of several sacred ways built among the temple complexes of Tikal, no doubt for astronomical as well as aesthetic reasons.

South Acropolis & Temple V

Due south of the Great Plaza is the South Acropolis. Excavation has hardly even begun on this huge mass of masonry covering two hectares. The palaces on top are from Late Classic times (the time of King Moon Double Comb), but earlier constructions probably go back 1000 years.

Temple V, just east of the South Acropolis, is 58m high and was built around AD 700. Unlike the other great temples, this one has rounded corners and one very tiny room at the top. The room is less than a meter deep, but its walls are up to 4.5m thick. The view (as usual) is wonderful, giving you a 'profile' of the temples on the Great Plaza. The restoration of this temple by a team of Guatemalan and Spanish archaeologists and historians was started in 1991.

Plaza of the Seven Temples

On the other side of the South Acropolis is the Plaza of the Seven Temples. The little temples, clustered together, were built in Late Classic times, though the structures beneath must go back at least a millennium. Note the skull and crossbones on the central temple (the one with the stela and altar in front). On the plaza's north side is an unusual triple ball court; another, larger version in the same design stands just south of Temple I.

El Mundo Perdido

About 400m southwest of the Great Plaza is El Mundo Perdido (the Lost World), a large complex of 38 structures with a huge pyramid in its midst. Unlike the rest of Tikal, where Late Classic construction overlays work of earlier periods, El Mundo Perdido holds buildings of many different periods. The large pyramid is thought to be essentially Preclassic (with some later repairs and renovations); the Talud-Tablero Temple (or Temple of the Three Rooms) is Early Classic; and the Temple of the Skulls is Late Classic.

The pyramid, 32m high and 80m along its base, has a stairway on each side. It had huge masks flanking each stairway but no temple structure at the top. Each side of the pyramid displays a slightly different architectural style. Tunnels dug into the pyramid by archaeologists reveal four similar pyramids beneath the outer face; the earliest (Structure 5C-54 Sub 2B) dates from 700 BC, making the pyramid the oldest Mayan structure at Tikal.

The central pyramid's flat top offers beautiful views and makes a great place for a picnic, weather permitting.

Temple IV & Complex N

Complex N, near Temple IV, is an example of the 'twin-temple' complexes popular among Tikal's rulers during the Late Classic period. These complexes are thought to have commemorated the completion of a *katun*, or 20-year cycle in the Mayan calendar. This one was built in 711 by King Moon Double Comb to mark the 14th katun of Baktun 9. The king himself is portrayed on Stela 16, one of the finest stelae at Tikal.

Temple IV, at 64m, is the highest building at Tikal. It was completed about 741, in the reign of King Moon Double Comb's son. From the base it looks like a precipitous little hill. A series of steep wooden steps and ladders take you to the top. The view is almost as good as from a helicopter – a panorama across the jungle canopy. If you stay up here for the sunset, climb down immediately thereafter, as it gets dark on the path quickly.

Temple of the Inscriptions (Temple VI)

Compared to Copán or Quiriguá, there are relatively few inscriptions on buildings at Tikal. The exception is this temple, 1.2km southeast of the Great Plaza. On the rear of the 12m-high roofcomb is a long inscription; the sides and cornice of the roofcomb bear glyphs as well. The inscriptions give us the date AD 766. Stela 21 and Altar 9, standing before the temple, date from 736. The stela had been badly damaged (part of it was converted into a *metate* for grinding corn!) but has now been repaired.

Warning: The Temple of the Inscriptions is remote from the other complexes, and there have been incidents of robbery and rape of single travelers and couples in the past. Though safety has been greatly improved at Tikal, ask a guard before you make the trek out here, or come in a group.

Northern Complexes

About 1km north of the Great Plaza is Complex P. Like Complex N, it's a Late Classic twin-temple complex that probably commemorated the end of a katún.

Complex M, next to it, was partially torn down by the Late Classic Maya to provide building materials for the causeway – now named after Alfred Maudslay – that runs southwest to Temple IV. Group H had some interesting graffiti within its temples.

Complexes Q and R, about 300m due north of the Great Plaza, are very Late Classic twin-pyramid complexes with stelae and altars standing before the temples. Complex Q is perhaps the best example of the twin-temple type, as it has been mostly restored. Stela 22 and Altar 10 are excellent examples of Late Classic Tikal relief carving, dated 771.

Complex O, due west of these complexes on the west side of the Maler Causeway, has an uncarved stela and altar in its north enclosure. An uncarved stela? The whole point of stelae was to record great happenings. Why did this one remain uncarved?

Museums

Tikal has two museums. **Museo Lítico**, the larger museum, is in the visitors center. It houses a number of stelae and carved stones from the ruins. Outside is a large relief map showing how Tikal would have looked during the Late Classic period, around AD 800. Admission is free.

The smaller **Museo Tikal** is just beyond the Jungle Lodge. It has some fascinating exhibits, including the burial goods of King Moon Double Comb, carved jade, inscribed bones, shells, stelae, ceramics and other items recovered from the excavations. Admission is US$1.50.

Both museums are open 9 am to 5 pm Monday to Friday, 9 am to 4 pm Saturday and Sunday.

Birding

Around 300 bird species (migratory and endemic) have been recorded at Tikal. Early morning is the best time to go birding, and even amateurs will have their share of sightings here. Ask at the visitors center about early-morning and late-afternoon tours led by accomplished birder Luis Antonio Oliveros. Bring binoculars if you have them, tread quietly and be patient and you will probably see some of the following birds in the areas specified:

• tody motmots, four trogon species and royal fly-catchers around the Temple of the Inscriptions

• two oriole species, keel-billed toucans and collared aracaris in El Mundo Perdido

• great curassows, three species of woodpecker, crested guans, plain chachalacas and three tanager species around Complex P

• three kingfisher species, jacanas, blue herons, two sandpiper species and great kiskadees at the Tikal Reservoir near the entrance; tiger herons in the huge ceiba tree along the entrance path

• red-capped and white-collared manakins near Complex Q; emerald toucanets near Complex R

Trails

The Sendero Benilj'a'a, a 3km trail with three sections, begins in front of the Jungle Lodge. Ruta Monte Medio and Ruta Monte Medio Alto (both one hour) are accessible year-round. Ruta Monte Bajo (35 minutes) is accessible only in summer. A short interpretive trail called *El Misterio de la Vida*

Maya (The Mystery of Maya Life) leads to the Great Plaza.

Organized Tours

All the hotels can arrange guided tours of the ruins, as well as tours to other places in the region such as Uaxactún, Ceibal, Yaxjá, Nakum. The Jungle Lodge is a good place to ask about this.

Places to Stay

Intrepid visitors used to convince park guards (with a US$5 'tip') to let them sleep atop Temple IV, but this is extremely rare these days; no one is in major concern. If you are caught in the ruins after hours, you'll likely be escorted out. Nowadays, the best way to catch solitude at the ruins and get an early glimpse of the wildlife is to camp at the entrance.

Other than camping, there are only three places to stay at Tikal. Most are booked in advance by tour groups. In recent years, travelers have logged numerous complaints of price gouging, unacceptable accommodations and 'lost' reservations at these hotels. And the value you get at these places compared to hotels in the rest of the country is laughable. It may be best to stay in Flores or El Remate and visit Tikal on day trips.

On the other hand, staying at Tikal enables you to relax and savor the dawn and dusk, when most of the jungle fauna can be seen and heard. If you'd like the thrill of staying overnight at Tikal, the easiest way is to forget about making reservations (which can be frustrating) and take a tour. Any travel agency can arrange one including lodging, meals, a guided tour of the ruins and airfare. The Adventure Travel Center (☎/fax 832-0162, viarealguate.net), 5a Avenida Nte 25-B, near the arch in Antigua, is one, and there are plenty of others. Reservations aren't necessary if you just want to camp.

Camping Cheapest of Tikal's lodgings is the official camping area by the entrance road and airstrip. Set in a large, open lawn with some trees for shade, it has tent spaces on the grass and also on concrete platforms under palapas; you can hang your hammock

here, too. Water for the toilets and showers is pretty dependable, since it's brought in. Camping is US$4.50 per person. The Restaurant Café Tikal, across the way near the museum, rents camping equipment at reasonable rates.

The Jaguar Inn (see below) has a smaller camping area with bathroom and shower facilities. Camping is US$3.25 per person with your own tent or hammock; they don't rent gear.

Hotels Largest and most attractive of these middling hotels is the *Jungle Lodge* (*Guatemala City* ☎ 476-8775, 477-0754, fax 476-0294, reservaciones@junglelodge.guate .com, www.junglelodge.guate.com), built originally to house the archaeologists excavating and restoring Tikal. It has 34 agreeable rooms in duplex bungalows, each room with private hot bath and two double beds, for US$48/60/70/80 single/double/triple/quad. In an older section are 12 much less attractive rooms with shared bath for US$20/25 single/double. Amenities include a swimming pool, large garden grounds and a restaurant/bar with breakfast for US$5, lunch or dinner for US$10.

Tikal Inn (*☎/fax 594-6944 or 926-0065*), past the Jaguar Inn as you walk away from the small museum toward the old airstrip, is the next best choice. It has 17 rooms in the main building, as well as bungalows, which are slightly nicer, plus gardens, a pool and restaurant. The rooms are simple and clean, and all have private hot bath and ceiling fan. The walls, however, extend only partway up to the roof, affording little conversational privacy. Rooms are US$27/35 in the main building, US$55/82 in the bungalows. The electricity operates only from 11 am to 10 pm.

The *Jaguar Inn* (☎ 926-0002, solis@ quetzal.net), to the right of the museum as you approach on the access road, has nine bungalow rooms with private bath and a ceiling fan for US$30/48/66/78 in high season; US$20/32/44/52 in low. Dorm beds are US$10 per person. The restaurant serves breakfast for US$3, lunch and dinner for around US$6.

Places to Eat

As you arrive in Tikal, look on the right-hand side of the road for the little comedores: *Comedor Imperio Maya, Comedor La Jungla Tikal, Comedor Tikal, Comedor Sagrado de Jesus* and *Tienda Angelita*. The Comedor Imperio Maya, first on the way into the site, seems to be the favorite. You can buy cold drinks and snacks in the adjoining shop. All the comedores are simple and rustic and serve huge plates of fairly tasty food at low prices. The meal of the day is usually roast chicken, rice, salad and fruit (enough to feed two people) for US$4. All of these places are open from around 5 am to 9 pm daily.

Across the street from the comedores, the *Restaurant Café Tikal*, in the visitors center, serves fancier food at fancier prices. *Lomito* (tenderloin of beef) and other meats are featured, at US$10 a portion. Plates of fruit cost less. All the hotels also have restaurants.

Picnic tables beneath shelters lie just off Tikal's Great Plaza; itinerant soft-drink peddlers stand by, but no food is sold. If you want to spend all day at the ruins without having to walk back to the comedores, carry food with you.

Getting There & Away

For transportation details to and from Flores/Santa Elena, see that section. Coming from Belize, you can get off the bus at El Cruce/Puente Ixlú. Wait for a northbound bus or minibus – or hitch a ride with an obliging tourist – to take you the remaining 35km to Tikal. Note that there is very little northbound traffic after lunch. If you come to Puente Ixlú in the afternoon, it's probably a good idea to continue to Flores or El Remate for the night rather than risk being stranded at El Cruce.

You don't need a car to get to Tikal, but a 4WD vehicle of your own can be useful for visiting Uaxactún. If you're driving, fill your fuel tank in Flores; no fuel is available at Tikal or Uaxactún.

Chicle & Chewing Gum

Chicle, a pinkish to reddish-brown gum, is actually the coagulated milky sap, or latex, of the sapodilla tree (Achras zapota), a tropical evergreen native to the Yucatán Peninsula and Central America. Chicleros (chicle workers) enter the forests and cut large V-shaped gashes in the sapodillas' trunks, as high up as 9m. The sap runs from the wounds and down the trunk into a container at the base. After being boiled, it is shaped into blocks for shipping. The cuts often kill the tree, and thus chicle harvesting tends to result in the serious depletion of sapodilla forests. Even if the tree survives the first round of cuts, a typical tree used for harvesting chicle has a life span of just 10 years.

First used as a substitute for natural rubber (to which the sapodilla is related), by about 1890 chicle was best known as the main ingredient in chewing gum.

As a result of war research for a rubber substitute during the 1940s, synthetic substitutes were developed for chicle. Now chewing gum is made mostly from these synthetic substitutes. However, in the northern reaches of the Petén, chicleros still live in the forest for months at a time harvesting the sap for gum. To check out some real chicle gum, visit www.junglegum.com.

– Tom Brosnahan

GUATEMALA

UAXACTÚN

Uaxactún (wah-shahk-**toon**), 23km north of Tikal along a poor, unpaved road through the jungle, was Tikal's political and military rival in Late Preclassic times. It was conquered by Tikal's King Great Jaguar Paw in the mid-4th century, and was subservient to its great sister to the south for centuries thereafter.

When you arrive at Uaxactún, sign your name in the register at the guard's hut (at the edge of the derelict airstrip). About halfway down the airstrip, roads go off to the left and to the right to the ruins.

Villagers in Uaxactún live in houses lined up along the airstrip. They make a living by collecting chicle, *pimienta* (allspice) and *xate* (**sha**-tay; a frond exported for floral arrangements) from the surrounding forest.

Ruins

The pyramids at Uaxactún were uncovered and stabilized so that no further deterioration would result; they were not restored. White mortar is the mark of the repair crews, who patched cracks in the stone to prevent water and roots from entering. Much of the work on the famous Temple E-VII-Sub was done by Earthwatch volunteers in 1974.

Turn right from the airstrip to reach Groups E and H, a 10- to 15-minute walk. Perhaps the most significant temple here is E-VII-Sub, among the earliest intact temples excavated, with foundations going back perhaps to 2000 BC. It lay beneath much larger structures, which have been stripped away. On its flat top are sockets for the poles that would have supported a wood-and-thatch temple.

About a 20-minute walk to the northwest of the runway are Groups A and B. At Group A, early excavators sponsored by Andrew Carnegie simply cut into the sides of the temples indiscriminately, looking for graves. Sometimes they used dynamite. This unfortunate work destroyed many of the temples, which are now in the process of being reconstructed.

The ruins are always open and accessible, and no admission is charged. However, the turnoff onto the Uaxactún road is inside the gate to Tikal, so you must pay the US$6.50 admission fee there.

Organized Tours

Tours to Uaxactún can be arranged at the hotels in Tikal. The Jungle Lodge, for example, offers a trip to Uaxactún departing daily at 8 am and returning at 1 pm, in time to meet the 2 pm buses back to Flores. The trip costs US$60 for one to four people, split among the number of people going, or US$15 per person for over four people.

Places to Stay & Eat

If you have your own gear, you can camp at one of several places. *Eco Camping*, at the entrance to the larger group of ruins, is an organized campground with basic cabins.

Posada y Restaurante Campamento El Chiclero, near the airstrip, is a primitive place with seven musty thatch-roofed rooms with walls going only part way up and screen the rest of the way. Rooms are US$4.50 per person, or you can pitch a tent. Bathrooms are shared, and there's no electricity. It's a 10-minute walk from the ruins. Trips can be arranged here to other places in the area, including Parque Nacional El Mirador-Dos Lagunas-Río Azul, La Muralla, Nakbé and Manantial.

Getting There & Away

During the rainy season (from May to October), you may find it difficult to get to Uaxactún. At other times of the year, ask in Flores or Tikal about the condition of the road. You may be advised to make the hour-long drive only in a 4WD vehicle.

A bus operates daily between Santa Elena and Uaxactún, stopping at Tikal on the way. The cost is US$2.50 for the three-hour ride from Santa Elena, or US$1 (one hour) from Tikal. The bus departs Uaxactún daily at 6 am and departs Santa Elena at 1 pm for the return trip.

If you're driving, fill your fuel tank in Flores; no fuel is available at Tikal or Uaxactún. You might also want to pack some food and drink, though beverages and snacks are available in the village at Uaxactún. You can

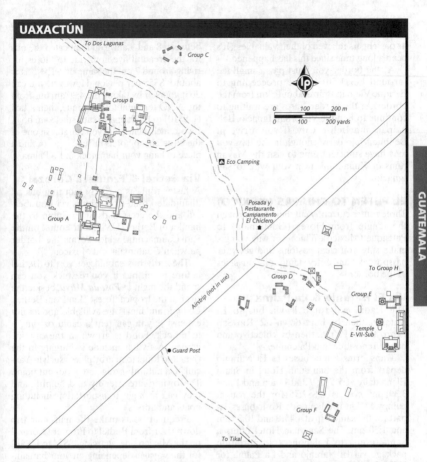

UAXACTÚN

To Dos Lagunas

Group C

Group B

Group A

Eco Camping

Posada y
Restaurante
Campamento
El Chiclero

To Group H

Airstrip (not in use)

Group D

Group E

Temple
E-VII-Sub

Guard Post

Group F

To Tikal

0   100   200 m
0   100   200 yards

GUATEMALA

hire a taxi from Flores to Uaxactún for about
US$50; bargain hard.

From Uaxactún it's another 104km to the
Río Azul ruins, or 88km to San Andrés.

EASTWARD TO BELIZE

It's 100km from Flores/Santa Elena east to
Melchor de Mencos, the Guatemalan town
on the border with Belize. You can take a
bus from Santa Elena to Melchor de
Mencos, where you can transfer to the Belizean side. Alternatively, the San Juan
Hotel shuttle bus leaves Santa Elena at
5 am and goes all the way to Belize City,
connecting with the boat to Caye Caulker
and Ambergris Caye. This shuttle enables
travelers to avoid spending the night in
seedy Belize City. See the Flores/Santa
Elena section for details on buses.

The road from Flores to El Cruce/Puente
Ixlú is good and fast. If you're coming from
Tikal, start early in the morning and get off
at El Cruce to catch a bus or hitch a ride
east. For the fastest, most reliable service,
however, it's best to be on that 5 am bus.

East of El Cruce the road goes to Melchor
de Mencos; the trip takes two hours. In the
past, there was guerrilla and bandit activity

along this road – there's an extremely remote chance that your bus could be stopped and its passengers relieved of their valuables. (It's been a long time since this has happened.)

At the border you must pay a small fee (around US$1.50) before proceeding to Benque Viejo in Belize, about 3km from the border. At the border, buses are waiting to continue to Benque Viejo, San Ignacio, Belmopan and Belize City. If you arrive in Benque Viejo early enough in the day, you may have sufficient time to visit the Mayan ruins of Xunantunich on your way to San Ignacio.

EL PETÉN TO CHIAPAS (MEXICO)

Three routes currently cut their way through the jungle from Flores (Guatemala) to Palenque (Mexico). Whichever way you go, make sure you clear customs and get your passport exit and entry stamps on both sides of the border.

Via El Naranjo & La Palma

The traditional route is via bus to El Naranjo, then by boat down the Río San Pedro to La Palma, then by colectivo and bus to Tenosique and Palenque.

Transportes Pinita buses to El Naranjo depart from the San Juan Hotel in Santa Elena daily at 5, 7, 8, 9 and 11 am and 1 and 3:30 pm; cost is US$2.75 for the rough, bumpy, 125km, five-hour ride. Rosío buses depart for the same trip at 4:45, 8 and 10:30 am and 1:30 pm. The San Juan Hotel offers a Santa Elena to Palenque transportation package via El Naranjo and La Palma for US$30 per person; departures at 5 am daily.

El Naranjo is a hamlet with a few thatched huts, large military barracks, an immigration post and a few basic lodgings. From El Naranjo you must catch a boat on the river around midday for the four-hour cruise to the border town of La Palma (US$20, bargain *hard*). From La Palma you can go by colectivo or bus to Tenosique (1½ hours), then by bus or combi to Emiliano Zapata (one hour, 40km) and from there by bus or combi to Palenque.

Going in the reverse direction, travel agencies in Palenque offer to get you from Palenque to La Palma by minibus in time to catch the boat to El Naranjo, which departs between 8 and 9 am. You then catch the bus for the dreadful five-hour ride to Flores, arriving around 7 pm the same day. The cost is about US$55 per person. However, you can do it yourself by taking the 4:30 am bus from the ADO terminal to Tenosique, then a taxi (US$10) to La Palma to catch the 8 am boat. If you catch a later bus, you can stay at one of the basic, cheap hotels in Tenosique or find a place to hang your hammock in La Palma.

Via Bethel & Frontera Corozal

A faster route is by early morning bus on dilapidated road from Flores via La Libertad and the crossroads at El Subín to the hamlet of Bethel (US$3, four hours) on the Río Usumacinta, which forms the border between Guatemala and Mexico.

The early bus should get you to Bethel before noon, but if you're stuck you can spend the night at *Posada Maya*, beside the river in the tropical forest 1km from Bethel. Lodging and meals are available, and it's not expensive; you can rent a cabin or sling a hammock. Food is grown in the organic garden. Activities include swimming in the river and tours to nearby places such as Yaxchilán, a natural spring and a lookout point. The owners are friendly and helpful, and they can arrange transportation including boats and horses.

Frequent boats make the half-hour trip down river from Bethel to Frontera Corozal on the Mexico side, charging US$4 to US$12 for the voyage, depending on your bargaining power and how many passengers are going.

Frontera Corozal (formerly Frontera Echeverría) has a restaurant and primitive accommodations, but you're better off taking one of the colectivos that wait for passengers to Palenque. The last colectivo tends to leave around 2 or 3 pm. The San Juan Hotel in Santa Elena also offers an all-inclusive transportation package to Palenque for US$30, departing daily at 5 am and arriving in Palenque by early afternoon.

From Frontera Corozal, a chartered boat to the Yaxchilán archaeological site might cost US$60, but sometimes you can hitch a ride with a group for US$10 or so; this is tough in the off-season. Buses from Frontera Corozal go to Palenque (US$5, 4½ hours).

Coming from Palenque, you can take a bus to Frontera Corozal (US$4, three hours), then a boat upstream (25 minutes to the Posada Maya, 35 minutes to the village of Bethel), either staying overnight at the Posada Maya or continuing on a bus to Flores.

In Palenque, travel agencies may insist that you can't do the trip on your own – that you must sign up for their US$30 trip – and that there is no place to stay overnight at the border. Not so! These organized trips save you some hassle, but you can do the same thing yourself for half the price. Just be sure to hit the road as early as possible in the morning.

Via Sayaxché, Pipiles & Benemérito

From Sayaxché, you can negotiate a ride on one of the cargo boats for the eight-hour trip (US$6.50) down the Río de la Pasión via Pipiles (the Guatemalan border post) to Benemérito, in Chiapas. These cargo boats leave when they have sufficient cargo and people. From Benemérito, proceed by bus or boat to the ruins at Yaxchilán and Bonampak, then onward to Palenque. There are also buses that run directly between Benemérito and Palenque (US$12, 10 hours).

SAYAXCHÉ & CEIBAL

The town of Sayaxché, 61km south of Flores through the jungle, is the closest settlement to a half dozen Mayan archaeological sites, including Aguateca, Altar de Los Sacrificios, Ceibal, Dos Pilas, El Caribe, Itzán, La Amelia and Tamarindito. Of these, Ceibal on the Río de la Pasión, is currently the best restored and most interesting ruins, partly because of its Mayan monuments but also thanks to the river voyage and jungle walk necessary to reach it.

Dos Pilas, presently under excavation, is not equipped to receive overnight visitors without their own camping gear. However, in good weather, you can make the trek in four hours on foot. From Dos Pilas, the minor sites of Tamarindito and Aguateca may be reached on foot and by boat, but they are unrestored, covered in jungle and of interest only to the very intrepid. Campgrounds are available at all these sites.

Sayaxché itself is of little interest, but its few basic services allow you to eat and stay overnight in this region.

Orientation & Information

The bus from Santa Elena drops you on the north bank of the Río de la Pasión. The main part of town is on the south bank. Frequent ferries cross the river; US$0.15.

The Banoro on the main street changes cash and traveler's checks at a weak rate. A block up the hill and to your right is a Banrural that will change money. The post office is way off the main drag near the radio station; head for the radio tower and ask passersby to steer you in the right direction.

Ceibal

Unimportant during the Classic Period, Ceibal grew rapidly thereafter, attaining a population of perhaps 10,000 by AD 900. Much of the population growth may have been due to immigration from what is now Chiapas, in Mexico, because the art and culture of Ceibal seems to have changed markedly during the same period. The Postclassic period saw the decline of Ceibal, after which its low ruined temples were quickly covered by a thick carpet of jungle.

Today, Ceibal is not one of the most impressive Mayan sites, but the journey to Ceibal is among the most memorable. A two-hour voyage on the jungle-bound Río de la Pasión brings you to a primitive dock. After landing, you clamber up a narrow, rocky path beneath gigantic ceiba trees and ganglions of jungle vines to reach the archaeological zone.

Smallish temples, many of them still (or again) covered with jungle, surround two principal plazas. In front of a few temples, and standing seemingly alone on paths deeply shaded by the jungle canopy, are magnificent stelae, their intricate carvings still in excellent condition. It takes about two hours to explore the site.

Organized Tours

Viajes Don Pedro (☎/fax 928-6109), on the riverbank, is run by the affable Pedro Mendéz. He can arrange transportation to any of the area sites. Half-day trips for one to three passengers to Ceibal or Dos Pilas are US$33; to Aguateca it's US$40. These prices are for transportation only, but guides can be contracted here too. Longer camping trips can be arranged, as can journeys to the Altar de Los Sacrificios and Yaxchilán and Bonampak, near the Mexican border.

Viajes Turísticos & Restaurant La Montaña (☎ 928-6169/14, fax 928-6168), just up from Banoro, is another outfit running tours to Ceibal (US$60 for up to five passengers) and Aguateca (US$70 for up to eight passengers), including guide. All-inclusive four-day, three-night camping trips visiting Ceibal, Dos Pilas and to Aguateca are also offered here for US$300 per person, minimum four people. Bookings can be made here for the Hotel Ecológico Posada Caribe (see Places to Stay & Eat, below).

Places to Stay & Eat

Hotel Guayacán (☎ 926-6111), just up from the dock on the south side of the river in Sayaxché, is basic and serviceable. Rooms cost US$13 single or double with shared bath, US$16 with private bath. The *Hotel Mayapán*, up the street to the left, has some cell-like rooms for US$2 per person. Upstairs are much better, cleanish rooms with private bath and fan for US$5.25/9.

The *Hotel Posada Segura* is the best budget option here. Clean rooms with good beds and fan are US$4 per person, shared bath, or US$7.75 per person, private bath. To get there, take your first right up from the river, follow this road until it dead ends, then hook a left.

The *Hotel Ecológico Posada Caribe* (☎ 928-6114/69, fax 928-6168, in Guatemala City ☎/fax 230-6588), on Laguna Petexbatún, has rooms that cost US$22 per person with kitchen privileges or US$54 per person with three meals a day.

Restaurant La Montaña serves tasty roasted chicken and other simple dishes at reasonable prices. Around the corner, *El Botanero Restaurant Café-Bar* is a dark, funky place chock full of atmosphere. It serves a variety of beef, chicken and seafood dishes starting around US$3.25. There's a full bar. *Restaurant Yaxkin* is typical of the other few eateries in town: basic, family-run and inexpensive.

Getting There & Away

Day trips to Ceibal are organized by various agencies and drivers in Santa Elena, Flores and Tikal; cost is about US$30 per person roundtrip. It can be done cheaper on your own, but this is significantly less convenient.

Transportes Pinita buses depart from Santa Elena at 5:30, 7, 8, 9 and 10:30 am and 1 and 3:30 pm for Sayaxché (US$1.50, two hours). From here you can arrange a tour with a travel agency (see Organized Tours, earlier) or strike a deal with one of the lancheros lingering by the river. From the river, it's less than 30 minutes' walk to Ceibal. You should hire a guide to see the site, as some of the finest stelae are off the plazas in the jungle. Most lancheros conveniently also serve as guides.

Buses leave Sayaxché for Flores from across the river at 5, 6 and 11 am and 1 pm. There is also a Fuentes del Norte departure to Guatemala City at 11 am (US$9, 14 hours).

REMOTE MAYAN SITES

Several sites of interest to archaeology buffs and adventure travelers are now open for limited tourism. Few of these sites can be visited without a guide, but many businesses in Flores and Santa Elena offer trips to sites deep in the jungle (see Organized Tours in those sections earlier). Few of these tours offer anything approaching comfort, and you should be prepared for buggy, basic conditions.

The ceremonial site of Yaxjá, on the lake of the same name, is about 48km east of El Remate. Scholars believe this site may have been a vacation spot for Maya nobility during the Classic period. The several sets of ruins here include a large plaza and two temples. A ruined observatory sits on Topoxté island in the middle of the lake.

El Perú, 62km northwest from Flores, lies along the Scarlet Macaw Trail. The trek starts in Paso Caballos and continues by boat along the Río San Pedro. Several important structures here have been dated to between AD 300 and 900. Archaeologists believe El Perú was an important commercial center.

The archaeological site of **El Zotz** is about 25km west of Tikal. Zotz means 'bat,' and you'll interact with plenty of them on a trek here. Among the many unexcavated mounds and ruins at the site is Devil's Pyramid, which is so tall that from its summit you can see over the canopy to the temples of Tikal. Trips to El Zotz can be extended to include a trek to Tikal.

El Mirador is buried within the farthest reaches of the Petén jungle, just 7km from the Mexican border. A trip here involves an arduous trek (60km roundtrip) in the most primitive conditions. The metropolis at El Mirador flourished between 150 BC and AD 150, when it was abandoned for mysterious reasons. The site holds the tallest pyramid ever built in the Mayan world: El Tigre is over 60m high, and its base covers some 18,000 sq meters. It's twin, La Danta (Tapir), though technically smaller, soars higher because it's built on a rise. From atop La Danta pyramid, some 105m above the forest floor, virgin canopy stretches as far as your eye can see. There are hundreds of buildings at El Mirador, but almost all of these structures are still hidden beneath the jungle canopy.

This trip is not for the faint of heart. For more on this incredible site, see the September, 1987 *National Geographic* article 'An Early Maya Metropolis Uncovered: El Mirador.' This is the most thorough, mainstream investigative report ever written about the site.

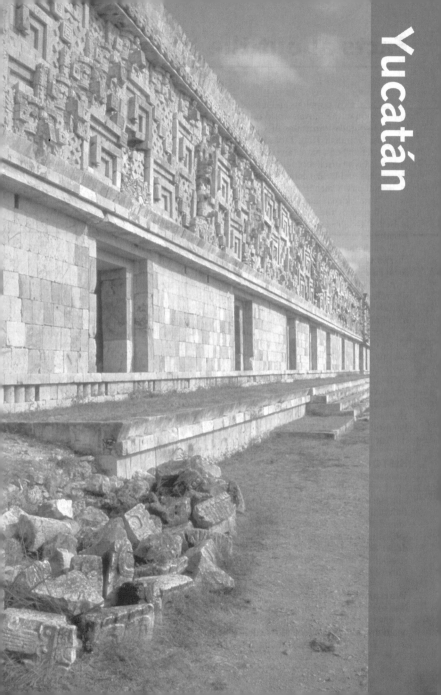

Facts about the Yucatán

The largest, most populous and most developed region of the Mayan world is in Mexico. The southeastern states of Campeche, Chiapas, Quintana Roo, Tabasco and Yucatán together boast more (around 1400) and bigger Mayan archaeological sites than Guatemala and Belize combined. The ruins of Bonampak, Chichén Itzá, Cobá, Palenque, Uxmal, Yaxchilán and other sites are equaled only by the great cities of Caracol in Belize, Tikal in Guatemala and Copán in Honduras.

Though the 'modern' Maya of Mexico cherish their ancient culture, most of them seem more distant from it than the Maya of highland Guatemala do. The exception to this rule is highland Chiapas, where Indian cultures are basically an extension of those found in Guatemala's highlands.

There is much more to Mexico than the Maya, of course. The country's prime international resort, Cancún, is here, and each of the region's colonial cities – Campeche, Mérida, San Cristóbal de Las Casas and Valladolid – has its particular charm.

Though this part of the Mayan world includes Chiapas, Tabasco and the Yucatán Peninsula, in this book it is all referred to as the Yucatán.

HISTORY

Geographically removed from the heart of Mexico, the colonists of the Yucatán Peninsula participated little in Mexico's War of Independence. Even though the Yucatán joined liberated Mexico, the peninsula's long isolation gave it a strong sense of independence, and this Mayan region desired little subsequent interference from Mexico City.

War of the Castes

Not long after gaining freedom from the Spanish, the Yucatecan ruling classes were again dreaming of independence, this time from Mexico, and perhaps union with the USA. With these goals in mind, and in anticipation of an invasion from Mexico, the *hacendados* (landowners) made the mistake of arming and training their Maya peons as local militias. Trained to use European weaponry, the Maya envisioned a release from their own misery and boldly rebelled against their Yucatecan masters.

The War of the Castes began in 1847 in Valladolid, a city known for its particularly strict and oppressive laws. The Maya were forbidden to enjoy the main plaza or the prominent streets and had to keep to the backstreets and the outskirts. The Maya rebels quickly gained control of the city in an orgy of killing, looting and vengeance. Supplied with arms and ammunition by the British through Belize, they spread relentlessly across the peninsula.

In little more than a year the Maya revolutionaries had driven their oppressors from every part of the peninsula except Mérida and the walled city of Campeche. Seeing the whites' cause as hopeless, the region's governor was about to abandon Mérida when the rebels saw the annual appearance of the winged ant. In Mayan mythology, corn (the staff of life) must be planted at the first sighting of the winged ant. If the sowing is delayed, Chac, the rain god, will be affronted and respond with a drought. The rebels abandoned the attack and went home to plant the corn. This gave the whites and mestizos time to regroup and receive aid from their erstwhile adversary, the government in Mexico City.

The Talking Cross

The counterrevolution against the Maya was without quarter and vicious in the extreme. Between 1848 and 1855 the Indian population of Yucatán was halved. Some Maya combatants sought refuge in the jungles of southern Quintana Roo. There they were inspired to continue fighting by a religious leader working with a ventriloquist, who in 1850 at Chan Santa Cruz made a sacred cross 'talk' (the cross was an important

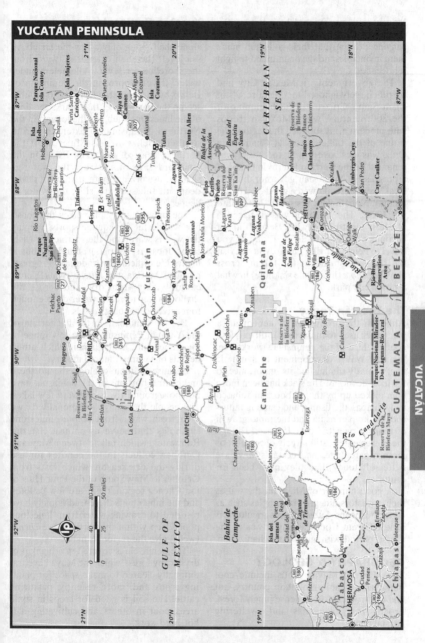

Mayan religious symbol long before the coming of Christianity). The talking cross convinced them that their gods had made them invincible, and they continued to fight for decades.

The governments in Mexico City and Mérida largely ignored the Maya rebels of Chan Santa Cruz until the beginning of the 20th century, when Mexican troops with modern arms subdued the region. The shrine of the talking cross at Chan Santa Cruz was destroyed, and the town was renamed Felipe Carrillo Puerto in honor of a progressive Yucatecan governor, but the local Maya were allowed a good deal of autonomy. Nonetheless, resistance lasted into the 1920s. The Yucatán was declared a Mexican 'territory' only in 1936 and did not become a state until 1974. Today, if you travel to Felipe Carrillo Puerto, you can visit the restored shrine of the talking cross above a *cenote* (limestone sinkhole) in what is now a city park.

The Yucatán Today

Although the production of henequen (a plant fiber used to make rope) still employs about a third of the peninsula's workforce, the post-WWII development of synthetic fibers greatly diminished its importance to the local economy. The slack has been more than picked up by the oil boom in Tabasco and Chiapas, the fishing and canning industries of the peninsula and the rapid growth of tourism over the past 15 years. Though the power elite is still largely of Spanish or mestizo parentage, the Yucatán's Maya are better off today than they have been for centuries.

A good number of Maya till the soil as their ancestors did, growing staples such as corn and beans. Subsistence agriculture is little different from the way it was in the Classic period, with minimal mechanization.

GEOGRAPHY & GEOLOGY

The Mexican Mayan lands include cool pine-clad volcanic mountain country, hot and dry tropical forest, dense jungly forest, broad grassy savannas and sweltering coastal plains.

Yucatán Peninsula

The Yucatán Peninsula is one vast, flat limestone shelf rising only a few meters above sea level. The shelf extends outward from the shoreline for several kilometers under water. If you approach the peninsula or Belize by air, you should have no trouble seeing the barrier reef that marks the limit of the limestone shelf. It's the longest in the Northern Hemisphere, extending from southern Belize to Isla Mujeres off the northern coast of Quintana Roo. On the landward side of the reef the water is shallow, usually no more than 5m or 10m deep; on the seaward side, the water is deeper.

The underwater shelf makes the coastline wonderful for aquatic sports, keeping the waters warm and the marine life (fish, crabs, lobsters, tourists) abundant, but it makes life difficult for traders; at Progreso, north of Mérida, the *muelle* (wharf) must extend 6.5km from dry land across the shallow water to reach water deep enough to receive oceangoing vessels.

The only anomaly in the flat terrain of the Yucatán Peninsula is the low range of the Puuc Hills, near Uxmal, which attain heights of several hundred meters.

Because of their geology, the northern and central portions of the peninsula have no aboveground rivers and very few lakes. The people there have traditionally drawn their fresh water from *cenotes*, limestone sinkholes that serve as natural cisterns. Rainwater, which falls between May and October, collects in the cenotes for use during the dry season, which lasts from October to May. South of the Puuc Hills, in the Chenes region, there are few cenotes, and the inhabitants there traditionally have resorted to drawing water from limestone pools deep within the earth. These *chenes* (wells) give the region its name.

The peninsula is covered in a blanket of dry thorny forest, which the Maya have traditionally cleared to make space for planting crops and, more recently, pasturing cattle. The soil is good for crops in some areas, poor in others, and cultivating it is hot, hard work.

Tabasco

West of the peninsula along the Gulf Coast is the state of Tabasco – low, well-watered and humid country that is mostly covered in equatorial rain forest. The relative humidity in some places averages 78%. The lush rain forest is endangered by farmers and cattle ranchers, who slash and burn it to make way for more crops and cattle, which in this climate are guaranteed to thrive.

Besides its agricultural wealth, Tabasco is one of Mexico's most important regions of petroleum production.

Chiapas

Chiapas is a huge state comprising several distinct topographical areas. The northern part of the state is lowland with low hills similar to those of Tabasco, and is well watered, sparsely populated and dotted with important Mayan cities such as Palenque, Toniná, Bonampak and Yaxchilán.

The central and south-central area is mountainous and volcanic, rising from several hundred meters in the west to more than 3900m in the southeast, near the Guatemalan border. Annual rainfall varies from less than 40cm at Tuxtla Gutiérrez, the state capital, to more than 200cm on the mountain slopes facing the Pacific Ocean. The high country around San Cristóbal de Las Casas is known locally as the *tierra fría* (cold country) because of its altitude and many cloudy days. The mountains in this area are covered in forests of oak and pine.

The Continental Divide follows the ridge of the Sierra Madre, which towers above the Pacific littoral. South and west of the ridge is the Pacific slope of the mountains and the coastal plain, which is known as the Soconusco. Rainfall there is abundant, as the weather arrives from the west and the wet clouds dump their loads as they ascend the high mountains. Cotton is the choice crop on the plain, but on the mountain slopes (up to 1400m) it's cacao and coffee.

CLIMATE
Yucatán Peninsula

The temperature is always hot on the peninsula, often reaching as high as 40°C (104°F) in the heat of day. From May to October, the rainy season makes the air hot and humid. From October to May it is hot and dry, though there are occasional showers even in the dry season. Violent but brief storms called *nortes* can roll in on any afternoon, their black clouds, high winds and torrents of rain followed within an hour by bright sun and utterly blue sky.

Tabasco & Chiapas

The low-lying state of Tabasco is always hot and muggy, but it's more pleasant in the dry season (October to May) than the rainy season. As on the Yucatán Peninsula, it's always hot; unlike the peninsula, the area is not seasonally crowded with tourists.

Mountainous central Chiapas can get lots of rain in summer, but at least it's cool at the higher altitudes. In winter the air is cool most of the time, warming up considerably on sunny days, though many days are overcast. In the tierra fría around San Cristóbal de Las Casas, mornings and evenings are usually chilly (a thrill after the sticky heat of Palenque!) and the nights downright cold (though frost is rare), especially if it's raining, which it often is from May to October.

The Soconusco is hot and humid all the time and frequently rainy in summer.

GOVERNMENT & POLITICS

In theory the United Mexican States (Estados Unidos Mexicanos) is a multiparty democracy headed up by an elected president, a bicameral legislature and an independent judiciary.

In practice, however, the gigantic, authoritarian Partido Revolucionario Institucional, or PRI ('el **pree**'), controlled all aspects of political life and society, including the government, the labor movement, the press and most of the small 'opposition' parties, from its founding in the 1930s.

With the municipal and congressional elections of July 1997 all that began to change. Widely condemned for corruption, mishandling of the economy and election fraud, the PRI was on the defensive. President Ernesto Zedillo was under pressure to make the elections fairer than any in

YUCATÁN

Mexican history. Instead of its normal absolute majority, the PRI received less than 40% of the vote. The right-of-center National Action Party (PAN) garnered 27%, the Party of the Democratic Revolution (PRD) 26%, with another 10% going to splinter parties. The PRI lost 12 seats in the senate and was forced to share power in the Chamber of Deputies, the lower house of congress that determines the country's budget.

The events of the '97 elections set the stage for the 2000 presidential race. President Zedillo was under even more pressure this time to ensure a fair contest. His party was no longer all-powerful, and the memory of the 1988 elections – in which Cuauhtémoc Cárdenas, son of the late president Lázaro Cárdenas, challenged the PRI's candidate for the nation's highest office but 'lost' when the PRI-controlled election computers mysteriously broke down during vote-counting – was still strong in the public's mind.

Zedillo called for a primary election within the PRI to choose the party's candidate, an unprecedented break from the practice of the outgoing president handpicking his successor. Thus was chosen Francisco Labastida Ochoa, Zedillo's minister of the interior. Labastida had served during the first three years of Zedillo's presidency as secretary of agriculture; he became interior minister only in January 1998, shortly after the massacre at Acteal in Chiapas forced the resignation of the previous interior minister.

Labastida's chief opponents were Cárdenas, in his third presidential bid with the PRD, and the PAN candidate, populist Vicente Fox Quesada, governor of the state of Guanajuato and the former head of Coca-Cola's Mexican and Central American operations.

As the race progressed, PAN strengthened its position by forging an alliance with the Green Party of Mexico. On July 2, 2000, in an election monitored closely by local and international observers (including former US president Jimmy Carter), Vicente Fox emerged victorious with 44% of the

Detail, Edificio de los Cinco Pisos, Edzná

vote. Labastida received 37%, and the PRI, after 71 years of dominance, was finally knocked out of the Mexican presidency.

The PRI won 209 of 500 lower-house seats in the July 2 vote, and 60 of 128 senate seats. The handover of the presidency takes place five months after the election; it should be extremely interesting to follow Mexico's progress during Fox's single six-year term. Among his proposals addressing the main concerns of the electorate – poverty and unemployment – Fox has suggested a second phase to the NAFTA agreements. He suggests that the US allow the free flow of Mexican workers across the border until the Mexican economy is strong enough to provide jobs for them at home. Whether this plan or his plans to curtail government corruption and the increasing power of drug cartels can be implemented is anyone's guess.

ECONOMY

Because it lacks plentiful water resources, the Yucatán Peninsula has minimal agriculture, with some cattle ranches. The important exception is the cultivation of henequen, a plant that yields fibers used to make rope and twine.

The export economy based on henequen thrived in the latter half of the 19th century. By WWI it was said that Mérida had more millionaires per capita than any other city in the world. The plantation owners were a de facto Yucatecan aristocracy and built opulent mansions along Mérida's Paseo de Montejo, many of which still stand. They decorated their homes with the artistic treasures of the world and sent their children off to the best schools of Europe.

With the invention of synthetic fibers such as nylon, henequen lost much of its importance, but it is still a significant part of the peninsula's agriculture.

Besides henequen, the Yucatán has some pig and chicken farms, and light industry around Mérida and Chetumal. Tourism is very important in the neighboring states of Yucatán and Quintana Roo.

Campeche is an important fishing port for lobster, shrimp and fish, much of the catch being for export. Towns along the northern coast of the peninsula also depend on fishing.

By far the richest sector of the Mexican economy is petroleum. The deposits beneath Tabasco and Veracruz are among the richest in the world. Campeche has significant petroleum reserves as well.

Farming, mining, forestry and oil exploration are important in Chiapas, as is tourism. Tuxtla Gutiérrez, the Chiapan capital, is one of Mexico's main coffee-producing regions. The cattle ranches in Chiapas and along the Gulf Coast in Tabasco are expanding into the rain forest, threatening the tropical ecosystem and triggering revolts by indigenous peoples who are being swept from their traditional lands.

POPULATION & PEOPLE

Over millennia, the Maya of the Yucatán and Chiapas have intermarried with neighboring peoples, especially those of central Mexico with whom they had diplomatic and commercial relations and the occasional invasion and conquest. During the 20th century they also have intermarried, to some degree, with the descendants of the conquering Spanish. People of mixed Mayan and Spanish blood are called *mestizos*. Most of Mexico's population is mestizo, but the Yucatán Peninsula has an especially high proportion of pure-blooded Maya. In many areas of the Yucatán and Chiapas, Mayan languages prevail over Spanish, or Spanish may not be spoken at all. In remote jungle villages some modern cultural practices descend directly from those of ancient Mayan civilization.

Thanks to the continuation of their unique cultural identity, the Maya of the Yucatán are proud without being arrogant, confident without the machismo seen so frequently elsewhere in Mexico, and kind without being servile. And, with the exception of those who have become jaded by the tourist hordes of Cancún, many Maya retain a sense of humor.

Facts for the Visitor

PLANNING

When to Go

The dry season is generally preferred for travel in the Yucatán because you needn't dodge the raindrops, the heat is not quite as muggy and, most important, it's winter in most of North America and Europe! November and early December are perhaps the best times, as there are fewer tourists and prices are low.

From mid December to April is the busy winter tourism season, when premium prices prevail (with surcharges around Christmas, New Year's and Easter). May, the end of the dry season, and June, when the rains begin, are the hottest and muggiest months. If you have a choice of months, don't choose those. July and August are hot, not too rainy and busy with the summer travel crowd. September and October are pretty good for travel, as the traffic decreases markedly and so do the rains.

Maps

For motorists in Mexico, the best road atlas is generally reckoned to be Guía Roji's *Generation 2000 Mexico Tourist Road Atlas*, available at bookstores in tourist areas and elsewhere (general information can be obtained by emailing guiaroji@guiaroji.com .mx). Guía Roji also publishes state and city maps for Mexico; be sure to check the publication date before buying.

Mexico's Secretaría de Comunicaciones y Transportes (SCT) also publishes a line of maps, including individual state maps at 1:350,000. They're sold in some bookstores in tourist areas. INEGI, the Mexican government's bureau of statistics and geography, produces decent state and area maps, available at their offices, which are usually in or near the federal government complex in larger cities and state capitals. Either know exactly what you're looking for or be ready to sort through several offerings before you find it. Both SCT and INEGI are slow to update their maps; unless you

are lucky enough to catch them in an update year, new roads and improvements are likely to be missing from the maps you buy (check the publication date).

TOURIST OFFICES

All large cities and resorts and some towns in Mexico have tourist offices, which may be run by the city, state or federal government. In May of 2000, the Mexican government closed all 13 of its tourism offices abroad. Plans are being discussed to replace them with the Consejo de Promoción Turís tica de México, an organization funded largely by hoteliers and airlines. In the meantime, US travelers might still be able to order brochures and maps and ask questions by calling ☎ 800-446-3942.

In Mexico, the government operates a 24-hour national toll-free tourist-assistance hot line at ☎ 01-800-903-92-00. Operators speak English and Spanish.

VISAS & DOCUMENTS

Visitors to Mexico should have a valid passport. Visitors of some nationalities have to obtain visas, but others (when visiting as tourists) require only the easily obtained Mexican government tourist card. Because the regulations sometimes change, it's wise to confirm them at a Mexican embassy or consulate before you go. Several Mexican embassies and consulates, and foreign embassies in Mexico, have websites with useful information on tourist permits, visas, travel with minors and so on (see Embassies & Consulates) but they don't all agree with each other, so you should back up any Internet findings with some phone calls. The Lonely Planet website (www.lonelyplanet .com) has links to updated visa information.

Passport

Though it's not recommended, US tourists can enter Mexico without a passport if they have official photo identification, such as a driver's license, plus some proof of their citizenship, such as a birth certificate certified by the issuing agency or their original certificate of naturalization (not a copy). Officials are used to passports and may delay people who have other documents. This applies to officials you have to deal with on reentry to the USA or Canada as well as to Mexican officials; the only proof of citizenship recognized by US or Canadian immigration is a passport or (for nonnaturalized citizens) a certified copy of your birth certificate. In Mexico you will often need your passport when you change money as well.

Citizens of other countries need to show a passport valid for at least six months after they arrive in Mexico.

Bar-code readers are being installed at Cancún's airport to cut processing time down to a promised 10 seconds. Once these are in place, it is likely that travelers not holding passports will have to stand in a separate (and much slower) line. This is aimed in part at the hordes of US college students who visit Cancún on spring break without passports, resulting in hours-long waits for all arrivals.

Visas

Citizens of the USA, Canada, EU countries, Australia, New Zealand, Norway, Switzerland, Iceland, Japan, Argentina and Chile are among those who do not require visas to enter Mexico as tourists. But they must obtain a Mexican government tourist card (see Travel Permits). Countries whose nationals *do* have to obtain visas include South Africa, Brazil and most Eastern European nations – check well ahead of travel with your local Mexican embassy or consulate.

For citizens of many countries, one of the requirements is possession of a valid US multiple-entry visa.

Travel Permits

The Mexican tourist card is a small paper document that you must get stamped by Mexican immigration (INM: Instituto Nacional de Migración) when you enter Mexico and must keep till you leave. The card is available free of charge at official border crossings, international airports and ports, and often from airlines, travel agencies and Mexican consulates. At the US-Mexico border you won't usually be given one automatically – you have to ask for it.

One section of the card – to be filled in by the immigration officer – deals with the length of your stay in Mexico. You may be asked a couple of questions about how long you want to stay and what you'll be doing, but normally you will be given the maximum 180 days if you ask for it. It's always advisable to ask for more days than you think you'll need, in case you are delayed or change your plans. Be sure to check that the official has written what you requested, especially if you are traveling with a companion. The official fee to make any changes to the card later is the same as the tourist fee to enter the country (read on).

Look after your tourist card; you will sometimes be asked to produce it. When you leave Mexico, you're supposed to turn it in. Look on the back side of the card and check whether you are still required to 'sing in the box.'

Tourist Fee Foreign tourists (of any age) and business travelers are charged a fee of 170 pesos (about US$18.50), called the Derecho para No Inmigrante (DNI, Nonimmigrant Fee). If you enter Mexico by air, the fee is included in the price of your air ticket.

If you enter by land you must pay the fee at one of the many Mexican banks listed on the back of your tourist card, at any time before you reenter the frontier zone on your way out of Mexico (or before you check in at an airport to fly out of Mexico). It makes sense to get the job done as soon as possible, and at least some Mexican border posts have on-the-spot bank offices where you can do so.

When paying at a bank, you need to present your tourist card or business visitor card, which will be stamped to prove that you have paid. This will probably be checked when you leave the country.

Tourist Card Extensions & Lost Cards If the number of days indicated on your tourist card is for some reason less than the 180-day maximum, its validity may be extended one or more times, at a cost of 170 pesos, up to the maximum time. To get a card extended you have to apply to the INM, which has offices in many towns and cities. You'll need your passport, tourist card, photocopies of the important pages of these documents and – at some offices – evidence of 'sufficient funds.' A major credit card is usually OK for the latter, or an amount in traveler's checks that could vary from between US$100 and US$1000 depending on which office you are dealing with.

Driver's License & Permits

If you're thinking of renting a vehicle in Mexico, take your driver's license and a major credit card with you. Mexican police are familiar with US and Canadian licenses. Those from other countries may be scrutinized more closely, but they are still legal. For more information on rentals, see the Yucatán Getting There & Around chapter. For the paperwork involved in taking your own vehicle into Mexico, see the Getting There & Away chapter at the beginning of this book.

Minors

If you are an adult traveling with a child under 18 years of age, the Mexican immigration officer will require you to show a notarized affidavit from the child's other parent permitting you to take the child into Mexico. This is to prevent separated, divorcing or divorced parents from absconding to Mexico with a child against the wishes – or legal actions – of the other parent. In the case of divorced parents, a custody document may be needed as well as the notarized consent form. If one or both parents are dead, or the traveler has only one legal parent, a notarized statement saying so may be required. These rules are aimed primarily at North Americans but apparently apply to all nationalities. If both parents are traveling together with the child or children, there's no problem and no affidavit is needed.

If you have any questions about this procedure, talk them over in advance of your trip with a Mexican diplomatic representa-

tive to find out exactly what you need to do. Don't wait until you're at the border or airport without an affidavit and the immigration officer refuses to permit you and the child to enter the country!

EMBASSIES & CONSULATES
Mexican Embassies & Consulates

Unless otherwise noted, details are for embassies or their consular sections.

Argentina (☎ 01-4821-7172) Larrea 1230, CP 1117 Capital Federal, Buenos Aires

Australia (☎ 02-6273-3963) 14 Perth Ave, Yarralumla, Canberra, ACT 2600; Consulate (☎ 02-9326-1311) Level 1, 135-153 New South Head Rd, Edgecliff, Sydney, NSW 2027

Austria (☎ 01-310-7383) Türkenstrasse 15, 1090 Vienna

Belgium (☎ 02-629-0777) Franklin Roosevelt 94, 1050 Brussels

Belize (☎ 2-30193, 2-31388, fax 2-78742) 18 N Park St, PO Box 754, Belize City

Brazil (☎ 061-244-1011) Av das Nacoes, QD 805, Lote 18, 70412-900 Brasilia

Canada (☎ 613-233-8988/6665) 45 O'Connor St, Suite 1500, Ottawa, ON K1P 1A4; Consulate (☎ 514-288-2502) 2055 rue Peel, Suite 1000, Montreal, QC H3A 1V4; Consulate (☎ 416-368-2875) Commerce Court West, 199 Bay St, Suite 4440, Toronto, ON M5L 1E9; Consulate (☎ 604-684-1859) 810-1130 W Pender St, Vancouver, BC V6E 4A4

Costa Rica (☎ 257-0633) Avenida 7a No 1371, San José

Denmark (☎ 3961-0500) Strandvejen 64E, 2900 Hellerup, Copenhagen

El Salvador (☎ 243-3458) Calle Circunvalación y Pasaje No 12, Colonia San Benito, San Salvador

France (☎ 01-53-70-27-70) 9 rue de Longchamp, 75116 Paris; Consulate (☎ 01-42-61-51-80) 4 rue Notre Dame des Victoires, 75002 Paris

Germany (☎ 030-327-7110) Kurfürstendamm 72, 10709 Berlin; Consulate (☎ 069-299-8750) Taunusanlage 21, 60325 Frankfurt-am-Main; Consulate (☎ 040-450-1580) Hallerstrasse 76-11, 20146 Hamburg

Guatemala (☎ 333-7254 to -7258) 15a Calle 3-20, Edificio Centro Ejecutivo, 7th Floor, Zona 10, Guatemala City; Consulate (☎ 331-8165, 331-9573) 13a Calle 7-30, Zona 9, Guatemala City

Honduras (☎ 232-0138) Avenida República de México 2402, Colonia Palmira, Tegucigalpa

Ireland (☎ 01-260-0699) 43 Ailesbury Rd, Ballsbridge, Dublin 4

Israel (☎ 03-516-3938) 25 Hemered St, 5th Floor, Trade Tower, 68125 Tel Aviv

Italy (☎ 06-44-11-51) Via Lazzaro Spallanzani 16, 00161 Rome; Consulate (☎ 02-7602-0541) Via Cappuccini 4, 20122 Milan

Japan (☎ 03-3580-8734) 2-15-1 Nagata-cho, Chiyoda-ku, Tokyo 100-0014

Netherlands (☎ 070-360-2900) Nassauplein 17, 2585 EB The Hague

New Zealand (☎ 04-472-5555) 8th Floor, 111-115 Customhouse Quay, Wellington

Nicaragua (☎ 505-278-4919) Carretera Masaya Km 4.5, 25 Varas Arriba (next to Optica Matamoros), Altamira, Managua

Norway (☎ 2243 1165) Karenslyst Allé 2, 0244 Oslo

Spain (☎ 91-369-2814) Carrera de San Jerónimo 46, 28014 Madrid; Consulate (☎ 93-201-1822) Avinguda Diagonal 626, 08021 Barcelona; Consulate (☎ 95-456-3944) Calle San Roque 6, 41001 Sevilla

Sweden (☎ 08-663-5170) Grevgatan 3, 11453 Stockholm

Switzerland (☎ 31-357-4747) Bernastrasse 57, 3005 Bern

UK (☎ 020-7499-8586) 42 Hertford St, London W1J 7JR

USA (☎ 202-728-1600) 1911 Pennsylvania Ave NW, Washington, DC 20006; Consulate (☎ 202-736-1000) 2827 16th St NW, Washington, DC 20009

There are Mexican consulates in many other US cities, especially in the border states. Check www.embassyofmexico.org for details.

Embassies & Consulates in Mexico

Embassies are in Mexico City. The following is a list of foreign consulates and consular agencies in the Yucatán.

Belgium (☎ 925-29-39) Calle 25 No 159 between Calles 28 and 30, Mérida

Belize (☎ 832-77-28) Avenida Álvaro Obregon 226, Chetumal (Belize has a vice consul in Mérida at the UK's consular office; see UK in this list)

Canada (☎ 983-33-60, fax 983-32-32) Plaza Caracol No 330, Zona Hotelera, Cancún

France (☎ 985-29-24) Casa Turquesa, Blvd Kukulcán (Km 13.5), Zona Hotelera, Cancún; (☎ 925-28-86, fax 925-70-09) Calle 33B No 528 between Calles 62 and 64, Mérida

Germany (☎ 984-18-98) Punta Conoco 36 (downtown), Cancún; (☎ 981-29-76) Calle 7 No 217, between Calles 20 and 20A, Colonia Chuburna de Hidalgo, Mérida

Guatemala (☎ 9-832-30-45) Retorno 4, Casa 8, Fraccionamiento Bahía, Chetumal; (☎ 9-632-04-91) 1a Calle Sur Pte 26, Comitán; (☎ 9-626-12-52) 2a Oriente 33, Tapachula

Honduras (☎ 944-82-06) Calle 54 No 280, Fraccionamiento del Norte, Mérida

Italy (☎ 984-12-61, fax 984-54-15) Calle Alcatraces 39 (downtown), Cancún

Netherlands (☎ 983-02-00) Presidente Inter-Continental, Blvd Kukulcán (Km 7), Zona Hotelera, Cancún; (☎ 924-31-22, ☎/fax 924-41-47, pixan@diario1.sureste.com) Calle 64 No 418, between Calles 47 and 49, Mérida

Spain (☎ 983-24-66, fax 983-28-70) Edificio Oasis, Blvd Kukulcán (Km 6.5), Zona Hotelera, Cancún; (☎ 927-15-20, fax 923-00-55) Calle 3 No 237, Fraccionamiento Campestre, Mérida

Switzerland (☎ 981-80-00, fax 981-80-80) Caesar Park, Blvd Kukulcán (Km 17), Zona Hotelera, Cancún

UK (☎ 985-01-00, fax 985-12-25) Royal Caribbean, Blvd Kukulcán (Km 16.5), Zona Hotelera, Cancún; (☎ 928-61-52, fax 928-39-62) Calle 58 No 450, at Calle 53, Fraccionamiento del Norte, Mérida; you can also get information about travel in Belize here

USA (☎ 983-02-72, fax 983-13-73) Plaza Caracol Two, 3rd Floor, No 320-323, Blvd Kukulcán (Km. 8.5), Zona Hotelera, Cancún; (☎ 872-61-52) 35 Norte No 650, Cozumel; (☎ 925-50-11, afterhours emergency ☎ 947-22-85, fax 925-62-19) Paseo de Montejo 453, at Avenida Colón, Mérida

Embassy & Consulate Websites Many Mexican embassies and consulates and foreign embassies in Mexico City have websites. Links to most of them can be found on mexico.web.com.mx/mx/embajadas.html.

Two particularly useful sites, with tourist information and data on Mexican visas and tourist permits, are those of the Mexican embassy in Washington, DC (www.embassy ofmexico.org) and the Mexican consulate in New York (www.consulmexny.org).

CUSTOMS

The normal customs inspection routine when you enter Mexico is to complete a customs declaration form (which lists duty-free allowances), then choose between going through a goods-to-declare channel or a nothing-to-declare channel. Those declaring items have their belongings searched, and duty is collected. Those not declaring items will sometimes be asked by customs agents to push a button on what looks like a traffic signal. The signal responds randomly: A green light lets you pass without inspection, a red light means your baggage will be searched, usually quickly and courteously.

If you arrive in the Yucatán via Mexico City you need to clear immigration (but not customs) in the capital before continuing to your destination.

MONEY
Currency

Mexico's currency is the *peso*; it is divided into 100 centavos. Mexican coins come in denominations of five, 10, 20 and 50 centavos and one, two, five, 10 and 20 pesos. Bills (notes) are in denominations of 10, 20, 50, 100, 200 and 500 pesos.

You may see prices written as '$100 m.n.' meaning *moneda nacional*, or Mexican pesos, to distinguish it from '$100 dlls.' (US dollars).

Iced-drink vendor, Mérida

JOHN ELK III

Exchange Rates

At the time this book went to press, the following exchange rates applied:

country	unit		pesos
Australia	A$1	=	$5.07
Belize	BZ$1	=	$4.76
Canada	CN$1	=	$6.29
euro	€1	=	$8.23
France	FFr1	=	$1.25
Germany	DM1	=	$4.21
Guatemala	Q1	=	$1.20
Italy	IL1000	=	$4.25
Japan	¥100	=	$8.62
New Zealand	NZ$1	=	$3.82
UK	UK£	=	$13.74
USA	US$1	=	$9.43

Exchanging Money

The peso is exchanged freely, so there is no black market. At the time of research the daily exchange rate averaged about 9.2 pesos to the dollar, and prices in the text are calculated from their peso amounts based on that rate.

Though banks and *casas de cambio* (exchange offices) change most major currencies, US dollars are always easiest. Bank automated teller machines (ATMs) give the best service (24 hours a day) and rates.

In such heavily touristed areas as Cancún and Cozumel you can often spend US dollars as easily as pesos at hotels, restaurants and shops. Many businesses in these areas post prices in pesos with a dollar equivalent alongside. At the time of research, these equivalents were usually 10 pesos to the dollar, which favored those paying in cash dollars. Be aware that using a credit card at these businesses will not get you the same savings! Some businesses in these areas accept dollars at an outrageously bad exchange rate; it's a good idea to carry dollars and pesos.

Traveler's Checks & Cash Even if you have a credit card or debit card, you should still bring along some major-brand traveler's checks (best denominated in US dollars) or – less desirable for security reasons – cash US dollars as a backup. If you don't have a credit card or debit card, use US-dollar traveler's checks. American Express is a good brand to have because it's recognized everywhere, which can prevent delays. American Express in Mexico City maintains a 24-hour hot line (☎ 5-326-3625) for lost American Express traveler's checks; you can call it collect from anywhere in Mexico.

ATMs Not so long ago automated teller machines were uncommon in Yucatán. Today, the majority of banks on the peninsula have at least one ATM out front.

ATMs are generally the easiest source of cash. Despite the handling charge that will normally appear on your account, you get a good exchange rate and avoid the commission you would pay when changing cash or traveler's checks.

Mexican banks call their ATMs by a variety of names – usually something like *caja permanente* or *cajero automático*. Each ATM displays the cards it will accept.

Credit Cards Major credit cards such as Visa, MasterCard, Eurocard and Access are accepted at all airline and car-rental companies and at the larger hotels and restaurants; American Express cards are often accepted at the fancier and larger places and at some smaller ones.

Many smaller establishments will readily accept your credit card, even for charges as little as US$5 or US$10. Cancún, for example, lives on credit cards and even has some telephones that accept them for long-distance (trunk) calls (these are expensive and best avoided).

Costs

Though Mexico is the cheapest country in the Mayan region, Cancún and Cozumel are the two most expensive places in the country, far more expensive than Mexico City or even Acapulco. Small towns such as Tizimín and Izamal, not being heavily touristed, are much cheaper. Larger cities such as Mérida and San Cristóbal de Las Casas offer a good range of prices, with good values for your money.

A single traveler staying in budget (fan-cooled) accommodations and eating two set meals a day in inexpensive restaurants may pay as little as US$13 per day in a town such as Izamal or Valladolid. For the same in downtown Cancún in high season the least you could get away with would be about US$37 (though staying in a hostel dorm room better than halves this). A rough Yucatán-wide average for these budget costs would be about US$20; if you'd prefer to spend more time relaxing and less time bargain hunting, figure on roughly US$30.

Other costs (snacks, bottled water, soft drinks, admission to archaeological sites, local transportation) can add another US$10 or more to these figures, depending on your itinerary (and thirst).

Sharing accommodations can cut costs considerably, as many Mexican hotels charge the same (or only slightly higher) rates for double occupancy as for single. Triples or quadruples are often only a few dollars more than doubles.

Travelers on middle-range budgets find excellent values for their money in the Yucatán: Good hotel rooms with private bath and air-conditioning cost US$25 to US$50 (double these figures for Cancún), and full meals in good restaurants run US$8 to US$15.

At the top end, airfares, car-rental rates and prices for luxury hotels and meals are usually lower than in Canada, Europe or the USA, but not by much.

Taxes

Mexico's Impuesto de Valor Agregado (Value-Added Tax), abbreviated IVA ('ee-bah'), is levied at 15%. By law the tax must be included in virtually any price quoted to you and should not be added afterward. Signs in shops and notices on restaurant menus often state *'IVA incluido.'* Occasionally (in expensive establishments) they state instead that IVA must be added to the quoted prices. Beware of scamming waiters who try to add a bogus IVA to your bill!

YUCATÁN

Impuesto Sobre Hospedaje (ISH, 'ee-**ess**-e-**ah**-che,' the Lodging Tax) is levied on the price of hotel rooms. Each Mexican state sets its own rate, but in most it's 2%.

Most budget accommodations include both IVA and ISH in quoted prices (though it's sometimes worth checking). In top-end hotels a price may often be given as, say, 'US$100 *más impuestos*' ('plus taxes'), in which case you must add about 17% to the figure. When in doubt, ask, '*¿Están incluidos los impuestos?*' ('Are taxes included?').

All prices in the Yucatán section of this book, to the best of our knowledge, include IVA and ISH.

Airport usage taxes are levied on every passenger on every flight. The tax on international flights departing Mexico is equivalent to approximately US$12; domestic departure taxes are less. Both are usually included in the cost of the ticket.

Student Discounts

Discounts for foreign students are virtually unknown. A few places offer small discounts on admission fees to students under 26.

POST & COMMUNICATIONS
Post

Almost every city and town (but not village) has an Oficina de Correos (Post Office), where you can buy postage stamps and send or receive mail.

If you are sending something by airmail from Mexico, be sure to clearly mark it with the words 'Por Avión.' An airmail letter sent to Canada or the USA may take anywhere from four to 14 days (but don't be surprised if it takes longer). Mail to Europe may take between one and three weeks, to Australasia a month or more.

Receiving Mail Receiving mail in Mexico can be tricky. You can send or receive letters and packages care of a post office if they're addressed like this:

Jane SMITH (last name in capitals)
Lista de Correos
City
State 00000 (post code)
MEXICO

When the letter arrives at the post office, the name of the addressee is placed on an alphabetical list called the *lista de correos*, which is updated daily. If you can, check the list yourself, because the letter might be listed under your first name instead of your surname.

To claim your mail, present your passport or other identification; there's no charge. The snag is that many post offices hold lista mail for only 10 days before returning it to the sender. If you think you're going to pick mail up more than 10 days after it has arrived, have it sent to you at Poste Restante, Correo Central, Town/City, State, Mexico. Poste restante holds mail for up to a month, but no list of what has been received is posted. Again, there's no charge for collection.

Telephone

Local calls are cheap, but domestic long-distance and international calls can be very expensive. Generally, using a phone card, either one issued by your home telephone company or a Ladatel card, at a public pay phone (see below) is the least expensive way to place a call in Mexico.

Public pay phones operated by Telmex are usually marked 'Ladatel' or 'Telmex.' 'Lada' stands for *larga distancia* (long distance), but these phones work for both local and long-distance (including international) calls. Nearly all Telmex pay phones work exclusively on *tarjetas telefónicas* (phone cards). The cards are sold at many kiosks and shops – look for the sign reading '*De Venta Aquí Ladatel*' – in denominations of 30, 50 or 100 pesos.

Most Telmex card phones can be used to dial toll-free numbers, making them good places from which to make eKno card calls (see Post & Communications in the regional Facts for the Visitor chapter). As this book goes to print, Mexico is the only country covered in it from which you can access the eKno service by phone. The access number from Mexico is ☎ 001-800-514-02-87.

A bit more expensive than a regular phone booth is a *caseta de teléfono* or *caseta telefónica* – a call station (sometimes in its own office, sometimes in a shop or restaurant) where an operator connects the call for you and you take it in a booth. Calling from your hotel can be very expensive, because hotels charge what they like for this service.

Prefixes, Codes & Costs All local Mexican phone numbers have been standardized to consist of seven digits. When calling from one city to another, the seven-digit number must be preceded by 01 and a single-digit area code (except when calling Mexico City and Guadalajara, which have no area code). This is true even if the city you are calling is within the same area code. All of the Mexican portion of the Ruta Maya lies within the area code 9.

So, to place a call from Mérida to the municipal tourist office in San Cristóbal de Las Casas, for example, you would first dial the long-distance prefix 01, followed by the area code 9, followed by the number, 678-06-65.

When dialing a call, you need to know what *prefijo* (prefix) and *claves* (country or area codes) to put before the number. If you are making a call in Mexico, the prefixes, codes and approximate costs of local and long-distance calls vary depending on where you are calling. General guidelines are as follows:

calls to city/town you are in – no need to dial a prefix or code; US$0.04 per minute

calls to other cities/towns in Mexico – dial ☎ 01 + area code; US$0.40 per minute

calls to USA or Canada – dial ☎ 00 + 1 + area code; US$1.30 per minute

calls to Europe – dial ☎ 00 + country code + area code; US$2.75 per minute

calls to Australasia – dial ☎ 00 + country code + area code; US$3.50 per minute

Telmex international calls are 33% cheaper on weekends until 4:59 pm Sunday, and weekdays between 7 pm and 6:59 am (to the USA and Canada), 6 pm to 5:59 am (Europe) or 5 am to 4:59 pm (Australasia).

If you need to speak to a domestic operator, call ☎ 020; for an international operator, call ☎ 090. For Mexican directory information, call ☎ 040. The country code for Mexico is 52.

To call a number in Mexico from another country, dial your international access code, then the Mexico country code – 52 – then the area code and number.

Mexican toll-free numbers – all ☎ 800 followed by five digits – always require the 01 prefix. Most US toll-free numbers are ☎ 800 or 888 followed by seven digits. In general you cannot call a toll-free number from outside the country where it is based, but in the US and Canada you can call any toll-free number in either of those two countries.

Collect Calls A *llamada por cobrar* (collect call) can cost the receiving party much more than if *they* call *you*, so it's cheaper for them if you find a phone where you can receive an incoming call, then pay for a quick call to the other party to ask them to call you back. Be forewarned: Collect calls from Mexico can be outrageously expensive. A collect call from Cancún to New York, for example, can cost as much as US$20 per minute. It's always a good idea to ask the operator for the per-minute rate before you place your collect call.

If you do need to make a collect call, you can do so from pay phones without a card. Call an operator at ☎ 020 for domestic calls, or ☎ 090 for international calls. Mexican international operators can usually speak English.

Credit Card Phones In Cancún, Cozumel and Mérida, you'll find phones with signs urging you to charge calls to MasterCard, Visa or American Express. Beware that very high rates – as high as US$23 for the first minute, US$8 per minute thereafter – are charged on these devices, which require dialing only 0 to contact an international operator.

Emergency In the event of a police, fire or medical emergency, dial ☎ 060 and you will immediately be connected to an emergency operator. Most of the operators speak English as well as Spanish. If the one who answers your call doesn't speak English, he or she will quickly connect you with someone who does.

YUCATÁN

Fax, Email & Internet Access

It's generally possible to send faxes from hotels in the Yucatán; the service is often available to guests. Where it's not, a tip will usually result in the service being rendered. Faxes can also usually be sent from Internet cafés, and there are many other businesses that provide the service; those that do generally post a 'Fax Público' sign in their window.

Internet cafés are proliferating rapidly in Mexico; there are sure to be many more than those listed in this book by the time you arrive. These cafés typically charge around US$3 to US$5 for 30 minutes on a computer. A useful website with listings of Mexican cybercafés is netcafeguide.com/mexico1.htm.

BOOKS

Lonely Planet also publishes Yucatán, which provides much more in-depth coverage of the three Yucatán Peninsula states. If you are going to be doing some diving or snorkeling, get Lonely Planet's Pisces guide Diving & Snorkeling Cozumel – it has beautiful, full-color underwater shots and detailed accounts of the possible dives and dive outfitters. The Pisces Guide to Caribbean Reef Ecology brims with bright color photos and introduces its subject with lively text.

NEWSPAPERS & MAGAZINES

The English-language Mexico City News is distributed throughout Mexico wherever tourists gather. Price varies with location, but it's usually about US$1.

Mexico has a thriving local Spanish-language press as well as national newspapers. Even small cities often have two or three newspapers of their own; Mérida's is El Diario de Yucatán.

For those interested in a nonestablishment view of events, La Jornada is a good national daily with a mainly left-wing viewpoint; it covers a lot of stories that other papers don't. Its website is www.jornada.unam.mx. Proceso is a weekly newsmagazine with a similar approach; its online edition can be read at proceso.com.mx.

BUSINESS HOURS

Stores generally open from 9 am to 2 pm, close for siesta, then reopen from 4 to 7 pm Monday to Saturday. In particularly hot locales such as Mérida and Chetumal, stores sometimes take a longer siesta but stay open later in the evening. Some may not be open Saturday afternoon.

Offices have similar Monday to Friday hours; those with tourist-related business might be open for a few hours on Saturday as well.

Some Mexican churches, particularly those that contain valuable works of art, are locked when not in use, but most churches are in frequent use. Be careful not to disturb services when you visit them.

Archaeological sites are usually open 8 am to 5 pm daily. Most museums have one closing day a week, typically Monday. On Sunday, nearly all archaeological sites and museums are free, and the major ones can get very crowded.

Banks are open Monday to Friday 9 am to 1:30 pm, though many have begun to keep longer hours and some are open Saturday. The opposite trend is occurring with post offices, many of which now close completely on Saturday (others are open only for sales of stamps). Weekday hours in most cases are from 9 am to 5 pm or shorter.

FOOD

Called by its Maya inhabitants 'the Land of the Pheasant and the Deer,' the Yucatán has always had a distinctive cuisine.

The resident chile is the habanero, and though small, it is one hot pepper. The habanero is a very important ingredient in achiote, the popular Yucatecan sauce, which also includes chopped onions, the juice of sour Seville oranges, cilantro (fresh coriander leaf) and salt. You'll see a bowl of achiote on most restaurant tables in the Yucatán. It looks rather innocent as salsas go, but the little green chunks of habanero are the tip-off.

One local hearty breakfast favorite is huevos motuleños, or eggs in the style of the town of Motul, east of Mérida. Fresh tortillas are spread with refried beans, then topped with an egg or two, then garnished with chopped ham, green peas and shredded cheese, with a few slices of fried banana on the side. It can be slightly *picante* or *muy picante*, depending on the cook.

An authentic Yucatecan lunch or supper might begin with *sopa de lima* and progress to a main course of *pollo pibil* – chicken marinated in achiote sauce, sour Seville-orange juice, garlic, black pepper, cumin and salt, then wrapped in banana leaves and baked. There are no nuclear chiles to blow your head off. A variant is *cochinita pibil*, made with suckling pig instead of chicken.

The Los Almendros restaurant in Ticul, Yucatán, claims to have created *poc-chuc*, slices of pork marinated in sour orange juice, cooked and served with a tangy sauce and pickled onions. A more traditional pork dish is *frijol con puerco*, the Mayan version of pork-and-beans, with black beans, tomato sauce and rice.

Another hearty dish is *puchero*, a stew made with chicken, pork, carrots, cabbage, squash (marrow) and sweet potato.

The turkey is native to the Yucatán and has been used as food for millennia. *Pavo relleno negro*, or dark stuffed turkey, is slices of turkey over a 'filling' made with pork and beef, all topped by a rich dark sauce.

Venison, also native to the Yucatán, is perhaps best as a *pipián de venado*, steamed in banana leaves à la pibil and topped with a sauce made with ground squash (marrow) seeds.

Among the lighter traditional dishes, *papadzules* consist of tortillas sprinkled with chopped hard-boiled eggs, rolled up and topped with a sauce that is made with squash or pumpkin seeds. *Salbutes* are the native tacos: fried corn tortillas topped with shredded turkey meat, avocado and pickled onions. *Panuchos* are similar, but are made with refried beans.

As for seafood, the all-time favorite is *pescado frito*, simple fried fish, but there's also *langosta* (lobster), usually just the tail. The most interesting seafood concoctions are the *ceviches*, cocktails made of raw or parboiled seafood in a marinade of lime juice, tomato sauce, chopped onion and cilantro. Cheapest is the *ceviche de pescado* made with whatever fish is in season and cheap in the markets. Other choices include *ceviche de camarones* (with shrimp) and *ceviche de ostiones* (with oysters).

At the open-air markets and cookshops you'll need to know some Spanish to read the menus: *higado encebollado* is liver and onions, *longaniza* is a spicy sausage, *pollo asado o frito* is roasted or fried chicken, *bistec de res* (or *puerco*) is a beef (or pork) steak, *puerco empanizado* is a breaded pork chop, and *bistec a la Mexicana* is bits of beef sautéed with tomatoes and hot peppers.

Getting There & Around

Following is general information for the Yucatán region. For specific information on each town or city, see the individual sections. For detailed information on flights to and from Cancún, see the introductory Getting There & Away chapter.

AIR
Cancún
Cancún's international airport is unquestionably the busiest airport in the region, with the most local and international flights.

Aerocaribe (in Cancún ☎ 884-20-00, www.aerocaribe.com), Mexicana's regional airline, covers destinations in the Yucatán Peninsula and beyond in a fleet of small and medium-size planes.

Cozumel
Some domestic and international flights to or from Cancún stop at Cozumel as well, giving it excellent air service.

Mérida
Most international flights to Mérida are connections through either Mexico City or Cancún; there is no nonstop international service, except for Aeroméxico's two daily flights from Miami.

Domestic service includes half a dozen Aerocaribe/Mexicana flights daily from Mexico City to Mérida, and one or two by Aeroméxico as well. Bonanza has flights to Cancún, Mérida, Palenque, Tuxtla Gutiérrez and Villahermosa.

Palenque
The small town of Palenque now receives scheduled flights by Aerocaribe from Bahías de Huatulco, Oaxaca, Tuxtla Gutiérrez, Cancún and Mérida.

Tuxtla Gutiérrez
Aviacsa, the Chiapan regional airline, has several daily nonstop flights to and from Mexico City, and also makes a daily nonstop run to Tapachula. The major airport for the region, however, is at the Tabascan capital of Villahermosa.

Villahermosa
Because of its oil wealth, Villahermosa has good domestic air links to Mérida, Cancún, Tuxtla Gutiérrez and Mexico City.

Departure Tax
A departure tax equal to about US$12 is levied on international travelers departing Mexico by air; this cost is usually included in the price of the ticket.

LAND
Mexico can be entered by land from the USA at 24 points. For details, see Lonely Planet's *Mexico*.

The most popular and easily accessible entry points to Mexico from Guatemala are at Tecún Umán/Ciudad Hidalgo, entering the Soconusco region of Chiapas from Guatemala's Pacific Slope, and at La Mesilla/Ciudad Cuauhtémoc, entering highland Chiapas from the southwestern highlands of Guatemala. More adventurous routes take you by country bus and riverboat from El Petén, Guatemala, down the Río Usumacinta or the Río de la Pasión to Yaxchilán in Chiapas. For information on these routes, see the chapter on El Petén, in the Guatemala section.

Bus
In Mexico the buses range from luxury-class air-conditioned cruisers to shabby but serviceable village buses. The various companies offer different levels of comfort and service, usually determined by price: the more you pay, the more comfortable the bus and the faster the trip. Luxury service is available on the busiest long-haul routes.

Except for short runs, it's usually not worth the savings to travel by 2nd-class bus when 1st-class service is available, unless you're really pinching pennies. That said, 2nd-class buses are a great place to soak up local atmosphere (including pitches for health products of dubious value), and they pass through lots of towns that the 1st-class buses blow by.

A general rule of thumb is that 1st class costs about 30% more and takes about a third less time. The price differential can be even smaller; the big differences are in comfort, security and time.

There are almost no international bus lines; usually you take one company's bus to the border, then change to the bus of another company. The exception is Chetumal, which receives buses from Belize, and the special fast service from Flores (Guatemala), near Tikal.

Here's a quick rundown on some of the bus lines of the Yucatán and the destinations they serve:

ADO (Autobuses de Oriente) – long-haul 1st-class routes between Mérida, Campeche, Palenque, Villahermosa, Veracruz, Mexico City and beyond.

ATS (Autotransportes del Sur) – service primarily in the southern peninsula, including frequent buses from Mérida to Cancún and Campeche. They also run buses to Bolonchén de Rejón, Celestún, Chiquilá, Ciudad del Carmen, Emiliano Zapata, Hecelchakán, Hopelchén, Izamal, Ocosingo, Palenque, Playa del Carmen, San Cristóbal de Las Casas, Tizimín, Tulum and Valladolid.

Mayab – mostly 2nd-class service between Mérida and Cancún, the Riviera Maya, Chetumal, Felipe Carrillo Puerto and many small towns on the peninsula.

Noreste – service to many small towns in the northeastern part of the peninsula, including Río Lagartos and Tizimín.

Omnitur del Caribe (Caribe) – deluxe service between Mérida and Chetumal via Felipe Carrillo Puerto.

Oriente (Autotransportes de Oriente) – frequent buses between Mérida and Cancún, stopping at Chichén Itzá and Valladolid; buses between Mérida and Cobá, Izamal, Playa del Carmen and Tulum.

Super Expresso – deluxe service between Mérida, Cancún, Chetumal and Ticul.

UNO – superdeluxe service on major routes, such as Mérida to Cancún and Mérida to Villahermosa and Mexico City.

Car & Motorcycle

Insurance It is foolish to travel without Mexican liability insurance. If there is an accident and you cannot show a valid insurance policy, you will be arrested and not permitted to leave the locale of the accident until all claims are settled, which could be weeks or months. Mexico's legal system follows the Napoleonic model, in which all persons involved in an incident are required to prove their innocence; trial is by a court of three judges, not by a jury. Your embassy can do little to help you in such a situation, except to tell you how stupid you were to drive without local insurance.

Mexican insurance is sold in US, Guatemalan and Belizean towns near the Mexican border. Approaching the border from the USA you will see billboards advertising offices selling Mexican policies. At the busiest border-crossing points (Tijuana, Mexicali, Nogales, Agua Prieta, Ciudad Juárez, Nuevo Laredo and Matamoros) there are insurance offices open 24 hours a day.

Prices for Mexican policies are set by law in Mexico, so bargain-hunting isn't easy. Instead of discounts (which cannot be offered), insurance offices offer incentives such as free guidebooks and/or maps, connections to automobile clubs and other treats.

Mexican motor-vehicle insurance policies are priced so as to penalize the short-term buyer with extremely high rates. You may pay almost as much for a one-month policy (which is approximately US$200, on average) as you would for a full year's policy.

Fuel At the time of writing fuel costs in Mexico were US$2.04 and US$2.24 per US gallon (US$0.54 and US$0.60 per liter) for the two grades of unleaded gas, Pemex Magna and Pemex Premium. Gasoline prices rise almost on a monthly basis, a baffling phenomenon given the fact that Pemex is a government-run enterprise in a country with huge oil reserves.

Car Rental Renting a car is a viable option for getting around the Yucatán if you are visiting some of the more out-of-the-way archaeological sites, especially if you have two or more people to share costs. Assume you will pay a total of US$40 to US$60 per day (tax, insurance and gas included) for the cheapest car offered, usually a bottom-of-the-line Volkswagen or Nissan.

You can book vehicles through the agencies listed in the Yucatán chapters, or through the foreign offices of the big-name international agencies. Doing the latter can sometimes get you lower rates, but be aware that most of these offices are only affiliated with the companies whose names they bear. In the event of a dispute, the big-name agency may bow out and leave you to try to settle with the Mexican firm.

Here are toll-free telephone numbers for some of the international firms that have offices in Yucatán:

company	in the USA	in Mexico
Avis	☎ 800-331-2112	☎ 01-800-707-77
Budget	☎ 800-527-0700	☎ 01-800-700-17
Dollar	☎ 800-800-4000	☎ 01-800-900-10
Hertz	☎ 800-654-3131	☎ 01-800-700-16
National	☎ 800-328-4567	☎ 01-800-003-95
Thrifty	☎ 800-367-2277	☎ 01-800-018-59

Quintana Roo

The state of Quintana Roo, Mexico's only Caribbean real estate, stretches north from the border with Belize to the extreme northeastern tip of the Yucatán Peninsula. The longest barrier reef in the Western Hemisphere runs almost this entire distance, stopping at Isla Mujeres. This and the other reefs along the coast, all bathed in the crystal-clear Caribbean waters teeming with tropical fish, provide a profusion of excellent diving and snorkeling sites ranking among the world's best. Quintana Roo is also home to several impressive Mayan ruins and to resorts of every size and flavor.

Owing in part to its geographic isolation and the effects of the War of the Castes, the region did not have an official name until 1902, when it was given the status of territory and named after Andrés Quintana Roo, the poet-warrior-statesman who presided over the drafting of Mexico's constitution. In 1974, largely as a result of the development of Cancún, 'QR' achieved statehood.

Cancún

• **population 400,000**

In the 1970s Mexico's ambitious tourism planners decided to outdo Acapulco with a brand new, world-class resort in Yucatán. The place they chose was a deserted sand spit offshore from the little fishing village of Puerto Juárez, on Yucatán's eastern shore. The name of the place was Cancún. The Mexican government built the resort as an investment in the tourism business. Vast sums were sunk into landscaping and infrastructure, yielding straight, well-paved roads, potable tap water and great swaths of sandy beach. Cancún's raison d'être is to shelter planeloads of tourists who fly in to spend one or two weeks in a resort hotel before flying home again. More than 2 million visitors descend on Cancún each year.

During their stay they can get by with speaking only English, spending only US

Highlights

- The clubs, resorts and white-sand beaches of Cancún's Zona Hotelera
- Cozumel, ranked Number 1 worldwide by many divers
- Playa del Carmen, a burgeoning beach resort with many European touches
- Tulum's Mayan ruins, with their stunning waterfront setting and nearby beach cabañas
- Banco Chinchorro, a huge coral atoll that has sunk many ships, making it heaven for wreck divers

dollars and eating only familiar food. In the daytime, group tourists enjoy the beaches, rent a car or board a bus for an excursion to Chichén Itzá, Xcaret or Tulum, or browse in air-conditioned shopping malls straight out of Dallas. At night they dance and drink in clubs and discos to music that's the same all over the world. They have a good time. This is the business of tourism.

ORIENTATION

Cancún is actually two places in one: Ciudad Cancún and the Zona Hotelera.

Ciudad Cancún

On the mainland lies Ciudad Cancún (often referred to as 'downtown'), a planned city founded as the service center of the resort. The main north-south thoroughfare is Avenida Tulum, a 1km-long tree-shaded boulevard lined with banks, shopping centers and restaurants. On the east side of the boulevard in the city center is the city hall, 'Ayuntamiento Benito Juárez.'

Those who are content to trundle out to the beach by bus or taxi can save pots of money by staying in Ciudad Cancún in one of the smaller, low- to medium-priced hotels, many of which have swimming pools. Restaurants in the city center range from ultra-Mexican taco joints to fairly smooth and expensive salons.

Zona Hotelera

The sandy island, Isla Cancún, is usually referred to as the Zona Hotelera (so-na ohte-le-ra). Boulevard Kukulcán, a four-lane divided avenue, leaves Ciudad Cancún and goes eastward out on the island several kilometers, passing condominium developments, a youth hostel, several moderately priced hotels, some expensive larger ones and several shopping complexes, to Punta Cancún (Cancún Point) and the Centro de Convenciones (Convention Center).

From Punta Cancún, the boulevard heads south for 13km, flanked on both sides for much of the way by mammoth hotels, shopping centers, dance clubs and many restaurants and bars, to Punta Nizuc (Nizuc Point), where it turns westward and rejoins the mainland. From there, the boulevard cuts through light tropical forest for several more kilometers to its southern terminus at Cancun's international airport.

Cancún International Airport is about 8km south of the city center. Puerto Juárez, the port for passenger ferries to Isla Mujeres, is about 3km north of the center. Punta Sam, the dock for the slower car ferries to Isla Mujeres, is about 5km north of the center.

As you head along the larger streets you will notice that many of the smaller ones coming off them seem to be repeated at the next block. These are actually continuous streets (usually one-way) that make two right-angle turns to form an open box. Just to keep it interesting, occasionally a third street with the same name will appear in between the two ends, as with the middle, pedestrian arm of Calle Palmera, off Avenida Uxmal.

INFORMATION

Tourist Offices

There is a tourist information booth on the right side of the international arrivals terminal at the airport, staffed sporadically. In Ciudad Cancún, the State Tourism Office (☎ 884-80-73) is at Avenida Tulum 26, just north of Ayuntamiento Benito Juárez (the city hall); it's open 9 am to 9 pm daily and usually has English-speakers on staff.

Immigration

For visa and tourist-card extensions, visit the Instituto Nacional de Migración (☎ 854-14-04), Avenida Náder 1 at Avenida Uxmal in Ciudad Cancún. The office handles extension requests from 9 am to noon Monday to Friday, sometimes keeping the same hours Saturday.

Consulates

Several countries maintain consulates in Cancún; see the list in the Yucatán Facts for the Visitor chapter.

Money

There are at least three banks in the Zona Hotelera: Banco Bilbao Vizcaya in Mayafair Plaza, across from the Fiesta América Cancún hotel; a Banamex with currency exchange and ATM next door in Plaza Terramar; and Bital, at the Centro de Convenciones, a full-service bank open 8 am to 7 pm Monday to Saturday. There are ATMs and *casas de cambio* (open long hours) inside practically all the malls and at Punta Cancún. Virtually all the resorts on the island will change money, but they offer poor exchange rates and sometimes limit

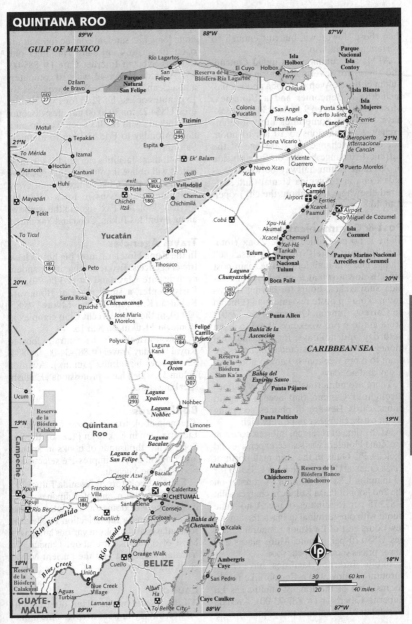

transactions to guests only. Exchange rates on the island are generally less favorable than those downtown, but not enough to warrant a special trip.

ATMs are common in Ciudad Cancún, and there are several banks on Avenida Tulum between Avenidas Cobá and Uxmal, including a Bancomer and a Banamex. Most banks are open 9 am to 5:30 pm weekdays, but they sometimes limit foreign-exchange transactions to 10 am to noon. For better exchange rates use one of the currency-exchange booths on the east side of Avenida Tulum halfway between Avenida Cobá and Avenida Uxmal (and scattered elsewhere throughout the city), open 8 am to 8 pm daily.

Post & Communications

There is no post office in the Zona Hotelera, but most hotels' reception desks sell stamps and will mail letters. The main post office is downtown at the west end of Avenida Sunyaxchén; hours for buying stamps and picking up poste restante mail (Oficina de Correos, Cancún, Quintana Roo 77500) are 8 am to 6 pm weekdays, 9 am to 1 pm Saturday and holidays; for international money orders and registered mail, hours are 8 am to 6 pm weekdays, 9 am to noon Saturday and holidays.

There are numerous Telmex pay phones throughout Cancún that accept prepaid phone cards. Beware of phones accepting credit cards; charges can be very high.

At the time of research, Internet access in the Zona Hotelera was scarce, expensive and sketchy. PC Guía, in the strip mall north of Plaza Quetzal (Km 8.5) charges US$3.25 for 15 minutes, US$8.75 an hour. A counter on the 2nd floor of Plaza Kukulcán charges a flat US$3.75 per 15 minutes of use. A no-name booth with one terminal in Plaza Terramar a few doors east of La Ruina restaurant charges US$0.10 per minute. More places and lower prices should appear soon.

Public Internet facilities have been sprouting in downtown Cancún like mushrooms. One of the longest standing is La Taberna Ciberb@r (☎ 887-73-00), Avenida Yaxchilán 23, an adjunct to a popular neigh-

borhood bar managed by friendly English-speaking people. They charge US$4.25 an hour for a fast satellite connection and are open 10 am to 4 am daily. The other old-timer is Sybcom Internet Café (☎ 885-00-55), Avenida Náder 42, with 10 computers and a clean private line. Rates are US$1 for 15 minutes or less, US$2.25 for 15 to 30 minutes, US$4.25 for 30 to 60 minutes; discount for students with ID. It's open 9 am to midnight Monday to Friday, 3 pm to midnight Saturday).

Both these facilities can send faxes, most hotels will oblige if you insist that you have a document that must be faxed right away, and many businesses in town offer fax service – look for 'Fax' signs in the windows along Avenidas Tulum, Cobá and Yaxchilán.

Travel Agencies

In the Zona Hotelera, most big hotels have travel agencies. Two reputable independent agencies are Mayaland (☎ 883-06-79), 225 Party Center, a small plaza at Boulevard Kukulcán Km 9; and Thomas Moore (☎ 885-02-66), in the Royal Yacht Club complex at Boulevard Kukulcán Km 16.

Downtown there's the centrally located Royal Holiday Travel (☎ 887-34-00, fax 884-58-92, royalh@telmex.com.mx), Avenida Tulum 33, which has a professional, English-speaking staff.

Bookstores

The main bookstore in the Zona Hotelera is Librería Dalí in Kukulcán Plaza on the 2nd floor; it has thousands of books in Spanish and English and an impressive selection of books on the Yucatán.

Fama, a bookstore at Avenida Tulum 105, near the southern end of Tulipanes, has a large variety of domestic and international magazines, and a fair selection of Mexican road atlases and books in various languages. Most of the books are about Cancún, the Yucatán Peninsula and the ancient Mayan civilization.

Laundry

All the resorts on the island offer laundry service, but if you want to save some money

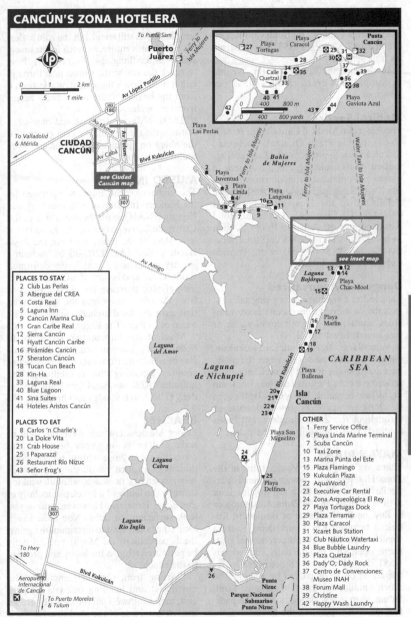

CANCÚN'S ZONA HOTELERA

To Punta Sam

To Punta Sam

Puerto Juárez

Ferry to Isla Mujeres

0   1   2 km
0   .5   1 mile

MEX 180

Av López Portillo

To Valladolid & Mérida

CIUDAD CANCÚN

Av Uxmal

Av Tulum

Av Cobá

Blvd Kukulcán

see Ciudad Cancún map

MEX 307

Av Amigo

Playa Las Perlas

Bahia de Mujeres

Ferry to Isla Mujeres

Water Taxi to Isla Mujeres

Playa Juventud

Playa Linda

Playa Langosta

see inset map

Laguna Bojórquez

Playa Chac-Mool

Laguna del Amor

Playa Marlin

Laguna de Nichupté

Blvd Kukulcán

CARIBBEAN SEA

Playa Ballenas

Isla Cancún

Playa San Miguelito

Laguna Cabra

Playa Delfines

Laguna Río Inglés

To Hwy 180

Blvd Kukulcán

Aeropuerto Internacional de Cancún

To Puerto Morelos & Tulum

Punta Nizuc

Parque Nacional Submarino Punta Nizuc

MEX 307

Inset map:
Playa Tortugas
Playa Caracol
Punta Cancún
Calle Quetzal
Playa Gaviota Azul
0   400   800 m
0   400   800 yards

YUCATÁN

PLACES TO STAY
2 Club Las Perlas
3 Albergue del CREA
4 Costa Real
9 Laguna Inn
9 Cancún Marina Club
11 Gran Caribe Real
12 Sierra Cancún
14 Hyatt Cancún Caribe
16 Pirámides Cancún
17 Sheraton Cancún
18 Tucan Cun Beach
28 Kin-Ha
33 Laguna Real
40 Blue Lagoon
41 Sina Suites
44 Hoteles Aristos Cancún

PLACES TO EAT
8 Carlos 'n Charlie's
20 La Dolce Vita
21 Crab House
25 I Paparazzi
26 Restaurant Río Nizuc
43 Señor Frog's

OTHER
1 Ferry Service Office
6 Playa Linda Marine Terminal
7 Scuba Cancún
10 Taxi Zone
13 Marina Punta del Este
15 Plaza Flamingo
19 Kukulcán Plaza
22 AquaWorld
23 Executive Car Rental
24 Zona Arqueológica El Rey
27 Playa Tortugas Dock
29 Plaza Terramar
30 Plaza Caracol
31 Xcaret Bus Station
32 Club Náutico Watertaxi
34 Blue Bubble Laundry
35 Plaza Quetzal
36 Dady'O; Dady Rock
37 Centro de Convenciones; Museo INAH
38 Forum Mall
39 Christine
42 Happy Wash Laundry

try Happy Wash Laundry, on Paseo Pok-Ta-Pok near the Hotel Suites Laguna Verde. Blue Bubble Laundry, on Boulevard Kukulcán at Km 7.5, charges US$1 per kilogram for bulk service.

In the city, the lavandería on Avenida Bonampak at Cereza charges US$1 per kilogram.

Medical Services

The American Medical Care Center (☎ 883-10-01), beside Plaza Quetzal, Boulevard Kukulcán Km 8, provides good medical attention. As its name suggests, it is American owned and operated. From downtown Cancún it's a 15-minute bus ride to the hospital.

Downtown the Hospital Total Assist (☎ 884-80-82), Claveles 5, next to the Hotel Antillano, just off Avenida Tulum, is open 24 hours. The Centro de IMSS (Social Security Center; ☎ 884-19-63) is on Avenida Cobá at Avenida Tulum.

Dangers & Annoyances

Cancún has a reputation for being safe, but as is the case everywhere, don't leave valuables unattended in your hotel room or beside your beach towel.

Vehicular traffic on Boulevard Kukulcán, particularly as it passes between the malls, bars and discotheques at Punta Cancún, is a serious concern. Pedestrians (many of them drunk) are regularly hit by cars. Traffic cops watching for speeders station themselves throughout the Zona Hotelera, but buses routinely speed and tailgate nonetheless.

MAYAN RUINS

There are two sets of Mayan ruins in the Zona Hotelera, and though neither is particularly impressive, both are worth a look if time permits. In the **Zona Arqueológica El Rey**, on the west side of Boulevard Kukulcán between Km 17 and Km 18, are a small temple and several ceremonial platforms, open 8 am to 5 pm daily; admission is US$1.75, and visitors are occasionally 'required' to be accompanied by a guide. The much smaller of the two sites is **Yamil Lu'um**, atop a beachside knoll on the parklike grounds separating the Sheraton Can-

cún and Pirámides Cancún towers. Only the outward-sloping remains of the weathered temple's walls still stand, but the ruin makes for a pleasant venture, as much for its lovely setting as anything else. Admission is free; to reach the site visitors must pass through either of the hotels flanking it or approach it from the beach – there is no direct access from the boulevard.

The tiny Mayan structure and chac-mool statue set in the beautifully kept grounds of the Sheraton Hotel are authentic and were found on the spot.

MUSEO INAH

The archaeological museum, operated by the National Institute of Anthropology and History (INAH), is on the south side of the Centro de Convenciones in the Zona Hotelera. Most of the items are from the Postclassic period (AD 1200–1500), including jewelry, masks and intentionally deformed skulls. There also is part of a Classic-period hieroglyphic staircase inscribed with dates from the 6th century, and the stucco head that gave the local archaeological zone its name of El Rey (The King).

Most of the informative signs are in Spanish only, but you can get a fractured-English information sheet at the ticket counter detailing the contents of the museum's 47 showcases. Open 9 am to 8 pm daily (US$2; free Sunday and holidays).

BEACHES

Under Mexican law you have the right to walk and swim on every beach in the country except those within military compounds. In practice, it is difficult to approach many stretches of beach without walking through the lobby of a hotel, particularly in the Zona Hotelera. However, unless you look suspicious or unless you look like a local (the hotels tend to discriminate against locals, particularly the Maya), you'll usually be permitted to cross the lobby and proceed to the beach.

Starting from Ciudad Cancún in the northwest and heading out Isla Cancún east, then southwest, all the beaches are on the left-hand side of the road (the lagoon is on your right). The first beaches are Playa Las Perlas, Playa Linda, Playa Langosta, Playa Tortugas and Playa Caracol; after rounding Punta Cancún, the beaches to the south are Playa Gaviota Azul, the long stretches of Playa Chac-Mool, Playa Marlin, the long stretch of Playa Ballenas and finally, at Km 17, Playa Delfines.

Delfines is about the only beach with a public parking lot; unfortunately, its sand is coarser and darker than the exquisite fine sand of the more northerly beaches.

Beach Safety
Cancún's ambulance crews respond to as many as a dozen near-drownings per week. The most dangerous beaches seem to be Playa Delfines and Playa Chac-Mool.

As experienced swimmers know, a beach fronting on open sea can be deadly dangerous, and Cancún's eastern beaches are no exception. Though the surf is usually gentle, undertow is a possibility and sudden storms (called *nortes*) can blacken the sky and sweep in at any time without warning. The local authorities have devised a system of colored pennants to warn beachgoers of potential dangers. Look for the pennants on the beaches where you swim:

Blue	Normal, safe conditions
Yellow	Use caution, changeable conditions
Red	Unsafe conditions; use a swimming pool instead

WATER SPORTS
For decent **snorkeling**, you need to travel to one of the nearby reefs. Resort hotels, travel agencies and various tour operators in the area can book you on day-cruise boats that take snorkelers to the barrier reef, as well as to others within 100km of Cancún. To see the sparse aquatic life off Cancún's beaches, you can rent snorkeling equipment for about US$10 a day from most luxury hotels.

For **diving**, try Scuba Cancún (☎ 883-58-46, 883-10-11, fax 884-23-36, scuba@cancun .com.mx, www.scubacancun.com.mx), Boulevard Kukulcán Km 5, a family-owned, PADI-certified operation with many years of experience. The bilingual staff are safety oriented and environmentally aware, and offer a variety of dive options (including cenote dives), as well as snorkeling and **fishing** trips, at reasonable prices.

Deep-sea fishing excursions can also be booked through a travel agent or one of the large hotels. Most of the major resorts rent **kayaks** and the usual water toys; a few make them available to guests free.

AquaWorld is an enormous, impersonal operation with a very poor environmental record. The company offers everything from diving and snorkeling tours to 'submarine' rides and equipment rental.

ORGANIZED TOURS
Most hotels and travel agencies work with companies that offer tours to surrounding attractions. Some of the places visited, and approximate prices, are: Chichén Itzá (US$64, includes buffet lunch and admission), Tulum and Xel-Há (US$64, includes admission), Xcaret (US$75, includes admission). Budget-conscious travelers can go to the bus station downtown and book a tour offering the same for less: Chichén Itzá (US$49), Xcaret (US$53), Tulum and Xel-Há (US$40).

PLACES TO STAY
As happens in other popular Yucatán destinations, the rates at some of Cancún's hotels change with the tourist seasons, and every hotelier's idea of when these seasons are is slightly different. Rate changes occur more at mid-range and top-end establishments, though during Semana Santa (Easter Week) rates can rise at budget hotels as well. Broadly, Cancún's high season is from mid-December through March. All prices quoted here are for that high season unless otherwise specified; off-season rates can be significantly lower.

When business is slow (as it was in the first months of Y2K), getting a significant discount can be as easy as showing hesitation about a place. It's always worth asking for a *promoción* (discount), regardless of season.

Places to Stay – Budget
Except for the first hostel described below, all budget accommodations are in Ciudad

YUCATÁN

Cancún. 'Budget' is a relative term; prices in Cancún are higher for what you get than anywhere else in the Yucatán.

Only a brief and inexpensive bus ride separates the beaches of the Zona Hotelera from the city.

Four kilometers from the bus station, *Albergue del CREA* (☎/fax 883-04-84, Blvd Kukulcán Km 3.2) is on the left-hand side of the road as you come from downtown. Built decades ago as a modern 600-bed complex in honor of youth, it is now dilapidated, with 300 beds still in use. The staff is friendly and the place reasonably priced for what you get: a single-sex dorm bed for US$8 (plus a US$6 deposit for a sheet and pillow). Camping on the lawn out back costs US$4.25 per person, with a locker and use of the hostel's shower and bathroom facilities. There is no age limit and space is usually available. The beach there is silty and shallow.

As this book was going to press, another hostel announced its opening. If they live up to their advertising, it should be a decent place to stay, with beds starting at US$10 a night. The hostel is four blocks northwest of the bus terminal, on the far arm of Palmera (off Avenida Uxmal). Check mexicohostels .com for further details.

Many of Cancún's cheap hotels are within a few blocks of the bus station. Go northwest on Avenida Uxmal to reach the first three described here.

Hotel El Alux (☎ 884-66-13, fax 884-05-56, Avenida Uxmal 21) is a block from the bus station. The 35 air-con rooms with hot shower, phone and TV go for US$29/36 single/double.

Across Uxmal is the 38-room *Hotel Cotty* (☎ 884-05-50, fax 884-13-19, Avenida Uxmal 44). Rooms with shower, air-con, cable TV, phone and two comfortable double beds cost US$29/32/34 double/triple/quad. There is off-street parking; 2nd-floor rear rooms get club noise from Avenida Yaxchilán.

A few steps farther on Uxmal is Calle Palmera and the *Hotel María Isabel* (☎ 884-90-15, Palmera 59), a clean, quiet, nine-room place. It is one of the cheapest hotels close to the bus station, and it shows. Rooms with private shower, so-so air-con and cable TV

cost US$26 double. A two-bedroom, two-bath unit runs US$57.

From Avenida Uxmal, walk south along Avenida Yaxchilán and take the first right, Punta Allen, to find *Casa de Huéspedes Punta Allen* (☎ 884-02-25, Punta Allen 8). This family-run guesthouse has several double rooms with bath and air-con for US$29 to US$33, light breakfast included.

The *Hotel Colonial* (☎/fax 884-15-35, Tulipanes 22) has 50 rooms facing a courtyard and offers a very good value at US$27 per double room without air-con, US$33 with air-con (US$7 per extra person).

Another fine hotel is the *Suites El Patio* (☎ 884-35-00, fax 884-35-40, cancun@ cancunsuites.com, cancun-suites.com), Avenida Bonampak at the northern end of Cereza, with 12 charming rooms for US$50 and a suite for US$55. There's off-street parking, a communal refrigerator, a TV room, a restaurant on the premises and a laundry across the street. The friendly owner speaks English, French and Spanish.

Around the corner from the bus station is the *Hotel Novotel* (☎ 884-29-99, fax 884-31-62, Avenida Tulum 75). Double rooms with fan only cost US$43, with air-con US$54; front rooms can be noisy.

The *Hotel Tulum* (☎ 884-18-90), at the corner of Avenida Tulum and Claveles, offers 22 rooms with air-con, cable TV, telephone and minibar for US$46/55/65 double/triple/quad.

On Avenida Tulum just south of Avenida Xcaret is *Hotel Cancún Handall* (☎ 842-66-66, fax 884-19-76), where air-con rooms cost US$41. Noise can be a problem, but the hotel is comfortable and clean.

Places to Stay – Mid-Range

Zona Hotelera In choosing a moderately priced hotel in the Zona Hotelera (that is, one that's under US$135 for two people), bear in mind that those close to Boulevard Kukulcán are close to cheap, convenient transportation.

The *Laguna Real* (☎ 883-28-99, fax 883-00-03, Quetzal 8), 100m off Blvd Kukulcán Km 7.7, is an excellent find. Its 36 air-con rooms feature two double beds (some have king-size beds), cable TV and use of all of the facilities at the seaside Gran Caribe Real and Costa Real resorts (there's free shuttle service to these resorts). There's also a pool on the premises. Rooms are US$100.

Just down the street is **Sina Suites** (☎ 883-10-17/8, fax 883-24-58, in the USA ☎ 877-666-9837, Quetzal 33), with 33 spacious suites with kitchen, 1½ baths, separate living room with sofa bed, bedroom with two double beds, satellite TV, a pool, bar and restaurant. Rates are US$80 to US$125.

The **Blue Lagoon** (☎ /fax 883-12-15, Quetzal 39) offers 24 one-bedroom suites with private balcony, air-con and TV. There's a pool and restaurant, and each suite is roomy and comfortable. A great find for US$65 double most of the year.

Between Kms 3 and 4 and facing the lagoon is the **Laguna Inn** (☎ 883-20-55, fax 883-20-61, in the USA ☎ 407-331-7355, fax 407-834-3337, Calle del Pescador, Lote D-8-3). It has 90 air-con rooms, each containing either two double beds or one queen-size bed. There's a pool, a tree-shaded courtyard and an inviting palapa bar-restaurant. Rooms cost US$90.

The popular **Cancún Marina Club** (☎ 883-15-61, 883-14-09, in the USA ☎ 800-448-8355, Blvd Kukulcán 5.5) has a very inviting pool, a pleasant restaurant-bar overlooking the lagoon and a water-sports center. Among the 75 rooms are 10 penthouses with Jacuzzis. Regular rooms are US$90.

Considering its location and amenities, the **Hoteles Aristos Cancún** (☎ 883-00-11, fax 883-00-78, in the USA ☎ 800-527-4786, intl .sales@aristoshotels.com, www.aristoshotels .com, Blvd Kukulcán 9.6) offers the best value of the Zona's moderately priced digs. Its 250 balconied guestrooms come with satellite TV, air-con and two double beds or one king-size bed. All rooms face the sea or the lagoon. Facilities include two pools (one for kids), two tennis courts, pool tables, two restaurants and three bars. Rooms are US$115.

Ciudad Cancún One of the best values in town, **Hotel El Rey del Caribe** (☎ 884-20-28, fax 884-98-57, reycarib@cancun.rce.com .mx, www.reycaribe.com), at the corner of Avenidas Uxmal and Náder, has 24 air-con suites with fully equipped kitchenettes and super-comfy beds. There's a lush courtyard, a lovely pool, a Jacuzzi and off-street parking. Rates are US$60 double (no extra charge for up to two children under 11); extra person US$10. The rooms at the back are very nice lodgings indeed.

El Rey is a true eco-tel that composts, uses solar collectors and cisterns, gardens with gray water, and has even begun using composting toilets. Its owners are educating other hotels and businesses in the area about such methods as well.

Directly across Pino from the bus station is the **Hotel Best Western Plaza Caribe** (☎ 884-13-77, fax 884-63-52, in the USA ☎ 800-528-1234, plazacbe@cancun.com.mx, www.bestwestern.com), between Avenidas Tulum and Uxmal, offering 140 comfortable air-con rooms and all the amenities for US$75 double. A pool and a restaurant are on the premises.

The very pleasant **Hotel Antillano** (☎ 884-15-32, fax 884-18-78), on Claveles just off Avenida Tulum, has a pool and 48 guestrooms with air-con and cable TV for US$48/55/63 single/double/triple.

Cheerful **Hotel Margaritas** (☎ 884-93-33, fax 884-13-24, Avenida Yaxchilán 41) has 100 guestrooms with air-con, TV and bath. There's a pool, a restaurant and a bar and attentive service, all for US$73 double (extra persons US$11 each).

Just across Yaxchilán, the **Hotel Suites Caribe Internacional** (☎ 884-3999, fax 884-1993, Avenida Sunyaxchén 36) has a small pool in a pleasant courtyard, secure parking and 80 standard rooms with air-con and cable TV for US$85 double. There are also numerous junior suites with two beds, sofa and kitchenette for US$110. These rates are negotiable depending on occupancy; ask for a discount!

Places to Stay – Top End

Rates in this category start at US$160 double; all of these resorts border the Caribbean. All guestrooms in this price category have air-con and satellite TV, and many

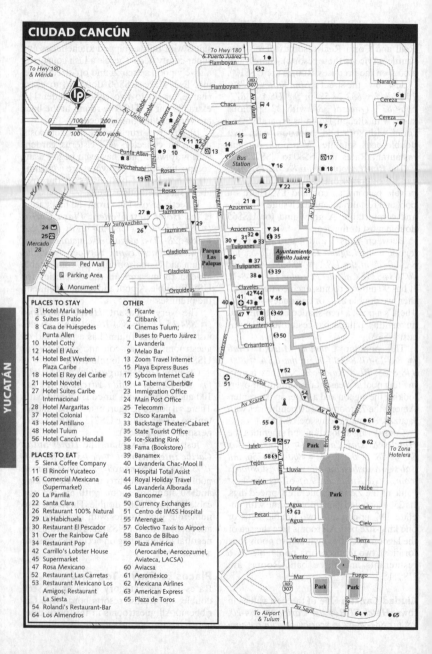

CIUDAD CANCÚN

To Hwy 180 & Puerto Juárez
To Hwy 180 & Mérida
To Zona Hotelera
To Airport & Tulum

Flamboyan
Flamboyan
Chaca
Chaca
Punta Allen
Nicchehabi
Rosas
Rosas
Azucenas
Azucenas
Jazmines
Jazmines
Gladiolas
Gladiolas
Orquídeas
Tulipanes
Tulipanes
Claveles
Claveles
Crisantemos
Crisantemos
Naranja
Cereza
Cereza
Bus Station
Parque Las Palapas
Ayuntamiento Benito Juárez
Mercado 28

Av Uxmal
Av Robie
Robie
Palmera
Palmera
Jaguel
Av Yaxchilán
Laurel
Cedro
Pino
Av Tulum
Margaritas
Margaritas
Abrances
Av Sunyaxchén
Tauch
Av Xcaret
Av Cobá
Av Cobá
Av Náder
Av Náder
Av Bonampak
Av Tankah
Av Yaxchilán
Av Yaxchilán
Av Sayil
Tejón
Tejón
Lluvia
Lluvia
Pecari
Pecari
Agua
Agua
Viento
Viento
Mar
Siena
Brisa
Nube
Nube
Cielo
Cielo
Tierra
Tierra
Fuego
Fuego
Jaleb
Merengue
Park
Park
Park
Park
Park

MEX 307
MEX 307

0   100   200 m
0   100   200 yards

Ped Mall
P Parking Area
⚓ Monument

PLACES TO STAY
3 Hotel María Isabel
6 Suites El Patio
8 Casa de Huéspedes Punta Allen
10 Hotel Cotty
12 Hotel El Alux
14 Hotel Best Western Plaza Caribe
18 Hotel El Rey del Caribe
21 Hotel Novotel
27 Hotel Suites Caribe Internacional
28 Hotel Margaritas
37 Hotel Colonial
43 Hotel Antillano
48 Hotel Tulum
56 Hotel Cancún Handall

PLACES TO EAT
5 Siena Coffee Company
11 El Rincón Yucateco
16 Comercial Mexicana (Supermarket)
20 La Parrilla
22 Santa Clara
26 Restaurant 100% Natural
29 La Habichuela
30 Restaurant El Pescador
31 Over the Rainbow Café
34 Restaurant Pop
42 Carrillo's Lobster House
45 Supermarket
47 Rosa Mexicano
52 Restaurant Las Carretas
53 Restaurant Mexicano Los Amigos; Restaurant La Siesta
54 Rolandi's Restaurant-Bar
64 Los Almendros

OTHER
1 Picante
2 Citibank
4 Cinemas Tulum; Buses to Puerto Juárez
7 Lavandería
9 Melao Bar
13 Zoom Travel Internet
15 Playa Express Buses
17 Sybcom Internet Café
19 La Taberna Ciberb@r
23 Immigration Office
24 Main Post Office
25 Telecomm
32 Disco Karamba
33 Backstage Theater-Cabaret
35 State Tourist Office
36 Ice-Skating Rink
38 Fama (Bookstore)
39 Banamex
40 Lavandería Chac-Mool II
41 Hospital Total Assist
44 Royal Holiday Travel
46 Lavandería Alborada
49 Bancomer
50 Currency Exchanges
51 Centro de IMSS Hospital
55 Merengue
57 Colectivo Taxis to Airport
58 Banco de Bilbao
59 Plaza América (Aerocaribe, Aerocozumel, Aviateca, LACSA)
60 Aviacsa
61 Aeroméxico
62 Mexicana Airlines
63 American Express
65 Plaza de Toros

YUCATÁN

have balconies with a sea view. Often the best room rates available are contained in hotel-and-airfare packages; shop around. Because the rates offered by each resort vary greatly depending on when and where guests book reservations, and because all of the resorts are conveniently located along Boulevard Kukulcán, the hotels are arranged by their location along the boulevard rather than by cost.

Km 2.5 The *Club Las Perlas* (☎ 883-20-22, fax 883-08-30, clperlas@cancun.rce.com.mx) boasts 194 rooms in a close grouping of three- and four-story buildings. The resort's location, at the end of the Zona Hotelera, means its beach is considerably quieter than those farther east and to the south. Rates typically start at US$170 double.

Km 4 The *Costa Real* (☎ 881-13-00, fax 881-13-99, in the USA ☎ 800-543-7556, real@bestday.com, www.real.com.mx) is a large, all-inclusive resort with attractive grounds and a shared-facilities agreement with the much more spectacular Gran Caribe Real to the east. Per-person double-occupancy rates are US$150.

Km 5.7 The *Gran Caribe Real* (☎ 881-73-00, fax 881-73-99, in the USA ☎ 800-543-7556, real@bestday.com) has 504 deluxe rooms (all with ocean views), 52 junior suites and two three-story, three-bedroom penthouse suites. All come with private terraces that overlook a dazzling swimming pool and 200m of beach. Room rates start at US$160. An all-inclusive plan runs US$170 per person, double occupancy.

Km 8.1 The self-contained *Kin-Ha* (☎ 883-23-77, fax 883-21-47, kinha3@mail.caribe.net.mx) has 162 rooms and suites in four buildings. All rooms feature a balcony and two double beds or one king-size bed. A travel agency, car rental, mini-market, bars and a gym are on the premises. Rooms are US$190, suites US$242.

Km 10 The *Sierra Cancún* (☎ 883-24-44, fax 883-34-86, in the USA ☎ 800-448-5028) features 54 standard rooms (mostly lagoon view), 204 mini-suites (all ocean-view), and a variety of larger suites. This Mexican-owned and -operated resort offers all the usual amenities for US$250 for two, meals included.

Km 10.3 The *Hyatt Cancún Caribe* (☎ 883-00-44, fax 883-15-14, in the USA ☎ 800-233-1234, www.hyatt.com) has a range of accommodations and amenities among its 206 lovely guestrooms and suites. Rooms start around US$180, villas around US$240, suites US$289.

Km 11.75 The *Pirámides Cancún* (☎ 885-13-33, fax 885-01-13, piramides@piramidescancun.com.mx, www.piramidescancun.com.mx) has 289 charming rooms and suites. The grounds are idyllic and the beach particularly deep. The resort 'shares' a real Mayan ruin with its neighbor to the south, the Sheraton Cancún. Room rates start at US$200.

Km 12.5 The *Sheraton Cancún* (☎ 883-19-88, fax 885-02-04, in the USA ☎ 800-325-3535, cancunrsvshecun@sybcom.com, www.sheraton.com/cancun) has tremendous appeal, from the elegant lobby to the immaculate gardens to the gorgeous tiled art in the restaurant. At US$200 a room, it's an excellent value.

Km 13.5 The *Tucan Cun Beach* (☎ 885-08-14, fax 885-18-50, ventasj@cancun.com.mx, www.inetcorp.net.mx/tucancun) is a fun, budget-minded all-inclusive resort with 319 guestrooms, decent food and an inviting pool with swim-up bar. Per-person rates most of the year hover around US$130.

PLACES TO EAT

Though you can find a meal in any price range in the Zona Hotelera, the best selection of budget and moderately priced eats is available in Ciudad Cancún, away from the big resorts.

Budget

Zona Hotelera For budget eats in the Zona Hotelera, try the food courts in every large mall. Facing Boulevard Kukulcán near Km 8.5 and comprising part of the Plaza Terramar is *La Ruina*; the highlights here are the delicious Mexican traditionals.

Nothing's priced over US$7 at outdoor *Restaurant Río Nizuc*, at the end of a short, nameless road near Boulevard Kukulcán Km 22. Octopus, conch and fish are served in various ways, and it's a nice place to settle in a chair under a palapa and watch convoys of snorkelers in sporty little boats pass by.

Ciudad Cancún The main market is set back from the street, west of the post office. Its official name is long; locals simply call it *Mercado 28* (that's 'mercado veintiocho'). The eateries are mostly in the inner courtyard. The likes of *Restaurant Margely*, *Cocina Familiar Económica Chulum* and *Cocina La Chaya* offer set meals for as little as US$3 and sandwiches for less.

The *Over the Rainbow Café* *(Tulipanes 30)* is a charming air-con café that specializes in crepes, none of which is more than US$3.25. There's also a fine variety of sandwiches, salads and pastries (most under US$4) and a good selection of coffee drinks. It's open 12:30 pm to 4 am Monday to Saturday, until 2 am Sunday. This is a pleasant and civilized place to end your day

El Rincón Yucateco *(Avenida Uxmal 24)*, across from the Hotel Cotty, serves excellent yet inexpensive Yucatecan food, with good comidas corridas for US$3.25. Air-conditioned *Restaurant Pop* is on Avenida Tulum about a block south of Avenida Uxmal. Few of the tasty salads, soups, pastas, fish and meat dishes are over US$6. Around the corner on Avenida Uxmal is *Santa Clara*, specializing in ice cream.

The *Restaurant Mexicano Los Amigos* *(Avenida Tulum 16)* is an open-air restaurant that serves up decent Mexican and American food for about US$4 to US$9. Next door and very similar is the *Restaurant Las Carretas*.

For your iced mocha, double latte, croissant or bagel with cream cheese fix, look no further than the tiny *Siena Coffee Company* *(Náder 328)*, a block north of Avenida Tulum.

A centrally located supermarket with a good selection of produce, meats, cheeses and cookies is *Comercial Mexicana*, at the corner of Avenida Tulum and Avenida Uxmal.

Mid-Range

Zona Hotelera The Zona Hotelera's mid-range choices are mostly franchised American and Mexican, some of the party-hardy stripe, serving upscale American fast food with some Mexican options. Try *Señor Frog's* *(Blvd Kukulcán Km 9.8)* or *Carlos 'n Charlie's* *(Blvd Kukulcán Km 5.5)*, where dishes range from US$10 to US$17. Plaza Flamingo and the Forum mall hold other options.

Ciudad Cancún The *Restaurant El Pescador* *(Tulipanes 28)* has been serving dependably good seafood meals for many years; most of the specialties cost US$14 or more.

Rolandi's Restaurant-Bar *(Avenida Cobá 12)*, between Avenidas Tulum and Náder just off the southern roundabout, is an attractive Italian eatery serving elaborate one-person pizzas (US$4 to US$7), spaghetti plates and more substantial dishes of veal and chicken (US$5 to US$8).

The *Restaurant 100% Natural* (Cien por Ciento Natural), on Avenida Sunyaxchén near Avenida Yaxchilán, is one of a chain of restaurants serving juice blends, a wide selection of yogurt-fruit-vegetable combinations and pasta, fish and chicken dishes. There's a bakery on the premises, and the place is very nicely decorated and landscaped. No item is over US$9. A branch in the Zona Hotelera on the north side of Plaza Terramar (Blvd Kukulcán Km 8.65) charges slightly higher prices.

Los Almendros, Avenida Bonampak near Avenida Sayil, is the local incarnation of Yucatán's most famous restaurant. Started in Ticul in 1962, it set out to serve country food for the bourgeoisie and claims to have invented *poc-chuc*, a dish of succulent pork cooked with onion and served in a tomato sauce made tangy with bitter oranges. Dishes cost from US$4 to US$6.

A long-standing favorite is *Rosa Mexicano* *(Claveles 4)*, the place to go for unusual Mexican dishes in a pleasant hacienda decor. Try the squid sautéed with three chiles, or garlic and scallions and shrimp in a *pipían* sauce (made of ground pumpkin seeds and spices). Dinner goes for US$10 to US$30.

La Parrilla *(Avenida Yaxchilán 51)* is a traditional Mexican restaurant popular with locals and tourists alike. Tasty *calamari al mojo de ajo* (squid in garlic sauce), steaks and sautéed grouper are all around US$8; mole enchiladas, US$5. Superb piña coladas run US$5.50.

Top End

Zona Hotelera The *Crab House* *(Blvd Kukulcán Km 14.8)* is a draw as much for its lovely view of the lagoon as for its seafood. The long menu includes many shrimp and fillet-of-fish dishes (mostly around US$18). Crab is priced by the pound

(US$10 to US$50), and set meals are offered for US$28 to US$54.

About 25m north of the Crab House is *La Dolce Vita*, facing the lagoon, one of Cancún's two fancy Italian restaurants; the other is *I Paparazzi (Blvd Kukulcán Km 18)*, overlooking Playa Delfines. Expect to pay around US$20 with beverage and tip at either.

Ciudad Cancún Elegant *La Habichuela (Margaritas 25)* is just off Parque Las Palapas in a residential neighborhood. Typical items are shish kebab flambé, lobster in champagne sauce and beef tampiqueña. Dinners average US$20 to US$25 but can run much higher if you pull out all the stops.

For lobster, head to the somewhat formal *Carrillo's Lobster House (Claveles 35)*, where dishes cost around US$30. There are numerous shrimp and fish dishes around US$10 to US$15.

ENTERTAINMENT

Most of Cancún's nightlife is loud and booze-oriented, and the dance clubs are as wild as you'll find anywhere. Most charge US$10 admission, some don't open their doors before 10 pm, and none are hopping much before midnight.

Dady'O (Blvd Kukulcán Km 9), opposite the Forum mall, is one of Cancún's hottest dance clubs. The setting is a five-level black-walled faux cave with a two-level dance floor and zillions of laser beams and strobes, and the beat is pure disco. Next door is *Dady Rock*, a steamy rock & roll club with live music.

Christine (Blvd Kukulcán Km 8.85) features a synchronized light, sound and video system and a different mix of music every night; it attracts a fair number of thirtysomethings. *La Boom (Blvd Kukulcán Km 3.8)* features Top 40 tunes played at many decibels. *Cat's (Blvd Kukulcán Km 8.75)*, on the south side of Plaza La Parrilla, is the one true reggae club in Cancún, with live music each evening; a hip-hop band usually plays on nights the house band is off.

For live Cuban music, there's *Melao Bar*, on Avenida Yaxchilán at Punta Allen, an intimate upstairs club where the atmosphere can be magical. There's no cover, but the performances often don't begin until after 11 pm. Another Cuban venue, with very few tourists, is *Merengue*, on Avenida Tulum near Avenida Cobá, next to the Hotel Cancún Handall, with two shows nightly, at 9:30 and 11:30 pm (closed Sunday). Cover is US$2.75; don't come casually dressed.

Gay & Lesbian Venues There's a significant gay scene in Ciudad Cancún, but it's not apparent until well after sunset. The *Backstage Theater-Cabaret (☎ 887-91-06, Tulipanes 30)* features drag shows, strippers (male and female), fashion shows and musicals. This is a very cool place, with terrific ambience and a joyful crowd. Admission is usually US$3.25.

Disco Karamba, above the Ristorante Casa Italiana, on the corner of Azucenas at Avenida Tulum, is famous for its frequent drink specials (closed Monday). *Picante*, set back from Avenida Tulum a few blocks north of Avenida Uxmal, is mainly for talkers, not dancers.

Dance Performances An excellent alternative to the party scene is the *Folkloric Ballet of Cancún (☎ 881-04-00 ext 193, fax 881-04-02, Blvd Kukulcán Km 8.8)*, inside the Centro de Convenciones. The first-rate show includes dances from various Mexican regions, including one with ancient Mayan ceremonial themes. Performances are nightly at 8 pm (arrive no later than 7:15 for good seats) and cost US$28 for the show and a drink, US$46 for a buffet dinner, drink and show (the food is delicious). Cocktails are at 6:30 pm, dinner at 7.

GETTING THERE & AWAY

Air

Cancún's international airport is the busiest in southeastern Mexico. Upon arrival, don't change money until after you've passed through Customs and Immigration, as the rate is poor. Turn left out of the arrivals area and make the short walk to the *departures* area; there are exchange windows offering better rates, as well as ATMs.

There are baggage lockers in the departure terminal just before the first gates (they may move to a more convenient location); they cost US$5.50 for 24 hours.

The general information number at the airport is ☎ 886-00-49.

Cancún is served by many direct international flights (see the Yucatán Getting There & Away chapter).

From Cancún, between Aerocaribe and Aerocozumel (both owned by Mexicana) there is one flight daily to Mexico City (US$130), Oaxaca (US$236), Tuxtla Gutiérrez (US$223) and Veracruz (US$111). The airlines have a total of two flights daily to Chetumal (US$88), two daily to Chichén Itzá (US$65), three daily to Villahermosa (US$145), three daily to Mérida (US$95) and eight daily to Cozumel (US$50).

They also provide service to Campeche (four flights a week, US$107); Palenque (three a week, US$173); Belize City (one Saturday, one Sunday, US$137); Flores, Guatemala (three a week, US$122); Guatemala City; and Havana, Cuba (two flights daily, US$174).

Aviacsa, a regional carrier based in Tuxtla Gutiérrez, has flights from Cancún to Mérida, Mexico City, Oaxaca, Tapachula, Tuxtla Gutiérrez, Villahermosa and points in Guatemala.

Aviateca runs flights from Cancún to Flores, Guatemala, and on to Guatemala City (US$329) several times a week. Several major international carriers also offer domestic flights from Cancún.

If you intend to fly from Cancún to other parts of Mexico, you are well advised to reserve your airline seat ahead of time to avoid any unpleasant surprises. Airline contact information is:

Aerocaribe & Aerocozumel (☎ 884-20-00, www.aerocaribe.com), Avenida Cobá 5, Plaza América (downtown)

Aeroméxico (☎ 884-10-97, www.aeromexico.com), Avenida Cobá 80, between Avenidas Tulum and Bonampak (downtown)

American Airlines (☎ 01-800-904-60-00, www.aa.com) airport counter only

Aviacsa (☎ 887-42-11, fax 884-65-99, www.aviacsa.com), Avenida Cobá 37 (downtown)

Aviateca (☎ 884-39-38, fax 884-33-28, www.grupotaca.com), Avenida Cobá 5, Plaza América (downtown)

Continental (☎ 886-00-40, fax 886-00-07, www.continental.com) airport counter only

LACSA (☎ 887-31-01, www.grupotaca.com), Avenida Cobá 5, Plaza América (downtown)

Mexicana (☎ 87-44-44 downtown, 24-hr toll-free ☎ 91-800-50-220, www.mexicana.com), Avenida Cobá 39 (downtown), Centro de Convenciones (Zona Hotelera; ☎ 883-48-81)

Northwest (☎ 886-00-46, www.nwa.com) airport counter only

Bus

Cancún's bus station occupies the wedge formed where Avenidas Uxmal and Tulum meet. Services are 2nd-class, 1st-class and any of several luxury flavors. Across Pino from the bus station, a few doors from Avenida Tulum, is the ticket office and miniterminal of Playa Express, which runs shuttle buses down the Caribbean coast to Tulum and Felipe Carrillo Puerto at least every 30 minutes until early evening, stopping at major towns and points of interest along the way.

The staff at the ADO Riviera information counter in the bus station are in touch with their routes and can tell you all about it.

Following are some of the major routes serviced daily:

Chetumal 382km, 6 hours; ADO 1st-class (US$15.25), 2nd-class (US$12.50); 28 buses total daily

Chichén Itzá 205km, 3 to 4 hours; 1st-class (US$10.25), 2nd-class (US$6.75); 15 buses total

Mérida 320km, 4 to 6 hours; buses at least every half hour (US$15.75)

Mexico City 1883km, 20 to 22 hours; one 1st-class (7:45 am) to Norte, three to TAPO (US$79)

Playa del Carmen – 68km, 45 minutes to 1¼ hours; Playa Express every 30 minutes until 4:30 pm, numerous others (US$2.75)

Puerto Morelos –36km, 40 minutes; Playa Express every 30 minutes until 4:30 pm, numerous others (US$1 to US$1.50)

Ticul 395km, 6 hours; eight Mayab 2nd-class (US$15)

Tizimín 212km, 3 to 3½ hours; eight buses total by Noreste and Oriente (US$6.50 to US$7)

Tulum 134km, 2¼ hours; Playa Express every 30 minutes, numerous others (US$5 to US$6)

Valladolid 160km, 2 to 3 hours; buses at least every half hour (US$7)

Villahermosa 947km, 12 hours; 13 buses total (US$38)

Car

Alamo (☎ 886-01-33), Avis (☎ 886-01-47), Executive (☎ 846-13-87), Hertz (☎ 886-01-50) and Mónaco (☎ 886-02-39) have counters at the airport. Bear in mind that you can receive better rates and have a better selection of vehicles if you reserve ahead of time.

Executive Car Rental (☎ 885-03-72, www .executive.com.mx), Boulevard Kukulcán Km 15.5, occasionally has vehicles long after the airport offices have rented out all of theirs. Weekly rates are available.

See the boxed text 'You Take the High Road?' in the Yucatán State chapter for details on the toll road west of Cancún.

GETTING AROUND
To/From the Airport

If you don't want to pay US$38 for a taxi ride into town, there are a few options. Comfortable shared vans charging US$8.25 leave from the curb in front of the international terminal about every 15 minutes, heading for the Zona Hotelera via Punta Nizuc. They head into town after the island, but it can take up to 45 minutes from the airport. To get downtown more directly and cheaply, head straight out of the terminal to the parking lot and past the flagpole. At the left side of the lot is the shell of a bus that now serves as a ticket booth for buses (US$4.25) that stop here every 20 minutes or so. They travel up Avenida Tulum and stop at the bus terminal downtown.

If you follow the access road out of the airport and past the traffic-monitoring booth (a total of about 300m), you can often flag down a taxi leaving the airport empty that will take you for less (try for US$4) because the driver is no longer subject to the expensive regulated airport fares. If you're willing to walk the 2km to the highway, you can flag down a passing bus, which is very cheap (US$0.45).

To return to the airport you can catch a colectivo taxi in front of the Hotel Cancún Handall on Avenida Tulum just south of Avenida Cobá. They operate between 3 am and 8 pm, charge US$3.50 per person and leave when full. Private taxis from town charge US$8 to US$10.

Bus To reach the Zona Hotelera from downtown, catch any bus with 'R1,' 'Hoteles' or 'Zona Hotelera' displayed on the windshield as it travels south along Avenida Tulum or east along Avenida Cobá. The fare each way is US$0.45.

To reach Puerto Juárez and the Isla Mujeres ferries, catch a Ruta 13 ('Pto Juárez' or 'Punta Sam'; US$0.40) bus at the stop in front of Cinemas Tulum, on Avenida Tulum north of Avenida Uxmal.

Taxi Cancún's taxis do not have meters. There is a sign listing official fares on the outside wall of the bus station; if you can't refer to it you'll probably have to haggle. From downtown to Punta Cancún is US$6, to the airport is US$12, to Puerto Juárez US$4.25.

Scooter Marina Punta del Este (☎ 883-12-10), Boulevard Kukulcán Km 10.3, rents Yamaha 100cc scooters for US$10 the first hour and US$5 each additional hour.

Around Cancún

ISLA MUJERES
• **population 8322**

Isla Mujeres (Island of Women) has a reputation as a backpackers' Cancún – a quieter island where many of the same amenities and attractions cost a lot less. That's not as true today – Cancún makes itself felt each morning as boatloads of package tourists arrive for a day's excursion. But Isla Mujeres continues to offer good values, a popular sunbathing beach, and plenty of dive and snorkel sites. Though its character has changed, the island's chief attributes are still a relaxed tropical social life and waters that are turquoise blue and bathtub warm.

History

Although many locals believe Isla Mujeres got its name because Spanish buccaneers kept their lovers there while they plundered galleons and pillaged ports, a less romantic but still intriguing explanation is probably more accurate. In 1517 Francisco Hernández de Córdoba sailed from Cuba to procure slaves for the mines there. His expedition came upon Isla Mujeres, and in the course of searching it the conquistadors located a stone temple containing clay figurines of Mayan goddesses. Córdoba named the island after the icons.

Today some archaeologists believe that the island was a stopover for the Maya en route to worship their goddess of fertility, Ixchel, on the island of Cozumel. The clay idols are thought to represent the goddess.

Orientation

The island is 8km long, 300m to 800m wide and 11km off the coast. The town of Isla Mujeres is at the island's northern tip, and the ruins of the Mayan temple are at the southern tip. The two are linked by Avenida Rueda Medina, a loop road that hugs the coast. Between them are a handful of small fishing villages, several saltwater lakes, a string of westward-facing beaches, a large lagoon and a small airport.

The best snorkeling sites and some of the best swimming beaches are on the island's southwest shore; the eastern shore is washed by the open sea, and the surf there is dangerous. The ferry docks, the town and the most popular sand beach (Playa Norte) are at the northern tip of the island.

Information

Tourist & Immigration Offices There's an island-sponsored tourist information office (☎ 877-07-67, ☎/fax 877-03-07, infoisla@qroo1.telmex.net.mex) on Avenida Rueda Medina between Madero and Morelos. One member of its friendly staff speaks English, the rest Spanish only. Open 8 am to 8 pm weekdays, 9 am to 2 pm weekends.

The immigration office is next door and open weekdays 8 am to 5 pm, weekends 8 am to noon.

Money Several banks are within a couple of blocks of the ferry docks, including a Bital on Avenida Rueda Medina directly across from the Zona Hotelera ferry dock. Most exchange currency, have ATMs and are open 8:30 am to 5 pm weekdays, 9 am to 2 pm Saturday.

Post & Communications The post office, on Guerrero at López Mateos, is open 9 am to 4 pm weekdays. Telmex pay phones are abundant; for the best rates, use a phone card.

The Café Internet, on Hidalgo near Abasolo, offers Internet access and email services; open daily 8 am to midnight. CompuIsla, on Abasolo just south of Juárez, provides Internet and email services from 8 am to 10 pm daily. They both charge about US$1.10 for up to 15 minutes, and get cheaper in half-hour increments.

Cosmic Cosas (see Bookstores) has four terminals and charges reasonable prices for

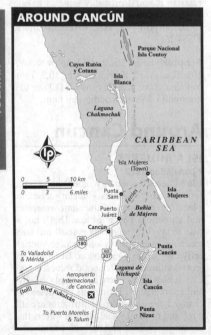

AROUND CANCÚN

Parque Nacional
Isla Contoy

Cayos Ratón
y Cotuna

Isla
Blanca

Laguna
Chakmochuk

CARIBBEAN
SEA

Isla Mujeres
(Town)

0   5   10 km
0   3   6 miles

Punta
Sam

Isla
Mujeres

Puerto
Juárez

Bahía
de Mujeres

Cancún

MEX
180

To Valladolid
& Mérida

MEX
307

Punta
Cancún

Aeropuerto
Internacional
de Cancún

Laguna de
Nichupté

Isla
Cancún

(toll) Blvd Kukulcán

To Puerto Morelos
& Tulum

Punta
Nizuc

Internet access. They also provide photography services with a digital camera from which you can email your photos (or upload them straight to the Web).

Bookstores Cosmic Cosas, at Matamoros 82, just north of Hidalgo, is a nifty store that buys, sells and trades English-language books (mostly novels, but also some travel guides and history). The store has a comfortable living room where visitors are welcome to relax and play board games. Owner Genevieve Pritchard enjoys offering tourist information as well. It's open 10:30 am to 10:30 pm daily.

Laundry Laundries in town will wash, dry and fold 4kg of clothes for US$2.70 to US$3.80. Among them are Lavandería Automática Tim Phó, on Juárez at Abasolo, and Lavandería JR, on Abasolo between Avenida Rueda Medina and Juárez. Lavandería Ángel, just off Hidalgo in Plaza Isla Mujeres, is the cheapest of the three unless you want colors washed separately. Most are open 7 am to 9 pm Monday to Saturday, 9 am to 1 pm Sunday.

Tortugranja (Turtle Farm)

Six species of sea turtle lay eggs in the sand along the island's calm western shore. Although they are endangered, sea turtles are still killed throughout Latin America for their eggs and meat, considered a delicacy. In the 1980s efforts by a local fisherman led to the founding of the Centro de Investigaciones and the Isla Mujeres Turtle Farm (☎ 877-05-95, Carretera Sac Bajo Km 5), which protects the turtles' breeding grounds and places their eggs in incubators, out of harm's way. Hatchlings live in three large pools for up to a year, at which time they are tagged for monitoring and released. Because most turtles in the wild die within their first few months, the practice of guarding them until they are a year old greatly increases their chances of survival. Moreover, the turtles that leave this protected beach return each year, which means their offspring receive the same protection. The Turtle Farm is a scientific facility, not an

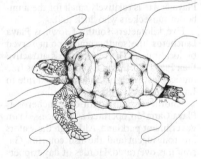

Sea turtles lay eggs on the beaches
of Isla Mujeres.

amusement center. But if you'd like to see several hundred sea turtles, ranging in weight from 150g to more than 300kg, this is the place. It's open 9 am to 5 pm daily; admission is US$2.20. Tours are available in Spanish and English. The facility is best reached by taxi (about US$2.30). If you're driving, bear right at the unsigned 'Y' south of town.

Mayan Ruins

At the south end of the island lie the severely worn remains of a temple dedicated chiefly to Ixchel, Mayan goddess of the moon and fertility. (The conquistadors found various clay female figures here; whether they were all likenesses of Ixchel or instead represented several goddesses is unclear.) In 1988 Hurricane Gilbert nearly finished the ruins off. Except for a still-distinguishable stairway and scattered remnants of stone buildings, there's little left to see other than the sea (a fine view) and, in the distance, Cancún. The ruins are beyond the lighthouse, just past Playa Garrafón (see Beaches). From downtown, a taxi costs US$4.

Beaches

Walk west along Calle Hidalgo or Guerrero to reach the town's principal beach, **Playa Norte**, sometimes called Playa Los Cocos or Cocoteros. The slope of the beach is gradual, and the transparent and calm waters are only chest-high even far from shore. But

Playa Norte is relatively small for the number of sunseekers who flock to it.

Five kilometers south of town is **Playa Lancheros**, the southernmost point served by local buses. The beach is less attractive than Playa Norte, but it sometimes has free musical festivities on Sunday. A taxi ride to Lancheros is US$1.85.

Another 1.5km south of Lancheros is **Playa Garrafón**, operated as a concession on government parkland. Although the waters are translucent and the fish colorful, Garrafón is overrated. Hordes of day-trippers from Cancún crowd the waters, and the reef

has been heavily damaged by hurricanes and careless visitors, which makes it less likely to inflict cuts but also reduces its color and the intricacy of its formations. Average visibility is 10m. The water can be very choppy, sweeping you into jagged areas. Although much of the park contains shallow reef, the bottom falls off steeply close to shore, so those without strong swimming skills should not venture too far. There is a swimming pool for the less adventurous.

Garrafón is open 8 am to 5 pm daily (get there early to avoid the mobs). Admission is US$11 and includes snorkeling gear. Taxis

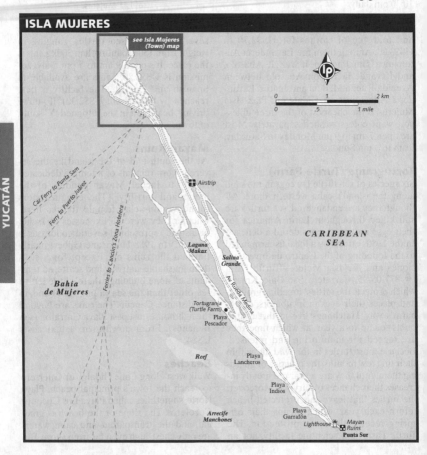

ISLA MUJERES

see Isla Mujeres (Town) map

Car Ferry to Punta Sam

Ferry to Puerto Juárez

Ferries to Cancún's Zona Hotelera

Bahía de Mujeres

Airstrip

Laguna Makax

Salina Grande

Av Rueda Medina

Tortugranja (Turtle Farm)

Playa Pescador

Reef

Playa Lancheros

Playa Indios

Arrecife Manchones

Playa Garrafón

Lighthouse Mayan Ruins

Punta Sur

CARIBBEAN SEA

0   1   2 km
0   .5   1 mile

YUCATÁN

from town cost about US$3.75. If you elect to walk, take some water – it's a hot two-hour trek.

Diving & Snorkeling

Within a short boat ride of the island are a handful of lovely reef dives, such as Arrecife Barracuda, La Bandera, Manchones Xico, El Jigueo and Arrecife Manchones. A popular nonreef dive is the one to a cargo ship resting in 30m of water 90 minutes by boat northeast of Isla Mujeres. Known as El Frío (The Deep Freeze) because of the unusually cool water found there, the site contains the intact hull of a 60m-long cargo ship thought to have been deliberately sunk.

At all the reputable dive centers you need to show your certification card and will be expected to have your own gear; any piece of scuba equipment is generally available for rent. Coral Scuba Diver Center (☎ 877-07-63, fax 877-03-71, coral@coralscubadivecenter.com, www.coralscubadivecenter.com), Matamoros at Avenida Rueda Medina, offers dives for US$29 to US$98; snorkel trips are US$14. Sea Hawk Divers (☎/fax 877-02-96), on Carlos Lazo just before Playa Norte, offers dives for US$45 to US$55 and snorkeling tours beginning at US$20.

The fishermen of Isla Mujeres have formed a cooperative that offers snorkeling tours of various sites, including the reef off Playa Garrafón (see the Beaches section, earlier), as well as day trips to Isla Contoy. Tours start at US$13. You can book through their office at the foot of Madero, in a palapa steps away from the dock.

Places to Stay

Each hotel seems to have a different 'high season'; prices here are for mid-December through March, when you can expect many places to be booked solid by midday (earlier during Easter week). Some places offer substantially lower rates in off-season periods.

Budget The *Poc-Na Hostel* (☎/fax 877-00-90), on Matamoros at Carlos Lazo, is a privately run youth hostel with campsites (US$2.50 per person). The fan-cooled dor-

mitories accommodate men and women together. A bunk and bedding cost US$4; you must put down a deposit for the bedding. Lockers are provided free. This is not the cleanest place, and a party atmosphere often prevails.

The *Hotel Marcianito* (☎ 877-01-11), on Abasolo between Juárez and Hidalgo, offers eight clean, fan-cooled rooms, each containing two beds and a hammock, for US$20. The *Hotel Vistalmar* (☎ 877-02-09, fax 877-00-96), on Avenida Rueda Medina between Matamoros and Abasolo, offers 30 very acceptable rooms for US$25/28 single/double with fan, US$31/34 with air-con.

The friendly *Hotel Caribe Maya* (☎ 877-06-84), on Madero between Guerrero and Hidalgo, has dark but comfy rooms with fan for US$20 double. *Hotel Las Palmas* (☎ 877-0965, Guerrero 20), across from the Mercado Municipal, offers basic but clean rooms with fan and bath for US$18 for one or two persons.

Hotel El Caracol (☎ 877-01-50), on Matamoros between Hidalgo and Guerrero, offers 18 clean basic rooms with insect screens, ceiling fans and tiled bathrooms; many have two double beds. The cost is US$28 double.

Hotel D'Gomar (☎ 877-05-41), on Avenida Rueda Medina between Morelos and Bravo, above a boutique and facing the ferry dock, has four floors of attractive, clean, double-bedded, air-con rooms for US$25 double.

Mid-Range The *Hotel Francis Arlene* (☎ /fax 877-03-10), on Guerrero between Abasolo and Madero, offers comfortable rooms (many with balconies and sea views) for US$52 with air-con.

Hotel Mesón del Bucanero (☎ 877-01-26, 800-712-35-10, fax 877-02-10, bucaneros@bucaneros.com, www.bucaneros.com), on Hidalgo between Abasolo and Madero, is above the restaurant of the same name. Its charming rooms all have TV, most have air-con, and various permutations of beds, balcony, tub and fridge result in rates ranging from US$32 to US$51 double, US$56 to US$67 triple or quad (lower in off-season).

Hotel Belmar (☎ 877-04-30, fax 877-04-29), on Hidalgo between Abasolo and Madero, is above the Pizza Rolandi restaurant and is run by the same friendly family. All rooms are comfy and well kept, and they're a bargain at US$55 double with air-con. There's also a suite with Jacuzzi for US$95.

The *Hotel Rocamar* (☎ /fax 877-01-01), on a slight hill at the eastern end of Guerrero, was the town's first real hotel, built decades ago. The 24-room, one-suite hotel has been updated, has a pool, and charges US$67/77/87 single/double/triple for fan-only rooms with good sea views; placs down-, room US$45 to US$51.

Top End The *Hotel Perla del Caribe* (☎ 877-04-44, in the USA ☎ 800-258-6454, fax 877-00-11), on Madero a block north of Guerrero right on the eastern beach, has a pool, restaurant and 91 nice rooms on three floors. All have balconies and air-con, most have wonderful sea views, for US$79 to US$90 double, depending on view.

The *Hotel Posada del Mar* (☎ 877-00-44, fax 877-02-66, in the USA ☎ 800-544-3005, hposada@cancun.rce.com.mx, www.posada delmar.com), on Avenida Rueda Medina between López Mateos and Matamoros, is a lovely newer place with 30 rooms in a three-story building (most with sea views) and 12 bungalows ringing a swimming pool. All have air-con. Doubles in bungalows cost US$64, rooms in the three-story building are US$75 (less from May to December).

Hotel Na Balam (☎ 877-02-79, fax 877-04-46, nabalam@cancun.rce.com.mx, www .nabalam.com), on Calle Zazil-Ha, faces Playa Norte on the northern tip of the island. Most of the 31 spacious, air-con rooms (including beachfront bungalows) have fabulous sea views and numerous nice touches. Rooms cost US$150, and there's a pool.

Places to Eat
At the time of research, the mercado municipal (town market) was being rebuilt. Before the remodel began, several places next to the market served simple but tasty and filling meals at the best prices on the island. Stay tuned.

La Casita Bakery, on Madero between Guerrero and Hidalgo, has good pastries and sandwiches. *Super Betino*, the market on the plaza, has limited groceries but a wide selection of junk food. *Panadería La Reyna*, on Madero at Juárez, is *the* place for breakfast buns and snacks.

Café Cito, a small place at Juárez and Matamoros, has a menu in both English and German, croissants, fruit, 10 varieties of crepes and good coffee. Come for breakfast (about US$5) or supper (about US$10). Closed 2 to 5:30 pm in high season.

Café El Nopalito, on Guerrero near Matamoros, is intimate, with beautifully painted tables and chairs. They specialize in healthful but fancy food, and serve delicious breakfasts for US$2.50 to US$4, as well as espresso, crepes, sandwiches and ice cream; open 8 am to 1 pm.

El Bucanero, on Hidalgo between Abasolo and Madero in the Hotel Mesón del Bucanero, is a fan-cooled restaurant with a pleasing ambience and a variety of nonalcoholic tropical shakes and drinks. The best deal is the *menú ejecutivo*: For about US$6.75 you can choose Mexican-style beef tips, fish fillet prepared to order, or bell peppers stuffed with meat, cheese or tuna; all come with soup, beans, rice and coffee.

Across the street, *Pizza Rolandi* serves pizzas and calzones cooked in a wood-fired oven. The menu also includes pasta, fresh salads, fish, good coffee and some Italian specialties. Most dishes are US$6 to US$8.

Popular with tourists, *El Balcón*, on Hidalgo below Abasolo, is an airy, casual 2nd-floor eatery serving good fruit drinks, and seafood dishes mostly under US$7. Try the rich *camarones a la Reina* if you have friend who can help out.

Entertainment
The nightlife of Isla Mujeres is fairly nonexistent Sunday through Thursday. On Friday and Saturday nights, if you're looking for a crowd, head to the beach bar of the *Hotel Na-Balam*, which offers live music and somewhat sedate dancing every week. Or try *Las Palapas Bar Restaurant* (also

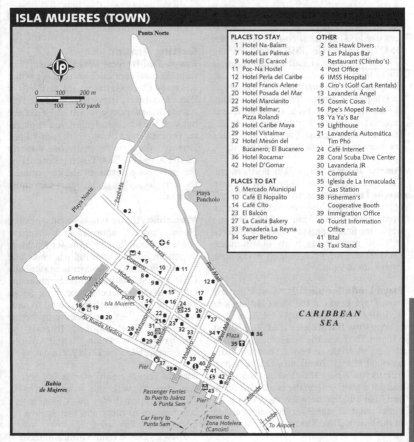

ISLA MUJERES (TOWN)

PLACES TO STAY	OTHER
1 Hotel Na-Balam	2 Sea Hawk Divers
7 Hotel Las Palmas	3 Las Palapas Bar
9 Hotel El Caracol	Restaurant (Chimbo's)
11 Poc-Na Hostel	4 Post Office
12 Hotel Perla del Caribe	6 IMSS Hospital
17 Hotel Francis Arlene	8 Ciro's (Golf Cart Rentals)
20 Hotel Posada del Mar	13 Lavandería Ángel
22 Hotel Marcianito	15 Cosmic Cosas
25 Hotel Belmar;	16 Ppe's Moped Rentals
Pizza Rolandi	18 Ya Ya's Bar
26 Hotel Caribe Maya	19 Lighthouse
29 Hotel Vistalmar	21 Lavandería Automática
32 Hotel Mesón del	Tim Phó
Bucanero; El Bucanero	24 Café Internet
36 Hotel Rocamar	28 Coral Scuba Dive Center
42 Hotel D'Gomar	30 Lavandería JR
	31 CompuIsla
PLACES TO EAT	35 Iglesia de La Inmaculada
5 Mercado Municipal	37 Gas Station
10 Café El Nopalito	38 Fishermen's
14 Café Cito	Cooperative Booth
23 El Balcón	39 Immigration Office
27 La Casita Bakery	40 Tourist Information
33 Panadería La Reyna	Office
34 Super Betino	41 Bital
	43 Taxi Stand

called Chimbo's), on Playa Norte behind the cemetery, where a band plays and the foreign youth of the island dance with abandon. **Ya Ya's Bar**, beside the lighthouse on Avenida Ruedas Medina at López Mateos, occasionally hosts a rock band. Even without one, it's a fine place to have a drink and kick back.

Getting There & Away

There are five main points of embarkation to reach Isla Mujeres. The following description starts from the northernmost port and progresses southeast. (See the Around

Cancún and Cancún's Zona Hotelera maps.) To reach Puerto Juárez or Punta Sam from downtown Cancún, catch a bus (US$0.40 to Puerto Juárez, US$0.50 to Punta Sam) displaying those destinations from in front of the Cinemas Tulum, on Avenida Tulum north of Avenida Uxmal.

Punta Sam Car ferries, which also take passengers, depart from Punta Sam, about 5km north of Cancún center, and take at least an hour to reach the island. Departure times are 8 and 11 am and 2:45, 5:30 and 8:15 pm from Punta Sam; from Isla Mujeres

YUCATÁN

they are 6:30 and 9:30 am and 12:45, 4:15
and 7:15 pm. Walk-ons and vehicle passengers pay US$1.35; a car costs US$14, a van
US$17, a motorcycle US$5.40 and a bicycle
US$4.35 (operator included in each fare). If
you're taking a car, be sure to get in line an
hour or so before departure time. Tickets go
on sale just before the ferry begins loading.

Passenger-only service (both slow and
express) between Punta Sam and Isla
Mujeres can be erratic. Puerto Juárez boats
are much more reliable and convenient.

Puerto Juárez About 3km north of the
Cancún city center and 2km south of Punta
Sam is Puerto Juárez, from which express
boats head to Isla Mujeres every 30 minutes
from 6 am to 9 pm (25 minutes, US$3.80 one
way). One final express departs Isla Mujeres
at 11:30 pm. Slower boats (45 minutes,
US$1.60 one way) run roughly every hour
from 7 am to 9 pm.

Playa Linda Terminal *The Shuttle* departs
from Playa Linda in the Zona Hotelera at
9:30, 10:45 and 11:45 am and 1:30 pm, returning from Isla Mujeres at 12:30, 3:30 and
5:15 pm. The roundtrip fare is US$14 and in-
cludes soft drinks on board. Show up at the
terminal at least 20 minutes before departure so you'll have time to buy your ticket
and get a good seat on the boat. It's a beige
and blue building between the Costa Real
Hotel and the channel, on the mainland side
of the bridge (Blvd Kukulcán Km 4).

Playa Tortugas The *Isla Mujeres Shuttle*
departs the Zona Hotelera from the dock
near Fat Tuesday's on Playa Tortugas beach
(Km 6.35) at 9:15 and 11:30 am and 1:45 and
3:30 pm, returning from Isla Mujeres at
10 am and 12:30, 2:30 and 5 pm, for US$7.70
one way.

Club Náutico Dock Sharing a parking lot
with the Xcaret bus terminal and located
next to the Fiesta Americana Coral Beach is
this new dock, from which the Watertaxi
whisks people to Isla Mujeres at 9 and
11 am and 1 and 3 pm, and back to the Zona
Hotelera at 10 am, noon and 2 and 5 pm.

The fare is US$8 one way, US$13.50
roundtrip; the trip takes 40 minutes.

Getting Around
Bus & Taxi By local (and infrequent) bus
from the market or dock, you can get within
1.5km of Playa Garrafón; the terminus is
Playa Lancheros. The personnel at the Poc-
Na youth hostel can give you an idea of the
bus's erratic schedule. Unless you're pinching pennies, you'd be better off taking a taxi
anyway – the most expensive one-way trip
on the island is US$4. Taxi rates are set by
the municipal government and are posted at
the ferry dock, though the sign is sometimes
defaced.

Motorbike If you rent a scooter or 50cc
Honda 'moped,' shop around, compare
prices and look for new or newer machines
in good condition, with full gas tanks and
reasonable deposits. Cost per hour is usually
US$5 or US$6 with a two-hour minimum,
US$25 all day, cheaper by the week. Shops
away from the busiest streets tend to have
better prices, but not necessarily better
equipment. Ppe's Moped Rentals, on
Hidalgo between Matamoros and Abasolo,
offers motorbikes for US$19.50 a day.

Bicycle For all transportation it's best to
deal directly with the shop renting it.
They're happier if they don't have to pay
commissions to touts, and the chances for
misunderstandings are fewer.

Bicycles can be rented from a number of
shops on the island, including Richas, next
door to Lavandería JR on Abasolo, which
charges US$1.65/5.70 an hour/day. Before
you rent, compare prices and the condition
of the bikes in a few shops, then arrive early
in the day to get one of the better bikes.
Most places ask for a deposit of about
US$10.

Golf Cart Those with impaired mobility
can rent golf carts (caravans of which can be
seen tooling down the roads). Some swear
by this as a way to get around the island.
Ciro's, on Guerrero north of Matamoros,
has a huge inventory of carts for US$13 an

hour, US$43 for a 9 am to 5 pm day. They rent scooters as well.

PARQUE NACIONAL ISLA CONTOY

From Isla Mujeres it's possible to take an excursion by boat to tiny, uninhabited Isla Contoy, a national park and bird sanctuary 25km north. Its dense foliage is home to more than 100 species, including brown pelicans, olive cormorants, turkey birds, brown boobies and red-pouched frigates, and subject to frequent visits by red flamingos, snowy egrets and white herons.

Bring mosquito repellent. There is good snorkeling both en route to and just off Contoy, which sees about 1500 visitors a month.

Getting There & Away

Coral Scuba Dive Center (☎ 877-07-63, fax 877-03-71), on Matamoros at Avenida Rueda Medina on Isla Mujeres, offers a day trip for US$35 that includes lunch and opportunities to snorkel and bird-watch.

The fisherman's cooperative (see Diving & Snorkeling, in the Isla Mujeres section) makes daily trips to Isla Contoy for US$40 per person. The tours include a light breakfast, a lunch (with barbecued fish caught en route), stops for snorkeling (gear provided), scientific information on the island and your choice of purified water or soft drinks. Try to book on one of the faster boats; this will give you more time for activities and less time on the hard seats. For reservations call ☎ 877-05-00 or book at your hotel.

ISLA HOLBOX
• population 1500

With its friendly fishing families and hammock-weaving cottage industry, Isla Holbox (hol-**bosh**) is a beach site not yet overwhelmed by gringos. It is 25km long and 3km wide, with seemingly endless beaches, tranquil waters and a galaxy of shells in various shapes and colors. There are also red flamingos and the occasional roseate spoonbill. As for drawbacks, the water is not the translucent turquoise common to Quintana Roo beach sites, because here the Caribbean waters mingle with those of the darker gulf. During the rainy season there are clouds of mosquitoes; bring repellent and be prepared to stay inside for a couple of hours each evening.

Places to Stay & Eat

Development has arrived on Holbox, and besides such modest places as the *Hotel Flamingo*, *Hotel Holbox* and the *Posada Amápola*, all priced at US$15 a night, there are several more upscale ones, such as the *Puerto Holbox Hotel* (☎/fax 873-05-01, info@holboxisland.com, holboxisland.com/hotel.html), with four balconied rooms with air-con for US$60 per night for up to four people.

The charming *Villas Delfines* (☎ 884-86-06, uniterra@prodigy.net.mx, www.holbox .com) is an eco-tel that composts waste, catches rainwater and uses solar power. Its fan-cooled beach bungalows run US$150 double including breakfast and dinner (less in off-season).

Besides the hotel restaurants there are local restaurants with fresh seafood, and transplants offering European fare as well.

Getting There & Away

The ferry for Holbox departs from the port village of Chiquilá. Direct buses from Cancún serve Chiquilá (3½ hours, US$5.25). Try to get there early; the small ferry (25 minutes, US$2.75) is supposed to depart for the island at 6 and 8 am, noon, and 2 and 5 pm, but does not always keep to this schedule. There is one bus a day from Valladolid to Chiquilá (2 hours, US$5) departing at 2:30 pm, which cuts it a bit close. You can hire a fishing launch (about US$25) to make the crossing, or camp out in Chiquilá.

Tulum Corridor

The coast of Quintana Roo is among the fastest-developing areas in Mexico. Because of the raging success of Cancún, developers have been rushing to build more leisure palaces along the beaches of the 'Mayan Riviera,' and environmental concerns often

YUCATÁN

take a back seat to the generation of tourism revenue.

The highway has been widened in almost the entire stretch from Cancún south to Tulum, and continues to be improved. The road to sleepy Xcalak has been paved. As a result, reefs continue to be damaged by sewage, careless divers and boaters; turtle hatcheries fall victim to resort hotels; and once-pristine stretches of coast become amusement parks for the wealthy tourist.

For the time being, however, there are still places to enjoy. Small, low-impact hotels stand alone on some stretches of beach. Several large reserves and parks have been created, including the Sian Ka'an and Banco Chinchorro Biosphere Reserves and the Parque Nacional Marino Arrecifes de Cozumel. These are protected from development and exploitation (even if enforcement is occasionally lax). And Playa del Carmen, though it continues to grow, is still a quiet, laid-back beach town compared with Cancún.

The barrier reef runs along this entire stretch of coastline, at times close enough to swim to from shore.

PUERTO MORELOS
• population 830

Puerto Morelos, 33km south of Cancún, is a quiet fishing village known principally for its car ferry to Cozumel. It has some good hotels, and travelers who spend the night here find it refreshingly free of tourists. A handful of scuba divers come to explore the splendid stretch of barrier reef 600m offshore, reachable by boat.

The reef is threatened by planned resort development in the mangroves nearby, but as of this writing, residents were still holding the developers off.

Two kilometers south of the turnoff for Puerto Morelos is the **Jardín Botánico Dr Alfredo Barrera**, with 3km of trails through several native habitats. The orchids, bromeliads and other flora are identified in English, Spanish and Latin. Open 9 am to 5 pm daily; US$2. Buses may be hailed directly in front of the garden.

Places to Stay & Eat

The *Posada Amor* (☎ 871-00-33, fax 871-01-78), 100m southwest of the plaza, is the longtime lodging here. Fan-cooled rooms range from US$16 to US$20 single, or from US$21 to US$35 double; the cheaper rooms have shared bath. Meals are available.

Hotel Hacienda Morelos (☎ /fax 871-00-15), 150m south of the plaza on the waterfront, has appealing, breezy rooms with sea views, kitchenettes and fan for US$73 double (extra persons US$16 each). They also have a pool and restaurant.

Farther to the south, beyond the ferry terminal, is the best place in town, the *Rancho Libertad* (☎ 871-01-81, in the USA ☎ 888-305-5225, fax in the USA 719-685-2332, www.rancholibertad.com). This mellow B&B has 15 charming guestrooms in one- and two-story thatched bungalows. All rooms have private bath and good ventilation; some have air-con. There's a pleasing beach, and room rates include breakfast for two and use of bikes and snorkel gear (as available). Upstairs rooms are US$56 double April to December (add US$21 during the high season). Downstairs rooms are US$46 (US$66 during high season). The hotel is managed by a team of friendly Americans and Austrians.

The best restaurant in town (with prices that reflect the fact) is *Johnny Cairo's* at Hotel Hacienda Morelos. Next to Hacienda Morelos is *Las Palmeras*, a good restaurant. *Los Pelícanos*, just off the southeast corner of the plaza, has a great setting overlooking the sea, but service and food aren't up to the prices.

Getting There & Away

Playa Express buses on the way between Ciudad Cancún and Playa del Carmen drop you on the highway. All 2nd-class and many 1st-class buses heading to or from Ciudad Cancún stop at Puerto Morelos. The plaza is 2km from the highway. Taxis are usually waiting by the turnoff to shuttle people into town, and there's usually a taxi or two near the square to shuttle them back over to the highway. The official local rate is US$1.25

each way, for as many people as you can stuff in; strive for it (gringo rate is US$2 each way).

The *transbordador* (car ferry; in Cozumel ☎ 9-872-09-50) to Cozumel leaves Puerto Morelos at 5 and 10 am and noon daily. Departure times are subject to change according to season or the weather; during high seas, the ferry won't leave at all. Unless you plan to stay awhile on Cozumel, it's hardly worth shipping your vehicle. You must get in line at least two hours before departure and hope there's enough space. The 2½- to four-hour voyage is US$55 per car, US$4.50 per person. Departure from Cozumel is from the dock in front of the Hotel Sol Caribe, south of town along the shore road.

PLAYA DEL CARMEN
• population 17,621

For decades Playa was a simple fishing village that foreigners passed through on their way to a ferry that would take them to Cozumel. But with the construction of Cancún, the number of travelers roaming this part of Yucatán increased dramatically, as did the number of hotels and restaurants serving them. Playa has overtaken Cozumel as the preferred resort town in the area; its beaches are better and nightlife groovier than Cozumel's, and the reef diving is just as good. Many of the town's accommodations are stylish European-owned and -managed inns, and several of its restaurants serve delicious French and Italian cuisine.

What's to do in Playa? Hang out. Swim. Dive. Shop. Eat. Drink. Walk the beach. Get some sun. Listen to beach bands. Dance in clubs. In the evening, Playa's pedestrian mall, Quinta Avenida (5th Avenue), is a popular place to stroll and dine, or drink and people-watch, or any combination of the above.

Though nudity is tolerated on the beach about 1km north of the town center, it is not recommended; with the construction boom in Playa has come a nefarious element, and rapes, robberies and thefts have become common in town and especially on remote patches of beach. Beware the shantytown north of town, where most of the construction workers live, and as always keep an eye out when walking deserted streets alone at night.

Orientation & Information

Playa is laid out on an easy grid. Pedestrian Quinta Avenida is the most happening street in town; the bus station and main plaza are at its intersection with Avenida Juárez. There's a helpful tourist information kiosk in the plaza.

There's an ATM across Quinta Avenida from the bus terminal. Bancomer has a branch with ATM four blocks west on Avenida Juárez, and Banamex has one at the corner of Calle 12 and 10 Avenida.

For medical treatment, try the Centro de Salud on 15 Avenida near Avenida Juárez.

Post & Communications The post office is at the corner of 15 Avenida and Avenida Juárez, a couple blocks inland from the main plaza.

The air-conditioned Supersónico Internet Café is on 10 Avenida south of Calle 4. It charges US$0.08 per minute and is open 9 am to midnight Monday to Saturday, 10 am to 10:30 pm Sunday. Capuchino net, on Calle 6 between 10 Avenida and Quinta Avenida, charges US$0.11 per minute and is open 8 am to 11 pm daily.

Bookstores If you're looking for some beach reading, try friendly La Librería, on Calle 8 between Quinta Avenida and 10 Avenida; behind the café tables they have new and used books in several languages and a section on Mayan history. The Coffee Press on Calle 2 at Quinta Avenida has a book exchange.

Water Sports

Scuba Tarraya (☎ 873-20-40, fax 873-20-60, g_millet@hotmail.com, gmillet@yuc1.telmex .net.mx), at the eastern end of Avenida Juárez in Restaurant La Tarraya, offers several options for **diving**, **snorkeling** and **fishing**, and rents out **kayaks**. Other dive centers are Aqua Venturas (☎/fax 873-09-69), Quinta

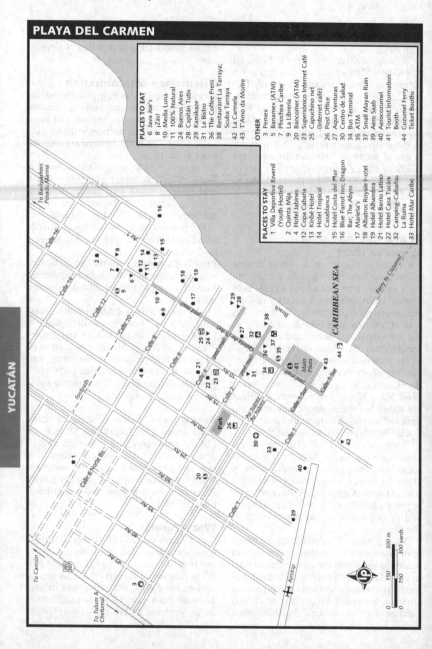

PLAYA DEL CARMEN

PLACES TO EAT
6   Java Joe's
8   ¡Zas!
10 Media Luna
11 100% Natural
24 Buenos Aires
28 Capitán Tutix
29 Kamikaze
31 Le Bistro
36 The Coffee Press
38 Restaurant La Tarraya;
    Scuba Tarraya
42 La Carmela
43 T'Amo da Morire

OTHER
3   Pemex
5   Banamex (ATM)
7   Phochea Caribe
9   La Librería
20 Bancomer (ATM)
23 Supersónico Internet Café
25 Capuchino net
    (Internet café)
26 Post Office
27 Aqua Venturas
30 Centro de Salud
34 Bus Terminal
35 ATM
37 Small Mayan Ruin
39 Aero Saab
40 Aerocozumel
41 Tourist Information
    Booth
44 Cozumel Ferry
    Ticket Booths

PLACES TO STAY
1   Villa Deportiva Juvenil
    (Youth Hostel)
4   Quinta Mija
4   Hotel Jabines
12 Copa Cabaña
13 Kinbé Hotel
14 Hotel Tropical
    Casablanca
15 Hotel Costa del Mar
16 Blue Parrot Inn; Dragon
    Bar; The Abyss
17 Marieta's
18 Albatros Royale Hotel
19 Hotel Alhambra
21 Hotel Barrio Latino
22 Hotel Casa Tucán
32 Camping Cabañas
    La Ruina
33 Hotel Mar Caribe

CARIBBEAN SEA

Ferry to Cozumel

To Backpackers
Posada Marina

To Cancún

To Tulum &
Chetumal

MEX 307

Airstrip

Main
Plaza

Park

To Cancún

YUCATÁN

0   150   300 m
0   150   300 yards

Avenida between Calles 2 and 4; the Abyss (☎ 873-21-64, abyss@playadelcarmen.com), at the Blue Parrot Inn, east end of Calle 12; and Phochea Caribe (☎/fax 873-10-24), Quinta Avenida between Calles 12 and 14.

Places to Stay

Playa del Carmen is developing and changing rapidly. You can expect many new hotels by the time you arrive, as well as a number of changes in the existing ones. The room prices given below are for the busy winter tourist season (roughly January to March). Prices at many places can be up to 30% lower at other times.

Budget The *Backpackers Posada Marina* hostel *(no telephone, playabackpackers@ hotmail.com)* is a bit distant from the center on Quinta Avenida at Calle 24, but it's a block from the beach and offers dorm beds for US$8 and private rooms for US$21, some with kitchenette. There's a pool, garden and communal cooking facilities.

The *Villa Deportiva Juvenil* hostel *(☎/fax 873-15-08)*, on Calle 8 at the end of 35 Avenida, offers cheap clean lodging (US$4.50 per bunk) and cabañas for US$22, but it's a trek to the beach, and the single-sex dorm bunks are worn.

A good bet is *Camping-Cabañas La Ruina* *(☎ /fax 873-04-05)*, on Calle 2 just off the beach, where you can pitch your tent or hang your hammock for US$5.50 per person (hammock rental available), or stay in a simple cabaña with two cots and ceiling fan for US$22 to US$27. A more comfortable cabaña with private bath is US$34 to US$49.

At the nine-room *Hotel Mar Caribe* *(☎ 873-02-07)*, Avenida 15 at Calle 1, you can get a clean, simple room with private bath for US$27 (fan only) to US$38 (with air-con). It's secure, and the *dueña* (proprietor) speaks French and some English.

The German-run *Hotel Casa Tucán* *(☎ /fax 873-02-83, casatucan@playadelcarmen .com)*, on Calle 4 between 10 and 15 Avenidas, features 12 rooms (a couple with kitchenettes), four cabañas, an apartment, swimming pool and a restaurant in the nice

tropical garden. All rooms are fan-only and are a good value at US$30 to US$36; the two-room apartment is US$60.

Marieta's, centrally located on Quinta Avenida between Calles 6 and 8, has a variety of rooms, some with kitchenettes or balconies, all centered around a relaxing, leafy courtyard. It can be noisy during the day. Rates range from US$33 to US$65.

The *Hotel Barrio Latino* *(☎/fax 873-23-84, posadabarriolatino@yahoo.com)*, on Calle 4 between 10 and 15 Avenidas, offers 14 clean, pleasant rooms with tiled floors, ceiling fan and hammocks. The friendly Italian owners speak English and Spanish and maintain strict security. Rooms are US$35 and there's off-street parking.

The *Hotel Jabines* *(☎ 873-08-61, fax 873-11-41)*, on Calle 8 between 15 and 20 Avenidas, has 16 ground-floor rooms with secure parking, cable TV and two or three beds per room for US$37 double with fan, US$42 with air-con.

Mid-Range The *Copa Cabaña* *(☎ 873-0218)*, Quinta Avenida between Calles 10 and 12, boasts 30 comfortable rooms with showers and a lush courtyard; some have air-conditioning. A double with one or two beds is US$49.

Italian-owned and -operated *Kinbé Hotel* *(☎ 873-04-41, fax 873-22-15, hotelkinbe@ playadelcarmen.com)*, on Calle 10 just before 1 Avenida, has 19 clean, modern rooms starting at US$55.

Around the corner on 1 Avenida *Hotel Costa del Mar* *(☎/fax 873-00-58)* has 38 pleasing rooms overlooking the beach for US$45 double with fan, US$55 with air-con. Simple cabañas with fans cost US$35.

Across 1 Avenida and north a bit, *Hotel Tropical Casablanca* *(☎/fax 873-00-57)* has a palapa restaurant-bar perched above the street, and both a swimming pool *and* a cenote. Rooms cost US$55 double with fan, US$65 with air-con.

The atmospheric *Quinta Mija* *(☎/fax 873-01-11)*, Quinta Avenida at Calle 14, has a tropical courtyard with a quiet bar. Twin rooms are US$58; condos with kitchenettes US$82. There's Internet access here.

YUCATÁN

Hotel Alhambra (☎ 873-07-35, fax 873-06-99, olas@cancun.com.mx), at the beach end of Calle 8, has 25 rooms, from fan-only to air-con with balcony and beach view. It has a private roof deck, and the owner speaks English, Spanish and French. Rooms are US$50 to US$110 depending on amenities.

Top End The *Albatros Royale Hotel* (☎ 873-00-01, fax 873-0002, in the USA ☎ 800-538-6802), next to the beach on Calle 8, has 31 lovely air-con rooms. Breakfast at a nearby restaurant is included. Rates are US$85 double with fan, US$95 with air-con

The friendly *Blue Parrot Inn* (☎ 873-00-83, fax 873-00-49, in the USA ☎ 888-854-4498), on the beach end of Calle 12, is the place most people wish they were staying when they wander up the beach and discover it. Many of its charming rooms have terraces or sea views, and there are also a number of beachside bungalows and villas. The inn's beachfront bar often features surfer bands. Rooms are US$90, bungalows US$130, villas US$200. Beachside palapa rooms are a good value at US$90.

Places to Eat

For a caffeine fix, head over to *The Coffee Press* on Calle 2 east of Quinta Avenida. They have a selection of gourmet coffees and teas, along with breakfasts and café food. Another good spot to feed that monkey is *Java Joe's*, on Quinta Avenida between Calles 10 and 12; they have some great coffee drinks.

Restaurant La Tarraya, at the beach end of Calle 2, is one of the few eateries in town that dates from the 1960s. It continues to offer good food at decent prices, including guacamole for US$1.50, fried fish for US$8 per kilogram and *pulpo* (octopus) for US$3.25.

Capitán Tutix, at the beach end of Calle 4, has live music most nights and is a good choice for fast Mexican food, decent pasta, acceptable seafood and a half-dozen veggie items. Main dishes are US$7 to US$12; check out the boat bar. *Kamikaze*, next door, serves the same purpose: decent, cheap food without leaving the beach.

Most tourists don't venture south of Avenida Juárez, and that's a pity because some of the best Mexican cuisine on the Yucatán Peninsula is served at *La Carmela*, on Avenida 10 three blocks south of Avenida Juárez. It's known for its succulent chicken smothered in dark mole and its white pork slow-cooked in a green tomatillo sauce, among other dishes. Specialties run US$10 to US$20. Dress nicely.

The best Italian food (in a town serving a lot of it) is at *T'Amo da Morire*, which overlooks the main plaza. Entrées cost US$7 to US$10. *Le Bistro*, on Calle 2 between Quinta Avenida and 10 Avenida, specializes in savory French home cooking. Meals at this simple, open-sided restaurant with 10 little wooden tables and excellent service are simply divine. Appetizers cost about US$5, entrées about US$7.

If you *love* beef head to *Buenos Aires*, on Quinta Avenida between Calles 4 and 6, tucked away down an alley behind two mediocre restaurants. It's famous in Quintana Roo for its steaks, ribs, burgers and other meaty items (US$5 to US$10), made only with Angus beef. Check your bill to see if the tip has already been added to it.

Media Luna, on Quinta Avenida between Calles 8 and 10, takes top honors in the veggie category, serving a wide variety of good dishes and drinks for breakfast, lunch and dinner. Prices for entrées range from US$8 to US$10. The same owners run *¡Zas!*, on Quinta Avenida north of Calle 12, where the international cuisine is interesting and delicious. A typical entrée costs US$8.

There's a branch of *100% Natural*, with its trademark fruit and vegetable juice blends and other healthy food, on Quinta Avenida at Calle 10.

Entertainment

The party's hearty at the Blue Parrot Inn's *Dragon Bar*, where Calle 12 meets the sand. Surfer bands play at the open-sided palapa bar during the day, and at night it's usually an Afro-Cuban band. A band starts up most nights at *Capitán Tutix* restaurant, near the beach end of Calle 4, playing reggae, rock, calypso or salsa. Neither of these places charges a cover.

Secondary music scenes, but not necessarily secondary party scenes, can be found along Quinta Avenida most nights.

Getting There & Away

Playa's little airstrip handles mostly small charter, tour and air taxi flights. Aerocozumel (☎ 873-03-50) has an office next to Playa's airstrip, as does Aero Saab (☎ 873-08-04). Flights to Cozumel are US$26; roundtrip to Chichén Itzá is US$139.

ADO, Maya de Oro, Altos, Riviera, Mayab and Oriente serve Playa's bus terminal, at the corner of Avenida Juárez and Quinta Avenida.

Cancún 68km, 45 minutes to 1¼ hours; frequent buses (US$2 to US$2.75)

Chetumal 315km, 5 hours; eight ADO (US$13), one ADO GL (US$15), one Mayab (US$10)

Chichén Itzá 272km, 3 hours; one Oriente (US$7), two Riviera (US$13); it's best to take an early bus to Ciudad Cancún, then transfer

Cobá 113km, 1½ hours; one Premier (US$4)

Mérida 385km, 5 hours; one Oriente (US$11), one Mayab (US$15), one ADO (US$16), 11 Riviera (US$16), one ADO GL (US$18)

Palenque 800km, 10 hours; one Altos (US$28), one Maya del Oro (US$37)

San Cristóbal de Las Casas 990km, 16 hours; one each by Maya de Oro (US$47) and Altos (US$35)

Tulum 63km, 1 hour; Playa Express (US$2.75) every 15 minutes, one Riviera (US$2.75), one Mayab (US$2)

Valladolid 169km, 3 hours; two Riviera (US$9.25), one Oriente (US$5.50); buses going to Mérida via Cancún stop at Valladolid, but it's faster to go on the *ruta corta* (short route) via Tulum and Cobá (see Cobá)

If you're heading to Cancún International Airport, there are two ways to save time and avoid backtracking: Book at a booth in the bus station a day in advance for a US$14 airport shuttle, or hire a taxi. You may need to pay as much as US$35 or US$40 for a cab, but if you form a group it can be worth it.

Ferries to Cozumel run nearly every hour on the hour from 4 am to 10 pm. The ride takes 45 minutes to an hour and costs US$7 one way.

ISLA COZUMEL
• population 70,000

Cozumel is a teardrop-shaped coral island ringed by crystalline waters 71km south of Cancún. It is Mexico's only Caribbean island and, measuring 53km by 14km, it is also the country's largest island. Called Ah-Cuzamil-Peten (Island of Swallows) by its earliest inhabitants, Cozumel has been a favorite destination for divers since 1961, when a Jacques Cousteau documentary on its glorious reefs appeared on TV. Today, no fewer than 100 world class dive sites have been identified within 5km of Cozumel, and at least a dozen of them are shallow enough for snorkeling. But except for the diving and snorkeling, there's little reason to visit Cozumel.

History

Mayan settlement here dates from AD 300. During the Postclassic period, Cozumel flourished as a trade center and, more importantly, a ceremonial site. Every Maya woman on the Yucatán Peninsula and beyond was expected to make at least one pilgrimage here to pay tribute to Ixchel, the goddess of fertility and the moon, at a temple erected in her honor at San Gervasio, near the center of the island.

At the time of the first Spanish contact with Cozumel (in 1518, by Juan de Grijalva and his men), there were at least 32 Mayan building sites on the island. According to Spanish chronicler Diego de Landa, Cortés a year later sacked one of the Mayan centers but left the others intact, apparently satisfied with converting the island's population to Christianity. Smallpox introduced by the Spanish wiped out half the 8000 Maya, and of the survivors, only about 200 escaped genocidal attacks by conquistadors in the late 1540s.

The island remained virtually deserted into the late 17th century, its coves providing sanctuary for several notorious pirates, including Jean Lafitte and Henry Morgan. In 1848 Indians fleeing the War of the

ISLA COZUMEL

see Playa del Carmen map

MEX 307

Playa del Carmen

Car Ferry to Puerto Morelos

Lighthouse

Punta Molas

Aguada Grande

Punta Norte

Isla de la Pasión

Laguna Xlapak

El Castillo Real

CARIBBEAN SEA

Santa Pilar

Airport

Playa Xhanan

Passenger Ferry Dock

see San Miguel de Cozumel map

San Miguel de Cozumel

San Gervasio

Playa Bonita

Playa la Ceiba

Carretera Transversal

Santa Rita

Car Ferry Dock

Presidente Intercontinental Cozumel

Club del Sol

San Benito

Red

Bahía Chankanaab

Fiesta Americana

Playa Los Cocos

Parque Chankanaab

Isla Cozumel

Playa Santa Cecilia

Punta Morena

Chen Río Restaurant

Playa Chen Río

Playa San Francisco

Allegro Resort

Parque Marino Nacional Arrecifes de Cozumel

El Cedral

Buena Vista

Playa de San Martín

Playa Palancar

Costera Sur

Punta Chiqueros

Cinco Puertas

Arrecife Palancar

Laguna de Columbia

Playa El Mirador

El Caracol

Playa Bush

Chun Chacab

Playa Encantada

Punta Celarain

Lighthouse

0   5   10 km
0   3   6 miles

Castes began to resettle Cozumel. At the beginning of the 20th century the island's now mostly mestizo population grew, thanks to the craze for chewing gum. Cozumel was a port of call on the chicle export route, and locals harvested chicle on the island. After the demise of chicle Cozumel's economy remained strong owing to the construction of a US air base here during WWII.

When the US military departed, the island fell into an economic slump, and many of its people moved away. Those who stayed fished for a livelihood until 1961,

when Cousteau's documentary broadcast Cozumel's glorious sea life to the world. The tourists began arriving almost overnight.

Orientation

It's easy to make your way on foot around the island's only town, **San Miguel de Cozumel**. The waterfront boulevard is Avenida Rafael Melgar; along Melgar south of the main ferry dock (the 'Muelle Fiscal') is a narrow sand beach. The main plaza is just opposite the ferry dock. Lockers are available for rent at the landward end of the Muelle Fiscal for US$2 per day, but they're not big enough for a full backpack. The airport is 2km north of town.

Information

At the time of research, Cozumel's tourist information office had closed, and no plans to open another were in the works. Tourist Police patrol the island; they are there mainly to keep the peace, but can be very informative and helpful. Their office (☎ 872-00-92) is in the Dirección de Seguridad Pública (Public Safety Headquarters), next door to the Palacio Municipal (City Hall), on Calle 13 Sur just off Avenida Melgar.

Money For currency exchange, try any of the banks near the main plaza shown on the map. All are open 8 or 9 am to 4:30 pm weekdays and on Saturday morning; Banca Serfin keeps longer hours. Many have ATMs.

The many casas de cambio around town may charge as much as 3.5% commission (versus the bank rate of 1%) to cash a traveler's check, but they keep longer hours. Most of the major hotels, restaurants and stores will also change money.

Post & Communications The post office, at Calle 7 Sur and Avenida Melgar, is open 9 am to 4 pm weekdays, 9 am to 1 pm Saturday (for stamp sales only). The Telcomm office next door handles faxes, money orders and such. The abundant Telmex pay phones around town are the least expensive way to place long-distance calls.

Internet Cozumel, on Calle 1 Sur at Avenida 10 Norte, offers eight computers for US$0.10 per minute, open 10 am to 10:30 pm Monday to Saturday. Coffee Net has a large air-con 2nd-floor facility in a courtyard off the north side of the main plaza. Internet access is US$9 an hour with a US$5 (which gets you a half hour) minimum. Open until 11 pm daily. A small branch on Avenida Melgar at Calle 11 Sur is open 9 am to 10 pm daily. Both serve coffee, soft drinks and snacks.

Bookstores The Gracia Agencia de Publicaciones, on the southeast corner of the plaza, sells English, French, German and Spanish books, and English and Spanish periodicals. Fama, a bookstore one block north along Avenida 5 Norte, carries books and periodicals in English and Spanish.

Laundry The washers at Margarita Laundromat, on Avenida 20 Sur near Calle 3 Sur cost US$1.75 per load (soap is US$0.50 extra); 10 minutes of dryer time is US$1. It's open daily.

Museo de la Isla de Cozumel

Exhibits at this fine museum, on Avenida Melgar between Calles 4 and 6 Norte, present a clear and detailed picture of the island's flora, fauna, geography, geology and ancient Maya. Thoughtful and detailed signs in English and Spanish accompany them. It's a good place to learn about coral before hitting the water and one not to miss before you leave the island. Admission is US$3; hours vary seasonally, but are roughly 9 am to 6 pm daily.

Glass-Bottom Boat Rides

The Palapa Marina (☎ 872-05-39), on Calle 1 Sur, between Avenidas 5 and 10, has a boat departing the Sol Caribe pier, south of San Miguel near the car ferry dock, at 9 am and 1 pm daily. The fare is US$15.

Around the Island

In order to see most of the island you will have to rent a bicycle, moped or car, or take a taxi. The following route will take you south from San Miguel, then counterclockwise around the island. There are some places along the way to stop for food and drink, but all the same it's good to bring water.

Several signs along the west coast of the island offer horseback riding. Asking price is US$16.50 an hour; bargain hard.

Parque Chankanaab This park on the bay of the same name is a very popular snorkeling spot, though there's not a lot to see in the water beyond a few brightly colored fish and some deliberately sunken artificial objects. The beach is a beauty, though, and 50m inland is a limestone

YUCATÁN

YUCATÁN

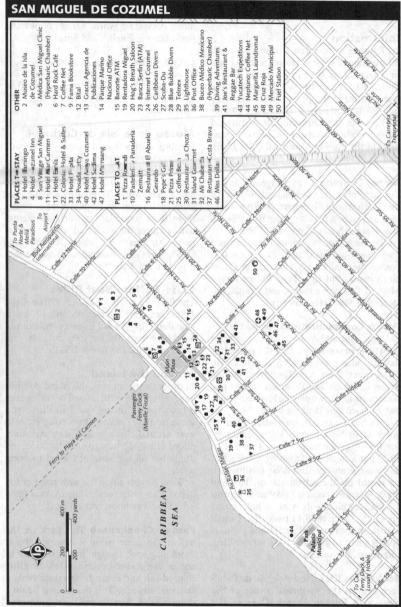

SAN MIGUEL DE COZUMEL

PLACES TO STAY
3   Hotel Flamingo
4   Hotel Cozumel Inn
8   Sun Village San Miguel
11 Hotel Mar Carmen
17 Hotel Mina
22 Colonial Hotel & Suites
33 Hotel Pepita
34 Posada Letty
40 Hotel Maya Cozumel
42 Hotel Safari Inma
47 Hotel Mary Tuang

PLACES TO EAT
1   Pizza Rolandi
10 Pastelería Panadería
    Zermatt
16 Restaurant El Abuelo
    Gerardo
18 Pepe's Grill
21 Pizza Prima
25 Coffee Bean
30 Restaurant La Choza
31 Island Gourmet
32 Mi Chabelita
37 Restaurant Costa Brava
46 Miss Dolla

OTHER
2   Museo de la Isla
    de Cozumel
5   Médica San Miguel Clinic
    (Hyperbaric Chamber)
6   Hard Rock Café
7   Coffee Net
9   Fama Bookstore
12 Bital
13 Gracia Agencia de
    Publicaciones
14 Parque Marino
    Nacional Office
15 Banorte ATM
19 Rentadora Miguel
20 Hog's Breath Saloon
23 Banca Serfín (ATM)
26 Internet Cozumel
27 Scuba-Du
28 Blue Bubble Divers
29 Telmex
35 Lighthouse
36 Post Office
38 Buceo Médico Mexicano
    (Hyperbaric Chamber)
39 Diving Adventures
41 Joe's Restaurant &
    Reggae Bar
43 Yucatech Expeditions
44 Neptuno; Coffee Net
45 Margarita Laundromat
48 Cruz Roja
49 Mercado Municipal
50 Fuel Station

lagoon surrounded by iguanas and inhabited by turtles. You're not allowed to swim or snorkel there, but it's picturesque nevertheless. The beach is lined with palapas and fiberglass lounge chairs, and snorkel and dive equipment is available for rent.

There's a small archaeological park on the grounds containing Olmec heads and Mayan artifacts, a small museum holding objects imported from Chichén Itzá, and a botanical garden with 400 species of tropical plants. There's also a restaurant and bar, several snack shops, and dressing rooms, lockers and showers included in the admission fee. It's open 9 am to 5 pm daily; US$7. A taxi from town costs US$8 one way.

Playas San Francisco & Palancar Playa San Francisco, 14km from San Miguel, and Playa Palancar, a few kilometers farther south, are the island's nicest beaches. San Francisco's white sands run for more than 3km; rather expensive food is served at its restaurant. If you want to scuba dive or snorkel at nearby Arrecife Palancar (Palancar Reef), you will have to sign on for a day cruise or charter a boat.

El Cedral This Mayan ruin is the oldest on the island. It's the size of a small house and not really worth visiting. If you must, it's 3.5km down a paved road (signed) that heads off to the left a kilometer or two south of Playa San Francisco's access road. El Cedral is thought to have been an important ceremonial site; today there is a small church next to the tiny ruin.

Punta Celarain The southern tip of the island has a picturesque lighthouse, accessible via a dirt track, 4km from the highway. To enjoy truly isolated beaches en route, climb over the sand dunes. There's a fine view of the island from the top of the lighthouse.

The East Coast The eastern shoreline is the wildest part of the island and highly recommended for beautiful seascapes. Unfortunately, except for Punta Chiqueros, Playa Chen Río and Punta Morena, swimming is dangerous on Cozumel's east coast because of riptides and undertows. Playa Chen Río has a restaurant by the same name, where you can enjoy a good *cocktel de pulpo* (octopus cocktail; US$4.50). Various preparations of conch, snapper, grouper and other seafood run US$5 to US$10.

To Punta Molas Beyond where the east coast highway meets the Carretera Transversal, intrepid travelers may take a poorly maintained, infrequently traveled road toward Punta Molas, the island's northeast point, accessible only by 4WD or on foot. About 17km down the road are the Mayan ruins known as El Castillo Real, and a few kilometers farther is Aguada Grande. Both sites are quite far gone, their significance lost to time. In the vicinity of Punta Molas are some fairly good beaches and a few more minor ruins. If you head down this road be aware of the risk: If your vehicle breaks down, you can't count on flagging down another motorist for help.

The best camping spot along the road is Playa Bonita. Playa Xhanan isn't nearly as pretty, and there are no sandy beaches north of it.

Diving & Snorkeling

In a recent reader survey, *Scuba Diving* magazine found Cozumel to be the most popular diving destination in the world. For many reasons, Cozumel's diving is unsurpassed; chief among them are fantastic year-round visibility (50m and greater) and a jaw-droppingly awesome variety of marine life.

There are no fewer than 100 dive centers on Cozumel and dozens more in Playa del Carmen. Prices vary, but in general, expect to pay about US$70 for a two-tank dive (less if you bring your own BCD and regulator), US$65 for an introductory 'resort' course and US$350 for PADI open-water-diver certification. Multiple-dive packages and discounts for groups or paying in cash can bring these rates down significantly. For more information, pick up a copy of Lonely Planet's Pisces *Diving & Snorkeling Cozumel*, with detailed descriptions of local dive sites and operators.

YUCATÁN

The dive shops listed here are in downtown San Miguel. Most also have facilities at hotels outside of town, and many offer snorkeling and deep-sea fishing trips as well as dives and diving instruction.

Blue Bubble Divers (☎ 872-44-83, ☎/fax 872-18-65, in the USA ☎ 800-878-8853, bbubbles@dicoz.com, www.cozumel-diving.net/blue_bubble), on Avenida 5 Sur at Calle 3 Sur; also offers gear storage, rinse and delivery service

Caribbean Divers (☎ 872-10-80, fax 872-14-26, caridive@cozumel.com.mx, www.cozumeldiving .net/caribbean_divers), on Calle 3 Sur just west of Avenida 5 Sur

Diving Adventures (☎/fax 872-30-09, in the USA ☎ 888-338-0388, diventur@cozumel.com.mx, www.divingadventures.net), on Calle 5 Sur near Avenida Melgar

Scuba Du (☎/fax 872-19-94, scubadu@cozumel .net, www.islacozumel.net/diving/scubadu), on Calle 3 Sur between Avenida Melgar and Avenida 5 Sur

Yucatech Expeditions (☎ 872-56-59, fax 872-14-17, www.cozumel-diving.net/yucatech), on Avenida 15 Sur between Calle Adolfo Rosado Salas and Calle 1 Sur; specializes in diving the region's caves and caverns

There are two hyperbaric chambers in San Miguel: Buceo Médico Mexicano (☎ 872-23-87, 872-14-30, fax 872-18-48), on Calle 5 Sur between Avenidas Melgar and 5 Sur, and Cozumel Hyperbaric Research (☎ 872-01-03), in the Médica San Miguel clinic on Calle 6 Norte between Avenidas 5 and 10 Norte.

The most prominent scuba destinations are the reefs. Some of the best are the kilometers-long Arrecife Palancar, where

stunning coral formations and a 'horseshoe' of coral heads in 70m visibility offer some of the world's finest diving; Arrecife Maracaibo, where the current and aquatic life offer experienced divers a challenge; Arrecife Paraíso, famous for its coral formations, especially brain and star coral; and Arrecife Yocab, shallow yet vibrantly alive and great for beginners.

Snorkelers: All of the best sites are reached by boat. A half-day tour will cost US$25 to US$48, but you'll do some world-class snorkeling. If you want to be penny-wise and fish-foolish, you can save on the boat fare and walk into the gentle surf at Playa La Ceiba, Bahía Chankanaab, Playa San Francisco and elsewhere.

Places to Stay – Budget

Camping To camp near the coast within the Parque Marino Nacional Arrecifes de Cozumel (☎ 872-46-89) you'll need to secure a permit from the office, hidden away upstairs in the Plaza del Sol, a shopping area on the southeast side of the main plaza. It's open 8 am to 5 pm weekdays. The best camping places are along the island's relatively unpopulated eastern shore.

For camping north of the Parque Marino Nacional, permits are available at the Oficina de Urbanismo y Ecología (☎ 872-51-95). This office is downstairs in the Palacio Municipal on Calle 13 Sur just off Avenida Melgar, open 8 am to 3 pm weekdays. You'll also need to go next door to the Seguridad Pública office to inform them of where you'll be camping (this is for your safety).

Hotels All hotel rooms come with private bath and fan, unless otherwise noted. Prices given are winter rates and may be lower at other times of year.

Hotel Cozumel Inn (☎ 872-03-14, fax 872-31-56), on Calle 4 Norte between Avenida Melgar and Avenida 5 Norte, has 20 rooms for US$22 double, US$28 with air-con. There's a pool on the premises.

Hotel Saolima (☎ 872-08-86), on Rosado Salas between Avenidas 10 and 15 Sur, has clean, pleasant rooms in a quiet locale for US$21, US$25 with air-con.

Hotel Marruang (☎ 872-16-78), on Calle Rosado Salas between Avenidas 20 and 25 Sur, is entered from a passageway across from the municipal market. Rooms go for US$20.

Posada Letty (☎ 872-02-57), at Avenida 15 Sur and Calle 1 Sur, offers no-frills rooms for US$20 to US$22. Half a block south on Avenida 15 Sur is *Hotel Pepita* (☎ /fax 872-00-98), with well-maintained rooms around a garden for US$25. All have two double beds, insect screens, refrigerators and air-con, and there's free morning coffee. A very good deal!

Tried and true, clean and comfortable, *Hotel MariCarmen* (☎ 872-05-81) is on Avenida 5 Sur half a block south of the plaza. Its 27 tidy air-con rooms rent for US$25.

Places to Stay – Mid-Range

Prices given are winter rates and may be lower at other times of year.

Hotel Flamingo (☎ 872-12-64) is on Calle 6 Norte between Avenidas 5 Norte and Melgar. The 22 rooms cost US$55 double with fan, US$83 with air-con.

Colonial Hotel & Suites (☎ 872-40-34, fax 872-13-87, bacocame@dicoz.com), down a passageway off Avenida 5 Sur near Rosado Salas, has studios and one-bedroom suites (some sleep four people) with kitchenette and air-con for US$57 to US$68. The similar *Hotel Bahía* (☎ 872-02-09, fax 872-13-87, bacocame@dicoz.com), facing the sea on Avenida Melgar at Calle 3 Sur, is under the same management and charges US$57/72 double/triple; suites are more. Its unmarked entrance is on Calle 3 Sur, just past the KFC.

Hotel Maya Cozumel (☎ 872-00-11, fax 872-07-81), on Calle 5 Sur between Avenida Melgar and Avenida 5 Sur, has rooms with air-con, fridge, TV for US$35/40/45 single/double/triple. There's also an inviting pool surrounded by lawn and bougainvillea. A very good value.

Sun Village San Miguel (☎ 872-03-23, fax 872-18-20, hmeson@prodigy.net.mx), on Avenida Benito Juárez between Avenidas Melgar and 5 Norte, has a pool and 96 air-con rooms, some with balconies. Rates are US$94/112 double/triple.

South of town (see the Isla Cozumel map) is the *Club del Sol* (☎ 872-37-77, fax 872-58-77, clubdelsol@cozunet.finred.com.mx, Carretera a Chankanaab Km 6.8), with 28 air-con rooms, some with kitchenettes, for a reasonable US$70 double.

Places to Stay – Top End

Beginning several kilometers south of town are the big luxury resort hotels. See the Isla Cozumel map for locations. The rates given here are winter 'rack' rates; most are lower in off-seasons. Whatever the season, if business is slow, most places are open to negotiation.

The *Presidente Intercontinental Cozumel* (☎ 872-03-22, fax 872-31-20, cozumel@interconti.com, www.interconti.com, Carretera a Chankanaab Km 6.5) has 253 guestrooms, many with sea views, set amid tropical gardens and swimming pools. Wild iguanas roam the grounds. Room rates start at US$312.

The *Fiesta Americana* (☎ 872-22-62, in the USA ☎ 800-343-7821, dive@fiestamericana.com.mx, www.fiestamericana.com, Carretera a Chankanaab Km 7.5) has 172 balconied oceanview rooms and 56 'jungle casitas' behind the main building, plenty of gardens and a spectacular swimming pool. Rates start at US$300. The hotel has a dive shop as well.

The *Allegro Resort* (☎ 872-34-43, fax 872-45-08, Carretera a Chankanaab Km 16.5) has 300 rooms in two-story, Polynesian-style thatched-roof villas for US$154 double. There are three restaurants on the grounds and a pool with a swim-up bar.

Places to Eat

Budget Cheapest of all eating places, with tasty food, are the little market *loncherías* next to the Mercado Municipal on Calle Rosado Salas between Avenidas 20 and 25 Sur. All offer soup and a main course for less than US$3, with a large selection of dishes available.

Restaurant Costa Brava, on Calle 7 Sur half a block off Avenida Melgar, is a no-frills spot serving cheap breakfasts (US$2.50 to

US$3.25) and such filling dishes as chicken tacos, grilled steak and fried fish for US$4 to US$10.

Mi Chabelita, Avenida 10 Sur near Calle 1 Sur and Rosado Salas, is an inexpensive eatery run by a señora who serves decent portions of decent food for US$3 or less.

The forthrightly named *Miss Dollar*, on Avenida 20 Sur near Calle Rosado Salas, earns its money by providing inexpensive meals to take out; you can also eat there. The pricey *Coffee Bean*, on Calle 3 Sur just off Avenida Melgar, serves the latest trendy jum rodpo. For pastries, try *Tusteleria y Panadería Zermatt*, Avenida 5 Norte at Calle 4 Norte.

Mid-Range The American owners at *Pizza Prima*, on Rosado Salas between Avenidas 5 Sur and 10 Sur, make their own pasta and serve fresh pizzas (US$6 to US$12) and excellent Italian specialties (US$8 to US$15). Open daily 4 to 11 pm.

Pizza Rolandi, on Avenida Melgar between Calles 6 and 8 Norte, serves good one-person pizzas cooked in a wood-fired oven for US$8 to US$10. Homemade pasta is also available.

The *Island Gourmet*, on Avenida 10 Sur at Calle Rosado Salas, is a casual corner joint that whips up some excellent seafood. Dishes cost US$6 to US$10; the coconut shrimp's a big seller.

The menu at *Restaurant El Abuelo Gerardo*, on Avenida 10 Norte at Avenida Juárez, is extensive and the prices reasonable. Beef or chicken fajitas (US$8) and fried fish (US$8) are popular. Guacamole and chips are on the house.

Restaurant La Choza, on Rosado Salas at Avenida 10 Sur, is an excellent and popular restaurant specializing in authentic regional cuisine. Entrées cost US$7 to US$10, and all include soup.

If you're looking for a bite before catching the ferry back to Playa, avoid Las Palmeras restaurant (the closest to the ferry dock). It's overpriced, the drinks are terrible, and waiters have been known to try to short-change patrons.

Top End Cozumel's traditional place to dine well and richly is *Pepe's Grill*, on Avenida Melgar just south of Rosado Salas. Entrées include New York steak (US$20), prime rib (US$21) and charcoal-broiled lobster with garlic (market price, typically around US$35).

Entertainment

Most of the year, Cozumel can't keep up with Playa del Carmen as a nightlife destination. But if you're here a couple of hours after sunset and looking for a happening scene, there are a few places to go. The *Hard Rock Café*, on Avenida Melgar near the main ferry dock, has live rock most nights of the week, as does the *Hog's Breath Saloon*, on Avenida 5 Sur half a block south of the main plaza. For reggae, head to *Joe's Restaurant & Reggae Bar*, on Avenida 10 Sur between Rosado Salas and Calle 3 Sur. For disco, there's only one name in town: *Neptuno*, Avenida Melgar at Calle 11 Sur, open Thursday, Friday and Saturday nights.

Getting There & Away

Air Cozumel has a surprisingly busy international airport, with numerous direct flights from other parts of Mexico and the US. Flights from Europe are usually routed via the US or Mexico City. From the US, Continental (☎ 01-800-900-5000, www.continental.com) and American (☎ 872-08-99) have direct flights from Dallas, Houston, and Raleigh-Durham, North Carolina. Mexicana (☎ 872-02-63) has nonstops from Miami, Mérida and Mexico City.

Aerocozumel (☎ 872-09-28), with offices at Cozumel airport, flies daily between Cancún and Cozumel (US$50 one way) and between Cozumel and Belize City (US$165 one way). Reserve in advance.

Ferry Passenger ferries run from Playa del Carmen, and car ferries run from Puerto Morelos. See those sections for details.

Getting Around

To/From the Airport The airport is about 2km north of town. You can take a minibus from the airport into town for less than

US$2 (slightly more to the hotels south of town), but you'll have to take a taxi (US$4 from town, US$8 from southern hotels) to return to the airport.

Taxi Fares in and around town are US$1.50 per ride; luggage may cost extra. There is no bus service.

Car Rates for rental cars run US$35 to US$55 per day, all inclusive, more during late December and January. You could probably haggle with a taxi driver to take you on a tour of the island, drop you at a beach, come back and pick you up, and still save money. If you do rent, observe the law on vehicle occupancy. Usually only five people are allowed in a vehicle. If you carry more, the police will fine you.

Shop around; there are plenty of agencies around the main plaza. If you agree on a price in dollars and then pay with a credit card, the exchange rate could go against you. Work out all details with the agency beforehand.

If you have rented a car on the mainland from an agency that promises to furnish you a car on Cozumel at no extra charge (while you leave your other rental in Playa del Carmen), be sure to make the Cozumel arrangements well in advance, or you're likely to find yourself paying to rent on the island.

There's a fuel station on Avenida Juárez five blocks east of the main square.

Motorcycle 'Mopeds' (actually small motorcycles or scooters; no pedaling possible!) are one way to tour the island on your own, and rental opportunities abound. The standard asking price is US$22 a day (US$27 for 24 hours), but you may be able to haggle down to as little as US$15 per day, gas, insurance and tax included. If someone approaches you as you're getting off the ferry offering mopeds for US$25 a day, reply 'ten dollars a day' and see what results.

To rent, you must have a valid driver's license, and you must leave a credit card slip or put down a deposit (usually US$100). There is a helmet law and it is enforced (the fine for not wearing one is US$25), although most moped rental people won't mention it. Before you sign a rental agreement, be sure to request a helmet.

The best time to rent is first thing in the morning, when all the machines are there. Choose one with a working horn, brakes, lights, starter, rearview mirrors and a full tank of fuel; remember that the price asked will be the same whether you rent the newest machine or the oldest rattletrap.

Don't plan to circumnavigate the island with two people on one moped. The well-used and ill-maintained machine may break down under the load, stranding you a long way from civilization with no way to get help.

Remember to wear sunblock or cover up. Bring a towel to toss on the moped's seat when parked – the black plastic can get blisteringly hot in the sun. Keep in mind that you're not the only one unfamiliar with the road here, and some of your fellow travelers may be hitting the bottle. Drive carefully.

Bicycle Bicycles typically rent for US$5.50 for 24 hours and can be a great way to get to Bahía Chankanaab and other spots on the flat island. Rentadora Miguel, on Rosado Salas off of Avenida Melgar, has a ton of bicycles and rents scooters as well.

XCARET

Once a precious spot with excellent snorkeling, open to all, Xcaret (shkar-**et**; ☎ 9-871-40-00), about 10km south of Playa del Carmen, is now a heavily Disneyfied 'eco-park,' run by the consortium that operates Garrafón on Isla Mujeres and Xel-Há down the coast. There are still Mayan ruins and a beautiful inlet on the site, but much of the rest has been created or altered using dynamite, jackhammers and other terraforming techniques. There are a cenote and 'underground river' for swimming, a restaurant, an evening show of 'ancient Mayan ceremonies' worthy of Las Vegas, a butterfly pavilion, a botanical garden and nursery, orchid and mushroom farms and a wild-bird breeding area.

Package tourists from Cancún fill the place every day, happily paying the US$39

YUCATÁN

admission fee (children under 11 US$24, under five free), plus additional fees for many of the attractions and activities, such as swimming with captive dolphins.

PAAMUL

Paamul, 87km south of Ciudad Cancún and 5km north of Puerto Aventuras, is a de facto private beach. Like many other spots along the Caribbean coast, it has signs prohibiting entry to nonguests, and parking is limited.

The attractions here are the beach and the great diving. The sandy beach is fringed with palms, but it holds many small rocks, shells and spiked sea urchins in the shallows offshore, so take appropriate measures. The large RV park here is a favorite with snowbirds; the 'BC' license plates you see here are from British Columbia, not Baja California. There is also an attractive alabaster sand beach about 2km north.

Scuba-Mex (☎ 9-874-17-29, fax 9-873-06-67, scubamex.com), run by a couple of friendly Texans, offers **diving** trips to any of 30 superb sites for a reasonable price and has dive packages and certification courses. Snorkel gear and booties in a limited number of sizes are available, but you're best off bringing your own. Kayaks and inner tubes are also available.

The *Paamul* (☎/fax 9-877-85-12, paamul@ playa.com.mx) has beachfront cabañas consisting of spacious, if worn, duplexes facing a protected bay with fine coral heads. Each cabaña has a private bathroom with hot water, a ceiling fan and two beds and costs US$65 double. Camping costs US$8 for two people per site. Numerous spaces for recreational vehicles go for US$17 a night with full hookups.

Giant sea turtles come ashore here at night in July and August to lay their eggs. If you run across one during an evening stroll along the beach, keep a good distance away and don't shine a flashlight at it, as that will scare it off. Do your part to contribute to the survival of the turtles, which are endangered; let them lay their eggs in peace.

If you intend to reach Paamul by bus, you'll have a 400m walk from the highway to the hotel and beach.

XPU-HÁ

Xpu-Há (shpoo-**ha**; ☎ 9-875-10-10, xpuhavta@ cancun.com.mx), a private ecopark 97km south of Cancún, offers a great many of the things the other three ecoparks on the coast offer, but the US$39 entry fee is all inclusive. Once in, visitors can eat and drink, kayak the park's cenotes, ride a catamaran or a bicycle, boogie board in the surf, snorkel and even scuba dive (following a free introductory lesson). There are some animal enclosures (deer, crocodiles), an aviary, a snake house and a botanical garden. Fully 97% of Xpu-Há's 37 hectares has been left in its natural state.

AKUMAL

Famous for its beautiful beach, Akumal (Place of the Turtles) does indeed see some sea turtles come ashore to lay their eggs in the summer, although fewer and fewer arrive each year thanks to resort development. Akumal is one of the Yucatán's oldest resort areas and consists primarily of pricey hotels and condominiums on nearly 5km of wide beach bordering four consecutive bays.

Activities

Although population is taking a heavy toll on the reefs that parallel Akumal, **diving** remains the area's primary attraction. The Akumal Dive Shop (☎ 9-875-90-32, fax 9-875-90-33, akumal@cancun.com.mx) and Akumal Dive Center (9-875-90-25, akumal dive@mail.caribe.net.mx) both run dive trips and deep-sea **fishing** excursions.

Places to Stay & Eat

For the lowdown on most of the lodgings available in Akumal or to make a reservation, call ☎ 800-448-7137 in the USA. There are few rooms in Akumal under US$100 per day.

Modern *Villa Las Brisas* (☎ /fax 9-876-21-10, fax 9-875-90-59), on the beach in Aventuras Akumal (whose turnoff is 2.5km south of Playa Akumal's), has one- and two-bedroom condos and a studio apartment – all under one roof. Rates run from US$73 to US$185 in high season. The owners speak

English, Spanish, German, Italian and some Portuguese.

The ***Hotel Club Akumal Caribe/Hotel Villas Maya*** (☎ *9-875-90-12, in the USA* ☎ *800-351-1622, fax in the USA 915-581-6709, clubakumal@aol.com, www.hotelakumal caribe.com*), offers bungalows starting at US$109 plus tax. All rooms have air-con, and there's a pool.

Las Casitas Akumal (☎ *9-875-90-71, fax 9-875-90-72, mexvac@aol.com*) has cabañas containing a kitchen, a living room, two bedrooms and two bathrooms. High-season rates run US$200 to US$235 depending on the size of the accommodations.

The ***Turtle Bay Bakery & Café***, to the left of the walled entrance as you're facing the beach, serves breakfasts and light meals for US$4.50 to US$5. They also sell pastries and various espresso drinks (including iced mochas). Just outside the entrance of Akumal is a grocery store that stocks a good selection of inexpensive food.

XCACEL

Xcacel (shkah-**cell**) is the name of an area with a beach on a somewhat turbulent bay. The only structure here is a beat-up building occasionally used by biologists studying the sea turtles that lay eggs in the sand. Because of the turtles, no camping is permitted; indeed, only the biologists are allowed into Xcacel after sunset. A guard is posted at the end of the long dirt road that links Xcacel to Hwy 307, and during the day he sometimes charges visitors US$2 to enter the area.

At the time of research the Spanish company Meliá was pushing a resort project here symptomatic of the environmental devastation of the entire Mayan Riviera by developers, and one that would almost certainly spell the end of turtle reproduction at Xcacel.

XEL-HÁ

Once a pristine natural lagoon brimming with iridescent tropical fish and ringed on three sides by untouched mangroves, Xel-Há (shell-**hah**) is now a private park with landscaped grounds, a dolphin enclosure

(yes, you can frolic with them for an extra price), numerous restaurant-bars and a gift shop. The fish are regularly driven off by the busloads of day-trippers who come to enjoy the beautiful site and swim in the pretty lagoon. A visit to Xel-Há is worth it only in the off-season (summer), or in winter either very early or very late in the day. Admission is US$45 including food, towel, snorkel gear, locker and use of sand chairs.

There is a small archaeological site on the west side of the highway 500m south of the park's turnoff, open 8 am to 5 pm daily for US$2, free on Sunday. The ruins, which are not all that impressive, date from the Classic and Postclassic periods.

CENOTE TOURS

About 1.5km south of Xel-Há is the turnoff for Cenote Dos Ojos, which provides access to the Nohoch Nah Chich cave system, the largest underwater cave system in the world. You can take guided snorkel and dive tours of some amazing underwater caverns, floating through illuminated stalactites and stalagmites in an eerie wonderland.

Hidden Worlds (☎ 9-875-40-59, buddy@ hiddenworlds.com.mx, www.hiddenworlds .com.mx) is an American-run outfit that gives two- to three-hour snorkeling tours for US$25 to US$40 including flashlights, wet suit, equipment and transportation to the cenotes on a unique 'jungle mobile.' The drive through the jungle is a unique experience in itself, and the guides are very knowledgeable and informative.

Dives are also available, for US$60 for one tank, US$80 for two tanks; equipment rental is extra. Tour times are 9 and 11 am and 1 pm daily, and you don't need to make a reservation, but it never hurts to call; English is spoken.

These are cavern (as opposed to cave) dives, and they require only standard openwater certification.

A cheaper way to see some of the cenotes is through the Dos Cenotes operation a short distance north of Hidden Worlds. It's run by the Mayan community who own the land. Entrance is US$9; to hire local guides with flashlights is US$24; for US$27 you get snorkeling gear as well. There's no fixed schedule. If you don't hire guides you'll have to provide all your equipment and find your own way to the cenotes. Even with the guides you're not likely to be told much. Dives are possible here as well.

TULUM
• population 3600

Tulum lies some 130km south of Cancún. Its main attractions are at water's edge: Mayan ruins, beautiful beaches and a profusion of cabañas for rent.

Orientation & Information

Approaching from the north the first thing you reach is Tulum Crucero, the junction of Hwy 307 and the old access road to the ruins; there are decent lodgings here, including a new youth hostel. The new access road is 400m farther south and leads another 400m to the ruins themselves. Another 1.5km south on the highway brings you to the Cobá junction; turning right (west) takes you to Cobá. The road to the left leads about 1km to the north-south road servicing the Zona Hotelera, the string of waterfront lodgings extending 10km southward from the ruins. This road eventually enters the Reserva de la Biósfera Sian Ka'an and continues for some 50km past Boca Paila to Punta Allen.

From the Cobá junction it's another 1.5km south on the highway to the town, Tulum Pueblo.

There are Telmex pay phones in town, but few along the coastal road. There are numerous currency-exchange booths but no banks in town. The booths with the best exchange rates are opposite the bus station.

Across the main street from the bus station and one block south is the Weary Traveler, providing fast Internet access (US$0.07 per minute) and travelers' information. John, the friendly operator, offers free luggage storage, as well as free incoming phone calls and faxes (up to two pages). There's a book exchange, coffee drinks for sale, and nightly movies. It's open 8 am to 11 pm daily.

Savana is another place offering Internet access, as well as copier, fax and telephone services. It's about four blocks north of the Weary Traveler, across the street. Access prices are similar, and they have a book exchange.

Tulum Ruins

The ruins of Tulum (Mayan for 'wall'), though well preserved, would hardly merit rave reviews if it weren't for their setting. The grayish-tan buildings dominate a palm-fringed beach lapped by turquoise waters. Even on dark, stormy days, the majestic cliff-top ruins overlooking vast stretches of pristine beach look fit for the cover of a magazine. But don't come to Tulum expecting anything comparable to Chichén Itzá or Uxmal. The buildings here, decidedly Toltec in influence, were the product of a Mayan civilization in decline.

Tulum is a prime destination for tour buses. To best enjoy the ruins, visit them either early in the morning or late in the afternoon, when the tour groups aren't there. Hours are 7 am to 5 pm daily; admission is US$2.75, parking US$2.25 and the shuttle to the site US$1.75 roundtrip (this is optional and saves you about a seven-minute walk).

History Most archaeologists believe that Tulum was occupied during the Late Postclassic period (AD 1200–1521) and that it was an important port during its heyday. When Juan de Grijalva sailed past in 1518, he was amazed by the sight of this walled city, its buildings painted a gleaming red, blue and yellow and a ceremonial fire flaming atop its seaside watchtower.

The ramparts that surround three sides of Tulum (the fourth side being the sea) leave little question as to its strategic function as a fortress. Several meters thick and standing 3m to 5m high, the walls protected the city during a period of considerable strife between Mayan city-states. Not all of Tulum was situated within the walls. The vast majority of the city's residents lived outside them; the civic-ceremonial buildings and palaces likely housed Tulum's ruling class.

TULUM RUINS

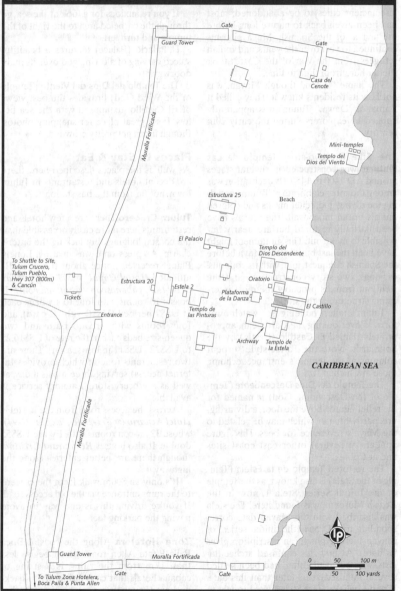

Gate

Guard Tower

Gate

Casa del Cenote

Mini-temples

Templo del Dios del Viento

Muralla Fortificada

Estructura 25

Beach

El Palacio

Templo del Dios Descendente

To Shuttle to Site,
Tulum Crucero,
Tulum Pueblo,
Hwy 307 (800m)
& Cancún

Tickets

Estructura 20

Estela 2

Oratorio

Plataforma de la Danza

El Castillo

Entrance

Templo de las Pinturas

Archway

Templo de la Estela

CARIBBEAN SEA

Muralla Fortificada

YUCATÁN

Guard Tower

Muralla Fortificada

To Tulum Zona Hotelera,
Boca Paila & Punta Allen

Gate

Gate

0   50   100 m
0   50   100 yards

The city was abandoned about 75 years after the Spanish conquest. It was one of the last ancient cities to be abandoned; most had been given back to nature long before the arrival of the Spanish. Maya pilgrims continued to visit over the years, and Indian refugees from the War of the Castes took shelter here from time to time.

The name 'Tulum,' though Mayan, was not how its residents knew it. They called it Zama, or 'Dawn.' 'Tulum' was apparently applied by explorers during the early 20th century.

The Site The two-story **Templo de Las Pinturas** was constructed in several stages around AD 1400 to 1450. Its decoration was among the most elaborate at Tulum, including the diving god, relief masks and colored murals on an inner wall. The murals have been partially restored but are nearly impossible to make out. This monument might have been the last built by the Maya before the Spanish conquest, and, with its columns, carvings, two-story construction, and the stela out front, is probably the most interesting structure at the site.

Tulum's tallest building is a watchtower fortress overlooking the Caribbean, appropriately named **El Castillo** (Castle) by the Spaniards. Note the Toltec-style serpent columns at the temple's entrance, echoing those at Chichén Itzá.

The **Templo del Dios Descendente** (Temple of the Descending God) is named for the relief figure above the door, a diving figure, partly human, which may be related to the Maya's reverence for bees. This figure appears at several other east coast sites and at Cobá.

The restored **Templo de la Estela** (Temple of the Stela) is also known as the Temple of the Initial Series. Stela 1, now in the British Museum, was found here. The stela was inscribed with the Mayan date corresponding to AD 564 (the 'initial series' of Mayan hieroglyphs in an inscription gives its date). At first this confused archaeologists, who believed Tulum had been settled several hundred years later than this date. It's now believed that Stela 1 was brought to Tulum from Tankah, 4km to the north, a settlement dating from the Classic period.

If you're anxious for a look at the sea, go through the corbeled arch to the right of the temple and turn left.

El Palacio (Palace) features a beautiful stucco carving of a diving god over its main doorway.

The **Templo del Dios del Viento** (Temple of the Wind God) provides the best views of El Castillo juxtaposed with the sea below. It's a great place for snapping photos, though it can get pretty crowded.

Places to Stay & Eat

As well as the places described here, there are decent hotels and restaurants in Tulum town, not far from the bus station.

Tulum Crucero There are a few hotels and restaurants here more easily accessible than the coastal lodgings, but lacking the latter's charm. As press time was nearing, Lonely Planet received notice about the new HI-affiliated *Hostel Copal* (☎ 871-24-81, ☎/fax 871-24-82, cabanascopal@hotmail.com). It boasts 10 rooms with four to six beds each at US$7 per bed (US$6 with HI card), and four rooms with private bath and two queen-size beds each at the rate of US$16.25 to US$22 (US$11 in low season). There are two restaurants (one of which provides Internet access) serving three meals a day, as well as a grocery store. Laundry service is available.

Across the access road from the hostel is *Hotel Acuario* (☎ 871-21-95, fax 871-21-94), whose 32 air-con rooms with TV are US$55 double. It also houses *Restaurant Cristina*, though there are better eateries along the highway.

It's only an 800m walk from the crucero to the ruins entrance via the old access road. If you're driving this is one way to avoid paying the parking fee.

Zona Hotelera Along the coastal Boca Paila-Punta Allen road, which begins less than 1km from the ruins, is a string of cabaña hotels that cater primarily to backpackers, though prices can be high for what you get. Most have simple restaurants but do not have telephones. Electricity is often either absent or shut off at 9 or 10 pm.

The cheapest way to sleep here is to have your own hammock and mosquito net; if you don't, several of the cheaper places rent them. In the cheapest places you'll have to supply your own towel and soap. See the boxed text for more tips on Tulum cabañas.

These places appear in the order you'd find them if you were to travel south on the coastal road from the ruins; not all establishments are listed.

Closest to the ruins is *Cabañas El Mirador*, with 28 cabins, (half with sand floors) most with beds (some with hammocks), but no fans or anything else. Costs run from US$4.50 for tents or a dormitory cabaña up to US$16 for the best. There's a beach out front and a decent restaurant above it, serving meals for US$4 to US$6, more for seafood. They'll store valuables. Next door is the indifferent *Cabañas Santa Fe*, which has 40 mostly thatch-roofed cabins with sides made of wooden poles on sandy floors.

Sharing a driveway with Cabañas Santa Fe and just south is *Cabañas Don Armando*, a 10-minute walk from the ruins. If you're coming via the road rather than the beach, note that the driveway is marked only by a Corona beer sign. Cabañas run US$11 to US$18. The poles have been filled in with concrete, which makes them more secure but prevents ventilation. Rates range with features such as lockable doors, hammocks and beds (you pay a deposit for key, sheets and pillows). Lighting is by candles.

The friendly *Cabañas Playa Condesa*, 500m farther south, has 18 comfortable cabañas (eight with private bath), each with a bed suspended by rope from the ceiling, mosquito netting, a concrete floor and slat-pole siding with good ventilation. Rates are US$14 to US$43. There's a restaurant, and power runs till midnight.

Two doors south, *Hotel Diamante K (in town of Tulum ☎ 871-23-76, fax 871-22-83)* offers rooms with wooden pole or bamboo siding, suspended beds and a table for a candle (the electricity goes off at 11:30 pm). Those with communal bath start at US$22;

Tips for Tulum's Cabañas

The waterfront cabañas south of the Tulum ruins are world famous with backpackers. The first four are side-by-side and within 1km of the ruins. Thereafter, they are mixed in with more expensive places and spread out over the next 10km. Here are a few tips to keep in mind if you intend to stay at one of them:

- Cabañas closest to the ruins are usually occupied by 10 or 11 am every day from mid-December through March and in July and August. Arrive early, or make a reservation the night before.

- Taxis are recommended to cover the distance between the cabañas and the bus station or the bus stops at Tulum Crucero and the Zona Arqueológica.

- The cheapest cabañas are made of sticks and built on sand (some have concrete floors). Bring a mosquito net to hang over yourself at night.

- Few of the flimsy, primitive cabañas can be reliably secured. Thieves lift the poles in the walls to gain entrance, or burrow beneath through the sand, or jimmy the locks. Never leave valuables unattended in a cabaña.

- Bring a pair of sandals or flip-flops. Most of the cabañas, even at the pricier places, have shared bathrooms. Shoes help you keep sand out of your bed and reduce the chance of catching athlete's foot.

with private bath, US$65. There are two communal rooms with beds for US$11 each, a much better deal than the comparably priced places already mentioned. The Diamante K has a small beach and a fine restaurant-bar and fills up even in the low season.

About 700m south, just south of the road that links the coastal road and Tulum town, is the popular *Papaya Playa (☎ 871-20-91, fax 871-20-92, sertrapote@hotmail.com)*. There are 13 sand-floor cabañas for US$20,

YUCATÁN

and four big rooms with private bath, furniture and beds for US$54. All have screened windows and ocean views, and there's a cozy bar and restaurant. Reservations are recommended. Teepees and hammocks slung between trees are available for US$5.50 each.

Cabañas Copal (☎ 871-24-81, ☎/fax 871-24-82, copal@tulum.cc) is the next place south and consists of three comfortable cabañas with concrete floors, private bath and ocean view for US$60 in high season. There are also 32 cheaper cabañas, with sand or cement floors, all with mosquito nets, firm mattresses and good ventilation, and ranging from US$20 to US$40 depending on location, beds, and flooring.

Next to the south and by now about 4km south of the ruins is the family-run **Cabañas La Conchita** (fax only 871-20-92; include 'attn La Conchita'), with eight rooms. These are a major step up from those described thus far. Most have cool, concrete walls, standard windows with some degree of sea view and lockable doors (good security). The beach here is lovely. Rates are a reasonable US$60 for most rooms, breakfast included.

The **Restaurant y Cabañas Nohoch Tunich** (☎ 876-94-07, fax 871-20-92, www.secom.net/nohochtunich) offers both appealing hotel rooms with porches and electricity until 11 pm, and thatch-and-board cabañas. Rooms are US$54 to US$65; cabañas start at US$22.

Next door is the upscale **Piedra Escondida Hotel y Restaurant** (fax only 871-20-92, piedraescondida@tulum-mexico.com), which offers eight hotel rooms with private bath and balconies or porches, all with good ventilation. Rates are US$76 much of the year, a bit more during the high season.

Hotel Cabañas La Perla, the next place to the south, offers six rooms and two cabañas. The rooms have private bath and rent for US$40 (one bed) and US$50 (two beds). The rustic cabañas have shared bath for US$20. La Perla shares a small beach with Nohoch Tunich and Punta Piedra.

South of La Perla approximately 500m is the **Maya Tulum** (in the USA ☎ 888-515-4580, www.mayantulum.com), which is in a different league from all the other places mentioned. Here you'll find 33 deluxe cabañas and two houses, a gorgeous beach nearby, a yoga room and a vegetarian restaurant. Rates run from US$60 to US$70 for a shared-bath cabaña, US$85 to US$115 for a cabaña with a private bath, and US$195 to US$235 for a house.

Getting There & Away

You can walk from Tulum Crucero to the ruins (800m). The cabañas begin about 600m south of the ruins and can be reached by taxi from Tulum pueblo. The fares are fixed and cheap. At the center of town you'll see the large sign of the Sindicato de Taxistas, on which the rates are posted. To the ruins it's US$2, to most of the cabañas US$4.

The bus station is toward the southern end of town (look for the two-story building with 'ADO' painted on it in huge letters). When leaving Tulum, you can also wait at Tulum Crucero for a Playa Express or regular intercity bus. Here are some distances and travel times for buses leaving Tulum:

Cancún 132km, 1 hour, US$5

Chetumal 251km, 3½ hours, US$8.50

Chichén Itzá 190km, 2½ hours, US$6.50

Cobá 45km, 30 minutes, US$2

Felipe Carrillo Puerto 98km, 1¾ hours, US$4

Mérida 320km, 5 hours via Cobá or 6 hours via Cancún, US$11

Playa del Carmen 63km, 45 minutes, US$2.75

Punta Allen 57km, 3 hours, US$5 (from the taxi cooperative in the middle of town)

Valladolid 106km, 2 hours, US$4.25

GRAND CENOTE

A little over 3km from Tulum on road to Cobá is Grand Cenote, a worthwhile stop on your visits between the Tulum and Cobá ruins, especially if it's a hot day. You can snorkel (US$4.50) or dive (US$6.50) among small fish in the caverns here if you bring your own gear.

COBÁ

Among the largest of Mayan cities, Cobá, 50km northwest of Tulum, offers the chance to explore mostly restored antiquities set deep in tropical jungles.

History

Cobá was settled earlier than Chichén Itzá or Tulum, and construction reached its peak between AD 800 and 1100. Archaeologists believe that this city once covered 50 sq km and held 40,000 Maya.

Cobá's architecture is a mystery; its towering pyramids and stelae resemble the architecture of Tikal, several hundred kilometers away, rather than the much nearer sites of Chichén Itzá and the northern Yucatán Peninsula.

Some archaeologists theorize that an alliance with Tikal was made through marriage to facilitate trade between the Guatemalan and Yucatecan Maya. Stelae appear to depict female rulers from Tikal holding ceremonial bars and flaunting their power by standing on captives. These Tikal royal females, when married to Cobá's royalty, may have brought architects and artisans with them.

Archaeologists are also baffled by the extensive network of *sacbeob* (stone-paved avenues) in this region, with Cobá as the hub. The longest runs nearly 100km from the base of Cobá's great pyramid Nohoch Mul to the Mayan settlement of Yaxuna. In all, some 40 sacbeob passed through Cobá, parts of the huge astronomical 'time machine' that was evident in every Mayan city.

The first excavation was by the Austrian archaeologist Teobert Maler in 1891. There was little subsequent investigation until 1926, when the Carnegie Institute financed the first of two expeditions led by Sir J Eric S Thompson and Harry Pollock. After their 1930 expedition, not much happened until 1973, when the Mexican government began to finance excavation. Archaeologists now estimate that Cobá contains some 6500 structures, of which just a few have been excavated and restored.

Orientation & Information

The village of Cobá, 2.5km west of the Tulum-Nuevo Xcan road, has a small cheap hotel and several small, simple and low-cost restaurants. At the lake, turn left for the ruins, right for the upscale Villa Arqueológica Cobá hotel.

The archaeological site is open from 6 am to 6 pm; admission costs US$2.75, free on Sunday. The parking lot for the site charges US$1 per passenger car.

Be prepared to walk at least several kilometers on paths, depending on how much you want to see. Dress for heat and humidity, and bring insect repellent and water; it's hot and there are no drinks stands within the site, only at the entrance (bug spray can also be bought here). Avoid the midday heat if possible. Most people spend around two hours at the site.

Within the site, near the juego de pelota, are bicycles for rent at US$2.75 for the day. These are useful if you really want to get around the farther reaches of the site. It helps to have some experience riding on rocky trails. If the site is unusually crowded it's probably best to walk.

You may want to buy a book on the site before coming to Cobá. Onsite signage and maps are minimal and cryptic. Guides near the entrance size you up and ask whatever they think you're worth, anywhere from US$7 to over US$23. At the time of research, the Nohoch Mul pyramid was the only one the public was allowed to climb.

Grupo Cobá

Walking just under 100m along the main path from the entrance and turning right brings you to the Templo de las Iglesias (Temple of the Churches), the most prominent structure in the Cobá Group. It's an enormous pyramid, and from the top you could get a fine view of the Nohoch Mul pyramid to the north and shimmering lakes to the east and southwest if you were allowed to climb it.

Back on the main path, you pass through the *juego de pelota* (ball court), 30m farther along. It's been restored quite well.

YUCATÁN

Grupo Macanxoc

About 500m beyond the juego de pelota, turn right for the Grupo Macanxoc, a group of stelae that bore reliefs of royal women who are thought to have come from Tikal. They are badly eroded, and it's a 1km walk; the flora along the way is interesting, however.

Conjunto de las Pinturas

Another 100m beyond the Macanxoc turnoff, a sign points left toward the Conjunto de las Pinturas (Group of Paintings). Go beyond this to the second sign and turn left to see the temple. It bears easily recognizable traces of glyphs and frescoes above the door and traces of richly colored plaster inside.

You approach the temple from the southeast. Leave by the trail at the northwest (opposite the temple steps) to see several stelae. The first of these is 20m along beneath a palapa. A regal figure stands over two others, one of them kneeling with his hands bound behind him. Sacrificial captives lie beneath the feet of a ruler at the base. Continue along the path past another badly weathered stela to the Nohoch Mul path and turn right.

Nohoch Mul

A farther walk of 800m brings you to Nohoch Mul (Big Mound), the Great Pyramid, built on a natural hill. Along the way, just before the track bends sharply to the left, a narrow path on the right leads to a group of badly weathered stelae. Farther along, the track bends between piles of stones – a ruined temple – before passing Templo 10 and Stela 20. The exquisitely carved stela bears a picture of a ruler standing imperiously over two captives. Eighty meters beyond stands the Great Pyramid.

At 42m high, the Great Pyramid is the tallest Mayan structure in the northern Yucatán. There are two diving gods carved over the doorway of the temple at the top (built in the Postclassic period, AD 1100–1450), similar to the sculptures at Tulum. The view is spectacular. Be advised that at least one person a year loses footing on the pyramid and dies somewhere on the way down. Wear snug shoes with traction. Most sandals are not recommended. Try zigzagging up the steps, making diagonal passes to either side of the stairway. This is an especially good technique if your feet are at all large, and can be useful throughout the Ruta Maya.

From Nohoch Mul, it's a 1.4km, half-hour walk back to the site entrance.

Places to Stay & Eat

There's no organized campsite, but you can try finding a place along the shore of the lake. Before you go swimming, consider the crocodiles living in the lake.

There are several small restaurants by the site parking lot. Buy your drinks at either *Restaurant El Faisán* or *Restaurant El Caracol*, both of which serve inexpensive meals. If you don't want to shell out US$2.25 on a liter of water, bring some from elsewhere.

In the village of Cobá, *Restaurant Las Pirámides* is nearest the lake, with good views and friendly service. *Hotel y Restaurant El Bocadito* (no phone) is also popular. The Bocadito rents rooms with fan and bath for US$6.50 to US$9, and they'll store luggage while you visit the ruins. The restaurant is very well run and serves a great *menú* for US$5. The owner, Don Francisco, is a very good source of information, especially about transportation. El Bocadito also serves as Cobá's bus terminal and taxi colectivo terminus.

For upscale lodging and dining there's Club Med's *Villa Arqueológica Cobá* (☎/fax 9-87-420-87, in the USA ☎ 800-258-2633), right next to the lake. There's a swimming pool and mediocre restaurant to complement the air-con rooms for US$53/61/83 single/double/triple. This is the most pleasant and best value among the Villas Arqueológicas on the Yucatán Peninsula and a nice place to relax.

Getting There & Away

There are several buses daily between Tulum and Cobá; four of them serve Playa del Carmen as well. The fare is US$1.20 to Tulum. Combis between Cobá and Tulum charge US$4 per person. There is frequent service to Valladolid (1 hour, 60km, US$2), Chichén Itzá (US$3.25) and Mérida (US$7.25) as well.

A more comfortable but expensive way to reach Cobá is by taxi from Tulum Crucero. Find some other travelers interested in the trip and split the cost, US$45 roundtrip, including two hours at the site.

The 31km road from Cobá to Chemax is arrow-straight and in excellent shape. If you're driving to Valladolid or Chichén Itzá this is the way to go.

Southern Quintana Roo

TULUM TO PUNTA ALLEN

The 50km stretch from Tulum Ruinas past Boca Paila to Punta Allen is rich with wildlife and encompasses part of the protected Reserva de la Biósfera Sian Ka'an. The beaches aren't spectacular, but there's plenty of privacy.

A white minivan makes the trip from Tulum Pueblo to Punta Allen twice daily, taking about three hours (see Getting There & Away in the Tulum section). Motorists: It's important to have plenty of fuel before heading south from Tulum, as there is none available on the Tulum-Punta Allen road.

Reserva de la Biósfera Sian Ka'an

Over 5000 sq km of tropical jungle, marsh, mangroves and islands on Quintana Roo's coast have been set aside by the Mexican government as a large biosphere reserve. In 1987 the United Nations appointed it a World Heritage Site – an irreplaceable natural treasure.

The reserve is home to howler monkeys, foxes, ocelots, pumas, crocodiles, eagles, raccoons, tapirs, peccaries, giant land crabs, jaguars and hundreds of species of birds. But there are no hiking trails through Sian Ka'an (Where the Sky Begins) and only two ways to get much out of the reserve. The first is to drive down one of the few roads that intersect the Tulum-Punta Allen road, pull to the side at a promising stretch and walk along the road for a while. Don't enter the forest – there's a good chance you'll become lost.

The other way is to enter the reserve with a professional guide. Aventuras Tropicales de Sian Ka'an (☎ 9-871-20-92 November to April, ☎/fax in the USA 218-388-9455 April to November, in the USA ☎ 800-649-4166, yucatan@boreal.org, www.boreal.org/yucatan), based in Punta Allen, runs outings combining sea kayaking, mountain biking, snorkeling, luxury camping, gourmet dining, quality hammock time and total immersion in a truly remote tropical wilderness. Most trips last four to eight days. Birding and ecosystem-study trips are also offered.

Punta Allen

Although it suffered considerable damage from the ferocious winds of Hurricane Gilbert in 1988, Punta Allen still sports a laid-back ambience reminiscent of the Belizean cayes. The area is known primarily for its bonefishing, and for that many people come a long way. There's also a healthy reef 400m from shore that offers snorkelers and divers wonderful sights. Between the reef and the beach there's lots of sea grass; that's a turnoff to a lot of people, but it provides food and shelter for numerous critters and is one of the reasons the snorkeling and diving are so good.

The *Cruzan Inn* (☎ 9-834-03-83, fax 9-834-02-92, fishcruzan@aol.com) has eight cabañas on stilts, each with private bath, two beds, mosquito netting and 24-hour lighting for US$50/75 double in low/high season. The couple who run it offer breakfast, lunch and dinner. They also offer snorkeling trips, gear included, for US$25, and they can arrange fishing and birding expeditions.

The *Ascension Bay Bonefish Club* (www.joefish.com) specializes in providing guided fishing expeditions. Packages with six full days of guided fishing, roundtrip transportation from Cancún, meals and accommodations go for US$2000 to US$2350.

Let It Be Inn (www.letitbeinn.com) has several thatched cabañas with tiled floors, private bath with hot water and sea-view porches with hammocks. The rate of US$60 double includes a hearty breakfast.

FELIPE CARRILLO PUERTO
• population 16,500

Now named for a progressive governor of Yucatán, this crossroads town 95km south of Tulum was once known as Chan Santa Cruz. It was the rebel headquarters during the War of the Castes, and it was here that the talking cross exhorted Maya rebels to fight (see The Talking Cross in Facts about the Yucatán's History section).

'Carrillo Puerto' offers the visitor little in the way of attractions, but it's a transit hub and the first town of consequence if you're arriving from the Mérida/Ticul/Uxmal area. There's a gas station on the highway and inexpensive air-con accommodations. At the time of research no bank in town would change money or cash traveler's checks.

The bus station is on the main plaza, which is a block west of Hwy 307 and two blocks south of the intersection of Hwy 295 (to Valladolid) and Hwy 184 (to Ticul and Mérida). The gas station is at Hwy 307 and Calle 69. Hwy 307 is also known as Calle 70 and Avenida Juárez.

The **Santuario de la Cruz Parlante** (Sanctuary of the Talking Cross) is five blocks west of the gas station on Hwy 307. There isn't much to see there, and the town's residents do not like strangers in the sanctuary; they will try to take your camera if they see you using it there. More interesting and accessible are the murals on the Casa de Cultura's outside wall, depicting the War of the Castes and the Maya's future redemption. The center occasionally has exhibits on the War of the Castes.

Places to Stay & Eat
The 30 air-con rooms of *El Faisán y El Venado* (☎ 834-07-02, Avenida Juárez 7812) feature private bath, firm mattresses, TV and ceiling fans for US$16 double; there's also a good, inexpensive restaurant. A few dozen meters south is the friendly *Restaurant 24 Horas*, with food a bit cheaper than El Faisán's.

South of the 24 Horas is the *Hotel San Ignacio*, with 12 air-con rooms for US$16 and an air-con restaurant called *Danburguer Maya*.

Getting There & Away
Most buses serving Carrillo Puerto are *de paso* (they don't originate there).

Cancún 230km, 3¼ hours, US$7.50 to US$9

Chetumal 155km, 2¼ hours, US$5

Mérida 310km, 5½ hours, US$10.50

Playa del Carmen 159km, 2½ hours, US$5.25 to US$6

Ticul 200km, 4½ hours, US$7.50; change there or at Muna for Uxmal

Tizimín 208km, 3½ hours, US$6.75

Tulum 96km, 1½ hours, US$4

Valladolid 160km, 2½ hours, US$5

Note that there are very few services such as hotels, restaurants or fuel stations between Felipe Carrillo Puerto and Ticul.

XCALAK & COSTA MAYA
The coast south of the Reserva de la Biósfera Sian Ka'an to the small fishing village of Xcalak (shka-**lak**) is often referred to as the Costa Maya. There are some ambitious plans for development of the area but as of this writing they hadn't yet come to fruition (translation: See it now before it's too late). Electric lines are approaching the town of Mahahual to the north (which is also witnessing construction of a cruise-ship pier), and the road linking Xcalak to Hwy 307 has been paved. Xcalak remains a relatively primitive part of Mexico, however. There are very few services, and most residents have electricity only six hours a day.

Xcalak's appeal lies in its quiet atmosphere, decaying Caribbean-style wooden homes, swaying palms and pretty beaches. Another draw is the little-explored **Reserva de la Biósfera Banco Chinchorro**, the largest coral atoll in the Northern Hemisphere, 40km northeast. In addition to its many natural beauties, the atoll is a wreck diver's paradise. So many ships have crashed into the ring of islands during adverse weather that parts of it resemble a ship graveyard. The barrier reef is much closer and provides some very interesting diving and snorkeling opportunities.

Aventuras Xcalak to Chinchorro Dive Center (dive@xcalak.com.mx, www.xcalak.com), in the Hotel Tierra Maya, offers dive and snorkel trips to Banco Chinchorro and other dive spots, and rents equipment. A few fine small hotels north of town have been operating quietly for several years.

Places to Stay & Eat

The six-room *Hotel Caracol* (no phone) is the town's only cheap place to stay, offering decent rooms with fan and cold-water private bath for US$9. Electricity is available from 6 to 10 pm. Look for the owner, Sra Mauricia Garidio, next door to the hotel.

The rest of the places to stay are on the old coastal road leading north from town; all rates are the higher winter prices. *Costa de Cocos* (☎ 9-831-01-10, ccocos@astro.net.mx, www.costadecocos.com), 1.5km north, has 14 appealing thatched cabañas with private bath, solar hot water, screened windows and 24-hour electricity. Rooms are US$75/120/150/184 single/double/triple/quad, breakfast and dinner included.

The *Hotel Tierra Maya* (☎ 9-831-04-04, in the USA ☎ 800-480-4505, fantasea@xcalak.com, www.xcalak.com/aventuras) is a modern beachfront hotel featuring six rooms (three quite large), each tastefully appointed and boasting lots of architectural details. All of the rooms have a balcony facing the sea, hot-water private bathrooms and mahogany furniture – the bigger rooms even have small refrigerators. There's electricity 24 hours and mangroves nearby. Rates are US$73 double occupancy for the smaller rooms, US$84 for the larger rooms.

The *Villa Caracol* (☎ /fax 9-838-18-72) features two 2nd-floor doubles plus four individual beach cabañas, each with two queen-size beds, purified water, a private bath, air-con and 24-hour electricity; US$98 double. Cabañas without air-con rent for US$68 double. Breakfast and dinner are an extra US$20 per person. Rates include unlimited use of snorkeling equipment, bicycles, paddleboats, fishing tackle and more.

There are a very few small restaurants near the center of town keeping sporadic hours. *Restaurant Bar Xcalak Caribe*, about one block south of the wharf and just across the street from the beach, is the best of these. Delicious fried fish is US$4.25 and a huge serving of lobster runs US$13.

Getting There & Away

From Hwy 307, take the signed turnoff for Mahahual. The turnoff is 68km south of Felipe Carrillo Puerto (1km south of Limones) and 46km north of Bacalar. About 55km east, a few kilometers before Mahahual, turn right (south) and follow the signs to Xcalak (another 60km).

Expect to stop more than once at military checkpoints; they're searching for contraband. The road passes through young mangroves and is frequented by diverse wildlife. Watch for the usual herons and egrets, as well as cranes, iguanas, peccaries and other critters.

Sociedad Cooperativa del Caribe buses depart Chetumal's main bus terminal for Xcalak (200km, 3 to 5 hours, US$4.50) daily at 6 am and 3:15 pm. From Felipe Carrillo Puerto catch a bus to Limones; from there buses to Xcalak (US$3.25) depart at 7:30 am and 4 pm.

LAGUNA BACALAR

A large, clear, turquoise freshwater lake with a bottom of gleaming white sand, Laguna Bacalar comes as a surprise in this region of tortured limestone and scrubby jungle.

The small, sleepy town of Bacalar, just east of the highway, 125km south of Felipe Carrillo Puerto, is the only settlement of any size on the lake. It's noted mostly for its old Spanish fortress and its popular swimming facilities.

The fortress was built above the lagoon to protect citizens from raids by pirates and Indians. It served as an important outpost for the whites in the War of the Castes. In 1859, it was seized by Maya rebels who held the fort until Quintana Roo was finally conquered by Mexican troops in 1901. Today, with formidable cannons still on its ramparts, the fortress remains an imposing sight.

It houses a museum exhibiting colonial armaments and uniforms from the 17th and 18th centuries. Open 10 am to 6 pm Tuesday to Sunday; US$0.50.

A divided avenue runs between the fortress and the lakeshore northward a few hundred meters to the balneario. There are some small restaurants along the avenue and near the balneario, which is very busy on weekends.

Costera Bacalar & Cenote Azul

The road that winds south along the lakeshore from Bacalar town to Hwy 307 at Cenote Azul is called the Costera Bacalar. It passes a few lodging and camping places along the way. Cenote Azul is a 90m-deep natural pool on the southwestern shore of Laguna Bacalar, 200m east of Hwy 307. (If you're approaching from the north by bus, get the driver to let you off here.) There's a restaurant that looks over the cenote; most meals here cost US$5 to US$8.

Hotel Laguna (☎ 9-834-22-06, fax 9-834-22-05), 2km south of Bacalar town along the Costera, is only 150m east of Hwy 307. Clean, cool and hospitable, it boasts a swimming pool and a restaurant and bar. Rooms cost US$34 double.

Only 700m south of the Hotel Laguna along the Costera is *Los Coquitos*, a very nice camping area on the lakeshore that charges US$2.75 per person. Bring your own food and water, as the nearest supplier is the restaurant at the Hotel Laguna.

Getting There & Away

Coming from the north, have the bus drop you in Bacalar town, at the Hotel Laguna or at Cenote Azul, as you wish; check before you buy your ticket to see if the driver will stop.

Departures from Chetumal's minibus terminal on Primo de Verdad at Hidalgo to the town of Bacalar are about once an hour from 5 am to 7 pm (39km, 40 minutes, US$1); some northbound buses departing from the bus terminal will also drop you near the town of Bacalar (US$1.25).

Heading west out of Chetumal, take Hwy 307 north 25km to the turn on the right marked for the Cenote Azul and Costera Bacalar.

CHETUMAL
• population 115,200

Before the Spanish conquest, Chetumal was a Mayan port for shipping gold, feathers, cacao and copper to the northern Yucatán Peninsula. After the conquest, the town was not actually settled until 1898, when it was founded to put a stop to the illegal trade in arms and lumber carried on by the descendants of the War of the Castes rebels. Dubbed Payo Obispo, the town changed its name to Chetumal in 1936. In 1955, Hurricane Janet virtually obliterated it.

During the rebuilding, the city planners laid out the new town on a grand plan with a grid of wide boulevards. In times BC (Before Cancún), the sparsely populated territory of Quintana Roo could not fulfill the plans for a grand city. Even when QR became a state in 1974, and Chetumal its capital, large lots were left empty in town. But the boom at Cancún brought prosperity to all, and the vacant lots are finally being filled in with buildings.

Chetumal is also the gateway to Belize. With the peso so low and Belize so expensive, Belize nearly empties out on weekends with shoppers coming to Chetumal's markets.

Orientation

Despite Chetumal's sprawling layout, the city center is easily manageable on foot. Once you find the all-important intersection of Avenida de los Héroes and Avenida Álvaro Obregón, you're within 50m of several inexpensive hotels and restaurants. The best hotels are only four or five blocks from this intersection.

Information

A tourist information kiosk (☎ 832-36-63), on Avenida de los Héroes, right in the center of town, is open 9 am to 1 pm and 4 to 9 pm Monday through Saturday.

The Guatemalan consulate (☎ 832-30-45) is at Retorno No 4, Casa 8, Fraccionamiento Bahía. To get there, take Héroes de Chapultepec east to where it ends at the water; the

CHETUMAL

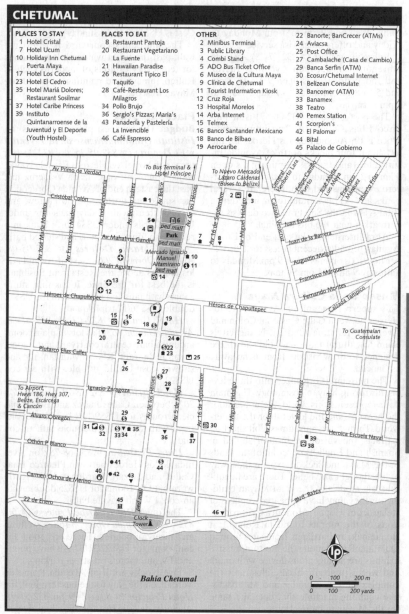

PLACES TO STAY
1 Hotel Cristal
7 Hotel Ucum
10 Holiday Inn Chetumal Puerta Maya
17 Hotel Los Cocos
23 Hotel El Cedro
35 Hotel Mariá Dolores; Restaurant Sosilmar
37 Hotel Caribe Princess
39 Instituto Quintanarroense de la Juventud y El Deporte (Youth Hostel)

PLACES TO EAT
8 Restaurant Pantoja
20 Restaurant Vegetariano La Fuente
21 Hawaiian Paradise
26 Restaurant Típico El Taquito
28 Café-Restaurant Los Milagros
34 Pollo Brujo
36 Sergio's Pizzas; Maria's
43 Panadería y Pastelería La Invencible
46 Café Espresso

OTHER
2 Minibus Terminal
3 Public Library
4 Combi Stand
5 ADO Bus Ticket Office
6 Museo de la Cultura Maya
9 Clínica de Chetumal
11 Tourist Information Kiosk
12 Cruz Roja
13 Hospital Morelos
14 Arba Internet
15 Telmex
16 Banco Santander Mexicano
18 Banco de Bilbao
19 Aerocaribe

22 Banorte; BanCrecer (ATMs)
24 Aviacsa
25 Post Office
27 Cambalache (Casa de Cambio)
29 Banca Serfin (ATM)
30 Ecosur/Chetumal Internet
31 Belizean Consulate
32 Bancomer (ATM)
33 Banamex
38 Teatro
40 Pemex Station
41 Scorpion's
42 El Palomar
44 Bital
45 Palacio de Gobierno

YUCATÁN

consulate is one block northwest on a street that doesn't quite connect to Boulevard Bahía. It's open 9 am to 4 pm Monday to Friday and offers quick visa service.

Belize's consulate (☎ 832-77-28), Avenida Obregón 226, between Avenidas Juárez and Independencia, is open 9 am to 2 pm and 5 to 8 pm Monday to Friday, 9 am to 2 pm Saturday.

The post office (☎ 832-00-57) is at Plutarco Elías Calles 2A. The immigration office is on Avenida de los Héroes on the left about four blocks north of Avenida Insurgentes (and the bus terminal); it's open 9 am to 2 pm Monday to Friday for tourist-card extensions and such. There are several banks and ATMs around town, including a Bital ATM in the San Francisco de Asís supermarket near the bus terminal.

Abra Internet, at the east end of Efraín Aguilar, provides decent access for US$3.25 per hour. It's open 9 am to 9 pm Monday to Saturday, 9 am to 1 pm Sunday.

Museo de la Cultura Maya

This superb museum, on Avenida de los Héroes between Calle Cristóbal Colón and Avenida Mahatma Gandhi, is the city's claim to cultural fame – a bold showpiece designed to draw visitors from as far away as Cancún.

The museum is organized into three levels, mirroring Mayan cosmology. The main floor represents this world, the upper floor the heavens, and the lower floor the underworld. Though the museum is a bit short on artifacts, the various exhibits (labeled in Spanish and English) cover all of the lands of the Maya and seek to explain their way of life, thought and belief. There are beautiful scale models of the great Mayan buildings as they may have appeared, replicas of stelae from Copán, Honduras, reproductions of the murals found in Room 1 at Bonampak, and artifacts from sites around Quintana Roo. Among the most impressive exhibits are an ingenious device with crank and wheels that graphically illustrates the complex Mayan calendar and an abacus-like counting machine that does the same for the Mayan numerical system.

Museum hours are 9 am to 7 pm Tuesday to Sunday, until 8 pm Friday and Saturday. Cost is US$5.50 (free Sunday).

The museum's courtyard is free (just walk past the ticket window). It has salons for temporary exhibits of moderns such as Rufino Tamayo and paintings reproducing Mayan frescoes.

Places to Stay

Budget The cheapest place in town is the *Instituto Quintanarroense de la Juventud y El Deporte* (☎ 832-05-25, fax 832-00-19), the youth hostel, on Heroica Escuela Naval which comes off of Calzada Veracruz just past the eastern end of Avenida Obregón. It has single-sex dorms and no curfew, and serves three meals a day, each for under US$2. Cost is under US$4 for a bunk in a room with four or six beds and shared bath.

Hotel María Dolores (☎ 832-05-08, Avenida Obregón 206), west of Avenida de los Héroes above the Restaurant Sosilmar, is the best for the price. It has tiny, stuffy rooms with fans and private bath for US$12 double, US$16/17 triple/quad.

Hotel Ucum (☎ 832-07-11, 832-61-86, Avenida Gandhi 167) has lots of plain rooms around a bare central courtyard and a good, cheap restaurant. Rooms with fan, TV and shower cost US$15 double, with air-con US$22.

Hotel Cristal (☎ 832-38-78, Calle Colón 207), between Calles Juárez and Belice, has clean rooms for US$9/11/14 single/double/triple with fan, US$23 a double with air-con and TV.

Hotel El Cedro (☎ 832-68-78), on Avenida de los Héroes between Plutarco Elías Calles and Lázaro Cárdenas, has slightly worn but OK rooms for US$25 double with air-con, TV and private bath.

The quiet *Hotel Caribe Princess* (☎/fax 832-09-00, Avenida Obregón 168) is well run and nicely appointed. There are good air-con rooms for US$27/31/37. All have phone and TV, and there's off-street parking.

Five blocks north of Avenida Primo de Verdad, on the way to the bus terminal, the *Hotel Príncipe* (☎ 832-47-99, fax 832-51-91, Avenida de los Héroes 326) has decent rooms, a restaurant and even a small swimming pool. Air-con rooms are US$32 single or double; they may waive the 12% IVA (tax) if you ask.

Mid-Range & Top End The *Hotel Los Cocos* (☎ 832-05-44, fax 832-09-20), Avenida de los Héroes at Calle Héroes de Chapultepec, has a nice swimming pool, a guarded parking lot and a popular sidewalk restaurant. Air-con rooms with TV cost US$54 double.

Two blocks north of Los Cocos along Avenida de los Héroes, near the tourist information kiosk, is the *Holiday Inn Chetumal Puerta Maya* (☎ 832-11-00, 832-10-80, fax 832-16-76, in the USA ☎ 800-465-4329, Avenida de los Héroes 171). Its comfortable rooms overlook a small courtyard with a swimming pool set amid tropical gardens; there's a restaurant and bar. Rates are US$92 double. This is the best in town.

Places to Eat

Across from the Holiday Inn and the tourist information kiosk is the Mercado Ignacio Manuel Altamirano and its row of small, simple eateries serving meals for US$2 or US$3. Similar is the upstairs area in the Nuevo Mercado Lázaro Cárdenas, on Calzada Veracruz.

Restaurant Sosilmar, on Avenida Obregón beneath the Hotel María Dolores, is bright and simple. Filling platters of fish or meat go for US$3 to US$6 (closed Sunday). A good pastry shop is the *Panadería y Pastelería La Invencible*, on Calle Carmen Ochoa de Merino west of Avenida de los Héroes.

West of the Sosilmar is *Pollo Brujo*, where a roasted half-chicken costs US$3. Take it with you or dine in the air-con salon. Be sure to sample their secret sauce.

Restaurant Vegetariano La Fuente (Calle Cárdenas 222), between Calles Independencia and Juárez, is a tidy meatless restaurant next to a homeopathic pharmacy. Healthy meals cost US$6 or less.

Café-Restaurant Los Milagros, on Calle Ignacio Zaragoza between Avenida de los Héroes and Avenida 5 de Mayo, serves meals for US$2 to US$4 indoors or outdoors. It's a favorite with Chetumal's student and intellectual set. The family-owned *Restaurant Pantoja*, Avenida Gandhi at Calle 16 de Septiembre, is a neighborhood favorite that opens early for breakfast and later provides enchiladas and other entrées for US$2 to US$3.

For your coffee fix try *Café Espresso*, 22 de Enero and Avenida Miguel Hidalgo, facing the bay. It has an upscale ambience and is open for breakfast and dinner. A good selection of omelets and other breakfasts runs US$2 to US$4. Dinner adds various cuts of meat to the menu, for US$4 to US$7.

To sample the typical traditional food of Quintana Roo, head for the *Restaurant Típico El Taquito* (Plutarco Elías Calles 220), at Avenida Juárez. In the airy, simple dining room, tacos cost US$0.50 each, slightly more with cheese, and the daily comida corrida is US$2.75. This is a good place to go with a jolly group of friends.

Maria's and *Sergio's Pizzas* (Avenida Obregón 182), a block east of Avenida de los Héroes, are actually the same full-service restaurant with two wood-paneled, air-con dining rooms. In Maria's, order one of the many wines offered, then a Mexican or continental dish (around US$7). In Sergio's, order a cold beer in a frosted mug and a pizza (US$6 to US$12).

Natural and artificial iced beverages in many flavors are available at *Hawaiian Paradise*, a modern juice bar on Lázaro Cárdenas a half block west of Avenida de los Héroes. The *concentrados* (slushies) consist of crushed ice and sweet fruit syrup. The *leches* (milk-based drinks) contain real fruit. The *naturales* contain juice only. A small costs US$0.60, a medium is US$0.80, and a large costs US$1.

If you're busing into town, stock up at the *Supermercado San Francisco de Asís* just west of the bus terminal.

Entertainment

There are two major clubs in town, and they happen to be next door to one another near the south end of Avenida Benito Juárez. At *El Palomar*, vocalists belt out

YUCATÁN

Mexican traditional songs from 1:30 to 10 pm daily. It is often packed, with attendees ranging in age from 18 to 60. *Scorpion's*, a black-walled club with a heavy disco beat, is popular with Chetumal's 18-to-25 crowd. Few tourists ever enter.

Getting There & Away

Air Chetumal's small airport is less than 2km northwest of the city center along Avenida Obregón. Mexicana's regional carrier Aerocaribe (☎/fax 832-66-75), Avenida Héroes 125, Plaza Baroudi Local 13, flies direct from Chetumal to Cancún and Mérida with onward connections.

Aviacsa (☎ 832-77-65, fax 832-76-54; at the airport ☎ 832-77-87, fax 832-76-98) flies to Mexico City. Its in-town office is on Avenida Cárdenas at 5 de Mayo.

For flights to Belize City (and on to Tikal) or to Belize's cayes, cross the border into Belize and fly from Corozal.

Bus The Terminal de Autobuses de Chetumal is about 2km north of the center near the intersection of Avenidas Insurgentes and Belice. ADO, Sur, Cristóbal Colón, Omnitur del Caribe, Maya de Oro, Mayab and Novelo's, among others, provide service. The terminal has lockers, a bus information kiosk, post office, international phone and fax services, exchange counter, cafetería and shops. East of the terminal is a huge San Francisco de Asís department store.

You can buy ADO tickets and get information about most bus services at the ADO office on Avenida Belice, just west of the Museo de la Cultura Maya.

Many local buses, and those bound for Belize, begin their runs from the Nuevo Mercado Lázaro Cárdenas, on Calzada Veracruz at Confederación Nacional Campesina (also called Segundo Circuito). To get there, go north on Avenida de los Héroes. From Avenida Primo de Verdad it's about ten blocks north to Segundo (2o) Circuito (turn right at the defunct Jeep dealership onto the wide divided Circuito), then three blocks east. From the mercado, Novelo's Belize-bound buses continue to the long-distance terminal and depart from there 15 minutes

after leaving the mercado. Novelo's tickets can be purchased at the mercado, on board the buses, or at the main terminal.

The minibus terminal, at the corner of Avenidas Primo de Verdad and Hidalgo, has minibuses to Bacalar and other nearby destinations. Departures listed below are from the main terminal unless otherwise noted.

Bacalar 39km, 45 minutes; hourly minibuses from the minibus terminal (US$1); three Sociedad Cooperativa daily, departing from the main terminal (US$3.75)

Belize City 160km, 3 to 4 hours; five Novelo's via Corozal and Orange Walk, departing from Nuevo Mercado between 10:45 am and 5 pm (departing main terminal 15 minutes later); also Venus Bus Lines, departing from Nuevo Mercado hourly between 4 and 10 am (US$5.50 to US$6.50)

Campeche 422km, 7 to 9 hours; one ADO at noon, one Sur (US$15 to US$17.25)

Cancún 382km, 5½ hours; many buses (US$11 to US$15.25)

Corozal (Belize) 30km, 1 hour with border formalities (US$2.25); see Belize City schedule

Escárcega 273km, 4 to 6 hours; 11 buses between 9 am and 9 pm (US$9 to US$11)

Felipe Carrillo Puerto 155km, 2 to 3 hours; many buses (US$4.50 to US$6.25)

Flores (Guatemala) 350km, 9 hours; Servicio San Juan and Mundo Maya at 7 am and 2 pm daily (US$35), continuing to Tikal (8 hours, US$41.25) and most then continuing to Guatemala City (15 hours, US$63)

Kohunlich 67km, 1 hour; take a bus heading west to Xpujil or Escárcega, get off just before the village of Francisco Villa and walk 5km to a hotel, then take a taxi to the site

Mérida 456km, 6 to 8 hours; 14 buses (US$11 to US$16.25)

Orange Walk (Belize) 91km, 2¼ hours; two Chell's daily, departing the Nuevo Mercado at 11:15 am and 12:15 pm (US$2); also Novelo's (US$3.25; see Belize City listing, above)

Playa del Carmen 315km, 4½ to 6 hours; many buses (US$10 to US$13)

Ticul 352km, 5 hours; eight buses (US$11.75 to US$13)

Tulum 251km, 3½ to 4 hours; many buses (US$7 to US$10)

Valladolid 407km, 7½ hours; two 2nd-class (US$10)

Veracruz 1037km, 16 hours; one 1st-class bus (US$43)

Villahermosa 565km, 7 to 9 hours; seven buses (US$15 to US$23)

Xcalak 200km, 3 to 5 hours; two Sociedad Cooperativa del Caribe 2nd-class, at 6 am and 3:15 pm (US$4.50)

Xpujil 120km, 2 to 3 hours; eight buses (US$3.50 to US$5)

Car & Motorcycle If you're driving west on Hwy 186 from Chetumal to Campeche state, note that the highway starts at the border with Belize and, several kilometers north, hits Hwy 307. Coming out of Chetumal, follow the signs for 307 and Mérida (not for Hwy 186) until you reach a junction signed for Campeche and Hwy 186.

Getting Around

Taxis from the stand at the bus terminal charge US$1.10 to the center (agree on the price before getting in). You may be able to catch one for less by walking out of the terminal to the main road (Avenida Insurgentes), turning left (east), and walking a little over a block to the traffic circle at Avenida de los Héroes. From here you can also catch the cheapest ride to the center (US$0.20), in an eastbound ('Santa María' or 'Calderitas') combi. The route will be circuitous. To reach the terminal from the center, head for the combi and taxi stands on Avenida Belice behind the Museo de la Cultura Maya. By combi, ask to be dropped off at the *glorieta* (traffic circle) at Avenida Insurgentes. Head left (west) to reach the terminal.

KOHUNLICH

The archaeological site of Kohunlich is being aggressively excavated, though most of its nearly 200 mounds are still covered in vegetation. The surrounding jungle is thick, but the archaeological site itself has been cleared selectively and is now a delightful forest park. Drinks are sometimes sold at the site. The toilets are usually locked and 'under repair.'

These ruins, dating from the Late Preclassic (AD 100–200) and the Early Classic

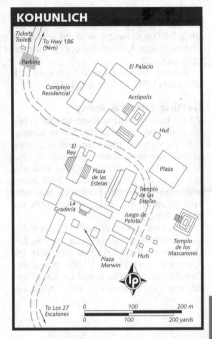

KOHUNLICH

Tickets, Toilets — To Hwy 186 (9km)

Parking

Complejo Residencial

El Palacio

Acrópolis

Hut

El Rey

Plaza de las Estelas

Plaza

Templo de las Estelas

La Gradería

Juego de Pelota

Templo de los Mascarones

Plaza Merwin

Huts

To Los 27 Escalones

0   100   200 m
0   100   200 yards

(AD 250–600) periods, are famous for the great **Templo de los Mascarones** (Temple of the Masks), a pyramid-like structure with a central stairway flanked by huge, 3m-high stucco masks of the sun god. The thick lips and prominent features are reminiscent of Olmec sculpture. Of the eight original masks, only two are relatively intact following the ravages of archaeology looters.

The masks themselves are impressive, but the large thatch coverings that have been erected to protect them from further weathering also obscure the view; you can see the masks only from close up. Try to imagine what the pyramid and its masks must have looked like in the old days as the Maya approached it across the sunken courtyard at the front.

A few hundred meters southwest of Plaza Merwin are the **27 Escalones** (27 Steps), the remains of an extensive residential area, with photogenic trees growing out of the steps themselves.

The hydraulic engineering used at the site was a great achievement; 90,000 of the site's 210,000 sq meters were cut to channel rainwater into Kohunlich's once enormous reservoir.

The site is open 8 am to 5 pm daily; admission is US$2.75 (free Sunday).

Getting There & Away

At the time of writing, there was no public transportation running directly to Kohunlich. To visit the ruins without your own vehicle, you need to start early, taking a bus to the village of Francisco Villa near the turnoff to the ruins, and from there either walk 5km to the Villas Ecológicas hotel and take a taxi the remaining 4km or walk the entire 9km.

Better still, take a taxi from Chetumal to the ruins, have the driver wait for you, and then return. Roundtrip taxi fare, with the wait, will cost about US$60 per party. Another means is to travel to Xpujil and book a tour from there. For US$30 per person you can visit Kohunlich and Dzibanché (see the Campeche chapter).

To return by bus to Chetumal or head west to Xpujil or Escárcega you must hope to flag down a bus on the highway; not all buses will stop.

SOUTH TO BELIZE & GUATEMALA

Corozal, 18km south of the Mexico-Belize border, is a pleasant, sleepy, laid-back farming and fishing town and an appropriate introduction to Belize. There are several hotels catering to a full range of budgets, and restaurants to match.

Buses run directly from Chetumal's market to Belize City via Corozal and Orange Walk. From Belize City you can catch westward buses to Belmopan, San Ignacio and the Guatemalan border at Benque Viejo, then onward to Flores, Tikal and other points in Guatemala. There are also buses from Chetumal to Flores and Tikal. See Chetumal Getting There & Away for details on all of these.

Yucatán State

Mérida

• **population 612,300**

The capital of the state of Yucatán is a prosperous city of narrow streets, colonial buildings and shady parks. Known throughout Mexico as the 'White City' because of the preponderance of quarried limestone and white paint used there, Mérida has been a center of Mayan culture in the Yucatán region since before the conquistadors arrived.

Today it is the peninsula's center of commerce as well, a bustling city that has benefited greatly from the maquiladoras that opened in the 1980s and '90s and the tourism that picked up during those decades. There are hotels and restaurants of every class and price range and good transportation services to any part of the peninsula and the country. The city can be your base for numerous excursions into the Mayan countryside that surrounds it.

Mérida's drawbacks are traffic, pollution and heat. Noisy buses pump clouds of noxious fumes into the air, and the region's high temperatures seem even higher in this city, where buildings catch the heat and hold it well into the evening. These sensory assaults do keep some from enjoying Mérida, while many others find it charming. You will have to judge for yourself.

HISTORY

Francisco de Montejo the Younger founded a Spanish colony at Campeche, about 160km to the south, in 1540. From this base he was able to take advantage of political dissension among the Maya, conquering Tihó (now Mérida) in 1542. By the end of the decade, most of the peninsula was under Spanish colonial rule.

When Montejo's conquistadors entered defeated Tihó, they found a major Mayan settlement of lime-mortared stone reminiscent of Roman architectural legacies in Mérida, Spain. They renamed the city and built

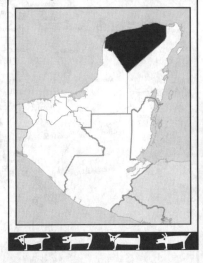

Highlights

• Mérida's opulent architecture and abundant cultural events
• Uxmal and the Ruta Puuc's fascinating variety of Mayan sites
• The limestone caverns of Grutas de Loltún
• The awesome Maya-Toltec architecture of Chichén Itzá
• Mexico's largest flamingo colony, near Río Lagartos

YUCATÁN

it into the colonial capital, dismantling the Mayan structures and using the materials to construct a cathedral and other stately buildings. Mérida took its colonial orders directly from Spain, not from Mexico City, and Yucatán has had a distinct cultural and political identity ever since.

With the conquest of the area complete, indigenous people became little more than slaves. Using religious redemption as their rationale, colonial governors and church leaders built their own little empires on the backs of the Indians. Their harsh rule created

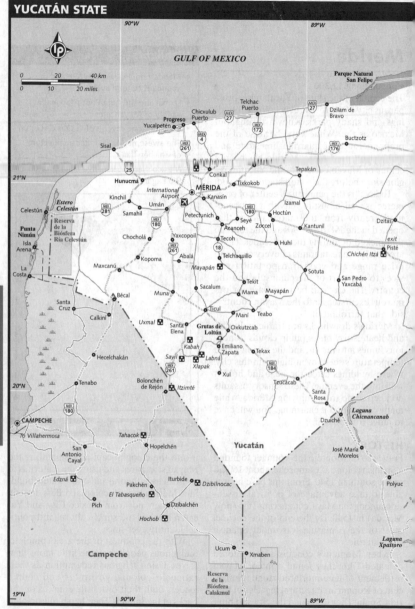

YUCATÁN STATE

GULF OF MEXICO

Parque Natural San Felipe

Dzilam de Bravo

Buctzotz

Telchac Puerto

Chicxulub Puerto

Progreso
Yucalpetén

Sisal

Conkal

Tepakán

Tikkokob

Hunucmá

MÉRIDA

Kanasín

Izamal

Hoctún

Kantunil

Dzitás

Kinchil

International Airport

Celestún

Estero Celestún

Reserva de la Biósfera Ría Celestún

Punta Nimún

Isla Arena

La Costa

Samahil

Umán

Petectunich

Seyé

Zoccel

Huhí

Chocholá

Yaxcopoil

Acanceh

Tecoh

Telchaquillo

Sotuta

San Pedro Yaxcabá

Chichén Itzá

exit

Pisté

Maxcanú

Kopoma

Abalá

Mayapán

Muna

Sacalum

Tekit

Mama

Mayapán

Bécal

Santa Cruz

Calkiní

Ticul

Maní

Teabo

Uxmal

Santa Elena

Grutas de Loltún

Oxkutzcab

Hecelchakán

Kabah

Emiliano Zapata

Tekax

Peto

Sayil

Labná

Xlapak

Xul

Tenabo

Bolonchén de Rejón

Itzimté

Tzucacab

Santa Rosa

CAMPECHE

To Villahermosa

Dzuiché

Laguna Chicnancanab

Tahacok

Yucatán

José María Morelos

San Antonio Cayal

Hopelchén

Edzná

Pakchén

Iturbide

Dzibilnocac

Polyuc

El Tabasqueño

Pich

Dzibalchén

Hochob

Laguna Xpaitoro

Campeche

Ucum

Xmaben

Reserva de la Biósfera Calakmul

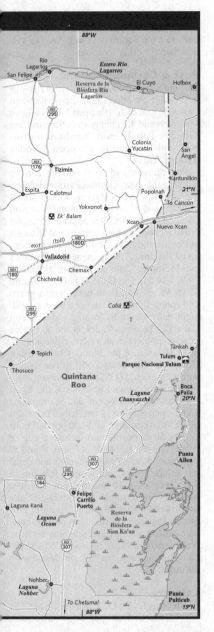

resentments that would eventually explode into rebellion.

When the Mexican War of Independence ended in 1821, the Spanish colonial governor of Yucatán resigned his post, and the peninsula enjoyed a brief two years as an independent nation before it finally threw in its lot with Mexico, joining the union of Mexican states in 1823.

Spanish control, harsh as it was, had prevented certain abuses of power from becoming too much of a problem in Yucatán. With colonial rule removed, local potentates were free to build vast estates, or haciendas, based on the newly introduced cultivation of sugarcane and henequen, and the lot of the indigenous peoples got even worse. Though the Indians were nominally free citizens in a new republic, their hacienda bosses kept them in debt peonage.

As the *hacendados* grew in power and wealth they began to fear that outside forces (the government in central Mexico, or the USA) might covet their prosperity. So the Méridan government organized armed forces and issued weapons to the soldiers, who were the same Indians being oppressed on the haciendas. Given the power to achieve their freedom, the Indians rebelled in 1847, beginning the War of the Castes.

Only Mérida and Campeche were able to hold out against the rebel forces; the rest of Yucatán came under Indian control. On the brink of surrender, the ruling class in Mérida was saved by reinforcements sent from central Mexico in exchange for Mérida's agreeing to take orders from Mexico City.

Though the Yucatán is certainly part of Mexico, there is still a strong feeling of local pride in Mérida, a feeling that the Mayab (Mayan lands) are a special realm set apart from the rest of the country.

ORIENTATION

The Plaza Grande, as *meridanos* call the main square, has been the center of Mérida since Mayan times. Most of the services visitors want are within five blocks of the square. Odd-numbered streets run east-west, and their numbers increase by twos going from north to south (eg, Calle 61 is a

YUCATÁN

block north of Calle 63); even-numbered streets run north-south, and increase by twos from east to west.

House numbers may increase very slowly, and addresses are usually given in this form: Calle 57 No 481 x 56 y 58 (between Calles 56 and 58).

Radiating outward from the main square are Mérida's colonial *barrios* (neighborhoods), many of which have a park and church side by side giving the barrio its name: For example, Iglesia de Santiago is next to Parque de Santiago in Barrio Santiago.

INFORMATION
Tourist Offices

The tourist information booths at the airport and the main bus station, Terminal CAME, are not of much use, but there are three helpful tourist offices downtown (two run by the state, one by the city) that provide brochures, maps and current information. The first of the state-run offices is in the entrance to the Palacio de Gobierno, on the Plaza Grande, open 8 am to 10 pm daily; a second is less than two blocks north, at the corner of Calles 60 and 57A on the northeast edge of Parque de la Madre (☎ 924-92-90, open 8 am to 8 pm daily.

The city tourist office (☎ 923-08-83), at the corner of Calles 59 and 62, is generally staffed with helpful English-speakers. Its hours are ostensibly 8 am to 8 pm daily, but it's often closed at siesta time.

Consulates

A number of countries have consulates in Mérida. See the Yucatán Facts for the Visitor chapter.

Money

Casas de cambio offer faster, better service than banks, though some charge fees. Try the Money Marketing Centro Cambiario in the Gran Hotel on Parque Hidalgo; Finex Money Exchange, just south of the cathedral; or Cambio La Peninsular, on the east side of Calle 60 between Calles 55 and 57.

Banks and ATMs are scattered throughout the city. There is a cluster of both along Calle 65 between Calles 60 and 62, one

block south of the Plaza Grande. Most are open 9 am to 5 pm weekdays, some open 9 am to 1 pm Saturday as well. See the Mérida map for other locations.

Post & Communications

The main post office (☎ 921-2561) is just north of the market, on Calle 65 between Calles 56 and 56A. It's open 8 am to 7 pm weekdays and, for stamps only, 9 am to 1 pm Saturday. Postal service booths at the airport and bus station are open Monday through Friday.

Buy phones and card phones can be found at the Plaza Grande, Parque Hidalgo, the airport, the bus stations, the corner of Calles 59 and 62 and Calles 64 and 57 and on Calle 60 between Calles 53 and 55, among other locations. There are several Internet places around town, and more are popping up all the time. Among them are Mayanet's two locations, Calle 60 between 51 and 53 (☎ 924-24-59), and Calle 41 between 30 and 32 (☎ 922-54-84). Both have decent prices and connections and are open 9 am to midnight daily. Centrally located Cybernet, on Calle 57A between Calles 58 and 60, has six or so computers in an air-con environment, open 10 am to 8 pm Monday to Saturday. Computer time costs US$0.10 per minute with a 15-minute (US$1.50) minimum.

Cibercafé Santa Lucí@, on Calle 62 at Calle 55, has good air-con and 56k modems and is open 8 am to 11 pm daily. Their rates of US$2.70 per hour, US$1.50 per half hour and US$0.05 per minute include a cup of coffee. Air-con La Net@, at Calles 58 and 57 (upstairs, ☎ 923-38-68 lanet@yahoo.com) has similar prices, and is open 9:30 am to 9 pm weekdays, 10 am to 4 pm Saturday. Near the bus terminals is CenterNet, Calle 64 between Calles 69 and 71, south of Parque de San Juan. It's small but no-nonsense, with air-con and fax and scanning services. Net access is US$1.60 an hour, US$0.95 per half hour; open 8 am to 8 pm Monday to Saturday.

Laundry

Lavandería La Fe, Calle 61 No 520, at Calle 64, charges US$3.90 per 3kg load to wash and dry your clothing; same-day service if you drop your clothes off in the morning. Open 8 am to 7 pm weekdays, 8 am to 5 pm Saturday. You also can drop off your clothing at Lavandería Flamingo, on Calle 57 between Calles 56 and 58, and pick it up in the late afternoon. It charges US$0.25 per shirt, US$0.35 for pants or US$0.20 for shorts, and US$0.05 for each undergarment (yes, it's US$0.10 for a pair of socks). Open 9 am to 6 pm Monday to Friday, until 3 pm Saturday.

Most hotels in the mid-range and above, including the Gran Hotel, offer overnight laundry service.

Medical Services
Hospital O'Horán (☎ 924-48-00), the largest hospital in Mérida, is near the Parque Zoológico Centenario on Avenida de los Itzáes. For most treatment (prescriptions, consultations) you're best off going to a private clinic. Ask at your consulate or one of the better hotels for a recommendation. In an emergency, call the Cruz Roja (Red Cross), ☎ 924-98-13.

Dangers & Annoyances
Guard against pickpockets, bag-snatchers and bag-slashers in the market district and in any crowd, such as at a performance. Buses drive fast along the narrow streets and don't slow down for anything; sidewalks are often narrow and crowded.

If you're driving, try to avoid the center until you're well oriented. Parking is very difficult, traffic is heavy, one-way streets are confusing, and on Sunday Calle 60 is closed. The police tow-trucks patrol frequently, and no-parking zones are not always clearly marked.

PLAZA GRANDE
This large but at times surprisingly intimate square is the most logical place to start a tour of Mérida. Also known as 'El Centro' (as in the center of town) or the Plaza Principal, the Plaza Grande was the religious and social center of ancient Tihó; under the Spanish it was the Plaza de Armas (parade ground), laid out by Francisco de Montejo

the Younger. The plaza is surrounded by some of the city's most impressive and harmonious colonial buildings, and its carefully tended laurel trees provide welcome shade. On Sunday hundreds of meridanos take their *paseo* (stroll) here. Various events take place around the plaza on weekly schedules; see Entertainment for details.

Cathedral
On the plaza's east side, at the former site of a Mayan temple, is Mérida's hulking, severe cathedral, begun in 1561 and completed in 1598. Some of the stone from the Mayan temple was used in its construction. The great crucifix at the east end of the nave is **Cristo de la Unidad** (Christ of Unity), a symbol of reconciliation between those of Spanish and Maya stock. To the right over the south door is a **painting of Tutul Xiú**, cacique of the town of Maní, paying his respects to his ally Francisco de Montejo at Tihó (de Montejo and Xiú jointly defeated the Cocomes; Xiú converted to Christianity, and his descendants still live in Mérida).

In the small chapel to the left of the principal altar is Mérida's most famous religious artifact, a statue called *Cristo de las Ampollas* (Christ of the Blisters). Local legend says the statue was carved from a tree that was hit by lightning and burned for an entire night without charring. It is also said to be the only object to have survived the fiery destruction of the town of Ichmul's church (though it was blackened and blistered from the heat). The statue was moved to the Mérida cathedral in 1645.

Other than these, the cathedral's interior is plain, its rich decoration having been stripped away by angry peasants at the height of anticlerical feeling during the Mexican Revolution.

The cathedral is open 6 am to noon and 4 to 7 pm.

Around the Plaza
South of the cathedral, housed in the former archbishop's palace, is **MACAY**, the Museo de Arte Contemporáneo Ateneo de Yucatán (Yucatán Contemporary Art Museum and Atheneum; ☎ 928-33-58). The

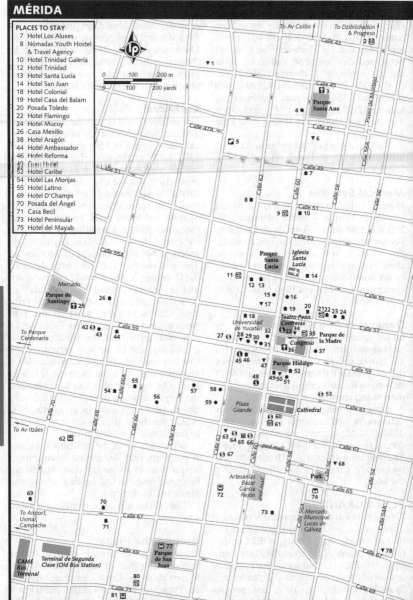

MÉRIDA

PLACES TO STAY
7   Hotel Los Aluxes
8   Nómadas Youth Hostel
    & Travel Agency
10 Hotel Trinidad Galería
12 Hotel Trinidad
13 Hotel Santa Lucía
14 Hotel San Juan
18 Hotel Colonial
19 Hotel Casa del Balam
20 Posada Toledo
22 Hotel Flamingo
24 Hotel Mucuy
26 Casa Mexilio
38 Hotel Aragón
44 Hotel Ambassador
46 Hotel Reforma
47 Gran Hotel
52 Hotel Caribe
54 Hotel Las Monjas
55 Hotel Latino
69 Hotel D'Champs
70 Posada del Ángel
71 Casa Becil
73 Hotel Peninsular
75 Hotel del Mayab

PLACES TO EAT	OTHER
1 Restaurant Kantún	2 Museo Regional de
6 La Casona	Antropología (Palacio
17 Pop Cafetería; Restaurante	Cantón)
Pórtico del Peregrino	3 Iglesia de Santa Ana
28 Café La Habana	4 Tourist Car Rental
30 Amaro	5 Consulate of Netherlands
34 Café y Restaurante WAO	9 Mayanet (Internet Access)
39 Los Almendros	11 Cibercafé Santa Lucí@
47 Café-Restaurant Express	15 Budget Car Rental
50 Giorgio's Pizza & Pasta	16 Executive, Hertz & National
63 Panificadora Montejo	Car Rental Offices;
68 Supermarkets	Turismo Bolontikú
78 San Francisco de Asís	21 La Net@
Supermarket	23 Lavandería Flamingo
	25 Iglesia de Santiago
	27 Banco Bilbao Vizcaya (ATM)
	29 Pancho's
	31 Popol-Nah
	32 La Bella Época
	33 Tourist Information Center;
	Café Peón Contreras
	35 Cybernet
	36 Iglesia de Jesús
	37 Plaza Cine International
	40 Iglesia La Mejorada
	41 Museo Nacional de
	Arte Popular
	42 Bital (ATM)
	43 Cinema 59
	45 City Tourist Office
	48 Palacio de Gobierno;
	State Tourist Office
	51 Cine Fantasio
	53 Bancapromex (ATM)
	56 Casa de las Artesanías
	57 Lavandería La Fe
	58 Olimpo (Cultural Center)
	59 Palacio Municipal
	60 Findex Money Exchange
	61 Museo de Arte
	Contemporáneo Ateneo de
	Yucatán (MACAY)
	62 Terminal Maaya K'iin
	64 Banorte (ATM)
	65 Casa de Montejo (Banamex)
	66 Bancrecer (ATM)
	67 Currency Exchange
	Prenda Oro
	72 Progreso Bus Station
	74 Main Post Office
	76 Noreste Bus Station
	77 Minibuses to Dzibilchaltún
	79 Oriente & Noreste
	Bus Station
	80 CenterNet
	81 Celestún Bus Terminal (Old
	ATS Terminal)

attractive museum holds permanent exhibits of Yucatán's most famous painters and sculptors, changing exhibits of local arts and artisanry and a cafeteria. Open 10 am to 6 pm Wednesday to Monday; US$2.20 (free Sunday).

The **Casa de Montejo**, sometimes called the Palacio de Montejo, is on the south side of the Plaza Grande and dates from 1549. It originally housed soldiers but soon was converted into a mansion that served members of the Montejo family until 1970. These days it shelters a bank, and you can enter it and look around whenever the bank is open (9 am to 5 pm weekdays, 9 am to 2 pm Saturday). If the bank is closed, content yourself with a close look at the facade, where triumphant conquistadors with halberds hold their feet on the necks of generic barbarians (who are not Maya, but the association is inescapable). Also gazing across the plaza from the facade are busts of Montejo the Elder, his wife and his daughter.

Across the square from the cathedral is Mérida's **Palacio Municipal** (City Hall). Originally built in 1542, it has twice been refurbished, in the 1730s and the 1850s. Adjoining it to the north is the **Olimpo**, Mérida's new municipal cultural center. Attempts to create a modern exterior for the building were halted by government order to preserve the colonial character of the plaza. The impressive ultramodern interior serves as a venue for music and dance performances as well as other exhibitions. Schedules for these and events around the city are posted inside.

On the north side of Plaza Grande, the **Palacio de Gobierno** houses the state of Yucatán's executive government offices (and one of its tourist information offices). It was built in 1892 on the site of the palace of the colonial governors. Inside are murals painted by local artist Fernando Castro Pacheco. Completed in 1978, they were 25 years in the making and portray a symbolic history of the Maya and their interaction with the Spaniards. The largest depicts corn, which the Maya held as sacred – the 'ray of sun from the gods.' It's open 7 am to 11 pm daily, and it's free.

YUCATÁN

WALKING UP CALLE 60

A block north of the Plaza Grande, just beyond Parque Hidalgo, rises the 17th-century **Iglesia de Jesús**, also called the Iglesia de la Tercera Orden. Built by the Jesuits in 1618, it is the sole surviving edifice from a complex of buildings that once filled the entire city block. Always interested in education, the Jesuits founded schools that later gave birth to the nearby Universidad de Yucatán.

North of the church is the enormous bulk of the **Teatro Peón Contreras**, built between 1900 and 1908, during Mérida's henequen heyday. Designed by Italian architect Luis Roncuroni, it boasts a main staircase of Carrara marble and a dome with frescoes by Italian artists. The main entrance to the theater is at the corner of Calles 60 and 57. A gallery inside the entrance often holds exhibits by local painters and photographers; usual hours are 9 am to 2 pm and 5 to 9 pm weekdays, 9 am to 2 pm weekends. To see the grand theater itself, you'll have to attend a performance.

Across Calle 60 from the theater is the main building of the **Universidad de Yucatán**. Though the Jesuits provided education to Yucatán's youth for centuries, the modern university was established in the 19th century by Governor Felipe Carrillo Puerto and General Manuel Cepeda Peraza. The story of the university's founding is rendered in a 1961 mural by Manuel Lizama. Ask for directions to the mural.

A block north of the university, at the intersection of Calles 60 and 55, is the pretty little **Parque Santa Lucía**, with arcades on the north and west sides. When Mérida was a lot smaller, this was where travelers would get on or off the stagecoaches that linked towns and villages with the provincial capital. Today the park is the venue for performances of Yucatecan music on Thursday at 9 pm. Also here on Sunday at 11 am is the **Bazar de Artesanías**, the local handicrafts market.

To reach the Paseo de Montejo, walk 3½ blocks north along Calle 60 from the Parque Santa Lucía to Calle 47. Turn right on Calle 47 and walk two blocks; Paseo de Montejo is on your left.

PASEO DE MONTEJO

The Paseo de Montejo was an attempt by Mérida's 19th-century city planners to create a wide boulevard similar to the Paseo de la Reforma in Mexico City or the Champs Élysées in Paris. Though more modest than its predecessors, the Paseo de Montejo is still a beautiful swath of green, relatively open space in an urban conglomeration of stone and concrete.

Europe's architectural and social influence can be seen along the paseo in the fine mansions built by wealthy families around the end of the 19th century. Many were torn down to make way for banks, hotels and other establishments. Most of those remaining are north of Calle 37, which is three blocks north of the Museo Regional de Antropología, and on the first block of Avenida Colón west of Paseo de Montejo.

MUSEO REGIONAL DE ANTROPOLOGÍA

The great white Palacio Cantón, on the corner of Paseo de Montejo and Calle 43, houses the Regional Anthropology Museum of Yucatán. The mansion was designed by Enrico Deserti, also responsible for the

Museo Regional de Antropología

Teatro Peón Contreras. Construction took place from 1909 to 1911. The mansion's owner, General Francisco Cantón Rosado (1833–1917) lived here for only six years before his death. No building in Mérida exceeds it in splendor or pretension. It's a fitting symbol of the grand aspirations of Mérida's elite during the last years of the Porfiriato, the period from 1876 to 1911 when Porfirio Díaz held despotic sway over Mexico.

The museum covers the peninsula's history since the age of mastodons. Exhibits on Mayan culture include explanations (in Spanish only) of forehead-flattening, which was done to beautify babies, and other practices such as sharpening teeth and implanting them with tiny jewels. If you plan to visit archaeological sites near Mérida, you can study the many exhibits here – lavishly illustrated with plans and photographs – covering the great Mayan cities of Mayapán, Uxmal and Chichén Itzá, as well as lesser sites. Open 8 am to 8 pm Tuesday to Saturday, 8 am to 2 pm Sunday; US$2.20 (free Sunday).

PARQUE CENTENARIO
About 12 blocks west of the Plaza Grande lies the large, verdant Parque Centenario, bordered by Avenida de los Itzáes, which leads to the airport and becomes the highway to Campeche. The park's zoo features the fauna of Yucatán. To get there, take a bus west along Calle 61 or 65. The park and zoo are open Tuesday to Sunday. Park hours are 6 am to 6 pm; zoo hours are 8 am to 5 pm. Both are free.

MUSEO NACIONAL DE ARTE POPULAR
The National Museum of Popular Art, on Calle 59 between Calles 48 and 50, six blocks northeast of the Plaza Grande, holds displays of the best of local arts and crafts. It will satisfy your curiosity about the embroidering of colorful huipiles, carving of ceremonial masks, weaving of hammocks and hats, turning of pottery, and construction of musical instruments. It's open 9 am to 6 pm Monday to Saturday. Admission is US$1.10.

ORGANIZED TOURS
Guided two-hour bus tours of Mérida, in English, are offered by Transportadora Turística Carnaval (☎ 927-61-19). Their Paseo Turístico bus departs from Parque Santa Lucía, Calle 55 at Calle 60, at 10 am and 1, 4 and 7 pm Monday to Saturday. Seating capacity is 30 people. You can buy your tickets (US$6) ahead of time at the nearby Hotel Santa Lucía.

You can choose from many group tours to sites around Mérida. Ask at your hotel reception desk for brochures, or consult any of the various travel agencies along Calle 60 (such as Turismo Bolontikú; ☎/fax 95-31-96, Calle 60 between Calles 55 and 57), in the lobbies of various hotels, or scattered elsewhere throughout the city. Some prices are: Celestún (US$40), Chichén Itzá (US$27; with drop-off in Cancún US$47), Uxmal and Kabah (US$27), Uxmal light-and-sound show (US$27), Ruta Puuc (Puuc Route; US$51) and Izamal (US$24). All prices are per person and most include transportation, guide and lunch; cheaper packages to some destinations are available as well.

For further information on Uxmal, Kabah and Ruta Puuc tours, see the Southwestern Yucatán State section. For details of the Sunday train excursion to Izamal, see the Eastern Yucatán section.

The helpful Nómadas Youth Hostel and Travel Agency (☎ 924-52-23, ☎/fax 928-16-97, nomadashostel@hotmail.com, www.hostels .com.mx, Calle 62 No 433) arranges a variety of tours, from do-it-yourself trips in your rented car or on public transportation (with written instructions) to nearly all-inclusive (some meals) trips in private buses. Many of the tours include lodging at other hostels as well as insurance. Nómadas will also help to match up travelers into groups for sharing cars and such, and can give suggestions (and rent the bicycles) for biking to outlying haciendas and other sites for the hardy.

SPECIAL EVENTS
For most of the month of February the Universidad de Yucatán celebrates its anniversary with free performances by the Ballet Folklórico, concerts of Afro-Cuban and *son*

music, and other manifestations of Yucatán's cultural roots.

Prior to Lent, in February or March, Carnaval features colorful costumes and nonstop festivities. It is celebrated with greater vigor in Mérida than anywhere else in Yucatán state. Also during the last days of February or the beginning of March (the dates vary) is Kihuic, a market that fills the Plaza Grande with handicrafts artisans from all over Mexico.

Between September 15 and October 15, the Cristo de las Ampollas (Christ of the Blisters) statue in the cathedral is venerated with processions.

Another big religious tradition is the Exposicíon de Altares, held the night of November 1, when the Maya welcome the spirits of their ancestors with elaborate dinners outside their homes. Although this custom is more apparent in the countryside, Mérida observes it with elaborate festivities in the center of town from 11 am November 1 until 11 am the next day.

PLACES TO STAY

Among the establishments in Mérida whose rates vary with season, there is no consensus as to what constitutes the high seasons (though most places raise prices for Semana Santa). July and August tend to be the busiest months, and you may want to book ahead then. When business is slow many hotels will discount, some without being asked (it never hurts to ask for a *promoción* if they don't). If you're arriving at the CAME bus terminal, check at the tourism desk for flyers offering hotel discounts. All rates given below are 'rack' (full price; a term used in Mexico as well).

Budget

Prices range from US$7 to US$20 for a small but clean double with fan and private shower a short walk from the plaza. All hotels should provide purified drinking water, usually at no extra charge. (Sometimes the water bottles are not readily evident, so ask for *agua purificada*.)

The *Nómadas Youth Hostel* (☎ 924-52-23, ☎/fax 928-16-97, nomadas1@prodigy .net.mx, www.hostels.com.mx, Calle 62 No 433), at Calle 51, is HI affiliated. There are 14 beds in two coed dorms, for $7 each (US$6.50 with hostel card), and a room with private bath and two double beds for $17/21/25 double/triple/quad. Guests have use of a full kitchen with fridge and purified water, 24-hour hot showers and hand-laundry facilities. Bring mosquito repellent and earplugs.

Basic foods are provided on an honor system (write down what you use and pay for it later), as is good Internet access. Luggage lockers are free while you stay, US$1 a day while you travel. For couch potatoes there's satellite TV; for active folk, there are bikes to rent, and the managers also run a full travel service (see Organized Tours, earlier). Between the two of them, the owners speak Spanish, good French and English and some Italian.

Cozy *Hotel Las Monjas* (☎/fax 928-66-32, Calle 66A No 509), just off Calle 63, is among the best deals in town. All 31 rooms have ceiling fans and sinks or private baths with hot and cold water. Doubles with one bed cost US$10, with two beds US$12. One room has air-con for US$14. Most rooms are tiny and dark, but they're clean. Rooms 30 and 12 are best for their superior ventilation.

The *Hotel Latino* (☎ 923-50-87, Calle 66 No 505), between Calles 61 and 63, offers 29 fan-cooled rooms with good mattresses and private hot-water bath for US$8/9 single/ double and two air-con rooms for US$13 per room. It's a bit noisy, though.

Hotel Mucuy (☎ 928-51-93, fax 923-7801, Calle 57 No 481) is between Calles 56 and 58. Its 24 tidy rooms on two floors face a long, narrow garden courtyard. Singles/doubles/ triples with ceiling fans and private showers cost US$16/20/23.

Casa Becil (☎ 924-6764, fax 924-24-24 – during office hours – Calle 67 No 550C), between Calles 66 and 68 near the main bus stations, is a friendly 13-room house with a high-ceilinged sitting room-lobby and small, sometimes hot, but clean rooms with private shower and fan for US$15 to US$19 double.

The *Hotel Flamingo* (☎ 924-77-55, fax 924-70-70, Calle 57 No 485), near Calle 58, offers 39 worn rooms with air-con, TV, telephone and private hot-water bath for US$17. There's a laundry service, restaurant, pool and a travel agency.

If you don't mind walking a few extra blocks and you really want to save money, try the **Hotel del Mayab** (☎ 928-51-74, fax 928-60-47, Calle 50 No 536A), between Calles 65 and 67, a block north of the Oriente and Noreste bus station. Streetside rooms can be noisy, but interior rooms with shower are quiet, and there's a swimming pool, all for US$12 double with fan, US$17 with air-con.

Clean, secure and very popular, **Hotel Santa Lucía** (☎ 928-26-62, ☎/fax 928-26-72, Calle 55 No 508), between Calles 60 and 62 facing the Parque Santa Lucía, has a pool and 51 decent doubles with air-con, TV and telephone for US$24/28 single/double.

The colonial **Hotel Trinidad** (☎ 923-20-33, fax 924-11-22, ohm@sureste.com, Calle 62 No 464), between Calles 55 and 57, is run by artists; it's quirky and a tiny bit run-down, but in a good way. It has a lovely, quiet courtyard, and each of the 19 fan-cooled guestrooms, priced from US$18 double with shared bathroom to US$25 double with private bathroom, has its own unique decor and charm. Guests can use the pool at the Trinidad's sister hotel, the **Hotel Trinidad Galería** (☎ 923-24-63, fax 924-23-19, Calle 60 No 456), at Calle 51. A former appliance showroom, it is farther-out in appearance and has a bar and art gallery (and some excellent artistic touches in rooms and public areas both). Presentable rooms with fan and private shower are US$23/28/33 single/double/triple.

The 45-room **Hotel Peninsular** (☎ 923-69-96, fax 923-69-02, Calle 58 No 519), between Calles 65 and 67, is in the heart of the market district and three blocks from the Plaza Grande. You pass through a long corridor to find a neat restaurant and a maze of rooms; most are spacious and have windows opening onto the interior. The hotel charges US$12 double with private bath and fan; US$17 with air-con. Throw in a swimming pool and you have a pretty good deal.

The neocolonial 30-room **Posada del Ángel** (☎ 923-27-54, fax 926-07-58, Calle 67 No 535), between Calles 66 and 68, is three blocks northeast of Terminal CAME and is quieter than most other hotels in this neighborhood. It's convenient, and rooms are priced at US$16/22/28 with fan, US$21/27/33 with air-con.

The **Hotel Reforma** (☎ 924-79-22, fax 928-32-78, hreforma@yuc1.telmex.net.mx, Calle 59 No 508), between Calles 60 and 62, has 50 rooms ringing a courtyard with a swimming pool. Each contains a TV, telephone and ceiling fan. Laundry service is available. Rooms with fan run US$21/24 single/double, or US$24/26 with air-con.

The **Hotel San Juan** (☎ /fax 924-17-42, Calle 55 No 497-A), near Calle 58, offers a pool, parking and 63 air-con rooms with phone, TV and private hot-water bath for US$25/29 single/double. This and the Hotel Santa Lucía are the best in this price range.

The **Hotel Aragón** (☎ 924-02-42, fax 924-11-22, www.hotelaragon.com, Calle 57 No 474), between Calles 52 and 54, offers 18 very clean air-con rooms on three floors overlooking a charming little courtyard for US$28 per room. Purified water, tea and coffee are available free 24 hours.

Mid-Range

Mérida's mid-range places provide surprising levels of comfort for what you pay. Most charge between US$35 and US$60 double with air-con, ceiling fan and private shower (and often TV and phone). Most have restaurants, bars and small swimming pools as well.

Posada Toledo (☎ 923-16-90, 923-57-35, ☎/fax 923-22-56, Calle 58 No 487), at Calle 57, three blocks northeast of the main plaza, is a colonial mansion with rooms arranged on two floors around the classic courtyard, a dining room (breakfast only) straight out of the 19th century, and small, somewhat modernized doubles with air-con for US$31 per room (US$33 triple occupancy). The newer, upstairs rooms are larger than the ground-floor rooms.

Just a block from the two main bus terminals, **Hotel D'Champs** (☎ 924-86-55, 800-

849-09-34, fax 923-60-24, Calle 70 No 543), at Calle 67, is in a classy old building with modernized interior. It has a massive open courtyard with pool and trees and 90 decent-sized rooms with TV, air-con and phones for US$51 double.

The *Gran Hotel* (☎ 924-77-30, fax 924-76-22, granh@sureste.com, www.wotw.com/mexico/yucatan/hotels/granhotel, Calle 60 No 496), between Calles 59 and 61, is in a grand old building nicely situated on the southern side of Parque Hidalgo. It has a pizza restaurant and money exchange. All 28 rooms have air-con and cost US$45/50 single/double.

A couple of doors east is *Hotel Caribe* (☎ 924-90-22, 800-712-00-03, fax 924-87-33, in the USA ☎ 888-822-6431, Calle 59 No 500), a favorite with visiting foreigners because of its central location, lovely courtyard with fountain and two restaurants, and third-floor pool. Rooms range in price from US$37 for a small single with fan to US$50 for a large double with air-con.

The *Hotel Colonial* (☎ 923-64-44, fax 928-39-61, in the USA ☎ 888-886-2982, hcolonial@finred.com.mx, Calle 62 No 476), at the corner of Calle 57, features 73 comfortable air-con rooms in a fairly modern building with a small pool for US$54 double, US$64 triple.

Romantic *Casa Mexilio* (☎/fax 928-25-05, in the USA ☎ 800-538-6802, info@turqreef .com, www.mexicoholiday/destinations/mexilio.html, Calle 68 No 495), between Calles 57 and 59, is Mérida's most charming pensión – a well-preserved historical house with pool and a maze of quiet, beautifully appointed rooms. Doubles with air-con are US$67, less with fan. All room rates include a good breakfast in the period dining room and are US$10 less in Mexilio's off-seasons. Some of the rooms have air-con. The owners have acquired another fine old house across the street and remodeled it into various dwelling configurations that include a large apartment with kitchen and private pool for $150. See the website for more details.

The *Hotel Ambassador* (☎ 924-2100, fax 924-2701, reser@ambassadormerida.com, www.ambassadormerida.com, Calle 59 No

546), at Calle 68, offers 100 comfortable, modern rooms with satellite TV for US$64 double, US$69 triple, US$72 for suites; try asking for a discount. There's a pool, a travel agency and a car-rental outfit, and laundry service is available.

Top End

Top-end hotels charge between about US$70 and US$150 for a double with air-con. Most will have a restaurant, bar, nightclub and swimming pool, and many will offer other services such as a newsstand, hairdresser and travel agency.

If you reserve your top-end room through your travel agent at home, you're likely to pay international-class rates. But if you walk in and ask about *promociones* (promotional rates), or – even better – look through local newspapers and handouts for special rates aimed at a local clientele, you can lower your lodging bill substantially.

Hotel Casa del Balam (☎ 924-21-50, fax 924-50-11, in the USA ☎ 800-624-8451, bal amhtl@finred.com.mx, www.yucatanadven ture.com.mx, Calle 60 No 488), at Calle 57, is wearing at the edges a bit, but is centrally located and has a great pool and large, quiet rooms with powerful air-con for US$92 double. They offer large discounts when things aren't busy.

Hotel Los Aluxes (☎ 924-21-99, fax 923-38-58, in the USA ☎ 800-782-8395, Calle 60 No 444), at Calle 49, has 109 rooms and is popular with tour groups. Rack rates are US$112 double in high season (April to June and July to August in this case), but they offer commercial and low-season rates of US$70.

Holiday Inn Mérida (☎ 925-68-77, fax 25-77-55, in the USA ☎ 800-465-4329, Ave-nida Colón 498), half a block west of Paseo de Montejo, has a plain boxy exterior and dull reception desk. The 213 air-con rooms start at US$97.

Across Avenida Colón from the Holiday Inn is a large building housing shops, travel agencies, airline offices and restaurants. Upstairs is the reception desk for the enormous *Fiesta Americana Mérida* (☎ 942-11-11, fax 942-11-12, in the USA ☎ 800-343-7821,

ventasmd@fiestaamericana.com.mx, www
.fiestaamericana.com, Calle 56A No 451), a
new neocolonial luxury hotel charging
US$145 to US$163 for its very comfortable
rooms and junior suites.

Crossing Avenida Colón again brings you
to Mérida's most expensive hotel, the 17-
story, 300-room *Hyatt Regency Mérida*
(☎ 942-02-02, fax 925-70-02, hyatt@sureste
.com, www.hyatt.com, Avenida Colón 344),
at Calle 60, 100m west of Paseo de Montejo
and about 2km north of the Plaza Mayor.
Rack rates range from US$178 to US$1130
(for the presidential suite and its VIP treatment); promotional deals can bring those
prices down. The lobby is impressive but
regular rooms are nothing special considering the prices.

PLACES TO EAT
Budget
Mérida's least-expensive eateries are in the
Mercado Municipal Lucas de Gálvez on
Calle 56A. Upstairs are places with tables,
chairs and more varied menus. Downstairs
at the north end are some taquerías where
you sit on a stool at a narrow counter. These
family-run joints include *El Chimecito*, *La
Temaxeña*, *Saby*, *Mimi*, *Saby y El Pelón*, *La
Socorrito* and *Reina Beatriz*. *Comidas corridas* (set meals, upstairs) are priced from
US$1.50. Main-course platters of beef, fish
or chicken with vegetables and rice or potatoes go for as little as US$2.50. The market
eateries are open from early morning until
early evening.

The best inexpensive breakfasts consist
of a selection of *pan dulces* (sweet rolls and
breads) from one of Mérida's several *panifi-
cadoras*, such as the *Panificadora Montejo*,
on the southwest corner of the main plaza,
where a full bag of breads usually costs
US$2 or so.

The air-con *Café y Restaurante WAO*,
on Calle 57A near Calle 58, offers lots of delicious food and friendly service at reasonable prices: around US$4 for poc-chuc,
chicken mole or chicken pibil, around US$2
for breakfast items.

There are two *supermarkets* side by side
on Calle 56 between Calles 63 and 65, and a

branch of the *San Francisco de Asís* market
chain at Calles 67 and 54A.

Mid-Range
Those willing to spend a little more money
can enjoy the pleasant restaurants on the
Parque Hidalgo at the corner of Calles 59
and 60. The least expensive and most pleasant of these is the *restaurant* in the courtyard of Hotel Caribe (see Places to Stay).
Meat, fish and chicken dishes are priced
from US$4 to US$7, but sandwiches and
burgers are less.

The 24-hour, air-con *Café La Habana*,
corner of Calle 59 and 62, is one of the most
popular restaurants in town. It serves decent
food at decent prices; breakfast items and
soups cost US$1.50 to US$3, sandwiches
US$2.40 to US$4.40, chicken US$3 to US$5
and seafood US$6 to US$7. There's a full
bar as well.

The *Café-Restaurant Express*, on Calle
60 near Calle 59, is a popular, noisy meeting
place, whose prices are on the high side for
OK food. It's one of the few places in town
where you can get a cappuccino. Also available are juices and shakes that go down
easily in the heat of the day. A few steps
north along Calle 60 from the Parque
Hidalgo is the *Cafe Peón Contreras*, with a
long, varied menu with breakfasts for
US$2.50 to US$4, pizzas for around US$6
and a combination plate of Yucatecan specialties for around US$8.

Pop Cafetería, on Calle 57 between
Calles 60 and 62, is plain, modern and cool.
The menu includes hamburgers and spaghetti, but smart diners will choose the
chicken mole (US$4) and some delicious
guacamole. Breakfast is offered as well.

Good pizza is served at *Giorgio's Pizza
& Pasta*, in the Gran Hotel building facing
the Parque Hidalgo. The pizzas cost US$3 to
US$7, the portions are generous, and the
outdoor tables present prime people-
watching opportunities.

Amaro, on Calle 59 between Calles 60 and
62, is a romantic dining spot, especially at
night. It's set in the courtyard of the house in
which Andrés Quintana Roo – poet, states-
man and drafter of Mexico's Declaration

of Independence – was born in 1787. The restaurant specializes in Yucatecan food and beer and also offers vegetarian and some continental dishes and pizzas. Most plates are between US$3 and US$6, and there's a full bar. Service and food are good, but beware of waiters adding a bogus 'service charge' or IVA (a tax already included in the menu price) to your bill. Open 9 am to 10 pm daily.

For the best seafood in town, head to *Restaurant Kantún*, on Calle 45 between Calles 64 and 66, a family-run, neighborhood place. Entrées are all prepared to order and superbly seasoned or sauced. Try the *Filium Normanda*, a fillet stuffed with smoked oysters and anchovies (US$7.50). There are a few meat dishes for nonfishy types, and you can eat very well for under US$10. The catch? They're open only from 11 am to 6 pm Thursday through Sunday.

Top End

The *Restaurante Pórtico del Peregrino*, on Calle 57 between Calles 60 and 62, has several pleasant, traditional dining rooms (some air-conditioned) around a small courtyard. Yucatecan dishes are the forte, but you'll find many continental dishes as well. A full meal costs US$12 to US$20.

La Casona, on Calle 60 between Calles 47 and 49, is a fine old city house with tables set out on a portico next to a small but lush garden; dim lighting lends an air of romance. Italian dishes and a few Yucatecan choices cost US$10 to US$20. Open for dinner only.

Los Almendros, on Calle 50A between Calles 57 and 59, serves a wide variety of authentic Yucatecan country cuisine and is famous for its zingy onion-and-tomato pork dish *poc-chuc*. This is hearty, stick-to-your-ribs food. Full meals cost US$9 to US$15.

ENTERTAINMENT
Concerts, Folklore & Drama

Mérida offers many folkloric and musical events in parks and historic buildings, put on by local performers of considerable skill. Admission is free except as noted. Check with one of the tourist information offices to confirm schedules and learn of special events.

Monday *Vaquerías* (traditional Yucatecan dances) are performed to live music in front of the Palacio Municipal (west side of Plaza Grande) from 9 to 10 pm (arrive early to get a good seat). The dance and music reflect a mixture of Spanish and Mayan cultures, and date from the earliest days of the Vaquería Regional, a local festival that celebrated the branding of cattle on neighboring haciendas.

Tuesday In Parque de Santiago (Calles 59 and 70) from 8:30 to 10:30 pm a big band plays dance music from the '40s and '50s for couples to whirl to. At the Teatro Peón Contreras (Calle 60 at Calle 57), the University's Ballet Folklórico (rated number three in the country) performs at 9 pm (US$9; tickets on sale at the theater).

Wednesday Open-air *teatro satírico*, behind the Palacio Municipal from 9 to 10 pm, gives performers the opportunity to air political and social issues and lambaste the government (or anyone else, for that matter!) with impunity (in Spanish only). The issues and references may be obscure, but it's always a lively – and often an uproarious – time.

Thursday Traditional Yucatecan serenades (featuring dance, poetry and Yucatecan musical trios) are performed in the Parque Santa Lucía, Calles 55 and 60, at 9 pm.

Friday Traditional Yucatecan serenades are performed in the courtyard of the University, Calles 57 and 60, from 9 to 10 pm (US$2.20; no performances during Semana Santa or month of August). *Estampas Yucatecas* (regional folk dances) are performed in the shop-lined Pasaje Picheta, west of the Palacio de Gobierno, from 8 to 9 pm.

Saturday 'Mexican Night,' at the southern end of Paseo de Montejo (where it meets Calle 47), features mariachi and other Mexican (as opposed to Yucatecan) music and folkloric dances. The festivities last from 7 pm to midnight and are very well attended. There are usually fireworks around 10:30.

Sunday 'Mérida en Domingo' is a series of concerts and special events taking place between 9 am and 9 pm in various venues. One highly recommended event is the reenactment of a colorful mestizo wedding, performed in Mayan with Spanish translation, from 6 to 7 pm at the Palacio Municipal. Sometimes a 1 pm show is given as well, featuring child performers in place of the later show's professional entertainers.

Last Saturday of each month 'Ponte Chula, Mérida' (Make Yourself Pretty, Mérida) features musical events (and food!) at various locales throughout the city.

The *Olimpo* cultural center (on the northwest side of the Plaza Grande) hosts frequent performances. Its bulletin board is a good source of event information.

Cinema

Many English-language films, some of fairly recent release, are screened in Mérida with Spanish subtitles. Buy your tickets (usually about US$2.75) before showtime, and well in advance on weekends. Theaters include popular *Cine Fantaslo*, Calle 59 at 60, between the Gran Hotel and Hotel Caribe; *Cinema 59*, Calle 59 between Calles 68 and 70; and the *Plaza Cine Internacional*, Calle 58 between 57 and 59.

Nightlife

For dancing to live salsa, head to *Pancho's* restaurant, on Calle 59 between Calles 60 and 62, or *La Bella Época* restaurant, around the corner on Calle 60.

SHOPPING

Mérida is *the* place on the peninsula to shop. Purchases you might want to consider include traditional Mayan clothing such as the colorful embroidered *huipiles* (women's tunics), panama hats woven from palm fibers, and of course the wonderfully comfortable Yucatecan hammocks.

Mérida's main market, the Mercado Municipal Lucas de Gálvez, is bounded by Calles 56 and 56A at Calle 67, southeast of the Plaza Grande. The surrounding streets are all part of the large market district, lined with shops selling everything one might need. Guard your valuables extra carefully in the market area. Watch for pickpockets, purse-snatchers and slash-and-grab thieves.

The Artesanías Bazar García Rejón, at the corner of Calles 65 and 60, is set up to attract tourists. You should have a look at the stuff here, then compare the goods and prices with independent shops outside.

Handicrafts

The Casa de las Artesanías, on Calle 63 between 64 and 66, is a government-supported market for local artisans selling just about everything: earthenware, textiles, wicker baskets, sandals, wind chimes, ceramic dolls, vases, purses and pouches, figurines of Mayan deities, and bottles of locally made liqueurs such as *licor de guanábana, anís* and *licor de manta*. Open 9 am to 8 pm Monday through Saturday, 10 am to 2 pm Sunday.

Popol-Nah, on Calle 59 between Calles 60 and 62, sells high-quality hammocks and guayaberas (they are the same quality as those found at Jack's, a nearby Yucatecan-clothing store, only much cheaper), as well as carved Mayan calendars and masks of Mayan gods, quilts, tablecloths, clothing, jewelry, panama hats, bags and earthenware.

A few doors west is Miniaturas Arte Popular Mexicano, with *lots* of miniature figurines of varying quality (but all easy to pack). Open 10 am to 2 pm and 4 to 8 pm, 'más o menos,' according to the sign.

Panama Hats

Locally made panama hats are woven from jipijapa palm leaves in caves, where humid conditions keep the fibers pliable when the hat is being made. Once exposed to the relatively dry air outside, the panama hat is surprisingly resilient and resistant to crushing. The Campeche town of Bécal is the center of the hat-weaving trade, but you can buy good examples of the hatmaker's art in Mérida.

The best-quality hats have a fine, close weave of slender fibers. The coarser the weave, the lower the price should be. Prices range from a few dollars for a hat of basic quality to US$50 or more for top quality. They can be found at the Casa de los Artesanías and Popol-Nah, among other places.

GETTING THERE & AWAY
Air

Mérida's modern airport is a 10km, 20-minute ride southwest of the Plaza Grande off Hwy 180 (Avenida de los Itzáes). It has car-rental desks and a tourist office that can help with hotel reservations.

Most international flights to Mérida are connections through Mexico City or Cancún. The only nonstop international services are Aeroméxico's daily flights from

Yucatecan Hammocks: The Only Way to Sleep

Yucatecan hammocks are normally woven from strong nylon, cotton or sisal string and dyed in various colors; there are also natural, undyed versions. In the old days, the finest, strongest, most expensive hammocks were woven from silk. These are rare now, usually special orders for wealthy local families. The most expensive hammocks you're likely to find are *de croché*, meaning very tightly woven. These can take several weeks to produce and can be double or triple the usual hammock price.

Some unscrupulous vendors misrepresent the material their hammocks are made from, claiming that nylon is silk, or cotton is sisal or a sisal-cotton blend. Make sure you're getting the material you're paying for.

Hammocks come in several widths. The *sencillo* (one-person hammock) has about 50 pairs of end strings (each pair consisting of at least four strands) and should run from about US$10 to US$14 for one of decent quality. Next come the *doble* (also called *número 4*), made with 100 to 110 pairs and costing US$15 to US$20; the *matrimonial/número 5* (150 pairs, US$18 to US$21); and finally the *matrimonial especial/número 8* (175 or more pairs, US$24 to US$28), which can hold three good-sized adults. Sizes above matrimonial are harder to find; you can always commission special orders directly from weavers. The prices given here are for hammocks of standard quality. De croché hammocks will cost more.

Hammocks fold up small, and larger hammocks are more comfortable, so consider the bigger sizes, but be sure that you're really getting the width you're paying for.

Peddlers approaching you on the street may quote very low prices, but street-sold hammocks are usually mediocre at best. Check hammocks very carefully. Look closely at the string; it should be sturdy, and tightly and evenly spun. Check the end loops; they should be fairly large and tightly wrapped in string. To be long enough for you, a hammock's body (not counting the end strings) should be as long as you are tall.

Open the hammock and look at the weave; it should be even, with few mistakes. Watch out for dirty patches and stains. Check the width. Any hammock looks very wide at first glance, but a matrimonial especial should be truly enormous, at least as wide as it is long, and probably wider.

Miami and Aviateca's flights to Guatemala City. Scheduled domestic flights are operated mostly by smaller regional airlines, with a few flights by Aeroméxico and Mexicana.

Aerocaribe (☎ 928-67-90) Paseo de Montejo 500, flies between Mérida and Cancún, Havana (Cuba), Chetumal, Ciudad del Carmen, Monterrey, Oaxaca, Tuxtla Gutiérrez (for San Cristóbal de Las Casas), Veracruz and Villahermosa.

Aerolíneas Bonanza (☎ 928-06-09, fax 927-7999) Calle 56A No 579, between Calles 67 and 69, flies roundtrips daily from Mérida to Cancún, Chetumal and Palenque.

Aeroméxico (☎ 920-12-60, 920-12-93) Hotel Fiesta Americana (Avenida Colón at Paseo Montejo), flies to Mexico City.

Aviacsa (☎ 925-68-90 at Hotel Fiesta Americana, ☎ 946-18-50 at airport) flies nonstop to Guadalajara, Tijuana, Mexico City and Villahermosa.

Aviateca (☎ 946-12-96) at the airport, flies to Tikal and Guatemala City several times a week.

Mexicana (☎ 946-13-22) Paseo de Montejo 493, has nonstop flights to Mexico City.

Bus

Mérida is the bus transportation hub of the Yucatán Peninsula. Take care with your gear on night buses and those serving popular tourist destinations (especially 2nd-class buses); Lonely Planet has received many reports of theft on the night runs to Chiapas and of a few daylight thefts on the Chichén Itzá and other lines.

Bus Stations Mérida has a variety of bus stations, and some lines operate out of (and stop at) more than one terminal. Tickets for departure from one terminal can often be bought at another, and destination overlap among lines is great. Following are some of the stations, bus lines operating out of them and areas served (see the Yucatán Getting There & Around chapter for further information on bus lines). Smaller terminals not mentioned here are included in the Bus Routes list.

CAME Bus Terminal Pronounced 'kah-meh,' and sometimes referred to as the 'Terminal de Primera Clase,' Mérida's main terminal is seven blocks southwest of the Plaza Grande, on Calle 70 between Calles 69 and 71. Come here for (mostly 1st-class) buses around the peninsula and to points well beyond, for example, Campeche, Cancún, Mexico City, Palenque, San Cristóbal de Las Casas and Villahermosa. Lines include ADO, Maya de Oro, Super Expresso and UNO. CAME has pay phones, an ATM and runs counters for tourist, bus and hotel information.

Terminal de Segunda Clase The old bus terminal, also known as Terminal 69 ('Sesenta y Nueve') or simply Terminal de Autobuses, is on Calle 69, just around the corner from CAME. ATS, Mayab, Omnitur del Caribe, Oriente, Sur, TRP and TRT run mostly 2nd-class buses to points in the state and around the peninsula, such as Campeche, Cancún, Chetumal and Felipe Carrillo Puerto.

Oriente & Noreste These two lines share a terminal on Calle 67 between Calles 50 and 52; LUS uses it as well. Oriente serves routes to Cancún via Chichén Itzá and Valladolid, and to Cobá, Playa del Carmen and Tulum; some of these buses depart from Terminal 69 as well. Noreste serves many small towns in the northeastern part of the peninsula, including Tizimín and Río Lagartos, and also has a small open-air terminal on Calle 50, around the corner from the shared terminal.

Parque de San Juan The Parque de San Juan, on Calle 69 between Calles 62 and 64, is the terminus for vans and Volkswagen combis going to Dzibilchaltún Ruinas, Muna, Oxkutzcab, Peto, Sacalum, Tekax and Ticul. Fares from here generally don't exceed US$2.

Progreso The separate bus terminal for Progreso is at Calle 62 No 524 between Calles 65 and 67.

Hotel Fiesta Americana This small 1st-class terminal on the west side of the hotel complex is aimed at guests of the luxury hotels on Avenida Colón, far from the center. Don't catch a bus to here unless you'll be staying at the Fiesta, Hyatt or Holiday Inn. ADO GL and Super Expresso have service between here and Cancún, Campeche, Chetumal and Playa del Carmen.

Celestún Bus Terminal This terminal is on Calle 71 between Calles 64 and 66.

Terminal Maaya K'iin From this small terminal on Calle 65 just west of Calle 50, Elite, a struggling, cut-rate 1st-class line serves many of the same destinations as the CAME terminal more cheaply, but not as reliably or comfortably.

Bus Routes The destinations served from Mérida include the following.

Campeche 195km (short route via Bécal), 2½ to 3 hours; 250km (long route via Uxmal), 4 hours; ATS every 20 to 30 minutes (US$6), 33 ADO (US$7.75)

Cancún 320km, 4 to 6 hours; six Oriente between 6 and 11:15 am (US$10), 21 Super Expresso 5:30 am to midnight (US$14), many other buses

Celestún 95km, 2 hours; 12 ATS from Celestún terminal (US$2.25)

Chetumal 456km, 6 to 8 hours; several deluxe Omnitur del Caribe and Super Expresso (US$16.25), three 2nd-class Mayab (US$11)

Chichén Itzá 116km, 2½ hours; Oriente at 5, 6 and 8 pm (US$4)

Cobá 270km, 5 hours; Oriente at 11 am and 1:15 pm (US$7.25)

Escárcega 345km, 5 hours; 1st-class Elite (US$11), Altos (US$12) and ADO (US$14)

Felipe Carrillo Puerto 310km, 5½ hours; Omnitur del Caribe (US$10.50)

Izamal 72km, 1½ hours; frequent Oriente (from Oriente & Noreste terminal; US$1.25)

Mayapán Ruinas – 48km, 1½ hours; 15 LUS 2nd-class between 5:30 am and 8 pm (from Oriente & Noreste terminal; US$1.50 one way, US$2.50 roundtrip)

Mexico City (Norte) 1360km, 20 hours; ADO at noon and 6:15 pm (US$64)

Mexico City (TAPO) 1550km, 20 hours; ADO GL at 3:30 and 4 pm (US$73)

Palenque 556km, 8 to 9 hours; Maya de Oro (US$20), ADO (US$23) and Elite (US$16.25) go directly to Palenque; others drop you off at Catazajá, the main highway junction 27km north of Palenque town (from Catazajá you can hitchhike or catch a bus or colectivo to Palenque)

Playa del Carmen 385km, 5 to 7 hours; eight ADO (US$15.75), three Elite (US$14.75), several others, including Oriente at 11am and 1:15 pm (US$11)

Progreso 33km, 45 minutes; Autoprogreso every 12 minutes from 5 am to 9 pm (US$0.90) from the Progreso bus terminal (see Bus Stations, above); for the same price, colectivo taxis (some with air-con) run from opposite the *Diario Yucatán* building on Calle 60 between Calles 63 and 65

Río Lagartos 261km, 4½ hours; Noreste at 9 am and 4 pm (US$6.75)

Ticul 85km, 1½ hours; frequent Mayab (US$3), three LUS (US$2.75) at 6:15 and 10:35 am and 4:30 pm; frequent minibuses (combis and vans) from Parque de San Juan (US$2.75)

Tizimín 210km, 2½ to 4 hours; five Noreste (US$5.50 for 2nd-class, US$6.75 for 1st-class) and five Oriente (US$6.50); or take a bus to Valladolid and change there for Tizimín

Tulum 320km, 5 hours via Cobá; or 450km, 6 hours via Cancún; a few Oriente (US$8.75) and ADO (US$11)

Tuxtla Gutiérrez 820km, 13 hours; one Maya de Oro (US$39), three Colón (US$28); or change at Palenque or Villahermosa

Valladolid 160km, 3 to 5 hours; many buses, including ADO (US$7), Oriente (US$5.25) and ATS

Villahermosa 560km, 9 hours; three ADO (US$26), one UNO (US$43)

Car

Rental car is the optimal way to tour the many archaeological sites south of Mérida, especially if you have two or more people to share costs. Assume you will pay a total of US$40 to US$60 per day (tax, insurance and gas included) for the cheapest car offered, usually a bottom-of-the-line Volkswagen or Nissan. Getting around town is better done on foot or with public transportation, so hold off renting your car until you've seen most of Mérida, or at least gotten well oriented. See Dangers & Annoyances earlier in this chapter for further Mérida driving tidbits, and 'You Take the High Road?' in the Eastern Yucatán State section for information on the toll highway heading east to Cancún.

Tourist Car Rental (☎ 924-9471, 924-6255, harrycaam@hotmail.com), Calle 60 between Calles 45 and 47, offers rates the big-name agencies often can't touch, especially if you offer to pay in cash. It's sometimes possible to get a VW for as little as US$25 a day, depending on demand, form of payment and length of rental.

Several other agencies have offices on Calle 60 between 55 and 57, at the airport and in and around the hotels on Avenida Colón. Among them are:

Budget (☎ 928-66-59) Calle 60; (☎ 946-13-23) airport; (☎ 925-68-77 ext 516) Holiday Inn

Executive (☎ 920-37-32) Calle 60; (☎ 946-13-87) airport

Hertz (☎ 924-28-34) Calle 60; (☎ 924-28-34) airport; (☎ 925-75-95) Hotel Fiesta Americana

National (☎ 923-24-93, 928-63-08) Calle 60; (☎ 946-13-94) airport; (☎ 925-75-24) Hotel Fiesta Americana

At any agency, be sure to check carefully the condition of the car, including the fuel level, against the diagram that usually accompanies the contract, before you agree to sign anything.

GETTING AROUND
To/From the Airport
Bus 79 ('Aviación') travels every 15 to 30 minutes between the airport and the city center for US$0.30. It follows a very roundabout route on its way to the airport; the best place to catch it is along Calle 70 just south of Calle 69, near the corner of the CAME terminal a few meters north of the taxi stand. The trip takes about half an hour; at one point the bus gets within 400m of the airport before veering off into a nearby neighborhood for 10 more minutes. When it finally reaches the air terminal, it pauses for a minute before heading back to the center.

Most arriving travelers use the Transporte Terrestre minibuses (US$8.75 per person) to go from the airport to the center. It is difficult getting a fair price for a regular taxi from the airport, but going the opposite way try for the local price of US$6.50.

To/From CAME Bus Terminal
To walk from CAME to the Plaza Grande, exit the terminal, turn left, then right onto Calle 69; the old Terminal de Autobuses will be on your right. Walk straight along Calle 69 for four blocks (through Parque de San Juan and around the church) to Calle 62. Turn left and walk the remaining three blocks to the plaza.

Bus
Most parts of Mérida that you'll want to visit are within five or six blocks of the Plaza Grande and are thus accessible on foot. Given the slow speed of city traffic, particularly in the market areas, travel on foot is also the fastest way to get around.

City buses are cheap at US$0.30 per ride (US$0.35 in a minibus), but routes are confusing. Most start in suburban neighborhoods, meander through the city center, and terminate in another distant suburban neighborhood. To travel between the Plaza Grande and the upscale neighborhoods to the north along Paseo de Montejo, catch a 'Tecnológico' bus or minibus on Calle 60 and get out at Avenida Colón; to return to the city center, catch any bus heading south on Paseo de Montejo that is displaying the destination 'Centro.'

The bus system is supplemented by colectivo minibuses, which are easier to use, as they run shorter and more comprehensible routes. The most useful is the Ruta 10 (US$0.35), which departs the corner of Calles 58 and 59, half a block east of the Parque Hidalgo, and travels along the Paseo de Montejo to Itzamná.

Taxi
Taxis in Mérida are not metered. However, to prevent price abuse, Mérida's taxi drivers belong to a union, the members of which have agreed on rates to various destinations. A broad sampling of those fixed rates is posted beside the taxi stand at the corner of Calles 60 and 57A (across from the Tourist Information Center). Most rides within city limits do not exceed US$5. Taxi stands can be found at most of the barrio parks. To call a taxi, dial ☎ 928-53-22 or 923-12-21; service

is available 24 hours. A dispatch fee of US$1 to US$2 (depending on the hour) is added to the fare for this service.

Around Mérida

The region around Mérida contains ancient ruins, colonial towns, decaying and restored haciendas, beaches and even a flamingo colony. It can largely be explored on day trips from Mérida, but you may want to spend more time at a place that captures your fancy.

DZIBILCHALTÚN

Dzibilchaltún (Place of Inscribed Flat Stones) was the longest continuously utilized Mayan administrative and ceremonial city, serving the Maya from 1500 BC or earlier until the European conquest in the 1540s. At the height of its greatness, Dzibilchaltún covered 80 sq km. Archaeological research in the 1960s mapped 31 sq km of the city, revealing some 8500 structures; few of these have been excavated and restored.

Enter the site along a nature trail that terminates at the modern, air-conditioned **Museo del Pueblo Maya**, featuring artifacts from throughout the Mexican-Mayan region. Exhibits explaining Mayan daily life and beliefs from ancient times until the present are labeled in Spanish and English. Beyond the museum, a path leads to the central plaza, where you will find an open chapel that dates from early Spanish times (1590–1600).

The **Templo de las Siete Muñecas** (Temple of the Seven Dolls), which got its name from seven grotesque dolls discovered here during excavations, is a 1km walk from the central plaza. It is most impressive for its precise astronomical orientation: The rising and setting sun of the equinoxes 'lights up' the temple's windows and doors, making them blaze like beacons and signaling this important turning point in the year.

The **Cenote Xlacah**, now a public swimming pool, is more than 40m deep. In 1958 an expedition sponsored by the US National Geographic Society sent divers down and recovered 30,000 Mayan artifacts, many of ritual significance. The most interesting of these are now on display in the site's museum. South of the cenote is Estructura 44, at 130m one of the longest Mayan structures in existence.

Dzibilchaltún is open from 8 am to 5 pm Tuesday through Sunday. Admission is US$5, free on Sunday. Parking costs US$1. Minibuses and colectivo taxis depart frequently from Mérida's Parque de San Juan, on Calle 69 between Calles 62 and 64, for the village of Dzibilchaltún Ruinas (15km, 30 minutes, US$0.75), only a little over 1km from the museum.

PROGRESO
• population 40,000

If Mérida's heat has you dying for a quick beach fix, or you want to see the longest wharf (7km) in Mexico, head to Progreso (also known as Puerto Progreso). Otherwise there's little reason to visit this dual-

---

Death of the Dinosaurs

North of Progreso, beneath the emerald green water and a layer of sediment up to 1km thick in spots, lies the crater of Chicxulub (chik-shoo-**loob**).

In 1980 Nobel Prize laureate Luis Alvarez and some colleagues put forth the theory that an asteroid or small comet hit the earth about 65 million years ago, causing severe climatic changes that resulted in the extinction of the dinosaurs. In 1991 the huge Chicxulub crater, estimated at between 180km and 200km in diameter, was identified as the most likely candidate for the site of impact.

In 1996 scientists discovered what they believe to be tiny pieces of the original meteor, which is thought to have measured up to 10km across. Tektites (beads of glass formed by meteors striking the earth) associated with the event have been found as far away as Haiti and Wyoming.

– Tom Brosnahan

purpose port-resort town. The beach is fine, well groomed and long, but nearly shadeless and dominated by the view of the wharf, giving it a rather industrial feel. Winds hit here full force off the Gulf in the afternoon and can blow well into the night. As with other Gulf beaches, the water is murky; visibility even on calm days rarely exceeds 5m. None of this stops meridanos from coming in droves on weekends, especially in the summer months. Even on spring weekdays it can be difficult to find a room with a view.

Progreso's street grid confusingly employs two different numbering systems 50 numbers apart. The city center's streets are numbered in the 60s (10s), 70s (20s) and 80s (30s). This text uses the high numbers. Even-numbered streets run east-west and decrease by twos eastward; odd ones, by twos northward. The bus station is on Calle 79 west of Calle 82, a block north (toward the water) from the main plaza. It's six short blocks from the plaza on Calle 80 to the Malecón (waterfront street) and *muelle* (wharf); along the way are two Banamexes, one with an ATM. All hotels and restaurants listed are no more than a total of 11 blocks north and east of the station.

Places to Stay & Eat

The *Hotel Miralmar* (☎ 935-05-52, Calle 77 No 124), at the corner of Calle 76, offers rooms with private shower, fan and one double bed for US$11, two beds and TV for US$15.25. Rooms on the upper floor are not as dungeonlike as the ground-floor rooms. The three bubble-shaped rooms may look a tad bizarre, but offer the best ventilation.

Six blocks northeast, at the corner of the Malecón and Calle 70 is the seaside *Tropical Suites* (☎ 935-12-63, fax 935-30-93), with 21 tidy rooms with shower ranging from US$13 for a viewless single with fan to US$30 for a sea-view double with air-con. Across the street is *Hotel Real del Mar* (☎ 935-07-98), featuring 15 air-con rooms with various configurations of beds and views starting at US$15 single and going up to US$31 double with sea view.

Restaurant Los Pelícanos, on the Malecón at Calle 70 by the Hotel Real del Mar,

has a shady terrace, sea views, a good menu and moderate prices, considering its location. Four blocks west is *Las Rocas*, at the corner of Calle 78, where a full fish dinner costs about US$5.

Closer to the Hotel Miralmar are the *Restaurant Mary Doly*, on Calle 75 between Calles 74 and 76, a homey place with good, cheap seafood, meat and breakfasts; and *Restaurant El Cordobes*, on the north side of the plaza, with similar prices and menu in a 100-year-old building with character.

Getting There & Away

Progreso is 33km due north of Mérida along a fast four-lane highway that's basically a continuation of the Paseo de Montejo. If you're driving, head north on the Paseo and follow signs for Progreso. Autoprogreso buses (US$0.90, 45 minutes) depart the Progreso bus terminal, Calle 62 between Calles 65 and 67, 1½ blocks south of the Plaza Grande, every 12 minutes from 5 am to midnight. For the same price colectivo taxis (some with air-con) run from opposite the *Diario Yucatán* building on Calle 60 between Calles 63 and 65 to Progreso's plaza.

CELESTÚN
• population 5200

Celestún is in the middle of a wildlife sanctuary abounding in resident and migratory waterfowl, with flamingos as the star attraction, and makes a good beach-and-bird day trip from Mérida. It's also a great place in which to kick back and do nothing for a few days, especially if you've become roadweary. Fishing boats dot the appealing white-sand beach that stretches to the north for kilometers, and afternoon breezes cool the town on most days.

Though the winds can kick up sand and roil the sea, making the already none-too-clear water unpleasant for swimming, they are less intense than in Progreso. Celestún is sheltered by the peninsula's southward curve, resulting in an abundance of marine life (and cheap seafood). It's a great place to watch the sun set into the sea, and if you are from a west coast anywhere you'll feel perfectly oriented. If you're not from a west coast, all you need to know is that Calle 11 is the road into town (due west from Mérida), ending at Calle 12, the dirt road paralleling the beach along which lie most of the restaurants and hotels.

Flamingo Tours

The status of the Ría Celestún Biosphere Reserve was in administrative limbo at the time of writing, and it may be reclassified as another sort of protected area, but its 59,130 hectares are still home to a huge variety of animal life, including a large flamingo colony.

Given the winds, the best time to see birds is in the morning, though from 4 pm onward they tend to concentrate in one area after the day's feeding, which can make for good viewing. There are two places to hire a boat for bird-watching: from the bridge on the highway into town about 1.5km from the beach, and from the beach itself.

Tours from the beach last 2½ to three hours and begin with a ride south along the coast for several kilometers, during which you can expect to see egrets, herons, cormorants, sandpipers and many other species of bird. The boat then turns into the mouth of the *ría* (estuary) and passes through a 'petrified forest,' where tall coastal trees once belonging to a freshwater ecosystem were killed by saltwater intrusion long ago and remain standing, hard as rock.

Continuing up the ría takes you under the highway bridge where the other tours begin, and beyond which lie the flamingos. Depending on the tide, the hour and the season, you may see hundreds or thousands of the colorful birds. Don't encourage your captain to approach them too closely; a startled flock taking wing can result in injuries and deaths (for the birds). In addition to taking you to the flamingos, the captain will wend through a 200m mangrove tunnel and go to one or both (as time and inclination allow) of the freshwater cenote/springs welling into the saltwater of the estuary, where you can take a refreshing dip (if you wore your bathers).

The cost for this tour is roughly US$71 per boatload (up to six passengers). Boats depart from several beachside spots. The operation leaving from Restaurant Celestún, at the foot of Calle 11, is the best organized, and the restaurant's beachfront palapa is a pleasant place to wait for a group to accumulate.

If you're prone to seasickness or on a budget, you may want to begin your tour from the bridge, where there is a parking lot, ticket booth and a place to wait for fellow passengers. For US$33 per boat (again up to six passengers) you get the latter part of the tour described earlier: flamingos, mangrove tunnel and spring. It's also possible to tour from the bridge south to the 'petrified forest' and back (also US$33), or combine the two (each lasts about 1¼ hours).

With either operation, bridge or beach, your captain may or may not speak English. English-speaking guides can be hired at the bridge; this reduces the maximum possible number of passengers, of course. Bring snacks, water and sunscreen for the longer tours, and cash for any of them. There is no bank in town, and neither credit cards nor traveler's checks are accepted by the tour operators.

Places to Stay

Celestún had five hotels at the time of research, with talk of more to come. All are located on Calle 12 within a short walk of each other. They are listed from north to south. Try to book ahead if you want a sea view, especially on weekends.

North of Calle 11 is the **Hotel San Julio** (☎ 916-20-62, in Mérida ☎ 923-63-09). It's old and a little beat-up, but the eight fan-cooled rooms with private bath are clean, and the hotel is right on the beach. A steal at US$9/10 single/double (if you use only one bed; US$11 double if two). Try for the front room.

Across the street and south a bit, the whitewashed **Hospedaje Sofía** (no phone) has eight spotless, fan-cooled rooms (three with TV), updated with new tile, fresh paint and other nice touches, for US$8/13.

On the same side of Calle 12, south of Calle 11, is **Hotel Sol y Mar** (☎ 916-21-60),

AROUND MÉRIDA

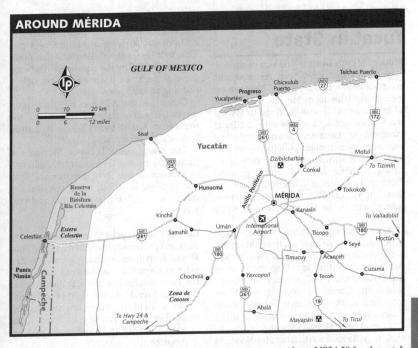

which offers 20 spacious and clean new rooms with TV for US$22 with fan, US$27 air-con. Crossing the street again, you'll find *Hotel Gutiérrez (916-20-41)*, a newer place under indifferent management. Its 18 fan-cooled, beachfront rooms are US$22; some lack mosquito screens.

Next door is *Hotel María del Carmen (☎/fax 916-20-51)*, with 14 clean and pleasant beachfront rooms. Each has two double beds and a private balcony facing the sea. The sole air-conditioned room costs US$27; the others are US$22.

Places to Eat

Celestún's specialties are crab and, of course, fresh fish. Service and decor vary from restaurant to restaurant in Celestún, but the menu for the most part does not, and most restaurants have outdoor areas on the beach. Eat early on weeknights or you may find every place closed.

Expect to pay about US$4.50 for the catch of the day, US$4.50 for delicious ceviche, US$3.25 for a conch or shrimp cocktail and US$4.50 for crab fried or served with mayonnaise. *Restaurant Celestún*, at the foot of Calle 11, offers good service, good food and pleasing decor, but *Playita*, *La Boya*, *Ávila* and others all have their own charm.

Getting There & Away

Buses from Mérida head for Celestún (95km, 2 hours, US$2.75) 12 times daily between 5 am and 8 pm from the terminal on Calle 71 between Calles 64 and 66, to Celestún's plaza, a block inland from Calle 12. Returning to Mérida, buses run from 5 am to 9 pm.

Companies such as Turitransmérida (in Mérida ☎ 924-11-99) offer day trips leaving Mérida at 9 pm and returning at 5 pm. For around US$40 they provide transportation, guide, a boat tour and lunch.

YUCATÁN

Southwestern Yucatán State

South of Mérida lies a region rich in ancient Mayan sites that have been restored and made accessible to the public. These can be seen in day trips from Mérida, though not all in one day. If time is short, go to Uxmal and Kabah, or take a whirlwind Ruta Puuc excursion (see Organized Tours). To give the area its propers, though, plan to stay over at least one night, whether you're driving or busing. Lodgings at Uxmal are expensive; those in Ticul are not. Transportation options for various itineraries are provided later, mostly in the Getting There & Away sections.

After exploring the archaeological wealth of this area you can head south on the inland route to Campeche, past Hopelchén to San Antonio Cayal (the turnoff to the ruins of Edzná) and finally to Campeche city. If your goal is the Caribbean coast, go southeast from Ticul and Oxkutzcab to Felipe Carrillo Puerto, then north to the coast or south to Chetumal and Belize. Another route to explore is the road south from Hopelchén to Xpujil, in eastern Campeche.

Organized Tours

Various companies offer Puuc Route tours. A typical tour departs Mérida at 9 am and visits Sayil, Xlapak, Labná and the Grutas de Loltún, returning by 6 pm. With lunch, entrance fees and guide service included, expect to pay about US$53 per person. To visit Kabah and Uxmal on a tour with the same features costs about US$27 per person.

Getting Around

Bus Some parts of the region have excellent bus service, others poor. The most problematic are the Ruta Puuc sites.

The daily Ruta Puuc whirlwind excursion run by ATS (Autotransportes del Sur; US$5) departs from Mérida's Terminal de Segunda Clase at 8 am and goes to the Ruta Puuc sites, Kabah and Uxmal, depart-ing from the parking lot of the Uxmal archaeological site on the return journey at 2:30 pm and arriving in Mérida by 4 pm. This 'tour' is transportation only; all other costs are borne by the passenger. The time spent at each site is enough to get only a nodding acquaintance.

Other than the ATS tour bus, there is no scheduled public transportation along the route from Kabah to Sayil, Xlapak, Labná, Loltún and Oxkutzcab.

The inland route between Mérida and Campeche passes Uxmal and Kabah, and most buses coming from the cities will drop you at those sites; but when you want to leave the sites, buses may be full and pass you by.

Car & Motorcycle Plan on at least two days and preferably three to make the Puuc Route loop from Mérida. Spend the first night at Uxmal and continue to Kabah and the Puuc Route sites the next day. You can return to Mérida for the night or to Uxmal, or go to Ticul. If you return via Yucatán State Hwy 18, you can stop for a visit to the ruins of Mayapán and a look at the pyramid in Acanceh.

There are three routes between Mérida and Campeche: the fastest and westernmost route, straight to Campeche on Hwy 180; the central route, which leads to the Uxmal ruins via the town of Muna; and the east-ernmost route, which takes you to the ruins at Mayapán via the town of Acanceh.

Fast Road to Campeche The western-most route leaves Mérida by Avenida de los Itzáes, passes the airport and travels through the towns of Umán, Chocholá, Kopoma and Maxcanú to Campeche.

To Uxmal via Muna The more interesting route heads southeast at Umán to Uxmal, Kabah and the Puuc Route.

It's 78km from Mérida to Uxmal via Hwy 180 southwest to Umán and then Hwy 261 to Muna and Uxmal. Hwy 261 continues south to Kabah and the junction with the road to the Puuc Route sites of Sayil, Xlapak and Labná. Past the junction Hwy 261 continues south to the town of Bolonchén de Rejón and then to Hopelchén, where you turn to reach the ruins of Dzibalchén. From Hopelchén the highway heads west toward the turn for Edzná and, beyond the turn, Campeche. This is a fairly well-traveled bus route, and if you don't have your own car, it is probably the way you'll come.

The urban conglomeration of Mérida extends almost to the suburb of Umán, 17km from the center. At Umán turn left and head south on Hwy 261 toward Muna. After 16km there's a bend in the road and, on the right-hand (west) side of the road, the hacienda of **Yaxcopoil**.

The hacienda's French Renaissance–style buildings have been restored and turned into a museum of the 17th century (8 am to 6 pm Monday to Saturday, 9 am to 1 pm Sunday; US$5). This vast estate specialized in the growing and processing of henequen. You can see much of what there is to see without paying the high museum admission fee.

Twenty-nine kilometers south of Yaxcopoil is **Muna**, an old town with several interesting colonial churches, including the former Convento de la Asunción and the churches of Santa María, San Mateo and San Andrés. Another 16km south of Muna is Uxmal; the highway passes the Hotel Misión Uxmal on the right and comes to the Hotel Hacienda Uxmal. Just across the highway from the hotel is the short entrance road (400 meters) to the ruins.

To Ticul via Acanceh The third, easternmost route south goes via Acanceh and the ruins of the old Mayan capital city of Mayapán before reaching Ticul. Take Yucatán State Hwy 18 southeast via Kanasin, Acanceh and Tecoh to Mayapán, then on to the provincial town of Ticul, which has several inexpensive hotels. From Ticul you can go directly to Uxmal via Muna or go southeast to Oxkutzcab, then west to the Grutas de Loltún and the Puuc Route sites of Labná, Xlapak, Sayil and Kabah before heading north and west to Uxmal. Trans-portation on this route is much more difficult without your own car. It might take the better part of a day to get from Mérida via the ruins of Mayapán to Ticul by bus. If you take this route you miss a visit to the hacienda of Yaxcopoil, but you get to see the ruins at Acanceh and Mayapán instead.

UXMAL

Some visitors rank Uxmal (oosh-**mahl**) among the top Mayan archaeological sites, somewhere below such marvels as Chichén Itzá and Tikal. While this may be stretching things, it's a large site with some fascinating structures in good condition, and visitors go away happy. Its setting in the Puuc Hills, which lent their name to the architectural patterns in this region, adds to its appeal.

History

Uxmal was an important city during the Late Classic period (AD 600–900) of a region that encompassed the satellite towns of Sayil, Kabah, Xlapak and Labná. Although Uxmal means 'Thrice Built' in Mayan, it was actually constructed five times.

That a sizable population flourished in this dry area is yet more testimony to the engineering skills of the Maya, who built a series of reservoirs and *chultunes* (cisterns) lined with lime mortar to catch and hold water during the dry season. First settled about AD 600, Uxmal was influenced by highland Mexico in its architecture, most likely through contact fostered by trade. This influence is reflected in the town's serpent imagery, phallic symbols and columns. The well-proportioned Puuc architecture, with its intricate, geometric mosaics sweeping across the upper parts of elongated facades, is unique to this region.

The scarcity of water in the Puuc Hills meant that Chac, the rain god or sky serpent, carried a lot of weight. His image is ubiquitous here in the form of stucco masks protruding from facades and cornices. There is much speculation as to why Uxmal was abandoned in about AD 900; drought conditions may have reached such proportions that the inhabitants had to relocate.

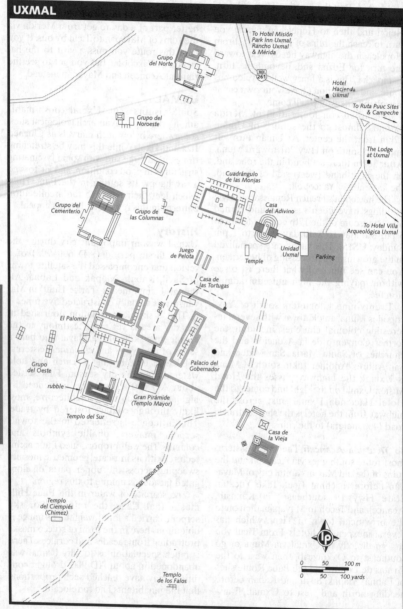

UXMAL

To Hotel Misión
Park Inn Uxmal,
Rancho Uxmal
& Mérida

Grupo
del Norte

MEX
261

Hotel
Hacienda
Uxmal

To Ruta Puuc Sites
& Campeche

Grupo del
Noroeste

The Lodge
at Uxmal

Cuadrángulo
de las Monjas

Grupo del
Cementerio

Grupo de
las Columnas

Casa
del Adivino

Unidad
Uxmal

To Hotel Villa
Arqueológica Uxmal

Juego
de Pelota

Temple

Parking

Casa de
las Tortugas

path

El Palomar

Grupo
del Oeste

Palacio del
Gobernador

rubble

Gran Pirámide
(Templo Mayor)

Templo del Sur

Casa de
la Vieja

San Simón Rd

Templo
del Ciempiés
(Chimez)

0   50   100 m
0   50   100 yards

Templo
de los Falos

Uxmal was rediscovered by archaeologists in the 19th century. The great American archaeologist John L Stephens and his British illustrator, Frederick Catherwood, wrote about and drew the site with accuracy, publishing their work in *Incidents of Travel in Central America, Chiapas & Yucatan*. Uxmal was first excavated in 1929 by Frans Blom. Although much has been restored, there is still a good deal to discover.

Information

Parking is US$1 per car. The site is entered through the modern Unidad Uxmal building, which holds an air-conditioned restaurant, a small museum, shops selling souvenirs and crafts, an auditorium, bathrooms and a Librería Dante. This bookstore has an excellent selection of travel and archaeological guides and general interest books on Mexico in English, Spanish, German and French; the imported books are very expensive.

The archaeological site is open 8 am to 5 pm daily; admission is US$8.25 (free Sunday and holidays) and includes the 45-minute *Luz y Sonido* (Light & Sound) show. This begins each evening at 8 pm in summer and 7 pm in winter and is in Spanish. Devices for listening to English, French, German or Italian translations (beamed via infrared) rent for US$2.75. Specify the language you need or it may not be broadcast. Cost for the show is US$3.25 if you don't have a ruins ticket, so hold on to the wristband you're issued.

Licensed guides offer their services for about US$38 for groups of up to 15. They will show you around for two to three hours, depending on interest. At least one guarantees his services thus: 'If you're not satisfied, you can sacrifice me.'

As you pass through the turnstile and climb the slope to the ruins, the rear of the Casa del Adivino comes into view.

Casa del Adivino

This tall temple (the Magician's House), 39m high, was built on an oval base. The smoothly sloping sides have been restored; they date from the temple's fifth incarnation. The four earlier temples were covered in the rebuilding, except for the high doorway on the west side, which remains from the fourth temple. Decorated in elaborate Chenes style (which originated farther south and takes its name from the many natural wells there), the doorway proper forms the mouth of a gigantic Chac mask.

The ascent to the doorway and the top is best done from the west side (though at the time of research the temple was being worked on and climbing it was not allowed). Heavy chains serve as handrails to help you up the steep steps.

From the top of the temple you can survey the rest of the site. Directly west is the Cuadrángulo de las Monjas. On the south side of the quadrangle, down a short slope, is a *juego de pelota* (ball court). Farther south stands the great artificial terrace holding the Palacio del Gobernador; between the palace and the ball court is the small Casa de las Tortugas. Other structures lie not quite visible beyond the Palacio del Gobernador; still more have been recaptured by the jungle and are now just verdant mounds.

Cuadrángulo de las Monjas

Archaeologists have not yet deciphered what this 74-room quadrangle was used for, but they guess that it might have been a military academy, royal school or palace complex. The long-nosed face of Chac appears everywhere on the facades of the four separate temples that form the quadrangle. The northern temple, grandest of the four, was built first, followed by the southern, then the eastern and then the western.

Several decorative elements on the facades show signs of Mexican, perhaps Totonac, influence. The feathered serpent (Quetzalcóatl, or in Mayan, Kukulcán) motif along the top of the west temple's facade is one of these. Note also the stylized depictions of the *na* (Mayan thatched hut) over some of the doorways in the northern building. The na motif alternates with stacks of Chac masks over the doors. Similar na depictions are over the doors of the southern building as well.

Chac masks at the Quadrángulo
de las Monjas, Uxmal

Juego de Pelota

Passing through the corbeled arch in the
middle of the south building of the quadrangle and continuing down the slope brings
you to the ball court. Turn left there and
head up the steep slope and stairs to the
large terrace.

Casa de las Tortugas

To the right at the top of the stairs is the
House of the Turtles, which takes its name
from the turtles carved on the cornice. Turtles were associated by the Maya with the
rain god, Chac. According to Mayan myth,
when the people suffered from drought so
did the turtles, and both prayed to Chac to
send rain.

The frieze of short columns, or 'rolled
mats,' that runs around the temple below

the turtles is characteristic of the Puuc style.
On the west side of the building a vault has
collapsed, affording a good view of the corbeled arch that supported it.

Palacio del Gobernador

The Governor's Palace, with its magnificent
facade nearly 100m long, has been called
'the finest structure at Uxmal and the culmination of the Puuc style' by Mayanist
Michael D Coe. Buildings in Puuc style
have walls filled with rubble, faced with
cement and then covered in a thin veneer of
limestone squares; the lower part of the facade is plain, the upper part festooned with
stylized Chac faces and geometric designs,
often latticelike or fretted. Other elements
of Puuc style are decorated cornices, rows
of half-columns (as in the House of the
Turtles) and round columns in doorways (as
in the palace at Sayil). The stones forming
the corbeled vaults in Puuc style are shaped
somewhat like boots.

Gran Pirámide

Though it's adjacent to the Governor's
Palace, to reach the Great Pyramid without
disobeying any signs you must retrace your
route down the hillside stairs and turn left
before reaching the ball court.

The 32m-high pyramid has been restored
only on its northern side. Archaeologists
theorize that the quadrangle at its summit
was largely destroyed in order to construct
another pyramid above it. That work, for
reasons unknown, was never completed. At
the top are some stucco carvings of Chac,
birds and flowers.

El Palomar

West of the Great Pyramid sits a structure
whose roofcomb is latticed with a pattern
reminiscent of the Moorish pigeon houses
built into walls in Spain and northern
Africa – hence the building's name (the
Dovecote, or Pigeon House). The nine hon-
eycombed triangular 'belfries' sit on top of a
building that was once part of a quadrangle.
The base is so eroded that it is hard for archaeologists to guess its function.

Places to Stay & Eat

Budget As there is no town at Uxmal – only the archaeological site and several top-end hotels – cheap food and lodging can be hard to come by.

Campers can pitch their tents 4km north of the ruins on Hwy 261 (the road to Mérida) at friendly *Rancho Uxmal* (☎ 9-972-02-77) for US$3.25 per person, which includes use of the pool, showers and toilets. The rancho also has 23 basic, serviceable guestrooms with shower and fan for US$27 double and a shady, welcoming restaurant serving three meals.

If there's no room at the rancho you can pitch a tent in the parking lot of the *Parador Turístico Cana Nah* (☎ 9-971-01-02) next door. For US$2.75 per person you can sleep near the highway and get access to un-heated showers, toilets and a nice pool.

The only other cheap lodging in the area are the rooms at Camping Sacbé, about 16km east of Uxmal (see Places to Stay in Kabah). If you don't want to return to Mérida for the night, make your way there or to Ticul.

The *Salon Nicté-Ha*, just across the highway from the road to the ruins, on the grounds of the Hotel Hacienda Uxmal, is an informal air-con restaurant open from 1 to 8 pm daily offering sandwiches, fruit salads and similar fare at prices slightly higher than those at the Yax-Beh (at Unidad Uxmal). There's a swimming pool for restaurant patrons.

Top End Mayaland Resorts' *The Lodge at Uxmal* (☎ 9-976-21-02, fax 9-976-21-27, in the USA ☎ 800-235-4079, uxmal1@sureste .com, www.mayaland.com), just opposite the entrance to the archaeological site, is Uxmal's newest, most luxurious hotel. Rooms with fan and all the comforts cost US$90 double, US$120 with air-con. There are two pools and a restaurant-bar with OK food.

A short walk east is *Hotel Villa Arqueológica Uxmal* (☎ /fax 9-976-20-20, in the USA 800-258-2633, in France 801 802 803, villauxm@sureste.com). Run by Club Med, it's an attractive hotel with swimming pool,

tennis courts, a restaurant and air-con guest-rooms for US$53/61/74 single/double/triple.

Another Mayaland Resort, *Hotel Hacienda Uxmal* (☎ 9-976-20-12, fax 9-976-20-11, in the USA 800-235-4079, mayaland@diario1.sureste.com, www.mayaland.com), 500m from the ruins and across the highway, originally housed the archaeologists who explored and restored Uxmal. High ceilings, wide, tiled verandas and a beautiful swimming pool make this an exceptionally comfortable place to stay. All rooms are air-conditioned. Simple rooms in the annex cost US$98 double; the standard rooms in the main building cost US$134. Unremarkable meals are moderately priced.

The hilltop *Hotel Misión Park Inn Uxmal* (☎ 9-976-20-22, fax 9-976-20-23, in the USA ☎ 800-448-8355, vmg@yuc1.telmex .net.mx, hotelesmision.com.mx) is 1km north of the turnoff to the ruins. All rooms have balconies, some with views of Uxmal, at US$91/103 double/triple. There's a restaurant and a lovely pool.

Getting There & Away

From Mérida's Terminal de Segunda Clase, it's 80km (1½ hours) to Uxmal. The inland route between Mérida and Campeche passes Uxmal, and most buses coming from either city will drop you there. But when you want to leave, passing buses may be full (especially Saturday and Monday) and may not stop.

If you're going from Uxmal to Ticul, first take a northbound bus to Muna (20 minutes, US$0.50) then catch another east to Ticul (30 minutes, US$0.75); the latter buses run every 45 minutes from 8 am to midnight. For buses to Kabah, the Puuc Route turnoff and points on the road to Campeche, flag down a southbound bus at the turnoff to the ruins.

Organized tours offered from Mérida (available through any travel agent) include the following itineraries and prices: Uxmal and Kabah (US$27), the Uxmal light-and-sound show (US$27) and Ruta Puuc sites (US$51). All tour prices are per person and include transportation, guide and lunch.

KABAH

The ruins of Kabah, just over 23km southeast of Uxmal, are right astride Hwy 261. The sign says 'Zona Arqueológica Puuc.' The guard shack/souvenir shop (selling snacks and cold drinks) and the bulk of the ruins are on the east side of the highway.

On entering, head to your right to climb the stairs of the structure closest to the highway, **El Palacio de los Mascarones** (Palace of Masks). The facade is an amazing sight, covered in nearly 300 masks of Chac, the rain god or sky serpent. Most of their huge curling noses are broken off; the best intact beak is at the building's south end. These noses may have given the palace its modern Mayan name, Codz Pop (Rolled Mat).

When you've had your fill of noses, head around back to check out the two restored **atlantes** (an atlas – plural 'atlantes' – is a male figure used as a supporting column).

These are especially interesting, as they're among the very few three-dimensional human figures you'll see at a Mayan site. One is headless and the other wears a jaguar mask atop his head. A third atlas stands by the office near the entrance; the two others that were discovered here are in museums.

Descend the steps near the atlantes and turn left, passing the small **Pirámide de los Mascarones**, to reach the plaza containing **El Palacio**. Its broad facade has several doorways, two of which have a column in the center. These columned doorways and the groups of decorative *columnillas* (little columns) on the upper part of the facade are characteristics of the Puuc architectural style.

Steps on the north side of El Palacio's plaza put you on a path leading a couple of hundred meters through the jungle to the **Templo de las Columnas**. This building has more rows of decorative columns on the upper part of its facade.

West of El Palacio, across the highway, a path leads up the slope and passes to the south of a high mound of stones that was once the **Gran Pirámide** (Great Pyramid). The path curves to the right and comes to a large restored **monumental arch**. It's said that the *sacbé*, or cobbled and elevated ceremonial road, leading from here goes through the jungle all the way to Uxmal, terminating at a smaller arch; in the other direction it goes to Labná. Once, all of the Yucatán Peninsula was connected by these marvelous 'white roads' of rough limestone.

At present, nothing of the sacbés is visible, and the rest of the area west of the highway is a maze of unmarked paths leading off into the jungle. Some of the structures (none as impressive as those east of the road) include the **Cuadrángulo del Oeste** (Western Quadrangle), with some decoration of columns and masks, and the **Templo de los Dinteles** (Temple of Lintels). This once had intricately carved lintels of tough sapodilla wood, but John L Stephens had them removed and shipped to New York for 'safekeeping,' where they were destroyed in a fire shortly after their arrival.

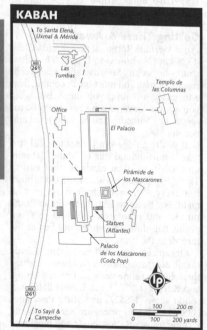

KABAH

To Santa Elena, Uxmal & Mérida

MEX 261

Las Tumbas

Office

El Palacio

Templo de las Columnas

Pirámide de los Mascarones

Statues (Atlantes)

Palacio de los Mascarones (Codz Pop)

MEX 261

To Sayil & Campeche

0   100   200 m
0   100   200 yards

Kabah is open 8 am to 5 pm daily. Admission is US$1.75.

Places to Stay & Eat

The quiet, well-kept *Camping Sacbé* (no phone, sacbehostel@hotmail.com) on the south side of the village of Santa Elena, 8km north of Kabah, has two simple but pleasant and clean rooms with a spotless shared bath for US$9.25 and two rooms with private bath for US$13.50 double. All rooms have fans; the owners are expanding the hotel and converting all rooms to private bath. Camping in a parklike setting costs US$2.75 per person. Good breakfasts and dinners are served at low prices. If you stay here, it is possible to catch a local bus to the Ruta Puuc ruins, and the owner, who speaks French, English and Spanish, will provide schedule information. As the book was going to press Camping Sacbé became affiliated with Hostelling International.

Getting There & Away

Kabah is 101km from Mérida, a ride of about two hours. The inland route between Mérida and Campeche passes Kabah, and most buses coming from the cities will drop you here.

To return to Mérida, stand on the east side of the road at the entrance to the ruins and try to flag down a bus. Buses in both directions are often full, however, and won't stop, so it may be a good idea to try organize a lift back with some other travelers at the site itself. Many visitors come to Kabah by private car and may be willing to give you a lift, either back to Mérida, or southward on the Puuc Route. If you're trying to get a bus to the Puuc Route turnoff, 5km south of Kabah, or to other sites along Hwy 261 farther south, stand on the west side of the highway.

LA RUTA PUUC

Just south of Kabah on Hwy 261, a road branches off to the east and winds past the ruins of Sayil, Xlapak and Labná, ending at the Grutas de Loltún. This is the Puuc Route, and its sites offer some marvelous architectural detail and a deeper acquaintance with the Puuc Mayan civilization.

If you make this excursion on Sunday, you will enjoy free admission to the archaeological sites; except for the Grutas, all sites are free on Sunday and holidays. Unfortunately, no scheduled public transportation serves this route, although there is one tour bus you can catch (see Getting Around, earlier in the Southwest Yucatán State section).

Sayil

The ruins of Sayil are 4.5km from the junction of the Puuc Route with Hwy 261, and are open 8 am to 5 pm daily; admission is US$1.75.

Sayil is best known for **El Palacio**, the huge three-tiered building with a facade some 85m long reminiscent of the Minoan palace on Crete. The distinctive columns of Puuc architecture are used here over and over, as supports for the lintels, as decoration between doorways and as a frieze above them, alternating with huge stylized Chac masks and 'descending gods.'

Taking the path south from the palace for about 400m and bearing left, you come to the temple named **El Mirador**, whose roosterlike roofcomb was once painted a bright red. About 100m beyond El Mirador, beneath a protective palapa, is a **stela** bearing the relief of a fertility god with an enormous phallus, now badly weathered.

Xlapak

From the entrance gate at Sayil, it's 6km east to the entrance gate at Xlapak (shla-pak). The name means 'Old Walls' in Mayan and was a general term among local people for ancient ruins. The site is open 8 am to 5 pm daily; admission is US$1.25.

If you're going to skip any of the Ruta Puuc sites, Xlapak should be it. The ornate **palace** at Xlapak is smaller than those at Kabah and Sayil, measuring only about 20m in length. It's decorated with the inevitable Chac masks, columns and colonnettes and fretted geometric latticework of the Puuc style. The building is slightly askew, looking like it doesn't know which way to fall. There's not much else here.

Labná

If Xlapak is the skippable Puuc site, Labná is the one not to miss. Its setting on a flat, open area is unique, and if no one has been through before you for a while, at each doorway you approach you're likely to startle groups of long-tailed mot-mots (clock birds) into flight. Between the birds and the vegetation growing atop the Palacio, you can almost imagine yourself one of the first people to see the site in centuries.

Archaeologists believe that at one point in the 9th century, some 3000 Maya lived at Labná. To support such numbers in these arid hills, water was collected in *chultunes*. At Labná's peak there were some 60 chultunes in and around the city; several are still visible. From the entrance gate at Xlapak, it's 3.5km east to the gate at Labná. The site is open 8 am to 5 pm daily; admission costs US$1.75.

El Palacio The Palace, the first edifice you come to at Labná, is one of the longest buildings in the Puuc Hills, and much of

El Arco, Labná

its interesting decorative carving is in good shape. On the west corner of the main structure's facade is a serpent's head with a human face peering out from between its jaws, the symbol of the planet Venus. Toward the hill from this is an impressive Chac mask, and nearby is the lower half of a human figure in loincloth and leggings.

The lower level has several more well-preserved Chac masks, and the upper level contains a large chultún that still holds water. The view of the site and the hills beyond from there is impressive.

From the Palace a limestone-paved **sacbé** leads to El Arco.

El Arco Labná is best known for its magnificent arch, once part of a building that separated two quadrangular courtyards. It now appears to be a gate joining two small plazas. The corbeled structure, 3m wide and 6m high, is well preserved, and the reliefs decorating its upper facade are exuberantly Puuc in style.

Flanking the west side of the arch are carved *na* (thatched structures) with multi-tiered roofs. Also on these walls, the remains of the building that adjoined the arch, are lattice patterns atop a serpentine design. Archaeologists believe a high roofcomb once sat over the fine arch and its flanking rooms.

El Mirador Standing on the opposite side of the arch and separated from it by the

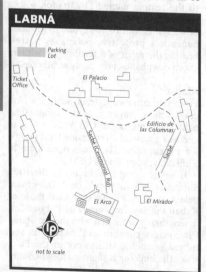

LABNÁ

Parking Lot

Ticket Office

El Palacio

Edificio de las Columnas

Sacbé (Ceremonial Rd)

Sacbé

El Arco

El Mirador

not to scale

sacbé is a pyramid known as El Mirador, topped by a temple. The pyramid itself is largely stone rubble. The temple, with its 5m-high roofcomb, is well positioned to be a lookout, thus its name. When John L Stephens saw El Mirador in 1840 it had a row of death's heads along the top and two lines of human figures beneath; over the center doorway was a colossal seated figure in high relief.

GRUTAS DE LOLTÚN

East of Labná 15km is the signed left turn to the Grutas de Loltún, which lie another 5km to the northeast. The road passes through lush orchards and some banana and palm groves, an agreeable sight in this dry region.

The Loltún Caves, one of the largest and most interesting cave systems in the Yucatán, provided a treasure trove of data for archaeologists studying the Maya. Carbon dating of artifacts found here reveals that the caves were used by humans 2500 years ago. Chest-high murals of hands, faces, animals and geometric motifs were apparent as recently as 20 years ago, but so many people have touched them that scarcely a trace remains. Today, visitors to the illuminated caves see mostly natural limestone formations, some of which are quite lovely.

Loltún is open 9 am to 5 pm daily; admission is US$4. To explore the labyrinth, you must take a scheduled guided tour at 9:30 or 11 am, or 12:30, 2, 3 or 4 pm, but they may depart early if enough people are waiting. The English-speaking guides may be willing to take you through at other hours if you offer a few dollars' tip. The guides, who are not paid by the government, expect a tip at the end of the hour-long tour (US$2 per person is common).

If you drove from Labná, you passed the *Restaurant El Guerrero* on your left just before the junction where the caves lie. If you're on foot, it's a walk of eight to 10 minutes (600m) along a marked path from the far side of the parking lot near the cave entrance. Tasty dishes are in the US$3.50 to US$5 price range and are accompanied by

enough sides to fill you up. Ask the price before ordering drinks. There is also a *parador turístico* serving food across the highway from the caves' parking lot.

Getting There & Away

Loltún is on a country road leading to Oxkutzcab (Osh-kootz-**kahb**), and there is usually some transportation along the road. Colectivos – often a *camioneta* (pickup truck) or *camión* (truck) – ply this route, charging US$1 for a ride (the price for locals is less, but it's hard to get). A taxi from Oxkutzcab may charge US$6 or so, one way, for the 7km ride.

Daily buses run frequently between Mérida and Oxkutzcab via Ticul. If you're driving from Loltún to Labná, turn right out of the Loltún parking lot, and take the next road on the right, which passes Restaurant El Guerrero's driveway. Do not take the road marked for Xul. After 5km turn right at the T intersection to join the Puuc Route west.

TICUL

• **population 27,000**

Ticul, 30km east of Uxmal and 14km northwest of Oxkutzcab, is the largest town south of Mérida in this ruin-rich region. It has decent hotels and restaurants, and good transportation. Although there is no public transportation available to the Puuc Route from here it is possible to stay the night in Ticul and catch a bus to Muna in time to catch a tour bus that travels from Muna to the Ruta Puuc ruins; see Getting There & Away. Ticul is also a center for fine huipil weaving, and ceramics made here from the local red clay are renowned throughout the Yucatán.

Because of the number of Mayan ruins in the vicinity from which to steal building blocks and the number of Maya in the area needing conversion to Christianity, Franciscan friars built many churches in the region that is now southern Yucatán state. Among them is the Iglesia de San Antonio de Padua at Ticul, construction of which dates from the late 16th century. Although looted on several occasions, the church has some original touches, among them the stone statues of friars in primitive style flanking the side entrances and a Black Christ altarpiece ringed by crude medallions.

Saturday mornings in Ticul are picturesque: Calle 23 in the vicinity of the public market is closed to motorized traffic, and the street fills with rickshaws transporting shoppers between the market and their homes.

Orientation & Information

Ticul's main street is Calle 23, sometimes called the Calle Principal, going from the highway northeast past the market and the town's best restaurants to the main plaza, or Plaza Mayor. A post office faces the plaza, as does a bank, and the bus station is less than 100m away. Catercorner to the Plaza Mayor is the newly built Plaza de la Cultura, all cement and stone but an agreeable place to take the evening breeze, enjoy the view of the church and greet passing townspeople.

Places to Stay

The *Hotel Plaza* (☎ 970-19-97, fax 972-00-26), on Calle 23 at Calle 26, is the best hotel in town, offering 22 rooms with air-con, telephone and cable TV for US$26. It also offers five rooms with fan for US$22.

The *Hotel Sierra Sosa* (☎ /fax 972-00-08, Calle 26 No 199A), just northwest of the plaza, has basic rooms for US$9.25/13.50 single/double with fan, US$14.25/18.50 with air-con. A few rooms at the back have windows, but most are dark.

The *Hotel San Miguel* (☎ 972-0382, Calle 28 No 215D) is near Calle 23 and the market. The friendly management offers worn rooms with fan and bath for US$5 single, US$7 (for one bed) or US$8.25 (for two beds) double.

Places to Eat

Ticul's lively market, on Calle 28A between Calles 21 and 23, provides all the ingredients for picnics and snacks. It also has lots of those wonderful market eateries where the food is good, the portions generous and the prices low. Across Calle 23 is *Super Salomón*, a small supermarket with a big variety of groceries and household items. For variety, try out some of the *loncherías* along Calle 23 between Calles 26 and 30.

For bread and sweet rolls, there's *El Buen Samaritano*, on Calle 23 west of Calle 26. For a sit-down meal, there's the cheap *Restaurant El Colorín (Calle 26 No 199B)*, half a block northwest of the plaza. Have a look at *La Carmelita*, on the opposite side of the Hotel Sierra Sosa, as well.

The *Jarro Café*, facing the main plaza, is an attractive Mexican-style café with cheap but decent food (US$1 to US$3) and numerous nonalcoholic beverages, none more than US$1.50.

Pizza La Góndola, on Calle 23 at Calle 26A, serves the best pizza in Ticul (US$4 to US$6), but it isn't really all that good. A half-dozen pastas are also available here. *Lonchería Mary* on Calle 23 east of Calle 28 is a clean, family-run place.

Restaurant Los Almendros (Calle 23 No 207), between 26A and 28, specializes in hearty Yucatecan food. The menu has photos and descriptions of the food. The *combinado yucateco* (Yucatecan combination plate), with a soft drink or beer, costs US$6.

Getting There & Away

Bus Ticul's bus station is on Calle 24 behind the massive church. Mayab runs between Mérida and Ticul (85km, 1½ hours, US$3) 22 times from 5 am to 8:30 pm. There are five buses to Felipe Carrillo Puerto (4 hours, US$7.25), frequent ones to Oxkutzcab (US$0.75) and nine a day to Chetumal (6½ hours, US$11). There are also five buses to Cancún each day (US$15). Super Expresso has less-frequent, 1st-class service to some of these destinations. All Ticul buses are *de paso* (originating elsewhere); seats aren't always available.

Minibuses (combis and vans) direct to Mérida's Parque de San Juan (1½ hours, US$2.75) depart from the intersection of Calles 24 and 25 as soon as they're full between 5 am and 7 pm. Combis for Oxkutzcab (16km, 30 minutes, US$0.75) leave

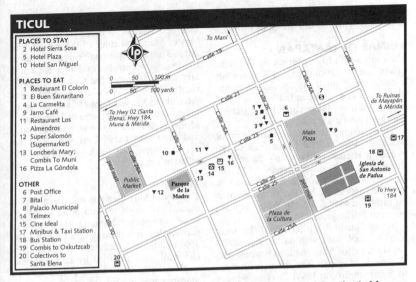

TICUL

PLACES TO STAY
2   Hotel Sierra Sosa
5   Hotel Plaza
10 Hotel San Miguel

PLACES TO EAT
1   Restaurant El Colorín
3   El Buen Samaritano
4   La Carmelita
9   Jarro Café
11 Restaurant Los
    Almendros
12 Super Salomón
    (Supermarket)
13 Lonchería Mary;
    Combis To Muni
16 Pizza La Góndola

OTHER
6   Post Office
7   Bital
8   Palacio Municipal
14 Telmex
15 Cine Ideal
17 Minibus & Taxi Station
18 Bus Station
19 Combis to Oxkutzcab
20 Colectivos to
    Santa Elena

from Calle 25A on the south side of the church between 7 am and 8:30 pm. From Oxkutzcab you can catch a minibus or pickup truck to Loltún (8km, about US$1); ask for the 'camión a Xul' ('shool'), but get off at the Grutas de Loltún.

Colectivo minibuses to Santa Elena (15km, US$0.75), the village between Uxmal and Kabah, depart from Calle 30 just south of Calle 25 between 6:15 am and 7:45 pm. They take Hwy 02 and drop you to catch another bus northwest to Uxmal (15km) or south to Kabah (3.5km). You may find it more convenient to take a combi or bus to Muna (see below) on Hwy 261 and another south to Uxmal (16km).

A good option for Ruta Puuc-bound travelers is to catch one of the early-morning buses from Ticul to Muna and pick up the ATS tour bus (US$5) for Labná, Sayil, Xlapak, Kabah and Uxmal at 9 am on its way from Mérida. It returns to Muna at 3 pm. Any of the buses leaving Ticul between 6 and 8 am for Muna (US$0.60) will get you there in time to catch the Ruta Puuc bus (all 2nd-class Mérida-bound buses stop in Muna). Combis for Muna (US$0.75)

leave from in front of Lonchería Mary on Calle 23 near Calle 28.

Car Those headed east to Quintana Roo and the Caribbean coast by car can take Hwy 184 from Ticul through Oxkutzcab to Tekax, Tzucacab and José María Morelos. At Polyuc, 130km from Ticul, a road turns left (east), ending after 80km in Felipe Carrillo Puerto, 210km from Ticul, where there are hotels, restaurants and a gas station (see the Quintana Roo chapter). The right fork of the road goes south to the region of Laguna Bacalar.

Between Oxkutzcab and Felipe Carrillo Puerto or Bacalar there are very few places to eat (those that you do find are rock-bottom basic), no hotels and few gasoline stations. Mostly you see small, typical Yucatecan villages, with their traditional Mayan thatched houses, *topes* (speed bumps) and agricultural activity.

Getting Around

The local method of getting around is to hire a *triciclo* (three-wheeled cycle), Ticul's answer to the rickshaw. You'll see them on

YUCATÁN

Calle 23 just up from the market, and the fare is less than US$0.50 for a short trip.

RUINAS DE MAYAPÁN

The route south from Mérida via the ruins of Mayapán to Oxkutzcab and Ticul reveals a landscape of small Mayan villages, crumbling haciendas surrounded by henequen fields, a ruined Mayan capital city and expanses of limitless scrubby jungle.

Those taking this route, whether by car or bus, should be careful to distinguish between the Ruinas de Mayapán – the ruins of the ancient city – and Mayapán – a Mayan village some 40km southeast of the ruins, past the town of Teabo. The ruins are right on the main road (Yucatán State Hwy 18) between Telchaquillo and Tekit.

About 2km past Telchaquillo (48km from Mérida), look for a sign on the right-hand (west) side of the road indicating the Ruinas de Mayapán. The site is open 8 am to 5 pm; admission US$1.25 (free Sunday and holidays).

History

Mayapán was supposedly founded by Kukulcán (Quetzalcóatl) in 1007, shortly after the former ruler of Tula arrived in Yucatán. His dynasty, the Cocom, organized a confederation of city-states that included Uxmal, Chichén Itzá and many other notable cities. Despite their alliance, animosity arose between the Cocomes of Mayapán and the Itzáes of Chichén Itzá during the late 12th century, and the Cocomes stormed Chichén Itzá, forcing the Itzá rulers into exile. The Cocom dynasty emerged supreme in all of northern Yucatán.

Cocom supremacy lasted for almost 2½ centuries, until the ruler of Uxmal, Ah Xupán Xiú, led a rebellion of the oppressed city-states and overthrew Cocom hegemony. The great capital of Mayapán was utterly destroyed and remained uninhabited ever after.

But there was no peace in Yucatán after the Xiú victory. The Cocom dynasty recovered and marshaled its forces, and struggles for power erupted frequently until 1542,

when Francisco de Montejo the Younger established Mérida. At that point the current lord of Maní and ruler of the Xiú people, Ah Kukum Xiú, offered to submit his forces to Montejo's control in exchange for a military alliance against the Cocomes, his ancient rivals. Montejo willingly agreed, and Ah Kukum Xiú was baptized as a Christian, taking the unoriginal name of Francisco de Montejo Xiú. The Cocomes were defeated and – too late – the Xiú rulers realized that they had signed the death warrant of Mayan independence.

The Site

The city of Mayapán was huge, with a population estimated to be around 12,000; its ruins cover several square kilometers, all surrounded by a great defensive wall. Over 3500 buildings, 20 cenotes and traces of the city wall were mapped by archaeologists working in the 1950s and in 1962. The workmanship was inferior to the great age of Mayan art.

Jungle has returned to cover many of the buildings, though you can see several cenotes (including Itzmal Chen, a main Mayan religious sanctuary) and some Chac masks, and you can still make out the large piles of stones that were once the Temple of Kukulcán and the circular Caracol. Though the ruins today are far less impressive than those at many sites, Mayapán is green and peaceful, and archaeologists are busily excavating and restoring more all the time.

Getting There & Away

Between 5:30 am and 8 pm LUS runs 15 2nd-class buses from the Oriente & Noreste terminal in Mérida that will drop you off at the Ruinas de Mayapán (1½ hours, US$1.50). These buses continue to Oxkutzcab (US$3.25 from Mérida), so you should be able to see the ruins and catch another southbound bus afterward. Double-check in Mérida; the routes are in flux, but you should at least be able to make a day trip to the ruins and back. Roundtrip fares bring the price down. From Oxkutzcab there are frequent buses and colectivos to Ticul.

If you're driving, leave Mérida on Calle 59, which runs one-way eastward. Turn right onto Circuito Colonias, a four-lane boulevard with railroad tracks running in its center, and go south until you reach a traffic circle with a fountain. Turn left and head due east on the road marked for Kanasín, Acanceh and Tecoh. You might stop on the way at Acanceh to visit the partially restored pyramid near the church (admission US$1.50).

After the ruins, the road heads south about 8km to Tekit (67km from Mérida). Turn right and go through the town square to find the road marked for Oxkutzcab. Another 7km brings you to Mama, with its particularly fortresslike church. At Mama the road forks: straight on to Oxkutzcab (27km), right to Chapab and Ticul (25km).

Eastern Yucatán State

The eastern portion of Yucatán state holds several delights for the visitor, including the easy pace of life in colonial Valladolid, the impressive Franciscan monastery in Izamal, and of course the awesome Mayan site of Chichén Itzá.

IZAMAL

• population 14,500

In ancient times, Izamal was a center for the worship of the supreme Mayan god, Itzamná, and the sun god, Kinich-Kakmó. A dozen temple pyramids were devoted to these or other gods. Perhaps these bold expressions of Mayan religiosity are why the Spanish colonists chose Izamal as the site for an enormous and impressive Franciscan monastery, which today stands at the heart of this small city.

The Izamal of today is a quiet, colonial gem of a provincial town, nicknamed La Ciudad Amarilla (The Yellow City) for the traditional yellow that most buildings are painted. It is easily explored on foot and makes a great day trip from Mérida.

You Take the High Road?

The region is traversed by Hwy 180 and its evil twin 180D, the *autopista de cuota*, a high-speed, high-cost highway that begins about 17km west of Cancún and ends at Kantunil, approximately 65km east of Mérida. Drivers, if you're burned out on *topes* (speed bumps) and traffic, and have more money than time, you'll like this empty and expensive concrete motorway. Otherwise, stick with Hwy 180.

The toll road's first exit coming from Cancún is Valladolid (US$14.75), then Pisté (for Chichén Itzá; another US$3.25). That's it, until you hit the end at Kantunil (US$8.75 from Valladolid or US$5 from Pisté). Driving straight through the entire 238km costs an ungodly US$23 and takes about two hours (if you obey the speed limit). There are gas stations and restaurants along the way, but there's very little to see.

Driving Hwy 180 takes approximately five hours to cover the same distance, and the route passes through several towns (some of them quite scenic) and over many speed bumps.

Things to See

When the Spaniards conquered Izamal, they destroyed the major Mayan temple, the Ppapp-Hol-Chac pyramid, and in 1533 began to build from its stones one of the first monasteries in the Western Hemisphere. Work on **Convento de San Antonio de Padua** was finished in 1561. Under the monastery's arcades, look for building stones with an unmistakable mazelike design; these were clearly taken from the earlier Mayan temple.

The monastery's principal church is the Santuario de la Virgen de Izamal, approached by a ramp from the main square. The ramp leads into the **Atrium**, a huge arcaded courtyard in which the fiesta of the Virgin of Izamal takes place each August 15.

At some point, the 16th-century **frescoes** beside the entrance of the sanctuary were completely painted over. For years they lay concealed under a thin layer of whitewash until a maintenance worker who was cleaning the walls discovered them a few years ago. The church's original altarpiece was destroyed by a fire believed to have been started by a fallen candle. Its replacement, impressively gilded, was built in the 1940s. In the niches at the stations of the cross are some superb small figures.

In the small courtyard to the left of the church, look up and toward the Atrium to see the original **sundial** projecting from the roof's edge.

Entry to the church is free. The best time to visit is in the morning, as it is occasionally closed during the afternoon siesta.

Three of the 12 **pyramids** have been partially restored so far. The largest is the enormous Kinich-Kakmó, three blocks north of the monastery. You can climb it for free.

Organized Tours

On Sundays at 8:15 am a special train leaves Mérida's railroad station (at Calles 55 and 50) for a day excursion to Izamal, arriving in the Yellow City at 10 am. A *calesa* (horse-drawn carriage) ride around the city and lunch are included in the price. The train reboards at around 3 pm, arriving back in Mérida at 5:20 pm. Cost is US$24 for adults, US$21 for children under 12. Book through a travel agency or contact Turismo Ferroviario directly at ☎ 926-17-22 or 926-20-57.

Minibus tours from Mérida to Izamal are offered by various companies. Most depart Mérida's Parque de Santa Lucía at 9 am and return by 5 pm.

Places to Stay & Eat

In front of the monastery are two budget hotels, *Hotel Kabul* and *Hotel Canto*, and several inexpensive eateries. The Canto is the more attractive of the two, with tiny skylights and colorful murals brightening the worn but clean rooms renting for US$5.50/8.75 single/double.

About eight blocks southwest on broad, quiet Avenida Zamná (Calle 39), between Calles 38 and 40, is the much nicer *Hotel Green River* (☎/fax 954-03-37, Avenida Zamna No 342). It has 16 air-con rooms with cable TV, minibar, purified water, telephone and private parking, all only 10 minutes' walk from the center of town. Rates are US$24 double. Try to get one of the newer rooms with good air-con.

Restaurant Kinich-Kakmó, on Calle 27 between Calles 28 and 30, is casual and extremely friendly, offering fan-cooled patio dining beside a garden. It specializes in traditional Yucatecan food, and you can have an absolute feast for less than US$10.

Getting There & Away

Oriente operates frequent buses between Mérida and Izamal (1½ hours, US$2.20) from its terminal in Mérida on Calle 67 between Calles 52 and 50. There are buses from Valladolid (2 hours, US$3) as well. Coming from Chichén Itzá you must change buses in Hóctun. Izamal's bus station is just one block west of the monastery.

Other departures from Izamal include an 8:30 am bus to Tizimín (US$4.75), as well as buses for Valladolid and Cancún (6 hours, US$7.25) at 6:30 am and 1 and 5 pm, and a 3 pm bus to Cobá (2½ hours, US$5), Tulum (3½ hours, US$6.25) and Playa del Carmen (4½ hours, US$8.50).

Driving from the west, turn north at Hóctun; from the east, at Kantunil.

CHICHÉN ITZÁ

The most famous and best restored of the Yucatán Peninsula's Mayan sites will awe even the most jaded visitor. Many mysteries of the Mayan astronomical calendar are made clear when one understands the design of the 'time temples' here.

At the vernal and autumnal equinoxes (March 20 to 21 and September 21 to 22), the sun produces a light-and-shadow illusion of the serpent ascending or descending the side of El Castillo's staircase. Chichén is mobbed on these dates, however, making it difficult to get close enough to see, and after the spectacle most of the site is closed to the public. The illusion is almost as good in the week preceding and following each equinox, and is re-created nightly in the light-and-sound show year-round.

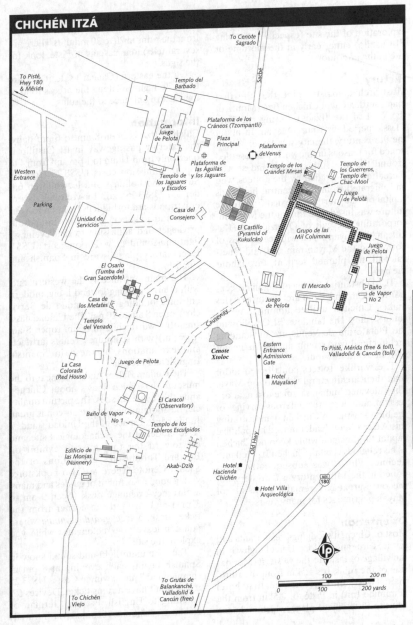

CHICHÉN ITZÁ

To Cenote Sagrado

To Pisté, Hwy 180 & Mérida

Templo del Barbado

Sacbé

Gran Juego de Pelota

Plataforma de los Cráneos (Tzompantli)

Plaza Principal

Plataforma de Venus

Templo de los Grandes Mesas

Templo de los Guerreros, Templo de Chac-Mool

Plataforma de las Águilas y los Jaguares

Templo de los Jaguares y Escudos

Western Entrance

Parking

Juego de Pelota

Casa del Consejero

El Castillo (Pyramid of Kukulcán)

Grupo de las Mil Columnas

Juego de Pelota

Unidad de Servicios

El Osario (Tumba del Gran Sacerdote)

El Mercado

Baño de Vapor No 2

Casa de los Metates

Templo del Venado

Juego de Pelota

Causeway

Cenote Xtoloc

Eastern Entrance Admissions Gate

To Pisté, Mérida (free & toll), Valladolid & Cancún (toll)

La Casa Colorada (Red House)

Juego de Pelota

Hotel Mayaland

Baño de Vapor No 1

El Caracol (Observatory)

Templo de los Tableros Esculpidos

Edificio de las Monjas (Nunnery)

Akab-Dzib

Hotel Hacienda Chichén

Hotel Villa Arqueológica

180

To Grutas de Balankanché, Valladolid & Cancún (free)

To Chichén Viejo

0   100   200 m
0   100   200 yards

YUCATÁN

Heat, humidity and crowds can be fierce; try to spend the night nearby and do your exploration of the site (especially climbing El Castillo) either early in the morning or late in the afternoon.

History

Most archaeologists agree that the first major settlement at Chichén Itzá (Mouth of the Well of the Itzáes), during the Late Classic period, was pure Mayan. In about the 9th century, the city was largely abandoned for reasons unknown. It was resettled around the late 10th century, and shortly thereafter was invaded by the Toltecs, who had migrated from their central highlands capital of Tula, north of Mexico City. Toltec culture was fused with that of the Maya, incorporating the cult of Quetzalcóatl (Kukulcán, in Mayan). You will see images of both Chac, the Mayan rain god, and Quetzalcóatl, the plumed serpent, throughout the city.

The substantial fusion of highland central Mexican and Puuc architectural styles makes Chichén unique among the Yucatán's ruins. The fabulous El Castillo and the Plataforma de Venus are outstanding architectural works built during the height of Toltec cultural input.

The warlike Toltecs contributed more than their architectural skills to the Maya. They elevated human sacrifice to a near obsession, and there are numerous carvings of the bloody ritual in Chichén demonstrating this. After a Maya leader moved his political capital to Mayapán while keeping Chichén as his religious capital, Chichén Itzá fell into decline. Why it was subsequently abandoned in the 14th century is a mystery, but the once-great city remained the site of Mayan pilgrimages for many years.

Orientation

Most of Chichén's lodgings, restaurants and services are ranged along 1km of highway in the village of Pisté, to the western (Mérida) side of the ruins. It's 1.5km from the ruins' main (west) entrance to the first hotel (Pirámide Inn) in Pisté, or 2.5km from the ruins to Pisté village plaza, which is shaded by a huge tree. Buses generally stop at the plaza; you can make the hot walk to and from the ruins in 20 to 30 minutes. There are several telephone casetas in Pisté; look for the signs.

On the eastern (Cancún) side, it's 1.5km from the highway along the access road to the eastern entrance to the ruins.

Information

Chichén Itzá is open 8 am to 6 pm daily; the interior passageway in El Castillo is open only from 11 am to 1 pm and from 4 to 5 pm. Admission costs US$8.25 (free on Sunday and holidays and for children under 13), US$3.25 extra for your video camera; tripods are forbidden. Hold on to your wristband ticket; it gives you in-and-out privileges and admission to that evening's light-and-sound show. Parking costs US$1. Explanatory plaques are in Spanish and English.

The main entrance is the western one, with a large parking lot and a big, modern entrance building (the Unidad de Servicios), open 8 am to 10 pm. The Unidad has a small but worthwhile museum (open 8 am to 5 pm) with sculptures, reliefs, artifacts and explanations of these in Spanish, English and French.

The Chilam Balam Auditorio, next to the museum, has video shows about Chichén and other Mexican sites. The picture quality can be abominable, but the air-con is great. In the central space of the Unidad stands a scale model of the archaeological site, and off toward the toilets is an exhibit on Edward Thompson's excavations of the Sacred Cenote. There are two bookstores with a good assortment of guides and maps, a currency-exchange desk (open 9 am to 3 pm) and, around the corner from the ticket desk, a free *guardaequipaje* where you can leave your belongings while you explore the site.

The 45-minute light-and-sound show in Spanish begins each evening at 8 pm in summer and 7 pm in winter. Cost is US$3.25 if you don't have a ruins ticket. Devices for listening to English, French, German or Italian translations (beamed via infrared) rent for US$2.75. Specify the language you need or it may not be broadcast.

Exploring the Ruins

El Castillo As you approach from the turnstiles at the Unidad de Servicios into the archaeological zone, El Castillo (also called the Pyramid of Kukulcán) rises before you in all its grandeur. The first temple here was pre-Toltec, built around AD 800, but the present 25m-high structure, built over the old one, has the plumed serpent sculpted along the stairways and Toltec warriors represented in the doorway carvings at the top of the temple.

The pyramid is actually the Mayan calendar formed in stone. Each of El Castillo's nine levels is divided in two by a staircase, making eighteen separate terraces that commemorate the eighteen 20-day months of the Vague Year. The four stairways have 91 steps each; add the top platform and the total is 365, the number of days in the year. On each facade of the pyramid are 52 flat panels, which are reminders of the 52 years in the Calendar Round.

To top it off, during the spring and autumn equinoxes, light and shadow form a series of triangles on the side of the north staircase that mimic the creep of a serpent (note the carved serpent's heads flanking the bottom of the staircase). The serpent ascends in March and descends in September.

The older pyramid *inside* El Castillo boasts a red jaguar throne with inlaid eyes and spots of jade, and also holds a chacmool figure. The entrance to the inner pyramid is at the base of El Castillo's north side; it's open only from 11 am to 3 pm and 4 to 5 pm. The dank air and steep, narrow stairway can make the climb a sweltering, slippery, claustrophobic experience.

Gran Juego de Pelota The great ball court, the largest and most impressive in Mexico, is only one of the city's eight courts, indicative of the importance the games held here. The court is flanked by temples at either end and bounded by towering parallel walls with stone rings cemented up high.

There is evidence that the ball game may have changed over the years. Some carvings

El Castillo, Chichén Itzá

YUCATÁN

JOHN ELK III

show players with padding on their elbows and knees, and it is thought that they played a soccerlike game with a hard rubber ball, the use of hands forbidden. Other carvings show players wielding bats; it appears that if a player hit the ball through one of the stone hoops, his team was declared the winner. It may be that during the Toltec period the losing captain, and perhaps his teammates as well, were sacrificed.

Along the walls of the ball court are stone reliefs, including scenes of decapitations of players. The court's acoustics are amazing – a conversation at one end can be heard 135m away at the other, and a clap produces multiple loud echoes.

Templo del Barbado & Templo de los Jaguares y Escudos

The structure at the northern end of the ball court, called the Temple of the Bearded Man after a carving inside of it, has some finely sculpted pillars and reliefs of flowers, birds and trees. The Temple of the Jaguars and Shields, built atop the southeast corner of the ball court's wall, has some columns with carved rattlesnakes and tablets with etched jaguars. Inside are faded mural fragments depicting a battle.

Plataforma de los Cráneos

The Platform of Skulls (*tzompantli* in Toltec) is between the Templo de los Jaguares and El Castillo. You can't mistake it, because the T-shaped platform is festooned with carved skulls and eagles tearing open the chests of men to eat their hearts. In ancient days this platform held the heads of sacrificial victims.

Plataforma de las Águilas y los Jaguares

Adjacent to the tzompantli, the carvings on the Platform of the Eagles and Jaguares depict those animals gruesomely grabbing human hearts in their claws. It is thought that this platform was part of a temple dedicated to the military legions responsible for capturing sacrificial victims.

Cenote Sagrado

A 300m rough stone road runs north (a five-minute walk) to the huge sunken well that gave this city its name. The Sacred Cenote is an awesome natural well, some 60m in diameter and 35m deep. The walls between the summit and the water's surface are ensnared in tangled vines and other vegetation. There are ruins of a small steam bath next to the cenote, as well as a modern drinks stand with toilets. See 'Dredging Chichén's Sacred Cenote' for the historical details.

Grupo de las Mil Columnas

Comprising the Templo de los Guerreros (Temple of the Warriors), Templo de Chac-Mool (Temple of Chac-Mool) and Baño de Vapor (Sweat House or Steam Bath), this group behind El Castillo takes its name (Group of the Thousand Columns) from the forest of pillars in front.

The platformed temple greets you with a statue of the reclining god, Chac, as well as stucco and stone-carved animal deities. The temple's roof, once supported by columns entwined with serpents, disappeared long ago.

Archaeological work in 1926 revealed the Temple of Chac-Mool beneath the Temple of the Warriors. You may enter via a stairway on the north side. The walls inside have badly deteriorated murals that are thought to portray the Toltecs' defeat of the Maya.

Just east of the Temple of the Warriors lies the rubble of a Mayan *baño de vapor* (sweat house), with an underground oven and drains for the water. The sweat houses were regularly used for ritual purification.

El Osario

The Ossuary, otherwise known as the Bonehouse or High Priest's Grave (Tumba del Gran Sacerdote), is a ruined pyramid southwest of El Castillo. As with most of the buildings in this southern section, the architecture is more Puuc than Toltec.

El Caracol

Called El Caracol (the Snail) by the Spaniards for its interior spiral staircase, this observatory is one of the most fascinating and important of all the Chichén Itzá buildings. Its circular design resembles some central highlands structures, although, surprisingly, not those of Toltec Tula. In a fusion of architectural styles and religious

Dredging Chichén's Sacred Cenote

Around 1900 Edward Thompson, a Harvard professor and US Consul to Yucatán, bought the hacienda that included Chichén Itzá for US$75. No doubt intrigued by local stories of female virgins being sacrificed to the Mayan deities by being thrown into the cenote, Thompson resolved to have the cenote dredged.

He imported dredging equipment and set to work. Gold and jade jewelry from all parts of Mexico and as far away as Colombia was recovered, along with other artifacts and a variety of human bones. Many of the artifacts were shipped to Harvard's Peabody Museum, but some have since been returned to Mexico.

Subsequent diving expeditions in the 1920s and '60s turned up hundreds of other valuable artifacts. It appears that all sorts of people, including children and old people, the diseased and the injured, and the young and the vigorous, were forcibly obliged to take an eternal swim in Chichén's Sacred Cenote.

imagery, there are Mayan Chac rain god masks over four external doors facing the cardinal directions. The windows in the observatory's dome are aligned with the appearance of certain stars at specific dates. From the dome the priests decreed the times for rituals, celebrations, corn-planting and harvests.

Edificio de las Monjas & Anexos

Thought by archaeologists to have been a palace for Mayan royalty, the Nunnery, with its myriad rooms, resembled a European convent to the conquistadors, hence their name for the building. The building's dimensions are imposing: Its base is 60m long, 30m wide and 20m high. The construction is Mayan rather than Toltec, although a Toltec sacrificial stone stands in front. Two smaller adjoining buildings are known as the Eastern Annex and the Southeastern Annex. The Nunnery is built in the Puuc style, while the Eastern Annex is Chenes and the Southeastern Annex is of the Itzáes.

Akab-Dzib

On the path east of the Nunnery, the Akab-Dzib is thought by some archaeologists to be the most ancient structure excavated here. The central chambers date from the 2nd century. 'Akab-Dzib' means 'Obscure Writing' in Maya and refers to the south-side Annex door, whose lintel

depicts a priest with a vase etched with hieroglyphics that have never been translated.

Chichén Viejo

Old Chichén comprises largely unrestored ruins, scattered about and hidden in the bush south of the Nunnery. The predominant architecture is Mayan, with Toltec additions and modifications. Though trails lead to the most prominent buildings, you may want to hire a guide.

Grutas de Balankanché

In 1959 a guide to the Chichén ruins was exploring a cave on his day off when he came upon a narrow passageway. The guide, whose name history records only as Gómez, followed the passageway for 300m, meandering through a series of caverns. In each, perched on mounds amid scores of glistening stalactites, were hundreds of ceremonial treasures the Maya had placed there 800 years earlier. In the years following the discovery, the ancient ceremonial objects were removed and studied. Eventually most of them were returned to the caves, placed exactly where they were found.

The caverns are 6km east of the ruins of Chichén Itzá and 2km east of the Hotel Dolores Alba on the highway to Cancún. Second-class buses heading east from Pisté toward Valladolid and Cancún will drop you at the Balankanché road. You'll find

YUCATÁN

the entrance to the caves 350m north of the highway.

As you approach the caves, you'll enter a botanical garden displaying native Yucatecan flora. In the entrance building is a little museum, a shop selling cold drinks and souvenirs, and a ticket booth. The museum features large photographs taken during the exploration of the caves and descriptions (in English, Spanish and French) of the Mayan religion and the offerings found in the caves. Also on display are photographs of modern-day Mayan ceremonies of Chac Ch'a Chaac, which continue to be held in all the villages in the Yucatán during times of drought and consist mostly of praying and numerous offerings of food to Chac.

Plan your visit for an hour when the compulsory 40-minute tour (minimum six people, maximum 30) with recorded narration will be given in a language you can understand: English is at 11 am, 1 and 3 pm; Spanish is at 9 am, noon 2 and 6 pm; and French is at 10 am. Tickets (US$4, US$2.25 Sunday) are sold daily between 9 am and 6 pm.

Places to Stay
Most of the lodgings convenient to Chichén and the caves are in the middle and top-end price brackets, but there are budget options. No matter what you plan to spend on a bed, don't hesitate to haggle in the off-season (May, June, September and October), when prices should be lower.

Budget There's *camping* at the agreeable Pirámide Inn, in Pisté (see Mid-Range). For US$4.50 per person you can pitch a tent or hang a hammock under a palapa, enjoy the Pirámide Inn's pool and watch satellite TV in the lobby. There are tepid showers, clean, shared toilet facilities and a safe place to stow your gear.

Posada Olalde, two blocks south of the highway by Artesanías Guayacán, is the best of Pisté's several small pensiones, offering seven clean, quiet and attractive rooms for US$13/17 double/triple. There are four even cheaper bungalows on the premises.

Posada Chac-Mool, just east of the Hotel Misión Chichén on the opposite (south)

side of the highway in Pisté, charges US$17 for a basic double with shower and fan. *Posada Novelo*, on the west side of the Pirámide Inn, charges the same for similar accommodations, but you can use the Stardust Inn's pool.

Hotel Posada Maya (☎ 9-851-02-11), a few dozen meters north of the highway (look for the sign), charges US$14 double for clean rooms with shower, fan and good beds. You can also hang a hammock here for US$4 a night. *Posada Poxil*, at the western end of town, charges the same for relatively clean, quiet rooms.

Mid-Range The *Hotel Dolores Alba* (☎ in Mérida 9-928-56-50, fax 9-928-31-63, www .doloresalba.com), on Hwy 180 at Km 122, is just over 3km east of the eastern entrance to the ruins and 2km west of the road to Balankanché, on the free highway to Cancún. It has 40 modern, air-con rooms facing two inviting swimming pools, and an air-con restaurant. The hotel will transport you to and from the Chichén ruins. Singles/doubles cost US$25/39.

The *Pirámide Inn* (☎ 9-851-01-15, fax 9-851-01-14, piramide@chichen.com.mx, www .piramide.inn.com) in Pisté, less than 2km from Chichén, was entirely renovated in 1999. All 42 rooms have air-con, and there's a book exchange and deep swimming pool. The restaurant serves international and vegetarian cuisine. Here, you're as close as you can stay to the archaeological zone's western entrance. Rooms cost US$44/49 double/triple.

Stardust Inn (☎ /fax 9-851-01-22), next to the Pirámide Inn, is an attractive place with two tiers of rooms surrounding a shaded swimming pool and restaurant. The 57 air-con rooms with TV cost US$48 double.

Top End All of these hotels have swimming pools, restaurants, bars, well-kept tropical gardens, comfortable guestrooms and tour groups coming and going. Several are very close to the ruins.

The *Hotel Mayaland* (☎ 9-851-01-28, fax 9-851-00-77, in the USA 800-235-4079, www mayaland.com), less than 100m from the eastern entrance to the archaeological zone, was built around 1923 and is the most gracious hotel in Chichén's vicinity. Rooms cost US$114/126 single/double.

Hotel Hacienda Chichén (in Mérida ☎ 9-924-21-50, fax 9-924-50-11, in the USA ☎ 800-624-8451, balamhtl@finred.com.mx, www.yucatanadventures.com.mx), about 200m farther from the entrance, is an elegant converted colonial estate that dates from the 16th century. It was here that the archaeologists who excavated Chichén during the 1920s lived. Their bungalows have been refurbished, new ones have been built and a swimming pool has been added. Bungalows cost US$70/80 double/triple, and have ceiling fans, air-con and private baths but no TVs or phones. Guests give it high marks.

Club Med's *Hotel Villa Arqueológica (☎ 9-851-00-34, fax 851-00-18, in the USA ☎ 800-258-2633, in France 801-802-803, chicchef01@clubmed.com)* is 300m from the east entrance. It is an exact clone of the villas at Cobá and Uxmal except the beds are larger and it somehow lacks their charm. The 40 air-con rooms are smallish but comfortable and cost US$65/76/93 single/double/triple.

On the western side of Chichén, in Pisté, *Hotel Misión Chichén-Itzá (☎ 9-851-00-22, fax 9-851-00-23, misionchichen@finred .com.mx)* is comfortable without being distinguished. Its 42 air-con rooms with cable TV cost US$75 double and are rather expensive for what you get.

Places to Eat

The *restaurant* in the Unidad de Servicios, at the western entrance to the archaeological zone, serves decent food at decent prices.

The highway through Pisté is lined with more than 20 small restaurants. The cheapest are the market eateries on the main plaza opposite the huge tree. The others are ranged along the highway from the town square to the Pirámide Inn. *Los Pájaros* and *Cocina Económica Chichén Itzá* are among the cheapest ones, serving sandwiches, omelets, enchiladas and quesadillas for around US$3. *Restaurant Sayil*,

facing the Hotel Misión Chichén, offers good values; bistec, cochinita or pollo pibil are US$2.75.

Restaurant Ruinas serves big plates of fruit for US$2 and hamburgers, sandwiches, fried chicken and spaghetti plates for around US$4. The *Stardust Inn* gets good reviews for its hearty US$3.25 breakfast.

The restaurant at the *Hotel Dolores Alba* specializes in Yucatecan food. Good pollo pibil costs US$5, fillet of red snapper US$7.

Across the street is the *Ik Kil Parque Ecoarqueológico*, an 'eco/archaeological park.' Basically, it's a wooden area with a cenote in the middle and a restaurant a short walk away. The cenote offers an absolutely divine plunge after a day of ruins-roaming (US$3.25 adults, US$1.75 kids). Buffet breakfast (US$4.50) is served from 9 am till noon, a buffet lunch (US$10) from noon till 5 pm. The food is very good.

The big *Restaurant Xaybe*, opposite the Hotel Misión Chichén, has decent food for about US$10 per person. Customers of the restaurant get to use its swimming pool free, but even if you don't eat here, you can still swim for about US$2.

Getting There & Away

Chichén's airstrip is north of the ruins, on the north side of the highway, 3km from Pisté's main plaza. Aerocaribe runs same-day roundtrip excursions by air from Cancún to Chichén Itzá, charging US$109 for the flight. Aerocozumel runs a similar service from Cozumel for US$118. More flight options should be available at a newly constructed international airport near Pisté.

Some of the fastest buses between Mérida, Valladolid and Cancún travel by the *cuota* (toll) highway and do not stop at Chichén Itzá. ADO has a ticket desk right in the souvenir shop in Chichén's Unidad de Servicios selling Oriente, Super Expresso and TRP tickets as well.

Six 2nd-class buses leave the ruins for Mérida between 9 am and 4:15 pm (US$4); eight for Valladolid and Cancún between 9:30 am and 4:30 pm (US$1.50 and US$9.25, respectively); one for Cobá and Tulum at

1:30 pm (US$3.25 and US$4.75, respectively); and two for Playa del Carmen, at 8:30 am and 1:30 pm (US$7).

First-class buses leave the ruins for Mérida at 3 and 7:15 pm (1½ hours, US$5.50), Valladolid at 11:15 am (30 minutes, US$2.25), Cancún at 4:30 pm (US$10.25), Cobá at 8 am (1½ hours, US$4.50), Tulum at 8 am and 2:45 pm (2½ hours, US$6) and Playa del Carmen at 2:45 and 4:30 pm (3½ hours, US$12).

Getting Around
Be prepared to walk at Chichén: from your hotel to the ruins, around the ruins, and back to your hotel, all under a broiling sun. When there's room, you can catch 2nd-class buses (see Getting There & Away) between Pisté and the ruins (US$0.50). For the Grutas de Balancanché, you can set out to walk early in the morning when it's cooler (it's 8km from Pisté, less if you're staying on the eastern side of the ruins) and then hope to hitch a ride or catch a bus for the return.

A few taxis are available in Pisté and sometimes at the Unidad de Servicios parking lot at Chichén Itzá (expect to pay US$2.75 from there into town), but you cannot depend on finding one unless you've made arrangements in advance. Despite a demand for them, taxis are fairly uncommon in these parts.

VALLADOLID
• population 53,000
Valladolid is small, manageable and affordable, with an easy pace of life, many handsome colonial buildings and several good hotels and restaurants. It's a fine place to stop, spend a day or three and get to know the real Yucatán, and makes a good base from which to visit the surrounding area, including Chichén Itzá.

History
Valladolid was once the Mayan ceremonial center of Zací (sah-**kee**). The initial attempt at conquest in 1543 by Francisco de Montejo, nephew of Montejo the Elder, was thwarted by fierce Mayan resistance, but the Elder's son Montejo the Younger ultimately took the town. The Spanish laid out a new city on the classic colonial plan.

During much of the colonial era, Valladolid's physical isolation from Mérida kept it relatively autonomous from royal rule. The Maya of the area suffered brutal exploitation, which continued after Mexican independence. Barred from entering many areas of the city, the Maya made Valladolid their first point of attack in 1847 when the War of the Castes began. After a two-month siege, the city's defenders were finally overcome. Many fled to the safety of Mérida; the rest were slaughtered.

Today Valladolid is a prosperous seat of agricultural commerce, with some light industry thrown in. It's a relaxed place, and many *vallisetanos* speak Spanish with the soft and clear Mayan accent.

Orientation & Information
The old highway passes through the center of town, though all signs direct motorists to the toll road north of town. To follow the old highway eastbound, take Calle 41; westbound, Calle 39.

Most hotels are on the main plaza, called Parque Francisco Cantón Rosado, or within a block or two of it. On the east side of the plaza is the Ayuntamiento (City Hall), where the tourist office (☎ 856-20-63 ext 15) has maps and somewhat accurate information and is open 9 am to 8 pm daily (except during siesta).

A few doors north is the main post office, open 8 am to 3 pm weekdays. Various banks, most with ATMs, are near the center of town and are generally open 9 am to 5 pm weekdays, 9 am to 1 pm Saturday.

Most Internet places in town charge a hefty US$0.11 per minute and have annoying software of one form or another. A happy exception is @lbert's PC, on Calle 43 near Calle 40, which charges US$1.65 a half hour. It's open from 9 am to 2 pm and 4 to 9 pm Monday to Saturday.

To preserve the colonial flavor of the center, Valladolid has limited the posting of signs by businesses to those approved by the city. This can sometimes make it difficult to find an establishment; you need to keep

VALLADOLID

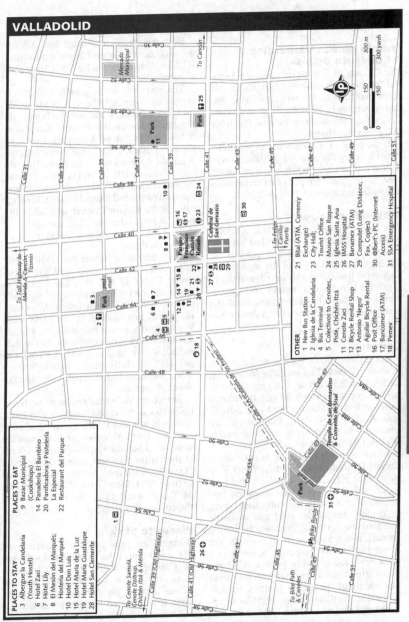

PLACES TO STAY
3   Albergue la Candelaria (Youth Hostel)
6   Hotel Zací
7   Hotel Lily
8   El Mesón del Marqués; Hostería del Marqués
10 Hotel Don Luis
15 Hotel María de la Luz
19 Hotel María Guadalupe
28 Hotel San Clemente

PLACES TO EAT
9   Bazar Municipal (Cookshops)
14 Panadería El Bambino
20 Panificadora y Pastelería La Especial
22 Restaurant del Parque

OTHER
1   New Bus Station
2   Iglesia de la Candelaria
4   Bus Terminal
5   Colectivos to Cenotes; Pisté, Chichén Itzá
11 Cenote Zací
12 Bicycle Rental Shop
13 Antonio 'Negro' Aguilar Bicycle Rental
16 Post Office
17 Bancomer (ATM)
18 Pemex
21 Bital (ATM, Currency Exchange)
23 City Hall; Tourist Office
24 Museo San Roque
25 Iglesia Santa Ana
26 IMSS Hospital
27 Banamex (ATM)
29 Computel (Long Distance, Fax, Copies)
30 @lbert's PC (Internet Access)
31 SSA Emergency Hospital

YUCATÁN

a keen eye out for small cardboard signs on open doors.

Templo de San Bernardino & Convento de Sisal

The Church of San Bernardino de Siena and the Convent of Sisal, 1.5km southwest of the plaza, are said to be the oldest Christian structures in Yucatán. They were constructed in 1552 to serve the dual functions of fortress and church.

If the convent is open, you can go inside. Apart from the likeness of the Virgin of Guadalupe on the altar, the church is relatively bare, having been stripped of its decorations during the uprisings of 1847 and 1910.

Museo San Roque

This church turned museum is less than a block east of the plaza. It is modest but very nicely done, with models and exhibits on the history of the city and the region, and displays of traditional Mayan religious offerings and ceremonies, masks and instruments, medicines, handicrafts and food. It's open from 9 am to 9 pm daily; a donation is requested.

Cenotes

Among the region's several underground cenotes is **Cenote Zací**, on Calle 36 between Calles 37 and 39. It's set in a park that also holds an open-air amphitheater, traditional stone-walled thatched houses and a small zoo. Zací is vast, dark, impressive and covered with a layer of algae and bat guano. It's open 9 am to sunset daily; US$1.

More enticing but less accessible is **Cenote Dzitnup** (also called Xkakah), 7km west of the plaza. It's artificially lit and very swimmable, and a massive limestone formation dripping with stalactites hangs from its ceiling. Across the road and a couple hundred meters closer to town is **Cenote Samulá**, which at the time of research was about to open to the public. A sneak preview revealed a lovely pool with *álamo* roots stretching down many meters from the middle of the ceiling to drink from it. The guide said there were *aluxes* (Mayan leprechauns) that were carved into the ceiling

centuries ago, but there was no light yet to confirm this.

Both cenotes sport eyeless fish. Admission to Dzitznup (open 7 am to 6 pm daily) is US$1.30; Samulá will be US$1.10 until it gains popularity.

The best route from the center of town is via the old colonial Calle 41A (Calzada de los Frailes), which leads past the Templo de San Bernardino and the convent. Keep them to your left as you skirt the park, then turn right on Calle 49. This opens into tree-lined Avenida de los Frailes and hits the old highway. Turn left (if you're on a bicycle, take the *ciclopista* – bike path – paralleling the road) and head toward Mérida. Turn left again at the sign for Dzitnup and follow the road for just under 2km; Samulá will be off this road to the right and Dzitnup a little farther on the left.

You can rent a bicycle for US$0.55 per hour from one of the shops on Calle 44 between Calles 39 and 41. Their signage is minimal; look for Antonio 'Negro' Aguilar's place (☎ 856-21-25, vinicio@chichen.com). He played pro baseball in the 1950s for a Washington Senators minor-league affiliate and is something of a character. His rentals include a lock, map and advice. Check out any bike carefully before putting money down. Pedaling to the cenotes should take about 20 minutes.

Taxis from Valladolid's main plaza charge US$8.70 for the excursion there and back, with an hour's wait (this is a local price; your rate may vary). You also can hop aboard a westbound bus, ask the driver to let you off at the Dzitnup turnoff, then walk the final 2km (20 minutes) to the site; or catch a colectivo taxi (US$0.55) from Calle 39 at Calle 44. There's a restaurant and drinks stand at the entrance to Dzitnup.

Places to Stay

Budget Near press time word was received of the opening of the HI-affiliated *Albergue la Candelaria* (☎/fax 85-22-67, fidery@sureste.com, Calle No 201-F), on the north side of the park across from Iglesia Candelaria. It is reported to have a full kitchen, self-service laundry area, a cable TV room and Internet access. The 40 beds (with private lockers) run US$7 each (US$6.50 with hostel card).

Hotel María Guadalupe (☎ 856-20-68, *Calle 44 No 188*), on Calle 44 between Calles 39 and 41, is a study in modernity in this colonial town. The eight simple rooms cost US$11 double with private shower and fan.

The *Hotel Lily* (☎ 856-21-63, *Calle 44 No 190*) is cheap and basic but reasonably priced with 20 rooms; with fan they're US$9.25 single and US$11 double for one bed, $15.75 for two. The one air-con room has three beds and costs US$24.

Hotel Don Luis (☎ 856-20-08, *Calle 39 No 191*), at the corner of Calles 39 and 38, is a motel-style structure with a palm-shaded patio, swimming pool, a restaurant serving three meals and acceptable rooms for US$11/13/15.20 single/double/triple with fan, US$12/14/17.40 with air-con.

Mid-Range & Top End All of the hotels listed here have restaurants, free secure parking facilities and swimming pools. The well-kept *Hotel Zací* (☎/fax 856-21-67, *Calle 44 No 191*), between Calles 37 and 39, has 48 rooms with colonial decor and TVs around a quiet courtyard with a bar. Rooms cost US$17/22/28 single/double/triple with fan, US$22/29/34 with air-con.

Agreeable *Hotel San Clemente* (☎/fax 856-22-08, *Calle 42 No 206*), with nearly identical decor, is at the southwest corner of the main plaza. The 64 rooms cost US$23/27 with air-con and cable TV.

The *Hotel María de la Luz* (☎/fax 856-20-71, *Calle 42 No 193*, email maria_luz@ chichen.com.mx, www.xaac.com.playacar /maria.html) on Calle 42 near Calle 39 at the northwest corner of the plaza, has serviceable air-con rooms around a pool for US$22 double, US$33 triple.

Best of the lot is *El Mesón del Marqués* (☎ 856-20-73, fax 856-22-80, h_marques@ chichen.com.mx, *Calle 39 No 203*), on the north side of the main plaza. It has two colonial courtyards, the best restaurant in town and guestrooms with air-con and ceiling fans. Rates are US$38 double for the older, smaller rooms, US$49 for the newer, bigger ones.

Places to Eat

Valladolid has several good bakeries, including *Panificadora y Pastelería La Especial*, on Calle 41 less than a block west of the plaza, and *Panadería El Bambino*, on Calle 39 a half block west of the plaza.

The *Bazar Municipal* is a collection of open-air market-style cookshops at the corner of Calles 39 and 40 (the northeast corner of the plaza), popular for their big, cheap breakfasts. At lunch and dinner, *comidas corridas* (set meals) cost US$2.20 – but ask before you order. Try Doña Mary, Sergio's Pizza, La Rancherita or El Amigo Casiano.

The *Hotel María de la Luz* (see Places to Stay, earlier) has breezy tables overlooking the plaza. The breakfast buffet costs US$3.80, the comida corrida is the same price. The comida corrida is only US$2 at the old-fashioned, high-ceilinged *Restaurant del Parque*; service is amiable if sometimes bumbling, and the menu's English translations are fun to read.

The best value in town is the *Hostería del Marqués*, the dining room of the Hotel El Mesón del Marqués, on the north side of the main plaza. A three-course meal with beer and tip costs about US$10. If you won't be visiting Campeche, try the superb *pan de cazón* (dogfish – a small shark – in layers of tortillas; a *campechano* specialty).

Getting There & Away

Bus Valladolid has two bus terminals: the convenient old one on Calle 39 at Calle 46, two blocks from the plaza, and a newer terminal five blocks farther northwest, on Calle 37 at Calle 54. Ticket agents claim that any bus stopping at one stops at the other, but you might want to check with your driver. To further complicate things, many 1st-class buses running between Cancún and Mérida don't go into town at all; instead they drop you near the off-ramp from the toll road, where, ideally, a bus will be waiting to shuttle you into town (at no extra charge). These shuttles drop you at the northwest corner of the plaza.

The principal services are Oriente and Expresso (2nd-class) and Super Expresso

YUCATÁN

(1st-class). Prices and travel times given are for 1st-class unless there is only 2nd-class service; in most cases 2nd-class costs about 30% less and takes at least one-third longer.

Cancún 165km, 2 hours; nine 1st-class (US$7), 15 2nd-class, 7:45 am to 10 pm

Chetumal 357km, 7½ hours; two 2nd-class (US$10)

Chichén Itzá 40km, 45 minutes; 17 2nd-class Mérida-bound buses from 7 am to 10 pm (US$1.50); ask driver to drop you at the turnoff to the ruins

Chiquilá (for Isla Holbox) 155km, 2½ hours; one 2nd-class at 2:30 pm (US$5)

Cobá 60km, 1 hour; three 1st-class (US$2.50), three 2nd-class

Izamal 115km, 2 hours; three 2nd-class (US$3)

Mérida 165km, 3 hours; nine 1st-class (US$7), 17 2nd-class

Playa del Carmen 169km, 3 hours; six 1st-class (US$9.25), three 2nd-class

Tizimín 51km, 1 hour; 10 2nd-class (US$1.75)

Tulum 106km, 2 hours; three 1st-class (US$4.25), three 2nd-class

Taxi Often faster and more comfortable than buses are the shared taxis (many of them Ford vans, some VW combis; look for air-con) that leave for various points as soon as their seats are filled. They congregate outside the old bus terminal, along the plaza and elsewhere in town, from about 7 am to 8:30 pm. Direct services to Mérida (from the terminal, US$5.50) and Cancún (from west side of the plaza, US$6.50) take 2 hours; with stops they're US$3.75. Pisté and Chichén Itzá (40 minutes) are US$2.25.

EK' BALAM

Due north of Valladolid, 17km along the road to Tizimín, is the turnoff for this archaeological site, 10.5km farther past fields and through hamlets teeming with pigs.

Ek' Balam is open 8 am to 5 pm; admission is US$1.30 (plus a tip if you follow the guide). Much is still covered by vegetation, but excavations and restoration continue to add to the sights, including an interesting ziggurat-like structure near the entrance, a fine arch and a ball court. Perhaps most impressive is the main pyramid, a massive, towering structure sporting a huge monster-mouth with 360° dentition.

The guide, Sr Anastasio Vaas, can show you cisterns, a subterranean entry, a *sacbé* (ancient ceremonial road, paved with limestone), several stelae with high relief carving and more. From the top of the pyramid, the landscape's flatness is broken only by a few small, tree-covered 'hills' on the horizon – which are not hills at all, but pyramids marking other once-great Mayan cities.

A roundtrip taxi ride from Valladolid with an hour's wait at the ruins will cost around US$18, though negotiation can bring this down.

TIZIMÍN
• population 38,000

Travelers bound for Río Lagartos change buses in Tizimín, a ranching center. There is little to warrant an overnight stay, but the tree-filled Parque Principal is pleasant, particularly at sundown.

Two great colonial structures – Parroquia Los Santos Reyes (Church of the Three Wise Kings) de Tizimín and its former Franciscan monastery (the ex-convento) – are worth a look. Five lengthy blocks from the plaza, northwest on Calle 51, is a modest zoo, the Parque Zoológico de la Reina.

Both Bital, on the southwest side of the parque, and Bancomer, at Calles 48 and 51, have ATMs.

Places to Stay & Eat

The *Posada María Antonia* (☎ 863-23-84, fax 863-28-57, Calle 50 No 408), on the east side of the Parque de la Madre, has three fan-cooled and nine air-con rooms at US$14.75 and US$15.75, respectively, for up to four people. You can place international calls at the reception desk. *Hotel San Jorge* (☎ 863-20-37, Calle 53 No 211) has basic rooms for US$17.50 double with fan, US$19.50 with air-con. Avoid room No 3.

Hotel San Carlos (☎ 863-20-94, Calle 54 No 407) has 27 clean, quiet rooms with TV and two double beds for US$16.25 double with fan, US$19 with good air-con. Carlos, the manager, speaks excellent English, is

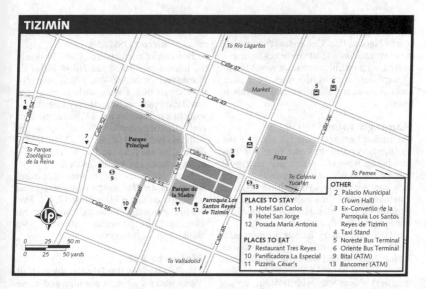

TIZIMÍN

To Río Lagartos

Calle 47

Market

Calle 49

Parque
Principal

To Parque
Zoológico
de la Reina

Calle 51

Plaza

To Colonia
Yucatán

To Pemex

Parque de
la Madre

Parroquia Los
Santos Reyes
de Tizimín

Calle 55

pedestrian mall

Calle 53

To Valladolid

0   25   50 m
0   25   50 yards

PLACES TO STAY
1 Hotel San Carlos
8 Hotel San Jorge
12 Posada María Antonia

PLACES TO EAT
7 Restaurant Tres Reyes
10 Panificadora La Especial
11 Pizzería César's

OTHER
2 Palacio Municipal
 (Town Hall)
3 Ex-Convento de la
 Parroquia Los Santos
 Reyes de Tizimín
4 Taxi Stand
5 Noreste Bus Terminal
6 Oriente Bus Terminal
9 Bital (ATM)
13 Bancomer (ATM)

very knowledgeable about the region and can arrange horseback rides, a popular activity here in cowboy country.

The *market*, a block west of the bus stations, has the usual cheap eateries. The bakery ***Panificadora La Especial*** is on Calle 55 down a pedestrian lane from the Parque Principal. Festive ***Restaurant Tres Reyes***, at the corner of Calles 52 and 53, opens early for breakfast and is a favorite of town notables. Lunch or dinner costs US$4.25 to US$7.50; try the excellent natural juices. Popular ***Pizzería César's***, on the south side of Parque de la Madre, serves pizza, pasta, sandwiches and burgers. Few items are over US$5.

Getting There & Away

Oriente (2nd-class only) and Noreste (1st- and 2nd-class) have bus terminals around the corner from one another, just east of the market.

Cancún 194km, 3 to 3½ hours; seven Oriente between 3:30 am and 8 pm (US$6.50), 10 Noreste 1st-class (US$7) and 2nd-class from 3 am to 6 pm

Cobá 111km, 3 hours; one Oriente at 12:30 pm (US$6.50), continuing to Tulum (US$7) and Playa del Carmen (US$9.25)

Izamal 109km; one Oriente at 11:20 am (US$4.75)

Mérida 180km, 2¼ hours; two Oriente at 6 and 11:20 am (US$6.50), 12 Noreste 1st-class (US$7) and 2nd-class between 5:45 am and 6 pm

Playa del Carmen 270km; two Oriente (US$9.25) at 8:30 am and 12:30 pm (see Cobá listing)

Río Lagartos 50km, 1 hour; seven Noreste between 5 am and 7:45 pm (US$2); some buses continue another 12 km west to San Felipe

Tulum 207km; see Cobá listing

Valladolid 51km, 1 hour; 14 Oriente between 4:30 am and 7 pm (US$1.75)

Taxis to Río Lagartos or San Felipe charge US$16.25.

RÍO LAGARTOS
• population 1900

The most spectacular flamingo colony in Mexico warrants a trip to this fishing village, 103km north of Valladolid, 52km north of Tizimín, lying within the Ría Lagartos Biosphere Reserve. The mangrove-lined estuary is also home to snowy egrets, red egrets, tiger herons, snowy white ibis, hundreds of other bird species and a small number of the crocodiles that gave the town its name (Alligator River).

YUCATÁN

The Maya knew the place as Holkobén, and used it as a rest stop on their way to the nearby lagoons (Las Coloradas) from which they extracted salt. (Salt continues to be extracted, on a much vaster scale now.) Spanish explorers mistook the inlet for a river and the crocs for alligators, and the rest is history.

Flamingo Tours

The brilliant orange-red birds can turn the horizon fiery when they take wing. For their well-being, however, please ask your boat captain not to frighten the birds into flight. You can generally get to within 100m of flamingos before they walk or fly away. Depending on your luck, you'll see either hundreds or thousands of them.

The four primary haunts, in increasing distance from town, are Punta Garza, Yoluk, Necopal and Nahochín (all flamingo feeding spots named for nearby mangrove patches). Prices vary with boat, group size (maximum five) and destination. The lowest you can expect to pay is around US$33; a full boat to Nahochín runs US$44 to US$55.

To hire a boat, negotiate with one of the eager men in the waterfront kiosks near the entrance to town. They speak English and will connect you with a captain (who usually doesn't). Alternatively, visit the Restaurante-Bar Isla Contoy (turn left when you reach the water) and hire Diego Núñez Martínez or his partner (call him Ismael). They speak English and Italian, have formal training as guides and naturalists, and are up on the area's fauna and flora. They also offer night rides looking for crocodiles and, from May through September, sea turtles. Call Holkobén Expeditions at ☎ 862-00-00 or email nunez@chichen.com.

Places to Stay

Most residents aren't sure of the town's street names, and signs are few. The road into town is Calle 10, whose northern end is the waterfront Calle 13. *Posada Leyli* (☎ *862-01-06*), on Calle 14 (two blocks south of Calle 10) at Calle 11, has six pleasant, fan-cooled rooms: two singles with shared bath cost US$11, two singles with private bath go for US$13, while two doubles with private bath cost US$18.50.

Two blocks north, where Calle 14 meets the lagoon, you'll find the *Hotel Villas de Pescadores* (☎ *862-00-48*), which offers 14 very clean new rooms with good cross-ventilation (all face the estuary), three suites with balconies, air-con, TV, sofa, minibar and kitchenette for US$49 and nine rooms with two beds and fan for US$27 or US$33 depending on floor and view. The owner rents bicycles and kayaks as well.

Nearly completed at the time of research was the *Hotel Hol Kobén* (www.riolagartos .com.mx) on Calle 14 at Calle 17. If it lives up to the manager's claims, it will be quite nice, and the projected rate of US$60 double quite reasonable.

Places to Eat

The *Restaurante-Bar Isla Contoy*, on Calle 19 at water's edge, is popular and serves seafood for US$4 to US$5. It's a good place to meet other travelers and form groups for the boat tours.

At the *Restaurant Los Negritos*, on Calle 10 near the entrance of town, the *filete de camarones* (grouper stuffed with shrimp and lots of mayonnaise) is the house specialty. The fried fish or *ceviche de pulpo* (octopus ceviche) costs US$5.

Getting There & Away

Noreste has five direct buses to Tizimín (50km, US$2) and five to Mérida (4½ hours, US$6.75) between 5:30 am and 3:30 pm; three to Cancún (US$7.20), at 11 am and 4 and 5 pm daily except Wednesday. Noreste also offers semidirect service to Tizimín (US$1.40) hourly from 5:30 am to 5:30 pm and to San Felipe (20 minutes, US$0.75), seven times per day between 6:30 am and 5:30 pm.

RESERVA DE LA BIÓSFERA RÍA LAGARTOS

If you'd like to explore the biosphere reserve, be sure to stop at its office south of town (☎ 863-43-90, rialarg@tizimin.com.mx, www.rialagartos.org.mx) at the crossroads for San Felipe and the Las Coloradas salt-extraction facility. Some areas require permission to enter; at times someone from the office is available to escort groups.

About 10km east (toward Las Coloradas) of the junction the road crosses the estuary via a wooden bridge where locals often fish by casting nets. A **croc** or two can sometimes be seen lurking in the water there. On the way to the bridge a **nature trail** leads into mangrove hummocks from the right side of the road. *Ría*, by the way, means 'estuary,' so the reserve's name, unlike the town's, is geographically correct.

SAN FELIPE

This seldom-visited fishing village 12km west of Río Lagartos makes a nice day trip from there. Birding and beach are the main attractions, just across the estuary at Punta Holohit.

At friendly, clean and cleverly constructed *Hotel San Felipe de Jesús* (☎ 863-37-38, fax 862-20-36, sanfelip@prodigy.net.mx) – turn left at the water and proceed 100m – six of the 18 rooms are large and have private balconies and water views. All rooms have good cross-ventilation and are super bargains at US$24 to US$35. The restaurant offers tasty seafood at low prices.

By public transportation you pretty much have to come through Río Lagartos (20 minutes, US$0.75); to save time, take a taxi from Tizimín. From San Felipe, buses to Tizimín (US$2) leave at 5:45, 8:30 and 10 am, noon, and 3 and 6 pm, and continue on to Valladolid (US$2.75). There are no taxis stationed in Río Lagartos or San Felipe.

Campeche State

Though it's the least visited of the three states on the Yucatán Peninsula, Campeche has a lot to offer the traveler and is proudly preparing to take its place among Mexico's top tourist destinations.

CAMPECHE

• population 182,000

In late 1999 UNESCO added the city of Campeche to its list of World Heritage Sites. *Campechanos* are rightly proud of this, and are doing an excellent job of improving the

---

Highlights

• The ruins, jungle and wildlife of the Calakmul Biosphere Reserve, Mexico's largest

• Campeche city's rich history, colonial center and pirate-repelling fortifications

• The picturesque ancient Mayan site, Edzná

• Bécal, a sleepy town where many of the residents make hats in caves

---

colonial heart of the city while retaining the best of the old (Mérida, take note!). Structures are being restored, repainted and, in some cases, reconstructed from scratch. Several sites were closed for such work at the time of research, but when they reopen they should be better than ever.

During Campeche's heyday, many wealthy Spanish families built mansions that still stand. Two segments of the city's famous wall have survived the times as well, as have no fewer than seven of the *baluartes* (bastions or bulwarks) that were built into it, and two perfectly preserved colonial forts guard the city's outskirts.

Adding to Campeche's charm is its location on the Gulf of Mexico. A broad waterfront boulevard provides the perfect place for cloud- and sunset-watching; add a thunderstorm rolling in off the Gulf and you have a sound-and-light show nonpareil.

History

Once a Mayan trading village called Ah Kim Pech (Lord Sun Sheep-Tick), Campeche was first entered by the Spaniards in 1517. The Maya resisted, and for nearly a quarter century the Spaniards were unable to conquer the region. Colonial Campeche was founded in 1531, but later abandoned owing to Mayan hostility. By 1540 the conquistadors, led by Francisco de Montejo the Younger, had gained enough control to establish a settlement that survived. They named it Villa de San Francisco de Campeche.

The settlement soon flourished as the major port of the Yucatán Peninsula, but it suffered from pirate attacks from an early date (see the boxed text 'Pirates!').

Today the local economy is largely driven by shrimping and offshore petroleum extraction, and the prosperity brought by these activities has helped fund the downtown area's renovation. Unfortunately, the benefits of this wealth have not yet trickled down to several of Campeche's poorer residential areas.

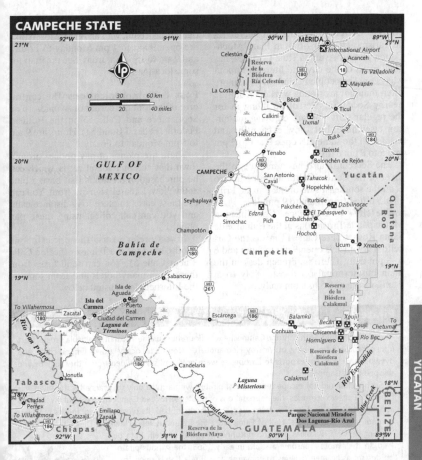

CAMPECHE STATE

Orientation

Though the bastions still stand, the city walls themselves have been mostly razed and replaced by Avenida Circuito Baluartes, which rings the city center just the way the walls once did. Many of the streets making up the circuit are paved with stone taken from the demolished wall. An ambitious plan to restore the entire wall is currently on hold.

According to the compass, Campeche is oriented with its waterfront to the northwest, but tradition and convenience hold that the water is to the west, inland is east

(we observe that rule in the following text). The center is on a grid of numbered streets; those running north-south have even numbers, east-west streets have odd numbers. Street numbers ascend by twos toward the south and the east.

A multilane boulevard with bicycle and pedestrian paths on its seaward side extends several kilometers in either direction along Campeche's shore, changing names a few times. The stretch closest to the city center is named Avenida Adolfo Ruiz Cortínez, and is commonly referred to as *el malecón* (the seafront drive).

Information

Tourist Offices The state-run Secretaría de Turismo (☎ 816-67-67), in Plaza Moch-Couoh just off Avenida Ruiz Cortínez, has good maps of the city and literature about what's on. The people behind the desk more often than not are young workers from the nearby Social Services office filling in for the regular staff who are enjoying the air-con elsewhere, but they're friendly and helpful all the same. It's open 9 am to 3 pm and 5 to 8 pm daily.

The Secretaría also has a module in the foyer of the Centro Cultural Casa Número 6, on the southwest side of the Parque Principal, staffed from 9 am to 9 pm daily.

The city's tourist office (Coordinación Municipal de Turismo) is in the Baluarte de Santa Rosa, where Calle 14 meets the Circuito. The office is open 9 am to 2 pm and 6 to 8 pm daily. There's a branch desk in the main bus terminal open ostensibly from 9 am to 1 pm and 5 to 8 pm daily.

Money It's hard to spit in Campeche without hitting a bank with an ATM. Most banks are open 9 am to 4 pm Monday to Friday, and 9 am to 1 pm Saturday. See the map for some locations.

Post & Communications The central post office is at the corner of Avenida 16 de Septiembre and Calle 53, in the Edificio Federal (Federal Building). Hours are 9 am to 5 pm Monday to Friday.

There are plenty of pay phones around town that accept Ladatel cards, which can be purchased in all stores that have a blue and yellow 'Ladatel' sign out front. You can use these cards to place long-distance calls, and you can call collect using these pay phones.

If you prefer to use the pricier phone booths, head for the Telmex office on Calle 8 near Calle 51. You can send faxes from there, from many hotels and from some of the Internet places listed below.

Pirates!

As early as the mid-16th century, Campeche was flourishing as the Yucatán Peninsula's major port under the careful planning of Viceroy Hernández de Córdoba. Locally grown timber, chicle and dyewoods were major exports to Europe, as were gold and silver mined from other regions and shipped from Campeche.

Such wealth did not escape the notice of pirates, who arrived only six years after the town was founded. For two centuries, the depredations of pirates terrorized Campeche. Not only were ships attacked, but the port itself was invaded, its citizens robbed, its women raped and its buildings burned. In the buccaneers' Hall of Fame were the infamous John Hawkins, Diego the Mulatto, Laurent de Gaff, Barbillas and the notorious 'Pegleg' himself, Pata de Palo. In their most gruesome assault, in early 1663, the various pirate hordes set aside their rivalries to converge as a single flotilla upon the city, where they massacred many of Campeche's citizens.

This tragedy finally spurred the Spanish monarchy to take preventive action, but it was not until five years later, in 1668, that work on the 3.5m-thick ramparts began. After 18 years of building, a 2.5km hexagon incorporating eight strategically placed *baluartes*, or bastions, surrounded the city. A segment of the ramparts extended out to sea so that ships literally had to sail into a fortress, easily defended, to gain access to the city.

With Campeche nearly impregnable, the pirates turned their attention to other ports and ships at sea. In 1717, the brilliant naval strategist Felipe de Aranda began a campaign against the buccaneers, and eventually made this area of the Gulf safe from piracy.

At the time of research Campeche had few Internet facilities, but more will certainly sprout rapidly. Telmex has three standup terminals in their office for demonstrating the Internet to the public; don't abuse the privilege. En Red Cibercafé, at the corner of Calle 12 and Avenida Circuito Baluartes Sur, charges US$1 for 30 minutes. It has air-con and sells coffee and sodas as well. The café is open 9:30 am to 11:30 pm Monday to Friday, 11:30 am to 9:30 pm Saturday and Sunday.

More low-key and professional, though a few blocks north of town center, is Cibernet (☎ 816-67-02, jogusa@latinmail.com), Calle 12 No 48 at Calle 45. It charges US$2.25 an hour for decent connections and is open 9:30 am to midnight weekdays, and 9:30 am to 3 pm and 6 to 10 pm Saturday.

Laundry Lavandería Tintorería Campeche is on Calle 55 between Calles 12 and 14. You can drop off clothing here in the morning and usually get it back cleaned, dried and folded in the afternoon. Cost is about US$4 for a large load. Open 8 am to 6 pm Monday to Friday, 8 am to 4 pm Saturday.

Medical Services The IMSS Hospital is at the corner of Avenida Circuito Baluartes Este and Avenida Central. In an emergency, call the Red Cross at ☎ 815-24-11.

Dangers & Annoyances The center's smooth cobblestone streets are slippery even when dry. When the slightest bit wet they can be like ice. Additionally, some sidewalks are quite high and have abrupt drops in odd places. Tread carefully!

Walking Tour

Seven of the eight bulwarks still stand, and all can be visited on a 2km walk around Avenida Circuito Baluartes, taking in other sights on the way. Because of traffic, some of the walk is not very pleasant; you might want to limit your excursion to the first three or four baluartes described, which house museums and gardens.

First stop, at the corner of Calles 10 and 63, the **ex-Templo de San José** is a visual delight. Its facade is covered in striking blue and yellow tiles, and one spire is topped by a lighthouse complete with weathervane. The former church was being remodeled at the time of research; it usually hosts art exhibitions, and on Tuesday evening at 7 pm free performances of folkloric dance and music.

A block west is the bizarre, ultramodern **Palacio Legislativo** (Congress Building). Undoubtedly meant to evoke a baluarte with slitted windows, it looks more like the Mothership landing. Just south along Calle 8 is its colonial inspiration, the **Baluarte de San Carlos**, which contains the modest Museo de la Ciudad. There's a good scale model of the old city, historical photos, specimens of dyewood and the like. You can visit the dungeon and look out over the sea from the roof. Open 8 am to 2 pm Monday, 8 am to 8 pm Tuesday to Saturday, 8 am to 1 pm Sunday; donation requested.

Head north back along Calle 8 to its intersection with Calle 59 to see the **Puerta del Mar** (Sea Gate), which provided access to the city from the sea before the area to the northwest was filled in. The gate was demolished in 1893 but rebuilt in 1957 when its historical value was realized. A short section of recently re-erected wall connects the gate to the **Baluarte de Nuestra Señora de la Soledad**, which holds the Museo de Estelas Maya. Many of the Mayan artifacts here are badly weathered, but the precise line drawing next to each stone shows you what the designs once looked like. The bulwark also has an interesting exhibition of colonial Campeche. Among the antiquities are 17th- and 18th-century seafaring equipment and armaments used to battle pirate invaders. You can visit the roof here as well. The museum is open 8 am to 6:30 pm Tuesday to Saturday, 8 am to 1 pm Sunday, and 8 am to 2 pm Monday. Admission is US$0.50.

Work has begun on a replica of the original Palacio Municipal in its original location in front of the Baluarte de Nuestra Señora.

Across Calle 8 from the baluarte is the **Parque Principal**, Campeche's main plaza. It's a pleasant place where locals go to sit and think, chat, smooch, plot, snooze, have their shoes shined or stroll and cool off after

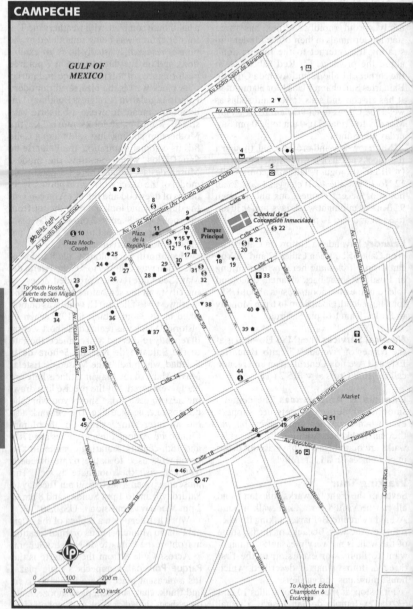

CAMPECHE

GULF OF MEXICO

PLACES TO STAY
3 Hotel Del Mar
7 Hotel Baluartes
16 Hotel Campeche
21 Posada del Ángel
27 Hotel Castelmar
28 Hotel Roma
29 Hotel América
34 Hotel del Paseo
37 Hotel López
39 Hotel Colonial

PLACES TO EAT
2 San Francisco de
   Asís Supermarket
13 Restaurant Marganzo
14 Restaurant del Parque
15 Café y Restaurant
   Campeche
19 Restaurant-Bar Familiar
   La Parroquia
30 Panificadora Nueva
   España
38 Nutri Vida

OTHER
1 Cines Hollywood
4 Post Office; Edificio Federal
5 Telmex
6 Baluarte de Santiago; Jardín
   Botánico Xmuch Haltún
8 Banco Santander Mexicano
   (ATM; Currency Exchange)
9 Baluarte de Nuestra Señora
   de la Soledad; Museo de
   Estelas Maya
10 Secretaría de Turismo
   (State Tourist Office)
11 Puerta del Mar
12 Inverlat Bank
17 Centro Cultural Casa No 6
18 Portales del Centro
20 Bital (ATM)
22 Banamex (ATM)
23 Baluarte de San Carlos;
   Museo de la Ciudad
24 Palacio Legislativo
25 Palacio de Gobierno
26 Palacio Municipal
31 BanCrecer (ATM)
32 Banca Serfin (ATM)
33 Iglesia Dulce Nombre
   de Jesús
35 En Red Cibercafé
36 Ex-Templo de San José
40 Lavandería Tintorería
   Campeche
41 Iglesia de San Juan de Dios
42 Baluarte de San Pedro
43 Main Bus Terminal
44 Picazh Servicios Turísticos
45 Baluarte de Santa Rosa
   (City Tourist Office)
46 Baluarte de San Juan
47 IMSS Hospital
48 Puerta de Tierra
49 Baluarte de San Francisco
50 Sur Champotón Terminal
   (Buses to Edzná)
51 Lerma & Playa
   Bonita Buses

the heat of the day. Come for the concerts on Sunday evenings.

On the park's southeastern side is **Centro Cultural Casa Número 6**, an old 18th-century building furnished with pieces from the 18th and 19th centuries that gives a good idea of how the city's high society lived back then. The center also contains several computer-interactive exhibits providing information about the main tourist attractions in the city and state of Campeche. It's open 9 am to 9 pm daily, and admission is free, as is a guided tour of the building (in Spanish only).

Stretching along the entire block on the park's east side is the attractive arcaded **Portales del Centro**, a shopping area that's another replica of the original Palacio Municipal. Construction was begun on the **Catedral de la Concepción Inmaculada**, on the north side of the plaza, in the mid-16th century shortly after the conquistadors established the town, but it wasn't finished until 1705.

Back on Calle 8 head north again for two blocks beyond the park – note the long stretch of **city wall** extending from the north side of the Baluarte de Nuestra Señora – to **Baluarte de Santiago**. It houses a minuscule yet lovely tropical garden, the Jardín Botánico Xmuch Haltún, with 250 species of tropical plants set around a lovely courtyard of fountains. Tours of the garden are given between 5 and 6 pm Monday to Friday. The garden is open 8 am to 8:30 pm Tuesday to Friday, 9 am to 2 pm and 4 to 8 pm Saturday, and 9 am to 1 pm Sunday. Admission is free.

Walk south on Calle 8 a few steps and turn left (inland) onto Calle 51. Follow it to Calle 18, passing the **Iglesia de San Juan de Dios** (1652) on the way. The **Baluarte de San Pedro** is in the middle of a complex traffic intersection at the beginning of Avenida Gobernadores. Within the bulwark is the Exposición Permanente de Artesanías, a regional crafts sales center, and an agency that will book tours of the city and region. The baluarte is open 9 am to 1 pm and 5 to 8 pm Monday to Friday. Admission is free.

If you're still game, head south from the Baluarte de San Pedro along Avenida Circuito Baluartes to the **Baluarte de San Francisco**, at Calle 57, and, a block farther at

Calle 59, the **Puerta de Tierra** (Land Gate). Linked to the gate by Campeche's other stretch of wall is **Baluarte de San Juan**, at Calles 18 and 65. From here you bear right along Calle 67 (Avenida Circuito Baluartes) to the intersection of Calles 14 and 67 and the **Baluarte de Santa Rosa**. Admission to the last three baluartes is free.

Museo de la Cultura Maya & Fuerte de San Miguel

Four kilometers south of Plaza Moch-Couoh a road turns left off the malecón and climbs for about 600m to the Fuerte de San Miguel, a colonial fortress now home to the Museo de la Cultura Maya. This museum holds objects found at Calakmul, Edzná and Jaina, an island north of the city used by the Maya as a burial site for the aristocracy.

Among the objects on display are stunning pieces of jade jewelry and exquisite vases, masks and plates. The star attraction is the jade burial mask from Calakmul. Also displayed are arrowheads, weapons, necklaces made of seashells and clay figurines.

The fort is itself a thing of beauty. In mint condition, it's compact and equipped with a dry moat and working drawbridge, and it's topped with several cannons. The views are great, too. The fort and museum are open 8 am to 7 pm Tuesday to Sunday. Admission is US$1, free on Sunday.

A motorized *tranvía* (trolley) leaves the Parque Principal at 9 am and 5 pm for the fort (US$1.75). For US$0.20 you can take one of the 'Lerma' or 'Playa Bonita' buses that depart from market (at the northeast edge of the center) and travel counterclockwise most of the way around the circuito, making several stops on the way, before heading down the malecón. Tell the driver when you board that you're going to the Batería de San Luis. The turnoff for the fort, Avenida Escénica, is across from the old San Luis artillery battery. The walk from the coastal road up the hill to the fort is strenuous.

Organized Tours

City tours (by tranvía) depart the Parque Principal daily at 9:30 am and 6 and 8 pm.

Cost is US$1.75. Tours to Edzná depart from the Puerta de Tierra at 9 am and 2 pm (see the Edzná Getting There & Away section later in this chapter). The Corazón Maya agency (☎/fax 811-37-88, tourcorazonmaya@hotmail.com, www.corazonmaya.cjb.net) operates out of Baluarte de San Pedro and offers archaeological tours to Calakmul, the Río Bec sites in eastern Campeche, and elsewhere.

Places to Stay

Campeche's weak suit is decent lodging at decent prices. Compared to much of the rest of the Yucatán, you don't get a lot for your money.

Budget Campeche's youth hostel, the *Villa Deportiva Universitaria* (☎ 816-18-02), is in a university sports complex on Avenida Agustín Melgar, which comes off the malecón 3.5km southwest of Plaza Moch-Couoh. Dormitory beds cost US$4 per night, and a cafeteria serves inexpensive meals (there's a supermarket just down the street as well). There's an 11 pm curfew; doors unlock at 7 am. Buses marked 'Avenida Universidad' will take you there. Ask the driver to let you off at the *albergue de juventud* or Villa Deportiva. Avenida Melgar heads inland between a Volkswagen dealership and a Pemex fuel station. The hostel is 150m up on the right. Enter through the farther, smaller black gate and keep turning right.

Of the cheapest hotels, only a couple are worth trying, and they're fairly dumpy. *Hotel Roma* (☎ 816-38-97), on Calle 10 between Calles 59 and 61, charges US$6.50/7 single/double with fan and hot-water bath. *Hotel Castelmar* (☎ 816-28-86, Calle 61 No 2), at Calles 8 and 61, has a courtyard with plants, and looks like someplace the protagonist in a James M Cain novel might hole up. Rooms are US$8.25.

The *Hotel Campeche* (☎ 816-51-83, Calle 57 No 2), above the Café y Restaurant Campeche, facing the Parque Principal, is inexpensive and centrally located. Rooms are US$7.75//9.50/12.25/14 single/double/triple/quadruple.

The *Hotel Colonial* (☎ 816-22-22, Calle 14 No 122) is popular with budget travelers. Some readers have complained of noise, others recommend it highly. Housed in what was once the mansion of Doña Gertrudis Eulalia Torostieta y Zagasti, former Spanish governor of Tabasco and Yucatán, the rooms have good showers with hot water for US$10.75/13.50 single/double with fan and one bed only, US$14.75 for two beds, US$18 for a triple. Add US$5 for air-con.

Posada del Ángel (☎ 816-77-18, Calle 10 No 307) is a good value with 14 spartan, modern, clean rooms with private bath for US$14/17.50/21/24 single/double/triple/quad with fan only, US$19.50/23/26/29 with air-con. Some sheets need replacing, so ask to see more than one room before registering.

Mid-Range The *Hotel América* (☎ 816-45-88, fax 816-05-56, hotelamerica@campeche .com.mx, www.campeche.com.mx/hamerica, Calle 10 No 252) is a converted colonial house with 49 spacious though somewhat spartan and noisy rooms ringing an interior courtyard. Singles are available with fan only for US$24. Doubles/triples with fan are US$34/39. A few doubles are available with air-con for US$43, but these rooms are not worth it (go elsewhere if you crave air-con).

The *Hotel López* (☎/fax 816-33-44, lopezh@elsitio.com, Calle 12 No 189) has a pleasant courtyard and rooms with fan for US$27, US$36 with air-con.

Top End One of the best values in town is *Hotel del Paseo* (☎ 811-01-00, 811-0077, fax 811-00-97, cslavall@etzna.uacam.mx, Calle 8 No 215), with 42 new air-con standard rooms and six suites, all with cable TV and phone. Rates are a very reasonable US$39/44 single/double, US$66 for a suite. There's a restaurant and bar, but no pool.

The *Hotel Baluartes* (☎ 816-3911, fax 816-2410, baluarte@campeche.sureste.com, Avenida 16 de Septiembre 128; enter from Calle 61), though showing its age a bit, offers good values. The trick is to get a room on one of the upper floors, the higher the better, with a good view of the sea or the city (the old wall and cathedral juxtaposed with the modern government buildings). Their perfectly serviceable rooms have good air-con and run US$41/46/55 single/double/triple, US$58 for suites. There is a restaurant, and the pool is clean and deep.

The 119-room *Hotel Del Mar* (☎ 816-22-33, fax 811-16-18, Avenida Ruiz Cortínez 51) was formerly a Ramada hotel. Rooms start at US$80 for a city view and go up to US$99 for a sea view. The hotel has two restaurants and a pool.

Places to Eat
While in town, be sure to try the regional specialty *pan de cazón*, which is dogfish – a small shark – cooked between layers of tortillas in a dark sauce. Another regional specialty is *camarones al coco*, consisting of shrimp rolled in ground coconut and fried. It's often served with marmalade, and when done right tastes much better than it sounds.

There is a *San Francisco de Asís* supermarket across Avenida Ruiz and west of the Baluarte de Santiago; the selection is broad and prices low.

The air-con *Restaurant Marganzo*, on Calle 8 between Calles 57 and 59, facing the Baluarte de Nuestra Señora de la Soledad, is popular. Breakfast costs US$3 to US$4, lunch and dinner run US$4 to US$10; the seafood menu is extensive. Alas the camarones al coco are not up to par.

Half a block north, at the corner of Calles 8 and 57 is *Restaurant del Parque*. This little place serves a big selection of meat and fish dishes accompanied by rice and salad for around US$3.50 to US$6 a platter. Try the 'Spaniel bread with meat' if you dare.

Around the corner on Calle 57, opposite the Parque Principal, *Café y Restaurant Campeche* is in the building that saw the birth of Justo Sierra, founder of Mexico's national university. It's simple, bright with fluorescent light and loud with a blaring TV. It's open for breakfast and dinner, and few dishes cost more than US$3.

The *Panificadora Nueva España*, on Calle 10 at Calle 59, has a large assortment of fresh baked goods at very low prices.

Every now and then a brave entrepreneur opens a natural-foods restaurant in Campeche, only to close soon after. *Nutri Vida (Calle 12 No 167)*, a health-food store serving up soy burgers and the like, was still going at last visit. It's open 8 am to 2 pm and 5:30 to 8:30 pm Monday through Friday, and 8 am to 2 pm Saturday.

Perhaps the best-known (though not the best) restaurant in town is the *Restaurant-Bar Familiar La Parroquia (Calle 55 No 8)* between Calles 10 and 12. The complete family restaurant-café-hangout, La Parroquia is open 24 hours and serves breakfast from 7 to 10 am for US$2 to US$3. Substantial lunches and dinners of traditional and regional dishes are almost all well under US$10.

Entertainment

On Saturday at 8 pm (weather permitting) from September to May, the state tourism authorities sponsor *Estampas Turísticas* – performances of folk music and dancing – in the Plaza Moch-Couoh. Also, every Sunday at 7 pm in the Parque Principal you can hear popular campechana music performed by the Banda del Estado (State Band). There's no cost to attend and it's a pleasant way to pass time. Arrive early for a good seat. Tuesday evening at 7 pm free performances of folkloric dance and music are given at the ex-Templo de San José, at the corner of Calles 10 and 63.

Cines Hollywood is a modern multiplex cinema just outside the circuito's northwest corner, a block from the water.

Getting There & Away

Air The airport is located at the end of Avenida López Portillo (Avenida Central), 3.5km east from the Plaza Moch-Couoh. Aeroméxico flies to Mexico City at least once daily for US$157. Aerocaribe flies four times a week to Cancún.

Bus Campeche's main bus terminal (sometimes called the ADO terminal) is on Avenida Gobernadores, 1.7km from Plaza Moch-Couoh, or about 1.5km from most hotels. The terminal has a restaurant and a tourist

information counter. The 2nd-class area is farther off the street in the same building.

Sur has a terminal for buses to Champotón on Avenida República across from the Alameda (which is south of the market). Rural buses for Edzná and other parts depart from here as well.

There have been reports of theft on night buses, especially 2nd-class buses to Chiapas; keep a close eye on your bags.

Daily buses from Campeche include:

Bolonchén de Rejón 116km, 3 to 4 hours; four 2nd-class (US$3.50)

Cancún 512km, 6 to 9 hours; two ADO direct (US$22) at 10 and 11:30 pm; also TRP buses, which may require a change at Mérida

Chetumal 422km, 6¼ to 9 hours; one 1st-class (US$17) at noon, one 2nd-class (US$13.50) at 10 pm

Edzná 55km, 1½ hours; buses leave at 7 and 10 am, then roughly hourly until 6 pm, from the back lot of the Sur Champotón terminal (US$1.50); see the Edzná section for further information

Escárcega 150km, 2½ hours; one Altos (US$6.75) at 10:10 pm, many 2nd-class buses

Hopelchén 86km, 2 hours; eight Sur 2nd-class (US$2.50)

Mérida (short route via Bécal) 195km, 2½ to 3 hours; (long route via Uxmal) 250km, 4 hours; 10 ADO 1st-class (US$7.75), ATS every 30 minutes (US$6)

Mexico City (TAPO) 1360km, 18 hours; one ADO (US$69) at 4 pm

Palenque 362km, 5 hours; three ADO (US$15), two Colón (US$13), two ATS (US$10); many other buses drop you at Catazajá (the Palenque turnoff), 27km north of Palenque village

San Cristóbal de Las Casas 820km, 14 hours; one Altos (US$22) at 10:10 pm, one Maya de Oro (US$27) at midnight

Veracruz 930km, 12 hours; one ADO (US$22) at 4 pm

Villahermosa 450km, 6 hours; 15 buses (US$16.50 to US$18.25); they'll drop you at Catazajá (for Palenque) if you like

Xpujil 306km, 6 to 8 hours; one ADO at noon (US$12.25), four ATS (US$9.50)

Car & Motorcycle If you're heading for Edzná, the long route to Mérida or the fast toll road going south, take Avenida Central and follow signs for the airport and Edzná. If you're taking the free route south you can just head down the malecón.

For the short route to Mérida you can head north on the malecón (which is more pleasant) or out Avenida Gobernadores.

Getting Around

Local buses all originate at the market. Most charge US$0.20 and go around the Avenida Circuito Baluartes counterclockwise before heading to their final destinations. Ask a local where along the circuito you can catch the bus you want.

Taxis have set prices for destinations on a sign posted in the back seat. Open the door and have a look, but agree on a price with the driver before you go. By the hour they are US$6.50. The fare between the bus terminal and the center is around US$1.75. Between the airport and the center is US$3.75. Colectivo taxis from the airport charge US$2.25 per person.

AROUND CAMPECHE
Edzná

The closest ruins to Campeche are about 53km to the southeast, at Edzná. This site covers more than 2 sq km and was inhabited from approximately 600 BC to the 15th century AD. Most of the visible carvings date from AD 550 to 810. Though a long way from such Puuc Hills sites as Uxmal and Kabah, some of the architecture here has elements of the Puuc style. What led to Edzná's decline and gradual abandonment remains a mystery.

The site is open 8 am to 5 pm daily. Admission is US$2.25, free on Sunday and holidays.

Beyond the ticket office is a palapa sheltering carvings and stelae from the elements. A path from here leads about 400m through vegetation to the zone's big draw, the main plaza, 160m long and 100m wide, surrounded by temples. On your right as you enter from the west is the **Nohoch Ná** (Big House), a massive, elongated structure that was topped by four long halls likely used for administrative tasks, such as the

collection of tributes and the dispensation of justice. The built-in benches facing the main plaza clearly were designed to serve spectators of special events in the plaza.

Across the plaza is the Gran Acrópolis, a raised platform holding several structures, including Edzná's major temple, the 31m-high **Edificio de los Cinco Pisos** (Five-Story Building). It rises five levels from vast base to roofcomb and contains many vaulted rooms. A great central staircase of 65 steps goes right to the top. Some of the weathered carvings of masks, serpents and jaguars' heads that adorned each level are now in the palapa near the ticket office.

The current structure is the last of four remodels and was done primarily in the Puuc architectural style. Scholars generally agree that this temple is a hybrid of a pyramid and a palace. The impressive roofcomb is a clear reference to the sacred buildings at Tikal in Guatemala.

In the Pequeña Acrópolis to the south of the main plaza is the palapa-protected **Templo de Mascarones** (Temple of Masks), which features carved portrayals of the sun god. The central motif is the anthropomorphic head of a Maya man whose face has been modified to give him the appearance of a jaguar.

Getting There & Away From Campeche, buses leave from the back lot of the Sur Champotón terminal at 7 and 10 am, then roughly hourly until 6 pm (55km, 1½ hours, US$1.50); it's a good idea to check the day before. Most drop you about 200m from the site entrance; ask before boarding. The last bus returning to Campeche passes near the site at 2 pm, so if you're roundtripping from the city you'll want to catch one of the two early buses.

Coming from the north and east, get off at San Antonio Cayal and hitch or catch a bus 20km south to Edzná. If you're headed north on leaving Edzná, you'll have to depend on hitching or the occasional bus to get you to San Antonio Cayal, where you can catch a Chenes Route bus north to Hopelchén, Bolonchén de Rejón and ultimately Uxmal.

JOHN ELK III

Edificio de los Cinco Pisos, Edzná

Coming by car from Campeche, take Avenida Central out of town and follow the signs to the airport and Edzná. If you drove to Edzná from the north and are headed to Campeche city, don't retrace your route to San Antonio; just bear left shortly after leaving the parking lot and follow the signs westward.

Picazh Servicios Turísticos (☎ 816-44-26, fax 816-27-60), Calle 16 No 348 between Calles 57 and 59 near the Puerta de Tierra in Campeche, runs tours to Edzná. For US$16.25 per person (minimum two persons), they'll pick you up from hotels near the center and drive you to the ruins and back. For US$22 per person, they'll give you a guided tour in Spanish or English (if you're by yourself, prices are US$25 and US$33). Entry to the site is not included in these prices. At the Puerta de Tierra ask for Profesor Zavala. Tours depart daily at 9 am and 2 pm.

North of Campeche

The short, western route to Campeche city from Yucatán state takes you past a couple of towns that may be of interest. You can reach them on the frequent 2nd-class buses running between Mérida and Campeche.

Bécal, 85km southwest of Mérida and just inside the border of Campeche state, is a center of the Yucatán's panama hat trade. The soft, pliable hats, called *jipijapas* by the locals, have been woven by townsfolk from the fibers of the huano palm tree in humid limestone caves since the mid-19th century. The caves – there's at least one on every block, generally reached by a hole in the ground in someone's backyard – provide just the right atmosphere for shaping the fibers, keeping them pliable and minimizing breakage. Each cave is typically no larger than a bedroom. About 1000 of the town's 3000 adult residents make their living weaving hats. The hats cost from US$10 to US$50, depending on quality. If you're shopping for a hat, be sure to visit the cooperative on the main street, a stone's throw from Bécal's dominating church.

Another 24km brings you to Hecelchakán, home of the **Museo Arqueológico del Camino Real** (also known as the Museo de Hecelchakán), where you will find some burial artifacts from the island of Jaina, as well as ceramics and jewelry from other sites. The museum is supposed to be open from 9 am to 6 pm Tuesday to Saturday (admission US$2), but the attendant seems to take long siestas. It's on the far left side of the plaza when you're facing the church.

The **Iglesia de San Francisco** dates from the 16th century, but its dramatic features – a massive octagonal dome and a pair of monumental bell towers – are 18th-century additions. It's the center of festivities on the saint's day, October 4. From August 9 to 18, a popular festival known as the Novenario is held in town, with bullfights, dancing and refreshments.

From Hecelchakán it's about 65km south to the city of Campeche.

East of Campeche

Coming south from Uxmal, Hwy 261 crosses the border into Campeche state and heads southwest for Bolonchén de Rejón. Just off the highway, 3km north of Bolonchén, is the archaeological zone of **Itzimté**, with its many unrestored buildings in the Puuc style. This is the southernmost limit of purely Puuc architecture; south of here the more elaborately decorative Chenes style predominates, named for the many natural wells in the region. The suffix *-chén* is often found at the end of town names hereabouts.

Continuing south, the road splits at Hopelchén. Heading west from here takes you to Campeche city; south and east, to Xpujil (some interesting places lie along this route).

Hopelchén This town contains no attractions, but has a decent hotel, *Hotel Arcos*, with rooms for US$5/7 single/double. The bus station is served exclusively by 2nd-class Autobuses del Sur. There are 12 buses daily to Campeche from 4:45 am to 7:45 pm (US$2), four to Mérida (7:35 am, 1:35, 4 and 6:30 pm, US$4), eight to Dzibalchén from 8:30 am to 8 pm (US$1) and one to Xpujil (8 pm, US$5.10).

Two kilometers west of Hopelchén on the Campeche road are the ruins of Tahacok (or Tohkok). The one ruined structure here, dating from Late Classic times, is on the north side of the highway. Its decoration is a blend of Puuc and Chenes styles.

El Tabasqueño & Hochob Two minor Mayan sites are relatively easy to access if you're on your way between Hopelchén and Xpujil in your own vehicle. Admission to both is free.

Northwest of Dzibalchén, **El Tabasqueño** boasts a temple-palace (Estructura 1) with a striking monster-mouth doorway flanked by Chac masks. The doorway is similar to the one atop the House of the Magician at Uxmal, though in Chenes style. Estructura 2 is a solid freestanding tower, an oddity in Mayan architecture. To reach El Tabasqueño, go south from Hopelchén 30km, turn right (south) to the village of Pakchén and follow an unpaved road another 4km to the site.

Five kilometers south of Chencoh is **Hochob**, which, though small, is among the most beautiful and impressive of Chenes-style sites. The Palacio Principal (Estructura 2) is faced with an amazingly elaborate Chenes monster-mouth doorway in surprisingly good condition. Estructura 1 is similar, though in worse condition. Estructura 5, on the east side of the plaza, retains part of its roofcomb. Estructura 6, to the west, is in ruins. To reach Hochob, turn right (south) about 500m west of Dzibalchén and drive the 9km to Chencoh on a rocky road, then the remaining 5km on a rough dirt road.

XPUJIL & VICINITY

The southeastern corner of Campeche holds many important Mayan archaeological sites, and exploration and restoration are making more wonders accessible to the public every year.

Orientation & Information

The hamlet of Xpujil (shpu-**heel**) lies at the junction of east-west Hwy 186 and Campeche Hwy 261 (not to be confused with Mexico Hwy 261), which leads north to Hopelchén (220km) and eventually Mérida. It is well positioned as a base from which to explore the area's sites, and is growing rapidly in anticipation of a tourist boom.

From the taxi stand on the south side of the junction, it is possible to hire drivers to take you to any of the archaeological sites along or off Hwy 186, including Calakmul. The drivers charge very reasonable fares, but be sure to agree on the price (including waiting time, about US$4.25 an hour) before you depart to avoid any surprises later.

Taxi fares in the following sections are from the Xpujil junction. Sites are listed in the order they're accessed from Hwy 186, going east to west. All are open from 8 am to 5 pm, and admission to all is free Sunday and holidays. Most charge US$7.50 extra for use of a video camera.

El Ramonal & Río Bec

The entrance to the collective farm Ejido 20 de Noviembre is 10km east of the Xpujil junction and signed 'Río Bec.' The unpaved ejido road south leads 5km to the collective itself and its U'lu'um Chac Yuk Nature Reserve. You can ask for directions to El Ramonal, the fairly impressive ruins within walking distance of the settlement, or look for the 'museum,' the fourth building on the right-hand side of the road, and ask there for guides to show you the sights.

They can also show you the various sites of Río Bec, about 13km farther down the road. Río Bec is the designation for an agglomeration of small sites, 17 at last count, in a 50-sq-km area southeast of Xpujil. Of these many sites, the most interesting is certainly Grupo B, followed by Grupos I and N.

Río Bec gave its name to the prevalent architectural style of the region, characterized by long, low buildings that look as though they're divided into sections, each with a huge serpent mouth for a door. The facades are decorated with smaller masks, geometric designs and columns. At the corners of the buildings are tall, solid towers with extremely small, steep, nonfunctional steps and topped by small temples. Many of these towers have roofcombs.

The best example is **Estructura I** at Grupo B, a Late Classic building dating from around AD 700. Though not restored, Estructura I has been consolidated and is in a condition certainly good enough to allow appreciation of its former glory. At Grupo I look for **Estructuras XVII and XI**. At Grupo N, **Estructura I** is quite similar to the grand one at Grupo B.

The road is passable only when dry, and even then you need a high-clearance vehicle. The way is unsigned as well; you're best off hiring a guide with or without his 4WD truck. A taxi to the ejido will charge around US$4.50 for drop-off service (and may be able to take you to El Ramonal); negotiate waiting time. Though it looks closer on the map, access to Río Bec from the road to Hormiguero is all but impossible.

Hormiguero

This site is reached by heading 14km south from Xpujil junction, then turning right and heading another 8km west (the roads are paved). Hormiguero (Spanish for 'anthill') is an old site, with some buildings dating as far back as AD 50. The city flourished during the Late Classic period, however.

Hormiguero has one of the most impressive buildings in the region. Entering the site you will see the 50m-long **Estructura II**, which has a giant Chenes-style monster-mouth doorway with much of its decoration in good condition. You'll also want to see **Estructura V**, 60m to the north; Estructura E-1, in the East Group, should be a sight once it is excavated.

At the time of research the site wasn't charging admission, but once improvements are finished this will undoubtedly change. A roundtrip taxi ride will run US$6.50.

Xpujil Ruins

Xpujil, 'Place of the Cattails' in Mayan, flourished during the Late Classic period from AD 400 to 900, though there was a settlement here much earlier. The site's entrance is at the edge of town on the north side of Hwy 186, at the turnoff for the airport, less than 1km west of the junction.

One large building and three small ones have been restored. Estructura I in Grupo I, built about AD 760, is a fine example of the Río Bec architectural style, with its lofty towers. The three towers (rather than the usual two) have traces of the impractically steep ornamental stairways reaching nearly to their tops, and several fierce jaguar masks (go around to the back of the tower to see the best one). About 60m to the east is Estructura II, an elite residence.

Xpujil is a far larger site than may be imagined from these buildings. Three other structure groups have been identified, but it may be decades before they are restored. Admission is US$1.75.

Becán

Becán, 8km west of the Xpujil junction, sits atop a rock outcrop; a 2km moat snakes its way around the entire city to protect it from attack. *(Becán* – literally 'path of the snake' – is Mayan for 'canyon' or 'moat.') Seven causeways crossed the moat, providing access to the city. Becán was occupied from 550 BC until AD 1000.

This is among the largest and most elaborate sites in the area. The first thing you'll come to is a plaza. Walk keeping it to your left to pass through a rock-walled passageway and beneath a corbeled arch. You will reach a huge twin-towered temple with cylindrical columns at the top of a flight of stairs. This is Estructura VIII, dating from about AD 600 to 730. The view from the top of this temple has become partially obscured by the trees, but on a clear day you should still be able to see structures at the Xpujil ruins to the east.

Northwest of Estructura VIII is Plaza Central, ringed by 30m-high Estructura IX (the tallest building at the site) and the better-looking Estructura X.

There are more ruins in the jungle to the west, including the Plaza Oeste, surrounded by low buildings, one of which is a ball court. Much of this area is still being excavated and restored, however, and is open to the public only intermittently.

Retrace your steps through the passageway to the plaza and cross it diagonally to the right, climbing a wooden staircase to the Plaza Sureste. Around this are Estructuras I through IV; a circular altar (Estructura III-a) lies on the east side. Estructura I has the two towers typical of the Río Bec style. You can go around the plaza counter-

clockwise and descend the stone staircase on the southeast side or go down the southwest side and head left. Both routes lead to the exit. Admission is US$2.25.

Chicanná

Almost 12km west of Xpujil junction and 800m south of the highway, Chicanná is a mixture of Chenes and Río Bec architectural styles buried in the jungle. The city was occupied from about AD 300 to 1100.

Enter through the modern palapa admission building, then follow the rock paths through the jungle to Grupo D and Estructura XX (AD 830), which boasts not one but two monster-mouth doorways, one above the other, the pair topped by a roofcomb.

A five-minute walk along the jungle path brings you to Grupo C, with two low buildings (Estructuras X and XI) on a raised platform; the temples bear a few fragments of decoration.

The buildings in Grupo B (turn right when leaving Grupo C) have some intact decoration as well, and there's a good roofcomb on Estructura VI.

Shortly beyond is Chicanná's most famous building, Estructura II (AD 750 to 770) in Grupo A, with its gigantic Chenes-style monster-mouth doorway, believed to depict the jaws of the god Itzamná, lord of the heavens, creator of all things. If you photograph nothing else here, you'll want a picture of this, best taken in the afternoon.

Take the path leading from the right corner of Estructura II to reach nearby Estructura VI.

Admission is US$2.25. Roundtrip taxi fare is US$2.75 plus US$4.25 per hour of wait.

Calakmul

Most Mayanists agree that Calakmul (Adjacent Mounds) is an important site – it's larger than Tikal, in Guatemala – but so far only a fraction of its 100-sq-km expanse has been cleared, and few of its 6500 buildings have been consolidated, let alone restored. Exploration and restoration are ongoing, however. The turnoff to Calakmul is 59km west of the Xpujil junction, and the site is 59km farther south on a paved road.

YUCATÁN

The ruins, at the heart of the vast, untrammeled Calakmul Biosphere Reserve, were discovered in 1931 by American botanist Cyrus Lundell. Like Tikal, they are surrounded by rain forest, which is best viewed from the top of one of the several pyramids. A visit to these ruins represents the best opportunity to explore the reserve without risk of getting lost in the jungle.

Calakmul was the leading city in a vast region known as the Kingdom of the Serpent's Head from about AD 250 through 750. Its perpetual rival was Tikal, and its decline began with the power struggles and internal conflicts that followed the defeat by Tikal of Calakmul's king Garra de Jaguar (Jaguar Claw).

As at Tikal, there are indications that construction occurred over a period of more than a millennium. Beneath Edificio VII, archaeologists discovered a burial crypt with some 2000 pieces of jade, and tombs continue to yield spectacular jade burial masks; many of these objects are on display in Campeche city's Museo de la Cultura Maya. Calakmul holds at least 120 carved stelae, though many are eroded.

Admission is US$2.50. A toll of US$2.50 per car (more for heavier vehicles) and US$1.25 per person is levied at the turnoff from the highway. From the parking lot to the ruins is a 500m walk. A roundtrip taxi ride from Xpujil with a two- to four-hour visit costs US$55.

Balamkú

Balamkú (also called Chunhabil) is 60km west of Xpujil junction (less than 3km west of Conhuas), then just under 3km north of the highway along a rough unpaved road. Discovered only in 1990, the site boasts an exquisite, ornate stucco frieze showing a jaguar flanked by two large mask designs and topped with images of a king in various forms. Another section has figures as well (look for the toad). The unusual design bears little resemblance to any of the known decorative elements in the Chenes and Río Bec styles and has mystified archaeologists.

The frieze is well preserved; a structure has been built over it, with skylights, but a flashlight can come in handy. Andrés, the knowledgeable, longtime caretaker, can explain (in Spanish) aspects of the site's archaeology, flora and fauna if he's not busy.

Excavation and research continue. At the time of research, admission was free.

Organized Tours

Guided tours from Xpujil are offered starting at about US$30 per person. This can be more convenient, if more expensive, than taxi travel. You can book through hotels in Xpujil.

See the Campeche city Organized Tours section for information on visiting Calakmul and other sites from there.

Places to Stay & Eat

About 350m west of Xpujil junction, the uncongenial *Restaurant-Hotel Calakmul* has cabins with shared bath for US$13 and several rooms with fan and private bath for US$26; you may have to make an effort to see more than one room.

At *El Mirador Maya* (☎/fax 9-871-60-05), about 1km west of Xpujil junction, there are eight bungalows and two rooms. The bungalows have a fan, private bath and two beds each, for US$22. The rooms have air-con and private bath with hot water for US$33 per room. There is a restaurant here as well.

There are a few eateries in Xpujil town on either side of the junction. The two-story house with blue trim across the highway and just up the hill from Hotel Calakmul serves delicious *barbacoa de borrego* (pit-baked lamb) for US$2.25 (US$0.75 beer!).

The *Chicanná Ecovillage Resort* (☎/fax 9-816-22-33) is 500m north of the highway and directly across it from the road to the ruins, almost 12km west of Xpujil junction. Large, airy rooms with private baths and ceiling fans are grouped mostly four to a bungalow and set amid well-tended grass lawns. Rates are US$91/100 single/double. The small dining room/bar serves decent but expensive meals.

Getting There & Away

Xpujil is 220km south of Hopelchén, 153km east of Escárcega and 120km west of Chetumal. Stopping in Xpujil are six buses daily to Escárcega, five to Campeche and two to Chetumal (you may be able to flag down others). No buses originate in Xpujil, so you must hope to luck into a vacant seat on one passing through. The bus station is just east of the Xpujil junction, on the north side of the highway.

The nearest gas station is 5km east of Xpujil.

ESCÁRCEGA

• **population 25,000**

Most buses passing through Escárcega stop here to give passengers a refreshments break, but unless you must break your journey to rest, there is no reason to stay in this town at the junction of Hwys 186 and 261, 150km south of Campeche and 301km from Villahermosa. Indeed, as most buses arrive in town full and depart in the same condition, you may find it difficult to get out of Escárcega if you break your trip here.

The town is spread out along 2km of Hwy 186 toward Chetumal. The ADO station is at the junction of the highways; the 2nd-class bus station is 1.7km east on Hwy 186. Most hotels are nearer to the Sur bus station than to the ADO; most of the better restaurants are near the ADO bus station.

Hotel Escárcega (☎ *824-0188, fax 824-0187*), on Hwy 186 about 400m east of the junction with Hwy 261 (not far from the ADO terminal), is probably the best place in town, which isn't saying much. Singles/doubles/triples with air-con are US$22/24/30; with fan, US$15/17/20. There are slightly less appealing places for less money. One is opposite the 2nd-class bus station, another is about 150m east of the Hotel Escárcega on Hwy 186.

HIGHWAY 186 TO PALENQUE

The 212km ride from Escárcega to Palenque takes you southwest on fast, straight Hwy 186. As you approach the Campeche-Tabasco border keep an eye out for egrets and great blue herons in the ponds flanking the highway and jaunty kingfishers perched on the wires above. Sometimes there seems to be one every kilometer or less.

By the time you reach the Río Chumpán, the traditional Mayan *na* have given way to board shacks with roofs of corrugated steel. As you enter the region of the Río Usumacinta the landscape becomes lush and green. A toll bridge (US$1.75 for cars) spans the Usumacinta, which forms the border between Tabasco state and Chiapas.

About 184km southwest of Escárcega you come to Catazajá, at the turnoff to Palenque, Ocosingo and San Cristóbal de Las Casas. Turn left (south) for Palenque, 27km south. If your goal is Villahermosa, then continue straight on Hwy 186.

YUCATÁN

Tabasco & Chiapas

Just east of the Isthmus of Tehuantepec – Mexico's narrow 'waist' – lie the states of Tabasco and Chiapas. Their differences define them: Chiapas is wealthy in natural resources but most of its people are poor, whereas Tabasco is oil-rich. Tabasco, with a long coastline on the Gulf of Mexico, is mostly well-watered lowland, hot and humid, but in its south start to rise the hills that become the cool, pine-clad Altos (Highlands) of Chiapas. Chiapas' indigenous history is Mayan; Tabasco's is chiefly Olmec.

There are river routes into neighboring Guatemala from both states.

Highlights

- Jungle-enshrouded Palenque, most romantic of Mayan cities
- The colonial highland town of San Cristóbal de Las Casas and nearby Mayan villages
- The Mayan ruins of Bonampak and Yaxchilán, deep in the Lacandón Jungle
- Villahermosa's Parque-Museo La Venta, a fascinating outdoor Olmec archaeological museum and zoo
- Remote, serene Laguna Miramar, the largest lake in the Lacandón Jungle

YUCATÁN

Tabasco

Tabasco is kept fertile by huge rivers that meander across it en route to the Gulf of Mexico. It was here, between about 1200 and 600 BC, that the Olmecs developed Mesoamerica's first great civilization. In recent years Tabasco's mineral riches, particularly petroleum, have brought great prosperity.

History

La Venta, the second great Olmec center (after San Lorenzo, Veracruz) was in western Tabasco. Olmec religion, art, astronomy and architecture deeply influenced all Mexico's later pre-Hispanic civilizations. The Chontal Maya who followed the Olmecs built a great ceremonial city called Comalcalco in northwest Tabasco.

Cortés, who disembarked on the Tabasco coast in 1519, initially defeated the Maya and founded a settlement called Santa María de la Victoria. The Maya regrouped and offered stern resistance until they were defeated by Francisco de Montejo, around 1540. Later, pirate attacks forced the original settlement to be moved inland from the coast, and it was renamed Villahermosa de San Juan Bautista.

After Mexico won independence from Spain, various local land barons tried to assert their power over the area, causing considerable strife. The economy languished until after the Mexican Revolution, when exports of cacao, bananas and coconuts started to increase.

In the 20th century, US and British petroleum companies discovered oil, and

TABASCO & CHIAPAS

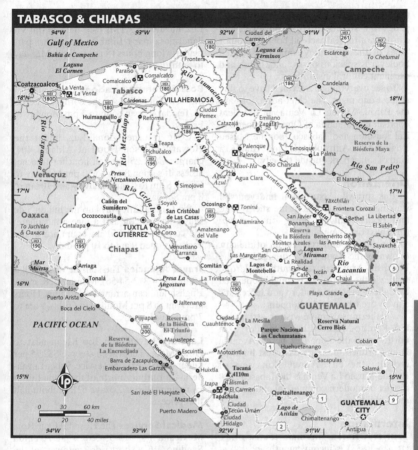

Tabasco's economy began to revolve around the resource. During the 1970s, Villahermosa became an oil boomtown, and profits from agricultural exports added to the good times. This prosperity has brought a feeling of sophistication that cuts right through the tropical heat, stamping Tabasco as different from neighboring Chiapas and Campeche.

Geography & Climate

Tabasco's topography changes from flatland near the seaside to undulating hills as you near Chiapas. Owing to heavy rainfall

of about 1500mm annually (mostly between May and October), there is much swampland, lush tropical foliage and sticky humidity. Outside of Villahermosa, Tabasco can be quite bug-infested (particularly near the rivers), so bring repellent. The state is rather sparsely populated, with 1.8 million people inhabiting 24,475 sq km.

VILLAHERMOSA

- **population 301,200**

Hot and crowded downtown Villahermosa is not quite the 'beautiful city' that its name implies, despite its location on the banks of the Río Grijalva. There are some pleasant pedestrian streets to stroll, however, and courtesy of the Tabasco oil boom the outer areas of the city enjoy some tree-shaded boulevards, spacious parks, fancy hotels and excellent cultural institutions.

To see everything here, you'll have to stay at least one night. The chief attractions are the Parque-Museo La Venta, an excellent open-air combination of Olmec archaeological museum and Tabasco zoo; the Museo Regional de Antropología; and Yumká, a kind of safari park outside the city.

Orientation

In this sprawling city you'll find yourself walking some distances in the sticky heat, and occasionally hopping on a *combi* (minibus) or taking a taxi.

The older commercial center of the city, known as the Zona Luz, extends from the Plaza de Armas in the south to Parque Juárez in the north, and is roughly bounded by Calles Zaragoza, Madero and Juárez. It's a lively area, busy with shoppers.

Villahermosa's main visitor attraction, the Parque-Museo La Venta, lies 3km northwest of the Zona Luz, beside Avenida Ruiz Cortines, the main east-west highway crossing the city. About 1km west of Parque-Museo La Venta is the Tabasco 2000 district of modern commercial and government buildings.

Information

Tourist Offices The main tourist office (☎ 316-36-33) is inconveniently located at the corner of Avenida de los Ríos just south of Paseo Tabasco in the Tabasco 2000 district in the northwest of the city. It's open 9 am to 3 pm and 6 to 9 pm Monday to Friday, 9 am to 1 pm Saturday. Staff are helpful and have lots of information on Tabasco state. To get there from the Zona Luz, take a 'Fracc Carrizal' combi from Madero just north of Parque Juárez, get off at the big traffic circle after you cross Avenida Ruiz Cortines, and walk one block to the left along Avenida de los Ríos.

There are small tourist offices at Parque-Museo La Venta and Rovirosa Airport.

Money There are many banks in the Zona Luz, most with ATMs (see the Central Villahermosa map). Bital, on Juárez, has particularly long hours (8 am to 7 pm Monday to Saturday).

Post & Communications The main post office, at Sáenz 131 on the corner of Lerdo de Tejada, is open 8 am to 3 pm Monday to Friday.

C@fé Internet Zona Luz, under the Howard Johnson Hotel at Aldama 404, charges US$1.25 per half hour for Internet access. It's open 9 am to 10 pm Monday to Friday, 8 am to 8 pm Saturday and 10 am to 8 pm Sunday.

Sin Cafe, a little ways up the hill on 5 de Mayo, has air-con and a nice atmosphere; the computers (US$1 an hour) are in the back. It's open 9 am to 10 pm daily.

Travel Agencies The staff at Viajes Villahermosa (☎ 312-54-56), Méndez 728, speak English and can arrange excursions. Hours are 9 am to 8 pm Monday to Friday, 9 am to 7 pm Saturday.

Laundry Lavandería Top Klean next to Hotel Madero charges a steep US$2.75 per kilogram for next-day service. Super Lavandería La Burbuja, north of the Zona Luz at Hermanos Bastar Zozaya 621, is about half that price.

Medical Services The Hospital Cruz Roja Mexicana (☎ 315-55-55) is at Avenida Sandino 716, a short ride southwest of the Zona Luz. Unidad Médica Guerrero Urgencias (☎ 314-56-97/98), at 5 de Mayo 44 in the center, is open 24 hours.

Parque-Museo La Venta

The Olmec city of La Venta, built on an island near where the Río Tonalá runs into the Gulf some 130km west of Villahermosa, flourished in the centuries before 600 BC. Danish archaeologist Frans Blom did the initial excavations in 1925, and work was continued by archaeologists from Tulane University and the University of California. Matthew Stirling is credited with having

Olmec head at Parque-Museo
La Venta, Villahermosa

JOHN ELK III

constrictors, peccaries and plenty more. Stop at the informative display (in English and Spanish) on Olmec history and archaeology as you go through. Parque-Museo La Venta (☎ 314-16-52) is open 8 am to 4 pm daily (US$1.75); the zoo is closed Monday. There is also a good indoor Museo de Historia Natural across from the entrance to the zoo. It's open 8 am to 4 pm Tuesday through Sunday (US$0.55).

The park is 3km from the Zona Luz. A 'Fracc Carrizal' combi (US$0.40) from Madero just north of Parque Juárez in the Zona Luz will drop you at the corner of Paseo Tabasco and Avenida Ruiz Cortines. Then walk 1km northeast along a pleasant lakeside path to the entrance. A taxi from the Zona Luz costs US$1.25.

CICOM & Museo Regional de Antropología

The Centro de Investigación de las Culturas Olmeca y Maya (CICOM) is a complex of buildings on the bank of the Río Grijalva. The complex includes a theater, research center and arts center, but its main attraction is the Museo Regional de Antropología Carlos Pellicer Cámara, named for the scholar and poet responsible for the preservation of the Olmec artifacts in the Parque-Museo La Venta.

The best way to tour the museum is to take the elevator to the top floor and work your way down. Although the museum's explanations are all in Spanish, they are accompanied by photos, maps and diagrams.

On the top floor, exhibits outline Mesoamerica's many civilizations, from the oldest Stone Age inhabitants to the relatively recent Aztecs. The middle floor concentrates on the Olmec and Mayan cultures, and the ground floor holds a room of particularly big Olmec and Mayan sculptures, plus temporary exhibits. The anthropology museum (☎ 312-63-44) is open 9 am to 7 pm Tuesday through Sunday (US$2.25).

CICOM is 1km south of the Zona Luz. You can walk there in about 15 minutes, or catch any 'CICOM' combi or microbus heading south on Madero or on the *malecón* south of Madero.

discovered, in the early 1940s, five colossal Olmec heads sculpted from basalt. The largest weighs over 24 tons and stands more than 2m tall. It is a mystery how the Olmecs managed to move these massive basalt heads some 100km to La Venta, without the use of the wheel.

When petroleum excavation threatened the La Venta site, the most significant finds – including three of the Olmec heads – were moved to Villahermosa to found the Parque-Museo La Venta, a fascinating outdoor museum and tropical zoo.

The museum section of the park includes a 1km-long trail through lush foliage past the 34 Olmec stone sculpture exhibits. Along the way many trees bear signs giving their names and species. Some harmless animals, such as coatis, roam freely. A giant ceiba (the sacred tree of the Olmecs and Maya) marks the starting point of the trail.

The park's zoo is devoted to animals from Tabasco and nearby regions: colorful macaws and toucans, pumas, ocelots, white-tailed deer, spider monkeys, crocodiles, boa

YUCATÁN

Museo de Historia

The History Museum, in a blue-tiled building at the corner of 27 de Febrero and Juárez, deals with Tabasco history. It's small but contains some interesting exhibits, including an early X-ray machine. Opening hours are 9 am to 8 pm Tuesday through Sunday (US$0.55).

Tabasco 2000

The Tabasco 2000 complex is a testimony to the prosperity oil has brought to Villahermosa, with its modern government buildings, chic boutiques in the Galerías Tabasco 2000 mall, convention center and pretty fountains. From the Zona Luz, take a 'Fracc Carrizal' combi from Madero just north of Parque Juárez.

Places to Stay

Budget The *Hotel del Centro* (☎ 312-59-61, *Pino Suárez 209*) is better kept than most

cheapies. Bright, clean singles/doubles with fan, TV and bathroom go for US$10.75/13.50, or US$19/22 with air-con.

Hotel San Miguel (☎ 312-15-00, *Lerdo de Tejada 315*) is small and cheap, renting its plain rooms with fan for US$8.75/10.75/13 single/double/triple, or US$18/21/24 for singles/doubles/triples with air-con and TV. Neighboring *Hotel Tabasco* (☎ 312-00-77, *Lerdo de Tejada 317*), charging US$7.50/9.75, is a step worse. *Hotel Oriente* (☎ 312-01-21, *Madero 425*), around the corner, is marginally better, though the front rooms are noisier. Rates are US$9.25/16.25, or US$22 for a room with TV and air-con.

Hotel San Francisco (☎ 312-31-98, *Madero 604*) is a considerable improvement; rooms with air-con and TV are US$15.75/19. Some have balconies, but this street can be *very* noisy. *Hotel Palma de Mallorca* (☎ 312-01-44, *Madero 516*) charges US$8.50/11 for singles/doubles with

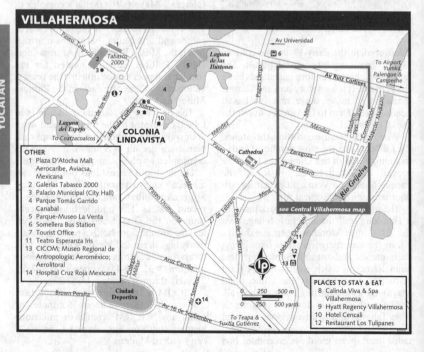

VILLAHERMOSA

OTHER
1 Plaza D'Atocha Mall:
   Aerocaribe, Aviacsa,
   Mexicana
2 Galerías Tabasco 2000
3 Palacio Municipal (City Hall)
4 Parque Tomás Garrido
   Canabal
5 Parque-Museo La Venta
6 Somellera Bus Station
7 Tourist Office
11 Teatro Esperanza Iris
13 CICOM; Museo Regional de
   Antropología; Aeroméxico;
   Aerolitoral
14 Hospital Cruz Roja Mexicana

PLACES TO STAY & EAT
8 Calinda Viva & Spa
   Villahermosa
9 Hyatt Regency Villahermosa
10 Hotel Cencali
12 Restaurant Los Tulipanes

see Central Villahermosa map

one bed and fan, US$11/14.50 for two-bed rooms with fan, and US$14.50/16.75 for air-conditioned rooms.

Hotel Madero (☎ *312-05-16, Madero 301*) is an old building with plans to remodel and add air-con to all rooms. At present, however, doubles with bath and fan are US$16.25 to US$19.50. Check your room: Some are a lot more pleasant and less stuffy than others.

Mid-Range Most middle-range hotels are in the Zona Luz. The 76-room *Hotel Miraflores* (☎ */fax 312-00-22, Reforma 304*), on a pedestrian street just off Madero, offers large, clean air-conditioned rooms with good bathrooms and about 60 TV channels for US$43/49 – if they're not too busy they may offer a few dollars' discount. The hotel has a restaurant, a coffee shop that also serves meals and a rather dire music bar.

Hotel Madan (☎ *314-05-24, Madero 408*) has 40 air-conditioned rooms with bath for US$29 to US$40, single or double. They should be fully renovated by the time you hold this book in your hands. It has a restaurant too. *Hotel Pakaal* (☎ *314-46-48, Lerdo de Tejada 106*) charges US$33/38 for fair-size air-conditioned rooms with bath and cable TV. Friendly *Hotel Don Carlos* (☎ *312-24-99, Madero 418*) charges US$38 for its older air-conditioned rooms, and has a restaurant, bar and parking.

Top End Most top-end hotels are close to the main east-west highway, which crosses northern Villahermosa as Avenida Ruiz Cortines.

The 99-room *Howard Johnson Hotel* (☎ */fax 314-46-45, ☎ 800-505-49-00, Aldama 404*) has small but comfortable rooms in the Zona Luz's pedestrian zone for US$61 single or double with one bed, US$70 with two beds.

Hotel Best Western Maya Tabasco (☎ *314-44-66, 800-237-77-00, Avenida Ruiz Cortines 907*) is 1km north of the Zona Luz. Comfy, modern rooms are US$123 single or double, and there are nice gardens with a large pool.

As an oil town, Villahermosa has no shortage of luxury hotels. Three of the best are located near the intersection of Paseo Tabasco and Avenida Ruiz Cortines (Hwy 180), a pleasant few minutes' walk from Parque-Museo La Venta. Poshest is the *Hyatt Regency Villahermosa* (☎ *315-12-34, Avenida Juárez 106, Colonia Lindavista*), with all the expected luxury services, including a swimming pool and tennis courts, from US$165, single or double.

Hotel Cencali (☎ */fax 315-19-99, ☎ 800-112-50-00*), also on Avenida Juárez in Colonia Lindavista, neighbors the Hyatt. The hotel's setting, away from noisy streets, is excellent. Modern air-conditioned rooms cost US$105 single or double, including buffet breakfast. There's a swimming pool in tropical gardens running down to the Laguna de las Ilusiones.

The *Calinda Viva & Spa Villahermosa* (☎ *315-00-00, 800-711-55-55*), at the corner of Avenidas Juárez and Ruiz Cortines, is a three-story, motel-style, white stucco building surrounding a large swimming pool. The comfortable rooms are US$115, single or double, but promotions often reduce this by 10% or 15%. The hotel boasts a spa with gym, sauna and massage services.

Places to Eat

Madero and the pedestrian streets of the Zona Luz (Lerdo de Tejada, Juárez, Reforma, Aldama) have lots of snack and fast-food shops.

Douglas Pizza (*Lerdo de Tejada 105*), opposite Hotel Pakaal, offers pizzas with a wide assortment of toppings, from around US$3.75 for *chicas* (small) to *grandes* for US$6.50 to US$9.75. There's a pleasant ambience, and pasta and salads too; open 4 to 11:30 pm Monday to Saturday, 2 to 9:30 pm Sunday.

Aquarius Restaurante Vegetariano (*Zaragoza 513*), near Parque Juárez, open 8 am to 5 pm daily, has many veggie offerings as well as some items that contain meat. Try the granola, yogurt, fruit and honey, the soy burgers or the mushroom cocktail (all US$1.60 to US$2.75). There's a

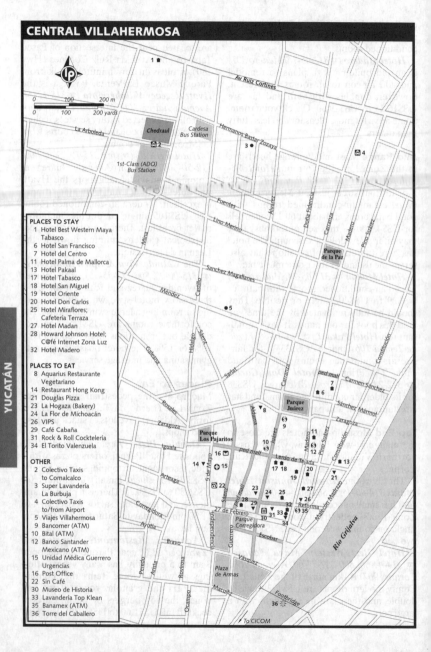

CENTRAL VILLAHERMOSA

PLACES TO STAY
1 Hotel Best Western Maya Tabasco
6 Hotel San Francisco
7 Hotel del Centro
11 Hotel Palma de Mallorca
13 Hotel Pakaal
17 Hotel Tabasco
18 Hotel San Miguel
19 Hotel Oriente
20 Hotel Don Carlos
25 Hotel Miraflores; Cafetería Terraza
27 Hotel Madan
28 Howard Johnson Hotel; C@fé Internet Zona Luz
32 Hotel Madero

PLACES TO EAT
8 Aquarius Restaurante Vegetariano
14 Restaurant Hong Kong
21 Douglas Pizza
23 La Hogaza (Bakery)
24 La Flor de Michoacán
26 VIPS
29 Café Cabaña
31 Rock & Roll Cocktelería
34 El Torito Valenzuela

OTHER
2 Colectivo Taxis to Comalcalco
3 Super Lavandería La Burbuja
4 Colectivo Taxis to/from Airport
5 Viajes Villahermosa
9 Bancomer (ATM)
10 Bital (ATM)
12 Banco Santander Mexicano (ATM)
15 Unidad Médica Guerrero Urgencias
16 Post Office
22 Sin Café
30 Museo de Historia
33 Lavandería Top Klean
35 Banamex (ATM)
36 Torre del Caballero

US$5 lunch buffet too, and they sell whole-wheat baked goods and vitamins.

The Hotel Miraflores' *Cafetería Terraza* *(Reforma 304)* is good, with decent prices – *antojitos* or a quarter chicken with fries and salad for US$3 to US$4.50, meats and fish US$5 to US$8.

VIPS (Madero 402) is a branch of a countrywide chain offering reliable Mexican and international food in very clean surroundings. Most main courses cost between US$4 and US$7.

Restaurant Hong Kong (5 de Mayo 433) is an upstairs Chinese restaurant serving a range of Cantonese and Mandarin food. A full meal, from wonton soup through a chicken dish to fortune cookie, costs US$5 to US$10.

El Torito Valenzuela (27 de Febrero 202) is a popular and convenient taquería, open from 8 am to midnight. Varied tacos cost US$0.50 to US$1 apiece and the daily *comida corrida* (set lunch) is less than US$4.35 for four courses.

Always busy in the late afternoon is *Rock & Roll Cocktelería (Reforma 307)*. A *cocktel* (fish or seafood, tomato sauce, lettuce, onions and a lemon squeeze) with crackers is yours for the rockin' price of US$5.50 to US$6.50.

Eating or drinking on the run? Try *La Hogaza*, a bakery on Juárez, for croissants, doughnuts, Danish pastries, yogurt or boxed juices; *La Flor de Michoacán* just across the street has fresh juices, *licuados*, frozen yogurt and fruit cocktails.

There's excellent coffee at the sidewalk *Café Cabaña* on Juárez.

The luxury hotels near the intersection of Avenida Ruiz Cortines and Paseo Tabasco all have good restaurants – the Hyatt Regency Villahermosa has a particularly high reputation. In Tabasco 2000, there are plenty of restaurants in the Galerías Tabasco 2000 mall, including an economical food court.

Overlooking the river near the Museo Regional de Antropología is *Restaurant Los Tulipanes*, open every day from 1 to 11 pm. Seafood and steaks, the specialties, cost between US$6 and US$10.

Entertainment

The *Teatro Esperanza Iris* (☎ 314-42-10), just north of CICOM, often stages folkloric dance, theater, cinema and music performances.

Live music, usually with dancing, is featured at several hotel bars including the Calinda Viva & Spa Villahermosa, Hyatt Regency Villahermosa, Hotel Cencali, Hotel Best Western Maya Tabasco and Hotel Miraflores.

Getting There & Away

Air Nonstop and one- or two-stop direct flights to/from Villahermosa include:

Cancún – Aerocaribe daily
Guadalajara – Aeroméxico daily
Havana, Cuba – Aerocaribe daily
Houston, Texas – Aeroméxico twice weekly
Mérida – Aerocaribe 3 times daily, Aviacsa daily
Mexico City – Aeroméxico, Mexicana, Aviacsa and Aerocaribe all daily
Monterrey – Aerolitoral 6 days weekly, Aeroméxico 5 days weekly
Oaxaca – Aerocaribe daily
San Antonio, Texas – Aerolitoral 5 days weekly
Tuxtla Gutiérrez – Aerocaribe daily
Veracruz – Aerocaribe twice daily, Aerolitoral 6 days weekly

Mexicana (☎ 316-31-32) is at Locales 5 & 6, Plaza D'Atocha Mall, Tabasco 2000. Aerocaribe (☎ 316-50-46) and Aviacsa (☎ 316-57-33) are on the mall at Locales 9 and 10 respectively. Aeroméxico and Aerolitoral (☎ 800-021-40-00) are inside the CICOM complex at Periférico Carlos Pellicer 511-2.

The phone numbers for the airport are ☎ 356-01-56/57.

Bus The 1st-class (ADO) bus station (☎ 312-89-00), Mina 297, is three blocks south of Avenida Ruiz Cortines and about 12 blocks north of the city center. It has a luggage room (US$0.20 per hour) and a selection of little eating places. Deluxe and 1st-class buses of UNO, ADO and Cristóbal Colón run from here, as well as a few 2nd-class buses by Colón's Altos service and AU.

YUCATÁN

Though Villahermosa is an important transportation point, many buses serving it are *de paso*, so buy your onward ticket as early as possible. Daily departures (most in the evening) include:

Campeche 380km, 6 hours; 13 buses (US$18 to US$22)

Cancún 875km, 12 hours; 10 buses (US$38 to US$47)

Chetumal 580km, 8 hours; 11 buses (US$23)

Mérida 560km, 9 hours; 13 buses (US$26 to US$43)

Mexico City (TAPO) 780km, 11 hours; 28 buses (US$41 to US$66)

Oaxaca 700km, 12 hours; three buses (US$30)

Palenque 140km, 2½ hours; 12 buses (US$6)

Playa del Carmen 850km, 12 hours; 10 buses (US$35)

San Cristóbal de Las Casas 305km, 7 hours; one bus (US$13), or go via Tuxtla Gutiérrez

Tuxtla Gutiérrez 285km, 6 hours; 10 buses (US$11 to US$15)

Veracruz 590km, 8 hours; 17 buses (US$20 to US$34)

Smaller companies have service to destinations within Tabasco from other terminals in Villahermosa.

Car Most car-rental companies have desks at Rovirosa Airport. Here are some city offices:

Advantage (☎ 315-50-48) Paseo Tabasco 1203

Budget (☎ 315-80-88) Malecón Madrazo 761

Dollar (☎ 313-35-84) Paseo Tabasco 600, next to the cathedral; (☎ 314-44-66) Hotel Best Western Maya Tabasco, Avenida Ruiz Cortines 907

Getting Around

Villahermosa's Rovirosa Airport is 13km east of the center along Hwy 186. A taxi between the airport and city costs US$9 and takes about 20 minutes. Alternatively, go to the road outside the airport parking lot and pick up a colectivo taxi into the city for US$0.70 per person. These terminate on Carranza half a block south of Ruiz Cortines, about 1km north of the Zona Luz. Take a

'Dos Montes' vehicle from there to return to the airport.

To get from the ADO bus station to the Zona Luz, take a 'Centro' combi (US$0.40) or a taxi (US$1), or walk 15 to 20 minutes. To walk, go out of the bus station's side (south) door, turn left onto Lino Merino and walk five blocks to Parque de la Paz, then turn right on Carranza.

From the Zona Luz to the ADO bus station, take a 'Chedraui' bus or combi north on Malecón Madrazo. Chedraui is a big store just north of the bus station.

Any taxi ride within the area between Avenida Ruiz Cortines, the Río Grijalva and Paseo Usumacinta costs US$1.25. Combi rides within the same area are US$0.40.

YUMKÁ

Yumká (☎ 56-01-07), 18km east of Villahermosa (4km past the airport), is the city's version of a safari park, divided into jungle, savanna and lake areas, representing Tabasco's three main ecosystems. Visits take the form of guided tours of the three areas (30 minutes each). You tour the lake by boat, and the savanna – which with its elephants, giraffes and hippos seems more African than Mexican – on a tractor-pulled trolley. In the jungle you'll see Tabascan species such as howler monkeys, jaguars, macaws and peccaries (the big cats are in enclosures!).

It's hardly a Kenya game drive, but if you fancy a dose of space, greenery and animals, go. Yumká is open 9 am to 5 pm daily, with the last trolley leaving at 4 pm (US$2.25, US$1 extra for the lake). Drinks and snacks are available. A taxi from the Zona Luz costs US$8.

COMALCALCO

The Chontal Mayan city of Comalcalco flourished during the Late Classic period between AD 500 and 900. *Comalcalcanes* traded the cacao bean with other Mayan settlements, and it is still the chief local cash crop.

Resembling Palenque in architecture and sculpture, Comalcalco is unique because it is built of bricks made from clay, sand and – ingeniously – oyster shells. Mortar was made with lime from the oyster shells.

As you enter the ruins, the substantial structure to your left may surprise you, as the pyramid's bricks look remarkably like the bricks used in construction today. Look on the right-hand side for remains of the stucco sculptures that once covered the pyramid. In the northern section of the Acrópolis are remains of fine stucco carvings.

Although the west side of the Acrópolis once held a crypt comparable to that of Palenque's Pakal, the tomb was vandalized centuries ago and the sarcophagus stolen. Continue up the hill to the Palacio and enjoy the breeze while you gaze down on unexcavated mounds.

Comalcalco is open 10 am to 5 pm daily (US$2.25, free Sunday and holidays).

Getting There & Away
The 55km journey from Villahermosa to Comalcalco town takes about 1¼ hours. Colectivo taxis leave from the street on the north side of the ADO bus station in Villahermosa every 20 minutes, charging US$2.50 per person. Frequent 2nd-class buses go from the Cardesa terminal on Hermanos Bastar Zozaya and from the Somellera bus station, northwest of the center on Avenida Ruiz Cortines. Taxis cost US$22.

The ruins are about 3km from Comalcalco town. You can cover the distance by taxi, or by a Paraíso-bound combi. Combis may go right to the ruins or they may drop you at the entrance, from which it's about a 1km walk.

AGUA SELVA
If you're hankering to get far off the beaten track, consider a trip to the Agua Selva ecotourism project in the remote, rugged hills of far southwest Tabasco. A series of rustic cabaña lodgings have been set up to help visitors enjoy the canyons, waterfalls and caves of the area, and the Early Classic period Zoque ruins and rock carvings of animals, people and geometric designs at Malpasito. There's transportation into the area from Huimanguillo, 67km southwest of Villahermosa. Villahermosa's main tourist office can provide enough information to set you on your way, and the inexpensive *Hotel del Carmen* (*Morelos 49*) in Huimanguillo has more details.

TO/FROM GUATEMALA VIA TENOSIQUE
The river route from Tabasco into Guatemala is along the Río San Pedro from La Palma in southeast Tabasco. Compared to the more commonly taken route via Frontera Corozal in Chiapas, the San Pedro gives you a longer river ride, but the connecting transportation is less convenient, especially from Palenque.

First you have to get to the town of Tenosique, served by 11 buses a day (3½ hours, US$8.50) from Villahermosa's ADO bus station. Starting from Palenque you must go first to the town of Emiliano Zapata (one hour by three daily ADO buses or by hourly Transportes Palenque colectivos from 5 am to 6 pm), then get another bus to Tenosique (one hour). A taxi from Palenque to Tenosique is about US$43.

From Tenosique, there are buses to La Palma (one hour) every two hours from 4:30 am to 4:30 pm, from Calle 31. A taxi (45 minutes) costs US$12.

A daily boat leaves La Palma at 8 am for the four-hour trip (US$25) through jungle and cleared land to the village of El Naranjo, Guatemala. Other boats may leave later in the day. El Naranjo has a few places to stay (basic rooms along the main street for US$3 to US$5, good rooms in *Posada San Pedro* by the river for US$23 to US$34). About five buses daily go to Flores (four hours, US$5). Coming from Guatemala, the scheduled boat leaves El Naranjo about 1 pm. If you miss the last bus out of La Palma, there should be trucks.

Tenosique and Emiliano Zapata have economical hotels.

Palenque travel agencies offer transportation packages (US$35 per person) for the approximately 11- to 13-hour Palenque-Flores trip, via Bethel (see Organized Tours in the Palenque section). However, you can do this same trip a bit cheaper by yourself if you're in a group that can split the cost of the Río Usumacinta boat ride.

Chiapas

Mexico's southernmost state has enormous variety reflected in its nature, ancient civilizations and modern indigenous peoples. At the center of Chiapas is San Cristóbal de Las Casas, a cool and tranquil colonial town surrounded by mysterious indigenous Maya villages. Two hours' drive west (though a new road being constructed through the mountains should cut this down to 40 minutes) – and nearly 1600m lower – the surprisingly modern state capital, Tuxtla Gutiérrez, has probably the best zoo in Mexico, devoted entirely to Chiapas' varied fauna. Only a few kilometers from Tuxtla is the 800m-deep Cañón del Sumidero, through which you can take an awesome boat ride.

About three hours north of San Cristóbal are the Agua Azul and Misol-Ha waterfalls, which are among Mexico's most spectacular. A little farther on are the ruins of Palenque, perhaps the most beautiful of all ancient Mayan sites. In the east of Chiapas is the Selva Lacandona (Lacandón Jungle), one of Mexico's largest areas of tropical rain forest. Within the jungle you can visit beautiful Mayan sites such as Yaxchilán and Bonampak, or lovely Laguna Miramar, a pristine lake. You can also cross the jungle-lined Río Usumacinta into Guatemala, en route to Flores and Tikal.

Three hours' travel southeast of San Cristóbal, near the border with Guatemala, is the lovely Lagos (or Lagunas) de Montebello region. Chiapas also has a steamy Pacific coast where you can explore the beaches and mangrove-fringed lagoons of La Encrucijada Biosphere Reserve or relax at laid-back Puerto Arista.

You'll find a reasonable touristic introduction to Chiapas on the Mundo Maya website (www.mundomaya.com.mx/portal).

Warning

Since the 1994 Zapatista uprising, the security situation in Chiapas has been volatile. Keep your ear to the ground about where it's not advisable to go, especially if you are thinking of leaving the main highways.

When traveling by bus, take care of your belongings (try not to fall asleep on a 2nd-class bus without someone watching your stuff). Traveling by bus is probably safer than driving yourself, however: We have heard of a few incidents in which private cars were held up and robbed, especially along the road to Bonampak/Yaxchilán.

Special Considerations

Make sure your tourist card is valid and keep it and your passport handy: They may be scrutinized at checkpoints. Dozens of foreigners have been expelled from Mexico for supposedly engaging in unauthorized political or journalistic activities or human-rights observation in Chiapas. Since 1998 Mexico has had a special category of FM3 visa for international observers; if the purpose of your visit is anything other than plain tourism, you can ask in advance at a Mexican consulate or embassy about visa requirements. Also, note that when you enter Mexico in Chiapas (from Guatemala) you will be given only 15 days on your visa; you can get extensions in Chiapas but they may be costly (and, at least in San Cristóbal, you'll only get 15 days more).

History

Chiapas has always been intimately connected with Guatemala. Pre-Hispanic civilizations lived in the area on either side of today's Chiapas-Guatemala border, and for most of the Spanish colonial era Chiapas was governed from Guatemala.

Pre-Hispanic Civilizations Central and coastal Chiapas came under Olmec influence. Izapa, near Tapachula, peaked between 200 BC and AD 200 and is thought to be a link between the Olmec and the Maya.

During the Classic era (approximately AD 250 to 900), coastal and central Chiapas were relative backwaters, but low-lying, jungle-covered eastern Chiapas gave rise to splendid Mayan city-states such as Palenque, Yaxchilán, Bonampak and Toniná, which flourished in the 7th and 8th centuries.

After the Classic Mayan collapse, highland Chiapas and Guatemala were divided among a number of often warring kingdoms, many with cultures descended from the Maya but some also claiming central Mexican Toltec ancestry. Coastal Chiapas, a rich source of cacao, was conquered by the Aztecs at the end of the 15th century and became their most distant province, under the name Xoconochco (from which its present name, Soconusco, is derived).

Colonial Era Central Chiapas was brought under Spanish control by the 1528 expedition of Diego de Mazariegos, who defeated the dominant, warlike Chiapa people, many of whom jumped to their death in the Cañón del Sumidero rather than be captured. Outlying areas were subdued in the 1530s and 1540s, though Spain never gained full control over the scattered inhabitants of the Lacandón Jungle. New diseases arrived with the Spaniards, and an epidemic in 1544 killed about half the indigenous people of Chiapas.

Administration from Guatemala for most of the Spanish era meant that Chiapas lacked supervision for long periods, and there was little check on colonists' excesses against the indigenous people.

The only real light in the darkness was the work of some Spanish church figures. Preeminent was Bartolomé de Las Casas (1474–1566), appointed the first bishop of Chiapas in 1545. Las Casas had come to the Caribbean as a colonist, but in 1510 he entered the Dominican order, and he spent the rest of his life fighting for indigenous rights in the new colonies. His achievements, including the passing of laws reducing compulsory labor (1542) and banning indigenous (though not black) slavery (1550), earned him the hostility of the colonists but the affection of the native people.

19th & 20th Centuries In 1821 newly independent Mexico annexed Spain's former Central American provinces (including Chiapas), but when Mexican emperor Agustín de Iturbide was overthrown in 1823, the United Provinces of Central America declared their independence. A small military force under General Vicente Filísola managed to persuade Chiapas to join the Mexican union, and this was approved by an 1824 referendum in Chiapas.

Since then, a succession of governors appointed in Chiapas by Mexico City, along with local landowners, have maintained a feudal-like control over the state. Periodic uprisings and protests bore witness to bad government, but the world took little notice until January 1, 1994, when a group calling itself the Ejército Zapatista de Liberación Nacional (EZLN; Zapatista National Liberation Army) briefly occupied San Cristóbal de Las Casas and nearby towns by military force.

The Zapatistas (see the boxed text), fighting for a fairer deal for indigenous peoples, won widespread support around and beyond Mexico but got no real concessions. In 2000, despite a tight Mexican army noose around their areas of strongest support in Chiapas and other harassment, they were still maintaining a mainly political campaign for democratic change. Hopefully, the recent elections in Mexico (which toppled the long-standing PRI stronghold in Chiapas and elected Pablo Salazar into the governor's position) will bring promised peace concessions to the state.

Geography & Climate

Chiapas' 74,000 sq km fall into five distinct bands, all roughly parallel to the Pacific coast. The heaviest rain in all of them falls from May to October.

The hot, fertile coastal plain, 15km to 35km wide, is called the Soconusco. Rising inland of the Soconusco is the Sierra Madre de Chiapas mountain range, mostly between 1000m and 2500m in height, though Tacaná volcano on the Guatemalan border reaches 4110m. The Sierra Madre continues on into Guatemala.

The Zapatistas

On January 1, 1994, an armed left-wing peasant group calling itself the Ejército Zapatista de Liberación Nacional (EZLN, the Zapatista National Liberation Army) sacked and occupied government offices in the Chiapas towns of San Cristóbal de Las Casas, Ocosingo, Las Margaritas and Altamirano. The Mexican army evicted the Zapatistas within a few days, with about 150 people killed. The rebels retreated to a remote forest hideout on the fringes of the Lacandón Jungle, having drawn the world's attention to Chiapas.

The EZLN's goal was to overturn a corrupt, wealthy minority's hold on land, resources and power in Chiapas, which had left many indigenous peasants impoverished, marginalized and lacking in education, health care and fundamental civil rights. Some say that the Mexican Revolution of 1910–20 never really happened in Chiapas.

Though the Zapatistas were militarily far outnumbered and outgunned, they attracted broad support and sympathy, and their leader, a masked figure known as Subcomandante Marcos, became a cult figure for many Mexicans.

During 1994, while Marcos waged a propaganda war from his jungle hideout, demanding justice and reform in Mexican politics, peasants took over hundreds of farms and ranches in Chiapas. Ultimately the government bought some of these properties from their previous owners and handed them over to the peasants.

In 1996 an agreement on indigenous rights was reached between EZLN and government negotiators at San Andrés Larraínzar, the main center of Zapatista support in the Chiapas highlands. The deal was to give limited autonomy to Mexico's indigenous peoples, but by 1997 it was clear that the government did not intend to turn the San Andrés accords into law.

Inland from the Sierra Madre is the wide, warm, fairly dry Río Grijalva valley, also called the Central Depression of Chiapas, 500m to 1000m high.

Next come the Chiapas highlands, Los Altos, mostly 2000m to 3000m high and also extending into Guatemala. San Cristóbal de Las Casas, in the Valle de Jovel in the middle of these uplands, is cool with temperatures between high single figures and the low 20s (°C) year-round.

The low-lying northern and eastern parts of the state include some of Mexico's few remaining areas of tropical rain forest.

The Zapatistas

There had been an amnesty since 1995, but the rebels, hemmed into a remote pocket of jungle territory near the Guatemalan border, remained encircled by government troops. They continued to wage a propaganda war, using the Internet and staging a series of high-profile conventions in La Realidad, 85km southeast of Ocosingo.

In 1997 and 1998, tension and killings escalated in Chiapas. The Zapatistas set up some 'autonomous municipalities,' ousting officials of the ruling PRI party, whom they said had been elected fraudulently. The Zapatistas' enemies formed paramilitary organizations to drive Zapatista supporters from their villages and oppose the autonomous municipalities. Many of these paramilitaries were aligned with the state government; some were led by prominent local PRI members.

Violence reached its worst point with the Acteal massacre in December 1997 (see 'Indigenous Peoples of Chiapas') and continued in 1998, partly as a result of the seizure of some autonomous municipalities by the army and police.

In 1999 the EZLN organized a nationwide 'consultation' in which the 2.85 million respondents overwhelmingly favored the enactment of the San Andrés accords and of special constitutional rights for indigenous people. Subcomandante Marcos appeared in public for the first time in two years at a meeting in La Realidad in May 1999. Participants were urged to join students', workers' and farmers' struggles in addition to becoming part of indigenous peoples' struggles.

The Mexican army had approximately 60,000 troops in Chiapas by 1999, along with many imposing new bases and roadblocks all over the place. But a blatant attempt to wipe out the rebels would cause a huge outcry; what the army seemed to be trying to do was grind Zapatista supporters into submission and draw the noose ever tighter around their heartland. In mid-1999 troops, police and paramilitaries launched a major campaign of intimidation, violence and detentions against dozens of pro-Zapatista villages in Las Cañadas and the Lacandón Jungle. Thousands fled their villages, and by late 1999 the number of Chiapas indigenous people displaced was estimated to be as high as 21,000.

Underlying – literally – the whole complicated conflict may be oil, large quantities of which are rumored to be sitting beneath several areas of eastern Chiapas.

Recent elections that took place in August 2000 ousted the longtime PRI government and could promise a more peaceful future, if newly elected governor Pablo Salazar's vows hold true. Other promises from the new government include calming religious conflicts and a development of industry in the mostly agricultural state.

To get the Zapatista point of view firsthand, you can visit the EZLN Internet site ¡Ya Basta! (www.ezln.org). You'll get plenty more background on this complicated situation from organizations such as Global Exchange (www.globalexchange.org) and SIPAZ (www.sipaz.org) and on the Mexico Channel site (www.trace-sc.com) under Politics. The Chiapas state government's position can be found on www.chiapas.gob.mx.

YUCATÁN

Economy

Chiapas has little industry but high agricultural output. It produces more coffee and bananas than any other Mexican state – chiefly from the fertile Soconusco and adjacent slopes. Tapachula is the commercial hub of the Soconusco.

Chiapas contributes 13% of Mexico's natural gas and 4% of its oil (oil was found in northwest Chiapas in the 1970s), and the Río Grijalva, flowing across the center of the state, generates more electricity than any other river in Mexico at several huge dams. But in this electricity- and water-rich state, half the homes have neither electricity nor running water, and rates of illiteracy and infant mortality are the highest in the country. Most *chiapanecos* are in fact very poor, and wealth is concentrated in a small oligarchy.

TUXTLA GUTIÉRREZ
• population 378,100 • elevation 532m

Chiapas' lively state capital has several things worth stopping for, among them one of Mexico's best zoos (devoted to the fauna of Chiapas) and easy access to exhilarating boat trips through the 800m-deep Cañón del Sumidero, though both of these trips could also be made in a long day trip from San Cristóbal de Las Casas.

Tuxtla Gutiérrez is toward the west end of Chiapas' hot, humid central valley. Its name comes from the Náhuatl word *tuchtlan* ('where rabbits abound'), and from Joaquín Miguel Gutiérrez, a leading light in Chiapas' early-19th-century campaign not to be part of Guatemala. The city was unimportant until it became the state capital in 1892.

Orientation
The city center is Plaza Cívica, with the cathedral on its south side. The main east-west street, here called Avenida Central, runs past the north side of the cathedral. As it enters the city from the west this same street is Boulevard Dr Belisario Domínguez; to the east it becomes Boulevard Ángel Albino Corzo.

East-west streets are called Avenidas, and are named Norte or Sur depending whether they're north or south of Avenida Central. North-south streets are Calles, and are called Poniente (Pte) or Oriente (Ote) depending whether they're west or east of Calle Central, which runs along the west side of Plaza Cívica. Each street name also has a suffix indicating whether it is east (Oriente, Ote), west (Poniente, Pte), north (Norte) or south (Sur) of the intersection of Avenida Central and Calle Central. So the address 2a Avenida Norte Pte 425 refers to the western (Pte) half of 2a Avenida Norte, with 425 being the street number.

Maps INEGI, at 1a Avenida Norte Ote 220A just east of 2a Ote Norte, sells 1:25,000 and 1:50,000 maps of many parts of Chiapas and other Mexican states, for US$3 each; open 8:30 am to 4:30 pm Monday to Friday.

Information
Tourist Offices The friendly Oficina Municipal de Turismo (City Tourism Office, ☎ 612-55-11 ext 214) is at Calle Central Norte and 2a Norte Ote, in the underpass at the northern end of Plaza Cívica. It's open 8 am to 8 pm Monday to Friday, 8 am to noon Saturday and Sunday, though exact hours may change throughout the year. They provide free luggage storage.

Chiapas' state tourism ministry, Sedetur, has a tourist information office (☎ 800-280-35-00) at Boulevard Domínguez 950. It's open 9 am to 9:30 pm daily.

Immigration The Instituto Nacional de Migración (☎ 611-42-42), 1a Calle Ote Norte 323, is open 9 am to 3 pm Monday through Friday. If you're heading into the highlands and need a visa extension, get it here as you'd likely get 30 or more days (rather than 15 in San Cristóbal).

Money Bancomer, at the corner of Avenida Central Pte and 2a Avenida Norte Pte, does foreign exchange 8:30 am to 5:30 pm Monday to Friday, 10 am to 2 pm Saturday. Bital, on the west side of Plaza Cívica, exchanges money 8 am to 7 pm Monday to Friday, 8 am to 7 pm Saturday. These and many other city-center banks have ATMs. Hecali, a shop on Calle Central Sur facing the cathedral, handles Western Union money transfers.

Post & Communications The post office, on a pedestrian-only block of 1a Avenida Norte Ote just off Plaza Cívica, is open 8 am to 5 pm Monday to Friday, 9 am to 1 pm Saturday. There are plenty of pay phones around the plaza.

Netcropper, 2a Avenida Norte Pte 427, is open 9 am to 9 pm daily and charges US$1.60 an hour for Internet access.

Laundry Lavandería La Burbuja, 1a Avenida Norte Pte 369, will wash and dry up to 3kg for US$3.25 (ready next day). It is open 8:30 am to 8 pm Monday to Saturday.

Magic Wash Lavandería, on 4a Calle Ote Norte and 1a Avenida Norte Oriente, has similar prices and is open from 8 am to 7:30 pm Monday to Friday and 8 am to 2 pm Saturday.

Plaza Cívica & Catedral

Tuxtla's broad, lively main plaza occupies two blocks, with the modern Catedral de San Marcos facing it across Avenida Central at the south end. On the hour the cathedral's clock-tower bells tinkle out a tune to accompany a revolving parade of apostles' images on one of its upper levels.

Zoológico Miguel Álvarez del Toro (ZOOMAT)

Chiapas claims the highest concentration of animal species in North America – among them several varieties of big cat, 1200 types of butterfly and over 600 birds. You can see 180 of these species – many of them in danger of extinction – in Tuxtla's zoo, where they're kept in relatively spacious enclosures on a forested hillside just south of the city.

Among the creatures here are ocelots, jaguars, pumas, red macaws, toucans, spider monkeys and a pair of quetzals. The zoo has a clear conservation message and is named after Miguel Álvarez del Toro, the eminent Chiapas conservationist and zoologist who founded it.

ZOOMAT (☎ 612-37-54) is open 9:30 am to 5:30 pm Tuesday through Sunday (free) and has a bookstore. To get there take a 'Cerro Hueco, Zoológico' colectivo (US$0.25) from the corner of 1a Ote Sur and 7a Avenida Sur Ote. They leave about every 20 minutes and take 20 minutes. A taxi is around US$1.50.

Parque Madero

This museum-theater-park area, 1.25km northeast of the city center, includes several sites of interest. The modern **Museo Regional de Chiapas** has archaeological and colonial history exhibits, and costume and craft collections, all from Chiapas. It is open 9 am to 4 pm Tuesday through Sunday (US$2, free on Sunday and holidays). Next door is the 1200-seat **Teatro de la Ciudad**. Nearby is the somewhat unkempt but shady **Jardín Botánico** (Botanical Garden), open 9 am to 6 pm Tuesday through Sunday (free).

Also in Parque Madero is a children's park, the **Parque de Convivencia Infantil**, open 10 am to 9 pm daily (though the rides seem to operate only on busy days such as Saturday and Sunday).

If you don't want to walk, take a colectivo along Avenida Central to Parque 5 de Mayo at the corner of 11a Calle Ote, then another colectivo north along 11a Calle Ote.

Places to Stay – Budget

Camping Three kilometers west of Plaza Cívica, beside a traffic circle with a large 'cow horn' sculpture, *La Hacienda Hotel & Trailer Park* (☎ 612-79-86, Boulevard Domínguez 1197) has all hookups for US$12 per RV site, a coffee shop and a tiny pool.

Hostel Tuxtla's youth hostel, the *Villa Juvenil Chiapas* (☎ 613-54-78, Boulevard Albino Corzo 1800) is part of a sports center nearly 2km east of Plaza Cívica. For a bed in a small, clean separate-sex dormitory you pay US$3.25. Meals cost US$1.60 each. You need no hostel card. From the city center, take a 'Ruta 1' colectivo east along Avenida Central to the yellow footbridge just before a statue of Albino Corzo.

Hotels Tap water in the cheaper hotels is *'al tiempo'* (not heated) but, since this is a hot town, it's not cold either.

There are many hotels on and near 2a Avenida Norte Ote, off the northeast corner of Plaza Cívica. *Hotel Casablanca* (☎ 611-03-05, 2a Avenida Norte Ote 251) has plain, small rooms, but they're very clean and the whole place is brightened by leafy indoor plants. Singles/doubles are US$8.75/13.50 with fan and shower, US$13.50/16.25 with TV too; doubles with air-con, TV and bath are US$25. The hotel has parking.

TUXTLA GUTIÉRREZ

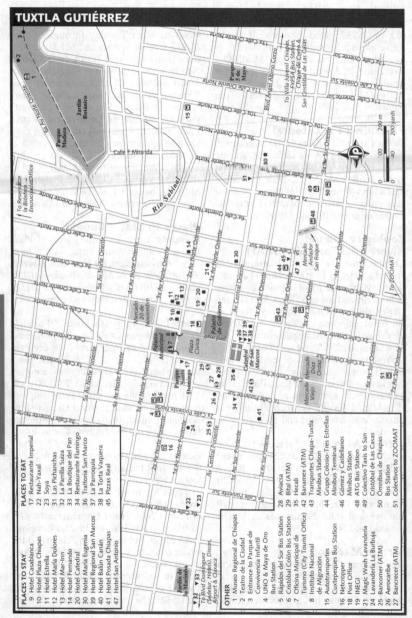

PLACES TO STAY
9 Hotel Casablanca
10 Hotel Plaza Chiapas
11 Hotel Estrella
12 Hotel María Dolores
13 Hotel Mar-Inn
14 Hotel Fernando
20 Hotel Catedral
30 Hotel María Eugenia
39 Hotel Regional San Marcos
40 Hotel Balún Canán
41 Hotel Posada Chiapas
47 Hotel San Antonio

PLACES TO EAT
17 Restaurante Imperial
22 Nah-Yaxal
23 Soya
31 Las Pichanchas
32 La Parrilla Suiza
33 La Boutique del Pan
34 Restaurante Flamingo
36 Trattoria San Marco
37 La Parroquia
38 La Torta Vaquera
45 Pizzas Real

OTHER
1 Museo Regional de Chiapas
2 Teatro de la Ciudad
3 Entrance to Parque de Convivencia Infantil
4 UNO & Maya de Oro Bus Station
5 Rápidos del Sur Bus Station
6 Cristóbal Colón Bus Station
7 Oficina Municipal de Turismo (City Tourist Office)
8 Instituto Nacional de Migración
15 Autotransportes Cuxtepeques Bus Station
16 Netcropper
18 Post Office
19 INEGI
21 Magic Wash Lavandería
24 Lavandería La Burbuja
25 Bancomer (ATM)
26 Aerocaribe
27 Bancrecer (ATM)
28 Aviacsa
29 Bital (ATM)
35 Hecali
42 Banamex (ATM)
43 Transportes Chiapa-Tuxtla Minibus Station
44 Grupo Colosio-Tres Estrellas Minibus Terminal
46 Gómez y Castellanos Minibus Station
48 ATG Bus Station
49 Colectivo Taxis to San Cristóbal de Las Casas
50 Ómnibus de Chiapas Bus Station
51 Colectivos to ZOOMAT

Hotel Plaza Chiapas (☎ 613-83-65, *2a Avenida Norte Ote 229*) has a shiny lobby but the bare rooms are nothing fancy. They're clean enough, with fan and private bath for US$9.75/12. Across the side street here, *Hotel María Dolores* (☎ 612-36-83, *2a Calle Ote Norte 304*) and *Hotel Estrella* (☎ 612-38-27, *2a Calle Ote Norte 322*) have unremarkable rooms with private bath for US$6.50/8.75 (or US$5.50/7.50 with shared bath, at the Estrella).

Half a block east, *Hotel Mar-Inn* (☎ 612-10-54, *2a Avenida Norte Ote 347*) has 59 decent rooms and wide plant-lined walkways, but its roof seems to trap in humidity. Singles/doubles with fan and bath are US$14/18.

Farther east again, rooms in the *Hotel Fernando* (☎ 613-17-40, *2a Avenida Norte Ote 515*) are plain but spacious and clean. Singles/doubles/triples with fan and bath are US$10.75/13/15. Parking is available. More toward the center, *Hotel Catedral* (☎ 613-08-24, *1a Avenida Norte Ote 367*) has decent, clean rooms with bath, fans, hot water and even cable TV at US$16.25/ 20/23 for singles/doubles/triples.

Toward the southeast, *Hotel San Antonio* (☎ 612-27-13, *2a Avenida Sur Ote 540*) is an amicable modern place with a small courtyard and clean rooms for good prices of US$7.50 with private bath and fan, or US$9.75 for twin beds. A few blocks west, *Hotel Posada Chiapas* (☎ 612-33-54, *2a Calle Pte Sur 243*) charges US$7.50/14 for clean but smallish rooms with fan, TV and bath, centered around a sunny courtyard.

Places to Stay – Mid-Range

The *Hotel Regional San Marcos* (☎ 613-19-40, *2a Calle Ote Sur 176*), a minute's walk from Plaza Cívica, has medium-size rooms with TV and bath for US$18.50/21 single/ double (US$22.50/26 with air-con). Bright, flower-patterned furniture and a recent paint job give the place a tiny sparkle.

Seven blocks east of the center, *Hotel Balún Canán* (☎ 612-30-48, *Avenida Central Ote 944*) has fairly pleasant rooms with air-con, bath and TV for US$23/28. Get one at the back, not on the noisy street.

La Hacienda Hotel (☎ 612-79-86, *Boulevard Domínguez 1197*), 3km west of Plaza Cívica, has clean doubles with fan for US$33.

Places to Stay – Top End

Most comfortable downtown is *Hotel María Eugenia* (☎ 613-37-67, fax 613-28-60, *Avenida Central Ote 507*). It has a good restaurant, pool, parking and attractive air-conditioned rooms with cable TV and bath for US$53/59.

Hotel Bonampak (☎ 613-20-50, fax 612-77-37, *Boulevard Domínguez 180*), 1.6km west of Plaza Cívica almost opposite the state tourist office, has comfortable air-conditioned singles/doubles/triples with cable TV for US$53/59/65. It boasts a pool, travel agency, parking and a copy of one of the famous murals at Bonampak ruins.

Tuxtla's most luxurious hostelry is the modern, 210-room *Hotel Camino Real* (☎ 617-77-77, *Boulevard Domínguez 1195*), which rises like some huge colored-concrete castle of the hospitality industry 1.5km west of Hotel Bonampak. The interior is spectacular, with a pool and waterfall in a large, verdant inner courtyard. Very comfortable air-conditioned singles/doubles cost US$97/ 109, and there are plenty of top-end facilities.

Hotel Flamboyant (☎ 615-09-99), on Boulevard Domínguez 1km west of the Camino Real, is in handsome modern Arabic style, with singles/doubles for US$85/99.

Places to Eat

The *Restaurante Imperial*, on Calle Central Norte facing the west side of Plaza Cívica, is a good, clean, busy place, convenient for the 1st-class bus station. A two-course comida corrida with lots of main-course choice is US$2.50, breakfast items (from cornflakes to eggs or hotcakes) are US$1 to US$2, and there's good chocolate to drink.

There's a row of popular restaurants with outdoor tables behind the cathedral; most are open from around 7 am to midnight. At *Trattoria San Marco* you can enjoy more than 20 varieties of pizza (US$1.85 to US$10.75), baguettes (US$3 to US$3.50), salads, *papas rellenas* (baked potatoes with toppings) or savory *crepas*. *La Parroquia*

YUCATÁN

next door specializes in *a la parrilla* grills, from spicy sausages to a T-bone for US$5 to US$7.50. *La Torta Vaquera* is popular for coffee, tacos (US$0.50) and quesadillas.

Restaurante Flamingo (1a Calle Pte Sur 17), down a passage off the street, is a quiet, efficient place with air-con and a dinerlike atmosphere, open 7 am to 10 pm daily. A full pancake breakfast, or an order of luncheon tacos or enchiladas, is yours for US$3.50. Most meat and fish dishes cost US$5.50 to US$8. For a decent-size meal at a small price, try *Pizzas Real (2a Avenida Sur Ote 557)*, opposite Hotel San Antonio, where a comida corrida of rice and two other dishes costs only US$1. One of the best values for comidas corridas in town (US$6) is served in the restaurant of the *Hotel María Eugenia (Avenida Central Ote 507)*.

A few blocks west of the center on Avenida Central Pte, *Soya* sells whole-wheat breads, fresh yogurt and yogurt ice cream (US$1), to which you can add fruits along with a range of tasty toppings. *Nah-Yaxal (6a Calle Pte Norte 124)*, round the corner, is a clean, bright vegetarian restaurant open 7 am to 10 pm Monday to Saturday, 8 am to 4 pm Sunday. Whole-wheat *tortas*, *antojitos* and an *energética* breakfast salad of fruit, granola, yogurt and honey go for US$1.50 to US$2.50 each, and the three-course lunch is US$4.

Three blocks farther west, *La Boutique del Pan*, on Avenida Central Pte facing the Jardín de la Marimba, is a bakery with a nice, bright café section where you can sit down for a pastry, sandwich or coffee. *La Parrilla Suiza (Avenida Central Pte 1013)*, on the next block, is popular for its *tacos al pastor* at US$0.50 each and grills up to US$3.50. It stays open until 4 or 5 am.

Farther west, the Hotel Bonampak's *Cafetería Bonampak* is very popular and reasonably priced.

Six blocks east of Plaza Cívica is *Las Pichanchas (Avenida Central Ote 837)*, a courtyard restaurant open noon to midnight daily, with a long menu of local specialties. Marimbas play in the afternoon and evening, and there's Chiapas folkloric dance in the evenings too. Try *chipilín*, a cheese-and-cream soup on a maize base, and for dessert, *chimbos*, made from egg yolks and cinnamon. In between, have tamales, vegetarian salads or *carne asada*. Three courses with drinks costs around US$12.

Entertainment

Popular free marimba concerts are held from 7 to 9 pm nightly in the Jardín de la Marimba, a pleasant park beside Avenida Central Pte eight blocks west of Plaza Cívica.

The city's most popular discos, both attracting a mixed-ages crowd, are *Baby Rock* (☎ 615-14-28), on Calzada Emiliano Zapata, west of the center off Boulevard Domínguez opposite the Camino Real hotel, and *La Uno* (☎ 615-29-57, Boulevard Las Fuentes 101), just outside the Camino Real's main door.

Shopping

The Casa de las Artesanías de Chiapas, unhandily located at Boulevard Domínguez 2035, 2km west of Plaza Cívica, sells a good range of Chiapas crafts; it's open 10 am to 8 pm Monday to Saturday, 10 am to 3 pm Sunday.

Getting There & Away

Air Aerocaribe flies to/from Mexico City, Oaxaca, Villahermosa, Veracruz, Tapachula, Mérida, Cancún, Guatemala and Havana (Cuba) all at least once daily; and to/from Palenque daily. Aviacsa flies several times daily to/from Mexico City, as well as several other destinations.

Aerocaribe (☎ 612-00-20, airport ☎ 615-50-30) is at Avenida Central Pte 206, one block from Plaza Cívica. Aviacsa (☎ 611-20-00, airport ☎ 615-10-11) is nearby at Avenida Central Pte 160.

Bus The Cristóbal Colón terminal (☎ 612-51-22) at 2a Avenida Norte Pte 268, two blocks west of the main plaza, is the primary bus station. Colón's 1st-class and 2nd-class (Altos) services and ADO's 1st-class buses operate from here. The 2nd-class line Rápidos del Sur is next door, and UNO and Maya de Oro deluxe services are across the street (though at time of research they were using the Colón/ADO terminal while remodeling). There's no baggage checkroom, but there are private ones outside on 2a Norte Pte: Look for *'Se guardan maletas'* or *'Se guardan equipaje'* signs.

Most 2nd-class companies' terminals are east of the center:

Autotransportes Cuxtepeques 10a Calle Ote Norte at 3a Norte Ote

Autotransportes Tuxtla Gutiérrez (ATG) 3a Avenida Sur Ote 712

Fletes y Pasajes (FYPSA) 9a Avenida Sur Ote 1882

Grupo Colosio-Tres Estrellas 2a Avenida Sur Ote 521

Ómnibus de Chiapas (OdC) 3a Avenida Sur Ote 884

Daily departures include:

Cancún 1110km, 16 hours; one Maya de Oro (US$43), one Colón (US$45), two ATG (US$38)

Comitán 175km, 3½ hours; Cuxtepeques every half hour (US$5.50), three Colón (US$6.50)

Mérida 820km, 13 hours; one Maya de Oro (US$39), one Colón (US$28), one ATG (US$24)

Mexico City (most to TAPO, a few to Norte) 980km, 17 hours; one UNO (US$76), two Maya de Oro (US$56), three Colón/ADO (US$48)

Oaxaca 540km, 10 hours; one Maya de Oro (US$26), two Colón (US$21), eight FYPSA (US$13.50)

Palenque 275km, 6 hours; three Maya de Oro (US$14), three Colón (US$12), five ATG (US$10)

Puerto Escondido 560km, 11½ hours; two Colón (US$23)

San Cristóbal de Las Casas 85km, 2 hours (new road will cut this to 40 minutes); six Maya de Oro (US$4), five Colón (US$3.50), five ATG (US$3), frequent Colosio–Tres Estrellas minibuses (US$2.75), OdC every half hour 6 am to 5 pm (US$2), frequent colectivo taxis (US$3.75) from 3a Avenida Sur Ote 847

Tapachula 390km, 8 hours; six Maya de Oro (US$19), 15 Colón (US$16), 20 Rápidos del Sur from 4 am to 2 pm (US$13.50)

Villahermosa 285km, 6 hours; two Maya de Oro (US$14.50), three Colón (US$12), one ATG (US$10)

Car Rental companies, most also with desks at the airport, include:

Álamo (☎ 612-52-61) 5a Avenida Norte Pte 2260

Arrendadora Express (☎ 612-26-66) Avenida Central Ote 725

Autos Gabriel (☎ 612-07-57) Boulevard Domínguez 780

Budget (☎ 615-06-83) Boulevard Domínguez 2510

Hertz (☎ 615-53-48) Hotel Camino Real

Getting Around

Tuxtla's Aeropuerto Francisco Sarabia (☎ 612-29-20), also called Aeropuerto Terán, is 3km south of Hwy 190 from a signposted turnoff 5km west of Plaza Cívica. Taxi desks in the airport ask US$4.50 to the city center; outside the airport gate you may get one for US$4.

All colectivos (US$0.25) on Boulevard Domínguez-Avenida Central-Boulevard Albino Corzo run at least as far as the Hotel Bonampak and state tourist office in the west, and 11a Calle Ote in the east. Official stops are marked by *'Parada'* signs, but they'll sometimes stop for you elsewhere. Taxi rides within the city cost US$1.25 to US$1.60.

CHIAPA DE CORZO
• **population 27,700** • **elevation 450m**

This pleasant colonial town on the Río Grijalva, 12km east of Tuxtla Gutiérrez, is the main starting point for trips into the Cañón del Sumidero.

History

Chiapa de Corzo has been occupied almost continuously since about 1500 BC. Its sequence of pre-Hispanic cultures makes it invaluable to archaeologists, but there's little to see in the way of remains.

In the couple of centuries before the conquistadors arrived, the warlike Chiapa – who dominanted western Chiapas at the time – had their capital, Nandalumí, across the Grijalva near the canyon mouth. When the Spaniards under Diego de Mazariegos invaded the area in 1528, the Chiapa, realizing defeat was inevitable, apparently hurled themselves by the hundreds to death in the canyon – men, women and children – rather than surrender.

Mazariegos founded a settlement that he called Chiapa de los Indios here, but a month later shifted his base to another new settlement, Villa Real de Chiapa (now San Cristóbal de Las Casas), where the climate and natives were more agreeable.

At Chiapa in 1863, liberal forces, organized by Chiapas state governor Ángel Albino Corzo, defeated conservatives supporting the French invasion of Mexico. The name of Corzo, who was also born in the town and died here, was added to Chiapa's in 1888.

Orientation & Information

Buses and minibuses to and from Tuxtla stop on the north side of Chiapa's spacious plaza, named for Albino Corzo. Chiapa's embarcadero for Cañón del Sumidero boat trips is two blocks south of the plaza along 5 de Febrero, the road on the plaza's west side.

There's a tourist information office a few steps down on Domingo Ruiz off the west side of the plaza, around the corner from the Banamex and its ATM.

Things to See & Do

Impressive **arcades** frame three sides of the plaza, a statue of General Corzo rises on the west side, and an elaborate castlelike brick fountain in Mudéjar-Gothic style, said to resemble the Spanish crown and known as **La Pila**, stands toward the southeast corner. The large **Templo de Santo Domingo de Guzmán**, one block south of the plaza, was built in the late 16th century by the Dominican order. Its adjoining convent is now the Centro Cultural (open 3:30 to 7:30 pm weekdays), holding an exposition of Mexican prints, folk dress and wares. Also here is the **Museo de la Laca**, which features the local craft specialty, lacquered gourds (open 10 am to 6 pm Tuesday to Sunday). Combined entry to both is US$2.

If you're around January 9 to 21, check out the Fiesta de Enero, when young men dress as women and dance the streets, representing maids distributing food to the poor during colonial times. Also, colorfully dressed masked men with blond wigs (representing blond conquistadors) take part in processions on Jan 15, 17 and 20. There are other festivities on other days; check the tourist office for specifics.

Places to Stay

Casa de Huéspedes Los Ángeles, at the southeast corner of the plaza, has basic singles/doubles with bath for US$8.75/10.75. *Hotel La Ceiba* (☎ 616-07-73, Domingo Ruiz 300), two blocks west of the plaza, has attractive rooms with air-con, fan and folksy decor for US$28/33, and an inviting pool.

Places to Eat

By the embarcadero are several *restaurants* with similar menus and loud music. All are equally overpriced, though the view of the river is nice.

Near the market on Coronel Urbina, across from the Museo de la Laca, are the standard ultracheap market *comedores*.

Restaurant Los Corredores, on 5 de Febrero at Madero, facing the southwest corner of the plaza, has good cheap breakfasts and plenty of reasonably priced fish plates. One block along Madero from here, and popular with tour groups, is the friendly *Restaurant Jardines de Chiapa (Madero 395)*, set around a garden patio, with main dishes for US$3.50 to US$4.50 and seafood up to US$6.

Ristorante Italiano Valle d'Aosta, on 5 de Febrero between the plaza and embarcadero, serves pizza and moderately priced Italian-style dishes.

Getting There & Away

Minibuses from Tuxtla Gutiérrez to Chiapa de Corzo are run by Gómez y Castellanos at 3a Avenida Sur Ote 380 and Transportes Chiapa-Tuxtla on 2a Avenida Sur Ote at 2a Ote Sur. Both depart every few minutes for the 20-minute, US$0.60 trip, and will also stop at Cahuaré embarcadero if you wish (see the Cañón del Sumidero section).

Buses to/from San Cristóbal de Las Casas don't pass through central Chiapa de

Templo de los Guerreros, Chichén Itzá, Yucatán

Santuario de la Virgen de Izamal, Yucatán

El Castillo (Pyramid of Kukulcán), Chichén Itzá

Bartering for a hammock, Mérida

Ball-court ring at Uxmal

Cuadrángulo de las Monjas, Uxmal

Noche de México dance, Mérida

Corzo, but most will stop at a gas station on Hwy 190 on the northeast edge of town. Microbuses (US$0.20) run between the *gasolinera* and the top end of the plaza.

CAÑÓN DEL SUMIDERO

The Cañón del Sumidero (Sumidero Canyon) is a daunting fissure in the earth a few kilometers east of Tuxtla Gutiérrez, with the Río Grijalva flowing northward through it. In 1981 the Chicoasén hydroelectric dam was completed at its northern end, and the canyon became a narrow, 25km-long reservoir with calm waters.

Fast motorboats carry visitors through the canyon between towering sheer rock walls. The fare per person for a roundtrip of about 2½ hours, in a boat holding 10 to 12 people, is US$7. There's a stop at the end of the reservoir, close to the dam, for food and refreshments.

Hwy 190 crosses the canyon mouth at Cahuaré, between Tuxtla and Chiapa de Corzo. Just east of the bridge and a few hundred meters off the highway is the Cahuaré embarcadero. You can board one of the open fiberglass *lanchas* (motorboats) here, or at the embarcadero in Chiapa de Corzo a couple of kilometers farther upstream, between roughly 8 am and 4 pm. Depending on traffic you may have to wait about an hour for a boat to fill up. Bring something to drink, something to shield you from the sun (though a hat will blow off) and, if the weather is not hot, some warm clothing.

It's about 35km from Chiapa de Corzo to the dam. Soon after you pass under Hwy 190 the sides of the canyon tower an amazing 1000m above you. Along the way you'll see a variety of bird life – herons, egrets, cormorants, vultures, kingfishers – plus probably a crocodile or two. The boat operators will point out a few odd formations of rock or vegetation, including one cliff face covered in thick, hanging moss resembling a giant Christmas tree.

At the end of the canyon, the fast, brown river opens out behind the dam. The water beneath you is 260m deep.

SAN CRISTÓBAL DE LAS CASAS
• population 99,300 • elevation 2100m

Hwy 190 from Tuxtla Gutiérrez seems to climb endlessly into the clouds before descending into the temperate, pine-clad Valle de Jovel, where lies the beautiful colonial town of San Cristóbal (cris-**toh**-bal).

San Cristóbal's rewards come from rambling its streets, discovering its many pretty nooks and crannies, visiting the unusual nearby indigenous villages (maybe on bicycle or horseback) and absorbing the unique atmosphere. San Cristóbal has a vaguely artsy, bohemian community of Mexicans and foreigners, a lively bar and music scene and wonderfully clear highland light. Accommodations and meals are inexpensive here.

San Cristóbal was catapulted into the limelight on January 1, 1994, when the Zapatista rebels, fighting for Chiapas' oppressed indigenous people, selected it as one of four towns in which to launch their revolution. The Zapatistas seized and sacked government offices in the town before being driven out within a few days by the Mexican army. They have since continued their struggle by mainly political means ever since from villages elsewhere in Chiapas, and with the brand new government recently voted in, changes (hopefully positive) may be taking place in the near future. It is no longer possible to treat the indigenous people of the San Cristóbal area as mere quaint objects of anthropological curiosity. If nothing else, the postcards and dolls representing Subcomandante Marcos (the Zapatista leader with the trademark black balaclava) are enough to make most visitors aware of Chiapas' political and economic struggles.

History

The Maya ancestors of the indigenous Tzotzil and Tzeltal people of the San Cristóbal area moved to these highlands after the collapse of lowland Maya civilization over 1000 years ago. Diego de Mazariegos founded San Cristóbal as the Spanish regional base in 1528.

For most of the colonial era San Cristóbal stayed a neglected outpost governed

YUCATÁN

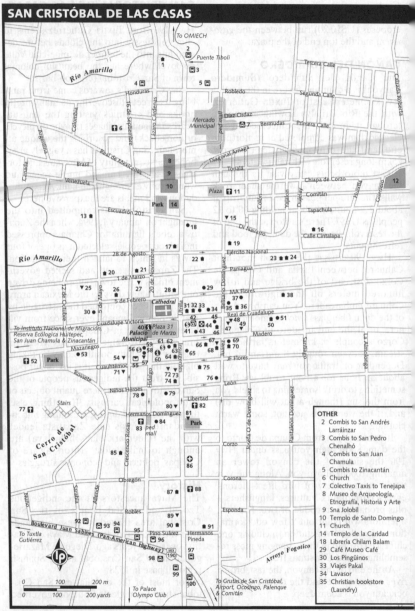

SAN CRISTÓBAL DE LAS CASAS

OTHER
2   Combis to San Andrés
    Larráinzar
3   Combis to San Pedro
    Chenalhó
4   Combis to San Juan
    Chamula
5   Combis to Zinacantán
6   Church
7   Colectivo Taxis to Tenejapa
8   Museo de Arqueología,
    Etnografía, Historia y Arte
9   Sna Jolobil
10 Templo de Santo Domingo
11 Church
14 Templo de la Caridad
18 Librería Chilam Balam
29 Café Museo Café
30 Los Pingüinos
33 Viajes Pakal
34 Lavasor
35 Christian bookstore
    (Laundry)

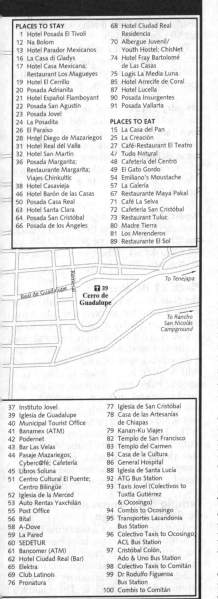

Real de Guadalupe

Kenedi

⌂ 39
Cerro de
Guadalupe

To Tenejapa

To Rancho
San Nicolás
Campground

ineffectively from Guatemala. Its Spanish citizens made their fortunes from wheat, while the indigenous people lost their lands and suffered diseases, taxes and forced labor. The church afforded some protection against colonist excesses. Dominican monks reached Chiapas in 1545 and made San Cristóbal their main base. One of them, Bartolomé de Las Casas (for whom the town is now named), was appointed bishop of Chiapas that year; he and Juan de Zapata y Sandoval, bishop from 1613 to 1621, are both fondly remembered. In modern times Bishop Samuel Ruiz, who retired in late 1999 after a long tenure, followed very much in the Las Casas tradition of support for the oppressed indigenous people – and earned the loathing of the Chiapas establishment for his pains.

San Cristóbal was the state capital from 1824 to 1892 but remained relatively isolated until the 1970s, when tourism began to be a significant factor in its economy. After a hiccup following the Zapatista uprising, tourism has bounced back.

Orientation

San Cristóbal is easy to walk around, with straight streets rambling up and down several gentle hills. The Pan-American Highway (Hwy 190) passes through the south side of town. Officially named Boulevard Juan Sabines, it's called 'El Bulevar' by locals.

Nearly all transportation terminals are on or just off the Pan-American. From the Cristóbal Colón bus terminal it's six blocks north up Insurgentes to the central square, Plaza 31 de Marzo, which has the cathedral on its north side.

Information

Tourist Offices The municipal tourist office (☎ 678-06-65) is in the north end of the Palacio Municipal, on the west side of Plaza 31 de Marzo. It is open 9 am to 2 pm and 5 to 8 pm Monday to Saturday.

More helpful is the tourist information office (☎ 678-65-70) of the Chiapas state tourism department, the Secretaría de Desarrollo Turístico (Sedetur). It's just off

YUCATÁN

Plaza 31 de Marzo at Hidalgo 1B and is open 8 am to 9 pm Monday to Saturday, 8 am to 2 pm Sunday. There's usually someone here who speaks English.

Immigration The Instituto Nacional de Migración (☎ 678-02-92), Diagonal El Centenario 30, is open 9 am to 2 pm Monday to Friday. Note: Extending your visa in San Cristóbal will give you only 15 more days, and costs US$17. You may be able to get 30 days or more in Tuxtla Gutiérrez, so it would be worth going there for any extensions,

Money Bancomex, on the main plaza, is efficient at currency exchange, and Bital bank, half a block west of the plaza on Mazariegos, is open long hours: 8 am to 7 pm Monday to Friday, 9 am to 1:30 pm Saturday. If the banks are shut, try Viajes Chincultik at the Posada Margarita, Real de Guadalupe 34, which has better rates than casas de cambio and is open daily.

Elektra, at Insurgentes 8, offers Western Union 'Dinero en Minutos' service.

Post & Communications The post office, on the corner of Cuauhtémoc and Rosas, one block west and one south of the main plaza, is open 8 am to 6 pm Monday to Friday, 9 am to 1 pm Saturday.

La Pared bookstore, Hidalgo 2, offers an inexpensiv e fax and phone service.

Cyberc@fé (☎ 678-74-88), in the Pasaje Mazariegos mall between Real de Guadalupe and Madero, charges US$1 for 15 minutes of Internet access. It has plenty of computers and some good coffee; open 9 am to 10 pm daily. Podernet on Real de Guadalupe has the same prices, but ChisNet (next to the youth hostel) is the cheapest, at US$1.75 per hour.

Bookstores & Libraries La Pared, Hidalgo 2, has the town's best selection of new and used books in English; come here to trade in your used book. Dana, the owner and long-time resident of San Cristóbal, is a good source of information on the region.

Librería Chilam Balam, in a courtyard at Utrilla 33, has a few guidebooks in English

and French, and lots of history and anthropology in Spanish. Libros Soluna, Real de Guadalupe 13B, has a few books on Chiapas and Mexico in English.

The 14,000 books at Na Bolom, Guerrero 33, make up one of the world's biggest collections on the Maya and their lands. It's open 10 am to 2 pm daily.

Laundry Lavasor, Real de Guadalupe 26, charges US$3.50 to wash and dry ?I y. It's open 8 am to 2:30 pm and 4:30 to 9 pm daily.

The Christian bookstore around the corner at Belisario Domínguez 9 will do laundry for only US$1 per kilogram and is open 9 am to 2 pm and 4 to 8 pm Monday through Saturday.

Medical Services Among the English-speaking doctors in San Cristóbal is general practitioner Dr Luis José Sevilla (☎ 678-16-26), Calle del Sol 2. There's a general hospital (☎ 678-07-70) on Insurgentes.

Plaza 31 de Marzo

The main plaza was the old Spanish center of town, used for markets until the early 20th century. Today it's a fine place to sit and watch the town life happen around you.

The cathedral, on the north side of the plaza, was begun in 1528 but completely rebuilt in 1693. Its gold-leaf interior has a baroque pulpit and altarpiece, and the detailed stonework on the west facade has recently been attractively picked out in yellow, red and white paint.

The Hotel Santa Clara, on the plaza's southeast corner, was the house of Diego de Mazariegos, the Spanish conqueror of Chiapas. It's one of the few secular examples of plateresque style in Mexico.

Templo & Ex-Convento de Santo Domingo

North of the center on Cárdenas, the Templo de Santo Domingo is the most beautiful of San Cristóbal's many churches – especially when its pink facade is floodlit at night. The church and adjoining monastery were built between 1547 and 1560. The church's baroque facade – on which can be seen the double-headed Hapsburg eagle, symbol of the Spanish monarchy in those days – was added in the 17th century. There's plenty of gold inside, especially on the ornate pulpit.

Chamulan women and bohemian types from elsewhere conduct a daily craft market around Santo Domingo and the neighboring Templo de La Caridad (built in 1712). You'll find local and Guatemalan textiles, leather bags and belts, homemade toys and dolls, hippie jewelry and more.

The Ex-Convento (Ex-Monastery) attached to Santo Domingo contains two interesting exhibits. One is the showroom of **Sna Jolobil**, a cooperative of 800 indigenous women weavers from the Chiapas highlands; showcased are some fine huipiles, skirts, rugs and other woven items. Prices run from a few dollars for smaller items to over US$700 for the best huipiles and ceremonial garments. Sna Jolobil is open 9 am to 2 pm and 4 to 6 pm Monday through Saturday.

The **Museo de Arqueología, Etnografía, Historia y Arte**, also in the ex-convento buildings, deals mainly with the history of San Cristóbal. It's open 10 am to 5 pm Tuesday through Sunday (US$2.25, Sunday and holidays free).

Mercado Municipal

The flavor of outlying indigenous villages can be sampled at San Cristóbal's busy municipal market, between Utrilla and Belisario Domínguez, eight blocks north of the main plaza, open Monday through Saturday till late afternoon. Many of the traders are villagers for whom buying and selling is the main reason to come to town.

Café Museo Café

This combined café and coffee museum, at MA Flores 10 (☎ 678-78-76), is a venture of Coopcafé, a group of 15,000 small-scale Chiapas coffee growers. In the café you can taste good organic local coffee along with limited breakfast and dessert items. The three-room museum covers the history of coffee and its cultivation in Chiapas. Coopcafé is part of the international 'fair trade' movement that aims to bring developing nations' commodity producers more of the profits from their products by promoting direct sales to the consumers.

Casa de las Artesanías de Chiapas

This has both an exhibition area, displaying the costumes and explaining the crafts of various villages around San Cristóbal, and a sales area with a good range of crafts from around Chiapas. It's on Niños Héroes at Hidalgo; open 10 am to 2 pm and 4 to 8 pm daily (free).

Templo del Carmen & Casa de la Cultura

El Carmen church stands on the corner of Hidalgo and Hermanos Domínguez. Formerly part of a nunnery (built in 1597), it has a distinctive arch-based tower built in 1680 to replace one destroyed by floods. Next door is the Casa de la Cultura, containing an art gallery, a library and the Bellas Artes auditorium.

Cerros de San Cristóbal & Guadalupe

The most prominent of the small hills over which San Cristóbal undulates are the tree-covered Cerro de San Cristóbal southwest of the center, reached by steps up from Allende, and the Cerro de Guadalupe, seven blocks east of the main plaza. Both are crowned by churches and afford good views, but you may encounter drunks on Cerro de San Cristóbal after about noon.

Organización de Médicos Indígenas del Estado de Chiapas (OMIECH)

This center in the north of town will interest anyone who's curious about the beliefs and lives of Chiapas' indigenous people. OMIECH (Organization of Indigenous Doctors of Chiapas) was set up in the 1980s to sustain the traditional Maya medicine of prayers, candles, incense, bones and herbs. Its Centro de Desarrollo de la Medicina Maya (Maya Medicine Development Center; ☎ 678-54-38, omiech@laneta.apc.org), at Avenida Salomón González Blanco 10, on the northward continuation of Utrilla, contains a museum (US$1) explaining how pulse-readers, herbalists, prayer specialists and other traditional practitioners work; a medicinal plant garden; and a *casa de curación* where cures are carried out. They sell herbal medicines as well. The center is open from 9 am to 2 pm and 3 to 6 pm Monday to Friday, and from 10 am to 4 pm Saturday and Sunday.

Horseback Riding

Almost any place you stay in San Cristóbal can arrange a four- or five-hour guided ride to San Juan Chamula for US$8 or US$9, or to the Grutas de San Cristóbal. You might want to ask about the animals: Are they full-size horses or just ponies, fiery or docile, fast or slow?

Language Courses

San Cristóbal has two prominent Spanish-language schools. Competition between them is keen and details of what they offer may change fairly rapidly. We've heard excellent reports from students at Instituto Jovel (☎/fax 678-40-69, jovel@sancristobal.podernet.com.mx, www.mexonline.com/jovel.htm), MA Flores 21. Most classes here are one-on-one, and you get three hours of instruction a day. Five days' tuition and seven days' accommodations with a Mexican family (with a private room and all meals) costs US$185 (US$145 if you take group classes).

Centro Bilingüe (☎/fax 678-37-23, spanish@mundomaya.com.mx, mundomaya.com.mx/centrob), at Real de Guadalupe 55 in the Centro Cultural El Puente, charges US$71.50/101.25 per week for 15 hours of group/private instruction (plus a US$50 registration fee); this includes several hours of chat sessions. A stay in a family house (with meals every day but Sunday) costs US$85/95 for a shared/private room.

Organized Tours

Na Bolom This beautiful colonial-style house, at Guerrero 33, belonged to Swiss anthropologist and photographer Gertrude (Trudy) Duby-Blom (1901–93) and her Danish archaeologist husband Frans Blom (1893–1963). While Frans researched the ancient Mayan sites, Trudy studied and protected the Lacandón people of eastern Chiapas. The house is full of archaeological and anthropological relics, books and photographs. Visits are by informal guided tour (US$2.75) in Spanish and English at 11:30 am and 4:30 pm daily.

Na Bolom is also the departure point for interesting tours to local villages and the Selva Lacandona, and offers lodging and meals (see Places to Stay – Mid-Range). You can find out more about Na Bolom at its website, www.ecosur.mx/nabolom.

Farther Afield Several agencies in San Cristóbal offer trips. All these destinations can be reached independently, but some people may prefer a tour with an informative guide. Typical day tours and prices per person (usually with a minimum of four people) are:

Chiapa de Corzo and Cañón del Sumidero 7 to 8 hours, US$23

Lagos de Montebello, Chinkultic ruins, Amatenango del Valle 9 hours, US$26

Palenque ruins, Agua Azul, Misol-Ha 14 hours, US$37

Toniná 9 hours, US$26

Agencies offering these kinds of tours include:

Kanan-Ku Viajes (☎ 678-61-01) Niños Héroes 2C

Viajes Chinkultic (☎ 678-09-57) Real de Guadalupe 34, in the Posada Margarita

Viajes Pakal Real de Guadalupe between Plaza 31 de Marzo and Belisario Domínguez

Another option is a three- or four-day trip to Laguna Miramar (see that section for details) or to Bonampak and Yaxchilán. The latter trip – also offered by Na Bolom – usually includes other stops such as Agua Azul, Palenque or Lacanjá in an all-inclusive price around US$175 per person.

Special Events

Semana Santa is celebrated with much churchgoing on Thursday evening and Via

Crucis processions on Good Friday morning; Saturday afternoon is the start of the annual town fair, the Feria de la Primavera y de la Paz (Spring & Peace Fair) with parades, bullfights and so on. Sometimes the celebrations of the anniversary of the town's founding (March 31) fall in the midst of it all too!

Also look out for events marking the feast of San Cristóbal (July 17 to 25) and the anniversary of Chiapas joining Mexico in 1824 (September 14), as well as other fiestas celebrated nationwide.

Places to Stay – Budget
In addition to camping and hostel options, there are dozens of budget hostelries in San Cristóbal. The municipal tourist office has lists.

Bus Station Area Places at the lower end of Insurgentes, near the bus stations, lack atmosphere. Just a 10-minute walk north puts you in the center of town.

Rooms at *Posada Insurgentes* (☎ 678-24-35, *Insurgentes 73*) are bare but reasonably modern, with shared baths, for US$5.50/10.75. *Hotel Lucella* (☎ 678-09-56, *Insurgentes 55*), opposite the Santa Lucía church, has OK rooms with bath for US$10.75/13. *Posada Vallarta* (☎ 678-04-65, *Hermanos Pineda 10*), half a block off Insurgentes, has bland, modernish rooms with bath and balcony for US$15.25/17.75.

The Center The *Albergue Juvenil/Youth Hostel* (☎ 678-76-55, *Juárez 2*) offers bunks in clean four- to eight-person rooms; cost is US$4 in rooms with their own bathroom, US$2.75 with shared bathrooms.

The *Hotel Real del Valle* (☎ 678-06-80, *Real de Guadalupe 14*) has a nice courtyard and 36 clean rooms costing US$16.25/20/23 single/double/triple. Close by, *Hotel San Martín* (☎ 678-05-33, *Real de Guadalupe 16*) has reasonable rooms with private bathroom for US$10.75/15/20.

Hotel Barón de las Casas (☎ 678-08-81, *Belisario Domínguez 2*) has just a few simple, clean singles/doubles with bath for US$12/15.75 along a wood-pillared patio.

Posada Margarita (☎ 678-09-57, *Real de Guadalupe 34*) has long been a budget travelers' halt. Decent, clean singles/doubles/triples/quads are US$6.50/9.75/13/17.50. The shared bathrooms are kept clean and there are plenty of them. There's a wide courtyard and a handy in-house travel agency, and a good restaurant under the same ownership next door.

Friendly *Logis La Media Luna* (☎ 678-16-58, *JF Flores 1*) has just a handful of singles/doubles around a nice yard with two hammocks. Most are US$10.75/16.25 but there are two with private bath and TV for US$22. Proprietress Luciana plans to offer free continental breakfast to all who stay here.

Two blocks below the main plaza at Insurgentes, the attractive, colonial-style *Hotel Fray Bartolomé de Las Casas* (☎ 678-09-32, *Niños Héroes 2*) has varied rooms around a wide, pillared courtyard with a dribbling fountain. It's an excellent value at US$19.50/23/28.25 for singles/doubles/triples.

Posada Adrianita (☎ 678-81-39, fax 678-12-83, *1 de Marzo 29*), built around two pretty courtyards, has comfortable singles/doubles for US$8.75/10.75 with shared bath or US$16.25/21.75 with private bath and TV. Rooms holding four or five people are US$27 to US$38.

East of the Center The *Rancho San Nicolás* (☎ 678-00-57) camping and trailer park is 2km east of the main plaza, along León. It's a friendly place with a grassy lawn, apple trees, a cafetería, horses grazing and hot showers. Cost is US$1.50 per person in a tent, US$3.25 in a cabin or US$2.25 in a medium-size trailer with full hookups.

Friendly Amparo will greet you at the safe and homey *Posada Casa Real* (☎ 678-13-03, *Real de Guadalupe 51*). There are eight nice, clean rooms and the cost is US$4.50 per person; there's an area to wash clothes in the pleasant upstairs open patio. The door is locked at 11 pm.

Tidy *Posada Jovel* (☎ 678-17-34, *Paniagua 28*) has rates of US$8.75/12 with shared bath, US$13/14.25 with private bath.

It has four superior new rooms across the street at US$16.25/19.50/22 double/triple/quadruple. *La Posadita (Paniagua 30)*, next door to the Jovel, has single/doubles/triples for just US$5.50/8.75/11.50.

North of the Center A couple blocks up from the cathedral, family-run *Posada San Agustín* (☎ 678-18-16, *Ejército Nacional 7*) has clean singles/doubles, all with windows, for US$8.75/14, with plenty of hot water and good views from the roof.

Hotel El Cerrillo (☎/fax 678-12-83, *Belisario Domínguez 27*) has a beautiful flowery courtyard and big rooms with shower for US$16.25/27 single/double. There's a very nice sitting room and guest kitchen.

La Casa di Gladys (☎ 678-57-75, *Cintalapa 6*) offers 16 rooms with shared bath at US$5.50/10.75 single/double. Dorm beds are only US$3.25. It's secure and clean, and there are plans to install a rooftop patio with views of city and mountains.

Up north past the Mercado Municipal and close to the combis to the outlying villages is *Hotel Posada El Tivoli* (☎ 678-81-50), on Lázaro Cárdenas at the Río Amarillo, where large and simple rooms cost just US$5 to US$6.50 with bath (TV is a bit more). It's a quiet area of town and some rooms even have a 'river view' (but don't expect too much).

Places to Stay – Mid-Range

The following is just a selection from the many choices. New hotels are opening all the time, often in attractive restored colonial buildings.

The pleasant *Posada San Cristóbal* (☎ 678-68-81, *Insurgentes 3*), a block south of the main plaza, has 10 airy, colorful rooms around a nice courtyard for US$22/30/37 single/double/triple.

Posada de los Ángeles (☎ 678-11-73, fax 678-25-81, *Madero 17*) is a colonial-style building with 20 pleasant rooms on three stories around two patios. Singles/doubles with TV and private bath are US$33/38. Indigenous costume prints add an attractive touch, and one patio contains a wood-and-glass-roofed restaurant.

The historic *Hotel Santa Clara* (☎ 678-11-40, fax 678-10-41, *Insurgentes 1*), on the main plaza, has sizable, comfortable rooms, a courtyard with caged red macaws, a restaurant, a bar/lounge and a pool. Singles/doubles/triples/quads are US$32/38/49/60.

El Paraíso (☎ 678-00-85, fax 678-51-68, *5 de Febrero 19*) has a cheery flower-filled courtyard and an amiable atmosphere. Comfortable singles/doubles cost US$34/46. The restaurant serves Mexican as well as a few European dishes.

Hotel Parador Mexicanos (☎ 678-15-15, fax 867-00-55, *5 de Mayo 30*) has big, comfortable rooms with cable TV for US$32/43/49 single/double/triple. A lobby lounge, restaurant, tennis court and verandas add to the appeal.

The modern *Hotel Arrecife de Coral* (☎ 678-21-25, *arrecife@sancristobal.podernet .com.mx, Rosas 29*) has several two-story buildings around grassy lawns. Quiet rooms with baths and TVs are US$36/41/46.

The museum/research institute *Na Bolom* (☎ 678-14-18, fax 678-55-86, *nabolom@ sclc.ecosur.mx, www.ecosur.mx/nabolom, Guerrero 33*) has good rooms with bath for US$38/52. Reservations are always a good idea.

Places to Stay – Top End

Hotel Diego de Mazariegos (☎ 678-06-21, fax 678-08-27, *5 de Febrero 1*) occupies two fine buildings either side of Utrilla one block north of the main plaza. The 74 rooms (US$43/54 single/double) are tastefully furnished and most have fireplaces.

Hotel Español Flamboyant (☎ 678-00-45, fax 678-05-14, *1 de Marzo 15*) is a remodeled old hotel (Graham Greene stayed here in the 1930s). Rooms are US$45/53 and there's a nice courtyard garden.

Hotel Casavieja (☎/fax 678-68-68, *MA Flores 27*) is located in an 18th-century house – very attractive and comfortable. Rooms are arranged around grassy, flowered courtyards, and there's a tidy restaurant. Rates are US$47/56.

Hotel Ciudad Real Residencia (☎ 678-10-53, *Juárez 1A*) is another converted colonial-style place, tastefully decorated with pretty bathroom tiling, wooden furniture and upstairs walkways. Rooms with TV are US$44/55/66, and there's a restaurant.

Hotel Casa Mexicana (☎ *678-06-98, fax 678-26-27, 28 de Agosto 1*), with its skylighted garden, fountains, plants, art and sculpture, exudes colonial charm. Rooms are agreeable, have views of the courtyard and cost US$47/60; suites are more.

Places to Eat

San Cristóbal offers a variety of cuisines and plenty of choice for vegetarians. Some eateries try to please everyone with long lists of multinational imitations; those with more focused efforts tend to be better.

Real de Guadalupe This is a good street for economical breakfasts. The pleasant *Cafetería* in Pasaje Mazariegos mall and the popular *Cafetería del Centro* (*Real de Guadalupe 15*) will both do eggs, toast, butter, jam, juice and coffee for US$2.

Restaurante Margarita (*Real de Guadalupe 34*), adjoining Posada Margarita, offers a broad choice of reliably good food. Breakfasts are US$1.75 to US$3.25, salads or spaghetti around US$3, antojitos US$3 to US$4.75, and chicken and meat dishes US$5 to US$6.

Just off Real de Guadalupe on Belisario Domínguez, the *Todo Natural* juice bar serves up big plates of fruit, yogurt and granola for US$1.60.

Insurgentes One and a half blocks south of the main plaza, *Restaurant Tuluc* (*Insurgentes 5*) scores with its efficient service, good food and reasonable prices. Most main courses cost US$2.50 to US$4.25, though pasta is less. It's open 7 am to 10 pm daily.

Good coffee and cakes are served in the little *Cafetería San Cristóbal*, on Cuauhtémoc just off Insurgentes. Mexican men bring along chess sets and newspapers to relax here.

The long-running *Madre Tierra* (*Insurgentes 19*) has an appetizing vegetarian menu with filling soups, whole-grain sandwiches, pizzas, salads, spinach cannelloni and other pasta. Most items are between

US$1.50 and US$3, there are big breakfasts for US$2.25, and the daily set menu costs US$5.50. *Panadería Madre Tierra*, a wholegrain bakery next door, sells breads, muffins, cookies, cakes, quiches, pizzas and frozen yogurt.

The cheapest meals in town are at *Los Merenderos*, a collection of food stalls just south of the Templo de San Francisco. Pick items that look fresh and hot. A full meal can be had for around US$1.50.

Farther down Insurgentes, little *Restaurante El Sol* does good, economical breakfasts and a US$2.50 comida corrida of four courses and coffee.

Madero There are about eight restaurants on Madero within a block of Plaza 31 de Marzo. One of the few that stand out is *Restaurante Maya Pakal* (*Madero 21A*), which serves a popular vegetarian comida of three courses and coffee or tea for US$3.50. Salads, pasta, pizza and other main dishes are mostly around US$2.50, and breakfasts are inexpensive too. It's open 7:30 am to 11 pm daily. A block farther east is the friendly, economical *El Gato Gordo* (*Madero 28*), popular with budget travelers. A typical breakfast here costs US$2, and there's a veggie comida for US$1.75. Crepes and pasta are around US$1 to US$2, and chicken and meat dishes, US$2.25 to US$2.75. Hours are 9 am to 10 pm every day but Tuesday.

Hidalgo & Rosas A block south of the main plaza, the upstairs restaurant of artsy *La Galería* (*Hidalgo 3*) serves pizza and pasta for US$3 to US$4.50 and a variety of other stuff.

A block west, carnivores flock into *Emiliano's Moustache* (*Rosas 7*) for tacos starting at US$0.50 each and meat *filetes* (US$3.50 to US$4.25). A specialty is the filling order of five tacos with combinations of meat, vegetable or cheese for US$2.25 to US$5.50. There are vegetarian possibilities too (including veggie tacos). It's open 9 am to 1 am daily.

Café La Selva (*Rosas 9*) is a pricey coffee shop run by an association of small-scale

Chiapas organic-coffee growers. Sit in the courtyard or in either of two clean, bright rooms to enjoy sandwiches and/or any of 36 types of coffee for US$2 to US$4; just be patient with the service. Like Café Museo Café (see earlier in this section), this association is a fair-trade venture.

North of the Center Among the few upscale restaurants in town is *Café-Restaurant El Teatro (1 de Marzo 8)*, which has a nice 2nd-floor location. The European-based menu includes crepes, fresh pasta, pizzas and desserts. Expect to spend US$10 to US$15 for a good full dinner here. The Hotel Casa Mexicana's *Restaurant Los Magueyes (28 de Agosto 1)* is another good choice in this price range.

The atmospheric *La Creación (1 de Marzo 14B)* does good sandwiches, salads, pasta and antojitos for US$2.50 to US$4. The specialty is *pechuga Creación*, a chicken, ham and mango *creación* (creation) served with vegetables for US$7.

La Casa del Pan (Dr Navarro 10) is an excellent bakery-restaurant with lots of vegetarian fare. A 'high-energy breakfast' of orange juice, fruit, yogurt, granola, organic Chiapas highland coffee and croissant or whole-grain bread is US$3.50. Whole-wheat sandwiches, organic vegan salads, *hojaldres* (vegetable strudels) and vegetarian antojitos are all between US$2 and US$3, pasta and pizzas a bit more. Hours are 8 am to 10 pm Tuesday through Sunday.

For unique ambience, eat at Na Bolom (see Places to Stay – Mid-Range). Everyone sits at one long wooden table in the Bloms' old dining room. Dinner is at 7 pm and costs US$8.50 – book an hour or two ahead. Lunch (1:30 pm) is the same price, and breakfast (7 to 10 am) costs US$4.25.

Entertainment

Thanks to San Cristóbal's traveler/student/bohemian scene, you can choose from half a dozen live music spots any night – though the musicianship isn't always the best!

About the funkiest nightspot is *Club Latino's*, at Madero and Juárez. It features live tropical music nightly from about

7:30 pm, and moderately priced food is served. *Madre Tierra (Insurgentes 19)* and *La Galería (Hidalgo 3)*, in its ground-floor patio-bar-gallery, both have live reggae, *son latino* or jazz almost nightly. *La Casa del Pan (Dr Navarro 10)* usually has something going on around 8 pm. *Bar Las Velas (Madero 14)*, popular with young locals, has a happy hour from 8 to 10 pm, and a reggae/rock/cumbia band around 11 pm; cover charge here is US$1.

A-dove (Hidalgo 2), popular with a youngish international crowd, features a variety of DJ music. It's open from 8 or 9 pm nightly except Monday, and cover charges are US$1 Friday and US$2 Saturday. There are usually two drinks for the price of one for some part of the night.

Restaurante Margarita (Real de Guadalupe 34) has a band nightly, and you may hear some unusual sounds at *La Creación (1 de Marzo 14B)* on weekends. The bar at the *Hotel Santa Clara* has music every night, and *Hotel Ciudad Real* on Plaza 31 de Marzo has music Wednesday through Friday.

San Cristóbal's one high-tech disco is *Palace Olympo Club (☎ 678-26-00, Prolongación Rosas 59)*, a couple of blocks south of the Pan-American Highway. It is open nightly except Monday.

The *Centro Cultural El Puente (Real de Guadalupe 55)* features a good, well-publicized program of movies. It also has a notice board where you may find out about other interesting goings-on.

There are fairly regular musical and theatrical performances at the *Casa de la Cultura* on Hidalgo.

Shopping

Most San Cristóbal shops are open 9 am to 2 pm and 4 to 8 pm Monday to Saturday. Hosts of them sell Chiapas indigenous crafts. Artistically speaking, the outstanding local *artesanías* are textiles such as huipiles, blouses and blankets, for Tzotzil weavers are some of the most skilled and inventive in Mexico. Another Chiapas specialty is amber jewelry (amber – fossilized tree resin – is mined near Simojovel, north of

San Cristóbal). Just be aware that lots of fake amber is sold by vendors walking the streets. A curiosity is little balaclava-wearing Subcomandante Marcos dolls, effigies of the EZLN leader.

The heaviest concentrations of craft shops are along Real de Guadalupe (prices go down as you move away from Plaza 31 de Marzo) and Utrilla (toward the Templo de Santo Domingo). Also near Santo Domingo are an inexpensive daily crafts market and the showroom of Sna Jolobil, a classy indigenous weavers' cooperative (see Templo & Ex-Convento de Santo Domingo).

The Casa de las Artesanías de Chiapas, at the corner of Niños Héroes and Hidalgo, sells a good range of Chiapas crafts at very good prices.

Food and everyday goods are the main stocks-in-trade at the Mercado Municipal.

Getting There & Away

Air San Cristóbal airport is about 15km out of town on the Ocosingo road. The only civilian passenger flights are daily to/from Mexico City by Aeromar. Taxi fare to San Cristóbal airport is US$3.50.

Bus, Combi & Taxi Sometime in early 2001 the new highway should be close to completion, cutting the travel time between San Cristóbal and Tuxtla Gutiérrez from almost two hours to about 40 minutes.

Cristóbal Colón, ADO and UNO (including Colón's Maya de Oro deluxe service and Altos 2nd-class service) share a terminal (☎ 678-02-91) at the junction of Insurgentes and the Pan-American Highway, south of the city about seven blocks. The baggage checkroom here charges US$0.50 per item for 24 hours.

The 2nd-class lines Autotransportes Tuxtla Gutiérrez (ATG), Transportes Lacandonia (TL), Andrés Caso Lombardo (ACL) and Dr Rodulfo Figueroa also have terminals nearby on the Pan-American Highway, as do various combi and colectivo taxi services to Comitán, Ocosingo and Tuxtla Gutiérrez. The combis and colectivos run all day from 6 am or earlier and leave when the vehicle is full. See the map for locations.

Daily departures from San Cristóbal de Las Casas include:

Cancún 1025km, 14 hours (via Chetumal, Tulum, Playa del Carmen); three from Colón terminal (US$37 to US$50), one ATG (US$35), also one ATG via Mérida (1045km, US$35)

Chiapa de Corzo 70km, 1½ hours; take a 2nd-class bus, combi or colectivo heading for Tuxtla Gutiérrez, but check first that it will let you off in Chiapa de Corzo

Ciudad Cuauhtémoc (Guatemala border) 170km, 2½ hours; six Altos (US$6.25), five ACL (US$3.75), leave early if you hope to get any distance into Guatemala the same day

Comitán 90km, 1½ hours; 10 from Colón terminal (US$3 to US$3.75), three ACL (US$2.25), combis (US$2.75) and colectivo taxis (US$3.25) from south side of Pan-American Highway

Mérida 735km, 11 hours via Campeche; two from Colón terminal (US$30 to US$35), one ATG (US$28)

Mexico City (TAPO) 1065km, 19 hours; six from Colón terminal (US$44 to US$84), one ATG (US$4)

Oaxaca 625km, 12 hours; two from Colón terminal (US$25 to US$31)

Ocosingo 88km, 1½ hours; four from Colón terminal (US$3 to US$4), six Figueroa (US$2 to US$3), eight ATG (US$3), 10 TL (US$2.25), combis (US$2.75) and colectivo taxis (US$3.75) from north side of Pan-American Highway

Palenque 190km, 5 hours; four from Colón terminal (US$7.50 to US$10), eight ATG (US$7.25), five Figueroa (US$7), 10 TL (US$5.50)

Puerto Escondido 645km, 13 hours; two Colón (US$26)

Tapachula 335km, 7 hours via Ciudad Cuauhtémoc, Motozintla; six from Colón terminal (US$12), three ACL (US$8)

Tuxtla Gutiérrez 85km, 2 hours; 10 from Colón terminal (US$3 to US$5.75), eight ATG (US$3), Figueroa at least every 40 minutes from 6:20 am (US$2.75), colectivo taxis (US$3.75) by Taxis Jovel

Villahermosa 305km, 7 hours; two from Colón terminal (US$14), four ATG (US$12)

Car Auto Rentas Yaxchilán (☎ 678-18-71), Mazariegos 36, is a Budget car-rental agency.

Getting Around

Combis (US$0.13) go up Rosas from the Pan-American Highway to the town center.

Taxis are fairly plentiful; a typical trip within the town costs US$1.25.

Los Pingüinos (☎/fax 678-02-02), 5 de Mayo 10B, rents bikes for US$6.50 for four hours or US$9 all day. It also conducts bicycle tours (see Organized Tours in the next section).

AROUND SAN CRISTÓBAL DE LAS CASAS

The indigenous villagers of the beautiful Chiapas highlands are descended from the ancient Maya and maintain some unique customs, costumes and beliefs.

Warning A few years ago the danger of armed robberies made it unsafe to walk between villages outside San Cristóbal. The word as we researched this edition was that walking or riding on horse or bicycle between villages was again safe – along the main roads, by day. You should still ask around yourself.

Special Considerations In some villages, particularly those nearest San Cristóbal, cameras are at best tolerated – and sometimes not even that. Some indigenous people apparently believe that appearing in

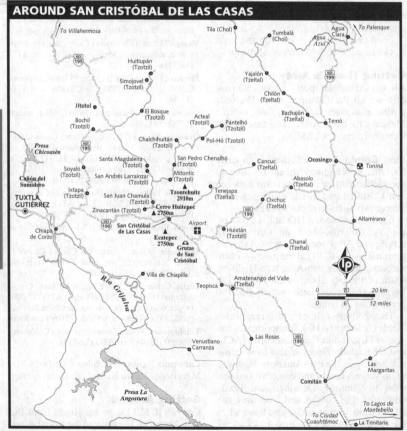

AROUND SAN CRISTÓBAL DE LAS CASAS

a photograph can put them in danger of losing their souls. Photography is banned in the church and during rituals at San Juan Chamula, and in the church and churchyard at Zinacantán. You may put yourself in physical danger if you take photos without permission. Always ask before taking a picture.

Markets & Festivals The villages' weekly markets are nearly always on Sunday. Proceedings start very early, with people arriving from outlying settlements as early as dawn, and wind down by lunchtime.

Festivals often give the most interesting insight into indigenous life, and there are plenty of them. Occasions like Carnaval (for which Chamula is famous), Semana Santa, el Día de los Muertos (Day of the Dead, November 2) and el Día de la Virgen de Guadalupe (December 12) are celebrated almost everywhere. At some of these fiestas a great deal of posh an alcoholic drink made from sugarcane – is drunk, and at Carnaval troops of strolling, posh-sozzled minstrels wander the roads strumming guitars, chanting, and wearing sunglasses (even when it's raining) and pointed 'wizard' hats with long, colored tassels.

Organized Tours A good guide can give you a feel for indigenous village life that you could never gain alone; these tours fascinate nearly everyone who joins them. All cost US$8 to US$10.

You can find Alex and Raúl (☎ 678-37-41) in front of San Cristóbal cathedral at 9:30 am daily. They give tours in either English or Spanish and limit their group sizes to 14 people. Trips to San Juan Chamula and Zinacantán last 4½ hours, and there are also tours available to less visited villages and other interesting sites.

Mercedes Hernández Gómez, a fluent English-speaker who grew up in Zinacantán, has been giving tours for many years. Groups can be large and are dosed with her personally 'spiritualized' messages; some like this, some don't. You can find Mercedes at 9 am almost daily near the kiosk in San Cristóbal's main plaza, twirling her colorful

umbrella. Other recommended village tours leave from Na Bolom (see Places to Stay – Mid-Range in San Cristóbal) at 10 am daily, lasting about six hours.

The friendly folk at Los Pingüinos (☎/fax 678-02-02), 5 de Mayo 10B, lead bicycle tours to little-visited, scenic country areas outside San Cristóbal. The trips (minimum two people) cost from US$22 per person for a three- to four-hour ride to US$24 for a five- or six-hour trip. The guides speak English, Spanish and German.

Getting There & Away Transportation to most villages leaves from points around the Mercado Municipal in San Cristóbal (see the San Cristóbal map for exact locations). Check latest return times before you set out: Some services wind down by lunchtime. Combis to San Juan Chamula (US$0.65) leave from Calle Honduras fairly frequently up to about 6 pm; for Zinacantán (US$0.75), combis go at least hourly, 6 am to 5 pm, from a yard off Robledo. Colectivo taxis to Tenejapa (US$1.50) leave from Bermudas. For San Andrés Larraínzar (US$1.30) and San Pedro Chenalhó (US$1.40), combis leave from yards north and south, respectively, of the Puente Tiboli bridge at the north end of Utrilla.

Reserva Ecológica Huitepec

The entrance to the Huitepec Ecological Reserve is about 3.5km from San Cristóbal on the road to San Juan Chamula. A 2km trail mounts 2700m Cerro Huitepec, rising from evergreen oak woods to rare cloud forest. The ascent takes about 45 minutes. The reserve has 60 resident bird species and over 40 winter visitors. It's open 9 am to 3 pm Tuesday through Sunday. The nonprofit conservationist association Pronatura (☎ 678-50-00), Juárez 11B, San Cristóbal, offers tours.

San Juan Chamula
• **population 2060**

The Chamulans put up strong resistance to the Spaniards in 1524 and launched a famous rebellion in 1869, attacking San Cristóbal. Today they are one of the largest

Indigenous Peoples of Chiapas

Of Chiapas' 3.6 million people, about 900,000 are indigenous (mostly Maya groups). In the countryside in various parts of the state, indigenous peoples speak the Chol, Chuj, Lacandón, Mam, Tojolabal, Tzeltal, Tzotzil and Zoque languages. Although all derived from ancient Mayan, most of these tongues are now mutually unintelligible, so local inhabitants use a second language such as Spanish or Tzeltal to communicate with other groups.

The indigenous people travelers will most likely come into contact with are the 310,000 or so Tzotzils who live in a highland area around San Cristóbal; their clothing is among the most colorful and elaborately worked in Mexico. You may also encounter the Tzeltals, numbering about 340,000, who inhabit the region between San Cristóbal and the Lacandón Jungle. Both of these groups are among Mexico's most traditional indigenous peoples.

Chiapas' indigenous peoples are 2nd-class citizens in economic and political terms, with some of the least productive land in the state. Their plight was the major reason behind the 1994 Zapatista uprising. But not everyone supports the Zapatistas, and violence between opposing indigenous factions has been an ugly side of the Zapatista upheaval. One series of revenge killings between pro-PRI and pro-Zapatista Tzotzils culminated in the 1997 massacre at the village of Acteal, north of San Cristóbal. Some 45 Zapatista-aligned people, mostly women and children, were gunned down by pro-PRI paramilitaries in a chapel.

Other Chiapas indigenous peoples include about 170,000 Choles, mainly in the north of the state, a few thousand Mexican Mames near the Guatemalan border between Tapachula and Ciudad Cuauhtémoc (around 300,000 other Mames are Guatemalans) and some 40,000 Zoques in the northwest.

Despite their problems, indigenous peoples' identities and self-respect survive with the help of traditional festivals, costumes, crafts and often ancient religious practices. These people remain suspicious of outsiders and may resent interference – especially in their religious practices. But they also will be friendly and polite if treated with due respect.

Tzotzil groups – about 80,000 strong. Their main village, San Juan Chamula, 10km northwest of San Cristóbal, is the center for some unique religious practices. A big sign at the entrance to the village strictly forbids photography in the village church or anywhere rituals are being performed. Nearby, around the shell of an older church, is the village's graveyard, with black crosses for people who died old, white for the young and blue for others. Near the old church is a small village museum, Ora Ton, open 9 am to 6 pm (US$0.55).

From dawn on Sunday, people stream into San Juan Chamula from the hills for the weekly market and to visit the church. Busloads of tourists also stream in, so you might prefer to come another day. Everyday necessities are the main goods traded at the Sunday market. Every day, vendors sell artesanías (mainly textiles) for the passing tourist trade.

The main church stands beside the main plaza. A sign tells visitors to obtain tickets (US$0.55) at the village tourist office, also on the plaza, before entering the church. Inside, the rows of burning candles, the clouds of incense and the worshipers kneeling on the pine-needle-carpeted floor make a powerful impression. Chanting curanderos may be rubbing patients' bodies with eggs or bones, or waving live chickens over them to 'absorb' any sickness. Saints' images are surrounded with mirrors and dressed in holy garments. Chamulans revere San Juan Bautista (St John the Baptist) above Christ, and his image occupies a more important place in the church. Coca-Cola also occupies an important place in the Chamulan cosmography – it facilitates burping in the church, which is believed to expel evil spirits.

Festivals in San Juan Chamula include Carnaval, ceremonies for Semana Santa, San Juan Bautista (June 22 to 25, with up to 20,000 people gathering to dance and drink on the 24th) and the annual change of *cargos*, or community leaders (December 30 to January 1).

Zinacantán
• population 2850
The road to the orderly village of San Lorenzo Zinacantán, 11km northwest of San Cristóbal, forks left off the Chamula road before descending into a valley. This is the main village of the Zinacantán municipality (population 40,000). Zinacantán people are Tzotzil, and the predominantly pink and purple colors of their costume are very distinctive.

A market is usually held only at fiesta times. The most important celebrations are for the festival of the Virgen de la Candelaria, around August 10.

The village has two churches. The central Iglesia de San Lorenzo has been rebuilt following a 1975 fire. Photography is banned in the church and churchyard. There's also a museum, Sna Jsotz'lebetik, with displays on Zinacantán customs, costumes and crafts; open 9 am to 6 pm daily, US$0.20.

Tenejapa
• population 1440
Tenejapa is a Tzeltal village 28km northeast of San Cristóbal, in a pretty valley with a river running through it. There are over 20,000 *tenejapanecos* in the surrounding area. A busy market fills the village center early on Sunday mornings. On the last Thursday of each month, the village leaders gather at the church in their ceremonial attire of wide, colorfully ribboned hats and long necklaces of silver coins, and there may be a market. Tenejapa women wear brightly brocaded or embroidered huipiles.

There are a few comedores in the main street and one basic posada, *Hotel Molina*, which isn't always open. The main festival is for the village's patron saint, San Ildefonso, on January 23.

Grutas de San Cristóbal
The *grutas* (caves) are in fact a single long cavern 9km southeast of San Cristóbal. The entrance is among pine woods a five-minute walk south of the Pan-American Highway, in the midst of an army encampment.

The first 350m or so of the cave have a wooden walkway and are lit. You can enter from 9 am to 4 pm daily (US$0.40). To get there, take a combi heading southeast along the Pan-American Highway from San Cristóbal and ask for 'Las Grutas.'

Amatenango del Valle
• population 3530
The women of this Tzeltal village by the Pan-American Highway 37km southeast of San Cristóbal are renowned potters. Amatenango pottery is still fired by a pre-Hispanic method, building a wood fire around the pieces rather than putting them in a kiln. In addition to the everyday pots and jugs that the village has turned out for generations, young girls now find a ready tourist market with *animalitos* – little animal figures that are inexpensive but fragile. If you visit the village, expect to be surrounded within minutes by girls selling these.

Amatenango women wear white huipiles with red and yellow embroidery, wide red belts and blue skirts.

From San Cristóbal, take a Comitán-bound bus or combi.

North of Chamula
Villages north of Chamula are in the thick of the Zapatista upheaval, and even though it has been a while since any serious incidents took place you should check on the security situation before venturing up there.

San Andrés Larraínzar is a hilltop Tzotzil and mestizo village 18km north from San Juan Chamula through spectacular mountain scenery. San Andrés is the main center of Zapatista support in the Chiapas highlands and was the site of the 1996 negotiations between the EZLN and Mexican government representatives that produced the San Andrés accords on indigenous rights (as yet unenacted). A weekly Sunday market is held.

In a valley some 27km northeast of San Juan Chamula is **San Pedro Chenalhó**, a Tzotzil village. It was in the politically divided Chenalhó municipality that escalating rivalry between pro-PRI and pro-Zapatista Tzotzil groups culminated in the 1997 massacre at Acteal, 20km northeast of San Pedro Chenalhó (see 'Indigenous Peoples of Chiapas'). At the time of writing thousands of pro-Zapatistas driven out of their own villages in the municipality were living as refugees at Pol-Hó near Acteal.

OCOSINGO
• **population 25,000** • **elevation 900m**
Around the halfway mark of the 180km journey from San Cristóbal to Palenque – a trip that takes you down from cool, misty highlands to steaming lowland jungle – is the growing town of Ocosingo, a busy market hub.

Ocosingo saw the bloodiest fighting in the 1994 Zapatista rebellion, when rebels who had wrecked and burned the town hall (at the western end of the main plaza) were cornered in the town's market by the Mexican army; about 50 of them were killed.

The market area, three blocks east down Avenida Sur Ote from the main plaza, is the liveliest part of town.

Near Ocosingo are the Mayan ruins of Toniná and a beautiful guest ranch that is one of the most enjoyable places to stay in Chiapas. Ocosingo is also the main jumping-off point for scenic Laguna Miramar.

Orientation & Information
Ocosingo spreads east (downhill) from Hwy 199, the San Cristóbal-Palenque road; bus terminals, combi stops and taxi stands are all close together on this road. Avenida Central runs from here to the central plaza, four blocks away. Banamex on the plaza has an ATM, but none of the banks in town will

change cash or traveler's checks; try Hotel Central.

Places to Stay
At the really cheap end there's **Hospedaje Las Palmas**, on the corner of Calle 2 Pte Norte and Avenida 1 Norte Pte – one block west and one north from the main plaza. It's an adequately clean, family-run place with a leafy courtyard; singles/doubles with shared bathrooms are US$4.25/6.50. **Hotel San José** (☎ 673-00-39, Calle 1 Ote 6), half a block north of the northeast corner of the main plaza, has small, dark but clean rooms with bathroom for US$8.75/10.

Hotel Central (☎ 673-00-24, Avenida Central 1), on the north side of the main plaza, has simple, clean rooms with fan, bath and TV that go for US$13/17.50/19.50 single/double/triple.

A few doors away up the side street, **Hotel Nakum** (☎ 673-02-80), previously known as the Hotel Margarita, charges US$16.25/19.50/22, with air-con extra. It was being remodeled when last checked.

Places to Eat
Ocosingo is known for its *queso amarillo* (yellow cheese), which comes in three-layered 1kg balls. The two outside layers are like chewy Gruyère, the middle is creamy.

You can get a decent comida for US$1.50 at comedores in the **mercado** on Avenida Sur Ote. There are also numerous **comedores** on Hwy 199 and Avenida 1 Norte, near the bus stations.

Restaurant La Montura (*Avenida Central 1*) has a prime location on the Hotel Central's veranda. It's good for a big breakfast (fruit, eggs, bread and coffee for US$3.25). Later in the day main dishes are around US$3.50 to US$6.50, and antojitos US$2.50 to US$4. **Restaurant Los Portales** (*Avenida Central 19*), a few doors east, offers traditional meals for US$2 to US$5. You walk through someone's living room to get to it.

On the opposite side of the plaza, **Restaurant y Pizzas El Desván** has a good upstairs location overlooking the square. Pizzas cost from US$5 to US$13, and there are other possibilities, including breakfasts. *Restaurant & Pizzería Troje*, a few doors away, does cheap *quesadillas*, and pizzas from US$5 to US$16.

Getting There & Away

Air Servicios Aéreos San Cristóbal (☎ 673-01-88) offers flights to Bonampak and Yaxchilán (around US$120 per person for four or five people) or San Quintín (from which you can reach Laguna Miramar).

Bus & Combi The main transportation terminals for Transportes Lacandonia (TL, 2nd-class buses), Autotransportes Tuxtla Gutiérrez (ATG, 2nd-class buses) and Cristóbal Colón (1st- and 2nd-class buses) are on Hwy 199 about five blocks west and two or three blocks north of the town's center; most buses are *de paso*.

Departures include the following:

Palenque 103km, 2½ hours; 10 Colón (US$6), five ATG (US$5), 12 TL (US$5)

San Cristóbal de Las Casas 88km, 1½ hours; eight Colón (US$4), 10 ATG (US$3), 10 TL (US$3.25), frequent combis and microbuses (US$2.75)

Tuxtla Gutiérrez 170km, 3½ hours; seven Colón (US$6 to US$8), 10 ATG (US$5.50)

Colón and/or ATG also run buses to Campeche, Cancún, Chetumal, Mérida, Mexico City and Villahermosa.

TONINÁ

• elevation 900m

The Mayan ruins of Toniná, 14km east of Ocosingo, don't match famous Palenque, 95km north, for beauty or extent, but they form a sizable site with large structures on terraces cut from a hillside, and they have a very interesting history.

The site was not excavated until 1979, and work is still being done at present. Archaeologists have concluded that it was Toniná that brought about Palenque's downfall. The prelude to Toniná's heyday was a change of dynasty in the late 7th century – from the long-standing Lords of the Lineage of the Underworld to the even unfriendlier-sounding Snake Skull-Jaguar Claw clan. The

new rulers demolished their predecessors' palaces and temples and declared war on Palenque about AD 690. At least three Palenque leaders were held prisoner at Toniná. One, Kan-Xul II, probably had his head chopped off here around AD 720.

Toniná reached its maximum splendor in the decade following its devastation of Palenque in 730. It became known as the Place of the Celestial Captives, for in some of its chambers were held the captured rulers of Palenque and other Mayan cities, destined to be either ransomed for large sums or decapitated. A recurring image in Toniná sculpture is that of captives before decapitation, thrown to the ground with their hands tied.

In around AD 900, Toniná was rebuilt again, in a simpler, austere style. But Jaguar Serpent, in 903, was the last Toniná ruler of whom any record has been found. Classic Mayan civilization was ending here, as it was elsewhere.

As you walk among the ruins, try to imagine many of the stone facings and interior walls covered in paint or frescoes, as they were during Toniná's prime.

Exploring the Ruins

A new **museum** near the entrance should be open by now; it contains the sarcophagus of Zots-Choj, a ruler of the Snake Skull-Jaguar Claw dynasty who took the throne in AD 842.

The path from the ticket office crosses a stream and climbs steps to a **juego de pelota** (ball court), on the edge of the large, flat **Gran Plaza**. The ball court was inaugurated in about the 780s under the rule of the female regent Smoking Mirror. A decapitation altar stands beside it.

At the left (south) end of the Gran Plaza stands the **Templo de la Guerra Cósmica** (Temple of Cosmic War), with five altars in front of it.

To the north rises a hillside terraced into a number of platforms. At the right-hand end of the steps that rise from the first to the second platform is the entry to a **ritual labyrinth** of passages (flick the light switch on as you go in).

On the third terrace is the **Palacio de las Grecas y de la Guerra** (Palace of the Grecas and War) – a *greca* being a band of geometrical decoration, in this case a zigzag X-shape in the stone facing of one of the walls. The zigzag may represent Quetzalcóatl and is also a flight of steps (you're not allowed to climb it!). To the right of the X is a rambling series of chambers, passages and stairways, believed to have been Toniná's administrative center.

Higher again, still toward the right-hand side of the stepped and terraced hillside, is Toniná's most remarkable sculpture, the **Mural de las Cuatro Eras** (Mural of the Four Eras). Created sometime between AD 790 and 840, this stucco relief of four panels (the first, from the left end, has been lost) represents the four suns, or eras of human history in Maya belief. At the center of each panel is the upside-down head of a decapitated prisoner. Blood spurting from the prisoner's neck forms a ring of feathers and, at the same time, a sun. In one panel, a skeleton dances in the underworld and holds a disembodied head with its tongue out. Below is a lord of the underworld who resembles an enormous rodent. This mural was created at a time when a great wave of destruction was running through the Maya world. The people of Toniná at this time believed themselves to be living in the fourth sun, the sun of winter, stillness, mirrors, the direction north and the end of human life.

Near the middle of the sixth level is a tomb with a stone sarcophagus, and toward the left end of the platform, stone steps descend into a narrow opening, the **Tumba de Treinta Metros** (Thirty-Meter Tomb). You'll need a flashlight (torch) to investigate this; it's not for the claustrophobic.

Above this is the acropolis, the abode of Toniná's rulers and site of its eight most important temples – four on each of two levels. The lower level has two smaller temples in the middle and the larger **Templo del Agua** (Temple of Water) on the left and **Templo del Monstruo de la Tierra** (Temple of the Earth Monster) on the right. The latter has Toniná's best-preserved roofcomb and was built around AD 713.

The topmost level has two tall temples behind and two smaller ones in front. The top of the right-hand (eastern), taller one, the **Templo del Espejo Humeante** (Temple of the Smoking Mirror), is 80m above the Gran Plaza. This temple was built, and its neighbor the Templo del Comercio (Temple of Trade) was ruined, by the 9th-century ruler Zots-Choj. In that era of the fourth and final sun and the direction north, Zots-Choj needed to raise this, Toniná's northernmost temple, higher than all the others, which necessitated a large artificial northeastward extension of the hill.

Around the left-hand smaller temple on this level, the **Templo de la Guerra** (Temple of War), can be seen stucco figures of prisoners. The views from up here are wonderful.

The ruins are open 9 am to 4 pm daily (US$2, free on Sunday).

Places to Stay

The relaxing, immaculately clean *Rancho Esmeralda* (fax 673-07-11, email ranchoes@ mundomaya.com.mx) is set amid rolling countryside just a 15-minute walk from the Toniná ruins (but a loop of about 6km by road). Its welcoming American owners, Glen Wersch and Ellen Jones, settled here in 1994 because the site's altitude is perfect for the macadamia grove they wanted to plant.

Their rustic but comfortable guest cabañas, set on grassy lawns, cost from US$24 to US$29 double, or US$40 for a family of four; they are lit at night by oil lamps. You can camp for US$4 per person, and RV parking is available (no hookups). Excellent meals are served (breakfast US$3.50 to US$4.50, dinner US$7).

Three- to four-hour horseback rides on the ranch's well-kept animals are popular at US$20 per person. You can also arrange day trips by plane to the ruins of Yaxchilán and Bonampak.

A taxi from Ocosingo to Rancho Esmeralda is US$4 or US$5. Alternatively, take a Toniná-bound combi from Ocosingo and get off after about 8km at a signed turnoff opposite a military base, from which it's about 1.5km along a dirt road to the rancho.

Getting There & Away

Combis to Toniná (US$1) leave from a stop that's opposite the Tianguis Campesino in Ocosingo. The last one back departs Toniná about 4 pm.

LAGUNA MIRAMAR

• elevation 400m

Beautiful, pristine Laguna Miramar, 100km southeast of Ocosingo, is the largest lake in the Lacandón Jungle. Surrounded by hills covered in rain forest and echoing with the roars of howler monkeys, the 16-sq-km lake has a pleasant temperature all year round. It has become known – and accessible – to the outside world thanks to a successful community ecotourism project by the village near its western shore, Ejido Emiliano Zapata.

A visit to Miramar is an unforgettable close encounter with nature. Ejido life in Emiliano Zapata – a poor but well-ordered, alcohol-free community founded in 1968 by Chol and Tzotzil settlers from northern Chiapas – is fascinating too. It is forbidden to bring alcohol or drugs into Emiliano Zapata.

You can visit Miramar in an organized group or on your own. In either case it's advisable to contact in advance Señor Fernando Ochoa, the architect of the ecotourism project, at Calle Dr Navarro 10, Barrio del Cerrillo, San Cristóbal de Las Casas (☎/fax 9-678-04-68, miramar@mundo maya.com.mx). Fernando, who speaks excellent English, takes groups to the lake and will provide other visitors with important information and advice.

When you reach Emiliano Zapata, ask for the *presidente de la laguna* (the villager in charge of lake matters) and/or the *comisariado*. Through them you must arrange details of your visit and pay for the services you need – US$10 per day for a guide to or around the lake, US$5 for a porter to or from the lake, US$10 per day for use of a *cayuco* (canoe), US$4 per person for a night's stay. The village is a spread-out place of huts and a few communal buildings on a gentle slope running down to the Río Perlas, which is the village's beautiful bathing place.

The 7km walk from village to lake takes 1½ hours. Guides will point out trees such as the *caoba* (mahogany) and what they call the *matapalo* (wood-killer), which leans on other trees as it grows and ends up strangling them. Around the lake you hear the incessant growls of howler monkeys, and you might see these and spider monkeys. Bird life includes macaws, toucans and prolific butterflies. Locals fish for *mojarra* (perch) in the lake, and will assure you that its few crocodiles are not dangerous.

It takes about 45 minutes to canoe across to Isla Lacan-Tun, a 6000-sq-meter island covered in overgrown pre-Hispanic remains from the Chol-Lacantún people, who were not conquered by the Spanish until the 1580s. The island was the site of their last stand.

Organized Tours

Fernando Ochoa's trips – for groups of three to eight – last four days (three nights) from San Cristóbal, and cost US$350 per person including flights from Ocosingo to San Quintín and back, equipment, good food, porters and all other fees at the ejido and lake.

Kanan-Ku Viajes (see Organized Tours in the San Cristóbal section) also offers Miramar trips, traveling by road and charging around US$150 per person (minimum four) for three days and two nights.

Places to Stay & Eat

At the lakeshore you can camp or sling a hammock under a palapa shelter. There are plans to build a small lodging for tourists in the village; meanwhile they can put people up in the Comisaría, a kind of village hall.

The food supplies in Emiliano Zapata's couple of stores are very basic; there are a few slightly better-stocked stores, and a couple of simple comedores, in neighboring San Quintín.

Getting There & Away

To reach Emiliano Zapata you must first get to the neighboring ejido, San Quintín, which has an airstrip and a large Mexican army base (San Quintín supports the PRI;

Emiliano Zapata is sympathetic to the Zapatistas). From the bus stop in San Quintín, walk five minutes along the airstrip and turn down a dirt road to the right opposite a complex of military buildings. From here it's a 15- or 20-minute walk to the middle of Ejido Emiliano Zapata.

The small planes of Servicios Aéreos San Cristóbal (☎ 673-01-88 in San Cristóbal) leave Ocosingo most mornings for San Quintín; call them for availability, current prices and return flights.

Four or five buses, microbuses or passenger-carrying trucks run daily to San Quintín from a stop a few meters south of the Tianguis Campesino in Ocosingo. Departure times vary, but there's nearly always something at 9 or 9:30 am from Ocosingo (often 10 or 11 am too), and something returning at midnight or 1 am from San Quintín. The five-hour, 130km trip costs US$5.50.

From Ocosingo you start out on the paved Altamirano road, then turn left onto a dirt road after about 7km. The roads across the mountainous territory east of Ocosingo pass along a number of river valleys known as Las Cañadas de Ocosingo. Inhabited mainly by Tzeltal indigenous people, this is one of the main areas of support for the Zapatista rebels. You may pass villages with signs proclaiming '*Territorio Rebelde Zapatista*' (Zapatista Rebel Territory) almost side by side with large military bases, and your documents will be checked at Mexican army checkpoints as you travel through. Keep your passport handy and make sure your tourist card is valid.

AGUA AZUL, AGUA CLARA & MISOL-HA

Three short detours off the Ocosingo-Palenque road lead to beautiful water attractions: the thundering cascades of Agua Azul, the turquoise Río Shumulha at Agua Clara and the spectacular waterfall of Misol-Ha.

All three can be visited in an organized day tour from Palenque – perhaps best if time is precious – but it's quite possible to go independently, and there are decent accommodations at Agua Clara and Misol-Ha.

The road between Ocosingo and Palenque has in the past been the scene of highway robberies, with bandits stopping vehicles and relieving travelers of their valuables. There seem to have been no recent incidents, but it's always wise to ask a few questions, especially if you're driving.

Agua Azul

The turnoff for the superb waterfalls of Agua Azul is about halfway between Ocosingo and Palenque. Scores of dazzling white waterfalls thunder into turquoise pools surrounded by jungle. (Note that the beautiful blue water color that gives the place its name may be evident only in April and May; silt can cloud the waters in other months, and it turns muddy during the height of the rainy season.)

On holidays and weekends the site is thronged; at other times you'll have few companions. A paved road leads 4.5km down from Hwy 199 to a parking lot and the cluster of comedores near the main falls. Admission is US$2.50 per car, US$0.75 for a person on foot.

The temptation to swim is great, but take extreme care – the current is deceptively fast and there are many submerged hazards such as rocks and dead trees. Use your judgment to identify slower, safer areas. Drownings are all too common here. You may also want to keep a close eye on your shoreside belongings.

About 2km downstream is another set of falls, Cascadas Bolón-Ahau, just before the river from Agua Azul flows into the Río Shumulhá.

Agua Azul is not a good place to stay. There's a camping/hammock-slinging area with a palapa shelter 100m down to the right opposite the parking lot. Cost is US$3 per tent and US$1.50 per hammock, and the facilities are grotty.

Agua Clara

Around 8km toward Palenque from the Agua Azul turnoff, another signed detour leads 2km by paved road to Agua Clara, an indigenous campesino-run community created to benefit the local people. Here the Río Shumulhá (or Tulijá) is a beautiful, broad, shallow expanse of turquoise water that's a delight to swim in (but test the current before choosing your spot). You can also rent a kayak or take a stroll across a hanging footbridge.

Agua Clara's hotel, *Sna Ajaw* (☎/fax 934-5-12-10 for information or bookings) has eight plain, clean rooms with fan for US$20/25; this includes a continental breakfast. Bathrooms are shared and have hot water. There are camping spots and a reasonably priced restaurant too. Call ahead of time to let them know you're coming.

Misol-Ha
About 20km from Palenque, the Río Misol-Ha drops 35m into a wide pool surrounded by lush tropical vegetation. The pool is safe for swimming, and a path behind the main fall leads into a cave with some smaller trickles of water.

The waterfall is 1.5km off Hwy 199, and the turn is signposted. To enter you pay US$0.75 per visitor.

The *Centro Turístico Ejidal Cascada Misol-Ha* (☎/fax 934-5-12-10 in Palenque) at the falls rents good wooden cabins with bathrooms and mosquito netting, at US$18 for one or two people or US$33 for a family cabin with kitchen. There's also a restaurant open till 6 pm.

Getting There & Away
Many travel agencies in Palenque offer daily trips to Misol-Ha and Agua Azul, with Agua Clara as a possible extra. See the list of agencies under Organized Tours in the Palenque section, then check out a few current deals. Most trips last around seven hours, spending half an hour at Misol-Ha and three hours at Agua Azul. The basic price is about US$8 including admission fees but not food. Add a dollar or two for extras such as breakfast or more comfortable vehicles. To do it independently, take almost any combi heading south at the

Maya-head statue in Palenque, or any 2nd-class bus along Hwy 199; they will drop you at any of the three intersections. The combi fare from Palenque to the Agua Azul *crucero* (junction) is US$2.50.

The distances from the highway to Misol-Ha and Agua Clara are manageable on foot. For the 4.5km between the Agua Azul crucero and Agua Azul itself, there are passenger-carrying *camionetas* (pickups) for US$0.75. Check out times of camionetas going back to the crucero, as it's uphill in that direction.

A taxi from Palenque to Misol-Ha with a one-hour wait costs around US$24; to Agua Azul with a two-hour wait should be US$46.

PALENQUE
• population 24,500 • elevation 80m
The ancient Mayan city of Palenque, with its superb jungle setting and exquisite architecture and decoration, is one of the marvels of Mexico. Modern Palenque town, a few kilometers to the east, is a sweaty, humdrum place with little attraction except as a base for visiting the ruins.

History
Palenque means 'palisade' in Spanish and has no relation to the ancient city's real name, which may have been Nachan, Chocan, Culhuacán, Xhembobel Moyos, Huehuetlapalla or Otolum.

Evidence from pottery fragments indicates that Palenque was first occupied more than 1500 years ago. It flourished from AD 600 to 800, and what a glorious two centuries they were! The city rose to prominence under Pakal, a clubfooted king who reigned from AD 615 to 683, and who lived to a ripe old age, possibly 80 to 100 years. In Mayan hieroglyphs he is represented by the signs for 'sun' and 'shield.'

During its golden age the city grew to some 20 sq km and included many handsome buildings characterized by mansard roofs and fine stucco bas-reliefs. Pakal's reign saw the construction of many of Palenque's finest plazas and buildings, including the superlative Temple of Inscriptions.

PALENQUE

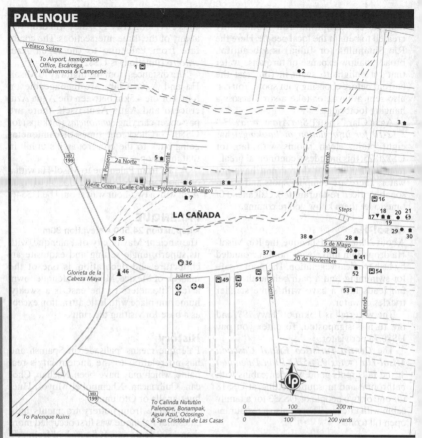

Pakal was succeeded by his son Chan-Balum, symbolized in hieroglyphs by the jaguar and the serpent. Chan-Balum continued Palenque's political and economic expansion, as well as the development of its art and architecture. He completed his father's crypt in the Temple of Inscriptions and presided over the construction of the Plaza of the Sun temples, placing sizable narrative stone stelae within each. One can see the influence of Palenque's architecture in the ruins of the Mayan city of Tikal in Guatemala's Petén region and in the pyramids of Comalcalco, near Villahermosa.

Not long after Chan-Balum's death Palenque started on a precipitous decline, due perhaps to ecological catastrophe, civil strife or invasion. After the 10th century Palenque was largely abandoned, its great buildings reclaimed by the fast-growing jungle.

Rediscovery of Palenque It is said that Hernán Cortés came within 40km of the ruins without any awareness of them. In 1773 Mayan hunters told a Spanish priest that stone palaces lay in the jungle. Father Ordóñez y Aguilar led an expedition to

PALENQUE

PLACES TO STAY
3 Posada Bonampak
4 Hotel Maya Tulipanes
5 La Posada
6 Hotel Chablis
7 Hotel Xibalba; Shivalva
   Viajes Mayas
8 Hotel La Cañada
9 Hotel Naj K'in
15 Hotel Lacroix
18 Posada Shalom
19 Hotel Nikte-Ha
25 Hotel Casa de Pakal
26 Hotel Chan-Kah
28 Hotel Kashlan
30 Hotel Regional
34 Hotel Vaca Vieja
35 Maya Palenque Hotel
37 Posada Los Ángeles
41 Posada Nacha'n Ka'an
42 Posada Kin
43 Posada Canek
45 Hotel Palenque
52 Posada Santo
   Domingo
53 Hotel Yun-Kax
55 Posada Charito

PLACES TO EAT
10 Café Te'El
11 Restaurant Virgo's
14 Restaurant Na Chan Kan;
   Na Chan Kan Travel Agency
17 Pizza Palenque
27 Restaurant Maya
32 Mara's
33 Los Farolitos; Fuente de Sodas

OTHER
1 Transportes Comitán-
   Lagos de Montebello
2 Mercado
12 Post Office
13 Palacio Municipal (Town Hall)
16 Colectivos Chambalu
20 Viajes Yax-Ha
21 Banamex (ATM)
22 Bancomer (ATM)
23 Tourist Office; Shivalva Viajes Mayas
24 Farmacia Central
29 Kim Tours
31 Viajes Misol-Ha
36 Pemex
38 Viajes Kukulcán
39 Autotransportes Río Chancalá
40 Lavandería
44 Cibernet
46 Maya Head Statue
47 Hospital General
48 Centro de Salud
49 Cristóbal Colón/ADO Bus Station
50 ATG Bus Station
51 Transportes Rodulfo Figueroa
   & Transportes Lacandonia Bus Station
54 Transportes Palenque

YUCATÁN

Palenque and wrote a book claiming that the city was the capital of an Atlantis-like civilization.

An expedition led by Captain Antonio del Río set out in 1787 to explore Palenque. His report was subsequently locked away in the Guatemalan archives, but a translation of it made by a British resident of Guatemala was published in England in 1822. This led a host of adventurers to brave malaria in their search for the hidden city.

Among the most colorful of them was the eccentric Count de Waldeck, who, in his 60s, lived atop one of the pyramids for two years (1831–33). He wrote a book complete with fraudulent drawings that made the city resemble those of great Mediterranean civilizations, causing all the more interest in Palenque. In Europe, Palenque's fame grew, and it was mythologized as a lost Atlantis or an extension of ancient Egypt.

Finally, in 1837, John L Stephens reached Palenque with artist Frederick Catherwood. Stephens wrote insightfully about the city's aqueduct system and the six pyramids he examined in detail. His was the first truly scientific investigation, and it paved the way for serious research by others.

Orientation

Hwy 199 meets Palenque town's main street, Juárez, at the Glorieta de la Cabeza Maya, an intersection with a large statue of a Maya chieftain's head, at the west end of the town. From here Juárez heads 1km east to the central square, El Parque. The main bus stations are on Juárez just east of the Maya head statue.

A few hundred meters south of the Maya head, the 7.5km road to Palenque Ruinas heads west off Hwy 199. This road passes the site museum after 6km, then winds on 1.5km to the site's main entrance.

Palenque town has plenty of places to stay, but there are others, including campgrounds, along the road to the ruins; many of these are beautifully situated, and most have restaurants. Combis (US$0.75) will stop anywhere along this road (see Getting There & Away under Exploring the Ruins). Yet other accommodations are on Hwy 199, south and north of the Maya head; these are mostly higher-end places.

Information

The helpful tourist office (no phone at this location, but call ☎ 345-03-56 for general information), on Juárez at Abasolo, has reliable town and transportation information and a few maps. It's open 9 am to 9 pm Monday to Saturday, 9 am to 1 pm Sunday.

The Instituto Nacional de Migración is 6km north on the highway out of town. Hours are 9 am to 3 pm and 5 to 7 pm Monday to Friday.

Bancomer, on Juárez 1½ blocks west of El Parque, changes money from 9 am to 3 pm Monday to Friday. Banamex is a little farther west on Juárez; both have ATMs. Some travel agencies, hotels and restaurants will change money, at less favorable rates.

The post office, at Independencia and Bravo one block from El Parque, is open 9 am to 4 pm Monday to Friday and 9 am to 1 pm Saturday. There are pay phones around El Parque, along Juárez and elsewhere. Cibernet Internet café (☎ 345-01-94), on Independencia just south of El Parque, is open 9 am to 9 pm daily. The cost is US$1 for each 15 minutes or part thereof.

A small shop right next to the Hotel Regional on Juárez sells a few books in English and Spanish on Mayan and Mexican culture and history. The *lavandería* on 5 de Mayo opposite Hotel Kashlan will wash and dry up to 3kg for US$4.25.

Palenque's Hospital General (☎ 345-07-33) is at the west end of Juárez, with the Centro de Salud (Health Center, ☎ 345-00-25) next door. There are several pharmacies along Juárez.

Exploring the Ruins

The 500 buildings of ancient Palenque are spread over 15 sq km, but only a relatively few, in a fairly compact central area, have been excavated. Everything you see here was built without metal tools, pack animals or the wheel.

The site stands at the precise point where the first hills rise out of the Gulf Coast plain, and the dense green jungle covering these hills forms a superb backdrop to Palenque's outstanding Mayan architecture. The forest is home to toucans, ocelots and monkeys; you may hear the howler monkeys, especially if you stay at a campground near the ruins.

As you explore the ruins, try to picture the gray stone edifices as they would have been at the peak of Palenque's power: painted bright red.

The best way to visit is to take a minibus or taxi (see Getting There & Away) to the main (upper) entrance, see the major ruins (the Templo de las Inscripciones, El Palacio and the Grupo de la Cruz), exploring nearby lesser ones as you please, then walk downhill through the jungle visiting minor ruins along and near the Arroyo Otulum, to the museum. From the museum you can catch a minibus back to town.

The archaeological site is open 8 am to 5 pm daily, the museum 7 am to 4 pm daily (US$2.50 for both, free Sunday and holidays). Parking at the site's upper lot is limited but free.

A good time to visit is when the site opens, as morning mist wraps the temples in a picturesque haze. At this time of day it's also cooler, and crowds tend to be thinner.

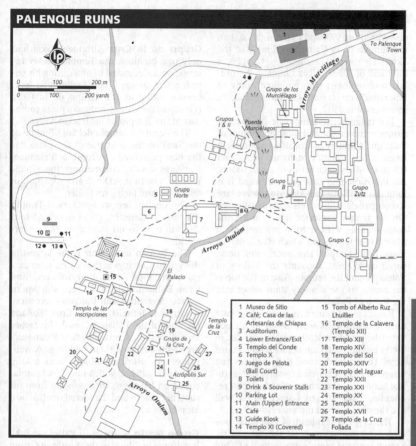

PALENQUE RUINS

1 Museo de Sitio	15 Tomb of Alberto Ruz
2 Café; Casa de las	Lhuillier
Artesanías de Chiapas	16 Templo de la Calavera
3 Auditorio	(Templo XII)
4 Lower Entrance/Exit	17 Templo XIII
5 Templo del Conde	18 Templo XIV
6 Templo X	19 Templo del Sol
7 Juego de Pelota	20 Templo XXIV
(Ball Court)	21 Templo del Jaguar
8 Toilets	22 Templo XXII
9 Drink & Souvenir Stalls	23 Templo XXI
10 Parking Lot	24 Templo XX
11 Main (Upper) Entrance	25 Templo XIX
12 Café	26 Templo XVII
13 Guide Kiosk	27 Templo de la Cruz
14 Templo XI (Covered)	Foliada

Between May and October, be sure to bring insect repellent.

Drinks, snacks, hats and souvenirs are available from stands outside the entrance, and there are cafés here and at the museum. Guide service is available from a kiosk by the entrance (a two-hour tour for up to seven people costs US$26).

Palenque's paths go up and down slopes that are sometimes slippery. Seniors and the disabled may need help, or may have to limit their visit to the main plaza.

An excellent source of information on Palenque, including news of latest archaeo-

logical discoveries, is the official Palenque website, www.mesoweb.com/palenque.

Warning There have been some muggings of tourists who ventured away from the main frequented parts of the Palenque site. On our last visit the site was patrolled by security guards, a positive sign, but stay alert if you go to outlying ruins such as the Templo del Jaguar or Grupo C.

Templo de las Inscripciones After you climb the slope to the ruins, the grand Temple of the Inscriptions comes into view to your right. Adjoining, to its right, is Templo XIII, in which a royal burial was discovered in 1993, and to the right of that, the Templo de la Calavera (Temple of the Skull). By the path, facing these temples, is the tomb of Alberto Ruz Lhuillier, the tireless archaeologist who revealed many of Palenque's mysteries – including Pakal's secret crypt in 1952.

The magnificent Templo de las Inscripciones is the tallest and most prominent of Palenque's buildings. Constructed on eight levels, it has a central staircase rising 25m (69 steep steps) to a series of small rooms; the tall roofcomb that once crowned it is long gone. Between the doorways are stucco panels with reliefs of noble figures. On the temple's interior rear wall are the three panels with a long inscription in Mayan hieroglyphs for which Ruz Lhuillier named the temple. The inscription, dedicated in AD 692, recounts the history of Palenque and the temple. Also at the top is the access to the slippery stairs down into the **tomb of Pakal**.

Pakal's jewel-bedecked skeleton and jade mosaic death mask were taken to Mexico City (the priceless death mask was stolen in 1985), but the stone sarcophagus lid remains here. This carved stone slab includes the image of Pakal encircled by serpents, mythical monsters, the sun god and glyphs recounting Pakal's reign. Carved on the wall are the nine lords of the underworld.

The crypt, a highlight of Palenque, was closed for maintenance at the time of research (and the temple itself roped off) but previously had opened from 10 am to 4 pm.

El Palacio Diagonally opposite the Templo de las Inscripciones is the Palace, an unusual structure harboring a maze of courtyards, corridors and rooms. Its tower, restored in 1955, has fine stucco reliefs on its walls, but is not open to visitors. Some of the lower chambers of the Palace have electric lights burning. Have a look inside!

Archaeologists and astronomers believe that the tower was constructed so that Maya royalty and the priest class could observe

the sun falling directly into the Templo de las Inscripciones during the winter solstice.

Grupo de la Cruz Although Pakal had only one building, the Templo de las Inscripciones, dedicated to him during his 68-year reign, his son Chan-Bahlum had four, known today as the Grupo de la Cruz (Group of the Cross), around a plaza southeast of the Templo de las Inscripciones.

The beautiful **Templo del Sol** (Temple of the Sun) on the west side of the plaza has the best-preserved roofcomb at Palenque. Carvings inside, commemorating Chan-Bahlum's birth in AD 635 and accession in 684, show him facing his father.

The smaller, less well-preserved **Templo XIV** has an interesting panel showing a lord dancing next to his mother in the underworld.

The **Templo de la Cruz** is the largest in this group. Carvings in the central sanctuary show the God L smoking tobacco, and Chan-Bahlum. Behind is a reproduction of a panel depicting Chan-Bahlum's accession.

On the **Templo de la Cruz Foliada** (Temple of the Foliated Cross), the arches are fully exposed, revealing how Palenque's architects designed these buildings. A well-preserved inscribed tablet shows a king (most likely Pakal) with a sun-shield emblazoned on his chest, corn growing from his shoulder blades and the sacred quetzal bird atop his head.

Grupo Norte North of El Palacio are the handsome buildings of the Northern Group and a **juego de pelota** (ball court). The crazy Count de Waldeck (see Rediscovery of Palenque, earlier in this section) lived in the so-called Templo del Conde (Temple of the Count), which was constructed in AD 647 under Pakal.

Northeastern Groups East of the Grupo Norte the path crosses the Arroyo Otulum. Some 70m beyond the stream, a right fork in the path will take you to **Grupo C**, a set of buildings and plazas on different levels, thought to have been lived in from about

JOHN ELK III

**The stone structures at Palenque were
once painted bright red.**

AD 750 to 800. Large trees now grow from
some of these buildings.

The main path descends via a series of
switchbacks that afford interesting looks at
stalactite-like formations among tree roots.
You continue past a series of falls and pools
to **Grupo B**, eventually reaching several
elongated buildings rising from terraces.
These structures were thought to have been
occupied as residences around AD 770 to
850; tombs were found beneath them.

The path continues to another residential
quarter, the **Grupo de los Murciélagos** (Bat
Group), then turns left down to the **Puente
Murciélagos** (Bat Bridge), a suspension
footbridge across the Arroyo Otulum.

Across the bridge and a little farther downstream, a path leads west to **Grupos I & II**, a
short walk uphill. These ruins, only partly

uncovered, are in a beautiful jungle setting.
The main path continues downstream to
the road, which you can follow to the right
(across a bridge) a short way to the museum.

Museo de Sitio Palenque's Site Museum
does a fine job of displaying finds from the
site and interpreting Palenque's history (entrance included with ruins admission). Next
door are a branch of Casa de las Artesanías
de Chiapas, selling some of Chiapas' best
handicrafts, and a pleasant but rather overpriced café.

Getting There & Away A paved footpath,
some parts shaded, runs beside the road
from the Maya head statue all the way to
the museum, about 6km.

Colectivos Chambalu, on Allende at
Hidalgo, and Transportes Palenque, on
Allende at 20 de Noviembre, operate combis
to the ruins about every 15 minutes from
around 6 am to 7 pm daily. The vehicles will
pick you up anywhere along the town-to-
ruins road, which helps campers and others
staying along that road. Fare is US$0.75.

A taxi from town to the ruins costs US$4.

Organized Tours

Several agencies in Palenque offer trans-
portation packages to Agua Azul, Agua
Clara and Misol-Ha; to Bonampak and Yax-
chilán; and to Flores (Guatemala), for Tikal.
See the sections 'To/From Guatemala via
Tenosique,' 'Agua Azul, Agua Clara &
Misol-Ha' and 'Bonampak, Yaxchilán & the
Carretera Fronteriza' for more information.

Agencies include:

Colectivos Chambalu Hidalgo at Allende

Kim Tours Juárez 27

Na Chan Kan (☎ 345-02-63) Hidalgo at Jiménez

Transportes Palenque Allende at 20 de Noviembre

Shivalva Viajes Mayas (☎ 345-04-11, 800-232-24-
00, fax 345-03-92, shivalva@tnet.net.mx) Juárez
at Abasolo; and Merle Green 9, La Cañada

Viajes Kukulcan (☎ 345-15-06) Juárez s/n

Viajes Misol-Ha (☎ 345-04-88) Juárez 103

Viajes Yax-Ha (☎ 345-07-67) Juárez 123

YUCATÁN

Places to Stay – Budget

In Town Best of the rock-bottom cheapies is the *Posada Bonampak* (☎ 345-09-25, *Domínguez 33*). Rooms are well kept and amply sized, and the rates are just US$5.50 for a single or double with a *cama matrimonial*, US$6 with twin beds.

Posada Canek (☎ 345-01-50, 20 de Noviembre 43) has largish rooms for US$11; most have private bath. Other rooms have dorm beds for US$5 per person. *Posada Charito* (☎ 345-01-21, 20 de Noviembre 15) and *Posada Santo Domingo* (☎ 345-01-46, 20 de Noviembre 119) have gloomy rooms with fan and shower for around US$7.75 double.

Hotel Yun-Kax (☎ 345-07-25, Corregidora 87), handily placed between the bus stations and town center, has clean rooms with shower, around a little patio, for US$7/9 for singles/doubles with fan or US$15 with air-con. Friendly *Posada Nacha'n Ka'an* (20 de Noviembre 25), a block north, offers clean, good-size rooms with ample bathrooms for US$8/10, and a cafetería for breakfast. Nearby, *Hotel Kashlan* (☎ 345-02-97, 5 de Mayo 117) has drab but clean rooms with fan and bath for US$16/22, and nicer air-con rooms for US$32.

Posada Los Ángeles (☎ 345-17-38), on Juárez almost opposite the bus stations, has bare rooms with fan and bathroom for US$7/8, or with air-con for US$18. There's secure parking here.

Nearer the town center, *Posada Shalom* (☎ 345-09-44, Juárez 156) is clean and modern with fan and bathroom for US$11/13. A couple of doors east, *Hotel Nikte-Ha* (☎ 345-09-34, Juárez 133) offers small, clean rooms with bath, air-con and TV for US$22 double. *Hotel Regional* (☎ 345-01-83, Juárez 119) has adequate rooms with shower and fan around a small plant-filled courtyard for US$11/14/17/22 single/double/triple/quad; try negotiating here.

The relatively new *Posada Kin* (☎ 345-17-14, Abasolo 1), south of Juárez, has clean, decent-size rooms with bathroom and fan, on four floors around a small patio, for US$13/16 including light breakfast. At the *Hotel Vaca Vieja* (☎ 345-03-88, 5 de Mayo 42), east of El Parque, clean, spacious doubles with bathroom and fan cost US$13.

Family-run *Hotel Lacroix* (☎ 345-00-14, Hidalgo 10), opposite the church near El Parque, has nice murals, a courtyard with potted tropical plants and adequate rooms with fan and shower for US$11/16.

North of Juárez, *Hotel Naj K'in* (☎ 345-11-26, Hidalgo 72) is a nice, family-run place where rooms with good bathrooms, hot water and fans cost US$11/17. Doubles with air-con are US$22.

La Posada (☎ 345-04-37, 2a Norte s/n), in the leafy La Cañada area, north of the Maya head intersection, is a quiet hangout with a grassy courtyard. Posted prices for the clean rooms with fan and bathroom are US$11/20/23 single/double/triple, but they'll often come down several dollars. There's a pizza restaurant here too.

On the Ruins Road One of the first places you will come to, 3km along the road, is the pleasant *La Aldea del Halach-Uinic* (☎ 345-16-93, email aldea@mexico.com, www.mundomaya.com.mx/laaldea), where you can camp for US$5 per tent. They also have simple palapa-roofed cabañas amid green gardens, each containing two rooms costing US$8 single, US$5.50 per additional person. Each room has two beds and two hammocks on a little porch. There's a small, clean pool, clean shared toilets and showers, and a restaurant.

A farther 1.5km along is *El Panchán*, a group of basic places to stay and eat in a beautiful rain forest setting. At *Beto's Café*, you can camp or sling your hammock under a palapa for US$1.50 per person. Beto's has inexpensive food too. At *Margarita & Ed Cabañas* (edcabanas@yahoo.com), cabañas with bathroom and mosquito netting cost US$11. They have two apartments as well with kitchen and fridge for US$15 (US$12 without kitchen).

Still in El Panchán, there are more cabañas at *Rakshita's*, which is also an exotically painted meditation center and an inexpensive vegetarian restaurant, serving curries, other Indian fare and sizable breakfasts for US$1.50 to US$2. *Don Mucho* is another popular restaurant here that offers good veggie dishes for US$1.50 to US$3.50.

For those really pinching pennies, a short distance up the ruins road from El Panchán is **Chaac Camping**, which charges US$1 per person to pitch a tent or rent a hammock. There are a few shabby cabañas here for around US$2.50, and also a loud restaurant-bar. Don't say we didn't warn you.

The closest place to the ruins to camp is **Mayabell Hotel Trayler Park**, just 400m from the site museum. The site has no phone but you can book a few days ahead at ☎ 345-01-25 or fax 345-07-67. For US$2 per person you get clean toilet and shower blocks and some shade. For the same price, there are palapas for slinging hammocks. The charge for a vehicle is US$1 to US$10, depending on size. There are also single/double/triple rooms with private bathroom at US$14/17/21 with fan, or US$33/38 with air-con. In the pleasant restaurant nothing costs more than US$2.50. Lockers cost US$0.50 per day. A taxi from town is US$4.50.

Management is not friendly here but the location is great, facilities are good, and it's a fine place to meet fellow travelers and exchange information.

Another option for campers is the green riverside **campground** at the Calinda Nututún Palenque (see Places to Stay – Top End), which charges US$6 per person.

Places to Stay – Mid-Range
In Town On Juárez near El Parque, **Hotel Casa de Pakal** (no phone) has small doubles with air-con and private bath for US$23. **Hotel Chan-Kah** (☎ 345-03-18, Juárez 2), overlooking El Parque, offers three rooms on each floor with a balcony. All rooms have bathroom, fan, air-con and TV and cost US$33/39 single/double. There's an elevator.

Hotel Palenque (☎ 345-01-88, 5 de Mayo 15), just east of El Parque, is the town's oldest hotel. It has been spruced up and offers rooms with bathroom and fan for US$27 double (US$31/33 triple/quadruple), or with air-con for US$33. They're set around a pretty garden courtyard.

Several mid-range hotels cluster in the leafy La Cañada area west of the center.

Hotel Maya Tulipanes (☎ 345-02-01, 800-714-47-10, fax 800-712-35-60, mtulipan@tnet.net.mx, Cañada 6) is the most comfortable and expensive. Air-con rooms with TV and phone go for US$57 double, US$63 triple (avoid the rooms fronting the street to the east unless you enjoy Mexican karaoke). There's a small pool and a nice restaurant. On the same street (which has at least three names) is **Hotel Chablis** (☎ 345-08-70, fax 345-03-65, Merle Green 7), where large rooms with air-con and fan cost US$35 double. There's a video bar for nighttime amusement.

Opposite the Chablis is **Hotel Xibalba** (☎ 345-04-11, shivlava@tnet.net.mx, Merle Green 9), with attractive air-con rooms for US$22/27. Rooms with fan run US$17.50/19.50. **Hotel La Cañada** (☎ 345-01-02, fax 345-13-02, Prolongación Hidalgo 12), is a collection of cottages at the eastern end of the same street, once a favorite with archaeologists working at the ruins. The large, fan-cooled rooms, many with huge ceramic bathtubs, cost US$22/24/28. There's a restaurant with set lunch or dinner for US$6.

On the Ruins Road About 4km from town the **Hotel Villas Kin-Ha** (☎ 345-05-33, fax 345-05-44) has palapa-roofed duplex concrete cabañas. The rooms aren't big but are pleasant enough, with fan and bathroom for US$40 double, US$45 triple. Add US$5 for air-con. The gardens hold a good-sized pool and open-sided palapa restaurant.

Places to Stay – Top End
The **Maya Palenque Hotel** (☎ 345-07-80), right by the Maya head intersection on the edge of town, has good air-con rooms with two double beds and cable TV for US$65 double. There's a pool and a restaurant.

On Hwy 199, 3.5km south of town and next to the Río Chacamax, the **Calinda Nututún Palenque** (☎ 345-01-00, fax 345-06-20, cnututun@tnet.net.mx) has modern buildings set in spacious jungle gardens shaded by palm trees. Large air-con rooms with bath cost US$70 double. There's an enticing pool and a deep swimming hole/balneario on the river.

YUCATÁN

Chan-Kah Resort Village (☎ 345-11-00, fax 345-08-20, chan-kah@tnet.net.mx), at Km 3.5 on the road to the ruins and 4km from the ruins entrance, is among the most attractive lodgings in Palenque. An enormous stone-bound swimming pool, lush jungle gardens, open-sided restaurant and other accoutrements all enhance the handsome wood-and-stone cottages that boast generous bathrooms, ceiling fans and air-conditioning, for US$87 double, US$93 triple.

Places to Eat

The cheapest fare in Palenque is at the taquerías along the eastern side of the park, in front of the church. Try *Los Farolitos* or neighboring *Fuente de Sodas* for a plate of tacos at US$2 to US$3.

Mara's has a prime location at Juárez and Independencia facing El Parque, with a handful of sidewalk tables and an abundance of whirring fans inside. Several set lunch and dinner menus go for US$3 to US$4. Set breakfasts are similarly priced. There's medium-priced à la carte fare too.

Restaurant Maya, at Independencia and Hidalgo on the northwest corner of El Parque, has been going since 1958. The food is standard and the hours long (7 am to 11 pm), with most main dishes costing US$3 to US$5. Breakfasts are sizable, and there are good set menus for US$2.75 to US$4.

Restaurant Na Chan Kan, facing the northeast corner of El Parque, is popular for its excellent pizzas (US$4 to US$6) and other fare including two-course set meals with a drink for US$3 to US$4.

Restaurant Virgo's (Hidalgo 5) offers 2nd-story open-air dining half a block west of the park. White pillars, a red-tile roof and plants set the scene. Try the *burritas al aguacate* (quesadillas with ham and avocado, US$2), or one of their pasta plates for US$2 to US$3. Meat dishes cost around US$3 to US$5. They serve wine too.

Pizza Palenque (Juárez 168) has surprisingly good pizzas from US$2.75 to US$8.

The organic coffee at little *Café Te 'El* (Hidalgo 68A), also known as Don Cafeto, is the best brew in town – just US$0.55 for

americano, US$0.70 for espresso, US$1.25 for cappuccino.

Getting There & Away

Air Palenque's airport is served by Aerocaribe (☎ 345-06-18), which has flights to/from Oaxaca (US$82), Bahías de Huatulco (US$236) and Mérida (US$135) daily, Tuxtla Gutiérrez (US$93) three or four days a week and Cancún (US$180) via Flores, Guatemala (US$99), three or four days a week.

Bus Buses serving Palenque – especially 2nd class night buses to/from Mérida – have a bad record for theft. Take special care of your valuables on these buses and don't accept drinks from strangers. Don't leave anything of value in the overhead rack or under seats, and stay alert. Your gear is probably safest in the luggage compartment under the bus, but watch as it is stowed and removed.

Westernmost of the main bus terminals on Juárez is the joint terminal (tel 345-13-44) of Cristóbal Colón (deluxe, 1st-class and 2nd-class buses) and ADO (1st-class). A block east is Autotransportes Tuxtla Gutiérrez (ATG, 2nd-class), and together half a block farther east are Transportes Rodulfo Figueroa (1st-class) and Transportes Lacandonia (TL, 2nd-class).

It's a good idea to buy your outward ticket a day in advance. Daily departures include:

Campeche 365km, 5 hours; four Colón/ADO (US$10.50 to US$14), one ATG (US$11)

Cancún 870km, 13 hours; four Colón/ADO (US$24 to US$34), two ATG (US$23)

Chetumal 495km, 7 hours; four Colón/ADO (US$14 to US$19.50), one ATG (US$12.50)

Mérida 545km, 8 hours; four Colón/ADO (US$15.50 to US$21), one ATG (US$15)

Mexico City (TAPO) 1010km, 16 hours; two ADO (US$47)

Oaxaca 815km, 15 hours; one ADO (US$35)

Ocosingo 103km, 2½ hours; 10 Colón/ADO (US$3.75 to US$5), nine ATG and 12 TL (all US$3 to US$4)

Playa del Carmen 805km, 12 hours; four Colón/ADO (US$23 to US$31), one ATG (US$21)

San Cristóbal de Las Casas 190km, 4 hours; 10 Colón/ADO (US$6 to US$8.25), five Figueroa (US$6.50), seven ATG (US$5.50 to US$6.50), nine TL (US$5)

Tulum 745km, 11 hours; three Colón/ADO (US$21 to US$28), one ATG (US$19)

Tuxtla Gutiérrez 275km, 6 hours; nine Colón/ADO (US$8.50 to US$11), nine ATG (US$7.50 to US$9), five Figueroa (US$9)

Villahermosa 140km, 2½ hours; 12 ADO (US$6), four ATG (US$4.25)

To/From Guatemala See this chapter's sections 'To/From Guatemala via Tenosique' (earlier) and 'Bonampak, Yaxchilán & the Carretera Fronteriza' (below).

Getting Around
The airport is a couple of kilometers north of the Maya head statue along Hwy 199. Yellow Transportación Terrestre cabs from airport to town cost US$3. In town, taxis wait at the northeast corner of El Parque and at the Colón/ADO bus station. They charge US$2 to the airport. You can call a taxi at ☎ 345-01-12.

BONAMPAK, YAXCHILÁN & THE CARRETERA FRONTERIZA
The ancient Maya cities of Bonampak and Yaxchilán, southeast of Palenque, have become much more accessible in the last few years because of a new paved road, the Carretera Fronteriza, which has been built parallel to the Mexico-Guatemala border almost all the way from Palenque to the Lagos de Montebello (though at research time a small stretch of the Carretera near the Lagos was still unpaved). There have been reports of bandits on some stretches around the ruins; check on these situations with a state tourism office before you go.

Both Bonampak, famous for its frescoes, and bigger Yaxchilán, with a peerless setting above the broad Río Usumacinta, are tucked amid thick tropical rain forest. Bonampak is 148km by road from Palenque; Yaxchilán is 173km by road then about 22km by boat along the Río Usumacinta.

Visiting this area independently is easier than some travel agencies would have you

think. Doing so doesn't necessarily work out cheaper than taking a tour, but it allows you time to explore this intriguing region and visit places such as the Lacandón village of Lacanjá Chansayab, which is located just 12km from Bonampak. You can cross into Guatemala at several points, including Frontera Corozal and Benemérito de las Américas. It's always worth bringing along insect repellent.

Organized Tours Several Palenque travel agencies offer day tours to Bonampak and Yaxchilán for around US$40 per person, transportation only (you pay for entry fees, food and drink). The trip, usually by van or minibus, lasts about 14 hours. Na Chan Kan agency offers a two-day trip for US$75 per person (minimum six) including camping at Lacanjá Chansayab and meals. There are also tours from San Cristóbal de Las Casas.

Some Palenque agencies also offer transportation packages to Flores, Guatemala (near Tikal) for US$35. The deal usually includes a van or minibus to Frontera Corozal, river launch to Bethel, Guatemala, and public 2nd-class bus from Bethel to Flores – about 12 hours altogether. Some agencies throw in a visit to Bonampak; a few offer Yaxchilán for extra.

See Organized Tours in the Palenque and San Cristóbal de Las Casas sections for details of agencies.

Getting There & Away Autotransportes Río Chancalá, at 5 de Mayo 120 in Palenque, runs combis to Frontera Corozal four times daily between 6 am and 2:30 pm (three hours, US$4.50), to Benemérito 14 times between 4:30 am and 4:15 pm, and to Chajul once (US$8.50). Transportes Comitán–Lagos de Montebello (☎ 345-12-60), also in Palenque, runs slower big buses to Frontera Corozal at noon (four hours), to Benemérito nine times between 4 am and 3:45 pm, and to Chajul five times daily. Fares are similar to the combis.

All the above-mentioned services stop at San Javier (US$3.50), 140km from Palenque, where a side road branches to Bonampak and Lacanjá Chansayab. They also stop at

Crucero Corozal, the intersection for Frontera Corozal. There are *comedores* at both intersections.

There are several military checkpoints along the Carretera Fronteriza. The road has been built, among other reasons, to stem the flow of drugs and illegal immigrants into Mexico, to tighten the noose on the Zapatista rebels and to increase tourism.

Bonampak

Bonampak's setting in dense jungle hid it from the outside world until 1946. Stories of how it was revealed are full of mystery, but it seems that Charles (or Carlos or Karl) Frey, apparently a young WWII conscientious objector from the US, and John Bourne, heir to the Singer sewing machine fortune, were the first outsiders to visit the site when Chan Bor, a Lacandón, took them there in February 1946.

Later in 1946 an American photographer, Giles Healey – who had apparently fallen out with Frey and Bourne during a 1945 expedition to film the Lacandones – was also led to the site by Chan Bor and found the Templo de las Pinturas with its famous murals.

The Bonampak site spreads over 2.4 sq km, but all the main ruins stand around the rectangular Gran Plaza. At different periods Bonampak was an enemy and an ally of more powerful Yaxchilán. The major surviving monuments were built under Bonampak's greatest ruler, Chan Muan II, who took the throne in AD 776 at a time of alliance with Yaxchilán. He was a nephew of the Yaxchilán ruler Escudo Jaguar II and was married to Yaxchilán royalty. The 6m-high Stela 1 in the Gran Plaza represents Chan Muan at the height of his reign. He also features in Stelae 2 and 3 on the Acrópolis, which rises from the south end of the plaza. Eight small temples near the top of the Acrópolis are Bonampak's most intriguing architectural feature seen from outside.

The masterly frescoes painted for Chan Muan *inside* the **Templo de las Pinturas** (Edificio 1) on the Acrópolis steps are what give Bonampak its fame (and its name: *bonampak* means 'painted walls' in Yucatecan Mayan and was coined by the 20th-century Mayanist Sylvanus Morley).

Diagrams outside the temple help interpret these murals, which were restored in the 1990s. **Room 1**, on the left as you face the temple, shows the consecration of an infant heir – probably Chan Muan II's son – who is seen held in arms toward the top of the right end of the room's south wall, which faces you as you enter. Lavish celebrations for this event are depicted elsewhere in the room. The central **Room 2** shows a battle on the south wall and, on the north wall, the torture (by fingernail removal) and sacrifice of prisoners – a scene presided over by Chan-Muan II in jaguar-skin battle dress. A severed head lies on one of the steps below him, beside the foot of a sprawling captive. **Room 3** shows a celebratory dance on the Acrópolis steps by lords wearing huge headdresses – and on its east wall three white-robed women puncture their tongues in a ritual bloodletting. By one interpretation, the prisoner sacrifices, the bloodletting and the dance may all have been part of the ceremonies surrounding the new heir – and the wars of Room 2 may have been conducted to gain the necessary captives.

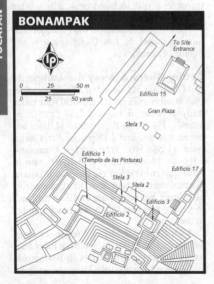

BONAMPAK

To Site Entrance

0   25   50 m
0   25   50 yards

Edificio 15

Gran Plaza

Stela 1

Edificio 1
(Templo de las Pinturas)

Edificio 17

Stela 3

Stela 2

Edificio 3

Edificio 2

Catedral de la Concepción, Campeche

Colorful architecture, Felipe Carrillo Puerto

On guard for pirates, Campeche

Tulum, home of the original Mayan beachcombers

On the street in San Cristóbal de Las Casas

Catedral, San Cristóbal de Las Casas

The magnificent Mayan city of Palenque flourished from AD 600 to 800.

The infant prince probably never came to rule Bonampak; the place was abandoned before the murals were finished, as Classic Maya civilization imploded.

The site is open 8 am to 4:45 pm daily (US$2.50, free Sunday and holidays). Refrescos and snacks are sold at a house by the entrance.

Places to Stay The nearest place to stay is *Camping Margarito*, 9km from Bonampak at the Lacanjá Chansayab turnoff. It costs US$1.50 to pitch your tent in their grassy camping area or US$5 to rent one, and US$2.50 to hang your hammock under their palapa or US$4 to rent one. Meals are only sometimes available.

Getting There & Away Bonampak is 12km from San Javier on the Carretera Fronteriza. The first 3km, to the Lacanjá Chansayab turnoff, is paved; the rest is good gravel/dirt road through the forest. On foot, you can opt for a jungle path from the Lacanjá Chansayab turnoff onward (about three hours). Camping Margarito, at the turnoff, should be able to supply a guide for about US$7. A taxi from San Javier to Bonampak and back, with time to visit the ruins, will cost around US$9. You may have to wait awhile at San Javier before one turns up, however. Hitching is possible.

Lacanjá Chansayab
• population 500 • elevation 320m
Just 12km from Bonampak is the largest village of the indigenous Lacandón people, Lacanjá Chansayab. This scattered settlement, with an inviting river pool for bathing, was founded around 1980 when the majority of Lacandones, who had previously lived dispersed around the Lacandón Jungle, settled here. At least four villagers have set up simple *campings* where you can pitch a tent and/or rent a hammock – ask for Carlos Cham Bor Kin near the entrance to the village, or Kin Bor, Vicente or Manuel. Vicente, for one, has a wooden building with hammocks already slung. You pay around US$1.50 to pitch a tent or US$2.50 to rent a hammock. The campings should be able to

provide a meal or two for a small number of visitors, but bring food supplies if you plan to stay more than a night. Your hosts will probably be able to cook for you. Camping Margarito (see Bonampak) is also nearby.

Villagers can guide you to Bonampak (around US$11) and to other places of interest in the nearby forests, such as the little-explored Maya ruins of Lacanjá, the 2.5km-long Laguna Lacanjá or the Cascadas Lacanjá waterfalls.

Lacanjá Chansayab is 6.5km by paved road from San Javier on the Carretera Fronteriza. A taxi is US$5 (US$1.25 if you can get it on a colectivo basis) but you might have to walk or hitch.

Frontera Corozal
• population 500 • elevation 200m
This spread-out, edgy frontier town (also called Frontera Echeverría) stretches back from the southwest bank of the Río Usumacinta, 15km by paved road from the Crucero Corozal junction on the Carretera Fronteriza. The broad Usumacinta, flowing swiftly between jungle-covered banks, forms the Mexico-Guatemala border here, and Frontera Corozal is an essential stepping-stone both for the ruins of Yaxchilán and for the village of Bethel on the Guatemalan bank. Bethel is a departure point for buses to Flores, near Tikal.

Corozal's townspeople are mainly indigenous Choles who moved from northern Chiapas to the Lacandón Jungle in the 1950s, '60s and '70s. After the Montes Azules Biosphere Reserve was declared in 1978, the Chol settlers agreed to congregate outside the reserve in Frontera Corozal.

Long, outboard-powered launches come and go from the river embarcadero, below a cluster of wooden buildings that includes several inexpensive *comedores*. Almost everything you'll need is on the paved street leading inland from here – including the immigration office, a couple of hundred meters along, where you should hand in or obtain a tourist card if you're leaving for or arriving from Guatemala. There's a telephone caseta in the restaurant of Escudo Jaguar (see Places to Stay).

Places to Stay A short distance along the road back from the river is *Escudo Jaguar* (☎ *01-5-201-64-40/1*), the area's most comfortable accommodation. Sizable, spotless rooms in pink palapa-roofed huts, with fans, bathrooms, mosquito nets and screens cost US$15/30 single/double, and there's a good restaurant (main dishes US$4 to US$6), which can close as early as 7:30 pm. You may also be able to camp here.

A couple of hundred meters farther inland along the road, *Posada Yhany* has primitive rooms for US$2.50/5, with fan and shared toilet. About three blocks farther back, then one block east, the *Yax Lum* community association and neighboring *Posada Tumbalá* have better posada rooms, at around US$3 with fan.

Getting There & Away Buses and combis stop two blocks east of Yax Lum at a small park beside the Auditorio Comunal. Ask directions from there to the accommodations or embarcadero. The last combi from Frontera Corozal to Palenque leaves at 3 pm.

If you can't get a bus or combi to Frontera Corozal, try getting one to Crucero Corozal, 20 minutes from San Javier, where you should be able to find a ride – maybe in the back of a *camioneta* (pickup) for US$1.

To/From Guatemala Speedy river *lanchas* (launches) go from Frontera Corozal to the village of Bethel, on the Guatemalan bank of the Usumacinta 40 minutes upstream. Ask at the Contratación de Lanchas office in Escudo Jaguar (see Places to Stay), open 8 am to 2 pm daily, or try going directly to the boat people at the riverside. The regular cost for up to four people in a boat is US$40; for five to 10 people it's US$60. It's possible to get bicycles, even motorcycles, on the launches.

Second-class Guatemalan buses leave Bethel for Flores at 12:30 and 2:30 pm (subject to change). The trip is a bumpy 4½ hours for around US$8.

Yaxchilán

A marvelous jungle setting above a loop of the Usumacinta makes Yaxchilán special.

Archaeologically, the site is famed for its ornamented building facades and roofcombs, as well as its stone lintels carved with conquest and ceremonial scenes. Don't forget to look at the undersides of the lintels, which often bear the most important carvings.

Conquests and alliances made Yaxchilán one of the most important cities in the Usumacinta region by the 7th century AD. It peaked in power and splendor between 681 and 800 under the rulers Escudo Jaguar I (Shield Jaguar I, 681–742), Pájaro Jaguar IV (Bird Jaguar IV, 752–768) and Escudo Jaguar II (777–800). Yaxchilán's inscriptions tell more about this 'Jaguar' dynasty than is known of almost any other Mayan ruling clan – but many of the important carvings are now in the Museo Nacional de Antropología in Mexico City and the British Museum in London. The names by which the rulers are known come from the hieroglyphs representing them: The shield-and-jaguar symbol appears on many Yaxchilán buildings and stelae. Pájaro Jaguar IV's hieroglyph is a small jungle cat with feathers on the back and a bird superimposed on the head. Yaxchilán was abandoned around AD 810.

The site is open 8 am to 4:45 pm daily (US$2.50, free Sunday and holidays). Refrescos are sold at a shack near the river landing.

As you walk toward the ruins, a signed path to the right leads up to the Pequeña Acrópolis, a group of ruins on a small hilltop. You can visit this later at the end of a circuit of the site. Continuing, you soon reach the convoluted passages of El Laberinto (Edificio 19), built between AD 742 and 752 during the interregnum between Escudo Jaguar I and Pájaro Jaguar IV. A flashlight (torch) is a big help in finding your way through this complicated two-level building. You emerge at the northwest end of the Gran Plaza.

Though it's hard to imagine anyone here ever wanting to be any hotter than they already were, Edificio 17 was apparently a sweathouse. About halfway along the plaza, Stela 1, flanked by weathered sculptures of a crocodile and a jaguar, shows Pájaro

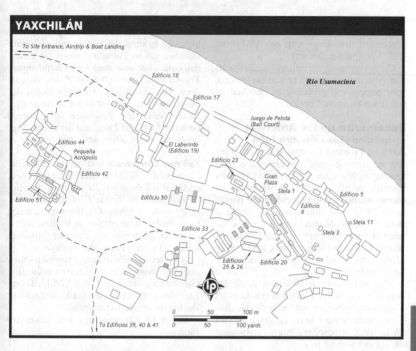

YAXCHILÁN

To Site Entrance, Airstrip & Boat Landing

Río Usumacinta

Edificio 18

Edificio 17

Juego de Pelota
(Ball Court)

Edificio 44

Pequeña
Acrópolis

El Laberinto
(Edificio 19)

Edificio 23

Edificio 42

Gran
Plaza

Stela 1

Edificio 5

Edificio 51

Edificio 30

Edificio
8

Stela 11

Edificio 33

Stela 3

Edificios
25 & 26

Edificio 20

0   50   100 m
0   50   100 yards

To Edificios 39, 40 & 41

Jaguar IV in a ceremony that took place in 761. Edificio 20, from the time of Escudo Jaguar II, was the last significant structure built at Yaxchilán. Stela 11, now at the northeast corner of the Gran Plaza, was originally found in front of Edificio 40. The bigger of the two figures visible on it is Pájaro Jaguar IV.

A grand stairway climbs from Stela 1 to Edificio 33, the best-preserved building at Yaxchilán, with about half its roofcomb remaining. The final step in front of the building is carved with many ball-game scenes. There are fine relief carvings on the lintels' undersides. Inside is a decapitated statue of Pájaro Jaguar IV; he lost his head to treasure-seeking 19th-century timber-cutters.

At the right-hand end of the clearing behind Edificio 33, a path leads into the trees. A short distance along this, a sign reading 'Edificios 39, 40, 41' points up to the left. Follow this, going left at a fork after about 100m, and in 10 minutes – mostly uphill – you reach the three buildings, on a hilltop. You can climb to the top of Edificio 41 for great views across the treetops.

Getting There & Away You can reach Yaxchilán by chartered plane from places such as Palenque and Ocosingo, or by boat from Frontera Corozal.

River launches take 40 minutes for the downstream trip from Frontera Corozal, and one hour returning upstream. Ask at the Contratación de Lanchas office at Escudo Jaguar (see Places to Stay in the Frontera Corozal section). The roundtrip price for a whole boat, holding 10 people, is US$70 including two or three hours at Yaxchilán. If there are only one or two of you, you might manage to reduce this to US$55, but it's better to try to join with a tour group. These come most days, sometimes several of them, arriving at Frontera Corozal as early as 8:30 am. You can try asking at Contratación de Lanchas or talking to the boat people by the river in the morning; in either case they may insist you obtain the group guide's agreement first. Expect to pay US$12 to US$16 per person this way.

Carry your passport and tourist card with you. Although you won't be leaving Mexico, your papers will probably be checked as you leave Frontera Corozal.

Benemérito de las Américas
• population 6000 • elevation 200m

South of Frontera Corozal you soon enter the area in Chiapas' far eastern corner known as Marqués de Comillas (for its Spanish former landowner). After oil explorers opened tracks into this jungle region in the 1970s, land-hungry settlers poured in from all around Mexico; now it's one of the most deforested parts of the Lacandón Jungle. Cattle and logging have made many of the settlers richer than they could have hoped to be back home.

The main town is Benemérito de las Américas, on the bank of the Río Salinas, an Usumacinta tributary that forms the Mexico-Guatemala border here. It has traces of 'Wild West' atmosphere but no attractions except as a staging post.

Benemérito's main street is a 1.5km-long stretch of the highway. A side street beside the Farmacia Arco Iris, toward the north end of town, leads 1.25km to the river. About 400m down this street is the Clínica/Hospital de Campo IMSS, with an Urgencias (Emergencies) department. There's a telephone caseta in Minisuper Marisol on the highway. Benemérito has no immigration post; pick up or hand in Mexican tourist cards at Frontera Corozal.

Places to Stay The *Hotel de Las Américas* (☎ 800-029-40-60), by the highway at the south end of town, looks a bit run-down. But the rooms are OK, costing US$12/14 single/double with bathroom and fan.

The alternative is one of the very basic posadas by the highway around the middle of town. *Hospedaje Siempre Viva* beside the Autotransportes Río Chancalá combi terminal has doubles with fan at US$5 or US$6.

Getting There & Away Autotransportes Río Chancalá has its combi terminal on the highway toward the north end of town. Combis run to Palenque about 14 times daily (the last at 4 pm) and Chajul once. There's a taxi stand (☎ 800-029-41-23) next door. The Transportes Comitán-Lagos de Montebello bus stop is about 350m south. Buses leave for Palenque nine times between 5 am and 2 pm, and for Chajul five times between 6:30 am and 3 pm.

To/From Guatemala You can hire a lancha for around US$120 to US$150 to take you up the Río Salinas and its tributary, the Río de la Pasión, to Sayaxché (Guatemala) in three to four hours. On the way, there's Guatemalan immigration at Pipiles. Infrequent cargo boats are cheaper (around US$8 per person) and take all day.

An alternative is to take a lancha a short distance downriver to Laureles on the Guatemalan side, for about US$12. From Laureles a bus reportedly leaves at 2 am for the five-hour ride to Sayaxché.

Sayaxché has lodgings and buses to Flores.

Carretera Fronteriza to Lagos de Montebello

South of Benemérito the Carretera Fronteriza heads 60km south before turning due west for the 150km stretch to Tziscao in the Lagos de Montebello.

At the time of research, about 30km of the road, from about 5km west of the Chajul turnoff to the Flor de Café turnoff, remained unpaved (but was being worked on). Public transportation from the east ran as far as the Chajul turnoff, and from the west as far as Ixcán, about 15km east of the Flor de Café turnoff. It's not too difficult to get lifts along the in-between bit. A bus from Benemérito to the *Crucero Chajul* (Chajul turnoff) takes 2½ hours for US$5. Combis or buses between Ixcán and Comitán (the Línea Comitán-Montebello bus station) run about hourly; the last departure from Ixcán can be as early as 2 pm. From Ixcán it takes 2½ hours (US$4) as far as Tziscao, 3½ hours (US$5) to Comitán.

By the time you travel, the whole Carretera Fronteriza may be paved, with public transportation going right through between Palenque and Comitán. On the other hand bridges may be down or fords impassable. The only sure way to find out if it's passable is to travel it!

East of Ixcán you're passing through jungle or semicleared jungle, crossing several tropical rivers. West of Ixcán starts the climb of over 1000m up to the much cooler, pine-clad highlands around the Lagos de Montebello. There are quite a lot of villages along the way.

COMITÁN

• population 62,300 • elevation 1635m

Comitán, a surprisingly pleasant, orderly town with what must be the cleanest streets in Mexico, is the jumping-off point for the Lagos de Montebello and the last place of any significant size as you travel Hwy 190 south to the Guatemalan border. The town holds attractive churches, and the peaceful ruins of Tenam Puente are close by. Nevertheless, few tourists come here.

The first Spanish settlement in the area, San Cristóbal de los Llanos, was set up in 1527. Today the town is officially called Comitán de Domínguez, after Belisario Domínguez, a local doctor who was a national senator during the presidency of Victoriano Huerta.

Orientation

Comitán is set on hilly terrain and has a wide, attractive central plaza. North-south streets are Avenidas and east-west ones are Calles.

Information

The municipal tourist office (☎ 632-19-31), upstairs in the Palacio Municipal on the north side of the main plaza, is open 9 am to 2 pm and 4 to 8 pm Monday to Friday. Hours vary with the seasons. The Delegación (Chiapas state) tourist office is a few doors east.

The Guatemalan consulate (☎ 632-04-91), at 1a Calle Sur Pte 26, is open 9 am to 4:30 pm Monday to Friday.

There's a branch of Banamex, with an ATM, at the Cristóbal Colón bus station. See the Comitán map for other banks and ATMs.

The post office, at 3a Avenida Pte Norte 5, is open 8 am to 3 pm Monday to Friday, 9 am to 1 pm Saturday. Café Inter Net, at Local 12, Pasaje Morales, offers email and Internet access for US$1.50 per half hour or US$2.25 an hour. It's open 9 am to 2 pm and 4 to 8 pm Monday to Saturday.

Things to See & Do

The **Casa de la Cultura**, on the southeast corner of the plaza, includes an exhibition gallery and auditorium. Nearby is the small **Museo Arqueológico de Comitán**, with local artifacts going back to 700 BC; open 10 am to 5 pm Tuesday to Sunday (free). There are misshapen pre-Hispanic skulls on display – deliberately deformed (or beautified, in the ancients' eyes) by squeezing infants' heads between two boards.

Casa Museo Dr Belisario Domínguez is a museum providing fascinating insights into medical practices and the life of the professional classes in early-20th-century Comitán. It's at Avenida Central Sur 35, half a block from the main plaza; open 10 am to 6:45 pm Tuesday to Saturday, 9 am to 12:45 pm Sunday (US$0.55).

For a nice walk into the nearby countryside and to check out the surrounding areas from the top of the tiny ruins of Junchabín, start at the plaza and head north about 10 minutes on Avenida Central Norte. Take the road on the right just past the white church and walk 15 minutes on the hilly road; soon you'll see a small blue-gated Christ altar set into the hillside. A little beyond on the left will be about 15 stone steps leading to a wood-and-wire gate. A hike up to the top of this hill rewards you with a 7m-high pyramid and some great views.

Places to Stay

Comitán has several cheap posadas with small, often dingy and severely plain rooms. One of the better ones is ***Posada Primavera*** *(☎ 632-20-41, Calle Central Pte 4)*, a few steps west of the main plaza. It charges

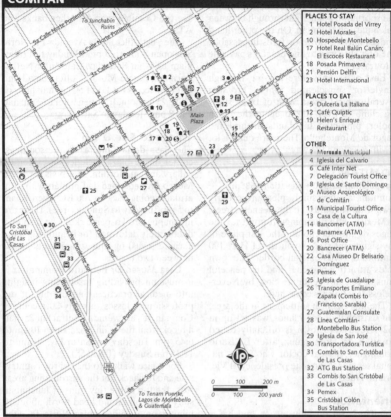

COMITÁN

PLACES TO STAY
1   Hotel Posada del Virrey
2   Hotel Morales
10 Hospedaje Montebello
17 Hotel Real Balún Canán;
    El Escocés Restaurant
18 Posada Primavera
21 Pensión Delfín
23 Hotel Internacional

PLACES TO EAT
5   Dulcería La Italiana
12 Café Quiptic
19 Helen's Enrique
    Restaurant

OTHER
3   Mercado Municipal
4   Iglesia del Calvario
6   Café Inter Net
7   Delegación Tourist Office
8   Iglesia de Santo Domingo
9   Museo Arqueológico
    de Comitán
11 Municipal Tourist Office
13 Casa de la Cultura
14 Bancomer (ATM)
15 Banamex (ATM)
16 Post Office
20 Bancrecer (ATM)
22 Casa Museo Dr Belisario
    Domínguez
24 Pemex
25 Iglesia de Guadalupe
26 Transportes Emiliano
    Zapata (Combis to
    Francisco Sarabia)
27 Guatemalan Consulate
28 Línea Comitán-
    Montebello Bus Station
29 Iglesia de San José
30 Transportadora Turística
31 Combis to San Cristóbal
    de Las Casas
32 ATG Bus Station
33 Combis to San Cristóbal
    de Las Casas
34 Pemex
35 Cristóbal Colón
    Bus Station

US$5.50/6.50 for dark singles/doubles with shared bathrooms and US$13 for one room with private bathroom. *Hospedaje Montebello* (☎ 632-35-72, *1a Calle Norte Pte 10*) has clean rooms around a courtyard for US$5 with bathroom.

Hotel Morales (☎ 632-04-36, *Avenida Central Norte 8*) looks something like an aircraft hangar, with small rooms perched around an upstairs walkway, but it's clean, and rooms with bath cost US$12/14. There are renovated rooms with color TV, too, for US$16.

Pensión Delfín (☎ 632-00-13), on the west side of the main plaza, has nice renovated rooms with TV and bath for US$17.75/21.50/30 single/double/triple and unrenovated but nevertheless spacious rooms for US$15.25/20/26, as well as a pleasant rear courtyard.

Hotel Internacional (☎ 632-01-10, *Avenida Central Sur 16*), a block from the plaza, has comfy singles/doubles for US$22/25. Also pleasant is *Hotel Posada del Virrey* (☎ 632-18-11, *Avenida Central Norte 13*), which has small rooms surrounding a courtyard with a fountain. Rooms, with TV, cost US$18/24.

Hotel Real Balún Canán (☎ 632-10-95, 1a Avenida Pte Sur 7) has small but comfortable rooms with TV and phone for US$19.50/22.

Places to Eat
Several reasonable places line the west side of the main plaza. The best is *Helen's Enrique Restaurant*, which serves good food with breakfasts for US$1.75 to US$4, antojitos for US$2 to US$4 and meat dishes for US$3.50 to US$6. Other places in the same row are more basic and cheaper. *Dulcería La Italiana* in Pasaje Morales does good cakes and sweet treats.

Trendy *Café Quiptic*, on the main plaza next to the church, is run by a group of campesino coffee growers and serves good Chiapas organic coffee. Breakfasts run US$2.25 to US$3, and there are good sandwiches, salads, cakes and other light eats.

Hotel Internacional has a good restaurant with prices a little higher than Helen's Enrique. For a more expensive meal amid international-style surroundings, try the Hotel Real Balún Canán, where *El Escocés Restaurant* is open until 11 pm and the *Disco Tzisquirin* until 1 or 2 am.

Getting There & Away
Air Aeromar flies to Mexico City twice daily. Their office is in the airport but at present they have no phone; use a travel agency to book flights. Transportadora Turística (☎ 632-29-69) offers hotel-to-airport (and vice versa) service for US$5.50; call ahead.

Bus Comitán is approximately 90km southeast down the Pan-American Highway from San Cristóbal, and 83km north of Ciudad Cuauhtémoc. The bus stations of Colón (deluxe, 1st-class and 2nd-class, ☎ 632-09-80) and Autotransportes Tuxtla Gutiérrez (ATG, 2nd-class, ☎ 632-10-44) are on the Pan-American Highway, which passes north-south through the western part of town, about a 20-minute walk from the

main plaza, or you can take a microbus. The highway here is named Boulevard Dr Belisario Domínguez and is called simply 'El Bulevar.' Daily departures include:

Ciudad Cuauhtémoc (Guatemalan border) 83km, 1¼ hours; seven Colón (US$3.25), nine ATG (US$2.25)

Mexico City (TAPO) 1155km, 20 hours; five Colón (US$48 to US$62)

San Cristóbal de Las Casas 90km, 1½ hours; 18 Colón (US$3 to US$3.75), also combis (US$2.25) from two stops on Boulevard Dr Belisario Domínguez between 1a and 2a Calle Sur Pte

Tapachula 245km, 5½ hours (via Motozintla); six Colón (US$9)

Tuxtla Gutiérrez 175km, 3½ hours; 18 Colón (US$6 to US$7.50)

Colón also serves Bahías de Huatulco, Pochutla, Puerto Escondido, Palenque and Villahermosa (via San Cristóbal).

The Línea Comitán-Montebello terminal, for buses and combis serving Lagos de Montebello and beyond, is on 2a Avenida Pte Sur, southwest of the central plaza.

Getting Around
'Centro' microbuses, across the road from the Colón bus station and passing the ATG bus station, will take you to the main plaza for US$0.30. Taxi rides around town cost about US$1.50.

TENAM PUENTE
Around 14km south of Comitán lie the peaceful hilltop ruins of Tenam Puente. Occupied from about AD 600 to 900, Tenam Puente (*tenam* means 'fortified place' in Nahuatl; *puente* is Spanish for 'bridge') flourished until the Early Postclassic period, when it was mysteriously abandoned. It was rediscovered in 1925 by Frans Blom and Oliver La Farge.

There are quite a few structures to see here; the highlight is the Acrópolis, which contains various platforms, temples and ball courts arranged around plazas and patios. The regional architecture shows a few influences from other areas such as the Guatemalan highlands, and materials originally uncovered at the site also suggest that Tenam Puente had a lively commercial economy. The site covers 2 sq km and the good views from points around the hilltop show the expanse of the Comitán Valley. Open 9am to 5 pm daily; admission is free.

Tenam Puente is about 11km south on Hwy 190 and 3km west off the highway past the town of Francisco Sarabia. Transportes Emiliano Zapata on 1a Calle Sur Poniente will take you there in combis, or you can take a taxi there and back for US$11 plus US$5 per hour wait (bargain for a rate).

LAGOS DE MONTEBELLO

The temperate forest along the Guatemalan border southeast of Comitán is dotted with 59 small lakes of varied colors – the Lagos (or Lagunas) de Montebello. The area is beautiful, refreshing, quiet and not hard to reach. Little-used vehicle tracks through the forest provide some good walks.

Some Mexican weekenders come down here in their cars, but the rest of the time you'll probably see only resident villagers and a handful of visitors. At one edge of the lake district are the Mayan ruins of Chinkultic.

Orientation

The paved road to Montebello turns east off Hwy 190 16km south of Comitán, just before the town of La Trinitaria. It passes Chinkultic after 30km, and enters the forest and the Parque Nacional Lagunas de Montebello 5km beyond. At the park entrance (no fee) the road splits. One road continues 3km north between lakes to end at Laguna Bosque Azul. The other heads east, passing turnoffs for several more lakes and the village of Tziscao (9km). Beyond Tziscao it becomes the Carretera Fronteriza, continuing east to Ixcán and ultimately Palenque.

Chinkultic

These dramatically situated ruins lie 2km north of the La Trinitaria–Montebello road. The access road is paved.

Chinkultic was on the far western edge of the ancient Mayan area. Dates carved here extend from AD 591 to 897 – the last of which is nearly a century after the latest dates at Palenque or Yaxchilán. Those years span Chinkultic's peak period. Of the 200 mounds scattered over a wide area, only a few have been cleared, but they're worth the effort.

LAGOS DE MONTEBELLO

1 Paso de Soldado
2 Campground
3 Chinkultic
4 Doña María Cabañas; El Pino Feliz
5 Albergue

The track brings you first to a gate. Here, take the path to the left, which curves around to the right. On the hill to the right of this path stands one of Chinkultic's major structures, E23. The path reaches a long ball court where several stelae – some carved with human figures – lie on their sides, some under thatch shelters.

Follow the track back to the gate and turn left until you can spot a few stone mounds to the right. On the hillside that soon comes into view is the partly restored temple, El Mirador. The path goes over a stream and steeply up to El Mirador, where there are superb views over the surrounding lakes and down into a gaping 50m deep *cenote* (well).

The Lakes

Lagunas de Colores The road straight on from the park entrance leads through the Lagunas de Colores, whose hues range from turquoise to deep green. The first of these lakes, on the right after about 2km, is Laguna Agua Tinta. Then on the left come Laguna Esmeralda and Laguna Encantada, with Laguna Ensueño on the right opposite Encantada. The fifth and biggest is Laguna Bosque Azul, on the left where the paved road ends.

Boys will probably offer you a ride on small horses from the end of the paved road. Two paths continue from here; go straight ahead for 800m to get to the *gruta*, a cave shrine. About 300m farther ahead and to the left is Paso de Soldado, a picnic site beside a small river.

Laguna de Montebello About 3km toward Tziscao from the park entrance, a track leads 200m left to Laguna de Montebello, one of the bigger lakes, with a flat, open area along its shore where the track ends.

Cinco Lagunas & Laguna Pojoj Three kilometers farther along the Tziscao road another track leads left to the Five Lakes. Only four are visible from the road, and the second, La Cañada, on the right after about 1.5km, is one of the most beautiful Montebello lakes; it's nearly cut in half by two

rocky outcrops. The track eventually reaches the village of San Antonio.

One kilometer farther along the Tziscao road from the Cinco Lagunas turnoff, a track leads 1km north to clear, deep blue Laguna Pojoj, with an island in the middle.

Laguna Tziscao This lake comes into view on the right 1km farther along the main road. The junction for Tziscao village, a pleasant, spread-out place, is a little farther, again on the right.

Places to Stay & Eat

A few hundred meters past the Chinkultic turnoff, you can rent a rustic cabin and eat good, inexpensive food at *Doña María Cabañas*, also called *La Orquidea*, beside the road. The elderly owner, Señora María Domínguez Figueroa, has been looking after travelers since the 1930s. She has also given a lot of help to Guatemalan refugees in the area. For the cabins, which have electric light but no running water, you pay US$2 per person; dinner is US$3, breakfast US$2.50. Next door is *El Pino Feliz*, a newer, rival set of cabañas charging US$3 per person.

Inside the national park, you can camp for free at *Laguna Bosque Azul*. There are cabañas here too, costing around US$3, and toilets. *Bosque Azul Restaurant* serves egg dishes for US$2.50 and *chiles rellenos* or meat dishes for around US$5.

Tziscao village has a hostel – the *Albergue* – where you pay US$1.25 to camp, US$3 per person in small cabañas or US$3.50 per person in small rooms; meals are available. The hostel lies on the shore of beautiful Laguna Tziscao. You can rent a rowboat, and Guatemala is just a few hundred meters away. Entering the village from the main road, turn right after about 600m at the sign 'Lago Tziscao Otel Cabañas Restaurant 400m.' It's actually 1km from there to the Albergue.

By far the best and most original lodgings in the area are at the *Hotel Parador–Museo Santa María* (☎/fax 632-51-16, *Carretera La Trinitaria–Lagos de Montebello Km 22*). This 19th-century hacienda, restored and decorated with period furniture and art, has six rooms at US$66 double. Its chapel has been turned into a religious art museum. There's a restaurant serving chiapaneco and international cuisine, and billiards in the bar. A sign points to 'Museo de Santa María' 22km from La Trinitaria on the Montebello road. It's 1.5km from highway to hotel.

Getting There & Away

If you wish, it's possible to make a quick day trip to Chinkultic and the lakes from San Cristóbal de Las Casas, by either public transportation or tour.

Buses and combis to the Lagos de Montebello go from the yard of Línea Comitán–Montebello (☎ 632-08-75) on 2a Avenida Pte Sur in Comitán. There are a number of different destinations, so make sure you get one that's going your way. Combis to Laguna Bosque Azul (US$1.75) run every few minutes until about 6:30 pm; to Tziscao (US$1.75) they go every hour, 5 am to 7:30 pm. Combis and buses bound for Ixcán or Flor de Café also pass Tziscao. All these will let you off at the turnoffs for Hotel Parador-Museo Santa María or Chinkultic, or at Doña María Cabañas (US$1.50).

The last vehicles back to Comitán from Tziscao leave at around 5 pm, and from Laguna Bosque Azul around 6 pm.

CIUDAD CUAUHTÉMOC
• population 1790

This 'city' amounts to little more than a few houses, a hotel and a comedor or two, but it's the last/first place in Mexico on the Pan-American Highway (Hwy 190). Comitán is 83km north. Ciudad Cuauhtémoc is the Mexican border post; the Guatemalan one is 4km south at La Mesilla. Colectivo taxis (US$0.75) ferry people between the two sides. There's a bank on the Guatemalan side of the border, and money changers on both sides. Expect to be charged small 'fees' of a couple of dollars by Guatemalan officials as you enter or leave their country.

Hotel Camino Real, above the Cristóbal Colón bus station in Ciudad Cuauhtémoc, has plain, dingy doubles with shared bath for US$12. There are better-looking hotels in La Mesilla.

Getting There & Away

Fairly frequent buses and combis run between Ciudad Cuauhtémoc, Comitán and San Cristóbal (see the Comitán and San Cristóbal sections for details). The Cristóbal Colón line also runs to Tuxtla Gutiérrez (US$9) six times daily, Mexico City (US$50 to US$62) once daily, and a few other destinations once each.

Guatemalan buses depart La Mesilla every half hour from 8 am to at least 4 pm for main points inside Guatemala, such as Huehuetenango (84km, 1½ to 2 hours, US$1.25), Quetzaltenango (also called Xela, 170km, 3½ hours, US$4) and Guatemala City (380km, 7 hours, US$5). Lago de Atitlán (245km, 5 hours) and Chichicastenango (244km, 5 hours) both lie a few kilometers off the Pan-American Highway. If there's no bus to your destination, take one to Huehuetenango, where you may be able to get an onward bus.

RESERVA DE LA BIÓSFERA EL TRIUNFO

The luxuriant cloud forests high in the remote El Triunfo Biosphere Reserve in the Sierra Madre de Chiapas are a bird-lovers' paradise in a bizarre world of trees and shrubs festooned with ferns, bromeliads, mosses, lichens and vines. The cool, damp forest is formed by moist air rising from the hot, humid lowlands to form clouds and rain on the highlands.

The Sierra Madre de Chiapas is home to over 30 bird species that are nonexistent or rare elsewhere in Mexico. El Triunfo is the one place in the country where it's fairly easy to see the resplendent quetzal. Other birds here include the extremely rare horned guan (big as a turkey, but dwelling high in trees), the azure-rumped tanager, the black guan, the blue-tailed and wine-throated hummingbirds and the blue-throated motmot.

Visits are controlled fairly strictly. Avoid the May-to-October wet season. For a permit and arrangements, contact – at least one month in advance – Alejandro Estrada Mendoza, Ecoturismo, Reserva de la Biósfera El Triunfo, Calle Argentina 389, Colonia El Retiro, CP 29040, Tuxtla Gutiérrez,

Chiapas (☎ 614-03-78, eltriunfo@infosel.net .mx). The minimum group size is six persons, and the minimum cost is about US$100 per person. For that you get one or two nights at the rustic Campamento El Triunfo, 1850m high in the heart of the reserve, guides who are expert bird-spotters and some help with transportation to/from Jaltenango (also called Ángel Albino Corzo), the nearest town, 130km south of Tuxtla Gutiérrez. Jaltenango is served by Autotransportes Cuxtepeques buses from Tuxtla Gutiérrez.

EL SOCONUSCO

The Soconusco is Chiapas' hot, fertile coastal plain, 15km to 35km wide. Its climate is hot and sweaty year-round, with plenty of rain from mid-May to mid-October. The steep-sided Sierra Madre de Chiapas, sweeping up from the plain, provides an excellent climate for bananas, coffee and other crops.

Tonalá
• population 29,600
Tonalá, on Hwy 200, is the jumping-off point for Puerto Arista. There's a tourist office (☎ 663-27-87) on the main street, Hidalgo, at 5 de Mayo, two blocks southeast of the main plaza, Parque Esperanza. *Hotel Tonalá (☎ 663-04-80, Hidalgo 172)*, between Parque Esperanza and the Colón bus station, is a reasonable, moderately priced choice if you have to stay here.

Cristóbal Colón (deluxe and 1st-class) and Transportes Rápidos del Sur (TRS; 2nd-class) share a bus station toward the northwest end of town on Hidalgo, six blocks from Parque Esperanza. There are frequent buses to Tuxtla Gutiérrez (3½ hours, US$6 to US$8), Escuintla (three hours, US$5 to US$7.50) and Tapachula (4½ hours, US$7.50 to US$10) from 5 or 6 am until at least midafternoon. Colón also runs three buses to Mexico City (US$45 to US$50) and one to Oaxaca (US$17).

For Puerto Arista, combis and microbuses (US$1) leave from Juárez and 5 de Mayo, one block southeast of the market, until 6 pm. Colectivo taxis run as late as

8 pm from Matamoros and 5 de Mayo, one block uphill from the combi stop. A taxi is around US$8; you can call a 24-hour radio cab at ☎ 663-06-20.

Puerto Arista
• population 760
Puerto Arista, 18km southwest of Tonalá, stretches lazily for about 2km along part of a 30km gray beach. Though the past few years have seen several substantial concrete buildings join its collection of palm shacks, it remains a sleepy place most of the time. On weekends a few hundred chiapanecos cruise in from the towns, and at Semana Santa and Christmas they come by the thousands, and the few permanent residents make their money for the year. The temperature's usually sweltering if you stray more than a few meters from the shore, and you get through a lot of refrescos while you listen to the crashing of the Pacific waves.

The ocean is clean here but take care: We've heard tales of riptides that can sweep you a long way out in a short time.

Puerto Arista's only real street, interchangeably called Boulevard Matamoros or Boulevard Zapotal, runs along the back of the beach. The road from Tonalá meets it at a T-junction by a lighthouse, the midpoint of town.

Places to Stay & Eat There are plenty of places in both directions from the lighthouse. The following is just a selection.

Head about 850m southeast from the lighthouse, then turn left (inland) near Hotel Lucerito to reach *José's Camping Cabañas (☎ 664-99-82)*. Run by a friendly Canadian, this has camping space and five cute cabañas in a coconut and citrus grove. The cabañas have mosquito screens, fans and electric lights, and cost US$5.50/8.75/12 for single/double/triple occupancy. You can camp for US$1.50 per person, and good food (including vegetarian) is available – about US$4 for a typical fish meal. The nearby Mexican-run *Maya Bell* has a similar setup.

Hotel Lucerito (☎ 663-01-82 ext 152) is one of the best hotels at this end of town, with air-con and TV in rooms for US$40,

YUCATÁN

and a pool. Just 150m southeast of the lighthouse, **Restaurant Playa Escondido** is typical of several beachfront comedores with a few basic little rooms. The bare abodes here are US$4.50 double, or US$6 with private bath. **Restaurant Ocmar**, a block southeast, does some of the best food in town and is not overly expensive.

Almost opposite the lighthouse, three-story **Hotel Lizeth** has doubles with fan for US$18, US$23 with air-con and TV. Add US$5 for triple or quadruple occupancy. Fronting the beach one block farther northwest, **Restaurant Hospedaje Brisas del Mar** has bare, medium-size rooms with fan and bath for US$17 triple.

The top hotel is **Hotel Arista Bugambilias** (☎ 663-01-82 ext 116, ☎ 663-06-75), almost 1km northwest of the lighthouse, with a pool, restaurant and bar in gardens fronting the beach, and air-conditioned rooms with TV for US$50 double.

Getting There & Away See the Tonalá section, earlier. The best place to pick up a Tonalá-bound combi, microbus, colectivo taxi or regular taxi is the T-junction by the lighthouse.

Reserva de la Biósfera La Encrucijada

This large biosphere reserve protects a 1448-sq-km strip of coastal lagoons, wetlands, forest and Mexico's tallest mangroves (some above 30m). It's a vital wintering and breeding ground for migratory birds and a well-preserved, important ecosystem. Inhabitants include one of Mexico's biggest populations of jaguars, plus ocelots, spider monkeys, white-tailed deer, four species each of sea and river turtle, river crocodiles, caimans, boa constrictors, green iguanas, fishing bats, anteaters, buzzards, fishing eagles, pelicans and lots of waterfowl.

A ride in a lancha through almost any part of the reserve will take you through towering mangroves and past palm-thatched lagoonside villages. You'll see plenty of birds any time of year.

The biosphere reserve maintains an office (☎ 647-00-84, closed Saturday and Sunday)

at Avenida Central 4 in the small town of Acapetahua, 6km southwest of Escuintla. It has another office (☎ 618-21-05) at Calle 3 Oriente Norte 1621, in Tuxtla Gutiérrez. Ask at either office about visits to the reserve's study, protection and vigilance center, Campamento La Concepción, which has guides available. La Concepción is a 25km lancha ride southeast from Embarcadero Las Garzas, which is 16km southwest of Acapetahua. Another *campamento* is being built at Las Garzas, where there are comedores.

Nearer to Embarcadero Las Garzas is Barra de Zacapulco, a small settlement on a sandbar between the ocean and a lagoon. Barra de Zacapulco has a handful of palapa comedores where a heaping plate of fresh prawns with salad and tortillas costs around US$3.25, and a coconut to drink is about US$0.50. There's a sea turtle breeding center nearby.

Places to Stay You can camp or sling a hammock at Barra de Zacapulco for a minimal fee. **Campamento La Concepción** (see above) has accommodations for up to 30 people. Southeast of La Concepción, in San José El Hueyate, 24km by a good dirt road from Mazatán, is the beachside **Centro Turístico San José El Hueyate** (☎ 625-39-40). This has 10 rustic cabañas holding five people each, and a restaurant. Lancha rides are available here too.

Hotel El Carmen on Acapetahua's main street, Avenida Central, has adequate rooms with bath for US$9 double. There are also hotels in Escuintla.

Getting There & Away To reach Embarcadero Las Garzas, first take a bus along Hwy 200 to Escuintla. Then get a colectivo taxi to Acapetahua (6km, US$0.50). Beside the railway in Acapetahua, get a combi or bus to Embarcadero Las Garzas (16km, US$1.25). These run about every 30 minutes.

From Embarcadero Las Garzas, a colectivo lancha to Barra de Zacapulco takes 25 minutes for US$2.25. The last lancha back to Embarcadero Las Garzas may leave Barra de Zacapulco as early as 3:30 pm, and the last combi from Embarcadero Las

Garzas to Acapetahua about 4:30 pm, but double-check these times.

A three-hour personal lancha tour from Embarcadero Las Garzas costs around US$120 to US$150.

TAPACHULA

• population 163,300

Mexico's southernmost city is an important gateway to Guatemala and a busy commercial center, overlooked from the northeast by 4110m Tacaná, the first of a chain of volcanoes stretching southeast into Guatemala.

Orientation

The central plaza, Parque Hidalgo, is the site of the tourist office, banks, cathedral and museum. Bus stations and places to stay are scattered around the central area.

Information

The tourist office (☎ 626-55-25 ext 140), on 8a Norte facing Parque Hidalgo, is open 9 am to 2 pm and 4 to 8 pm Monday to Friday, 9 am to 1 pm Saturday and Sunday. Hours may vary widely, however, depending on who's working.

The Instituto Nacional de Migración (☎ 625-04-66) is at Carretera del Antiguo Aeropuerto Km 1.5, about 2.5km south of the center; it's open 8 am to 3 pm Monday to Friday.

The Guatemalan consulate (☎ 626-12-52), at 2a Oriente 33, is open 9 am to 1:30 pm and 3 to 5 pm Monday to Friday.

There are banks with ATMs around Parque Hidalgo (see the Tapachula map). Elektra, on 4a Norte at 3a Poniente, offers Western Union 'Dinero en Minutos' service.

The post office, east of the center on 1a Oriente, is open 9 am to 6 pm Monday to Friday, 9 am to 1 pm Saturday and holidays.

Globali@ cybercafé, at Calle Central Oriente 16B, charges US$1.50 per half hour and is open 9 am to midnight Monday through Saturday, 9 am to 9 pm Sunday.

AeroPromociones y Viajes del Centro (☎ 626-88-18), at 4a Norte 18B, is a handy air-ticket agency.

The Cruz Roja Mexicana (Mexican Red Cross, ☎ 626-76-44, 626-19-49) at the corner of 1a Oriente and 9a Norte has ambulances and an *urgencias* (emergencies) section. Sanatorio Soconusco (☎ 626-50-74), 4a Norte 68, handles urgencias too.

Museo Arqueológico del Soconusco

The Soconusco Archaeological Museum facing the west side of Parque Hidalgo displays some of the best finds from the nearby Izapa ruins, including stone sculptures and a gold-and-turquoise-encrusted skull. It's open 11 am to 6 pm Tuesday to Sunday (US$2.25).

Places to Stay

Budget The *Hospedaje Las Américas* (☎ 626-27-57, 10a Norte 47), four blocks from Parque Hidalgo, has a leafy patio and offers clean singles/doubles with fan and curtained-off bathroom for US$6.50/7.50, US$9.75 for two-bed doubles.

Hotel La Amistad (☎ 626-22-93, 7a Pte 34), a bit nearer Parque Hidalgo, has clean rooms with bath and fan, around a nice leafy patio, for US$8/10.75, but is often full.

Posada del Parque (☎ 626-51-18, 8a Sur 3) has rooms that are clean, but muggy despite fans. Singles/doubles with small curtained-off bathrooms cost US$9.75/ 10.75, US$14.50 for twin beds, US$17 with air-con.

Around the corner from the Cristóbal Colón bus station is *Hospedaje Chelito* (☎ 626-24-28, 1a Norte 107). Clean, good-size singles/doubles/triples with TV, fan and bathroom cost US$16/18.50/21; doubles/ triples with air-con and cable TV are US$21.50/25. Attached is a small café.

Mid-Range The *Hotel Santa Julia* (☎ 626-31-40, 17a Oriente 5), next door to the Cristóbal Colón bus station, has clean air-conditioned singles/doubles with TV, phone and bath for US$27/30.50.

Hotel Fénix (☎ 625-07-55, 4a Norte 19), a block from Parque Hidalgo, has good re-modeled rooms at US$39/49 with air-con and cable TV; unremodeled rooms go for US$18/22.50 with fan, or US$30.50/38 with air-con.

The modern *Hotel Don Miguel* (☎ 626-11-43, 1a Pte 18) is the best city-center hotel

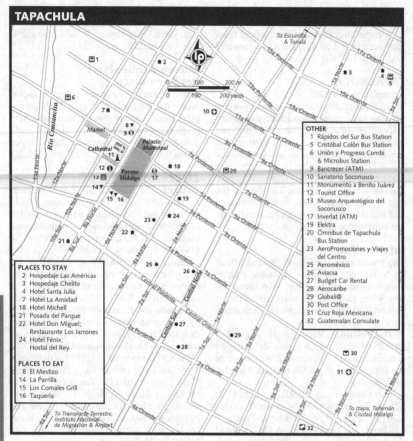

TAPACHULA

OTHER
1 Rápidos del Sur Bus Station
5 Cristóbal Colón Bus Station
6 Unión y Progreso Combi & Microbus Station
9 Bancrecer (ATM)
10 Sanatorio Soconusco
11 Monumento a Benito Juárez
12 Tourist Office
13 Museo Arqueológico del Soconusco
17 Inverlat (ATM)
19 Elektra
20 Ómnibus de Tapachula Bus Station
23 AeroPromociones y Viajes del Centro
25 Aeroméxico
26 Aviacsa
27 Budget Car Rental
28 Aerocaribe
29 Globali@
30 Post Office
31 Cruz Roja Mexicana
32 Guatemalan Consulate

PLACES TO STAY
2 Hospedaje Las Américas
3 Hospedaje Chelito
4 Hotel Santa Julia
7 Hotel La Amistad
18 Hotel Michell
21 Posada del Parque
22 Hotel Don Miguel; Restaurante Los Jarrones
24 Hotel Fénix; Hostal del Rey

PLACES TO EAT
8 El Mestizo
14 La Parrilla
15 Los Comales Grill
16 Taquería

To Escuintla & Tonalá
To Izapa, Talismán & Ciudad Hidalgo
To Transporte Terrestre, Instituto Nacional de Migración & Airport

YUCATÁN

and is often full. Rooms are clean and bright with air-con and TV for US$40/50. There's a good restaurant here too.

Just half a block off Parque Hidalgo, *Hotel Michell* (☎ 625-26-40, 5a Pte 23) has reasonable rooms with air-con, TV and desks for US$31/37/46.50 single/double/triple.

Places to Eat

Several restaurants line the south side of Parque Hidalgo. *Los Comales Grill* stays open late and serves a bit of everything: egg dishes (US$1 to US$2.25), main dishes

(US$3 to US$8), tacos and tortas. Tacos are cheaper two doors along at the *Taquería*. Across the street, *La Parrilla*, does tasty *tortas a la parrilla* for US$2.25, good plates of fruit salad for US$2.75, thirst-quenching fruit drinks such as *agua de maracuyá* (passion-fruit juice) and reasonably priced tacos, meat and chicken dishes.

Breakfast at the Hotel Fénix's air-conditioned *Hostal Del Rey (4a Norte 17)* is a nice way to begin the day. An early meal of pancakes or eggs, fruit or juice, and coffee is US$3.50. Later you may want soup, salad or antojitos (each around US$3), or *aves* or carne for US$5 to US$7.50.

The Hotel Don Miguel's air-conditioned *Restaurante Los Jarrones* is another of the best and most popular places in town, similarly priced.

El Mestizo, on 7a Pte near Parque Hidalgo, is a cleanish, economical place open to the street, serving a range of Chinese and Mexican dishes for US$1.50 to US$2.25.

Getting There & Away

Air Aviacsa (☎ 626-14-39), Central Norte 18, flies daily nonstop to/from Tuxtla Gutiérrez and Mexico City.

Aeroméxico (☎ 626-20-50), 2a Norte 6, flies daily nonstop to/from Mexico City.

Aerocaribe (☎ 626-98-72), 2a Oriente 4, flies daily to/from Mérida via Tuxtla Gutiérrez and Veracruz.

Bus Cristóbal Colón (☎ 626-28-81), on 17a Oriente 1km northeast of Parque Hidalgo, operates deluxe, 1st-class and 2nd-class buses. The main 2nd-class bus stations are Rápidos del Sur (RS; ☎ 626-11-61), at 9a Pte 62, and Ómnibus de Tapachula (OT), at 7a Pte 5.

Transportation to/from the Guatemalan border is covered in the Talismán & Ciudad Hidalgo section. Other departures include:

Comitán 245km, 6 hours (via Motozintla); six Colón (US$9)

Escuintla 85km, 1½ hours; 11 Colón (US$3.25), 37 RS (US$1.50), 52 OT (US$1.50)

Guatemala City 300km, 7 hours; two Colón (US$24)

Mexico City (TAPO) 1110km, 19 hours; seven Colón (US$53 to US$61)

Oaxaca 670km, 13 hours; two Colón (US$27 to US$32)

San Cristóbal de Las Casas 335km, 7½ hours; six Colón (US$12)

Tonalá 220km, 4½ hours; 14 Colón (US$9 to US$10.50), 37 RS (US$7.50), 14 OT (US$5.50)

Tuxtla Gutiérrez 390km, 8 hours; 18 Colón (US$16 to US$25.50), 37 RS (US$11)

Colón also runs one or two daily buses to Palenque, Bahías de Huatulco, Pochutla and Puerto Escondido.

Getting Around

Tapachula's airport (☎ 626-22-91) is 20km southwest of the city off the Puerto Madero road. Transporte Terrestre (☎ 625-12-87), 2a Sur 68, charges US$5 per person from the airport to any hotel in the city, or vice versa. A taxi is about US$11.

There's a Budget Car Rental (☎ 626-09-82) on Central Sur near Central Oriente.

AROUND TAPACHULA
Izapa

The Izapa ruins are important to archaeologists as a link between the Olmecs and the Maya (see History in the Facts about the Region chapter), but of limited interest to the nonenthusiast. Pre-Hispanic Izapa flourished from approximately 200 BC to AD 200. The Izapa carving style – typically seen on stelae with altars placed in front – shows descendants of Olmec deities, with their upper lips unnaturally lengthened. Early Mayan monuments from north Guatemala are similar.

At each of the three groups of remains, the caretaking family will get you to sign a visitors book and ask you for a small tip.

Izapa is 11km east of Tapachula on the Talismán road. The sign pointing toward the northern part of the site, left of the road coming in from Tapachula, is invisible from that direction; watch instead for the small pyramids. Some restoration has been done at this part of the site, which has a few low pyramids, a ball court and several carved stelae and altars.

From the northern area, go 700m back toward Tapachula and take a signposted dirt road to the left. After 800m, past houses with 2000-year-old sculptures lying in their gardens, you reach a fork with signs to Izapa Grupo A and Izapa Grupo B, each about 250m farther. Grupo A is a set of weathered stela-and-altar pairings around a small field. Grupo B is a couple of grass-covered mounds and more stone sculpture, including three curious ball-on-pillar affairs.

To get there, take a Unión y Progreso combi from 5a Pte 53 in Tapachula. The fare is US$0.65.

Talismán Bridge & Ciudad Hidalgo

The road from Tapachula heads 9km northeast past Izapa to the international border at Talismán bridge, opposite El Carmen, Guatemala. A branch south off the Talismán road leads to another cross-border bridge at Ciudad Hidalgo (37km from Tapachula), opposite Ciudad Tecún Umán. There are hotels and places to change money at both borders. Both crossings are open 24 hours.

The Guatemalan border posts may make various small 'unofficial' charges as you go through; you could try asking them for a receipt to keep them honest. Also, it may be a good idea to have Guatemalan quetzals at this point, unless you feel confident with the street money changers who will besiege you while you're crossing.

Getting There & Away Combis of Unión y Progreso leave for Talismán from 5a Pte 53 in Tapachula every few minutes, 5 am to 10:30 pm (US$0.65). They pass the Cristóbal Colón bus station as they leave town. A taxi from Tapachula to Talismán takes 20 minutes and costs around US$7.50.

Ómnibus de Tapachula buses from 7a Pte 5 in Tapachula make the 45-minute journey to Ciudad Hidalgo about every 15 minutes (or when full) from 5 am to 7:30 pm, and at 8:15, 9:15 and 10:15 pm, for US$1. Cristóbal Colón runs a daily bus to/from Mexico City (20 hours, US$55) from Ciudad Hidalgo.

Many of the longer-distance buses leaving the Guatemalan side of the border head for Guatemala City (about five hours away) by the coastal slope route through Retalhuleu and Escuintla. If you're heading for Lake Atitlán or Chichicastenango, you need to get to Quetzaltenango (Xela) first, for which you may have to change buses at Retalhuleu or Malacatán on the Talismán-San Marcos-Quetzaltenango road.

Language

Spanish is the most commonly spoken language of the countries of La Ruta Maya. English is the official language of Belize, although both Spanish and a local creole are widely spoken. Groups of people throughout the region speak Mayan languages and dialects.

For more Spanish words and phrases, get a copy of Lonely Planet's *Latin American Spanish phrasebook*.

For Spanish words pertaining to food and restaurants, see the Menu Guide following this Language chapter.

A basic guide to Mayan language follows the Spanish section of this chapter.

Spanish

Pronunciation

Pronunciation of Spanish is not difficult. Many Spanish sounds are similar to their English counterparts, and the relationship between pronunciation and spelling is clear and consistent. Unless otherwise indicated, the English words used below to approximate Spanish sounds take standard American pronunciation.

Vowels Spanish vowels are generally pronounced consistently and have close English equivalents:

a   is like 'a' in 'father'
e   is somewhere between the 'e' in 'met' and the 'ey' in 'hey'
i   is like 'ee' in 'feet'
o   is like 'o' in 'note'
u   is like 'oo' in 'boot'; it is silent after 'q' and in the pairings 'gue' and 'gui,' unless carrying a diaeresis, as in *güero* (blond, fair)

Diphthongs A diphthong is one syllable made up of two vowels. Here are some diphthongs in Spanish, and their approximate pronunciations:

ai   as in 'hide'
au   as in 'how'
ei   as in 'hay'
ia   as in 'yard'
ie   as in 'yes'
oi, oy as in 'boy'
ua   as in 'wash'
ue   as in 'well'

Consonants Many consonants are pronounced much the same as in English, but there are some exceptions:

c   is pronounced like 's' in 'sit' when before 'e' or 'i'; elsewhere it is like 'k.'
ch always as in 'choose.'
g   as the 'g' in 'gate' before 'a,' 'o' and 'u'; before 'e' or 'i' it is a harsh, breathy sound like the 'h' in 'hit' (see also 'u').
h   always silent.
j   a harsh, guttural sound similar to the 'ch' in the Scottish 'loch.'
ll as the 'y' in 'yellow.'
ñ   nasal sound like the 'ny' in 'canyon.'
q   as the 'k' in 'kick'; always followed by a silent 'u.'
r   pronounced with the tongue quickly touching the palate and flapping down, almost like the 'tt' of 'butter.' At the beginning of a word or following 'l,' 'n' or 's,' it is often rolled strongly.
rr a strongly rolled 'r.'
x   like English 'x' as in 'taxi,' usually. Sometimes when followed by 'e' or 'i,' it is pronounced like the Spanish 'j.' Note that in Mayan words 'x' is pronounced like English 'sh.'
z   the same as the English 's.'

A few other minor pronunciation differences exist, but the longer you stay in the region, the more of them you'll pick up. Note that ñ is considered a separate letter of the alphabet and follows 'n' in alphabetically organized lists and books, such as dictionaries and phone books. The same is true for **ch**, **ll** and **rr**, though these conventions are changing.

LANGUAGE

Stress Three general rules govern which syllable of a word to stress.

- For words ending in a vowel, 'n' or 's,' the stress goes on the next-to-last syllable:

naranja	na-**rahn**-ha
joven	**ho**-ven
zapatos	sa-**pa**-tos

- For words ending in a consonant other than 'n' or 's,' the stress is on the final syllable:

estoy	es-**toy**
ciudad	syoo-**dahd**
catedral	ka-teh-**dral**

- Any deviation from these rules is indicated by an accent:

Mérida	**meh**-ree-da
árbol	**ahr**-bol
Cortés	cor-**tess**

Exceptions to these rules are usually words foreign to the Spanish language. Note that written accents often do not appear on capital letters, though they are pronounced.

Gender

Nouns in Spanish are either masculine or feminine. Nouns ending in 'o,' 'e' or 'ma' are usually masculine. Nouns ending in 'a,' 'ión' or 'dad' are usually feminine. Some nouns can be either masculine or feminine, depending on the ending; for example, *viajero* is a male traveler, *viajera* is a female traveler. In the following text the masculine form is given first, followed where relevant by the feminine ending: *muchachos/as*. Adjectives agree with nouns in number and gender.

Greetings & Civilities

Hello/Hi.	*Hola.*
Good morning.	*Buenos días.*
Good afternoon.	*Buenas tardes.*
Good evening/night.	*Buenas noches.*
Bye, see you.	*Hasta luego.*
Goodbye.	*Adiós.*
Pleased to meet you.	*Mucho gusto.*
How are you?	
(to one person)	*¿Cómo está usted?*
How are you? (to more than one person)	*¿Cómo están?*
How's it going?	*¿Qué tal?*
Well, thanks.	*Bien, gracias.*
Very well.	*Muy bien.*
Very badly.	*Muy mal.*
Please.	*Por favor.*
Thank you.	*Gracias.*
You're welcome.	*De nada.*
Good luck!	*¡Buena suerte!*
Forgive me, excuse me.	*Disculpe, discúlpeme, perdóneme.*
Excuse me (when needing to get past).	*Con permiso.*
What is your name?	
	¿Cómo se llama usted? (formal)
	¿Cómo te llamas? (informal)
My name is…	*Me llamo…*
Where are you from?	
	¿De dónde es usted? (formal)
	¿De dónde vienes? (familiar)

People

I	*yo*
you (familiar)	*tú*
you (formal)	*usted*
you (pl, formal)	*ustedes*
he/it	*él*
she/it	*ella*
we	*nosotros/as*
they	*ellos/as*
my wife	*mi esposa*
my husband	*mi esposo, mi marido*
my brother/sister	*mi hermano/a*
Sir/Mister	*Señor*
Madam/Mrs	*Señora*
Miss	*Señorita*
pal, friend	*compañero/a, amigo/a*

Useful Words & Phrases

Yes.	*Sí.*
No.	*No.*
Maybe.	*Quizás.*
What did you say?	*¿Mande?* (colloq)
	¿Cómo?
good/OK	*bueno*
bad	*malo*
better	*mejor*

best	lo mejor
more	más
less	menos
much	mucho/a
very little	poco/a or poquito/a
I am...	Estoy...(location or temporary condition)
here	aquí
tired	cansado/a
sick/ill	enfermo/a
happy	contento/a
sad	triste
I am...	Soy...(permanent state)
a worker	trabajador
married	casado

Can I take a photo?
        ¿Puedo sacar una foto?
Of course/Why not/Sure.
        Por supuesto/Cómo no/Claro.
How old are you?
        ¿Cuántos años tiene?
How does one say...?
        ¿Cómo se dice...?
What does...mean?
        ¿Qué significa...?
Where are the toilets?
        ¿Dónde están los servicios/baños?

Buying

How much?	*¿Cuánto?*
How much does it cost?	
	¿Cuánto cuesta?
	¿Cuánto se cobra?
	¿Cuánto vale?
I want...	*Quiero...*
I do not want...	*No quiero...*
I would like...	*Quisiera...*
Give me...	*Deme...*
What do you want?	*¿Qué quiere usted?*
Do you have... ?	*¿Tiene...?*
Is/are there... ?	*¿Hay...?*

Nationalities

American	(norte)americano/a
Australian	australiano/a
British	británico/a
Canadian (m & f)	canadiense
English	inglés/inglesa
French	francés/francesa
German	alemán/alemana

Languages

I speak...	Yo hablo...
I do not speak...	No hablo...
Do you speak...?	¿Habla usted...?
Spanish	español
English	inglés
German	alemán
French	francés
I understand.	Entiendo.
I do not understand.	No entiendo.
Do you understand?	¿Entiende usted?
Please speak slowly.	Por favor hable despacio.

Crossing the Border

birth certificate	certificado de nacimiento
border (frontier)	la frontera
car-owner's title	título de propiedad
car registration	registración
customs	aduana
driver's license	licencia de manejar
identification	identificación
immigration	inmigración
insurance	seguro
passport	pasaporte
temporary vehicle import permit	permiso de importación temporal de vehículo
tourist card	tarjeta de turista
visa	visado

Getting Around

north	norte (Nte)
south	sur
east	este
east (in an address)	oriente (Ote)
west	oeste
west (in an address)	poniente (Pte)
street	calle
boulevard	bulevar, boulevard
avenue	avenida
road	camino
highway	carretera
corner (of)	esquina (de)
block	cuadra
to the left	a la izquierda
to the right	a la derecha
forward, ahead	adelante
straight ahead	todo recto or derecho

LANGUAGE

this way	*por aquí*
that way	*por allí*
Where is…?	*¿Dónde está…?*
a long-distance phone	*un teléfono de larga distancia*
the airport	*el aeropuerto*
the bus station	*el terminal de autobuses, central camionera*
the post office	*el correo*
bus	*camión* or *autobús*
bus (long distance)	*flota, bus, camioneta*
minibus	*colectivo, combi*
train	*tren*
taxi	*taxi*
ticket sales counter	*taquilla*
waiting room	*sala de espera*
baggage check-in	*(recibo de) equipaje*
toilet	*sanitario*
departure	*salida*
arrival	*llegada*
platform	*andén*
left-luggage room/ checkroom	*guardería* (or *guarda) de equipaje*
How far is…?	*¿A qué distancia está…?*
How long? (How much time?)	*¿Cuánto tiempo?*

Driving

gasoline	*gasolina*
fuel station	*gasolinera*
unleaded	*sin plomo*
fill the tank	*llene el tanque; llenarlo*
full	*lleno* or *'ful'*
oil	*aceite*
tire	*llanta*
puncture	*agujero*

How much is a liter of gasoline?
        ¿Cuánto cuesta el litro de gasolina?
My car has broken down.
        Se me ha descompuesto el carro.
I need a tow truck.
        Necesito un remolque.
Is there a garage near here?
        ¿Hay un garaje cerca de aquí?

Highway Signs

Though Mexico mostly uses the familiar international road signs, you should be prepared to encounter these other signs as well:

camino en reparación	road repairs
conserve su derecha	keep to the right
curva peligrosa	dangerous curve
derrumbes	landslides or subsidence
despacio	slow
desviación	detour
disminuya su velocidad	slow down
escuela (zona escolar)	school (school zone)
hombres trabajando	men working
no hay paso	road closed
no rebase	no passing
peligro	danger
prepare su cuota	have toll ready
puente angosto	narrow bridge
raya continua	continuous white line
topes or *vibradores*	speed bumps
tramo en reparación	road under repair
un solo carril a 100 m	one-lane road 100 meters ahead
vía corta	short route (often a toll road)
vía cuota	toll highway
vía libre	free route

Dangers & Annoyances

Watch out!	*¡Cuidado!*
Help!	*¡Socorro! ¡Auxilio!*
Fire!	*¡Fuego!*
Thief!	*¡Ladrón!*
I've been robbed.	*Me han robado.*
They took my…	*Se me llevaron…*
money	*el dinero*
passport	*el pasaporte*
bag	*la bolsa*
Where is…?	*¿Dónde hay…?*
a police officer	*un policía*
a doctor	*un doctor*
a hospital	*un hospital*
Leave me alone!	*¡Déjeme!*
Don't bother me!	*¡No me moleste!*
Get lost!	*¡Váyase!*

Accommodations

hotel	*hotel*
guesthouse	*casa de huéspedes*
inn	*posada*
room	*cuarto, habitación*
room with one bed	*cuarto sencillo*
room with two beds	*cuarto doble*
room for one person	*cuarto para una persona*
room for two people	*cuarto para dos personas*
double bed	*cama matrimonial*
twin beds	*camas gemelas*
with bath	*con baño*
shower	*ducha* or *regadera*
hot water	*agua caliente*
air-conditioning	*aire acondicionado*
blanket	*manta, cobija*
towel	*toalla*
soap	*jabón*
toilet paper	*papel higiénico*
the check (bill)	*la cuenta*

Where is…?	*¿Dónde hay…?*
a hotel	*un hotel*
a boardinghouse	*una pensión*
a guesthouse	*un hospedaje*
I am looking for…	*Busco/ Estoy buscando…*
a cheap hotel	*un hotel barato*
a good hotel	*un hotel bueno*
a nearby hotel	*un hotel cercano*
a clean hotel	*un hotel limpio*

Are there any rooms available?
¿Hay habitaciones libres?
What is the price?
¿Cuál es el precio?
Does that include taxes?
¿Están incluidos los impuestos?
Does that include service?
¿Está incluido el servicio?

Money

money	*dinero*
traveler's checks	*cheques de viajero*
cash	*efectivo*
bank	*banco*
dollars	*dólares*
exchange bureau	*casa de cambio*
credit card	*tarjeta de crédito*

exchange rate	*tipo de cambio*
ATM	*caja permanente* or *cajero automático*

I want/would like to change some money.
Quiero/quisiera cambiar dinero.
What is the exchange rate?
¿Cuál es el tipo de cambio?
Is there a commission?
¿Hay comisión?

Telephones

telephone	*teléfono*
telephone call	*llamada*
telephone number	*número telefónico*
telephone card	*tarjeta telefónica*
area or city code	*clave*

local call	*llamada local*
long-distance call	*llamada de larga distancia*
prefix for long-distance call	*prefijo*
long-distance telephone	*teléfono de larga distancia*
coin-operated telephone	*teléfono de monedas*
card-operated telephone	*teléfono de tarjetas telefónicas*
long-distance telephone office	*caseta de larga distancia*

tone	*tono*
operator	*operador/a*
person to person	*persona a persona*
collect (reverse charges)	*por cobrar*
dial the number	*marque el número*
please wait	*favor de esperar*
busy	*ocupado*
toll/cost (of call)	*cuota/costo*
time & charges	*tiempo y costo*
(don't) hang up	*(no) cuelgue*

Times & Dates

Monday	*lunes*
Tuesday	*martes*
Wednesday	*miércoles*
Thursday	*jueves*
Friday	*viernes*
Saturday	*sábado*
Sunday	*domingo*

LANGUAGE

yesterday	*ayer*
today	*hoy*
tomorrow (also at some point, or maybe)	*mañana*
right now (meaning in a few minutes)	*horita, ahorita*
already	*ya*
morning	*mañana*
tomorrow morning	*mañana por la mañana*
afternoon	*tarde*
night	*noche*
What time is it?	*¿Qué hora es?*

Numbers

0	*cero*
1	*un, uno* (m), *una* (f)
2	*dos*
3	*tres*
4	*cuatro*
5	*cinco*
6	*seis*
7	*siete*
8	*ocho*
9	*nueve*
10	*diez*
11	*once*
12	*doce*
13	*trece*
14	*catorce*
15	*quince*
16	*dieciséis*
17	*diecisiete*
18	*dieciocho*
19	*diecinueve*
20	*veinte*
21	*veintiuno*
22	*veintidós*
30	*treinta*
31	*treinta y uno*
32	*treinta y dos*
40	*cuarenta*
50	*cincuenta*
60	*sesenta*
70	*setenta*
80	*ochenta*
90	*noventa*
100	*cien*
101	*ciento uno*
143	*ciento cuarenta y tres*
200	*doscientos*

500	*quinientos*
700	*setecientos*
900	*novecientos*
1000	*mil*
2000	*dos mil*

Ordinal Numbers As with other adjectives, ordinals must agree in gender and number with the noun they modify. Ordinal numbers are often abbreviated using a numeral and a superscript 'o' or 'a' in street names, addresses, and so forth: Calle 1ª, 2º piso (1st Street, 2nd floor).

1st	*primero/a*
2nd	*segundo/a*
3rd	*tercero/a*
4th	*cuarto/a*
5th	*quinto/a*
6th	*sexto/a*
7th	*séptimo/a*
8th	*octavo/a*
9th	*noveno/a*
10th	*décimo/a*
11th	*undécimo/a*
12th	*duodécimo/a*
20th	*vigésimo/a*

Spanish-Language Schools

Studying at home before you leave for the Mayan region might get you up to speed in Spanish, but for learning the language quickly and well there's nothing like studying in your destination country. Not only will you be sure to pick up local idioms, you'll also absorb the cultural intricacies that provide context for the proper usage of your new knowledge. Many schools offer programs that allow you to stay with a local family while you study – the ultimate in total immersion.

Language schools can be found throughout Guatemala and the Yucatán, but several towns are especially well known for them, most notably Antigua and Quetzaltenango in Guatemala and San Cristóbal de Las Casas in Chiapas. See those sections of this book for further details.

Modern Mayan

Since the Classic period, the two ancient Mayan languages, Yucatecan and Cholan, have subdivided into 35 separate Mayan languages (Yucatec, Chol, Chorti, Tzeltal, Tzotzil, Lacandón, Mam, Quiché, Cakchiquel etc), some of them unintelligible to speakers of others.

Writing today is in the Latin alphabet brought by the conquistadors – what writing there is. Most literate Maya are literate in Spanish, the language of the government, the church, schools and the media; they may not be literate in Mayan.

As with Japanese, Chinese, and other languages, more than one system of transliteration is in use for rendering Mayan in the Latin alphabet; some are based on the early efforts of priests, others on more modern linguistic analysis. You will sometimes see place names spelled differently from one road sign to the next, for example, 'Majajual' and 'Mahahual.'

PRONUNCIATION
There are a number of rules to remember when pronouncing Mayan words and place names. The Mayan vowels are relatively straightforward:

a   is like 'a' in 'father'
e   is like 'e' in 'met'
i   is like 'ee' in 'feet'
o   is like 'o' in 'note'
oo is same as 'o' but held longer
u   is like 'oo' in 'boot'

It's the consonants that give problems. Remember the following:

c   is always hard, like 'k.'
j   is always an aspirated 'h' sound. So *jipijapa* is pronounced **hee**-pee-**haa**-pah and *abaj* is pronounced ah-**bahh**; the 'hh' sound is like the 'h' sound from 'half.' The letter 'h' is used in place of this 'j' in many transliterations.
u   is 'oo' except when combining with another vowel to form a diphthong, in which case it is like English 'w.' Thus

baktún is pronounced bahk-**toon**, but *Uaxactún* is pronounced wah-shahk-**toon** and *ahau* is pronounced ah-**haw**.

x   is like English 'sh,' a shushing sound.

Consonants followed by an apostrophe (b', ch', k', p', t') are similar to normal consonants but pronounced more forcefully and 'explosively.' An apostrophe following a *vowel* signifies a glottal stop, *not* a more forceful vowel.

In written Mayan place names, Spanish rules for indicating stress are often followed (see earlier in this chapter). This practice varies; in this book we have tried to include accents as much as possible. Here are some general pronunciation examples:

Abaj Takalik	ah-**bahh** tah-kah **leek**
Acanceh	ah-kahn-**keh**
Ahau	ah-**haw**
Dzibilchaltún	dzee-beel-chahl-**toon**
Kaminaljuyú	kah-mee-nahl-hoo-**yoo**
Oxcutzkab	ohsh-kootz-**kahb**
Pacal	pah-**kahl**
Pop	pohp
Tikal	tee-**kahl**
Uaxactún	wah-shahk-**toon**
Xcaret	shkah-**reht**
Yaxchilán	yahsh-chee-**lahn**

QUICHÉ
An estimated 1.8 million Quiché Maya live in Guatemala, and Quiché is widely spoken throughout the Guatemalan highlands. Travelers to this region will have plenty of opportunity to practice some of the common terms and phrases listed below.

Greetings & Civilities
Good morning.	*Saqarik.*
Good afternoon.	*Xb'eqij.*
Good evening/night.	*Xokaq'ab'.*
Goodbye.	*Chab'ej.*
Bye. See you soon.	*Kimpetik ri.*
Thank you.	*Maltiox.*
How are you?	*Uts awech?*
Excuse me.	*Kyunala.*

More Useful Words & Phrases
What is your name?	*Su ra'b'i?*
My name is...	*Nu b'i...*

LANGUAGE

Where is a...?	*Ja k'uichi' ri...?*	19	*b'elejlajuj*
bathroom	*b'anb'al chuluj*	20	*juwinak*
hotel	*jun worib'al*	30	*lajuj re kawinak*
police officer	*ajchajil re tinamit*	40	*kawinak*
doctor	*ajkun*	50	*lajuj re oxk'al*
bus stop	*tek'lib'al*	60	*oxk'al*
Do you have...?	*K'olik...?*	70	*lajuj re waqk'al*
coffee	*kab'e*	80	*waqk'al*
boiled water	*saq'li*	90	*lajuj re o'k'al*
copal	*kach'*	100	*o'k'al*
a machete	*choyib'al*	200	*lajuj k'al*
rooms	*k'plib'al*	400	*omuch'*
We have it.	*K'olik.*		
We don't have it,	*K'otaj*		

MAM

Mam is spoken in the department of Huehuetenango, in the western portion of the country. This is the indigenous language you'll hear in Todos Santos, nestled among the Cuchumatanes Mountains.

vegetables	*ichaj*
blanket	*k'ul*
soap	*ch'ipaq*
good	*utz*
bad	*itzel*
open	*teb'am*
closed	*tzapilik*
hard	*ko*
soft	*ch'uch'uj*
hot	*miq'in*
cold	*joron*
sick	*yiwab'*
north (white)	*saq*
south (yellow)	*k'an*
east (red)	*kaq*
west (black)	*k'eq*

Greetings & Civilities

Luckily, in Mam you need only know two phrases for greeting folks, no matter the time of day:

Good morning/afternoon/evening.
Chin q'olb'el teya (informal singular).
Chin q'olb'el kyeyea (informal plural).

Goodbye.	*Chi nej.*
Bye. See you soon.	*Chi nej. Ak qli qib'.*
Thank you.	*Chonte teya.*
How are you?	*Tzen ta'ya?*
Excuse me.	*Naq samy.*

Numbers

1	*jun*
2	*keb'*
3	*oxib'*
4	*kijeb'*
5	*job'*
6	*waq'ib'*
7	*wuqub'*
8	*wajxakib'*
9	*b'elejeb'*
10	*lajuj*
11	*julajuj*
12	*kab'lajuj*
13	*oxlajuj*
14	*kajlajuj*
15	*o'lajuj*
16	*waklajuj*
17	*wuklajuj*
18	*wajxaklajuj*

More Useful Words & Phrases

What is your name?	*Tit biya?*
My name is...	*Luan bi...*
Where are you from?	*Jaa'tzajnia?*
I am from...	*Ac tzajni...*

Many words in Mam have been in disuse for so long that the Spanish equivalent is now used almost exclusively.

Where is a...?	*Ja at...?*
bathroom	*baño*
hotel	*hospedaje*
police officer	*policía*
doctor	*médico/doctor*

Where is the bus stop?	
Ja nue camioneta?	
(literally, where does the bus stop?)	
Is there somewhere we can sleep?	
Ja tun kqta'n?	

Do you have...?	*At...?*
coffee	*café*
boiled water	*kqa'*
a machete	*machete*
rooms?	*cuartos*
We have it.	*At.*
We don't have it.	*Nti'.*

How much is/are the...?	*Je te ti...?*
fruits and vegetables	*lobj*
blanket	*ponch* (short for poncho)
soap	*jabón*

good	*banex* or *g'lan*
bad	*k'ab'ex* or *nia g'lan*
open	*jqo'n*
closed	*jpu'n*
hard	*kuj*
soft	*xb'une*
hot	*kyaq*
I am...	*At...*
cold	*xb'a'j* or *choj*
sick	*yab'*
north (white)	*okan*
south (yellow)	*eln*
east (red)	*jawl*
west (black)	*kub'el*
white	*saq*
yellow	*q'an*
red	*txa'x* (also the word for raw)
black	*q'aq*

Menu Guide

Antojitos

Many traditional Mexican dishes fall under the heading of *antojitos* ('little whims') – savory or spicy concoctions that delight the palate. Many of these same snacks are found in Guatemala, where they are also sometimes called *refacciones*.

burrito – any combination of beans, cheese, meat, chicken or seafood, seasoned with salsa or chile and wrapped in a wheat-flour tortilla

chilaquiles – scrambled eggs with chiles and bits of tortillas

chile relleno – *poblano* chile stuffed with cheese, meat or other foods, dipped in egg whites, fried and baked in sauce

chuchitos – a Guatemalan *tamal* (see below) stuffed with spicy meat

enchilada – ingredients similar to those used in tacos and burritos but wrapped in a corn tortilla, dipped in sauce and then baked or fried

machaca – cured, dried and shredded beef or pork mixed with eggs, onions, cilantro and chiles

papadzul – corn tortillas filled with hard-boiled eggs, cucumber or squash seeds and covered in tomato sauce

quesadilla – flour tortilla topped or filled with cheese and occasionally other ingredients and then heated

queso relleno – 'stuffed cheese,' a mild yellow cheese stuffed with minced meat and spices

taco – a soft or crisp corn tortilla wrapped or folded around the same filling as a burrito

tamal – steamed corn dough stuffed with meat, beans, chiles or nothing at all, wrapped in corn husks

tostada – flat, crisp tortilla topped with meat or cheese, tomatoes, beans and lettuce

Sopas (Soups)

birria – a spicy-hot soup of meat, onions, peppers and cilantro, served with tortillas

chipilín – cheese and cream soup on a corn base

gazpacho – chilled vegetable soup spiced with hot chiles

menudo – popular soup made with spiced tripe

pozole – hominy soup with meat and vegetables (can be spicy)

sopa de arroz – not a soup at all but just a plate of rice; commonly served with lunch

sopa de lima – 'lime soup,' chicken stock flavored with lime and filled with pieces of crisped corn tortilla

sopa de pollo – bits of chicken in a thin chicken broth

Huevos (Eggs)

huevos estrellados – fried eggs

huevos fritos – fried eggs

huevos motuleños – local dish of the Yucatecan town of Motul; fried eggs atop a tortilla spread with refried beans and garnished with diced ham, green peas, shredded cheese and tomato sauce, with fried bananas *(plátanos)* on the side

huevos rancheros – ranch-style eggs; fried eggs laid on a tortilla and smothered with spicy tomato sauce

huevos revueltos – scrambled eggs; *con chorizo* is with spicy sausage, *con frijoles* is with beans, *estilo mexicano* is with tomatoes, onions, chiles and garlic

Pescado, Mariscos (Seafood)

The variety and quality of seafood from the coastal waters of the Yucatán and Belize is excellent.

Lobster is available along Mexico's Caribbean coast and in Belize, particularly on the cayes. Campeche (Mexico) is a major shrimping port, and much of its total catch is exported.

All of the following types of seafood are available in seafood restaurants most of the year. Clams, oysters, shrimp and prawns are also often available as *cocteles* (cocktails).

abulón – abalone
almejas – clams
atún – tuna
cabrilla – sea bass
camarones – shrimp
camarones gigantes – prawns
cangrejo – large crab
cazón – dogfish (a small shark)
ceviche – raw seafood marinated in lime juice and mixed with onions, chiles, garlic, tomatoes and cilantro (fresh coriander leaf)
dorado – dolphin (the fish, not the mammal)
filete de pescado – fish fillet
huachinango – red snapper
jaiba – small crab
jurel – yellowtail
langosta – lobster
lenguado – flounder or sole
mariscos – shellfish
ostiones – oysters
pan de cazón – a specialty of Campeche consisting of *cazón* (see above) layered with corn tortillas in a dark sauce
pescado – fish after it has been caught (see *pez*)
pescado al mojo de ajo – fish fried in butter and garlic
pez – fish alive in the water
pez espada – swordfish
sierra – mackerel
tiburón – shark
tortuga or *caguama* – turtle
trucha de mar – sea trout

Carnes y Aves (Meats & Poultry)

asado – roast, roasted
barbacoa – literally 'barbecued,' but by a process whereby the meat (or fish) is covered and placed under hot coals
birria – barbecued on a spit
bistec – beefsteak; sometimes any cut of meat, fish or poultry
bistec de res – beefsteak
borrego – sheep
cabrito – kid
cabro – goat
carne al carbón – charcoal-grilled meat
carne asada – tough but tasty grilled beef
carnitas – deep-fried pork
chicharrones – deep-fried pork skin

chorizo – pork sausage
chuletas de puerco – pork chops
cochinita – suckling pig
codorniz, chaquaca – quail
conejo – rabbit
cordero – lamb
costillas de puerco – pork ribs or chops
guajolote – turkey
hígado – liver
jamón – ham
milanesa – breaded, crumbed
milanesa de res – breaded beefsteak
patas de puerco – pig's feet
pato – duck
pavo – turkey, a fowl native to Yucatán that figures prominently in Yucatecan cuisine
pibil – Yucatecan preparation in which meat is flavored with *achiote* sauce, wrapped in banana leaves and baked in a *pib* (pit oven)
poc-chuc – slices of pork cooked in a tangy sauce of onion and either sour oranges or lemons
pollo – chicken
pollo asado – grilled or roasted chicken
pollo con arroz – chicken with rice
pollo frito – fried chicken
puerco – pork
tampiqueño, tampiqueña – 'in the style of Tampico,' with spiced tomato sauce
tocino – bacon or salt pork
venado – venison

Frutas (Fruit)

anona – custard apple or cherimoya, a foul-smelling but delicious fruit
coco – coconut
dátil – date
fresas – strawberries; any berries
guayaba – guava
higo – fig
hocote – a small fruit that looks like a diminutive avocado; it ranges from green to orange and is eaten with lime and nutmeg
limón – lime or lemon
mango – mango
melocotón – peach
melón – melon
naranja – orange

papaya – try it with lime, chile and salt; superb!

piña – pineapple

plátano – in Mexico this is any banana; in Guatemala it refers to the plantain, a type of banana edible only when cooked (in Guatemala, the familiar, immediately edible banana is called a *banano)*

toronja – grapefruit

uva – grape

Legumbres, Verduras (Vegetables)

Vegetables are rarely served as separate dishes but are often mixed into salads, soups and sauces.

aceitunas – olives

ajillo – a small onion akin to a scallion

calabaza – squash or pumpkin

cebolla – onion

champiñones – mushrooms, also called *hongos*

chícharos – peas

ejotes – green beans

elote – corn on the cob; commonly served with a slice of lime from steaming bins on street carts

jícama – a popular root vegetable that resembles a potato crossed with an apple; eaten fresh with a sprinkling of lime, chile and salt

lechuga – lettuce

pacaya – a squashlike staple among the highland Maya of Guatemala

papa – potato

tomate – tomato, often called *jitomate* in Mexico

zanahoria – carrot

Dulces (Desserts, Sweets)

choco bananos – in Guatemala, chocolate-covered bananas; also sold with chocolate and peanuts *(maníes)*

flan – custard, crème caramel

helado – ice cream

nieve – Mexican equivalent of the American 'snow cone': flavored ice with the consistency of ice cream

paleta – flavored ice on a stick

pan dulce – sweet rolls, usually eaten for breakfast

pastel – cake

postre – dessert, after-meal sweet

Other Foods

achiote – a sauce of chopped tomato, onion, chiles and cilantro, used widely in Yucatán

atole – a hot drink made with corn, milk, cinnamon and sugar

azúcar – sugar

bolillo – French-style bread rolls

crema – cream

fiambre – a traditional salad type dish eaten in Guatemala on All Saints' Day; made from assorted meats, seafood and vegetables (most notably beets) in a vinegar base

guacamole – mashed avocados mixed with onion, chile sauce, lemon, tomato and other ingredients

leche – milk

mantequilla – butter; intestinal upset from butter gone rancid in this hot climate has generated its jocular colloquial name 'meant-ta-kill-ya'

mole poblano – a popular hot sauce from Puebla, Mexico, made from more than 30 ingredients, including bitter chocolate, various chiles and many spices; often served over chicken or turkey

mosh – a hot oat concoction similar to oatmeal or porridge; served as part of breakfast in Guatemala and also a popular offering of street vendors

pimienta negra – black pepper

poporopo – neon-colored popcorn balls

queso – cheese

sal – salt

salsa – any sauce; often one made with chiles, onion, tomato, lemon or lime juice and spices

tapado – a fish and plantain stew served on Guatemala's Caribbean coast

Café (Coffee)

café americano/solo – black coffee with nothing added except sugar

café con leche – coffee with hot milk

café con crema – coffee with cream served separately

café sin azúcar – coffee without sugar; ordering this keeps the waiter from adding heaps of sugar to your cup, but it doesn't mean your coffee won't taste sweet – sugar is often added to and processed with the beans

nescafé – instant coffee (also called *café instantáneo* or *café soluble*); if instant is all that's available, you'll often be told *'agua para café,'* or you may be asked if you want *'leche para café,'* hot milk into which you can mix the coffee powder

At the Table

carta – menu (see also *lista*)

copa – glass

cuchara – spoon

cuchillo – knife

cuenta – bill

lista – menu; short for *lista de precios* (see *menú*)

menú – fixed-price meal, as in *menú del día*; in fancier places can also mean 'menu' (usually *carta* or *lista*)

plato – plate, dish

propina – the tip

servilleta – table napkin

taza – cup

tenedor – fork

vaso – drinking glass

Glossary

abrazo – embrace, hug; in particular, the formal, ceremonial hug between political leaders

aceite de frenos – brake fluid

alux – Mayan for gremlin, leprechaun, benevolent 'little people'

Apartado Postal – post office box, abbreviated *Apdo Postal*

Ayuntamiento – Town Council or City Hall (see *Palacio Municipal*); often seen as 'H Ayuntamiento (*Honorable Ayuntamiento*)

barrio – district, neighborhood

billete – bank note (unlike in Spain, where it's a ticket)

boleto – ticket (bus, train, museum etc)

bolo – Guatemalan term for a drunk

caballeros – literally 'horsemen,' but corresponds to 'gentlemen' in English; look for it on toilet doors

cacique – Indian chief; also used to describe provincial warlord or strongman

cafetería – literally 'coffee shop,' it refers to any informal restaurant with waiter service; it does not usually mean a self-service restaurant, as it does in the US

cajero automático – automated bank teller machine (ATM)

callejón – alley or small, narrow or very short street

camión – truck, bus

camioneta – bus or pickup truck

casa de cambio – currency exchange office; offers exchange rates comparable to banks and is much faster to use

caseta de larga distancia – long-distance telephone station, often shortened to *caseta*

cazuela – clay cooking pot, usually sold in a nested set

cenote – large natural limestone sinkhole or cave, often used as a water source (or for ceremonial purposes) in the Yucatán

cerveza – beer

Chac – Mayan god of rain

chac-mool – Mayan sacrificial sculpture

chapín – a citizen of Guatemala

charro – cowboy

chicle – chewing gum; also, a substance processed from the sap of the sapodilla tree, used to make chewing gum

chiclero – a person who extracts chicle from the sapodilla tree

chultún – artificial Mayan cistern found at Puuc archaeological sites south of Mérida

Churrigueresque – describes buildings constructed in the Spanish baroque architectural style of the early 18th century, with lavish ornamentation; named for architect José Churriguera

cigarillo – cigar

cigarro – cigarette

cofradía – in Guatemala, refers to a religious brotherhood

colectivo – jitney taxi or minibus that picks up and drops off passengers along its route

comal – hot griddle used to cook tortillas

combi – a Volkswagen van that's used as a *colectivo*

completo – full up, a sign you may see on hotel desks in crowded cities

conquistador – any of the Spanish explorer-conquerors of Latin America

copal – a tree resin used as incense in Mayan ceremonies

correos – post office

curandero – Indian traditional healer

damas – ladies, the usual sign on toilet doors

dzul, dzules – Mayan for foreigners or 'townfolk,' that is, not Maya from the rural countryside

ejido – in Mexico, communally owned Indian land once taken over by landowners but returned to the local people under a program started by President Lázaro Cárdenas

encomienda – Spanish colonial practice of putting Indians under the 'guardianship' of landowners, practically akin to medieval serfdom

estación ferrocarril – train station

ferrocarril – railroad
finca – estate, ranch, farm
frenos – brakes

galón – US gallon (fluid measure of 3.79L); gallons are sometimes used as a measurement in Belize and Guatemala
gringo/a – a mildly pejorative Mexican term applied to a male/female visitor from the US or Canada; sometimes applied to any visitor of European heritage
gruta – cave
guardarropa – cloakroom, place to leave parcels when entering an establishment
guayabera – man's thin fabric shirt with pockets and appliquéd designs, often worn in place of a suit jacket and tie at formal occasions

hacendado – landowner
hacienda – country estate, ranch; also 'Treasury,' as in Departamento de Hacienda (Treasury Department)
hay – pronounced like 'eye,' meaning 'there is' or 'there are'; you're equally likely to hear *no hay* ('there isn't' or 'there aren't')
henequen – the fibers of an agave plant (grown particularly around Mérida in Yucatán), used to make rope; also the plant itself
hombre – man
huipil – woven white dress featuring intricate, colorful embroidery; found in the Mayan regions

IMSS – Instituto Mexicana de Seguridad Social, the Mexican Social Security Institute; operates many of Mexico's larger public hospitals (in Guatemala the corresponding institution is the IGSS)
IVA – *impuesto al valor agregado* or 'ee-vah'; a value-added tax that can be as high as 15% and is added to many items in Mexico

Kukulcán – Mayan name for the Aztec-Toltec plumed serpent Quetzalcóatl

ladino – a person of mixed Indian and European race (Guatemala); see also *mestizo*

larga distancia – long-distance telephone, abbreviated as Lada; see also *caseta de larga distancia*
lavandería – laundry; a *lavandería automática* refers to a coin-operated laundry (laundromat)
leng – colloquial Mayan term for coins (Guatemalan highlands)
libra – pound (a weight equal to 0.45kg); pounds are used as a measurement in Belize and sometimes in Guatemala
lista de correos – general delivery in Mexico; literally 'mail list,' the list of addressees for whom mail is being held, displayed in the post office
llantas – tires
lleno – full (can apply to fuel tank)
lonchería – from English *lunch*; a simple restaurant that may serve meals all day, not just lunch (you often see loncherías near municipal markets)

machismo – maleness, masculine virility; an ever-present aspect of Mexican society
malecón – waterfront boulevard
manzana – apple; also a city block
mariachi – small ensemble of Mexican street musicians; strolling mariachi bands often perform in restaurants
mecapal – a forehead tumpline made of thick leather; still used by rural Maya as a means of carrying heavy loads
mestizo – a person of mixed Indian and European blood (Mexico); the word now more commonly means 'Mexican' (see also *ladino*)
metate – flattish stone on which corn is ground with a cylindrical stone roller
milla – mile (a distance equal to 1.61km); miles are used as a measurement in Belize and sometimes in Guatemala
mordida – 'bite,' or bribe; usually paid (to a traffic policeman, for example) to keep the wheels of bureaucracy turning
mudéjar – Moorish architectural style
mujer – woman

onza – ounce (a weight equal to 28.35g); ounces are used as a measurement in Belize and sometimes in Guatemala

Palacio de Gobierno – building housing the executive offices of either a state or regional government

Palacio Municipal – City Hall, seat of the municipal government

palapa – thatch-roofed shelter with open sides

parada – bus stop, usually for city buses

pie – foot (a length equal to 0.3m); feet are used as a measurement in Belize and sometimes in Guatemala

pinchazo – automobile tire repair shop (Guatemala)

pisto – colloquial Mayan term for money, quetzala (Guatemalan highlands)

Plateresque – describes buildings constructed in a 16th-century Spanish architectural style using elaborate decoration reminiscent of silverwork

PRI – Institutional Revolutionary Party, the controlling force in Mexican politics for more than half a century

propina – a tip, gratuity

puro – cigar

Quetzalcóatl – plumed serpent god of the Aztecs and Toltecs

rebozo – long woolen or linen scarf covering the head or shoulders

retablo – altarpiece (often ornately gilded and carved); also a small painting on tin, wood, cardboard, glass etc, placed in a church to give thanks for answered prayers or other divine intercession

retorno – 'return'; in Cancún and some other cities in the Yucatán, a U-shaped street that starts from a major boulevard, loops around and 'returns' to the boulevard a block away

roofcomb – a decorative stonework lattice atop a Mayan pyramid or temple

rutelero – jitney

sacbé, sacbeob – ceremonial limestone avenue or path between or within great Mayan cities

sacerdote – priest

sanatorio – hospital, particularly a small private one

sanitario – literally 'sanitary'; usually means toilet

serape – traditional woolen blanket

stela (pl **stelae**) – standing stone monument(s), usually carved

supermercado – supermarket, ranging from a small corner store to a large, American-style supermarket

taller – shop, workshop or studio; a *taller mecánico* is a mechanic's shop, usually for cars, while a *taller de artesanía* is a crafts shop or studio

teléfono monedero – coin-operated tele phone (Guatemala)

templo – temple, also a church (anything from a wayside chapel to a cathedral)

tequila – clear, distilled liquor produced, like pulque and mezcal, from the maguey cactus

Tex-Mex – Mexican-American cuisine (also music, culture) originating in southern Texas

típico – typical or characteristic of a region; particularly used to describe food

topes – speed bumps found in many Mexican towns, sometimes indicated by a highway sign bearing a row of little bumps

viajero – traveler

vulcanizadora – automobile tire repair shop (Mexico)

War of the Castes – bloody Mayan uprising that took place in the Yucatán during the mid-19th century

xate – a low-growing palm native to Guatemala's Petén region and exported for use in floral arrangements, particularly in the US

xateros – men who collect xate

Xinka – a small, non-Maya indigenous group living on Guatemala's Pacific Slope

zócalo – Aztec for 'pedestal' or 'plinth,' but now used to refer to a town's main plaza (Mexico)

zotz – bat (the mammal) in many of the Mayan languages

Acknowledgments

THANKS
Thanks to all the following travelers (and to any we've missed!) who took the time to write to us about their experiences in Belize, Guatemala and the Yucatán.

Anders Aarkrog, Masoud Afarinkia, Paul Altomonte, Vicente Alvarez, Lotta Andersson, Brian Andreasen, James Andrick, Giuseppe Anzalone, Bianca Arens, Jörg Ausfelt, Jan Bailey, Myriam Baum, Taylor Beavers, Chuck Behrens, Matthew K Belcher, Rob Bell, Steve Bell, Martin Belzile, Charles Bennett, Caryl Bergeron, Béatrice Blaise, Joel Bleskacek, Adam Blissett, Claire Bonnet, Nicole Boogaers, Theo Borst, Stephan Bössler, Annemarie Breeve, Peter Brennan, Heather Brown, James Brown, Ciara Browne, Steve Burton, Eric Calder, Elizabeth Canter, John Carlisle, Alexandre Chatin, Evelyne Chauis, Paula Cipolla, Michelle Clark, Jennifer Compton, David J Connor, Gianluigi Contin, Thomas P Coohill, Michelle Cooper, Elisabetta Corva, Francesc Costa, Jean-François Cousin, Colleen Coyle, Steve Creamer, Clare Cronan, Ingrid Dauh, Susanne de Raaij, Sylvia de Verga, Dean Desantis, Adolf Descalzi, Joseph-Ambroise Desrosiers, Elke Ditscheid-Göller, Bernard Dix, MG Dixon, Clement Djossen, Stéphane Doutriaux, J Winslow Dowson, Daniel Drazan, Annabella Dudziec, Linda A Dufresne, Roel Duijf, Jerry Eldred, Jocelyn Elliot, Kari Eloranta, Doron Ezra, Lisa Falloon, Daniel Finkbeiner, Jerry D Finley, Franesa Fiore, Artemis Fire, R Steve Fox, William F Frank, Lill Tove Fredriksen, Barbara Fricke, Eileen Fruggiero, Ulf Gäbler, Caroline & Mark Galanty, Rafael Jiménez García-Pascual, Elissa Gershon, Clive Giddings, Tracy R Glass, Ian Gleave, Javier Gonzalez-Ustes, Caroline Goodman, Roberto Gotta, Emanuel Graef, Pamela Grist, Suzette Hafner, Susan Hall, Marion C Halmos, Mary Anne Hamer, Rhonda Hankins, Steve Harris, Colin Harvey, Ayman Hasson, Andrea Hazard, Michelle Hecht, KJ Herman, Matthias Herrlein, Gary Hickman, Allan Hindmarch, Dean R Hoge, Dorsey Holappa, Derek Hollinsworth, Paul Hopcraft, Camilla Hult, Nancy Hummel, Maury Hurt, Mary Ellen Jarvis, Tim Jeffries, Ginger Johnson, Tim Johnson, Jerven Jongkind, Tom Josephs, Isabelle K.Y. Jost, Tim San Jule, Alexander Jurk, Rikke Kamstrup, Tom Kegelman, David Kerkhoff, Hans Kerres, Samyra Keus, Zella King, Paul-Michael Klein, Esther Kobel, Raghu Krishnan, Randall R Krueger, Rainer Kugler, Louise La Valliére, Charles & Thelma L'Anson, Sean Lawson, Katalyne Lens, Steven Lidgey, Iris Lohrengel, Gaute Losnegård, To Man Mak, Yoshi Makino, Alessandro Marcolin, Anna Marron, Bob Mason, Christopher Mathis, Alexander Matskevich, Barrie McCormick, Stephanie Mills, Conrad Milne, Ramon Mireles, Alexis Morgan, Kat Morgenstern, Jennifer Morrissey, Julie Morse, Juraj Neidel, Michael Newton, Hugo Nielsen, Salena Noel, Karin Offer, Fernando Miguel Moreno Olmedo, Frank E Orgain, Louise Palmer, Ned Palmer, Eric Patrick, Patrik Paulis, Jane Anemærke Pedersen, Antonio Perez, Arnd Peterhoff, Karen Petersen, Ilse Pijl, David Plotz, Brigitte Poels, Andreas Poethen, Julio Puig, Jeannine Pulsfort, M Philippe Queriaux, Ben Radford, Hanna Ramberg, Laila Rasmussen, Ingrid Rauh , Bob Redlinger, Yolanda Ribas, Brane Ribic, Lisa Roberts, Paul Roberts, Stefan Roemer-Blum, Steve Rogowski, Geoffrey Rollins, Cheri Rosenthal, Hanna Rosin, Leo Ross, Fernando Sanchez Cuenca, Marietta Sander, David Schaffer, Jed Schlosberg, Stephen Schmidt, Emanuel Schnidrig, Wanda Schooley, Thomas Schwarz, Peter Schweitzer, Devin Scott, Terry Scott, Kelly Shields, Elena Shtromberg, Aisha Siddiqi, Amy Sillman, Michael S Singer, Bo Sjoholm, Tijn Sleegers, Donald M Smith, Shirley Smith, Janne Solpark, Stan Spacey, Giulliame Stephane, Paul Steng, Jill Strudwick, Hilary Tempest, Dino ten Have, Tim C Thatcher, Lisette Thresh, Louri Lynn Throgmorton, Jason Throop, Cecile Tiano, Dogan Tirtiroglu, Thomas Todl, Sheila Tratt, Mike & Pauline Truman, Karena Ulede, BL Underwood, Henk van der Berg, Joeke van Waesberghe, Michael Vestergaard, Joanne Viveash, Kathryn Wagner, Lidka Washington, Lindsey Webb, David Weinberg, Jim Whitaker, John T Widdowson, Geert Wijnhoven, Dave & Ann Williams, Bill Willoughby, Claudia Wink, Eva Wortman, Michael Wray, Iris Wüest, Susan Yanow, Camil Züloura

Lonely Planet Guides by Region

Lonely Planet is known worldwide for publishing practical, reliable and no-nonsense travel information in our guides and on our Web site. The Lonely Planet list covers just about every accessible part of the world. Currently there are 16 series: Travel guides, Shoestring guides, Condensed guides, Phrasebooks, Read This First, Healthy Travel, Walking guides, Cycling guides, Watching Wildlife guides, Pisces Diving & Snorkeling guides, City Maps, Road Atlases, Out to Eat, World Food, Journeys travel literature and Pictorials.

AFRICA Africa on a shoestring • Botswana • Cairo • Cairo City Map • Cape Town • Cape Town City Map • East Africa • Egypt • Egyptian Arabic phrasebook • Ethiopia, Eritrea & Djibouti • Ethiopian Amharic phrasebook • The Gambia & Senegal • Healthy Travel Africa • Kenya • Malawi • Morocco • Moroccan Arabic phrasebook • Mozambique • Namibia • Read This First: Africa • South Africa, Lesotho & Swaziland • Southern Africa • Southern Africa Road Atlas • Swahili phrasebook • Tanzania, Zanzibar & Pemba • Trekking in East Africa • Tunisia • Watching Wildlife East Africa • Watching Wildlife Southern Africa • West Africa • World Food Morocco • Zambia • Zimbabwe, Botswana & Namibia
Travel Literature: Mali Blues: Traveling to an African Beat • The Rainbird: A Central African Journey • Songs to an African Sunset: A Zimbabwean Story

AUSTRALIA & THE PACIFIC Aboriginal Australia & the Torres Strait Islands •Auckland • Australia • Australian phrasebook • Australia Road Atlas • Cycling Australia • Cycling New Zealand • Fiji • Fijian phrasebook • Healthy Travel Australia, NZ & the Pacific • Islands of Australia's Great Barrier Reef • Melbourne • Melbourne City Map • Micronesia • New Caledonia • New South Wales • New Zealand • Northern Territory • Outback Australia • Out to Eat – Melbourne • Out to Eat – Sydney • Papua New Guinea • Pidgin phrasebook • Queensland • Rarotonga & the Cook Islands • Samoa • Solomon Islands • South Australia • South Pacific • South Pacific phrasebook • Sydney • Sydney City Map • Sydney Condensed • Tahiti & French Polynesia • Tasmania • Tonga • Tramping in New Zealand • Vanuatu • Victoria • Walking in Australia • Watching Wildlife Australia • Western Australia
Travel Literature: Islands in the Clouds: Travels in the Highlands of New Guinea • Kiwi Tracks: A New Zealand Journey • Sean & David's Long Drive

CENTRAL AMERICA & THE CARIBBEAN Bahamas, Turks & Caicos • Baja California • Belize, Guatemala & Yucatán • Bermuda • Central America on a shoestring • Costa Rica • Costa Rica Spanish phrasebook • Cuba • Cycling Cuba • Dominican Republic & Haiti • Eastern Caribbean • Guatemala • Havana • Healthy Travel Central & South America • Jamaica • Mexico • Mexico City • Panama • Puerto Rico • Read This First: Central & South America • Virgin Islands • World Food Caribbean • World Food Mexico • Yucatán
Travel Literature: Green Dreams: Travels in Central America

EUROPE Amsterdam • Amsterdam City Map • Amsterdam Condensed • Andalucía • Athens • Austria • Baltic States phrasebook • Barcelona • Barcelona City Map • Belgium & Luxembourg • Berlin • Berlin City Map • Britain • British phrasebook • Brussels, Bruges & Antwerp • Brussels City Map • Budapest • Budapest City Map • Canary Islands • Catalunya & the Costa Brava • Central Europe • Central Europe phrasebook • Copenhagen • Corfu & the Ionians • Corsica • Crete • Crete Condensed • Croatia • Cycling Britain • Cycling France • Cyprus • Czech & Slovak Republics • Czech phrasebook • Denmark • Dublin • Dublin City Map • Dublin Condensed • Eastern Europe • Eastern Europe phrasebook • Edinburgh • Edinburgh City Map • England • Estonia, Latvia & Lithuania • Europe on a shoestring • Europe phrasebook • Finland • Florence • Florence City Map • France • Frankfurt City Map • Frankfurt Condensed • French phrasebook • Georgia, Armenia & Azerbaijan • Germany • German phrasebook • Greece • Greek Islands • Greek phrasebook • Hungary • Iceland, Greenland & the Faroe Islands • Ireland • Italian phrasebook • Italy • Kraków • Lisbon • The Loire • London • London City Map • London Condensed • Madrid • Madrid City Map • Malta • Mediterranean Europe • Milan, Turin & Genoa • Moscow • Munich • Netherlands • Normandy • Norway • Out to Eat – London • Out to Eat – Paris • Paris • Paris City Map • Paris Condensed • Poland • Polish phrasebook • Portugal • Portuguese phrasebook • Prague • Prague City Map • Provence & the Côte d'Azur • Read This First: Europe • Rhodes & the Dodecanese • Romania & Moldova • Rome • Rome City Map • Rome Condensed • Russia, Ukraine & Belarus • Russian phrasebook • Scandinavian & Baltic Europe • Scandinavian phrasebook • Scotland • Sicily • Slovenia • South-West France • Spain • Spanish phrasebook • Stockholm • St Petersburg • St Petersburg City Map • Sweden • Switzerland • Tuscany • Ukrainian phrasebook • Venice • Vienna • Wales • Walking in Britain • Walking in France • Walking in Ireland • Walking in Italy • Walking in Scotland • Walking in Spain • Walking in Switzerland • Western Europe • World Food France • World Food Greece • World Food Ireland • World Food Italy • World Food Spain **Travel Literature:** After Yugoslavia • Love and War in the Apennines • The Olive Grove: Travels in Greece • On the Shores of the Mediterranean • Round Ireland in Low Gear • A Small Place in Italy

Lonely Planet Mail Order

onely Planet products are distributed worldwide. They are also available by mail order from Lonely Planet, so if you have difficulty finding a title please write to us. North and South American residents should write to 150 Linden St, Oakland, CA 94607, USA; European and African residents should write to 10a Spring Place, London NW5 3BH, UK; and residents of other countries to Locked Bag 1, Footscray, Victoria 3011, Australia.

INDIAN SUBCONTINENT & THE INDIAN OCEAN Bangladesh • Bengali phrasebook • Bhutan • Delhi • Goa • Healthy Travel Asia & India • Hindi & Urdu phrasebook • India • India & Bangladesh City Map • Indian Himalaya • Karakoram Highway • Kathmandu City Map • Kerala • Madagascar • Maldives • Mauritius, Réunion & Seychelles • Mumbai (Bombay) • Nepal • Nepali phrasebook • North India • Pakistan • Rajasthan • Read This First: Asia & India • South India • Sri Lanka • Sri Lanka phrasebook • Tibet • Tibetan phrasebook • Trekking in the Indian Himalaya • Trekking in the Karakoram & Hindukush • Trekking in the Nepal Himalaya • World Food India **Travel Literature:** The Age of Kali: Indian Travels and Encounters • Hello Goodnight: A Life of Goa • In Rajasthan • Maverick in Madagascar • A Season in Heaven: True Tales from the Road to Kathmandu • Shopping for Buddhas • A Short Walk in the Hindu Kush • Slowly Down the Ganges

MIDDLE EAST & CENTRAL ASIA Bahrain, Kuwait & Qatar • Central Asia • Central Asia phrasebook • Dubai • Farsi (Persian) phrasebook • Hebrew phrasebook • Iran • Israel & the Palestinian Territories • Istanbul • Istanbul City Map • Istanbul to Cairo • Istanbul to Kathmandu • Jerusalem • Jerusalem City Map • Jordan • Lebanon • Middle East • Oman & the United Arab Emirates • Syria • Turkey • Turkish phrasebook • World Food Turkey • Yemen **Travel Literature:** Black on Black: Iran Revisited • Breaking Ranks: Turbulent Travels in the Promised Land • The Gates of Damascus • Kingdom of the Film Stars: Journey into Jordan

NORTH AMERICA Alaska • Boston • Boston City Map • Boston Condensed • British Columbia • California & Nevada • California Condensed • Canada • Chicago • Chicago City Map • Chicago Condensed • Florida • Georgia & the Carolinas • Great Lakes • Hawaii • Hiking in Alaska • Hiking in the USA • Honolulu & Oahu City Map • Las Vegas • Los Angeles • Los Angeles City Map • Louisiana & the Deep South • Miami • Miami City Map • Montreal • New England • New Orleans • New Orleans City Map • New York City • New York City City Map • New York City Condensed • New York, New Jersey & Pennsylvania • Oahu • Out to Eat – San Francisco • Pacific Northwest • Rocky Mountains • San Diego & Tijuana • San Francisco • San Francisco City Map • Seattle • Seattle City Map • Southwest • Texas • Toronto • USA • USA phrasebook • Vancouver • Vancouver City Map • Virginia & the Capital Region • Washington, DC • Washington, DC City Map • World Food New Orleans **Travel Literature:** Caught Inside: A Surfer's Year on the California Coast • Drive Thru America

NORTH-EAST ASIA Beijing • Beijing City Map • Cantonese phrasebook • China • Hiking in Japan • Hong Kong & Macau • Hong Kong City Map • Hong Kong Condensed • Japan • Japanese phrasebook • Korea • Korean phrasebook • Kyoto • Mandarin phrasebook • Mongolia • Mongolian phrasebook • Seoul • Shanghai • South-West China • Taiwan • Tokyo • Tokyo Condensed • World Food Hong Kong • World Food Japan **Travel Literature:** In Xanadu: A Quest • Lost Japan

SOUTH AMERICA Argentina, Uruguay & Paraguay • Bolivia • Brazil • Brazilian phrasebook • Buenos Aires • Buenos Aires City Map • Chile & Easter Island • Colombia • Ecuador & the Galapagos Islands • Healthy Travel Central & South America • Latin American Spanish phrasebook • Peru • Quechua phrasebook • Read This First: Central & South America • Rio de Janeiro • Rio de Janeiro City Map • Santiago de Chile • South America on a shoestring • Trekking in the Patagonian Andes • Venezuela **Travel Literature:** Full Circle: A South American Journey

SOUTH-EAST ASIA Bali & Lombok • Bangkok • Bangkok City Map • Burmese phrasebook • Cambodia • Cycling Vietnam, Laos & Cambodia • East Timor phrasebook • Hanoi • Healthy Travel Asia & India • Hill Tribes phrasebook • Ho Chi Minh City (Saigon) • Indonesia • Indonesian phrasebook • Indonesia's Eastern Islands • Java • Lao phrasebook • Laos • Malay phrasebook • Malaysia, Singapore & Brunei • Myanmar (Burma) • Philippines • Pilipino (Tagalog) phrasebook • Read This First: Asia & India • Singapore • Singapore City Map • South-East Asia on a shoestring • South-East Asia phrasebook • Thailand • Thailand's Islands & Beaches • Thailand, Vietnam, Laos & Cambodia Road Atlas • Thai phrasebook • Vietnam • Vietnamese phrasebook • World Food Indonesia • World Food Thailand • World Food Vietnam

ALSO AVAILABLE: Antarctica • The Arctic • The Blue Man: Tales of Travel, Love and Coffee • Brief Encounters: Stories of Love, Sex & Travel • Buddhist Stupas in Asia: The Shape of Perfection • Chasing Rickshaws • The Last Grain Race • Lonely Planet ... On the Edge: Adventurous Escapades from Around the World • Lonely Planet Unpacked • Lonely Planet Unpacked Again • Not the Only Planet: Science Fiction Travel Stories • Ports of Call: A Journey by Sea • Sacred India • Travel Photography: A Guide to Taking Better Pictures • Travel with Children • Tuvalu: Portrait of an Island Nation

Index

Bold indicates maps.

Bold indicates maps.

Bold indicates maps.

Bold indicates maps.

Boxed Text

MAP LEGEND

ROUTES

City Regional

Freeway	Pedestrian Mall
Toll Freeway	Steps
Primary Road	Tunnel
Secondary Road	Trail
Tertiary Road	Walking Tour
Dirt Road	Path

TRANSPORTATION

Train		Bus Route	
Metro		Ferry	

HYDROGRAPHY

River; Creek	Spring; Rapids
Canal	Waterfalls
Lake	Dry; Salt Lake

ROUTE SHIELDS

Mexico Highway · State Highway

Carretera Nacional · Carretera Interamericana

BOUNDARIES

International
State; District
County
Disputed

AREAS

Beach	Cemetery	Golf Course
Building	Forest	Reservation
Campus	Garden; Zoo	Sports Field
	Park	Plaza
		Swamp; Mangrove

POPULATION SYMBOLS

✪ NATIONAL CAPITAL National Capital	● Large City Large City	○ Small City Small City
◉ State Capital State Capital	● Medium City Medium City	○ Town; Village Town; Village

MAP SYMBOLS

▲ Place to Stay		▼ Place to Eat	● Point of Interest

Airfield	Church	Museum	Skiing - Downhill
Airport	Cinema	Observatory	Stately Home
Archeological Site; Ruin	Dive Site	Park	Surfing
Bank	Embassy; Consulate	Parking Area	Synagogue
Baseball Diamond	Footbridge	Pass	Tao Temple
Battlefield	Gas Station	Picnic Area	Taxi
Bike Trail	Hindu Temple	Police Station	Telephone
Border Crossing	Hospital	Pool	Theater
Bus Station; Terminal	Information	Post Office	Toilet - Public
Cable Car; Chairlift	Internet Café	Pub; Bar	Tomb
Café	Lighthouse	RV Park	Trailhead
Campground	Lookout	Shelter	Tram Stop
Castle	Mission	Shipwreck	Transportation
Cathedral	Monument	Shopping Mall	Volcano
Cave	Mountain	Skiing - Cross Country	Winery

Note: not all symbols displayed above appear in this book

LONELY PLANET OFFICES

Australia
Locked Bag 1, Footscray, Victoria 3011
☎ 03 8379 8000 fax 03 8379 8111
email talk2us@lonelyplanet.com.au

UK
10a Spring Place, London NW5 3BH
☎ 020 7428 4800 fax 020 7428 4828
email go@lonelyplanet.co.uk

USA
150 Linden Street, Oakland, California 94607
☎ 510 893 8555, TOLL FREE 800 275 8555
fax 510 893 8572
email info@lonelyplanet.com

France
1 rue du Dahomey, 75011 Paris
☎ 01 55 25 33 00 fax 01 55 25 33 01
email: bip@lonelyplanet.com
www.lonelyplanet.fr

World Wide Web: www.lonelyplanet.com *or* AOL keyword: lp
Lonely Planet Images: lpi@lonelyplanet.com.au